Dictionary
of the
Middle Ages

American Council of Learned Societies

The American Council of Learned Societies, organized in 1919 for the purpose of advancing the study of the humanities and of the humanistic aspects of the social sciences, is a nonprofit federation comprising sixty-seven national scholarly groups. The Council represents the humanities in the United States in the International Union of Academies, provides fellowships, supports research-and-planning conferences and symposia, and sponsors special projects and scholarly publications.

Constituent Societies with Founding Dates

American Philosophical Society, 1743

American Academy of Arts and Sciences, 1780

American Antiquarian Society, 1812

American Oriental Society, 1842

American Numismatic Society, 1858

American Philological Association, 1869

Archaeological Institute of America, 1879

Society of Biblical Literature, 1880

Modern Language Association of America, 1883

American Historical Association, 1884

American Economic Association, 1885

American Folklore Society, 1888

American Society of Church History, 1888

American Dialect Society, 1889

American Psychological Association, 1892

American Philosophical Association, 1900

American Schools of Oriental Research, 1900

Association of American Law Schools, 1900

American Anthropological Association, 1902

American Political Science Association, 1903

Association of American Geographers, 1904

Bibliographical Society of America, 1904

Hispanic Society of America, 1904

American Sociological Association, 1905

American Society of International Law, 1906

Organization of American Historians, 1907

American Academy of Religion, 1909

College Forum (of the National Council of Teachers of English), 1911

Society for the Advancement of Scandinavian Study, 1911

College Art Association, 1912

National Communication Association, 1914

History of Science Society, 1924

Linguistic Society of America, 1924

American Association for the History of Medicine, 1925

Medieval Academy of America, 1925

American Musicological Society, 1934

Economic History Association, 1940

Society of Architectural Historians, 1940

Association for Asian Studies, 1941

American Society for Aesthetics, 1942

American Association for the Advancement of Slavic Studies, 1948

American Studies Association, 1950

Metaphysical Society of America, 1950

American Society of Comparative Law, 1951

Renaissance Society of America, 1954

Society for Ethnomusicology, 1955

American Society for Legal History, 1956

American Society for Theatre Research, 1956

International Center of Medieval Art, 1956

Society for French Historical Studies, 1956

African Studies Association, 1957

Society for the History of Technology, 1958

Society for Cinema and Media Studies, 1959

American Comparative Literature Association, 1960

Law and Society Association, 1964

Latin American Studies Association, 1966

Middle East Studies Association of North America, 1966

Association for the Advancement of Baltic Studies, 1968

American Society for Eighteenth-Century Studies, 1969

Association for Jewish Studies, 1969

Sixteenth Century Society and Conference, 1970

Dictionary Society of North America, 1975

Society for American Music, 1975

German Studies Association, 1976

Society for Music Theory, 1977

Society of Dance History Scholars, 1979

National Council on Public History, 1980

Grammarian and Students in a Late Medieval Manuscript. *Medieval education experienced a series of renewals from the monastic revival of the Carolingian renaissance to the rise of urban cathedral schools in the 12th century. Grammar was always paramount, and elsewhere (as on a Chartres Cathedral carving) Grammatica herself is sometimes shown wielding the rod of discipline.* BIBLIOTHÈQUE NATIONALE DE FRANCE.

Dictionary
of the
Middle Ages

WILLIAM CHESTER JORDAN, *Editor in Chief*

SUPPLEMENT 1

CHARLES SCRIBNER'S SONS®

THOMSON
★
™
GALE

New York • Detroit • San Diego • San Francisco • Cleveland • New Haven, Conn. • Waterville, Maine • London • Munich

Dictionary of the Middle Ages, Supplement 1

William Chester Jordan

For permission to use material from this product, submit your request via Web at www.gale-edit.com/permissions, or you may download our Permissions Request form and submit your request by fax or mail to:

Permissions Department
The Gale Group, Inc.
27500 Drake Rd.
Farmington Hills, MI 48331-3535
Permissions Hotline:
248 699-8006 or 800 877-4253, ext. 8006
Fax: 248 699-8074 or 800 762-4058

The *Dictionary of the Middle Ages* was produced with support from the National Endowment for the Humanities.

LIBRARY OF CONGRESS CATALOGING-IN-PUBLICATION DATA

Dictionary of the Middle Ages.
Includes bibliographies and index.
1. Middle Ages—Dictionaries. I. Strayer, Joseph Reese, 1904–1987

D114.D5 1982 909.07   82-5904

ISBN 0-684-19073-7 (set)

ISBN 0-684-16760-3 (v. 1)   ISBN 0-684-18169-X (v. 7)
ISBN 0-684-17022-1 (v. 2)   ISBN 0-684-18274-2 (v. 8)
ISBN 0-684-17023-X (v. 3)   ISBN 0-684-18275-0 (v. 9)
ISBN 0-684-17024-8 (v. 4)   ISBN 0-684-18276-9 (v. 10)
ISBN 0-684-18161-4 (v. 5)   ISBN 0-684-18277-7 (v. 11)
ISBN 0-684-18168-1 (v. 6)   ISBN 0-684-18278-5 (v. 12)
          ISBN 0-684-18279-3 (v. 13)

ISBN 0-684-80642-8 (supp. 1)

Printed in the United States of America
10 9 8 7 6 5 4 3 2 1

Associate Editors

Editorial Staff

Preface

The *Dictionary of the Middle Ages* (1982–1989) was an extraordinary project for its time. Nevertheless, dramatic changes in medieval studies in the twenty-five years since the *Dictionary* was conceived have lent considerable force to the many suggestions that it be supplemented. Continuing research on old subjects has turned up new information leading to radically revised and seemingly more persuasive interpretations than those offered in the original. Additionally, the original *Dictionary*, although it aimed at comprehensiveness, reflected a very strong bias in North American scholarship toward northwestern Europe—in particular, toward northern France and England. Phenomena that were common to the whole of Europe were sometimes treated as if they occurred only in the English Midlands, Normandy, or the Île de France. There is no article on charity in the original *Dictionary*. Curiously, there is also none on poverty. Medieval thinking on the virtues and the vices was scarcely represented, and there were no entries explicitly devoted to conversion, demons, the devil, humanism, just price, the liturgical year, natural law, or women—to name just a few. Related to the skewed coverage of so many articles, the original version ignored topics that now would be required reading. Childbirth, civic ritual, ecology, gender, race, and sexuality were new or virtually unknown as topics of genuinely serious scholarly interest in the 1970s, when the *Dictionary* was planned.

This supplementary volume is an attempt to address the problems and lacunae of the original *Dictionary*. It includes not only all the topics proposed above but also a range of wider cultural associations. We have broadened the scope of the original to include such topics as the course of medieval studies and "cultural medievalism" over the past six hundred years. And we have even included a few "debunking" articles to dispel from young minds some of the myths (such as Pope Joan and the chastity belt) that may still linger in the popular consciousness.

With the assistance of former Scribner publisher Karen Day and John Fitzpatrick, the managing editor of the original project; the capable cooperation of two associate editors, Joel Kaye of Barnard College and Lynn Staley of Colgate University; and the efforts of a number of graduate students at Princeton University who did a great deal of the cross-checking, a list of topics was assembled. The editors then assigned lengths to the various entries. We chose not to contract for less than five hundred words, concluding that the shortest articles in the original *Dictionary* were among the least successful.

We also put together an atelier or *équipe* of authors with specialties in fields that were poorly represented in the original *Dictionary*. The names of the members of the atelier, their present affiliations, and a general but not exhaustive description of their fields follow: On German and early medieval topics, we retained Scott Bruce of the History Department of the University of Colorado at Boulder. Elspeth Carruthers of the University of Illinois at Chicago is the author of a considerable number of entries on central Europe. It was to Adam Davis of Denison University that we turned for help on many ecclesiastical matters. Emily Kadens of the University of Chicago Law School contributed entries on technical legal subjects and jurists. Christopher MacEvitt, a professor in the Religion Department at Dartmouth College, was responsible for entries on popes, crusades, and related issues. Jarbel Rodriguez, a historian at San Francisco State University, wrote extensively on Spanish topics.

Scholarly participation was solicited especially at conventions like the Annual Meeting of the Medieval Academy of America and the International Congress of Medieval Studies (in Kalamazoo, Michigan). The Academy and the Congress also spread the word on their Web sites, and we wish to acknowledge Richard Emmerson, the Executive Secretary of the Academy, and Paul Szarmach, the Director of the Medieval Institute at Western Michigan University, for doing so. These preliminary efforts paid off handsomely. In general, the response was exceptionally good. The editors, individually and collectively, honed their skills at persuasion and indeed became quite adept at not crossing the delicate line between getting a slow writer to finish and provoking him or her to the fearful words, "Find someone else." Almost every entry was read by at least two people, often three. This meant that there was a great deal of feedback that authors received, not counting the queries, cuts, and modifications that copy editors suggested. Here, too, the editors learned how to be diplomats, although, being scholars themselves, they were aware of how difficult it was for their peers to cut the length of essays and of painstakingly assembled bibliographies. One youngish writer put it nicely: what fell to the cutting room floor would not be lost forever; he would put the excised information to use in stories he would someday tell his grandchildren. (We apologize in advance to the grandchildren.)

Despite the complications involved in the coordination of so many scholars in this enterprise, it did successfully come to fruition. The unsung heroes of the enterprise were the support staff, especially Anna Grojec, Roberta Klarreich, Lisa Vecchione, and Mark Mikula. It was they who arranged for individual author contracts, logged in entries, made sure authors were acknowledged, distributed the entries to referees, applied gentle pressure to delinquents, toned down the referees' and editors' comments on some entries, so as not to offend the authors, and made sure people were paid. Their coolness under fire, even when one author demanded his "moolah" more quickly, was fantastic. It is worth noting that the writing, reviewing, and editing of this volume were all conducted entirely in the electronic domain—a first for Scribners and a far cry from the innumerable postal communications that occurred for every single article in the original *DMA.*

The result of all this effort, the *Dictionary of the Middle Ages, Supplement 1,* will, we hope, become as valued a reference tool as its great predecessor.

WILLIAM CHESTER JORDAN
PRINCETON UNIVERSITY
JUNE 2003

Articles

ABORTION
Margaret Schleissner

ACCIAIUOLI
Adam Jeffrey Davis

ACCURSIUS
Emily Kadens

ADALBERT, ST.
Elspeth Jane Carruthers

ADMIRAL
Jarbel Rodriguez

ALBERICUS DE ROSATE
Kenneth Pennington

ALBERTANO DA BRESCIA
James M. Powell

ALEXANDER IV, POPE
Christopher Hatch MacEvitt

ALEXANDER DE VILLA DEI
Adam Jeffrey Davis

ALFONSO V OF ARAGON
Jarbel Rodriguez

ALLITERATIVE LITERATURE
Christine Chism

AMSTERDAM
Emily Kadens

ANDREA DA BARBERINO
Adam Jeffrey Davis

ANIMALS, ATTITUDES TOWARD
Lisa J. Kiser

ANNE OF BOHEMIA
William Chester Jordan

ANSGAR, ST.
Scott G. Bruce

ANTAR
Christopher Hatch MacEvitt

ANTHONY OF EGYPT, ST.
Jaclyn Maxwell

ANTWERP
Emily Kadens

ARCHAEOLOGY
Pam J. Crabtree

ARCHITECTURE, DOMESTIC
Kim Bowes

ARTHURIAN ROMANCES
Thomas Hahn

ASTRAL MAGIC
Adam Jeffrey Davis

ASTROLOGICAL ICONOGRAPHY
Christopher Hatch MacEvitt

ATHEISM
Adam Jeffrey Davis

ATHENS
Christopher Hatch MacEvitt

AUTOBIOGRAPHY AND CONFESSIONAL
LITERATURE
Laurence de Looze

BANNOCKBURN, BATTLE OF
William Chester Jordan

BARTHOLOMAEUS ANGLICUS
Adam Jeffrey Davis

BATHS AND BATHING
Christopher Hatch MacEvitt

BEDOUIN
Christopher Hatch MacEvitt

BERNARD OF PARMA
Emily Kadens

BERNARD OF PAVIA
Emily Kadens

BIBLICAL COMMENTARIES
Karlfried Froehlich

BIOGRAPHY
Thomas J. Heffernan

BLUES AND GREENS
Christopher Hatch MacEvitt

BOBBIO
Adam Jeffrey Davis

BODY, THE
Sarah Stanbury

BOETHIUS OF DACIA
Adam Jeffrey Davis

BOGURODZICA
Adam Jeffrey Davis

BOHEMIAN ART
Evelin Wetter

BOLESŁAW I CHROBRY OF POLAND,
KING
Elspeth Jane Carruthers

BOLESŁAW III KRZYWOUSTY OF
POLAND, KING
Elspeth Jane Carruthers

BRIAN BORU
Dáibhí ó Cróinín

BRUNHILD
Kevin Uhalde

BULGARUS
Emily Kadens

BURSFELD, ABBEY OF
Jarbel Rodriguez

BYLINY
William Chester Jordan

CALUMNY OATH
Emily Kadens

CAPITAL PUNISHMENT
Emily Kadens

CAPITULATIONS
Jarbel Rodriguez

CAROLINGIAN RENAISSANCE
Christopher Hatch MacEvitt

CARTOGRAPHY
Benjamin Weiss

CASIMIR III THE GREAT OF POLAND,
KING
William Chester Jordan

CASIMIR IV THE JAGIELLONIAN OF
POLAND, KING
William Chester Jordan

CASPE, COMPROMISE OF
Jarbel Rodriguez

CASTLE-GUARD
Christopher Hatch MacEvitt

CATHERINE OF SIENA, ST.
Renate Blumenfeld-Kosinski

CHARITY
Neil S. Rushton

CHARLES IV, EMPEROR
Scott G. Bruce

CHASTITY BELT
William Chester Jordan

CHILDBIRTH AND INFANCY
Monica H. Green

CHILDHOOD AND ADOLESCENCE
Anne E. Lester

CHINA
James D. Ryan

CHRISTOPHER, ST.
Christopher Hatch MacEvitt

CINQUE PORTS
Jonathan A. Bush

CIOMPI, REVOLT OF THE
Christopher Hatch MacEvitt

CLARE, ST.
Adam Jeffrey Davis

COLONNA FAMILY
Christopher Hatch MacEvitt

COMITATUS
Christopher Hatch MacEvitt

COMMERCIALIZATION
Richard Britnell

COMMUNES, 1200–1500
Steven A. Epstein

CONRAD I OF GERMANY, EMPEROR
Elspeth Jane Carruthers

CONRAD III OF GERMANY, EMPEROR
Scott G. Bruce

CONRAD IV OF GERMANY, EMPEROR
Scott G. Bruce

CONRADIN
Scott G. Bruce

CONVERSION
James Muldoon

CORBIE, ABBEY OF
Scott G. Bruce

CORVEY, ABBEY OF
Scott G. Bruce

CUMANS/KIPCHAKS
William Chester Jordan

DALIMIL'S CHRONICLE
William Chester Jordan

DANDOLO, ENRICO
Christopher Hatch MacEvitt

DEGUILEVILLE, GUILLAUME DE
Jarbel Rodriguez

DEMANDA DO SANTO GRAAL
Adam Jeffrey Davis

DEMONS
John Block Friedman

DEVIL
John Block Friedman

DHIMMĪS
Paula Sanders

DIES IRAE
Adam Jeffrey Davis

DIPLOMATICS
Emily Kadens

DIRC VAN DELFT
Emily Kadens

DISEASE
Michael McVaugh

DRACONTIUS, BLOSSIUS AEMILIUS
Jarbel Rodriguez

DROIT DU SEIGNEUR
William Chester Jordan

DUNSTAN, ST.
Paul E. Szarmach

DURAND OF HUESCA
Adam Jeffrey Davis

ECOLOGY
Richard C. Hoffmann

EDESSA, COUNTY OF
Christopher Hatch MacEvitt

EDMUND OF ABINGDON, ST.
William Chester Jordan

ELIAS OF CORTONA
Adam Jeffrey Davis

ELIZABETH OF HUNGARY, ST.
William Chester Jordan

EPIC GENRE
Joyce Tally Lionarons

ESPIONAGE
Ivana Elbl

ETIQUETTE AND MANNERS
Kathleen Ashley

EUGENIUS III, POPE
Christopher Hatch MacEvitt

EUGENIUS IV, POPE
Christopher Hatch MacEvitt

EUNUCHS
Paula Sanders

EUSKARA
Kevin Uhalde

EXETER BOOK
Patrick W. Conner

EZZELINO DA ROMANO
Christopher Hatch MacEvitt

FALL, THE
Adam Jeffrey Davis

FERDINAND III OF CASTILE, KING
Jarbel Rodriguez

FINNSBURH FRAGMENT
Jarbel Rodriguez

FIREARMS
Kelly DeVries

FITZRALPH, RICHARD
Adam Jeffrey Davis

FRANKS
Christopher Hatch MacEvitt

FRAXINETUM
Scott G. Bruce

FREDEGUNDA
Kevin Uhalde

FRISIAN LITERATURE
Oebele Vries

GENDER, THEORIES OF
Ruth Mazo Karras

GENIUS
Adam Jeffrey Davis

GHOSTS
Mark Gregory Pegg

GNOSTICISM
Mark Gregory Pegg

GODFREY OF BOUILLON
Christopher Hatch MacEvitt

GODRIC OF FINCHALE, ST.
Dominic D. Alexander

GOSCELIN OF ST. BERTIN
Paul Antony Hayward

GOTHIC ARCHITECTURE
Stephen Murray

GOTHIC ART
M. B. Shepard

GRÁGÁS
Jarbel Rodriguez

GRATIAN
Kenneth Pennington

GREGORY X, POPE
Christopher Hatch MacEvitt

GUESCLIN, BERTRAND DU
William Chester Jordan

GYNECOLOGY
Monica H. Green

HAGIOGRAPHY, ISLAMIC
Josef W. Meri

HAGIOGRAPHY, JEWISH
Susan L. Einbinder

HEBREW LANGUAGE
Angel Sáenz-Badillos

HELL, CONCEPTS OF
Richard K. Emmerson

HENRY I OF GERMANY, EMPEROR
Elspeth Jane Carruthers

HENRY II OF GERMANY, EMPEROR
Elspeth Jane Carruthers

HENRY V OF GERMANY, EMPEROR
Elspeth Jane Carruthers

HENRY VI OF GERMANY, EMPEROR
Elspeth Jane Carruthers

HENRY VII OF GERMANY, KING
Scott G. Bruce

HENRY THE NAVIGATOR OF PORTU-
GAL, PRINCE
Jarbel Rodriguez

HERMANN OF SALZA
Christopher Hatch MacEvitt

HILĀL, BANŪ (SĪRAT BANŪ HILĀL)
Christopher Hatch MacEvitt

HILARY OF ORLÉANS
Jan M. Ziolkowski

HONORIUS III, POPE
Christopher Hatch MacEvitt

HORSES AND HORSEMANSHIP
C. M. Gillmor

HOSPITALLERS
Christopher Hatch MacEvitt

HUBERT DE BURGH
Jonathan A. Bush

HUMANISM
James Simpson

HUMBERT OF ROMANS
Adam Jeffrey Davis

HYGIENE, PERSONAL
Michael McVaugh

HYPATIA
Kevin Uhalde

IDUNG OF PRÜFENING
Scott G. Bruce

IMMACULATE CONCEPTION OF THE
VIRGIN
Alexandra Cuffel

INSURANCE
James M. Murray

JACQUES DE RÉVIGNY
Emily Kadens

JAMES I OF ARAGON, KING
Jarbel Rodriguez

JEAN RENART
Adam Jeffrey Davis

JEROME OF PRAGUE
Scott G. Bruce

JOAN, POPE
William Chester Jordan

JOHANNES BASSIANUS
Kenneth Pennington

JOHANNES DE LIGNANO
Adam Jeffrey Davis

JOHN OF SACROBOSCO
Adam Jeffrey Davis

JOHN XXIII, ANTIPOPE
Adam Jeffrey Davis

JOSEPH OF VOLOKOLAMSK, ST.
T. Allan Smith

JUGLARÍA
Jarbel Rodriguez

JUST PRICE
Joel Kaye

KALĪLA WA-DIMNA
Christopher Hatch MacEvitt

KALISZ, STATUTES OF
William Chester Jordan

KRAKÓW
William Chester Jordan

LAS NAVAS DE TOLOSA, BATTLE OF
Jarbel Rodriguez

LATIFUNDIA
Kevin Uhalde

LATIN LITERATURE: SECULAR LYRICS
Jan M. Ziolkowski

LAW, CRIMINAL PROCEDURE
Kenneth Pennington

LAW, FEUDAL
Kenneth Pennington

LE FRANC, MARTIN
Jarbel Rodriguez

LIBRI FEUDORUM
Emily Kadens

LISBON
Jarbel Rodriguez

LITURGICAL YEAR, EASTERN
George E. Demacopoulos

LITURGICAL YEAR, WESTERN
Richard W. Pfaff

LOUIS IV THE BAVARIAN, EMPEROR
Scott G. Bruce

LOVE AND COURTSHIP
Lynn Staley

LUND
William Chester Jordan

MAIOLUS
Scott G. Bruce

MANFRED OF SICILY, KING
Christopher Hatch MacEvitt

MANOR AND MANORIALISM
William Chester Jordan

MANUFACTURING AND INDUSTRY
John H. Munro

MANUSCRIPT COLLECTIONS
Don C. Skemer

MANUSCRIPT ILLUMINATION,
BYZANTINE
Georgi Parpulov

MARRIAGE, CHRISTIAN
James A. Brundage

MARTIN OF TOURS, ST.
Kevin Uhalde

MATHEMATICS, ISLAMIC
J. L. Berggren

MATILDA, EMPRESS
Lois L. Huneycutt

MATTER
Guy Guldentops and Carlos Steel

MEDICINE, ISLAMIC
Danielle Jacquart

MEDIEVAL STUDIES
Paul Freedman

MEDIEVALISM
Kathleen Verduin

MERCEDARIANS
Jarbel Rodriguez

MERCHANTS
Kathryn L. Reyerson

MERTON CALCULATORS
Edith Dudley Sylla

MIDDLE AGES
Emily Kadens

MIESZKO I OF POLAND, KING
Elspeth Jane Carruthers

MONSTERS AND THE MONSTROUS
John Block Friedman

MORISCOS
Mark D. Meyerson

MUSICUS
Alice V. Clark

NATURAL LAW
Kenneth Pennington

NATURE
Guy Geltner

NICHOLAS II, POPE
Christopher Hatch MacEvitt

NICHOLAS III, POPE
Christopher Hatch MacEvitt

NICHOLAS IV, POPE
Christopher Hatch MacEvitt

NOTARIES
Kathryn L. Reyerson

NOVEL (BYZANTINE LAW)
Leonora Neville

NUMEROLOGY
Anne Berthelot

OBLATES AND OBLATION
Scott G. Bruce

OLD AGE
Joel T. Rosenthal

OLDRADUS DE PONTE
Kenneth Pennington

OLEŚNICKI, ZBIGNIEW
Adam Jeffrey Davis

ORIGINAL SIN
Kevin Uhalde

ORIGINALITY IN ARTS AND LETTERS
Celia Chazelle

ORSINI FAMILY
Christopher Hatch MacEvitt

OTTO II OF GERMANY, EMPEROR
Elspeth Jane Carruthers

OTTO IV OF GERMANY, EMPEROR
Elspeth Jane Carruthers

OTTOMAN ART AND ARCHITECTURE
Rachel Milstein

OVENS
Kevin Uhalde

PAGANISM AND PAGAN GODS,
SURVIVAL OF
Peter Dinzelbacher

PATRONAGE, ARTISTIC
Elizabeth J. Moodey

PATRONAGE, LITERARY
Martin Aurell

PEACEMAKING
Geoffrey Koziol

PEDRO III "THE GREAT" OF ARAGON,
KING
Jarbel Rodriguez

PERAULT, WILLIAM
Jarbel Rodriguez

PERCY FAMILY
Matthew Strickland

PERSIAN LANGUAGE
Vera B. Moreen

PETER DES ROCHES
Jonathan A. Bush

PETRUS ALFONSI
Jarbel Rodriguez

PHILOSOPHICAL GENRES
Stephen Lahey

PHYSICIANS
Michael McVaugh

PIERRE DE BELLEPERCHE
William Chester Jordan

PILGRIM SOUVENIRS
Diana Webb

PILGRIMAGE, CELTIC
Diana Webb

PIRATES AND PIRACY
Clifford R. Backman

PLANCTUS MARIAE
Alice V. Clark

POLLUTION AND TABOO
Mark Gregory Pegg

POOR CLARES
Katherine Ludwig Jansen

PORNOGRAPHY
Michael Uebel

PORTUGUESE LITERATURE
Isabel de Sena

POVERTY
Teofilo F. Ruiz

PROBABILITY
Edith Dudley Sylla

PRODROMIC POEMS
Elizabeth Jeffreys

QUEENS AND QUEENSHIP
Lois L. Huneycutt

RACE
Jeffrey J. Cohen

RADEGUNDA, ST.
Kevin Uhalde

RAPE
Henry Ansgar Kelly

RELIGION, POPULAR
John Shinners

RIBĀT
Christopher Hatch MacEvitt

RICARDUS ANGLICUS
Emily Kadens

RITUAL, CIVIC
Walter Prevenier

ROLANDINUS DE PASSAGERIS
Kenneth Pennington

ROUTIERS
William Chester Jordan

RUDOLF OF HABSBURG
Scott G. Bruce

SABIANS
Christopher Hatch MacEvitt

SACRAMENTS AND SACRAMENTAL
THEOLOGY
Ian Christopher Levy

SATIRE
Jan M. Ziolkowski

SAVONAROLA, GIROLAMO
Christopher Hatch MacEvitt

SCHOOLS
Jo Ann Hoeppner Moran Cruz

SERVANTS
Susan Mosher Stuard

SEXUALITY
Ruth Mazo Karras

SEXUALITY, MEDICAL
Joan Cadden

SIGNS, THEORY OF
Brigitte Miriam Bedos-Rezak

SONG OF IGOR'S CAMPAIGN
William Chester Jordan

SOUL AND BODY
Caroline Walker Bynum

STANISŁAW, ST.
William Chester Jordan

STEPHEN OF ENGLAND, KING
William Chester Jordan

SÜSSKIND VON TRIMBERG
Scott G. Bruce

SYRIAN CHRISTIAN ARCHITECTURE
Christopher Hatch MacEvitt

TAKLA HAYMANOT, ST.
Christopher Hatch MacEvitt

TANNENBERG/GRUNWALD, BATTLE OF
William Chester Jordan

TAXATION: GERMANY, ITALY, IBERIA
William Chester Jordan

TEMPLARS
Christopher Hatch MacEvitt

TERTULLIAN
Jaclyn Maxwell

TEUTONIC KNIGHTS
Scott G. Bruce

TEXTILES, BYZANTINE
Christopher Hatch MacEvitt

TOLLS
William Chester Jordan

TONSURE
Kevin Uhalde

TORQUEMADA, JUAN DE
Jarbel Rodriguez

TORQUEMADA, TOMÁS DE
Jarbel Rodriguez

TOURNAI
Emily Kadens

TRANSUBSTANTIATION
Gary Macy

TRINITARIANS
Jarbel Rodriguez

TYRANTS AND TYRANNICIDE
Adam Jeffrey Davis

ULFILA
Jaclyn Maxwell

UPPSALA
Scott G. Bruce

URBAN IV, POPE
Christopher Hatch MacEvitt

UTRAQUISM
William Chester Jordan

VATICAN LIBRARY
Edward D. English

VIOLENCE
Peter Haidu

VIRTUES AND VICES
Richard G. Newhauser

VOIVODE
William Chester Jordan

WALLACE, WILLIAM
Jarbel Rodriguez

WENCESLAS, ST.
William Chester Jordan

WIDOWHOOD
P. J. P. Goldberg

WILLIAM OF DROGHEDA
Jonathan A. Bush

WILLIAM OF ST. AMOUR
William Chester Jordan

WILLIAM II (RUFUS) OF ENGLAND,
KING
William Chester Jordan

WILLIAM I OF SICILY, KING
Christopher Hatch MacEvitt

WILLIAM II OF SICILY, KING
Christopher Hatch MacEvitt

WOMEN
Ruth Mazo Karras

ZADONSHCHINA
William Chester Jordan

ZURARA, GOMES EANES DE
Jarbel Rodriguez

Dictionary
of the
Middle Ages

Dictionary of the Middle Ages

SUPPLEMENT 1

ABORTION—ZURARA, GOMES EANES DE

ABORTION. According to Roman law a fetus was a thing, not yet human. But as early as A.D. 200, the jurist Julius Paulus specified punishment (by exile for the upper classes or by the mines for the lower classes) for those who administered a drink producing abortion. If death resulted to the consumer, the abortifacient provider was given the death penalty. There was no punishment for abortion with consent of the father if the mother was not injured and potions were not used. The Hebrew Bible (Exodus 21: 22–23) prescribed only a civil punishment for accidental abortion, unless the mother was killed, in which case the penalty was a "life for a life." The Septuagint (a Greek translation of the Old Testament from the third century B.C.) mistranslated this passage to distinguish between a developed (formed) and an undeveloped fetus, a fully formed fetus being considered a life. Early Christian thought was influenced by the first-century Jewish philosopher Philo, who interpreted this passage as including intentional abortion by parents and infanticide. Church fathers such as Augustine and Jerome accepted the distinction between an unformed and a formed fetus, based on Aristotle's view that ensoulment occurs after forty days if the fetus is male and after eighty days if the fetus is female. Moreover, the Augustinian view that sexual activity was acceptable only for the purpose of procreation within marriage meant that early Christians condemned abortion as a violation of that purpose.

While Roman and Germanic law was concerned with the use of evil magic *(maleficium)* by those who gave abortions, early-fourth-century church councils as well as the sixth-century bishop Caesarius of Arles also penalized women who procured them. Penitentials, written from the eighth to the eleventh centuries to aid priests in assessing penances, treated giver and consumer as equally guilty. Some, like Bishop Regino of Prüm, made distinctions based on social class or motivation, discriminating between a woman motivated by poverty and one motivated by vanity or fornication. Others punished not only the accomplice but also those who distributed knowledge about abortion.

Despite strong opposition to abortion in religion and law, references to abortion in medical writing (often produced in ecclesiastical settings like monasteries or cathedral schools) abound. Recipes are found both within treatises and inserted between texts, most often without authors' commentaries or apologies. While recipes for emmenagogues (to provoke the menses) may have been understood as abortifacients, it is important to remember that according to humoral pathology, menstruation is necessary to preserve a woman's health (because of her cold and moist nature, she is unable to "concoct" harmful by-products of digestion) and in order for conception to occur. Influenced by Greek, Roman, and Islamic sources, medical texts describe potions, vaginal suppositories, substances to be inhaled, and baths, as well as exercise and magic, such as amulets. Most writers warn against surgical procedures. The Hippocratic oath prohibited administering an abortifacient. Another Hippocratic treatise, *On the Nature of the Child,* recounted the case of a slave girl who leaped repeatedly, touching her heels to her buttocks, in order to expel the fetus. In the first century A.D., Soranus distinguished between contraceptives and abortifacients, writing that according to some, abortion should not be used to conceal extramarital sex or to preserve a woman's beauty but only when birth would be impeded by a physical defect or endanger the life of the mother. Later writers such as Theodorus Priscianus in the fourth century, Abū Abkr Muḥammad ibn Zakarīya al-Rāzī (Rhazes) in the ninth, and Ibn Sīnā (Avicenna) in the eleventh echoed this medical-ethical justification for abortion: concern for the mother's safety. Following this tradition, the author of *Book on the Conditions of Women* from the *Trotula* treatises on women's medicine and beauty care writes, "Galen says that women who have narrow vaginas and constricted wombs ought not have sexual relations with men lest they conceive and die. But all such women are not able to abstain, and so they need our assistance." In only a single known case was information regarding abortion consciously suppressed in a medical text. An entire chapter on abortifacients was omitted from Constantine the African's eleventh-century translation of Ibn al-Razzāz al-Jazarī's *Provision of the Voyager,* known as the *Viaticum* in Latin, either by Constantine himself or a scribe.

Reservations about transmitting information on abortion were voiced in late medieval vernacular translations of medical and scientific texts because of fear of misuse by prostitutes and others wishing to conceal illicit sexual relations. A fifteenth-century German translation of *Secreta mulierum,* a compendium of natural lore about female sexuality and reproduction attributed to Albertus Magnus, adopts a misogynous male perspective, reviling evil women and prostitutes who induce abortion through running and jumping and strenuous sexual activity. Echoing the ancient fear of "evil magic" *(maleficium),* the commentary cautions against old witches who counsel young daughters on how to cause abortion by poisoning the womb. A nearly contemporaneous German translation of the *Trotula* by Dr. Johannes Hartlieb addressed to married people recommends that the chapter on contraceptives and abortifacients be written in cipher lest it be used for wantonness.

Midwives were often suspected of witchcraft due to their knowledge of potions that caused abortion. Thus the *Malleus maleficarum* (Hammer of the witches, 1486) of Henry Institoris and James Sprenger claims "That Witches who are Midwives in Various Ways Kill the Child Conceived in the Womb, and Procure an Abortion; or if they do not do this Offer New-born Children to Devils." In the late fifteenth century in Germany, city ordinances regulating midwives and midwives' oaths included intentional and accidental abortion. Especially after the adoption of the *Carolina,* a legal code created by the emperor Charles V in the 1530s, midwives had to give legal testimony and interrogate women jailed in cases of suspected abortion. Midwives themselves were prosecuted for aiding in or failing to report abortions. A Nuremberg ordinance of 1522 specified that midwives must be accompanied by three or four female persons when burying a child to guard against infanticide or abortion.

Whereas abortion was condemned or criminalized in medieval religious and legal thought, medical writing treated it for the most part impartially, as an objective matter of fact. Not until the late Middle Ages did some scientific writers censure or even demonize women who attempted abortion.

BIBLIOGRAPHY

PRIMARY WORKS

Institoris, Heinrich, and Jacob Sprenger. *Malleus maleficarum.* Translated by Montague Summers. 1928. Reprint, New York: Dover, 1971.

The Trotula: A Medieval Compendium of Women's Medicine. Edited and translated by Monica H. Green. Philadelphia: University of Pennsylvania Press, 2001.

SECONDARY WORKS

Demaitre, Luke. "Domesticity in Middle Dutch 'Secrets of Men and Women.'" *Social History of Medicine* 14 (2001): 1–25. Analyzes attitudes toward sexological information in a group of fourteenth- and fifteenth-century Middle Dutch translations and adaptations of *Secreta mulierum* and *Trotula.*

Green, Monica H. "Constantinus Africanus and the Conflict between Religion and Science." In *The Human Embryo: Aristotle and the Arabic Tradition.* Edited by G. R. Dunstan. Exeter: University of Exeter Press, 1990. The suppression of the chapter on abortifacients in Constantine's translation of Ibn al-Razzāz al-Jazarī's *Zad al-musafir.*

Greilsammer, Myriam. "The Midwife, the Priest, and the Physician: The Subjugation of Midwives in the Low Countries at the End of the Middle Ages." *Journal of Medieval and Renaissance Studies* 21 (1991): 285–329.

Noonan, John T. *Contraception: A History of Its Treatment by Catholic Theologians and Canonists.* Enl. ed. Cambridge, Mass.: Harvard University Press, 1986. Authoritative and broad in scope. Treats abortion as well as contraception.

Riddle, John M. *Contraception and Abortion from the Ancient World to the Renaissance.* Cambridge, Mass.: Harvard University Press, 1992.

Wiesner, Merry E. "Early Modern Midwifery: A Case Study." In *Women and Work in Preindustrial Europe.* Edited by Barbara A. Hanawalt. Bloomington: Indiana University Press, 1986. Surveys primary sources on the regulation of midwives in Nuremberg.

MARGARET SCHLEISSNER

[See also **DMA:** Contraception, European; Contraception, Islamic; Trota and Trotula; **Supp:** Childbirth and Infancy; Sexuality; Women.]

ACCIAIUOLI, Florentine merchant banking family. Along with the larger Bardi and Peruzzi companies, the Acciaiuoli company was one of the wealthiest and most powerful of the hundreds of Florentine merchant banking companies during the late thirteenth and early fourteenth centuries. The Florentine chronicler Giovanni Villani called the Bardi, the Peruzzi, and the Acciaiuoli "the pillars of Christian trade," and a modern scholar has labeled them "super-companies" on account of their size, the range of their economic activities, and their wide geographical reach. Originally from Brescia, the Acciaiuoli family migrated to Florence in the twelfth century. The company had major branches in Naples, Sicily,

France, Avignon, and England and along the eastern shore of the Adriatic Sea, especially Dubrovnik, where the company sold wheat and barley from southern Italy. The company had as many as forty-three factors working abroad in 1341, almost as many as the Peruzzi company. Unlike the Peruzzi and Bardi companies, the Acciaiuoli company was not significantly engaged in the wool trade. It was, however, heavily involved in the grain trade of southern Italy and a wide range of other activities, from manufacturing and merchandise trading to banking and money changing. By 1343, the Acciaiuoli, Peruzzi, and Bardi companies faced an economic crisis from which they would never recover. A number of factors contributed to their financial collapse: turmoil in Florence caused by wars, famines, and economic depression; high Florentine taxation; the loss of business in Rome due to strained relations between Florence and the papacy; and the default of Edward III of England on his loan repayments.

Much of the economic power of the Acciaiuoli stemmed from their prominent role in Florentine politics. As one of the most influential Florentine patrician families during the late thirteenth and early fourteenth centuries, members of the Acciaiuoli family were constantly being elected to the Signoria and the *balia* priorates. Moreover, much of Florence's electoral power lay in the hands of the Acciaiuoli and a handful of other patrician families. Indeed, between 1282 and 1532, the Acciaiuoli served ninety-one times in the Signoria; only six other families served more. While the Acciaiuoli company was very much a family operation, it did have shareholders who were not members of the family, and some family members chose not to involve themselves in the family business. Nonetheless, family loyalty mattered, and even those family members not directly engaged in the family business often found ways to provide or receive support from the company.

Even after the Acciaiuoli company went bankrupt in 1345, the family continued to play a major role in Florentine politics. One of the most prominent members of the family was Niccolò Acciaiuoli, who went to Naples in 1331 to oversee the family's interests there and in 1348 became grand seneschal and virtual ruler of the kingdom under Queen Joanna I. In 1434 Agnolo Acciaiuoli helped the Medici overcome the Albizzi. Although Agnolo was later found to be disloyal to the Medici and was exiled, most of the Acciaiuoli family was loyal to the Medici and was rewarded with important civil and ecclesiastical posts. Donato Acciaiuoli, a prominent diplomat and humanist, served as *gonfaloniere* (chief magistrate) of Florence in 1473 and gave the official eulogy for Cosimo

Niccolò Acciaiuoli. *Fresco by Andrea del Castagno from the* Famous Men and Women *series of 1448. Florence, Uffizi.* © ARTE & IMMAGINI SRL/CORBIS-BETTMANN. REPRODUCED BY PERMISSION.

de' Medici. Donato also wrote commentaries on Aristotle, published a Latin translation of some of Plutarch's *Lives,* and translated Leonardo Bruni's *Historia Florentini populi* (History of the Florentine people) into Italian.

BIBLIOGRAPHY

Hunt, Edwin S. *The Medieval Super-Companies: A Study of the Peruzzi Company of Florence.* Cambridge, U.K.: Cambridge University Press, 1994.

Sapori, Armando. *The Italian Merchant in the Middle Ages.* Translated by Patricia Ann Kennen. New York: Norton, 1970.

Tocco, Francesco Paolo. *Niccolò Acciaiuoli: Vita e politica in Italia alla metà del XIV secolo.* Rome: Instituto Palazzo Borromini, 2001.

ADAM JEFFREY DAVIS

[See also **DMA:** Banking, European; Trade, Western European.]

ACCURSIUS (*ca.* 1185–*ca.* 1266) was the creator of the standard gloss on the books of the Roman (civil) law. Born near Florence, he moved to Bologna to study civil law in the 1220s, at an older age than most students. By 1229 he is mentioned as a doctor of law, and at around the same time he began both to teach and to work on the gloss. Ever since the birth of the Bologna school of Roman law, much of the work of the jurists had focused on writing explanatory glosses on the texts of the civil law corpus. Accursius undertook the monumental task of assembling, choosing, and editing this accumulation of scholarship. While he modeled his work on the apparatus of his teacher Azo and, to a lesser extent, on that of Hugolinus, he also included glosses from twelfth-century jurists like Johannes Bassianus, Pillius, and Placentinus, all the way back to the early glossators Bulgarus and Irnerius. All told, the Accursian apparatus contains some 97,000 entries. Known as the *Glossa ordinaria*, it also quickly came to be called the *Magna glossa*, or great gloss, due to its size. Although he also wrote some of his own glosses, the work was in general not original. Accursius often copied verbatim from Azo and Hugolinus. The work's value came rather from its assimilation of around a hundred years of learning and from its completeness. Every part of the civil law corpus was glossed, including the *Libri feudorum* (Books of fiefs), which was added to the older Roman law in the mid-thirteenth century.

When it was published, the Accursian gloss almost immediately became the standard, or ordinary, gloss. It was copied or printed in the margins alongside virtually every copy of the civil law published between the mid-thirteenth and the seventeenth centuries. In part because of its intimate association with the text of the law and in part because a belief grew up that no one could understand the law without the aide of the gloss, Accursius's apparatus took on an authority of its own. Verona, for instance, passed a law in 1328 that the interpretation offered in the gloss was binding in the absence of a statute or long-standing custom. If the gloss contained several opinions, among them one by Accursius himself, the Accursian interpretation was given special deference. Indeed, so great was the authority of the gloss that a medieval maxim stated, "What the gloss does not recognize, the court does not recognize." Not merely a scholarly or pedagogical tool, the gloss also provided practitioners with explanations of abstract legal concepts and doctrines that they could use in litigation.

Although remembered primarily for the gloss, Accursius also wrote several summae, including one on the feudal law. In addition to teaching and scholarship, he practiced law and consulted in lawsuits. This work and some not particularly savory ventures, such as money lending to students and accepting bribes from students taking exams, brought him a substantial fortune. He had four sons; the three who lived to adulthood all became jurists. His son Franciscus assumed his father's chair at Bologna. The elder Accursius is also sometimes called Franciscus, so it is necessary to take care not to confuse father and son.

BIBLIOGRAPHY

Colliva, Paolo. "Documenti per la biografia di Accursio." In *Scritti minori*. Milan: A. Giuffrè, 1996. Edition of documents that shed light on the life of Accursius.

Feenstra, Robert. "Quelques remarques sur le texte de la Glose d'Accurse sur le Digeste Vieux." In *Fata iuris romani: Études d'histoire du droit*. Leiden, Netherlands: Leiden University Press, 1974.

Genzmer, Erich. "Zur Lebensgeschichte des Accursius." In *Festschrift für Leopold Wenger*. Vol. 2. Munich: C. H. Beck, 1945. Criticism of the Kantorowicz biography.

Kantorowicz, Hermann. "Accursio e la sua biblioteca." *Rivista di storia del diritto italiano* 2 (1929): 35–62, 193–212. Complete biography, although out of date in some particulars.

Rossi, Guido, ed. *Atti del Convegno internazionale di studî accursiani*. Milan: A. Giuffrè, 1968. Three volumes of studies in various languages on Accursius.

EMILY KADENS

[See also **DMA:** Law, Civil—Corpus Iuris, Revival and Spread; Law, Schools of; **Supp:** Johannes Bassianus; *Libri Feudorum*.]

ADALBERT, ST. (*ca.* 956–997), bishop of Prague. Originally named Woyciech, or Vojtěch, the future bishop was born into the aristocratic Slavnik family in Bohemia. At his consecration he took the name of his teacher, Adalbert, the first archbishop of Magdeburg. In 982 he was elected to be the second bishop of the new see of Prague. There Adalbert was frustrated by the persistence of pagan practices in his see, and he took refuge in Rome, where he developed close relations with the German emperor Otto III and joined the abbey of Sts. Boniface and Alexius. The Bohemian duke Boleslav II protested to the pope and emperor about Adalbert's abandonment of his episcopacy, and Adalbert eventually returned to his duties in Prague. His tenure as bishop remained tumultuous, however. Adalbert eventually so alienated the aristocrats of Prague that he was forced to return to Rome, and after members of his family were massacred in 995 by Boleslav in what seems to have been a dynastic dispute, Adalbert's exile became permanent.

In 997 Bolesław I Chrobry enlisted Adalbert to convert the pagan Prussians, and not incidentally extend the duke's political authority eastward. With papal permission, Adalbert began his mission, evangelizing briefly and with limited success among the Polanians in Gdansk and then sailing on to Samland to preach to the Prussians, who promptly martyred him. Bolesław recovered Adalbert's body and enshrined his relics under the altar at Gniezno.

In 1000, encouraged by the pope, Otto III made a pilgrimage to visit his friend Adalbert's relics at Gniezno, which he elevated to be the first metropolitan see in Poland. Although Polish rulers had been Christian since the conversion of Mieszko I in 966, this administrative reform fortified Poland's political as well as religious status. Otto and Bolesław sealed the occasion with an exchange of relics, with Otto receiving a portion of Adalbert's body.

Adalbert's precise role in the elimination of the Slavonic tradition from Poland remains disputed. His own family in Bohemia had adhered to the Slavonic rite, but certain sources depict him as forcibly eradicating the Slavic liturgy and even killing Slavic clergy. Other sources describe his attitude toward orthodoxy in a much more benign light. Either way, the Slavic rite would continue to be practiced in Poland for decades after his death.

Adalbert's cult developed first in Poland but then spread to Bohemia as well. The Bohemian duke Břetislav took advantage of the pagan rebellion that erupted after the death of Mieszko II in 1034 not only to capture Kraków and Gniezno but also to translate Adalbert's relics forcibly from Gniezno to Prague. According to a twelfth-century Bohemian chronicle, Adalbert resisted translation, rendering those attempting to move his body blind and dumb. Only after the duke and his men promised to be better Christians did the saint allow his relics to be transported.

Once returned to Prague, Adalbert became, along with St. Wenceslas, a protector of the Czech people. This in no way diminished his status in Poland as a martyred saint, which continued to grow in the twelfth century as the movement to convert and conquer the Prussians intensified.

BIBLIOGRAPHY

PRIMARY WORKS

Adam of Bremen. *Hamburgische kirchengeschichte.* Edited by Bernhard Schmeidler. Scriptores rerum Germanicarum in usum scholarum ex Monumentis Germaniae historicis. Hannover and Leipzig, Germany: Hohnsche, 1917. Edition with German translation of *Gesta Hammaburgensis ecclesiae pontificum.*

Bielowski, August, ed. *Monumenta Poloniae Historicae: Pomniki Dziejowe Polski.* 6 vols. Lvov, Poland: Nakładem Własnym, 1864–1893. See especially "Passio Sancti Adalperti Martiris," volume 1, and "Chronica principum Polonie," volume 3.

Canaparius, Joannes. *Das Leben des Bischofs Adalbert von Prag.* Translated by Hermann Hüffer. Berlin: W. Besser, 1857. Life of Adalbert.

Cosmas of Prague. *Die Chronik der Böhmen des Cosmas von Prag.* Edited by Bertold Bretholz and Wilhelm Weinberger. Monumenta Germaniae Historica, Scriptores rerum germanicarum, n.s., 2. Berlin: W. Besser, 1923. German edition of *Cosmas's Chronica Boemorum.*

Warner, David A., ed. and trans. *Ottonian Germany: The Chronicon of Thietmar of Merseburg.* Manchester, U.K., and New York: Manchester University Press, 2001.

SECONDARY WORKS

Łowmiański, Henryk. "The Slavic Rite in Poland and St. Adalbert." *Acta Poloniae Historica* 24 (1971): 5–21.

Vlasto, A. P. *The Entry of the Slavs into Christendom: An Introduction to the Medieval History of the Slavs.* Cambridge, U.K.: Cambridge University Press, 1970. See especially the chapter "The Western Slavs."

Wolverton, Lisa. *Hastening toward Prague: Power and Society in the Medieval Czech Lands.* Philadelphia: University of Pennsylvania Press, 2001.

ELSPETH JANE CARRUTHERS

[See also **DMA**: Adalbert, St. (*d.* 981); Otto III, Emperor; Slavs, Origins of; **Supp**: Bolesław I Chrobry of Poland, King; Mieszko I of Poland, King; Paganism and Pagan Gods, Survival of; Wenceslas, St.]

ADMIRAL, from the Arabic *amîr* (commander or leader) and *al* (of). In the Islamic world *amîr-al* preceded many titles, and Christian writers took it to be one word, which they then assimilated and reproduced in their own tongues.

The first Christian admirals (*amiratus* or *admiralius* in Latin) appeared in the kingdom of Sicily, where after the Norman Conquest (1071), Christian knights were given the titles once held by Muslim emirs. The office was originally an administrative post in charge of fiscal administration and the organization of naval as well as land forces. Indeed, some of the earlier admirals distinguished themselves by fighting on land.

In the first half of the twelfth century, admirals in Sicily—multiple men held the title concurrently—were associated with diverse offices in the curia ranging from treasurers to chamberlains, as the title was not exclusively linked to naval officers. Most of the officeholders were Greek, reflecting the expertise in administration that the office demanded and in which the Greeks excelled.

Among these admirals, there was usually a grand admiral who was the chief minister of the crown and who coordinated the other admirals. Beyond their fiscal and military duties, these men distinguished themselves in other areas. The *amiratus amiratorum* (admiral of admirals) George of Antioch founded the church of La Martorana in Palermo, and his successor, Maio of Bari, built the church of San Cataldo. Even more notable was Eugenius of Palermo, who won fame as a political philosopher and man of letters. By the end of the twelfth century, however, the office had declined to an honorary position or to the naval role now associated with it, as the first of the true naval admirals, Margaritus of Brindisi, emerged to lead the Sicilian fleet during wartime.

SPREAD BEYOND SICILY

Taking the Sicilian example, other Mediterranean maritime powers soon adopted the office. By the early thirteenth century, most of the Italian city-states and the Crown of Aragon had admirals and even vice-admirals, as did Castile. The different polities usually adapted the office to meet their own local needs. In Venice, for example, the *armiraio* was in charge of the arsenal where the Venetian galleys were built. Other polities tasked their admirals with the organization of royal fleets, the licensing of corsairs for privateering duties, and the prevention of piracy. Eventually, the admirals' duties extended into the sphere of law, as they exercised legal jurisdiction over most naval matters. These included settling mercantile disputes, imposing and maintaining discipline within the fleet and its sailors, and presiding in other cases that had to do with the sea.

The northern European powers took longer to incorporate admirals into their military ranks, but France had one by the late 1240s, and the title first appears in England in 1295, when two of the household knights of Edward I were identified as admirals. In 1300 the English appointed their first admiral of the fleet, Gervase Alard, and there was an admiral of England by the time of Henry V (*r.* 1413–1422). The English admirals were not only tasked with leading the fleet in combat but also with all the logistics attached to naval warfare, including impressing ships and crews; gathering all the supplies, ammunition, and weapons; and even refitting ships that might not be ready for combat.

English and French admirals were likely to be drawn from the upper aristocracy and often lacked significant naval experience. For instance, when the Hundred Years War began, the earls of Arundel and Suffolk were among the nobles who held the title, and the first admiral of England was Thomas Beaufort, the duke of Exeter and

uncle to the king. These men relied on deputies who advised them on naval matters. Their Mediterranean counterparts, on the other hand, were often career seamen or at the very least had some degree of experience fighting naval battles. Thus, when the War of the Sicilian Vespers broke out (1282), Peter III of Aragon quickly replaced his illegitimate son as admiral of the fleet with the more experienced Roger de Lauria and Conrad Lancia. Roger de Lauria, in particular, would reward that decision with some of the most decisive naval victories of the entire medieval period.

NAVAL WARFARE

In a naval battle, an experienced and skilled admiral could often make the difference between victory and defeat. In spite of the fact that medieval battles often degenerated into disorganized affairs with leaders exercising a very small degree of control once the action began, there were still a lot of tactical and strategic decisions that a good admiral could make to increase his chances of success. Naval battles were fought by fleets of galleys and auxiliary ships, which attempted to grapple with one another and capture the enemy vessels. Before clashing, the archers and crossbowmen on board harassed the enemy with missile fire. Sometimes galley fleets bound the individual ships together to form a solid line through which the enemy could not break and to create a more stable platform on which to fight. When the two fleets finally came together, it was up to the embarked infantry to carry the day, as knights fought one another on the rolling decks much as they fought on land.

The admiral could affect the outcome mostly by the decisions he made before battle. Among the most important decisions was figuring out where to fight. Depending on the strengths of his fleet, an admiral could opt to fight in the open water or near the coast or even to beach his galleys and fight with his ships grounded—a useful tactic that gave the ships a lot of stability and easy access to reinforcements. Crew preparation and discipline were also critical, since having a subordinate break line or attack out of order could crush any chance for victory. Deciding what types of troops to have on board could also make a difference. Heavily armored knights, for instance, were of limited use on pitching and rolling decks and were often defeated when the enemy deployed light infantry. Resourceful admirals also employed trickery and innovations. For example, oil was sprayed by Castilian ships against the English at the battle of La Rochelle (1372); when lit, the oil set the English galleys afire. The wind, tide, and even the sun could provide useful allies to those admirals who knew how to use them. Consequently, the kingdoms that enjoyed the service of competent admirals ruled the seas at the expense of their neighbors.

BIBLIOGRAPHY

Brooks, F. W. *The English Naval Forces, 1199–1272*. 1932. Reprint, London: Pordes, 1962.

Jamison, Evelyn. *Admiral Eugenius of Sicily: His Life and Work*. London: Oxford University Press, 1957.

Lane, Frederic C. *Venice: A Maritime Republic*. Baltimore: Johns Hopkins University Press, 1973.

Lewis, Archibald, and Timothy J. Runyan. *European Naval and Maritime History, 300–1500*. Bloomington: Indiana University Press, 1985.

Prestwich, Michael. *Armies and Warfare in the Middle Ages: The English Experience*. New Haven, Conn.: Yale University Press, 1996. See esp. ch. 11, "The Navy."

Pryor, John H. "The Naval Battles of Roger of Lauria." *Journal of Medieval History* 9 (1983): 179–216.

Takayama, Hiroshi. *The Administration of the Norman Kingdom of Sicily*. Leiden, Netherlands: Brill, 1993.

JARBEL RODRIGUEZ

[See also **DMA**: Navies, Western.]

ADOLESCENCE. See **Childhood and Adolesence.**

AGE AND AGING. See **Old Age.**

ALBERICUS DE ROSATE (*ca.* 1290–1360), an influential jurist, was born in Rosciate, near Bergamo, and studied in Padua under Oldradus de Ponte, Riccardus Malumbra, and Ranieri di Forlì. He knew and sought counsel from Bartolo de Sassoferrato. Although he wrote an impressive number of legal works in Roman and canon law, he did not have a teaching career but instead practiced law as an advocate after returning to Bergamo around 1310. Albericus played a significant role in the political life of Bergamo by helping to revise the city statutes of 1331. He was the Visconti's ambassador on many diplomatic missions and served at the papal court in Avignon from 1335 to 1341. Albericus also had a literary bent, as seen in his translations of Jacopo della Lana's commentary on Dante's *Commedia* into Latin. He died on 14 September 1360 in Bergamo.

Albericus's commentaries on Roman and canon law circulated widely and were printed frequently in the fifteenth and sixteenth centuries. The *Dictionarium iuris tam civilis quam canonici* was his most popular work. It was one of the first dictionaries of legal terms in the European *ius commune* and served as a foundation for later reference works. His major works of Roman law were commentaries on the Digest and Code of canon law. Because of his interest in local statutory law, he wrote a treatise on the interpretation of statutes that was widely cited. In canon law he wrote a commentary on the *Liber sextus* of Pope Boniface VIII.

Like his near contemporary Dante Alighieri, he was a vigorous supporter of the German emperor's authority and power. In his commentary on the Digest, Albericus produced an extended and nuanced discussion of the emperor's *potestas absoluta* (absolute power). He defined absolute power as the right of the emperor to exercise his authority arbitrarily, though he also stipulated that this authority must be exercised legally. This definition made Albericus perhaps the first jurist to grant the emperor such unbridled power. He argued that the emperor occupies the office of God on earth and could confiscate the goods of his subjects even without cause. When discussing papal and imperial power, he relied on Dante's *Monarchia* and John of Paris's *De regia potestate et papali*.

As a jurist, Albericus represented a position that was unusual in the Middle Ages. He advocated a strict separation of church and state, exalted imperial authority, and granted the pope the same authority within the church as the emperor exercised in the secular world.

BIBLIOGRAPHY

PRIMARY WORKS

Commentaria in Digesto et Codice. 1585–1586. Reprint, Bologna: A. Forni, 1974–1982.

Commentarium super sextum librum Decretalium. In *Recueil des traites des illustres iurisconsultes*. 1585.

Dictionarium iuris tam civilis quam canonici. 1481. 1583 edition reprint, Turin, Italy: Bottega d'Erasmo, 1971.

SECONDARY WORKS

Cremaschi, G. "Contributi alla biografia di Alberico da Rosciate." *Bergomum* 50 (1956): 3–102.

Prosdocimi, Luigi. "Alberico da Rosciate e la giurisprudenza italiana del secolo XIV." *Bergomum* 49 (1955): 1–7. (Also in *Rivista di storia del diritto italiano* 29 (1956): 67–78.

———. "Alberico da Rosate." In *Dizionario biografico degli Italiani*. Edited by Alberto M. Ghisalberti. Vol. 1. Rome: Istituto della enciclopedia italiana, 1960.

Weimar, P. "Albericus de Rosate." In *Lexikon des Mittelalters*. Edited by Robert Auty et al. Vol. 1. Munich, Germany: Artemis, 1977.

KENNETH PENNINGTON

[See also **DMA:** Law, Canon: After Gratian; Law, Canon: To Gratian; Law, Civil—Corpus Iuris, Revival and Spread; Law Codes: 1000–1500.]

ALBERTANO DA BRESCIA (**Albertanus of Brescia,** *ca.* 1195–after 1251), author of social treaties and sermons. Little is known of his early life and education. He had three sons, Vincent, Stephen, and John, the last of whom was a surgeon. Aldo Checchini argued on the basis of legal citations and his use of rhetoric in his treatises that Albertano studied at the University of Bologna, but an examination of evidence regarding his writings and career associates him with notaries and *causidici* (professional legal counselors) rather than lawyers. He first appears in 1226 in a document renewing the Lombard League, where he is referred to as a judge. In 1238, he was named captain to defend the important town of Gavardo, near Lake Garda, against the forces of the Holy Roman Emperor Frederick II. Forced to surrender, he was imprisoned for some months in Cremona, where he began his writing career.

His treatise *De amore et dilectione Dei et proximi et aliarum rerum et de forma vitae* (On love and delight in God and in neighbor and other matters concerning the rule of life; 1238) revealed his debt to Seneca's *Ad Lucilium* as well as to Christian conceptions of life under the aegis of religious rules. In 1243, while in Genoa in the company of a fellow Brescian, Emmanuel de Madiis (di Maggi), he delivered a sermon to a confraternity of notaries, in which he emphasized their place in public life. In 1245, he expanded on this in his treatise *De doctrina dicendi et tacendi* (On teaching about speech and silence). He wrote his best-known work, *Liber consolationis et consilii* (The book of consolation and counsel), a penetrating investigation of the causes of human violence, in 1246. Finally, in 1250, he delivered four sermons explaining the meaning of their rule to a confraternity composed of his fellow *causidici* in Brescia. From the beginning, his chief goal was to set forth a rule of life *(propositum)* that would provide the foundation for a good society. He drew on deep reading, especially in Seneca, Cicero, Augustine, the Wisdom literature of the Old Testament, and a number of twelfth-century authors. In many ways, the confraternities of his time served as a model, but he also drew on his experience of communal life in Brescia. Central to his thought was the importance of moral restraint based on voluntary participation in a community, which encapsulated an early theory of consent. In his *De doctrina dicendi et tacendi,* he explored the role of an emerging professionalism in public life. His *Liber consolationis et consilii* provided a dramatic and insightful dialogue about the urban vendetta. His Brescian sermons opened a window on thirteenth-century confraternity life and helped to explain how Albertano's thought achieved a synthesis through his practical experience. Although he influenced such major figures as Geoffrey Chaucer, Brunetto Latini, the author of *Le ménagier de Paris,* Christine de Pizan, and John Gower, there is abundant evidence of his much broader impact on society. The numerous translations of his treatises into French, German, Tuscan, Venetian, Spanish, Dutch, and other languages and the widespread circulation of his works demonstrate the value placed on them well into the late fifteenth and early sixteenth centuries.

BIBLIOGRAPHY

PRIMARY WORKS

Albertano da Brescia. *Sermo Januensis.* Translated, with introduction and notes, by Oscar Nuccio. Brescia, Italy: Industrie Grafiche Bresciane, 1994.

———. *The Four Sermons of Albertanus of Brescia: An Edition.* Edited with translation, notes, and introduction by Gregory W. Ahlquist. M.A. thesis, Syracuse University, 1997.

———. *Liber de doctrina dicendi et tacendi: La parola del cittadino nell'Italia del Duecento.* Edited by Paola Navone. Florence, Italy: Edizioni del Galluzzo, 1998. Contains bibliography.

SECONDARY WORKS

Checchini, Aldo. "Un giudice del secolo decimoterzo: Albertano da Brescia." *Atti del reale istituto veneto di scienze, lettere, ed arti* 71 (1911–1912): 1423–1495.

Graham, Angus. "Albertanus of Brescia: A Preliminary Census of Vernacular Manuscripts." *Studi Medieval* 41 (2000): 891–924.

Powell, James M. *Albertanus of Brescia: The Pursuit of Happiness in the Early Thirteenth Century.* Philadelphia: University of Pennsylvania Press, 1992. Contains bibliography.

Spinelli, Franco, ed. *Albertano da Brescia: Alle origini del razionalismo economico, dell'umanesimo civile, della grande Europa.* Brescia, Italy: Grafo, 1996.

JAMES M. POWELL

ALEXANDER IV, POPE (1199–1261). Related to the influential di Segni family, which had already produced two popes (Innocent III and Gregory IX), Rainaldo (or Rinaldo) dei Conti became Pope Alexander IV on 12 December 1254 in Naples, where the mayor had locked the city gates to force the cardinals to proceed with the election. Rainaldo, who inherited the county of Jenne from his father, began his ecclesiastical career sometime before 1209, when he was *magister* in the cathedral chapter of Anagni. By 1219 he was a chaplain for Honorius

III and, soon after, for his uncle Hugolino of Ostia. When Hugolino became Gregory IX in 1227, he elevated Rainaldo to the cardinalate; four years later Rainaldo succeeded his uncle as the cardinal-bishop of Ostia and as the protector of the Franciscan order, a position he kept even when pope. As papal chamberlain, he was familiar with the challenges facing the papacy, dealing frequently with Emperor Frederick II. His experience, politics of compromise, personal piety, and collegiality, a quality particularly lacking in his predecessor Innocent IV, made Rainaldo an appealing successor in 1254.

As pope, Alexander inherited a struggle to drive the Hohenstaufen from power. Although his predecessors had successfully ended Hohenstaufen rule in Germany, Manfred, a legitimated son of Frederick II, ruled Sicily and aspired to control all of Italy. He had broken the agreements made with Innocent IV, so on 25 March 1255 Alexander excommunicated the Hohenstaufen prince. Manfred, however, defeated a papal army in September at Foggia, gaining control over the rest of southern Italy and Sicily, and on 10 August 1258 he was crowned king in Palermo. As overlord of Sicily, Alexander refused to acknowledge Manfred's authority and declared Edmund, the young son of Henry III of England, king of Sicily. Henry III rashly agreed to pay the papacy's debts in return, an exchange he later realized was more expensive than he had originally thought. Furthermore, he supported Henry's brother, Richard of Cornwall, as king of Germany—despite the fact that Alexander was the guardian of Conradin, Conrad IV's son, who had a claim to both Germany and Sicily. Alexander also struggled to maintain authority over Rome itself. In the spring of 1257 Manfred's ally Brancaleone returned to power in Rome and established a commune similar to those found in northern Italian cities. Manfred himself became a candidate for senator of Rome in 1261 after he defeated the Florentines in the battle of Montaperti on 4 September 1260.

Alexander's career, however, cannot be reduced to his struggle against Manfred. He curtailed the abused papal right of provisions, which allowed the pope to nominate successors to vacant positions. In 1256 he reopened negotiations with the Empire of Nicaea on reunion of the churches and began planning for a crusade against the Mongols. Alexander also authorized the successful crusade against Ezzelino da Romano and his brother Alberich. Continuing his support of the Franciscan legacy, he canonized Clare of Assisi in 1255, only two years after her death. He himself founded the Augustinian Hermits in 1256 and enthusiastically enforced the friars' right to teach at the University of Paris in 1256, a controversy that led to the exile of the noted teacher William of St. Amour for his opposition and to years of hostile feelings in Paris. Alexander IV died at Viterbo on 25 May 1261, having uncertain authority in Rome and seeing Manfred triumphant throughout Italy.

BIBLIOGRAPHY

Bourel de la Roncière, Charles. *Les registres d'Alexandre IV: Recueil des bulles de ce pape publiées ou analysées d'après les manuscripts originaux des archives du Vatican.* 3 vols. Paris: A. Fontemoing, 1903–1953.

Sibilia, Salvatore. *Alessandro IV (1254–1261).* Anagni, Italy: A cura della Cassa rurale ed artigiana di Anagni, 1961.

Thomson, Williel R. "The Earliest Cardinal-Protectors of the Franciscan Order: A Study in Administrative History, 1210–1261." *Studies in Medieval and Renaissance History* 9 (1972): 21–80.

CHRISTOPHER HATCH MacEVITT

[See also **DMA:** Gregory IX, Pope; Guelphs and Ghibellines; Hohenstaufen Dynasty; Nicaea, Empire of; Paris, University of; Provisions, Ecclesiastical; Sicily, Kingdom of.]

ALEXANDER DE VILLA DEI (Alexander of Villedieu, *ca.* 1170–*ca.* 1250), the author of popular metrical treatises on a variety of subjects, was born in Villedieu, in lower Normandy. He studied in Paris and collaborated with two friends, Ivo and Adolphus, on a massive collection of notes on grammar that they put into verse. The bishop of Dol shortly called upon Alexander to tutor his two nephews in grammar. Drawing upon the notes he and his friends had put together, Alexander prepared a rhymed grammar for the bishop's nephews with the hope that it would facilitate their memorization of the rules of grammar. The result was Alexander's famous *Doctrinale puerorum,* a grammar textbook of 2,645 leonine hexameters, finished around 1199. Along with the *Graecismus* of Evrard of Béthune, the *Doctrinale* became the standard way students learned Latin grammar for centuries to come. Approximately 250 manuscript copies of the *Doctrinale* survive from 1259 to 1526, and 267 separate printed editions from 1470 to 1588. In the introduction to the *Doctrinale,* Alexander was quite candid about having incorporated material, sometimes verbatim, from Priscian, Donatus, and dozens of other authors (many of them from the twelfth century), simply recasting their work in metrical form. By using mnemonic verses in the instruction of grammar, Evrard and Alexander popularized a new approach to teaching, one that carried over into other subjects that were part of the university curriculum, including arithmetic, biblical studies, and music.

By 1202 Alexander had completed another poem, the *Ecclesiale,* a verse *computus* (or book on how to reckon church festivals) that also describes the liturgical year and deals with a range of other subjects. It is clear from the *Ecclesiale* that Alexander bitterly opposed the school at Orléans, where the curriculum emphasized the ancient classical authors. Alexander also composed a popular metrical treatise on arithmetic, the *Carmen de algorismo.* Much of this treatise is drawn from a translation of *Kitāb al mukhtaṣar fī-ḥisāb al-jabr w'al-muqābala* (Compendious book on calculation by completion and balancing) by the ninth-century Muslim mathematician Muḥammad ibn Mūsā al-Khwārizmī. Alexander also composed a metrical treatise on the computation of the calendar, the *Massa compoti,* and a metrical summary of the Bible, the *Summarium biblicum.* It has been suggested that an influential musical treatise written in poetic form and contained in a manuscript held by the Vatican Library is also likely the work of Alexander. The treatise, which appears to have been used to teach young choirboys, deals primarily with plainchant but also has much to say about use of the B-flat and *musica falsa* (the introduction of chromatic notes into modal music; the earliest known reference to this term), which had only recently come into being with the introduction of polyphony. It would not be surprising if the musical treatise was authored by Alexander, since it is similar to his other treatises, and Alexander is known to have spent his later years as the choirmaster of the cathedral of St. Andrew in Avranches, where he died.

BIBLIOGRAPHY

Alexander de Villa Dei. *Das Doctrinale des Alexander de Villa-Dei.* Edited by Dietrich Reichling. 1893. Reprint, New York: Burt Franklin, 1974. A critical edition of the *Doctrinale,* a description of the numerous manuscript copies, and an analysis of the text.

———. *Ecclesiale.* Edited and translated by L. R. Lind. Lawrence: University of Kansas Press, 1958.

Waite, William G. "Two Musical Poems of the Middle Ages." In *Musik und Geschichte: Leo Schrade zum sechzigsten Geburtstag.* Cologne, Germany: Arno Volk Verlag, 1963. Argues that a musical treatise is the work of Alexander de Villa Dei.

ADAM JEFFREY DAVIS

[See also **DMA:** Calendars and Reckoning of Time; Grammar; Mathematics; **Supp:** Liturgical Year, Western.]

ALFONSO V OF ARAGON (**Alfonso IV in Catalonia,** 1396–1458).

Alfonso V was born in Castile, the eldest son of Ferdinand de Antequera, who was the youn-

ger brother of Henry III of Castile. In 1410, Martin I of Aragon died heirless, triggering a succession crisis. Ferdinand emerged victorious, and the Compromise of Caspe awarded him the throne in 1412. In 1416, however, Ferdinand died, and Alfonso succeeded him at the age of twenty. His reign witnessed the expansion of Aragonese power into Naples and other parts of Italy but also rancorous divisions at home, especially in Catalonia, and a loss of prestige and influence in his native Castile, which his family had essentially ruled during the royal minority of John II. Alfonso also played a decisive role in ending the Great Schism that divided the papacy between Rome and Avignon when he withdrew his support for Benedict XIII.

The early years of Alfonso's reign were marked by repeated efforts to establish working relationships with his numerous realms. The results were mixed. In Valencia he found a kingdom willing to work with him and to grant him the resources in money and materiel that his numerous enterprises required. Catalonia was at the other extreme, constantly refusing to grant the king monetary aid and frustrating his designs, as the Catalans sought to protect and expand their constitutional rights.

Hoping to win Catalonia over, Alfonso sought a mutually agreeable objective and found one in the Catalans' old nemesis, Genoa. By 1420 he was ready to proceed against Genoese interests in Sardinia and Corsica. Sardinia, already part of his realm, was pacified in a brief campaign, but Corsica would not give in so easily and remained in Genoese hands.

In Sardinia, Alfonso received word from Queen Giovanna II of Naples offering to make him her heir in return for military aid against the Angevins and their allies. In July 1421, Alfonso entered Naples as the heir to the throne. However, he would soon receive a lesson in the complexities of Italian politics, as Naples rebelled in favor of the Angevins in 1423.

At the height of the Neapolitan crisis, Alfonso was forced to return to Spain, as the rashness of his younger brothers threatened to undermine his influence in Castile. Castile became a prolonged struggle, and by the end of the decade Alfonso decided to give up his power there so that he could devote his energies to Italy. He departed for Naples in 1432. He would never set foot in Spain again.

For the next ten years his forces fought to gain control of the elusive kingdom. Alfonso was even captured and became the prisoner of the duke of Milan. It was a fortuitous setback, as Alfonso and the duke entered into an alliance that divided Italy between them. In 1443 he entered Naples and was crowned king.

The last part of his reign was marked by efforts to revive the Neapolitan economy and bureaucracy, wrecked by years of war; to keep his brothers' Castilian ambitions in check; and to maintain his authority over his Aragonese kingdoms, where his prolonged absence was beginning to take a toll. Catalonia, in particular, was growing divided along social lines and would explode into civil war in 1462, following decades of royal neglect. Alfonso meanwhile stayed in Naples, trusting his governors, his wife Maria, and his brother John to run the kingdoms. In June 1458 he died, leaving no legitimate heirs, and was succeeded by John—part of the price of being away from his kingdom, subjects, and wife for most of his reign.

BIBLIOGRAPHY

Bisson, Thomas. *The Medieval Crown of Aragon*. Oxford: Clarendon Press, 1986. Excellent introduction to Alfonso's reign.

Ryder, Alan. *The Kingdom of Naples Under Alfonso the Magnanimous: The Making of a Modern State*. Oxford: Clarendon Press, 1976.

————. *Alfonso the Magnanimous: King of Aragon, Naples, and Sicily, 1396–1458*. Oxford: Clarendon Press, 1990. A highly readable and impeccably researched biography of Alfonso V.

JARBEL RODRIGUEZ

[See also **DMA:** Angevins: France, England, Sicily; Aragon, Crown of (1137–1479); Castile; Italy, Fourteenth and Fifteenth Centuries; Naples.]

ALLITERATIVE LITERATURE in English was written throughout the medieval period, from the seventh-century Anglo-Saxon Cædmon's *Hymn* to the early-sixteenth-century Scottish *Gologras and Gawain*. However, it is less a discrete literary tradition than a process of continual experimentation, reinvention, and cross-fertilization with other literary forms. These forms include most notably rhythmical prose; English chronicle history; Latin historical, biblical, and scholastic traditions; and French courtly romance, Anglo-Norman romance, and English insular romance.

TWO MEDIEVAL VIEWS OF ALLITERATIVE WRITING

Several medieval English writers situate alliterative writing as distinctive among other forms of writing, while raising new questions about its practice. The "Life of St. Kenelm" in the *South English Legendary* (*ca.* 1280) tells how a child-king's murder is exposed by a line of alliterative writing direct from God. St. Kenelm is killed by his treacherous sister and buried secretly beneath a thornbush in a remote valley in the Welsh Marches. However, years later and far away in Rome, as the pope is holding Mass, a white dove alights and drops a beautiful piece of writing on the altar. The pope, expert in the Latin most usually associated with the word of God, nevertheless cannot read this writing until some Englishmen at the papal court interpret it for him: "Þe writ was iwrite pur Engliss as me radde it þere, / And to telle it wiþoute ryme þis wordes riȝt it were / In Clent Coubach Kenelm, kynges bern / Liþ vnder an þorn, heued bireued'" (That writing was written in pure English, as men read it there, / and these are the correct words of it, told without rhyme here: "In Cowbach valley, Kenelm, king's son / lies beneath a thornbush, his head riven from him"). In this story, the dove assumes the same shape as the murdered Kenelm's departing soul (as well as that of God's spirit), and so the writing is almost like the saint's own voice, telling of his death from beyond a desolate grave. But what makes the incident even more compelling is the way the *Legendary* breaks off its brisk and lilting end-rhymed seven-stress line to perform the alliterative difference of these golden letters. This thirteenth-century saint's life dramatically presents alliterative writing as a quandary: gorgeous, sanctified, desolate, and peculiarly English. It becomes the divine ratification of the tale's English regionalizing imperatives.

The "Life of St. Kenelm" differentiates English alliterative writing from Latin while bringing them into a productive congress with each other; at the same time, it infuses alliterative writing with both celestial power and regional homeliness. Later, Chaucer's *Canterbury Tales* makes several provocative assumptions about the differences between alliterative literature and other forms of Middle English writing, when it contrasts northern alliteration against southern end-rhymed, syllabic verse. Chaucer's stern Parson disclaims northern alliterative frivolity and then goes on to discard southern rhyming poetry as well: "I am a Southren man; / I kan nat geeste [tell stories] 'rum, ram, ruf,' by lettre, / Ne, God woot, rym holde I but litel bettre." Instead, the Parson chooses to tell "a merry tale in prose" that turns out to be not a merry tale at all but a serious sermon. The Parson was a key witness for many earlier twentieth-century scholars who wanted to define fourteenth-century alliterative literature through precisely these oppositions—northern versus southern, alliteration versus rhyme, poetry versus prose. Scholars such as R. W. Chambers associated late medieval alliterative writing with English nationalism and with native English resistance to continental cultural influences. James Root Hulbert further argued that late medieval alliterative literature expressed northern provincial baronial resistance to the fourteenth-century English monarchy, which based its major apparatus of government in the south and cultivated a French-influenced courtliness.

Yet what is interesting in the Parson's speech is that he emphatically positions himself as a distant outsider to all these literary traditions in order to dismiss them. Since the late twentieth century, scholars have been more willing to get involved and have complicated the Parson's oppositions. If alliterative writing is northern or provincial, it is also shows both interest in and familiarity with London (*St. Erkenwald* and *Piers Plowman,* for example) and the royal court itself (*Sir Gawain, Pearl,* and *Morte Arthure*). And the metrical diversity of alliterative verse incorporates rhyme schemes of all kinds, internal and end rhymed, sometimes taking alliteration, rhyme, and a host of other prosodic features to staggering extremes. Finally and most interestingly, alliterative literature moves easily between poetry and prose forms, showing an openness to influence that nurtured medieval alliterative literature throughout its thousand-year flowering.

Alliterative literature is striking for its diversity of forms, genres, and strategies and for its enormous stylistic flexibility. *Piers Plowman* (A-version, *ca.* 1370; B-version, *ca.* 1377; and C-version, before 1388) can move in a blink from slangy colloquialism to stately erudition, while *Beowulf* (before 1000) and the alliterative *Morte Arthure* (*ca.* 1360–1410) can dramatize shattering battles and plangent burials with equal dexterity. Alliterative literature spans formal and informal poetry, rhythmic prose, and drama. The York Corpus Christi pageant (1376–1569) shows dramatic alliterative originality, and the Wakefield-Master's plays interweave rhyme and alliteration to tremendous effect. Alliterative literature appears in virtually every medieval literary genre: historical epic, biblical and Christian epic, chivalric romance, English chronicle history, lyric, debate poem, dream vision, didactic, political satire and social commentary, saint's life, and prophecy. In the fifteenth century, alliterative poetry became very popular among Scottish writers, who extended the form to beast fable and political allegory.

PRODUCTION, AUTHORSHIP, AND AUDIENCE

Alliterative literature is also famous for the difficulties it has posed modern scholars. As a literary form it is most often associated with English vernacular writing, but elaborate alliterative poetic forms are found in early Welsh heroic-age and later court-centered ceremonial poetry (often accompanied by internal rhyme) and in post-twelfth-century Irish bardic poetry (interwoven

with syllabic patterns and rhyme). Alliterative passages enliven Peter of Langtoft's Anglo-Norman *Chronicle* (*ca.* 1280–1307), and the fourteenth-century devotional writer Richard Rolle even bent Latin to alliterative rhythms.

Manuscript survival for alliterative literature has been sporadic, and we therefore cannot accurately map the popularity or social pervasiveness of alliterative writing. Most alliterative texts survive only in single and late manuscript exemplars, and most are anonymous, separated from their original provenances, scribally emended, and translated between regions and dialects. They are therefore only tenuously dateable.

Most alliterative poetic works cannot be pinned to original provenances. Scholars have argued persuasively for the involvement of monastic and clerical establishments and their libraries, the royal court and its functionaries, and the clerical and household staff of the provincial gentry. Precise authorship is a mystery as well, though evidently many were clerically trained, widely read, and multilingual in French and Latin. They were probably not paid for their literary work; there is little evidence throughout much of the period for any systematic patronage of writers or poets. Professional minstrel authorship is possible for early Middle English works but more unlikely by the fourteenth century. We are luckier with alliterative rhythmical prose: it is often clerically produced, associated with didactic themes, homily, and exhortation, and we tend to know more about its authors, from Aelfric and Wulfstan in the eleventh century through to Richard Rolle in the fourteenth.

Original audiences are also unknown. Many formal poems invoke an implied audience and milieu, usually aristocratic, and often address the didactic, historical, devotional, and romance themes that interested the nobility (to judge from what we can ascertain about the content of their libraries). However, the actual manuscripts that survive are modest and workmanlike, very unlike the conspicuous and lavish manuscripts commissioned by the royal court and aristocracy for their libraries and private collections. The informal tradition seems to direct itself to many possible audiences: *The Parlement of the Thre Ages* (*ca.* 1350) begins with an engaging description of a poacher at his work, and there is evidence that William Langland's *Piers Plowman* was eagerly read by the artisans and laborers who organized the rising of 1381. Vernacular literacy was increasing in the fourteenth and fifteenth centuries, when many alliterative manuscripts were produced. In London and other urban centers, professional print shops began to supplement monastic scriptoria as sites of book production. This bespeaks a widening interest in literature of all kinds by readers in different social situations and may help explain the wide diversity of late medieval alliterative literary forms and topics.

THE ALLITERATIVE TRADITION AND ITS DISCONTENTS

Alliterative literature has traditionally been seen as oppositional to the literary trends that eventually achieved cultural dominance, exemplified most importantly by the Chaucerian tradition. Early-twentieth-century scholarship tried to establish a unified alliterative tradition spanning Old English, early Middle English, and late Middle English writings. J. P. Oakden's two-volume metrical and dialectical study found significant continuities between alliterative works from different periods, while R. W. Chambers posited a lost but unbroken oral alliterative tradition, sustaining the native strain and emerging at key moments into written form. Unfortunately, there are significant breaks in the alliterative manuscript record, gaps created by the Norman Conquest and the two-hundred-year demotion of English as a culturally authorized language. Between 1066 and the late fourteenth century, French and Latin replaced English as languages of aristocratic culture, literature, learning, religious doctrine, politics, and legal process. Throughout the period, therefore, many writers were functionally trilingual, and recent scholarship has stressed the complex interplay of English, French, and Latin in a range of differing social milieus. To complicate matters further, at this time English was changing linguistically, losing its case endings and evolving new syntactical and phrasal structures. During this period, Latin continued to be associated with the church and religious practice, though meeting increasing vernacular resistance as the fourteenth century progressed. From the thirteenth century on, French (in a dialect called Anglo-Norman) gradually lost its cultural dominance among the nobility, fading as a language of baronial culture in direct proportion to the contemporaneous ongoing losses of English aristocratic holdings in France. However, Anglo-Norman continued to be associated with civic and legal records well into the fifteenth century. English gradually garnered cultural legitimacy throughout the fourteenth century, but it really began to gain ground only after Henry IV deposed Richard II in 1399 and had to prop up his authority by courting wider English-speaking constituencies. This regime change coincides with the energetic production of a new English literary culture, visible in Chaucerian literary traditions as well as in the reappearance of English alliterative manuscripts. It is not accidental that most of late medieval alliterative poetry survives in fifteenth- and sixteenth-century manuscript copies.

However, this reemergence of literary English was late, and as a result there are large gaps in our knowledge of thirteenth- and early-fourteenth-century English literary history. After the Norman Conquest, classical Anglo-Saxon poetry virtually vanished, leading to a century of sporadic Anglo-Saxon antiquarianism. There is evidence in particular locations that clerks and writers were struggling to preserve what they could of their vanishing Anglo-Saxon literary history, and in so doing, they began to evolve new forms of alliterative verse. At this time rhythmical prose became a dominant influence on alliterative writing. The Peterborough *Chronicle* entry of 1087 shows familiarity with Anglo-Saxon rhythmical homily, echoing Wulfstan's diction as it formulates its own alliterative line. Very few texts of alliterative poetry survive from this period, but we do have the classically elegant *Durham* (*ca.* 1104?) and a century later, we find that *The Soul's Address to the Body* within the Worcester Fragments (*ca.* 1200) has already adapted to the increasingly analytical state of English by evolving a longer more supple and improvisational poetic line. These works look forward to Layamon's *Brut* (*ca.* 1190) as well as backward to Anglo-Saxon poetry and prose.

However, there are essentially no surviving exemplars of alliterative poetry between Layamon's *Brut* and the mid-fourteenth century. Then suddenly around 1350, alliterative poetry begins to appear in a variety of forms. Exemplars range from halting and experimental (*Joseph of Arimathie* and the *Alexander* fragments; both 1350–1370) to enormously sophisticated and powerful (*Piers Plowman* and *Sir Gawain and the Green Knight; ca.* 1360–1395). Some scholars have called this apparent rebirth an "Alliterative Revival" and then set about trying to explain it, either positing a self-conscious reinvention of alliterative form or seeking for intertextual references in surviving manuscript collections for evidence of lost alliterative writing to fill the apparent 150-year gap. Controversy about the Alliterative Revival dominated scholarship until the last two decades of the twentieth century, when the critical focus shifted. Since then, scholarship has lost interest in a continuous alliterative tradition and instead has drawn attention to what Elizabeth Salter calls flexible "alliterative modes and affiliations," emphasizing the porousness of these texts as they shift metrical forms over time and across regions, seizing upon formal and thematic external influences.

CHARACTERISTICS OF ALLITERATIVE POETRY

Because of alliterative poetry's capacity to shift forms, it has been difficult to come to firm conclusions about its defining features. New metrical theories have appeared every decade. In the early 1990s, drawing on important work by Marie Borroff, Thorlac Turville-Petre, Thomas Cable, Hoyt Duggan, and David Lawton, Ralph Hanna proposed three key characteristics for late medieval alliterative poetry.

The first is a four-stress line or two two-stress half-lines (usually called the a-line and the b-line) with a caesura (or pause) between them. One- and three-stress lines, however, occur regularly in important alliterative texts such as Langland's *Piers Plowman, Sir Gawain and the Green Knight,* and *The Siege of Jerusalem* (*ca.* 1380–1400), as well as in the more metrically experimental *Joseph of Arimathie.* While still paying attention to stresses, scholars such as Hoyt Duggan and Thomas Cable have discerned regularities in the patterns of unstressed syllables (or dips) employed in each half-line.

The second characteristic is metrical heteromorphism between the different parts of the line. This means that the a-line and the b-line must vary in their metrical patterns of stresses and dips, usually through the patterned interpolation of varying numbers of unstressed syllables between the stressed syllables. Certain patterns become characteristic of the a-line, while others become characteristic of the b-line. Many combinations are therefore possible, and as a result, the whole alliterative line gives an impression of enormous flexibility and variation, even as it exhibits the poet's skill at negotiating very complicated metrical demands. This demand for heteromorphism excludes poetry that falls into more regularly syllabic patterns.

Third is alliteration. This binds half-lines into lines and sometimes, in poems such as *Morte Arthure,* collocations of lines into tour de force multiline displays of alliterative lexical prowess. Generally speaking, alliteration weighs most heavily upon the first stressed syllable of the second half-line. The defining patterns are the classical Anglo-Saxon aa/ax and ax/ax, but increasingly in Middle English poetry more numerous variations become possible: double alliteration like ab/ab and ab/ba, split alliteration like aa/bb, alliteratively enriched lines of aaa/aa, and even rhythmically correct xx/xx lines without any alliteration at all. In the formal poetry, each consonant sound (and consonant combination sound such as *st, sp,* or *sc*) can only alliterate with itself. In Anglo-Saxon and much Middle English poetry, any initial vowel can alliterate with any other vowel, but in late and particularly ornate fourteenth- and fifteenth-century alliterative poetry, same-vowel alliteration begins to predominate, hinting at an evolving literary consciousness of the pleasure of the reading eye, as well as the listening ear. Yet alliteration seems to be as much ornamental as central in some instances, and many poems characterized as alliterative do not alliterate regularly or adhere to the "classical" Anglo-Saxon patterns of aa/ax. Alliteration, though it gives the literature its name, may be the least indispensable criterion for its practice.

Aside from these three parameters, there are few holds barred. While formal alliterative verse often forswears rhyme and strophic division, much alliterative poetry experiments freely, with quatrains (four-line units), stanzas, strophes, bobs (two-syllable lines), and wheels (abab rhyming, four-line, four-stress stanzas). Poets seem determined to up the metrical ante. One of the most tasking forms was also the most popular: the thirteen-line stanza exemplified by *The Three Dead Kings* (before 1426), *The Awntyrs of Arthure* (1400–1430), and *Somer Sonday* (1370–1420). *The Three Dead Kings* incorporates a challengingly repetitive rhyme-scheme of *a b a b a b a b c d c c d* and a strenuous alliterative scheme of *a a b b c c d d d d x f f,* resulting in possibly the most metrically challenging poetic form in the English language.

ALLITERATIVE POETRY AND RHYTHMIC PROSE

Alliterative poetry tends to exhibit a more rigid and challenging prosodic structure than the freer phrasal rhythms of alliterative prose. However, in medieval alliterative literary practice, poetry and prose forms cannot be firmly separated from each other. There was a constant intercourse between alliterative poetic and prose forms, and influence frequently moved in both directions. For example, the Anglo-Saxon homilist Aelfric (*ca.* 955–*ca.* 1010/1015), abbot of Eynsham, drew upon classical Anglo-Saxon poetic practice in the terse and elegant rhythmical phrases of his prose Catholic homilies and in exhortatory sermons such as *De falsis deis.* But when Wulfstan, archbishop of York and bishop of Worcester, adapted *De falsis deis* for his larger, less learned audience of recent Danish settlers, he felt free to hammer his points home, regardless of metrical correctness. He interpolated phrases for clarity and rhetorical effect, blurring Aelfric's well-defined half-lines while still retaining a free and powerful two-stress rhythm. And while Anglo-Saxon poetry essentially died as a widespread literary form after the Norman Conquest, the tradition of rhythmical prose exemplified by Aelfric and Wulfstan survived in the Worcester area and very likely influenced Layamon. Possibly a priest at Erneleye, Layamon wrote an idiosyncratically alliterative poetic Arthurian epic, *The Brut* (ca. 1200–1225), which was not only informed by Aelfric but also drew on Geoffrey of Monmouth's Latin prose *Historia regum Britanniae* (1137) and its French poetic version, Wace's *Brut* (1155).

Later, in the second half of the fourteenth and the early fifteenth century, the most substantial alliterative poems can be divided into two modes that reflect this intercourse between alliterative prose and poetry. One mode is formal, hyperpoetic, metrically "purist," and often historically oriented, exemplified by *Sir Gawain and the Green Knight, The Siege of Jerusalem, The Wars of Alexander, The Morte Arthure*, and *The Destruction of Troy*. The other mode is more informal, generating an alliterative line so metrically flexible that it verges on the colloquial freedom of rhythmical prose, exemplified by the most important late medieval alliterative poem, *Piers Plowman*, and its imitators, *Pierce the Ploughman's Crede, Richard the Redeless, Mum and the Sothsegger*, and *The Crowned King*. Although the formal mode seems more closed and "poetic" and the informal mode more open and "proselike," both modes are alert to late medieval political, social, and religious currents; make use of a wide range of other medieval sources; and appeal to a variety of possible audiences. Doubtless this continual social involvement, whether historically mediated or urgently contemporary, helps to explain the thousand-year survival of this rich and unmanageable literature.

BIBLIOGRAPHY

Barr, Helen, ed. *The Piers Plowman Tradition*. London: J. M. Dent, 1993.

Borroff, Marie. *"Sir Gawain and the Green Knight": A Stylistic and Metrical Study*. New Haven, Conn.: Yale University Press, 1962.

Brewer, Derek, and Jonathan Gibson, eds. *A Companion to the Gawain-Poet*. Cambridge, U.K.: D. S. Brewer, 1997.

Cable, Thomas. *The English Alliterative Tradition*. Philadelphia: University of Pennsylvania Press, 1991.

Chambers, R. W. *On the Continuity of English Prose from Alfred to More and His School*. Oxford: Oxford University Press, 1932.

Greenfield, Stanley B., and Daniel G. Calder. *A New Critical History of Old English Literature* New York: New York University Press, 1986.

Hanna, Ralph. *William Langland*. Aldershot, U.K.: Variorum, 1993.

Hewitt-Smith, Kathleen M., ed. *William Langland's "Piers Plowman": A Book of Essays*. New York: Routledge, 2001.

Houwen, L. A. J. R., and A. A. MacDonald. *Loyal Letters: Studies on Mediaeval Alliterative Poetry and Prose*. Groningen, Netherlands: Egbert Forsten, 1994.

Kubouchi, Tadao. *From Wulfstan to Richard Rolle: Papers Exploring the Continuity of English Prose*. Cambridge, U.K.: D. S. Brewer, 1999.

Lawton, David, ed. *Middle English Alliterative Poetry and Its Literary Background*. Cambridge, U.K.: D. S. Brewer, 1982.

Levy, Bernard S., and Paul E. Szarmach, eds. *The Alliterative Tradition in the Fourteenth Century*. Kent, Ohio: Kent State Press, 1981.

Oakden, J. *Alliterative Poetry in Middle English*. 2 vols. Manchester, U.K.: Manchester University Press, 1930–1935.

O'Brien O'Keeffe, Katherine. *Visible Song: Transitional Literacy in Old English Verse*. Cambridge, U.K.: Cambridge University Press, 1990.

Pearsall, Derek. *Old and Middle English Poetry*. London: Routledge and Kegan Paul, 1977.

Salter, Elizabeth. *English and International: Studies in the Literature, Art, and Patronage of Medieval England*. Cambridge, U.K.: Cambridge University Press, 1988.

Scattergood, John. *The Lost Tradition: Essays on Middle English Alliterative Poetry*. Dublin: Four Courts Press, 2000.

Tavormina, M. Teresa, and R. F. Yeager. *The Endless Knot: Essays on Old and Middle English in Honor of Marie Borroff*. Cambridge, U.K.: D. S. Brewer, 1995.

Turville-Petre, Thorlac. *The Alliterative Revival*. Cambridge, U.K.: D. S. Brewer; Totowa, N. J.: Rowman and Littlefield, 1977.

———, ed. *Alliterative Poetry of the Later Middle Ages: An Anthology*. London: Routledge, 1989.

Wallace, David, ed. *The Cambridge History of Medieval English Literature*. Cambridge, U.K.: Cambridge University Press, 1999.

CHRISTINE CHISM

[See also **DMA**: Anglo-Saxon Literature; *Beowulf*; *Brut*, The; *Gawain and the Green Knight, Sir*; Langland, William; Middle English Literature: Alliterative Verse; Middle English Literature: Prosody and Versification; *Pearl*.]

AMSTERDAM went from uninhabited marshland to one of Europe's leading cities in only a few centuries. At the juncture of the Amstel River and the IJ, a bay of the Zuider Zee, the location of present-day Amsterdam was either inundated or barren swampland until around 1200, when settlers from more inland areas began the process of drying out parcels of land. Land reclamation and improvement was a communal task, requiring organization and manpower, and the archaeological evidence suggests that dike building and the creation of a permanent settlement began simultaneously in the early thirteenth century. Somewhat later, the inhabitants built a dam across the mouth of the Amstel to control flooding, and in 1275 what was by then probably a small village appeared in the documentary record as "Amsterdam"—in other words, the dam on the Amstel.

Growth was slow in the thirteenth and early fourteenth centuries. It was only around 1300, years later than the other major cities of Holland that Amsterdam would eventually surpass, that the village received a charter of privileges from the count of Holland, and only around 1334 did the town acquire its own parish priest. Not until after 1400 did the city build a town hall. At about the same time the Old Church, or St. Nicholas Church (which had been built around 1300), was split into two parishes, and a second church, the New Church, was established. By the end of the fifteenth century the population had only reached about nine thousand. The need to reclaim and then maintain land before it could be settled limited the speed of the town's expansion. Furthermore, the land around Amsterdam could not support agriculture sufficient to feed an urban population, forcing the townspeople to turn to trade. It was this activity that after the mid-fourteenth century led to the city's rapid rise.

Three factors aided Amsterdam's development into a trading metropolis. First, in 1323, the count of Holland made the city one of the two places to pay a toll on imported beer. Thus much of the beer entering the county, mostly from Hamburg, began to be shipped through Amsterdam. This spurred the second factor, the movement of the Hanseatic trading route from Utrecht and the IJssel River towns in the south to the more northerly route through Amsterdam. Over the course of the late fourteenth century, the Utrecht route declined, and Amsterdam became the new shipping entrepôt of the region. Finally, the invention and improvement of the cog, a shallow-drafted oceangoing ship with a large capacity, made the use of the northern Amsterdam route more economical. Responding to these changes, the Amsterdammers first began to ship bulk goods to and from Germany, England, and France and then slowly became merchants in their own right. By the end of the fifteenth century, Amsterdam had surpassed the other cities of Holland as a trading power.

The fifteenth century saw the city take on the form and institutions that would characterize it during the early modern period. By 1480 the government had evolved into a tripartite structure made up of four governing burgomasters who ran the city's day-to-day affairs, a council of aldermen who dealt primarily with judicial affairs, and a closed patrician advisory council of thirty-six prominent citizens (known as the Vroedschap), who were named for life. Between 1425 and the end of the sixteenth century, the surface area of the town was not increased, and what had been a thinly populated and partially rural space within the defensive walls became a crowded urban center.

BIBLIOGRAPHY

Israel, Jonathan. *The Dutch Republic: Its Rise, Greatness, and Fall, 1477–1806.* Oxford: Clarendon Press, 1995. Although this magisterial work deals primarily with a later era, its introductory chapters provide an excellent background to the political and cultural development of Holland and Amsterdam in the fifteenth century.

Mak, Geert. *Amsterdam: A Brief Life of the City.* Translated by Philipp Blom. London: Harvill Press, 1999. Not a scholarly book but an accessible introduction to the history of the city nonetheless.

Van Gelder, Roelof, and Renée Kistemaker. *Amsterdam, 1275–1795: De ontwikkeling van een handelsmetropool.* Amsterdam: Meulenhoff Informatief, 1983. A good start in readable Dutch.

EMILY KADENS

ANDREA DA BARBERINO

ANDREA DA BARBERINO (*ca.* 1370–after 1431), a prolific Florentine writer of prose romances. Born near Florence, Andrea da Barberino was married three times and widowed twice and appears never to have had children. He became one of the great Italian writers of chivalric prose literature. His works were composed just prior to the rise of the Medici in Florence.

Most of his stories were reworkings of older literary models. His most famous work, *I reali di Francia* (The royals of France), for instance, takes characters and episodes from a number of thirteenth-century French romances, such as those of Adenet le Rois. Many of Andrea's romances are closely based on French and Franco-Italian Carolingian-cycle epics and invoke the legends of Roland, Guillaume d'Orange, Renaut, Huon d'Auvergne, and Doon de Maïence. But Andrea's epic romances are characterized by a lay, secular tone that contrasts with the nationalist religious fervor of the chanson de geste tradition. Thus, while Andrea conserves many of the plots and characters of the traditional literature, he modernizes them in various ways, incorporating new styles and language taken from contemporary chronicles, bestiaries, and travel literature. He showed a particular interest, for instance, in geography, and his stories are littered with place-names. Some of his geographical references indicate a familiarity with the new Latin translation of Ptolemy's *Cosmographia*. Andrea's interest in detail is also reflected in his knowledge of genealogy and the names of different animal species, perhaps evidence of his familiarity with bestiaries. Verisimilitude, in short, appears to have been one of Andrea's central aims, in contrast with later works of chivalric literature produced in Renaissance Italy, which tended to spring more from pure fantasy. Historical, geographical, and genealogical detail animates Andrea's narrative and provides his stories with a greater sense of realism. Moreover, Andrea appears to have sought to cast his chivalric romances as entertaining pseudohistories.

There is still some question about which works can definitively be attributed to Andrea. It has only recently been shown, for instance, that *La storia del re Ansuigi,* the lost *Prima Spagna,* and a prose version of *Rinaldo* were all written by Andrea. His most famous works are *I reali di Francia* and *Guerrino il meschino* (Guerrino the lowly). *Guerrino il meschino* recounts the adventures of the upright Guerrino, who finds his parents and frees them from prison and discovers that he is of noble blood rather than a slave, as he had been told. Based on various Carolingian legends, *I reali di Francia* is a comprehensive epic filled with chivalry and heroics that tells the story of the French royal house from Fiovo, the son of Constantine, to Charlemagne. In short, *I reali di Francia* is framed as a medieval dynastic chronicle. A striking feature of *I reali di Francia* is the way in which Andrea depicts vivid battle scenes while also developing his characters and their motivations, often by having them deliver long orations just before or after a battle sequence. Andrea also used his romances as a vehicle for exploring various philosophical questions that interested him, such as the role of fortune in human affairs, the importance of a good reputation, and the proper relationship between justice and mercy.

Andrea's other works include *Aspramonte,* which is a continuation of the six books of *I reali di Francia; Secondo Spagna;* the seven-part *Storie Nerbonesi,* which is a reworking of the chansons de geste from the Guillaume d'Orange cycle; and *La storia di Aiolfo del Barbicone,* which is a reworking of the French *Aiol.* Andrea probably also authored the anonymous prose *Storie di Rinaldo da Montalbano* and *La storia di Ugone d'Avernia.* It is far less likely that he wrote either *Rambaldo* or *Girone il Cortese.* Andrea may also have written some pieces in verse, although he clearly preferred writing in prose.

Andrea had a significant influence on later-fifteenth- and sixteenth-century chivalric texts in Italy and elsewhere. His works served as popular sources for later literary works, inspiring future literary characters, plots, and narrative styles. Some later texts made clear allusions to Andrea's works, sometimes even copying passages verbatim. But while Andrea's influence was clearly felt, he was also criticized by some Latin humanists who dismissed his works on account of their popularity with "unlearned audiences." Andrea was also criticized for having written in vernacular prose as opposed to the heroic verse form, the octave. Increasingly, however, scholars have highlighted just how learned Andrea's style and language actually were. He had read far more widely than previously thought and incorporated into his stories elements from the Bible, Ovid, Arthurian romances, Dante, and numerous chansons de geste and Breton lays and romances, including Chrétien de Troyes's *Cligès,* Marie de France's

Lai de Lanval, the prose *Conte de la Charette* (Tale of the cart), and *Tavola ritonda* (Round table). Many of his plots and protagonists were modeled on classical or classical-cycle works. Andrea possessed some knowledge of Latin, at least enough to cite passages from the Latin liturgy and make use of the new Latin translation of Ptolemy. It is possible that Andrea's works never circulated in manuscript form during his own lifetime, since no manuscript of his works can be dated to before 1433, when it is thought that he died. But Andrea's works were clearly popular in the fifteenth and sixteenth centuries and remained so even after the appearance of the celebrated works by Matteo Boiardo, Ludovico Ariosto, and Torquato Tasso. The works of Andrea da Barberino have been reprinted, translated, and adapted in numerous editions, and versions of them have even been used as subject matter for Italian puppet shows.

BIBLIOGRAPHY

Allaire, Gloria. *Andrea da Barberino and the Language of Chivalry.* Gainesville: University Press of Florida, 1997.

Andrea da Barberino. *I reali di Francia.* Introduction by Aurelio Roncaglia, edited by Fabrizio Beggiato. Rome: Casini, 1967.

————. *L'Aspramonte.* Edited by Luigi Cavalli. Naples, Italy: Rossi, 1972.

Grendler, Paul F. "Chivalric Romances in the Italian Renaissance." In *Studies in Medieval and Renaissance History.* Edited by J. A. S. Evans and R. W. Unger. Vol. 10 (old series, vol. 20). New York: AMS Press, 1988. Contextualizes Andrea within the Italian chivalric romance tradition.

ADAM JEFFREY DAVIS

[See also **DMA:** Italian Literature: Epic and Chivalric.]

ANIMALS, ATTITUDES TOWARD. Attitudes toward animals were more diverse in the medieval period than in our own. Animals and human perceptions of them played a central role in medieval culture in part because people in every geographical area and every social station lived in close proximity to the animal world, and their economic success often directly depended on complex interactions with animals, both domestic and wild. Medieval Europe's agricultural economy required that humans employ the labor of animals in the plowing of fields, for example, and in transporting goods and people from one location to another. Moreover, animals were used to guard human property from theft and depredation (sometimes by other animals) and were themselves consumed as food. Animals served as the raw materials for certain articles of clothing, and parts of their bodies were important in the production of medicines, parchment, and pens. In short, the economic value of animals and animal products was inestimably great in the medieval period, and as we can tell from the evidence in legal documents and records alluding to business transactions, their market value was carefully calculated and monitored throughout the medieval period.

Yet to understand more thoroughly human attitudes toward animals in the medieval period, we need to move beyond considerations of their economic value alone. Medieval people inherited and created on their own a variety of interpretive frameworks within which to analyze animal behavior and relate it to human life. The Bible supplied an influential and authoritative set of attitudes and symbolic meanings concerning the animal world; Genesis, for example, reported that Adam had dominion over the animals and gave them their names. In both the Old and the New Testaments, specific animals were given symbolic meaning, as in the well-known metaphorical use of wolves and snakes to refer to any wicked, predatory individual acting against the innocent. Christ himself was figured as a sacrificial lamb, providing Scripture—and thus medieval thought—with one of its most enduring metaphors.

Classical, non-Christian culture also had an impact on medieval attitudes toward animals, as themes from ancient pastorals, eclogues, and epics, especially those romanticizing rural life, found their way into the works of learned medieval poets. In addition, the insights of ancient natural historians and agriculturalists provided medieval people with a rich and enduring stock of animal lore as well as advice concerning animal husbandry. Finally, the native Celtic, Germanic, and Slavic folkloric traditions of Europe provided medieval culture with some of its most persistent beliefs about animals, passed on in oral form but eventually showing up as recurring motifs in written texts. Since attitudes toward animals vary among medieval subcommunities, each of which produced and consumed distinctive sorts of writing about the natural world, it is useful to approach the topic by noting some of the most important genres in which animal lore appears and by generalizing about each genre's characteristic vision of animals and their behavior. It must be remembered, however, that at times these genres—and the audiences to whom they were directed—overlapped significantly.

THEOLOGICAL, SCIENTIFIC, AND ACADEMIC WRITINGS

St. Augustine (354–430) insisted—as did later influential theologians, such as St. Thomas Aquinas

(1224–1274)—that animals had neither souls nor rationality, thus being distinctively different from and inferior to humans. Nonetheless Augustine provided, in *On Christian Doctrine,* a strong rationale for investigating and interpreting the animal world. He urged Christians to seek an understanding of the natural creatures mentioned in Scripture, for animals, along with all other objects created by God, should properly be read as signs given to humanity for moral and theological guidance. This theological sanctioning of natural knowledge encouraged the systematic collection of animal lore in works by medieval natural philosophers and encyclopedists such as Isidore of Seville (*ca.* 560–636), Vincent of Beauvais (*ca.* 1190–*ca.* 1264), Albertus Magnus (*ca.* 1200–1280), Thomas of Cantimpré (*ca.* 1201–*ca.*1270/ 1272), Alexander Neckham (1157–1217), and Bartholomaeus Anglicus (*d.* 1272), among others. These writers not only summarized classical material concerning animal behavior, husbandry, and medicinal use, but in some cases they also added their own views, based on direct observation. Indeed, Albertus Magnus qualifies as one of Europe's greatest medieval analysts of nature.

BESTIARIES

Bestiaries, prevalent primarily in the twelfth and thirteenth centuries, were ultimately derived from Latin translations of the second century A.D. Greek *Physiologus,* a didactic work that takes note of many of the animals mentioned in the Bible, offering short descriptions along with moralizations designed to draw parallels between animals (their appearances, habitats, and behavior) and various doctrines of salvation history. Christ's fulfillment of the Law, for example, is figured by the phoenix's resurrection from its own ashes, and his Harrowing of Hell is shown to have parallels with the behavior of the water snake, which was believed to enter the mouths of crocodiles in order to disembowel them from within. Bestiaries preserved some of this theological lore, but they added to it by increasing the number of animals covered, so that native European creatures found a place in these reference works alongside the more exotic beasts of Scripture. Bestiaries also widened their descriptive functions by adding supplementary information—some of it entirely fictional—about animal behavior and habitats, and they increased their moral and ethical commentary by drawing strong parallels between animal behavior and human virtues and vices. Finally, though often lavishly illustrated, bestiaries were emotionally rather detached from the natural world they described, serving as catalogues of moral successes and failures. Essentially monastic productions, they were used in part as sources of sermon exempla, and in this way their views were widely disseminated in oral form.

BEAST FABLES AND BEAST EPICS

Just as widespread as bestiaries but different in their specific use of animal themes, medieval fables and beast epics flourished throughout the Middle Ages. These works were also didactic in that the animals presented within them were characters in fictional narratives expressly designed to edify readers or listeners about vice, virtue, and appropriate social and political behavior. From their beginnings, however, these genres demonstrated close observation of animal life, genuine affection for it, and a sense of the permeability of animal-human boundaries. Medieval beast fables derived from the classical Aesopic tradition; indeed the original Aesopic fables continued to be copied and adapted throughout the Middle Ages and were incorporated within collections that contained fables of medieval authorship as well. A staple of the grammar school curriculum, fables—like the longer beast epics they inspired—should be viewed as central to the formation of medieval people's attitudes toward the animals around them. Essentially, fables and beast epics rely on the stereotyping and the extensive anthropomorphizing of animals. Foxes, which figure prominently in both traditions, are thus seen as devious and vulgar animals, with a penchant for committing theft, while lions are seen as noble beasts, strong though somewhat vain and self-involved; mice are resourceful but often poor and oppressed; wolves are predatory on the small and the weak, though easily fooled by more intelligent creatures; oxen are dim-witted and of peasant status.

Beast epics and fables reflected medieval culture's social attitudes regarding gender roles, distinctions among social classes, power relations among the church and the state, and other matters, thus helping that culture work through solutions to its social problems. But these narratives also exhibit human attempts to understand the dynamics of animal behavior. That is, although fables and beast epics employed animal lore largely for the purposes of analyzing, "naturalizing," and at times satirizing human social constructs, the very use of those constructs to explore the animal world reveals the desire to understand animals better, to satisfy a curiosity about why animals do what they do. Indeed, the best medieval fabulists and beast epic writers based their narratives on the close observation of animal behavior in its natural environment and set them in realistically conceived landscapes; we meet Reynard the Fox and Ysengrimus the Wolf (to name the eponymous heroes of two beast epic

cycles that were popular in the late medieval period) among the familiar plowed fields, meadows, hedgerows, woodlots, and farms of rural medieval Europe. Moreover, the medieval beast fables and epics demonstrate the medieval capacity to take pity on animal suffering and to vilify those responsible for it; scenes of violence were often designed to encourage readers to identify with the physically injured parties. Indeed, the animals in these narratives provided occasions for medieval Europeans to consider issues such as vice, virtue, justice, oppression, and equality—as well as the bond of mortality and physical vulnerability that links humans to their animal cousins.

HAGIOGRAPHY

Although the medieval authors of saints' lives often employed bestiaries and local folklore about animals in the construction of their narratives and thus expressed a wide range of views about the animal world, they tended to observe some fixed conventions, rooted in Biblical and patristic sources, about animal-saint relations. Predominant among these is the convention that animals demonstrate God's approval of human sanctity: he works through animals by having them aid saints in achieving their social or ascetic goals and by having them serve as nature's witnesses to the saints' extraordinary holiness. Saints always have the potential to control the natural world, the behaviors of its animals included. In hagiographic narratives, saints often successfully command wild animals to carry out domestic tasks, such as plowing, or to abandon their predatory or destructive tendencies (lions, wolves, and even insects are commonly the recipients of these commands). If a wild animal attacks a saint or a saint's property, it is often shown later doing penance for its wrongdoing by becoming a servant to the holy one. Saints sometimes wield a cross as an effective weapon against animals believed to have demonic affiliations (snakes, wolves, and dragons being common examples). In general, wild animals are most often portrayed as tame in the presence of saints, as eager providers of food and protection. St. Benedict (*ca.* 480–*ca.* 547), for example, is said to have been fed daily by a crow, which brought bread to sustain him. Celtic saints' lives show extreme examples of such animal-human symbiosis: St. Colman, an Irish saint of the seventh century, is said to have had a fly that served as a living place marker in books that he had open on the table, a mouse that woke him up every morning, and a rooster that reminded him, by crowing, of the hours at which he was required to say the divine office.

There is also a widespread convention that saints acted as protectors of animals hunted by humans or other beasts. St. Martin of Tours (*ca.* 316–397), for instance, is said to have ordered hunting dogs to stop pursuing a tired rabbit, and St. Francis (*ca.* 1182–1226) is shown to have demonstrated great charity toward animals by freeing them from the snares of trappers. Saints are even reported to have resurrected dead animals, in a gesture reminiscent of Christ's raising of Lazarus. It is generally profitable, in fact, to think of saints' interactions with animals as imitations and extensions into the animal world of Christ's behavior toward humans in Scripture. In the hagiographic tradition, then, attitudes toward animals are complex, for the prevalent theme of domination and control of animals is mingled with an undercurrent of tender affection for them.

TREATISES ON HUNTING, FALCONRY, AND HERALDRY

The European aristocracy expressed its elevated status through the social practice of hunting and the adoption of animal symbolism in heraldic devices. Animals involved in hunting and falconry (deer, boars, dogs, hawks, and falcons) gained prestige and value by this association, and information about their types, breeding, medical care, and training was passed down orally and in treatises such as the *Livre de chasse* (The book of hunting) of 1387–1389. Aristocratic behavior during the hunt included highly ritualized ways of taking down and dismembering the prey. Animal symbolism in heraldry evinces a kind of totemistic use of animals, with noble families representing themselves as linked to the imagined nobility of certain beasts (such as the lion, the greyhound, or the eagle) and to the powers traditionally identified with them.

OTHER GENRES

Numerous other medieval literary genres employ motifs involving animals. Medieval debate poetry, originally associated with the universities, sometimes features animals in verbal contests, in which the debaters comically pit their stereotypical traits against one another, as in the English poem *The Owl and the Nightingale* (*ca.* 1189–1216). Medieval romances, which began as productions for noble audiences but eventually ended up in the hands of the lower gentry and the mercantile population, at times show animals in major roles: they may be helpers of the heroes and their families as they overcome hardship, formidable adversaries in the heroes' development of their knightly identities, or objects of the hunt. Medieval travel literature, such as Gerald of Wales's (1146–1223) descriptions of his journeys in Ireland and Wales and Sir John Mandeville's *Travels* (*ca.* 1356), imaginatively created animal-human or animal-plant hybrids to underscore the cultural and geographical strangeness of remote or alien places. These genres freely adapted attitudes toward animals derived from bestiaries, heraldic tradition, fables, theology, and folkloric sources. Finally, it is worth noting that legal records from the late Middle Ages and the early modern period preserve accounts of animals and insects put on trial (and often executed) for theft, murder, sexual transgressions, and other crimes. These records, which suggest that some communities extended their moral codes to include the animal kingdom, show a form of anthropomorphism reflecting confidence in the idea that all living things were governed by a single, divinely inspired moral framework.

BIBLIOGRAPHY

Albertus Magnus. *On Animals: A Medieval Summa Zoologica.* Translated by Kenneth F. Kitchell Jr. and Irven Michael Resnick. 2 vols. Baltimore: Johns Hopkins University Press, 1999.

Carnes, Pack. *Fable Scholarship: An Annotated Bibliography.* New York: Garland, 1985.

Cummins, John. *The Hound and the Hawk: The Art of Medieval Hunting.* New York: St. Martin's Press, 1988.

Evans, E. P. *The Criminal Prosecution and Capital Punishment of Animals: The Lost History of Europe's Animal Trials.* London: Heinemann, 1906.

George, Wilma, and Brunsdon Yapp. *Naming of the Beasts: Natural History in the Medieval Bestiary.* London: Duckworth, 1991.

Hassig, Debra. *Medieval Bestiaries: Text, Image, Ideology.* Cambridge and New York: Cambridge University Press, 1995.

Klingender, F. D. *Animals in Art and Thought to the End of the Middle Ages.* Edited by Evelyn Antal and John Harthan. Cambridge, Mass.: MIT Press, 1971.

Linzey, Andrew, and Tom Regan, eds. *Animals and Christianity: A Book of Readings.* New York: Crossroads, 1990.

McCulloch, Florence. *Mediaeval Latin and French Bestiaries.* Rev. ed. Chapel Hill: University of North Carolina Press, 1962.

Salisbury, Joyce E. *The Beast Within: Animals in the Middle Ages.* New York: Routledge, 1994.

L'uomo di fronte al mondo animale nell'alto Medioevo: 7–13 aprile, 1983. 2 vols. Settimane di studio del. Centro Italiano di studi sull'alto Medioevo. Spoleto: Presso la sede del Centro, 1985. Contains essays on animals in agriculture, warfare, hagiography, fable traditions, iconography, and daily life.

Yamamoto, Dorothy. *The Boundaries of the Human in Medieval English Literature.* Oxford and New York: Oxford University Press, 2000.

Ziolkowski, Jan M. *Talking Animals: Medieval Latin Beast Poetry, 750–1150.* Philadelphia: University of Pennsylvania Press, 1993.

LISA J. KISER

[See also **DMA:** Albertus Magnus, St.; Animals, Draft; Animals, Food; Beast Epic; Bestiare d'amour; Bestiary; Fables; Francis of Assisi,

St.; Gerald of Wales; Hagiography, Western European; Heraldry; Hunting and Fowling, Western European; Isidore of Seville, St.; Mandeville's Travels; Renard the Fox; Ysengrimus; **Supp:** Nature.]

ANNALES SCHOOL. See **Medieval Studies.**

ANNE OF BOHEMIA (1366–1394).

The daughter of the emperor Charles IV, Princess Anne of Bohemia was born in Prague. At the age of fifteen she came to England to wed the sensitive fourteen-year-old King Richard II. The marriage was celebrated formally and in a series of joyous festivities in January 1382. It was evidently a happy marriage, although it produced no heir. After Anne died at the age of twenty-eight, the grief-stricken king is supposed to have ordered Sheen Castle, where she died, razed to the ground. The lonely king also had Anne interred at Westminster Abbey, where he too hoped to be laid to rest—and eventually was (after temporary interment elsewhere).

These bare facts have been the stuff of legend, with Anne and Richard fictionalized as the ideal medieval aristocratic couple—she the cultivated imperial princess with the lilting central European accent and a bustling retinue of imitators and admirers, he the quintessential debonair chevalier. It is believed, for example, that Anne introduced the habit of riding sidesaddle, the explanation being that this made the lovers' companionate and romantic ride together possible. (Given the nature of female aristocratic dress, cross-saddle riding is considered to have been too uncomfortable.)

In fact, very few details are known about Anne or her relations with the king or others who interacted with her in England. She is widely credited with having been the conduit for Wyclifite ideas that traveled to Bohemia, but otherwise traditional scholarship has made her into something of a nonentity. Some recent scholarship, however, posits her influence on several of the major figures of late-fourteenth-century vernacular literature and courtly art—Chaucer, the Pearl Poet, and the sorts of artists who, for example, produced the famous Wilton Diptych. The arguments are plausible in that they cohere with an emerging scholarly consensus that late medieval aristocratic women were critically important as a potential and greatly expanded audience for vernacular literature. But a great deal more work needs to be done before these conclusions will meet general approbation.

BIBLIOGRAPHY

Saul, Nigel. *Richard II.* New Haven, Conn: Yale University Press, 1997. Represents the traditional scholarly relegation of Anne to a minor figure in the court culture of Richard II's reign.

Thomas, Alfred. *Anne's Bohemia: Czech Literature and Society, 1310–1420.* Minneapolis: University of Minnesota Press, 1998.

Wallace, David. *Chaucerian Polity: Absolutist Lineages and Associational Towns in England and Italy.* Stanford, Calif.: Stanford University Press, 1997.

WILLIAM CHESTER JORDAN

[See also **DMA:** Richard II; **Supp:** Women.]

ANSGAR, ST. (**Anskar,** *ca.* 801–865).

Ansgar was a monk of Corvey who became known as the Apostle of the North for his efforts to extend the limits of Latin Christendom as a missionary to the pagan kingdoms of the Danes and the Swedes. He was also the first archbishop of the diocese of Hamburg (later Hamburg-Bremen). Knowledge of his background and missionary activities comes primarily from the account of his life (*Vita Anskarii,* or *Life of St. Ansgar*) composed shortly after 865 by his pupil and companion Rimbert, who succeeded him as archbishop of Hamburg-Bremen.

Ansgar entered the abbey of Corbie as a child and eventually rose to the rank of master of the school. In 815 several monks of the community, including Ansgar, were sent to inhabit New Corbie (Corbeia nova), later known as Corvey, an imperial foundation built in their vicinity by the emperor Louis I (the Pious). Ansgar's first opportunity for missionary activity presented itself when the Danish king Harald Klak converted to Christianity in the early 820s and traveled to Mainz for baptism. Archbishop Ebo of Rheims attempted to shore up the king's commitment by sending a group of monks and priests back with him to the Danish court. The learned Ansgar was among those chosen to accompany the king.

The success of medieval Christian missionaries in pagan lands often depended on the compliance and assistance of local kings and rulers. The mission to Denmark was no exception. Under Harald's protection, Ansgar and his companions preached and taught among the Danes. Their return to Corvey two years later may have coincided with the exile of the king. A mission to Sweden followed in 829. With the permission of King Bern, Ansgar and his companion Witmar, another monk of Corbie, spent six months preaching among the Swedes. Upon his return in 831, Ansgar became archbishop of the newly founded diocese of Hamburg, traveled to Rome to receive the pallium, and was entrusted with continuing the mission to the Danes and the Swedes, a task that occupied him for the rest of his life. Civil war in the pagan kingdoms and the sack of Hamburg by Vikings in 845 hampered Ansgar's missionary efforts, and his work remained unfinished when he died in 865.

Rimbert's *Life of St. Ansgar* presents the idealized portrait of a missionary bishop and illuminates early medieval conversion strategies in the far north. Rimbert emphasized the need for diplomacy with pagan kings and their magnates as well as the benefit to missionaries of traveling with merchants better acquainted with local customs and politics. There are several accounts of Ansgar purchasing young boys and providing them with a Christian education in the hope that they would continue his missionary work. Rimbert also discussed the importance of the moral character of priests in newly converted territories and the provisioning of new churches with the books and liturgical vessels necessary for the establishment and maintenance of Christian worship.

BIBLIOGRAPHY

Haas, Wolfdieter. "Foris apostolus—intus monachus: Ansgar als Mönch und 'Apostel des Nordens.'" *Journal of Medieval History* 11 (1985): 1–30.

Jankuhn, Herbert. "Das Missionsfeld Ansgars." *Frühmittelalterliche Studien* 1 (1967): 213–221.

Rimbert. "Vita Anskarii." In *Quellen des 9. und 11. Jahrhunderts zur Geschichte der Hamburgischen Kirche und des Reiches,* 5th ed. Edited by W. Trillmich. Ausgewählte Quellen zur deutschen Geschichte des Mittelalters, no. 11. Darmstadt, Germany: Wissenschaftliche Buchgesellschaft, 1978, pp. 3–133. (English translation: *Anskar, The Apostle of the North, 801–865, Translated from the Vita Anskarii by Bishop Rimbert, His Fellow Missionary and Successor.* Translated by Charles H. Robinson. London: Society for the Propagation of the Gospel in Foreign Parts, 1921).

Wood, Ian. *The Missionary Life: Saints and the Evangelisation of Europe, 400–1050.* Harlow, U.K., and New York: Longman, 2001.

SCOTT G. BRUCE

[See also **DMA**: Birka; Denmark; Missions and Missionaries, Christian; Rimbert, St.; Sweden; **Supp**: Corbie, Abbey of; Corvey, Abbey of.]

ʿANTAR. The hero of an epic poem that draws on pagan, Islamic, and Persian folklore, ʿAntar legendarily lived in the sixth century before the coming of Islam. The *Sīrat ʿAntar* is one of the most famous epics of the Arab world, considered by some as second only to the *Thousand and One Nights* in narrative style and in the variety of scenes it depicts. The first manuscript of the epic

appeared only in the nineteenth century; the poem's oral character makes it difficult to speak of the *Sīrat ʿAntar* as a discrete poem with a single author. Rather, it is a collection of episodes to which any number of oral poets may have contributed. The stories of ʿAntar that survive were probably composed between A.D. 1000 and 1350, although the earliest mention of ʿAntar appears in a dialogue between a Jew and a Muslim, dated about the year A.D. 800. The stories have continued to be popular throughout the Arab world, although unlike the stories of the Banū Hilāl, the stories are now generally read from texts rather than recited.

The legendary ʿAntar is the son of an Abyssinian slave girl and a member of the ʿAbs tribe. As a child, he has prodigious strength, and at age nine kills a wolf but remains a slave, herding camels. He is characterized as "black and swarthy like an elephant, flat-nosed, bleareyed, harsh featured and shaggy haired." He eventually gains recognition from his father and his tribe by his strength and courage. He seeks his cousin ʿAbla in marriage, but to prove himself worthy he has to accomplish extraordinary feats, becoming the hero of the tribe. While many of his triumphs are achieved at the behest of his wife, "ʿAntar loved his horse ʿAbjar more than he loved ʿAbla." ʿAntar also has a heroic sword, az̲-Z̲āmī, made from a meteorite.

ʿAntar rescues his prospective wife, ʿAbla, from innumerable kidnappings and enslavements and battles opponents throughout the Arabian peninsula, as well as in Iraq and Persia. ʿAntar's exploits even attract the attention of the Byzantine emperor, for whom the Arab hero leads a Greek army against the Franks. ʿAntar finally is killed by a poisoned arrow from the hand of his archenemy Wizr ibn Jābir, whom the hero had defeated repeatedly but always mercifully released. After his death, the ʿAbs tribe is defeated and scattered by other Arab tribes who had tired of ʿAntar's long supremacy, and ʿAbla is killed by her second husband because of her constant unfavorable comparisons of him to ʿAntar.

ʿAntar has no children from his long-sought marriage with ʿAbla but fathers other notable progeny in his adventures, the foremost of whom is ʿUnaitira. Like her father, she is dark skinned and larger than most men. She assumes leadership of the regrouped ʿAbs tribe and leads an attack on ʿAbla's murderer. Then with two other illegitimate sons of ʿAntar, al-Jufrān and al-Ghaḍanfar (sons of Byzantine and Frankish liaisons), she defeats all Arab tribes. The three siblings are accompanied by ʿAntar's skeleton mounted on a camel and periodically ask if he is satisfied with the vengeance they inflicted in his name. When all of the Arab tribes are defeated, the three bury their father's corpse. Al-Jufrān and al-Ghaḍanfar return home, and ʿUnaitira converts to Islam and dies fighting the holy war.

BIBLIOGRAPHY

Abel, A. "Formation et construction du *Roman d'Antar.*" In *Poesia epica e la sua formazione.* Rome, 1970.

Dhuhnī, M. *Sirat ʿAntarah.* Cairo: Dār al Maʿārif, 1979.

Heath, Peter. *The Thirsty Sword: Sīrat ʿAntar and the Arabic Popular Epic.* Salt Lake City: University of Utah Press, 1996.

Norris, H. T., trans. *The Adventures of ʿAntar.* Warminster, U.K.: Aris and Phillips, 1980.

CHRISTOPHER HATCH MACEVITT

[See also **DMA:** Arabia: Pre-Islamic Arabia; Arabic Poetry; *Thousand and One Nights;* **Supp:** Hilāl, Banū *(Sīrat Banū Hilāl).*]

ANTHONY OF EGYPT, ST. (*ca.* 250–356), was admired during his own lifetime and became famous afterward for his ascetic endeavors. He and Pachomius, also an Egyptian, are known as the founders of Christian monasticism. Anthony's biography, attributed to St. Athanasius (*ca.* 293–373), bishop of Alexandria, had a great influence on the developing genre of Christian hagiography. Famously, this text played a role in Augustine's conversion in 386 (*Confessions* 8.6–8.12). This instance reveals the strong impression that Anthony's story could make on its readers; it also shows that the text had already been translated into Latin and was well known among some circles in Trier and Milan. Scholars debate the degree to which the *Life of Anthony* tells us about Anthony, versus how much it tells us about the author's ideal picture of an ascetic, with its careful depiction of Anthony's orthodox doctrine and his obedience to the clergy. Several letters attributed to Anthony survive, revealing a more philosophical bent to early Egyptian monastic life than is depicted in the hagiography. At any rate, the protagonist of the *Life of Anthony* became an influential model of the ascetic Christian life.

According to the narrative, Anthony grew up in a moderately wealthy, Coptic-speaking Christian family in a village in Upper Egypt. After his parents died, the teenaged Anthony was inspired when he heard the Gospel's exhortation to sell one's belongings, give to the poor, and follow Christ (Matt. 19:21). He did just this, leaving his younger sister in a community of virgins in order to begin his ascetic life. Anthony did not introduce ascetic practices to Christianity; he began by visiting and imitating other ascetics in his village who practiced various

The Temptation of St. Anthony. *The travails of the ascetic saint have been a popular theme for many centuries. This engraving is by Martin Schongauer (d. 1491).* THE LIBRARY OF CONGRESS.

types of self-denial. Anthony's practices included a strict diet of bread, salt, and water; all-night vigils; celibacy; and sleeping on the ground, which helped to fortify him for frequent psychological and physical attacks by demons. Next, he moved away from the other ascetics, at first residing in an empty tomb, then moving to an abandoned fort, and finally to a cave in a desert mountain. At each stage, would-be disciples and admirers disrupted Anthony's solitude and compelled him to serve as an adviser to novice ascetics, cure the sick, and exorcise demons. He left the desert twice, once in 311, to support Christians facing persecution, and later to denounce Arianism. The *Life* includes several lengthy sermons by Anthony devoted, not surprisingly, to ascetic discipline and battles with demons. Although the *Life* portrays Anthony as illiterate, he was able to hold his ground in debates with Greek philosophers who came to the desert to talk to him. Speaking through interpreters, the Christian ascetic impressed the philosophers with his arguments as well as his fine manners. Before his death at the age of 105, he requested that his burial place remain secret, in order to prevent the veneration of his body. A monastery grew at the place of his cave in the desert—and there is still a Coptic Orthodox monastery, Deir Mar Antonios, on the site. Groups of semi-independent hermits, striving to follow Anthony's example, became an important part of Eastern Orthodox monasticism.

BIBLIOGRAPHY

Athanasius, St. *Athanasius: The Life of Antony and the Letter to Marcellinus.* Translated by Robert C. Gregg. New York: Paulist Press, 1980.

Bolman, Elizabeth. *Monastic Visions: Wall Paintings in the Monastery of St. Antony at the Red Sea.* New Haven, Conn.: American Research Center in Egypt/Yale University Press, 2002.

Brakke, David. *Athanasius and the Politics of Asceticism.* Oxford: Clarendon Press; New York: Oxford University Press, 1995.

Rousseau, Philip. "Antony as Teacher in the Greek *Life.*" In *Greek Biography and Panegyric in Late Antiquity.* Edited by Tomas Hägg and Philip Rousseau. Berkeley: University of California Press, 2000.

Rubenson, Samuel. *The Letters of Saint Antony: Monasticism and the Making of a Saint.* Minneapolis, Minn.: Fortress Press, 1995. Commentary and translations of the letters attributed to Anthony.

JACLYN MAXWELL

[See also **DMA:** Athanasius of Alexandria, St.; Hagiography; Hermits, Eremitism; Monasticism, Origins.]

ANTWERP (French: Anvers; Flemish: Antwerpen). Located along the eastern bank of the Schelde River, accessible from the North Sea, Antwerp is the second-largest city in modern Belgium and one of the world's major seaports. For approximately a century prior to the religious wars of the late sixteenth century, Antwerp was the leading commercial center of northern Europe. Visitors marveled at its riches. It housed one of the first stock exchanges, gave birth to the newspaper, and was home to painters like Bruegel and Quinten Matsys, the humanist Justus Lipsius, the scientists Mercator and Ortelius, and Europe's largest printing house, run by Christophe Plantin. Yet this golden age could hardly have been foreseen in the small, regional port that Antwerp still was in the late fourteenth century.

Although archaeological evidence indicates that there had been a Gallo-Roman settlement near site of the modern city during the second and third centuries, there may not have been continuous habitation in the area until end of the Merovingian period, when we hear of missionary activity by St. Eligius in 645, St. Amand around 650, and, in the early eighth century, St. Willibrord. In 836 the Vikings destroyed the town, which was soon rebuilt.

The Schelde formed the western border of the Holy Roman Empire, and in the second half of the tenth century (*ca.* 973) the emperor Otto II created the margravate of Antwerp to protect that boundary. Geographically Antwerp was part of the duchy of Brabant, but politically it was only slowly integrated into the duchy because the margrave of Antwerp held his land in fief directly from the emperor and because the town was overshadowed by the more powerful and self-consciously Brabantine cities Brussels and Louvain. Furthermore, in the twelfth and thirteenth centuries Antwerp's economy was more closely tied to the towns of the county of Flanders, like Ghent, with whom it shared the Schelde River traffic and an early-developing cloth industry.

Over the course of the thirteenth and early fourteenth centuries, Antwerp attracted increased trade. Anglo-Flemish wars made Brabantine markets more interesting for English wool merchants, and the growing cloth industries of the towns of Brabant needed Antwerp's port. In response, both the dukes of Brabant and the counts of Flanders attempted to bring Antwerp more directly under their own control. Although Antwerp was far smaller than Louvain and Brussels, the count of Brabant gave it a representative on the council that supervised the duchy and granted it special trading rights. But the combination of Antwerp's growing role as a trading center and its closer connections with Brabant threatened the older commercial cities of Flanders, and in 1356 the count of Flanders annexed the town and subordinated it to Flemish interests. This put an abrupt end to Antwerp's first glimmers of prosperity and spelled the death of its cloth industry.

The annexation left Antwerp with only its twice-yearly fairs, but these were to prove the foundation of its future wealth. The merchants of Bruges treated the Antwerp fairs as branch markets under their control. This brought in new customers tied into the international commercial network of Bruges. The consequent rise in the international standing of the Antwerp fairs attracted new merchant groups like the Dutch, the southern Germans, and the London Merchant Adventurers who did not have a strong foothold in the traditional Bruges markets. Fortuitous floods in 1375–1376 and 1404 made Antwerp accessible to large seagoing vessels and made it an even more attractive destination at just the moment that Bruges's access to the North Sea was silting up. By 1470, Antwerp had lured away most international merchants from Bruges, and the prosperity that would soon make it one of the leading cities of Europe was already becoming apparent.

In addition to the wealth brought in by trade, Antwerp benefited from the favoritism of the counts of Burgundy, who had brought most of the Low Countries under their control during the fifteenth century. That century saw a flourishing of the arts that foreshadowed the greatness of the golden age. The construction of the magnificent Gothic Church of Our Lady (which would in the sixteenth century become the cathedral) was completed, and its choir became internationally famous. During the second half of the century, painters began coming to Antwerp, attracted by its affluence. By the last quarter of the century, Antwerp was already a major printing center.

BIBLIOGRAPHY

Acker, Jan van. "Anvers aux XVe et XVIe siècles." *Annales: Économies-Sociétés-Civilisations* 16 (1961): 248–278.

———. *Anvers: d'escale Romaine à port mondiale.* Antwerp and Brussels: Editions Mercurius, 1975. Useful for the political history.

Isacker, Karel van, and Raymond van Uytven, eds. *Antwerp: Twelve Centuries of History and Culture.* Antwerp: Fonds Mercator, 1986.

Prims, Floris. *Geschiedenis van Antwerpen.* 10 vols. Brussels: Standaard Boekhandel, 1927–1948. Still the authoritative history of the city in ten volumes, of which the first five deal with the medieval period.

Wee, Herman van der. *The Growth of the Antwerp Market and the European Economy (Fourteenth-Sixteenth Centuries).* 3 vols. The Hague, Netherlands: Nijhoff, 1963.

Werveke, Hans van. *Bruges et Anvers: Huit siècles de commerce flamand.* Brussels: Éditions de la Librarie Encyclopédique, 1944. The last two works are seminal studies on the economic development of the city.

EMILY KADENS

[See also **DMA:** Bruges; Flanders and the Low Countries; Ghent.]

ARCHAEOLOGY

INTRODUCTION AND HISTORY

While historians' primary data are derived from written sources, archaeologists use material remains to study the past. Material remains include three kinds of evidence: 1) artifacts such as pottery, weapons, and tools; 2) immovable items, known as "features," such as buildings, ditches, and fortifications; and 3) environmental data, sometimes termed "ecofacts," such as pollen and animal bones, which can provide information on past environments, diet, and health. Many medieval features, including cathedrals, fortifications, and half-timbered houses, continue to form part of the modern European landscape. As early as the 1580s, the Renaissance antiquarian William Camden made a study of the surviving prehistoric, Roman, and medieval monuments of Britain. His survey, published in the seminal work *Britannia*

(1586), represents one of the first attempts to use material remains to study the medieval past. Camden's work illustrates the antiquarian interest in the study of the material remains of past societies that developed throughout Europe in the sixteenth, seventeenth, and eighteenth centuries. Antiquarians in the Mediterranean world focused their research on the architecture, sculpture, and other artifacts of classical antiquity, while those in northern and central Europe, especially in regions that were never part of the Roman Empire, studied prehistoric and medieval remains. During this period, archaeological methods and chronologies were not well developed, and antiquaries often attributed all ancient buildings and artifacts to the earliest historically known societies in a particular region. As a result, French antiquities, regardless of their age, were often attributed to the Celts, while those from Sweden were seen as the work of the Goths.

While Camden's work centered on visible monuments, the majority of medieval remains, including building foundations, pottery and glass fragments, and animal bones, are recovered through excavations. Excavations of medieval sites also began in the early modern period. Perhaps the most famous of these is the opening of the tomb of the Frankish ruler Childeric I (*d.* 481/ 482) in Tournai, Belgium, in 1653. In the nineteenth century, especially in France, interest in medieval archaeology grew as a result of concerns about the destruction of medieval monuments and a fascination with the contents of buried early medieval tombs. Throughout Europe, the nineteenth century was also a period of growing nationalism. Outside the Mediterranean world, the Migration Period and the early Middle Ages were seen as a period of ethnogenesis, leading to an increased interest in Viking archaeology in Scandinavia, early Slavic archaeology in central and eastern Europe, and Anglo-Saxon archaeology in England. The situation in the Mediterranean world was quite different. In Italy, nineteenth-century scholars traced their heritage back to the Roman Empire, and the Lombardic graves of the Migration Period were seen as material remains of outside invaders. Similarly, in Greece, archaeological attention focused primarily on classical antiquity and the early Byzantine period. As of 2003, medieval archaeology as a discipline is poorly developed in Greece.

During the later nineteenth and early twentieth centuries archaeologists developed methods of stratigraphic excavation and recording that are still in use. However, the modern discipline of medieval archaeology was born in the aftermath of World War II, when the destruction of portions of many modern cities revealed their medieval and Roman predecessors. The number of medieval excavations has increased dramatically since the 1960s, as urban redevelopment threatens the cores of many medieval cities. In many European countries far more money is spent on medieval archaeology than is spent on all of prehistory.

Medieval archaeologists study the period from the decline of the Western Roman Empire in the fifth century to the beginnings of the voyages of discovery and the modern world in approximately 1500. The archaeology of the Middle Ages is essentially a hybrid discipline, drawing on both historical and archaeological evidence, and medieval archaeologists can be found in departments of history, art history, archaeology, and anthropology throughout Europe and North America. Only a small number of universities, most notably the University of Aarhus in Denmark, have separate departments of medieval archaeology.

Since the quality and quantity of documentary evidence is limited for the Migration Period and the early Middle Ages, most archaeologists who study the barbarian migrations of the fifth and sixth centuries, the Viking period (*ca.* 750–1050) in Scandinavia and the British Isles, and early medieval Europe outside the Roman frontiers were trained as prehistorians. As such, their interests tend to focus on settlement patterns, subsistence practices, and technology. These data can be used to reconstruct the day-to-day lives of early medieval people. Since written records are so limited for much of the early medieval world, basic questions such as what people ate and where they lived can be answered only through archaeological research. Archaeologists working in later medieval Europe are more often trained as historians or art historians. These scholars have access to a far wider range of documentary evidence and are more often located within departments of history or art history. They have often focused their research on such questions as the architectural history of castles and cathedrals, the development of cities, and the archaeology of pilgrimage. The differences in approach can be illustrated by the history of archaeological research at two of the most important long-term medieval excavations in the British Isles—West Stow and Wharram Percy.

The West Stow excavations are typical of the kinds of medieval excavations conducted by archaeologists trained as prehistorians. West Stow is an early Anglo-Saxon village in eastern England that was occupied from about 420 to about 650. There are no historical documents that refer to the Anglo-Saxon settlement at West Stow in any way; all the information about the site was derived from the material remains recovered through excavation. Major goals of the West Stow research included understanding the layout of the Anglo-Saxon village, its dates of occupation, the forms of the houses, and the economy that supported the villagers. The results were presented in a multivolume site report that resembles the reports that are typically produced from prehistoric excavations.

The history of the Wharram Percy excavations is entirely different. The research at Wharram Percy was begun by Maurice Beresford, a medieval economic historian, in 1948. Beresford was interested in the problem of rural depopulation in the later Middle Ages and its relationship to enclosure, late medieval economic changes, and the Black Death. Beresford began by examining Ordnance Survey maps of northern England for parish names that were no longer matched by villages. The name Wharram Percy was accompanied by the isolated church of St. Martin. Preliminary excavations at the site confirmed that Wharram Percy was, in fact, a deserted medieval village. However, Beresford had no formal training in archaeology. In 1953 the direction of the excavation was taken over by John Hurst, who was then a postgraduate research student in prehistoric archaeology, but who had no formal training in the archaeology of the Middle Ages. This was the beginning of a forty-year partnership between Beresford and Hurst. Throughout the course of the research, however, analyses of historic documents such as maps, cartularies (books that record landowners' possessions), account books, and inventories went hand in hand with excavation.

EARLY MEDIEVAL ARCHAEOLOGY

Archaeologists who study the early medieval period have traditionally been concerned with the transformation of the post-Roman world, including the migration of barbarian tribes both within and outside the Roman Empire. Relatively few settlement sites dating from the fifth to eighth centuries A.D. have been excavated anywhere in Europe. As a result, much of the archaeological record for the Migration Period comes from burials and cemetery sites. Since many pagan graves contain grave goods such as jewelry, weapons, and pottery, they are major sources of information for population movements and social organization. For example, the excavation of the *Reihengräber* (literally, graves in rows) in southern and western Germany, which began in the middle of the nineteenth century, has shed light on the chronology and material culture of the Merovingian Franks.

A crucial problem facing all archaeologists working in the Migration Period is correlation of the archaeological record with the limited historical sources for the era.

Archaeological cultures are groups of artifact types, such as styles of metalwork decoration or types of pottery, that repeatedly occur together. These archaeological cultures do not always correspond to the tribes or ethnic groups described in the documentary sources. The attempts to use archaeology to reconstruct the early history of the Slavs illustrate this problem. Today, over half of Europe is occupied by peoples speaking Slavic languages, and we know that Slavic peoples may have been even more widespread in the early Middle Ages. The initial westward expansion of the Slavs appears to be associated with the westward movement on the Huns. However, it has been difficult archaeologically to identify the homeland of the Slavs in eastern Europe in the fifth century.

An archaeological question that is closely related to the barbarian migrations of the fifth and sixth centuries is the question of the transformation of the Western Roman Empire. In the first half of the twentieth century, the Belgian historian Henri Pirenne suggested that the Mediterranean remained a Roman lake even after the barbarian migrations of the fifth century until maritime trade was interrupted by the seventh-century Islamic conquest of North Africa. Pirenne argued that the decline in commerce caused by the Islamic advance affected all of western Europe, including the Carolingian empire. For the past twenty-five years, archaeologists have attempted to use archaeological data to assess the Pirenne thesis by examining the evidence for trade and commerce from the fifth to the tenth centuries in the Mediterranean region and the North Sea. On the one hand, archaeological evidence from Italian sites such as Luni indicates that both trade and urbanism began to decline long before the Arab conquests of the seventh and eighth centuries. On the other hand, an increasing body of archaeological data suggests that widespread trade networks developed along the coats of the North Sea and the Baltic Sea from the seventh century onward.

One group of early medieval sites, the "emporia," has received particular archaeological attention since the 1970s. Most emporia are dated to the seventh to ninth centuries. They served as centers for long-distance and regional trade and may also have played a role in the political consolidation of early medieval kingdoms in northern Europe. The emporia are located along the North Sea and Baltic Sea coasts and include such sites as Hamwih (Saxon Southampton), Eoforwic (Anglian York), Ipswich, and London in England; Quentovic in France; Ribe in Denmark; Dorestad in the Netherlands; Haithabu in Germany; Birka in Sweden; Wolin in Poland; and Staraya Logoda in Russia. Many of the emporia have been the foci of major programs of archaeological excavation and research, yielding valuable new evidence for the development of trade and specialized crafts during the early Middle Ages in northern Europe. Although some of the emporia, such as Hamwih and Ipswich, are located on the sites of later medieval towns and cities, most of these sites ceased functioning as major ports of trade in the ninth century. Others, including Quentovic, were abandoned and never reoccupied.

Historic documents and coins indicate that Quentovic was the major early medieval Frankish port. It also served as a port of entry for Anglo-Saxon pilgrims on their way to Rome. The place-name means the "market on the River Canche," but the exact location of Quentovic was not identified until 1984. Initial archaeological fieldwork at the modern hamlet of Visemarest in northern France, approximately 4.5 miles (7 kilometers) from the mouth of the Canche, revealed Carolingian pottery. Ten seasons of test excavations by Manchester University in cooperation with the French antiquities authorities revealed the extent of the site, as well as the location of the early medieval waterfront, burial mounds, and a workshop for the manufacture of jewelry. Additional large-scale, open-area excavations will be needed to reveal the details of the layout of this emporium and its role in regional and long-distance trade.

Ipswich is located on the sheltered head of the Orwell River estuary in eastern England. The town is located around nine miles (15 kilometers) from Sutton Hoo, the burial ground for the royal house of East Anglia, and it is possible that the site was founded by the East Anglian royal house in the late sixth century. Archaeological evidence from the seventh-to-ninth-century features at Ipswich indicates that the economy of the town was based on craft production and international trade. Evidence for a number of craft activities was recovered from the emporium-period features, but pottery production was, by far, the most important industry in Middle Saxon Ipswich. Unlike most other English pottery of the period, Ipswich ware was wheel made and kiln fired. This pottery was widely distributed throughout eastern England during the Middle Saxon period, providing strong evidence for regional trade at this time. The pottery evidence from seventh-to-ninth-century Ipswich also indicates that foreign traders were present at the site during this period. Imported items that have been recovered from Ipswich include German lava millstones and wine that appears to have been imported from Germany in wooden barrels. Thus, the archaeological evidence from Ipswich indicates that the emporium was a center for international as well as regional trade.

The site of Dorestad in the Netherlands is one of the most extensively excavated of all the early medieval emporia. Although excavations began at the site as early as the nineteenth century, a major program of excavation between 1967 and 1977 revealed approximately seventy-four acres (30 hectares) of the early medieval settlement. Dorestad is located at the point where the Lower Rhine, the Lek, and the Kromme Rijn Rivers diverge, a focal point in the communication system. Excavations revealed an extensive harbor and trading area that was occupied between approximately 675 and 875. Crafts practiced at Dorestad included woodworking and bone and antler working. Evidence for long-distance trade includes lava quern stones from the Eifel Mountains in Germany and imported pottery. Even some of the cereals consumed at Dorestad may have been imported. The archaeological evidence from Dorestad points to both specialized craft production and regional and long-distance trade. In contrast to the Pirenne thesis, the archaeological data from all the emporium sites indicate that sophisticated systems of craft production and exchange had been established throughout northern Europe by the seventh century and that these trading sites continued to flourish until the ninth century.

URBAN ARCHAEOLOGY

Although many medieval churchyards, cemeteries, farms, and villages have been excavated during the past fifty years, since World War II medieval archaeology has been dominated by a series of large-scale urban excavation projects. The study of the growth and development of medieval cities has been one of the greatest achievements of modern medieval archaeology. As noted above, the destruction caused by World War II opened many inaccessible areas of European cities to archaeological exploration. In addition, urban redevelopment since the 1960s has allowed for additional urban research. While antiquities laws vary from country to country, many European countries require archaeological research before new construction can be built in historically sensitive areas, such as city centers. Major medieval archaeological excavations have been conducted in cities across Europe, from Dublin to Novgorod in Russia. These excavations have shed new light on the medieval roots of modern European cities.

Any discussion of medieval urban archaeology in Europe must begin with the pioneering work of Martin Biddle at the Winchester excavations (1961–1971). Winchester began its life as the Roman town of Venta Belgarum and briefly served as the capital of England in the eleventh century. While local historians had always thought that the modern town of Winchester retained its Roman street plan, Biddle's excavations conclusively demonstrated that the modern street plan is, in fact, late Saxon in date. In addition, Biddle's excavations at the Brook Street (Tanner Street) site shed new light on the day-to-day lives of medieval leather workers.

Medieval archaeology has also contributed to our understanding of the history of later medieval cities in Europe. Major programs of excavation and research have been carried out at Lübeck in Germany, Tours in France, Novgorod in Russia, Prague in the Czech Republic, and Trondheim in Norway. The excavations at Trondheim, formerly known as Nidaros, are particularly important because they trace the development of the town from a small tenth-century trading place to a major center of pilgrimage and specialized craft production.

Some of the most spectacular later medieval remains have been recovered from the excavation of the city of Novgorod in Russia. From the twelfth to the fifteenth century, Novgorod served as a capital of northwestern Russia. The excavations, which began in 1932 and have continued for over sixty years, revealed entire blocks of the medieval town. In addition to the typical medieval artifacts made of pottery, metal, and stone, the Novgorod excavations produced many preserved organic materials including wood, bone, leather, and birchbark. The excavators recovered many medieval musical instruments and over 700 birchbark documents dating to the eleventh through fifteenth centuries. Linguistic analysis revealed that these documents were written in a dialect that is different from common Russian and is more closely related to the western Slavic languages.

ARCHAEOLOGY AND MEDIEVAL ARCHITECTURE

As noted above, the modern European landscape includes many churches, castles, and other structures that were built during the Middle Ages. Systematic study of these standing medieval buildings can contribute to our understanding of medieval technology and culture. Archaeological surveys of standing medieval churches and castles have been carried out in many regions of Europe. However, the study of extant medieval architecture has made a particularly important contribution to the study of the archaeology of the Crusader Kingdom of Jerusalem. Earlier surveys of ecclesiastical buildings within the Crusader Kingdom have recently been supplemented by a detailed survey of all the standing nonecclesiastical buildings in the region dated between 1099 and 1291 (the period of Christian control). Since relatively few excavations have taken place at crusader sites, architectural surveys of town walls, castles, rural dwellings, wells and aqueducts, and mills provide much of our information about the nature of Frankish settlement in the Holy Land. For example, architectural surveys combined with excavational data have challenged the notion that Frankish settlement in the Kingdom of Jerusalem was largely confined to towns. As the costs of archaeological excavation continue to rise, nonexcavational approaches to the collection of archaeological data will play an increasingly important role in medieval archaeology.

NEW DIRECTIONS

Many of the major medieval excavation projects of the 1970s and 1980s focused primarily on questions of economic behavior. Rural excavations were concerned with settlement patterns and subsistence activities. An outstanding example of economically oriented rural archaeology is the work of Thomas McGovern at the western settlement of the Viking colony in Greenland. McGovern's excavations in the western settlement emphasized the recovery of animal bones and other environmental data that could shed light on Norse animal husbandry and hunting practices. In particular, the Greenland research focused on the economic, social, and environmental causes of the failure of the western settlement in the mid-fourteenth century.

Many major urban excavations also focused on economic questions, especially issues of craft production and regional and long-distance trade. While these questions were of particular importance in the study of the emporia, later medieval urban excavations also focused on economic issues. For example, the long-term excavations at Lübeck, a major Hanseatic town on the Baltic in Germany, revealed evidence for the production of high-quality glazed ceramics and, from the late thirteenth century onward, bakery ovens that were used to supply oceangoing ships. In addition, domestic artifacts, along with historic documents, were used to identify the full range of social and economic classes that inhabited Lübeck during the Middle Ages.

The economic approach to medieval archaeology generated a wealth of new data on subsistence activities and trading patterns. However, economic archaeology can lead to a one-dimensional view of medieval life. Theoretical changes in the field of archaeology in the 1980s led to an increased interest in the archaeological study of noneconomic activities such as religion and ritual, politics, and gender. In addition, environmental archaeology has been transformed from the simple study of past human subsistence practices to a broader interest in the interrelationship between humans and their physical, bi-

ological, and social environments. Since the 1980s, medieval archaeologists have attempted to use material remains to address a broader range of questions about the medieval world.

One of the most important of these recent studies is Roberta Gilchrist's examination of the social construction of gender in later medieval monastic communities in England. Gilchrist's research reveals important differences in the material remains associated with male monasteries and nunneries. In particular, Gilchrist notes the greater enclosure of monastic women when compared with religious men.

Another important new direction is the archaeological study of pilgrimage. In peacetime, pilgrimage was the main reason that long journeys were undertaken during the Middle Ages. Studies of pilgrims' souvenirs recovered from the city of London reveal visits to the shrine of St. Thomas Becket (ca. 1118–1170) in Canterbury, to the sepulcher of St. James (d. A.D. 44) at Compostela in Spain, and to the holy city of Rome. Souvenirs have also allowed archaeologists to reconstruct the routes traveled by these medieval pilgrims.

An excellent example of the contemporary approach to the study of the complex relationships between medieval people and their environment is seen in the research on early medieval farmsteads in Iceland sponsored by the North Atlantic Biocultural Organization (NABO), an international and interdisciplinary group of scholars who study the archaeology of the North Atlantic region. Their research in Iceland, including the excavation of the Viking Age farmstead at Hofstaðir, seeks to study the complex interactions between humans and the Icelandic landscape at the time of the initial Viking colonization. In regions of Europe with longer settlement histories, medieval archaeologists have collaborated with prehistorians to study long-term patterns of rural settlement.

THE FUTURE OF MEDIEVAL ARCHAEOLOGY

The future of medieval archaeology depends, to a great extent, on the nature and speed of economic development within Europe. In rapidly growing countries, such as Ireland, archaeologists can barely stay one step ahead of the bulldozers. The number of sites that have been excavated in Ireland has increased tenfold since 1990. The pace of development allows little time for reflection. Sites are excavated, artifacts are processed, and reports are written. Many of the reports become part of what is known as the "gray literature" of archaeology. These reports are available in government records offices, but not in books, journals, and magazines that are accessible to scholars and the general public. In addition, when construction and redevelopment take place within city centers, it is the medieval archaeological remains that are most often threatened, since Roman and prehistoric materials are often protected by meters of later accumulations. Medieval archaeological sites are important historical resources, and it is crucial that some of these sites are preserved intact for future generations of archaeologists.

BIBLIOGRAPHY

GENERAL WORKS ON MEDIEVAL ARCHAEOLOGY

Barford, P. M. *The Early Slavs: Culture and Society in Early Medieval Eastern Europe.* London: British Museum Press, 2001.

Barry, T. B. *The Archaeology of Medieval Ireland.* London: Routledge, 1988.

Crabtree, Pam J., ed. *Medieval Archaeology: An Encyclopedia.* New York: Garland, 2000.

Edwards, Nancy. *The Archaeology of Early Medieval Ireland.* Philadelphia: University of Pennsylvania Press, 1990.

Fehring, Günter. *The Archaeology of Medieval Germany: An Introduction.* London: Routledge, 1991.

Fitzhugh, William W., and Elizabeth I. Ward. *Vikings: The North Atlantic Saga.* Washington, D.C.: Smithsonian Institution Press, 2000.

Lock, Peter, and G. D. R. Sanders, eds. *The Archaeology of Medieval Greece.* Oxford: Oxbow, 1996.

Pringle, Denys. *Secular Buildings in the Crusader Kingdom of Jerusalem: An Archaeological Gazetteer.* Cambridge, U.K.: Cambridge University Press, 1997.

Randsborg, Klavs. *The First Millennium A.D. in Europe and the Mediterranean: An Archaeological Essay.* Cambridge, U.K.: Cambridge University Press, 1991.

SITE REPORTS

Beresford, Maurice, and John Hurst. *Wharram Percy: Deserted Medieval Village.* English Heritage Series. London: Batsford, 1990.

Biddle, Martin. "The Study of Winchester: Archaeology and History in a British Town, 1961–1983." In *British Academy Papers on Anglo-Saxon England.* Edited by E. G. Stanley. Oxford: Oxford University Press, 1990.

Brisbane, Mark A., ed. *The Archaeology of Novgorod Russia: Recent Results from the Town and Its Hinterland.* Monograph Series 13. Lincoln, Nebr.: Society for Medieval Archaeology, 1992.

Hall, Richard A. *Book of York.* English Heritage Series. London: Batsford, 1996.

Hill, David, David Barrett, Keith Maude, Julia Warburton, and Margaret Worthington. "Quentovic Defined." *Antiquity* 64 (1991): 51–58.

McGovern, T. H. "Cows, Harp Seals, and Churchbells: Adaptation and Extinction in Norse Greenland." *Human Ecology* 8, no. 3 (1980): 245–277.

Wade, Keith. "Ipswich." In *The Rebirth of Towns in the West, A.D. 700–1050.* Edited by R. Hodges and B. Hobley. London: Council for British Archaeology, 1988.

West, Stanley. *West Stow: The Anglo-Saxon Village.* East Anglian Archaeology Report 24. Ipswich, U.K.: Suffolk County Planning Department, 1985.

SPECIAL STUDIES

Amorosi, T., J. Woollett, S. Perdikaris, and T. H. McGovern. "Regional Zooarchaeology and Global Change: Problems and Potentials." *World Archaeology* 28 (1996): 126–157.

Gilchrist, Roberta. *Gender and Material Culture: The Archaeology of Religious Women.* London: Routledge, 1994.

Hodges, Richard. *Dark Age Economics: The Origins of Towns and Trade, A.D. 600–1000.* London: Duckworth, 1982.

Hodges, Richard, and David Whitehouse. *Mohammed, Charlemagne, and the Origins of Europe: Archaeology and the Pirenne Thesis.* London, Duckworth, 1983.

Stopford, Jennie, ed. *Pilgrimage Explored.* Rochester, N.Y.: York Medieval Press, 1999.

PAM J. CRABTREE

[See also **DMA:** Barbarians, Invasions of; Crusades and Crusader States; Novgorod; Pilgrimage, Western European; Vikings.]

ARCHITECTURE, DOMESTIC.

Principally pertaining to places of human habitation, the category of domestic architecture in all premodern periods embraces a much wider range of structures than we might today term "houses." In both legal and functional terms, the western medieval "house," particularly in its rural forms, included under its umbrella barns, gardens, granaries, and artisan's quarters. Owing largely to the recent contributions of archaeology, the study of domestic architecture now includes the houses of both the wealthy and the poor in their rural and urban manifestations. These houses provide more than a history of one type of building. Through plans and artifacts, records of sale and wills, houses have been most profitably used to trace a variety of social histories, such as the evolution of family structure, changes in ideas of privacy and individuality, and even the history of land ownership and exploitation.

LATE ANTIQUITY

Domestic architecture in the final centuries of antiquity saw both the continued expression of Roman types of habitation and, simultaneously, the breakdown of those forms, reflecting monumental changes in wealth and lifestyles. In Britain, France, Spain, and to a lesser extent Italy, the largest and most sumptuous Roman villas date to the first half of the fourth century. These

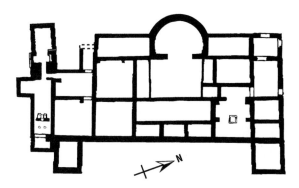

Fig. 1. Plan of a Late-Antique Villa at Lullingstone, Kent. *Note the apsed hall characteristic of northern Roman architecture.* BASED ON D. NEAL, *LULLINGSTONE ROMAN VILLA* (LONDON: ENGLISH HERITAGE, 1991).

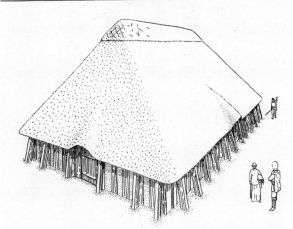

Fig. 2a. Alternative Reconstructions of an Anglo-Saxon House from Cowdery's Down, Hampshire. *Hypothetical exterior views. Illustrations by Anthony Kersting.* ARCHAEOLOGICAL JOURNAL.

rural estates typically consisted of a main living block with baths, with separate quarters for servants, agricultural activities, and the collection of rents and crops. In southern Gaul and Hispania, the living blocks of such villas were often arranged around a courtyard, while British and northern Gallic examples were frequently laid out as horizontal blocks fronted by a porch or corridor, as in the villa of Lullingstone, in Kent (fig. 1). Many villas are best known for their rich floor mosaics, as this art form flourished in symbiosis with the rise and enrichment of these rural estates. Late antique villas were similarly marked by the aggrandizement of their dining and reception rooms, whose rich decoration and use of elaborate apsed architectural forms seem to have acted as a backdrop for the elaborate receptions staged by increasingly powerful landowners. Even the small Lullingstone villa included a large apsed hall that occupied a significant portion of its domestic fabric.

In urban contexts, fewer examples of wealthy homes have come to light, lending support to the notion that aristocratic display in late antiquity increasingly took place in the countryside. What examples survive, such as the so-called House of the Valerii on the Caelian Hill in Rome, paint a picture similar to that found in villas. Here wealthy aristocrats may have not only received visitors and clients but heard judicial cases and made political decisions. This indicates that the great reception halls of private houses may have taken over the functions of the increasingly decrepit public basilicas, appropriating to the home that which was previously proper to the public sphere.

The houses of the lower classes, particularly the rural peasantry, are poorly understood during the High Imperial period. During late antiquity, however, they become impossible to ignore, and beginning with the final decades of the fourth century, lower-class housing becomes the most commonly detected type of habitation in the archaeological record. In both city and country, the most common site of lower-class housing was in fact the aristocratic home, converted to multifamily use. The rooms and courtyards of these large houses were subdivided, hearths were built over their mosaic floors, and industrial installations, such as glass and metal furnaces or wine presses, were constructed alongside living spaces. The material wealth of the inhabitants of these converted houses varied enormously—some having access to imported wine, while others were forced to make do with handmade pottery—raising important, as yet unresolved questions about the changes in the nature of wealth and poverty during this critical period.

Fig. 2b. Reconstruction of an Anglo-Saxon House from Cowdery's Down, Hampshire. *Little has survived of the early "long houses," and the construction of the common medieval hall is the subject of conjecture. Illustration by Anthony Kersting.* ARCHAEOLOGICAL JOURNAL.

SIXTH TO NINTH CENTURY

Very few new aristocratic houses of the Roman West are known after the mid-fifth century. The most notable exceptions are residences associated with the Gothic kings, such as the large rural estate at Monte Barro in northern Italy, thought to be the residence of a Lombard lord; the so-called palace of Theodoric in Ravenna; or the seventh-century Visigothic palaces of Pla de Nadal and Recopolis in Spain. Rather, it is the rural peasant house that, beginning in the late sixth century, appears most frequently in the material record. These peasant houses could appear within converted villas or as part of a larger village. In southern Gaul, Hispania, and Italy,

these were most frequently single-room houses, partially excavated into the ground (termed "sunken huts," *fonds de cabanes,* or *Grubenhäuser*). These might measure anywhere from about sixteen to fifty-six feet (five to seventeen meters) in length. In Germania, Scandanavia, Anglo-Saxon England, and the Lowlands, the typical housing unit was composed of a long, rectangular house, accompanied by one or more outbuildings, including sunken huts or granaries, all enclosed by a perimeter fence. In all cases, the building materials were generally similar, with wooden posts used as the principal support, timber and grass materials used for roofs, and mud, beaten earth, sticks, and occasionally dry stone masonry used

Fig. 3. Model of 9th-Century Houses Built in the Forum of Nerva, Rome. This period seems to mark the return
of housing on a grander scale. ELECTRA. REPRODUCED BY PERMISSION.

for side walls. With only a few exceptions, mortared masonry does not appear in domestic architecture until the ninth or tenth century.

The general appearance of these long houses is surprisingly consistent, with one important functional distinction. In parts of Scandinavia, the southern Baltic countries, coastal Germany, and the Netherlands, long houses tended to be of the so-called mixed type, divided into a central room with a hearth for gathering, eating, and sleeping, with a second, smaller room intended for stock animals. In other parts of early medieval Europe, including Britain, animals seem to have been housed separately, and the long house was given over solely to eating, sleeping, and assembly, such as in the sixth- to seventh-century houses unearthed at Cowdery's Down in Hampshire (fig. 2). The determination of functional types, as well as specific architectural detail, rests heavily on archaeological data open to a range of interpretation (see the variety of reconstructions offered by the Cowdery's Down excavators). In any case, these long houses formed the origin of the medieval hall, the heart of the medieval house and of domestic life until the sixteenth century.

Until the late twentieth century little was known of urban housing during the early Middle Ages.

Recent archaeological and archival research in Rome, however, has indicated that that city's *insulae,* or multistoried Roman-period apartment buildings, continued to function through late antiquity and the early Middle Ages. Most new houses, however, were built into the ruins of earlier buildings, using spoliate materials and including a small garden and perhaps one or two outbuildings. Documentary sources likewise describe Roman urban houses as composed of a house, garden, and outbuildings, indicating that Roman, and probably other early medieval urban houses, strongly resembled their rural cousins.

The Carolingian period marked the return of the monumental aristocratic house in palaces such as Aachen and Ingelheim. While the former example included an apsed audience hall modeled on late Roman and Byzantine examples, Ingelheim's hall was of rectangular form, a more monumental version of the halls ubiquitous in Germanic and Scandinavian housing. On a more modest scale, two well-to-do houses of ninth-century date have been recently found in the Forum of Nerva in Rome (fig. 3). Their two-story plan, accessed by an exterior staircase and built of spoliate materials, is one of the earliest examples of what would become the characteristic Roman townhouse. In the rural environment, the creation of fortified homes built with mortared masonry

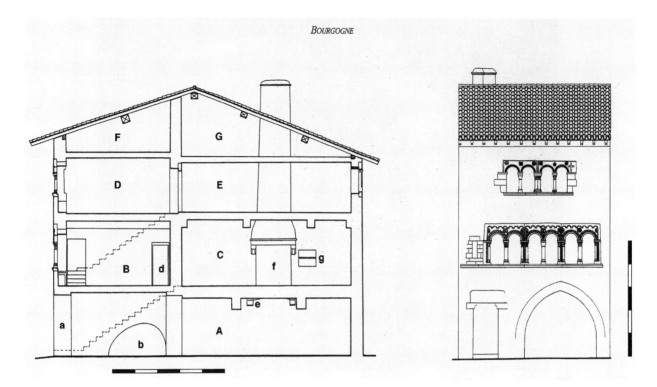

BOURGOGNE

Fig. 4. Town House in Cluny. *This 12th-century example at 9, rue de Merle, has a ground-level workshop and sleeping quarters above. Illustration by J. D. Salvêque. Print provided by New York Public Library.* CNRS EDITIONS. REPRODUCED BY PERMISSION.

marked a similar departure from earlier trends, but one whose study more properly belongs to the study of castles and fortifications generally.

TENTH TO FOURTEENTH CENTURY

The reappearance and subsequent expansion of masonry construction after the ninth century and advances in timber roof construction, coupled with the growth of towns, generally fostered the development of the urban townhouse. Usually the homes of wealthy merchants, these houses quickly adopted the Romanesque and later Gothic architectural vocabulary of their day, but like their humbler rural cousins, they continued to accommodate a variety of functions under one roof, including industrial activities and shops. The relatively strong spatial division between living and work spaces and the liminal position of the hall between the two are likewise characteristic. An example typical of the French townhouse is that at 9, rue de Merle, in Cluny, which dates to the twelfth century (fig. 4). Arranged as a simple, narrow rectangle, the house had three stories connected by internal staircases. The bottom floor opened onto the street and served as workshop and vending space, while the hall and principal sleeping chamber were located on the second floor. The upper-story facade was articulated with rounded columns and capitals in Romanesque style.

Of course, not all urban houses were as fine as the Cluny example, and a more modest plan, with a ground-floor hall flanked by two story blocks on either side, containing, respectively, apartments and service quarters, is commonly found in small English towns.

The larger houses of the aristocratic classes, both in town and country, display many of the same features, particularly use of the ground floor for service areas and of the second story for the hall. In plan, however, these houses consisted of a number of freestanding buildings, often grouped around an internal court. Such a house might have one or more halls, upper-story apartments, and a chapel. The kitchen in such residences was typically detached for fireproofing reasons. Both rural and urban houses might include one or more towers, although these often provided the appearance, rather than the functional fabric, of defensive architecture.

It is in these aristocratic houses that the evolution of the hall is most clearly traced. In the twelfth century, halls often assumed a three-aisled plan, the large span of their roofs requiring intermediary supports. With advances in timber construction techniques in the thirteenth century, particularly trussing systems, these supports were gradually removed, permitting the construction of expansive, uninterrupted spaces. At one

Fig. 5. Great Hall, Penshurst, Kent. *Sir John de Pulteney's great hall served as the principal public apartment of a rural manor house. Photo by A. Kersting.* YALE UNIVERSITY PRESS. REPRODUCED BY PERMISSION.

end of the hall, a raised dais held the high table for the lord and his family, while the hearth was set in the hall's center. Fireplaces with wall chimneys, while present in castle architecture as early as the twelfth century, did not become widespread until the later Middle Ages. The hall windows were typically large and were often preceded by deep embrasures in which private conversations and meetings might be held outside the main gathering. One particularly fine surviving example is the hall at Penshurst in Kent, built in the 1340s (fig. 5).

While the ninth century may have witnessed fundamental changes in both the form and materials of urban architecture of the upper classes, village architecture and rural village culture of the high and later Middle Ages was generally more conservative, retaining many of its

early medieval traits. The large-scale village excavations of Wharram Percy in England and Rougiers in southern France have provided two different pictures of rural medieval houses. The houses of Wharram Percy, including its manor house, were much like the long houses of the Anglo-Saxon period in materials and simple rectangular form. However, unlike their early medieval predecessors, most of the Wharram houses were of the so-called mixed type, with animals and humans finding space under the same roof, reflecting the general popularity of this type of housing over the whole of high medieval Europe. The topographic situation of Rougiers, one of the so-called *villages perchés* set atop a steep hill, produced radically different forms. Two-storied houses were composed of several rooms arranged linearly. Hearths were generally located just outside the house, as interior fireplaces with hoods or chimneys were rare in village housing until the later Middle Ages. The result at Rougiers was that most of the household's collective activity probably took place outdoors rather than in the hall.

LATE MEDIEVAL DEVELOPMENTS

The simple one- to two-roomed village house was extraordinarily long-lived and persisted in many areas through the eighteenth century. The appearance of farms, multistructure residences built around a small court, sometimes complete with fortifications, was an important facet of later medieval rural development in England, France, and Germany but never fully replaced the single-room rural house.

More fundamental changes appeared in urban houses and the homes of the wealthy, namely the reduction and eventual disappearance of the hall. The timing of this change varied enormously, and the persistence of halls well into the early modern period indicates not only the gradual pace of that change, but also the potent symbolic character the hall continued to carry. Already in thirteenth-century England, halls increasingly appeared on the ground floor, sharing space with an ever-larger array of more intimate meeting spaces, the most important of which was the family living room. The amount of house space given over to the solar (a more private, family chamber) and other sleeping quarters likewise increased, and the kitchen was incorporated into the house fabric. The gradual disappearance of the central hearth (such as that still preserved at Penshurst) and the increasing frequency of its replacement with the wall fireplaces over the fourteenth and fifteenth centuries similarly meant that high hall ceilings were no longer functionally necessary to prevent fire, thus permitting the construction of additional living spaces above the hall. By the sixteenth century, many residential halls were reduced to elaborate vestibules. The disappearance of the hall and with it the gathering of family and extra-family groups as the nexus of domestic life thus marked both an architectural and social watershed.

BIBLIOGRAPHY

Chapelot, Jean, and Robert Fossier. *Le village et la maison au Moyen Âge.* Paris: Hachette littérature, 1980.

Coates-Stephens, Robert. "Housing in Early Medieval Rome, 500–1000 A.D." *Papers of the British School in Rome* 64 (1996): 239–259.

Esquieu, Yves, and Jean-Marie Pesez, eds. *Cent maisons médiévales en France: Du XIIe au milieu du XVIe siècle: Un corpus et une esquisse.* Paris: CNRS éditions, 1998.

Mercer, Eric. *English Vernacular Houses: A Study of Traditional Farmhouses and Cottages.* London: H. M. Stationery Office, 1975.

Percival, John. *The Roman Villa: An Historical Introduction.* London: Batsford, 1976.

Wood, Margaret. *The English Mediaeval House.* New York: Harper and Row, 1994.

KIM BOWES

[See also **DMA:** Castles and Fortifications; Villages: Community; Villages: Settlement; **Supp:** Archaeology.]

ARCHITECTURE, SYRO-JACOBITE. See **Syrian Christian Architecture.**

ARTHURIAN ROMANCES. Since the 1980s, Arthurian romance has arguably given those who study the Middle Ages more to say, to one another and to those outside the academy, than any other feature of medieval culture. Bibliographies and general estimates suggest that scholars published more than twenty thousand separate articles and books on matters Arthurian in the last two decades of the twentieth century, and this number does not take into account the lively conversations that have erupted among medievalists and specialists in other fields (for example, art history, film studies, cultural studies, American studies) about the treatment of Arthur in post-medieval visual and written materials. Scholarship now takes as legitimate topics of study not merely the works of Chrétien, Wolfram, and Malory but also poetry and visual art ranging from the romances of Tasso and Spenser through Tennyson, the Pre-Raphaelites, T. H. White, and Marion Zimmer Bradley to the motives and sponsorship of academic work itself. This escalation of scholarship and spread of interest have not settled the issues that perplexed or preoccupied earlier generations of experts. Though it has inevitably built upon or borrowed from foundational studies produced in the nineteenth and twentieth centuries, recent work has frequently turned away from the pursuit of the "real" Arthur or the genuine origins of Arthurian romance, seeking instead to make sense of particular, sometimes peculiar, versions of these stories, according to the local interests, conditions, and audiences that sponsored them.

Earlier investigations of Arthurian romance often bore an uncanny resemblance to the Grail quest. Experts sought to discover the font from which all Arthurian meaning arose, whether through history (linguistic and tribal identities, group rivalries, archaeological remains), literary and cultural traditions (bardic tales, Celtic legends, myth, or religion), or textual recuperation (the scientific reconstruction of the original words or the author's intentions of surviving romances). Jessie L.

Weston's celebrated study *From Ritual to Romance* (1920) conveys in its title this contrast of an authentic core meaning embedded beneath the sundry, sometimes dazzling but often misleading surfaces of later retellings. Though large numbers of scholars rejected Weston's "solution" to the meaning of Arthurian romance, almost all adopted the same model, proposing some single essence or source that inspired or accounted for the meaning and appeal of Arthurian romance in various national traditions. Like the *Conte du Graal* itself, these approaches reflect an almost allegorical opposition of surface and depth, or husk and kernel: the goal of such research has often been to strip away what seem "arbitrary distortions" imposed by particular writers and readers, whether these take the form of deliberate or inadvertent scribal insertions, local fantasies or preoccupations, or generic and stylistic peculiarities associated with audience or period tastes. The object of this questing might be termed "Arthurity": a kind of literary DNA that inhabits, energizes, and authenticates all genuinely Arthurian materials, whether this is embodied in the "real" Arthur as a figure of history, in an unchanging nucleus of meanings, or in the original words of an author or text.

REASSESSMENTS OF MAJOR TEXTS

Revaluations of Arthurian romance since the 1980s have frequently distrusted this "deep" Arthurity, regarding it not as an essence inhabiting artistic achievement or core sources but as an effect, a cultural phenomenon produced through the particular interests or material conditions that sponsored the writing and reading of these stories. Work on two of the earliest and most influential literary writers, Geoffrey of Monmouth and Chrétien de Troyes, illustrates this line of study. Geoffrey's Latin *History of the Kings of Britain* (*ca.* 1140), the ultimate source for much Arthurian romance, has been called the single most influential book written in the Western Middle Ages. The hostile reception expressed by a number of Geoffrey's near contemporaries—that his book was nothing more than a tissue of fables and lies masquerading as history—remarkably anticipates a common twentieth-century response to his *History*. Earlier scholarship frequently regarded Geoffrey as an author who, whether through naïveté, pedantry, or sheer mendacity, stands as an imperfect or unreliable witness to the changeless core of authentic Arthurian lore. Recent interpretations, however, have moved away from this view of Geoffrey as merely an imperfect medium for the transmission of a "Celtic mother lode"; far from functioning as distortions or distractions, in such readings Geoffrey's "inventions" serve as the very means by which the *History* establishes the meaning and appeal of Arthurity in unprecedented ways.

Geoffrey's standing among the *moderni*—the self-consciously intellectual "new men" of his time—inevitably inflects his work. He is a "border writer," at once a cleric and a courtier who moved between spiritual and secular domains, and an author at home in at least four languages, speaking Welsh, English, and French, while writing a cosmopolitan Latin for a multicultural Anglo-Norman elite. His *History* creates literate paradigms for popular tales that may have circulated in Wales, Brittany, and elsewhere; in the course of fashioning a coherent narrative of Arthurian adventures, it endows his Arthurian stories with a chivalric ethos that reflects the remarkable changes in lordship, warfare, and social organization that marked twelfth-century Britain. Geoffrey does not treat his Celtic sources as authentic or original in some timelessly ahistorical way; instead he reshapes them to create a novel "modern" Arthurity clothed in nostalgic traditionalism. His Arthurian eclecticism enjoyed an astonishing popularity: besides its unsurpassed influence on Arthurian writing to the present time, the Latin *History* itself survives in more than two hundred manuscripts, with many versions differing radically from one another. Among the noteworthy initiatives of the last decades of the twentieth century was the project to catalog and edit all the manuscripts of Geoffrey's *History*. The objective here was not to recover Geoffrey's original text or a "master" version of it but rather to acknowledge its dispersed, invented Arthurity by publishing separate editions of each distinctive version. In this way, twenty-first-century readers may appreciate Geoffrey's eclectic handling of his sources and the diversity that marked the reading experience for medieval audiences encountering this foundational Arthurian narrative.

Chrétien de Troyes, who wrote nearly fifty years after Geoffrey's *History* appeared, has generally been regarded not as a mere fable monger but as an artistic genius whose five surviving Arthurian romances establish a "classical" ideal. Traditional literary history accordingly classified later verse and prose writings as "postclassical," and literature in other languages as "second tier" (with a few possible exceptions, like the German writers Wolfram von Eschenbach and Gottfried von Strassburg). Earlier scholarship typically concentrated on recovering Chrétien's authentic words and intentions, often seeking a "best manuscript" that most closely preserved the original version. The groundbreaking publication of *The Manuscripts of Chrétien de Troyes* (in French and English) sets up an alternative view of the author, for it provides modern readers extensive access to the material contexts in which medieval audiences read and reacted to Chrétien. Rather than eliminating "bad" readings as inauthentic or highlighting only exceptionally beautiful illustrations, these volumes have deployed modern technology to reproduce marginal notations, embedded instructions to readers, flourishes, doodles, drawings, incomplete illuminations—all the elements that allow us to assess how medieval manuscripts conveyed their meaning to the eyes, hands, and minds of earlier readers, writers, and performers. In effect, these volumes constitute a do-it-yourself kit for interpreting this influential writer, providing modern readers with the resources to reconstruct the competing "Chrétiens" available to medieval audiences. Recent editions of Chrétien's romances have increasingly abandoned the attempt to have a qualified expert provide ordinary readers with a text that approximates the original. In equipping audiences with competing readings from surviving manuscripts, both "good" and "bad," editors are not leveling all meanings, suggesting that we cannot choose a preferred interpretation; instead, their work has made apparent that, for medieval as for modern readers, the interpretation of an author like Chrétien and the Arthurity that his writings contain depends upon dynamic processes and conflicted choices. Though such practices complicate the experience of reading, they acknowledge that the understanding and enjoyment of Arthurian romance rests not on the learned opinion of experts but on the engagement of mixed readerships. Inexpensive editions of Chrétien, offering dual texts (medieval and modern) or contemporary translations, have proliferated in French, English, and other languages, accelerating the transition of Arthurian romance from the preserve of the academy to wider and more varied readerships.

Chrétien's status not as timeless genius but as a continuously and contentiously read author has motivated some of the most striking and influential criticism published since the 1980s. Manuscript evidence and literary imitation suggest that he may have found his most responsive readers (and imitators) not in France but in Britain or Picardy. This attention to material conditions and patterns of reading, in bringing to light the array of reactions and rewritings Chrétien inspired, has recast later romances as works distinctive in appeal and context rather than as mere pendants to canonical writings and major authors. The very titles under which earlier scholars studied these texts—the *First Continuation,* the *Second Continuation,* branches, supplements, "epigonic" imitations or derivatives—conveys their status as "postclassical" or "second-tier" literatures. In taking up issues that supplement source studies and formal or aesthetic analysis, recent critiques of individual romances and larger cycles (including the Grail stories) have revealed the spectrum of interests and shapes that comprise medieval Arthurity; by unpacking the particular habits and beliefs of writers and readerships, such research has permitted us to understand such poetry and prose not as anemic reworkings but as energetic ripostes to mainstream writings, Arthurian and non-Arthurian alike.

The reassessment of Arthurian romance in medieval England points up some of these changes. The meaning and achievement of Sir Thomas Malory's *Morte Darthur* was, in its first scholarly edition, often judged according to the text's degree of faithfulness to its French originals. Revised editions and the vast body of scholarship that has appeared on *Morte,* have highlighted Malory's distinctive position as a transitional author whose encyclopedic, mass-produced romance reflects the social, political, military, and literary circumstances of the late fifteenth century. Malory's nearly complete neglect of earlier English Arthurian romances (more than thirty of which survive) has sometimes been taken as an affirmation of their status within earlier scholarship as callow, uninteresting, feeble counterfeits of their French "originals." The publication of many of these romances in editions accessible to students and nonspecialists by the Middle English Texts Series has encouraged both reading and performance and has been accompanied by revisionary studies of their cultural status and appeal. To appraise the romance of *Sir Tristrem,* for example, as a deficient retelling of its literate source, Thomas de Bretagne's *Tristan,* misses the English poem's idiosyncratic exuberance and theatricality. Likewise, the surviving cluster of Gawain romances (like *Dame Ragnelle* and *The Carl of Carlisle*) mark out a familiar landscape whose features set off the exceptionally literary qualities of *Sir Gawain and the Green Knight.* Recent studies of *Sir Gawain* that have taken up socially embedded themes—for example, those linked to gender and identity, such as the portrayal of women, sexual temptation, knighthood, fellowship, same-sex bonding, and rivalry—have frequently depended for their force on the similarities and differences of popular romances.

OTHER ARTHURIAN ADAPTATIONS

The divergent, sometimes contradictory Arthurs of Geoffrey of Monmouth, Chrétien, Malory, *Dame Ragnelle,* and *Sir Gawain and the Green Knight* demonstrate the versatility of the medieval Arthurian mythos, even as they make clear the continuous and multiform creation of Arthurity. This quality depends not on the origins or essence of a particular narrative but on a set of shifting yet clearly recognizable traits that writers insert (or efface) in order to enhance their work. The stories of Tristan and the Grail quest stand as the most striking instances of material that may at first have circulated independently but that was ultimately, for the sake of prestige or appeal, drawn to the core of Arthurian romance. Among the most extravagant examples of inserted Arthurity are the opening and closing episodes of Wolfram von Eschenbach's *Parzival:* the poem begins with Gahmuret, the father of Parzival, leaving Anjou for Zazamanc, where he falls in love with the black queen, Belakane, and fathers a child. This son, Feirefiz, returns to *Parzival* toward its conclusion, to fight and then bond with his half brother the Grail knight and ultimately to go off to India, where he becomes the ancestor of Prester John. Wolfram has clearly invented a newly global Arthurity, one that implies universal claims not just for Christianity but, perhaps even more boldly, for the chivalric ethos of Europe. A Dutch romance, *Moriaen,* has its hero travel from the land of the Moors and fight and then bond with Gawain, Lancelot, and Parsival; eventually this trio returns to Moor-land to witness the marriage of Moriaen's father, an Arthurian knight, and his mother. The author has demonstrated great ingenuity (perhaps under the influence of Wolfram's *Parzival*) in endowing an otherwise unknown anecdote of racial encounter and racial exoticism with the validating cachet of Arthurity. Chaucer similarly "Arthurizes" the Squire's Tale, where he introduces "Gawayn, with his olde curteisye" into a story of eastern wonder; on the other hand, Chaucer eradicates Gawain from his retelling of the *Ragnelle* story in the Wife of Bath's Tale, apparently concluding that too much Arthurity might overwhelm the distinctive twist he gives to his romance.

Postmedieval appropriations of Arthurian romance—in film, popular and classical music, theater, visual and plastic media, and writing in every register—have constituted a major field of study since the 1980s. Far from viewing such artifacts as merely derivative or inauthentic, medievalists and those in later fields have come to view such work as commentary and interrogation that often supplements scholarly understanding of medieval Arthurian romance and that illustrates the multifaceted, deep-seated appeal of the genre. Although postmedieval creations plainly declare their Arthurity through their self-conscious, purpose-built character, they point up the parallel process through which the models they imitate came into being. The surge in research by medievalists (separately or in collaboration with those in other fields and disciplines) concerning more recent productions has demonstrated that only a detailed knowledge of medieval Arthurian romance can bring the layered nature of the modern fully into view.

BIBLIOGRAPHY

GUIDES, HANDBOOKS, BIBLIOGRAPHIES

Archibald, Elizabeth, and A. S. G. Edwards, eds. *A Companion to Malory.* Cambridge, U.K.: D. S. Brewer, 1996. Essays taking account of the main problems and recent scholarship.

Brewer, Derek, and Jonathan Gibson. *A Companion to the Gawain Poet.* Woodbridge, U.K.: D. S. Brewer, 1997. Review of recent research and interpretation on this much-studied romance and three linked poems.

Krueger, Roberta L., ed. *Cambridge Companion to Medieval Romance.* Cambridge, U.K.: Cambridge University Press, 2001. Comparative and general essays, written by experts for the general reader, placing Arthurian romance in national and generic contexts.

Lacy, Norris J., ed. *Medieval Arthurian Literature: A Guide to Recent Research.* New York: Garland, 1996. Overviews of recent trends and publications by a group of experts, organized by national literatures; extensive bibliographies but no index.

———. *New Arthurian Encyclopedia.* Rev. ed. New York: Garland, 1996. Convenient and reliable one-volume guide, arranged alphabetically.

Lupack, Alan, ed. *New Directions in Arthurian Studies.* Cambridge, U.K.: D. S. Brewer, 2002. Conference essays addressing recent work, five on medieval materials, six on postmedieval subjects.

Palmer, Caroline, ed. *The Arthurian Bibliography.* Vol. 3, *1978–1992.* Cambridge: D. S. Brewer, 1998. Comprehensive listing of materials published on medieval Arthurian literature, with full, detailed indices.

PRIMARY WORKS

Busby, Keith, Terry Nixon, Alison Stones, and Lori Walters, eds. *Les Manuscrits de Chrétien de Troyes / The Manuscripts of Chrétien de Troyes.* 2 vols. Amsterdam and Atlanta: Rodopi, 1993. Indispensable, lavishly produced study (more than 1,000 pages and 800 illustrations) of the material contexts in which romances were produced and transmitted throughout the Middle Ages, with illuminating essays on a wide range of topics by a broad array of scholars.

CRITICAL AND HISTORICAL STUDIES

Cazelles, Brigitte. *The Unholy Grail: A Social Reading of Chrétien de Troyes's "Conte du Graal."* Stanford, Calif.: Stanford University Press, 1996. Drawing upon recent literary and historical research, argues that the Grail's meaning for medieval audiences depended not on ancient myths or timeless symbols but particular cultural contexts.

Duggan, Joseph J. *The Romances of Chrétien de Troyes.* New Haven: Yale University Press, 2001. Study of Chrétien's five romances and the status of their literary achievement.

Krueger, Roberta L. *Woman Readers and the Ideology of Gender in Old French Verse Romances.* Cambridge, U.K.: Cambridge University Press, 1993. Demonstrates how the interests of particular audiences, as patrons and readers, inevitably shapes the meaning of romance, with gender as perhaps the single most important feature of identity.

Schmolke-Hasselmann, Beate. *The Evolution of Arthurian Romance: The Verse Tradition from Chrétien to Froissart.* Translated by Margaret

Middleton. Cambridge, U.K.: Cambridge University Press, 1998. Largely unrevised version of *Der Arturische Versroman von Chrestien bis Froissart* (Tübingen, Germany: Max Niemeyer, 1980), with substantive foreword and supplemental bibliography by Keith Busby; groundbreaking study that reads later poetic romances not as derivative imitations of Chrétien but in terms of the interests of audiences and cultural contexts in late medieval France and England.

Sterling-Hellenbrand, Alexandra. *Topographies of Gender in Middle High German Arthurian Romance.* New York: Garland, 2001. Wide-ranging reading of German romance using recent research in women's history and gender studies.

WEB SITES

The Camelot Project. A comprehensive site with links to the texts of many Arthurian romances, with reliable entries on major and minor authors, characters, and titles and with lavish illustrations, medieval to contemporary. Sponsored by the University of Rochester.

The Charrette Project. Offers access to the critical edition of Chrétien's *Le Chevalier de la Charrette* (known as the *Lancelot*), produced by Alfred Foulet and Karl D. Uitti in the Classiques Garnier series (Paris: Bordas, 1989), to transcriptions and images of the eight surviving manuscripts of the romance, as well as critical and historical materials and a variety of search engines. Sponsored by Princeton University and a number of allied institutions.

TEAMS Middle English Texts. Online access, without charges or subscriptions, to all texts published through this series, including dozens of English Arthurian romances prepared in accurate, comprehensible editions by eminent scholars. Sponsored by the Consortium for the Teaching of the Middle Ages and the University of Rochester.

THOMAS HAHN

[See also **DMA:** Arthurian Literature; Chrétien de Troyes; *Gawain and the Green Knight, Sir;* Geoffrey of Monmouth; Malory, Sir Thomas; Wolfram von Eschenbach.]

ASTRAL MAGIC. The lines that separated astral magic from astrology were often blurred during the Middle Ages. It was Isidore of Seville (*d.* 636) who, more than anyone else, sought to draw a distinction between "superstitious" astrology and "natural" astrology. Although Isidore has often been called a critic of astrology, he actually did much to promote its legitimacy as a science by drawing a distinction between its permissible and impermissible forms. According to Isidore, forecasting the position of the heavenly bodies was a form of natural astrology and thus was harmless. Engaging in divination using the stars, however, was a form of dangerous superstition and magic. Whereas astrology was generally used to learn one's destiny, the central aim of astral magic was to change that destiny.

As Arabic treatises on astral magic, many ascribed to the mythical Hermes Trismegistus, were translated into Latin during the twelfth and thirteenth centuries, the practice received a significant boost. The most important

of these treatises was known in the West as *Picatrix,* which in its Arabic form had been titled *Ghāyat al-ḥakīm* (The goals of the scholar) and was attributed to Maslama al-Majrītī (*d.* 1008). At the request of Alfonso X the Learned, king of Castile and Léon, this Arabic astrological treatise was translated into Spanish, and by 1256 it had been translated into Latin.

Astral magic was practiced in a variety of ways. Most often, an image was created bearing the sign of a particular constellation or planet. The power of that constellation or planet was thereby believed to be transmitted to Earth, where it could be used to perform magic. In some cases, the image of a constellation was engraved on an amulet that was worn, thereby capturing the stars' influence for its wearer. In other cases, the image was engraved on a rock or piece of metal and then buried. According to Thābit ibn Qurra (*ca.* 836–901), if one wanted to get rid of scorpions, for instance, one engraved an image of a scorpion on a piece of metal and, when the constellation Scorpio was present in the sky, buried the piece of metal in the place from which one wanted scorpions to disappear. It was also believed that the power of the heavenly bodies could be conjured up through prayer. Astral magic manuals provided prayer formulas for particular planets and particular situations. The person reciting the prayer addressed the planet by name, showered it with flattery, and implored it to come to his aid. In Chaucer's "Franklin's Tale," for example, Aurelius pleads with Apollo, the sun god, for help in convincing Lucina, the empress of the sea and rivers, to bring about a flood.

Some medieval physicians practiced a form of astral medicine. In general, medical schools taught students which signs of the zodiac governed which parts of the human body. Surgeons were mindful of the dominant constellation at the time they performed surgery, since it was widely accepted that this had a bearing on the medical procedures they performed. But astral medicine went further, seeking to transfer the power of the stars into the powders and liquids used for treating illnesses. Some physicians tried curing maladies by using medals with images of particular constellations on them.

Medieval treatises that gave instructions on how to practice astral magic listed a wide range of applications. The power of the stars was thought to be able to do everything from winning someone's favor to destroying unwanted lust, inflicting illness on an enemy, improving harvest yields, and turning up lost objects. Performed correctly, astral magic was thought by some to be capable of bringing about just about any desired effect. But it was necessary to know the precise formula for harnessing the energy of particular celestial bodies.

During the High Middle Ages, astral magic was viewed with mistrust by the church. Admittedly, there had been a long tradition of tension between Christianity and astrology, particularly during periods when Christians were surrounded by pagans. During the early Middle Ages, various attempts were made to make astrology appear more acceptable. Reconceived as a Christian science, astrology was used by Christians to counter what they viewed as "pagan superstitions." But in the view of many churchmen, the kind of astral magic that emerged in the twelfth century, largely derived from Arabic texts, was a vestige from pagan times. Astral magic undercut the belief both in God's omnipotence and man's free will by presupposing that all future events proceed by necessity according to the stars. Matters that ordinarily were considered under divine control were suddenly placed within the power of astrology.

Astral magic threatened to make all branches of astrology appear suspect. Some, such as Henry of Langenstein, Nicole Oresme, and John Gerson, wrote treatises that sought to explain natural phenomena without recourse to the stars. Gerson singled out for attack the practice of engraving stones with astrological images. The prominent churchman Pierre d'Ailly (1350–1420) openly defended the use of astrology to predict future events, even arguing that it could be used to approximate the arrival of the Antichrist. But in a treatise that appeared in 1410, *De legibus et sectis contra superstitiosos astronomos* (On the laws and the sects, against the superstitious astrologers), he criticized astral magic as false astrology. There was, in other words, a range of opinions about astrology more generally, but those who practiced astral magic were, in the eyes of many, undeserving of being called astrologers. It was not until Marsilio Ficino and Giovanni Pico della Mirandola in the later fifteenth century that astral magic found public defenders and was in a sense rescued from the fringes.

BIBLIOGRAPHY

Flint, Valerie I. J. *The Rise of Magic in Early Medieval Europe.* Princeton, N.J.: Princeton University Press, 1991.

Kieckhefer, Richard. *Magic in the Middle Ages.* Cambridge, U.K., and New York: Cambridge University Press, 1990.

Pingree, David, ed. *Picatrix, the Latin Version of the Ghāyat al-Hakīm.* London: Warburg Institute, University of London, 1986.

Smoller, Laura Ackerman. *History, Prophecy, and the Stars: The Christian Astrology of Pierre d'Ailly, 1350–1420.* Princeton, N.J.: Princeton University Press, 1994.

ADAM JEFFREY DAVIS

[See also **DMA:** Ailly, Pierre d'; Alfonso X (the Learned); Astrology/ Astronomy; Gerson, John; Henry of Langenstein; Magic, Bookish (Western European); Oresme, Nicole.]

ASTROLOGICAL ICONOGRAPHY.

Astrology, the belief that the stars and the planets cause, affect, or foretell events on earth, has held an ambiguous position in the Western tradition since the classical period. Often viewed as pernicious by rulers and established religions because of its claims to predict the future, astrology and its iconography nevertheless remained a part of Latin, Byzantine, and Islamic cultures from antiquity to the early modern period, leaving a double heritage. It became a part of magical and alchemical lore, but the close observation of the course of the stars and planets it inspired formed the basis for later scientific astronomy.

Astrological iconography can be divided into two rough categories—images of the planets, including the sun and the moon, and images of the zodiac and other constellations. The zodiacal symbols we are familiar with were largely developed in classical antiquity, and the names we use are roughly similar to those in ancient Latin. The images of the planets in the classical period derived from the Olympian gods for whom they were named, but in the medieval period artists developed new ideas of how the planets should be represented. Mercury, for example, came to be depicted as a bearded man seated holding a scroll. The appearance of similar astrological images in diverse locations—for example, the zodiacal circle with an image of the personified sun in the center, found in synagogues in Palestine, such as at Beit Alpha in the Galilee and at Hammat Tiberias, as well as in pagan and secular contexts in Tunisia, Italy, Greece, and Germany—suggests that astrological iconography was open to numerous interpretations. Astrological symbols were also an essential part of the iconography of Mithraic shrines, such as the temple on the island of Ponza, where the zodiac was aligned to commemorate the solar eclipse of 14 August 212. In antiquity, astrology was also a science, and the appearance of the zodiac on buildings such as the Tower of the Winds in Athens likely represented the cosmos and the passage of time rather than any astrological meaning.

The Islamic tradition absorbed classical ideas of astrology as well as its iconography, but, with the exception of the constellations depicted in the cupola of the bath at the Umayyad desert palace of Quṣayr ʿAmra, astrological iconography tended to be restricted to the illustration of astrological manuscripts. While Arabic names in some cases differed from the Greco-Roman tradition, the iconography of the zodiac remained largely the same.

Although condemned by Christian thinkers, such as Augustine, astrology and its iconographic language gained quick admittance to the Christian tradition. Late antique Christian calendars, such as the fourth-century terracotta example from the oratory of St. Felicity in Rome, displayed the zodiac and the planets as symbols of the days and months. In the Carolingian period, manuscripts of Aratus's astrological poem *Phainomena* in various Latin translations were often illustrated with images of the zodiac and other constellations. A luxury manuscript made in the early ninth century preserved the date of 18 March 816 in its illustration of the planets, perhaps the date the manuscript was commissioned or an important date in the life of the artist or patron. But early medieval scholars were perhaps more interested in astrology as a science. The Aratus illustrations served more than just a decorative function. Diagrams, often with images of planets and constellations, were an essential part of rethinking and developing astrological knowledge inherited from antiquity.

Astrological iconography could even be found illustrating sacred texts. Jerome's prologue to the Pentateuch, found in the Vivian Bible, produced for the Carolingian emperor Charles the Bald, was decorated with a large initial *D* in which were eleven signs of the zodiac plus the sun and the moon. The images symbolized the universe whose creation was described within the text. Astrological symbols in textiles, notably the eleventh-century coronation mantle of Emperor Henry II, also drew on the iconography established in Carolingian astrological texts and star catalogs. The images of the zodiac and other constellations suggested that Henry had the wisdom of the stars, like Solomon, and reigned over the empire as God ruled over the heavens. Inscriptions woven into the robes made clear that the images also had a predictive, not just representative character.

Zodiacal symbols first appeared in monumental architecture in the twelfth century, adorning church facades in northern Italy and southern France. Some scholars have suggested that their appearance in ecclesiastical architecture reflects contemporary interest and redefinition of time as an intellectual and scientific concept. The ring of the zodiac around the portal of the church may also have linked the entrance of the church to the gate to heavenly Jerusalem. Images of the planets and the constellations also commonly appeared on ceilings in both secular and ecclesiastic settings, often representing both the visible sky and the invisible celestial realm.

The annular image of the universe in the zodiacal circle was adapted to depict a fully Christian cosmography, beginning in twelfth-century commentaries on the Apocalypse. The personified sun in the center was replaced by an image of Christ as ruler of the universe. Angels praising God occupied the outer ring instead of the symbols of the zodiac.

The zodiacal imagery in the famous fifteenth-century *Très riches heures* of the duke of Berry reveals how astrology and medical knowledge were linked. The book of hours shows a naked man surrounded by a zodiacal mandorla (known as *homo signorum*), with the signs of the zodiac linked to various parts of his body. As established in classical medicine, each part of the body was linked to a zodiacal constellation, which in turn linked the four elements (earth, fire, water, air) and the four humors of the body (bile, blood, choler, phlegm). Medical operations such as bloodletting were thus best undertaken at a time when the influence of a sympathetic star would aid the operation.

Individual elements of astrological iconography developed a variety of other meanings as well. The emperor Augustus used his birth sign, Capricorn, as a symbol of his authority on his coins, signaling that he was destined by the stars to rule. The scorpion in the late Middle Ages became one of the attributes used to identify personified dialectic, as well as the Jewish nation, often appearing on a banner held by a personified synagogue or by Jews in crucifixion or other biblical scenes.

Astrological iconography gained further prominence in the Renaissance, spurred by the renewed interest in Neoplatonic thought and hermetic doctrines. While the practice of astrology has evolved over the last two millennia, its iconography remains perhaps the most easily recognized of classical antiquity.

BIBLIOGRAPHY

Aurigemma, Luigi. *Le signe zodiacal du Scorpion dans le traditions occidentales de l'Antiquité gréco-latine à la Renaissance.* Paris: Mouton, 1976.

Beck, Roger. *Planetary Gods and Planetary Orders in the Mysteries of Mithras.* Leiden, Netherlands: E. J. Brill, 1988.

Bober, Harry. "The Zodiacal Minature of the *Très riches heures* of the Duke of Berry." *Journal of the Warburg and Courtauld Institutes* 11 (1948): 1–34.

Blume, Dieter. *Regenten des Himmels: Astrologische Bilder in Mittelalter und Renaissance.* Berlin: Akademie Verlag, 2000.

Carboni, Stefano. *Following the Stars: Images of the Zodiac in Islamic Art.* New York: Metropolitan Museum of Art, 1997.

Cohen, Simona. "The Romanesque Zodiac: Its Symbolic Function on the Church Façade." *Arte Medievale,* 2d ser., 4 (1990): 43–54.

Gettings, Fred. *The Secret Zodiac*. London: Routledge and Kegan Paul, 1987.

Gundel, Hans Georg. *Zodiakos: Tierkreisbilder im Altertum*. Mainz, Germany: Verlag Philipp von Zabern, 1992.

Kamborian, Kelly. "Children of the Planets: Medieval Astronomical Imagery." In *Survival of the Gods: Classical Mythology in Medieval Art*. Providence, R.I.: Brown University Press, 1987.

CHRISTOPHER HATCH MACEVITT

[See also **DMA:** Astrology/Astronomy.]

ATHEISM. In antiquity the latinized *atheus* (from the Greek *atheos*) could either refer to the denial of the existence of a god or gods or designate impious views about the divine. Christians and pagans exchanged charges of atheism even while recognizing that their atheistic opponents believed in a divinity. The divinity of their opponents, however, was not in their eyes the true divinity, and this rendered their opponents atheists. Atheism was invoked less frequently in the Middle Ages. Many scholars in the past assumed that during this "age of faith" people did not possess the mental categories that would have permitted them to be atheists, and some have been reluctant to apply the construct of atheism to the Middle Ages, fearing that they would be charged with anachronism.

But scholars have increasingly recognized that impiety, doubt, skepticism, and sometimes outright atheism did in fact exist during the thirteenth and fourteenth centuries, sometimes independently of heretical movements. Religious doubts and denials about orthodox doctrine came from all sectors of society, including nobles, townspeople, peasants, and the clergy, even if these voices of skepticism were a small minority. Sermons preached to popular audiences are a good indication of the forms of unbelief that preachers tried to combat. The late-thirteenth-century Dominican Giordano da Rivalto, for instance, referred to the generic sinner who was so addicted to concupiscence that he suppressed his reason and convinced himself that no God existed. Giordano, in this instance, drew a connection between unbelief and the power of the passions. In other cases, unbelief was attributed to book learning. For a later period, Carlo Ginzburg has shown the impact that print had on the cosmology of a semiliterate miller. Some preachers referred to the "madmen" who questioned how God could exist given all of the misfortune in the world. These skeptics, living in a time of growing uncertainty, questioned whether prayer (and by implication God's power) was truly as efficacious as it was supposed. Others had a diffi-

cult time believing in specific doctrines, such as the Eucharistic miracle, the existence of an afterlife, and the resurrection. The Gospels, they said, were merely invented stories. In the eyes of many preachers, such doubts were the workings of the devil as he tried to pull Christians away from their God. It was largely the dangers of unbelief that first galvanized the apostolic mission of mendicant preachers during the thirteenth century.

But unbelief was not always expressed by actively negating an orthodox doctrine or asserting a counterbelief. It was also sometimes manifested as religious apathy, as episcopal visitation records and preachers' sermons show. Some Christians simply never attended church or, if they did, spent the time playing dice and gossiping. Others never confessed or received Communion and showed no interest in listening to preachers' sermons. The Christian message, in other words, did not resonate equally with every medieval Christian. Some believed in Christianity less than others. Nor were all unbelievers necessarily ignorant of doctrine and faith. The more that some Christians (peasants included) learned about Christianity, the more some of them questioned the tenets of the faith.

Religious skepticism was often the product of popular heretical movements such as Catharism, which taught that matter was evil and that Jesus did not really undergo human birth and death. But it sometimes appeared in regions that were free of heresy, popping up rather spontaneously. There was a history of anticlericalism, for instance, long before the emergence of Catharism. Many of the ideas that Catharism drew upon had a long history and did not originate with the Cathars. Rationalism, materialism, and skepticism, in short, were forces that the church had to reckon with during the Middle Ages.

Some orthodox medieval theologians were concerned about the problem of unbelief. When Anselm of Canterbury wrote his famous ontological proof for the existence of God in the *Proslogion* (1077–1078), he laid out a complex set of rational arguments that he hoped would satisfy even the doubting, skeptical fool. Even before the validity of Anselm's reasoning was attacked by Guanilo, a monk from the abbey of Marmoutier, it is clear that Anselm wished to provide arguments for proving God's existence so that Christians would be armed should they encounter an unbeliever. By the thirteenth century, when Thomas Aquinas presented his different kind of proof for the existence of God, a new body of translated works by Aristotle, other classical pagans, and Jewish and Islamic philosophers had appeared, making the central doctrines of Christianity appear more susceptible to questioning. It was as important as ever to be able to demonstrate that the truths of Christian doctrine could be known by the created intellect. Thirteenth-century theologians were aware of the danger not only of popular heresies such as Catharism and Waldensianism but also of intellectual heresies such as the Trinitarian views of the Calabrian abbot Joachim of Fiore, who had attacked the Trinitarian teaching of Peter Lombard. The church was quick to attack the pantheist materialism of David of Dinant, who argued that God is the principal material of all realities. The Paris master Amaury of Bène, whose body was exhumed and burned four years after his death, attracted a following by teaching that God is the formal principal of all, identical with all that exists, including evil. When it came to notions about God, the medieval church had to worry about popular ignorance, doubts about specific aspects of doctrine, religious apathy, and a wide range of heretical ideas, not all of them linked to specific heretical movements. Already with Duns Scotus in the thirteenth century and William of Ockham in the fourteenth, one senses a retreat from using reason in the service of theology and a redefinition of the proper relationship between faith and reason. In the fifteenth century Nicholas of Cusa's doctrine of "learned ignorance"—the notion that the most learned humans are those who recognize how entirely incapable they and all humans are of constructing a concept of God—represented a radically different antidote to religious skepticism from the one proposed earlier by Anselm and Aquinas.

BIBLIOGRAPHY

Faire Croire: Modalités de la diffusion et de la réception des messages religieux du XIIe au XVe siècle. Rome: École Français de Rome, 1981.

Ginzburg, Carlo. The Cheese and the Worms: The Cosmos of a Sixteenth-Century Miller. Translated by John Tedeschi and Anne Tedeschi. Baltimore: Johns Hopkins University Press, 1980.

Murray, Alexander. "Piety and Impiety in Thirteenth-Century Italy." Studies in Church History 8 (1972): 83–106.

Niewöhner, Friedrich, and Olaf Pluta, eds. Atheismus im Mittelalter und in der Renaissance. Wiesbaden, Germany: Harrassowitz Verlag, 1999.

Reynolds, Susan. "Social Mentalities and the Case of Medieval Scepticism." Transactions of the Royal Historical Society. 6th ser., 1 (1991): 21–41.

Wakefield, Walter L. "Some Unorthodox Popular Ideas of the Thirteenth Century." Medievalia et Humanistica. n.s., 4 (1973): 25–35.

ADAM JEFFREY DAVIS

[See also **DMA:** Cathars; Heresies, Western European; Heresy.]

ATHENS. Subsequently the home of Byzantine archbishops, French crusaders, and Catalan mercenaries, Athens remained an important Mediterranean city throughout the medieval period. By the late third century A.D., the city walls enclosed only the Acropolis and the area immediately north of it, much reduced from its classical size. Sacked by Alaric in 396, Athens remained a flourishing town with a large pagan population until Justinian I closed the schools of philosophy in 529. In 662 the city was still large enough to host Emperor Constans II for the winter, but little is known about Athens for the following three centuries. By 1000, the city showed signs of increased economic activity, perhaps as a result of the Byzantine reconquest of Crete in 961. Around 1175, Michael Choniates became archbishop of the city, and his sermons reminded the citizens of their classical past, while his letters bewailed Athens's rustic character and constantly reminded others of his misfortune in living there.

In 1204 Michael surrendered the city to the forces of Boniface of Montferrat, which were participating in the Fourth Crusade. Boniface granted Athens to Otho de la Roche, along with Thebes and Boeotia. Athens became a duchy within the Frankish kingdom of Thessaloniki. With the Franks came a new law code, the Assizes of Romania, and Latin clergy. Otho established Cistercians in the monastery of Daphne but was excommunicated by Pope Honorius III for seizing property from churches and treating Greek priests as serfs.

When Guy II, fifth duke of Athens, died in 1308 with no direct heir, his successor was his cousin Walter of Brienne. Unsatisfied with its remuneration, the mercenary Catalan company employed by Walter turned against him. At the battle of Skripou on 15 March 1311, Walter and the great majority of Frankish knights of Thebes and Athens lost their lives to the Catalan mercenaries, who then took over the duchy. While the Catalan royal family of Sicily claimed the title of duke of Athens and sent a vicar general to govern the area, the mercenaries ran the duchy as a corporation. In documents, the Catalans called themselves "the company of the Franks residing in the duchies of Athens and Neopatras." The governing structure of the company included captains, who were both judges and military leaders; time in office was limited to three years. Some castles were hereditary grants, but castellans, appointed by the company, controlled others. Barcelona's law code replaced the Assizes of Romania. Local Greeks still held some authority and served on the town council. Under the Catalans, the area seems to have gone into economic decline.

By 1370 the cohesive character of the company had disappeared, as the original members had died, and local anarchy prevailed. Aragon annexed Athens in 1380, but in 1388, Nerio Acciaiuoli, lord of Corinth and member of a Florentine banking family, seized the city. By this time, the Turks had conquered northern Greece, and Nerio was forced to pay tribute to Evrenoz Bey, ruler of Thessaly. When Nerio died in 1394, he gave Athens to the cathedral church of St. Mary, better known as the Parthenon, and in the following ten years, the city passed to the Turks, to the Venetians, and finally, to Nerio's illegitimate half-Greek son, Antonio. Antonio once more encouraged trade in the city, and he ruled peacefully over it until his death in 1435. By 1456, the city was in Turkish hands.

BIBLIOGRAPHY

Frantz, Alison. "From Paganism to Christianity in the Temples of Athens." *Dumbarton Oaks Papers* 19 (1965): 185–206.

Lock, Peter. *The Franks in the Aegean, 1204–1500.* London and New York: Longmans, 1995.

Setton, Kenneth M. "The Catalans in Greece, 1311–1380." In *The History of the Crusades.* Volume 3: *The Fourteenth and Fifteenth Centuries.* Edited by Harry W. Hazard. Madison: University of Wisconsin Press, 1975.

CHRISTOPHER HATCH MACEVITT

[See also **DMA:** Alaric; Assizes of Romania; Boniface of Montferrat; Catalan Company; Justinian I; Latin States in Greece; *Morea, Chronicle of.*]

AUTOBIOGRAPHY AND CONFESSIONAL LITERATURE. The study of autobiographical writing from premodern periods is fraught with methodological problems. Because the term "autobiography" is an invention of the eighteenth century, there is serious contention as to whether it can be applied to earlier centuries. There is similar controversy regarding the nature of the individual in the Middle Ages. Although one tradition of scholars has asserted that a consciousness on the part of an individual of his or her uniqueness is a preeminently modern phenomenon, some recent thinkers have argued that this distinction has been greatly exaggerated and may not hold with great regularity. In any event, what one determines to be autobiographical texts in the Middle Ages will vary according to one's conception of both what autobiography is and how the individual was perceived in the medieval world. For those who would deny that the individual in his or her particularity existed as such before the modern period, "medieval autobiogra-

phy" would seem to be an oxymoron; but for a scholar such as Georg Misch, writing in the mid-twentieth century, the study of medieval autobiography ran to many volumes because there were, in his estimation, so many examples (Misch included as "autobiography" the forewords, epilogues, and personal digressions by such figures as Cassidorius, Gregory of Tours, Bede, and Abbot Suger of St. Denis). For the reader who accepts that autobiographical and confessionary literature have considerable overlap, St. Augustine of Hippo's seminal *Confessions* (begun in 397) will be central to any consideration of medieval autobiography, while for a critic who cleaves the two, Augustine's work, though confessional, might not necessarily be considered an autobiography. A variety of viewpoints should not cause us to despair, however. It simply means that with each new consideration of what constitutes autobiographical writing and how subjectivity surfaces in medieval texts, one has to revisit the question of what constitutes medieval autobiography.

AUGUSTINE AND BOETHIUS

We certainly know that confessional literature existed in the Middle Ages, and if we view autobiography as a way of reading rather than a fixed generic taxonomy, we will be comfortable with the fact that not only Augustine's *Confessions* but many other medieval works have been read as autobiography by modern readers. Augustine's great work illustrates both the pluses and the problems of this kind of reading. Most scholars would accept that autobiography comprises a recording *(graphé)* of a life *(bios)* by the person who has lived it *(auto)* and as a result implies a double stance in which the present writing-self commemorates a past written-self according to known narrative molds. As such, then, the first nine books of St. Augustine can certainly be read as autobiographical. St. Augustine of Hippo was a product of the late Roman Empire; born in modern-day Algeria, he migrated to Rome and even to Milan before ending his life back in North Africa as archbishop of Hippo. Converted to Christianity in 386, Augustine rereads in the *Confessions* his earlier experiences from the standpoint of the "New Man" born again as a Christian; aware that the way humans are caught in sequential time (which is also, he argues, to be caught in narrative and language) is a condition of their fallen state, Augustine exploits both the molds of the traditional classical memoir and the radical new biblical textuality.

A reading as mere autobiography fails to do justice to Augustine's great work, however. First, the notion of confession in the early Christian church includes not only a recitation of one's (sinful) experiences but also the praise of God and a declaration of one's faith; second, and more seriously, books 9–13 of Augustine's *Confessions* seem to leave autobiography behind as they turn to discussions of time, sequentiality, and memory, ending with an explication of Genesis in the final book. Modern readers in their determination to read Augustine's work as autobiography have often considered these final books a ghastly mistake; but books 9–12 make overt a feature latent in the earlier books—namely, that Augustine's concern is for man's collective experience and man's relationship to God, time, and eternity. The move from the story of one man's origin to the biblical origin of all things is therefore integral to the work as a whole, and to understand the *Confessions* as autobiography and nothing more would be gravely to misunderstand the totality of the work.

The other pillar of early medieval autobiographical or confessional writing is from the next century: the celebrated *Consolation of Philosophy* written in 524 by Anicius Severinus Boethius. Boethius, like Augustine, converted to Christianity, but in this work, avidly read, translated, and imitated throughout the Middle Ages, he does not make explicit appeal to Christian thinking. Written from his jail cell, into which he says he was unjustly cast and from which he will be led to his execution in 524, the *Consolation* presents, over the course of five books, Boethius's reconciliation with his fate. After an apology in which Boethius bemoans the injustice of his situation (book 1), Lady Philosophy appears in his cell and for the next four books conducts "therapy sessions" of a sort. Philosophy describes their meetings as medicine for what she considers Boethius's sick mind. She is determined, above all, to destroy what she deems his false notion, that he is the victim of bad luck (the allegorized goddess *fortuna*). She argues that he, like all men, always possesses free will and that God merely *foresees* (*pro-videns*, whence "providence") what a person will freely choose. Though Boethius's dialogue is exteriorized as a debate with Lady Philosophy, the real conversation is between Boethius and his inner self as he faces his imprisonment and impending death. The greatest proof that he has returned to intellectual health is of course the written work we read since, it is implied, only a philosophically "healed" Boethius would be capable of authoring books 2–5.

MEDIEVAL AUTOBIOGRAPHICAL WRITING

Both Augustine's *Confessions* and Boethius's *Consolation* had enormous influence on subsequent medieval writers. Augustine's work, in particular, is in the background of almost all medieval confessional and/or auto-

biographical writing; in the fifth century, for example, several writers titled their works *Confessio* (from *confiteor*, meaning "to acknowledge," "to cede"). The twelfth-century autobiographical text by the abbot Guibert of Nogent is a prime example of Augustine's continuing influence. Though called *Monodiae* (1115) by Guibert—the title comes from Isidore of Seville's *Etymologies*, in which he defines *monodia* as a "song of one alone singing"—this Latin text goes by various names other than the one given to it by its author: *Vita sua* (His life), *Memoirs*, and *Autobiography*. That Guibert knew Augustine's *Confessions* well is indisputable, and there are some similarities in terms of his treatment of religious matters, the figure of the mother, sexuality, and the Book of Genesis. Guibert's work has been mined for the portrait it gives of daily life during the twelfth-century renaissance, despite the somewhat skewed and partisan stance of the writer.

Similarly partisan is another twelfth-century Latin autobiography, the *Historia calamitatum* (Story of calamities), which recounts the life of the philosopher, scholar, and Parisian teacher Peter Abelard. Abelard comes across as a brilliant and arrogant man, intellectually pugilistic at all times. The work is famous for the scandalous tale of how Abelard tutored and seduced his pupil Heloise, as well as for the description of the castration meted out to him by Heloise's uncle, Fulbert, as punishment. In the oldest and most authoritative manuscript, now in the library of Troyes, France, the *Historia* is followed by a consolation written in Heloise's voice, then an exchange of letters between Abelard and Heloise in which they cover a wide range of issues; the manuscript also contains two additional letters of an impersonal nature and a *regula* (rule) for the nuns under Heloise's direction when she became an abbess at Argenteuil. The fact that these texts were preserved in the convent over which Heloise ruled—and it must be added that the Troyes manuscript dates from 150 years after the events—has led to various views regarding authorship. Scholars have advanced three distinct possibilities: first, that Abelard authored the *Historia*, after which Heloise preserved it along with their letters; second, that Heloise authored both the *Historia* and the letters; and third, that a later writer authored both the *Historia* and the correspondence. These questions throw into relief the way in which a theory regarding the autobiographical nature of a work is also always a theory of the author and authorship: in the case of the first theory the *Historia* can be considered an autobiography, while in the case of the second and the third it must be viewed as an autobiographical fiction.

AUTOBIOGRAPHY IN LITERATURE

Many literary works of the Middle Ages raise the question of whether they can (or should) be read as autobiographical. Even highly stylized creations, such as troubadour poetry, have been subjected to autobiographical readings, and late medieval manuscripts of troubadour love poetry often included prose accounts of the troubadours' lives (*vidas*) based on what was implied in the love poems. Modern scholars are less wont to attribute an autobiographical dimension to troubadour (or trouvère) lyric poems; indeed, to do so would be to accept that some of the most powerful lords of Europe, such as William VII of Poitiers and Thibaut of Champagne, regularly trembled in the presence of their ladies or could be scared off by a shepherd. Similar questions have been raised about the thirteenth-century *Roman de la Rose,* the medieval "best-seller" that made a full-dress narrative out of the lover figure familiar from lyric poetry. Begun by Guillaume de Lorris (*ca.* 1237), the first part insists on a one-to-one correspondence between the lover-protagonist's dream and the author's real life; but Guillaume de Lorris never finished the work, and when one of the greatest intellectuals of the late thirteenth century, Jean de Meun, took up Guillaume de Lorris's first-person tale nearly fifty years later, part of the literary fun was the illogic of his being able to continue to narrate Guillaume's life autobiographically, since the *bios* was no longer his own.

One of the recurring features of much medieval narrative that flirts with autobiography is that it patently cannot represent lived experience yet claims to do precisely that. Dante's *Divine Comedy* (*ca.* 1313) insists that the namesake author-narrator's trip through hell, purgatory, and heaven really took place over Easter weekend in 1300. Indeed, it seems that in the fourteenth century there was a pan-European vogue for what has been called the "pseudo-autobiography," in which major writers inserted themselves as protagonists or secondary figures into their narratives: a partial list of such works would include Guillaume de Machaut's *Livre dou voir dit* (True tale) and Jehan Froissart's *La prison amoureuse* (Prison of love) in France, the *Frauendienst* in Germany, Juan Ruiz's *El libro de buen amor* (The book of good love) in Spain, and Geoffrey Chaucer's *Canterbury Tales,* John Gower's *Confessio Amantis,* Will Langland's *Piers Plowman,* and the anonymous poem "Pearl" in England. Late medieval writers continued to exploit the potentially autobiographical aspects of both lyric and narrative: the lyric poems of Rutebeuf, Petrarch, Eustache Deschamps, Charles of Orléans, and Thomas Hoccleve have all been subjected to autobiographical readings, as have François Villon's raucous works, including his *Grand testament.* In France Christine de Pizan, often called the "first feminist," follows in the Machaut-Froissart tradition, though with less humor than her male counterparts.

The literary works just mentioned are, for the most part, quite playful. But the High and late Middle Ages also included a tradition of political autobiography and confessional literature. First are the memoirs of major political figures and churchmen. In the twelfth century Gerald of Wales wrote an extraordinary autobiography in which, rather than writing directly in the first person, he created a fictive narrator who writes—"in the scholastic style," he says—a third-person account of his "friend" Gerald of Wales. Better known is the lighthearted treatment of court intrigues in the *Nugae* (Trifles) of John of Salisbury, also from the twelfth century. In the late fourteenth and fifteenth century a tradition of mystical autobiographical literature arose in various parts of Europe. Women are well represented as authors of these introspective, visionary mystical works. The English *Book of Margery Kempe* is often celebrated as the first true autobiography by a woman in the Christian West; well known also are Mechthild von Magdeburg, Julian of Norwich, and Marguerite Porete; in Spain Teresa of Ávila's spiritual autobiography was destined to have a great influence during the Counter-Reformation.

With Teresa of Ávila (1515–1582) we touch the end of the Middle Ages. The sixteenth century would retain many of the currents inherited from the medieval period while widening the scope still more to include autobiographies by artists and soldiers.

BIBLIOGRAPHY

PRIMARY WORKS

Abelard, Peter. *Historia calamitatum: Texte critique avec une introduction.* Edited by J. Monfrin. Paris: J. Vrin, 1959.

Augustine of Hippo, St. *Confessions.* 2 vols. Translated by William Watts. 1631. Reprint, Cambridge, Mass.: Harvard University Press, 1950–1951.

Boethius, Anicius Severinus. *De consolatione philosophiae.* Edited and translated by E. K. Rand, H. F. Stewart, and S. J. Tester. Cambridge, Mass.: Harvard University Press, 1978.

Giraldus Cambrensis (Gerald of Wales). *Opera.* 8 vols. Edited by J. S. Brewer. Wiesbaden, Germany: Kraus Reprints, 1964–1966.

TRANSLATIONS

Abelard, Peter. *The Letters of Abelard and Heloise.* Translated by Betty Radice. Harmondsworth, U.K.: Penguin, 1974.

Augustine of Hippo, St. *Confessions.* Translated by Henry Chadwick. Oxford: Oxford University Press, 1991.

Benton, John F., ed., and C. C. Swinton Bland, trans. *Self and Society in Medieval France: The Memoirs of Abbot Guibert of Nogent*. New York: Harper and Row, 1970.

Boethius, Anicius Severinus. *The Consolation of Philosophy*. Translated by Richard Green. New York: Bobbs-Merrill, 1962.

Gerald of Wales. *The Autobiography of Giraldus Cambrensis*. Edited and translated by H. E. Butler. London: J. Cape, 1937.

BIOGRAPHY AND CRITICISM

Brown, Peter. *Augustine of Hippo*. Los Angeles: University of California Press, 1967.

De Looze, Laurence. *The Pseudo-Autobiography in the Fourteenth Century: Juan Ruiz, Guillaume de Machaut, Jean Froissart, Geoffrey Chaucer*. Gainesville: University Press of Florida, 1997.

Misch, Georg. *Geschichte der Autobiographie*. 4 Vols. Bern: A. Francke, 1949–1969.

Vance, Eugene. "Augustine's *Confessions* and the Grammar of Selfhood." *Genre* 6 (1973): 1–28.

Zink, Michel. *The Invention of Literary Subjectivity*. Translated by Davis Sices. Baltimore: Johns Hopkins University Press, 1999.

MEDIEVAL AUTHORSHIP AND AUTOBIOGRAPHY

Minnis, A. J. *Medieval Theory of Authorship: Scholastic Literary Attitudes in the Later Middle Ages*. 2d ed. London: Scolar Press, 1988.

Morris, Colin. *The Discovery of the Individual, 1050–1200*. New York: Harper and Row. 1972.

Spitzer, Leo. "Note on the Poetic and the Empirical 'I.'" *Traditio* 4 (1946): 414–422.

Zumthor, Paul. "Autobiographie au Moyen Âge?" In *Langue, texte, énigme*. Paris: Seuil, 1975.

LAURENCE DE LOOZE

[See also **DMA:** Abelard, Peter; Augustine of Hippo, St.; Boethius, Anicius Manlius Severinus; Guibert of Nogent; *Roman de la Rose*.]

BANNOCKBURN, BATTLE OF. On 23 June 1314 advance troops of the English army of King Edward II were approximately two kilometers south of Stirling Castle, the last stronghold of English power in Scotland. Since the death of Edward I in 1307, English fortunes in the northern realm had plummeted, and Robert Bruce, the Scottish commander, was determined to prevent a resurgence. The opportunity looked good. Stirling Castle's commander needed reinforcements and intended to surrender if they did not arrive by the Feast of the Nativity of St. John the Baptist, 24 June. Edward II, however, was intent on relieving Stirling.

What Edward's troops encountered, well camouflaged by trees and brush, was a small but spirited Scottish army and "irregular" supporters. The boggy terrain abutting the River Forth and the smaller Bannock, a rivulet, or burn, hampered the English over the next day and a half. Though more and more English committed to the battle, it became ever more hopeless, for the large contingent of English cavalry in the relatively confined and inhospitable setting could neither maneuver with effect nor avoid throwing other contingents of the army into disarray. There was little coordination among the various units (archers, horse, infantrymen). Thus, the initial preponderance in numbers—perhaps twenty thousand or more English against about five thousand Scots—actually worked to the northerners' advantage by exacerbating the English troops' confusion on the battlefield. In the event, a Scottish infantry (or irregular) assault from high ground on the west (Gillies Hill) routed the English. A fortunate few fled and survived the bogs as well. Many drowned trying to make their escape. And large numbers were impaled by Scottish pikemen or were simply hacked to pieces—nobles, knights, and common soldiers alike. Edward II led what was left of his shattered army in retreat.

The battle of Bannockburn has a remarkable status in the historiography and mythography of Scotland. The tale of a vastly outnumbered group of "patriots," poorly armed and without significant cavalry, but fighting for their country's "independence" and holding their own against the flower of a great royal army is a central part of the story of the making of Scotland's collective identity. The confirmation of Robert Bruce as king of Scotland in the aftermath of the battle seems to support this understanding of Bannockburn in Scottish history, even though strife between Lowland and Highland Scots continued, the bitter war with the English persisted, and on more than one occasion the military campaigns of the Bruces suffered terrible setbacks, as in the ineffectual invasion of English-controlled Ireland in 1315 by Edward Bruce (Robert's brother). It could be argued that Scottish dynastic independence from the English crown was not effectively achieved for another generation and that the emergence of Scottish collective identity was a longunfolding and not straightforward process that took another century or more.

BIBLIOGRAPHY

Armstrong, Peter. *Bannockburn 1314: Robert Bruce's Great Victory*. Oxford: Osprey Publishing, 2002.

Reese, Peter. *Bannockburn*. Edinburgh: Canongate Books, 2000.

WILLIAM CHESTER JORDAN

[See also **DMA:** Edward II of England; Robert I of Scotland.]

BARTHOLOMAEUS ANGLICUS (*d.* 1272), Franciscan minister provincial and encyclopedist. Bartholomaeus Anglicus was born in England, probably some time before 1200. Little is known about his early years. At some point he moved to Paris, where he studied theology and presented cursory lectures on the Bible. By 1230, Bartholomaeus had entered the Franciscan order and had been appointed *lector* at the Franciscan *studium provinciale* in Magdeburg, Saxony, the furthest outpost of the Franciscans in the northeast. In this capacity, Bartholomaeus would have taught theology and the art of preaching to the student friars. By around 1245, he had completed the encyclopedia that would make him famous, *De proprietatibus rerum* (On the property of things). In 1247, Bartholomaeus was elected minister provincial of the Franciscans in Austria. It is possible that Bartholomaeus is the same Franciscan referred to in medieval sources as Bartholomaeus of Prague, who served as minister provincial of Bohemia in 1255–1256 and then served as papal legate to Poland and to Bohemia and its territories. Bartholomaeus Anglicus was elected minister provincial of Saxony in 1262 and died in 1272.

Along with the encyclopedias of the Dominicans Vincent of Beauvais and Thomas of Cantimpré, Bartholomaeus's *De proprietatibus rerum* was one of the great encyclopedias compiled during the thirteenth century. The encyclopedia covers every imaginable subject, including God and the angels, human anatomy and physiology, astronomy and geography, plants and animals, music, colors, odors, and tastes. The encyclopedia sought to contain in a single, easy-to-use book the increasingly wide spectrum of knowledge found in rich thirteenth-century libraries. It is divided into nineteen thematic chapters, with entries within chapters arranged alphabetically. In the encyclopedia's preface, Bartholomaeus explicitly stated that his aim was to educate those who were "simple and young, [and] who on account of the infinite number of books cannot look into the properties of each single thing about which Scripture deals." Written with a student audience in mind, the encyclopedia circulated rapidly (more than one hundred manuscripts survive) and was particularly useful as a pedagogical tool, serving as an elementary explication of the spiritual meaning found in the natural world. As a practical and accessible source of information, the encyclopedia also provided material for preachers to use in their sermons; it was even sometimes cited in thirteenth-century sermons and sermon aids. It is quite possible that Bartholomaeus intended the encyclopedia to serve as a reference tool for the Franciscan preachers he helped train. The encyclopedia drew heavily from the Bible as well as the gloss of Gilbert of Portiers, the *Sententiae* of Peter Lombard, the natural sciences of Aristotle, and the encyclopedias of Pliny and Isidore of Seville. Bartholomaeus was particularly indebted to the *Etymologiae* of Isidore of Seville, the standard-bearer of the medieval encyclopedic tradition. But in the *De proprietatibus rerum*, Bartholomaeus combined Isidore's etymological approach to the liberal arts with the newer scholastic approach of collecting, ordering, and assimilating all knowledge into a unified and divinely ordained whole, or *summa*. The most influential portions of Bartholomaeus's encyclopedia were those dealing with medicine and physiology, where he drew from new translations of Aristotle, Hippocrates, and Galen, as well as various Arabic writers, most notably Avicenna. During the fourteenth century there were several translations of Bartholomaeus's encyclopedia into the vernacular, indicative of the growing belief that vernacular languages were capable of conveying the kinds of technical and scholarly information contained in an encyclopedia. In 1372, at the request of King Charles V of France, Jean Corbechon carried out a French translation of Bartholomaeus's encyclopedia. In 1398, John Trevisa, translated the encyclopedia into English for Lord Berkeley, a translation that Shakespeare would later use. During the Middle Ages, Bartholomaeus was widely known as the "Master of Properties."

BIBLIOGRAPHY

Bartholomaeus Anglicus. *On the Properties of Soul and Body.* Edited by R. James Long. Toronto: Toronto Medieval Latin Texts, 1979.

———. *On the Properties of Things: John Trevisa's Translation of Bartholomaeus Anglicus* De proprietatibus rerum. Edited by M. C. Seymour et al. 3 Vols. Oxford: Clarendon Press, 1975–1988.

Binkley, Peter, ed. *Pre-Modern Encyclopaedic Texts: Proceedings of the Second COMERS Congress, Groningen, 1–4 July 1996.* Leiden, Netherlands: Brill, 1997.

Seymour, M. C., et al. *Bartholomaeus Anglicus and His Encyclopaedia.* Aldershot, U.K.: Variorum, 1992.

ADAM JEFFREY DAVIS

[See also **DMA:** Encyclopedias and Dictionaries, Western European.]

BATHS AND BATHING. One of the fundamental social institutions of the ancient world, bathing was not merely a matter of hygiene but a social and physical ritual involving mental and physical exercise and conversation with friends and family, as well as the pleasures of the warm water and massage. While bathing was a part of the classical Greek gymnasium, it was subordinate to exercise and usually involved cold water and a large basin, rather than heated rooms and large bathing pools. The invention of the hypocaust, a system of heating that used subfloor conduits, in the second century B.C. (the earliest use was in the Stabian Baths in Pompeii) allowed the development of enormous Roman bath complexes with hot and cold pools. Many Roman houses, both rural and urban, also contained private bathing rooms, sometimes only a simple chamber adjoining the kitchen, others freestanding buildings with many of the same amenities as large public baths.

Yet even in the ancient world, baths had a reputation as places where vice and immorality flourished. In Aristophanes's *The Clouds,* Right Logic chastises young men for going to the baths instead of to the gymnasium. Marcus Aurelius considered it a disgusting habit that corrupted the body. The critiques of late antique Christian leaders echoed and sharpened the concerns of earlier pagan moralists, but the great bath complexes of the Roman world continued to function into the seventh century, particularly in Constantinople. They eventually closed because of a decline in urban populations and economy as well as a change in moral sensibilities.

The growth in small privately run baths in late antiquity and the early medieval period suggests that the earlier ethos of public nudity and mixed-sex socializing gave way to a greater emphasis on personal privacy, modesty, and small-group socializing. In late antiquity many baths, particularly in the East, where they were most common, lost their athletic areas *(palestras).* The Jewish community of Sardis converted the *palestra* there into the largest synagogue of the ancient world, while the baths continued to function next door. By the end of the seventh century, the large public baths were shut down or converted to other purposes, but smaller local baths continued to serve the public. The public baths of the Anatolian city of Amorion, while briefly abandoned in the mid-seventh century, continued to be used until the sack of the city in 838. Many of the public baths in Byzantium may have been run by monasteries or churches, a pattern also seen in early medieval Italy. The Kosmoteira monastery, built in the twelfth-century Thrace region, had two baths—one for the monks and one for the public.

Perhaps more than anywhere else, the Islamic world inherited Roman attitudes toward bathing, as washing and bathing were religious obligations for Muslims. The medieval Islamic bathhouse *(hammam)* was, like Byzantine baths, smaller than the public baths of the Roman period, but like them it continued to be a center for so-

cial as well as hygienic purposes. Other elements of the bath evolved: for example, the large cold pool of the Roman bath *(frigidarium)* disappeared as part of the bath experience, and individuals bathed in smaller rooms attached to the large central steam room. Baths were sometimes built as part of a religious complex and used for ritual purposes as well as for revenue for charity.

For Jewish communities, the *miqveh* (plural, *miqva'ot*), a pool that employed naturally collected water (as from a spring or from rainwater), allowed individuals to ritually purify themselves following polluting events, such as menstruation. *Miqva'ot* have been found in archaeological sites throughout Europe and the Middle East. Jewish polemical texts, however, suggest that many communities observed a variety of purifying rituals that diverged from normative rabbinic prescriptions, such as using warm-water baths or sprinkling the body with water rather than fully immersing it.

In the medieval West public bathing also continued, but on a smaller scale. In Lombard Italy, Arechis II of Salerno built an aqueduct and baths in the 770s, but in the rest of Italy the construction and maintenance of urban baths often fell to the bishops. Although some baths were established to cater to the poor, such as the one built in Lucca in 720, public bathing generally may have become more of an aristocratic activity. Attended by impressive retinues, Lombard elites made just as much of a social spectacle out of bathing as did the ancient Romans. Unlike Roman bathers, however, Lombards and other medieval Christians preferred to wash themselves instead of relying on a slave, relative, or friend. Few baths from this period have survived or been excavated, but one found at the foot of the Palatine Hill in Rome, dated to the tenth or eleventh century, shows that hypocaust technology survived into the medieval period. Even monasteries had baths—the monastery of St. Gall had four baths in its eighth-century plan, although excessive bathing was one of the complaints of ninth-century monastic reformers. By the thirteenth century, cities throughout Europe had small baths for their populations; Paris had twenty-six public baths, most of them steam houses.

Bathing was also a domestic ritual, one that held connotations of pleasure, relaxation, and ease. Manuscript illustrations show couples or groups bathing together while they ate and watched entertainment; bathing appears as a frequent precursor to a seduction scene in French fabliaux. This association of bathing and sexual immorality was not ignored by moralists and preachers; some argued that even bathing alone exposed the Christian to sensual temptations. Secular moralists, however, advocated the saying *mens sana in corpore sano,* "a healthy mind in a healthy body." Bathing, whether in a tub, at hot springs, or in a steam bath, was frequently a part of medical treatment, recommended for ailments ranging from liver abcesses to a broken leg, and appeared in all standard medical texts of the Early and High Middle Ages. Conrad of Megenberg's *Buch der Natur* (1349) advocated frequent bathing. In northern and Slavic Europe, as well as Russia, the tradition of the steam bath predominated. The Jewish traveler Ibrāhīm ben Yaʿqūb in 973 noted the popularity of the sauna in Saxony and Bohemia.

Therapeutic natural baths also flourished in medieval Europe. The Florentine humanist Poggio Bracciolini in 1414 was astonished to find public mixed bathing in a large bath complex in Baden, near Zurich. The numerous mineral baths around the Bay of Naples continued to be used for medicinal purposes from antiquity to the early modern period. An early-thirteenth-century poem by Peter of Eboli described the different pools and their distinctive properties. The text served as a guide for those going to the baths and survives in twenty manuscript copies, many with extensive illustrations.

The bubonic plague that struck Europe in 1347 and periodically returned until the seventeenth century changed attitudes toward water, hygiene, and bathing. Fear of infection led to a sense of the porosity of human skin, and water more than anything else had the ability to cross the thin membrane that protects the body. Cleanliness came to be achieved less through immersion than through the washing of face and hands and frequent changes of underclothes. It is from this early modern period of uncertainty and fear of disease that the stereotype of the "dirty" Middle Ages developed, which remains one of the enduring misconceptions of the medieval world in the popular mind.

BIBLIOGRAPHY

Asher, Catherine. "The Public Baths of Medieval Spain: An Architectural Study." In *Medieval Mediterranean: Cross Cultural Contacts.* Edited by Marilyn J. Chiat and Kathryn L. Reyerson. St. Cloud, Minn.: North Star Press, 1988.

Berger, Albrecht. *Das Bad in byzantinischen Zeit.* Munich: Institut für Byzantinistik und neugriechische Philologie der Universität, 1982.

Grotzfeld, Heinz. *Das Bad im arabisch-islamischen Mittelalter.* Wiesbaden, Germany: Otto Harrassowitz, 1970.

Lillich, Meredith Parsons. "Cleanliness with Godliness: A Discussion of Medieval Monastic Plumbing." In *Studies in Medieval Stained Glass and Monasticism.* London: Pindar Press, 2001.

Magdalino, Paul. "Church, Bath, and *Diakonia* in Medieval Constantinople." In *Church and People in Byzantium.* Edited by Rosemary

Morris. Birmingham, U.K.: Centre for Byzantine, Ottoman, and Modern Greek Studies, 1986.

Magnusson, Roberta J. *Water Technology in the Middle Ages.* Baltimore: The Johns Hopkins University Press, 2001.

Squatriti, Paolo. *Water and Society in Early Medieval Italy:* A.D. *400–1000.* Cambridge, U.K.: Cambridge University Press, 1998.

Vigarello, Georges. *Concepts of Cleanliness: Changing Attitudes in France since the Middle Ages.* Translated by Jean Birrell. Cambridge, U.K.: Cambridge University Press, 1988.

Yegül, Fikret K. *Baths and Bathing in Classical Antiquity.* Cambridge: Massachusetts Institute of Technology Press, 1992.

CHRISTOPHER HATCH MacEVITT

[See also **DMA:** Black Death; Conrad of Megenberg; **Supp:** Hygiene, Personal.]

BEDOUIN. A Latin term usually applied to Arab nomads of the Middle East and Egypt. The word derives from the Arabic *badw* or *badawī,* meaning "nomad." In the pre-Islamic period, nomadic groups were also referred to as *aʿrab,* a term used for nomads and oasis dwellers but not for Arabic speakers generally. It can be difficult to uncover the role of nomadic groups in the ancient and medieval periods, for aside from a few short inscriptions, little literary material has been written from the perspective of nomadic communities. Pagan, Christian, and Islamic writers cast the nomad as barely human and as a continual threat to civilized society, a perspective that has continued to influence historiography to the present.

Although the subject is still debated, many prehistorians believe that nomadic pastoralism developed after the discovery of agriculture and represents a sophisticated system designed to make use of marginal and infertile land. Some scholars even suggest that Arab groups did not turn to nomadism until sometime in the first few centuries A.D. Annual migrants spent the summers in oases or other well-watered areas and in the winter traveled a circuit of established pasturage sites for their sheep, goats, or camels. As exploiters of marginal land, nomadic groups were small and had a symbiotic relationship with settled communities in more productive areas. The Bedouin needed settled communities with which to trade meat or dairy products from their flocks for grain and items of manufacture. Recent archaeological studies argue for a reversal of traditional ideas of conflict between nomads and settled communities. In the Negev Desert of southern Israel, the decline in urban centers in the seventh and eighth centuries did not increase nomadism, as traditional interpretations of nomadic life would suggest, but instead encouraged nomads to settle permanently in agricultural settlements. Unable to rely on the large settlements for trade and grain, nomadic groups were forced to settle and farm for themselves, often in marginal areas.

Little information has survived about women in medieval Bedouin culture. Modern studies suggest that Bedouin women were closely involved in domestic economy, playing important roles as herders and water-carriers. This gave them greater status and access to the world outside the domestic realm. The organization of Bedouin communities, where related kin groups often lived in close proximity, also allowed women greater freedom from seclusion than urban or rural women. Historians, however, cannot assume that modern Bedouins are coterminous with their medieval antecessors, and medieval Bedouin women may have lived very different lives than their twentieth-century counterparts.

In the Islamic period, the trope of nomads sweeping out of the desert "like locusts" to bring destruction to civilization had its appeal; the fourteenth-century writer Ibn Khaldūn attributed destruction of civilized life in the Maghrib to the rampages of the Banū Hilāl tribe in the eleventh century. Yet Bedouin poetry had a profound effect on the Arabic literary tradition. In the pre-Islamic period, poets commonly employed *ruwāt* (singular *rāwī*), professional performers who recited their poetry at fairs and festivals. The growth of Islam and the subsequent importance of writing led scholars to write down Bedouin poetry, which was still being collected in the early Abbasid period. Oral poetry continued to be a vital part of Bedouin culture into the twentieth century. In modern Bedouin communities, poetry in particular is part of the vocabulary of the individual and is used to express both personal emotions (grief, sorrow, love) and social relations among groups (feuds, reconciliations, alliances).

In the crusader period, nomadic groups within the boundaries of the Kingdom of Jerusalem (called *bedevini*) were considered seigneurial property, which did not mean that they were enslaved or even enserfed, but that the lord had exclusive right to tax and trade with the tribe.

The subject of Arab nomadism is receiving more attention, but historians still have little sense of the cultural and political relationship between nomads and sedentary communities for much of the medieval period.

BIBLIOGRAPHY

Abu-Lughod, Leila. *Veiled Sentiments: Honor and Poetry in a Bedouin Society.* Berkeley: University of California Press, 1986.

Avni, Gideon. *Nomads, Farmers, and Town-Dwellers: Pastoralist-Sedentist Interaction in the Negev Highlands, Sixth–Eighth Centuries C.E.* Jerusalem: Israel Antiquities Authority, 1996.

Shahîd, Irfan. *Byzantium and the Arabs in the Sixth Century.* Washington, D.C.: Dumbarton Oaks, 1995.

Shaw, Brent D. *Rulers, Nomads, and Christians in Roman North Africa,* Aldershot, U.K., and Brookfield, Vt.: Variorum, 1995. Several relevant articles are collected here.

CHRISTOPHER HATCH MacEVITT

[See also **DMA:** Arabia; Ghassanids; Khaldūn, Ibn; Lakhmids; **Supp:** Hilāl, Banū *(Sīrat Banū Hilāl).*]

BERNARD OF PARMA (**Bottono, de Botone,** *d.* 1266), scholar of canon law. Born in the late twelfth or early thirteenth century in Parma, Bernard studied canon law in Bologna under Tancred and later became a teacher there. One of his students was Guillaume Durand, whose *Speculum iudiciale* (published 1271–1276) would for many generations be the standard text on canon law procedure. Bernard became a canon of the cathedral of Bologna and by 1247 had begun serving as a chaplain to Popes Innocent IV and Alexander IV.

Bernard wrote several works of canon law, but he is best known for his gloss on the Gregorian decretals. The gloss was quickly accepted as the standard, or ordinary, gloss and was often copied or printed alongside the main text. The Gregorian decretal collection, also known as the *Liber extra,* was issued by Pope Gregory IX in 1234. It was the second part of what would become the accepted corpus of canon law. The *Liber extra* collected and organized the papal letters, or decretals, that had been promulgated since the publication in about 1140 of the first standard canon law book, the *Decretum* of Gratian. Due in part to its superior organization and its papal imprimatur, the *Liber extra* was a widely used law book in the later Middle Ages, and the gloss that generally traveled with it had a correspondingly significant impact. Bernard produced his first recension of the gloss some time between 1234 and 1241. He continued to revise the glosses until about 1263. At least four recensions have been identified in various manuscripts.

A gloss is not a systematic work but rather a series of brief, individual commentaries on the main text designed to clarify and supplement both single words and larger legal concepts. The glosses are only partly Bernard's own work. Many of the commentaries were borrowed from Bernard's predecessors, especially his teacher Tancred of Bologna, Laurentius Hispanus, and Vincentius Hispanus. However, the gloss also shows Bernard's expertise in the canon law and his familiarity with the Roman law and with the standard methods of biblical analysis of his day. Nevertheless, it does not represent a coherent and developed legal theory.

Bernard also wrote two other works. The *Casus longi* provided a short study of the judicial case with which each decretal dealt. The *Summa super titulis decretalium* was a short treatise on each chapter of the *Liber extra* that was in large part an updating of the works of Tancred and Bernard of Pavia. The *Summa* became an important teaching and reference work in the schools and among practitioners.

BIBLIOGRAPHY

Kuttner, Stephan. "Notes on the 'Glossa ordinaria' of Bernard of Parma." *Bulletin of Medieval Canon Law.* 11 (1981): 86–93.

Kuttner, Stephan, and Beryl Smalley. "The 'Glossa ordinaria' to the Gregorian Decretals." *English Historical Review* 60 (1945): 97–105.

Le Bras, G., Ch. Lefebvre, and J. Rambaud. *L'âge classique (1140–1378).* Paris : Sirey, 1965.

Orliac, Paul. "Bernard de Parme." In *Dictionnaire de droit canonique.* Vol. 2. Paris: Letouzey et Ané, 1937.

EMILY KADENS

[See also **DMA:** Decretals; Decretists; Gratian; Gregory IX, Pope; Law, Canon: After Gratian; **Supp:** Bernard of Pavia.]

BERNARD OF PAVIA (Papiensis) (also known as Balbus, *d.* 1213), one of the most important canonists of the twelfth century. Born in Pavia around the mid-twelfth century, Bernard studied canon law at Bologna, perhaps under Huguccio, arguably the most significant canonist of his age. Bernard taught at Bologna in the 1170s, then worked at the papal curia, but about this period in his life little is known. In 1187 he was named provost of the cathedral of Pavia. In 1191 he became bishop of Faenza and in 1198 bishop of Pavia, where he remained until his death in 1213.

Bernard published his legal works at a fertile moment in the development of canon law. Around 1140 the *Decretum* of Gratian had appeared, which provided a widely accepted attempt to codify and systematize the sources of canon law—including the papal decretals (or letters) that had accumulated over the centuries, as well as excerpts from the works of the church fathers, canons of church councils, the Bible, and bits and pieces of Roman law. The systemization of the law by Gratian's *Decretum* made gaps in canon law evident, which in turn led to an explosion of papal decrees. The collection, or-

ganization, and study of decretals so dominated the last decade of the twelfth and the first decades of the thirteenth centuries that the scholars of that age were known as decretalists. Bernard of Pavia was foremost in their ranks.

His most important work was the *Breviarium extravagantium,* published around 1190. The title derives from the work's goal: to give excerpts (thus "brief") of the decretals issued since the publication of the *Decretum* (thus "extra-vagantes," or those decretals "wandering about," i.e., not collected). The *Breviarium* made two improvements on earlier collections. First, Bernard included only those portions of a decretal that were relevant to the legal issue rather than incorporating the entire text. Second, he organized the work in five books, each devoted to a single legal topic. Book 1 concerns ecclesiastical judges, and book 2 deals with procedure in courts Christian (canon law courts). Book 3 handles monks, clerics, and ecclesiastical property. Book 4 concerns marriage—a topic of great importance in the canon law of medieval Europe. Finally, book 5 sets out a penal code. This order became the standard one used in all canon law collections after the appearance of the *Breviarium* and can be remembered by the mnemonic: *judex* (judge), *judicia* (judgments), *clerus* (clergy), *connubia* (marriages), *crimen* (crime). The *Breviarium* became the first textbook of decretal law in the canon law course at the University of Bologna. It was eventually joined by four other textbooks, which collectively were known as the *Quinque compilationes* (Five compilations). The *Breviarium* came to be called the *Compilatio prima* (First compilation).

The *Breviarium* may not have been Bernard's first attempt at collecting decretals. A short work, the *Collection in Ninety-five Titles (Parisiensis secunda),* compiled around 1177 to 1179, has also been ascribed to him, though his authorship has been questioned. Bernard also wrote glosses to the *Decretum,* which served as the standard (ordinary) gloss until the work of Johannes Teutonicus replaced it around 1216. More significant than these works was the *Summa decretalium,* written between 1191 and 1198 while Bernard was bishop of Faenza. Despite its name, this was actually a manual of the whole of canon law designed to be used as a textbook in the schools. In addition, Bernard also wrote summae on marriage and on ecclesiastical elections (*Summa de matrimonio* and *Summa de electione*), a glossary of the *Breviarium,* a life of St. Lanfranc, and commentaries on Ecclesiastes and the Song of Songs.

BIBLIOGRAPHY

EDITIONS

Friedberg, Emil, ed. *Quinque compilationes antiquae nec non collectio canonum lipsiensis.* 1882. Reprint, Graz, Austria: Akademische Druck-u. Verlagsanstalt, 1956. Incomplete edition of the *Compilatio prima.*

———. *Die Canones-Sammlungen zwischen Gratian und Bernhard von Pavia.* 1897. Reprint, Graz, Austria: Akademische Druck- u. Verlagsanstalt, 1958. Edition of the *Collection in Ninety-five Titles.*

Laspeyres, Ernst Adolph Theodor, ed. *Bernardus Papiensis Faventini Episcopi Summa decretalium.* 1860. Reprint, Graz: Akademische Druck- u. Verlagsanstalt, 1956. Includes editions of the *Summa decretalium,* the *Casus decretalium,* the *Summa de electione,* and the *Summa de matrimonio.*

SECONDARY SOURCES

Fransen, Gérard. "Les diverse formes de la Compilatio Ia." In *Scrinium Lovaniense: mélanges historiques, historische opstellen Étienne van Cauwenbergh.* Gembloux: J. Duculot, 1961.

Hanenburg, Jacoba. "Decretals and Decretal Collections in the Second Half of the Twelfth Century." In *Tijdschrift voor Rechtsgeschiedenis* 34 (1966): 522–599.

Kuttner, Stephan. *Repertorium der Kanonistik (1140–1234).* Vatican City: Biblioteca Apostolica Vaticana, 1937.

Le Bras, Guillaume. "Bernard de Pavie." In vol. 2 of *Dictionnaire du droit canonique.* Edited by R. Naz. Paris: Library Letouzey, 1937.

Lefebvre, Charles. "Les gloses à la Compilatio Ia." *Studia Gratiana* 20 (1976): 135–156.

EMILY KADENS

[See also **DMA:** Decretals; Decretists; Gratian; Law, Canon: After Gratian; **Supp:** Bernard of Parma.]

BIBLICAL COMMENTARIES. The genre of Christian biblical commentary is based on the methods of textual scholarship by which Greek classical literature, especially Homer, was transmitted in the Hellenistic schools from the third century B.C. onward. Alexandrian Jewish tradition applied the same procedures to the biblical canon as early as the first century B.C. Its outstanding representative was Philo, whose works of philosophically oriented biblical interpretation were largely preserved by sympathetic Christian readers. The earliest Christian biblical interpretation was oral and served practical purposes. The first literary pieces of sustained commentation had polemical and apologetic aims. Among them are exegeses of Gospel passages by the gnostic Heracleon. The actual creator of the Christian biblical commentary was Origen of Alexandria, whose scholia, annotations, and commentaries on most books of the Bible set standards and influenced the entire tradition after him. Origen understood himself as a teacher of a higher education for all intellectually interested Christians. Many of his commentaries come in the form of homilies delivered to congregations. But the Christian biblical commentary was a school product, and it was in the "schools" of bishops and ascetics that the Greek Christian commentary tradition had its primary location. Among the earliest Latin commentaries is a third-century Apocalypse commentary by Victorinus of Pettau. It was soon followed by the extensive exegetical work of the four luminaries of the Western church: Ambrose, Jerome, Augustine, and Gregory the Great.

PATRISTIC AND EASTERN CHRISTIAN COMMENTARY

The method of Christian patristic commentary followed the rules of Hellenistic philology. It included textual criticism, elucidation of vocabulary and grammar, explanation of the *realia,* rhetorical and literary analysis, and application. The latter rested on the conviction of the historical revelation of the same God in the Old and New Testaments and was an attempt to see both Testaments in a continuous stream of meaning where words and events of the Hebrew Scriptures functioned as prophetic anticipations of the Christocentric message of the New Testament and by extension of the church, through which God made salvation available to both Jew and Gentile. This "typology" remained characteristic of Christian exegesis. Hermeneutically, the final step of the interpretive process involved the expectation of a spiritual ascent. Origen used a Neoplatonic anthropological model of body, soul, and spirit to distinguish three levels of meaning in the Scriptures. The goal was spiritual understanding that would leave the letter of the text behind and lead the soul back to God. In all subsequent exegesis the basic division between literal and spiritual sense was maintained, but in the West, the spiritual sense was subdivided into allegory (doctrinal content, including typology), tropology (moral content), and anagogy (the goal concept). This "fourfold sense," first documented in John Cassian in the fifth century, informed the theory of biblical interpretation throughout the Middle Ages.

In its golden age (fourth and fifth centuries), the Greek-speaking church experienced the consolidation of orthodoxy. Biblical commentaries reflected the polemics of the time, especially the rivalry between the school of Antioch with an emphasis on historical-moral interpretation (Diodore of Tarsus, Theodore of Mopsuestia, John Chrysostom, Theodoret of Cyr) and the Alexandrians with their insistence on allegory and spiritual reading (Athanasius, Didymus the Blind, Cyril of Alexandria). The time of Emperor Justinian saw the emergence of a new form of biblical commentary, the *catena* (chain).

Catenae are serial collections of biblical texts *(lemmata)* followed by explanatory excerpts from a limited number of sources. The original purpose of this genre, which dominated the Greek commentary production through subsequent centuries, seems to have been the support of doctrinal orthodoxy. The study of the *catenae* has become a major focus of research since it allows scholars to identify fragments of patristic commentaries otherwise lost. Work in this area is complicated, however, by the fact that earlier *catenae* were later expanded; it is difficult to separate the layers. The earliest name connected with the production of *catenae* is Procopius of Gaza (*ca.* 475–*ca.* 538). His chains (Octateuch, Kings, Chronicles, Isaiah) often identify the authors of the excerpts by specific *sigla* (abbreviations). Later names connected with the compilation of *catenae* are John Drungarios (*ca.* 700), for the Prophets and Luke, and Niketas of Herakleia (eleventh century) for the Psalms, the Gospels, and the Pauline Epistles. Original commentaries from the Byzantine era are rare. We have commentaries from the seventh century, mainly able compilations, by Gregory of Akragas on Sirach, Georgios Choiroboskos on the Psalms and the Song of Songs, and John of Damascus on the Pauline Epistles. Basilios of Neopatrai wrote on the Prophets in the tenth century. In the eleventh and twelfth centuries Theophylact of Ochrid and Euthymios Zigabenos were productive exegetes. The Book of Revelation, which in the East was not universally accepted as canonical until the eleventh century, found imaginative interpreters in Oikoumenios and Andrew of Caesarea during the sixth century. On the latter's exposition Arethas of Caesarea (*ca.* 895) based his widely used commentary.

Most non-Byzantine Christian churches developed a commentary tradition of their own in interaction with that of the Greek church. In Armenia, early commentaries were translations of Greek works, first of the Antiochian school, later of the Alexandrian tradition as well. Certain patristic writings are preserved only in Armenian. Ełišē (Elishe; fifth century), probably the first indigenous commentator, wrote on Genesis, Joshua, and Judges. As a special feature, Armenian biblical interpretation, frequently in the form of *catenae,* included allegorical expositions of the Eusebian canon tables. The great medieval theologians Nersēs Šnorhali, Nersēs Lambronacʻi, Vardan Arewelcʻi, and Grigor Tatʻewacʻi were prolific commentary writers in the twelfth, thirteenth, and fourteenth centuries. Syrian Christianity had a distinguished history. Among its great fourth-century theologians, Ephraem wrote commentaries in the Antiochian style on Genesis and Exodus that are preserved in Syriac; the one on Tatian's *Diatessaron* (Gospel harmony) is ex-

Folio from Collatio *IV of John Cassian. The 5th-century exegete is the earliest known expositor of the fourfold method of allegorical interpretation. This is an 8th-century manuscript. Cod. Vat. Lat. 5766, fol. 4r.*

tant in Armenian translation. Narsai wrote expository homilies in the fifth century. Other Syrian exegetes such as Philoxenus of Mabbug or, in Islamic times, Theodore bar Konai and Īshōʻdad of Merv, continued the East Syrian Nestorian tradition of Edessa and the school of Nisibis. For them, Theodore of Mopsuestia was "the Commentator." The Syriac expositions of the entire Bible by Dionysius Bar Ṣalibi and Barhebraeus represent the West Syrian "Jacobite" tradition.

THE EARLY MIDDLE AGES IN THE WEST

With the transformation of the classical educational system through the barbarian invasions of western Europe, commentary writing in the style of the great Fathers declined steeply. The exceptions to this trend dem-

Incipit of Bede's **Ecclesiastical History of the English People.** *Despite Bede's fame as a historian, witnessed by this 8th-century manuscript portrait, more than half of his copious writings are biblical commentaries.* © DAVID REED/CORBIS-BETTMANN. REPRODUCED BY PERMISSION.

onstrate that the basic locus of Christian schooling was shifting to the monasteries. Under the Ostrogothic rule in Italy, Cassiodorus promoted the preservation of the literary heritage by having patristic and classical writings copied at his monastery of Vivarium near Naples in the sixth century. His own commentary on Psalms, indebted to Augustine, remained a standard source throughout the Middle Ages, and his monks preserved the Romans commentary of Pelagius in a doctrinally revised version. Pope Gregory the Great wrote his classic *Moralia in Job* at the request of his monks in Rome during the Lombard threat. In Visigothic Spain, Isidore of Seville stands out as the most important biblical encyclopedist of the patristic age. His educational zeal extended beyond the clerical students under his care to the cultural elite of a Christian Spain. His main work, the *Etymologies,* presents the entire knowledge of his time on the basis of the derivation of words and names.

The hallmark of Latin Christianity in Ireland was an indigenous monastic culture that developed soon after the introduction of Christianity in the sixth century. It produced a rich exegetical literature, including biblical glosses and commentaries, most of them anonymous. Early Irish commentaries were mostly of the gloss type, not continuous interpretations. They frequently employed a question-answer format and sought to display erudition. What seems characteristic is an interest in Latin grammar, curiosity about narrative details, a lack of interest in doctrinal polemics, and immense admiration for the patristic tradition. As early as the seventh century, an Irish monk, Lathcen, composed a condensation of Gregory's *Moralia.*

Irish monasticism left important traces in the culture of the Middle Ages. It influenced the development of Christianity in Britain, especially in the kingdom of Northumbria with its center at York. For the southern kingdom of Kent, missionized directly from Rome in 597, Bernhard Bischoff has drawn attention to an exegetical school at Canterbury connected with Archbishop Theodore, a learned Greek monk from Asia Minor, and Abbot Hadrian in the late seventh century. Recently published commentaries from this circle show that Greek learning was alive there and that even the heritage of Antiochene biblical philology had a place from which it could influence western Europe. From Canterbury Theodore's contemporary Benedict Biscop went to his native Northumbria to found the two abbeys of Wearmouth (674) and Jarrow (682), which was to house his first-rate library. Here the Venerable Bede found the tools for his comprehensive scholarly activity in the eighth century. Almost all of Bede's many biblical commentaries are now available in critical editions. Bede was aware of the Irish commentary tradition and shared its interest in *realia.* He knew Greek and used it for textual criticism. He also made extensive use of the Western Fathers. His commentaries, however, were not mere compilations but careful verse-by-verse expositions with the clear goal of inculcating Christian values, informing and edifying his readers in conscious dependence on the tradition. The large number of extant manuscripts attest to his enduring popularity throughout the Middle Ages.

In the Frankish realm, Charlemagne's zeal for education ended a period of cultural stagnation. By his legislation he promoted schools at cathedrals and monasteries, which led to a new flowering of ecclesiastical culture, including biblical studies. Latin grammar and rhetoric were taught, the biblical text was revised, and biblical interpretation flourished. The political ideology of the Carolingian rulers drew on biblical sources, especially the historical books of the Old Testament. Wigbodus, who wrote an encyclopedic commentary on the Octateuch, the first eight books of the Old Testament, at the request of Charlemagne, seems to have been a pacesetter in the wave of commentaries written in response to this new situation. His "official" model, integrating the patristic sources creatively into a running interpretation of single biblical books, was very influential. Claudius of Turin, an independent mind with close ties to the Carolingian court, followed this lead in numerous commentaries. Charlemagne surrounded himself with able theologians. Foremost among them was Alcuin of York, whom he asked to head his palace school and later the abbey of St. Martin at Tours, where Alcuin's revision of the Latin Bible was copied in the new Carolingian script, securing for it the widest distribution. He also was a prolific commentator. His *Questions and Answers on Genesis,* which popularized patristic exegesis and showed a special interest in the symbolism of numbers, follows the form of the Irish tradition. One of his pupils was Hrabanus Maurus, the abbot of Fulda, who authored some of the most successful commentaries of the period. Other monastic commentators include Walafrid Strabo of Reichenau, Paschasius Radbertus of Corbie, Angelomus of Luxeuil, and, somewhat later, Christian of Stavelot in Belgium. At the school of Auxerre in Burgundy the Irish grammarian Murethach stood at the beginning of a succession of important ninth-century teachers and exegetes: Haymo, Heiric, and Remigius. The identification of their works is rendered difficult by the confusion about authorship in the tradition. Among Irish authors on the Continent, Josephus Scottus commented on Isaiah, Sedulius Scottus on Matthew and the Pauline Epistles, and John Scottus Eriugena, a brilliant thinker whose knowledge of Greek allowed him to introduce Christian Neoplatonic sources into the West, authored a major commentary on the Gospel of John, using the Greek Fathers. The philosophical vision of the world in his main work, *De divisione naturae,* is based on a careful exegesis of Genesis 1–3.

Most Western writers knew the Eastern Fathers only through a few Latin translations: Rufinus's and Jerome's adaptations of Origen, some of Chrysostom's homilies, Theodore of Mopsuestia's commentaries on Psalms 1–40 and the Pauline Epistles, and Didymus the Blind's notes on the Catholic Epistles. Even for the Western Fathers, exegetical anthologies such as Paterius's excerpts from Gregory the Great or Florus of Lyons's commentary on the Pauline Epistles, compiled from Augustine's writings, regularly replaced the originals. It was not until the thirteenth century that new translations of Greek authors became available and Thomas Aquinas could draw on a wider range of sources for his *Catena aurea* on the four Gospels.

Alcuin of York. A later rendering of the leading Carolingian translator and commentator. CORBIS-BETTMANN. REPRODUCED BY PERMISSION.

THE HIGH MIDDLE AGES

In the eleventh century, monastic writers were at the forefront of the theological controversies, and monasteries remained the centers of biblical studies. Grammar, rhetoric, and dialectic formed the educational basis of an intimate life with the Bible. It included memorization of biblical texts, especially the Psalter, exposure to expository homilies, and the practice of *lectio divina,* personal meditation on the sacred text. Lanfranc of Bec used the Bible for grammar lessons, but, like many other monastic authors of the period, he also commented on the Psalms and the Pauline Epistles. Bruno of Segni left an extensive expository corpus on many books of the Bible. Monastic commentaries were leisurely and lengthy. The most famous work of this genre, Bernard of Clairvaux's commentary on the Song of Songs (1135–1148), covered only two chapters in eighty-six sermons. Bernard's method was that of a "spiritual tropology," which applied the text directly to the inner aspirations of his monks. He inspired other Cistercians such as Gilbert of Hoyland, William of St. Thierry, and Ethelred of Rievaulx. There were also innovations. Rupert of Deutz wrote independent commentaries on the Gospel of John and the Apocalypse. His main work, entitled *De Sancta Trinitate et operibus eius* (On the Holy Trinity and its works), is a commentary on the historical books of the Bible as the unfolding of the history of salvation. He also started the trend to give the Song of Songs a Mariological interpretation: the bride is the Virgin Mary. Honorius Augustodunensis pursued the same symbolism in his *Sigillum Sanctae Mariae* (St. Mary's seal) but used also the traditional interpretation (the bride is the church) in his widely read commentary. The rich commentary on Psalms 1–78 by Gerhoh of Reichersberg already cited contemporary exegetes among its sources.

In the twelfth century, the abbey of St. Victor in Paris was a center of biblical studies at a time of changing intellectual climate. Its library and scriptorium played a key role in the dissemination of exegetical literature, and Victorine scholars made decisive contributions to the theory and practice of biblical commentation. Hugh of St. Victor's entire work, guided by Augustine and Jerome, focused on the Bible. His educational program envisioned the liberal arts as the basis of all Bible study and stressed the importance of the historical content *(historia)* as well as the linguistic form of the text *(littera et sensus),* without giving up the monastic insistence on the ascent of the soul *(sententia).* He wrote detailed running commentaries on the historical books of the Old Testament and on Ecclesiastes. Andrew of St. Victor left commentaries on a large number of Old Testament books, which have recently begun to appear in critical editions. His main interest was philological, determining the precise meaning of the text by exact translation and analysis. Andrew knew Hebrew. In addition to Jerome he used Josephus and other Jewish sources and consulted Jewish scholars of the northern French school. Later exegetes frequently drew on his commentaries when they expounded the literal sense of an Old Testament passage.

A key factor in the cultural change was the increasing importance of cathedral schools, especially in France (Reims, Laon, Chartres, Paris, Troyes), and the emergence of the university as an institution in the early thirteenth century. Cathedral schools trained the secular clergy at a time of intellectual awakening, when the desire for education was urgent and the demand for preaching was high. The Bible remained the primary textbook for this task even at the universities where basic education was provided by the faculty of arts, and theology was only one of the three "higher" faculties. Thus the setting for the production of biblical commentaries was changing. Commentaries became the tools as well as the fruits of a specific form of academic instruction. The clearest example of this shift is the emergence of the *Glossa ordinaria* to the Bible, a twelfth-century compilation making available the exegetical tradition for every verse of a biblical book and cumulatively of the entire Bible. In *Glossa* manuscripts, every page displayed a window with several verses of biblical text in large letters surrounded by comments written between the lines and in the margins. We know the names of some early compilers of the *Glossa* at Laon: Anselm for the Psalms, the Pauline Epistles, and perhaps the Gospel of John; Radulphus for the Minor Prophets and Matthew; Gilbert the Universal for the Pentateuch and the Major Prophets. It seems that Gilbert of Poitiers played a key role in advancing the project and that Paris became the center of its distribution.

For critics of glossing, such as Robert of Melun, the alternative was lecturing on topical questions. Abelard, one of the most successful teachers of the period, built such *quaestiones* directly into his commentary on Romans. Since the late twelfth century, lecturing on the Bible in schools generally meant lecturing on the glossed Bible, including the Jeromian and other prologues to each biblical book. From a number of the Paris masters at the turn of the century we have such lectures on most books of the Old and New Testament. They come in several forms: as notes taken down by students *(reportatio),* as drafts revised by the master *(ordinatio),* and as polished publications under various designations *(lectura, expositio, glosulae).* Teachers such as Peter Lombard, Peter Comestor, Peter the Chanter, and Stephen Langton also provided instruments for the use of the Bible by preaching clerics. Peter Lombard systematized Bible doctrines by topics in his *Sentences;* Peter Comestor's *Historia scholastica,* a brief summary of the history covered by the Bible, was for generations every beginner's reading. Peter the Chanter's "Summa Abel" inaugurated the genre of *distinctiones,* alphabetical lists of biblical terms and their various spiritual meanings, and Stephen Langton's system of chapter division has remained in place to this day. Not surprisingly, the thirteenth century turned out to be the "age of tools." In the 1220s and 1230s, teamwork by the Dominicans of St. Jacques in Paris produced the *Postilla super totam Bibliam,* an update of the *Glossa ordinaria,* which had been printed under the name of Hugh of St. Cher. The Dominican Nicholas of Gorran assembled a similar work later in the century, and the Franciscan William Brito compiled a biblical dictionary around 1260. Hugh of St. Cher also supervised the publication of the first comprehensive concordance of the Latin Bible completed at St. Jacques in 1230.

Biblical commentary writing itself did not turn into new directions until the Reformation, but there were major changes in the setting of biblical studies. In the universities, the introductory courses on the glossed

Bible were generally assigned to graduate students and rarely left literary traces. The masters in the faculties of theology, on the other hand, were obliged to lecture on their choice of specific books of the Bible. Manuscripts of such lecture courses have been preserved in large numbers. Most of these writers, if known, were members of the new mendicant orders, Franciscans, Dominicans, and Augustinians, whose training continued to be Bible centered and was carried out in seminaries *(studia)* as well as at the theological faculties. For the next 150 years after 1220, commentary writing was firmly in the hands of the mendicants, with some notable exceptions such as William of Auvergne, John of Abbeville, Odo of Chateauroux, and Henry of Ghent, who were secular masters. These commentaries attempted to be scholarly, often including *quaestiones,* scientific observations, and philosophical or pastoral deliberations. Under the influence of the reception of Aristotle, the *accessus,* which treated intention, subject matter, literary procedure, usefulness, and philosophical classification at the beginning of a commentary, was replaced by a discussion of its "four causes": the material (subject matter), efficient (author), formal (literary style and genre), and final cause (contribution to the Christian life). This change indicates a hermeneutical reorientation: "divine" writings could now be appreciated as works of an (inspired) human mind and analyzed like other literature. The focus shifted from the divine to the human author, and the new definition of the literal sense was "that which the author intended." Among the Dominicans, Albertus Magnus and Thomas Aquinas left a significant amount of biblical commentaries, among them Thomas's influential *Expositio in Job ad litteram* (1261/1264).

Other thirteenth-century Dominican commentators include Guerric of St. Quentin, Roland of Cremona, William of Alton, Peter of Tarentaise, Peter of Scala, and John of Varzy; in the early fourteenth century, Dominic Grima, Robert Holcot, and Nicholas Trevet. On the Franciscan side, academic course lectures are extant from the pen of both Alexander of Hales and Bonaventure (Gospel of Luke). Along with them, John of La Rochelle, William of Middleton, Thomas Docking, Matthew of Aquasparta, and by extension Robert Grosseteste deserve mention. Grosseteste commissioned a Hebrew Psalter with a new interlinear translation. He also mastered Greek and used it in his major works on Genesis and the Psalms. The Franciscan Spirituals, whose ideas were influenced by the biblical meditations of Joachim of Fiore, had among its sympathizers Peter John Olivi, whose many biblical commentaries for the most part still await publication.

THE LATER MIDDLE AGES

The fourteenth century saw the appearance of Nicholas of Lyra's massive *Postillae perpetuae super totam Bibliam* (1322–1332), a literal exposition of the entire Bible, which established itself as a standard tool for commentators up to and beyond the Reformation of the sixteenth century. Lyra, a Franciscan, was a proficient Hebraist who used rabbinical and contemporary Jewish sources, such as Rashi. He was also concerned about spiritual understanding, as his shorter *Postilla moralis* (1339) demonstrates. Among Christian Hebraists, Andrew of St. Victor was especially useful for him, but he probably knew of others as well, such as Herbert of Bosham, Raymond Martini, and William de la Mare. Paul of Burgos, a converted Jew, wrote *Additiones* to Lyra's *Postillae.* Prominent among later Dominicans was Meister Eckhart, whose commentaries on Genesis, Exodus, Wisdom, and the Gospel of John are not being studied as much as his sermons. In the fifteenth century, both Denis the Carthusian and John of Hagen provided comprehensive commentation on the whole Bible. Such efforts were aimed at preachers, who also appreciated expositions of the Ten Commandments, the Lord's Prayer, and the seven penitential psalms as pastoral aids.

Throughout the Middle Ages, commentaries on specific biblical sections remained popular. Major commentaries on the Hexaemeron (the six days of creation described in Genesis) began with Basil the Great, Gregory of Nyssa, and Ambrose. In the High Middle Ages, the genre served as a vehicle of philosophical and scientific discussions of creation (Thierry of Chartres, Albertus Magnus, Thomas Aquinas, Bonaventure, Robert Grosseteste, Giles of Rome). The biblical canticles, which were a regular part of the liturgy of the hours and frequently appeared at the end of Psalter manuscripts, were often separately expounded. The same holds true of the ark of Noah (Genesis 6:14–16), Moses's Tabernacle (Exodus 25–30:21), the praise of the "strong woman" (Proverbs 31:10–31), and the twelve jewels (Revelation 21:19–20).

Reformist thought nourished by strong convictions about the Bible became more radical in the fourteenth century. John Wyclif based his criticism of the ecclesiastical establishment on biblical arguments. He used his biblical lectures at Oxford to write a comprehensive *Postilla super totam Bibliam* (1371/1376). One of his last works, *Opus evangelicum* (1383/1384), is a commentary on Gospel texts central to his call for reform. As part of his program, he promoted the translation of the Bible into English and wrote several expository pieces in the vernacular. John Hus, who was burned at the stake for his alleged Wyclifite sympathies, taught at Prague. Of his academic lectures on the Bible, expositions of a group of Psalms and of the Catholic Epistles have been preserved. Martin Luther, an Augustinian friar, began his career at the new university of Wittenberg in 1513 with a traditional lecture course on the Psalter. The autograph notes of his lectures provide glimpses of the Reformation to come.

JEWISH COMMENTARY

The literature of Jewish tradition in Mishnah, Midrash, and Talmud was by nature commentary on the Hebrew Bible. Here already multiple interpretations, later systematized in the acronym PARDES, were in use: *peshat* (plain sense), *derash* (homiletical exposition), *remez* (hint; sometimes allegory), *sod* (secret; symbolic interpretation). Running expositions of biblical books first appeared in Gaonic circles whose topical *responsa* to questions prepared the way. In the tenth century Saadiah Gaon provided his own Arabic translation and commentary on the Pentateuch and other biblical books following Islamic models. His reasoned exposition defended rabbinic learning against the rational biblicism of the Karaites. The verse-by-verse explanation of the Minor Prophets by the ascetic Daniel al-Qūmisī in the late ninth century is perhaps the first surviving commentary in Hebrew. Japheth ben Ali expounded the whole Bible in Karaite style.

From the middle of the tenth century, Spain became the center of Jewish intellectual life and commentary writing. Linguistic studies and lexicography flourished and reached high levels of sophistication. The commentaries pursued *peshat,* some even involving literary criticism: Moses Gikatilla, Judah ben Samuel ibn Balʿam, and the great Abraham ben Meïr ibn Ezra. Ibn Ezra, who used the "eye of reason," was interested in plausibility and the harmony of Bible and science. In his *Guide for the Perplexed* (*ca.* 1185–1190), Moses Maimonides, the foremost representative of Spanish philosophical exegesis, attempted to find rational and cultural explanations for the commandments of the Torah. Moses Naḥmanides added the sensitivity for literary structure, a penchant for pietistic admonition, and mystical symbolism, which subsequently blossomed in the cabala and its classic document, the *Zohar.*

In a climate of intensive Talmudic studies, an influential school of biblical commentators emerged in northern France, with Rabbi Solomon ben Isaac (Rashi) as its shining peak in the eleventh century. Rashi also annotated the entire Talmud. His biblical commentaries explore *peshat* but utilize materials from the rabbinic tradition as well. They greatly influenced Jewish and Christian interpreters. Among the former, Joseph Kara, Samuel ben Meir (Rashi's grandson), and Joseph Bekhor Shor stand out as commentary writers. Slightly later, the Kimḥi family from Andalusia inaugurated an equally famous school of commentators in southern France, beginning with Joseph Kimḥi. David Kimḥi was its most important representative. His numerous commentaries, similar in style to Rashi's, remain much appreciated classics of the scholarly biblical commentary in the Jewish tradition.

BIBLIOGRAPHY

SOURCES

Corpus christianorum: Series latina. Turnholt, Belgium: Brepols, 1953–.

Corpus christianorum: Series graeca. Turnholt, Belgium: Brepols, 1977–.

Corpus christianorum: Continuatio mediaevalis. Turnholt, Belgium: Brepols, 1994–.

Corpus scriptorum christianorum orientalium. Louvain, Belgium: L. Durbecq, 1903–.

Migne, Jacques-Paul, ed. *Patrologia latina.* 221 vols. Paris: Migne, 1844–1864. Available at http://pld.chadwyck.com.

———. *Patrologia graeca.* 161 vols. Paris: Migne, 1856–1866.

REPERTORIES

Blumenkranz, Bernhard, in collaboration with Gilbert Dahan and Samuel Kerner. *Auteurs juifs en France médiévale: Leur œvre imprimée.* Toulouse, France: E. Privat, 1975.

Lapidge, Michael, and Richard Sharpe. *A Bibliography of Celtic-Latin Literature, 400–1200.* Dublin: Royal Irish Academy, 1985.

Reinhardt, Klaus, and Horacio Santiago-Otero. *Biblioteca bíblica ibérica medieval.* Madrid: Centro de estudios históricos, 1986.

Stegmüller, Friedrich. *Repertorium biblicum medii aevi.* 11 vols. Madrid: Consejo Superior de Investigaciones Cientificas, Instituto Francisco Suarez, 1950–1980.

STUDIES

Beck, Hans Georg. *Kirche und theologische Literatur im Byzantinischen Reich.* Munich: Beck, 1959.

Bischoff, Bernhard, and Michael Lapidge, eds. *Biblical Commentaries from the Canterbury School of Theodore and Hadrian.* Cambridge, U.K.: Cambridge University Press, 1994.

The Cambridge History of the Bible. Volume 2: *The West from the Fathers to the Reformation.* Edited by G. W. H. Lampe. Cambridge, U.K.: Cambridge University Press, 1969.

Dahan, Gilbert. *L'exégèse chrétienne de la Bible en Occident médiéval, XIIe–XIVe siècle.* Paris: Cerf, 1999.

De Lubac, Henri. *Medieval Exegesis.* Translated by Marc Sebanc. 2 vols. Grand Rapids, Mich.: W. B. Eerdmans, 1998.

Gorman, Michael M. *Biblical Commentaries from the Early Middle Ages.* Florence: Edizioni del Galluzzo, 2002.

Hayes, John H., ed. *Dictionary of Biblical Interpretation*. 2 vols. Nashville: Abingdon Press, 1999.

Riché, Pierre, and Guy Lobrichon, eds. *Le Moyen Âge et la Bible*. Paris: Beauchesne, 1984.

Saebo, Magne, ed. *Hebrew Bible, Old Testament: The History of Its Interpretation*. Volume 1: *From the Beginnings to the Middle Ages (until 1300)*. Part 2, *The Middle Ages*. Göttingen, Germany: Vandenhoeck and Ruprecht, 1999.

Smalley, Beryl. *The Study of the Bible in the Middle Ages*. 3d ed. Oxford: Blackwell, 1983.

KARLFRIED FROEHLICH

[See also **DMA**: Alcuin of York; Bede; Bible, Glosses and Commentaries (Irish); Biblical Interpretation; Isidore of Seville, St.; John Scotus Eriugena; Nicholas of Lyra; Origen; Schools, Cathedral; Schools, Jewish; Schools, Monastic; Talmud, Exegis and Study of; Universities; Wyclif, John; **Supp**: Hebrew Language.]

BIOGRAPHY in the western Middle Ages fuses Greek and Roman models and the Christian Gospels. The word is derived from the Greek and is first used by Damascius, a fifth-century Athenian Neoplatonic philosopher, who wrote a biography of the philosopher Isidore of Alexandria. Although the word is not recorded before the sixth century, the genre in the west is at least a millennium older since the desire to celebrate great deeds is a natural one.

CLASSICAL BIOGRAPHY

The earliest biographies were composed to celebrate heroic exploits. They followed no fixed format, nor were there rules to govern rhetoric or organization. Indeed among the Romans there was considerable ambivalence about whether biography was principally a mode of literary or historical writing. The use of chronology in biography first appeared in Xenophon's celebration of Alexander the Great in his *Cyropaedia* and his *Agesilaus* and in the *Evagoras* (*ca.* 365 B.C.) of Isocrates. These three works depict the heroic virtue of their subjects in their deeds.

The Peripatetic school under Aristotle sharpened the focus of biography. Notable members of this school sought broader subject matter and inquired into motive and personality, believing character was revealed in action. Cornelius Nepos's *De viris illustribus*, Plutarch's *Parallel Lives*, Suetonius's *De viris illustribus*, and Philostratus's *Life of Apollonius of Tyana* were critical to Christian medieval biographers and singled out by St. Jerome as worthy of reverence. The ancients believed deeds were pregnant with virtue. Roman biography limits psychological scrutiny. Horace observed that one should imitate manners, not the psychology behind them. Roman biographers, however, like Suetonius, notably in his *Nero,* were unsparing of their subjects and could depict them in the most unflattering light.

The chief task of the classical biographer was to provide a window into the subject's character, to extol virtue and castigate vice. Philo of Alexandria remarked that virtue was uncommon among men and it was thus the biographer's task to praise those instances when it was palpable. The biographer's goal was to proclaim such virtue as an example worthy of imitation, since only one's reputation among the living conferred immortality. The titles of these biographies are best rendered as "in praise of" rather than "life of" the subject. For example, Philostratus's *Life of Apollonius of Tyana* is more correctly rendered *In Praise* [or *Respect*] *of Apollonius of Tyana,* the latter use underlying the epideictic quality of the composition.

CHRISTIAN GOSPELS

The four Gospels provided medieval biography with the principal touchstone against which all merit was measured, the life of Christ. Christian biography differs from its classical forebears in that it locates the highest and most unimpeachable virtue in the figure of Christ. Even in the pagan biographies of the philosophers, neither the biographer nor his audience believed the philosopher contained all of the best of human virtue. For the Christian, on the other hand, the Gospel depiction of Christ contained the only model one needed to imitate.

The Gospels proclaim Jesus as Messiah and God. Miraculous anecdotes in the four Gospels demonstrate his divinity, illustrate the perfection of his life, fill the audience with awe, and promote a desire to follow him. In short, the Gospels are cultic documents designed to spread the good news, broaden interest in Christianity, and change behavior. Unlike their ancient predecessors, Christian biography, from its beginning, idealized its subjects and effaced unique details through a rhetoric of generalization. Christian philosophers argued that all should strive to be like Christ. Lives that conformed to this ideal show explicit parallels between the subject and Christ. Such biographical idealizing is a subgenre of biography called hagiography, literally holy writing. All Christian biography from its inception to the eleventh century at least is informed by the tradition of hagiography.

THE MARTYRS

The earliest biographies in the western medieval tradition, written from the beginning of the second century to the early fourth, are the stories of martyrs. These brief sketches are almost always anonymous and depict a courtroom confrontation between the Roman presiding official and the accused Christian. They do not treat the life of the subject outside of the particular episode. This biographical form was intended to stiffen the resolve of the persecuted community through an illustration of the virtue of the martyr in imitation of Christ and to depict the corruption of the Roman state. They were influenced by the Roman transcripts of such interrogations.

Among the best representatives of this narrative form are the *Martyrdom of Polycarp* (156), Letter of the Churches of Lyons and Vienne (177), and the Acts of the Scillitan Martyrs (180). Occasionally the persecutions gave rise to autobiographical narratives of enormous power, like the *Passio Perpetuae et Felicitatis* (Passion of Perpetua and Felicitas, 203), which depicts the young matron Perpetua in a Carthaginian prison days before her execution. Also circulating during the late second century were apocryphal extracanonical works such as the *Infancy Gospel of Thomas* (*ca.* 140–170), the *Epistula Apostolorum* (Epistle of the Apostles, *ca.* 160), and the *Acts of Peter* (*ca.* 150–200). These narratives are fictions posing as historical truth and address the popular desire to learn more than the four Gospels tell about the life of Jesus. The growing Christian population also wanted additional biographical details about other New Testament leaders. This led to the composition of apocryphal works such as the *Acts of John* (*ca.* 150–200) and the *Acts of Paul and Thecla* (*ca.* 180–200), an account of Paul's conversion of the woman Thecla and their travels. This fictional biography is indebted to Greek romance, as are many saints' lives, for example, the popular *Life of St. Eustace and His Companions* (*ca.* 450).

THE ASCETICS

With the conversion of Constantine and the end of the persecutions in Rome around 313, the focus of Christian biography turned from martyrs to those who followed the daily life of Christ literally, as virgins, miracle workers, and renunciates. This was the age of bloodless martyrdom, and asceticism was the gospel preached in these lives. The virtuous life was that which turned its back on the world. The *City of God* of Augustine of Hippo, written in the early fifth century, is the learned counterpart to the more dramatic life sketches of the biographers. The *Life of St. Anthony* by Athanasius of Alexandria (*ca.* 357), which portrayed the desert-dwelling hermit, served as a model for the life of the ascetic. St. Jerome, indebted to the Roman models for his biographies—indeed, he called his work *De viris illustribus,*

echoing Suetonius—wrote vivid and influential portraits of individuals from St. Peter to himself. Jerome intended to show that Christians were just as capable of producing heroic individuals as the ancients. He wrote biographies of the ascetics Paul, Hilarion, and Malchus, highlighting the fantastic element.

BISHOPS AND ABBOTS

For the Latin West, however, there was no more crucial biography than the Gallo-Roman Sulpicius Severus's *Life of St. Martin of Tours* (396). Sulpicius was learned in the Latin rhetorical tradition, knew Athansius's *Life of Anthony,* and constructed a life fusing the qualities of the holy man, ascetic, monk, and bishop. Sulpicius acknowledges in the preface that he is interested in recording for posterity only the "outstanding" events of his subject's life. Sulpicius's depiction of Martin's episcopal ministry, although likely the progenitor of a host of bishops' lives, from *Vita Augustini* (Life of St. Augustine [of Hippo]) by Possidius of Calama in the early fifth century to Gervase of Canterbury's thirteenth-century *Life of St. Thomas of Canterbury,* found in his *History of the Archbishops of Canterbury,* emphasized Martin the miracle maker. Possidus portrayed Augustine as the shepherd of the flock and the tireless protector of orthodoxy. Gervase depicted Thomas Becket as a man faithful to God even if that meant incurring the wrath of his patron, Henry II. The lives of abbots of the monastic orders, including Benedict of Nursia, Columba of Iona, Columbanus, Benedict of Aniane, Boniface, and Bernard of Clairvaux, allow us to follow the origin, evolution, and reform of the monastic tradition in the West.

The next wave of biographies of founders of religious orders occurred in the thirteenth century with the biographies of St. Francis and St. Dominic. Thomas of Celano, the earliest of Francis's biographers, wrote two very popular biographies, one around 1228, the other from 1246 to 1247, including much of the material that was to become the staple of legends surrounding Francis. St. Dominic, founder of the Dominicans, was less fortunate in his biographers. There are, however, two early texts, both of which mix encomium with historical detail. Jean de Mailly's *Life of St. Dominic* (*ca.* 1243) illustrates the miraculous significance of Dominic from birth, while Thomas Agni of Lentini provides biographical details of Dominic within a sermon.

ROYAL BIOGRAPHY

Royal biography first appears in the ninth century with Einhard's *Vita Caroli Magni* (Life of Charlemagne, *ca.* 830–833), perhaps the best royal biography of the age. It is modeled on Suetonius's *Life of Augustus*. Both men's deaths are foretold by natural phenomena, and like Augustus, Charlemagne has a limp. Since Einhard was a member of Charlemagne's court and a confidant of the emperor, his biography provides a multifaceted and intimate portrait that alternates between the public and private life of the emperor: Charlemagne as warrior, father, builder, and pious believer. Although writing an encomium to his patron, Einhard avoids the miracle making and piety we find in hagiographies of the same time. Asser's *Annales rerum gestarum Alfredi* (Life of King Alfred, ca. 893) is the earliest biography of an English monarch. Although written within half a century of Einhard's work, it employs a radically different narrative style. Asser's *Life* reads like entries in a historical annal, the events of Alfred's reign summarized and presented episodically. St. Margaret, queen of Scotland and wife of Malcolm III, was fortunate to have a biographer of the ability of Turgot, bishop of St. Andrews. In his biography he reveals the public and private life of this remarkable woman, showing her work in the reformation of the church, her literacy and its positive impact on monastic libraries, and her charity to the poor and dispossessed.

Suger, abbot of the monastery of St. Denis and confidant of Louis VI (the Fat), wrote his biography, *Vita Ludovici Grossi*. Like many another royal biography from the twelfth and thirteenth centuries, it is a *gesta*, a record of Louis's deeds. In the prologue he refers to it as "the deeds [*gesta*] of Louis, the most serene king of the French." The *gesta* is unlike modern biographies in not drawing causal connections between events or deriving motivation from the deeds. Suger's short chapters depict the actions of the chivalric hero. The chivalric king, doer of mighty deeds, was a favorite biographical study, and Suger's depiction of Louis has close analogs in William of Poitiers's *Gesta Guillelmi ducis Normannorum* (The deeds of William the Conqueror, ca. 1071–1077), William of Apulia's hexameter *Gesta Roberti Wiscardi* (The deeds of Robert Guiscard, 1096–1099), and Otto of Freising's *Gesta Friderici* (The deeds of Frederick Barbarossa, ca. 1157–1160). Jean de Joinville's *Histoire de St. Louis* (Life of St. Louis), a biography of the French King Louis IX, depicts him in dialogue with the author and seeks to make the subject more approachable. Although royal biographies were chiefly in prose, John Barbour's massive *Bruce* (1375) is a history in verse of the kingship of Robert I (the Bruce) written for Barbour's patron Robert II of Scotland, the Bruce's grandson. It is an early testimony to the Bruce's political and military exploits, particularly in the conflict between the Scots and the English in such battles as Bannockburn.

Frequently the most interesting biographical writing in the Middle Ages was done within larger historical studies, separate biographies being uncommon. For example, one of the greatest historians of medieval England, William of Malmesbury, included vivid biographical sketches in his *Gesta rerum anglorum* (Deeds of the English kings, ca. 1118–1125), and *Gesta pontificum anglorum* (Deeds of the English bishops, ca. 1125). His *Historia novella* (New history, ca. 1143) is a study of the tumultuous years of the empress Matilda's struggle with King Stephen. It contains details that we get nowhere else, such as the preparation of Henry I's body in Rouen Cathedral before its internment and its subsequent burial in England.

Such brief portraitlike representations remained popular for centuries. Similar examples exist in Spain in *Generaciones y semblanzas* (Generations and portraits) by Fernán Pérez de Guzmán and Hernando del Pulgar's *Claros varones de Castilla* (Illustrious men of Castile). Guzmán and Pulgar both are intellectual descendants of Plutarch, intending their brief sketches to crystallize an essential quality of the individual. Guzmán's work consists of thirty-six vignettes of important Spanish contemporaries, principally individuals associated with the courts of Henry III and John II. Pulgar, court secretary to both Henry IV and Ferdinand and Isabella, wrote twenty-four sketches notable for the quality of their prose and their distillation of an individual's true essence.

One of the greatest biographies of the Middle Ages was Anna Komnena's *Alexiad* (1148). Anna's father, Alexios I Komnenos, was the emperor of Byzantium, and the *Alexiad* is a story of his exploits *(gesta)*. It is learned, filled with allusions to classical texts, and written by a woman proud of her learning; Anna writes: "I was not ignorant of letters, for I carried my study of Greek to the highest pitch . . . to recount the deeds done by my father." There were other distinguished female biographers in the Middle Ages. Christine de Pizan, one of the most notable French authors of the fifteenth century, exhibits independence of mind and pride in her sex in *Cité des dames* (Book of the city of women, 1404–1405). She is the author of *Le ditié de Jehanne d'Arc* (The poem of Joan of Arc, 1429), a tribute written in the face of considerable hostility, and one of the great royal biographies, *Livre des fais et bonnes meurs du sage roy Charles V* (Book of the deeds and the good behavior of the wise king Charles V, 1404). The latter, Christine's first major prose work, was commissioned by Charles's brother Philip II (the Bold) of Burgundy and celebrates the king who brought her family to the French court from Italy.

It was intended as a model for Charles's grandson, Louis of Guyenne, and as an object lesson in avoiding the mistakes of Charles's son, Charles VI. Christine's work has a historical solidity gleaned from her intimate knowledge of the court, where her father was a royal physician, and thus the work has more authority than that of Jean Froissart, for example. The work is in three sections: how a king should govern himself, sketches of the royal family, and Charles's intellectual interests.

Christine's verses on Joan of Arc predate Joan's trial, whose transcripts provide the first real information we have about Joan. These transcripts are important biographical records and were compiled in an interesting manner. At the end of each day of the infamous trial, which lasted from January 1431 until Joan's death the following May, four scribes, who were taking her statements, collated their transcripts, creating a single text. That compilation was later translated from French into Latin by Thomas de Courcelles, a professor of theology at the University of Paris in the fifteenth century. This curious biographical study is invaluable, since it is the only source of information about the nature of Joan's voices and visions.

The principal contributions of Italian medieval biography are the various lives of Dante. The first of these is a brief sketch by a contemporary, the Florentine historian Giovanni Villani, written most likely about 1346. It appears in his larger *Chronica Fiorentina* (Florentine chronicle), a universal history beginning with the tower of Babel and continuing to his day. The sketch of Dante begins with his death in 1321, briefly mentions his publications, including the *Divine Comedy,* and gives one or two interesting scraps of information about his personality. A more extensive life of Dante is found in Boccaccio's *Trattatello in laude de Dante* (Life of Dante), written probably in 1362. Although indebted to classical models, Boccaccio protests his lack of ability to write such a work. He mentions Dante's mother's dream in which she has a premonition of her child's greatness, but he also provides historical details of Dante's life and discusses his melancholy appearance, devotion to study, love of fame, and unhappy marriage. Other notables who took up the life of Dante were Filippo Villani (nephew of Giovanni) and the great Hellenist Leonardo Bruni Aretino. Giannozzo Manetti, a diplomat and scholar, wrote biographies of Dante, Petrarch, and Boccaccio. The precocious humanist Francesco Filelfo was the last of Dante's late medieval/early Renaissance biographers.

BIBLIOGRAPHY

Amt, Emilie. *Women's Lives in Medieval Europe: A Sourcebook.* New York: Routledge, 1993

Binfield, Clyde, ed. *Sainthood Revisioned: Studies in Hagiography and Biography.* Sheffield, U.K.: Sheffield Academic Press, 1995.

Boyarin, Daniel. *Dying for God: Martyrdom and the Making of Christianity and Judaism.* Stanford, Calif.: 1999.

Brown, Peter. *Society and the Holy in Late Antiquity.* Berkeley: University of California Press, 1982.

Cameron, Averil, ed. *History as Text: The Writing of Ancient History.* London: Duckworth, 1989.

Cox, Patricia. *Biography in Late Antiquity: A Quest for the Holy Man.* Berkeley: University of California Press, 1983.

Delehaye, Hippolyte. *The Legends of the Saints.* Translated by Donald Attwater. New York: Fordham University Press, 1962.

Gransden, Antonia. *Historical Writing in England.* 2 vols. London: Routledge and Kegan Paul, 1974–1982.

Hägg, T. "Socrates and St. Anthony: A Shortcut through Ancient Biography." In *Understanding and History in Arts and Sciences.* Edited by R. S. Karsten, E. J. Kleppe, and R. B. Finnestad. Vol. 1. Oslo: Acta Humaniora Universitatis Bergensis, 1991.

Head, Thomas, ed. *Medieval Hagiography: An Anthology.* New York: Routledge, 2001.

Heffernan, Thomas J. *Sacred Biography: Saints and Their Biographers in the Middle Ages.* New York: Oxford University Press, 1988.

LaCapra, Dominic. *History and Criticism.* Ithaca, N.Y.: Cornell University Press, 1985.

Leo, Friedrich. *Die griechisch-römische Biographie nach ihrer litterarischen Form.* Leipzig, Germany: Teubner, 1901.

Misch, Georg. *A History of Autobiography in Antiquity.* 2 vols. Translated by E. W. Dickes. Cambridge, Mass.: Harvard University Press, 1950.

Momigliano, Arnaldo, ed. *The Conflict between Paganism and Christianity in the Fourth Century: Essays.* Oxford: Clarendon, 1963.

———. *The Development of Greek Biography.* Expanded edition. Cambridge, Mass.: Harvard University Press, 1993.

Ridyard, Susan J. *The Royal Saints of Anglo-Saxon England: A Study of West Saxon and East Anglian Cults.* Cambridge, U.K., and New York: Cambridge University Press, 1988.

Uytfanghe, Marc Van. "Biographie II (Spirituelle)." In *Reallexikon für Antike und Christentum* Supplement 1. Stuttgart, Germany: Anton Hiersemann, 2001.

Winslow, Donald J. *Life-Writing: A Glossary of Terms in Biography, Autobiography, and Related Forms.* Honolulu: University of Hawaii Press, for the Biographical Research Center, 1995.

Young, Frances M. *Biblical Exegesis and the Formation of Christian Culture.* Cambridge, U.K., and New York: Cambridge University Press, 1999.

THOMAS J. HEFFERNAN

[See also **DMA:** Biography, French; Biography, Secular; Hagiography; Historiography, Western European; Martyrdom, Christian; Martyrology; *and individual biographers;* **Supp:** Autobiography and Confessional Literature; Hagiography, Islamic; Hagiography, Jewish.]

*A **Victorious Charioteer.** A 3d-century mosaic.* THE ART ARCHIVE. ARCHAEOLOGICAL MUSEUM MADRID/DAGLI ORTI. REPRODUCED BY PERMISSION.

BLUES AND GREENS. Circus factions prominent in the history and politics of late antiquity, the Blues and Greens, along with the less important Reds and Whites, were part of Roman and Byzantine urban life from the time of Augustus to the twelfth century. They were originally formed as groups to rent horses and equipment for the chariot races in Rome.

Professional chariot racing was, in its origins, a Roman sport, closely linked to political power. The Circus Maximus in Rome was located next to the imperial palace on the Palatine Hill, and this design was perpetuated in other imperial palaces throughout the Roman world. The circus was not only a place of entertainment but also the primary locale where the urban populace could express its political opinion. Petitions were submitted there to the emperor, who could maintain a close relationship with the city by strategically granting the requests of his subjects.

Late antiquity was the heyday of the circus factions for several reasons. Chariot racing, by this period found throughout the Roman Empire, had become more popular due to the disappearance of other forms of entertainment—namely the gymnasium in the East and gladiatorial games everywhere. The hippodrome may also have gained importance as the emperor increasingly remained in Constantinople and stopped leading the army in battle. The daily victories of the chariot races over which the emperor presided substituted for the imperial triumphs formerly celebrated when the emperor returned from war. The circus factions dramatically changed in the fifth century, when they expanded to include theater (pantomimes and actors) and amphitheater performers (Empress Theodora's father, for example, was bear keeper for the Greens). According to Alan Cameron, theater professionals introduced two novelties to the circus factions: a penchant for violence and rioting, which had long been associated with the theater, and organized chanting, a professional activity originally intended to stir up the audience's enthusiasm for particular performers. The transfer of chanting to the hippodrome led to the increased importance of the circus factions, as they now became responsible for chanting acclamations of the emperor. This role gave them an importance in late antiquity they did not previously have, and the factional riots of that period, though still not fully explained, stem from this new role. The riots began from a variety of causes, some political, some economic, and some perhaps simply from rivalry of sports fans. Indeed, Cameron argues that the closest parallel for the factions in the modern world are soccer hooligans. The great Nika riot in 532 began when Emperor Justinian I refused to free two men, one a Green and one a Blue, who had survived a bungled execution, but frustration over Justinian's financial exactions also fed popular anger. The riot that followed lasted several days, destroyed large parts of the city, and led to the death of 30,000 people by contemporary estimates. The factions also proclaimed a rival emperor to Justinian, who was prepared to flee the city but for the advice of Empress Theodora. The circus factions also played an important role in the revolt that dethroned Maurice and established Phokas as emperor in 602. Most riots, however, did not have specific political goals.

Previous scholarship linking the factions to certain neighborhoods, to urban militias, or to religious groups has now been discredited. The circus factions did indeed help defend their cities at certain crucial junctures, but this was not in any way a regular or defined role for the factions but one taken on in a time of emergency. At one time a faction comprised several hundred people, but by no means were entire cities divided between factions, as some sources suggest. A census in Constantinople in 602 put the number of Greens at 1,500 and the Blues at 900.

The idea that the circus factions declined in the middle Byzantine period is now contested. The factions cooperated with Constantine V in his attacks on iconodule monks (monks who thought religious icons were useful tools for worship) in the eighth century. The ninth-century *De ceremoniis* (Book of ceremonies) detailed the roles specified for the factions in imperial ceremonies, but the paucity of sources obscures other roles that the factions may have played in this period. However, the factions were no longer linked to violence as they were in late antiquity. The disappearance of the circus factions came in the twelfth century, when the Komnenian imperial family moved from the Great Palace next to the hippodrome to the Blachernae Palace on the outskirts of Constantinople, thus severing the link between imperial power and the hippodrome.

BIBLIOGRAPHY

Cameron, Alan. *Circus Factions: Blues and Greens at Rome and Byzantium.* Oxford: Clarendon Press, 1976.

Roueché, Charlotte. *Performers and Partisans at Aphrodisias in the Roman and Late Roman Periods.* London: London Society for the Promotion of Roman Studies, 1993.

Whitby, Michael. "The Violence of the Circus Factions." In *Organised Crime in Antiquity.* Edited by Keith Hopwood. London: Duckworth, 1999.

CHRISTOPHER HATCH MACEVITT

[See also **DMA:** Demes; Justinian I; Roman Empire, Late.]

BOBBIO, an abbey and diocese in the Trebbia Valley of northern Italy, in present-day Emilia-Romagna. The abbey was founded in 614 by the Irish saint Columbanus. When the Lombard ruler Agilulph converted to Catholicism under the influence of both his Catholic wife and the preaching of Columbanus, he donated the district of Bobium (or Ebovium) to the Irish saint. The territory had belonged to the patrimony of St. Peter before it was conquered by the Lombards. The abbey of Bobbio, built next to an old, ruined church dedicated to St. Peter, was the first abbey founded in the Lombard kingdom. Its first and most famous abbots after Columbanus were St. Atala (*d.* 637) and St. Bertulf (*d.* 640). Although its importance appears to have waned in the later Middle Ages, during the seventh century, the abbey served as a center of the Catholic mission to convert the Arians of northern Italy. As the only Irish outpost in northern Italy, Bobbio also linked the pope in Rome to Ireland and its community of monastic scholars. Inspired by the work of their brethren in Italy and the memory of St. Columbanus, a number of Irish monks and bishops moved to Bobbio, while others bequeathed their libraries to the famous abbey.

The abbey received its first privilege of exemption from the papacy in 628. Within a few decades of its founding, the Benedictine Rule had been introduced into the abbey, and it later formally joined the Congregation of Monte Cassino. From its founding, the abbey of Bobbio had an impressive collection of illuminated manuscripts brought from Ireland, and by the ninth century its library held more than 750 manuscripts. The library's most famous holdings included what is known as the Bobbio Missal (*ca.* 911), the Antiphonary of Bangor, and the palimpsests of Ulfila's Gothic version of the Bible. Gerbert of Aurillac (*ca.* 945–1003), later Pope Sylvester II and abbot of Bobbio, used the abbey's rich library collection to write his famous work on geometry.

The library contained a number of works of Aristotle and Demosthenes in Greek, classical grammars, and an illuminated manuscript of Vergil's *Aeneid*.

Even before Charlemagne made generous donations to the abbey, Bobbio owned considerable tracts of land, but its temporalities were further enlarged during the eighth century. Recognizing the strategic location of the abbey's territory and its diverse and valuable lands, in 1014 Emperor Henry II convinced Pope Benedict VIII to create a new episcopal see at Bobbio. Peter Aldus, the abbot of the monastery, was the first to serve as bishop. The first bishops of Bobbio served simultaneously as abbot and diocesan and lived in the abbey. Over time, however, the two offices became independent of each other, and tensions arose between the two institutions. Bobbio was eventually made a suffragan see of Genoa. In 1230 Piacenza conquered the commune of Bobbio, and during the fourteenth century it came under the control of the Visconti family.

BIBLIOGRAPHY

Clarke, H. B., and Mary Brennan, eds. *Columbanus and Merovingian Monasticism*. Oxford: B. A. R., 1981.

Piazza, Andrea. *Monastero e vescovado di Bobbio: Dalla fine del X agli inizi del XIII secolo*. Spoleto: Centro Italiano di Studi Sull'Alto Medioevo, 1997. A study of the relationship between the bishopric and monastery of Bobbio during the eleventh and twelfth centuries.

ADAM JEFFREY DAVIS

[See also **DMA:** Columbanus, St.; Sylvester II, Pope; Visconti.]

BODY, THE. The Apostle Paul, writing in the middle of the first century A.D., laments the central problem of the body in words that would be echoed by Christian writers for centuries to come: "For I know that nothing good dwells in me, that is, in my flesh. . . . I see in my members another law at war with the law in my mind and making me captive to the law of sin which dwells in my members. . . . Wretched man that I am! Who will deliver me from this body of death?" (Rom. 7:18, 23–24). In Paul's "war" the spirit, on the side of right, opposes body, the site of vulnerability and desire. The one who will deliver him is, of course, Christ, whose incarnation and sacrifice mirrors Paul's private crisis. The doctrine of Christ's incarnation voices a profound ambivalence about flesh, implying as it does that the body is both a sacred vessel and sinful flesh in need of salvation. Throughout the Middle Ages this ambivalence had profound impact in shaping the understanding and prac-

Arm Reliquary of the Apostles. *Precious containers demonstrate the medieval respect for physical relics. This late-12th-century reliquary in silver, gilt, and champlevé enamel on a core of oak is a Romanesque example from Lower Saxony.* © THE CLEVELAND MUSEUM OF ART, GIFT OF THE JOHN HUNTINGTON ART AND POLYTECHNIC TRUST, 1930.79. REPRODUCED BY PERMISSION.

tices of the human life cycle, from reproduction, gender, and sexuality to death and the afterlife. Anxieties about the body as a site of decay and sexual pollution also informed the medieval sense of universal history, which in many particulars mirrored human ontology. Beginning in an act of original sin, a doctrine articulated for posterity by St. Augustine of Hippo (354–430), human history was understood to end with the resurrection of the body, when perfected flesh would be reunited with the stainless soul.

The repression of the body and its pleasures was fundamental to the earliest Christian practice and appears to have emerged in response to the bodily ethics that

Voluptas (Pleasure). This seductive Gothic statue from the vestibule of Freiburg cathedral shows the late medieval willingness to depict the allure of the flesh in a moral context. MFG. BILDVERLAG GASS. REPRODUCED BY PERMISSION.

governed Roman cultural ideology. In the final centuries of its empire, Rome embraced a virile aesthetic that accepted bodily pleasure, though it argued for its careful regulation, understanding body to be an unruly and subordinate partner to the rational soul. In the same period, however, contempt for the body was increasingly voiced by pagans and Jews, who also developed concomitant interest in practices of asceticism. Christianity's dramatic renunciation emerged in part out of this widespread ascetic movement; it may also have expressed a radical social protest against Roman tolerance of sensuality. As St. Clement of Alexandria, a Christian writing at the end of the second century, explained, pagans trained their instincts to pursue rational ends, whereas Christians repressed instincts altogether, aiming to experience no desire at all. By the late sixth century, when the period of the Middle Ages nominally begins, the body had become the site of intense regulation: clerical celibacy was widely

practiced; among the laity, contraception and abortion were condemned and homosexuality shunned, even as virginity was increasingly idealized, taking as its icon the compassionate and maternal virginity of the Virgin Mary.

THE BODY IN MEDIEVAL ISLAM

From its origins Islam, which incorporated elements of Christianity and Judaism, also subordinated body to soul, even though it did not adopt the doctrine of original sin. Repression of the body was particularly marked in Sufism, which began as an Islamic ascetic movement in the seventh century and developed into a mystical movement in the eighth and ninth centuries. The inferior in the body-soul dialectic, body was also equated with the female. In writings of the Sufi poet Rūmī (1207–1273), the impure feminine *nafs,* or bodily urges, oppose the higher masculine spirit. Unlike Christian thinking, however, Islamic writings on the body often celebrate male sensuality. In the late Middle Period, Sufi writings increasingly describe erotic mystical union, often couched in homoerotic terms. Defining universal history, the body was also central to Islamic thinking about death and the afterlife. Human history began with the creation of Adam and Eve and will end with the resurrection of the body on the day of the final judgment.

BODY, CLASS, AND GENDER IN MEDIEVAL CHRISTIANITY

A singular feature of Western disciplines of the body was the equation of body with the lower classes, as well as with the feminine. To be a peasant was to be defined by corporeality and sexuality, whereas to be an aristocrat was to be identified with the superior qualities of mind and spirit. In constructs that date from antiquity, spirit also was to flesh as man was to woman—a hierarchy that endured throughout the Middle Ages and continues to have profound and lasting impact. For Aristotle, gendered differences of form and matter were inscribed in the biology of reproduction. Men were active, women passive; men produced the sperm, which was the efficient cause of reproduction; women, in contrast, provided the receiving matter: "The female always provides the material, the male provides that which fashions the material into shape . . . thus the physical part, the body, comes from the female, and the soul from the male" (*Generation of Animals,* 2.4.738^b 20–23). The equation of flesh with the female underwrote the logic of the Fall, instigated by Eve. It also served as fodder for misogynist writings; if flesh was inherently sinful and if woman was flesh, therefore woman was intrinsically suspect and a threat to the social order. The female body was signified

Pietà. *The sufferings of Christ received new emphasis in the 14th century. This carved wood version of* ca. *1400–1425, formerly in a beguinage church, is now in the Stedelijk Museum, Amsterdam.* PHOTOGRAPH BY JOANNA E. ZIEGLER. REPRODUCED BY PERMISSION.

by two dramatically contrasting tropes: Eve's appetite and sensuality on the one hand and Mary's virgin maternity on the other.

Some devotional practices of late medieval women may also have developed in specific response to the equation of the body and the feminine, and it may be that the very carnality that was identified with woman became a paradoxical source of empowerment. Since women were more intimately associated with care of the body than men—as midwives, as nurturers and providers of food, as lactating mothers—that access to physical experience may have translated into a rich resource for new kinds of devotional expression. Often union with Christ was described in physical and even erotic terms. The Italian mystic Angela of Foligno (*ca.* 1248–1309), like numerous other mystics, describes being called by Christ to place her mouth at the wound on his side to drink his blood. Documents from the late twelfth and thirteenth centuries also record new somatic responses to religious experience, many of them affecting an imitation of Christ's suffering, that were almost exclusively associated with women. These included experiences of miraculous lactations and pregnancies, uncontrollable tears, bodies that did not decay after death, renunciation of

food with miraculous survivals, and the five visible wounds of the stigmata. The male scribes and clerics who recorded these lives appear to have taken them as authentic manifestations of a direct link with God.

CHRIST'S BODY IN THE LATE MIDDLE AGES

It was not only women who found new possibilities for redemption through their bodies, however. The Christian West in the late Middle Ages in general gave extraordinary importance to the body, with particular emphasis on Christ's infancy, his Passion (his torture and crucifixion), and Mary's virginity. In multiple ways Christ's body emerged as a symbol, often a contested one, for private interpersonal relationships as well as for clerical and political systems of social regulation. Lyrics on the passion direct the reader to observe Christ's suffering and experience similar pain, presenting compassionate suffering as a communal spiritual good. The pietà, a new form that appeared in the fourteenth century, also glorifies the graphic physical suffering of Christ and the emotional pain of Mary. The popularity of the pietà as a form suggests that people responded powerfully to its invitation to compassion. In the late Middle Ages, Christians looked to Christ's incarnation and suffering and their own similar humanity as a site for redemption.

The new attention to the body and new focus on ethics of compassion were indebted in part to the widespread influence of the Franciscan order (founded in 1209). Indeed, St. Francis was the first of numerous Christians to report receiving the stigmata, or the gift of Christ's wounds. Franciscan arguments in favor of the sanctity of marriage and the humanity of Christ may themselves have emerged in response to Catharism—a dualistic heresy widespread in southern France from the twelfth to the early fourteenth century—the central tenet of which was that the material world opposed the world of spirit. Cathars opposed marriage, baptism, and communion—sacraments of the body—and argued against the incarnation of Christ. For orthodox Christians, the humanity of Christ was always a fundamental precept, one that sharpened in the face of opposition.

Christ's humanity also underwrote belief in the power of relics and the cult of the Eucharist. Relics, evidentiary fragments from Christ's life or the lives of the saints, sometimes took the form of material objects, such as the piece of Christ's Crown of Thorns for which Louis IX of France (St. Louis, 1214–1270) commissioned the gem-like private chapel Ste. Chapelle in 1241; more often they were purported to be actual body parts of Christ or of Christian martyrs, such as fingers, skulls, or bits of flesh or even bits of Christ's holy foreskin, a sign of his humanity that achieved cultic status. Often secreted in exquisitely crafted housings, or reliquaries, a prized relic would often become the singular treasure of a particular church or monastery and even the specific object of pilgrimage. At the end of a pilgrimage to Canterbury, for example, the pilgrim, for a fee, would be taken to see the bejeweled casket housing the bones of St. Thomas Becket, martyred in 1170. A pilgrimage to an important reliquary site carried the hope of a cure for physical ailments; it might also carry a promise of speedy progress of the soul through purgatory toward heaven. Symbolic capital aiding the resurrection of the pilgrim's body, relics were also important sources of church and monastic revenues.

The heightened importance of the Eucharistic rite during the mass in the late Middle Ages also attests to a new importance of the symbolic body in the ritual life of late medieval communities. The Eucharist, derived from the Last Supper as described in Matthew 26:26–28, is a rite of incorporation, or symbolic cannibalism, in which the believer physically ingests and becomes one with God and the community. Through a process of transubstantiation, bread was believed to turn into Christ's body and consecrated wine into his blood. Accounts of late medieval mystics frequently record their eagerness for communion and ecstatic pleasure on witnessing or eating the host. The church's bloody attempts to repress heresies that denied transubstantiation, such as the Cathars in the thirteenth century or the Lollards, active in England in the fourteenth and fifteenth, bespeak the crucial importance of this rite to clerical authority. In the late Middle Ages, Christ's body, particularly as represented in the host, became a potent and contested symbol for the power of clergy and for the relationship of individuals to the larger community. The importance of the host was particularly evident in a wave of accusations across Europe in the late Middle Ages against Jews who tried to torture consecrated wafers (the desecration of the host). Jews suffered greatly from these accusations from 1290 onward.

RESURRECTION OF THE BODY

While many of the miracles and renunciations associated with Jesus and Mary dramatized the bodily concerns of daily life—ordinary physical pain and suffering, childbirth and nurturance, sexuality—Christianity's central miracle supersedes human mortality. Christ's incarnation, the act in which a god takes on human form, was understood as a contract that promised men and women eternal life. Concerns about oneself and one's loved ones in the afterlife were universal, becoming particularly clamorous in the late Middle Ages; virtually all surviving bequests in fifteenth-century England contain provision for prayers to be said for the soul of the deceased or of others. Central to the promise of medieval eschatology, both Christian and Islamic, was the proviso that body and soul would reunite at the Resurrection. Particulars about the form in which the self would be resurrected, however, were debated by Christian theologians with particular intensity in the twelfth and thirteenth centuries—whether, for instance, the body will rise in one or two sexes, what age or color our body will be, or whether we will eat, taste, and smell in heaven. Obsessions with resurrection also led to expressions of contempt with life (the theme of *contemptus mundi*). Some late medieval tomb sculptures called *transi tombs* show the body of the deceased in a state of putrefaction in order to emphasize the triumph of spirit over decaying flesh.

The focus on particulars underscores the body's crucial role in the definition of personhood. On this the wisdom of the philosophers agreed with popular belief. St. Thomas Aquinas (*ca.* 1224–1274), who used the body-soul dichotomy to argue for the philosophical necessity of bodily resurrection, asserted clearly that the soul was not the whole person; "he" was not his soul. In the late Middle Ages, Christian liturgy as well as the religious practices of ordinary lay people indicate that the body, in its capacities to suffer or desire, was a site both of despair and also of hope—and also a key symbol for social regulation. Devotional practices, cults of relics, the rite of the Eucharist, and debates over the Resurrection reveal the multiple ways that the body's most troubling habits and appetites could be transformed into currency, both symbolic and literal, with the church as the body's most important broker.

BIBLIOGRAPHY

PRIMARY WORKS

Aristotle. *Generation of Animals.* Translated by A. L. Peck. Loeb Classical Library. Cambridge, Mass.: Harvard University Press, 1943.

SECONDARY WORKS

Beckwith, Sarah. *Christ's Body: Identity, Culture, and Society in Late Medieval Writings.* New York: Routledge, 1993. An anthropological and literary approach to the use of Christ's body as a sign and tool for social order.

Brown, Peter. *The Body and Society: Men, Women, and Sexual Renunciation in Early Christianity.* New York: Columbia University Press, 1988.

Bugge, John. *Virginitas: An Essay in the History of a Medieval Ideal.* The Hague, Netherlands: Nijhoff, 1975.

Bynum, Caroline Walker. *Fragmentation and Redemption: Essays on Gender and the Human Body in Medieval Religion.* New York: Zone, 1991. Examines embodied spirituality of late medieval women.

Kantorowicz, Ernst. *The King's Two Bodies.* Princeton, N.J.: Princeton University Press, 1957. Considers the relationship between the King's body and the body politic in medieval West.

Kay, Sarah, and Miri Rubin, eds. *Framing Medieval Bodies.* Manchester, U.K., and New York: Manchester University Press, 1994. Interdisciplinary essay collection.

Laqueur, Thomas. *Making Sex: Body and Gender from the Greeks to Freud.* Cambridge, Mass.: Harvard University Press, 1990. Addresses the constructions of sexuality and ancient and medieval one-sex models.

LeGoff, Jacques. "The Body." In his *The Medieval Imagination.* Translated by Arthur Goldhammer. Chicago: University of Chicago Press, 1988. Overview of the repression of the body in Christianity.

Lomperis, Linda, and Sarah Stanbury, eds. *Feminist Approaches to the Body in Medieval Literature.* Philadelphia: University of Pennsylvania Press, 1993. Essay collection.

Rubin, Miri. *Corpus Christi: The Eucharist in Late Medieval Culture.* Cambridge, U.K.: Cambridge University Press, 1991.

Schimmel, Annemarie. "'I Take Off the Dress of the Body': Eros in Sufi Literature and Life." In *Religion and the Body.* Edited by Sarah Coakley. Cambridge, U.K.: Cambridge University Press, 1997.

Smith, Jane Idleman, and Yvonne Yazbeck Haddad. *The Islamic Understanding of Death and Resurrection.* Albany: State University of New York Press, 1981.

SARAH STANBURY

[See also **DMA:** Antifeminism; Aquinas, St. Thomas; Augustine of Hippo, St.; Cathars; Death and Burial, in Europe; Francis of Assisi, St.; Islam, Religion; Lollards; Mass, Liturgy of the; Medicine, History of; Mysticism, Christian: Continental (Women); Mysticism, Islamic; Passion Cycle; Relics; Resurrection Cycle; Resurrection, Islamic; Rūmī; **Supp:** Gender, Theories of; Sexuality; Soul and Body; Transubstantiation.]

BOETHIUS OF DACIA (*fl.* thirteenth century), philosopher and leader of "heterodox Aristotelians." Little is known about the early life of Boethius except that he came from Denmark. By 1270 he was a master in the faculty of arts at the University of Paris. It is possible that Boethius entered the Dominican order at some point in the later 1270s, since a list of his writings appears in the Stams Catalogue of Dominican works. Although he was not summoned to appear before the royal inquisition in November of 1276 as Siger of Brabant and others were, what some viewed as Boethius's radical Aristotelianism stirred up controversy in Paris during the early 1270s. At least 13 of the 219 articles that the bishop of Paris, Étienne Tempier, formally condemned on 7 March 1277 originated with Boethius. Most controversial about Boethius were his efforts to defend the autonomy of philosophical reason.

In addition to writing commentaries on the works of Aristotle, Boethius wrote works that dealt with logic, speculative grammar, ethics, and metaphysics. In *De summo bono* (On the supreme good), he argued that the highest good for the speculative intellect is knowledge of truth and taking delight in that knowledge. The highest good for the practical intellect is right action and taking pleasure in doing good. Boethius was also one of the most important medieval theoreticians of grammar. His grammatical treatise *De modis significandi* (On the modes of signification) explored the interplay between philosophy and grammar. According to Boethius, one needed to be a grammarian in order to understand the modes of signification, or the ways in which words signify meaning. At the same time, one could not understand the properties of objects without being trained in philosophy. Thus Boethius argued for the need to combine an understanding of philosophy and grammar so as to be able to derive modes of signification from the properties of objects. In *De aeternitate mundi* (On the eternity of the world), Boethius sought to show the compatibility between the philosophical view of the world as being eternal and the Christian belief that the world had a beginning. In contrast to Bonaventure, John Peckham, and others, Boethius joined Thomas Aquinas in arguing that it was impossible to demonstrate that the world had had a beginning using reason alone. Boethius did not challenge the Christian argument that the world had a beginning but rather posited that any such beginning could not have occurred through natural causes and principles. This attempt to allow for both arguments, the one based on reason and the other on faith, has sometimes made Boethius appear a defender of the doctrine of double truth. But Boethius never denied the superiority of faith over reason. Instead, he argued that although reason is not sufficient to prove that the universe had a beginning, it is nonetheless possible that the world did have a beginning if, in creating the universe, God somehow suspended or contravened the laws of nature.

BIBLIOGRAPHY

Boethius of Dacia. *On the Supreme Good, On the Eternity of the World, On Dreams.* Translated by John F. Wippel. Toronto: Pontifical Institute of Mediaeval Studies, 1987.

Celano, Anthony J. "Boethius of Dacia: 'On the Highest Good.'" *Traditio* 43 (1987): 199–214.

Corpus Philosophorum Danicorum Medii Aevi. Vols. 1, 2, 4, 6, 8. Edited by Géza Sajó, Jan Pinburg, Heinrich Roos, Niels G. Green-Pedersen, Gianfranco Fioravanti, and S. Ebbesen. Copenhagen: Gad, 1969–1979. A critical edition of Boethius's works.

Hissette, Roland. *Enquête sur les 219 articles condamnés à Paris le 7 mars 1277.* Louvain, Belgium: Publications Universitaires de Louvain, 1977.

ADAM JEFFREY DAVIS

[See also **DMA**: Aristotle in the Middle Ages; Grammar; Philosophy and Theology: Thirteenth-Century Crisis.]

BOGURODZICA (Mother of God), a Polish hymn dedicated to the Virgin Mary that most likely originated in the thirteenth or fourteenth century. *Bogurodzica* is one of the first documents written in the Polish language and represents the earliest preserved document of Polish poetry. Although the composer of *Bogurodzica* is unknown, one scholar has hypothesized that it was written by a Dominican friar who, given the high artistry of the composition, was probably a trained musician. Legends have associated the authorship of the hymn's text with St. Adalbert of Prague (St. Wojcieh), the eleventh-century bishop and patron of Poland.

The earliest extant example of the hymn dates from the fifteenth century. In total, there are sixteen extant manuscripts of the hymn from the fifteenth through the eighteenth centuries. The language of the text is archaic and bears little resemblance to modern Polish. Written in the first person plural ("we"), the text addresses the Virgin Mary directly, asking her to intercede and grant happiness to her people both on earth and in heaven. Although the hymn makes no mention of Polish "national" identity and is primarily spiritual in character, it later became something of a national anthem and has sometimes been called Poland's *carmen patrium* (song of the mother country). On several occasions *Bogurodzica* has served as a battle hymn. In 1410, for instance, Polish troops were said to have sung the hymn as they fought the Teutonic knights in the Battle of Grunwald. Then in 1444, Polish soldiers fighting the Turkish army at Varna were also said to have sung the hymn. During the sixteenth century *Bogurodzica* was the coronation anthem used during the crowning of Polish kings. It was printed in the introduction to Jan Łaski's *Statutes of the Polish Kingdom* (1506). To this day, the hymn is still sung in some Polish churches and monasteries, where it is included in the vespers and Marian services.

Some scholars have explored the possibility of Byzantine origins for the Polish hymn, comparing it to earlier Slavic church literature and its metrical structure to that of hymns in the Byzantine liturgy. The hymn's music has also been linked to the songs of the medieval troubadours and trouvères, most notably Jehan de Braine's thirteenth-century *Par dessor l'ombre d'un bois* (Beneath the shade of a wood). *Bogurodzica* also bears a resemblance to certain medieval liturgical dramas. The song is mostly written in the syllabic style (as opposed to the melismatic, in which a group of notes is sung on a syllable) and is in the Dorian mode with some hints of the pentatonic scale. Over time, four distinct versions of the hymn's melody have appeared. The original hymn contained two strophes, but at least ten strophes were added at later times.

BIBLIOGRAPHY

Feicht, Hieronim. "Bogurodzica." In *Studia nad Muzyką Polskiego Średniowicza.* Kraków: PWM Edition, 1975.

Kilar, Wojciech, ed. *Bogurodzica na chór mieszany i orkiestre: Partytura (Bogurodzica for Mixed Choir and Orchestra: Score).* Kraków: Polskie Wydawn Muzyczne, 1978. Musical score with Polish text and an English translation.

Trochimczyk, Maja. "Sacred/Secular Constructs of National Identity: A Convoluted History of Polish Anthems." In *After Chopin: Essays in Polish Music.* Edited by Maja Trochimczyk. Los Angeles: Polish Music Center at USC, 2000.

Woronczak, Jerzy, ed. *Bogurodzica*. Wrocław, Poland: Nakład Narodowy im. Ossolińskich, 1962.

ADAM JEFFREY DAVIS

[See also **DMA:** Poland; **Supp:** Adalbert, St.]

BOHEMIAN ART. The checkered history of the dukedoms—and later the kingdoms—of Bohemia was, like that of the neighboring Roman Empire, shaped by numerous dynastic changes. Thus, until modern times, it was necessary for the rulers to legitimate their own position by presenting themselves as the rightful end to a line of predecessors. All the art forms owe a substantial portion of their iconographic as well as stylistic origins to the need for this type of representation.

THE PŘEMYSLID DYNASTY

Beginning in the tenth century, the Bohemian dukes of the Přemyslid dynasty were able to consolidate their rule. Prague, with its main castle overlooking the Vlatva River, became the focal point of their realm. The circular Church of St. Vitus, built by Duke Wenceslas I (*r.* 922–929/935) on the grounds of the Hradčany castle complex, was Prague's first significant stone structure and symbolized the city's prominent position. The appearance of the church can only be surmised on the basis of archaeological evidence, as it had already been pulled down by 1067. The four-apse building served as a burial church for the remains of St. Vitus, in the tradition of both ancient memorial structures and the Church of the Holy Sepulcher in Jerusalem. It is the most prominent in a line of rotundas that were built by the sovereigns of Bohemia in their castles from the ninth or tenth century to the twelfth century.

Wenceslas I was murdered in 929 or 935 and laid to rest in the St. Vitus Rotunda. Following his canonization Wenceslas became the patron saint of Bohemia, thereby making the church a martyrium of its own founder. Throughout the entire Middle Ages the burial place of Wenceslas remained a most important cult site, enclosed first within the Church of St. Vitus, then within the Romanesque (and subsequently Gothic) Cathedral of St. Vitus. For a number of rulers, it became the most important visual symbol of the legitimacy of their sovereignty.

The first work to serve this purpose, however, was a manuscript illumination, the Vyšehrad Codex (Prague, Statní knihovna Ceské republiky, Ms. XIV A 13), written and illuminated in 1085 on the occasion of the coronation of the first king of Bohemia, Vratislav II (*r.* 1061–1092). Subsequently, there followed the creation of a whole group of such manuscripts. The oldest extant Bohemian mural, dated to 1134 and painted on the dome of the Chapel of St. Catherine in Znojmo, pairs a Christological cycle with a genealogy of the Přemyslid dynasty.

To the east of the Church of St. Vitus, Mladá Maria, a sister of Boleslav II (*r.* 967–999), founded the Benedictine Convent of St. George. The church of the convent—the second main church of the Hradčany—is the oldest example of Ottonian architecture in Bohemia. In the period from 1220 to 1228, during the church's final Romanesque building phase, an apse was added to house the remains of the Bohemian patron saint Ludmilla (*d.* 921), wife of the first Christian prince of Bohemia, Bořivoj (*d. ca.* 894), and grandmother of St. Wenceslas. The most impressive late-Romanesque church in Bohemia, however, is the basilica (known in German as Maria Reich) of the Benedictine monastery Třebíč (*ca.* 1250). The three-aisled, vaulted basilica has a choir with three stepped apses, a western gallery, a two-tower facade, and a northern porch with an elaborate portal. The basilica's architectural system consists throughout of polygonal, single engaged shafts and ribs.

The Cistercian order, active in Bohemia since 1142, vigorously supported the kings in their building programs. The lasting regard given the order was made evident during the thirteenth century by the foundation of numerous monasteries and convents. As in the rest of the Holy Roman Empire, patrons aspired to replicate the achievements of French cathedral architecture. The Cistercian convent Porta Coeli in Moravian Tišnov was founded by Constance of Hungary (*ca.* 1180–1240), the widow of Přemsyl Otokar I (*r.* 1197–1230), and conceived as their burial place. Master builders and sculptors, who previously worked in the service of the House of Babenberg in Austria, were called in, and they produced a High Gothic figured-portal. The choice of the French style was clearly a question of prestige.

In addition to the creation of the monasteries of Žďár nad Sázavou and Vyšší Brod, the construction in 1263 of the monastery of Zlatá Koruna was initiated through the essential patronage of Přemsyl Otokar II (*r.* 1253–1278). In considering the art of Otokar's court, one must keep in mind that his sovereignty extended far beyond Bohemia and Moravia (the core lands of the Bohemian crown) and reached, with the inclusion of the duchies of Styria, Carinthia, and Carniola, nearly to the Adriatic. Artistic activity sponsored in these areas must, therefore, also be included in an evaluation of the cultural achievements of his rule.

Chapel of the Holy Cross, Castle Karlštejn. *The painted saints that surround this giant reliquary are by Master Theodoric and workshop.* NATIONAL GALLERY, PRAGUE. REPRODUCED BY PERMISSION.

THE ERA OF THE HOUSE OF LUXEMBOURG

While architecture was the primary artistic means of symbolically representing the sovereign under the Přemyslids, under the Bohemian kings of the House of Luxembourg the other artistic genres attained equal standing. King John (Jan) of Luxembourg (*r.* 1310–1346)—who gained the Bohemian crown through marriage to Elizabeth (Eliška; 1292–1330), daughter of the second-to-last Přemyslid king, Wenceslas (Vaclav) II (*r.* 1278–1305)—sent his son, Charles IV of Germany (*r.* 1346–1378), the future King of Bohemia and Holy Roman Emperor, to be educated at the court of the French kings. Following the example presented by Paris, Charles IV built Prague into the center not only of Bohemia but also of the Holy Roman Empire. As the largest urban expansion of the Middle Ages, the formation of the new part of the city of Prague included the

construction of numerous sacred buildings. The pictorial and decorative arts were fostered early on as well. The yearly presentation of the crown jewels and relics of the Holy Roman Empire attracted additional masses of pilgrims to the flourishing city.

The most ambitious project was the construction, beginning in 1344, of the Cathedral of St. Vitus, built on the site of the Church of St. Vitus. Mathieu d'Arras, who was educated in southern France, headed the project. After Mathieu's death in 1352, Peter Parler (1330–1399) was called in from Schwäbisch Gmünd. Although the ground plan and elevation of the choir had already been determined, the light-filled upper stories—especially the triforium undulating rhythmically in and out—the reticulated vault spanning the bays, and the ingenious tracery of the windows manifest Parler's seminal individuality. Ancestral memory *(memoria)* was kept alive on three levels in the choir: new sarcophagi for the

Přemyslid ancestors were made for the ambulatory chapels; the famous busts of Charles IV, his family, and royal household were placed above the triforium openings; and higher still, on the outside of the triforium, placed, as it were, above the contemporary level, one finds busts of Jesus, Mary, and Bohemian saints. The richest decoration was given to the Chapel of St. Wenceslas, consecrated in 1367. Located on the south side of the cathedral, the chapel has walls of precious stones, paintings, and above all, reliquaries and ornamental vestments. The focus of these decorations, however, was the tomb of Charles IV (later destroyed) in the sanctuary.

The site most complex in meaning is the Castle Karlštejn, the renovation of which was begun in 1348. The castle's main function, to house the imperial treasure, is already reflected in the building's arrangement. The Great Tower housing the Chapel of the Holy Cross, behind the altar of which the relics and royal regalia were kept, looks from the outside to be an impregnable fortress. If the mural cycle on the Apocalypse in the Chapel of the Virgin in the Small Tower still reflects the idea of the Church Militant *(ecclesia militans),* then the decoration of the Great Tower joins dynastic notions with the idea of the Church Triumphant *(ecclesia triumphans).* On one side of the staircase, murals depict a cycle of the life of St. Wenceslas, while on the opposite side appears the life of St. Ludmilla. The murals conclude with a representation of the royal family with church dignitaries. Above the entryway lintel one sees depicted an event that had once transpired in the chapel: the liturgical placement *(dispositio)* of pieces of the Cross and other relics by Charles IV.

The Chapel of the Holy Cross itself is like an inward-turning and monumental reliquary. A painted area and jewel encrustations form a socle level above which rises an All Saints cycle: panel paintings produced by the court painter Master Theodoric *(fl.* mid-fourteenth century), which at first seem naive but, precisely because of this, take on an expressive quality. An idea of how the two chapels looked when furnished with goldsmith work and ornamental vestments is still offered by the secular treasure room of the Kunsthistorisches Museum, Vienna, where objects like the small, engraved relic box for a piece of St. John the Baptist's garment *(ca.* 1370) (Vienna, Kunsthistorisches Museum) were taken after the Hapsburgs came to power in Bohemia.

The high level of achievement attained by the decorative arts in Bohemia is also made manifest by works from other sources, such as the reliquary for a thorn from Christ's crown of thorns (Prague, 1347–1349) (Baltimore, Walters Art Gallery) or the Antependium of Pirna

The Crucifixion. *From the Missal of Sbinko of Hasenburg (Sbynek Zajíc z Hazenburka), 1409.* ÖSTERREICHISCHE NATIONALBIBLIOTHEK, VIENNA, COD. 1844, FOL. 149V. REPRODUCED BY PERMISSION.

(Prague, before 1350) (Dresden, Kunstgewerbemuseum).

When assessing the development of the architectural, pictorial, and decorative arts in central Europe, fundamental consideration should be given to the fact that Charles IV, by means of wise marital and territorial politics, was able to extend his jurisdiction to include the dukedoms of Silesia and the March of Brandenburg. At the same time, he controlled large parts of Franconia and was able to rely on allies in the empire. This situation is reflected in the art of the period. In 1343 the first archbishop of Prague, Ernst of Pardubice, commissioned a panel of the enthroned Madonna for a church in Silesian Kłodzko (Berlin, Gemäldegalerie). Of exceeding quality, the image evinces the influence of Italy, especially of Bolognese painting, on the art of Prague during the middle of the century. The altarpiece for the High Altar of the Cathedral of Brandenburg an der Havel, documented to 1375, can be interpreted as a manifestation of the March of Brandenburg's inclusion in the Kingdom of Bohemia.

Christ on the Mount of Olives. *The Trebon Altarpiece (ca. 1380).*
© RADOVAN BOCEK. REPRODUCED BY PERMISSION.

The work echoes the art of the Court of Prague not only in style and motif but also in that it depicts the Bohemian saints Wenceslas, Sigismund, and Vitus. Especially in light of the later destruction of church decoration in the core regions of the Kingdom of Bohemia, such objects take on great importance, even if they do not always attain the level of quality reached at the main artistic center, as for example in the work of the Master of the Retable from the monastery of the Augustinian Canon Regulars at Wittingau (*ca.* 1380) (Prague, Národní galerie).

PRAGUE AS THE CENTER OF THE "BEAUTIFUL STYLE," *CA.* 1400

While Charles IV's patronage aimed at programmatic, outward effects, the patronal ambitions of his son, King Wenceslas IV of Germany (1361–1419), reflected Wenceslas's interests as a bibliophile collector. His most prominent undertaking was the luxurious illumination of the six-volume, Middle High German Bible translation, the Wenceslas Bible (Vienna, Österreichische Nationalbibliothek, Cod. 2759–2764), on which, over an extended period of time, a long line of illuminators worked.

During Wenceslas's reign, a school of sculptors—originating in the Parler family's activities in architectural sculpture—developed in Prague, out of which came image types like the so-called Beautiful Madonna or Beautiful Vesperbild. The Beautiful Madonna from Český Krumlov (Vienna, Kunsthistorisches Museum) combines, with the highest refinement of aesthetic means, an idealized linear beauty, reflected in elaborate and balanced plays of drapery, with a naturalism that allows the pressure of the Virgin's finely fingered hands to leave a mark on the bare skin of the Christ child. Such creations made from the locally occurring limestone of Prague were highly prized as cult images and exported far abroad. How influential such works were across artistic genres is shown by comparing them with an image of St. John in the Missal of Sbinko of Hasenburg (Vienna, Österreichische Nationalbibliothek, Cod. 1844, fol. 149v), or with one of the works of silk embroidery exported from Prague to Danzig (Lübeck, St. Annen-Museum).

THE HUSSITE REBELLION AND REFORMATION ART IN BOHEMIA

Such luxurious aesthetic creations ultimately became the target of the rage that had turned against the social and religious abuses of the times. The death at the stake of Bohemian church reformer John (Jan) Hus in 1415 during the Council of Constance was seen as martyrdom and resulted in unrest. This led in 1419 to violent attacks on the old-church communities in Prague as well as central and southern Bohemia, causing large-scale destruction of sacred decorations and furnishings. Nevertheless, contrary to earlier assumptions, artistic production continued. Typical now, however, was a reduction of linear beauty through conscious restraint and self-control, paired with grisly subject matter, as demonstrated by the depiction of the martyrdom of St. Catherine on a panel from Námešt (*ca.* 1420/30) (Brno, Moravská galerie) or by the so-called Raigern Altarpiece, dated to around 1430, with its extensive depiction of the carrying of the Cross and the Crucifixion (Brno, Moravská galerie and Prague, Národní galerie).

THE PERIOD OF THE JAGIELLONIAN KINGS

In 1471, following a phase of political isolation in Bohemia, the Bohemian estates elected as their king Vladislav II (*r.* 1471–1516) of the Polish-Lithuanian Jagiełło dynasty. Thus began not only a consolidation of civil and spiritual life but also a renewal or restoration

Władisław (Wenceslas) Hall, Prague Castle. *Completed by Benedikt Ried in 1500, this hall is one of the great nonliturgical spaces of the age.*
© RADOVAN BOCEK. REPRODUCED BY PERMISSION.

of the kingdom *(renovatio regni).* This is evident in the borrowing of architectural forms from the period of Charles IV for the Powder Tower of Matej Rejsek (Matthias Rejsek, 1445–1506), begun in 1475 in Prague's Old Town and intended as an homage to the new king. The renewal is even more obvious in the redecoration of the Chapel of St. Wenceslas, whose former walls were covered around the turn of the fifteenth century with a mural cycle of the life of St. Wenceslas by the workshop of the Master of the Leitmeritz Panel.

By 1485 Vladislav had already moved into the refurnished royal castle on the Hradčany grounds. Called in from Frankfurt, the stonemason Hans Spiesz (*d.* 1511) enlarged the castle, according to Vladislav's demands for ostentatious splendor, a sensibility highly developed in him because of his origins in Kraków. The new royal oratory in the Cathedral of St. Vitus had been built before the arrival of Spiesz, by Benedikt Ried from Pientzing

(*ca.* 1454–1534). Its architectural form is that of a gallery woven of naturalistic branch ribs and marked by a hanging boss in the vault (1490–1493). Ried's major work, however, is the Wenceslas Room in Prague castle. Completed in 1500 it was one of the largest secular spaces of its time. Without an interior vertical support system, the room is daringly covered with entwined ribs that carry the wide span of the vaulting.

The commissions and building projects were, however, completed during the absence of the king, who in 1490 attained the crown of Hungary and moved to Ofen (Buda) with his entire court. Even his son, Louis II of Hungary (*r.* 1516–1526), who would die young at the Battle of Mohács, was to reside mainly in Ofen. With the exception of the decoration of a few important building complexes like the royal castle at Křivoklat, court art was limited to projects funded by various high officials in the service of Bohemian nobility. Representative of these kinds of patrons are the Rosenberg family, with their own association of builders on lands in South Bohemia, and the Lev family of Rožmitál, for whom the Master I. P., a carver in the tradition of the so-called Danube School, labored. A city like Kutná Hora, where the royal mint was located, stands out due to its richly illuminated graduals (e.g., Vienna, Österreichische Nationalbibliothek, Cod. 15.501; Cod. s.n. 2657) and its Church of St. Barbara, with twined-rib vaulting and a pyramid-shaped roof characteristic of Benedikt Ried (completed 1548). The breadth and meaning of the artistic exchange characteristic of this phase can truly only be grasped, however, when the perspective is extended beyond Bohemia and Moravia to the centers of Hungary. Especially the upper part of Hungary (the current Slovakia) is important in this context, as its cities—such as Levoča in Szepes or Kosice—were located on heavily traveled trade routes and, in consequence, were well-to-do.

BIBLIOGRAPHY

Bachmann, Erich, ed. *Gothic Art in Bohemia.* Oxford: Phaidon, 1977. A good overview.

Bachmann, Erich, et al., eds. *Romanik in Böhmen: Geschichte, Architektur, Malerei, Plastik, und Kunstgewerbe.* Munich, Germany: Prestel, 1977. A general survey.

Benešovska, Klára, ed. *King John of Luxembourg (1296–1346) and the Art of His Era: Proceedings of the International Conference.* Prague: Konia Latin Press, 1998.

Chamonikolasová, Keliope, ed. *L'art gotique tardif en Bohème, Moravie et Silesie 1400–1550.* Brussels: Palais de Charles Quint, 1998.

Crossley, Paul. *The Politics of Presentation: The Architecture of Charles IV of Bohemia.* In *Courts and Regions in Medieval Europe.* Edited by Sarah Rees Jones, Richard Marks, and A. J. Minnis. York, U.K.: York Medieval Press, 2000. Concise analysis of the programmatic foundations and their spatial arrangement.

Dvořaková, Vlasta, Josef Krása, Anežka Merhautov, and Karel Stejskal. *Gothic Mural Painting in Bohemia and Moravia, 1300–1378.* London: Oxford University Press, 1964.

Fajt, Jirí, ed. *Magister Theodoricus, Court Painter to Emperor Charles IV: The Pictorial Decoration of the Shrines at Karlštejn Castle.* Prague: National Gallery, 1998. Best monograph of this painter with corresponding iconographic and programmatic analyses. Original Czech edition published in 1997.

Homolka, Jaromír, Josef Krása, Václav Mencl, Jaroslav Pešina, and Josef Petráň. *Pozdně gotické umění v Čechách.* Prague: Odeon, 1978. Comprehensive essay by Czech art historians about late Gothic art in Bohemia, limited to the core lands of the Bohemian crown.

Kaufmann, Thomas Da Costa: *Court, Cloister, and City: The Art and Culture in Central Europe, 1450–1800.* Chicago: University of Chicago Press, 1995.

Legner, Anton, ed. *Die Parler und der schöne Stil, 1350–1400: Europäische Kunst unter den Luxemburgern.* 5 vols. Cologne, Germany: Schnütgen-Museum und Kunsthalle Köln, 1978–1981. Comprehensive reference work.

Popp, Dietmar, and Robert Suckale. *Die Jagiellonen: Kunst und Kultur einer Europäischen Dynastie an der Wende zur Neuzeit.* Wissenschaftliche Beibände zum Anzeiger des Germanischen Nationalmuseums, Bd. 21. Nuremberg, Germany: Germanisches Nationalmuseum, 2002. Recent anthology with contributions in English, French, and German.

Rosario, Iva. *Art and Propaganda: Charles IV of Bohemia, 1346–1378.* Woodbridge/Suffolk, U.K.: Boydell, 2000.

Snyder, James. *Northern Renaissance Art: Painting, Sculpture, the Graphic Arts from 1350 to 1575.* New York: Abrams, 1985.

Wetter, Evelin. *Bohmische Bildstickerei um 1400: Die Stiftungen in Trient, Brandenburg, und Danzig.* Berlin: Gebr. Mann, 2001. Example-based study of the wide distribution of Bohemian art in central Europe.

EVELIN WETTER
TRANSLATED BY ANSELM HUELSBERGEN

[See also **DMA:** Bohemia-Moravia; Gems and Jewelry; Glass, Western European; Gothic Art: Painting and Manuscript Illumination; Gothic, International Style; Jagiełło Dynasty; Prague: Přemyslid Dynasty; **Supp:** Charles IV, Emperor; Gothic Architecture; Gothic Art; Wenceslas, St.]

BOLESŁAW I CHROBRY OF POLAND, KING

(**the Brave,** *r.* 992–1025). The eldest son of Mieszko I, the Piast duke responsible for consolidating the territory of medieval Poland, Bolesław succeeded his father as sole ruler after Mieszko's death in 992. Bolesław continued his father's program of territorial expansion, and although his gains proved ephemeral, at various points during his reign, he ruled an area that included Bohemia, Moravia, and parts of Slovakia, and for a brief time he occupied Kiev.

The most significant political relationship of Bolesław's early career was his close friendship with the German emperor Otto III. Otto's program of imperial renewal *(renovatio imperii Romanorum)* culminated in his pilgrimage to Gniezno, where Bolesław had interred the relics of St. Adalbert (Vojtěch), the martyred missionary to the Prussians. Otto placed his own crown on Bolesław's head and, according to Gallus Anonymous, addressed him as "fratrem et cooperatorem imperii," thereby elevating him to the status of imperial friend and ally. On this same occasion a synod reorganized the Polish church, raising Gniezno to the rank of archiepiscopal see with three subordinate sees in Kraków, Kolobrzeg, and Wrocław, an act that greatly enhanced the status of Piast Poland. In a gesture that affirmed Poland's continued political independence, Otto confirmed the grant made by Mieszko in the *Dagome Iudex* that had placed Poland under direct papal authority.

When Otto III died prematurely in 1002, Bolesław's close diplomatic bond with the German crown ended, and he began a relentless campaign of expansion and warfare. He took control of Lusatia, Meissen, and Milzen. Then in 1003 the dynastic crisis in Bohemia gave Bolesław the opportunity to seize Prague and the throne until Henry II forced him out for refusing to render homage. Henry then entered into a scandalous alliance with the pagan Lutici in 1003 and forced Bolesław to give up all claims to Lusatia, Milzen, and Bohemia. Conflict again erupted over Lusatia in 1007, resulting in a more favorable peace in 1013 that allowed Bolesław to hold both Lusatia and Milzen as fiefs from Henry. A final phase of war from 1015 to 1018 ended with the treaty of Budziszyn, which confirmed that Bolesław would retain control over both territories, possibly no longer as fiefs from the emperor. His imperial treaty freed Bolesław to focus on the east, and in 1018 he easily captured Kiev, putting his son-in-law Svyatopolk on the throne. Bolesław wrote immediately to the German and Byzantine emperors to inform them of his victory and departed in 1019 with plunder and prisoners, which suggests he was more interested in making a gesture of power than in pursuing permanent expansion. He did, however, seize the Grody Czerwieńskie.

During the interregnum after the death of Henry II, Bolesław became the first Piast ruler to be crowned king, only a few months before his own death in June 1025. Although Bolesław made important territorial gains, he did so by alienating powerful neighbors, which would eventually contribute to the collapse of the Piast state during the reign of his son and successor, Mieszko II.

BIBLIOGRAPHY

PRIMARY WORKS

Gallus Anonymous. *Galli Anonymi Cronicae et gesta ducum sive principum polonorum.* Edited by Karol Maleczyński. Monumenta Poloniae Historica, new ser., vol. 2. Kraków, Poland: Academia Litterarum Polonica, 1952.

Thietmar of Merseburg. *Die Chronik des Bischofs Thietmar von Merseburg und ihre Korveier Überarbeitung.* Edited by Robert Holtzmann. Monumenta Germaniae Historica, Scriptores rerum Germanicarum, new ser., vol. 9. Berlin: Weidmann, 1935.

SECONDARY WORKS

Dvornik, F. *The Slavs in European History and Civilization.* New Brunswick, N.J.: Rutgers University Press, 1962.

Halecki, Oskar. *A History of Poland,* 9th ed. New York: D. McKay, 1976.

Vlasto, A. P. *The Entry of the Slavs into Christendom: An Introduction to the Medieval History of the Slavs.* Cambridge, U.K.: Cambridge University Press, 1970.

ELSPETH JANE CARRUTHERS

[See also **DMA:** Bohemia-Moravia; Otto III, Emperor; Piast Dynasty; Poland; **Supp:** Adalbert, St.; Henry II of Germany, Emperor; Kraków; Mieszko I of Poland, King.]

BOLESŁAW III KRZYWOUSTY OF POLAND, KING (*r.* 1102–1138). The reign of Bolesław Krzywousty ("the wry-mouthed") of the Piast dynasty ended centralized ducal authority in the early Polish state, guaranteeing the magnates' continued aggrandizement of power at the cost of Piast control. Bolesław's father, Władysław Hermann, had ruled in name only. Real power rested with the palatine Sieciech, whom Władysław's sons, Zbigniew and Bolesław, encouraged by the magnates, forced into exile. Before he died in 1102 Władysław divided Poland between his two sons equally instead of designating a senior prince, eroding ducal control and ensuring struggle between the brothers. Bolesław eventually expelled Zbigniew from Poland in 1107, later blinding him for treason and possibly killing him.

Bolesław's central political goal was to recover Pomerania, lost to Piast authority since the pagan revolt of 1066. In 1109 he conquered seven Pomeranian cities, including Nakło, but was distracted from further gains by the German ruler Henry V, who was seeking retribution for Bolesław's part in Henry's unsuccessful campaign against Hungary the previous year. Bolesław repulsed Henry's invasion and launched a campaign against Henry's ally Bohemia, negotiating a treaty in 1111.

Details about the later part of Bolesław's reign are vague. Between 1113 and 1123 he gradually gained control over Pomerania, conquering the eastern portion by about 1116 before concentrating on the west. He partitioned the territory, annexing part to Great Poland, appointing local representatives to govern the area around the Vistula basin and subordinating the prince of western Pomerania to Polish suzerainty.

To reinforce Polish ecclesiastical authority there, Bolesław financed a mission by bishop Otto of Bamberg in 1124, enlisting him again in 1127 after a relapse to paganism. The latter campaign misfired due to Otto's return as an imperial, not Polish, representative, which resulted in the loss of Wolin to German ecclesiastical authority. To control eastern Pomerania, Bolesław established new dioceses in Kujavia and Lubusz, the latter for planned expansion of the Polish church.

A series of setbacks, including Bolesław's failed campaign in 1132 to challenge the royal succession in Hungary (which provoked repeated Czech attacks on Silesia), culminated in Bolesław's summons by the kings of Bohemia and Hungary to the imperial court. Anticipating the worst, Bolesław made concessions to the emperor in the Merseburg agreement of 1135, in which he settled matters with Bohemia and Hungary and acknowledged his vassalage to the emperor as lord of Pomerania and Rügen, agreeing to pay tribute owed since 1123.

In 1138, realizing his death was imminent, Bolesław devised a succession plan intended to prevent further unrest while protecting ducal authority. He replaced the seniorate system customary since Casimir I (the Restorer) with an arrangement in which the eldest of the dynasty would receive the title *princeps,* or senior prince, along with substantial central holdings that included Kraków, eastern Great Poland, and western Kujavia, as well as important political and military rights. The remaining territories were divided as independent hereditary duchies among Bolesław's four younger sons. This compromise gave rise almost immediately to disputes among the dynastic branches for the *princeps* title, further benefiting the very magnates Bolesław had wished to constrain.

BIBLIOGRAPHY

Davies, Norman. *God's Playground, a History of Poland.* Vol. 1. New York: Cambridge University Press, 1982.

Gallus Anonymous. *Galli Anonymi Cronicae et gesta ducum sive principum polonorum.* Edited by Karol Maleczyński. Monumenta Poloniae Historica, new ser., vol. 2. Kraków, Poland: Academia Litterarum Polonica, 1952.

Manteuffel, Tadeusz. *The Formation of the Polish State: The Period of Ducal Rule, 963–1194.* Translated by Andrew Gorski. Detroit, Mich.: Wayne State University Press, 1982.

ELSPETH JANE CARRUTHERS

[See also **DMA:** Otto of Bamberg, St.; Piast Dynasty; Poland; **Supp:** Henry V of Germany, Emperor.]

BRIAN BORU (941–1014). Born in Bóruma, the ford across the river Shannon a mile upstream from Killaloe, Brian Boru was the third son to Cennétig of the Uí Toirdelbaig branch of the Déis Tuaiscirt (later called Dál Cais), who occupied the territory of East Clare and part of East Limerick. Brian's grandfather was the first of his line to attain the kingship of that people. Though Cennétig enjoyed no great success as a war leader, by the time of his death in 951, the Déis Tuaiscirt were on the map as a political force. Brian's elder brother, Mathgamain, who succeeded Cennétig after his older brother was killed, was the real driving force behind the rise of the

Dál Cais, and he consolidated their power considerably. Dál Cais success against the Vikings of Limerick enabled Mathgamain to claim the Munster kingship at Cashel and thereby strengthen his position. Most important, his career proved (especially to his brother Brian) that the old structures of traditional kingship and power could be cast aside.

Mathgamain's career, however, ended prematurely, and Brian succeeded his murdered brother within two years as ruler of Munster. The arrival of Máelsechlainn mac Domnaill (Máelsechnaill II) as high-king of Ireland in 980 marked the beginning of a great rivalry between the two. Máelsechnaill was a scion of the Uí Néill kings, descended from Niall of the Niall Hostages (the supposed founder of the high-kingship of Ireland). Brian, by contrast, was an upstart claimant. In fact, Máelsechnaill's predecessor was the first man to be described by contemporary sources as *ard-rí Érenn* (high-king of Ireland), but Brian is termed by the same annalists *ard-rí Gaídel Érenn, Gall, Bretan, Auguist iarthair tuaiscirt Eorpa uile* (high-king of the Irish of Ireland and of the Vikings and of the Welsh, the Augustus of all of northwest Europe). This exalted terminology reflected more than a propaganda war: in the more than ten years since Máelsechnaill's accession to power he and Brian had faced each other with ever-increasing rivalry. The fluctuating nature of the military hostilities led eventually in 997 to an arrangement in accordance with which they divided Ireland between them. Brian's military success against the Vikings of Dublin in 999/1000, however, emboldened him, and he challenged Máelsechlainn for the full title of high-king, leading a Munster army to Athlone in 1002. When Máelsechlainn failed to field an army against him, he submitted to Brian. Strange to say, the two appear to have enjoyed remarkably cordial relations in the decade that followed.

In the years following his bloodless victory, Brian led armies north to seek the submission of the northern Irish kings but each time retreated without forcing the issue. By 1005, however, he was back again at Armagh, where his secretary signed Brian's name into the famous Book of Armagh (believed to be St. Patrick's own Bible) with the grandiloquent title *imperator Scottorum* (emperor of the Irish). Clearly, the title of "king of Ireland" was no longer sufficient to convey the measure of Brian's ambition. An alliance of the Vikings of Dublin with the men of Leinster in 1013, perhaps emboldened by Danish success in England, led to a renewal of the hostilities. Brian had been victorious against the same grouping at the battle of Glenn Máma in 997, but at the battle of Clontarf in 1014 the Dál Cais, though triumphant in the end, suffered severe losses, and Brian himself—though not a participant in the battle at age 73—was struck down.

Although Brian's reputation as a political and military innovator has been much exaggerated, he was the first Irish king to deploy naval forces on a large scale (sources refer to his *cablach mór,* or large fleet), and he was the strategic superior of his contemporaries. He was also careful to secure ecclesiastical support, as exemplified by his reception at Armagh. But Brian was neither a lawmaker nor a reformer of the church, and he introduced no new type of monarchy or secure method of succession. He left Ireland largely as he had found it.

BIBLIOGRAPHY

Byrne, Francis John. *Irish Kings and High-Kings.* London: Batsford, 1973.

Ryan, John. "Brian Boruma, King of Ireland." In *North Munster Studies: Essays in Commemoration of Monsignor Michael Moloney.* Edited by Etienne Rynne. Limerick, Ireland: Thomond Archaeological Society, 1967.

DÁIBHÍ Ó CRÓINÍN

[See also **DMA:** Ireland; Uí Néill.]

BRUNHILD (*ca.* 545/550–614). Born to Visigothic royalty, Brunhild was married to a Merovingian king, Sigibert I of Austrasia. Together they supported poets like Venantius Fortunatus and saints' cults like that of St. Martin. According to Venantius, the queen facilitated Gregory of Tours's elevation to bishop. Not surprisingly, Brunhild cuts an admirable figure in the writings of both Gregory and Venantius, quite different from the "second Jezebel" who terrorizes later sources. Gregory's portrait was especially flattering compared with his depiction of Fredegunda, whose husband, King Chilperic I of Soissons, murdered Brunhild's sister, his wife before Fredegunda. So began a notorious and luridly embellished blood feud between the two queens. Although Fredegunda arranged the assassination of Brunhild's husband in 575, and one seventh-century source claims that Brunhild reciprocated with Chilperic's murder a decade later, neither queen by any means restricted her activities to protecting children or avenging relatives. Brunhild was deeply enmeshed in the violent contest over cities and boundaries that dominated the political world in which she lived. In 613 she tried to preserve Theodoric's domain undivided for her great-grandson Sigibert II, but all was lost to Chlothar II, Fredegunda's son. According to a later source, he charged Brunhild with the murders of ten kings. She was tortured and dragged to pieces by a wild horse (Chronicle of Fredegar, 4.42).

By the time of her death, she had served as either nominal or *de facto* regent for four of her offspring, although her authority was usually mitigated by powerful nobles. They controlled the court, at least initially, when her five-year-old son Childebert II became king of Austrasia in 575. Meanwhile, Brunhild was briefly married to Merovech, a stepson of Fredegunda, but mostly looked out for her own interests until Childebert came of age in 585. She made good use of her personal wealth and alliances: she helped a friend into a highly prized bishopric, tormented her opponents with legal charges and exile, and successfully avoided plots on her life. Examples of her correspondence with Visigothic nobles and Byzantine royalty survive.

King Guntram of Burgundy, who adopted her son Childebert as heir in 577, suspected that Brunhild was involved with the pretender Gundovald, with whom she shared some notable acquaintances. After Childebert's death in 595 his territory passed to Brunhild's young grandsons—the kingdom of Burgundy to Theodoric II and Austrasia to Theodebert II—while Brunhild acted as their regent. Pope Gregory the Great complimented her skill at both childrearing and governance and praised her part in Augustine of Canterbury's initial mission to England.

Around 602, after Theodebert had come of age, nobles forced Brunhild out of Austrasia, so she settled in with Theodoric, whom she persuaded to war against his brother. She probably discouraged him from marrying a Visigothic princess but did not prevent him from having concubines. This led directly to Brunhild's notoriety. Bishop Desiderius of Vienne openly criticized her grandson's behavior and was deposed by a church council and later stoned to death. Columbanus, whose monastery at Luxeuil possibly enjoyed Brunhild's support, refused to bless Theodoric's illegitimate children; he was driven from the kingdom. Unlike Fredegunda, who died peacefully in 597, Brunhild survived to have her reputation ruined by hagiographers.

BIBLIOGRAPHY

Martindale, J. R. *The Prosopography of the Later Roman Empire:* Volume 3: A.D. *527–641.* Cambridge, U.K., and New York, Cambridge University Press, 1992. See the entry on "Brunichildis" for references to primary sources.

Nelson, Janet L. "Queens as Jezebels: The Careers of Brunhilde and Balthild in Merovingian History." In *Medieval Women.* Edited by Derek Baker. Oxford: Published for the Ecclesiastical Society by B. Blackwell, 1978.

Wood, Ian. *The Merovingian Kingdoms, 450–751*. London and New York: Longman, 1993. See especially chapter 8.

KEVIN UHALDE

[See also **DMA:** Gregory of Tours, St.; Merovingians; Venantius Fortunatus; **Supp:** Fredegunda; Martin of Tours, St.; Queens and Queenship.]

BULGARUS (*d.* 1166) was the foremost of the second generation of teachers of Roman law in Bologna. Unfortunately, although his teachings were to have a great impact on the development of law in the West, very little is known for certain about Bulgarus's life. He is assumed to have been born in Bologna toward the end of the eleventh century. He studied civil (Roman) law in his native town under Irnerius, the founder of the Bolognese school. From his teacher he learned a dialectical approach to the law that characterized the jurists of the twelfth and early thirteenth centuries. These scholars, known as glossators because one of their characteristic interpretative activities was the creation of explanatory glosses, undertook the task of assimilating and understanding the newly recovered corpus of Roman law.

Bulgarus began teaching around 1115. He was a contemporary of three other Bologna jurists, Martinus Gosia, Hugo da Porta Ravennate, and Jacobus, who together were known as the Four Doctors and whose eminence ensured for Bologna the leading place among law schools in Europe. Of this group, Bulgarus and Martinus were the most renowned. They are traditionally held to have represented opposing schools of thought, with Martinus in favor of interpreting the law equitably and Bulgarus in favor of a strict reading of the letter of the law. Ultimately Bulgarus's viewpoint won out and was promulgated by his famous student Johannes Bassianus.

The Doctors were not mere scholars. They played an important role at the Diet of Roncaglia in 1158, advising the emperor Frederick I on his regalian rights in northern Italy—his right as emperor to pass laws, levy taxes, mint coins, and so on—and upholding his claim to those rights. Bulgarus also served as a papal judge-delegate during the period from 1151 to 1159, and he argued the rights of the count of Barcelona against the count of Baux before the emperor in Turin in 1162. He also seems to have acted as a private judge and notary.

All of the extant works attributed to Bulgarus relate to his teaching. He wrote many glosses on the Roman law and was the first to create an apparatus, or sustained series of glosses covering an entire section of the text, in this case on the last title of the *Digest* of Justinian, *De*

diversis regulis iuris antiqui (Various rules of early law). He also wrote *summulae,* or short treatises of several paragraphs dealing with a particular section of a title. These *summulae* were actually extended glosses that originally were written in the margin of the legal text but were sometimes also copied separately. Bulgarus seems to have been the first jurist to address the issue of procedure in a letter he wrote to Cardinal Aimericus, the papal chancellor from 1123 to 1141. Finally, Bulgarus is credited with originating the system of mock disputes known as the *Quaestiones disputatae* (Disputed questions). Once a week, Bulgarus's students would gather in his school and argue each side of the legal problem raised by a set of facts offered by the professor. The professor himself would judge the dispute. These disputations were a critical part of the students' training and would become a fixture in legal education.

BIBLIOGRAPHY

Kantorowicz, Hermann. "The *Quaestiones disputatae* of the Glossators." *Tijdschrift voor Rechtsgeschiedenis* 16 (1939): 1–67.

———. *Studies in the Glossators of the Roman Law: Newly Discovered Writings of the Twelfth Century*. Rev. ed. Aalen, Germany: Scientia Verlag, 1969.

Paradisi, B. "Bulgaro." In *Dizionario biografico degli Italiani*. Vol. 15. Rome: Instituto della Enciclopedia Italiana, 1972.

EMILY KADENS

[See also **DMA:** Irnerius; Law, Civil—Corpus Iuris, Revival and Spread; Law, Schools of; Martinus Gosia; **Supp:** Johannes Bassianus.]

BURSFELD, ABBEY OF. The Benedictine abbey of Bursfeld in Hanover was founded by Duke Henry of Nordheim at the end of the eleventh century. Gifted with numerous lands and privileges, the abbey also came under the influence of the venerable and powerful monastery of Corvey, which provided Bursfeld with its first abbot, Almericus, and its first group of monks. The generosity of its patrons and the guiding hand of Almericus and those who followed him in the abbacy ensured that Bursfeld thrived, becoming a center of education and monastic piety. By the fourteenth century, however, the grandeur that Bursfeld had once known began to decline, obscured by problems in the monastery and the lack of effective leadership. This decline reached its nadir between 1331 and 1424, when the great abbey could not even manage to keep its own books. No records were kept for almost a century, and only a handful of monks remained as the monastery fell into disrepair.

In the early fifteenth century, the church found itself in the midst of the Great Schism, representative of a wider crisis within the church. Responding to the ongoing abuses and neglect that had become increasingly common, and of which Bursfeld was but one example, leading ecclesiastics undertook a comprehensive program of reform that was developed and approved as part of the Council of Constance (1414–1418) and later the Council of Basel (1431–1449). One of the leading reformers was John Dederoth, abbot of Clus. In 1433 Otto, duke of Brunswick, commissioned Dederoth to try to save and reform Bursfeld. Dederoth was an experienced reformer, having already restored a strict Benedictine discipline to Clus after he had forced the previous abbot out in 1430. Under his direction, Bursfeld not only recovered and prospered but eventually became the center of a monastic reform movement that would, at its height, include almost 140 monasteries.

From Bursfeld, Dederoth moved on to reform the abbey of Reinhausen. Other monasteries followed, but Dederoth died in 1439, leaving the work to John of Hagen, his able successor as abbot of Bursfeld. John of Hagen's most important contribution was the formation of a union among the monasteries in the Bursfeld circle. Between 1445 and 1446 the Council of Basel granted John the right to form the Bursfeld Congregation, a group of Benedictine monasteries that adhered to the same strict program of discipline and reform as well as liturgy that Dederoth had introduced at Bursfeld. In 1446 the union, consisting of six monasteries, had its first joint chapter meeting. In 1449 additional privileges were granted, including the right to include male and female monasteries. The abbot of Bursfeld was also charged with convoking and presiding over the annual meetings, making visitations and being the final arbiter of discipline and punishment for all the houses in the union.

The Bursfeld Congregation received additional support in 1451, when the papal legate, Nicholas of Cusa, placed it under his protection, ratifying many of its privileges and approving the Ordinarius of Bursfeld, the official rule of the congregation. Nicholas was also responsible for bringing additional houses into the congregation as he actively lobbied to have irresponsible and weak abbots replaced with monks from Bursfeld and encouraged other houses to join with it. Additional papal approval followed in 1461. Armed with these significant privileges as well as a growing popularity, Bursfeld became the guiding force for Benedictine reform in Germany prior to the Reformation.

BIBLIOGRAPHY

Berlière, D. Ursmer. "Les origines de la Congrégation de Bursfeld." *Revue Bénédictine* 16 (1899): 360–369; 385–413; 481–502.

JARBEL RODRIGUEZ

[See also **DMA:** Benedictines; Councils, Western (1311–1449); **Supp:** Corvey, Abbey of.]

BYLINY (singular, *bylina*) are long stories, in poetic form, that have been recited and sung in Russian for centuries. Every medieval European culture of which we have extensive knowledge preserves evidence of epic-length vernacular poetic storytelling either by professionals (bards, jongleurs, etc.) or by ordinary people. The evidence is often quite vague as to the circumstances of recitation and the length, character, and stability of the story lines. Yet scholars assume that this kind of storytelling was usually a very public form of collective entertainment, one of the most important, given the scarcity of alternatives. The content of the stories was also constantly being adapted to changing circumstances. Each story, if enduringly popular, grew and shrank in the retelling around a more stable core narrative, but even that was not entirely fixed. The stories were inspired by fairy tales, troubling or inspiring historical events, and controversial heroes and villains. In most cases, they had a strong chronological linearity to them.

Authors who composed written works on the themes of these stories, it seems reasonable to suppose, used the stories as raw material but also changed them as they saw fit—sometimes translating them from the vernacular to the learned language, sometimes expanding them with material garnered from other literary and chronicle sources, sometimes knitting various versions together, and sometimes interrupting or de-emphasizing the narrative for didactic, moral, lyrical, or other purposes. In turn, the written works, as their content became widely known, might contribute new material to the ever-changing oral stories.

Cultures in which widespread literacy has come late and where the adoption of new technologies for popular entertainment has been slow have tended to preserve this oral form of epic poetic story making and storytelling. Much work has been done on traditions in Wales, Brittany, the southern Slav lands, and of course, outside of Europe in the Arabic Near East and India, partly in an attempt to recover a putative medieval (or even ancient) substratum for some of the stories whose ostensible subjects go back to, or whose settings are placed in, remote times. Where complementary evidence exists, the success of these attempts may be evaluated systematically, and doubts have been raised about the reliability of the information recovered from the stories. The uncertainties are multiplied where there is little or no complementary evidence.

In Russia the tradition of the *byliny* lived on deep into the modern period, including the Soviet era. Given the subject matter of the earliest recorded *byliny* (tainted by being fixed, as it were, by the very act of recording), it is surmised that the genre probably originated in the Kievan Rus period. Entire cycles of stories drew their inspiration from events and characters at the court of Prince Vladimir I (977–1015), the first Christian ruler, and from the exploits of the Cossack warrior Ilya of Murom, who is reputed to have led some of the resistance to the Mongol invasion in the early thirteenth century.

Byliny on Vladimir's reign and Ilya's struggles were still being recited and sung in the twentieth century. The genre and its practitioners, however, had almost fallen into obsolescence by the end of the century. In many cases, only the written (scholarly) reconstructions of *byliny* now survive; they no longer represent points in a living tradition.

BIBLIOGRAPHY

Arant, Patricia M. *Compositional Techniques of the Russian Oral Epic, the Bylina.* New York: Garland Publishers, 1990.

Bailey, James, and Tatyana Ivanova, trans. *An Anthology of Russian Folk Epics.* Armonk, N.Y.: M. E. Sharpe, 1998.

WILLIAM CHESTER JORDAN

[See also **DMA:** Kievan Rus; Slavic Languages and Literatures; Vladimir, St.]

CALUMNY OATH *(juramentum calumniae).* The medieval calumny oath was a procedural mechanism borrowed from Roman law to deal with the problem of frivolous and dishonest litigation. In late antique Roman law, it consisted of an oath, the *sacramentum de calumnia,* taken in imperial courts by each litigant and their lawyers, swearing that their case was put forth in good faith and without the intention to abuse the court's procedure.

As Roman law disappeared from early medieval legal proceedings, so did the calumny oath. Although Germanic customary procedure relied heavily on oaths, swearing that one's case had merit did not reappear until the eleventh century, when northern Italian and south-ern French courts rediscovered the Roman law. By the late twelfth century the calumny oath had become common enough in ecclesiastical courts (the primary users of Roman law in the Middle Ages) that decretal collections like the *Compilatio prima* of Bernard of Pavia (*ca.* 1190) and the Decretals of Gregory IX (1234) devoted whole titles to it. Thirteenth-century procedural treatises, like those of Tancred and Guillaume Durand, also gave considerable space to the proper use of the oath. By the thirteenth century, even accounts of the procedure of customary courts, such as that found in the *Établissements of St. Louis,* included mention of the calumny oath.

According to the learned works, the calumny oath was to be taken by the major actors on each side of the litigation immediately after the commencement of *litis contestatio*—the point at which the issues were joined and the trial proper began. The plaintiff swore that he believed he had a good cause, that he would not knowingly act falsely or unjustly, and that he would not suborn witnesses, use bribery to sway the outcome, or protract the litigation through legal chicanery. The defendant swore that he in good faith believed he could justly deny the charge and did not pursue the suit merely to obstruct the plaintiff and that he had evidence to support his defense. Both sides also swore that they would not give false testimony or produce falsified evidence as proof. Refusing to take the oath meant losing one's case.

Mentions of the calumny oath in practice are sparse in the thirteenth century. Although it was in theory a required part of the procedure at least in civil cases (there was disagreement about whether it should be used in criminal cases), it appears that in practice it was employed only when one party requested it, and that may not have been often.

By the thirteenth century, one of the main unresolved issues was whether lawyers, too, had to take the oath. Until the 1230s, they would swear it only when acting as proxies for their clients but not as a guarantee of their own behavior. After the 1230s, a related procedure appeared, requiring advocates in some jurisdictions to take an oath similar to the calumny oath upon admission to the bar.

Also related to the calumny oath are the oath of verity *(iuramentum de veritate),* sworn only in cases concerning spiritual matters, like litigation over tithes, in which the calumny oath was considered inappropriate, and the oath of wickedness *(iuramentum de malitia),* which either party could request at any point in the litigation upon suspicion that the opposing party acted dishonestly or unjustly.

BIBLIOGRAPHY

Brundage, James A. "The Calumny Oath and Ethical Ideals of Canonical Advocates." In *Proceedings of the Ninth International Congress of Medieval Canon Law.* Edited by Peter Landau and Joers Mueller. Vatican City: Biblioteca Apostolica Vaticana, 1997.

Budischin, Hans Jörg. *Der gelehrte Zivilprozess in der Praxis geistlicher Gerichte des 13. und 14. Jahrhunderts im deutschen Raum.* Bonn, Germany: Röhrschied, 1974.

Lefebvre, Charles. "Le 'juramentum calumnaie' de droit canonique aux XIIe et XIII siècles." In *Ephemerides juris canonici* 4 (1948) 564–586.

Schlosser, J. "Prozeßeide der Kleriker im Verfahren vor dem weltlichen Zivilgericht während des späten Mittelalters." In *Festschrift Hermann Krause* (1975) 43–65.

EMILY KADENS

[See also **DMA:** Decretals; Law, Civil—Corpus Iuris, Revival and Spread; Law, Procedure of, 1000–1500; Oath.]

CAPITAL PUNISHMENT. The prevalence of the death penalty as punishment for crimes in the Middle Ages seems to have depended upon the theory of justice prevalent at a given time and place. In general, when society considered crime a private matter between the aggressor and the victim and the public's only goal was to maintain peace in the community, capital punishment was significantly less important than when the prince bore the responsibility for exercising justice and penalties were meant to have an exemplary nature.

During the late Roman Empire, punishment of crime was a duty of the state, and capital punishment was ordained for crimes as varied as murder, female adultery, bigamy, counterfeiting, interference with maritime commerce, and religious deviance. The government employed spectacular forms of public cruelty to put the accused to death, including impalement and drowning. The only factor mitigating the profligate use of capital punishment was the possibility of an imperial pardon. The concept of pardon depended upon a system of punishment that vested authority over justice in the hands of a sovereign. It would disappear in the early Middle Ages, only to reappear as a lordly privilege in the twelfth century with the reemergence of centralized government, public justice, and the renewed study of the Roman law.

Under the early Germanic kings, customary German ideas of justice replaced those of the Roman world. Traditional Germanic law treated most crimes, even murder, as private matters between the perpetrator and the victim or the victim's family. The public authority's only concern was to ensure that the first offense did not lead to an uncontrollable cycle of violence as each party wreaked vengeance for succeeding wrongs. The solution was to institute a detailed system of money damages, known as composition payments, by which the perpetrator symbolically bought back the victim's right of vengeance. Two-thirds of the damages, called the *faidus,* went to the victim or his family, and the remaining third, the *fredus,* went to the sovereign. The law established a scale of payments depending upon the specifics of the crime and the status of the victim.

The composition for murder was known as wergild, or "man price." The payment of the wergild fell not only on the criminal but also on his family. If neither the perpetrator nor the family could pay, the guilty person was obligated to pay with his body by becoming a slave of either the victim's family or a third-party redemptor who agreed to pay the composition. The family had the right to put the slave to death. In practice, thus, the death penalty for private crimes fell disproportionately on the poor and unfree who could not pay the wergild.

Public crimes, meaning crimes against the sovereign, were punishable by death even during the high point of the wergild system. These crimes included treason, counterfeiting, desertion, and cowardice in battle. During the Merovingian period, violence against the king was also punishable by death on the theory that the king had no wergild, and thus no composition was possible.

Under the first Carolingian kings, the desire to restore order in a violent age by centralizing power in the hands of the sovereign led to the multiplication of crimes for which capital punishment was mandated. In addition to the traditional public crimes, the capitularies of Charlemagne and Louis the Pious added religious deviation and brigandage, or theft by professional robbers. The punishments were intended to be public, severe, and exemplary in order to deter others.

From the tenth century, as the Carolingian empire disintegrated into ever smaller units of governance, the right of justice passed from the kings to counts, dukes, and other important Carolingian functionaries and then in the following century to local lords like castellans and eventually even to town magistrates. The ability to punish was a source of power and money, so lords and towns squabbled over the possession of the right of justice, leading to a division between high justice and low justice. The former tended to be held by more important lords and covered crimes in which blood was spilled as well as those subject to capital punishment. These amounted to murder, rape, arson, counterfeiting, brigandage, theft from a home, and the traditional crimes of lèse-majesté against the sovereign. Low justice was the right to adjudicate petty crimes. High justice in particular permitted lords to assert their power by demonstrating their ability to maintain the public peace, and the right of high justice was a significant source of income because of the high fines and even forfeiture of the property of the criminal. Lords holding jurisdiction over high justice thus had an incentive to increase the number of crimes for which capital punishment was ordained. An additional important impetus for the use of capital punishment was the church's violent repression of heresy. The first known case of heresy being treated as a capital offense occurred in 1022, when thirteen heretics from Orléans were burned at the stake. In keeping with a view inherited from Augustine, churchmen were not permitted themselves to shed blood, so the condemned heretics were given over to the secular authorities for punishment. Only the Waldensians opposed the death penalty regardless of who carried it out. Thus, while the church refused to bloody its hands with the actual putting to death of heretics, it did not condemn capital punishment as wrong because it accepted the secular power's right to act as vicar of God and punish those who menaced the peace of the community.

Capital punishment was intended to serve as a warning to future criminals. The executions were carried out publicly and with great, sometimes excessive cruelty. Cadavers were left hanging from the scaffolding until they putrefied or were cut into pieces and scattered, or the death was preceded by public torture.

The type of capital punishment employed differed by crime, gender, and social status. Hanging was the most common form of death for men, but women were usually burned at the stake or buried alive. In England, the members of the upper class would be beheaded. Forgers and counterfeiters would be boiled alive. Other forms of capital punishment used in the Middle Ages included drowning, stoning, casting from rocks, being broken on the wheel, and being dragged behind horses. Being a cleric could save a criminal from death. Since it was not always easy to know for certain who could claim the protection of the church and since traditionally only the clergy could read Latin, in England the so-called benefit of clergy was proved by being able to read a verse from the Fifty-first Psalm. As literacy spread, the ability to read this verse, known as the "neck verse," saved the lives of many lay people as well. The English benefit of clergy was only abolished in 1705.

BIBLIOGRAPHY

Carbasse, Jean-Marie. *Histoire du droit pénal et de la justice criminelle.* Paris: Presses Universitaires de France, 2000. Excellent overview of criminal justice and punishment.

Imbert, Jean. *La peine de mort.* Paris: Presses Universitaires de France, 1989.

La peine: Europe avant le XVIIIe siècle. Transactions of the Jean Bodin Society for Comparative Institutional History. Vol. 56, part 2. Brussels: De Boeck, 1991. A collection of essays about crime and punishment in various parts of Europe during the premodern period.

Laurence, John. *A History of Capital Punishment.* 1932. Reprint, Port Washington, N.Y.: Kennikat Press, 1971. Focused on England.

Megivern, James J. *The Death Penalty: An Historical and Theological Survey.* New York: Paulist Press, 1997.

Nash, Camille. *Death Comes to the Maiden: Sex and Execution 1431–1933.* London and New York: Routledge, 1991. Discusses the special punishments reserved for women.

EMILY KADENS

[See also **DMA:** Law, Civil—Corpus Iuris, Revival and Spread; Law, German: Early Germanic Codes; Wergild.]

CAPITULATIONS. Warfare between Christians and Muslims in the Middle Ages was a common occurrence. In the course of the Crusades, the Spanish Reconquest, and other conflicts, their soldiers fought one another hundreds of times in minor skirmishes, pitched battles, and sieges of fortresses and cities. In this martial environment mechanisms for bringing truces or peace were essential. In the Iberian Peninsula, these treaties or capitulation pacts followed a recognizable pattern and formed the basis for an important aspect of the relations between the two religious groups.

Treaties of capitulation between Christians and Muslims differ from other surrender and truce treaties in several important respects, especially in the stipulations about religious freedoms granted to the vanquished, the exchange of captives, and possible tributes to be paid. Capitulations were also an opportunity for the conversion of mosques to churches and for victory ceremonies, which the conquerors often staged for their entry into the city. The treaties helped to define the boundaries and conditions that would prevail after the conquest, during which time Christian settlers, administrators, and troops migrated into areas with large and well-established Muslim populations.

One of the earliest kings to master the treaties of capitulation was James I (the Conqueror) of Aragon in the thirteenth century. Possessing a deep understanding of Muslim sensibilities, James understood that his treatment of the vanquished would determine how much the local population would cooperate with him after the conquest. As a result, the surrender pacts surrounding the conquest of the kingdom of Valencia are marked by a high degree of decorum and respect extended to the defeated Muslims. Many of these capitulations also included the very important stipulation that the Muslims would be allowed to practice their religion freely and that even the call to prayer would be respected—in the capitulation of Játiva (1244) this appears in the very first line of the treaty. The residents were also taken under royal protection, which made any attack against them an attack against the crown. The Muslims were often given legal privileges, which included the right to have intrafaith cases heard before their own qadis instead of before Christian judges. Once all the points of the document were agreed to, oaths were taken, with the Muslims swearing on the Koran; sometimes the whole community took part in the oath-swearing ceremony.

In some capitulations the local Muslim elites were allowed to stay in control of their lands and castles and to remain as leaders of their communities. Under such an arrangement, a system of clientage and tribute was established as Muslim elites turned over part of their income to the crown and served with troops in time of war. Consequently, those who had once been enemies were now allies. However, even this military service was often carefully defined as part of the capitulation pact.

Once the city had agreed to surrender, the final preparations were made for the entrance of the king or commander and his entourage. Some of these ceremonies were rather ornate affairs, with pavilions and chapels set up outside the city walls, as occurred when Granada fell in 1492. A typical ceremony began with the transfer of power as the citadel, towers, and gates were handed over to the conquerors. If the defeated had negotiated from a position of relative strength, they might have been able to keep some of the fortresses under their command. The king's entrance into the city followed. This had the potential to be a tense event, as the conquered city was filled with angry people, and monarchs sometimes moved in with large bodies of troops for protection. Priests would lead the king and soldiers into the city, chanting hymns and carrying crosses and relics. Sometimes the conquerors would kiss the newly acquired ground in an act of thanksgiving. If there had been Christian captives in the city, as became increasingly common from the thirteenth century onward, these were usually incorporated into the ceremony.

One of the most symbolic and religiously charged acts occurred during the ceremonies that converted mosques into churches. Capitulation accords often specified which mosques would fall under Christian control and be converted to churches, but sometimes, as in Toledo in 1086, the Christians simply converted whichever mosques they wanted. The process consisted of a ritual cleansing, which, according to the Christians, eliminated the contamination of Mohammed and his followers. An altar was then built, priests were assigned to minister in it, and the mosque, now a church, was consecrated, usually to the Virgin Mary. Few if any physical changes were made to the building, and most of these changes were cosmetic, consisting of new frescoes and paintings. The consecration to the Virgin sometimes meant that the converted church ended up serving both the Christian and Muslim communities, as Mary, or Myriam, was holy to both.

Capitulation agreements were usually beneficial to both sides. For the Christians, it gave them title to their conquest and lordship over the lands that had once belonged to their ancestors. The king could use the new territories to reward his nobles, who were always hungry for land, and to encourage colonists to settle in them. The tributes were also welcomed by a crown that was often starved for money and resources. From the Muslim point of view, capitulations were seen as efforts to buy time until they could again gain military superiority and reclaim the land they were now giving up. The capitulation was only a temporary setback, allowed under Muslim law. Muslim cities were often careful to surrender peacefully, instead of being overrun in an assault, so that they could negotiate the best terms possible. A city that surrendered peacefully could expect to receive protection. On the other hand, a city that was taken by force of arms could expect slavery for its citizens and the threat of a conquering army loose within its walls.

BIBLIOGRAPHY

Burns, Robert I. "How to End a Crusade: Techniques for Making Peace in the Thirteenth-Century Kingdom of Valencia." *Military Affairs* 35 (1971): 1–15.

Burns, Robert I., Paul E. Chevedden, and Míkel de Epalza. *Negotiating Cultures: Bilingual Surrender Treaties in Muslim-Crusader Spain under James the Conqueror.* Leiden, Netherlands: Brill, 1999. The best source on the topic.

Harris, Julie A. "Mosque to Church Conversions in the Spanish Reconquest." *Medieval Encounters* 3 (1997): 158–172.

Nieto Soria, José Manuel. *Ceremonias de la realeza: Propaganda y legitimación en la Castilla Trastámara.* Madrid: Nerea, 1993. Particularly useful for victory ceremonies.

JARBEL RODRIGUEZ

[See also **DMA:** Reconquest; Spain, Christian-Muslim Relations; **Supp:** James I of Aragon, King.]

CAROLINGIAN RENAISSANCE. Now viewed in the context of a number of "renaissances" identified by scholars in the course of Western cultural history, the Carolingian renaissance is no longer seen as the sole savior of civilization between late antiquity and the twelfth century. Nor is it considered a renaissance in the traditional sense of a revival of classical languages and learning. From the perspective of the Carolingian monarchs and the scholars and churchmen whom they supported, their endeavors are better described as a reformation.

ECCLESIASTICAL REFORMS

The efforts of the early Carolingians and Anglo-Saxon and Irish missionaries to reform the Frankish church in the mid-eighth century mark the beginning of the reform movement. They sought the establishment of the ideal society as envisioned by the late antique fathers of the church—fully Christianized, where every rank in society fulfilled its obligations. Although the Christian church had been established in Gaul since the second century, pagan practices still flourished, and a large portion of the population was only nominally Christian. Furthermore, the disappearance of effective royal authority under the Merovingian dynasty in the late seventh and early eighth centuries had led to the effective dissolution of the institutions of the Frankish church—lands were alienated, and councils ceased to be held regularly, or at all. Ironically, some of the devastation of cities, bishoprics, and monasteries that led to the decline of the church, particularly in southern Francia, was the result of efforts by the progenitors of the Carolingian family to dominate the Merovingian kings.

With the encouragement of the Anglo-Saxon missionary Boniface, in 742 Carloman, the mayor of the palace of Austrasia from 741 to 747, called the first council of the Frankish church to be gathered in decades. Although only seven bishops attended, the council was a first step toward the reestablishment of an effective ecclesiastical hierarchy and institution. This council was followed by others held in the domains of both Carloman and his brother Pepin, who in 751 became the first Carolingian king. These early councils were concerned not only with ensuring that bishops knew and followed the canons of the church and that monks and nuns obeyed the strictures of the rule governing their community but also with lay moral issues, such as enforcing Christian restrictions on marriage. In this, however, the Carolingians were echoing the concerns of legislation enacted by the Merovingians before them. Carolingian concern for the church drew on a long tradition of similar Merovingian intervention. Yet royal support for strengthening the church and clerical morality did not translate into a church independent of royal control and abuse. The Carolingians continued, and even expanded, the custom of expropriating church lands for secular use. They did not hesitate to appoint bishops and lay abbots whose interests in the maintenance of the Christian church were minimal.

Assumption of kingship in 751 and strengthened authority both at home and over neighboring lands gave the Carolingians the opportunity to extend their reforms further. Charlemagne's decree of 789, the *Admonitio generalis,* commanded that all priests learn to read Latin, emphasizing that priests served as moral exemplars to their communities and insisting on the importance of preaching in addition to administering the sacraments. Furthermore, Charlemagne urged that bishops should establish a network of primary schools for children throughout the kingdom, an ambitious, if unrealized, goal. The emphasis on Latin marks a turning point in the language and culture of western Europe—some have called it "the birth of medieval Latin." From the Carolingian perspective, good Latin was essential to being a good Christian. Without good Latin, the priest did not know what he was saying when he chanted the liturgy or performed the sacraments, and through ignorance he could corrupt the teachings of the church. Boniface told the story of a priest who was found baptizing children "in the name of the fatherland and the daughter" *(in nomine patria et filia)* instead of "in the name of the Father and the Son" *(in nomine patris et filii).* Good Latin was also necessary to copy manuscripts correctly, for scribes ignorant in Latin were more likely to make errors, a particular problem when copying the holy books of the Bible.

For the Carolingians, as well as many modern scholars, the only good Latin was the classical Latin of Cicero and other great writers of Rome's golden age. Yet Latin had continued to be used through the early medieval period and had changed over the centuries—new words crept in from other languages, and the rules of grammar changed. While it was once thought that Latin had disappeared as a living language by the Carolingian period and that those who used it learned Latin as a second language, scholarship since the 1990s has emphasized the vitality of Late Latin into the ninth century. Indeed, Carolingian emphasis on "correct" classical Latin may well have killed the language as a spoken common tongue and forced the creation of early Romance languages.

While the classicizing Latin of the eighth and ninth centuries earned the period the title "renaissance," scholars now suggest that the Carolingians saw Latin as a way to access the texts of Christian late antiquity, not pagan classical antiquity. Alcuin of York revived the study of logic, which in antiquity had not been one of the more important of the seven liberal arts. Using late antique sources such as Cassiodorus's *Institutiones,* the works of Boethius, and the pseudo-Augustinian *Categoriae decem,* Alcuin fashioned the art of logic as an important intellectual tool for discussing Christian doctrine.

The Carolingian renaissance was also marked by the composition of new material, often biblical commentaries and theological treatises but including poetry, saints' lives, and princely biographies. Alcuin sought to produce a standardized version of the Bible, as the centuries since Jerome had produced his Vulgate edition had introduced a variety of errors into the text. Alcuin noted that this endeavor was supported by Charlemagne, and such standardization fits in well with other royal efforts to standardize liturgical and monastic practices. The Carolingians, who maintained close relations with the papacy, sought to replace local liturgical practices with the standard liturgy of Rome. The insistence on liturgical standardization bore intellectual fruit; the development of musical notation, which first appears in the early ninth century, was probably in response to the need to teach the Roman Gregorian chant to priests and monks all over Francia. The Rule of St. Benedict was also made the rule for all monasteries in the kingdom, overriding idiosyncratic rules established by the founders of the monasteries. Such standardization not only provided a convenient administrative tool but also created a sense of a single Catholic church, saying the same prayers and following the same rules as those elsewhere in Francia and Christendom.

SCHOLARSHIP

Perhaps the scholar who showed the full intellectual vigor of the Carolingian renaissance was John Scottus Eriugena, an Irish scholar at the court of Charles the Bald. Learned in Latin as well as Greek, Eriugena translated treatises from Gregory of Nyssa and Maximus the Confessor, introducing valuable strands of Platonic thought to the Latin church. But Eriugena was not just a translator—his five-book masterpiece, the *Periphyseon,* is a dialogue between a teacher and his student that runs some seven hundred pages in modern print, a vast learned exploration of the relationship between the creator and the created that drew heavily on Greek Platonic thought. While much of the scholarly activity of the Carolingian renaissance has been ascribed to a school founded by Alcuin at the court of Charlemagne at Aa-

chen, there is little evidence for such a school. Aachen, however, did become a seat of learning after Charlemagne's conquest of the Lombard kingdom in northern Italy in 774. A stream of Lombard scholars, such as Paul the Deacon, joined the king at Aachen, as well as Anglo-Saxon scholars such as Alcuin. Most scholars, however, stayed at the court for only a few years, being rewarded with abbacies and bishoprics in other parts of the kingdom. Aachen thus must have been intellectually lively but always with a changing cast of scholars. While in Charlemagne's day the majority of scholars were foreign, by the time of his grandson Charles the Bald most of the scholars in Francia were native born.

The classics did play a role in Carolingian learning, just a lesser one than previously thought. While Carolingian poets used nicknames drawn from the classical past, such as Flaccus, a nickname for Alcuin, and referred to Charlemagne's court of Aachen as the "new Athens" or the "new Rome," in reality they looked far more often to figures such as the sixth-century poet and bishop Venantius Fortunatus for inspiration. Alcuin's poetry in fact betrays the influence of only one classical author—Vergil. Einhard based his biography of Charlemagne—the first secular biography in centuries—on Suetonius's *Lives of the Caesars.* Most of the classical texts in existence have survived through copies made by Carolingian scribes. Charlemagne collected in his library such classical authors as Lucan, Terence, Statius, Claudian, Juvenal, Tibullus, Horace, Martial, Cicero, and Sallust.

The fact that Carolingian interest was in late antiquity rather than classical antiquity made their cultural and religious revival no less of an achievement. The impact of Carolingian emphasis on books and education can be seen in the production of manuscripts: some eighteen hundred manuscripts survive from the period 400 to 800, but from the ninth century alone, approximately seven thousand survive. This increase in manuscript production stimulated the development of a new writing style. At the monastery of Corbie developed the style of handwriting known as "Carolingian miniscule," a form of lowercase writing that is the source for the shape of printed letters today. This script was precise, clear, and readable, making it easily copied without mistakes as well as more efficient in terms of the number of strokes necessary to create each letter.

The Carolingian renaissance is somewhat of a misnomer—it was not so much a renaissance as a reformation, more an extension of late antique and early medieval learning and education than a revival of classical literature. Scholarship since the 1980s has shown that into the late seventh century both the lay and clerical elites of Merovingian Gaul were expected to be literate. Carolingian latinity was built firmly on a well-established Merovingian base. If a "dark age" did proceed this renaissance, it was a brief one. In its own era, the Carolingian renaissance impacted a relatively small association of Frankish elites and drew heavily on the intellectual resources of Anglo-Saxon England and Lombard Italy, where the study of the church fathers and the classics of Latin literature had continued unabated. The library attached to the cathedral of York was large and well known throughout western Europe for its collection of classical and patristic texts. Such evidence has led some scholars to postulate the existence of a Northumbrian renaissance of the early eighth century, which served to spur Charlemagne's reforms, just as an interest in ecclesiastical reform in Visigothic Spain served as another precursor. Constructing such a string of "renaissances" could be seen as an impediment to acknowledging the strong intellectual continuities between late antiquity and the early medieval period. The impact of the Carolingian renaissance, however, went far beyond its limited origins. The edited sacred texts, biblical commentaries, standardized liturgies, histories, and poetry became the bedrock texts for Latin Christian culture of the following several centuries.

BIBLIOGRAPHY

Bullough, D. A. "Albinus deliciosus Karoli regis: Alcuin of York and the Shaping of the Early Carolingian court." In *Institutionen, Kultur und Gesellschaft in Mittelalter: Festschrift für Josef Fleckenstein.* Edited by Lutz Fenske, Werner Rösener, and Thomas Zotz. Sigmaringen, Germany: J. Thorbecke, 1984.

Devisse, Jean. *Hincmar, archevêque de Reims, 842–882.* 3 vols. Geneva: Droz, 1975–1976.

McKitterick, Rosamond. *The Carolingians and the Written Word.* Cambridge, U.K.: Cambridge University Press, 1989.

———, ed. *Carolingian Culture: Emulation and Innovation.* Cambridge, U.K.: Cambridge University Press, 1994.

Nees, Lawrence. *A Tainted Mantle: Hercules and the Classical Tradition at the Carolingian Court.* Philadelphia: University of Pennsylvania Press, 1991.

Nelson, Janet. "On the Limits of the Carolingian Renaissance." *Studies in Church History* 14 (1977): 51–69. Reprinted in Janet Nelson, *Politics and Ritual in Early Medieval Europe.* London: Hambledon Press, 1986.

Sullivan, Richard E., ed. *The Gentle Voices of Teachers: Aspects of Learning in the Carolingian Age.* Columbus: Ohio State University Press, 1995.

Treadgold, Warren, ed. *Renaissances before the Renaissance: Cultural Revivals of Late Antiquity and the Middle Ages.* Stanford, Calif.: Stanford University Press, 1984.

Wallace-Hadrill, J. M. *The Frankish Church.* Oxford: Clarendon Press, 1983.

Wood, Ian. "Administration, Law, and Culture in Merovingian Gaul." In *The Uses of Literacy in Early Mediaeval Europe.* Edited by Rosamond McKitterick. Cambridge, U.K.: Cambridge University Press, 1990.

CHRISTOPHER HATCH MACEVITT

[See also **DMA:** Alcuin of York; Benedictine Rule; Boniface, St.; Carolingian Latin Poetry; Carolingians and the Carolingian Empire; Charlemagne; John Scottus Eriugena; Merovingians.]

CARTOGRAPHY. There is no medieval term to describe the process of drawing maps. The word "cartography" dates only to the beginning of the nineteenth century and is consequently something of an anachronism when applied to maps from the Middle Ages. In modern usage the term implies a systematic method of drawing pictures of the world, one that is based on a body of mathematical knowledge about projecting maps and has widely shared conventions of drawing and illustration. The lack of a medieval term points out both the rarity of maps in the Middle Ages and the diversity of the material that has been brought together in modern studies of medieval maps.

Maps were not common in the Middle Ages. Many tasks that are now accomplished with small maps or maplike diagrams—giving directions or recording land surveys, for example—were recorded in written accounts during the Middle Ages, if they were preserved at all. A few survivors notwithstanding, it appears that the habit of drawing sketch maps for daily use or quick reference was uncommon in the millennium before 1500. By contrast, most surviving maps from the Middle Ages depict large regions of the earth or the entire world. Those maps fall into several distinct groups—schematic diagrams of the world, narrative world maps, and nautical charts—which, despite some shared conventions, served different needs and derived from very different intellectual contexts.

Modern cartography is based on the idea that each spot on the surface of the earth is defined by a unique pair of numbers that refer to a specific place on a grid that covers the whole sphere—latitude and longitude. This idea of a geographical coordinate system has its origins in the work of ancient mathematicians and astronomers, most notably Claudius Ptolemy (active second century A.D.). The idea was known in the Islamic world throughout the Middle Ages and in Christian Europe from at least the thirteenth century, but it was very rarely used in Europe to make maps during the thousand years between 400 and 1400. To some degree, that lack reflects a paucity of available data. Latitude and longitude are both traditionally derived from astronomical observation. Since little ancient astronomical data was available during the Middle Ages and not many new observations were made until the fourteenth century, it would have been difficult to construct such an astronomically based map in the first place. More important, there seems to have been little expectation in medieval Europe that a map should be a faithful, scaled-down representation of the surface of the earth. Instead, for most of the medieval period, maps and geographical diagrams served most often as explanatory pictures for ideas about the shape and features of the earth and its place in a Christian cosmos. World maps in particular often carried implicit and sometimes very explicit messages about the Christian basis of geographical thought. In the so-called Psalter map, for example, a small world map of the thirteenth century, a large figure of Jesus Christ presides over the map of the world.

TYPES OF MAPS IN THE EARLY AND HIGH MIDDLE AGES

Very little is known about mapmaking in the early Middle Ages. Only a handful of maps or diagrams survive from the period between 500 and 1000, and it is difficult to derive any but the most vague conclusions from them. In general, though, neither the Byzantine world nor the Latin West showed much interest in the more mathematical aspects of ancient mapping. The works of Ptolemy and other astronomically influenced writers fell completely out of circulation in western Europe, and only the sparest references to them survive in the Byzantine world. Instead, geographical thought was dominated by descriptive geography of the sort found in ancient writers like Pliny the Elder, usually as transmitted through the works of late antique encyclopedists such as Isidore of Seville.

The "maps" associated with such texts are really diagrams, often meant to illustrate the idea that the world can be divided into zones, "climates," or continents (depending on the text). These pictures were often extremely schematic. The most common type is a circular diagram with an inscribed *T,* known in modern literature as an *O-T* (or *T-O*) map. The circle represents the ocean, surrounding the continents of Europe, Asia, and Africa, which are divided by a *T* that represents the Mediterranean Sea and the Nile and Tanais Rivers (or the Don). The implied, and sometimes explicitly marked, center of the circle is the city of Jerusalem. The prominent place given Jerusalem is a reminder of the almost metaphorical nature of such diagrams. *O-T* diagrams play a central role in the modern literature about early medieval maps, but a few chance survivals from this peri-

od hint at other traditions. The Cotton Map, a tenth- or eleventh-century Anglo-Saxon world map (named after its eighteenth-century owner), seems to reflect the influence of now lost Roman exemplars, and the plan of St. Gall, a ninth-century diagram of an ideal monastery in Switzerland, hints at the survival of Roman surveying techniques. Such maps were probably unusual even when first made, but they do provide hints of a more complicated story that has otherwise been lost.

The number of surviving maps increases dramatically after about 1100. The great majority are still diagrams of the *O-T* variety, but the period also sees the emergence of navigational charts and elaborate, encyclopedic world maps, as well as the beginnings of a revival of regional and local mapping. The world maps (called *mappae mundi* at that time and this) come in all sizes, from a few inches to several feet in diameter. Nonetheless, most share important traits. Nearly all are circular, and most are built around the framework of an *O-T* diagram. The larger *mappae mundi,* such as the Hereford map (late thirteenth century), housed at Hereford Cathedral, functioned as visual encyclopedias of God's creation as much as they were geographical descriptions. Most bear long texts explaining cosmological and geographical ideas as well as brief notes of historical, religious, or anthropological interest. In the later period such maps often bear astronomical and astrological information as well. The basic structure of the maps was extremely flexible, allowing mapmakers to incorporate new information as it entered circulation.

The thirteenth century saw the appearance of nautical charts of the Mediterranean, known as "portolan charts." The origin of these charts is a mystery, as the earliest surviving example, the *Carta Pisana,* (late thirteenth century), is clearly the product of a mature tradition. The maps are constructed around networks of compass bearings called rhumb lines (the compass was in use by the thirteenth century), and there seems to be a relationship between the maps and the books of sailing directions (or *portolani*) that contain information about the distance and direction between ports around the Mediterranean Sea. The modern name of the maps derives from that association. Whether the maps were actually used in navigation is another mystery, as the surviving examples were most likely never taken to sea. The portolans are remarkable both for their accuracy—they are the only medieval maps with instantly recognizable geographical outlines—and the persistence of the traditional form. Chart-making workshops in Italy and the western Mediterranean, especially in the Majorcas and Catalonia, maintained the basic format of the maps over several centuries, making minor adjustments and slowly increasing the geographical range of the charts. Some examples from the fourteenth century include the coast of northwest Europe and the British Isles; in the fifteenth century, some charts also began to show information derived from the Portuguese explorations of the coast of West Africa. Information from portolan charts found its way onto *mappae mundi*. There are also a few world maps, such as the so-called Catalan atlas (drawn in Majorca about 1375), that have the narrative content and cosmological overtones of the large circular *mappae mundi* but are built around an expanded portolan chart.

There is very little evidence about local and regional maps from any period of the Middle Ages. The great fame of some, such as Matthew Paris's thirteenth-century map of Britain merely points out the rarity of surviving examples. The list of local maps in J. B. Harley and David Woodward's *History of Cartography* counts barely a dozen examples before 1400 and only several dozen before 1500. Important among the surviving regional maps are a series of fourteenth-century Italian maps of the Holy Land, probably by Pedro Vesconte, one of which is especially remarkable for being built around a grid. There is also a group of fourteenth-century local maps from northern Italy, especially of the area around the Po River. All of the surviving regional maps are far enough apart in time and space that it is difficult to discern patterns of development, though some from the fourteenth and fifteenth centuries are related to the portolan tradition.

FIFTEENTH-CENTURY DEVELOPMENTS

Although its immediate influence can be overstated, the reintroduction of Ptolemy's *Geography* to western Europe at the beginning of the fifteenth century was of central importance to later European cartography. The text provided a theoretical explanation of the geometrical problems associated with projecting maps as well as a large body of geographical data. Some of the more expensive *Geography* manuscripts also came with a set of maps that could serve as models for copying. The earliest translation from Greek into Latin, made at Florence by Jacopo d'Angelo da Scarperia (about 1406), was notably flawed, though it remained the only available translation for more than a century. Despite the garbled text, the Latin version provided impetus for experiments in geographical mapping, experiments that were often associated with astronomy, which was also in a period of renewed activity. Mapmaking experiments using a coordinate system and some of Ptolemy's data began as early as the 1420s, especially in and around Vienna.

Only a very small number of people had the competence or interest to pursue the technical implications of Ptolemy's text—perhaps a few dozen over the course of the entire fifteenth century. More common was the incorporation of information from Ptolemy's lists of place names onto world maps. As early as the 1410s, the French cardinal Guillaume Fillastre commissioned a map for his manuscript *De situ orbis* by the ancient geographer Pomponius Mela, which shows strong influence from Ptolemaic models. In a more traditional context, the large circular world map drawn by the Venetian monk Fra Mauro around 1450 shows evidence of close critical reading of the *Geography*.

The regional maps included in many copies of the *Geography* may well have inspired the creation of modern versions of such maps. Several such modern maps appear in *Geography* manuscripts of the second half of the fifteenth century, though whether they were originally made for inclusion in the *Geography* is unknown. Still, the assimilation of the lessons and the data of the *Geography* was a long process. Despite the early experiments, the coordinate system did not become a standard tool for the making of new maps until the first third of the sixteenth century.

A CAVEAT

Survival rates for maps, indeed for any large-format single-sheet items, are tiny. For every map that survives, dozens did not. Even in the age of printing, when it became possible to produce hundreds of copies of any individual map, many early printed sheet maps survive in only one or two copies. Maps that are protected by being in books, such as *O-T* diagrams, have had a much better chance of surviving over the centuries, a fact that has perhaps skewed our sense of the range of medieval mapmaking. Entire genres of medieval maps, including painted wall maps, maps on fabric, and banners, are known only from passing references in descriptions or probate inventories. Similarly, most surviving maps are associated with courtly or monastic owners, but there is a certain amount of evidence documenting map ownership (especially portolan charts) in the probate inventories of fourteenth- and fifteenth-century Italian merchants. Although most of the surviving maps from the Middle Ages have been published and studied in detail, much information about ownership and distribution of maps—especially in the later Middle Ages—remains to be gleaned from archives.

BIBLIOGRAPHY

Durand, Dana Bennett. *The Vienna-Klosterneuburg Map Corpus of the Fifteenth Century: A Study in the Transition from Medieval to Modern*

Science. Leiden, Netherlands: E. J. Brill, 1952. Out of date in its premises and conclusions, but the only major study of early-fifteenth-century technical cartography in a Ptolemaic mode.

Edson, Evelyn. *Mapping Time and Space: How Medieval Mapmakers Viewed Their World.* London: British Library, 1999.

Harley, J. B., and David Woodward, eds. *The History of Cartography.* Volume 1: *Cartography in Prehistoric, Ancient, and Medieval Europe and the Mediterranean.* Chicago: University of Chicago Press, 1987.

Harvey, P. D. A. *Medieval Maps.* London: British Library, 1991.

———. *Mappa mundi: The Hereford World Map.* Toronto and Buffalo, N.Y.: University of Toronto Press, 1996.

International Geographical Union, Commission on Early Maps. *Mappemondes, A.D. 1200–1500: Catalogue.* Edited by Marcel Destombes. Amsterdam: N. Israel, 1964.

BENJAMIN WEISS

[See also **DMA:** Astrology/Astronomy; Exploration by Western Europeans; Geography and Cartography, Islamic; Geography and Cartography, Western European; Isidore of Seville, St.; Mappa Mundi; Navigation: Western European; Portolan Chart.]

CASIMIR III THE GREAT OF POLAND, KING

(1310–1370), king of Poland from 1333. After the death of an older brother in 1312, Casimir was in line for the throne. His mentor was the learned churchman and future archbishop of Gniezno, Jaroslaw. Casimir's marriage in 1325 to the newly baptized Aldona-Ona, the daughter of Duke Gediminas of Lithuania, promised a resolution of the conflict-ridden relations between Christian Poland and pagan Lithuania, and this pacification was symbolized at the wedding by the Lithuanian ruler's repatriation of perhaps thousands of Polish prisoners of war. Casimir succeeded to the throne on the death of his father, Władysław (Ladislaus) I, in 1333.

Casimir had a number of mistresses, with whom he seemed to get on better than his canonical spouses. Aldona-Ona was the first of his three wives, none of whom bore him a son, moving Casimir, with the consent of the nobles, to nominate his nephew, Louis of Hungary, as his heir. Casimir, however, did have a number of daughters and grandchildren whom he effectively used, through marriage, to cement alliances in Europe. He needed friends. The Bohemian king protested Casimir's accession, claiming the throne as his own, and the Teutonic Knights laid claim to territories that Casimir regarded as crown lands. In the first decade and a half of his reign, he managed to negotiate his way out of these difficulties, pointedly ceding claims to lands such as Silesia under Bohemian domination and parts of eastern Pomerania under that of the Teutonic Knights in return for the renunciation of the Bohemian claim to the Polish crown and the Knights' cession of other districts.

Twice in the 1340s Casimir's forces invaded eastern Galicia and in the wake began the incorporation of large new territories into Poland. Together with the concessions he wrested, through negotiation, from other princes or by marriage alliance, he almost doubled the size of the medieval kingdom, which he protected in an active castle-building campaign. His prestige grew over time, not least because of his patronage of the church and his promotion of education (he was effectively the founder in 1364 of what would become the Jagiellonian University of Kraków). He encouraged substantive and procedural legal and judicial reform aimed in part at the systematization of legal practice. He also supported policies, such as offering protection to the Jews and granting urban foundation charters, which turned out to be of real economic value. Late in his long reign he was something of an elder statesman, called upon for advice and even to arbitrate international disputes.

BIBLIOGRAPHY

Knoll, Paul W. *The Rise of the Polish Monarchy: Piast Poland in East Central Europe, 1320–1370.* University of Chicago Press, 1972. A thoughtful general introduction to Casimir's reign.

WILLIAM CHESTER JORDAN

[See also **DMA:** Poland; **Supp:** Kraków; Teutonic Knights.]

CASIMIR IV THE JAGIELLONIAN OF POLAND, KING

(1427–1492; grand duke of Lithuania, 1440–1492; king of Poland, 1447–1492). At the age of ten Władysław (Ladislaus) III (*b.* 1424; *r.* 1434–1444) succeeded to the Polish throne. His slightly younger brother, Casimir, began to play an important role in eastern European politics at the age of thirteen as a result of the assassination of Grand Duke Sigismund of Lithuania in 1440. Poland and Lithuania (the patrimony of Władysław and Casimir's father, Władysław II Jagiełło) were associated states. The effect of the dynastic union that came about from Władysław and Casimir's father's marriage to the Polish queen Jadwiga, however, was undermined by a compromise wrought from violent conflict that allowed the Lithuanians to maintain partial autonomy under a viceroy or independent grand duke "allied" by kinship. With Sigismund's death Władysław saw an opportunity to install his brother as viceroy in Lithuania, a move that could be interpreted as an attempt to shore up the union and limit the effective independence of the Lithuanian aristocracy from Polish royal control. Disgruntled Lithuanian nobles instead pledged loyalty to Casimir as grand duke; some of them possibly expected that this would lead to the dissolution of the union.

In the event, they were wrong. To be sure, Władysław III was distracted by other serious problems, especially the Turkish threat. His crusade against the Turks met a bitter end on 10 November 1444 at the battle of Varna, where Władysław himself fell. Thereupon, Casimir emerged as the most likely candidate for election (the constitutional process) to the Polish throne. He appears to have worked diligently to achieve the prize and was crowned king on 25 June 1447. The price he paid was a high one, however. Neither his Lithuanian noble subjects nor his Polish ones wanted their independence curtailed by the restrengthening of the union, and they managed to wrest from Casimir confirmation of their considerable privileges—the Lithuanians in the aftermath of creating him grand duke, the Poles somewhat later (November 1454), at a particularly difficult point in his reign.

Although the Turks continued to be a threat, the two major enemies Casimir faced were the Teutonic Knights and Muscovite Rus'. The Knights, who ruled Prussia, had managed to come into conflict with influential lords across Europe, including the pope and the Holy Roman Emperor. In 1454 their perceived highhandedness toward their own subjects sparked revolt. Prussian burghers and rural elites sought help from Casimir, who proceeded to incorporate Prussia into his domains while promising to respect the privileges of the upper estates. The move was premature. The Poles were defeated in September 1454, but Casimir was determined to rectify the situation. (It was at this point, November 1454, that he confirmed the privileges of the Polish nobility.) On 17 September 1462 the victory of Casimir's forces over the Knights gave him the clear advantage, and ultimately he succeeded in incorporating West Prussia ("Royal Prussia") into his domains, while confirming the remainder of the Prussian lands and their institutions to the Knights. But this rump state was clearly only a client of the crown.

Muscovite Rus' meanwhile was expanding its power considerably and dominating ever more of the principalities surrounding it. Novgorod in 1478 and Tver in 1485 fell under Moscow's power, a development of immense importance, since these principalities had periodically been allied with the Lithuanian state. The last years of Casimir's reign saw the first signs of the melting away of the eastern lands of the Grand Duchy, a process that would become a flood with Muscovite encroachments after his death.

BIBLIOGRAPHY

Stone, Daniel. *The Polish-Lithuanian State, 1386–1795*. Seattle: University of Washington Press, 2001. The most up-to-date major synopsis in English, although many matters remain controversial.

WILLIAM CHESTER JORDAN

[See also **DMA:** Jagiełło Dynasty; Lithuania; Muscovy, Rise of; Poland.]

CASPE, COMPROMISE OF (1412). On 31 May 1410 Martin I (*r.* 1395–1410), king of Aragon, died. His only son and heir had died the previous year. Martin had remarried after the death of his son in the hopes of conceiving another heir, but this effort had failed, and he also failed to name a successor. His death ended the long reign of the count-kings of Aragon, who had ruled since 1137, and threw the royal succession into chaos. The resulting interregnum plunged the peninsular realms of the Crown of Aragon (Catalonia, Aragon, and Valencia) into a crisis. Its resolution would forever change the political landscape of not only Aragon but of all Spain.

Five major contenders claimed the throne when Martin died. The early favorite was James, count of Urgell, a powerful Catalan noble and a descendant of Alfonso IV (*r.* 1327–1336). The second claimant was Frederick, count of Luna, Martin's illegitimate grandson, who, although he seems to have been Martin's choice as successor, was only nine years old. Louis of Anjou, the French descendant of another Aragonese king, John I (*r.* 1387–1395), was the third claimant. Alfonso, Duke of Gandia, and later his son, also made a bid for the throne. Finally, Ferdinand of Trastámara (also known as Ferdinand of Antequera), uncle of the king of Castile and regent, and the most powerful noble of that kingdom, rounded out the claimants. His claim came through his grandfather Pedro IV the Ceremonious (*r.* 1336–1387).

The interregnum created a serious social and political crisis that degenerated into violence, especially in Valencia and Aragon. As James and Ferdinand emerged as the two most serious challengers for the throne, followers of James of Urgell murdered the archbishop of Saragossa, who supported Ferdinand of Antequera. Catalonia managed to keep the peace and was influential in beginning the process that would lead to the election of the next king. With the help of the antipope Benedict XIII, the three realms each selected three representatives who would in turn elect the new king from among the claimants. The electors met at the Hospitaller fortress of Caspe on the Ebro River. Among them was the Dominican friar Vincent Ferrer, who, along with Benedict, was a staunch supporter of Ferdinand. With the help of Ferrer and Benedict and the threat of Castilian troops, which had already entered Valencia and Aragon to quell disturbances, Ferdinand was elected as the new king on 28 June 1412, bringing an end to the succession crisis. James of Urgell, after an initial pledge of fealty to the new king, went into open revolt in 1413. In a short time, however, Ferdinand's forces captured him, and he was sentenced to life imprisonment.

Modern Catalan historians have viewed the Compromise of Caspe as the beginning of Castilian hegemony over the peninsula and the end of the Crown of Aragon. Although the Compromise was probably the best possible outcome that contemporaries could hope for, there is little doubt that it gave the Trastámaras unmatched influence in Iberia. By 1469, the two branches of the House of Trastámara were again united when Ferdinand II of Aragon married his cousin Isabella of Castile, opening the way for the union of the two kingdoms.

BIBLIOGRAPHY

Bisson, Thomas N. *The Medieval Crown of Aragon: A Short History.* Oxford: Clarendon Press, 1986. Pages 134–136 provide a short but useful English introduction to the topic.

Dualde Serrano, Manuel, and Jose Camarena Mahiques. *El Compromiso de Caspe.* Saragossa, Spain: Institución "Fernando el Católico," Ayuntamiento de Caspe, 1976.

JARBEL RODRIGUEZ

[See also **DMA:** Aragon, Crown of (1137–1479); Valencia; Vincent Ferrer, St.]

CASTLE-GUARD, the obligation to provide garrisons for royal and baronial castles. This institution must be distinguished from that of castellans, officials holding authority over a castle and its dependent lands, either in their own name or on behalf of a lord or sovereign. While most recent considerations of castle-guard have focused on Norman and Angevin England, the recent decline in interest in military history has left it a neglected subject. The traditional definition of castle-guard emphasized its feudal nature; certain lands given in fief came with the obligation to provide garrison service for the lord's castle. Recent reconsideration of the definition of feudalism has to some extent disconnected castle-guard from land tenure. Castle-guard, as with other military and fiscal obligations, evolved as a service imposed whenever and wherever possible and thus is best understood on a local basis.

By the twelfth century, garrison obligations became fixed, particularly in France and England. When garrison duty was expected both in time of war and in peacetime, the obligation was often commuted to a monetary payment, which the lord might choose to use for other purposes at times when a garrison was not needed. If the service was expected only in wartime, however, it was more likely to be performed in person or by a substitute paid by the person owing castle-guard. Magna Carta stipulated that commutation of service for payment could not be extracted without the agreement of the man providing the service, suggesting that some lords may have demanded high fees instead of able bodies. Service was for a given time, perhaps two months; castles staffed by castle-guard thus had a rotating garrison, with fewer staff during the winter, when martial activities were less common. Despite the inadequacies of the system, royal English summons to perform castle-guard continued to be issued until 1327. However, many castles, such as the Tower of London, never had castle-guard as part of their garrisoning strategies.

Some studies of castle-guard have artificially separated feudal garrison services from other types of garrisoning. Castle-guard in Saxony as well as in France may have been imposed on free men of wealth, rather than on nobles who received land from the king or lord. Garrisoning in eleventh- and twelfth-century Hungary was one of many military duties tenants owed, while in the Christian kingdoms of Spain, citizens of frontier towns were often obligated to man the city walls and guard fortresses, a duty called *castellaria.* Although castles were found throughout western Europe and the Mediterranean, castle-guard was not. The scarcity of military manpower in the Latin east, for example, caused garrisoning duties to be included with other forms of military service, for the field army was made up of those who also had to garrison castles. Furthermore, the existence of the military orders, which held many of the larger castles in the Latin east, and the extensive use of mercenaries eliminated much of the need for castle-guard.

In the twelfth and thirteenth centuries, castle-guard was often commuted into a tax or cash payment, depending on circumstances. Castle-guard was most effective on frontiers. Frequent raids made castle garrisons a constant concern for border lords, but for effective service the lord needed a tight cluster of dependent lands established nearby. Otherwise lords depended on mercenaries to garrison castles. By the late Middle Ages, castle-guard survived only as a tax or money payment, rarely as military service performed without pay.

BIBLIOGRAPHY

Fügedi, Erik. *Castle and Society in Medieval Hungary (1000–1437).* Translated by J. M. Bak. Budapest, Hungary: Akadémiai Kiadó, 1986.

Prestwich, Michael. "The Garrisoning of English Medieval Castles." In *The Normans and Their Adversaries at War.* Edited by Richard P. Abels and Bernard S. Bachrach. Woodbridge, U.K.: Boydell Press, 2001.

Reynolds, Susan. *Fiefs and Vassals: The Medieval Experience Reinterpreted.* Oxford: Clarendon, 1994.

Suppe, Frederick. "The Persistence of Castle-Guard in the Welsh Marches and Wales: Suggestions for a Research Agenda and Methodology." In *Normans and Their Adversaries at War.* Edited by Richard P. Abels and Bernard Bachrach. Woodbridge, U.K.: Boydell Press, 2001.

CHRISTOPHER HATCH MACEVITT

[See also **DMA:** Castellan; Castles and Fortifications; Feudalism.]

CATHERINE OF SIENA, ST. (1347–1380), one of the great medieval mystics, known not only for her intimate connection to Christ but also for her active involvement in the care of the sick, charity, and the political events of her time. The twenty-third child of a Sienese dyer, at age six Catherine had her first vision of Christ in papal garb, a vision that forever shaped her view of the papacy. Her youth was marked by extreme piety, ascetic practices, and a refusal to marry. She took a vow of virginity and created an "interior cell" for her religious life within her family. A vision of St. Dominic led her to pursue a compromise between the cloister and the world by joining, in 1363, the Third Order of the Dominicans. Soon she was surrounded by a faithful group of followers, the Bella Brigata. In 1367 Christ wed her in a mystical marriage, often represented in art. She also exchanged hearts with Christ and saw herself living in Christ's heart, with her lips sucking his wound. Her increased ascetic practices, such as going without food for long periods of time, and her intense mystical experiences did not prevent her from pursuing a more active charity. She cared for the sick in the Hospital of Santa Maria della Scala and the leprosy hospital S. Lazzaro, where she herself contracted the disease and was miraculously cured.

In 1374 Raymond of Capua, eventually master general of the Dominican order, became her spiritual adviser and confessor. Later, he wrote her *vita* and tirelessly worked for her canonization. In 1375, while in Pisa, trying to avert Pisa's joining the antipapal league, she reportedly received the stigmata. In her *vita* Raymond depicts this event as similar to St. Francis's stigmatization. Imitating Francis's role for the Franciscans, Catherine could thus become the stigmatized saint for the Dominicans.

Her involvement in contemporary politics also increased during this period. In 1376 she traveled to Avignon, the seat of the papacy since 1309. She also wrote a number of letters to Pope Gregory XI, urging him to return the papacy to Rome, to organize a crusade, and to work for the reform of the church. These three themes were the guiding threads of most of her correspondence. Many of her letters are rhetorical masterpieces, using striking images and impassioned language. She stressed the pastoral responsibility of the clergy and decried clerical corruption. She also tried to work for peace between the city-states, especially Florence, and the pope.

In January 1377 Pope Gregory XI finally returned to Rome, where he died in March 1378. After a tumultuous election, Bartolomeo Prignano of Bari was confirmed as Pope Urban VI in April. A few weeks later his tyrannical rule alienated the cardinals, who, claiming to have voted "under duress" the first time, left Rome and proceeded to elect another pope, the Frenchman Robert of Geneva, as Clement VII in September. The existence of two popes and two papal courts, one at Rome and one at Avignon, created the Great Schism that was to divide the church until the Council of Constance in 1417. Ending the Schism became the all-consuming task of Catherine's last years. She wrote letters to rulers, urging them to adhere to Urban, as well as many letters to Urban exhorting him to moderation while unquestioningly supporting his right to the papacy. In 1378 she moved to Rome and made herself a "martyr for the Schism," eating less and less, displaying more and more penitence, trying to intervene with ever greater urgency in the deadlocked situation of the divided church. In April 1380, weakened from fasting and after a last public act of confession, Catherine died.

In addition to being a great mystic and tireless political activist, Catherine was one of the most accomplished early Italian authors. Though initially unable to read and write, she dictated her works to her followers and to Raymond of Capua. Her writings consist of about 380 letters, covering the years 1370 to 1380; the *Dialogue of Divine Providence,* dictated between the fall of 1377 and October 1378; and twenty-four *Prayers,* written down by her followers between December 1378 and the time of her death. The *Letters* are addressed to a wide range of people: popes, cardinals, kings, queens, and local political leaders, but also ordinary Italians to whom she offered spiritual guidance. The *Dialogue,* a transcript of an enraptured dialogue she held with a divine interlocutor in front of her followers, centers on the image of the

St. Catherine of Siena Receiving the Stigmata. *This miniature from Bibliothèque municipale de Poitiers shows the saint trampling a demon.* BIBLIOTHÈQUE MUNICIPALE DE POITIERS, MANUSCRIT 55 (334), FOLIO 175.

Catherine. Her feast day is 30 April. In 1866 she was named copatron of Rome (with Sts. Peter and Paul) and, in 1939, of Italy (with St. Francis of Assisi). In 1970 Pope Paul VI declared her a doctor of the church.

Catherine is often depicted in art. In addition to paintings and sculpture there was an early popular tradition of drawings on paper, reportedly in thousands of copies, chronicling Catherine's life and deeds, which were hung in churches and which people could take home for personal devotion. Catherine was a beloved figure whose cult grew quickly. She is most often shown with a crown of thorns and a crucifix, sometimes with a scourge or holding a heart, a lily, or a book. Other popular motifs are her stigmatization and the mystical marriage with Christ. Some paintings highlight her political role, such as her leadership in Pope Gregory XI's return to Rome.

St. Catherine stands out among the mystics of her time through her extremely affective relationship with Christ, rich in stunning images; her intellectualized doctrine of penitence and divine providence evident in the *Dialogue*; and her extraordinary devotion to the unity of the church.

BIBLIOGRAPHY

PRIMARY WORKS

Catherine of Siena. *The Dialogue.* Edited by G. Cavallini. Translated by Suzanne Noffke. New York: Paulist Press, 1980. (Translation of *Dialogo della divina provvidenza.*)

———. *The Prayers of Catherine of Siena.* Translated by Suzanne Noffke. New York: Paulist Press, 1983. (Translation of *Le orazioni.*)

———. *The Letters of Catherine of Siena.* Edited by G. Cavallini. Translated by Suzanne Noffke. Vol. 1, Binghamton, N.Y.: Medieval and Renaissance Texts and Studies, 1988. Vol. 2, Tempe, Ariz.: Center for Medieval and Renaissance Studies, 2000.

Raymond of Capua. *The Life of Catherine of Siena.* Translated by Conleth Kearns. Wilmington, Del.: Michael Glazier, 1980.

SECONDARY WORKS

Atti del simposio internazionale Cateriniano-Bernardiniano, Siena, 17–20 aprile 1980. Edited by Domenico Maffei and Paolo Nardi. Siena: Accademia Senese degli Intronati, 1982.

Atti del simposio internazionale di Studi Cateriniani, Siena-Roma, 24–29 aprile, 1980. Rome: Curia Generalizia O. P., 1981. An important collection of essays on Catherine of Siena.

Cavallini, Giuliana. *Catherine of Siena.* London and New York: Geoffrey Chapman, 1998. An excellent study of Catherine's thought by the editor of some of her works.

Noffke, Suzanne. *Catherine of Siena: Vision through a Distant Eye.* Collegeville, Minn.: Liturgical Press, 1996. Contains an extensive annotated bibliography of works in English.

bridge and is structured by four requests she makes to Christ: for her to experience true penitence, for church reform, for peace in the world, and for divine providence to embrace all humans. Her works were disseminated widely, translated, and printed in many editions.

Soon after her death Raymond of Capua began to work for Catherine's canonization. He wrote her life, the *Legenda maior,* between 1385 and 1395. Thomas Caffarelli, another Dominican, composed another biography, *Legenda minor,* early in the fifteenth century. Since 1374, a collection of miracles associated with Catherine had been in circulation. All these documents played a role in the official canonization proceedings initiated by Francesco Bembo, bishop of Castello in Venice. Twenty-six witnesses to Catherine's saintliness were heard, their testimony transcribed in the *Processo castellano* (1411–1416). But due to the Schism and its slow resolution, it was not until 1461 that Pope Pius II canonized

Scott, Karen. "St. Catherine of Siena, 'Apostola.'" *Church History* 61 (1992): 34–46.

RENATE BLUMENFELD-KOSINSKI

[See also **DMA:** Canonization; Dominicans; Hagiography, Western European; Mysticism; Schism, Great.]

CHARITY. Historians have often characterized charity in medieval western Europe as inadequate and indiscriminate and have suggested that for benefactors the main object of giving to the poor was increasing their own chances of salvation. What has been termed the "purchase of paradise" certainly played a role in the motives for charitable giving among philanthropic individuals and institutions in medieval society, but contemporary concepts of the poor and charity were always more complex than this. Perceptions of poverty and charity changed in several fundamental ways over the course of the Middle Ages, as did the reality of poor relief funded by the landowning classes.

MEDIEVAL CONCEPTS OF THE POOR AND CHARITY

Writing at the beginning of the fourteenth century, Robert Mannyng of Brunne in his didactic treatise *Handlyng Synne* recounts the story of a rich man, Piers, who finds himself facing the judgment of a heavenly host in a dream. All that can be found to counterbalance his manifold sins of covetousness is an instance of his throwing a loaf of bread at a beggar for want of a better missile:

> The fair angels said, "what do we find?
> Of him we find no good deeds
> made unto God, except a loaf
> Which at the poor man Piers did *drofe*."
> (*Handlyng Synne*, p. 142, lines 5655–5658)

Despite the bread being given "with no good will," it nevertheless, as a marginal act of charity, saves Piers from damnation. On waking, the chastised Piers takes the next opportunity to give one of his cloaks to a beggar—who then immediately sells it to raise some cash, much to the indignation of Piers. However, falling asleep again Piers sees God wrapped in the cloak. Piers is informed by the Almighty that giving to the poor is as good as giving to God: "What you gave him in charity, / Was really given unto me" (p. 144, lines 5737–5738). Piers awakes and pledges his wealth to good causes in order that he can live a life of poverty:

> Blessed be all poor men
> For God Almighty loveth them,
> And well it is for the poor who are here,
> They are with God both true and dear.
> (p.144, lines 5741–5744)

Encapsulated in this story are several aspects of the traditional medieval patristic concept of the poor and their place and role in society. First, the didactic is aimed at the rich. The lesson to be learned is that in order to avoid the unpleasantness of a space in purgatory reserved for covetous sinners, those with wealth should give to those without in the form of alms. Second, the inference that both beggars were perhaps undeserving of Piers's charity is deemed irrelevant to the worthiness of the gift (even when hurled at the recipient). Third, the poor are made representatives of God or Christ on Earth and the natural inheritors of the kingdom of Heaven.

This last point was a commonplace tradition derived largely from the fundamental patristic works of late antiquity. St. Thaschus Cyprian (*d.* 258), St. Ambrose (*d.* 397), St. Gaudentius *d.* 410), St. Augustine of Hippo (*d.* 430), St. John Chrysostom (*d.* 407)—the list of church fathers elaborating on the biblical lesson that Christ was represented on Earth by the poor is long and almost without stricture. Peter Chrysologus, a fifth-century bishop of Ravenna, summed up the patristic attitude: "a beggar's hand is Christ's poor box, for whatever a poor person accepts Christ accepts." By the twelfth century the *Pauperes Christi* had become an ingrained concept, finding its ultimate expression in the Franciscan movement of the thirteenth century. The rules of St. Francis informed brethren of the order that they were to:

> go confidently after alms, serving God in poverty and humility, as pilgrims and strangers in this world. Nor should they feel ashamed, for God made himself poor in this world for us. This is that peak of the highest poverty which has made you . . . heirs and kings of the kingdom of heaven, poor in things but rich in virtues . . . for the sake of our Lord Jesus Christ wish never to have anything else in this world. (Lambert, *Franciscan Poverty*, pp. 38–40)

A popular Franciscan exemplar of the 1270s described how Christ was liable at any time to disguise himself as a poor man in order to test the almsgiving commitment of the rich. The moral of the story being that *all* paupers should be viewed as the embodiment of Christ on earth; thus providing them with charity would constitute direct remuneration against sin come Judgment Day.

The *Secunda secundae* of the *Summa theologiae* of Thomas Aquinas (1224–1274) provides a more altruistic theory of charity, where the emphasis is placed upon the genuine compassion present in the provider of poor relief, rather than the reward to be expected as a benefactor to the poor. Acts of caring for the poor were to proceed

St. Martin of Tours. *The legend of the Roman soldier-saint who shared his cloak with a beggar is here depicted in a stained glass roundel from the Rhineland (ca. 1490–1500).* PHOTOGRAPH BY NEIL S. RUSHTON. REPRODUCED BY PERMISSION.

in a Christian attitude of benevolence without expectation of reciprocity or temporal rewards from God. Love for the poor involved not only the donation of money or material goods but also love for the poor as fellow human beings. Benefactors of the poor were advised to take the example of St. Martin of Tours (*d.* 397), who was willing to cut his cloak in two so that a beggar might receive his unquestioning charity. Aquinas's lengthy disquisition conforms to the traditional patristic conceptual framework, whereby the worthiness or otherwise of a person begging for alms was not an issue that should concern the almsgiver.

Following Aquinas, it was certainly the givers of alms—the rich—who were the main concern of most medieval didactic literature and sermonizing. This was based upon the assumption that one of the primary methods of lubricating the passage through purgatory was for the rich to ensure that almsgiving had formed a fundamental part of their daily lives.

The concept of purgatory, though present from late antiquity, seems not to have become wholly articulated

until the twelfth century—and not fully sanctioned by the Roman church until the Second Council of Lyon in 1274. But it was the rich person's desire to escape the worst excesses of a purificatory interlude in purgatory that fueled most discussions of almsgiving throughout the later Middle Ages. Robert Mannyng of Brunne's version of the bread-throwing story was one of many, aimed primarily at expostulating the ability to find Grace through the provision of charity to the poor.

Didactic literature tended to treat the poor as an amorphous social group, largely existing as a means by which those reading the treatises could alleviate purgatorial suffering—through providing one or more of the charitable seven works of mercy (feeding the hungry, giving drink to the thirsty, clothing the naked, receiving strangers, tending the sick, visiting prisoners, and burying the dead).

But despite the continuity of the patristic tradition of holy poverty in literary texts into the post–Black Death period and the continued assurances by writers

Souls Being Raised Up from Purgatory. This 15th-century Carthusian manuscript from Mount Grace Priory in England shows the power of prayer (at the altar, above) and almsgiving (distributing bread, below). THE BRITISH LIBRARY. REPRODUCED BY PERMISSION.

that charity of any kind would pay off come Judgment Day, there was a clear and obvious shift in contemporary attitudes to the poor and poor relief throughout Europe in the later Middle Ages. Michel Mollat suggests that fear and loathing of the poor was already commonplace by the later twelfth century, and he cites one of the All Saints' Day sermons of Peter of Blois (*ca.* 1135–1211), in which Peter shouted to the crowd in a skewed imitation of Christ's sermon on the mount: "Blessed are the poor in spirit . . . but not all of them." It certainly seems—assuming social values can be discerned at all accurately from literary and legal texts—that by 1300 there was a change in the perception of the poor. In Nicole Bozon's *Les Contes moralisés* (*ca.* 1300), for example, for every conception of the poor as representatives of innocence, there is a warning about providing for the unworthy among them. And the English *Book of Vices and Virtues* (*ca.* 1325) was translating ideas from a French text of the thirteenth century when admonishing that it was a "grete synne" to give any sort of charity to "harlotes and to mynstralles."

It would thus certainly be a mistake to think that writers in the High Middle Ages were not concerned

about differentiating between the recipients of alms. Brian Tierney has lucidly delineated the debate—concerning the identity of those deserving of charity—among canonists of the twelfth century following in the wake of Gratian, whose ideas were to be a decisive reference for the rest of the Middle Ages. But it is nevertheless true that by the fourteenth century there was an increased urgency to define the different kinds of poor in terms of their legitimacy as recipients of relief. Much of the rhetoric was aimed at the friars, whose voluntary poverty had been under attack from as early as the 1250s by the likes of the Parisian academic William of St. Amour, and from the 1320s by the papacy itself. In England the apostolic poverty of the friars was attacked most vehemently by Richard Fitzralph in the immediate post–Black Death period and by the Lollards later in the century. David Aers discusses the Lollard claim that the friars were leeching wealth from the country and depriving the true poor of charity: "And thus they deprive poor men with their false begging; they take falsely from them their worldly goods, by which they should sustain their life and body, and they deceive rich men of their alms, and maintain or persuade them to live in falseness, against Jesus Christ" (*Community, Gender, and Individual Identity*, pp. 25–26).

But the friars composed an articulate response to this kind of criticism of their voluntary poverty. In 1380 Richard of Maidstone was able to draw on the full weight of John Chrysostom in his rebuttal of Lollard criticism. Alms were to be given to any beggar who asked for them and not just the infirm, blind, and incapacitated. Such alms were conferred on Christ himself, who was being represented by the friars. According to Maidstone, Chrysostom fully condoned able-bodied beggars on the proviso that they prayed for the donor's soul, which of course the friars were only too willing to do. In Italy, the Franciscan Bernardino of Siena and St. Antoninus, the Dominican bishop of Florence, were influential advocates of the voluntary poverty of the friars and were able to disseminate the doctrine and defend their orders against criticism through constant rounds of preaching. Studies of testamentary bequests from Valladolid, the Lyonnais, Paris, London, Florence, and Norwich in the later Middle Ages demonstrate that the friars remained among the most popular recipients of posthumous bequests from all levels of will-making society, suggesting that their populist preaching on the legitimacy of voluntary poverty was at least a partially successful counter to the voices of reform.

But in many ways, medieval debates over the legitimacy of the friars' right to poor relief obscures from view

Caritas. This etching by Pieter Bruegel the Elder (d. 1569) shows the distribution of bread and other charitable works in a 16th-century town. MUSEUM BOIJMANS VAN BEUNINGEN, ROTTERDAM. REPRODUCED BY PERMISSION.

a parallel set of perceptions of the poor in general. The poorest sections of society were defined by an entrenched social hierarchy in whose interest it was to categorize the poor in their own terms and for their own social purposes.

In the wake of the demographic catastrophe of the Black Death, rhetoric opposing charity for the "able-bodied poor" increased markedly. The difficulty of procuring laborers to work the land encouraged a belief among the landholding classes that those poor who survived the epidemic were more prone to laziness and sedition. In his study of charity in late medieval Florence, John Henderson points out that the Florentine chronicler Matteo Villani (d. 1363) was outraged that "men and women no longer wanted to work at their normal trade because of the incredible abundance of everything. . . . And the cost of labor and manufacture in any craft or trade increased inordinately to twice its previous level" (*Piety and Charity in Late Medieval Florence,* p. 300). So it is little surprise that attitudes hardened to

the poor who were not sick, disabled, or too old to work. The rhetoric of those expected to bestow charity to the poor began to quickly discard patristic teaching that valued the sanctity of all poor people and the benefit to the rich of giving unquestioning charity to all who asked for it.

In the immediate aftermath of the Black Death governmental legislation began to supplement religious writings in outlining an attitude toward the able-bodied poor. In the 1349 Ordinance of Labourers, the English government was in little doubt that if a person was able-bodied, then they were not due any form of charity:

Because that many valiant Beggars, as long as they may live of begging, do refuse to labour, giving themselves to idleness and vice, and sometimes to theft and other abominations; none, upon the said pain of imprisonment, shall, under the colour of pity or alms, give anything to such, who may labour, or presume to

■ anniversary distributions ▨ weekly distributions and accommodation

The Changing Ratios of Types of Charitable Provision at Westminster Abbey, 1300–1540.

favour them in their sloth, so that thereby they may be compelled to labour for their necessary living.

Yet, the patristic ideals of charity were not easily loosened from medieval society. Writers with as divergent ideological platforms as William Langland, Agnolo di Tura, Phillipe de Mézières, and St. Antoninus all condoned a patristic ideal of charity while at the same time suggesting various policies for imposing discrimination in almsgiving.

These parallel ideologies of unquestioning charity in the patristic mold and the newer ethos of discriminatory charity were not only captured in secular and religious literature. They can also be discerned in the practical reality of the various systems of charitable provision functioning during the Middle Ages, where they often operated in tandem.

MEDIEVAL SYSTEMS OF CHARITABLE PROVISION

Most forms of charity during the Middle Ages were dispensed by the church, hospitals, confraternities, cor-

porations, or individuals. It is the lack of centralized, state-subsidized forms of relief that have most often led to historiographical criticisms of medieval charity. It is frequently argued that measured systems of welfare that genuinely helped the poorest members of society were not generally instituted until the Reformation. While it is true that European states did not introduce centrally funded and administered systems of poor relief until the sixteenth century, those uncoordinated forms of relief that existed before 1500 were nevertheless providing substantial amounts of charity in a variety of ways. However, both the methods and the quantity of charitable provision underwent fundamental changes in the wake of the socioeconomic dislocations of the mid-fourteenth century.

This can be shown by reference to the distributions of charity made by Westminster Abbey in England. In the pre–Black Death period the Benedictine monks acquired substantial estates from the foundation of Queen Eleanor of Castile (1244–1290), from which part of the proceeds were to go toward the funding of an anniversary distribution of charitable provision. These anniversary distributions frequently exceeded the £100 mark and were always given out in pennies. This would have occasioned thousands of applicants turning up at the abbey almonry outside the west gate of the main precinct in the hope of alms. In the Great Famine year of 1315 the anniversary was accorded an extra £50, demonstrating a direct reaction on the part of the monks to the effects of dearth and hardship among those members of society always likely to fall into poverty in the case of harvest failure. But these large set-piece distributions of charity, although aiding the plight of the benefactor's soul in its afterlife purgation, were not the most effective means to relieve poverty. A certain level of indiscriminate charity at such mass distributions was inevitable. The poor of Westminster and London were much more likely to find genuine relief in the smaller, but more regular weekly distributions supplied at the abbey almonry from various funds.

In the aftermath of the Black Death both the levels and types of charity administered at the abbey changed. The overall amounts of annual charity in the later fourteenth century were reduced to an average of around £108 from the pre–Black Death level of around £178, while greater proportions of this reduced amount were now diverted to funding weekly distributions of charity and the accommodation of the poor, sick, and elderly within the almonry. Part of this change was due to the demographic disaster caused by the plague, which meant that there were simply now fewer poor to relieve. But the changed priorities of charity also conformed to the new orthodoxy regarding the poor and their relief that had gained prevalence after 1348. Throughout the rest of the Middle Ages until the abbey's suppression in 1540 the monks attempted to manage their ever-increasing charitable funds so that the majority of it was expended on the known, local, and "deserving" poor. When charitable funds were (due to royal endowments) at their highest in the sixteenth century, approximately 81 percent was being expended on accommodating the poor, elderly, and sick or on weekly charitable provision as opposed to the old style anniversary doles.

Anniversary distributions of charity were, however, still carried out on a scale large enough to encourage several hundred or even thousands of applicants at a time until the Dissolution. This was partly due to the constraints imposed on the abbey by benefactors' grants, but it also demonstrated that patristic attitudes toward charity were still at least tacitly accepted alongside the more recently established strictures that indiscriminate charity encouraged able-bodied begging and should therefore be condemned.

Florentines Helping the Impovershed outside the City Walls. *Depicting the famine of 1329, this miniature by Domenico Lenzi is from* Il Libro del Biadaiolo. BIBLIOTECA LAURENZIANA, FLORENCE, TEMPI 3, C. 58R. © BIBLIOTECA MEDICEA LAURENZIANA. REPRODUCED BY PERMISSION.

A study of the 1535 taxation of the English church, known as the *Valor Ecclesiasticus,* has shown that, although few monasteries could match Westminster Abbey's charitable resources, most houses in England were providing the different types of charity—anniversary distributions versus weekly distributions and accommodation—at ratios similar to those of the royal abbey. The total monastic provision has been estimated at between £10,630 and £13,265, a substantial amount of poor relief that was not matched by secular funding until the beginning of the seventeenth century.

Monastic charity provided considerable amounts of poor relief in England throughout the Middle Ages. In many other parts of Europe, however, monastic charity seems to have diminished after the thirteenth century, with its place being taken by hospitals and confraternities. The greatest period of hospital foundation in the medieval West was during the twelfth century. This was during a period of renaissance in canonical learning, and writers such as Gerhoh of Reichersberg were keen that the traditional charitable institutions of late antiquity be restored in cities and in the countryside. By 1200 most urban areas in western Europe had at least one hospital, and many others existed in remoter rural areas, often sited along highways and pilgrimage routes. Many of these hospitals, although often episcopal or secular foundations, were administered by regular canons and were frequently governed by the rule of St. Augustine, making them in some respects special types of monasteries, carrying out many of the functions of a religious house. But usually a hospital foundation-charter confirmed that the raison d'être of such institutions was to feed and shelter the poor, infirm, and elderly. This concept soon became the subject of regulation by the church, which prescribed the adoption of official hospital statutes at the Fourth Lateran Council in 1215. These statutes were primarily concerned with the religious life and administration of hospitals and focused on ending corruption. But it is clear that, during the twelfth and thirteenth centuries, the means-testing of the potential recipients of hospital charity was not the primary concern of the founders and governors. Some hospitals, such as the reformed En Colom hospital in Barcelona (1236), even stipulated in their foundation ordinances that vagabonds were to be sheltered within its walls. This conformed with patristic attitudes toward the poor and the concept that charity was due to all who asked for it.

There was a certain amount of specialization in medieval hospitals. Most particularly, thousands of *leprosaria* (the chronicler Matthew Paris thought there were as many as 19,000 in Europe by the mid-thirteenth century) were founded in the late eleventh and twelfth centuries and could most often be found outside the gates of cities. These catered exclusively to lepers, segregating them from society but allowing inmates to live an institutionalized existence with a certain amount of funding and care. There were also hospitals exclusively for the blind at Paris, Chartres, and London, and many hospitals were designated exclusively for the sick or for abandoned children. However, the majority of hospitals founded in the pre–Black Death period were not defined as institutions that exclusively served ill or disabled patients and could usually offer only rudimentary medical treatment to inmates. More often hospitals were designed and perceived as refuges for the poorest members of society, who were as likely to be healthy but homeless as sick and in need of institutional care. These hospitals could be very large indeed: the Hôtel-Dieu in Paris had beds for more than 400 inmates, while those at Nüremberg and Regensburg could accommodate 200 and 250 people respectively. But more usually urban hospitals accommodated between 12 and 30 inmates, as at Narbonne, Genoa, Lisbon, and Hamburg, while rural hospitals could be even smaller, such as the Catalan hospital of Lleida with only seven beds or the numerous small hospitals with less than twelve beds that proliferated in rural Anjou and Poitou.

In the post–Black Death period hospitals, like other institutions and individual landlords, were deprived of resources due to falling rents and land values. This meant that in general fewer beds were available for the poor than was the case prior to around 1350. Although the dramatic population decline due to the plague may have meant there were fewer poor to accommodate in hospitals, it is still true that there was a severe curtailment of charitable provision in hospitals throughout Europe to the detriment of those most in need. The well-studied French hospitals at Meaux, Montbrison, and Tonnerre all follow a pattern familiar throughout Europe of falling revenues after 1350 followed by reductions in expenditure through the fourteenth and fifteenth centuries and the subsequent contraction of inmate numbers. In some towns such as Aix-en-Provence the smaller hospitals simply ceased to exist.

However, the ideological shift in attitudes toward the poor and charity that accompanied the socioeconomic dislocations of the post–Black Death period allowed the administrators of hospitals to change their priorities of admittance in order to avoid the accumulation of debt. This meant that while many of the older hospitals were suffering economic hardship, it was still possible for new types of more selective institutions to be founded. During the course of the fourteenth and fifteenth centuries both new and old hospitals were able to increasingly restrict their facilities to the "deserving" poor. This usually consisted of the sick and elderly rather than the destitute and vagabonds, and frequently the foundation ordinances of new institutions would specify that those receiving accommodation were to be the "local" poor.

In cities and towns these hospitals became increasingly administered by the governing lay corporations rather than religious orders. In the Holy Roman Empire the great majority of urban hospitals founded in the post–Black Death period were endowed by lay benefactors, either individuals or corporations, rather than religious organizations, and the subsequent management of these hospitals was conducted by city governments. Municipal authorities even acquired hospitals from the orders, such as in Gdańsk in 1382 when the city corporation assumed control of the Hospital of the Holy Spirit from the Teutonic Order, in order that more rigid controls could be imposed on its administration. In the fourteenth and fifteenth centuries frequent complaints were made that hospitals run by the religious orders in the empire were badly administered and more concerned with installing fee-paying lodgers (so-called corrodians) than with looking after the poor and sick. The reaction by secular authorities was to initiate programs of hospital provision in the form of *Gasthaüser*—small-to-medium-sized tightly regulated hospitals exclusively for the sick, lame, old, and local poor. By the mid-fifteenth century towns such as Lübeck, Cologne, Bremen, Hamburg, Frankfurt, Lüneburg, Freiburg im Breisgau, Rostock, Emden, and Münster all had at least one secular-run *Gasthaüse* where a century before most hospitals had been administered by various religious orders.

These hospitals were frequently to be found on the margins of cities and towns, partly through their evolution from earlier *leprosaria* (which were always outside the city gates) but also, in the case of new foundations, because of the constraints of resources and the need to build on less expensive real estate. This was certainly the case for St. Gertrude's Hospital in Emden, East Frisia, where in 1505 the town administrators were compelled to move the fifteenth-century *Gasthaüse* from a central location in the town to outside the northern gate due to falling income from the endowment and bequests. The pattern of shrinking resources available for *Gasthaüser* in the late fifteenth and early sixteenth century was a common problem in German towns and cities. It was exacerbated by many secular-run hospitals frequently falling victim to administrative corruption and poor management, so that by the Reformation municipal hospitals in the empire were often being criticized for the same shortfalls for which hospitals managed by religious orders had been censured since the fourteenth century.

Throughout medieval western Europe there were also thousands of lay associations, usually known as confraternities or religious guilds, many of which had charitable functions. Among the most intensively studied of European confraternities are those of Florence, where there were more than 160 in operation at one time or another during the later Middle Ages. Many of these were little more than small religious confraternities existing for the religious benefit of their members, but at least three Florence associations had, among their expenses, considerable charitable responsibilities. These were known as the Misericordia, the Spedale del Bigallo (later called the Compagnia della Vergine Maria), and the Madonna di Orsanmichele. The documentary sources of the confraternity of Orsanmichele demonstrate the methods used by this wealthy association for the relief of the poor

in the city and the changing institutional attitudes toward poverty and charity.

The earliest records of Orsanmichele are statutes dating from the end of the thirteenth century, which show that at this time most of the company's charity was directed at the voluntary poor of Florence, that is, the friars. The "wretched" were also due alms, however, and it is clear that at this time a patristic view of the poor and charity was an orthodoxy accepted by the confraternity. The first surviving account rolls for Orsanmichele date from 1324 to 1325 and show that by this time priorities had changed somewhat. From an income of almost 15,000 lire, approximately 12,750 lire were distributed as charity, but the friars in Florence received only 2 percent, and general distributions to beggars accounted for only 4 percent. The remainder was given as *limosina per la città* (alms throughout the city) to named individuals who had been designated as deserving recipients of the confraternity's charity by its members. A majority of these recipients were women—between 66 and 77 percent through the year—and of the men who received alms many were employed when the cash was given to them. This is suggestive of a company policy that not only supplied charity to the worthy poor, such as the sick, widows, and young mothers, but also condoned the provision of relief to the able-bodied, but working poor as part of a general system of welfare.

In years of particular dearth the fraternity of Orsanmichele joined forces with the city commune and other confraternities to supply charity as an emergency reaction. The chronicler Domenico Lenzi described how, during the famine of 1328–1329, people would flock to Florence from the surrounding countryside, swelling the number of poor in the city and putting immense pressure on the resources of all the charitable organizations. During the spring of the extremely severe famine year of 1347 Orsanmichele was dealing with as many as 9,000 people per day in search of alms, an obligation that increased the fraternity's charitable spending to more than 11,000 lire that year.

Orsanmichele continued to provide large amounts of poor relief for a generation after the first outbreak of the Black Death, although the priorities of provision became increasingly directed at the respectable poor within the city and less at the able-bodied working poor and beggars. By the end of the fourteenth century, however, the fraternity was spending much more of its falling income on religious devotions than on poor relief, and by 1429 only 1.1 percent of its expenditure was distributed as charity. By the fifteenth century the confraternity had ceased to be a major charitable institution in the city, and its place had been taken by a number of substantial new or refounded hospitals.

Both the intellectual concept of charity and the reality of poor relief changed during the course of the Middle Ages, most noticeably during the fourteenth century as a result of the socioeconomic dislocations caused by the Black Death. Canonists were certainly discussing the issue of discrimination in charitable giving prior to 1348, but it was not until the demographic catastrophe caused by the plague that the ideology, policy, and logistics of charity became fundamentally altered. The patristic view of the poor as holy representatives of Christ on Earth became tempered by a new ethos that alms were due only to the "deserving" poor, and able-bodied beggars became increasingly more likely to be flogged than given aid. However, the old patristic idea of charity never subsided completely. Churchmen, aristocrats, and wealthy merchants were as keen at the end of the Middle Ages (and beyond) to pay alms to have large numbers of poor at their funerals and anniversaries as they had been at the beginning. Charity based on Christian compassion remained throughout the period of the Middle Ages one of the best ways for the rich to mitigate the pains of purgatory and supplied one of the only strategies of survival for the always numerous poor.

BIBLIOGRAPHY

PRIMARY WORKS

Aquinas, St. Thomas. *Summa Theologiae*. Edited and translated by Thomas Charles O'Brien. London: Eyre and Spottiswoode, 1974.

Langland, William. *The Vision of Piers Plowman*. Edited by Terence Tiller. London: BBC, 1981. B-text.

Mannyng, Robert, of Brunne. *Handlyng Synne*. Edited by Idelle Sullens. Medieval and Renaissance Texts and Studies 14. Binghamton, N.Y.: Center for Medieval and Early Renaissance Studies, State University of New York at Binghamton, 1983.

SECONDARY WORKS

Aers, David. *Community, Gender, and Individual Identity: English Writing 1360–1430*. London: Routledge, 1988. Contains a discussion of attitudes to poverty and almsgiving in *Piers Plowman*.

Brodman, James William. *Charity and Welfare: Hospitals and the Poor in Medieval Catalonia*. Philadelphia: University of Pennsylvania Press, 1998. The best study of medieval Spanish hospitals.

Fehler, Timothy G. *Poor Relief and Protestantism: The Evolution of Social Welfare in Sixteenth-Century Emden*. Brookfield, Vt.: Ashgate, 1999. Includes a discussion on medieval systems of poor relief in the small town of Emden, Germany.

Geremek, Bronislaw. *Poverty: A History*. Translated by Agniezka Kolakowska. Oxford: Blackwell, 1994. A general study of perceptions of the poor and charity in medieval and Early Modern Europe.

Harvey, Barbara. *Living and Dying in England, 1100–1540: The Monastic Experience*. Oxford: Clarendon, 1993. Contains an insightful chapter on monastic charity at Westminster Abbey.

Henderson, John. *Piety and Charity in Late Medieval Florence*. Chicago: University of Chicago Press, 1994. Excellent study of the confraternities and hospitals of late medieval Florence.

———. *The Renaissance Hospital in Florence and Italy*. New Haven, Conn.: Yale University Press, 2003. New, comprehensive study of the development of the hospital in Italy from the later Middle Ages into the Renaissance.

Lambert, Malcolm David. *Franciscan Poverty: The Doctrine of the Absolute Poverty of Christ and the Apostles in the Franciscan Order, 1210–1323*. London: S.P.C.K., 1961. Seminal study of Franciscan poverty.

Le Goff, Jacques. *The Birth of Purgatory*. Translated by Arthur Goldhammer. Chicago: University of Chicago Press, 1984. Lucid discussion of the concept of purgatory in the High Middle Ages.

Mollat, Michel, ed. *Efitudes sur l'histoire de la pauvreté*. 2 vols. Paris: Publications de la Sorbonne, 1974. Collection of essays studying poverty and charity throughout the Middle Ages, mostly concentrating on French examples.

———. *The Poor in the Middle Ages*. Translated by Arthur Goldhammer. New Haven, Conn.: Yale University Press, 1986. Standard study of poverty in western Europe from late antiquity to the sixteenth century.

Pope, Stephen J. "Aquinas on Almsgiving, Justice, and Charity: An Interpretation and Reassessment." *Heythrop Journal* 32 (1991): 167–191. Good discussion of Aquinas's ideas on charity.

Ramsey, Boniface. "Almsgiving in the Latin Church: The Late Fourth and Early Fifth Centuries." *Theological Studies* 43 (1982): 226–259. Examination of early patristic attitudes to almsgiving.

Rawcliffe, Carole. *Medicine for the Soul: The Life, Death, and Resurrection of an English Medieval Hospital*. Stroud, U.K.: Sutton, 1999. In-depth survey of St. Giles's Hospital in Norwich.

Rosenthal, Joel Thomas. *The Purchase of Paradise: Gift Giving and the Aristocracy, 1307–1485*. London: Routledge and Kegan Paul, 1972. An analysis of chantry foundations and testamentary evidence in England.

Rubin, Miri. *Charity and Community in Medieval Cambridge*. Cambridge, U.K.: Cambridge University Press, 1987. Study of St. John's Hospital in Cambridge that includes a wide-ranging discussion of medieval concepts of poverty.

Rushton, Neil. "Monastic Charitable Provision in Tudor England: Quantifying and Qualifying Poor Relief in the Early Sixteenth Century." *Continuity and Change* 16, no. 1 (2001): 9–44. Examination of monastic charity at the end of the Middle Ages in England.

Rushton, Neil S., and Wendy Sigle-Rushton. "Monastic Poor Relief in Sixteenth-Century England." *Journal of Interdisciplinary History* 32 (2001): 193–216. Statistical analysis of monastic charity recorded in the *Valor Ecclesiasticus* of 1535.

Tierney, Brian. *Medieval Poor Law: A Sketch of Canonical Theory and Its Application in England*. Los Angeles: University of California Press, 1959. Unsurpassed study of charity in medieval canon law.

NEIL S. RUSHTON

[See also **DMA:** Black Death; Friars; Hospitals and Poor Relief, Western European; Mendicant Orders; Purgatory, Western Concept of; **Supp:** Poverty.]

CHARLES IV, EMPEROR (1316–1378). Charles IV, Holy Roman Emperor, was born in Prague, the son of John of Luxembourg and Elizabeth of Bohemia. He was baptized Wenceslas after the tenth-century saint, in the tradition of the Bohemian dynasty. In 1323 at the age of seven the young prince accompanied his father to the court of Charles IV of France. The French king became his godfather, and the boy adopted his name during the ceremony of confirmation. Charles spent his youth in France, where he received a formal education at the French court and the University of Paris.

Charles returned to Bohemia in 1333 and ruled alongside his father until the latter's death in 1346. That same year, the German princes deposed the excommunicated emperor Louis IV the Bavarian and with the support of the papacy elected Charles in his place. The death of Louis in 1347 ensured a peaceful succession. Charles immediately began a program of cultural reform and urban renewal in Prague that was strongly influenced by his experience in France. In 1348 he founded Prague University, the first institution of its kind in central Europe, on the model of the universities of Paris and Bologna. He promoted the bishopric of Prague to an archbishopric. He also fostered the cult of St. Wenceslas by composing an account of his life and by constructing a sumptuous chapel to the saint in St. Vitus's Cathedral in emulation of Ste. Chapelle in Paris. Unlike most rulers of his time, the emperor fostered a literary culture and composed an autobiography. The kingdom of Bohemia grew apace with the city of Prague. Charles was married four times, and each marriage added new territories to his kingdom and new allies to his court. Charles eventually traveled to Rome in 1355 to be crowned by the pope.

The most innovative and lasting contribution of Charles's reign was the Golden Bull *(chrysobullon).* Issued in 1356, this document fundamentally altered the constitution of the Holy Roman Empire by limiting the number of electors participating in the election of the king of the Romans to seven princes: the archbishops of Cologne, Mainz, and Trier; the king of Bohemia; the duke of Saxony; the margrave of Brandenburg; and the count-palatine by the Rhine. No other princes or church officials were allowed to participate in the election. A majority vote from the electoral princes assured the lawful succession of the candidate and his right to receive the imperial crown from the hands of the pope (who was otherwise excluded from the election process). The Golden Bull became the most important constitutional document in the Holy Roman Empire and retained its legal authority until the early nineteenth century. The new electoral system seemed to herald the end of hereditary succession, but Charles lobbied successfully for the election of his son Wenceslas, who was crowned king of the Romans in 1376, at the age of fifteen. Charles died two years later in Prague, on 29 November 1378.

BIBLIOGRAPHY

Charles IV. *Karoli IV Imperatoris Romanorum vita ab eo ipso conscripta; et, Hystoria nova de Sancto Wenceslao Martyre / Autobiography of Emperor Charles IV and His Legend of St. Wenceslas.* Edited by Balázs Nagy and Frank Schaer. Budapest, Hungary, and New York: Central European University Press, 2001.

Crossley, Paul. "The Politics of Presentation: The Architecture of Charles IV of Bohemia." In *Courts and Regions in Medieval Europe.* Edited by Sarah Rees Jones, Richard Marks, and A. J. Minnis. York, U.K.: York Medieval Press, 2000.

Stoob, Heinz. *Kaiser Karl IV, und seine Zeit.* Graz, Austria: Styria, 1990.

SCOTT G. BRUCE

[See also **DMA:** Chrysobullon; Elections, Royal; Prague; **Supp:** Louis IV the Bavarian, Emperor; Wenceslas, St.]

CHASTITY BELT. Ever so slowly, museums are reclassifying so-called chastity belts as simply large belts, girdles, hunting-dog collars, or farm animal harnessings. It is hard to imagine how credence was ever gained for the belief that medieval husbands and lovers, even if they fantasized about the possibility in the very late Middle Ages (an alleged picture is dated 1405), compelled their wives and mistresses to wear contraptions that would preserve their chastity while they were away on business, on a quest, or at war—and for years at a time. How could such a mechanism have been designed to permit the normal activities of urination, evacuation, menstruation, and hygiene, yet prevent both anal and vaginal sexual penetration? What materials would be needed? Wood, cloth and leather would not suffice; they could too easily be removed. Metal, then? How could serious chafing be avoided (even with the addition of soft cloth or pliant leather)—for by definition a device that absolutely preserved chastity needed to be worn day and night, day in and day out, and, in the case of crusaders' wives and mistresses left at home, for years at a time? Assuming that such a contraption could be designed, there had to be a way to remove it when the lover or husband returned. But if it were fitted with a lock to which he had the key, it would have been possible for the woman to hire a locksmith to free her from the contraption. The obvious absurdity of the so-called chastity belt notwithstanding, some late medieval fantasists, many modern writers of historical romances set in the Middle Ages, and even some curious historical studies assume that sexual concerns for purity or for male control of women's bodies in the Middle Ages stimulated the widespread use of "chastity belts."

Chastity belts are available in contemporary sex shops for fetishistic practices and pornography. Of course, some of these are but alleged to be reproductions of "authentic" medieval contraptions. Indeed, the very phrase "chastity belt" for a device intended to prevent a woman from engaging in sexual relations (or for one meant to be used in fetishistic sexual play) does not have a rich history in the modern vernacular languages. The phrase in medieval Latin sources, *cingulum castitatis*, however, occurs fairly frequently among clerical authors but has a completely different connotation. Christians are urged to put on or gird themselves with chastity or virginity much as they are urged, following St. Paul's injunctions in Ephesians 6: 11–17, to "take unto [themselves] the whole armour of God," to have their "loins girt about with truth," and to have on the "breastplate of righteousness." Their "feet" should be "shod with the preparation of the gospel of peace." Other accoutrements include the "shield of faith," "the helmet of salvation," and the "sword of the Spirit." It is possible that the extraordinary admiration of virginity and chastity in the Middle Ages together with the various "tests" (such as ordeals) for these in medieval romances gave rise to the persistent belief that women, especially aristocratic women, were regularly tormented with chastity belt contraptions throughout the period.

BIBLIOGRAPHY

Dingwall, Eric. *The Girdle of Chastity: A Medico-Historical Study.* Paris: Divan, 1922. One of the curious studies mentioned above (and once kept locked, at least in Princeton University's library).

Doctor Caufeynon [pseud.]. *La ceinture de chasteté: Son histoire, son emploi autrefois et aujourd'hui.* Paris: Société parisienne d'editions, 1904. Another of those curious studies, this one by a pseudonymous author.

Kelly, Kathleen. *Performing Virginity and Testing Chastity in the Middle Ages.* London and New York: Routledge, 2000.

Migne, J.-P., comp. *Patrilogiae cursus completus, series latina.* 221 vols. Paris: Garnier, 1844–1864. Word and phrase searches of this source attest to the medieval metaphorical usage of the phrase "chastity belt."

WILLIAM CHESTER JORDAN

[See also **Supp:** Sexuality.]

CHILDBIRTH AND INFANCY. Surrounded by both joys and anxieties, childbirth united women and men across classes, regions, and religions in medieval Europe even as differences of class, region, and religion produced divergent practices and concerns. The history of childbirth and the postpartum period in medieval Europe is inherently difficult to reconstruct as it was embedded in the lives of women and the household, neither of which normally generated public documents. Nevertheless, creative uses of a variety of source materials have considerably expanded our understanding of the practices and attitudes related to childbirth and the care of the mother and neonate.

DANGERS OF CHILDBIRTH

A study of Florence in the early fifteenth century has shown that close to one-fifth of all young married women died from childbirth-related causes. Paleopathological investigations (studies that employ scientific diagnostic techniques to assess mortality and morbidity in the past) have confirmed that the childbearing years (approximately ages nineteen to thirty-nine, or twenty-five to thirty-five in one study of northern England, where the age at first marriage was later) were indeed the years of highest differential mortality between men and women. Death may have been due not only to complications in labor but to perinatal infections and preexistent conditions, such as tuberculosis, that weakened a woman's ability to sustain the demands of birth. Given the absence of reliable mechanisms of birth control and consequently high birthrates (it is likely that the "average" medieval woman carried at least six pregnancies to term, and in many cases the number was much higher), the potential dangers of childbirth must be multiplied several times over for any given woman. Repeated childbirth also increased the mother's probability of dysfunctions later in life, such as uterine prolapse and incontinence.

MEDICAL KNOWLEDGE AND PROFESSIONAL CARE

While women—kinswomen, neighbors, and in the later Middle Ages, specialized midwives—seem to have had primary responsibility for childbirth throughout Europe, men were certainly interested parties and can be located in various peripheral roles. The general medical learning of literate male practitioners granted them authority to advise in matters of fertility, and by the late Middle Ages male physicians and surgeons were both supervising normal births (especially of the upper classes) and intervening in difficult ones.

Almost every general medical compendium contained a few chapters on difficult birth, uterine prolapse, and retention of the afterbirth, yet detailed instructions on the management of childbirth were to be found in only two texts. The first, the *Gynaecia*, by the late antique writer Muscio, derived from a Greek text by the second-century physician Soranus. Muscio itemized the characteristics of the good midwife and the information she needed to manage normal births. He also addressed pathological conditions, including malpresentations of the fetus that were illustrated by a series of figures that sometimes circulated independently of the main text. The other source of detailed obstetrical instructions was a tenth-century surgical text by Abu 'l-Qāsim al-Zahrāwī (in Latin, Albucasis), which addressed malpresentations of the fetus and mechanisms to extract the dead fetus and the afterbirth. Both Muscio's illustrations and al-Qāsim's text circulated among physicians and surgeons through the end of the Middle Ages.

Midwives were clearly professionalized in the Mediterranean world of late antiquity, where they were responsible for women's gynecological as well as obstetrical needs. With the slow disintegration of the urban environments that supported medical specialization, however, the midwife disappeared, although the concept of the midwife remained, enshrined in Roman law and in such canon law texts as Gratian's *Decretum*. (The legal figure of the *honesta matrona*, "honorable, upstanding matron," who served certain functions in ecclesiastical proceedings, such as testing for virginity, was explicitly distinguished from the midwife and should not be confused with her.) In more common use, such as in saints' lives, the term "midwife" seems to have applied to any woman who assisted at birth, not specialized practitioners. The twelfth-century Italian medical writer Trota saw herself and her audience not as midwives but as caretakers of women's general medical conditions; basic obstetrical procedures are barely mentioned in her text. Research on medical practitioners or female occupations in areas as diverse as eastern Spain and urban Flanders has produced no women claiming "midwife" as an occupational title up through the mid-fourteenth century. Data from France (whose medical practitioners have been most extensively studied) do not yield any *ventrières* prior to 1292 and then only in the metropolis of Paris. The shift toward specialized midwifery, at least in northern Europe, arose out of two different forces. As urban centers matured, concerns for poor relief led municipalities to hire midwives to provide free or subsidized services to women, beginning around the turn of the fourteenth century. Formal licensing, insofar as it concerned mid-

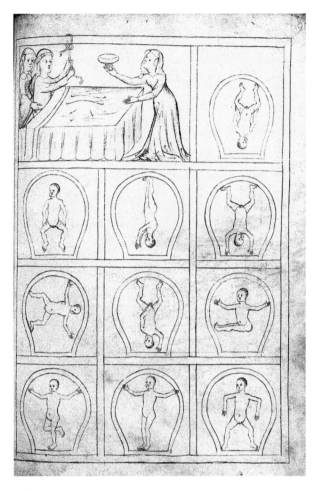

The Fetus in Utero. BODLEIAN LIBRARY, OXFORD, MS LAUD MISC. 724, S. XV, FOL. 97.

wives' medical knowledge, was established in Germanic areas only much later, the earliest known example coming from Brussels in 1424. Even here, concern focused more on their moral character and their willingness to defer to the medical expertise of physicians than on their own competence in obstetrics.

The other kind of licensing, that instigated by the church, had a different motivation: concern that the newborn might die before it had received baptism, a sacrament usually administered about a week after birth. After the Fourth Lateran Council in 1215, baptism of the newborn took on new urgency and became the only sacrament that could be performed by a layperson, even a woman. Priests were instructed to teach laypeople emergency baptism formulae. As specialist midwives emerged, the clergy soon recognized the need to train them. Thomas of Cantimpré, writing in the mid-thirteenth century, incorporated obstetrical material from Muscio into his encyclopedia for parish priests. In France, church leaders targeted midwives for special su-

Cesarean Section. *This German woodcut of 1483 depicts the birth of the Antichrist.* THE WELLCOME TRUST. REPRODUCED BY PERMISSION.

pervision to ensure their knowledge of baptism formulae. A 1311 Paris synod instructed that every vill (a township or parish) should have skilled midwives *(obstetrices peritae)* who were sworn to perform emergency baptisms. By 1365 a Meaux synodal collection details procedures for electing and examining either one or two midwives per parish. Surprisingly, no similar data for either municipal midwives or ecclesiastical appointments have yet been found for southern Europe.

Another striking outgrowth of the concern for baptism was the development of cesarean section. A better term for the procedure as it was practiced in the later Middle Ages would be *sectio in mortua* ("cutting open of the dead woman") since it was performed when the woman had already died. It was assumed that any child born this way would die soon after its mother. The concern was only to save its immortal soul, which explains why it took so long for medical writers to take note of the procedure.

OTHER AIDS IN CHILDBIRTH

Medical interventions, even at their most efficacious, could have done little to alleviate the dangers of such common obstetrical emergencies as hemorrhaging and acute infections. Another kind of aid was needed. Chanting, religious charms, wearing inscribed amulets and scrolls, or even eating inscriptions written on apples or cheese helped ensure safe deliverance of mother and child. The most common was the so-called *peperit* charm, which listed, first, Mary's birth of Christ *(Maria peperit Christum),* then Anna's birth of Mary and Elizabeth's of John the Baptist. Also common was the *Sator arepo tenet opera rotas,* an ancient magical palindrome often written in the form of a square. Despite their general popularity (birth paraphernalia were confiscated from numerous monasteries in England at their dissolution in the sixteenth century), there was some skepticism about their utility. The author of a late-fourteenth- or early-fifteenth-century Middle English gynecological text, *The Knowing of Woman's Kind in Childing,* included a charm-inscribed scroll in his list of birth aids but warned that these were no substitute for the direct ministrations of a midwife.

A number of saints had reputations as protectors in childbirth: the Virgin Mary, Mary Magdalene, St. Anne, St. Leonard, and above all St. Margaret of Antioch. In Margaret's legend, she was swallowed by a dragon only to emerge miraculously from the beast's belly. As an early thirteenth-century English version of her life suggested, "In the house where a woman is lying in labour, as soon as she recalls my name and my passion, Lord, make haste to help her and listen to her prayer, and may no deformed child be born in that house."

THE EVENT OF BIRTH

Evidence for the actual conduct of birth is slim. Artistic depictions of childbirth (such as the birth of the Christ child or Mary herself) usually show a serene postpartum scene, where the mother is lying peacefully in bed as the child is bathed and swaddled; few actually depict women in the throes of labor. Most unusual is the detailed account of the labor of Isabel de la Cavalleria, a noble lady of Zaragoza. Isabel, having just been widowed, asks a notary to witness the birth so that there be no suspicion of deceit in the birth of the heir. Besides two midwives, there are two other male witnesses as well as a man (perhaps her kinsman) who holds Isabel in his lap during the delivery of the child.

Even before the development of professionalized midwives, it seems to have been highly unusual for a woman to give birth alone or with just one attendant.

How women without networks of kinswomen and neighbors fared is harder to determine. We know virtually nothing about the management of childbirth in rural areas, although as in urban communities home birth was most common. Some hospitals were established for pregnant women from the thirteenth century on. While the majority seem to have been for poor women or, as was said of St. Bartholomew's in London, for "[single] women who have done amiss," in Douai a hospital was established in 1274 solely for use by female citizens of the town. Such institutions were hospitals not in the modern sense of advanced medical care facilities but rather in the sense of hospices that offered primarily food and shelter. The charter for the hospital in Douai, for example, includes no reference to the provision of midwifery care, and it is only in 1378 that we find the first record of midwives appointed to work at the maternity hospital of the Hôtel Dieu in Paris.

Postpartum conditions of the mother were discussed at greater length in medical treatises than was birth itself. Failure of the afterbirth to descend was recognized as demanding emergency intervention, as was failure of the lochia to flow. Trota's *Treatments for Women* has a famous description of how to repair tears in the perineum, and problems with milk production, vaginal pain, and uterine prolapse also merited attention.

LYING-IN AND CHURCHING

A period of postpartum seclusion seems to have been observed throughout western Europe among Christian women. (Jewish and Muslim women likely had similar practices, though little work on their traditions has thus far been published.) The so-called lying-in period involved approximately four to six weeks of confinement in the home or other domestic setting, which corresponded approximately to the duration of the lochial flow from the uterus after childbirth. It seems to have been motivated not only by a concern to seclude the recently delivered mother and relieve her of regular household duties but also to protect the newborn infant. A regulation from Douai from 1293 invokes banishment for any woman who does not complete the full lying-in period.

At least for certain classes, the lying-in period involved visits by neighbors and kinswomen, an obligation mentioned several times by Christine de Pizan in her 1405 conduct guide for women, *Livre des trois vertus* (Book of the three virtues). We find similar rituals among aristocratic and bourgeois women in northern Italy at the same period, where enormous investments

St. Margaret. *The patron saint of childbirth is here shown emerging from a dragon's belly.* VICTORIA AND ALBERT MUSEUM, LONDON/ART RESOURCE, NY. REPRODUCED BY PERMISSION.

were made in clothes for the new mother, bed linens, trays, and other domestic furnishings. The lying-in period ended, for Christian women, with the ceremony of churching (also called "purification"), which seems to have become a more important rite for women in northern Europe, where it generated its own liturgy, than in the south. This rite, the only one specifically for women,

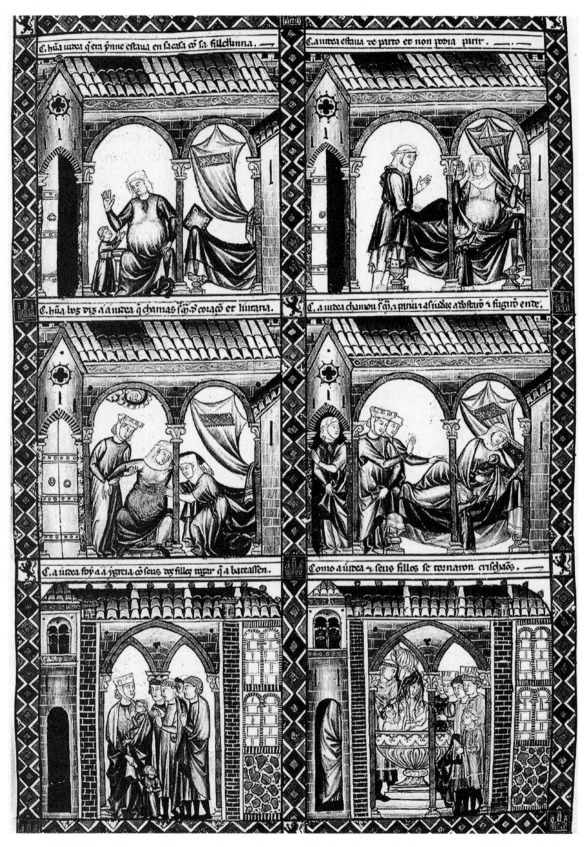

Pregnancy, Childbirth, and Baptism. *Miniatures from a 13th-century MS of* Las Cantigas de Santa María. *Real Biblioteca de lo Escorial.*
THE ART ARCHIVE/REAL BIBLIOTECA DE LO ESCORIAL/DAGLI ORTI. REPRODUCED BY PERMISSION.

was sometimes withheld by the clergy as a way of policing women who had conceived outside of marriage. In England, the ceremony of churching was often accompanied by a feast put on by the father to celebrate and commemorate the birth of his heir.

Artistic depictions from throughout Europe suggest that swaddling of the newborn was a universal practice. A description of swaddling and care of the newborn from the ninth-century Persian physician al-Rāzī was inserted into the popular *Trotula* texts and circulated throughout Europe. Provisions for a wet nurse (yet another factor that distinguished upper- from lower-class women), would often have been made prior to the birth, more often by the father than the mother. We also know something about wet-nursing through debates or regulations about the practice across religious lines; a council in Sens in the thirteenth century, for example, forbade Christian women from nursing Jewish children. In the Muslim world, wet-nursing was assumed to create a permanent relationship with the child, which, especially in the case of male children, allowed the nurse a wider circle of intimate social relations when the child was grown. There were some medical debates about the virtues of mother's milk versus that of a wet nurse since the physiology of milk production suggested that the woman nursing was bound to have an effect on the child. Yet maternal milk was not seen as inherently better: both Italian writers and the author of the Middle English *Knowing of Woman's Kind* argued that the milk of the newly birthed mother (what we now call the colostrum) was not good for the child, the English author noting that the child should not nurse from its mother until it had nursed from nine other women.

Wet-nursing, while it was the only alternative to maternal feeding, nevertheless probably contributed to high neonatal death rates, as, naturally, did abandonment. Data from fourteenth- and fifteenth-century Florence, where foundling hospitals were established, show female foundlings suffered higher rates of abandonment and then of death when placed in the care of wet nurses. Girls put out to nurse by their parents, however, survived better. The best nurses were those whose own children had died or had been given up to another, cheaper nurse or even a foundling hospital to make way for a "more worthy" child from a wealthy family. Like most other aspects of the social practices and ideological views surrounding childbirth and infancy in medieval Europe, this had consequences that went far beyond the mere biology of procreation.

BIBLIOGRAPHY

PRIMARY WORKS

Barratt, Alexandra, ed. *The Knowing of Woman's Kind in Childing: A Middle English Version of Material Derived from the "Trotula" and Other Sources.* Turnhout, Belgium: Brepols, 2001.

Cabré, Montserrat, trans. "Public Record of the Labour of Isabel de la Cavalleria. January 10, 1490, Zaragoza." *The Online Reference Book for Medieval Studies.* http://orb.rhodes.edu/birthrecord.html.

Green, Monica H., ed. and trans. *The "Trotula": A Medieval Compendium of Women's Medicine.* Philadelphia: University of Pennsylvania Press, 2001.

SECONDARY WORKS

Baumgarten, Elisheva. "'Thus Sayeth the Wise Midwives': Midwives and Midwifery in Thirteenth-Century Ashkenaz." *Zion* 65 (2000): 45–74. In Hebrew with English summary.

Elsakkers, Marianne. "In Pain You Shall Bear Children (Gen. 3:16): Medieval Prayers for a Safe Delivery." In *Women and Miracle Stories: A Multidisciplinary Exploration.* Edited by Anne-Marie Korte. Leiden, Netherlands: Brill, 2001.

Giladi, Avner. *Infants, Parents, and Wet Nurses: Medieval Islamic Views on Breastfeeding and Their Social Implications.* Leiden, Netherlands: Brill, 1999.

Grauer, Anne L. "Life Patterns of Women from Medieval York." In *The Archaeology of Gender: Proceedings of the Twenty-Second Annual Conference of the Archaeological Association of the University of Calgary.* Edited by Dale Walde and Noreen D. Willows. Calgary: University of Calgary Archaeological Association, 1991.

Klapisch-Zuber, Christiane. *Women, Family, and Ritual in Renaissance Italy.* Translated by Lydia G. Cochrane. Chicago: University of Chicago Press, 1985.

Lee, Becky R. "Men's Recollections of a Women's Rite: Medieval English Men's Recollections Regarding the Rite of the Purification of Women after Childbirth." *Gender and History* 14 (2002): 224–241.

Musacchio, Jacqueline Marie. *The Art and Ritual of Childbirth in Renaissance Italy.* New Haven, Conn.: Yale University Press, 1999.

Rieder, Paula M. "The Implications of Exclusion: The Regulation of Churching in Medieval Northern France." *Essays in Medieval Studies* 15 (1998): 71–80.

Schäfer, Daniel. *Geburt aus dem Tod: Der Kaiserschnitt an Verstorbenen in der abendländischen Kultur.* Hürtgenwald, Germany: Guido Pressler, 1999.

Taglia, Kathryn. "Delivering a Christian Identity: Midwives in Northern French Synodal Legislation, c. 1200–1500." In *Religion and Medicine in the Middle Ages.* Edited by Peter Biller and Joseph Ziegler. Rochester, N.Y.: York Medieval Press, 2001.

MONICA H. GREEN

[See also **DMA:** Baptism; Family; Medicine, History of; **Supp:** Abortion; Childhood and Adolescence; Gynecology; Women.]

CHILDHOOD AND ADOLESCENCE. During the Middle Ages the stages of early life that stretched from infancy through teething to boyhood or girlhood and up to adolescence were distinguished and commented on by numerous medieval writers. Similarly, most authorities distinguished the period of adolescence from both childhood and full adulthood. Adolescence possessed its own pressures, legal restrictions, and obligations that defined it as a separate period of life. The greatest challenge to understanding the concept of childhood during the Middle Ages concerns the issue of sentiment and the emotional attachment individuals felt toward children. Some historians, most notably Philippe Ariès, have concluded that the concept of childhood and the distinct culture associated with it did not exist during the Middle Ages but rather is a consequence of modern sentimentality. Medieval sources, however, speak otherwise. Adults clearly cultivated feelings for their own children and often cared for the children around them. Moreover, as the texts describe, they often indulged memories of and reflected upon their own childhoods.

The sources for the study of childhood and adolescence appear at first rather limited. Children left no deliberate records of their experiences of growing up. References in texts and archaeological evidence to leather shoes, milk horns, binding clothes, and toys form the clues to the everyday life of children. Richer descriptions of childhood can be gleaned from memoirs and autobiographical accounts, such as those offered by Augustine of Hippo in his *Confessions* or in the *Memoirs* of Guibert of Nogent. Saints' lives and biographical texts, such as John of Lodi's *Life of St. Peter Damian* (late eleventh century) and Eadmer of Canterbury's *Life of Anselm* (early twelfth century) give vivid descriptions of the exemplary childhoods of saints. Sermons and preachers' guides designed to offer advice to all strata of society also have words directed toward children that are useful for discerning expectations of behavior. The *ad status* collections of thirteenth-century preachers such as Gilbert of Tournai, John of Wales, and Humbert of Romans all make specific mention of children or direct advice and admonitions specifically to children in their audiences. The treatise *De proprietatibus rerum* (ca. 1240) by Bartholomaeus Anglicus devotes a lengthy book to childhood, detailing its various stages. Although often more difficult to interpret, references in legal sources such as charters, inquests, coroners' rolls, and Byzantine and Islamic law codes and juridical literature also shed light on experiences of childhood during the Middle Ages. To this should be added numerous medieval Islamic medical and pediatric manuals devoted to child development drawn from early Greek sources such as Galen and Hippocrates.

STAGES OF CHILDHOOD

There is abundant evidence that people in the Middle Ages were aware of and concerned about the risks of childbirth and infancy. Bearing children was one of the main responsibilities of a wife and the focus of the family. The birth of heirs had profound consequences for the distribution of familial property and the continuance of family lines and professions, as well as for religious and political ties. Concern for a child's spiritual wellbeing is reflected in the practice of infant baptism. In the early Middle Ages babies were baptized on the vigil of Easter or Pentecost, but from the twelfth century onward there was greater pressure to have an infant baptized in the days following birth. A rough estimate is that one in three infants survived to childhood. Indeed, there is an entire genre of medieval Islamic texts devoted to the consolation of bereaved parents who had lost a child, demonstrating the deep emotional effects of the realities of child mortality. Although a source of comment among Islamic and Christian authors alike, the majority of infants from peasant and middle-class households were nursed at home by their mothers. Aristocratic houses often employed nurses both to feed infants and to care for them as they grew. Honey was often rubbed on the gums of a newborn to stimulate the child's interest in feeding. A nursing horn—a hollowed cow's horn with a skin covering on the smaller end, filled with animals' milk or water—was used when mother's milk was not available or during the process of weaning. Muslim writers also refer to a special cup with a handle from which an infant could suck to aid the weaning and teething process.

Sermons, scholastic treatises, and legal texts employed different terms to distinguish among the various stages of childhood. *Infantia,* or infancy, typically lasted for the first two years of life, although some medieval authors described it as the period stretching from birth to the age of seven. In nonaristocratic households, babies were wrapped in cloth or strips of linen and often placed in cradles near the area where their mothers worked, most frequently near the hearth. Here the child was rocked, sung to, and fed, nearly always under the watchful eye of a mother or sibling. In contrast, Muslim and Byzantine authors recommended swaddling infants, a practice that was found among the Western aristocracy as well.

The second stage of childhood corresponded to the small-child stage, *parvulus,* as the tenth-century bishop Rather of Verona described it, which coincided with teething *(dentium plantatura)* and lasted from ages two to seven. During this time children for the most part remained in the constant presence of their parents. In an urban context they were with parents and guardians in workshops and kitchens, while rural peasant children joined their mothers, fathers, and siblings in the fields and in the household and farm complex. There are several descriptions both in pastoral texts and in coroners' inquests of children chasing birds in a newly planted field, reaching for ducks in a nearby pond, and falling into wells. Royal and noble children prove an exception, as they often spent long periods of their childhood away from their parents. Eleanor of Castile and Edward I of England's four children were in the care of their uncle and grandmother when the couple spent four years on crusade (1270–1274). Despite such physical absences there is considerable evidence that royal and noble parents exchanged letters with their children and were deeply concerned with their upbringing, well-being, and education as future kings, queens, and lords with multifold political responsibilities. Royal children were made aware of their future duties through didactic literature, ceremonial processions, early coronations, and other modes of cultural consumption that reinforced their elite identity. Children were also used to strengthen diplomatic ties through strategic betrothals and to solidify political alliances and future commitments, as in the case of Edward I of England, who gave his infant son as a pledge to be raised in the court of the French king Louis IX. On occasion very young boys were even taken into battle as observers, set close enough to the action to be at considerable risk. In Byzantium children were used as political captives and to seal peace agreements.

Pueritia (boyhood or girlhood) stretched approximately from the ages of seven to fourteen for boys and seven to twelve for girls and was a time when early apprenticeship began for many children. After the age of seven, children became an integrated part of the productive household. They performed simple but necessary tasks, such as feeding animals, gathering wood, working in the fields at harvest, and supervising younger children. This was also a time when ideas and attitudes about religion, self-identity, and socioeconomic markers began to be observed and internalized. For example, inquest records suggest that children accompanied their parents when pawning items of value for cash in times of economic pressure. In the process, they may have heard and internalized the comments made by their parents about the differences between themselves and those lending money at interest. These may have consisted of harsh critiques of the "Jewish usurers," which parents may have uttered after the conclusion of such a transaction. Similarly, there are references to critiques and stereotypes of Christian behavior that were taught to Jewish children

at an early age. Children learned ways of life and habits of thought from their parents that would influence their behavior and opinions as they grew to adulthood. In Islamic society, age seven was considered the "age of discernment," when a child was able to distinguish between good and evil and to grasp the meaning of Islam.

Pueritia was also the period when schooling began for many children, although it is difficult to estimate the number of boys and girls who began to learn their letters and the differences caused by gender in this respect. In fourteenth-century Flanders, for example, boys learned up to three languages including French, Flemish, and Latin. Girls were instructed in the vernacular but were also taught to read the Psalter. Grammar and logic, considered the basics of any education, were typically the first subjects children learned in the Christian West. Byzantine education stressed rote memorization, particularly of the psalms, whereas study of the Koran was emphasized in the Islamic tradition. A noted component of schooling was discipline; children learned to listen and to speak in turn. The link between discipline and education is reflected visually in the personification of Grammar, depicted with a branch in hand ready to beat her small pupil into obedience, on an archivolt of Chartres Cathedral. The rhetoric of physical punishment in many medieval sources, however, should not be taken to reflect its use so much as its prescription by a few authorities.

Medieval children also engaged in activities typical of modern childhood play. Children played games, both structured board games and word games employed in their schooling, and are depicted jumping, and running and playing leapfrog. Several thirteenth-century German poems describe children playing peekaboo, while the English *Ancrene Riwle* of the same period describes a peasant mother and child playing hide-and-seek. Games involving imagined worlds and places also occupied children's playtime. Indeed, an important marker of childhood as a separate period of life can be seen in the distinct culture of children. Lists of import duties levied on toys such as rattles, dolls, puppets, and carved figurines, among other items, complement the archaeological evidence for a culture of childhood play. The Islamic treatise by al-Ghazālī (written between 1095 and 1106) describes a puppet theater enjoyed by children, while another Muslim author, al-Qurashī, mentions a toy market in Baghdad during the early tenth century.

ABANDONMENT AND CIVIC CARE

For those who either found themselves parents before their own adolescence was over or could not or did not want to care for another child, abandonment, in several guises, was a solution. Although there were cases of exposure and infanticide, by the later Middle Ages synodal legislation, penitential literature, and customary law from most regions of Europe forbade such practices altogether, sometimes prescribing harsh punishments. During the central Middle Ages parents often chose to give children to monasteries as a holy offering, or oblation. Some oblates were given because their parents did not have the means to care for them, especially if they were deformed or unhealthy, but most were given as gifts, sealing a religious association between the family and a monastic community. In contrast, children in Byzantium were prohibited from entering a monastery until the age of ten. By the thirteenth century oblation was coming under increasing criticism, and the practice declined. Concomitantly, as urban centers rapidly expanded, unwanted and excess children became a social and charitable concern for civic authorities and the church hierarchy alike. The first foundling home was established in the eighth century under Archbishop Datheus of Milan and provided specifically for abandoned infants. Around 1160 Guy of Montpellier founded the Order of the Holy Spirit to receive and care for unwanted children. In 1201 Innocent III patronized the order, and thereafter the number of foundling hospitals greatly increased. In an urban context, when one or both parents died, orphans were often provided for by civic institutions that ensured their maintenance and administered their inheritance until they reached the age of legal maturity, typically twelve for girls and fourteen or fifteen for boys.

ADOLESCENCE

Although the word *adolescentia* was used more variously than is implied by the modern English word "adolescence," there were signs and markers that distinguished it as a unique period of life consistent with a modern understanding of the adolescent phase. Legal and medical treatises define the start of adolescence for girls as the age of menarche. For boys, as the *Sachsenspiegel* (1220–1235) of Eike von Repgowe relates, "if he has hair in his beard, and below, and under each arm, then you should know that he has come of age." The Byzantine legal tradition in contrast did not explicitly acknowledge a period of adolescence, and children were considered minors until age twenty-five. Adolescence is most clearly defined in records from the later medieval period, specifically contracts of apprenticeship. Rural apprenticeship went mostly unrecorded. Children were brought up working in the fields and with animals from a young age and were given greater responsibilities as they grew older. The goad-boy is perhaps the archetypical example of the rural apprentice to the plowman. In urban centers apprenticeship was typically contracted between the family of a teenage boy or girl and an artisan or merchant who taught the arts of a trade. Apprentice contracts record young women and men beginning their training between the ages of twelve and fifteen and often continuing in this capacity until their mid-twenties. Girls were usually apprenticed to women and trained in specific industries, such as the textile trades; production of foodstuffs, including baking and making of ale; luxury decorations; and silk work. Young men were usually trained in more prestigious and prosperous trades, eventually practicing as metalworkers, apothecaries, money changers, drapers, and merchants. Orphans were often contracted in apprenticeships or, more commonly, as servants, depending on their familial origins, and in Byzantium occasionally as slaves. For aristocratic boys adolescence coincided with the period before knighthood, typically bestowed at age seventeen, a period Georges Duby describes as *juventus,* or "youth," which could also persist late into the twenties. Young aristocratic women experienced similar training once they were betrothed and sent to live in the household of their future spouse.

There were also psychological markers that defined this stage of young adulthood, in the opinion of some scholars. This is most clearly evidenced in the medieval concern with adolescent conversions. In northern and southern Europe teenagers were given several days to think through their choice to convert from one religion to another. The autobiographical account of the conversion of Herman-Judah to Christianity provides a rich description of the psychological and social pressures attendant on adolescence and the freedoms and self-definition associated with conversion. Young women as well as young men were prey to the pressures of conversion, not only from Judaism to Christianity but also within Christianity to the monastic life or to a heretical sect such as the Cathars or Waldensians.

Recent scholarship has shown, in part as a response to Philippe Ariès's dismissal of childhood as a concept applicable to the Middle Ages, that there was a distinct culture and phase of life associated with childhood as well as adolescence. Indeed, once it is critically sought, medieval childhood appears clearly and distinctly in numerous different types of evidence.

BIBLIOGRAPHY

Antoniadis-Bibicou, H. "Quelques notes sur l'enfant de la Moyenne Époque byzantine (du VIeme au XIIeme siècle)." *Annales de démographie historique* 28 (1973): 77–84.

Ariès, Philippe. *Centuries of Childhood: A Social History of Family Life.* Translated by Robert Baldick. New York: Vintage, 1962.

Boynton, Susan. "The Liturgical Role of Children in Monastic Customaries from the Central Middle Ages." *Studia Liturgica* 28 (1998): 194–209.

Brown, Elizabeth A. R. "The Prince Is Father of the King: The Character and Childhood of Philip the Fair of France." *Mediaeval Studies* 49 (1987): 282–334.

Cunningham, Hugh. "Histories of Childhood." *American Historical Review* 103 (1998): 1195–1208.

DeMause, Lloyd, ed. *The History of Childhood.* New York: Psychohistory Press, 1974. See especially Chapter 3, "Survivors and Surrogates: Children and Parents from the Ninth to the Thirteenth Centuries," by Mary Martin McLaughlin.

Egan, Geoff. "Children's Pastimes in Past Time—Medieval Toys Found in the British Isles." In *Material Culture in Medieval Europe: Papers of the "Medieval Europe Brugge 1997" Conference, 7.* Edited by Guy de Boe and Frans Verhaeghe. Zellik, Belgium: Instituut voor het Archeologisch Patrimonium, 1997: 413–421.

Gil ʿAdi, Avner. *Children of Islam: Concepts of Childhood in Medieval Muslim Society.* New York: St. Martin's Press, 1992.

Guibert of Nogent. *Self and Society in Medieval France: The Memoirs of Abbot Guibert of Nogent (1064?–c. 1125).* Edited by John F. Benton and translated by C. C. Swinton Bland. New York: Harper and Row, 1970.

Hanawalt, Barbara A. "Childrearing among the Lower Classes of Late Medieval England." *Journal of Interdisciplinary History* 8 (1977): 1–22.

———. *Growing Up in Medieval London: The Experience of Childhood in History.* New York: Oxford University Press, 1993.

———. "Medievalists and the Study of Childhood." *Speculum* 77 (2002): 440–460.

Hooper, Bari. "A Medieval Depiction of Infant-Feeding in Winchester Cathedral." *Medieval Archaeology* 40 (1996): 230–233.

Jordan, William Chester. "Adolescence and Conversion in the Middle Ages: A Research Agenda." In *Jews and Christians in Twelfth-Century Europe.* Edited by Michael A. Signer and John Van Engen. Notre Dame, Ind.: University of Notre Dame, 2001.

Moffatt, Ann. "The Byzantine Child." *Social Research* 53 (1986): 705–723.

Nicholas, David. "Child and Adolescent Labour in the Late Medieval City: A Flemish Model in Regional Perspective." *English Historical Review* 110 (1995): 1103–1131.

Orme, Nicholas. "The Culture of Children in Medieval England." *Past and Present* 148 (1995): 48–88.

———. *Medieval Children.* New Haven, Conn.: Yale University Press, 2001.

Parsons, John Carmi. *Eleanor of Castile: Queen and Society in Thirteenth-Century England.* New York: St Martin's Press, 1995.

Parsons, John Carmi, and Bonnie Wheeler, eds. *Medieval Mothering.* New York: Garland, 1996.

Patlagean, Evelyne. "L'enfant et son avenir dans la famille byzantine (IVe–XIIe siècles)." *Annales de démographie historique* 28 (1973): 85–93.

Reyerson, Kathryn L. "The Adolescent Apprentice/Worker in Medieval Montpellier." *Journal of Family History* 17 (1992): 353–370.

Schultz, James A. "Medieval Adolescence: The Claims of History and the Silence of German Narrative." *Speculum* 66 (1991): 519–539.

Shahar, Shulamith. *Childhood in the Middle Ages.* London and New York: Routledge, 1990.

Sommerville, C. John. "Toward a History of Childhood and Youth." *Journal of Interdisciplinary History* 3 (1972): 439–447.

Swanson, Jenny. "Childhood and Childrearing in *ad status* Sermons by Later Thirteenth Century Friars." *Journal of Medieval History* 16 (1990): 309–331.

Willemsen, Annemarieke. "Medieval Children's Toys in the Netherlands: Production, Sale and Trade." In *Material Culture in Medieval Europe: Papers of the "Medieval Europe Brugge 1997" Conference, 7.* Edited by Guy de Boe and Frans Verhaeghe. Zellik, Belgium: Instituut voor het Archeologisch Patrimonium, 1997: 405–412.

Wilson, Adrian. "The Infancy of the History of Childhood: An Appraisal of Philippe Ariès." *History and Theory* 19 (1980): 132–153.

Wood, Diana, ed. *The Church and Childhood.* Oxford: Blackwell, 1994.

ANNE E. LESTER

[See also **DMA:** Family; Games and Pastimes; Inheritance, Western European; Schools, Grammar; **Supp:** Childbirth and Infancy; Oblates and Oblation; Schools.]

CHINA was little known in Europe prior to the thirteenth century. Chinese civilization developed in the fertile basins of the Huang He and Yangtze Rivers, and when the Chin dynasty (221–206 B.C.) created the Chinese empire by uniting several kingdoms, it already equaled half the land area Rome would control some three centuries later. China expanded geographically, and despite its occasional lack of political unity and the imposition of barbarian regimes, it experienced nothing comparable to the eclipse of learning Europe suffered after the Roman Empire collapsed. During the first millennium A.D., Chinese civilization was characterized by continuity in literature, philosophy, and the arts, and early in the Sung dynasty (960–1279) the invention of printing facilitated diffusion of those accomplishments. Medieval Europe knew little about China and nothing of these developments until the thirteenth century, when China was incorporated into the Mongol empire and direct contact with eastern Asia became possible.

ROMAN, BYZANTINE, AND ARAB CONTACT WITH CHINA

The Hellenistic world knew much about China, and the Byzantine Empire had intermittent contact with eastern Asia, but that knowledge was not preserved in western Europe. After Greek merchants discovered monsoon wind patterns in the first century A.D., voyages between the Red Sea and India became common and trade with Asia expanded. Because China was the source of silk, a highly valued luxury, Roman merchants and their wares traveled to China, and merchants, mercenaries, and adventurers provided information about Asia to Hellenistic geographers, such as the renowned Claudius Ptolemy of Alexandria in the second century. Most of this new lore concerning China remained in Greek, however. Earlier Latin authors like Pomponius Mela and Pliny the Elder in the first century A.D. had recounted fantastic descriptions of imagined Asian realms peopled by monstrous races, werewolves, cannibals, and Amazons. They knew of China only as an eastern land of the Seres, whence silk came. Writers of late antiquity and the early medieval period, unable to use Greek sources, relied on their fanciful works. Thus two-thirds of the third-century *Polihistor* of Gaius Julius Solinus was based directly on Pliny's *Natural History* and added nothing to the scant information about China recorded therein.

Although the *Etymologies* of Isidore of Seville, compiled from these sources in the seventh century, taught the medieval West virtually nothing about China, even as he was writing, sporadic contact continued between that land and the Levant. Trade with China decreased after silkworm eggs were smuggled to Constantinople in 552, but Theophylactus Simocatta, a Byzantine scholar, could write a reasonably accurate account of China about 628. Ambassadors from Constantinople visited the Tang dynasty four times between 643 and 719, hoping to involve China in joint war upon the Arabs. In the mid-eighth century, however, Arabs made Turkistan subject to Islam, and Byzantium's direct contact with China ended. As their trade grew, Arabs established a colony in Canton as early as 700, and subsequently Arab geographers wrote accurate descriptions of China and Asia, but their works had little impact in medieval Europe. Through most of the medieval period Europeans thought of Asia as the locus for the earthly paradise and accepted as fact fables handed down from antiquity. They saw Asia as a region where wonders and monsters abounded, the source of the four biblical rivers that watered the earth.

EUROPEAN CONTACT WITH THE MONGOL WORLD

This ignorance changed with the rise of the Mongol Empire in the thirteenth century. The Mongols first appeared in the Europe in 1222, when Genghis Khan sent troops to reconnoiter steppe lands north of the Caspian and Black Seas. Confronted by combined forces of Kip-

chak nomads and Russians in 1223, the Mongols annihilated them. Genghis ordered an invasion of eastern Europe to complete his conquest of the Eurasian steppe, but his death and the struggle to complete the conquest of the Chin Empire in northeast China delayed the attack. After the Chin fell in 1234, his successor, Ögödai, launched armies that overwhelmed the Kipchak khans, defeated the Russian princes, and sacked their cities. In 1241 the Mongols fell on both Hungary and Poland, crushing the Hungarians at Mohi and wiping out a combined Polish-German army led by Henry of Silesia at Liegnitz. Rumors from the east were deeply frightening as preparations were made to resist the Tartars, characterized as foul beasts from hell, a race of monsters out of far Asia. But the Mongols abruptly withdrew when news of the death of Ögödai reached them. Nevertheless, peril from Asia had been brought to Europe, and its rulers now sought accurate information about this threat.

In 1245, on the eve of the First Council of Lyons, Pope Innocent IV sent groups of mendicant friars east, charged with delivering letters to the Mongols and gathering data about them. The leader of one of these was John of Plano Carpini, whose *History of the Mongols* was much read and widely copied in the thirteenth century. Another Franciscan, William of Rubruck, lived among the Mongols from 1253 to 1255 and wrote a detailed account of his journey. Both men sojourned in Mongolia, but neither visited China. Only after 1260, when Kublai, founder of the Yuan dynasty, became great khan, did Europeans venture into China. As he was completing his conquest of the Sung dynasty, to bring all China under his authority, his brother Hulagu overthrew Muslim power in Baghdad in 1258 and created the Persian *il-khânate,* opening the overland route between the Middle East and China. Over the following decades a small but steady stream of merchants and missionaries made their way east, sending back reports that gave Europe its first glimpse of the vast Chinese realm, fueling imaginations for generations to come.

EUROPEANS IN CHINA IN THE THIRTEENTH CENTURY

Among the earliest merchants were Niccolo and Maffeo Polo, brothers from Venice who visited Kublai's court in the 1260s. According to Marco Polo, the khan sent his father and uncle west as emissaries to the papal court, with a request that a hundred learned men be sent from Europe to demonstrate the superiority of the Christian faith. It may well be doubted whether Kublai sought missionaries, but he surely solicited Westerners who could serve him in administering newly conquered territory. The Mongols made extensive use of outsiders—

Western and Nestorian Christians, Tibetan Buddhists, and Muslims—in governing China, and when Marco accompanied his father east in 1271, he apparently served as an administrator in Yangchow for some years before leaving China in 1292. Emissaries from the *il-khâns* reiterated Kublai's request for Western wise men several times before Pope Nicholas IV sent a delegation of Franciscans to China in 1289. Only their leader, John of Monte Corvino, completed the trip, arriving at Khanbalik (modern Beijing) in 1294, shortly after the great khan's death. When he presented the pope's letters to Kublai's successor, Temur Oljeitu (Chenzong), he was granted a generous stipend, which he used to establish a Catholic presence in China. He built two churches in Khanbalik, in which choirs of boys, whom he had purchased, baptized, and instructed, sang the canonical hours in Latin. John also enjoyed the patronage of Italian merchants, such as Peter of Lucalongo, with whom he had traveled to China, but he could not contact Europe for more than a decade because of war between Mongol factions in central Asia. When letters John sent in 1305 and 1306, reporting his successes, were carried to Pope Clement V in 1307, the pope created an archiepiscopal see for Khanbalik, encompassing the entire Mongol empire, and sent ordained bishops to China to consecrate John its first archbishop.

THE MISSION TO CHINA

Missionary activity in China can be sketched from letters sent home by missionaries and from the testimony of travelers to China. One missionary, Odoric of Pordenone, worked there from 1325 to 1328 before returning to Europe to recruit additional friars for the China mission, an activity cut short by his death in January 1331. On his arrival in Italy he dictated his *Relatio* (1330), a narration of wonders seen on his mission journeys. Another, Friar John of Marignolli, sent to China by Benedict XII in 1339 in response to an embassy from the khan, left his narrative among the pages of a chronicle of Bohemia he compiled in the 1350s for Emperor Charles IV. The mission in China grew quickly after reinforcements arrived in 1313. In addition to the archiepiscopal see of Khanbalik, there was a bishopric in Zaitun, near modern Quanzhou, a port city three months' journey from the capital. There Franciscans built two churches and established a *fundaco,* an inn with warehouse facilities, for Western merchants. Franciscans also had houses in Hangchow (staffed by four friars when Odoric visited there) and at Yangchow. Although letters always pleaded that more be sent, there were a fair number of friars in China who preached through translators, but they made few converts among the Chinese. The

Franciscans served as clergy for foreigners resident in China under Mongol rule, such as the Christian Alans, some 30,000 bodyguards of the khan, and the Armenian and Italian merchants, some of whom married and reared families in China.

This Western presence in China was relatively short-lived, however. The window of opportunity for merchants and missionaries opened by the Mongol Empire closed after the Yüan were expelled from China in 1368. Even before that Mongol regimes bordering Europe had adopted Islam and as the Mongol Empire began to disintegrate, Eurasia was jolted by bubonic plague, a pandemic that reached Europe in 1348. Few Westerners arrived in China in the two decades preceding 1368, and none were welcome after.

EUROPEAN TRAVEL LITERATURE AND MEDIEVAL KNOWLEDGE OF CHINA

Although missionary letters and Marignolli's recollections were soon forgotten and had to be rediscovered centuries later, travel reports concerning Asia were popular and widely circulated in the fourteenth and fifteenth centuries. The most important of these was Marco Polo's *Description of the World,* apparently composed in collaboration with Rusticello da Pisa, a writer of romances Marco met in 1299 while they were prisoners of war in Genoa. This account of what Marco did and saw traveling to, in, and from China was widely read. Written in Franco-Italian, it was translated into Latin, French, several Italian dialects, German, Czech, and Gaelic, and over 150 copies survive in several manuscript traditions. Another popular travel narrative was Odoric of Pordenone's *Relatio,* briefer than Polo's book but also much copied. These works expanded Western geographical knowledge of China, naming and describing Chinese cities, giving their approximate locations, and supplying much political, economic, and ethnographical detail. Their reports of teeming populations, commerce based on paper currency, and unimaginably huge walled cities with myriad bridges became reservoirs of data concerning China, from which authors of spurious accounts, such as *The Travels of Sir John Mandeville,* probably written about 1360, copied their material. Mandeville's *Travels,* a clever compilation attributed to a fictitious knight, was accepted as the authentic record of an Asian journey. Also often copied, the *Travels* further popularized Polo's and Odoric's books, and cartographers and geographers of the late Middle Ages and Renaissance did draw new information concerning China from those accounts. The Venetian Fra Mauro, for example, used Polo's book in compiling his 1459 *mappa mundi,* or world map, revered as one of the outstanding achievements of late medieval cartography. Similarly, Pierre d'Ailly, author of the encyclopedic *Imago mundi* (Image of the world; 1410), used Polo and Odoric in his descriptions of China. *Imago mundi* also demonstrates the limited use to which newly acquired knowledge about China was put. D'Ailly's sixty chapters were gleaned from all manner of sources, but he relied heavily on Pliny, Solinus, and Isidore of Seville and strove to identify the location of the mythical monstrous races they had reported. D'Ailly also incorporated Hellenistic learning when he later supplemented *Imago mundi* with instructions on map production using latitude and longitude, based on Ptolemy's *Geography,* just translated from Greek into Latin in 1406/1407. *Imago mundi,* which summarized all Europe then knew concerning China and the rest of the world, has survived in some 200 manuscripts, copied before its first printing (about 1483). Christopher Columbus owned copies of both *Imago mundi* and Polo's *Description of the World* and made notes in the margins of both as he planned how to reach China by sailing west. By the close of the medieval period China and all of Asia were still imperfectly understood in the West, but enough had become known to excite popular imagination and help inspire the age of exploration.

BIBLIOGRAPHY

PRIMARY WORKS

Dawson, Christopher. *Mission to Asia.* 1955. Reprint, Toronto: University of Toronto Press, 1980. The classic translation of Plano Carpini, Rubruck, and the letters from China, and readily accessible.

Polo, Marco. *The Book of Ser Marco Polo the Venetian.* Edited and translated by Henry Yule, revised by Henri Cordier. 3d ed. 1903. Reprint, New York: Dover, 1993. A standard and still useful compendium.

Ruysbroeck, Willem van. *The Mission of Friar William of Rubruck: His Journey to the Court of the Great Khan Möngke, 1253–1255.* Translated by Peter Jackson, edited by Peter Jackson and David Morgan. London: Hakluyt Society, 1990. The introduction is replete with useful insights, the translation a new standard.

The Travels of Sir John Mandeville. Translated by C. W. R. D. Mosley. New York: Penguin, 1983.

Wyngaert, P. Anastasius van den, ed. *Itinera et relationes Fratrum Minorum saeculi XIII et XIV.* Volume 1 of *Sinica Franciscana.* Florence: Ad Claras Aquas, 1929. A volume containing critical editions (in Latin) of all Franciscan sources concerning the mission to the Mongols, including John of Plano Carpini, William of Rubruck, the letters from China, Odoric of Pordenone, and John of Marignolli.

SECONDARY WORKS

Abu-Lughod, Janet L. *Before European Hegemony: The World System* A.D. *1250–1350.* Oxford: Oxford University Press, 1989.

Bentley, Jerry H. *Old World Encounters, Cross-cultural Contacts, and Exchanges in Pre-modern Times.* Oxford and New York: Oxford University Press, 1993.

Critchley, John. *Marco Polo's Book.* Aldershot, U.K.: Variorum, 1992.

Curtin, Phillip D. *Cross-cultural Trade in World History.* Cambridge, U.K.: Cambridge University Press, 1984.

de Rachewiltz, Igor. *Papal Envoys to the Great Khan.* Stanford, Calif.: Stanford University Press, 1971.

Franke, Herbert, and Denis Twitchett, eds. *The Alien Regimes and Border States, 907–1368.* Volume 6 of *The Cambridge History of China.* Edited by Denis Twitchett and John K. Fairbank. Cambridge, U.K., and New York: Cambridge University Press, 1994.

Larner, John. *Marco Polo and the Discovery of the World.* New Haven, Conn., and London: Yale University Press, 1999.

Morgan, David. *The Mongols.* London: Blackwell, 1986.

Phillips, J. R. S. *The Medieval Expansion of Europe.* 2d ed. Oxford and New York: Clarendon Press, 1998.

Phillips, William D., Jr., and Carla Rahn Phillips. *The Worlds of Christopher Columbus.* Cambridge, U.K., and New York: Cambridge University Press, 1992.

Rossabi, Morris. *Kublai Khan: His Life and Times.* Berkeley: University of California Press, 1988.

Semour, M. C. *Sir John Mandeville.* Aldershot, U.K.: Variorum, 1993.

JAMES D. RYAN

[See also **DMA:** Ailly, Pierre d'; Black Death; Byzantine Empire: History (330–1025); Exploration by Western Europeans; Franciscans; Genghis Khan; Geography and Cartography; Hulagu; Islam, Conquests of; John of Plano Carpini; Mandeville's Travels; Mappa Mundi; Missions and Missionaries, Christian; Mongol Empire; Navigation: Indian Ocean, Red Sea; Polo, Marco; Silk; Uljaytu Khudabānda.]

CHRISTOPHER, ST. Among the most popular of saints in both Eastern and Western Christianity, St. Christopher has had a number of different stories attached to his name. The oldest texts, probably composed in the fourth century, identify Christopher as a North African named Reprobus (which was simply Latin for "evildoer") who was captured by the Roman army and joined their ranks. He converted to Christianity and was martyred under the emperor Diocletian. Robert Woods has argued that St. Christopher's cult became conflated with that of St. Menas, a popular saint with a shrine in western Egypt. His story can be read as a metaphor for the trials of the soul taking on Christianity, as everyone begins as a "reprobus" until becoming a "Christophoros," or "Christ-bearer."

By the ninth century, the legend of Christopher had spread throughout the Christian world. In many ac-

verted to Christianity by a hermit, he refused to fast or pray but agreed to carry people across a river, being either a giant or blessed with extraordinary strength. One day he carried a child who grew increasingly heavy as he progressed until his weight was almost unbearable. The child revealed himself to be Christ, and the heavy burden was the weight of the world, which Jesus himself carried. Christopher's subsequent preaching led to martyrdom.

Images of the saint were popular across Christendom. One of the earliest is a sixth-century icon of the saint in the monastery of St. Catherine in Sinai. In the Tyrol, a brotherhood of St. Christopher was founded for guiding travelers over the Arlberg Mountains. He is considered the patron saint of travelers and pilgrims and was often associated with protection from floods. In the later Middle Ages, it was believed that seeing an image of St. Christopher would ensure that you would not fall or faint that day or, in some traditions, even die. For that reason, an image of St. Christopher is often found at the entrance of many late medieval churches, such as the cathedral of Seville. His feast was kept on 25 July in the West and on 9 March in the Orthodox church. Following the reforms of the Second Vatican Council, the feast of St. Christopher was removed from the list of worldwide feasts, but contrary to popular belief he is still a recognized saint.

BIBLIOGRAPHY

SOURCES

Halkin, François. *Hagiologie byzantine: Textes inédits publiés en grec et traduits en français.* Brusssels: Société des Bollandistes, 1986.

"Passio Sancti Christophori, martyris." *Analecta Bollandiana* 10 (1891): 393–405. Earliest Latin life.

Van Hooff, G. "S. Christophori Martyris Acta Graeca Antiqua." *Analecta Bollandiana* 1 (1882): 121–148.

STUDIES

Whaite, H. C. *St. Christopher in English Medieval Wallpainting.* London: E. Benn, 1929.

Woods, David. "St. Christopher, Bishop Peter of Attalia, and the Cohors Marmaritarum." *Vigiliae Christianae* 48 (1994): 170–186.

CHRISTOPHER HATCH MACEVITT

[See also **DMA:** Hagiography, Byzantine; Hagiography, Western European.]

CINQUE PORTS, the confederation of ports in southeastern England that received broad privileges from the crown in exchange for maritime and other services. Lore has it that the original three ports were Dover, Sandwich,

St. Christopher. *Legends and false etymologies led to the occasional depiction of the saint with a dog's head.* COURTESY OF BYZANTINE AND CHRISTIAN MUSEUM, ATHENS, GREECE. REPRODUCED BY PERMISSION.

counts of his life, he is a giant; in the Byzantine tradition he is reputed to have a dog's head, for the earliest *vita* remarked that he came from the land of the dog-headed people—originally an authorial aside showing knowledge of Herodotus. In Europe "dog-headed" became *caneus* or "doglike," which was further corrupted to mean he was from the land of Canaan. His name, Christopher, originally taken in baptism, was given a literal meaning. In the influential thirteenth-century *Golden Legend* of Jacobus de Varagine, Christopher was a Canaanite pagan king who dedicated himself to serve only the strongest and bravest in this world. Having been con-

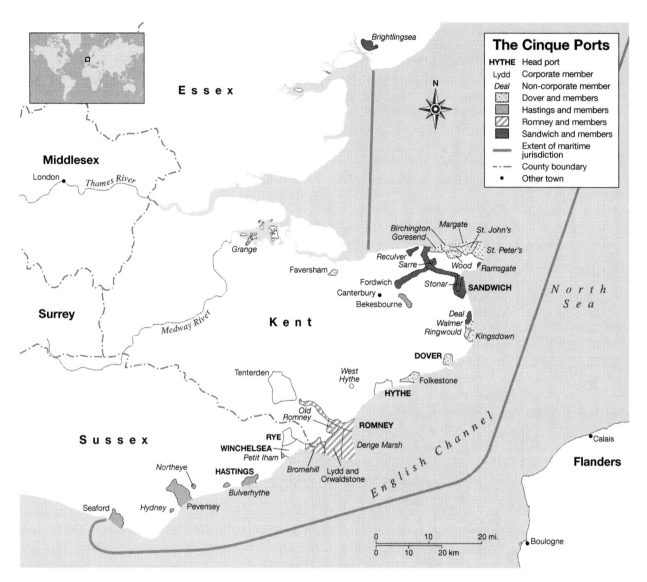

The Cinque Ports

HYTHE Head port
Lydd Corporate member
Deal Non-corporate member
Dover and members
Hastings and members
Romney and members
Sandwich and members
Extent of maritime jurisdiction
County boundary
• Other town

XNR PRODUCTIONS/THE GALE GROUP.

and Romney, then Hythe and Hastings, and that Rye and Winchelsea, termed the "Ancient Towns," joined time out of mind. To these "Head Ports" were added thirty other coastal, riparian, and hinterland towns, termed "limbs" or "members," with lesser legal rights and extending into Essex. Literature on the Cinque Ports dates back centuries, some of it written by maritime enthusiasts exploring the relationship of the ports' fleets to the fledgling royal navy, some by local historians arguing for the antiquity of the Ports' legal status. The first known royal charter to the Cinque Ports as an entity is from 1260. But the term "Cinque Ports" is found a full century earlier, when the king had already begun to treat the towns as a confederation formally responsible for "ship service" of fifty-seven ships for fifteen days yearly at their expense and longer at the king's expense, and

more generally for safeguarding crucial trade and transit routes to the Continent. From the thirteenth century, the crown appointed a royal official, a "lord warden," based in Dover Castle and charged with managing royal interests. Under this arrangement, the Cinque Ports seemingly were involved in almost every political and military crisis, especially after the fall of Normandy, with France now controlling the south coast of the Channel. They were crucial if inconstant allies of Henry III's guardians, Simon de Montfort, and Edward II. While their fleets are no longer viewed as the precursor to a national navy, the Cinque Ports participated in campaigns in 1173, 1190, 1196, 1217, 1282, 1293, 1297, 1340, 1347, 1460, and 1471. In between, they engaged in "their traditional occupation of more or less licensed piracy" (Powicke, *King Henry III,* vol. 2, p. 448).

Whether the Cinque Ports' value lay in their naval resources, their taxable wealth from trade and fishing, their shipbuilding capacity, their location at what they described as "the Gates that open and shutt to the perill or safety of this Kingdome," or something else, the crown plainly valued them and was willing to reward them with unusual privileges. Their rights were confirmed in reissues of Magna Carta and more fully in an important 1278 charter, later confirmed many times. Cinque Port merchants were subject to their own customs in their own courts, most important the "Court of Shepway." Sometimes claims to autonomy went too far. In 1312 Chief Justice Bereford chastised counsel by recalling that Cinque Port immunity "was contrary to all manner of reason, for, indeed, it would be inconsistent with reason to try actions arising in the most distant parts of England in their franchise Court of Shepway." But most Cinque Port litigants answered only in their courts, whose results were not reviewable by the Court of King's Bench, and neither shire nor eyre had jurisdiction over the Cinque Ports. Their freemen were immune from tolls and customs. The Head Ports sent representatives to local assemblies called "Guestlings" and "Brodhulls" and to national assemblies and parliaments as early as 1205, in 1225 and 1265, and regularly from 1322. A contemporary treatise, speaking theoretically, explained that Cinque Port representatives, or "barons," were to be paid, fined, and otherwise given parliamentary precedence above other borough representatives.

The paradox is that while the Cinque Ports' privileges imply naval importance, there is no modern consensus that they actually were of such value and, if so, when that was. According to N. A. M. Rodger, not only were the Cinque Ports not the "main component of English naval power, but . . . there is no evidence that they ever did . . . [supply the required fifty-seven ships with twenty-one men for a fortnight], and no period in their history (except possibly the 1050s) in which we know of a real naval requirement for a large number of small ships serving for very short periods" (*Safeguard of the Sea*, p. 125). Nor was the importance based on other maritime contributions, for the Cinque Ports did not significantly provide sailors, ferry services for the king, flotillas to transport the army, or payments in lieu of any of these services. Even under Edward I, at the height of their maritime importance, the Cinque Ports were "hardly distinguished from other ports" (*Safeguard*, p. 126). "Only once in eight centuries of corporate existence did the Ports' ships alone perform a notable naval feat: the raid on Boulougne in January 1340 which . . . indirectly contributed to the victory of Sluys later that year" (Rodger, "Naval Service," p. 648).

More likely, the Cinque Ports provided modest or behind-the-scenes functions. They supplied small ships for coastal patrol and for watching the coast of Flanders, probably as early as Saxon times. After 1200, the portsmen frequently gave the crown strategic and naval counsel. However, they were probably best known not for patriotic service but for their "violence and indiscipline" and their especially "indiscriminate piracy." (Rodger, "Naval Service," pp. 644, 646, 647). If so, the Cinque Ports' value may have derived not from naval glory but from "their repeated disloyalty, their willingness to be bought by enemies at home and abroad." As Rodger observes, "it was worth successive sovereigns trying to buy their support, but it was not primarily naval service that they were buying" (Rodger, *Safeguard*, p. 126).

Whatever the basis of the Cinque Ports' value, its decline began earlier than was once thought. Spurred by relentless action of the Channel in depositing shingle and silt, the spiraling cost of warships, repeated destruction by other pirates as well as rival towns and French raiders, royal taxes and naval mishaps, and the Cinque Ports' own involvement in piracy, the decline began before 1400, probably by 1300, and perhaps in the thirteenth century. Together, the late origin, early decline, and diminished heyday suggest correction is needed to the ancient history of the Cinque Ports.

The second puzzle is that the Cinque Ports retained their privileged status for many centuries, even after any maritime importance was gone, and when other franchises throughout the kingdom came under long-term attack by the crown and common lawyers. The Head Ports each retained two seats in parliament, and Henry VIII added representation for tiny Seaford. All eight constituencies were often able to maintain their precarious independence from magnates and officials in selecting their barons. In legal proceedings, Cinque Port courts continued to apply their own substantive and procedural rules, and the jurisdiction grew to include a form of equity. In criminal cases, the Cinque Ports, remarkably for a local jurisdiction, could try felonies. K. M. E. Murray concludes that the confederation clung "to its privileges for very life with a most rigid conservatism . . . but in the limited field of defense of chartered liberties it supplied a need, as is seen in the continuing allegiance of its members" ("Faversham and the Cinque Ports," pp. 82–83).

Long after every Head Port aside from Dover had lost all practical maritime significance, the Cinque Ports were able to retain legal privileges, including most admiralty jurisdiction, which survived the abolition of their general civil jurisdiction (1856) and of local admiralty jurisdiction everywhere else (1835), into the twentieth century.

BIBLIOGRAPHY

Bartlett, Robert. *England under the Norman and Angevin Kings, 1075–1225.* Oxford: Clarendon Press, 2000. See pages 259–261.

Bateson, Mary, ed. *Borough Customs.* London: B. Quaritch, 1904. Surveys the evidence for local customs on pages xxi–xxii, xxiii–xxiv, xlvii–xlix, lv.

Hull, Felix, ed. *A Calendar of the White and Black Books of the Cinque Ports, 1432–1955.* London: H.M.S.O., 1966. Describes the deliberations of the Guestlings and Brodhulls.

Murray, K. M. E. *The Constitutional History of the Cinque Ports.* Manchester, U.K.: Manchester University Press, 1935. The best overall work on the Cinque Ports.

———. "Faversham and the Cinque Ports." *Transactions of the Royal Historical Society,* 4th ser., 18 (1935): 53–84.

———. "Dengemarsh and the Cinque Ports." *English Historical Review* 54 (1939): 664–673.

Powicke, F. M. *King Henry III and the Lord Edward.* 2 vols. Oxford: Clarendon Press, 1947. See volume 1, pages 8–9, 169; volume 2, pages 420, 426 n.3, 447–448, 462, 476.

Rodger, N. A. M. "The Naval Service of the Cinque Ports." *English Historical Review* 111 (1996): 636–651. The leading naval account.

———. *The Safeguard of the Sea: A Naval History of Britain, 660–1649.* London: HarperCollins, 1997.

JONATHAN A. BUSH

[See also **DMA:** Edward I of England; England: Norman-Angevin; England: 1216–1485; Magna Carta; Navies, Western; Normands and Normandy; Parliament, English; Simon de Montfort; **Supp:** Pirates and Piracy.]

CIOMPI, REVOLT OF THE. A rebellion of wool workers that emerged from the conflicts of fourteenth-century republican Florence (*il tumulto,* as it was known in Italian) was one of a number of urban and rural revolts that shook western Europe in the late fourteenth century. These uprisings, such as the peasant revolt in England in 1381 and the urban movements in Flanders in 1379, while addressing different concerns, derived much of their impetus from the drastic changes wreaked upon Europe in the preceding decades. The European economy was devastated by a combination of catastrophes, from the start of the Hundred Years War in the 1340s to the bankruptcy of Italian business houses. In Florence alone the majority of trading houses had collapsed by 1346, including the three largest. The most disastrous blow was the bubonic plague that swept across Europe in 1348. The catastrophic loss of population, up to two-thirds in some areas, brought on a variety of social and economic pressures, increasing tensions between merchants and workers, lords and their serfs, and rulers and their subjects.

Fourteenth-century Florence was governed by a "guild-republic," in which civic officials were chosen by committees of guild leaders drawn from the twenty-one major and minor guilds of the city. The majority of the city's working communities did not belong to any guild and had no voice in governing the city. The Florentine elites were divided into two factions. The conservative aristocratic party allied itself with the papacy, while the liberal party opposed the expansion of papal power in northern Italy and supported the incorporation of a wider section of Florence's population into the government. While the liberal faction dominated Florence politically, the conservatives retained control over the Parte Guelfa, a semigovernmental institution devoted to ensuring that nobody of Ghibelline ancestry or beliefs participated in Florentine government. The power to denounce families as Ghibelline gave the conservatives considerable influence in the city. By the spring of 1378, tensions within Florence had reached a snapping point. Florence's liberal government had involved the city in a war with the papacy since 1375, a policy the Parte Guelfa detested. The conservatives began to undermine the liberal government by denouncing dozens of their supporters as Ghibellines, inflaming partisan tensions.

The revolt of the Ciompi, the wool workers, began as part of this elite factionalism. Several historians argue that Salvestro de'Medici and the liberal party instigated the first revolts as a way to attack the Parte Guelfa, and indeed the residences of the conservative elite were among the first targets of the revolt. But the Ciompi were not simply pawns of the elite factionalism; they quickly displayed an agenda of their own. The first disturbance began on 22 June 1378 and was largely an attack on the Parte Guelfa led by furriers and other guild members, although the *popolo minuto,* as those who did not have a role within Florentine government were called, did participate. In response to the uprising, civic leaders offered some reforms, notably the right of appeal against denunciation as a Ghibelline. Violence broke out again on 20 July, and members of the Parte Guelfa were again the targets. That evening the leaders of the revolt, both Ciompi and guild members, gathered to develop common goals for the revolt but were unable to agree. The next day the guilds and the Ciompi presented their different demands to the civic officers. The guilds insisted that all those who had been banned by the Parte Guelfa since 1358 be restored to their civic rights. The

Ciompi, however, laid out an ambitious platform of fiscal and political reform. They sought the establishment of new guilds for themselves and the rest of the *popolo minuto.* They also demanded that no forced loans be imposed on the city and that the communal debt (the *monte*) be paid. Florence taxed its population through these forced loans, by which the population would lend money to the government, in return receiving a share, which paid interest. Such a system benefited the wealthy, who could buy up shares in the *monte* from poorer citizens, often at a quarter of their value.

The following day (22 July) the civic officers fled the Signoria (the executive council of Florence), handing over the center of Florentine government to the rebels. The new Ciompi government established three new guilds, one for the wool workers (the Ciompi), one for the dyers, and one for the doublet makers. Included in these three groups were other workers, leading some historians to suggest that under the Ciompi government nearly the entire adult male population of the city participated in the public life of the commune. This is perhaps an exaggeration, but certainly an unprecedented percentage of the male population was enfranchised. A new constitution provided that the main magistracies of the city would be evenly divided between three groups: the new guilds, the lesser guilds, and the leading guilds.

By the end of August, however, divisions appeared among those leading the revolt over how far to push their reforms. The radical wing of the Ciompi was displeased with the compromises of the new government, which included levying a forced loan on the city. The armed radicals gathered, demanding the forced loan be revoked and a moratorium of two years be declared on debts. They also sought to establish their eight leaders as a permanent part of civic government similar to the Parte Guelfa but devoted to protecting the interests of the poor. Michele di Lando, the Ciompi gonfaloniere of justice, crushed this movement on 31 August and dissolved the guild of the Ciompi. The two surviving new guilds were joined with the lesser guilds, and the city magistrates were divided between the lesser guilds, now comprising sixteen guilds, and the major ones, of which there were seven.

This regime survived until 1382, when the leading wool merchants, taking advantage of the disgrace of two of the leading members of the government, led the *parlamento,* or citizens' meeting, to expel them and elect a new leader, who then rolled back the reforms of 1378. The government grew increasingly conservative over the next several years and consolidated civic power in the hands of the mercantile elites. Leading families who championed the moderate cause were expelled from the city or lost their privileges as magnates, leading to the formation of a ruling class relatively untroubled by factional and ideological divides.

The revolt of the Ciompi cannot be classified only as a workers' rebellion. Instigated by aristocrats such as Salvestro de'Medici, *il tumulto* included dyers and craftsmen from other industries, whose interests and goals differed from those of the Ciompi themselves. While other disenfranchised groups, such as the large group of day laborers in many industries, likely participated in the revolt, no attempt was made to incorporate their interests into the reforms. The reforms of the Ciompi, while brief, thus mark a break with the past but not a complete one. The institution of a guild for the wool workers democratized the government of Florence to a degree unmatched in the Middle Ages or Renaissance. They preserved, however, the same system of government that had come before, based on guild associations, and endeavored to maintain a sense of continuity.

BIBLIOGRAPHY

PRIMARY WORKS

Scaramella, Gino, ed. *Il tumulto dei Ciompi: Cronache e memorie.* Bologna, Italy: N. Zanichelli, 1917.

SECONDARY WORKS

Brucker, Gene A. "The Ciompi Revolution." In *Florentine Studies: Politics and Society in Renaissance Florence.* Edited by Nicolai Rubenstein. Evanston, Ill.: Northwestern University Press, 1968.

Mollat, Michel, and Philippe Wolf. *The Popular Revolutions of the Late Middle Ages.* Translated by A. L. Lytton-Sells. London: Allen and Unwin, 1973.

Najemy, John M. "*Audiant omnes artes:* Corporate origins of the Ciompi Revolution." In *Il tumulto dei Ciompi: Un momento di storia florentina ed europea.* Florence, Italy: Leo S. Olschki, 1981.

Roncière, Charles-M. de la. "Pauvres et pauvreté à Florence au XIVe siècle." In *Études sur l'histoire de la pauvreté.* 2 vols. Edited by Michel Mollat. Paris: Publications de la Sorbonne, 1974.

Ravel, Emilio. *Il tumulto dei Ciompi: 1378, i primi compagni.* Florence, Italy: Bonechi, 1978.

Stella, Alessandro. *La révolte des Ciompi: Les hommes, les lieux, le travail.* Paris: Éditions de l'école des haute études en sciences sociales, 1993.

CHRISTOPHER HATCH MacEVITT

[See also **DMA:** Florence; Guelphs and Ghibellines; Guilds and Métiers; Peasants' Rebellion; **Supp:** Acciaiuoli.]

CIVIC RITUAL. See **Ritual, Civic.**

CLARE, ST.

CLARE, ST. (1194–1253), cofoundress of the Poor Clares (or Order of Poor Ladies) and first abbess of S. Damiano. The "little plant of St. Francis," as she referred to herself, was born into a noble family at Assisi on 16 July 1194, the daughter of Favarone and Ortolana. The third child of five, Clare reportedly led a modest and virtuous life as a child and adolescent, spending most of her time at home. She refused a marriage proposal that had been arranged by her uncle. Sometime between 1210 and 1212, Clare first met St. Francis, probably on her own initiative. According to Thomas of Celano, Clare's conversion followed a detailed plan that had been laid out by Francis. On Palm Sunday in 1212, richly clothed, Clare went into Assisi to celebrate the Lord's triumphal entry into Jerusalem. That night she secretly left her parents' house and fled to the Portiuncula, where Francis and the brethren received her. As part of her conversion, Clare put aside her rich clothes and donned a simple tunic and veil. Francis cut off her hair, thereby consecrating her to the Lord. After selling her goods and distributing the proceeds to the poor, Clare moved for a short time to the nunnery of S. Paolo della Abbadesse. Without a dowry, she worked at the monastery as a servant, just as Francis had done for a short time at a monastery near Gubbio. Members of Clare's family were horrified by what she had done and tried to convince her to return to the world, even attempting without success to physically drag her from the monastery. After about two weeks at the nunnery, Clare moved to the church of Sant'Angelo in Panzo, where she was joined by her sister, Agnes, who had also decided to devote her life to God. On Francis's advice, the two sisters soon moved to S. Damiano, the church that Francis had helped repair. Joined by a number of female companions, Clare and the sisters living at S. Damiano became the first community of the Order of Poor Ladies, the second order of St. Francis. It was here that Clare remained for the forty-three years until her death.

At first the community at S. Damiano had no written rule except a short *forma vitae* given to them by Francis. The sisters engaged in various forms of work, particularly the cloth trade, but they gave to the poor everything they made. As the community at S. Damiano grew, Francis recognized a need for someone to oversee the government of the convent. Despite her protests, in 1215 Francis imposed upon Clare the title of abbess. Francis may also have given Clare this title as a result of the Fourth Lateran Council's prohibition of the creation of new orders. By giving Clare such a title, the community appeared part of the Benedictine tradition. But Clare did not wish her community to be subsumed by

The **Santa Chiara Dossal** *(detail). This earliest known panel painting of a contemporary female saint depicts miracles from the life of Clare. Assisi, the Church of Santa Chiara.* SCALA/ART RESOURCE, NY. REPRODUCED BY PERMISSION.

the Benedictine Order, and in 1215 she petitioned Pope Innocent III and received from him a privilege of poverty *(privilegium paupertatis),* which granted the sisters at S. Damiano the right to possess neither revenue nor property.

In 1219 Cardinal Hugolino, who had been appointed protector of the Order, provided four convents of Poor Clares, including the one at S. Damiano, with a set of constitutions that was essentially a modified version of the Benedictine Rule. While the constitutions were particularly strict with regard to the sisters' enclosure, they did not require the absolute evangelical poverty that was of such importance to Clare, nor did they stipulate that the sisters would be dependent upon the Franciscan Order. For this reason, Clare believed that the constitutions were contrary to the example and stated wishes of St. Francis. In 1228 when Hugolino (now Pope Gregory IX) visited Clare at S. Damiano, he tried to convince her that she should not insist upon strict poverty, arguing that it was impractical for the sisters to completely renounce all property. If Clare was worried about the vow of poverty that she had taken, the pope reassured her that he would be happy to absolve her of it. But Clare was not satisfied with this answer and boldly replied, "I never want to be absolved from following Christ." Gregory IX, who had been a close friend of St. Francis, appears to have been swayed by Clare's firm adherence to the Franciscan ideal. That same year he confirmed the Poor Clares' *privilegium paupertatis* first granted by Innocent III.

On 6 August 1247 Innocent IV provided a new set of constitutions for the monasteries of the Order of S. Damiano, this time based on the Rule of St. Francis rather than the Rule of St. Benedict. Once again, however, Clare found herself at odds with the papacy over the issue of poverty. She wished sisters to have the option of living in absolute poverty, whereas the pope argued that the community would have to hold goods in common in order to be self-supporting. Three years later, when the pope promulgated a bull declaring that no Poor Clare could be forced to accept the constitutions he had earlier promulgated, Clare set about writing her own Rule, thereby becoming the first woman to write a rule for religious women. For many years toward the end of her life Clare was ill and confined to her bed. Just before she died, however, the pope confirmed her Rule for the Poor Clares.

In addition to her Rule, Clare was the author of several letters and an autobiographical testament, the authenticity of which has sometimes been questioned. She was canonized on 15 August 1255 by Pope Alexander IV. Information about her life and miracles is contained in the Acts of the Process of Canonization, as well as in two of the *Vitae* of Thomas of Celano, a Franciscan contemporary. During the thirteenth century, communities of Poor Clares were established all over Europe.

BIBLIOGRAPHY

Armstrong, Regis J., ed. and trans. *Clare of Assisi: Early Documents.* New York: Paulist Press, 1988.

Armstrong, Regis J., and Ignatius C. Brady, trans. *Francis and Clare: The Complete Works.* New York: Paulist Press, 1982.

Bartoli, Marco. *Clare of Assisi.* Translated by Sister Frances Teresa, OSC. London: Darton, Longman and Todd, 1993.

Goobergh, Edith van den, and Theo H. Zweerman. *Light Shining through a Veil: On Saint Clare's Letters to Saint Agnes of Prague.* Louvain, Belgium: Peeters, 2000.

Kreidler-Kos, Martina. *Klara von Assisi: Schattenfrau und Lichtgestalt.* Tübingen, Germany: A. Francke Verlag, 2000.

Kuster, Niklaus. "'Das Armutsprivileg Innozenz' III und Klaras Testament: Echt Oder raffinierte auml;lschungen?" *Collectanea Franciscana* 66:1–2 (1996): 5–95.

Leclercq, Jean. "Sainte Claire et la spiritualité nuptiale." *Hagiographica* 1 (1994): 227–234.

L'hermite-Leclercq, Paulette. "Autour de Sainte Claire d'Assise: Publications récentes." *Revue Mabillon* 8 (1997): 295–300.

Maleczek, Werner. *Das "Privilegium Paupertatis" Innozenz' III und das Testament der Klara von Assisi.* Rome: Instituto storico dei Cappuccini, 1995.

ADAM JEFFREY DAVIS

[See also **DMA:** Franciscans; Women's Religious Orders; **Supp:** Poor Clares; Poverty.]

COLONNA FAMILY.

COLONNA FAMILY. An ancient aristocratic Roman family, the Colonna family was in origin lesser nobility from the Alban hills south of Rome. Like the Orsini, their inveterate enemies, the Colonna derived their power from both ecclesiastical and secular positions. The family ruled Palestrina, Colonna, and Zagarola outside of the city; controlled the fortified mausoleum of Augustus and Montecitorio in Rome; and often held the office of senator. With the exception of few periods, a Colonna was usually found numbered among the cardinals, protecting the family's interests in the church. Giovanni the Elder became the first Colonna cardinal in 1192, and Innocent III made his nephew Giovanni the Younger cardinal-priest of S. Prassede. The latter Giovanni brought the column on which Christ was flogged to S. Prassede from Jerusalem in 1222, a relic that was a pun on his family name. In 1240, Giovanni joined the partisans of Emperor Frederick II of Germany, establishing a tradition of Colonna support for the empire against the papacy. As a result of their imperial inclinations, no Colonna were members of the cardinalate or held high ecclesiastical office from 1245 to 1278. Furthermore, Senator Matteo Rosso Orsini destroyed many of the Colonna strongholds in Rome. Paradoxically, they returned to power under the Orsini pope Nicholas III, to whom they were related by marriage. Nicholas created Giacomo Colonna cardinal-deacon of S. Maria in Via Lata and his brother Giovanni senator in 1278. Giacomo's sister, Margherita, inspired by St. Francis and St. Clare, established a convent in the family's castle near Palestrina, which after her death the family moved to the Roman church of S. Silvestro in Capite.

A feud between the Colonna and Boniface VIII threatened the family's position and added further strife to Boniface's already troubled papacy. Annoyed by Colonna negotiations with his enemies James II of Aragon and Frederick III of Sicily, Boniface intervened in a family feud and insisted that Giacomo share the family wealth with his brothers Matteo, Ottone, and Landolfo. In response, Stefano Colonna seized the papal treasury on its way to Rome on 3 May 1297. The pope demanded the return of the treasure and the establishment of papal garrisons on Colonna territory, and when the Colonna refused (though they did return the treasure), Boniface issued the bull *In excelso throno,* excommunicating the two cardinals as well as other family members. The Colonna, supported by Fra Jacopone da Todi and other Spiritual Franciscans, responded with a public declaration that Boniface's election was invalid because of the uncanonical resignation of Celestine V. In September, Boniface declared war on the Colonna cardinals, entrusting the papal armies to their brother Landolfo, and in December 1297 declared a crusade against them. Their strongholds captured and Palestrina razed, the two cardinals appeared clad in mourning to cast themselves upon Boniface's mercy in 1298. He pardoned them but did not restore their titles or properties, giving them instead to Landolfo, the Orsini family, and Boniface's own relatives. Sciarra Colonna and Guillaume de Nogaret took Boniface captive at Anagni on 7 September 1303, demanding among other things the reinstatement of Sciarra's Colonna relatives. Two days later the pope was released by townspeople, but he died a month later in Rome. Clement V reappointed Pietro and Giacomo to the cardinalate in 1305, and Stefano reestablished the family's secular position in Rome, partly through attacks on Boniface's relatives, and was made imperial vicar in 1326. The family was again split in 1328 by the feud between Emperor Louis IV the Bavarian and Pope John XXII; Stefano defended the papacy's interest while his brother Sciarra was at the emperor's side when he was crowned in Rome.

Perhaps because of their Ghibelline sympathies, the family only produced one pope—Odo Colonna, who became Martin V. Elected at the Council of Constance on 11 November 1417, his pontificate eventually ended the Great Schism. He took the name Martin in honor of Martin of Tours, on whose feast day he was elected. He returned to Rome in 1420, to a city decimated by plague, war, and the long absence of its papal rulers. Under Martin's rule, the city began to recover, and large parts of the Papal States returned to obedience to the pope. Martin made his nephew Prospero cardinal in 1430, as well as giving many other civil and ecclesiastical benefits to his family. Under his patronage, Queen Joanna of Naples made his brother Giordano duke of Amalfi and prince of Salerno. Martin died in Rome on 20 February 1431. His successor, Eugenius IV, demanded the return of papal treasure entrusted to the Colonna, pushing the family to rebel. The Orsini, as papal allies, destroyed Palestrina in 1437, forcing the Colonna to submit.

The family particularly suffered under Sixtus IV (1471–1484), who was a close ally of the Orsini. The Orsini plundered the Colonna palace in Rome with papal permission, and Lorenzo Oddone Colonna was beheaded. The family continued imperial support; Ascanio Colonna was at the side of Charles V when he captured and sacked Rome in 1527, though he tried to minimize the damage to his native city. His son Marcantonio, however, commanded the papal forces at the battle of Lepanto and received a near imperial triumphal entry into Rome afterward. Julius II put an end to aristocratic feuding in Rome in the early sixteenth century, and the Colonna and other Roman aristocrats never had the independence they once enjoyed. The family continued to play a prominent role in the church and secular government of Rome through the early modern period; the last Colonna cardinal died in 1803.

The Colonnas also contributed to the intellectual history of the early Renaissance. Giovanni Colonna was a close friend of Petrarch's and wrote several historical works, including *Lives of the Roman Pontiffs from St. Peter to Boniface VIII.* At his death in 1348, Petrarch wrote the sonnet "Rotta è l'alta Colonna" in his honor. Egidius Colonna, often better known as Giles of Rome, was an important theologian of the later thirteenth and early fourteenth centuries who wrote several important treatises on the authority of the church. In the sixteenth century, Vittoria Colonna was a noted poet and romantic interest of Michelangelo.

BIBLIOGRAPHY

Barone, Guilia. "Margherita Colonna e le clarisse di S. Silvestro in Capite." In *Roma anno 1300.* Edited by Angiola Maria Romanini. Rome: L'Erma di Bretschneider, 1983.

Bretano, Robert. *Rome before Avignon: A Social History of Thirteenth-Century Rome.* New York: Basic Books, 1974.

Celletti, Vincenzo. *I Colonni principi de Paliano.* Milan: Ceschina, 1960.

Cherubini, Paolo. "Tra violenza e crimine di Stato: La morte di Lorenzo Oddone Colonna." In *Un pontificato ed una città: Sisto IV (1471–1484).* Edited by Masimo Miglio, Francesca Niutta, Diego Quaglioni, and Concetta Ranieri. Vatican City: Associazione Roma nel Rinascimento, 1986.

Rehberg, Andreas. *Kirche und Macht im Römischen Trecento: Die Colonna und ihre Klientel auf dem kurialen Pfründenmarkt (1278–1378)*. Tübingen, Germany: Max Niemeyer, 1999.

Ross, W. Braxton, Jr. "Giovanni Colonna, Historian at Avignon." *Speculum* 45 (1970): 533–563.

CHRISTOPHER HATCH MACEVITT

[See also **DMA:** Egidius Colonna; Rome; **Supp:** Eugenius IV, Pope; Orsini Family.]

COMITATUS. A Latin word meaning "escort" or "retinue," *comitatus* is usually used to describe groups of warriors in late antique and early medieval Europe, who by oaths of loyalty bound themselves to a common leader. The term first appeared in the second century A.D. when the Roman author Tacitus, in his work *Germania,* described free warriors who bound themselves to follow a lord into battle. The lord in turn shared with them the booty of the battlefield as well as the hospitality of his hall. Scholars have long seen the *comitatus* as an essential part of early Germanic societies. Some have used the concept of the *comitatus* to explain features of Celtic societies, as well as to explore the emergence of vassalage and feudalism in later medieval Europe.

The concept of the *comitatus* is perhaps most useful as a way to understand how the bonds of warrior society were described and imagined by writers looking upon it from afar, rather than as a description of how warrior societies actually functioned. Tacitus's description of the society and ethos of the Germans was part of a common language of behaviors typically ascribed to a wide variety of barbarian societies by Roman authors. Likewise, the most convincing descriptions of the *comitatus* and its cultural world are found in Anglo-Saxon epics and poetry, such as *Beowulf* and *The Battle of Maldon.* Such texts, however, were not the product of a pagan Germanic culture but of a Christian Anglo-Saxon one for which the *comitatus* was part of a long-lost ideal of the warrior rather than a component of contemporary society. Archaeological and historical evidence suggests that, contrary to the literary description of the life of the *comitatus,* most military retainers received land from their lords and lived independently and did not need to "repay glowing mead" consumed while living in the lord's hall by valiant deeds on the battlefield. That is to say, the social relationships between Anglo-Saxon soldiers and their leaders resembled those in contemporary Frankish kingdoms more closely than they resembled those described by Tacitus or by the author of *Beowulf.*

The value of the *comitatus* for understanding the later development of feudalism and vassalage in medieval Europe has also declined. Recent work has questioned the usefulness of these terms and suggested that the institutions they describe did not evolve from the personal ties of the early medieval period, such as the bonds of the *comitatus,* but were a product of the legal culture of the twelfth and thirteenth centuries. Nevertheless, the ideals of bravery and loyalty, the social bonds created by gift giving, and other social values encapsulated by the concept of the *comitatus* reveal much about the values of Anglo-Saxon society.

BIBLIOGRAPHY

Evans, Stephen S. *The Lords of Battle: Image and Reality of the Comitatus in Dark-Age Britain.* Woodbridge, U.K., and Rochester, N.Y.: Boydell Press, 1997.

Fanning, Steven. "Tacitus, Beowulf, and the *Comitatus.* " *Haskins Society Journal* 9 (1997): 17–38.

CHRISTOPHER HATCH MACEVITT

[See also **DMA:** Anglo-Saxons, Origins and Migrations; *Beowulf;* Feudalism.]

COMMERCIALIZATION. For as long as historians have shown any interest in medieval society, they have known that money and trade transformed ways of life between 400 and 1500. The recent emphasis on commercialization and on the importance of medieval monetary history has reiterated old truths, even if with an enhanced attention to measurement and description. A return to the commonplaces of the nineteenth and earlier twentieth centuries is only superficially conservative, however, since it has to confront a new and taxing set of problems.

EVALUATING MEDIEVAL ECONOMIC DEVELOPMENT

In the middle decades of the twentieth century Michael Postan, Georges Duby, and others reacted against older traditions of commercial history that, in their view, understated the significance of the vast noncommercial sectors of medieval production, especially farming for household consumption, both on peasant holdings and on larger estates. They interpreted commercial development rather as an epiphenomenon dependent upon more fundamental agrarian development. They also adopted interpretations of economic history that stressed the essential modernity of sustained economic growth and characterized "preindustrial society" by its propensity to stagnate. Postan criticized both vapid use of the concept of "the rise of a money economy" (which could be regarded as commercialization under a different name) and the assumption of continuous advances in productivity and welfare (to which historians writing about commercialization are occasionally prone). He considered that during the twelfth and thirteenth centuries population growth, chiefly sustained by subsistence farming and kin support, was able to wipe out any productivity gains induced by commercial enterprise. Doubts concerning the significance of commerce and urbanization for the course of economic development resulted in the systematic downgrading of medieval economic achievement by comparison with that of more recent centuries, when productivity growth unambiguously outstripped the growth of population in many parts of the world.

Historians since the 1970s have reacted against these views for a variety of reasons, some of which are scientifically justifiable. Many of the more pessimistic arguments were founded on an inadequate base of observation, and those who propounded them were so concerned with economic fluctuations that they often failed to give due weight to the ongoing institutional and technological change induced by commercial expansion.

Increased concern with commercialization has not led to any final consensus about how medieval economic development should be evaluated. Some arguments (notably those of Gunnar Persson) imply that commercially induced productivity gains, contrary to the pessimistic view, were in fact able to offset the debilitating effects of growing population and permit slowly increasing income per head of the population. Some have allowed that growth of this kind occurred, particularly in the period from about 1170 to 1250, but suppose that the benefits were very unequally spread and that a pessimistic account of the implications of population growth remains valid, especially for the late thirteenth and early fourteenth centuries. A minimalist commitment to the hypothesis of commercialization deploys it merely to plug some weaknesses in the pessimist argument, notably its difficulty in explaining how large numbers of peasant smallholders and townsmen were able to sustain their families. The long-term institutional gains from commercial development are more difficult to gainsay, though it must be admitted that many of the new institutions that came into being (local trade regulations, guild regulations, usury laws) were later judged to be incompatible with the continuing growth of trade.

Evidence in favor of commercial growth, especially in the twelfth and thirteenth centuries, is unambiguous. It is easily demonstrated that town life increased not only in former Roman towns but also in many wholly new locations. Venice is the best example of a major city on a new site, but there are many examples among the lower ranks of medieval towns. Newcastle upon Tyne, in eastern England, grew from nothing in 1066 to rank as England's fourth wealthiest town by 1334. The growth of international trade, led by Italian and German Hanseatic merchants, has been well studied for over a hundred years. The implications of that expansion for regional economies—English wool, Flemish cloth, Baltic fish and timber products, French wine and salt, Italian textiles and metalware as well as reexported Oriental goods—are no new discovery. The way in which monetization of the countryside permitted changes in landlord-tenant relations has also long been a principal theme in accounts of the decay of serfdom and the rise of urban liberties.

Those using such evidence to counter pessimistic interpretations of the period nevertheless face the major difficulty that formerly adequate levels of description no longer pass muster. The argument that commercial growth increased productivity and average incomes depends upon a comparison between measures of output and measures of population, and those are measures we do not possess even at a single moment, let alone as time series. Postan argued vigorously in the 1960s against the "lure of aggregates"—the temptation to use the fragmentary and often perplexing local evidence of medieval records to construct aggregate figures upon which to base arguments. He attempted to get around this problem by tracing a general history of declining productivity and increasing poverty in large numbers of documented local contexts. The trouble with this methodology and the principal reason why it has been challenged is that unless a large number of local studies all tell the same tale, the probability of any valid generalization is low. Historians have readily found counterexamples to those upon which Postan relied. Bruce Campbell, for example, has found evidence of rising productivity in East Anglia (eastern England) in response to commercial stimuli. These counterexamples have greatly reduced the validity of generalizations about the economy as a whole from local evidence. Debates about the quality of medieval economic development drive historians toward modeling the economy with aggregate measures whose calculation inevitably depends upon ingenious estimates. Unfortunately, however, the more sophisticated these calculations are, the more likely they are to be viewed with suspicion, particularly by historians with no stake in the debates that engender them.

Up to a point, the commercialization hypothesis can be argued persuasively without any far-fetched calculations of aggregate output or population growth. The chief arguments here turn on the supply and use of money. Not only did the quantity of silver in circulation rise during the twelfth and thirteenth centuries, mostly from central European deposits, but gold currencies were effectively revived from the mid-thirteenth century onward. On this evidence it appears certain that the volume of monetized trade increased more rapidly than population. In England, for example, currency in circulation is estimated to have increased by at least 3.5 times between about 1086 and 1300, and perhaps by 4.8 times, but only the most extravagant estimates of population increase suggest an increase of this order, and it is more likely that numbers did little more than double. Most historians would also accept the strong probability that throughout Europe urban populations increased more than population as a whole, which implies that a greater proportion of the population was dependent upon commerce for its livelihood. It seems very likely that the implied commercial expansion encouraged many improvements in productivity, though there is bound to be debate about their magnitude. Considering how hotly historians have debated standards of living in the period from 1780 to 1848, when nobody doubts that trade was increasing and levels of innovation were high, it is not surprising that there is no consensus about the thirteenth century. Some hypotheses currently in play may remain permanently contested for want of reliable data, but such intransigent problems can be a potent stimulus to original research in relevant and related areas.

EFFECTS OF COMMERCIALIZATION

There can be no doubt, meanwhile, of the far-reaching importance of the institutional changes induced by commercial growth. This is a large topic, and it is difficult to define its bounds. There was undoubtedly a strong relationship, for example, between the monetization of social relationships, the increasing resort to negotiated outcomes, and the increasing use of written contracts and bonds. The growth of monetized relationships also made possible new forms of taxation, with far-reaching implications for relationships between rulers and their subjects. For the purpose of appreciating the course of economic change, the most relevant institutional changes are those affecting the money supply, credit, and the organization of trade, since without them it is unlikely that commercialization could have occurred as it did. These institutions offer a rich but poorly explored field for comparative history, since although they have a family resemblance across Europe, there were also complex regional differences. Institutional change, together with some improvements in transport, encouraged both local and mercantile trade by reducing the costs of trading and increasing the security of traders.

Two institutions vital to the growth of trade were the market and the fair, the former being a daily or weekly event, the latter annual. Though medieval European markets and fairs had close analogs in the ancient world, their forms were new and of lasting significance. In medieval Europe, markets were held every seventh day in accordance with the Christian week, whereas Roman markets had been held every eighth day. The most significant markets were undoubtedly those in towns, retailing food, fuel, clothing, basketry, and other goods to local inhabitants, but a striking feature of European commercialization between the ninth and the fourteenth centuries was the proliferation of minor markets in tiny boroughs and even in villages. About 200 Polish markets have been identified before 1300, but only a quarter of these were in urban settlements. The spreading markets stimulated local trade and contributed to the monetization of social relations in both rural and urban society. Fairs spread mercantile trade over greater distances, and some attained international importance. The fairs of Champagne nurtured the development of trade between the Mediterranean and northwestern Europe during the twelfth and thirteenth centuries. By 1300 many minor fairs of only local importance connected rural and small-town communities with broader currents of trade. The development of markets and fairs was associated with the multiplication of commercial regulations and new business methods, in particular, new forms of partnership and new credit arrangements, which in turn encouraged the creation of new administrative and judicial procedures for policing trade and resolving disputes. The great fairs fostered the growth of a distinctly mercantile law that had no analogies in the older law codes.

The cultural impact of commercialization was profound. Its study has to some extent been impeded by deeply entrenched historical narratives that focus on the sixteenth century as a turning point in the development of modern commercial relations. There is enough work on Italian merchants, however, to establish that their education, training, and mode of operations were attuned to a distinctly commercial way of life from the twelfth and thirteenth centuries onward. The growth of a commercial and calculating ethic can be related to the development of rational and scientific thought. By the late thirteenth century leading canon lawyers had cleverly accommodated many commercial practices previously prohibited, and in so doing they moved toward modern interpretations of the nature of profit and interest. Even away from the main urban regions in northern Italy and northern France, the growth of commercial relations encouraged new uses of literacy, new concepts of profit and loss, and the adoption of new moral principles relating to commercial operations.

As an explanation of medieval social change, the argument for commercialization is distinguished chiefly by its stress on the creativity with which different ranks of people, from craftsmen to kings, innovated in response to changing opportunities. Monetary explanations can be absorbed into this interpretation as a special case, on the grounds that silver and gold had to be produced, minted, and traded. Though this perception of the period must always retain some validity, the emphasis to be placed on it is bound to remain contested by historians committed to the overriding importance of more impersonal changes, such as population growth or class conflict.

BIBLIOGRAPHY

Britnell, Richard H. *The Commercialisation of English Society, 1000–1500.* 2d ed. Manchester, U.K.: Manchester University Press, 1996.

Britnell, Richard H., and Bruce M. S. Cambpell, eds. *A Commercialising Economy: England 1086 to c. 1300.* Manchester, U.K.: Manchester University Press, 1995.

Duby, Georges. *Rural Economy and Country Life in the Medieval West.* Translated by Cynthia Postan. Columbia: University of South Carolina Press, 1968.

Kaye, Joel. *Economy and Nature in the Fourteenth Century: Money, Market Exchange, and the Emergence of Scientific Thought.* Cambridge, U.K.: Cambridge University Press, 1998.

Kowaleski, Maryanne. *Local Markets and Regional Trade in Medieval Exeter.* Cambridge, U.K.: Cambridge University Press, 1995.

Masschaele, James. *Peasants, Merchants, and Markets: Inland Trade in Medieval England, 1150–1350.* New York: St. Martin's, 1997.

Murray, Alexander. *Reason and Society in the Middle Ages.* Oxford: Clarendon Press, 1978.

Persson, Karl G. *Pre-industrial Economic Growth: Social Organization and Technological Progress in Europe.* Oxford: Blackwell, 1988.

Postan, M. M., and H. J. Habakkuk, gen. eds. *The Cambridge Economic History of Europe.* 8 vols. Cambridge, U.K.: Cambridge University Press, 1941–1989. See volumes 1–3.

Spufford, Peter *Money and Its Use in Medieval Europe.* Cambridge, U.K.: Cambridge University Press, 1988.

———. *Power and Profit: The Merchant in Medieval Europe.* London: Thames and Hudson, 2002.

RICHARD BRITNELL

[See also **DMA:** Banking; Demography; Fairs; Guilds and Métiers; Markets, European; Mints and Money; Trade.]

COMMUNES, 1200–1500. Communes were usually sworn associations devoted to governing a city, though similar institutions also existed in some rural villages. The main purpose of any commune was to secure the liberties of its members. Hence one of the major issues concerning urban communes is to define what liberties men and women living in cities wanted—liberties such as the right to own property and to make legally binding contracts and wills. Other powers in medieval societies, ecclesiastical and secular lords, had the power to grant or withhold these liberties. Liberty may have been at first a legal or political issue, but economic and other concerns soon surfaced. Communes were spontaneously created local institutions, and to speak of a communal movement across much of Europe is to generalize about a rich array of local experiments in self-help. The history of communes is not the vast story of medieval urbanization but the narrower subject of how, in some places, autonomous cities appeared for the first time since antiquity.

Towns existed across much of medieval Europe, though there were none in Iceland and few in Scandinavia and eastern Europe. In the Byzantine Empire, which still controlled much of the southern Balkans in 1200, older traditions guaranteed the state absolute control over city government, and hence there were no communes. In the remnant of the crusader states some faint signs of urban self-government would appear in the thirteenth century in places like Acre and Tyre, but there too royal power was predominant in urban government. As a general rule, the communal movement was strongest in those places that lacked a strong central authority or where towns were powerful enough to assert their claims against such authorities. Hence the Low Countries and northern Italy were strongholds for communes, as were parts of northern Germany, especially where the imperial cities succeeded in establishing self-determination. In the increasingly centralizing monarchies like France, England, Castile, and Naples, the self-governing rights of the cities came under increasing pressure, especially in the capitals where monarchs lived. Church lordships, most clearly in Rome but also in cities across Europe, also experienced a wide variety of successes and failures in maintaining their authority over cities. To complicate this picture even further, in some places communes like Florence were successful in subduing neighboring free cities and turning their own communes into effective ministates. For all these reasons the context of communes in the later Middle Ages requires a close look at chronology and regions in order to chart the vicissitudes of the communal movement.

LIBERTIES

At around 1200 communes flourished across Europe. Self-governing towns existed because the urban political class needed to secure freedoms in order to live as they chose. These freedoms appear as a bundle of limited rights that extracted their holders from particular claims of a lord. The dominant sources of authority in secular society remained those hereditary lords, from kings down to counts, who exercised jurisdictional powers over the land and those who lived on it. People living in towns did not want to be unfree, as were so many of the peasants across rural Europe. The dominant model for interpreting the communal movement sees it as a collection of local efforts to establish liberties inside feudal society. This does not mean that cities and their communes always existed in an antagonistic relation to feudal lords. On the contrary, beginning in the late eleventh century the warrior aristocracy was capable of seeing its self-interest in founding cities and granting privileges to communes. Self-governing cities often needed the help of strong regional rulers to protect their rights. Naturally these relations sometimes became violent as communes rebelled against lords. Communes and lordships represented different, practical solutions to the same problems of security and liberty. Local examples will flesh out the myriad ways medieval people found to work out their solutions.

People in towns required above all that they were personally free, not at the beck and call of a lord. Townspeople were not serfs. As such, they needed to possess their land, houses, warehouses, and shops, as freeholds or under a fixed rent to the landowner. Tenure had to be clear and subject to the rules of a market where people were free to buy and sell land, as their own needs required. Townspeople needed the liberty to make contracts that were enforced in courts following agreed-upon mechanisms for settling disputes. These rights to personal liberty, contracts, and courts were at the heart of the commune's purpose. Other necessary liberties flowed from these essential needs. People needed the right to leave property by testament, wanting their heirs to be free from a lord's exactions. Communes needed to raise funds in order to defend the towns, and so the right to tax was a fundamental part of the commune's power. Some taxes the members of the commune paid, while others were assessed on strangers who came to the city to do business. Part of the commune's purpose, in addition to securing political rights, was to foster the economic welfare of its members. Communes benefited from the right to coin money and control tolls and customs duties. After all, the commune's officers were either its own members or paid employees, close students of their own self-interest.

This issue of economic welfare concerned on one level the common good and broad questions like tariffs, tolls, and a reliable currency. The commune was also engaged in efforts to secure the food and water supply and its quality. The claims of particular businesses also merited attention. Often the big merchants, those engaged in long-distance trade in the town's main products or desired imports, dominated the commune. In a trading city like Barcelona, Venice, or Lübeck, these merchants in effect became the commune. Elsewhere, locally powerful merchants, like those in the cloth business in Florence or Ghent, expected the commune to protect their economic interests. Hence the commune became a clearinghouse for determining just which economic liberties would be protected and at whose expense. Although all the people living in a city were in some broad sense citizens of the commune, equality was not a strong value in the medieval commune. The politically active class, large in some cities and small in others, actually determined the extent of the liberties enjoyed by privileged groups (like guilds) or all the inhabitants. The final tension in the commune was between privileges for the favored and a general sense of the claims of merit. Being a member of a powerful family or group always mattered, but the commune, by fostering the welfare of its members, was also supposed to encourage the entrepreneurial spirit. And so the image of the poor boy who prospered, as Dick Whittington and his cat did in London, helped to justify the commune's existence. The opportunities for the increasing numbers of the poor were never the same as those for the rich, so the communal liberties counted differently for various levels of urban society, and within those economic levels the rights of women, Jews, and Muslims also varied.

THIRTEENTH-CENTURY COMMUNES

From the rise of the communes in the late eleventh and twelfth centuries, in the south (Provence and northern Italy), executive authority was usually in the hands of a committee of officials called consuls. These consuls, whose title if not exact functions harkened back to ancient Rome, came from the ranks of the big merchants and the nobles who had taken up urban life. Nearly everywhere the bishop remained an alternative source of power and executive authority left over from times when the bishop was the most reliable protector of the local population. A major part of the story of the commune is the gradual shifting of power to secular officials like the consuls. Before the commune established its own seat of authority, the palazzo, or palace, of the commune (or, in the north the city hall), official business often took place in the bishop's residence.

Struggles to control the consulate and the rise of factionalism led to a new solution to the problem of the commune's executive. By the 1190s the podesta had appeared in most Italian cities, except in Venice, where the doge provided some of the same functions. The job of the podesta, as it evolved over the course of the thirteenth century, became a professional post for a city manager. A podesta, usually serving along with the consuls or similar officials called, for example, *anziani* (elders) and selected by them, remained in office for a short period of time, generally one year. Increasingly the podesta was a trained lawyer because the most important asset he brought to the commune was impartial justice. For this reason communal law almost always required that he not be a member of the commune but a stranger from some other town. The job of the podesta became itinerant, as officeholders traveled from position to position with different communes, accompanied by a small staff of lawyers, notaries, servants, and a cook. The commune provided the team with an official residence, and the palazzo of the podesta became the seat of justice, an alternate palazzo of the commune.

In effect a city manager, the podesta became a profession passed on from father to son, and manuals appeared helping to train the next generation. The most famous of these manuals, *Liber de regimine civitatum* (Book on administering cities), written by James of Viterbo probably in the 1260s, offered a range of advice on legal, bureaucratic, and even military matters. Just as the podesta was supposed to ensure impartial justice, he also seemed to be an ideal commander of the commune's forces, since he would have the interests of the entire commune at heart, not just a faction or leading family. Even administering justice might be dangerous; in 1230 the podesta of Genoa was assaulted by a mob while he was trying to hang some pirates. This official escaped with a broken leg; in Bologna in 1269 another angry mob burned down the podesta's palazzo.

A reform that brought stability to some communes, the podestaria became a less effective tool for stability, as factions devised ways to evade its authority. Besides the local animosities among powerful families, two political issues swept across the thirteenth-century communes in the south. The first, the struggle between the Ghibelline supporters of the German emperors and the Guelph adherents of the papacy, bitterly divided some cities like Pistoia or led to the triumph of one faction over the other. In practice this political struggle evolved in local contexts and meant that the most powerful group, the Ghibellines, would hire a Ghibelline podesta from a city allied to this interest. Such an official was unlikely to conciliate the local Guelphs.

Another political split inside the commune cut across these divisions. The traditional elites of the commune, the magnates or nobles, the old families dominant in politics and the economy, witnessed over the course of this century the rise of the *popolo,* the rest of the population engaged in trades and professions. In turn the *popolo* itself was not always united but endured splits of its own between the richest, the *popolo grasso,* and the ordinary folk, the *popolo minuto,* the little people. Somewhere at the bottom of this hierarchy lived the growing ranks of the truly voiceless, the poor. The fates of individual communes depended on the how lords and bishops, Guelphs and Ghibellines, magnates and *popolo,* struggled for political supremacy. There were almost as many results as cities, and often the situation was quite fluid. The Visconti family used the office of archbishop of Milan to subvert the commune and establish their own faction's authority.

The rise of the *popolo* was accompanied by yet another new official, the captain of the people, first appearing in Parma in 1244. As commander of that part of the communal militia controlled by the *popolo,* the captain became a powerful force in city politics. In 1257 in Genoa the people elected Guglielmo Boccanegra as their captain, and he became the chief executive of the commune, even subordinating the podesta. The nobles overthrew him in 1262. In cities like Siena and Florence, the *popolo* waged a slower and more successful campaign to gain authority and positions in the various deliberative bodies of the commune. Often the *popolo,* organized into guilds set up on the basis of trade or profession, insisted that membership in these groups was a prerequisite for a political voice in the commune. The most successful leaders of the *popolo* faced the temptations of crossing over and joining the magnates or setting themselves up as city lords or signori.

One late-thirteenth-century development that had an impact across Europe was the recovery of Aristotle's political thought and the parallel efforts of canon lawyers and theologians to supply a legal and theoretical framework for the commune's right to exist. Thinkers like Baldus constructed a new model of sovereignty that saw the legitimacy of the commune as resting on local consent in the context of a lapsed or waning imperial authority. Local people, in communes and subordinate guilds, were free to make laws to govern their own affairs. Even where communes did not flourish, these new justifications for civic liberty and a renewed interest in Aristotle's polis paved the way for thinking about politics without lordship.

Northern European communes did not experience the podestaria, but the problems of factionalism and popular participation in running the city's affairs were issues everywhere. Another issue in the north was the growing power of national monarchies, so the kings of England and France were in a position to impose some order and rules on their capital cities, London and Paris, respectively. In London the mayor (from 1215) and aldermen, selected on the basis of geographical units called wards, supervised the internal affairs of the city, but the king was their lord, and through his sheriffs and royal courts he exercised considerable judicial authority over the commune and kept control of taxes. By around 1230, enjoying the freedom of the city by birth, by membership in the right guild, or by purchase, the politically active class divided responsibility over London with the king, who often lived in nearby Westminster and whose tower dominated the city. Beyond their capitals, lords also founded hybrid communes, where they granted varying degrees of self-government to new or growing settlements while retaining some lordly privileges and income from these places.

The policy of the French monarchy over the course of the thirteenth century was generally hostile to free communes, especially in Paris. King Louis IX's long-term provost of the guilds of Paris, Étienne Boileau, left behind a rich record of his activities in the 1260s. The king's provost controlled urban finances, regulated the guilds, administered justice, and with the royal power behind him, reduced the vestiges of communal traditions to insignificance by the late thirteenth and early fourteenth centuries. The places to look for the vibrancy of communal traditions in the north are those communes that were more successful in fighting lordly encroachments or where that outside power was weak or nonexistent. Two southern cities, Nîmes and Montpellier, had strong mayors and town councils. The commune of Toulouse succeeded in extracting itself from weakening lordly power in the thirteenth century, while the communes of Troyes and Provins had to strike deals with the still formidable counts of Champagne. In some places where factionalism was rampant, like Rouen, the position of rector, similar to the podestaria, turned to a noncitizen professional to establish order.

The earliest independent town councils appeared in Germany in Utrecht (1196), Lübeck (1201), and Cologne (1216). The struggles between papacy and empire in Germany offered cities there a chance to establish their liberties to balance lordly powers, secular and episcopal, that remained significant in most places until the 1270s. In most German cities that had communes the merchant and business elites dominated town councils, and there were as yet no signs of a rising of the people. In the Rhineland cities, the chief communal officials, the burgomasters, challenged the jurisdictional claims of the still powerful bishops and archbishops. Between 1258 and 1305 the council in Cologne ruled along with the archbishop, but the trend was for the big merchants and major guilds to supplant episcopal power and keep most of the people from having an effective political voice.

In the Low Countries, especially Flanders, many of the oldest communes had virtually complete control over their governments. Yet people may not have concluded that their liberties were safer under self-rule. A problem in some of these communes, like St. Omer, was that the city council chose its own members and the bailiff, the representative of executive authority, had become a figurehead. A narrow business and mercantile elite did not always respect the liberties of all the citizens of the commune. In these cloth-manufacturing, protoindustrial towns like Arras and Ghent, the commune often chose the short-term painless route of borrowing rather than taxing to pay for routine expenditures as well as wars. A pattern developed in which those local taxes that were collected, mainly excises on necessities, were farmed out to the wealthy, who made enormous profits as a result of political connections. The ordinary citizens, who paid most of the taxes, witnessed this transfer of wealth and resented it. In Ghent, the workers in the cloth industry had no political voice, and the commune was in the hands of a group called the Thirty-Nine, who replenished their own ranks without elections. In these circumstances the commune, instead of being the defender of liberties, in some places became just another repressive political institution.

THE FOURTEENTH-CENTURY CRISIS

The period from the 1290s to the 1390s witnessed a series of political and demographic crises affecting the survival of communes. A Malthusian crisis appeared in parts of Europe, soon to be exacerbated by famines and revolts in the early fourteenth century, in which population levels were running into limits on the food supply. In 1347 the catastrophic bubonic plague arrived in Europe, devastated local populations, and raised expectations among the survivors about communal liberties and self-government. Only by the 1390s did the period of immediate crisis seem to be ending, but many free communes had succumbed to lordship or even more narrow oligarchy.

Two bellwether events occurred in Florence and Venice. By the Ordinances of Justice in 1293 the Florentine commune banned the nobles from government, which rested on membership in the guilds. This model of a commune, common across Europe, allowed people a political voice through their occupations and in their status as self-employed and as employers of others. The subsequent struggles in Florence and elsewhere were over which workers had guilds and membership in which guilds carried the right to participate in government. In Venice in 1297 the so-called closing of the Great Council restricted membership in the main political body to those families, around 200 and now clearly defined as noble, who were already in it. Every male from a privileged family had a right to a seat on the council for life. Oligarchy in one form or another, defined by occupation, nobility, or membership in a faction, became more prevalent across Europe, as families and trades in a time of crisis secured their own liberties at the expense of the common good.

In the north a turning point occurred in 1302 at the Battle of Coutrai, where an alliance of Flemish towns defeated the French nobility. As a slow and uneven result of this war, communes like Ghent and Bruges were increasingly free to manage their own affairs, and more members of guilds acquired a political voice. The red thread though these developments is that as economic and demographic growth tapered off, disputes about communal rights became more violent. In Zurich a revolution resulted in 1336 with a noble, Rudolph Brun, serving as burgomaster for life and a city council divided between nobles and members of guilds. The durable communes in some Swiss cities remained a legacy of these medieval experiments in self-rule. In Ghent, Jacob van Artevelde presided over a regime from 1338 to 1345 that allowed the weavers a greater voice in the commune. This regime faced the economic difficulties the wool industry experienced at the beginning of the great war between England and France. Artevelde was assassinated in 1345, and Ghent returned to a more narrow oligarchy dominated by the count of Flanders's allies.

In Rome the papacy had never allowed any significant degree of self-rule. But for much of the fourteenth century the popes were in Avignon, and in 1347 a revolt by Cola di Rienzo established a popular regime that the nobles soon defeated. Returning in 1355, after the bubonic plague, Rienzo came to a much-depleted city, where he again attempted to set up a government. Rienzo died in the subsequent disorders, and papal government resumed. As first tribune and then senator, Rienzo evoked the glorious days of the city of Rome, but the

fourteenth century had no room for this classical model. Yet the theme of an absent or temporarily weakened central authority leaving a space for the resumption of communal liberties was not limited to Rome. After the capture of King John II of France by the English at the battle of Poitiers in 1356, the leading merchants of Paris made Étienne Marcel the de facto mayor of the city and head of a popular regime and thus gave the capital its first taste of self-rule. These events in Paris became tangled up with the larger revolt of the French peasants in 1358. In the end Parisians were unwilling to make common cause with the peasants, Marcel was assassinated, and royal authority returned to Paris.

Struggles inside communes, the ambitions of kings and lords, and the rising expectations of the survivors of the bubonic plague all fostered increasing turmoil in the later fourteenth century. In Florence in 1378 a revolt of the wool workers (Ciompi) during a period of economic stress brought about a popular regime that created new guilds and greatly increased the level of participation in the commune's affairs. The radical phase of this regime lasted only two months and was betrayed by its leader, Michele di Lando, a wool carder. The Florentine oligarchy learned to keep a more vigilant eye on troublemakers and sources of discontent. In England in 1381 the poor and voiceless of London, Cambridge, and a few other southern cities took the opportunity of the great Peasants' Revolt to strike back at urban oligarchies as well as royal and even university authority. Here too the revolt failed because the balance of power remained decisively in the hands of traditional authorities. Those communes surviving into the fourteenth century would not extend the liberties of their "members" to the entire population. Some communes, now calling themselves republics, retained the oligarchic features of this system of government and never pretended to be democracies.

THE FIFTEENTH-CENTURY SCENE

The period from the 1390s to the 1490s witnessed continued warfare and repeated, if gradually less severe, outbreaks of plague. Signs of economic and demographic recovery by midcentury may have contributed to less social tension inside communes, as did the increased vigilance and policing powers of city officials. Factionalism inside communes remained a serious problem. For example, Barcelona had developed a stable communal government that shared power among the rich, the employers organized in guilds, and even the workers. Yet even here, disputes between the Biga (beams) party and the Busca (thorns) cut across class and economic divisions and produced a series of disorders beginning in the

1430s. Only a rare commune like Venice had figured out a way to devise a system of government that contained factional disputes. Genoa repeatedly handed itself over to foreign rulers (France in 1396, Milan in 1421 and 1464) in a fruitless effort to contain local disputes by appealing to an impartial outside power.

In many parts of Europe the ambitions of monarchs, secular lords like the dukes of Bavaria, Burgundy, and Milan, and even strong communes like Florence meant that some cities found themselves incorporated into larger states that severely restricted their autonomy. In Italy more and more formerly free communes fell under the rule of despotic lords (signori). Florence in 1405 purchased the imperial rights over the weakened and depopulated commune of Pisa. Even Florence found its communal institutions cleverly manipulated and eventually subverted by the Medici family. Communes that had fought for their liberties in the eleventh and twelfth centuries succumbed to lordship again for a variety of reasons. The "New Monarchies" of the fifteenth century subordinated their own towns and posed too formidable a challenge to the independence of smaller city-states. Many free communes had failed to earn the loyalty of the voiceless, the majority of the population excluded from office but not taxes. Guild-dominated regimes tightened their own privileges in the face of war and economic uncertainty. The century that witnessed a revived interest in the politics of ancient Greece and Rome ironically lacked a strong theoretical base for defending even narrow oligarchy against aristocratic or monarchic forms of government.

Nevertheless, in some places like the Low Countries, the Swiss cantons, and some German city republics, the legacy of the communal era remained a living alternative to the claims of national monarchies. After successfully ending (for a time) Medici lordship over their city, the Florentine people in 1495 set up the most inclusive communal government ever devised in this period. Their Grand Council offered membership, based on a complicated set of "grandfather" rules, to 20 percent of adult males. No medieval commune had ever been so broad based. This one, served by Niccolo Machiavelli, was not destined to last long in a Europe increasingly hostile to autonomous cities where liberty was the core value.

BIBLIOGRAPHY

GENERAL STUDIES

Black, Antony. *Guilds and Civil Society in European Political Thought from the Twelfth Century to the Present.* Ithaca, N.Y.: Cornell University Press, 1984.

Jones, Philip. *The Italian City State, 500–1300.* Oxford: Clarendon Press, 1997.

Michaud-Quantin, Pierre. *Universitas: Expressions du mouvement communautaire dans le Moyen-Âge latin.* Paris: J. Vrin, 1970.

Nicholas, David. *The Growth of the Medieval City: From Late Antiquity to the Early Fourteenth Century.* London: Longman, 1997.

———. *The Later Medieval City, 1300–1500.* London: Longman, 1997.

Reynolds, Susan. *An Introduction to the History of English Medieval Towns.* Oxford: Clarendon Press, 1977.

Schulz, Knut, *"Denn sie lieben die Freiheit so sehr": Kommunale Aufstände und Entstehung des europäischen Bürgertums in Hochmittelalter.* Darmstadt, Germany: Wissenschaftliche Buchgesellschaft, 1992.

Waley, Daniel. *The Italian City Republics.* 3d. edition. London: Longman, 1988.

STUDIES OF INDIVIDUAL COMMUNES OR CITIES

Bensch, Stephen P. *Barcelona and Its Rulers, 1096–1291.* Cambridge, U.K.: Cambridge University Press, 1995.

Bowsky, William M. *A Medieval Italian Commune: Siena under the Nine, 1287–1355.* Berkeley: University of California Press, 1981.

Epstein, Steven A. *Genoa and the Genoese, 958–1528.* Chapel Hill: University of North Carolina Press, 1996.

Herlihy, David. *Pisa in the Early Renaissance: A Study of Urban Growth.* New Haven, Conn.: Yale University Press, 1958.

Lane, Frederic C. *Venice: A Maritime Republic.* Baltimore: Johns Hopkins University Press, 1973.

Lansing, Carol. *The Florentine Magnates: Lineage and Faction in a Medieval Commune.* Princeton, N.J.: Princeton University Press, 1991.

Nicholas, David. *The Metamorphosis of a Medieval City: Ghent in the Age of the Arteveldes, 1302–1390.* Lincoln: University of Nebraska Press, 1987.

STEVEN A. EPSTEIN

[See also **DMA:** Commune; Consuls, Consulate; Guilds and Métiers; Italy, Rise of Towns in; Podesta; Urbanism, Western European; **Supp:** Ciompi, Revolt of the.]

CONRAD I OF GERMANY, EMPEROR

(*r.* 911–918). The reign of Conrad I is often dismissed as a short interlude between the Carolingian and Ottonian dynasties. Conrad is blamed for his failure to curtail the autonomy of the duchies, thereby creating impediments to royal authority in Germany that would not be fully overcome until the reign of Otto I. In fact Conrad inherited impediments with the throne, most prominently the piecemeal demise of central Carolingian authority. Rule over a unified Carolingian Empire had ended during the reign of Charles III the Fat, when East Frankish nobles defected and chose Arnulf of Carinthia as king in 887. This trend toward local aristocratic authority continued during the minority rule of Arnulf's son, Louis the Child, when a coalition of lay and ecclesiastical nobles governed as regents. The erosion of Carolingian power was completed with the sudden death of Louis the Child in 911, which ended the East Frankish branch of the Carolingian dynasty.

Despite the potential for a succession crisis with the change in dynasty, Conrad's election was surprisingly smooth. With the exception of magnates from Lorraine (Lotharingia), the notables supported the election of Conrad, duke of Franconia. In so doing, they were not completely overlooking Carolingian traditions of inheritance: although from the Conradine house, Conrad was related to the East Frankish Carolingians on his mother's side. That Conrad was the first East Frankish king to be anointed reflected obvious concern to bolster the legitimacy of his reign, but the sacral nature of German kingship became a legitimating element for subsequent rulers.

Conrad had three major goals as ruler: to recover Lorraine, to defend his kingdom against the Magyars, and to reduce the growing independence of the dukes. He failed on all three counts, but not for lack of effort.

After launching three unsuccessful campaigns, in 913 Conrad gave up on trying to regain Lorraine, which had allied itself temporarily with the Carolingian West Frankish ruler. His efforts against the Magyars were similarly frustrated: whereas magnates in Bavaria and Swabia deflected the invaders, Conrad was notably unable to do so. His diplomatic strategies to control the duchies yielded more success. He offset the growing independence of Swabia by marrying the sister of its duke, Erchanger, and he stabilized relations with Saxony by signing a truce in 915 with Duke Henry, later his successor as Henry I, acknowledging his rank and position.

Like his diplomatic efforts, Conrad's reliance on the church failed to prevent the continued rise of ducal autonomy. In fact it may have exacerbated the situation by alienating lay nobles in the duchies, including those who had initially supported his election. However, in addition to his anointment, the alliance between rulers and ecclesiastics became a tool for building the royal and imperial authority of his Saxon and Salian successors. By his death on 23 December 918, Conrad had saddled his chosen successor, Henry, the duke of Saxony, not only with a legacy of internal dissension from competing independent duchies and external threat by Magyar invasions but also with instruments to overcome it.

BIBLIOGRAPHY

Arnold, Benjamin. *Medieval Germany, 500–1300: A Political Interpretation*. Houndsmills, U.K.: MacMillan, 1997.

Barraclough, Geoffrey. *The Origins of Modern Germany*. 2d ed. 1947. Reprint, New York: Norton, 1984.

———, ed. and trans. *Mediaeval Germany, 911–1250*. 2 vols. 1938. Reprint, Oxford: B. Blackwell, 1961.

Goetz, Hans-Werner. "Der letzte 'Karolinger'? Die Regierung Konrads I. Im Spiegel seiner Urkunden." *Archiv für Diplomatik* 26 (1982): 56–125.

Reuter, Timothy. *Germany in the Early Middle Ages, c. 800–1056*. London and New York: Longman, 1991.

ELSPETH JANE CARRUTHERS

[See also **DMA:** Carolingians and the Carolingian Empire; Germany: 843–1137; Otto I the Great, Emperor; **Supp:** Henry I of Germany, Emperor.]

CONRAD III OF GERMANY, EMPEROR

(1093–1152), was king of Germany from 1138 to 1152, a period of transition between Salian and Hohenstaufen rule in the aftermath of the investiture conflict. The younger brother of Frederick II of Swabia, Conrad III was elected antiking by the Hohenstaufen party in opposition to Lothar III. When Lothar died in 1137, the imperial insignia was in the hands of his son-in-law and heir apparent, Henry X (the Proud), duke of Bavaria and Saxony, but the German princes refused to accept him as king because he was arrogant and powerful. They found in Conrad III a more acceptable candidate for the crown. With the support of the German princes and the Roman curia, he was elected at Coblenz on 7 March 1138 and later crowned by a papal legate at Aachen. Conrad III was the first king of Germany in two centuries not to be crowned emperor.

Domestic troubles occupied Conrad III in the early years of his reign. The king aroused opposition by forbidding his princes to hold more than one duchy. When Henry the Proud rebelled, Conrad III stripped him of his family duchies of Bavaria and Saxony. Henry died in 1139, but opposition continued until 1142, when a resolution was reached in the king's favor: Henry's son, Henry the Lion, reclaimed the duchy of Saxony but lost his family's claim to Bavaria.

Conrad III was the first German king to take part in a crusade to the Holy Land. The results were disastrous. Inspired by the preaching of Bernard of Clairvaux and the example of King Louis VII of France, Conrad III and many German princes took the cross in late 1146. The goal of the Second Crusade was the liberation of the county of Edessa, which had fallen to Muslim forces in 1144. Odo of Deuil, the royal chaplain in the entourage of Louis VII, wrote a firsthand account of the crusaders' progress through Anatolia. The expedition was fraught with peril. Harried by Muslim armies in the mountain passes and suffering heavy losses from starvation and disease, Conrad III and the German army retreated to Constantinople and sailed to Jerusalem. There they joined the forces of Louis VII in a halfhearted and unsuccessful siege of Damascus (1148). The Second Crusade ended in utter failure. When the German king and the surviving princes abandoned the Holy Land in early 1149, the county of Edessa remained in Muslim hands.

Political turmoil greeted Conrad III upon his return to Germany. In 1149, a popular antipapal faction in Rome led by the preacher and reformer Arnold of Brescia offered Conrad the imperial crown. Conrad refused their invitation so as not to alienate his ally Pope Eugenius III, who had been forced to flee the city. The pope in turn urged the monarch to march on Rome and accept coronation by his hand. Before he had the opportunity to act on this request, Conrad III died on 15 February 1152. He remains a transitional figure in the medieval German monarchy, his pale achievements soon eclipsed by the reign of his successor, Frederick I Barbarossa.

BIBLIOGRAPHY

Conrad III. "Constitutiones." In *MGH Legum, sectio IV: Constitutiones et acta publica imperatorum et regum.* Vol. 1. Edited by L. Weiland. Hannover: Hohnsche, 1893.

Fuhrmann, Horst. *Germany in the High Middle Ages, c. 1050–1200.* Translated by Timothy Reuter. Cambridge, U.K., and New York: Cambridge University Press, 1986.

Lubich, Gerhard. "Beobachtungen zur Wahl Konrads III und ihrem Umfeld." *Historisches Jahrbuch* 117 (1997): 311–339.

Odo of Deuil. *De profectione Ludovici VII in orientem: The Journey of Louis VII to the East.* Edited and translated by Virginia Gingerick Berry. New York: Cambridge University Press, 1948.

SCOTT G. BRUCE

[See also **DMA:** Arnold of Brescia; Bernard of Clairvaux, St.; Crusades and Crusader States: To 1192; Germany: 1138–1254; Henry the Lion; **Supp:** Edessa, County of; Eugenius III, Pope.]

CONRAD IV OF GERMANY, EMPEROR

(1228–1254), was the son of Holy Roman Emperor Frederick II and Isabelle II of Brienne. Conrad spent the earliest years of his life at his father's court in Sicily. In 1235 the emperor brought the boy with him on a campaign to Germany to suppress an uprising led by his eldest son, Henry VII. After the defeat and imprisonment of the rebel, Frederick appointed Conrad as his representative in Germany. To secure the support of the German princes, he granted new rights of exemption that increased their control over lands and revenues. In 1237 the princes elected Conrad king of the Germans and his father's successor as Holy Roman Emperor. This action strengthened ties of loyalty and support between the emperor and his princes in the aftermath of the rebellion. It also undermined the role of the pope in the promotion of German kings to emperors, which further deteriorated the relationship between the Hohenstaufen dynasty and the papacy.

Throughout the 1240s, civil war and papal hostility troubled the regency of the young king in Germany. The emperor chose Archbishop Siegfried III of Mainz to act as regent until his son reached the age of majority but deposed him in 1241 when Siegfried's territorial ambitions led to unrest in the Rhineland. The papacy posed an even greater threat to stability in Germany. After a short-lived truce with the emperor, Pope Innocent IV excommunicated him at the Council of Lyons in 1245 on charges of breaking the peace. He also appointed and financed two antikings in Germany, Landgrave Henry Raspe of Thuringia and Count William of Holland, but neither of them was successful in unseating the prince.

Before his death in late 1250, Frederick composed a will naming Conrad as his heir to the kingdoms of Germany, Italy, Sicily, and Jerusalem. The new emperor was confronted immediately by the hostile attention of Innocent IV. The pope encouraged the Sicilians to rebel against him, renewed his support of the antiking William of Holland in Germany, and actively sought a western prince to champion the papal cause against Hohenstaufen claims. He offered the crown of Sicily to Richard, earl of Cornwall, and to Charles of Anjou, the brother of Louis IX, but both men refused to become involved in the battle between the emperor and the pope. Conrad responded with an invasion of Italy to crush the enemy of his father once and for all. After several inconclusive campaigns, his reign came to a sudden and untimely end in 1254, when he died from a fever. The loss of Frederick and Conrad in such a short span of time was devastating for the German princes and crushed the grand ambitions of the Hohenstaufen dynasty. Loyalists placed their fading hope in Conrad's infant son, Conradin, whose attempt to reclaim the kingdom of Sicily in 1268 resulted in his death and marked the final downfall of the Hohenstaufen line.

BIBLIOGRAPHY

Abulafia, David. *Frederick II: A Medieval Emperor*. London: Allan Lane, 1988.

Runciman, Steven. *The Sicilian Vespers: A History of the Mediterranean World in the Later Thirteenth Century*. Cambridge, U.K.: Cambridge University Press, 1958.

Thorau, Peter. "Konrad IV." In *Lexikon des Mittelalters*. Edited by Robert Auty et al. Vol. 5. Munich and Zurich: Artemis Verlag, 1991.

SCOTT G. BRUCE

[See also **DMA:** Frederick II of the Holy Roman Empire, King of Sicily; Germany: 1138–1254; Hohenstaufen Dynasty; Holy Roman Empire; Innocent IV, Pope; **Supp:** Conradin; Henry VII of Germany, King.]

CONRADIN (1252–1268), the short-lived son of Conrad IV and grandson of Frederick II, was the last legitimate king of the Hohenstaufen dynasty. When his father died in 1254, the two-year-old boy became the rightful heir to the kingdoms of Sicily and Jerusalem. He spent his youth in southern Germany in the care of his mother, Elizabeth, and her brothers, Louis and Henry of Bavaria. When false rumors of Conradin's death circulated in the south, his uncle Manfred, an illegitimate son of Frederick II, claimed the title of king of Sicily and was crowned on 10 August 1258. By 1261 Manfred had wrested control of the entire Italian peninsula from the papacy and its supporters. At the invitation of Pope Urban IV, Charles I of Anjou marched on Italy to oust the Hohenstaufen king. In 1266, Manfred died in battle, and Charles usurped Conradin's rightful claim to the kingdom of Sicily.

After their defeat by Charles I of Anjou, Manfred's family and allies placed their hope in the last Hohenstaufen prince, Conradin. Now aged fifteen, the boy was eager to claim his birthright and announced his plans to march on Italy. Pope Clement IV attempted to dissuade Conradin's Italian partisans by threatening excommunication to anyone who recognized his imperial claim or provided him with aid. In late 1267, Conradin set out from Bavaria with a modest army. The German princes were reluctant participants in the march. Conradin's personal entourage was made up primarily of Italian loyalists drawn from Manfred's supporters and the antipapal Ghibellines, who supplied soldiers and gold for his campaign. In the summer of 1268, the young prince pushed south to Rome, where the citizens greeted him with great enthusiasm, but his military successes did not last. On 23 August 1268, Charles defeated Conradin's forces at the Battle of Tagliacozzo and put the leaders of his army to flight. Conradin was captured soon after the battle,

and his royal blood cost him his life. It was more prudent for Charles to have Conradin put to death than to grant him clemency and thereby risk a future challenge to his power in Italy. Conradin was charged with robbery and treason and executed at Naples on 29 October 1268. The last imperial hopes of the Hohenstaufen dynasty died with him.

BIBLIOGRAPHY

Geldner, Ferdinand. "Konradin und das alte deutsche Königtum: Opfer der hohenstaufischen Italienpolitik." *Zeitschrift für bayerische Landesgeschichte* 32 (1969): 495–524.

Runciman, Steven. *The Sicilian Vespers: A History of the Mediterranean World in the Later Thirteenth Century*. Cambridge, U.K.: Cambridge University Press, 1958.

SCOTT G. BRUCE

[See also **DMA:** Hohenstaufen Dynasty; Sicily, Kingdom of; **Supp:** Manfred of Sicily, King; Urban IV, Pope.]

CONVERSION. The concept of religious conversion is central to the history of Christianity and to that of Europe. The term, however, spans a wide spectrum of religious and cultural experience. At one end of the spectrum stands the dramatic experience of a St. Paul, the first-century persecutor of Christians who was struck down and blinded on the road to Damascus, an experience that led to his becoming a Christian. At the other end of the spectrum there is the scene of all the members of a pagan society, led by its king, accepting baptism in appreciation for the assistance of the Christian God in defeating their enemies.

What these two quite distinct experiences share is a defining experience that serves as a pivot, so to speak, on which the life of an individual or entire society turns. This reflects the primary meaning of the term "conversion" a turning away. When applied to a religious experience, conversion describes the turning away from an old way of life and god or gods to a new way of life and the Christian God, in other words, a significant transformation in the way of life of the individual or society. The term also implies motion, that is, like Paul, the convert is on a journey. The dramatic event redirects the spiritual traveler from the wrong path to the right one. The baptism that follows the defining event marks the end of the old life and the beginning of the new one but not the end of the spiritual journey. For the rest of his life, the convert should deepen his understanding of God and strive to imitate Christ in his daily life.

Although the baptism of an entire society, accompanied by the destruction of traditional idols and sacred places and the imposition of Christian standards of behavior, is often termed conversion, it is quite different from the process whereby an individual accepts the Christian God. The former emphasizes external conformity to Christian standards rather than a profound internal transformation. In this situation, baptism marks only the beginning of the process of transformation, a process that some contemporary scholars, such as Ian Wood, have termed "Christianization" rather than conversion. In the process of Christianization, the people, once baptized, are organized into parishes under the direction of a resident priest who sees to their instruction in Christian doctrine and trains them in the rituals and practices of the Christian church.

The process of Christianization usually included a close relationship between religious and secular leaders. To some extent, this reflected the role of the king in pagan society as the representative of the gods. Once Christianized, the ruler lost his sacred status but gained the role of protector of the church and the faithful and the enforcer of Christian standards of behavior. Implementing these standards would cause significant changes in the life of the newly Christian society, so the support of secular authorities was essential. For example, Christian teaching forbade marriages between closely related individuals and banned polygamy and divorce, all of which directly affected political and social relations in the newly Christianized society. The internalization of Christian teaching and its implementation as the operating principles of a society, the consequence of Christianization, was therefore a continuous process spanning several generations.

EARLY CONVERSION

In the first three centuries of the Christian era, the emphasis was on the conversion of individuals and small groups as the followers of Christ traveled throughout the Roman world. The first converts were members of the Jewish communities found in trading cities throughout the Roman world. Such individuals readily understood the message that Christ's apostles preached even when they rejected it, because it was rooted in the Jewish religious tradition. Those who did accept it became converts, turned away from the synagogue, turned to Christ as the promised Redeemer, and gradually adopted the Christian way of life.

The second group of early converts, gentiles, consisted of pagans who found the traditional beliefs of the Mediterranean world unsatisfying. While such individuals might not have any acquaintance with Jewish thought, they could understand the Christian message in terms of the other religious movements, mystery religions, for example, that had emerged in the ancient world and provided a strong sense of community in a time when the bonds of the old civic communities were dissolving. The Christians and the potential converts shared a common cultural background, the world of the Mediterranean city-state, the civilized world in the view of Greek and Roman thinkers. This meant that the transition from Judaism or paganism to Christianity was not as culturally profound a transformation as the subsequent transition from barbarian and pagan society to Christian society was to be.

CONVERSION OF ENTIRE SOCIETIES

It was not until the fourth century that Christian missionaries began to make serious efforts at preaching to those who lived outside of the city-state culture of the ancient world. This gradually led to a new approach to the task of bringing newcomers to the faith. This approach, Christianization, focused not on individuals but on entire societies and often began with a dramatic event that enabled the missionary to convince a ruler to accept baptism. Once the ruler accepted Christianity, his people would follow. More clergy would come to instruct the newly baptized and to establish parishes and dioceses. The process of Christianization was not simply a matter of adopting Christian teachings and rituals, however. Many of the peoples the missionaries approached were barbarians in Roman terms, that is, seminomadic or migratory societies, not city-state dwellers. The institutional structure of the church, based as it was on the city-state world of the Mediterranean, required potential Christians to become agriculturists and take up a settled way of life, to become civilized in the literal sense of the term as well.

The story of Christianization has tended to focus on the dramatic actions of particular individuals, heroic Christian missionaries and enlightened pagan rulers whose efforts led to striking results, the baptism of entire peoples. In fact, of course, the process was a great deal more complex than these stories suggest. Current scholarship demonstrates that mass conversions did not occur among people who had no previous contact with Christianity. Intermediaries had to prepare the ground in order for the message to be understood.

Among the most important intermediaries between pagans and Christians were women, especially the Christian wives of pagan rulers. While from the perspective of a pagan royal family, a marriage alliance with a powerful Christian royal family might mean nothing more than a traditional form of alliance, from the Christian perspective, such a marriage could be a vehicle for introducing Christianity to the highest levels of a pagan society.

The careers of two individuals during the fourth century illustrate an important aspect of the new religious situation that faced Christian preachers who sought to win converts. The first was the emperor Constantine I; the second was the Gothic missionary Ulfila. Constantine is often described as having converted to Christianity and beginning the process of converting the Roman Empire to Christianity. The story of his seeing a vision that inspired him to employ the Greek letters chi and rho on the banners that his troops carried into the battle of Milvian Bridge in 312, where he defeated his last competitor for the imperial title, was the model for a number of subsequent conversion stories. Christians in his service identified the Chi-Rho with Christ and apparently convinced Constantine that he owed his victory to the intervention of the Christian God. He then issued the Edict of Milan in 313, legalizing Christianity within the empire and restoring property seized from Christians during the persecution of the emperor Diocletian.

Constantine did not, however, receive baptism at that point, doing so only on his deathbed. Furthermore, the Edict of Milan did not establish Christianity as the official religion of the empire. That occurred only in 392, when Theodosius outlawed paganism. It is not even clear what Constantine actually believed. Critics have suggested that he did not distinguish Christ clearly from *Sol Invictus,* the Unconquered Sun, the deity he and his soldiers had worshipped. Furthermore, he continued to see himself as a religious leader, keeping with the tradition of his predecessors, even calling the first church council, the First Council of Nicaea, in 325 in order to settle disputes within the church. He also had Christians such as Bishop Eusebius of Caesarea, author of the first history of the church, at his court. Gradually, a significant number of Romans appear to have adopted Christianity, many out of devotion and others because it was socially and politically rewarding to do so. Eusebius pointed out that there were many devout converts, such as Constantine's mother, Helena, who played a significant role in the subsequent growth of Christianity in the Roman world.

MISSIONARIES AND THE CHRISTIANIZATION OF BARBARIANS

The other important fourth-century figure in the Christianization of Europe was the Goth Ulfila, famous for translating the Bible into the language of the Goths. He was apparently a member of a Christian Gothic family residing in Constantinople in the mid-fourth century until imperial officials encouraged him to return and preach to his own people across the Danube. While that task was not very successful initially, his translation of the Bible eventually played a significant role in the Christianization of the barbarians. Ulfila's translation was the first in a long line of biblical translations that often were the first written texts in various languages.

Ulfila's career illustrates two important aspects of the missionary work that was to characterize medieval Christianity. In the first place, missionaries rarely, if ever, approached a society that did not already have some awareness of Christianity. The experience of Ulfila demonstrates that the barbarians beyond the boundaries of the Roman world were not entirely unaware of Christianity. He was himself after all from a Christian family, and his mission was as much to serve the already Christian population among the Goths as it was to win new members to the faith. Just as other elements of Roman culture gradually penetrated the barbarian world by way of Roman merchants, soldiers, and officials, so too Christianity had begun to penetrate this world as well. In the second place, missionaries such as Ulfila received support and encouragement from the imperial court, foreshadowing a role that medieval rulers often played. The Christianization of neighboring barbarians was often a way of stabilizing borders and expanding royal power. If Christian rulers were no longer descended from gods or the high priests of the state religion, they could still provide a great deal of assistance to the church in the form of support for missionaries.

In the wake of the collapse of Roman imperial authority in western Europe, new approaches to Christianization developed. In some cases the model was a lone missionary who braved the wrath of a pagan society to preach the Gospel. Like the story of Ulfila, however, such stories generally failed to appreciate the larger context within which the missionary operated. One example of this was the career of the fourth-century St. Patrick. Patrick was a slave in Ireland who escaped, became a priest, and then returned to Ireland to preach. He thus knew something of the people and their beliefs. It is also clear that there were Christians in Ireland before Patrick and that there were pagans there long after his death. There were also other missionaries working there as well, although their experiences have not been recorded with the detail that Patrick's were. Furthermore, although Ireland lay outside the Roman Empire, there had been trade and other contacts between Ireland and the Roman world, contacts that would have led to some awareness of Christianity among the Irish. The scene of the saint confronting the rulers of Ireland at Tara at midsummer and convincing them to become Christians, one that underscored the conception of Christianization as a process that operated from the top of society downward as the newly Christian rulers led their subjects to the baptismal font, was a later story, a story that schematized the process of Christianization rather than described what actually happened.

Elsewhere, women, especially the Christian wives of pagan rulers, played an important intermediary role in initiating Christianization. Clovis, king of the Franks, accepted baptism about 496 at the urging of his Christian wife Clotilda. Such marriages were common as barbarian tribes moved into regions of the old Roman Empire populated by Christians. From the king's perspective, such an alliance was politically useful, winning the support of a conquered people. From the Christian perspective it meant access to the highest levels of a pagan society. If the king would accept baptism, his subjects would follow.

The most detailed and thoughtful treatment of Christianization in the early Middle Ages, Bede's *Ecclesiastical History of the English Church and People,* reflected many of the themes found elsewhere. Bede stressed the role of great individuals and dramatic moments in the process. He may have understated the role of the surviving British Christians and the earlier contacts of the English with the continent in the process of Christianization in order to highlight a particular understanding of the process. Bede's discussion of the process begins with the coming of the Roman monk Augustine to the kingdom of Kent in 597. The pope, Gregory I, sent Augustine there because he knew that the king was married to a Frankish Christian princess, Bertha, an indication of regular contact between England and the continent. Although the queen had brought chaplains with her, no effort had been made thus far to spread Christianity, but their presence meant that the king of Kent, Ethelbert, was acquainted with Christianity and that his court could be used as a base for missionaries.

The process of Christianization that Bede described focused on efforts to convert rulers. His *Ecclesiastical History* described the negotiations in which King Ethelbert had to engage with his nobles before taking the decisive step of adopting his wife's religion, an experience repeated elsewhere as other missionaries spread out through England and confronted local rulers. Bede also suggests that acceptance of the missionaries' message by local leaders was facilitated by the fact that many individuals, moved by the virtuous lives of the missionaries, had already accepted baptism. In other words, the Christianization of a society was not simply a matter of royal decree but a matter of negotiation that involved a broad spectrum of the population and required the development of a consensus among the leading men of the kingdom before the new religion could be accepted.

Bede's *Ecclesiastical History* also provides a famous discussion of the ways in which missionaries could ease the passage from paganism to Christianization. He included in his history, letters from Pope Gregory I to Augustine and his successor Mellitus about a variety of problems the missionaries faced when dealing with the realities of the society in which the converts lived. One of the most important of these issues concerned those places that had been pagan sacred spaces. The pope pointed out that once pagan idols and other relics of the pagan past had been eliminated, the spaces could be consecrated to Christian uses. The conversion, so to speak, of formerly pagan places, rituals, and other practices to Christian use was characteristic of early medieval Christianization. Furthermore, as Bede pointed out in great detail, the process was not a neat, clean passage from paganism to Christianity but a complicated series of negotiations and compromises that only gradually and over several generations Christianized the English.

The Christianization of Europe, that is, the adoption of a way of life in accord with the rules of the Christian church, was therefore a long, never quite finished, process during the Middle Ages. Especially in rural areas along the outer edges of Christian society, pre-Christian beliefs and practices continued to play a part in people's daily lives even in the early modern era. The goal was to bring individuals to the level of spiritual life that is identified with the *Confessions* of Augustine of Hippo. The process was more than a spiritual transformation, however. The missionaries to the barbarian peoples of Europe not only had to preach Christian doctrine but also had to bring the barbarians to the civilized level of existence so that they could incorporate the institutional structure of the church, the parish and diocese. In order to become Christians, the barbarians had to become civilized, that is, give up their hunter-gatherer or pastoral way of life and become settled agriculturists.

OBSTACLES TO CHRISTIANIZATION

The complex process of Christianization in England that Bede describes occurred elsewhere as well, as missionaries came to terms with other local practices and customs that could be adapted to Christian use. The adoption of some elements of Christian life, marriage laws, for example, met resistance in some places such as Ireland, where church law forbidding divorce was generally ignored. Elsewhere, for several centuries clerics continued to record the survival of pagan practices, especially among the rural population of western Europe, and their efforts to eliminate them.

Resistance to Christianization was not limited to the rural population, however. Throughout Christian Europe there were Jewish communities that retained their identity and beliefs, and in Spain there were also Muslim communities that had come under Christian rule as the latter reconquered Spain from the Muslims. These communities posed a serious problem for the churchmen who wished to convert them, because their members possessed a body of religious learning and organizational structures that enabled them to defend themselves against Christian missionaries.

While forcing nonbelievers to accept baptism and, where necessary, Christianization might seem an obvious solution to the problem of non-Christians living in Christian society, theologically this was not possible, because conversion had to be a voluntary act and could not be coerced. At the same time, however, it was permissible to place restrictions on public expressions of Judaism, to require Jews to attend sermons designed to demonstrate that Christ was the promised redeemer, and to provide economic incentives for conversion.

Although theologians denied the validity of forced conversions, Christian mobs sometimes attacked Jewish communities and forced them to convert or die. The most famous example of this kind of popular violence occurred in Spain in 1391. One consequence was the creation of a number of converts eventually known as New Christians. These converts and their descendants were never fully accepted by established Christians, those whose ancestors had converted centuries earlier. They were mistrusted because their enemies believed that they had become Christians only to avoid being killed and continued to practice Judaism secretly in their homes.

TO A CHRISTIAN EUROPE AND BEYOND

By the early thirteenth century, the processes of Christianization and conversion had created the foundation of medieval European society. The Fourth Lateran Council in 1215 marks the point at which the process of Christianization was for the most part complete. The decrees of the council outlined the basic principles of European Christian society and assumed that the ecclesiastical and secular institutions required to enforce adherence to those principles were in place.

The medieval church's missionary experience had two important long-term consequences. In the first place, as Catholic missionaries went from Europe to the Americas after 1492, they brought with them fifteen hundred years of missionary experience that guided them in their approach to the peoples of the Americas. To a great extent, these missionaries saw themselves as replicating the experience of those who had Christianized and civilized the barbarian peoples of early medieval Europe, because the peoples of the Americas appeared to the missionaries to be at the same level of development as the barbarian peoples of Europe in the early Middle Ages. Their focus was therefore on repeating the experience of those missionaries who had Christianized entire barbarian societies by converting the rulers.

In the second place, the process of Christianization received strong criticism from Protestant reformers who argued that the Christian religion from Constantine to Gregory I had became corrupt under the leadership of the bishops of Rome. Among the signs of corruption was Gregory's toleration of practices associated with the pagan past of the new Christians. From the Protestant perspective medieval Christianity, the product of Christianization, resulted from the corruption of Christianity rather than from the conversion of nonbelievers. Protestant missionaries in the Americas therefore rejected the medieval approach to conversion, that is, the Christianization of entire peoples, in favor of what they understood as the conversion methods found in the early church. Seen in this light, conversion efforts in the Americas were a test of the validity of the original conversion practices and therefore of the validity of the Protestant version of Christianity.

BIBLIOGRAPHY

PRIMARY WORKS

Augustine, St. *Confessions*. Translated by Henry Chadwick. Oxford and New York: Oxford University Press, 1991.

Bede, St. *A History of the English Church and People*. Translated by Leo Sherley-Price. Harmondsworth, U.K.: Penguin, 1968.

Eusebius. *The History of the Church from Christ to Constantine*. Translated by G. A. Williamson. London and New York: Penguin, 1989.

SECONDARY WORKS

Abulafia, Anna Sapir. *Christians and Jews in Dispute: Disputational Literature and the Rise of Anti-Judaism in the West (c. 1000–1150)*. Aldershot, U.K.: Ashgate, 1998.

Armstrong, Guyda, and Ian N. Wood, eds. *Christianizing Peoples and Converting Individuals*. Turnhout, Belgium: Brepols, 2000.

Brown, Peter. *The World of Late Antiquity: From Marcus Aurelius to Muhammad*. London: Thames and Hudson, 1971.

Fletcher, Richard. *The Barbarian Conversion: From Paganism to Christianity*. Berkeley: University of California Press, 1999.

Kedar, Benjamin Z. *Crusade and Mission: European Approaches toward the Muslims*. Princeton, N.J.: Princeton University Press, 1984.

Morrison, Karl F. *Understanding Conversion.* Charlottesville: University Press of Virginia, 1992.

Muldoon, James, ed. *Varieties of Religious Conversion in the Middle Ages.* Gainesville: University Press of Florida, 1997.

Nock, A. D. *Conversion: The Old and the New in Religion from Alexander the Great to Augustine of Hippo.* Oxford: Clarendon Press, 1933.

Russell, James C. *The Germanization of Early Medieval Christianity: A Sociohistorical Approach to Religious Transformation.* New York: Oxford University Press, 1994.

Wood, Ian N. *The Missionary Life: Saints and the Evangelisation of Europe, 400–1050.* Harlow, U.K., and New York: Longman, 2001.

JAMES MULDOON

[See also **DMA:** Bede; Clovis; Constantine I, the Great; Councils (Ecumenical, 325–787); Councils, Western (1215–1274); Eusebius of Caesarea; Gregory I the Great, Pope; Missions and Missionaries, Christian; New Christians; Patrick, St.; **Supp:** Paganism and Pagan Gods, Survival of; Ulfila.]

CORBIE, ABBEY OF. Between 657 and 661, Queen Balthild and her son Chlothar III founded a monastic community at Corbie in the valley of the Somme upstream from Amiens in northern France. At her request, Abbot Waldebert of Luxeuil sent a group of monks to inhabit the new abbey. Luxeuil had been Columbanus's first foundation in Merovingian Gaul. Over the course of the seventh century, it rose to prominence as a center of monastic learning. Theodofrid, the first abbot of Corbie, had been a monk of Luxeuil and instituted its customs in the fledgling community. Little is known about the internal life of the abbey in this period, but early charters and privileges mention that the monks followed the *regula mixta,* a conflation of the rules of Benedict and Columbanus.

With rich endowments and royal immunities from taxes, Corbie throve during the Carolingian period. The statutes of Abbot Adalhard (822), a cousin of Charlemagne, estimated provisions for an exceptionally large community of 350 monks, 150 lay servants, and 12 resident poor. Both Adalhard and his predecessor, Maurdramnus, cultivated a vibrant intellectual life fueled by the intense activity of the monastic scriptorium. Over 400 manuscripts survive from early medieval Corbie, the earliest of which were copies of originals carried from Luxeuil, Italy, Northumbria, and Ireland. The didactic interests of abbots and teachers guided the choice of texts and the growth of the collection. The Corbie scriptorium maintained the highest standards of manuscript production. Texts of all kinds were copied both for internal use and for export to other monastic libraries. These included liturgical books, sacred histories, biblical com-

mentaries, hagiography, patristic works, and grammatical and computistical studies, as well as secular histories by Livy and Gregory of Tours. Annotations in these manuscripts, particularly those concerned with Christian doctrine and the study of grammar, indicate that the monks not only studied them for their content but also used them as models for their own compositions.

The writings of Abbot Paschasius Radbertus embodied the intellectual fervor fostered at Corbie. Paschasius entered the community under Abbot Adalhard and in 822 assisted him in founding a daughter house at Corvey in Saxony. Paschasius was abbot of Corbie for seven years before resigning to devote himself to contemplation and study. During this time, he wrote a biblical commentary, hagiographical works, and theological treatises, including his *De corpore et sanguine Domini,* the first substantive explanation of the presence of Christ in the Eucharist. Statements in this work aroused opposition, but its orthodoxy proved to be unassailable.

The collapse of Carolingian power contributed to the waning of Corbie's influence, but the remarkable output of its scriptorium has had a lasting impact on the study of early medieval book culture, beginning with Jean Mabillon, a former monk of Corbie, who used manuscripts from its library to illustrate the development of Latin script in his *De re diplomatica* (1681). Many of these manuscripts were sold and dispersed before the suppression of the abbey in 1790.

BIBLIOGRAPHY

Corbie, abbaye royale: Volume du XIIIe centenaire. Lille, France: Facultés catholiques de Lille, 1963.

Ganz, David. *Corbie in the Carolingian Renaissance.* Sigmaringen, Germany: Jan Thorbecke, 1990.

SCOTT G. BRUCE

[See also **DMA:** Columbanus, St.; Paschasius Radbertus of Corbie, St.; **Supp:** Corvey, Abbey of.]

CORVEY, ABBEY OF. In 822, Emperor Louis the Pious and Abbot Adalhard of Corbie founded the first monastic community in the Saxon territories near the town of Höxter in the diocese of Paderborn in Westphalia. The emperor appointed Adalhard as the spiritual father of the new community. The abbot summoned monks from Corbie to inhabit the foundation, which became known as New Corbie (Corbeia nova) and later simply as Corvey. Royal privileges from 823 provided the brethren with an endowment of imperial land and gave them immunities from external interference. In 833, Louis the Pious further strengthened the economic base of the abbey by granting the monks the right to mint coins, the earliest known privilege of this kind to a monastery.

These fortuitous beginnings allowed Corvey to grow and prosper. Between the ninth and twelfth centuries, child oblation—the practice of giving a child to a monastery for life—swelled the ranks of the monastic community. Corvey's *Liber vitae,* a chronological list of the names of individuals who joined the abbey between 822 and 1146, indicates that child oblates accounted for the majority of new monks. This pattern of recruitment was also evident at other successful religious communities in this period, such as St. Remi and St. Gall. Gifts of land made on the occasion of the entry of oblates accounted for a considerable portion of Corvey's income until the waning of the practice in the twelfth century.

Like its namesake, Corvey was renowned for its scriptorium and monastic school. Manuscripts of the *Institutiones* of Cassiodorus and the *De nuptiis Philologiae et Mercurii* (The marriage of Philology and Mercury) of Martianus Capella suggest that the liberal arts, particularly grammar, rhetoric, and dialectic, were a primary component of the monastic curriculum. The monks of Corvey showed a remarkable interest in secular history as well. Their library preserved the oldest copy of the first five books of the *Annales* of Tacitus. Moreover, in the later tenth century, Widukind of Corvey composed the earliest history of the Saxon peoples *(Res gestae Saxonicae)* at the abbey. Widukind was a monk from an aristocratic background who was interested in promoting the deeds of the Saxon tribes. His work is of primary importance for the history of the reigns of Henry I and Otto I.

Corvey was one of the northernmost centers of Christian culture in post-Carolingian Europe. It was the staging ground for the missions of Ansgar, who was a teacher at Corvey in the ninth century before setting out to preach to the pagan peoples of Denmark and Sweden. He later became the first archbishop of Hamburg-Bremen and was succeeded in this office by a number of Corvey monks. The translation of the relics of St. Vitus from St. Denis to Corvey in 836 provided a local focus for Saxon devotion to the cult of the saints. Monks of the abbey also composed numerous lives of northern saints, the most famous of which was Rimbert of Corvey's *Vita Anskarii.* Rimbert wrote this account of the life of Ansgar to commemorate the sanctity and missionary zeal of the indigenous "Apostle of the North" for his brethren at Corbie.

From the tenth to the twelfth centuries, the abbey benefited considerably from the attention of the Ottonian and Salian kings because it was favorably located at a ford in the Weser River on the Hellweg, the royal road frequented by German rulers and their entourages. Like other imperial monasteries, Corvey was expected to use a portion of its abundant income from landholdings to provide accommodation and provision for the itinerant German court. Some emperors took an active interest in the internal life of the community. In 1014, for instance, Henry II instituted a reform of the abbey at the request of Bishop Meinwerk of Paderborn. Corvey supported the German monarchy into the early thirteenth century. Like many Carolingian foundations, the fortunes of the abbey and the reputation of its school declined toward the end of the Middle Ages.

BIBLIOGRAPHY

Bernhardt, John W. *Itinerant Kingship and Royal Monasteries in Early Medieval Germany, c. 936–1075.* Cambridge, U.K.: Cambridge University Press, 1993.

Kaminsky, Hans Heinrich. *Studien zur Reichsabtei Corvey in der Salierzeit.* Cologne, Germany, and Graz, Austria: Böhlau Verlag, 1972.

Schmid, Karl, and Joachim Wollasch. *Der Liber Vitae der Abtei Corvey: Bestandteil des Quellenwerkes Societas et Fraternitas.* 2 vols. Wiesbaden, Germany: Ludwig Reichert, 1983–1989.

Semmler, Joseph. "Corvey und Herford in der benediktinischen Reformbewegung, des 9. Jahrhundert." *Frühmittelalterliche Studien* 4 (1970): 289–319.

Wiesemeyer, Helmut. "La fondation de l'abbaye de Corvey a la lumière de la 'Translatio sancti viti': Interprétation d'une source en bas-latin du IXe siècle." In *Corbie, abbaye royale: Volume du XIIIe centenaire.* Lille, France: Facultés catholiques de Lille, 1963.

SCOTT G. BRUCE

[See also **DMA:** Missions and Missionaries, Christian; Rimbert, St.; Saxony; Widukind of Corvey; **Supp:** Ansgar, St.; Corbie, Abbey of; Oblates and Oblation.]

CUMANS/KIPCHAKS.

CUMANS/KIPCHAKS. The inhabitants of the Eurasian steppe formed an astonishingly diverse array of ethnic and linguistic groups, and much effort has gone into trying to distinguish among or equate the Cumans, Kipchaks, Polovtsians, Pechenegs, and other peoples. The traditional distinction between Cumans and Kipchaks claims that Cumans were Turkic-speaking or ethnically Turkic nomads living in the western zones of occupation of a confederation of peoples known as Kipchaks. Such a classification scheme, still found in some modern scholarship, should however probably not be given too much credence, even if it does replicate the terminology of some of the earliest sources. The identities ascribed by contemporaries were themselves part of a simplifying effort to create conceptual boundaries in the face of the mixing occasioned by intermarriage, casual sexual relations, and ceaseless migration. While the relationship between Cuman and Kipchak is hard to determine, for convenience's sake, Cuman is the designation that will be employed in the discussion that follows.

Besides the ordinary nomadic occupations of herding and the like, Cumans hired themselves out as guides, go-betweens, and mercenaries. They participated in raids, sometimes against erstwhile allies in Rus (an area roughly equivalent to modern-day Muscovy). Relatively large numbers of them made inroads into Transylvania and became somewhat more sedentary. Though "related" to the Hungarians, they were often at odds with them militarily. Formal acceptance of Christianity occurred under Prince Barč in 1227, followed by the appointment of a bishop for the adherents and the establishment of a closer—and friendlier—relationship with the Hungarians under King Béla IV (r. 1235–1270). It is not clear, however, that Christianization went very far. The papacy was suspicious that the Cumans remained pagans even as they succeeded in maneuvering themselves into positions of power over Christians in greater Hungary.

The Mongol incursions into Rus and eastern Europe beginning in the 1220s drove the Cumans further into the arms of the Hungarians. Yet, old suspicions died hard; not even the existence of a common enemy in the Mongols could paper over all differences. On the eve of the Mongol invasion of Hungary (1240–1241), a particularly violent confrontation led to the murder of the Cuman prince and the estrangement of the Cuman settlers and the Hungarians. Many Cumans resumed their nomadism or simply moved away, only to suffer terribly from the ferocious Mongol attacks.

In 1245, after the Mongol threat abated, Béla again permitted bands of Cumans to settle and help repopulate his devastated county. Thereafter Cumans began to play an important role in Hungary; they may have constituted 7 to 8 percent of the population. Stephen (Stephen V; r. 1270–1272), Béla's son, married a Cuman princess. Cumans served as bodyguards, and Stephen's son, Ladislas IV (r. 1272–1290), despite occasionally fighting pitched battles with bands of Cumans, sometimes employed them in his own armies. He seems also frequently to have been a pawn in aristocratic and ethnic struggles involving Cumans. It was widely feared in ecclesiastical circles that, partly because of his Cuman mistress, he was in danger of going pagan; yet, he was assassinated in a Cuman plot.

Hungarian and Cuman distrust continued long after the Middle Ages came to an end, but Cuman assimilation did ultimately occur, including on the linguistic level. Despite some often wildly romantic claims to the contrary, little has survived of the Cuman language except a number of loan words in Hungarian, most often related to "horse-breeding, hunting, eating and fighting" (Berend, p. 265).

BIBLIOGRAPHY

Berend, Nora. *At the Gate of Christendom: Jews, Muslims, and "Pagans" in Medieval Hungary, c. 1000–c. 1300*. Cambridge, U.K.: Cambridge University Press, 2001. Valuable on the role of the Cumans in European politics.

Hildinger, Erik. *Warriors of the Steppe: A Military History of Central Asia*. New York: Sarpedon, 1997. A somewhat popular history of the Steppe peoples, emphasizing one important aspect of their lives.

WILLIAM CHESTER JORDAN

[See also **DMA:** Russia, Nomadic Invasions of.]

DALIMIL'S CHRONICLE (early fourteenth century) is the first chronicle written in Czech that charts Bohemian history down to the second decade of the fourteenth century. Its author is unknown, but a case has been made for Henry (Heinrich, Jindrich) of Warnsdorf, commander of the Hospitaller Commanderie of Zittau, which is now in eastern Germany, near the border of the Czech Republic, but was in Bohemia in the Middle Ages. The chronicle is in rhymed verses. There is a great deal of historical information, but the chronicle is also full of tales of origin and legendary and fabulous material, some of it borrowed from Latin sources and much of it frankly moralizing, testifying to the author's hope that the stories would be read at least in part for their didactic value. It does not endorse "frivolous" knightly activities but lays stress on fundamental values such as piety and courage. The telling of the story of Zdislava, duchess of Lemberk, for example, who died at the age of thirty-two in 1252 and though considered a saint was not formally canonized until 1995, lays stress on her strict devotional practices within her marriage, her eager support and (probably) confraternal affiliation with the new Dominican order, her endowment of and physical labor in building the sanctuary of Saint Lawrence, and her care for the sick and refugees from the Mongol incursions of the early thirteenth century. The chronicler reports her miracles, including raisings from the dead at St. Lawrence, the church that is now codedicated to her.

The chronicle is most often known for its vehement anti-German sentiments. Their presence prevented it from enjoying a modern scholarly printing in 1832, when the Prague censor turned down the request of the distinguished editor Venceslav (Vaclav) Hanka. The charge that it was too virulently anti-German must have arisen in part because of the chronicler's gleeful depiction of the disfiguring of medieval Germans. Hanka succeeded, however, in getting his scholarly edition published in Leipzig in 1848, and there have been multiple editions since, including the medieval German language version. Recent interpretations of *Dalimil's Chronicle* focus less on the hilarity and/or horror of his ethnic "prejudices" than on discerning what the author's descriptions suggest about the tensions among Latin, German, and Czech writers and the aristocratic and ecclesiastical courts that supported them.

BIBLIOGRAPHY

Bartlett, Robert. *The Making of Europe: Conquest, Colonization, and Cultural Change, 950–1350*. Princeton, N.J.: Princeton University Press, 1993. Illustrates how the chronicle's anti-German sentiments fit into a pattern of ethnic slurs.

Dalimil's Chronicle. Edited by J. Jiriček. *Fontes rerum Bohemicarum* 3. Prague: 1882. 5–224.

Thomas, Alfred. *Anne's Bohemia: Czech Literature and Society, 1310–1420*. Minneapolis: University of Minnesota Press, 1998.

WILLIAM CHESTER JORDAN

[See also **DMA:** Chronicles; Chronicles, French]

DANDOLO, ENRICO, doge of Venice (*ca.* 1107–1205). Crafty, blind, and vigorous into his nineties, Enrico Dandolo has fascinated historians since his death; his role in the diversion of the Fourth Crusade to Constantinople has been a source of considerable historiographical debate. He was not the first Dandolo with links to the Crusades and Byzantium. His grandfather Domenico and his father, Vitale, had been ambassadors to Constantinople, and both had joined the Venetian Crusade against Tyre, which was fought from 1123 to 1124. His father also became a judge, the highest office in Venice after the doge, and his uncle Enrico was patriarch of Grado.

Although little contemporary evidence survives, later historians suggest that Enrico was born around 1107; the future doge, however, does not appear in the written record until 1164. Disputes between his uncle the patriarch and Doge Pietro Polani led to the exile of the entire family in 1147, though they returned two years later. Joining the expedition against Byzantium in 1171 in response to the arrest of all Venetians in Constantinople and the seizure of their property by the emperor Manuel I Komnenos, Enrico served as an ambassador from the Venetian fleet to the imperial court. He traveled frequently throughout the Mediterranean, to Alexandria, probably to the Levantine coast, and several times to Constantinople, largely on political and diplomatic missions, not as a merchant. In 1176 he followed the example of his brother and father and became a judge in the Venetian government. In 1184 he returned to Constantinople as a representative of the doge to the Venetian community recently resettled in the imperial capital. Enrico went blind sometime in the mid-1170s from a blow to the head, although later legend posited that he was blinded by a Byzantine emperor who foresaw his role in destroying the empire.

On 1 June 1192, Enrico was anointed doge of Venice, an understandable choice given the prominence of Enrico's family and his own distinguished service to the city. The oath of office he swore is the oldest surviving, and his compilation of Venetian law was one of the basic legal texts of the city. Not all his actions were beneficial. Dandolo devalued the Venetian currency, but he also minted the *grosso,* the first large silver coin in western Europe since antiquity. His greatest accomplishments came with the Fourth Crusade. In February 1201 Dandolo negotiated an agreement with representatives from the counts of Champagne and Blois to transport 33,500 men to the Holy Land as part of the Fourth Crusade. The cost was 85,000 marks; in addition, Venice agreed to pay for fifty ships themselves. All told, Venice assembled at least 17,000 men and five hundred vessels for the Crusade, an enormous fleet. Although Dandolo himself took the cross in September 1202, the other Venetians who participated were chosen by lot. Whether they later voluntarily took the cross is unknown.

The planned Crusade faced its first crisis when only approximately 11,000 of the 33,500 crusaders expected showed up in Venice. The payments they owed to the city far exceeded their ability to pay. Dandolo offered to postpone the debt if the crusaders would help conquer the Adriatic port of Zara, which had long resisted Venetian claims of dominion. Many crusaders were reluctant to accept, as Zara was ruled by the king of Hungary, who had taken the cross and therefore was under ecclesiastical protection. Dandolo accompanied the fleet to Zara and assisted in its successful conquest. Outraged at this diversion of the Crusade, Pope Innocent III excommunicated the Venetians, including Dandolo.

At Zara, Dandolo agreed to a plan to divert the Crusade to Constantinople to place Alexios, son of the deposed and blinded Isaac II Angelos, on the Byzantine throne. The crusaders wintered in Zara and set out for Constantinople in April 1203; they attacked the imperial city on 5 July. Dandolo himself led the Venetian forces on a seaborne assault on the city. The emperor Alexios III Angelos, who had deposed Isaac II, fled the city on the night of 17 July after a destructive crusader assault, and Byzantine officials released Isaac II from jail and restored him to the throne. He crowned his son Alexios (IV) as his coruler, and the crusaders soon became the prop for the new uncertain Angelos emperors. Their regime did not last long. In January 1204, an anti-Latin faction led by Alexios Doukas deposed Alexios IV, whom they killed the following month. The crusaders were left with large sums unpaid by the deposed Alexios and the possibility that their Crusade might collapse.

The crusaders decided to seize Constantinople in repayment of their debts. In March, Dandolo reached agreement with the other crusader leaders concerning the division of spoils and the election of a new emperor should they capture the city. The second siege of the city began on 9 April 1204; Dandolo was influential in preparing the crusader forces. The first attack on the city focused on the sea walls on the Golden Horn, where Dandolo and his troops had had great success during the first siege of the city. The Byzantines, however, had prepared for the possibility of an attack there, and the crusaders suffered a resounding defeat. An attack three days later succeeded in breaching the sea walls, and Alexios V Doukas fled. The city, never before conquered by a foreign army, belonged to the crusaders. The fires they had set, however, to aid in their attack destroyed much of the city. After days of plunder and rape, the crusaders assembled in Dandolo's new palace to elect an emperor. The election of a Frankish emperor—Baldwin of Flanders—meant by the terms of the agreement that the patriarch was to be a Venetian. The pillaging of the city amply repaid Venice's debt, and through Dandolo's diplomatic skills, Venice gained three-eighths of the divided Byzantine Empire.

Dandolo was among the most influential leaders in the new Latin empire, mediating conflicts among the Frankish leaders. By supporting Boniface of Montferrat's claim to Thessaloniki, the doge won for Venice the island of Crete, an essential part of the Venetian empire for centuries to come. He died of an inguinal hernia in May 1205, following the crusader defeat at Adrianople. Byzantine chroniclers vilified him as an inveterate enemy of Byzantium.

BIBLIOGRAPHY

Madden, Thomas. "Venice and Constantinople in 1171 and 1172: Enrico Dandolo's Attitude towards Byzantium." *Mediterranean Historical Review* 8 (1993): 166–185.

———. *Enrico Dandolo and the Rise of Venice.* Baltimore: Johns Hopkins University Press, 2003.

Necker, Karl-Hartmann. *Dandolo: Venedigs kühnster Doge.* Vienna: Böhlau, 1999.

Queller, Donald E., and Thomas F. Madden. *The Fourth Crusade: The Conquest of Constantinople.* Philadelphia: University of Pennsylvania Press, 1997.

CHRISTOPHER HATCH MACEVITT

[See also **DMA:** Angelos; Constantinople; Crusades and Crusader States: Fourth; Doukas; Groat; Manuel I Komnenos; Venice.]

DEGUILEVILLE, GUILLAUME DE

DEGUILEVILLE, GUILLAUME DE (*ca.* 1295–after 1358). The Cistercian monk Guillaume de Deguileville was one of the most influential writers of the fourteenth century, yet only few basic facts are known about his life. He was born around 1295, possibly in Paris. In his early twenties he entered the Cistercian monastery of Chaalis near Senlis, in north central France, where he spent almost forty years.

In 1331 Deguileville wrote *Pèlerinage de vie humaine* (Pilgrimage of the life of man), the first of three major allegorical works. The manuscript, however, was stolen and circulated without his permission, and he disavowed this first draft. In 1355 he finished a second version of the poem that surpassed the first by more than 6,000 lines; it now totaled almost 25,000 lines and included new characters and situations and expanded many of the previous details and explanations. The work begins with the narrator reading the *Roman de la Rose*—which had greatly influenced Deguileville—and then proceeds to a dream vision in which the narrator makes a pilgrimage to the Heavenly Jerusalem. Along the way he is helped by such allegorical figures as Nature, Charity, and Grace Dieu while Idleness, the Seven Deadly Sins, and other evil characters try to impede his progress. The dream ends with Jerusalem unattained as Death approaches to take the narrator, only to be stopped by the narrator's awakening.

The same year Deguileville finished the second version of the *Pèlerinage de vie humaine,* he also completed the *Pèlerinage de l'âme,* which was translated and adapted into English as the *Pilgrimage of the Soul* or *The Book of Grace Dieu.* The *Pèlerinage de l'âme* follows a soul in its spiritual wanderings after death. The soul escapes eternal damnation only through the intercession of the Virgin

Mary and must then spend time in purgatory. The sentence in purgatory is spent learning and asking questions about Christian doctrine. Finally, after it has paid its dues, the soul makes its way to the gates of Heaven. Three years later, Deguileville finished his trilogy with the *Pèlerinage de Jhesucrist* (Pilgrimage of Jesus Christ), essentially a verse version of the Gospels that, like the others, relies on allegories.

The three poems have survived in at least eighty-six manuscripts from all over Europe, attesting to their wide popularity. They were translated into many of the western European vernaculars including German, Castilian, and English. John Lydgate (*ca.* 1370–*ca.* 1450), an accomplished poet in his own right and a prodigious translator, provided the Middle English adaptation of the *Pèlerinage de vie humaine* in 1426. Many of the manuscripts are beautifully decorated with miniatures, designed to help the reader understand the allegorical representations. The wide circulation the poems received help to explain the tremendous influence that Deguileville had upon his contemporaries and later writers. His influence on Chaucer is unquestioned, and he has been credited with inspiring Spenser, Milton, and John Bunyan, among others, although in some of these cases the relationship has been questioned.

BIBLIOGRAPHY

PRIMARY WORKS

Lydgate, John. *The Pilgrimage of the Life of Man.* Edited by F. J. Furnivall and with an introduction by K. B. Locock. London: Early English Text Society, 1899–1904. Middle English adaptation of *Le pèlerinage de vie humaine.*

Stürzinger, J. J., ed. *Le pèlerinage de vie humaine de Guillaume de Deguileville.* London: Nichols, 1893.

———. *Le pèlerinage de l'âme de Guillaume de Deguileville.* London: Nichols, 1895.

———. *Le pèlerinage de Jhesucrist de Guillaume de Deguileville.* London: Nichols, 1897.

SECONDARY WORKS

Faral, Edmond. "Guillaume de Deguileville, moine de Chaalis." *Histoire littéraire de la France* 39 (1952): 1–132.

Hagen, Susan K. *Allegorical Remembrance: A Study of the Pilgrimage of the Life of Man as a Medieval Treatise on Seeing and Remembering.* Athens: University of Georgia Press, 1990.

Phillips, Helen. "Chaucer and Deguileville: The *ABC* in Context." *Medium Aevum* 62 (1993) 1–19.

Potz McGerr, Rosemary, ed. *The Pilgrimage of the Soul: A Critical Edition of the Middle English Dream Vision.* New York: Garland, 1990.

JARBEL RODRIGUEZ

[See also **DMA:** Allegory; Chaucer, Geoffrey; Cistercian Order; Exegesis, Middle English; Lydgate, John; Middle English Literature; *Roman de la Rose;* Visions.]

DEMANDA DO SANTO GRAAL, the Portuguese version of the romance of the Holy Grail. Beginning with Alfonso VIII of Castile's marriage to Eleanor of England in 1170, contacts intensified between English courts and those on the Iberian Peninsula. By the early thirteenth century, Arthurian literature was being diffused through various parts of the peninsula. Pedro II of Aragon (*r.* 1196–1213) was likened to King Arthur. Galician-Portuguese poets made reference in their poems to the Arthurian legends.

The legend of the Holy Grail was first introduced in the peninsula in its French form, becoming popular among the thirteenth-century aristocratic elite in the courts of Lisbon, Toledo, Pamplona, and Barcelona. The earliest known translation of the legend into Portuguese was done by João Vivas, appearing in 1313 at the end of the Portuguese *Liuro de Josep Abaramatia* (Book of Joseph of Arimathea). A sixteenth-century manuscript copy of this early translation still survives. The text corresponds more or less to the *Estoire del Saint Graal* (History of the Holy Grail), the first part of a Grail trilogy (although this first part was actually written after the other two parts) commonly referred to as the first branch of the vulgate version of the Arthurian legend (because its author claimed to have translated the text from Latin into French). The text begins with some preliminary remarks by the author and then proceeds to tell the history of Joseph of Arimathea and the Grail, the conversion of Evalac and Seraphe, the story of the Turning Island and Solomon's ship, Joseph and his conversion of the pagans of Great Britain, the adventures of their descendants to the time of King Arthur, and finally Lancelot's visit to his father's tomb and his killing of the lions that guard it. The Portuguese version follows the French story with some slight abbreviations, extensions, and omissions. The language of the text, clearly that of the early fourteenth century and not that of the sixteenth century, displays the influence of the *trovadores,* who had recited oral versions of the story before it was written down and translated. The Grail romance may well have been translated into Portuguese before it was translated into Castilian, although a parallel Castilian text appears to have derived from the same source as the Portuguese version.

Also extant is an early fifteenth-century manuscript of the Portuguese *Demanda do Santo Graal.* This text is based on the third branch of the French post-Vulgate story of the Grail (a revised version of the earlier vulgate version), which includes the *Queste del Saint Graal* (Search for the Holy Grail) and *Mort Artu* (Death of Arthur). The narrative begins with the announcement of Galahad's arrival at Arthur's court and ends with the deaths of Arthur, Guenevere, Lancelot, and Mark. It appears that this Portuguese *Demanda* and a parallel Spanish *Demanda del Sancto Grial,* while independent of each other, did derive from a common source. In all likelihood, neither one derived directly from the French but rather from a lost Galician-Portuguese version of the French. The Spanish and Portuguese translations and adaptations of the Grail romance had a significant influence on chivalric romances composed on the peninsula during the fourteenth and fifteenth centuries.

BIBLIOGRAPHY

A demanda do Santo Graal. Edited by Irene Freire Nunes. Lisbon: Imprensa Nacional-Casa da Moeda, 1995. A critical edition of the Vienna manuscript (ms 2594) of the *Demanda* from the early fifteenth century. This supersedes the two earlier and problematic editions by A. Magne.

Bogdanow, Fanni. *The Romance of the Grail: A Study of the Structure and Genesis of a Thirteenth-Century Arthurian Prose Romance.* Manchester: Manchester University Press, 1966. A classic work that provides helpful context.

Lida De Malkiel, María Rosa. "Arthurian Literature in Spain and Portugal." In *Arthurian Literature in the Middle Ages.* Edited by Roger Sherman Loomis. Oxford: Oxford University Press, 1979.

Miranda, José Carlos Ribeiro. *A demanda do Santo Graal e o ciclo arturiano da vulgata.* Porto, Portugal: Granito, 1998.

ADAM JEFFREY DAVIS

[See also **DMA:** Arthurian Literature, Spanish and Portuguese.]

DEMONS. The word "demon" comes originally from the classical Greek *daimon,* a guardian spirit or being below the gods in status. For medieval authors demons were evil spirits serving as Satan's assistants, having fallen from heaven with him in rebelling against God and now existing on earth and in middle air. Demons replicated on earth the many legions and hierarchies of the fallen angels from which they had metamorphosed. One authority, Johann Weyer in his *De praestigiis daemonum* (The deception of demons, 1563), calculated their exact number at 7,405,926.

An alternative to this view of demons as fallen angels was popular in Jewish thought and apocryphal texts such as the second-century-A.D. *Book of Enoch.* Introducing an intermediate stage in their lineage, this explanation claimed that demons resulted from copulation between

Demon Leading Woman to St. Benedict. *Part of a temptation scene from a mid-12th-century capital at St. Madeleine, Vézelay.* PHOTOGRAPH COURTESY OF JOHN FRIEDMAN. REPRODUCED BY PERMISSION.

the fallen angels and mortal women. Whatever their origins, however, just as with Satan himself, demons exist only by God's will.

In the later Middle Ages, at the commands of a priest or bishop uttering formulas incorporating descriptions of Christ's power over demons in Matthew 8:16 and 28–32 (where the evil spirits entered the bodies of swine), demons were believed driven from churches and even persons. Exorcisms of people possessed by demons were often conducted in churches next to the altar, with a priest speaking the Gospel phrases and then applying relics or holy water to the affected person's body.

In didactic literature and in popular culture, demons could also be vanquished by a steadfast monk like Benedict or a hermit like the Desert Father St. Anthony, who, as reported in Jacobus de Varagine's *Golden Legend,* "conquered by his faith the demon of lust; when the devil appearing to him in the form of a black child, prostrated himself before Anthony, he pronounced himself overcome by the saint." Charms and conjurations using Christ's name and the names of saints like Benedict, who

Devils Seizing the Soul of a Rich Sinner. *The soul (*spiritus,* breath) is shown escaping from the sinner's mouth. Mid-12th-century capital from Ste. Madeleine, Vézelay.* PHOTOGRAPH COURTESY OF JOHN FRIEDMAN. REPRODUCED BY PERMISSION.

Demon in the Guise of a Toad Oversees Hell-Mouth with Damned Souls. *This miniature is from a French Blockbook Apocalypse of ca. 1470.* NEW YORK PUBLIC LIBRARY (COURTESY ASTOR, LENOX, AND TILDEN FOUNDATIONS).

successfully resisted such demonic assaults, were believed to expel demons from domestic buildings.

Demons most commonly appear in medieval literature and art as the tempters, assailants, and scourges of mortals. They do Satan's work in daily life, seducing mankind and figuratively or literally stealing souls, which they were ever alert to carry off, according to Gregory the Great's *Dialogues.* And they cluster around the bedside of the sick and the dying, ready to seize the soul as it escapes the body through the mouth, as in the story of the evil rich man carved on a capital at Vézelay. Sometimes devils even carry off the body. Edmund Leversedge in his *Vision* of 1465 describes how on his sickbed "ii. devellys wold hafe carid my body away and borne hit with hem" if he had not been saved by the prayers of relatives in the room.

In keeping with their descent through human and angelic mating in Jewish thought, demons make sexual attacks on both men and women. Accounts of such be-

havior appear in the second-century *Book of Jubilees* (5:1–5), among other places, and continue into the Midrashic period in works such as the eighth-century *Pirkei de Rabbi Eliezer.* Such male demonic attackers of sleeping women were called incubi and in their female form succubi, though the thirteenth-century Scholastic William of Auvergne, bishop of Paris, doubted demons had the capacity actually to impregnate mortal women; he felt that this intercourse and impregnation was illusory and that, obtaining human semen mysteriously, demons inseminated women by blowing it into the uterus. William was followed at greater length by Weyer, who proposed various naturalistic explanations, such as the weight of bedclothes for a person's belief that he or she had been attacked and sexually possessed in bed by demons.

While they had no specific visual attributes in scripture, demons were dramatically and variously depicted in medieval art and literature from a fairly early period. They appear in the famous mosaic in San Apollinare Nuovo at Ravenna (*ca.* 556–569). By the ninth century representations of demons were quite common, and there are several in the Stuttgart Psalter; they were also very popular with sculptors working in French Romanesque cathedrals.

Demons normally have a humanoid shape, though they can inhabit objects or animals like the toad. Typical physical features are horns and flame-shaped tufts of hair. The latter feature seems to derive from the fourth-century Latin version of Athanasius's *Life of St. Anthony,* where a demon has "locks which were also strewn about like flames." From the twelfth century onward, besides flamelike hair and horns, demons often had batlike wings, tails, clawed feet, and a covering of hair, fur, or feathers recalling their original feathered angelic status. In keeping with their infernal connections, demons are often fire red, coal black, or occasionally green; in Byzantine tradition they are dark blue. In their roles as hunters or punishers of souls they often carry chains, ropes, or ordinary domestic culinary implements with which to torment their prey, such as flesh hooks used to lift out and examine pieces of meat from cooking cauldrons, maces and billhooks, agricultural tools such as the rake or pitchfork, or the tridentlike tool used to prod a soul on a carved capital at Autun.

Late-medieval demons typically are associated with strong, unpleasant smells in their more comic manifestations. In Dante's *Inferno* a devil makes a trumpet of his anus, while in the fifteenth-century English *Castle of Perseverance* the stage directions specify the demon Belial is to have "gunne-powder brennynge In pypys in his handis and in his eris, and in his ers." Imagery from smelting and mining is often used to portray demons, especially the smell of sulfur. Indeed, in Germanic tradition, demons were believed to dwell in mines and to plague their workers.

During the late Middle Ages philosophical writers were increasingly interested in the spirit world and its role in human affairs. For example, a thirteenth-century Polish mathematician and philosopher connected with the papal court, Witelo, in his *De natura daemonum* organized the world according to categories of animals, men, demons, and noncorporeal intelligences. Thus men are higher than animals but lower than demons and can be affected by them.

The possible role of demons in magical conjurations and the occurrences of marvels also provoked much discussion. Jean de Meun in the *Roman de la Rose* forcefully denied that demons caused natural disasters: "Some say

Devils Seizing Sinner with Trident and Fork. *Capital from nave of Autun cathedral, mid-12th century.* PHOTOGRAPH COURTESY OF JOHN FRIEDMAN. REPRODUCED BY PERMISSION.

that demons bring all this [violent storms] about / With hooks and cables or with teeth and nails, / But such an explanation is not worth two turnips." Aristotelian rationalists like Nicole Oresme attempted to replace the influence of demons in the performance of marvels and the like with simple explanations of causality. Nonetheless, as works like Johann Weyer's *De praestigiis daemonum* attest, demons, largely through their connection with witchcraft, remained a popular subject of speculation down through the seventeenth century.

BIBLIOGRAPHY

Brown, Peter. "Sorcery, Demons, and the Rise of Christianity: From Late Antiquity into the Middle Ages." In *Religion and Society in the Age of St. Augustine.* London: Faber and Faber, 1972.

Kiessling, Nicolas. *The Incubus in English Literature: Provenance and Progeny.* Pullman: Washington State University Press, 1977.

Legros, Huguette. "Le diable et l'enfer: Représentation dans la sculpture romane." In *Le diable au Moyen Âge: Doctrines, problèmes moraux, représentations.* Paris and Aix-en-Provence: CUER MA, 1979.

Obrist, Barbara. "Les deux visages du diable." In *Diables et Diableries: La représentation du diable dans la gravure des XVe et XVI siècles*. Edited by Florian Rodari and Jean Wirth. Geneva: Cabinet des estampes, 1976.

Palmer, Barbara D. "The Inhabitants of Hell: Devils." In *The Iconography of Hell*. Edited by Clifford Davidson and Thomas H. Seiler. Kalamazoo, Mich.: Medieval Institute Publications, 1992.

Paschetto, Eugenia. "Il *De natura daemonum* di Witelo." *Atti della accademia delle scienze di Torino* 109 (1975): 231–271.

Russell, Jeffrey Burton. *Lucifer, the Devil in the Middle Ages*. Ithaca, N.Y.: Cornell University Press, 1984.

Seiler, Thomas H. "Filth and Stench as Aspects of the Iconography of Hell." In *The Iconography of Hell*. Edited by Clifford Davidson and Thomas H. Seiler. Kalamazoo, Mich.: Medieval Institute Publications, 1992.

Walzel, Diana Lynn. "Sources of Medieval Demonology." *Rice University Studies* 60, no. 4 (1974): 83–99.

JOHN BLOCK FRIEDMAN

[See also **DMA:** Angel/Angelology; **Supp:** Devil; Hell, Concepts of.]

DEVIL. In the Middle Ages the devil *(diabolus),* also called Satan (or, less commonly, Lucifer, Beelzebub, Leviathan, or Behemoth), was understood as a personal adversary of God and man. Though the Old Testament was vague about the devil's origins, he was early connected with a rebellious angel driven out of heaven with his followers by the archangel Michael and his minions after a conflict ensuing from the sin of pride.

Partly on the basis of the verse "how art thou fallen O Lucifer king of the morning" (Isaiah 14:4), this angel was named Lucifer by St. Jerome and others. After his expulsion from heaven, the devil was thought to interfere in the lives of men, first in the guise of the serpent tempting Eve in Paradise and later by entering into conflict with Jesus, only to be vanquished by him. The well-known Temptation in the Desert scene carved on a mid-twelfth-century capital at Autun Cathedral carefully portrayed the devil's vestigial wings from his former angelic state. Finally he would be chained up in hell, for the end of Satan's power was thought to be predicted in Revelation 12.

How such an evil being came into the world—especially if God was the First Mover and innately good—was not fully explained by theologians, and attempts to answer the question led ultimately to heresies such as Pelagianism or dualism. If the devil and evil were uncreated, then the devil's origins and importance could be comparable to those of God. If, on the other hand, the devil was created by God out of himself, then God must be partially bad, an untenable view.

Jesus Tempted by Satan in the Desert. *Mid-12th-century capital from the cathedral of Autun.* PHOTOGRAPH COURTESY OF JOHN FRIEDMAN. REPRODUCED BY PERMISSION.

A tradition developed in the apocryphal *Acts of Pilate,* which forms part of the *Gospel of Nicodemus* (thirteenth century), emphasizing a series of victories over Satan. In the most dramatic of these, Jesus in the interval between the Passion and the Resurrection directly overcomes the devil in a verbal and sometimes physical conflict called the Harrowing of Hell or *Descensus ad inferos* (a nonbiblical legend current in works such as Jacobus de Varagine's *Golden Legend*). After his triumph he exits the gates of hell to lead the patriarchs, such as Adam and Isaiah, up to heaven.

Support for calling the devil Leviathan or Behemoth and making him as deceived by the "bait" of Christ comes from *Moralia in Job,* especially its chapters devoted to commentary on verses 41:1–2 and 40:15, where the lines "Canst thou draw out Leviathan with an hook or his tongue with a cord which thou lettest down? Canst thou put an hook into his nose?" and "Behold now Behemoth" served as the locus for discussion. The idea is developed, for example, as an allegory in Honorius Augus-

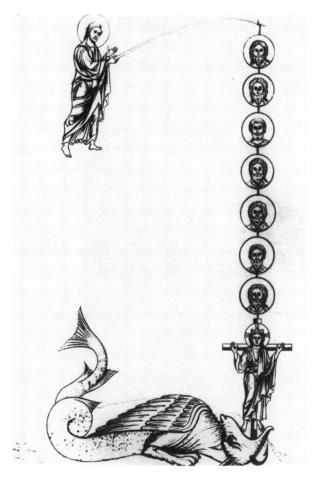

Fishing for Leviathan. *Allegory in which God captures the devil through the "hook" of Jesus's cross (with the genealogy of Jesus depicted along the fishing line. From a MS (now destroyed) of the* Hortus deliciarum *of Herrad of Landsburg (Hohenburg). Photo from Gérard Cames,* Allégories et symboles dans l'Hortus deliciarum *(Leiden: Brill, 1971). Print provided by the Library of Congress.* BRILL ACADEMIC PUBLISHERS.

Devil with Attendant Demon and Flamelike Hair. *Tympanum lintel, lower right, from Conques (Aveyron) mid-12th century.* PHOTOGRAPH COURTESY OF JOHN FRIEDMAN. REPRODUCED BY PERMISSION.

todunensis where "God presiding in heaven lowered a hook into the sea of this world with the plan of taking Leviathan through his son Christ. The line to which this hook is attached is the genealogy of Christ, the hook itself is Christ's divinity, the fishing pole is the holy cross, and the bait is Christ's humanity." This allegory is presented visually in Herrad of Hohenberg's encyclopedia *Hortus deliciarum* (*ca.* 1180).

More commonly, Satan was imagined to be humanoid but hideous in appearance—as ugly after his fall as he had been beautiful before it. One especially detailed portrait of the devil appears in the *Vision of Tundale* (from 1149), where the narrator sees a figure whose size overshadowed that of every kind of beast:

> [He] was very black, like a raven, with a body of human shape from its feet to its head, except

that it had many hands and a tail. This horrible monster had no less than a thousand hands, and each hand was a thousand cubits long and ten cubits wide . . . [with] twenty fingers connected to it . . . very long claws . . . [of] iron . . . and in his feet were just as many claws.

Like medieval demons, Satan often has flamelike hair and the staring, burning eyes *(igneos oculos)* described in Hildegard of Bingen's *Liber Scivias;* these features appear in a frontal portrait of him from the mid-twelfth-century tympanum at Conques. From the twelfth century onward he usually has batlike wings, and though he has human hands, his feet are clawed like those of a bird. In color he is totally black or, less often, red and covered with hair. He sometimes carries a flesh hook or goad, and in the late Middle Ages he is often represented with hideous faces on his knees and belly, often covering yet enhancing his genitalia, as in the Holkham Bible Picture Book.

There is a good deal of scatology associated with Satan in the Middle Ages, and this grows more prevalent

Hell. *Depicted in a manuscript of the* Pèlerinage de la vie humaine *by Guillaume Deguielville, Artois, 1410. Brussels, Bibliothèque Royale Albert 1er, MS 10176, fol. 149.* PHOTOGRAPH COURTESY OF JOHN FRIEDMAN. REPRODUCED BY PERMISSION.

in Lutheran and Counter-Reformation propaganda. For example, the devil and his demon assistants are often shown defecating on sinners in hell.

By the mid-twelfth century, there had been significant developments in the conception of Satan owing to a political and religious preoccupation with the dualism inherent in the thought of the Albigensian heretics active in southern France. The notion of a personal struggle between two elemental forces, primary in the late antique Gnosticism suppressed by the early church, was revived by the Albigensians, or Cathars, who believed that evil in the guise of Satan was an independent force in the cosmos and that the devil—himself a fallen angel—had created the physical universe as a sort of way station for souls in the process of transmigrating from the body. In

some extreme dualist forms, Catharism was reputed to make Satan God's direct rival and a sort of god himself. Its intellectual focus on the principle of evil and the strength of the Albigensians in southern France and the crusade against them proclaimed by Innocent III in 1208 brought the heresy wide attention and interested writers and artists in the idea of a struggle between Satan and ordinary mortals, a saint, or Christ.

By the end of the Middle Ages there was a pronounced interest among artists in the life of the desert father St. Anthony, whose *Vita* was a record of continuous temptation and physical attack by demons or Satan. Thus, it was common to portray scenes of the saint being tempted by a Satan seemingly divine in form and power. According to the *Golden Legend* the devil once appeared

Devil with Multiple Faces and Flesh Hook Devouring Souls. *Miniature from the Holkham Bible, ca. 1330. London, British Library Additional MS 47682, fol. 11v.* PHOTOGRAPH COURTESY OF JOHN FRIEDMAN BY PERMISSION OF BRITISH LIBRARY.

to St. Anthony "with a body of such height that his head seemed to touch the sky."

Satan was also associated with the popular medieval figure of the Antichrist central to Christian eschatology, the study of the Last Things. Sent by (or embodying) the devil just before the end of the world to thwart God's kingdom, this great adversary would appear and seem to be Christ, initiating a series of persecutions of true Christians. Figuring large in the writings of Gregory the Great, especially his *Moralia in Job,* the Antichrist is sometimes shown as a youthful and benign-seeming Christ, his diabolic nature given away by his cross-legged sitting position (associated with tyrants) and the plagues he visits on the world until his final overthrow at the true Second Coming. There will then be a great struggle and Christ and Michael will permanently triumph over the devil.

BIBLIOGRAPHY

PRIMARY WORKS

Athanasius. "Vita S. Antonii." In *Patrologia Latina.* Edited by Jacques-Paul Migne. Vol. 26, col. 16.887. Paris: Garnier, 1844–1902. (Also available as computer database, Alexandra, Va.: Chadwyck-Healey, 1995.)

Gardiner, Eileen, ed. and trans. *Visions of Heaven and Hell Before Dante.* New York: Italica, 1989. (Includes a translation of *Tundale's Vision.*)

Hildegard of Bingen. "Sanctae Hildegardis Scivias sive Visionum ac Revelationum Libri Tres." In *Patrologia latina.* Edited by Jacques-Paul Migne. Vol. 197, col. 709. Paris: Garnier, 1844–1902.

Honorius Augustodunensis. "Speculum Ecclesiae." In *Patrologia latina.* Edited by Jacques-Paul Migne. Vol. 172, col. 957. Paris: Garnier, 1844–1902.

Wyzewa, Teodor de, trans. *La légende dorée / Jacques de Voragine.* Paris: Perrin, 1925.

SECONDARY WORKS

Bazin, Germain. "The Devil in Art." In *Satan.* Edited by Bruno de Jésus-Marie. New York: Sheed and Ward, 1952.

Emmerson, Richard. *Antichrist in the Middle Ages: A Study of Medieval Apocalypticism, Art, and Literature.* Seattle: University of Washington Press, 1981.

Erich, Oswald A. *Die Darstellung des Teufels in der christlichen Kunst.* Berlin: Deutscher Kunstverlag, 1931.

Koppenfels, Werner von. *Esca et Hamus: Beitrag zu einer historischen Liebesmetaphorik.* Munich: Verlag der Bayerischen Akademie der Wissenschaften, 1973.

Legros, Huguette. "Le diable et l'enfer: Représentation dans la sculpture romane." In *Le diable au moyen âge (doctrine, problèmes moraux, représentations).* Senefiance no. 6. Aix-en Provence: CUERMA; Paris: H. Champion, 1979.

Marchand, James W. "Leviathan and the Mousetrap in the Nidhrstigningarsaga," *Scandinavian Studies* 47 (1975): 328–338.

Massing, Jean-Michel. "Étude iconographique de l'agression de St. Antoine de Grünewald." In *Grunewald et son oeuvre: Actes de la Table Ronde organisée par le Centre National de la Recherche Scientifique à Strasbourg et Colmar du 18 au 21 octobre 1974.* Strasbourg, France: Société pour la conservation des monuments historiques d'Alsace Société Schongauer, 1976.

McGuire, Brian P. "Man and the Devil in Medieval Theology and Culture." *Cahiers de l'Institut du Moyen Âge grec et latin* 18 (1976): 18–78.

Obrist, Barbara. "Les deux visages du diable." In *Diables et diableries: La représentation du diable dans la gravure des XVe et XVIe siècles.* Edited by Florian Rodari and Jean Wirth. Geneva, Switzerland: Cabinet des estampes, 1976.

Russell, Jeffrey Burton. *Lucifer: The Devil in the Middle Ages.* Ithaca, N.Y.: Cornell University Press, 1984.

JOHN BLOCK FRIEDMAN

[See also **DMA:** Albigensians; Anastasis; Angel/Angelology; Antichrist; Cathars; Dualism; *Golden Legend;* **Supp:** Anthony of Egypt, St.; Demons; Fall, The; Hell, Concepts of; Monsters and the Monstrous.]

DHIMMĪS were the non-Muslim peoples of the Islamic world who became a part of the Islamic polity (though not the religious community) by virtue of the contract of *dhimma* (protection). They are also referred to in Islamic texts by the terms *ahl al-dhimma* and *dhimma*. The world in which Islam arose and spread was populated by polytheist Arabs, Jews, and Christians. Although no provision was made for the assimilation into the early Islamic state of idolatrous Arabs (who were given the stark choice of conversion or death), Jews and Christians were accorded a place by virtue of their status as "people of the book" *(ahl al-kitāb),* monotheist religious communities who were considered by the Koran and the prophet Muḥammad *(d.* 632) to be the recipients of divinely revealed scriptures. The Koranic verse that defined the special status of monotheist non-Muslims was IX, 29: "Fight those who do not believe . . . among those who have been given the Book, until they pay the *jizya.*" Originally a nonspecific levy, the *jizya* developed into a poll tax imposed on non-Muslim adult males. Thus, the fundamental requirements for attaining *dhimmī* status were to practice a revealed religion, to submit to Muslim political rule, to accept the contract of *dhimma,* and to pay the poll tax *(jizya)* to the Muslim governing authority. The requirement to pay the poll tax was the only obligation mentioned explicitly in the Koran.

Initially, the *dhimma* was extended only to Jews and Christians, a policy for which there was precedent both in Koran and prophetic tradition *(ḥadīth).* But the category of *ahl al-dhimma* expanded along with the empire. When Iran was conquered, its large Zoroastrian population came to be included in the category of *dhimmīs,* because the caliph ʿUmar I (634–644) believed that the prophet Muḥammad had accepted *jizya* from them and ordered the conquerors to treat them like "people of the book." Using this episode as a precedent, Muslim jurists included the Zoroastrians among the *dhimmīs* and considered the Avesta, the Zoroastrian oral tradition that was committed to writing shortly before the rise of Islam, to be a revealed book. The early Muslim conquerors of India in the eighth century treated the Hindus as *dhimmīs,* although Muslim jurists disagreed on the question of whether they should be granted the status of *ahl al-dhimma.* The Ḥanafī legal school (one of the four orthodox schools of Muslim law), which later became established in India, distinguished between Arab and non-Arab idolators, permitting *dhimmī* status to be accorded to the latter but not the former. *Dhimmīs* were thus distinguished from Arab idolators, from Christians and Jews who lived outside of the lands of Islam *(ḥarbīs),* and

from foreigners who were given permission to live temporarily within the lands of Islam *(mustaʾmins).*

Islamic tradition credits the caliph ʿUmar I with establishing the regulations that govern the *dhimmīs'* relationship to the Islamic state. These regulations are laid out in a document called the Pact of ʿUmar. The content of the Pact includes many restrictions, some of which are derived from early Muslim conquest treaties and others that seem to be adapted from Byzantine laws regarding Jews. The Pact of ʿUmar prohibited non-Muslims from building new churches or synagogues or from repairing existing houses of worship. *Dhimmīs* agreed to refrain from public displays of religion (a condition that was of more consequence for Christians than for Jews) and neither to proselytize nor prevent their coreligionists from converting to Islam. They were not allowed to ride horses (a sign of elite status) or bear arms.

Nevertheless, adherence to the Pact of ʿUmar varied at different times and places. In practice, many of these provisions were ignored by both *dhimmīs* and Muslim governments, generally being observed more strictly in times of political, economic, or social stress and instability. At such times, Muslim rulers would issue decrees that reiterated the stipulations of the Pact of ʿUmar. For example, *dhimmīs* were required to wear distinctive dress. Insisting that local populations wear their traditional dress (including the *zunnār,* a distinctive belt) during and immediately after the conquest. Over time, however, distinctions in dress became less obvious as the Arabs were assimilated into local populations through marriage. In mid-ninth-century Baghdad, however, at a time of unrest, the caliph issued a decree ordering the *dhimmīs* to wear a honey-colored badge to distinguish them from Muslims. On the other hand, there is ample evidence that in Egypt during the eleventh and twelfth centuries, it was very difficult to tell *dhimmīs* from Muslims by appearance alone.

Scholars have long debated whether many of the Pact of ʿUmar's provisions were intended to humiliate the *dhimmīs.* Originally, they were probably meant largely to clarify boundaries between the conquered and the conquerors. But at least by the time of the early Abbasid caliphate in the mid-eighth century, medieval Muslims had come to believe that the purpose of both the *jizya* and the stipulations of the Pact of ʿUmar was, in fact, to humiliate non-Muslim populations. As time went on, there was increasing emphasis in law, commentary, and practice on the social and symbolic humiliation of the *dhimmīs.* While the *jizya* held symbolic significance both for *dhimmīs* and for Muslims, it was also a crushing financial burden for non-Muslim communities.

Paying the poll tax for poor coreligionists was a major objective of fund-raising among *dhimmīs*. Nonetheless, *dhimmīs* never endured the severe economic and social restrictions that characterized the status of Jews in Christian Europe. They owned land and participated fully in the economic life of the larger Muslim society. Although they preferred to live among their coreligionists, Jews and Christians were not segregated in separate quarters and often lived in the same apartment compounds with Muslims. They were technically prohibited from holding public office but nonetheless frequently served Muslim governments. In addition, they remained relatively autonomous, regulating their own internal religious and communal affairs.

BIBLIOGRAPHY

Atiyah, Aziz S., ed. *The Coptic Encyclopedia.* 8 vols. New York: Macmillan, 1991. Comprehensive and authoritative on a wide range of subjects concerning the Christian communities of Egypt.

Cahen, Cl. "Dhimma." In *Encyclopaedia of Islam.* Edited by H. A. R. Gibb et al. New ed. Leiden: Brill, 1960–.

Cahen, Cl., and Halil Inarcik. "Djizya." In *Encyclopaedia of Islam.* Edited by H. A. R. Gibb et al. New ed. Leiden: Brill, 1960–.

Cohen, Mark R. *Under Crescent and Cross: The Jews in the Middle Ages.* Princeton, N.J.: Princeton University Press, 1994. A detailed and well-documented comparison of Jewish experience in Christendom and Islam; engages important historiographical questions.

———. "What was the Pact of ʿUmar? A Literary-Historical Study." *Jerusalem Studies in Arabic and Islam* 23 (1999): 100–157. The most complete and up-to-date study, including historiographical survey and Arabic texts of about thirty different versions of the Pact.

Friedmann, Yohanan. "Medieval Muslim Views of Indian Religions" *Journal of the American Oriental Society* 95:2 (April–June 1975): 214–221. See notes for additional bibliography.

Goitein, S. D. *A Mediterranean Society: The Jewish Communities of the Arab World as Portrayed in the Documents of the Cairo Geniza.* 6 vols. Berkeley and Los Angeles: University of California Press, 1967–1993. The classic history of the Jewish communities of Egypt from about the tenth to the thirteenth centuries, based on documentary evidence. Comprehensive.

Lewis, Bernard. *The Jews of Islam.* Princeton, N.J.: Princeton University Press, 1984. An excellent, very readable introduction providing broad chronological, geographical, and thematic coverage.

Stillman, Norman A., comp. *The Jews of Arab Lands.* Philadelphia: The Jewish Publication Society of America, 1979. Translated and annotated documents accompanied by a very useful, clear historical introduction.

Stillman, Yedida Kalfon. *Arab Dress: from the Dawn of Islam to Modern Times.* Edited by Norman A. Stillman. Leiden and Boston: Brill, 2000. The most recent and authoritative work on the subject. See especially Chapter 5, "The Laws of Differentiation and the Clothing of Non-Muslims" (101–116).

Tritton, A. S. *The Caliphs and Their Non-Muslim Subjects: A Critical Study of the Covenant of ʿUmar.* [London]: F. Cass, 1970). Reprint of 1930 edition. Dated but still useful.

PAULA SANDERS

[See also **DMA**: Islam, Conquests of; Jewish Communal Self-Government: Islamic World; Jews in the Middle East; ʿUmar I ibn al-Khaṭṭāb.]

DIES IRAE ("day of wrath"), the sequence (also referred to as a hymn or prose) used in Offices and Masses for the dead. The sequence's name refers to the opening words of the first verse, "Dies irae dies illa" ("That day will be a day of wrath"), which are taken from the biblical text in Zephaniah (1:15–16). The original text of the *Dies irae* probably had seventeen rhymed stanzas, with several lines added later. Several of the lines appear to have come from the rhymed trope of the responsory *Libera me, Domine,* sung at the Absolution following the Mass. Indeed, the sequence begins with the same melodic phrase as the responsory.

The sequence first appeared in Italian missals and so appears to have originated in Italy. At least two thirteenth-century manuscripts contain the sequence: a Franciscan missal from 1253 to 1255 and an addition inserted at the end of the Breviary from the treasury of St. Damiano at Assisi, commonly referred to as the Breviary of St. Clare. The insertion of the sequence is dated to around 1250, while the breviary itself is dated 1228. Thus, it would appear that the *Dies irae* was first introduced into the Catholic liturgy by the Franciscans sometime during the thirteenth century. The person most frequently cited as the author of the *Dies irae* is the thirteenth-century Franciscan Thomas of Celano (*d. ca.* 1257), who was a friend and biographer of St. Francis and author of another sequence, the *Sanctitatis nova signa,* sung on the feast of St. Francis. The earliest reference to Thomas as the author of the sequence is found in the late-fourteenth-century *Liber Conformitatum,* a treatise on the ways Francis sought to imitate God, written by the Franciscan Bartholomew of Pisa (de Rinonico). A seventeenth-century historian of the Franciscan Order, Luke Wadding, also argued in favor of Thomas's authorship. Various others have been mentioned as possible authors: on the Franciscan side, St. Bonaventure and Cardinal Matthew d'Acquasparta and, on the Dominican side, Humbert of Romans and Cardinal Latino Orsini (or Frangipani) (*d.* 1296). Even Pope Gregory I the Great (*d.* 604) has sometimes been mentioned as the possible author. The strongest evidence, however, points to Thomas of Celano or a contemporary Franciscan.

Over time, the sequence spread from Italy to other parts of Europe and was adopted by the church.

Cast in the first person singular, the *Dies irae* may have originated as a personal meditation. The poet asks, "What shall I, frail man, be pleading? Who for me be interceding, when the just are mercy needing?" ("Quid sum miser tunc dicturus? Quem patronum rogaturus, cum vix justus sit securus?") With fear and trembling, the poet describes the Day of Judgment. "O what fear man's bosom rendeth, when from heaven the judge descendeth, on whose sentence all dependeth!" ("Quantus tremor est futurus, quando judex est venturus, cuncta stricte discussurus!") Blushing with guilt, he confesses that he is a sinner and appeals to God for mercy so that he might be saved: "Guilty, now I pour my moaning, all my shame with anguish owning: Spare, O God, thy suppliant groaning" ("Ingemisco, tamquam reus: Culpa rubet vultus meus: Supplicanti parce deus.") The poet appeals to Jesus in unusually personal terms saying, "Think, kind Jesus, my salavation, caused thy wondrous incarnation—leave me not to reprobation" ("Recordare Jesu pie, quod sum causa tuae viae, ne me perdas illa die").

The *Dies irae* was originally an Advent hymn, but it was later adopted as the sequence for the Mass for the Dead. In the Roman missal, the sequence is also used on All Souls' Day, for an anniversary Mass, or when Mass is celebrated on the third, seventh, or thirtieth day after death or burial.

BIBLIOGRAPHY

Clop, Eusèbe. "La prose 'Dies irae' et l'ordre des Frères Mineurs." *Revue du Chant Grégorien* 16 (1907–1908): 46–53.

The Roman Missal in Latin and English for Masses for the Dead, Including the Rite of Absolution. Collegeville, Maine: Liturgical Press, 1966. Contains both the Latin text of the sequence and an English translation.

Van Dijk, S. J. P., and J. Hazelden Walker. *The Origins of the Modern Roman Liturgy: The Liturgy of the Papal Court and the Franciscan Order in the Thirteenth Century.* Westminster, Md.: Newman Press, 1960.

Vellekoop, Kees. *Dies Irae Dies Illa: Studien zur Frühgeschichte einer Sequenz.* Bilthoven, Netherlands: A. B. Creyghton, 1978.

ADAM JEFFREY DAVIS

[See also **DMA:** Mass, Liturgy of the.]

DIPLOMATICS. Archival documents are a rich and important source of information about the medieval world. Documents consist of a heterogeneous assortment of generally brief, nonliterary, noneducational, nondevotional texts concerned with legal, judicial, and administrative matters. Tens, even hundreds, of thousands of these survive from the Middle Ages, their number increasing in each successive century. They encompass matters as diverse as papal bulls, land sales, apprenticeship contracts, rent rolls, bills of lading, judicial decisions, testaments, census lists, legislative texts, and orders to administrative officers. Providing a framework within which to study these documents is the role of the technical-historical field of diplomatics, which derives its name from the Latin "diploma," or official document. Diplomatics overlaps with several other technical-historical subjects, including paleography (the study of handwriting), codicology (the study of the codex, or book), sigillography (the study of seals), prosopography (the study of names), and chronology (the study of dating). These fields often provide essential information for the interpretation of documents, and a diplomacist, or student of documents, needs some training in them as well.

The subject matter of diplomatics has been variously defined. At its narrowest it is taken to include only acts and charters, highly formulaic documents written in an epistolary form that record a legal action. Contracts, donations, and royal grants of privileges are all examples of this genre. At its broadest, diplomatics can be said to include the study of all documents that are found in archives, a category that might include texts as diverse as letters, mortuary rolls, and all manner of ledgers and registers. Although each sort of document takes a different form, diplomatics provides a system that can be applied to the study of any sort of archival document. The essential principles of diplomatics encompass three elements of the document: its physical appearance and state of preservation, the actors involved in the transaction and in the production of the document, and the words of the text. To illustrate these elements, we will use the example of the charter, the most common medieval document found in archives.

PHYSICAL APPEARANCE AND STATE OF PRESERVATION

Charters are conserved in a variety of states. In many instances, we have the actual clean copy that was authenticated and delivered to one of the parties involved as proof of the transaction or that was stored in a public archive for safekeeping. We might also have a rough draft, sometimes with corrections, or even mere notes taken in preparation for writing the draft. Conversely, the document might exist in a copy, either authentic or nonauthentic, such as a copy the issuer might keep for his own records or an official copy, called a *vidimus,* often made because the original had deteriorated. The text of charters was also frequently copied into cartularies, made up by the recipients, or registers, made by the issuers. Normally in book and occasionally in roll form, these functioned as a sort of filing system recording documents being sent out (registers) or received (cartularies). A charter in any state might also, of course, be a forgery, and one of the principal functions of diplomatics is to provide the historian with the technical knowledge to identify falsifications.

The handwriting of a charter, though properly the subject of paleography, helps identify the date of the charter and the issuer. Royal or papal acts, for example, used a more formal writing, known as a chancery script, than did most urban scriptoria. Prior to writing, the scribe may have lined the parchment and delineated the margins, and lining patterns can point to particular writing centers as the likely place of production. The actual text of the document is only written on the recto side of the charter, but the verso can harbor important information as well. Sometimes a scribe will make his sign, or *seing manuel,* which may permit the historian to identify who wrote the text. Often there will be archival information giving a very brief summary of the contents to enable the archivist of the monastery or chancellery to organize and locate the many charters in the institution's possession. Rarely one might find an indication of how much the recipient paid to have the document drawn up—for such things were never free. These *mentions hors teneur,* or information outside the text itself, whether on the verso or in the margins alongside the text, can be extremely informative and should be carefully observed.

Finally, a charter will have some form of authentication. Popes and, in the early Middle Ages, kings signed documents with a monogram, a sort of stylized signature. Between the early Middle Ages and the late twelfth century, the decline in literacy and centralized authority meant that documents coming from an authority less than a pope, emperor, or (usually) king could not be guaranteed to be authentic. One strategy to ensure transactions would be honored was to provide a list of witnesses who could be called upon later to attest to them. Such people had no monogram and were generally illiterate, so the signature was replaced by a mark made by the signatory or merely by the word "signum" (signed) followed by the witness's name, written by the scribe rather than by the signatory. Such witness lists can be of tremendous use to historians in identifying and dating individuals they encounter in other sources.

Seals came into widespread use in northern Europe during the eleventh and twelfth centuries. Medieval seals were made of wax or metal (such as the lead ball, known as a bulla, appended to papal documents) and had a design that represented perhaps more the presence than the signature of the seal owner. They could be stuck on the charter after it had been folded (a letter close) or hung from the bottom (a letter patent).

The two final forms of authentication are the chirograph and the notary. To make a chirograph, a scribe wrote two or more copies of the same charter on a single piece of parchment. He then wrote a legend, often the word "chirographum," along the border between the copies, and cut them apart through the legend, usually along an indented or wavy line. One copy was kept in a public archive, any others were given to one or both of the interested parties. If a question of authenticity arose, the original exemplars would be matched up. The notarial system derived from Roman law and became important first in southern Europe from the late eleventh century and in northern Europe beginning in the thirteenth century. The notary was a person trained to draw up documents and registered with a high official—pope, emperor, or king. At the behest of the parties, he would make a record of the transaction and record it in his notarial book. Then he would draw up a document attesting to the transaction, signing it with his personal *seing manuel.*

THE ACTORS AND THE PRODUCTION OF THE DOCUMENT

It can sometimes be difficult to sort out the parties involved in making a document. A donation to a monastery, for instance, might be made in the name of a nobleman, yet the charter recording it was likely written by the recipient monastery. A contract might be made between two merchants, yet the document would be issued by the town aldermen. Writing was expensive in the Middle Ages: labor, parchment, ink, and sealing wax, not to mention various taxes and fees on document production, ensured that no document would be written unless some party, usually the beneficiary of the transaction, wanted and was able to pay for it. Furthermore, a charter without some authority supporting it was a waste of money. Consequently, behind each charter were at least two important parties (who may in some cases be identical): the beneficiary, who was often the document's recipient *(destinatarius),* and the document issuer who gave it authority. The ability of the act to inspire confidence depended on the identity of the issuer. One of the indications of the growing importance of literacy in the Middle Ages is the emergence of issuers of progressively lower social rank.

In addition to the recipient and issuer, other parties figure into charters. The person who performs the juridical action recorded, such as the seller of land, is called the disposant. Listed witnesses also frequently appear, especially prior to the thirteenth century. Documents sometimes provide information about people who had no stake in the action; for instance, a previous owner of land might be named in order to identify the property.

Finally, one of the most important parties is rarely even mentioned: the scribes and redactors who composed and wrote the document. We know more about the functioning of large chancelleries like those of the papacy, kings, and bishops than we do of the small writing centers that emerged in towns, businesses, and lesser noble courts from the twelfth century. In general, however, the process of writing a document involved several steps. A clerk conveyed, either orally or in writing, the details of the legal action to a redactor, who drew up a draft using all the appropriate formulas. A scribe wrote out a fair copy of the draft, which might then be checked by a corrector. Another scribe might record the details of the act in a register. The sealer *(sigillarius)* appended the correct seal once all the necessary fees had been paid. In small chancelleries the same scribe might be responsible for all of these steps, but in large writing centers, the work was divided among specialists. Paying attention to evidence of the drafting process—corrections, changes in handwriting, notes in the margin or on the verso—can enrich the historian's understanding of medieval literacy and administrative organization.

THE TEXT OF THE DOCUMENT

Charters were highly formulaic texts that followed the Roman rhetorical style laid out in the *ars dictaminis* (literally, the art of dictating, since medieval authors often dictated to scribes rather than wrote). The exact order and wording of the formulas in a given document are collectively known as its dictamen. The dictamen consists of three main sections: the beginning, or protocol; the body; and the conclusion, or eschatocol. Each section is further broken up into subparts. For example, imagine a charter that reads:

> [PROTOCOL] In the name of the Holy Trinity, greeting. We, Count Robert of N, [BODY] because that which is not committed to writing is too often snatched away by the wind of forgetfulness, we have ordered it to be made known to all those present and future who will see or hear this act read that in honor of the

memory of our mother, we have given to the monastery of N five bunders and three verges of land lying in the parish of N, bordered on the east by the homestead of Gilbert the Old and on the west by the homestead of the widow of Johan the Clerk. [ESCHATOCOL] In witness of this that it may remain ever steadfast and assured, we cause our seal to be appended to this present letter. Given and done in the year of the incarnation of Our Lord thousand one hundred seventy-two the day before the Annunciation to the Virgin.

This example contains many of the most common formulae. The invocation ("In the name of . . .") and the salutation ("greeting") show the influence of the epistolary rhetoric out of which charter formulas grew. With the intitulation ("we, Count Robert") the issuer introduces himself. "N" (plural NN) stands for *nomen,* or name, and is used as a generic place holder. Stemming from the rhetorical *captatio benevolentiae,* the preamble, or *arenga* ("that which is not committed to writing . . ."), makes known the purported reason for drawing up the document. As writing became more common, *arengae* tended to drop out. Next the author puts his prospective audience on notice: "made known to all those present and future." Following this notification, a document might include some background information about the act. In this example, the narration relates that the donation was made in memory of the count's mother. The body of the charter commences with words of disposition: "we have given" and includes all the necessary legal and geographical details. The text ends with a corroboration, attesting to the intent of the donor to uphold the transaction ("in witness of this . . ."), and finally the date. Dating can be extremely complicated. It might be based on the calendar of saints' days or on the reign of a monarch or on months and days. It can be very explicit or only provide a year. Sometimes charters are undated or are dated only in reference to an event: for instance, "two years after the great flood." Additionally, different regions of Europe calculated the new year in different ways. Some used 1 January, others Epiphany (6 January), others Easter, and so on. Since Easter is a movable feast, dates early in the year might fall in the following year according to our modern calendar. In the example above, the date is 24 March, which in Easter dating would be in 1173 (new style) since Easter that year fell on 8 April, and Easter in 1172 fell on 16 April.

Clearly, making profitable use of medieval archival documents requires a certain amount of technical know-how, but it can also provide researchers with valuable insights. *Arengae* tell us about attitudes toward writing.

The details of transactions permit the reconstruction of ownership patterns, land use, prices, and institutional and administrative structures. Witness lists tell us about relationships in feudal courts, in villages, on manors, and in towns. Narrations can offer biographical information. The corroboration clauses disclose legal customs. Documents are also a rich source of philological material. They provide, for instance, many Latin neologisms, and the vernacular words used within Latin documents are among the earliest written uses of the spoken languages.

BIBLIOGRAPHY

Bautier, Robert-Henri. *Chartes, sceaux et chancelleries: Études de diplomatique et de sigillographie médiévales.* 2 vols. Paris: Ecole des Chartes, 1990. A collection of essays by one of France's leading diplomacists.

Bedos-Rezak, Brigitte. "Diplomatic Sources and Medieval Documentary Practices: An Essay in Interpretative Methodology." In *The Past and Future of Medieval Studies.* Edited by John Van Engen. Notre Dame, Ind.: University of Notre Dame Press, 1994.

Boyle, Leonard E. "Diplomatics." In *Medieval Studies: An Introduction.* Edited by James M. Powell. Syracuse, N.Y.: Syracuse University Press, 1976. The only extensive discussion of diplomatic technique in English, with an excellent bibliography.

Bresslau, Harry. *Handbuch der Urkundenlehre für Deutschland und Italien.* 2d ed. 2 vols. Leipzig, Germany: Veit, 1912–1931.

Caenegem, R. C. van. *Introduction aux sources de l'histoire médiévale.* Translated by B. van den Abeele. Turnhout, Belgium: Brepols, 1997. Pages 91 through 175 are particularly useful concerning the various sorts of documents found in archives.

Cárcel Ortí, Maria Milagros, ed. *Vocabulaire international de la diplomatique.* 2d ed. Valencia, Spain: University of Valencia, 1997.

Clanchy, M. T. *From Memory to Written Record: England, 1066–1307.* 2d ed. Oxford: Blackwell, 1993. An outstanding work that shows how the study of documents can be used to further a larger cultural history.

De Boüard, A. *Manuel de diplomatique française et pontificale.* 2 vols. Paris: Picard, 1925–1952.

Fichtenau, Heinrich. *Arenga: Spätantike und Mittelalter im Spiegel von Urkundenformeln.* Graz, Austria: Böhlhaus Nachf, 1957. Example of how document formulas can be used to study the worldview of a period.

Genicot, Léopold. *Les actes publics.* Turnhout, Belgium: Brepols, 1972.

Giry, Arthur. *Manuel de diplomatique.* Paris: Hachette, 1894.

Guyotjeannin, Oliver, Jacques Pycke, and Benoît-Michel Tock. *Diplomatique médiévale.* Turnhout, Belgium: Brepols, 1993. The most recent overview of diplomatics.

Murray, James M. *Notarial Instruments in Flanders between 1280 and 1452.* Brussels: Palais des Académies, 1995. Although focused on Flanders, contains a useful introduction on charters and notarial documents in general.

EMILY KADENS

[See also **DMA:** Charter; Codicology, Western European; Paleography, Western European; Scriptorium; Seals and Sigillography.]

DIRC VAN DELFT (or van Delf, *ca.* 1365–?) was a Dutch Dominican and one of the ablest writers of Middle Dutch. Very little is known about his life. Judging from his patronym, he was born in Delft, in the province of Holland. He entered the Dominican house in Utrecht, where he must have demonstrated scholastic excellence because he was sent to study at a university, though it is unknown where. He eventually became a doctor of theology, and at the time he may have been the only Dutchman holding such a high degree. In 1399, Dirc was serving as vicar of the Dominican convents of Ghent and Ypres, charged with maintaining discipline, when in December of that year his patron, Duke Albert of Bavaria, count of Holland, summoned him to the Hague to be the court chaplain. As chaplain, Dirc would have preached, heard confessions, celebrated the liturgy, and acted as an adviser on political and diplomatic matters. While chaplain, Dirc also appears to have lectured at the German universities of Cologne and Erfurt. When Duke Albert died in 1404, Dirc disappears from the record entirely, though one scholar tentatively assigned to him authorship of a group of sermons preached to Dominican nuns in Flanders and preserved in a manuscript in Bruges. His death date is unknown.

Dirc van Delft's place in the history of Middle Dutch literature is assured by a single extant work, the *Tafel van den Kersten Ghelove* (Handbook—literally, "Table"—of the Christian faith), written in 1403 and dedicated to Duke Albert. A work written in 1401 for Albert's wife, Margaret of Cleves, has not survived. Dirc was a master of the Dutch vernacular, applying his Latin rhetorical training to the writing of his mother tongue. His prose style is considered among the best of medieval Dutch authors. The work itself is a monumental encyclopedia of Christian theology, ethics, practice, and liturgy written to be accessible to a lay, aristocratic public. It consists of two large parts: the Winter Piece and the Summer Piece. The Winter Piece discourses first on God, nature, man, virtues, sin, and creation and then relates the life of Christ from the marriage of Joseph and Mary to the Sermon on the Mount. The Summer Piece begins with Christ's crucifixion and ascension and then discusses the orders of the church, works of mercy, the seven sacraments, and the sins and ethical ideals of aristocratic life. The work concludes with discussions of death and the Last Judgment.

Dirc based his work upon Latin sources like the *Compendium theologicae veritatis* (Compendium of theological truth), a summa written by the thirteenth-century Dominican Hugh Ripelin of Strasbourg, and Thomas Aquinas's *Summa theologiae.* He apparently did not consult other Middle Dutch didactic works. Unlike many medieval vernacular authors, Dirc was not merely slavishly translating. Instead he reworked his sources and added illustrations drawn from contemporary life in order to make scholastic learning accessible and meaningful to his lay audience.

Numerous manuscripts of the *Tafel* survive, including the lushly illustrated dedication copy given to the duke and a Middle Low German translation. Although written for a courtly audience, the work appears to have been popular primarily in nunneries and Beguine communities and was used as a reference work by clergy.

BIBLIOGRAPHY

Axters, Stephanus Gérard. *De moderne devotie.* Vol 3 of *Geschiedenis van de vroomheid in de Nederlanden.* 4 vols. Antwerp, Belgium: De Sikkel, 1956–1960. Discusses the sermon manuscript on pages 316–317.

Daniëls, L. M. Fr. *Meester Dirc van Delf: Zijn persoon en zijn werk.* Utrecht: N. V. Dekker en van de Vegt en J. W. van Leeuwen, 1932. Still the standard work.

Delft, Dirk van. *Tafel van den Kersten Ghelove.* Edited by L. M. Fr. Daniëls. 3 vols. Antwerp, Belgium: Centrale Boekhandel "Neerlandia," 1937–1939. The only edition of the *Tafel.*

Oostrom, F. P. van. *Court and Culture: Dutch Literature, 1350–1450.* Translated by Arnold J. Poerans. Berkeley: University of California Press, 1992. The only recent study of Dirc.

EMILY KADENS

[See also **DMA:** Dutch Literature.]

DISEASE. "Disease" is a notoriously fluid, relative term; diseases can be variously constructed by professional consensus, legislative fiat, or even public sentiment. There was a not dissimilar fluidity in medieval ideas about what caused disease, what diseases were, and what they meant. For these and other reasons, it is usually close to impossible for the modern student to equate medieval names for diseases with modern ones, at least with any real confidence. Indeed, the physical symptoms that seemed characteristic to a practitioner in the Middle Ages are very often meaningless or irrelevant to a modern diagnostician. Retrospective diagnosis therefore offers very little certainty; even the traditional identification of the *magna mortalitas* of 1347–1350 with bubonic plague has recently been called into question.

CAUSES OF DISEASE

At the beginning of the fourteenth century, the Montpellier master Arnald of Villanova outlined the scholastic physician's understanding of disease *(morbus)*. One way to categorize diseases was in terms of the five ways in which they might be caused. Some diseases were regional, induced by the physical characteristics of the local environment: renal and vesical calculus were common where the water was sandy or clayey, dysentery where it was salty and nitrous; quinsy was frequent where tubers and fungi were common foods. Other diseases were epidemic, arising from causes corrupting the air or water or foods of a locality—causes like corpses and the vapors they emitted. Hereditary diseases were instilled by parents in generation: common experience, said Arnald, shows that phthisis, lepra, and tinea can be diseases of this kind. Then there were contagious diseases, which were impressed upon a healthy person who approached too close to someone already suffering from one of them: these included lepra, scabies, variola, febres pestilentiales, and ophthalmia, among others. Contagion did not, however, necessarily imply communication of physical "seeds" of disease. Sufferers from contagious disease were widely supposed to emit a poisonous miasma, evil vapors that could awaken an infection in healthy individuals who had an inherent susceptibility to the same illness. Finally, diseases sometimes arose from the particular reactions of individuals to their environment or their regimen—people vary enough so that in circumstances where one person is attacked by a quotidian fever, his neighbor may suffer from a tertian, and so forth.

KINDS OF DISEASES

An alternative way to classify diseases set out by Arnald was in terms of the kind of effect they have upon the body. Some diseases are called consimilar because they affect either the "consimilar members"—the parts of the body that are composed throughout of similar material, such as bones, muscles, skin, or nerves—or the body as a whole. Their effect is complexional, that is, they create a qualitative imbalance, or *discrasia,* in the member; they heat or chill it abnormally. Naturally the physician needs to discriminate among these *discrasie:* they may be of greater or lesser degree; they may affect just a part of the body or, like a fever or a general edema, the entire body; they may arise from different humors, as some hot *discrasie* are choleric and others sanguine; and so forth—for these differences determine how seriously the patient is affected and what kind of treatment will be needed.

Other diseases affect the nature and healthy functioning of the "official members"—members composed of dissimilar materials, like the liver, the heart, the eyes, the feet—and are therefore called *morbi officiales.* They affect not the complexion of these members but their composition, altering their size or their form (as when the arch of the foot is flattened, causing the patient to walk with difficulty) or their structure (for example, when they suffer from unnatural growths like tumors, warts, or calculi, all of which are unhealthy insofar as they interfere with the normal functioning of the body) or their position, as in the case of dislocations.

A third group of diseases, sometimes called *morbi communi,* involves what is called *solutio continuitatis,* a break or rupture in the integrity of an official or consimilar member. Sometimes the break is due to a loss of flesh, as in an ulcer or a fistula; sometimes it is simply a break, as in fractures of a bone or tears in cartilage. In general, *solutiones continuitatis* are treated by manual operation or manipulation, techniques that are the province of surgeons, while *morbi consimiles* are treated with medication; *morbi officiales* often require both sorts of treatment.

DIAGNOSING DISEASES

Writing probably in the 1260s, Roger Bacon complained that

> the Latins do not have a sufficient number of diagnoses of diseases [*divisiones morborum*]; because only Avicenna gives diagnoses, and, to some extent, Rhazes. . . . Rhazes put the diagnoses of diseases among the first duties in the practice of medicine, so that the causes and symptoms of any kind of illness might be clearly recognized, for example among the varieties of quartan fever or the varieties of dysentery, and of other things, because each variety comes from a different cause and has its own definite symptoms and its own cure.

And in fact, in the course of the thirteenth century medical practitioners became increasingly concerned to differentiate among diseases—often, as Bacon suggested they ought, drawing on the *Canon* of Avicenna to make new distinctions.

The case of surgery illustrates this tendency very well. The surgical textbooks of the first part of the century cover *solutiones continuitatis* like fractures, wounds, and abscesses as well as a limited number of other complaints (above all, scrofula, quinsy, hernia, hemorrhoids, and bladder stone). By the end of the century, however, drawing on Avicenna and Rhazes, surgical writers were describing many new diseases—scabies, gutta rosacea— and distinguishing among different forms of the older ones, like hernia. To be sure, it was not always clear to the surgeons how the diagnostic signs provided by the

Arabic authors were to be matched up with their own clinical experience, but in the end they created a compromise between the diseases they read about and the diseases they confronted in their practice. This same expansion of the diagnostic vocabulary is to be found in medicine as well as surgery: Arnald of Villanova includes "the kind of scabies that the Arabs call baras, which is like impetigo," among his list of hereditary diseases.

Roger Bacon (who was not a physician) understood perfectly well that diagnosing or identifying a disease and its cause meant identifying its treatment as well; the "meaning" of a disease has a therapeutic as well as a pathological dimension. But for the practitioner in the Middle Ages there was a third dimension to its meaning, a prognostic one that had been passed on since Hippocrates's day: if you were able to put a precise name to a disease it meant that you would thereby be able to anticipate accurately its future course. That ensured not just that you would be able to administer the necessary medicines at critical moments but that you would win your patient's trust—for being able to predict the progress of an illness provided a convincing demonstration of your mastery of the disease, and as practitioners were (and are still) well aware, patients who have confidence in their physician are more likely to recover than those who do not. A disease, then, was more than a static set of symptoms: it had a future and an anticipated outcome.

A SPECIFIC DISEASE AND ITS MEANING: LEPRA

Although it is rarely possible to equate medieval diseases with modern ones, in the case of medieval lepra we are on reasonably sure ground: some bony remains in medieval graveyards seem to reveal signs of actual leprosy (Hansen's disease). No doubt not all those labeled as leprosi in the Middle Ages suffered from this disease, but it was apparently a real and widespread pathological condition; the leprosaria, or leper hospitals, constructed so widely in the twelfth and thirteenth centuries were a response to an actuality. It has been calculated that there were nearly 20,000 such hospitals in Europe by 1300, implying the existence of more than half a million lepers in the population, though for some still uncertain reason the incidence of the disease dropped rapidly in the next century. Its prevalence and the anguish produced by a chronic and disfiguring condition make lepra an interesting case study in how not only physicians but also the laity responded to disease.

In determining whether a patient was leprous, a physician first asked questions to see whether heredity or contagion made the diagnosis a likely one. But there were other direct diagnostic indications: the physical signs, of course, the destruction of the extremities; the behavior of the sufferer (was he irascible, aggressive, violent?); and certain tests that were believed to be indicative of the disease—the grittiness of the patient's blood when rubbed between thumb and finger, for example. If leprosy seemed the probable diagnosis, there then arose the issue of prognosis: physicians tried to distinguish between the incipient stage of the disease, which was hoped to be curable, and established leprosy, which was almost universally understood to be incurable, though that did not inhibit them from trying to offer treatment. In keeping with the growing prominence of diagnosis, the laity came gradually to accept the judgment of physicians as determinative; from the late thirteenth century on we find individuals suspected of leprosy by their fellow citizens seeking certification of their health (or at least of their freedom from leprosy) from established medical practitioners.

This kind of certification was so important because of the evolution of public attitudes toward the disease. In the twelfth century it tended to be seen as divine punishment for sinfulness, and its sufferers as proper objects of compassion. In the course of the thirteenth century, however, a growing conviction of leprosy's naturalness and communicability transformed charity to the sick into suspicion and ostracism, and leper hospitals changed from being charitable shelters to being a means of excluding the sick from society. Under these conditions, a physician's certificate of healthiness was eagerly sought after. Leprosy was unusual in its attribution to sin; while the church certainly accepted that (in the words of the Fourth Lateran Council) "bodily infirmity is sometimes caused by sin" and stressed the importance of a patient's confession before being treated by a physician, in individual cases illness was normally explained as due to a physical rather than a moral cause. The universality of the epidemic of 1347–1350 encouraged an explanation in terms of the collective sinfulness of humanity, yet even here physical explanations were common—and became routine as the disease continued to recur.

BIBLIOGRAPHY

Amundsen, Darrel W. "The Medieval Catholic Tradition." In *Caring and Curing: Health and Medicine in the Western Religious Traditions.* Edited by Ronald L. Numbers and Darrel W. Amundsen. New York: Macmillan, 1986.

Cohn, Samuel K., Jr. "The Black Death: End of a Paradigm." *American Historical Review* 107 (2002): 703–738.

Demaitre, Luke. "The Description and Diagnosis of Leprosy by Fourteenth-Century Physicians." *Bulletin of the History of Medicine* 59 (1985): 327–344.

———. "The Relevance of Futility: Jordanus De Turre (fl. 1313–1335) on the Treatment of Leprosy." *Bulletin of the History of Medicine* 70 (1996): 25–61.

Nutton, Vivian. "The Seeds of Disease: An Explanation of Contagion and Infection from the Greeks to the Renaissance." *Medical History* 27 (1983): 1–34.

Siraisi, Nancy G. *Medieval and Early Renaissance Medicine: An Introduction to Knowledge and Practice.* Chicago and London: University of Chicago Press, 1990.

Touati, François-Olivier. *Maladie et société au moyen âge: La lèpre, les lépreux et les léproseries dans la province ecclésiastique de Sens jusqu'au milieu du XIVe siècle.* Brussels: DeBoeck, 1998.

———. "Contagion and Leprosy: Myth, Ideas, and Evolution in Medieval Minds and Societies." In *Contagion: Perspectives from Pre-Modern Societies.* Edited by Lawrence I. Conrad and Dominik Wujastyk. Aldershot, U.K.: Ashgate, 2000.

Welborn, Mary Catherine. "The Errors of the Doctors According to Friar Roger Bacon of the Minor Order." *Isis* 18 (1932): 26–62.

MICHAEL McVAUGH

[See also **DMA:** Arnald of Villanova; Bacon, Roger; Hospitals and Poor Relief; Leprosy; Medicine, Schools of; Plagues, European; Rāzī, Abū Bakr Muḥammad ibn Zakariyā al- (Rhazes); Sīnā, Ibn; **Supp:** Hygiene, Personal; Physicians.]

DIVORCE. See **Marriage, Christian.**

DRACONTIUS, BLOSSIUS AEMILIUS (*fl.* fifth century A.D.), was one of the most distinguished of the Christian Roman poets who lived under the Vandals in North Africa, yet we know very little about his life. Dracontius was probably born in Carthage, but the possible date of his birth could be any time between 420 and 460, most likely around 450. Even his family lineage is contested; some scholars have claimed that he came from a high-ranking Roman family, possibly senatorial, while others have suggested that his mother was a Vandal. As a young man he studied under the grammarian Felicianus, learning rhetoric, Latin literature, and possibly Greek. He also seems to have received legal training, as he followed his education with a successful legal practice.

The turning point in his life came in the early 480s, when he wrote a panegyric about a foreign prince—possibly the Byzantine emperor Zeno or the Ostrogothic king Odoacer. His sovereign, the Vandal ruler Gunthamund (*r.* 484–496), considered the text tantamount to treason and in 484 had Dracontius and his family imprisoned. While in prison he wrote an apology to Gunthamund, *Satisfactio ad regem Gunthamundum,* that did little to soften the monarch's heart. Dracontius remained in prison until Gunthamund died in 496. His successor, Thrasamund (*r.* 496–523), finally released the poet after more than a dozen years in captivity. The grateful Dracontius responded by writing a laudatory piece about Thrasamund, which has not survived. The imprisonment is the only part of Dracontius's life that we have any certainty about, and almost all other events in his life have been reconstructed based on this twelve-year period. Consequently, the last years of Dracontius's life are also shrouded in mystery.

Dracontius's major works were *De laudibus Dei* and a collection of epyllia (short epic poems). He wrote *De laudibus* while in prison. Consisting of three books, the work praises God's gifts to man, including the Creation and the Redemption. The Catholic Dracontius also takes several shots at Arianism, a move either heroic or foolish, considering that the ruling Vandals were staunch and intolerant Arians. Of the epyllia, four have survived—*Hylas, De raptu Helenae, Medea,* and *Orestis tragoedia*—the first three in a wider collection of Dracontius's work entitled the *Romulea.* These works are remarkable for the amazing breadth of classical knowledge they display, easily drawing on Greek myths and Roman styles. The epyllia, however, were also shaped by the poet's religious upbringing, and it is not uncommon to see a clash between the classical elements and Dracontius's own Christian faith in his writings. Additionally, Dracontius's Latin shows evidence of barbarian influences, adding a tangible Germanic flavor to his works. In his accomplishments, Dracontius presents the modern scholar with an intriguing and welcome problem: the possibility that the destruction of knowledge and education often associated with the Vandal invasions may not have been as thorough as usually believed. In the mid-seventh century, the Visigothic bishop Eugenius of Toledo converted and adapted some of Dracontius's works, opening them up for a new readership.

BIBLIOGRAPHY

Bright, David F. *The Miniature Epic in Vandal Africa.* Norman: University of Oklahoma Press, 1987.

Díaz de Bustamante, J. M. *Draconcio y su carmina profana: Estudio biográfico, introducció y edición crítica.* Santiago de Compostela: Universidad de Santiago, Secretariado de Publicaciones, 1978.

Vollmer, F. *Fl. Merobaudis reliquiae, Blossii Aemilii Dracontii carmina, Eugeni Toletani episcopi carmina et epistulae.* In *Monumenta Germaniae Historica, Auctorum Antiquissimorum XIV.* Berlin, 1905.

JARBEL RODRIGUEZ

[See also **DMA:** Eugenius II of Toledo; Latin Literature; Odoacer; Roman Empire, Late; Vandals; Vergil in the Middle Ages; Zeno the Isaurian.]

DROIT DU SEIGNEUR. Many modern writers of historical fiction imagine a Middle Ages in which lords had a special right that inhered in them as lords, hence the phrase "droit du seigneur," which literally means nothing more than the "the lord's right." More suggestive and describing the same putative right is the Latin phrase *ius primae noctis,* or "right of the first night." Allegedly, that is, lords claimed the right to have sex with any of their serfs' brides on the latters' wedding nights.

It is doubtful that this allegation arose out of a misunderstanding of the customary levies on servile marriages that were paid to lords and were a ubiquitous feature of the seigneurial regime, though this has been argued. More likely is that a lord in some circumstances somewhere made such a claim, possibly after the rape of a servile girl or after making an advance to one, perhaps the bride herself, at the wedding party of one of his serfs. It is easy to imagine a rumor spreading that lords in general were making such claims. Catalonia in the late fifteenth century is as good a place as any in which to imagine this situation arising, for rustics in that region did in fact charge (in 1462) that their lords were making the claim. The lords collectively answered the charge with a denial, but the king of Aragon, in case any such claim was made in the future, made it legally unenforceable in 1486. There are a very few early modern examples of rustics elsewhere believing that lords wanted or tried to exercise this so-called right of the first night.

Critics of feudalism in the Enlightenment had a field day denouncing a political, economic, and social system that allegedly encouraged, tolerated, or at least universally recognized the legitimacy of this right. Moreover, because these critics regarded the droit du seigneur as a widespread and integral aspect of feudal society, they could come to absurd conclusions, such as that the lineage of most of a country's people could be traced back to aristocratic liaisons with servile women by right of first night. In fact, a nonexistent right has been regarded as characteristic and indeed emblematic of the Middle Ages.

BIBLIOGRAPHY

Boureau, Alain. *The Lord's First Night: The Myth of the Droit de Cuissage.* Translated by Lydia Cochrane. Chicago: University of Chicago Press, 1998.

Freedman, Paul H. *The Origins of Peasant Servitude in Medieval Catalonia.* Cambridge, U.K.: Cambridge University Press, 1991.

Litvack, Frances Eleanor Palermo. *Le Droit du Seigneur in European and American Literature: From the Seventeenth through the Twentieth Century.* Birmingham, Ala.: Summa, 1984.

Schmidt, Karl. *Jus primae noctis: Eine geschichtliche Untersuchung.* Freiburg im Breisgau, Germany, and St. Louis: Herder, 1881.

WILLIAM CHESTER JORDAN

[See also **Supp:** Sexuality.]

DUNSTAN, ST. (*ca.* 909–988). Abbot of Glastonbury in the 940s, Dunstan was exiled to St. Peter's at Ghent, in 956, then recalled and appointed to hold the see of Worcester and London in plurality; soon thereafter he became archbishop of Canterbury, in which position he served from 960 until his death on 19 May 988. Along with Ethelwold of Winchester (*ca.* 908–984) and Oswald of Worcester (*d.* 992), Dunstan was one of the three leaders of the Benedictine Revival (or "Renaissance"), a resurgence of monasticism that marked the late tenth century. Dunstan taught Ethelwold, whom current scholarship considers the most ideological of the reformers.

The author known as "B," no longer thought to be Byrhtferth but rather more likely an Englishman with continental connections who may have known Dunstan personally, offers the first life of Dunstan some seventeen years after Dunstan's death. Ill proportioned as a whole, often obscure in style, and sometimes simply wrong, this *vita* nevertheless gives a fair amount of information about Dunstan's personal life and the court intrigues that surrounded him, all within the conventions of hagiography. To be sure, Dunstan had a good start. Heorstan and Cynethryth, his father and mother, were well off and well connected. The family owned significant estates, notably around Glastonbury, and his uncle Ethelhelm was archbishop of Canterbury. Dunstan rose to prominence during the reign of Ethelstan, and when the king died in 939, he suffered the envy and the lies of some in the court, which resulted in expulsion. He avoided the temptation to marry and became a monk and eventually abbot of Glastonbury. As many a saint, Dunstan is successful in encounters with the devil, who comes variously as bear, dog, and fox, and he has visions and utters prophecies. Yet within the hagiographic framework one learns important facts; for example, that Irish monks visited Glastonbury and that Dunstan, exiled by King Edwy (*r.* 955–959), whose personal conduct Dunstan disapproved of, went to Gaul (St. Peter's at Ghent), which ultimately became a model for Anglo-Saxon church reform. A special theme in B's account is the portrayal of Dunstan as a man of arts and letters, who pursued sacred studies, painting, and harp playing. Dunstan designed a stole, corrected scribes, and gave sermons. On one occasion his harp, by itself, played a holy anthem, which terrified those in the house where Dunstan was having dinner. Comparatively few of his apparent literary productions have survived. "St. Dunstan's Classbook" (Oxford, Bodleian Library, Auct. F.4.32) depicts Dunstan kneeling before Christ, with a distich written above him presumably by him (see Ramsay et al., opposite p. 190). "Hand D" in the manuscript is thought to be Dunstan's. Some Latin acrostics survive, and it is an attractive speculation, but nothing more, that some of the unattributed vernacular homilies might in fact be by Dunstan.

B does not give much information about Dunstan as archbishop, his later career, or most disappointingly, his role in the promulgation of the *Regularis concordia* (or "Rule of agreement," which bound together the monasteries restored by Ethelwold, Oswald, and Dunstan himself). Yet he does assert that the light of Dunstan's teaching filled all of England "as the sun and the moon."

Adelard of Ghent wrote the second life in the early eleventh century. In the next century William of Malmesbury (*ca.* 1090–1143), Osbern of Canterbury (*d.* between 1088 and 1093), and Eadmer of Canterbury (*ca.* 1060–*ca.* 1130) wrote *vitae* that attest to a flourishing cult well after the Anglo-Saxon period. In addition, two triforium windows at Canterbury cathedral (Christ Church) remember Dunstan with scenes from his life.

BIBLIOGRAPHY

Dales, Douglas. *Dunstan: Saint and Statesman.* Cambridge, U.K.: Lutterworth, 1988. An accessible biography set against the social and religious background.

Ramsay, Nigel, Margaret Sparks, and Tim Tatton-Brown, eds. *St. Dunstan: His Life, Times, and Cult.* Woodbridge, U.K.: Boydell, 1992. An authoritative collection of sixteen essays by various hands.

Whitelock, Dorothy, ed. *English Historical Documents.* Volume 1: *Ca. 500–1042.* General editor, David C. Douglas. London: Eyre Methuen, 1979. Item 234 contains a translation of sections from B's life of Dunstan.

PAUL E. SZARMACH

[See also **DMA:** Benedictine Rule; Benedictines; Ethelwold and the Benedictine Rule.]

DURAND OF HUESCA (Osca) (*ca.* 1160–*ca.* 1224), an early Waldensian who converted and founded the

Pauperes catholici (Poor Catholics). Born in Aragon, Durand was among the first disciples of Waldes, the founder of the Waldensians. Durand was likely with Waldes in 1179 at the Third Lateran Council when the Waldensians failed to win papal support for the right to preach. An anonymous Waldensian polemic against the Cathars entitled *Antiheresis* and written around 1191 to 1192 has been attributed to Durand. In addition to attacking the radical dualism of the Cathars, the treatise also defended the Waldensians' orthodoxy and their right to preach, citing God's alleged direct call to Waldes to preach. In short, the *Antiheresis* provided a collection of theological "talking points" for the Waldensians in their arguments with both the Cathars and the Catholics.

During the late twelfth and early thirteenth centuries, the Waldensians were a motley group, with some members more flagrantly heretical than others. Durand appears to have been part of a more moderate group that never strayed far from orthodoxy. In 1207, after meeting with representatives of the church at Pamiers, Durand and a group of Waldensians converted, formally submitting to Catholic authority. In a subsequent trip to Rome, Durand obtained the pope's permission to continue leading an apostolic life and return to Languedoc to fight heresy as the prior of a new group, the Poor Catholics. Although they were not clerics and did not follow a monastic rule, the Poor Catholics led austere lives of poverty, prayer, chastity, fasting, and obedience. They wore sandals to distinguish themselves from the heretical Waldensians, who went barefoot. By submitting to the ecclesiastical hierarchy and repudiating the Donatist doctrines that had begun to spread among the Waldensians, Durand and his followers won the right to preach against heresy and lead evangelical lives, as they had sought to do as Waldensians. There were, in other words, significant continuities between Waldes's original vision of an evangelical vocation of wandering preaching and that which emerged in the form of the Poor Catholics. Durand may have hoped that most Waldensians would follow his lead in submitting to Rome once they saw that the pope would support their apostolic mission. But unlike Durand, most Waldensians felt that they could not fulfill their mission if they were under the control of the local ecclesiastical hierarchy. Although the pope supported Durand and the Poor Catholics, prelates who perhaps felt threatened by the Poor Catholics' piety, learning, and popularity as preachers complained to the pope that the Poor Catholics were consorting with their former coreligionists, the Waldensians, and were practically indistinguishable from them.

Around 1222 and 1223 Durand composed *Liber contra Manicheos,* in which he presented excerpts from a Cathar treatise, refuted the Cathar arguments point by point, and then substituted them with orthodox doctrine. Taking up theological, christological, moral, and institutional issues, Durand's central aim was to show that there was no basis in the Scriptures for the Cathars' dogma. Through preaching and the writing of polemical texts, Durand and the Poor Catholics sought to wipe out what the Albigensian Crusade had not.

BIBLIOGRAPHY

Durand de Huesca. *Une somme anti-Cathare: Le Liber contra Manicheos de Durand de Huesca.* Edited by Christine Thouzellier. Louvain, Belgium: Spicilegium Sacrum Lovaniense, 1964.

Rouse, Mary A., and Richard H. Rouse. "The Schools and the Waldensians: A New Work by Durand of Huesca." In *Christendom and Its Discontents: Exclusion, Persecution, and Rebellion, 1000–1500.* Edited by Scott L. Waugh and Peter D. Diehl. Cambridge, U.K.: Cambridge University Press, 1996.

Selge, Kurt-Victor. *Die ersten Waldenser, mit Edition des Liber Antiheresis des Durandus von Osca.* 2 vols. Berlin: Walter de Gruyter, 1967.

Thouzellier, Christine. *Catharisme et Valdéisme en Languedoc à la fin du XIIe et au début du XIIIe siècle.* 1969. Reprint, Marseille: Laffitte, 1982.

———, ed. *Un traité Cathare inédit du début du XIIIe siècle d'après le "Liber contra Manicheos" de Durand de Huesca.* Louvain, Belgium: Bibliothèque de l'Université, 1961.

ADAM JEFFREY DAVIS

[See also **DMA:** Cathars; Donatism; Waldensians.]

ECOLOGY is a postmedieval concept of the interdependence of living organisms and their environment, living and nonliving. In modern thinking this necessarily includes humans in relation to nonhuman nature. Medieval Europeans thought otherwise, normally separating God from his creation and man from the rest of the physical world. Francis of Assisi tested theological limits with his notion that God, man, and animate and inanimate nature shared common being, but not even he imagined an "ecosystem," now understood as an assemblage of organisms and their environment acting as a unit, or the "landscape" as an assemblage of ecosystems (woodland, river, marsh, etc.) interacting less directly. Medieval consciousness affected how contemporaries perceived and recorded natural phenomena but less so the ecological situations in which they necessarily lived.

Scholars trying to reconstruct past ecological relationships have begun to call themselves "environmental historians," but much knowledge about ecological relations in medieval Europe was achieved by people unaware of that name. Environmental history makes critical use of written records, material relics (structures, artifacts, plant and animal remains), and results from archaeoscience (tree rings, ice cores, soil profiles) to establish conditions in the past.

HUMANS AND ECOSYSTEMS IN MEDIEVAL EUROPE

In each of Europe's three big geoclimatic regions, seasonal norms of temperature and precipitation act on distinctive topographies to set dynamic stages for preindustrial human societies. Environments commonly posed relatively predictable situations to which durable human societies found ways to adapt, often partly by adjusting natural conditions to their purposes.

South of the Alps and related ranges, Mediterranean Europe has thin soils and steep relief, leaving relatively few and small areas of level ground between the mountains and the sea. Short, fast rivers carry few nutrients to narrow continental shelves. Infertile Mediterranean waters support high species diversity but relatively low biomass. During warm and dry summers most land plants stop growing, while cool, wet winters favor grasses. These conditions influenced the choice of crops, agricultural routines, and the movement of livestock. Following ancient experience, medieval Mediterranean farmers worked their land in fall and winter, planted half their arable each year to use two years' accumulated soil moisture, and harvested their wheat as its seeds matured in early summer. Deeply rooted grapes and olives could handle the summer drought but respectively little or no winter freezing. Stormy winter brought herders and livestock down from chilling upland pastures to greening lowland vegetation (vertical transhumance).

Atlantic or maritime Europe is a mostly flatter landscape with a climate moderated as far east as Poland by prevailing westerly flows off the ocean. Mean temperatures at sea level rarely go much over seventy degrees Fahrenheit (twenty degrees Celsius) or much below freezing. Winter cold kept out the olive, calling for other sources of edible oils, but did not force livestock indoors. Atlantic Europe is humid the year round, so its often deep soils commonly support dense natural woodlands and the growth of summer cereals. The danger was too much water: saturated soils; leaching of soluble nutrients below the reach of grasses; seasonal flooding, erosion, and deposition. Large, low-gradient rivers run all year, pouring nutrient-rich water on to wide continental shelves, where abundant aquatic life could support large-scale fisheries.

Neither the Atlantic nor the Mediterranean moderate conditions in continental Europe. North of the Alpine-Balkan mountain ranges and east of the Bohemian upland and likewise to the southwest on the high plateau *(meseta)* of interior Portugal and Spain, climates are typically extreme, regularly going over eighty degrees Fahrenheit (twenty-five degrees Celsius) in summer and averaging below freezing in the winter. The saying "ten months of winter, two months of hell" comes from central Spain, not eastern Poland. Frozen soil harmed traditional winter wheat and favored rye. Livestock had to be housed and fed or else moved long distances from summer to protected winter pastures (horizontal transhumance or nomadism).

Like all farming, the traditional agricultures of medieval Europe were artificial ecosystems adapted to meet human cultural needs from available living and nonliving elements of the environment. Formation of agroecosystems was the greatest single ecological change in Europe's preindustrial human history, with stable relations established around the Mediterranean in the Bronze Age but agricultural coevolution continuing in the north throughout the Middle Ages. Agroecosystems are grossly simplified food chains, comprising a few chosen plant varieties whose growth humans subsidize and manage for high yield of human consumables. Annual grasses (cereal grains) rapidly cycle nutrients to mature in a single growing season. In nature these plants are soon replaced by more diverse, longer-lived flora, so agriculturists must work to keep the system simple. From an ecological perspective, agricultural practices and technologies are the means whereby each human community defines and sustains its particular niche.

By dry farming of light soils for winter grains in annual rotation with fallow and by summer use of upland pastures, traditional Mediterranean agriculturalists succeeded within regional climatic constraints. Their practices risked soil erosion from heavy fall rains on bare fallow and newly sown ground and overgrazing on fragile hill slopes. Intense land use by large human populations during the twelfth and thirteenth centuries followed by stormier conditions during a fourteenth-century phase of climatic cooling caused major sedimentation of Mediterranean estuaries. Despite defects, this agroecosystem sustained growing rural populations through all the central medieval centuries, although enlarged Italian cities had to subsidize half their cereal needs with imports from more thinly populated Apulia and Sicily.

Solutions early medieval northern Europeans devised for permanent farming in often wet and seasonally cold regions posed reciprocal hazards. The moldboard plow let farmers restore leached nutrients to the soil surface and adjust field profiles to manage runoff and infiltration. Heavy soils and dependable precipitation allowed each parcel to produce two years in three, so raising total output, especially of spring-sown cereals (barley, oats) well suited for use in beverages (ale) and the animal feed needed by a more energy-intensive and carnivorous society. Pasturing livestock on local fallow and stubble recycled some nutrients, but those lost by consumption elsewhere were only partly replaced through spreading barn litter, herbage cut from waste ground, marl, or urban wastes. Where additional resources were lacking, as in areas of dense peasant settlement, or other considerations took priority, soil fertility slowly fell. Equilibrium was also encouraged when farmers plowed the fallow to keep down weeds, maintained each peasant's arable in scattered plots, used wild resources, and rationed access to commons (stinting).

Coevolution of human agrarian economies with regional environments continued during the later Middle Ages, especially where people had access to special resources, techniques, or opportunities: field legumes (peas, beans, clover) raised fertility while feeding animals and even humans; market demand from towns or elsewhere changed production decisions. Innovations came more easily in lord-run than peasant agriculture and, when adopted for other motives, could as well diminish as improve local sustainability. But progressive microadaptations to local soils, water, and climate helped shape alternative subsistence strategies and challenge Europeans' earlier obsession with cereal grains.

Trees grew naturally almost everywhere in temperate Europe, forming woodlands of various density and species composition. Medieval woods were rarely pristine. "Wilderness" devoid of human imprint was always more a cultural construct than an ecological fact. Medieval Europeans used native woodland species as sources of human food, animal fodder, raw materials, and energy, and these uses changed the woodland.

In some places woodland provided a reserve of temporary plow land, cut and burned for a few years' cultivation of fertile ash, then left to regenerate for many years as "forest fallow." Woodland was pasture, too, supporting especially swine and cattle—natives of wooded habitats—on new growth of most plants and seasonally abundant fruits of oak and beech.

The fundamental distinction in woodland exploitation was between timber (*silva maior, Oberwald,* etc.) and coppice (*silva minuta, Niederholz,* etc.). Timber woods held big, old trees, commonly oaks or beeches, sometimes conifers, yielding logs for heavy construction and not, except for logging waste, fuel. After a cut, regenerating timber took 50 to 150 years, for most of which

time the land could also provide pasture, game habitat, and gathering resources (herbs, honey, etc.). Up to about the year 1000 timber was generally available in Europe, so records are few, but from the thirteenth century landowners carefully managed these valuable assets.

Coppice epitomizes medieval humanized woodland, providing fuel and raw materials for an advanced preindustrial economy. Coppice exploits the natural capacity of most woody vegetation (but few conifers) to respond to cutting by putting forth new shoots. After only a few years' growth these could serve—depending on species—as wattle, rods, stakes, poles, or bundles or blocks of fuel wood, or they could be made into lighter, pure-burning charcoal. Coppice needs protection against browsing animals, either by fencing or by making the initial cut some distance off the ground, forming a pollard with sprouts from its top. Productive pollards can live for centuries and coppice stools (the underground portion) indefinitely, so surviving medieval oak and ash coppices are likely the oldest living things in, for instance, Britain and Sardinia. Managerial skills called "woodmanship" were older still, though literate elites rarely mentioned them.

Plantation forestry, a late medieval development for intensified production of conifers, remained uncommon.

Medieval coevolution between humans and woodlands tended toward rough and contingent equilibria. In Mediterranean Europe most individual woodlands survived independent narratives of depletion and regrowth. Northern Europe experienced a great deforestation during the tenth through thirteenth centuries, but from around 1200 most remaining woods were protected and managed for various essential human purposes.

ECOLOGIES OF CHANGE, NATURAL AND HUMAN

Natural forces and human activities alike repeatedly disrupted ecological balances during the Middle Ages. Changes cascading from such events confirm the complex linkages between medieval Europeans and their environment. Among dynamic natural occurrences, some in the atmospheric and microbiological environments are so far best studied, combining scientific and traditional historical evidence.

During the growing season of 536, tree ring sequences from numerous European and other regions of the Northern Hemisphere show a sudden halt in vegetative growth, which lasted ten to fifteen years. Human observers from the Mediterranean to East Asia described a "dry fog" in the atmosphere which perceptibly cut the solar heat and light and cereal yields. Scientists now find such "dust veil events" result from large volcanic eruptions or impacts of extraterrestrial objects, but no particular occurrence in 535 and 536 has so far been verified. Subsequent conditions are consistent with an extended period of reduced solar radiation to the earth's surface: widely reported storms and cold in 536 and 537 and following years; crop failures; a great drought in Italy in 539; from 542 a deadly epidemic spread across the Mediterranean and into western Europe. It becomes harder clearly to connect these developments with such later sociopolitical changes as the subsistence crises of the late 530s that triggered Slavic migrations into the Balkans, the mid-sixth-century collapse of British resistance to Anglo-Saxon invaders, and the decline of the entire European population to a postclassical low shortly after 600.

The first half of the fourteenth century experienced comparable and drawn-out environmental peculiarities. Growth rates of oak trees in Europe collapsed in 1318 and remained low until 1353. Human reports of terribly wet and cold weather from 1314 to 1317 were followed by crop failures and epidemics among domestic animals, which in turn brought human famine and mortalities. Extremely high human population levels likely exacerbated some of these effects, but the unprecedented death rates of the Black Death (1347–1351) have not convincingly been linked to prior malnutrition or densities. The Black Death—a new disease with high incidence and mortality rates—then did shock Europe into a century of demographic free fall, nearly wiping out a half millennium of human increase. Historians have long thought this an epidemic of the plague bacillus (Yersinia pestis), which normally lives in a complex relationship with rodent hosts and the rat flea as primary vector, but recent researchers bothered by discrepancies between modern medical descriptions of plague and eyewitness medieval reports of symptoms and incidence speculate about some otherwise unknown disease or combination of diseases.

Ascertaining the nature and effects of relatively short-term events in the atmosphere and biosphere at the start of the fourteenth century is complicated by the simultaneous onset of a probably global climatic phase, the so-called Little Ice Age, which brought several long periods of distinctly lower mean annual temperatures over the next five hundred years. A cooling trend set in at northwestern Europe from the 1290s and spread southeastward, affecting the Mediterranean and central Europe after the 1320s. Climatic change brought generally greater storminess, but its regional consequences were strongly influenced by prior weather patterns and

human adaptations. For instance, after more than two successful centuries in Greenland, Norse settlers found that newly shorter, chillier summers grew less winter fodder for their livestock, and longer winters with heavier sea ice put seasonal concentrations of marine mammals beyond their reach. They abandoned the more exposed Western Settlement around 1350 and disappeared from their southern farms in the fifteenth century. Their Icelandic cousins suffered deaths by starvation of animals and humans but survived by shifting economic emphasis from livestock to the cod fishery. In the Alps glaciers surged forward over long-standing human structures, while in many mountains people gave up their highest grain fields.

Annals, chronicles, and other local sources further document extreme environmental events—floods, landslides, volcanic eruptions, outbreaks of locusts, epidemics—with large and long-term effects on human communities. For instance, the 1362 storm flood called the "Great Drowning" (Grosse Manndränke) in Friesland swept livestock, people, villages, and some 40 percent of the land (more than a hundred square kilometers) from the island of Strand. Research into these phenomena is, however, just beginning.

Human environmental impacts are not peculiar to industrial and postindustrial societies. Medieval Europeans brought about large ecological changes, some on purpose and others quite by accident. The largest single medieval assault on natural ecosystems was agricultural colonization, a process encapsulated in the Anglo-French term assart, meaning to grub out trees and create permanent plowland. Clearances began as early medieval barbarians accepted the grain-based dietary culture of the "civilized" Mediterranean and then from the tenth century became a great wave driven by subsistence needs of a growing population. A biogeographic revolution turned European woodlands into agricultural landscapes. Compared with 1000, forested area in France fell 57 percent by 1300; cultivated land in Poland doubled by 1500. A gradual process in southern and western Europe was more abrupt farther east, where most cutting came in a rush during the twelfth and thirteenth centuries.

Clearance had several ecological consequences, only some of them intended. It meant to replace diverse old-growth natural vegetation with an artificial flora of selected annual grasses that concentrated solar energy into seeds humans had learned to consume. As human farmers captured more energy from the transformed landscape, they changed the environment for all other organisms. From the eleventh century woodland-adapted domestic animals such as pigs and cattle were replaced in European herds and diets by sheep and goats, creatures better suited for spaces between agricultural land uses. Removing woody cover set off violent runoff, floods, and large-scale soil erosion and deposition; sometimes this created new landscapes far from where humans had intervened. Central Mediterranean estuaries became malarial marshes. Like the clearances, medieval drainage projects served agricultural needs while destroying complex wetland habitats and communal resources for multiple human uses, not always without local resistance. Some new farmland proved unsustainable. Gravity drainage of raised bogs in Holland caused the dried peat to oxidize and settle at a rate of one meter per century. By around 1300 Dutch fields once well above sea level were sinking below it, necessitating dikes to hold the sea back and wind-powered pumps to lift rain and river water out. Drained acidic sands in Brandenburg lost fertility under cereal crops and were abandoned as grain prices and demand for farmland fell in the later Middle Ages.

Medieval Europeans hunted wild animals for material needs (meat, hides, bone, etc.), to reduce competition (vermin), for leisure recreation, and to show off high social rank. The cliché that only noble elites could and did hunt must always be tested against well-dated regional evidence, often ambiguous. Early medieval peasants in northern France and late medieval villagers in several Mediterranean areas certainly consumed wild game. Only in the late fourteenth century did general laws bar western commoners from hunting outside elite game preserves (forests, parks, chases). Besides habitat loss, hunting (and fishing) pressure contributed to medieval extirpations of local and regional animal populations. Large carnivores, bears and wolves, were driven into the most mountainous parts of continental western Europe and other impressive species taken as trophies until none (the aurochs) or few (the bison) survived. Among fur bearers the native beaver was so persecuted as to be wholly unfamiliar to most later medieval naturalists. Likewise the largest freshwater and migratory fishes that early medieval elites and ordinary people enjoyed eating and giving as gifts slowly dwindled until in many places, as a London record from 1386 put it, "salmon and sturgeon are completely destroyed."

Wild animals were preserved when elite social interests became engaged in their management. Since Carolingian times monarchs set up their own "forests" (foresta), special jurisdictions to protect and nourish selected species, notably deer, which the king found of recreational and gustatory value. Fallow deer, for instance, occur almost exclusively at royal sites in France, where local peasant tenants were drafted to improve their habitat. Nobles emulated monarchs with their own private hunting reserves.

Medieval elites introduced exotic animals to European landscapes, at times with large ecological effects. Anglo-Norman aristocrats brought fallow deer and pheasants to England in the twelfth century. The rabbit, first introduced from North Africa to Spain by the Romans, was by that time common across Mediterranean Europe, while northern landowners actively sought their own stocks. Rabbits reached central Poland and Hungary by 1500, displacing the indigenous European hare from most settled areas. Meanwhile the common carp spread during the tenth to twelfth centuries from its native range in the Balkans into the upper Danube and Rhine basins and around 1200 more quickly into west-flowing watersheds of France. Both rabbits and carp fit into complex cultural contexts of food taboos, multiple uses, and intentionally modified landscapes (rabbit warrens and fish ponds). Both also soon developed feral populations in natural ecosystems under stress from human agricultural development.

Human manipulation of watercourses for transport, power generation, or irrigation; urbanization; disposal of human waste and emissions from manufacturing activities; and regional specialization in large-scale production and export of primary products (live cattle, wool, grain) all also affected landscapes and ecosystems in the Middle Ages. While medieval Europeans did work toward what might now be called sustainable uses of their environment, changing human impacts and natural forces together shaped continual ecological coevolution.

BIBLIOGRAPHY

Bechmann, Roland. *Trees and Man: The Forest in the Middle Ages.* Translated by Katharyn Dunham. New York: Paragon House, 1990.

Fagan, Brian. *The Little Ice Age: How Climate Made History, 1300–1850.* New York: Basic Books, 2000.

Grove, A. T., and Oliver Rackham. *The Nature of Mediterranean Europe: An Ecological History.* New Haven, Conn.: Yale University Press, 2001.

Guillerme, André E. *The Age of Water: The Urban Environment in the North of France, A.D. 300–1800.* College Station, Tex.: Texas A&M University Press, 1988.

Keys, David. *Catastrophe: An Investigation into the Origins of the Modern World.* New York: Ballantine, 2000.

Rackham, Oliver. *Trees and Woodland in the British Landscape.* London: Dent, 1976.

Simmons, I. G. *Environmental History: A Concise Introduction.* Oxford: Blackwell, 1993.

Smil, Vaclav. *Energy in World History.* Boulder, Colo.: Westview, 1994.

Squatriti, Paolo, ed. *Working with Water in Medieval Europe: Technology and Resource Use.* Leiden, Netherlands: Brill, 2000.

RICHARD C. HOFFMANN

[See also **DMA:** Agriculture and Nutrition; Animals, Food; Black Death; Climatology; Fisheries, Marine; Forest Law; Forests, European; Hunting and Fowling, Islamic; Hunting and Fowling, Western European; **Supp:** Animals, Attitudes Toward; Nature.]

EDESSA, COUNTY OF. Founded by an unusual combination of perspicacity and luck, the county of Edessa began its life as a Frankish-Armenian condominium and vanished fifty-three years later, divided among various Turkish emirs. The only Frankish principality in the Levant without a seacoast, the county stretched across what is now southeastern Turkey, dominating crucial routes between Antioch and northern Mesopotamia. Largely high, dry plateau suitable for some grains and herding, the county was divided by the Euphrates River, which provided a fertile valley suitable for intensive agriculture.

In October 1097, the French crusader Baldwin of Boulogne first conquered the fortress of Tell Bashir in western Syria at the advice of his Armenian ally Bagrat. Baldwin soon acquired a small territory between the Euphrates and Antioch and a reputation for defeating the Turks. T'oros, the Greek ruler of the city of Edessa, one of the largest cities in northern Syria, invited Baldwin to come to the city in March 1098. T'oros adopted the crusader as his son under public pressure and died at the hands of an angry mob less than a month after Baldwin arrived in the city. The crowd immediately proclaimed Baldwin the ruler of the city, and the county was effectively founded. Baldwin had few Frankish troops at his side, but he skillfully manipulated local factions to maintain his rule. In September 1100, he claimed Jerusalem after the death of his brother Godfrey of Bouillon, who was the first Frankish ruler of the city, and handed over the county to his first cousin once removed, Baldwin of Bourg.

Baldwin of Bourg (hereafter Baldwin II) established the county institutionally. Expelling many of the local Armenian rulers of towns and castles, Baldwin II replaced them with Frankish relatives and supporters. Despite this policy, Armenian lords continued to rule in some parts of the county, particularly Gargar. Baldwin II was captured by a Turkish emir at the Battle of Harran in 1104 and did not gain his release until 1108. During

his captivity, Edessa was ruled by Tancred of Antioch and his relative Richard of Salerno, who were unwilling to return it to Baldwin. Both sides called on Turkish allies, and a protracted civil war was avoided only through the intervention of Baldwin I of Jerusalem.

Baldwin II subsequently inherited Jerusalem as he had Edessa and in turn gave the county to his own cousin Joscelin of Courtenay. Joscelin's fierceness in battle and close relationships with local Christian communities won him acclaim from indigenous chroniclers. When Joscelin fell hostage to Balak in 1122, a group of intrepid Armenians sneaked into the castle where he was being held to release him. Joscelin escaped while the Armenians and other Frankish prisoners, including Baldwin II of Jerusalem, seized the fortress. Balak died not long afterwards, and Baldwin II was released by his successor.

Joscelin died in 1131 and was succeeded by his half-Armenian son, Joscelin II. The second Joscelin confronted a much different world than his father. The atabeg of Mosul, Zangī, was uniting much of northern Syria under his leadership. Both Joscelin and Raymond of Antioch were increasingly dependent on the armies of John II Komnenos to prevent Zangī from attacking them. Such protection did not come without a price, however. John had demanded that Raymond admit a Byzantine patriarch to Antioch and allow a garrison to take up residence in the citadel. Joscelin feared that similar demands might be placed on him. With his reluctant Frankish allies in tow, John seized Al-Atharib and attacked Shaizar in 1138. The two Frankish princes sullenly refused to participate in the siege, and John was forced to retreat by the approach of Zangī's army. On John's next visit to Syria, he demanded hostages from Joscelin to enforce his good behavior.

Byzantine protection of Edessa and Antioch provided Frankish northern Syria with a degree of protection that quickly disappeared following the death of John in 1143 and the subsequent return of the Byzantine army to Constantinople. Zangī attacked the city of Edessa on 24 December 1144 while Joscelin was away from the city and quickly captured it. His troops massacred the Frankish population but spared the local Christians and their churches. Two years later, Joscelin, who still ruled a considerable territory west of the Euphrates, briefly recaptured the city with Armenian help but soon lost the city to Zangī's son, Nūr-al-Dīn, who massacred Franks and local Christians alike.

The loss of the city shocked both the Latin East and Western Christendom and led to the Second Crusade. Led by the kings of France and Germany, the Crusade attacked independent Damascus, forcing the former

Frankish ally into Nūr-al-Dīn's growing empire. The crusade did nothing to recover Edessa or curb Nūr-al-Dīn's power. Joscelin himself was captured in 1150 and died nine years later, blinded in an Aleppan jail. His wife, Beatrice, sold the remaining portion of the county to the Byzantine emperor, but the Turks seized even these fortresses within a year.

Although the shortest-lived of all the crusader states, Edessa with its large local Christian population and landlocked locale was a very different place from Antioch or Jerusalem. It is difficult to establish the level of Frankish settlement in Edessa, although historians suggest it was limited, as virtually no archaeological work has been done on the crusader period. While cursory architectural surveys suggest considerable Frankish fortification and building, little detailed work has been done to separate Frankish style and technique from that of Byzantine, Islamic, or indigenous builders. The counts of Edessa, however, had considerable influence over local Christian churches; Baldwin II encouraged the Armenian patriarch Barsegh I to settle in Edessa, while Joscelin demanded that the Jacobite patriarchal election of 1129 take place in the Latin church of Tell Bashir under his supervision. Armenian lords continued to hold authority in some parts of the county, while in the cities local councils also wielded considerable authority. An Armenian inscription placed on the walls of Edessa in 1122 attested to the authority of a local Armenian leader named Vasil.

BIBLIOGRAPHY

SOURCES

Matthew of Edessa. *Zhamanakagrut'yun.* Edited by Mambre Melik'-Adamyan and Nerses Ter-Mik'ayelyan. Erevan, Armenia: Erevani Petakan Hamalsaran, 1991.

———. *Armenia and the Crusades, Tenth to Twelfth Centuries.* Translated by Ara Edmond Dostourian. New York: University Press of America, 1993.

Michael the Syrian. *Le chronique de Michel le Syrien.* Edited and translated by J.-B. Chabot. Brussels: Culture et Civilisation, 1963.

STUDIES

Amouroux-Mourad, Monique. *Le comté d'Edesse, 1098–1150.* Paris: Librairie orientaliste Paul Guethner, 1988.

Beaumont, Andre Alden. "Albert of Aachen and the County of Edessa." In *The Crusades and Other Historical Essays.* Edited by Louis J. Paetow. New York: F. S. Crofts, 1928.

Cahen, Claude. *La Syrie du Nord a l'époque des croisades et la principauté franque d'Antioche.* Paris: Librairie orientaliste Paul Guethner, 1940.

Dédéyan, Gérard. "Le rôle politique et militaire des Arméniens dans les États croisés pendant la première partie du XIIe siècle." In *Die Kreuzfahrerstaaten als multikulturelle Gesellschaft.* Edited by Hans Eberhard Mayer. Munich: R. Oldenbourg Verlag, 1997.

MacEvitt, Christopher. "Christian Authority in the Latin East: Edessa in Crusader History." In *Crusades and Crusading in the Middle Ages.* Edited by Susan Ridyard. Woodbridge, U.K.: Boydell and Brewer, Forthcoming.

CHRISTOPHER HATCH MACEVITT

[See also **DMA:** Baldwin I of Jerusalem; Crusades and Crusader States; Edessa; Matthew of Edessa.]

EDMUND OF ABINGDON, ST. (1175?–1240).

Edmund Rich was born at Abingdon near Oxford perhaps as early as 1170 or more likely a few years afterward, but no later than 1180. His early life was conspicuous for its piety. How many of the details, including the rigorous fasting and the wearing of a hair shirt even as a child, are true and not hagiographical embellishments is uncertain.

The central event in the evolution of Edmund's personal style of devotion occurred during the period of his initial studies at Oxford, when he had a vision of the Christ child, who chided him for not at first recognizing him as such. Moved by this encounter, the hagiographers tell us that the youth from then on nightly inscribed the words "Jesus of Nazareth" on his forehead in remembrance, and he also vowed chastity, symbolized by a kind of spiritual marriage between himself and the Virgin Mary. The hagiography says that the future saint wore a ring as a token of his dedication. It was alleged that he placed another on the finger of one of the Virgin's statues in the church of St. Mary's, Oxford. Edmund also engaged in long periods of personal prayer and slept little. When he did rest, he did so mostly only kneeling or sitting.

Edmund continued his education at Paris and began to teach logic and dialectic, but as a consequence of another vision, if the hagiographers are to be believed, he transferred his zeal to theology, ultimately teaching the subject at Paris and Oxford. In the early 1220s he took office as treasurer of Salisbury Cathedral. A gifted speaker, he preached the Crusade in England under papal license in 1227 and, probably owing to his noticeable vigor in doing so and the fame of his devotions, seemed an ideal candidate to Pope Gregory IX for the see of Canterbury in the wake of a disputed election. On 2 April 1234 he was consecrated archbishop.

As archbishop, Edmund was a zealous defender of the prerogatives of his office, and he also supported baronial demands for reform in government, especially pressuring King Henry III to repudiate his so-called Poitevin favorites in a successful effort to avoid civil war early in his archiepiscopacy. Later he struggled with the king over quasi-jurisdictional and fiscal matters like the exercise of prerogative wardship. Yet, it was hostility to his allegedly authoritarian rule at Canterbury that most disturbed his archiepiscopacy. At one time, Edmund even excommunicated the monks of Christ Church, Canterbury, and their prior for disobedience.

In the late summer or autumn of 1240 Edmund left England for negotiations in Rome on various disputes in which he was involved; it would have been his second trip there during his archiepiscopacy. At some stage he took shelter at a small priory in Soisy, not far from the Cistercian abbey of Pontigny, perhaps after deciding to abandon the journey because of illness and reports of disorder in Italy. He had not been exiled to France, as his apologists, not least the Capetian rulers of that kingdom, later implied; nor was his death at Soisy the equivalent of a martyr's, as they also implied. In any case, despite what must have been ambivalence on the part of the English crown, Edmund's canonization was pronounced orally on 16 December 1246; the formal bull was promulgated on 11 January 1247. His elevation was owed primarily to his rigorous pious devotions, his benefactions (including dowries for poor girls), and the miracles associated with his cult and certainly not to any perceived defense of the church against secular tyrants' encroachments. The French royal family participated in the translation of his relics at Pontigny in 1247, however, emphasizing their earlier welcome of the putative exile. The English king, Henry III, visited Edmund's tomb in 1254 in order to venerate the saint. Edmund's cult continued to flourish at Pontigny well into modern times, even in the face of the French government's anticlericalism in the late nineteenth century.

BIBLIOGRAPHY

Edmund of Abingdon, St. *Speculum religiosorum; and Speculum ecclesie [by] Edmund of Abingdon.* London: Oxford University Press for the Academy, 1973. An edition of Edmund's most popular work, the devotional tract *Speculum ecclesie.*

Lawrence, C. H. *St. Edmund of Abingdon: A Study in Hagiography and History.* Oxford: Clarendon Press, 1960. The best modern biography, with Latin versions of various relevant texts appended.

Paris, Matthew. *The Life of St. Edmund.* Translated and edited by C. H. Lawrence. Oxford: A. Sutton, 1996.

WILLIAM CHESTER JORDAN

[See also **DMA:** Henry III of England.]

ELIAS OF CORTONA (*ca.* 1180–1253), the minister general of the Franciscan order (1232–1239) and one of the earliest companions of St. Francis. Elias was born in Castel Britti, or Brittignano, a village near Assisi. According to the Franciscan chronicler Salimbene, Elias's family name was Bonusbaro or Bombarone. Elias's father was a mattress maker. As a young man, Elias apparently worked for his father and also taught young boys in Assisi. Little is known about the circumstances surrounding his joining Francis, but Elias probably joined the order around 1211. By 1218, he was leading a group of evangelizing friars in Palestine, where they established a Franciscan province. In 1219 he was named the first provincial of the Syrian province, but a year later he accompanied Francis from Syria back to Italy.

When Peter Catani, whom Francis had earlier named as his successor, died on 10 March 1221, Francis appointed Elias as "the father of the other brethren." It is clear from this that Elias had won the confidence and trust of the saint. Although Francis continued to exert influence within the order, all formal administrative responsibilities lay with Elias, who acted as vicar of the order. According to Thomas of Celano in *Vita prima,* a few days before Francis died on 3 October 1226 he reserved a special, personal blessing for Elias. It was Elias who wrote the letter to the order announcing the news of the saint's death and the appearance of the stigmata, which had been kept a secret for two years. The letter, which Elias signed "Brother Elias, a sinner," is the only text from Elias that is extant. Immediately following Francis's death, Elias began raising money for the building of a great basilica at Assisi to enshrine the saint's remains. In the meantime, Francis was temporarily buried at the small church of S. Giorgio, where he had preached his first sermons. At the Chapter General meeting in 1227, contrary to expectations, Giovanni Parenti, provincial of Spain, was elected minister general of the order rather than Elias.

But for the next few years, Elias kept busy raising funds for the basilica in Assisi, designing the building (which was actually three buildings: a church for friars, a separate church for the laity, and a convent to house the friars), commissioning the artwork for the interior, and personally overseeing the construction of the building. By 1230, the lower church of the basilica, which Pope Gregory IX declared to be *caput et mater* (head and mother) of the Franciscan order, was virtually finished. Controversy, however, engulfed the translation of the saint's body to the new shrine. With dozens of bishops and hundreds of friars gathered from all over Europe to witness the translation of the saint, a procession took place but no body was moved. As it turned out, Elias, who from the start had been obsessed with ensuring the safety of the saint's body (even hiring armed guards to watch over it as it lay at the church of S. Giorgio), had arranged for a secret burial a few days before. Those who had traveled far for the translation were disappointed, and Elias's image was hurt by the fiasco even though he may have acted in the best interest of the saint. A number of Elias's remaining supporters then failed in a bold attempt to get him elected minister general. For a short time Elias withdrew from public view to lead a penitential life in a hermitage. By 1232, however, he had sufficiently repaired his image within the order to become minister general in a highly contested election.

For almost seven years, Elias ruled the order, stirring up controversy at almost every turn. In an effort to reduce the power of provincial ministers and increase the minister general's power, Elias created new provinces. He held virtually no general chapters during his seven-year generalship, and he dispatched agents to conduct visitations of the Franciscan convents in the provinces to ensure that the vow of poverty was being observed. Complaints were leveled at these much-hated agents for, among other things, collecting money for Elias's pet project, the Assisi basilica. Those hostile to Elias were primarily from the clerical and academic elements within the order. They were upset that he appointed so many lay brothers to high offices. Opponents of Elias also argued that he violated the Franciscan Rule and set a poor example by living a life of luxury and ambition. In 1239 Haymo of Faversham, who led the opposition against Elias, appealed to Pope Gregory IX to have Elias removed, and after the pope was unsuccessful in convincing the Franciscan to resign voluntarily, Elias was deposed.

Elias's generalship convinced many Franciscans of the need to constrain the power of the minister general's office. More important, though, the inconsistency between Elias's alleged close relationship with St. Francis and his later conduct as minister general sharpened a debate that was only just beginning to emerge about the meaning of poverty as a Franciscan ideal. Following his deposition, Elias retired to Cortona and began supporting the excommunicated emperor Frederick II, even going to Constantinople and Cyprus on a diplomatic mission on his behalf. Pope Gregory IX personally excommunicated Elias for consorting with the excommunicated emperor, but Elias continued to devote much energy to the erection of a church and convent in Cortona dedicated to St. Francis, much as he had done with the basilica in Assisi. Several efforts by the Franciscans to repair relations between Elias and the church failed. Shortly before his death on 22 April 1253, however,

Elias realized that his end was near, and he repented, was absolved, and received Holy Communion, at last reconciled with the church.

Although he had many enemies, particularly the intellectuals and the early disciples of Francis, who felt that Elias betrayed the saint's ideals, it has been shown that many of the Franciscan chronicles portrayed Elias unfairly, particularly in their depiction of the years during St. Francis's lifetime. Later Spirituals, a group of Franciscans who espoused the ideal of absolute poverty, blamed Elias for bringing great tribulation upon the order. Instead of acknowledging the special relationship between St. Francis and Elias, chroniclers regarded Elias as the arch-traitor of the saint. Elias rarely even received credit for the monumental church at Assisi, which he did so much to build.

BIBLIOGRAPHY

Accrocca, Felice. "Un apocrifo la 'Lettera enciclica di frate Elia sul transito di S. Francesco?'" *Collectanea Franciscana* 65:3–4 (1995): 473–509.

Brooke, Rosalind B. *Early Franciscan Government: Elias to Bonaventure.* Cambridge, U.K.: Cambridge University Press, 1959.

Cusato, Michael. "Elias and Clare: An Enigmatic Relationship." In *Clare of Assisi: Investigations.* Edited by Mary Francis Hone. St. Bonaventure, N.Y.: Franciscan Institute Publications, 1993.

Lempp, Edouard. *Frère Élie de Cortone: Étude biographique.* Paris: Librairie Fischbacher, 1901.

Moorman, John. *A History of the Franciscan Order: From Its Origins to the Year 1517.* Chicago: Clarendon Press, 1968.

ADAM JEFFREY DAVIS

[See also **DMA:** Francis of Assisi, St.; Franciscans.]

ELIZABETH OF HUNGARY, ST. (1207–1231).

Elizabeth, the daughter of Andrew II of Hungary, was sent as a four-year-old to the household of the landgrave of Thuringia, to whose eldest son she was betrothed. The first years in her new home, the great castle of the Wartburg, do not seem to have been happy. Her excess of girlish piety, as it was perceived, was off-putting to some of the household. When the man who was supposed to be her future husband died in 1216, the arrangements that had brought her to Thuringia were renegotiated, and she was betrothed to the new heir, Ludwig. Their marriage was celebrated in 1221, when he inherited the landgraviate. All these arrangements owed much to the complex political alliances that characterized the difficult opening years of the thirteenth century in Germany, when rival claimants to the German crown and, subsequently, papal-imperial rivalries disrupted social and economic life.

Elizabeth, only fourteen when she married, probably did not fully recognize the depth and meaning of these political struggles, though their indirect impact on her life had been and would continue to be profound. Ludwig, a young man of twenty-one at his accession, generally indulged his wife's pious gestures, and they appear to have been quite happy. She bore him three children, the third being born shortly after Ludwig died in 1227 while in Italy on his way to crusade. Ludwig's younger brother assumed the regency. At twenty, Elizabeth was a widow with three young children and very vulnerable.

The details of her life in the next several months are not entirely clear. Her children were taken under the protection of kin as she prepared herself to continue with greater vigor certain ascetic practices that her spiritual adviser, a member of the new Franciscan order, had urged on her. The fact that her uncle, the bishop of Bamberg, took an interest in her offered her some protection from other parties who wanted to enlist her and her family in their political schemes, but the bishop himself also wanted to see her remarry to political advantage. She steadfastly refused. It is not unlikely that she had taken a vow, while still married, to remain chaste if she were widowed.

Increasingly she began to distribute her personal fortune as alms to the poor. Although the Franciscan vision of radical poverty was attractive to her, the people nearest to her, in agreement with churchmen in general, did not find absolute mendicant poverty appropriate for women. Elizabeth's confraternal association with the Franciscan order (what would later be termed, joining the Third, or Tertiary, Order) in Easter Week 1228, soon after she was widowed, also attests to her strong admiration for Franciscan values. Nonetheless, she was encouraged to retain her considerable fortune and to use it selectively, as she had been doing. This encouragement came from one special source, a new spiritual adviser, Conrad of Marburg. Conrad was not a Franciscan but an administratively experienced churchman who shared their zeal. Conrad, who had solemnized Elizabeth's association with the Franciscans, was already spoken of with awe because of his relentless inquisition into "heretical depravity" in the Rhineland under a general papal license in 1227.

Under Conrad's influence, Elizabeth persisted in her charitable works, which included founding a hospice for the sick at Marburg in 1228, but what was striking about Conrad's guidance was his insistence on ascetic practices. He himself was an ascetic of renown. Under his tutelage, Elizabeth achieved even greater renown. The severity—moderns may say savagery—of the discipline he imposed on her, including penitential beatings and diminished communication with other women in her circle, was extraordinary by any reckoning. Her reputation both for pious generosity and for extreme asceticism, however, helped initiate popular recognition of her as a holy woman. Undoubtedly her ascetic practices and her ministrations to the diseased inmates of the hospice at Marburg hastened her death, on 17 November 1231, at the age of twenty-four. Miracles proliferated at her tomb. Conrad strenuously labored for her canonization, which took place in 1235.

Two stories—one legendary, the other true—testify to the widespread fascination with and admiration for Elizabeth. One, a fairly common topos, tells of her carrying out acts of charity while still married by bringing bread to the needy. When her husband, who sometimes thought she overdid this sort of thing, came upon her on the way, the bread miraculously turned into roses before he recognized what she was doing (hence her depiction holding roses in the common iconography). Jean de Joinville, the friend and biographer of St. Louis (Louis IX of France), reports the other. He tells how Louis's mother, Blanche of Castile, venerated St. Elizabeth and how, when she met the holy woman's son ("a young German lad of eighteen"), kissed him on the forehead ("as a pure act of devotion"), believing that his pious mother frequently kissed him there herself.

BIBLIOGRAPHY

Joinville, Jean de, and Geoffre de Villehardouin. *Chronicles of the Crusades*. Translated by Margaret R. B. Shaw. Baltimore: Penguin, 1963.

Klaniczay, Gábor. *Holy Rulers and Blessed Princesses: Dynastic Cults in Medieval Central Europe*. Translated by Éva Pálmai. Cambridge, U.K., and New York: Cambridge University Press, 2002.

Obbard, Elizabeth Ruth. *Poverty, My Riches: A Study of St. Elizabeth of Hungary, 1207–1231*. Southampton, U.K.: St. Austin, 1997. A reverential biography, whose interpretations should be interrogated.

WILLIAM CHESTER JORDAN

[See also **DMA:** Franciscans; Wartburgkrieg.]

EPIC GENRE. Aristotle defined the epic in his *Poetics* as a long narrative poem in a single meter that concerns itself with noble characters and is presented in elevated diction and style. He ranked tragedy higher than epic as a genre; however, by the Renaissance most scholars and poets had reversed this hierarchy, considering the epic the most important of poetic genres. Aristotle based his definition on the Homeric poems, the prototypes of the classical epic; these, together with Vergil's *Aeneid,* provided the basis for the epic conventions that came to define the genre in later centuries. Epic conventions are typical motifs used initially by Homer in the *Iliad* and the *Odyssey* and imitated by Vergil in his *Aeneid,* which were in turn imitated by the composers of medieval Latin epics and incorporated into vernacular epics of the late medieval and early modern periods. Such conventions include a statement of the argument of the poem at the outset; the invocation of the Muse; the custom of beginning the narrative *in medias res* ("in the middle of things," usually at an important point in the action); the use of extended, often quite complex "epic" or "Homeric" similes; catalogs of warriors, ships, armies, or other items; a protracted scene describing the arming of the hero; and the hero's descent into the underworld.

PRIMARY AND SECONDARY EPICS

Modern literary critics make a distinction between "primary" (also called "oral" or "folk") and "secondary" ("literary" or "art") epics. Primary epics are poems dating from before the advent of writing in a particular culture; they were composed and performed orally, making use of metrical formulas that provided a poetic vocabulary for the bard, or *scop,* and thus allowed him to create an epic that would adhere to the metrical rules of poetry in the very act of performing the poem. Classical epics considered primary include Homer's *Iliad* and *Odyssey;* medieval epics thought to have been originally composed in this fashion include the Old English *Beowulf* (of disputed date; manuscript *ca.* 1000), the French *Chanson de Roland* (Song of Roland, *ca.* 1100), the Middle High German *Nibelungenlied* (*ca.* 1200), and the Spanish *Cantar de Mío Cid* (*ca.* 1140). The fact that we have received these oral epics in written form, however, means that they have been heavily influenced by scribal, Latinate (and therefore almost certainly Vergilian) culture. Traces of their oral character can be discerned in their written form, but because they have been consciously reshaped by literate authors or scribes, such poems are perhaps better described as "orally derived" rather than truly "oral-formulaic" in their composition. In some cases, as in the *Nibelungenlied,* epics that may have originally been orally composed have not only been revised but also consciously updated to reflect medieval courtly culture.

Secondary epics are literary creations, composed in written form by specific authors, often in imitation of the primary epics, and designed to be read or recited verbatim. Vergil's *Aeneid,* which was composed in imitation of Homer, is an example of a classical secondary epic, while the fourteenth-century Middle English alliterative *Morte Arthure* may be cited as an example of a medieval secondary epic.

Classical and medieval epics are linked by their common use of the figure of the epic hero, who may be defined as a man (and epic heroes are almost invariably male; perhaps the sole exception is Kudrun in the thirteenth-century Middle High German epic of the same name) who is of exceptional physical and social stature, national or even international importance, and historical or legendary significance. His actions require immense courage and sometimes supernatural strength or abilities; in addition, those actions are generally significant not only for the hero himself but also for the entire nation or people whom he represents.

LATIN EPICS

Both Aristotle's *Poetics* and the Homeric epics were largely unknown to the Middle Ages; therefore, medieval ideas of the epic genre were based on classical Latin poetry, including Vergil's *Aeneid,* Statius's *Thebaid,* and Lucan's *Pharsalia.* In addition, the Book of Job from the Old Testament was sometimes regarded by medieval commentators as an epic narrative, in part on the basis of the mistaken idea that it had originally been written in hexameters, the meter of classical epic poetry. This categorization is found initially in Isidore of Seville (seventh century) and is repeated and elaborated on by Bede (eighth century) and Hrabanus Maurus (ninth century). Of the Latin poets, Vergil in particular was admired, studied, and imitated; the manuscripts of his poetry were glossed extensively, and the interpretive tradition developed within those glosses, with their decidedly medieval cast, transformed the *Aeneid* for readers in the Middle Ages into what may arguably be called the most important medieval epic. Christopher Baswell divides the interpretations developed in the Vergilian glosses into three categories: "allegorical" interpretations, which focused primarily but not exclusively on Aeneas's descent into the underworld and which read the poem in terms of moral symbolism and Christian typology, opening the way for later allegorical epics; "romance" interpretations, which generally focused on the story of Dido and Aeneas and opened the way for the epic treatment of romantic themes; and "pedagogical" interpretations, which attempted to understand Vergil in his own world and provided extensive grammatical, historical, geographical, mythological, and religious information, much of which made its way into medieval retellings of the story of Troy.

When medieval Latin writers imitated the epic form, adapting it to their own interests, they were thus influenced not only by the *Aeneid* itself but also by the interpretations found in the Vergilian glosses. Latin epics of the Middle Ages include, in the fourth century, a Vergilian epic narrating the Gospel by the Spanish poet Juvencus and Prudentius's *Psychomachia,* an allegorical account of the war between Virtues and Vices. Fifth-century Christian epics include Dracontius's *De laudibus Dei,* which retells the story of the Fall, and Sedulius's *Carmen pascale,* concerning Christ's Passion. By the tenth century, however, more secular influences on the Latin epic came into play: vernacular heroic poetry provided the inspiration for the German *Waltharius,* and the French *Ecbasis captivi* recalls the beast fable. The story of Troy provided the basis for two epics of the twelfth century, Simon de Chévre d'Or's and Joseph of Exeter's respective epics entitled *Ylias,* while Walter of Châtillon's *Alexandreis* is an epic narration of the story of Alexander the Great. At the same time, satiric poetry took epic form in John of Hauville's *Architrenius* (Archlamenter), Nigel of Canterbury's beast epic *Speculum stultorum* (Mirror of fools), and in *Ysengrimus,* an anonymous beast epic featuring Reynard the Fox.

VERNACULAR EPICS

The primary vernacular epics of the Middle Ages, although sharing certain characteristics with the Latin epics, also differed from them, most notably in their lack of the familiar epic conventions. Because such primary epics were not originally composed in imitation of the Latin epics (despite their inevitable revision by Latin-trained scribes), the lack of these characteristic conventions has resulted in differences among scholars as to whether such vernacular literary works may be classified as epics at all and, if so, which poems merit the term. In fact, some scholars, such as J. B. Hainsworth, assert that virtually none of the vernacular poems can properly be called epic because of their omission of the formal characteristics of the genre. Others, most notably W. P. Ker but also Richard M. Dorson in his introduction to Felix Oinas's *Heroic Epic and Saga,* go to the other extreme, invoking a somewhat vaguely defined "epic spirit" in order to extend the genre to include predominantly prose works such as the Icelandic sagas (recorded primarily in thirteenth- and fourteenth-century manuscripts) and the Irish *Táin bó Cúailgne* (Cattle raid of Cooley; earliest manuscript *ca.* 1100). However, the majority of modern scholars agree that certain primary vernacular

works—including *Beowulf,* the *Nibelungenlied,* the *Cantar de Mio Cid,* and the *Song of Roland*—may be at least loosely defined as epics, and most restrict the classification to narrative poetry.

In addition to the primary epics, secondary epics were composed in most of the European vernaculars during the Middle Ages, including the direct descendants of the classical languages: Greek epic continued in the tenth century with the story of *Digenis Akritis;* medieval Italian epics from the fourteenth century include Dante's *Commedia* and Boccaccio's *Teseida.* Such vernacular secondary epics, composed as they were by literate poets, generally exhibit the same classical—primarily Vergilian—influences as their medieval Latin counterparts. By contrast, the Islamic world produced little epic poetry. The Koranic condemnation of fiction as "lies" ensured that Arabic narrative—written almost exclusively in prose rather than verse—was made up for the most part of heavily didactic, often allegorized stories or informative essays. The Persian tradition, however, includes Abū 'l Qāsim Firdawsī's *Shāhnāma* (Book of kings; tenth century), a narrative poem of epic proportions that was developed in isolation from the Homeric or Vergilian traditions, drawing from pre-Islamic sources (modified to exclude any elements offensive to its Islamic audience); to this can perhaps be added the fourteenth-century Turkish epic *Dede Korkut.*

EPIC AND ROMANCE

Modern scholars generally attempt to differentiate between epic and the genre that succeeded and largely displaced it in medieval narrative poetry: romance. Both genres comprise long narrative poems in a single meter, but they differ in content and in tone. A medieval romance may be defined as a narrative (either in poetry or prose) concerned primarily with the adventures of a knight and often, although not exclusively, dealing with love and courtesy. Unlike the actions of the epic hero, those of the romance hero are important to him as an individual but are not generally related to the fortunes of his society as a whole. In addition, while the epic observes narrative unity, the romance is often episodic and looser in its structure. W. P. Ker states that the distinction between the two genres "corresponds in general history to the difference between the earlier 'heroic' age and the age of chivalry," adding that "whatever Epic may mean, it implies some weight and solidity; Romance means nothing, if it does not convey some notion of mystery and fantasy" (*Epic and Romance,* pp. 3–4). He notes that the two differ primarily in their favorite types of episode and in the "commonplaces of adventure":

No kind of adventure is so common or better told in the earlier heroic [i.e., epic] manner than the defence of a narrow place against odds. . . . The favourite adventure of medieval romance is something different,—a knight riding alone through a forest; another knight; a shock of lances; a fight on foot with swords . . . then, perhaps, recognition—the knights belong to the same household and are engaged in the same quest. . . . In the older kind the parties always have good reasons of their own for fighting; they do not go into it with the same sort of readiness as the wandering champions of romance. (*Epic and Romance,* pp. 5–6)

The distinction between genres is not always as easy for modern scholars to make as Ker implies, however, and such a distinction may not have been made at all by many medieval poets and readers. Although scholars agree that the *Song of Roland* is epic, other chansons de geste—for example, the *Pèlerinage de Charlemagne* (Charlemagne's pilgrimage), the *Chanson de Guillaume, Girart de Roussillon, Renaud de Cambrai,* and *Ami et Amile*—are variously regarded as epic or romance. The same may be said of some of the Middle High German "courtly epics," including Wolfram von Eschenbach's *Parzival,* Hartmann von Aue's *Iwein,* and Gottfried von Strassburg's *Tristan,* as well as certain medieval narratives in English, such as Layamon's *Brut.* The blurring of genres even extends to Latin literature: the eleventh-century *Ruodlieb* is today most often regarded as a romance; however, it is written in the standard epic meter of Latin hexameters, contains numerous allusions to the *Aeneid,* and features several epic conventions, most notably epic similes and a catalog. Its author may well have considered himself to be writing an epic.

Other authors mixed genres deliberately. Geoffrey Chaucer's fourteenth-century *Troilus and Criseyde,* for example, appears to consist of a conscious hybrid of genres: although Chaucer calls the poem a "tragedye," he uses elements of epic, romance, drama, history, and fabliau in combination, along with a generous admixture of lyrical forms. Epic elements include a statement of purpose at the beginning, the invocation of the Muse, and numerous allusions to both Latin epic poetry and Dante's *Commedia.* When toward the end of Book 5 Chaucer's narrator bids the poem to go forth and kiss the footprints of "Virgile . . . , Omer, Lucan, and Stace," he is not only echoing Statius but also implicitly including his poem as one among theirs. Yet the mixture of genres in *Troilus and Criseyde* precludes its being categorized as any one in particular; in Barry Windeatt's words, the work is "distinctively and essentially *sui generis.*"

By the early modern period, the mixture of epic and romance developed in the Middle Ages had evolved into a subgenre of its own, the so-called romance epic, exemplified by Ludovico Ariosto's *Orlando furioso* (Roland insane), Torquato Tasso's *Gerusalemme liberata* (Jerusalem delivered), and Edmund Spenser's *Fairie Queene.* Other forms of vernacular epic continued to flourish, however, reaching their culmination in John Milton's *Paradise Lost.*

BIBLIOGRAPHY

Astell, Ann W. *Job, Boethius, and Epic Truth.* Ithaca, N.Y.: Cornell University Press, 1994.

Bailey, Matthew. "Oral Composition in the Medieval Spanish Epic." PMLA 118 (2003): 254–269.

Baswell, Christopher. *Virgil in Medieval England: Figuring the "Aeneid" from the Twelfth Century to Chaucer.* Cambridge, U.K.: Cambridge University Press, 1995.

Draper, R. P., ed. *The Epic: Developments in Criticism.* Houndmills, U.K.: Macmillan, 1990.

Duggan, Joseph J., ed. *Oral Literature: Seven Essays.* New York: Barnes and Noble, 1975.

Foley, John Miles. *Traditional Oral Epic: The Odyssey, Beowulf, and the Serbo-Croation Return Song.* Berkeley: University of California Press, 1990.

Hainsworth, J. B. *The Idea of Epic.* Berkeley: University of California Press, 1991.

Jackson, Guida M., ed. *Encyclopedia of Traditional Epics.* Santa Barbara, Calif.: ABC-CLIO, 1994.

Ker, W. P. *Epic and Romance: Essays in Medieval Literature.* London: Macmillan, 1931.

Lord, Alfred B. *The Singer of Tales.* Cambridge, Mass.: Harvard University Press, 1960.

Murdoch, Brian. *The Germanic Hero: Politics and Pragmatism in Early Medieval Poetry.* London: Hambledon, 1996.

Oinas, Felix, ed. *Heroic Epic and Saga: An Introduction to the World's Great Folk Epics.* Bloomington: Indiana University Press, 1978.

Tillyard, E. M. W. *The English Epic and Its Background.* 1954. Reprint, New York: Oxford University Press, 1976.

Von Grunebaum, G. E. "The Hero in Medieval Arabic Prose." In *Concepts of the Hero in the Middle Ages and Renaissance.* Edited by Norman T. Burns and Christopher J. Reagan. Albany: State University of New York Press, 1975.

Windeatt, Barry, ed. *Troilus and Criseyde.* Oxford: Clarendon Press, 1992.

JOYCE TALLY LIONARONS

[See also **DMA:** Beast Epic; *Beowulf; Cantar de Mío Cid;* Chansons de Geste; Chaucer, Geoffrey; Dante Alighieri; Latin Literature; Medievalism; *Nibelungenlied; Roland, Song of;* Saga; Troy Story; Vergil in the Middle Ages.]

ESPIONAGE. Various ways of intelligence gathering can be traced to the earliest periods of human history. The objective was to secure information on diverse issues ranging from basic geographical, political, and economic realities to specific data on military situations, diplomatic matters, and domestic problems. Unlike other forms of information gathering, espionage relies on covert, rather than overt means. It operates on the premise that the desired information is not obtainable through an open inquiry or that the inquiry itself must be kept secret. Spying is regarded as criminal by most societies, and spies tend to face stiff penalties.

There is abundant evidence that in the medieval period spying was widespread and considered essential to military, political, and also personal success. However, only Byzantium and some Islamic states boasted institutionalized intelligence organizations. Building on the Roman *frumentarii* tradition, professionals—such as the *agentes in rebus* of early Byzantium or members of the Mamlūk *quassad*—combined dispatch, intelligence, counterintelligence, and secret police functions. In addition to these services, however, both Byzantium and the Muslim powers employed a less formal network of informants and spies, both at home and abroad. The emperor Justinian I (*r.* 527–565) and his empress, Theodora I, stood out in the skillful and extensive use of all forms of espionage, but later Byzantine rulers likewise maintained sophisticated spy networks and elaborate counterespionage measures.

In medieval western Europe spying was seldom a specialized activity carried out by professional experts. Those who traveled frequently—merchants, clerics, artists, soldiers, and diplomats—could find themselves occasionally or regularly entrusted with covert information gathering, even as their primary occupation was quite unrelated to spying. Women, particularly those transient or socially marginalized, such as army followers, performers, or courtesans, were known to supplement their earnings by acting as spies, messengers, or information brokers.

In the later Middle Ages, most embassies, or at least some of their staff members, were assumed to have secret agendas well removed from what was considered morally acceptable for an ambassadorial party. According to Philippe de Commines, writing late in the fifteenth century, diplomats and spies were essentially the same. Espionage was often the true objective of ostensibly diplomatic missions. In 1412, for example, the king of Portugal dispatched a high-profile embassy to the widowed queen of Sicily to negotiate her marriage to his second-born son—but its true goal was to gather extensive intelligence on the northern Moroccan city of Ceuta, which the Portuguese eventually conquered in 1415. The embassy stopped in Ceuta on both legs of the journey and, under the pretext of a layover, spied out the city so well that one of the embassy's leaders, the prior of Crato, was able to create a three-dimensional model of the fortifications and the surrounding landscape.

Spying was highly situational because, as Comynes pointed out, "friendship among princes does not endure forever," and the messenger from one's ally could be regarded as an agent of the enemy the next day. Foreign merchants, Jews, intellectuals, and clerics were particularly vulnerable to charges of spying because they habitually exchanged news through a network of correspondents. Should hostilities erupt, a previously innocent exchange of information could suddenly become an act of espionage. Because of their access to information, these groups were moreover expected to act as spies both by their patrons or home authorities and by those they were potentially spying on. Foreign merchants were assumed to supply their home governments with information. The Republic of Venice codified this expectation by requiring its citizens returning from abroad to submit written reports, *relazioni,* to the Senate.

While military, diplomatic, and commercial espionage are the most frequently considered forms of illicit intelligence gathering, most spying activity took place to promote the political interests of individuals or families, rather than states. Roman aristocratic families were known to have maintained extensive networks of informants planted in the households of their rivals. The practice certainly survived the fall of Rome and is documented not only in Byzantium and the Islamic states but also in the early medieval West.

In the high and late medieval period both narrative and documentary evidence provides an ever-increasing number of examples of informants, agents, and double agents spying on behalf of their masters for money, career advancement, or out of personal loyalties. In 1439, for example, Queen Leonor of Portugal greatly offended her subjects when she ordered, in the middle of the night, the physical removal of the women of her household she suspected of spying for her political rival Dom Pedro, the eldest brother of her late husband. Medieval chronicles abound in such stories of conflicting loyalties and obligations.

Loss of favor and position was one possible punishment for spying. The medieval legal codes and edicts, however, usually call for much more severe penalties, very often death. Death could be meted out either for the act of espionage itself or because spying meant treason and treason was a capital offense. Even those who aided spies could face execution. In reality, the treatment of real and suspected spies was highly uneven. In the course of the Hundred Years War, there are examples of spies being lynched by outraged mobs, executed by the royal authorities, or left to languish in prison without trial; conversely, they were at times pardoned or even employed and promoted by their captors. Skilled or well-positioned spies could represent a valuable commodity, not to be disposed of lightly.

Medieval espionage poses an interesting challenge to the normative morality of both Christianity and chivalric honor, both of which frowned on the deception and lies inherent in spying. Yet both mirrors of princes (books of counsel for nobles) and chivalric manuals refer to espionage matter-of-factly as a necessity of life and politics. As Christine de Pizan put it in *The Book of Deeds of Arms and of Chivalry* (*ca.* 1410): "With respect to spying on one's enemies, . . . it is very profitable to have wise spies who know well how to discover the strategy of the adversaries. For such as these know how by gifts and promises to intervene and by ruse to attract one or several, even from the council of the other side, if possible, so that they can learn the whole plan of action" (p. 47). Need and pragmatism clearly overrode finer considerations of morals and honor.

BIBLIOGRAPHY

PRIMARY WORKS

Christine de Pizan. *The Book of Deeds of Arms and of Chivalry.* Translated by Sumner Willard and edited by C. Cannon Willard. University Park: Pennsylvania State University Press, 1999.

SECONDARY WORKS

Alban, J. R., and C. T. Allmand. "Spies and Spying in the Fourteenth Century." In *War, Literature, and Politics in the Late Middle Ages.* Edited by C. T. Allmand. Liverpool, U.K.: Liverpool University Press, 1976.

Amitai-Preiss, Reuven. "Mamlūk Espionage among Mongols and Franks." *Asian and African Studies* 22 (1988): 173–181.

Arthurson, Ian. "Espionage and Intelligence from the Wars of the Roses to the Reformation." *Nottingham Medieval Studies* 35 (1991): 134–154.

Ballard, Mark, and C. S. L. Davies. "Étienne Fryon: Burgundian Agent, English Royal Secretary, and 'Principal Counsellor' to Perkin Warbeck." *Historical Research* 62, no. 149 (1989): 245–259.

Crook, David. "The Confession of a Spy, 1380." *Historical Research* 62, no. 149 (1989): 346–350.

Dvornik, Francis. *Origins of Intelligence Services: The Ancient Near East, Persia, Greece, Rome, Byzantium, the Arab Muslim Empires, the Mongol Empires, China, Muscovy.* New Brunswick, N.J.: Rutgers University Press, 1974.

Sheldon, Rose Mary, Col. "Toga and Dagger: Espionage in Ancient Rome." *MHQ: A Quarterly Journal for Military History* 12 (autumn 2000): 28–33.

————. *Espionage in the Ancient World: An Annotated Bibliography of Books and Articles in Western Languages.* Foreword by Thomas Durrell-Young. Jefferson, N.C.: McFarland, 2003.

Tai, Emily Sohmer. "Spies." In *Trade, Travel, and Exploration in the Middle Ages: An Encyclopedia.* Edited by J. B. Friedman and K. Mossler Figg. New York and London: Garland, 2000.

IVANA ELBL

[See also **DMA:** Postal and Intelligence Services, Byzantine.]

ETIQUETTE AND MANNERS. Rules for social comportment were codified at courts of the High Middle Ages and continued to influence conduct into the early modern period. Most discussions of social behavior were addressed to specific subgroups, defined by age, profession, rank, or gender. They combined diverse sources, including stories, sayings, and proverbs from Christian and classical traditions as well as contemporary anecdotes and customs. Books written to explain courtly manners are usually called "courtesy books"; manuals with a wider social range are termed "conduct books." However, discussions of etiquette and manners drawing on a recurrent set of sources are found in many genres of medieval literature.

Audiences for instruction in manners could differ from those originally targeted. In the late Middle Ages, for example, as the bourgeoisie adopted lifestyles previously enjoyed by the aristocracy, they purchased courtesy books to guide them in acquiring upper-class manners. Likewise, works addressed to children appear in manuscripts owned by adults, and texts about female conduct appear to have been read by males. The texts themselves may appear narrowly prescriptive, but they were diversely appropriated and creatively used.

CODES OF BEHAVIOR

The importance of manners was first systematically articulated in tenth- and eleventh-century cathedral schools, which offered aspiring clerics a curriculum combining *litterae et mores* (literature and proper conduct). Students trained at these schools then moved to ecclesiastical courts, where "courtier bishops" exhibited the ideals of physical beauty, refined speech, decorum in dress, graceful movement, and charm, as well as the social virtues of moderation, gentleness, affability, and humility. The elegantly disciplined body was seen as the outer correlative of inner nobility—it was "virtue made visible."

In the twelfth century, this model of elegant behavior was adopted as the basis of aristocratic identity in worldly courts. The ideal knight, or chevalier, was no longer just an efficient military man but had to demonstrate chivalric virtues of using arms in defense of the faith and the vulnerable, of loyalty to his vows, and of refined manners. Many aspects of courtly life were ritualized and codified, including dining, receiving guests, interacting with the opposite sex, leisure activities such as tournaments and hunting, and preparing the knight for battle. The anonymous but very popular northern French work *Ordene de chevalerie* (composed before 1250) explains in detail what is symbolized by each action in the ceremony of making a knight, from the initial cleansing bath to the white robe, red cloak, two-edged sword, and gold spurs in which the knight is dressed, culminating in the *colée,* or light blow, with which he is dubbed knight. In every case, the aim of the external behavior was to reveal the internal values that constituted the noble subject. Opposed to the upper classes characterized by courtesy were the lower classes, or *villains,* inevitably identified by their unmannerly behaviors.

In the new courtly context, codes of behavior were elaborated that included women, often drawing on Ovidian literature that playfully discussed how to win or reject a lover. The Latin poem *Facetus moribus et vita* (The art of courtly living) offered advice on proper dress and behavior in various careers as well as the politics of love that influenced innumerable vernacular works of courtesy from the twelfth century onward. Andreas Capellanus also wrote a witty treatise on the rules of love (*De amore,* modeled on the classical poet Ovid's *Ars amatoria*) explaining that the peasant who loves naturally, like the animals, cannot win courtly love, which depends on *probitas morum*—the refinement of manners. The thirteenth-century French allegorical and didactic narrative *Roman de la Rose* fictionalized the courtly pursuit of love with its attendant etiquettes so memorably that many authors of later centuries, including Geoffrey Chaucer, found it an irresistible source.

Noble lovers also became protagonists in a new literary genre, the romance. Besides offering entertainment, romances could be didactic or instructional in their portrayal of courtly etiquette and manners. The twelfth-century northern French author Chrétien de Troyes was the first and certainly the most influential writer of the courtly romance; his works based on the Arthurian legend were translated from French and disseminated throughout Europe. Chrétien used the trope of "virtue made visible" to characterize many of his heroes and heroines, most notably Érec and Énide, whose physical beauty and social graces mirror their spiritual courtesy. His grail knight, Perceval, who has been brought up by his mother in the woods, must be socialized into proper knightly conduct. Perceval's naive and gauche behavior allows Chrétien to comically rehearse the elements of the chivalric code, such as speaking appropriately, protecting women, and supporting the church. In Germany, the thirteenth-century poet Gottfried von Strassburg wrote a version of the Tristan and Isolde legend that also represented his protagonists as the epitome of courtly breeding. Tristan, whose prowess as musician, linguist, rhetorician, and diplomat are more important to the story than his fighting skills, epitomizes the intelligent courtier who is master of social decorum. Through their display of courtly manners, romances could have the ideological role of creating the desire for noble identity, although the most sophisticated narratives (such as those by Chrétien and Gottfried) simultaneously explore and even critique the values implicit in courtly etiquette.

ETIQUETTE MANUALS

The twelfth century also saw the first examples of formal etiquette manuals, with table manners as the favorite subject. These guides to mealtime behavior were probably indebted to earlier monastic rules, but they were greatly amplified to provide instruction to young males being brought up in noble households. One of the first, *Disciplina clericalis,* was written in Latin by a Spanish cleric, Petrus Alfonsi, who was physician to two kings, Alfonso I of Aragon and Henry I of England, in the early twelfth century. His rules for courtly eating may strike us as amusingly basic, but they were endlessly repeated in vernacular courtesy books of the later Middle Ages. Diners are instructed "not to eat the bread before the first course is placed onto the table, otherwise you will be considered as lacking in self-control. Do not put such a large piece into your mouth that the crumbs fall out left and right, otherwise you will be considered a glutton. . . . Drink only when your mouth is empty, otherwise you will be regarded as a drunkard." The Latin *Urbanus magnus* was another twelfth-century work from which many later etiquette books borrowed passages, especially those describing proper and improper table manners. Another type of etiquette book addressed to adults focused on estate management and included seating protocols for meals in noble households.

While clerical writers were responsible for many didactic works that fused social and moral precepts, parents also wrote advice to their children about how to lead a good life. Some texts, like the French king Louis IX's letters to his son and daughter, were produced in royal society, and the paired thirteenth-century German treatises *Die Winsbekin* (Mother to daughter) and *Der Winsbeke* (Father to son) assume a courtly or knightly context. However, the bulk of conduct literature from the fourteenth and fifteenth centuries was probably acquired and read by members of the middle classes. In the thirteenth-century anonymous *Urbain le courtois,* the narrative voice is that of a father instructing his son; many other widely disseminated books of nurture, including *Stans puer ad mensam* (Rules of breeding; a popular text about table manners) and *How the Wise Man Taught His Son,* use the voice of fatherly wisdom for boys. Others, such as the fourteenth-century Italian *Dodici avvertimenti che deve dare la madre alla figliuola quando la manda a marito* (Twelve warnings that a mother must give her daughter when she gets married) and the English *How the Good Wife Taught Her Daughter,* represent female advice for daughters—although the point of view and the anonymous author were probably male. The "children" addressed likewise may include household servants. Widely disseminated during the later Middle Ages, these works brought the aristocratic program of disciplined manners to the affluent urban classes who wished to create new elite identities for themselves.

The advice in such works is gendered, with males urged to adopt behaviors that would advance them socially. They should adopt cleanliness, avoiding black uncut nails, dirty ears, and nose picking; have an honest demeanor, a firm gaze, and controlled speech when conversing with other men; be genial and attentive to successful men at table; and follow all the rules of dining etiquette (wipe grease from your lips so that it does not get into the common cup; do not scratch, break wind, loosen your belt, eat with an open mouth, pick your teeth with the knife, and so on). Manners and moderation should be the guide in all things, for "manners make man."

The "well-taught" boy will also develop the courtly skills of playing musical instruments and dancing and will read to learn eloquence. William Caxton's *Book of Courtesy* recommends the English authors John Gower, Chaucer, Thomas Hoccleve, and John Lydgate. Peter Idley's *Instructions to His Son* likewise encourages education, in this case study of the law, as an important component in the balanced and successful life of a country gentleman. In the fifteenth century as in the eleventh, *litterae et mores* offered cultural capital to males seeking to achieve elite social status and prosperity.

CONDUCT BOOKS FOR WOMEN

Most late-medieval conduct books addressed to women also caution against the dangers of immoderate behavior such as ill-advised speech and extravagant dress, but they especially warn against too much public exposure on the streets, at church, in the market, at taverns, and at other entertainments. Robert of Blois in his *Chastoiement des dames* (late thirteenth century), for example, lists twenty-one points of etiquette for women that guard their body and reputation, including the requirement that a woman let no man except her husband kiss her or touch her breast, that she should accept no gifts from other men for they will damage her honor, and that she should not squabble, shout, or curse, for those actions mark her as lacking in good sense and courtesy.

The most comprehensive and best-known conduct books of the fourteenth century are two French treatises written for women, one for his teenage bride by an elderly husband (known as the *Ménagier de Paris*) and the other for his daughters by their father (*Le livre du Chevalier de la Tour Landry,* or the *Book of the Knight of the Tower*). They bolster their instructions in etiquette and manners with colorful exempla—either contemporary anecdotes or traditional stories—that provide guidance in the right and wrong ways for females to act. As in most medieval behavioral manuals, there is no tension between the social and the spiritual; following his advice will ensure both the salvation of his daughters' souls and the honor of their earthly bodies, the *Book of the Knight of the Tower* says.

Unlike Robert of Blois's behavioral advice, which treats church mainly as an arena for the woman's demonstration of social courtesy, these manuals both begin by explaining the significance of religious ritual for the woman's soul and her reputation. The *Ménagier* includes instruction on private prayers, discussion of proper responses at Mass, and a surprisingly full explanation of the process of repentance, explicating the meaning of the seven sins (in all their branches) and their remedies. This is followed by a memorable section on how the young wife should treat her husband and another on details of running an affluent urban household—including a calendar of gardening, advice on dealing with servants, menu planning, food acquisition, and finally a large recipe collection. Spanning the duties of the bourgeois wife from worship to food preparation, the manual embeds advice on manners within a concept of how each material practice will have the appropriate spiritual and moral as well as social effect.

When consumed by nonaristocrats, the courtly literature on etiquette and manners seems to turn the aristocratic equation on its head. Rather than external behaviors mirroring and manifesting an inner, innate nobility, those behaviors now act to produce and justify a gendered elite identity that the bourgeoisie, in particular, sought during the later Middle Ages. The late medieval texts thus convey a sense of agency and possibility, for the advice enables the user to gain control over his or her life. Ostensibly confined within an estate and gender, in fact, people of the fourteenth and fifteenth centuries were aware of the fluidity of social identities.

Codes of etiquette and manners could be used either to reinforce or to challenge the existing social structures. We see this tension between opposing possibilities in the fifteenth-century French works of Christine de Pizan, the first professional woman writer, who among her wide literary output wrote a conduct book for women, the *Livre du trésor de la cité des dames* (Treasure of the city of ladies; 1405). Christine organizes her discussion of women's behavior by the estate or social category to which each belongs, with two-thirds of her book devoted to princesses and noblewomen. The final third gives advice to women of the upper bourgeoisie, to widows, to chaste women both young and old, to wives of artisans and laborers, to servants, to the truly destitute, and even to prostitutes. The conservative message of her book is that there is an appropriate set of behaviors for women in each class or category and that they should be content with living according to those expectations—most of which subordinate women to male power and maintain the social hierarchy.

Along with its pragmatic reinforcement of the status quo, however, Christine's manual contains an eloquent subtext that empowers women to take control of their own destinies, make constructive decisions, and through their own efforts (both moral and material) increase the honor of "ladies and the whole world of women," as she says in her conclusion. Her book thus conveys one of the powerful messages of late medieval culture—that through careful self-cultivation in etiquette and manners we can achieve the good and virtuous life.

BIBLIOGRAPHY

PRIMARY WORKS

Alfonsi, Petus. *The "Disciplinus clericalis" of Petrus Alfonsi.* Edited by Eberhard Hermes. Translated by Paul R. Quarrie. London: Routledge and Kegan Paul, 1977.

Andreas Capellanus. *The Art of Courtly Love.* Edited by Frederick W. Locke. Translated by John Jay Perry. New York: Frederick Ungar, 1957.

The Babees Book. Edited by Frederick J. Furnivall. 1868. Reprint, New York: Greenwood Press, 1969.

Caxton's Book of Curtesye. Edited by Frederick J. Furnivall. 1868. New York: Kraus Reprint, 1981.

Christine de Pizan. *The Treasure of the City of Ladies: or The Book of the Three Virtues.* Translated by Sarah Lawson. Harmondsworth, U.K.: Penguin, 1985.

Early English Meals and Manners. Edited by Frederick J. Furnivall. 1868. Reprint, Detroit: Spring Press, 1969.

Elliott, Alison Goddard, ed. and trans. "The *Facetus*: Or, the *Art of Courtly Living.*" *Allegorica* 2, no. 2 (1977): 27–57.

The Goodman of Paris (Le Ménagier de Paris). Translated by Eileen Power. London: Routledge, 1928.

The Good Wife Taught Her Daughter, The Good Wyfe Wold a Pylgremage, and The Thewis of Gud Women. Edited by Tauno F. Mustanoja. Helsinki: Annales Accademiae Scientiarum Fennicae, 1948.

Idley, Peter. *Peter Idley's Instructions to His Son.* Edited by Charlotte D'Evelyn. New York: Modern Language Association, 1935.

La Tour-Landry, Geoffroy de. *The Book of the Knight of the Tower.* Translated by William Caxton. Edited by M. Y. Offord. London: Oxford University Press, 1971.

Robert of Blois. *Robert de Blois: Son oeuvre didactique et narrative.* Edited by John Fox. Paris: Nizet, 1950.

SECONDARY WORKS

Ashley, Kathleen, and Robert L. A. Clark, eds. *Medieval Conduct.* Minneapolis: University of Minnesota Press, 2001.

Bumke, Joachim. *Courtly Culture: Literature and Society in the High Middle Ages.* Translated by Thomas Dunlap. Woodstock, N.Y.: Overlook Press, 2000.

Hentsch, Alice A. *De la littérature didactique du moyen âge s'adressant spécialement aux femmes.* 1903. Reprint, Geneva: Slatkine Reprints, 1975.

Jaeger, C. Stephen. *The Envy of Angels: Cathedral Schools and Social Ideals in Medieval Europe, 950–1200.* Philadelphia: University of Pennsylvania Press, 1994.

Krueger, Roberta L. "Courtesy Books." In *Medieval France: An Encyclopedia.* Edited by William W. Kibler, Grover A. Zinn, and Lawrence Earp. New York: Garland, 1995.

Nicholls, Jonathan. *The Matter of Courtesy: Medieval Courtesy Books and the Gawain-Poet.* Woodbridge, U.K.: Brewer, 1985.

Parsons, H. Rosamund. "Anglo-Norman Books of Courtesy and Nurture." *PMLA* 44 (1929): 383–455.

Riddy, Felicity. "Mother Knows Best: Reading Social Change in a Courtesy Text." *Speculum* 71 (1996): 66–86.

Scaglione, Aldo D. *Knights at Court: Courtliness, Chivalry, and Courtesy from Ottonian Germany to the Italian Renaissance.* Berkeley: University of California Press, 1991.

Sponsler, Claire. "Courtesy Books and Good Governance." In *Drama and Resistance: Bodies, Goods, and Theatricality in Late Medieval England.* Minneapolis: University of Minnesota Press, 1997.

KATHLEEN ASHLEY

[See also **DMA:** Capellanus, Andreas; Chivalry; Chrétien de Troyes; Christine de Pizan; Courtesy Books; Courtly Love; *Roman de la Rose;* Schools, Cathedral; **Supp:** Love and Courtship.]

EUGENIUS III, POPE

EUGENIUS III, POPE (*d.* 1153). Perhaps belonging to the aristocratic Pisan family of Paganelli di Montemagno, Eugenius III was the first Cistercian pope and is most remembered for authorizing the Second Crusade. Named Bernardo either at baptism or when he became a disciple of Bernard of Clairvaux, he was first a canon at the cathedral of Pisa and later joined the new order of the Cistercians in 1135. He became the abbot of the newly reformed Cistercian monastery of Tre Fontane, an ancient monastery built on the site of St. Paul's martyrdom outside of Rome. When that monastery was handed over to the Cistercians to be reformed. Bernardo quickly became prominent in Roman ecclesiastical politics, and on 15 February 1145 he was elected pope, following the death of Lucius II only days earlier. A letter from Bernard of Clairvaux expressed his astonishment at his disciple's elevation, implying that he might not be capable of doing the job. He consequently wrote *De consideratione,* a book of advice for his disciple to help him in his new job.

Eugenius immediately fled Rome with the cardinals who elected him to escape the attacks of a newly formed antipapal commune in the city. The pope established his court in Viterbo, and it was here that news reached him of the fall of Edessa in the Levant to the Muslim leader Zangī on 24 December 1144. The conquest of the city shocked Western Christendom. Eugenius's response came on 1 December 1145, when he issued the bull *Quantum praedecessores,* calling for a new crusade to recapture Edessa. With him at the time was a delegation of bishops from the Armenian patriarch, who may have encouraged Eugenius to issue it. The bull, reissued 1 March 1146 in a slightly different form, defined the previously vague notion of the Crusade indulgence, making clear that the indulgence granted remission only of temporal punishment for sins, not divine punishment after death.

The plans for the Crusade gathered momentum in 1146 when Eugenius commissioned his teacher Bernard of Clairvaux to preach the Crusade in northern France. Eugenius himself traveled north to France in 1147 to promote the Crusade, there issuing the bull *Divina dispensatione,* which widened the crusade to incorporate German attacks on the Wends, Slavic tribes east of the River Elbe, a move probably urged by Bernard of Clairvaux. Eugenius also included a call for a crusade against Tortosa and Tarragona in Spain. The crusade did not attack Zangī or attempt to recapture Edessa and was largely considered a failure, a fact the pope himself recognized. Eugenius intervened in another struggle when he supported Theobald, archbishop of Canterbury, after King Stephen of England had banished him and confiscated his lands. Eugenius placed the kingdom under interdict in 1148, and the king and archbishop were subsequently reconciled.

Eugenius spent little time in Rome. He returned to Rome briefly in 1145 but retired to Trastevere, then outside the city, forced out by the anticlerical preaching of Arnold of Brescia. He returned again in 1149, protected by the armies of Roger II of Sicily, but failed to assert his authority and again retreated. In 1153, he returned a third time, this time with Frederick Barbarossa of Germany, but died at Tivoli on 8 July that same year.

BIBLIOGRAPHY

Constable, Giles. "The Second Crusade as Seen by Contemporaries." *Traditio* 9 (1953): 213–279.

Horn, Michael. *Studien zur Geschichte Papst Eugens III (1145–1153).* Frankfurt am Main: Peter Lang, 1992.

John of Salisbury. *Historia pontificalis.* Edited and translated by Marjorie Chibnall. London: Nelson, 1956.

CHRISTOPHER HATCH MACEVITT

[See also **DMA:** Bernard of Clairvaux, St.; Cistercian Order; Crusades and Crusader States: To 1192; Edessa; Wends.]

EUGENIUS IV, POPE (*ca.* 1383–1447). Gabriel Condulmaro was born to a mercantile family of Venice around 1383. He became a canon in Verona while still a teenager under the patronage of his uncle, Angelo Correr. When he became Pope Gregory XII, Correr made Gabriel bishop of Siena and then a cardinal in 1408. Under Pope Martin V, Gabriel became the legate for Ancona in 1419 and for Bologna in 1423. He was removed from these duties in 1424 for allying with the Florentines against Milan, contrary to Martin's instructions to remain neutral.

Gabriel was elected pope on 3 March 1431. He immediately faced a revolt by the Colonna family and was forced to flee Rome in 1434. Papal troops destroyed the town of Palestrina, stronghold of the Colonna, in 1436, and Eugenius reestablished a measure of authority in the Papal States. A greater threat to papal authority was the Council of Basel (1431–1437), a continuation of the Council of Constance (1414–1418), which had ended the Western Schism by taking upon itself authority over the church. From Florence and Bologna, Eugenius negotiated with the council over how to rule the church. He hoped to summon a council in Bologna to discuss union with the Byzantine church (Greek Orthodoxy), but the council refused to be dissolved and to reconvene at the pope's pleasure. Both the council and the pope sent envoys to the Byzantines, but the latter discounted the council's claims of authority.

Eugenius sought support from secular princes to dissolve the Council of Basel, and in September 1438 he transferred the council to Ferrara, a site more congenial to the Byzantines. The Council of Basel in response suspended Eugenius from office, taking supreme authority on itself, but the rival council of Ferrara proceeded without them. Eugenius had to pay the maintenance costs of the Greek delegation, numbering approximately seven hundred men, as well as for their transportation to Italy. As a result of this, as well as his uneasy authority in the Papal States and the financial actions of the council of Basel, the pope found himself broke. In January 1439 the council was transferred to Florence, partly due to promises of financial support from the city. On 6 July 1439 union was finally achieved between the Latin and Greek churches after more than a year of discussion, and Eugenius achieved his greatest triumph. This was followed by a union with a branch of the Armenian church on 22 November 1439, with the Copts on 4 February 1439, with a branch of the Syrian church on 30 August 1444, and with the Chaldeans and Maronites on 7 August 1445. The Crusade that was to be the Byzantine reward for the union finally set out in 1444 but was disastrously defeated by the Turks at Varna on 10 November. The remaining doctors and bishops at Basel deposed Eugenius and on 5 November 1439 elected Amadeo VIII of Savoy pope, who took the name Felix V. The council was still in existence when Eugenius died on 23 February 1447 in Rome, but it had lost most of its support. While Eugenius successfully preserved papal authority and temporarily restored unity to the Christian world, he did so by sacrificing the goals of reform for which the councils of Constance and Basel stood.

BIBLIOGRAPHY

Gill, Joseph. *Eugenius IV, Pope of Christian Union*. Westminster, Md.: Newman Press, 1961.

Stieber, Joachim W. *Pope Eugenius IV, the Council of Basel, and the Secular and Ecclesiastical Authorities in the Empire: The Conflict over Supreme Authority and Power in the Church*. Leiden: Brill, 1978.

CHRISTOPHER HATCH MACEVITT

[See also **DMA**: Councils, Western (1311–1449); Ferrara-Florence, Council of; **Supp**: Colonna Family.]

EUNUCHS played important and similar roles in political, court, and social life in both the Byzantine and Is-

lamic Empires. The eunuch institution was known in the Roman Empire in late antiquity and flourished later under Byzantium. Its importance began to decline in the late eleventh century with the advent of the Komnenian dynasty. In the lands that came to be part of the Islamic world, the eunuch institution was already in existence at the time of the Arab conquests and was well established by Abbasid times (750–1258). Eunuchs seem to have reached the apogee of their power and influence from the Fatimid caliphate in Egypt (969–1171) onward, and their presence as a significant group in the Islamic world lasted until the end of the Ottoman Empire.

Eunuchs were created through either castration alone (removal of the testicles through compression or excision) or both castration and emasculation (amputation of the penis). Emasculated eunuchs were rare—due no doubt to the high mortality rate—and very expensive. Owning them, therefore, was a sign of high status and significant wealth. The most coveted eunuchs were those who had been castrated before puberty and therefore showed none of the secondary sexual characteristics of postpubescent males. In addition, eunuchs castrated after puberty were thought popularly to be sexually obsessed.

In the Islamic tradition, the *ḥadīth* ("report" of what the prophet Muḥammad said or did) literature is largely silent on the issue of eunuchs, although one *ḥadīth* is reported in which the prophet Muḥammad forbade a companion to castrate himself in order to live a celibate life. No text, however, forbids owning eunuchs. Jurists condemned castration, but they made little comment about it in the long run, since most castrations took place outside the lands of Islam. Even the chief architect of Islamic jurisprudence, Muḥammad ibn Idrīs al-Shāfiʿī (*ca.* 767–820), owned eunuchs. The tension between revulsion at and condemnation of castration and the reality of eunuchs as important social and political actors found expression in the Islamic world in the terminology used to designate eunuchs. The term *khāṣī* ("castrated man") was much less common in usage than a number of euphemisms, including *khādim* and *ṭawāshī*, both meaning "servant." In Byzantium, the term *eunouchos* connoted a range of meanings that went well beyond "castrated male," and its meaning changed over time. Until the ninth century, "eunuch" referred both to men who were incapable of procreating and those who had voluntarily withdrawn from the world and reproduction. From the tenth century on, the term *ectomios* ("cut" or "castrated") became common, probably referring to the surgical removal of the testicles in childhood.

Castration was forbidden in Byzantium as it was within the Islamic Empire. There is abundant evidence, however, that castration did take place inside the borders of both empires. Indeed, Muslims considered the Byzantines to have invented the practice, and so close was the association of Byzantium with castration in the minds of medieval Muslims that eunuchs in the Islamic world played a crucial role in guarding the frontier between Islam and Byzantium, ostensibly because of their antagonism toward the location of their mutilation.

Byzantine eunuchs were largely slaves and non-Romans; many were imported from the Caucasus, the lands of Islam, and the Slavic countries. It was not unknown, however, for a Roman to be castrated for religious reasons, and some eunuchs were even members of prominent Byzantine families. In the Islamic world, eunuchs were invariably of slave origin, though like other high-status slaves, they were likely to be manumitted at some point in their lives. Eunuchs serving in harems were fully emasculated, reflecting a persistent anxiety that merely castrated eunuchs might still be capable of sexual intercourse, even if they were sterile. Eunuchs castrated before puberty were assumed to have no sexual desires and were therefore considered to be ideal guardians for women and young boys. They were also entrusted with the education of the ruling elite, especially under the Mamluk sultanate (1250–1517) and particularly with the education of mamlūk youths in the barracks. In this context, they were ordinarily referred to as *agha* or *ustādh*.

In both Byzantine and Islamic cultures, eunuchs protected the highly charged space around emperors, caliphs, and sultans. Eunuchs were closely associated with the rulers (be they caliph or sultan), and throughout the Islamic Middle Ages they typically served as rulers' bodyguards. They also mediated between the living and the dead. Eunuchs played a very important role as guardians of the tombs of prophets and saints and, in particular, the tomb of the prophet Muḥammad in Medina. Reflecting the role they played in the household of their master, they also served as guards of household tombs, with the provision that the initial group of eunuch guards would be composed of the tomb founder's freedmen and that these guardians would subsequently be buried there. Eunuchs, particularly those who served in the Citadel (the seat of government in Cairo from the twelfth century onward) and in Medina, themselves owned eunuchs and established endowments to support their own eunuch freedmen. Eunuchs had networks of their own and, in the Mamluk period, often contributed to a fund intended to support "unemployed" eunuchs, that is, those who were exiled from Cairo.

Eunuchs served in a similarly wide range of capacities in Byzantium, where they were closely linked to the emperors, guarded the women of the court, and served in various capacities in the domestic realm. By the later Byzantine period, aristocratic women and members of the imperial family were increasingly willing to take part in political affairs. As a consequence, eunuchs decreased in political importance and served in low-ranking positions. Outside of the imperial court, they also cared for the sick and the dead. They served as monks, priests, bishops, and church officials in the religious hierarchy, where hagiographical literature presents a generally positive view of eunuchs as celibates, in sharp contrast to the secular literary tradition, which was ordinarily hostile, characterizing eunuchs as harsh, unpleasant, and deceitful. In both Byzantium and Islam, eunuchs' special status as a "third sex" appears to have allowed them to move across boundaries that otherwise were not crossed, and in both empires they played important roles as cultural, political, and social mediators.

BIBLIOGRAPHY

Ayalon, David. *Outsiders in the Lands of Islam: Mamluks, Mongols, and Eunuchs.* London: Variorum Reprints, 1988.

———. *Islam and the Abode of War: Military Slaves and Islamic Adversaries.* Aldershot, U.K., and Brookfield, Vt.: Variorum, 1994. Along with the preceding volume, a collection of Ayalon's articles.

———. *Eunuchs, Caliphs and Sultans: A Study in Power Relationships.* Jerusalem: Magnes Press, The Hebrew University, 1999. See especially Appendix A, which lays out comprehensively Ayalon's argument for the synonymy of the terms *khāṣī* and *khādim*. He argues directly with many scholars on this important point, including the author of the authoritative article in the *Encyclopaedia of Islam* (new edition). Extensive bibliography.

Hopkins, Keith. *Conquerors and Slaves.* Cambridge and New York: Cambridge University Press, 1977. See especially chapter 4, pages 172 to 196, on eunuchs in the Roman Empire.

Kazhdan, Alexander P. "Eunuchs." In *Oxford Dictionary of Byzantium.* Edited by Alexander P. Kazhdan. New York: Oxford University Press, 1991.

Marmon, Shaun. *Eunuchs and Sacred Boundaries in Islamic Society.* New York: Oxford University Press, 1995.

Pellat, Charles. "Khāṣī: In the Central Islamic Lands." In *Encyclopaedia of Islam.* Edited by H. A. R. Gibb et al. New ed. Leiden: Brill, 1960–.

Ringrose, Kathryn M. "Living in the Shadows: Eunuchs and Gender in Byzantium." In *Third Sex, Third Gender: Beyond Sexual Dimorphism in Culture and History.* Edited by Gilbert Herdt. New York: Zone Books, 1994. Includes a discussion of the history of the term "eunuch" in late antique and Byzantine sources.

———. "Eunuchs as Cultural Mediators." *Byzantinische Forschungen* XXIII (1996): 75–93.

Tougher, Shaun F. "Byzantine Eunuchs: An Overview, with Special Reference to Their Creation and Origin." In *Women, Men, and Eu-*

nuchs: Gender in Byzantium. Edited by Liz James. London and New York: Routledge, 1997.

———, ed. *Eunuchs in Antiquity and Beyond.* London: Classical Press of Wales and Duckworth, 2002.

PAULA SANDERS

[See also **DMA:** Abbasids; Byzantine Empire; Fatimids; Mamluk Dynasty; Shāfiʿī, Al-; Slavery, Islamic World; **Supp:** Gender, Theories of; Sexuality.]

EUSKARA, a language spoken in the Basque country *(Euskal Herria),* which during the Middle Ages included the provinces of Biscay, Guipúzcoa, Álava, and Navarre in modern Spain and Labourd, Low Navarre, and Soule in modern France. The ancient geographical extent of Euskara was probably larger. Julius Caesar and Strabo commented on the peculiarity of Aquitanians, who were distinguished in part by their language. This alone does not make Euskara speakers out of the ancient Aquitanians, but some Roman inscriptions include personal names whose elements closely resemble Euskaran words, for example, *andere, neseato,* and *gison,* approximating Basque words for "woman," "girl," and "man," respectively. Place names from the same general region provide a similar sort of evidence, which, taken together, makes the extinct language of the Aquitanians the only plausible relative of Euskara currently known and the likely source for the etymology of the Latin term *vasco* (pl., *vascones),* modern "Basque." By contrast, a once very popular notion related Euskara to the vanished language of the Picts, based on what were believed to be Pictish inscriptions. These were the basis for speculations regarding a common linguistic, cultural, and ethnic heritage, as well as some odd theories about the mysterious druids. The discovery that the inscriptions actually belong to a language family no more or less obscure than Gaelic virtually extinguished this line of inquiry among scholars.

Although no comparisons can be made between Euskara and vanished languages like Pictish, other research has long established beyond doubt that Euskara is not Indo-European. Very few non-Indo-European languages are extant in Europe. Among them, Estonian, Finnish, and Hungarian are interrelated, and their arrival in Europe is historically documented. Euskara shows some similarities to these languages, such as agglutination (elements added to a word stem rather than placed in apposition). These, however, are merely superficial. Moreover, by the time the Aquitanian inscriptions were carved, Euskara was already an old language. Its antiquity is demonstrated in part by its conservatism—in terms of syntax, grammar, and morphology, present-day Basque has changed little, compared with other languages, from its earliest significant literary record in the sixteenth century.

Furthermore, because linguists believe that languages only evolve socially, there must once have been other languages closely related to Euskara, but there are no traces save those few already mentioned. Besides possible northern relatives among Aquitanian and Pictish, there have been inquiries into Euskara's southern relations. By the sixteenth century, theories circulated that the entire Iberian Peninsula once spoke Euskara, and the restriction of the language to the Bay of Biscay and the western Pyrenees was due to the successive incursions of the Carthaginians and the Romans. Such "Vasco-Iberist" arguments were deeply grounded in political agendas and had little or nothing to do with either history or linguistics; indeed, there were people willing to make almost identical claims on behalf of Castilian. The place-name evidence brought to bear on the matter is quite inconclusive on its own, and yet, nevertheless, the argument for a prehistoric supremacy of Euskara throughout the Iberian Peninsula had adherents well into the twentieth century. The most expansive late medieval theory included far more than Iberia in the sweep of Euskara. This endeavor correlated local place names with biblical place names in Armenia, and it explained the relationship by attributing Iberia's settlement to Tubal, son of Japheth, son of Noah. According to such biblical arguments, the pedigree of Euskara could be traced directly back to the tower of Babel.

Some of the scholars who supported such theories themselves spoke Euskara, but until the mid-sixteenth century they published exclusively in Spanish. The first to write about Euskara in Euskara was Bernard (or Bernat) Etxepare (known in French as Dechepare), from the region of Low Navarre. His *Linguae vasconum primitiae* was completed in 1545 and also became the first book printed in Euskara. The other monumental literary project of the sixteenth century was again by a French Basque, a Protestant minister from Labourd named Joannes de Leizarraga (or Lissarague), who published an unabridged translation of the New Testament into Euskara in 1571. Other, earlier evidence of Euskara on the Iberian Peninsula is slim and often indirect. What are believed to be Euskaran words appear in two places among the tenth-century *Glosas Emilianenses,* from a manuscript famous for also containing the earliest Spanish writing. Just as vernacular elements might appear in personal names in Roman inscriptions, so vernacular terms for places and natural landscape features often appear in otherwise Latin-language documents of the Middle Ages. For example, the *Reja de San Millán* from 1025 includes a list of Basque towns and villages. More compelling but also more difficult to confirm is a 1055 charter recording a donation by a lord and his wife to the monastery of Ollazabal, in the province of Guipúzcoa. Written in Latin, it registered some personal names and boundary descriptions in what seems to have been Euskara, although later copyists who did not know Euskara garbled the unfamiliar words.

In the thirteenth century, Ferdinand III allowed inhabitants of the Riojan valley to speak Euskara in the Castilian court. A century later, around 1349, it was illegal to speak Euskara, Hebrew, or Arabic in some marketplaces. Euskara vocabulary lists appear in travel literature throughout the medieval period. Thus Aymeri Picaud in 1140 included the Euskara for "flesh," "house," "wheat," "bread," "king," "lady," and other useful words in his *Codex Calixtinus,* a guide to Santiago de Compostela, the most popular western pilgrimage site after Rome. Other writers such as Lucio Marineo Siculo, an early strong defender of the Vasco-Iberist theory, and Rabelais created word lists in the sixteenth century. The most curious glossary, however, is from a seventeenth-century Icelandic manuscript that testifies, in some scholars' view, to a pidgin based mainly on Euskara that was spoken by fishermen as far from Biscay as Newfoundland.

BIBLIOGRAPHY

Bakker, Peter, et al. *Basque Pidgins in Iceland and Canada.* San Sebastián, Spain: Disputación Foral de Gipuzkoa, 1991.

Caro Baroja, Julio. *Sobre la lengua vasca y el vasco-iberismo.* 2d ed. San Sebastián, Spain: Editorial Txertoa, 1979.

Collins, Roger. *The Basques.* 2d ed. Oxford and Cambridge, Mass.: Blackwell, 1990.

Echenique Elizondo, María Teresa. *Historia lingüística vasco-románica.* Rev. ed. Madrid: Paraninfo, 1987.

Hualde, José Ignacio, Joseba A. Lakarra, and R. L. Trask, eds. *Towards a History of the Basque Language.* Amsterdam Studies in the Theory and History of Linguistic Science, ser. 4. Current Issues in Linguistic Theory, vol. 131. Amsterdam and Philadelphia: J. Benjamins Pub. Co., 1995.

Iragaray, A. *Una geografía diacrónica del euskara en Navarra.* Pamplona, Spain: Ediciones y Libros, 1974.

Michelena, Luis. *Sobre historia de la lengua vasca.* Edited by Joseba Adoni Lakarra. 2 vols. San Sebastián, Spain: Seminario de Filología Vasca "Julio de Urquijo," 1988.

Michelena, Luis, and Ibon Sarasola. *Textos arcaicos vascos; Contribución al estudio y edición de textos antiguos vascos.* San Sebastián, Spain: Disputación Foral de Guipúzcoa/Universidad del País Vasco, 1990. Reprint of two works (Michelena's *Textos* and Sarasola's *Contribución*) in one volume.

Tovar, Antonio. *Mitología e ideología sobre la lengua vasca: Historia de los estudios sobre ella.* Madrid: Alianza, 1980.

Trask, R. L. *The History of Basque.* London and New York: Routledge, 1997.

Zubiaur Bilbao, J. R. *Las ideas lingüísticas vascas en el s. XVI: Zaldiba, Garibay, Poza.* San Sebastián, Spain : Cuadernos Universitarios, 1990.

KEVIN UHALDE

[See also **DMA**: Basques.]

EXETER BOOK. The first description of the Exeter Book is found in a list of books and treasures drawn up at Exeter Cathedral, where this codex is said to be "a large English book with everything written out in the manner of poetry." The Exeter Book is indeed a large manuscript, presently containing 131 folios measuring about 12.5 inches by 8.6 inches, written in a single monumental script that has been dated to the mid-tenth century. The Exeter Book is the repository of a collection of Old English poetry that is remarkable both for the number of poems it contains and for the variety of literary genres these poems comprise. The manuscript has remained at Exeter in the Cathedral library since at least 1072, where it is cataloged as MS. 3501. Its place of origin remains a matter of discussion among scholars. Patrick W. Conner offers evidence that the manuscript was written in the monastic institution located at Exeter since the seventh century, but Richard Gameson argues for its origin at Christ Church, Canterbury, and Robert Butler refines the evidence for a Glastonbury attribution for the origin of the book.

In addition to a number of shorter poems mostly known only to specialists, the manuscript also contains a number of the best-known and most remarkable examples of Old English, preconquest poetry. While none of the poems in the manuscript was originally given a title, the conventional titles established in Krapp and Dobbie's 1936 edition of the Exeter Book remain in general use. The first poem in the manuscript is *Christ,* different portions of which include the *Advent Lyrics,* Cynewulf's *Christ II,* and an elaborate poem on the Christian Apocalypse and Judgment Day. *Guthlac* follows, a composite poem in two parts usually labeled "Guthlac A" and "Guthlac B," the composition of the former having been dated to the period of the tenth-century Benedictine reformation, and the latter possibly having been composed by Cynewulf about the same time. *The Phoenix* offers a retelling in Old English of the life cycle of the phoenix, the marvelous bird that regenerates itself through immolation and rebirth from its own ashes, and includes an

The Exeter Book. *Folio 76r, containing the end of Cynewulf's Juliana; his runic signature can be seen on line 5 (C, Y & N), line 6 (E, W & U), and line 7 (L, F).*

allegorical application following the description of the bird's life. The Exeter Book also contains a sequence of three other bestiary poems, *The Panther, The Whale,* and *The Partridge,* with but eight words intact in the last of these, the final leaf of the gathering having been lost. *Juliana* is a poetic retelling of the martyrdom of St. Juliana and, like *Christ II,* contains Cynewulf's runic signature. All of the so-called Anglo-Saxon elegies are found in this manuscript, including *The Wanderer, The Seafarer, The Ruin, The Wife's Lament,* and *The Husband's Message,* as well as poems that express elegiac sentiments, such as *The Riming Poem, Deor,* and *Wulf and Eadwacer. Widsith,* a poem consisting largely of catalogs of early rulers and peoples ostensibly visited by Widsith, a *gléoman,* or court poet, is found here, too. The Exeter Book is furthermore the repository of a collection of nearly one hundred riddles on profane as well as sacred subjects, composed, like everything else in the manuscript, in traditional Old English alliterative lines.

The overarching critical issue for the Exeter Book concerns the nature of the collection itself and whether individual poems should be read in the context of the collection or some part of it, as a sonnet is read within the context of the sequence in which it is found, or whether the poems should be taken as independent of each other, like works in an anthology. Kenneth Sisam first attempted to see a pattern in the collection of entries. Patrick W. Conner (1993) has contributed to this discussion in his reconstruction of the processes that led to the compilation of the Exeter Book based on material evidence of the manuscript. Conner marshals physical support for the idea that the codex was comprised of three sections, or "booklets," which are more or less organized internally but not in relation to each other. The first booklet contains the two long, compound poems *Christ* and *Guthlac.* The second booklet contains an elaborate sequence of shorter poems, possibly with affinities to late Carolingian Latin poetry. The third booklet is occupied almost entirely with two collections of riddles, interspersed with shorter poems, including *Deor, Wulf and Eadwacer,* and *The Wife's Lament,* all of which appear to have been annexed to earlier copies of the riddles collections. The relationships of the texts of the third booklet have been explored by Mercedes Salvador. Bernard J. Muir, whose edition of the Exeter Book was published in 2003, describes it as a single, unstructured anthology.

John Josias Conybeare first drew general attention to the Exeter Book in a series of short articles with extracts from some of the poems, which he published in the journal *Archaeologia* in 1814. These and other materials concerning Old English poetry generally were published in *Illustrations of Anglo-Saxon Poesie* in 1826, a work planned by Conybeare but published posthumously by his brother. Conybeare's work occasioned sufficient interest that, in 1831, the British Museum commissioned Robert Chambers to make a careful transcription of the codex, preserving even the character of the script insofar as was possible. The first edition of the codex was accomplished in 1842 by Benjamin Thorpe. In 1933, a full collotype facsimile was published of the manuscript, *The Exeter Book of Old English Poetry,* edited by R. W. Chambers; the work of distinguished scholars of the time prefaced the facsimile, and these began the process of critically examining it. Two important editions depended upon this facsimile. William S. Mackie edited *The Exeter Book* from it in 1934, and George Phillip Krapp and Elliot Van Kirk Dobbie edited it in 1936. The latter is currently the edition most often consulted and cited by scholars. John Pope published a series of articles between 1969 and 1981 that called into question the collation of the manuscript established by R. W. Chambers in the 1933 facsimile and established a new collation for the manuscript. Patrick W. Conner (1993) and Bernard J. Muir refined this collation slightly in their respective works. In 2003, Bernard Muir published an electronic facsimile of the manuscript with an accompanying edition and a full apparatus. This new development in the virtual representation of the manuscript will undoubtedly encourage further scholarship on the codex and its contents.

BIBLIOGRAPHY

Butler, Robert M. "Glastonbury and the Early History of the Exeter Book." In *Old English Literature in Its Manuscript Context.* Edited by Joyce Tally Lionarons. Morgantown: West Virginia University Press, 2004.

Chambers, R. W., Max Förster, and Robin Flower, eds. *The Exeter Book of Old English Poetry.* London: Percy Lund, Humphries for the Dean and Chapter of Exeter Cathedral, 1933.

Conner, Patrick W. *Anglo-Saxon Exeter: A Tenth-Century Cultural History.* Woodbridge, U.K.: Boydell Press, 1993.

———. "Exeter's Relics, Exeter's Books." In *Essays on Anglo-Saxon and Related Themes in Memory of Dr. Lynne Grundy.* Edited by David Hook. London: King's College Medieval Studies, 2000.

Gameson, Richard. "The Origin of the Exeter Book of Old English Poetry." *Anglo-Saxon England* 25 (1996): 135–185.

Klinck, Anne L. *The Old English Elegies: A Critical Edition and Genre Study.* Montreal: McGill-Queen's University Press, 1992.

Krapp, George Philip, and Elliott Van Kirk Dobbie, eds. *The Exeter Book.* New York: Columbia University Press, 1936.

Muir, Bernard J., ed. *The Electronic Exeter Anthology of Old English Poetry.* Exeter, U.K.: University of Exeter Press, 2003.

Old English Newsletter (1968–). A survey of each year's scholarship on the poems of the Exeter Book is presented in "The Year's Work in Old English Studies," published in the winter issue of the *Newsletter.*

Pope, John C. "Palaeography and Poetry: Some Solved and Unsolved Problems of the Exeter Book." In *Medieval Scribes, Manuscripts, and Libraries.* Edited by M. B. Parkes and A. G. Watson. London: Scholar Press, 1978.

Salvador, Mercedes. "The Key to the Body: Unlocking Riddles 42–46." In *Naked before God: Uncovering the Body in Anglo-Saxon England.* Edited by Benjamin C. Wither. Morgantown: West Virginia University Press, 2003.

Sisam, Kenneth. *Studies in the History of Old English Literature.* Oxford: Clarendon Press, 1953.

Williamson, Craig, ed. *The Old English Riddles of the Exeter Book.* Chapel Hill: University of North Carolina Press, 1977.

PATRICK W. CONNER

[See also **DMA:** Anglo-Saxon Literature; England, Anglo-Saxon; Old English Language; Riddles.]

EZZELINO DA ROMANO, Lord of Parma

(1194–1259). One of the most powerful of the *signori,* or city tyrants, of northern Italy in the thirteenth century, Ezzelino was born on 25 April 1194 in the March of Treviso. The estates of the da Romano family, whose paternal ancestor had settled in the area in the eleventh century, were centered around Bassano. Ezzelino inherited his family's rivalry with the d'Este family of Verona and in 1228 allied with enemies of the d'Este and drove them out of Verona. He quickly expanded his authority throughout the area, although Azzo d'Este VII continued to be a threat throughout most of Ezzelino's life. Once Ezzelino joined the imperial camp, it was not long before Azzo joined the side of the papacy and the Italian communes. Frederick II tried to heal the feud by arranging a marriage between Ezzelino's brother Alberich's daughter and Azzo's son Rinaldo, but this only made Alberich more likely to switch sides.

In 1236 Ezzelino joined the emperor Frederick II in his campaign to force the cities of the Lombard League to acknowledge his authority. With the emperor's help he seized Vicenza that same year and Padua the following, and these three cities largely remained under his control until his death. Unlike other *signori,* Ezzelino held no titles to validate his power, either from the emperor or from the cities he ruled. He fought against the Lombard League with Frederick II at the battle of Cortenuova on 27 November 1237 and that same year married Frederick's illegitimate daughter Selvaggia. Ezzelino was essential to Frederick's ambitions in northern Italy and later to those of his naturalized son Manfred of Sicily. As a result of Ezzelino's Hohenstaufen alliance, the papacy saw him as a threat. He was excommunicated in 1254, and in 1256 Alexander III proclaimed a crusade against him. His brother Alberich was added to the crusade in 1258. The crusade against Ezzelino received support from both the people and government of Venice, where Filippo Fontana, archbishop of Ravenna, preached the crusade to great effect. Filippo was also the military leader of the crusade and captured Padua with Venetian help in 1256. After this victory, however, the crusade lost its momentum; Ezzelino captured the papal legate, Philip Fontana, as well as the city of Brescia in 1258. In September of 1259, after attempting to seize Milan, he himself was captured, not by crusaders but by fellow *signore* Uberto da Pallavicino. He died two months later, on 7 October, of injuries sustained during his capture. A priest attended his deathbed, and he died within the church.

The quantity of crusade propaganda produced against Ezzelino makes it difficult to analyze his career. Many historians accept the multiple accusations of massacres and tortures imputed to him and hold him up as the very model of tyranny. Certainly, Ezzelino was merciless toward his political rivals. Despite the accusations of violence, some evidence suggests that Ezzelino preserved local traditional governance and was even popular among urban populations. The accusations of heresy are more difficult to fathom. Ezzelino certainly employed an astrologer and may have even plundered churches, but this was not unusual. If he did harbor heretics, as the papacy suggested, then perhaps he had strayed over the fine line of what was acceptable.

BIBLIOGRAPHY

PRIMARY WORKS

Maurisio, Gerardo. *Cronica dominorum Ecelini et Alberici fratrum de Romano.* Edited by Giovanni Soranzo. *Rerum italicarum scriptores* (2). Vol. 8, pt. 4. Città di Castello, Italy: Tipo della casa editrice S. Lapi, 1914.

SECONDARY WORKS

Cracco, Giorgio, ed. *Nuovi studi ezzeliniani.* 2 vols. Rome: Istituto storico italiano il Medio Evo, 1992.

Housley, Norman. *The Italian Crusades: The Papal-Angevin Alliance and the Crusades against Christian Lay Powers, 1254–1343.* Oxford: Clarendon, 1982.

CHRISTOPHER HATCH MACEVITT

[See also **DMA:** Frederick II.]

FALL, THE. The story of the Fall of Man from Genesis 3:1–7 was of central importance in the development of the Christian doctrine of original sin. Although Jesus only once mentioned the story of Adam and Eve in the New Testament, St. Paul laid great emphasis on what he viewed as the critical connection between human sinfulness and Adam and Eve's transgression in the Garden of Eden. According to the apostle, human sin and death were punishments inherited by humanity for Adam's act of disobedience. Setting up a typology between Adam and Christ (the new Adam), Paul suggested that the universal salvation embodied by Christ was a corollary to the universal sin brought about by Adam. Paul's interpretation of the Fall and its place in the history of humankind was to have a profound and lasting influence on Christian thought.

PATRISTIC, JEWISH, AND MEDIEVAL INTERPRETATIONS

The early church fathers, who were deeply interested in the sources of human sin, drew heavily upon the Pauline notion that the corrupted, damaged, and broken state of human nature was a direct consequence of Adam's sin. According to St. Augustine, the entire human race not only sinned through Adam (being in him when he sinned), but all humans contracted the original sin through concupiscence, "the begetting of the flesh." Sexual desire was itself both proof of original sin and its punishment. The catastrophic, corrupting consequences of Adam's disobedience—mortality, physical suffering, concupiscence, and sin—were universal and inevitable for all future generations.

There was much debate in the Middle Ages over the nature of free will before and after the Fall. Because of original sin, humans would no longer be born in the same condition in which Adam was created nor would they have the same type of free will that Adam had had before his transgression. But the free will that humans had lost through Adam's sin was also thought to have been regained through Christ's life and death. Christ's Incarnation was viewed as a kind of second creation, repairing the damage done by the first Adam. Thus various medieval Christian theologians pointed to the paradox that the Fall in some ways made Christ's Incarnation necessary, thereby rendering the Fall a *felix culpa,* or fortunate crime.

There was also significant discussion among theologians in the twelfth and thirteenth centuries about how original sin was transmitted from one generation to another. Most theologians believed that the Fall had made propagation sinful and that henceforth propagation could not occur without sin. At the moment of conception, all of the iniquities and sins associated with original sin were transmitted to the unborn child through "the unclean seed." Although there was no strong tradition in Jewish thought of sin having been inherited from Adam's act of disobedience, there was a notion that each human being possessed in his or her nature *yezer ha-ra* (evil inclination) and *yezer ha-tov* (good inclination). Several of the apocryphal books also appear to have parallels with notions found in Paul, such as the idea that death is a punishment for Adam's disobedience. In the Fourth Book of Ezra and the Apocalypse of Baruch (both probably written by Jews in the first century A.D.) and in some later rabbinic commentaries, the cosmological consequences of Adam's sin were stressed. But rabbinic Judaism as a whole never developed a concept of the Fall as having permanently stained and corrupted human nature.

VERSIONS OF THE STORY

A number of versions of the Adam and Eve story were available during the Middle Ages, many of them inspired by the Old Testament apocrypha and pseudepigrapha. Several Latin versions of the *Vita Adae et Evae* (The life of Adam and Eve) were available as early as the eighth century, and these versions were later translated into English, German, and early Middle Irish. In the *Vita Adae et Evae,* Satan told Adam about his own earlier fall. Jealous of Adam and Eve, Satan had refused to bow down to Adam, saying that he was born before Adam and was superior to him. For his insubordination, Satan was expelled from heaven. Wandering the earth, he decided to enter the serpent in an attempt to bring about the downfall of Adam and Eve.

The theological implications of the Fall were also treated in three anonymous early Middle High German poems composed between 1050 and 1200: the *Wiener Genesis,* the *Vorauer Genesis,* and the *Anegenge.* Following a long Latin exegetical tradition, the poems explored such issues as the link between the serpent and the devil, Eve's role as temptress, the centrality of the sin of pride, and the effects of the Fall on Adam and Eve. The poems contain numerous extrabiblical elements, such as the notion that Adam and Eve lost their "garments of paradise" as a result of the Fall, but many of these elements belonged to a familiar and deep-rooted exegetical tradition.

The various versions of the *Vita Adae* spurred the creation of new legends that further filled in the history of Adam and Eve before and after the Fall. Especially popular were the legends of the Holy Rood, the English versions of which probably first appeared during the eleventh century. In these legends, Eve and Seth go to paradise to ask the guardian angel for the healing oil of life for Adam, who is dying. Seth is unable to get the oil, but he is given three pips of cedar, cypress, and pine instead. Returning to find that his father has died, Seth places the pips under Adam's tongue. From the three pips buried with Adam, three rods grow. The story goes on to show how much of biblical history is intertwined with the rods. Ultimately, one of the rods grows into the tree that is used to make the cross on which Christ is crucified. Both the *Vita Adae* and the Holy Rood legends connected the story of Eden with the life of Christ.

DRAMATIC AND VISUAL REPRESENTATIONS

The story of the Fall was also the subject of medieval plays, although here too the biblical narrative was greatly amplified and given new meaning. The twelfth-century Anglo-Norman liturgical drama *Mystère d'Adam* focuses on the awful consequences of man's disobedience and depicts Adam and Eve as they confront those frightening consequences. Although the two sinners appear contrite and are shown atoning for their sins, God drives them from paradise and angrily condemns them to hell. Indeed, the dramatist has devils arrive on stage to put chains on the necks of Adam and Eve and drag them to hell, whence smoke and terrifying sounds bellow. Other medieval plays were less gloomy in their dramatization of the Fall. The English N-Town play of the Fall, for instance, freed Adam and Eve of moral responsibility for their actions, suggesting that the serpent had appeared to them as an angel, thereby leading them to believe that it was sent from God. Thus they were not so much sinners as victims of Satan's craftiness. The English Chester play depicts the Fall as the result of forgetfulness not willed disobedience or evil on the parts of Adam and Eve. If the Fall was to be understood as a fortunate crime in bringing about the Redeemer, it followed that Adam and Eve should not receive too much blame. At times, they were even portrayed as innocent intermediaries in a cosmic struggle between God and Satan.

Visual images of the Eden story also abounded during the Middle Ages. Medieval visual depictions often showed the way the Genesis story functioned typologically with episodes from the New Testament. The tree of fruit was understood as prefiguring the cross, Eve's role as a sinful woman was interpreted to be the inverse corollary of Mary's role as the mother of God, and Adam's failure to obey God was taken to foreshadow Christ's ability to resist the devil's temptation in the wilderness.

EVE

In the patristic and medieval traditions, Eve was depicted as weak, fickle, easily deceived, sensuous, and sinful. Already in 1 Timothy 2:11–15, the story of Adam and Eve was used to justify women's submission to men. Several church fathers created a typology between Mary and Eve just as they did with Christ and Adam, with Mary representing obedience and life and Eve representing disobedience and death. Moral responsibility for the Fall was often placed on Eve's shoulders. Since Eve was viewed as the representative of her gender, the guilt for her transgression involved all women by association. St. Jerome and others suggested that Eve was virginal before the Fall and that through her sin, sexuality had been introduced into the world. Medieval writers frequently invoked Eve's sin to justify the subjection of women to their husbands. It was against the backdrop of this long misogynistic tradition that Christine de Pizan, writing in defense of women in the fifteenth century, invoked the story of Eve's creation to argue that since the first woman was created from a man's rib, women should stand beside their husbands as companions and not lie at their feet like slaves. Without Eve, Christine pointed out, there would have been no Mary, and so more was gained than lost through Eve's transgression.

BIBLIOGRAPHY

Anderson, Gary A. *The Genesis of Perfection: Adam and Eve in Jewish and Christian Imagination.* Louisville, Ky.: Westminster John Knox Press, 2001.

Barr, James. "The Authority of Scripture: The Book of Genesis and the Origin of Evil in Jewish and Christian Tradition." In *Christian Authority: Essays in Honour of Henry Chadwick.* Edited by G. R. Evans. Oxford: Clarendon Press, 1988.

Evans, J. M. *Paradise Lost and the Genesis Tradition.* London: Clarendon Press, 1968. A study of the precursors to Milton's *Paradise Lost.*

Jones, Lee. "Oure First Moder: Eve as Representative and Representation in Medieval Thought." *Limina* 2 (1996): 77–86.

Murdoch, Brian. *The Fall of Man in the Early Middle High German Biblical Epic: The "Wiener Genesis," the "Vorauer Genesis," and the "Anegenge."* Göppingen, Germany: Verlag Alfred Kümmerle, 1972.

———. *Adam's Grace: Fall and Redemption in Medieval Literature.* Cambridge, U.K.: D. S. Brewer, 2000.

Okuda, Hiroko. "Obedience or Disobedience? Medieval Dramatizations of the Fall of Man." *Poetica* 25–26 (1987): 52–72.

Pagels, Elaine. *Adam, Eve, and the Serpent.* New York: Random House, 1988.

ADAM JEFFREY DAVIS

[See also **DMA:** Anegenge; Antifeminism; Biblical Poetry, German; Chester Plays; Jeu d'Adam; N-Town Plays; **Supp:** Original Sin.]

FERDINAND III OF CASTILE, KING (*ca.* 1201?–1252), was the son of Alfonso IX of León (*r.* 1188–1230) and Berenguela, daughter of Alfonso VIII of Castile (*r.* 1158–1214). They had married (1197) in an effort to bring peace between Castile and León, but Innocent III quickly annulled the marriage (1204) due to their consanguinity, again throwing Castilian-Leonese relations into chaos. When Alfonso VIII died, his eleven-year-old son, Henry I (*r.* 1214–1217), succeeded him. But Henry's reign was short-lived; he died in an accident in 1217, making Berenguela the heir to the throne. She quickly passed the right of succession to Ferdinand. Alfonso IX, encouraged by rebellious Castilian nobles, now saw an opportunity to once again unite Castile and León under one ruler, himself, even if it meant having to wrest the Castilian crown from his son. His brief invasion of Castile (1218) ended in a peace agreement between Ferdinand and his father. With peace at hand, Ferdinand set himself to return order to his kingdom, and he also married Beatrice of Swabia, the granddaughter of Frederick Barbarossa, in 1219.

In 1212, when Ferdinand was still a boy, his grandfather Alfonso VIII had won a great victory over the Muslim Almohads at the Battle of Las Navas de Tolosa. Subsequent turmoil within the Christian ranks, highlighted by the death of Alfonso VIII and the bickering between Castile and León, had prevented the successful exploitation of Muslim weakness following the battle. By the mid-1220s, however, the Christian kings were ready to continue with their reconquest of Iberia. The collapse of Almohad power in North Africa greatly facilitated this task, as Ferdinand and Alfonso IX began a two-pronged attack against the Muslim cities. In 1230, Alfonso IX died, and Ferdinand inherited León, although not without some difficulties, and united it with Castile to form a powerful kingdom that would come to dominate the peninsula. Military success followed as he slowly but surely captured the major Muslim cities (and many smaller ones) of Andalusia in a campaign spanning over twenty years. In the process, he established for himself a reputation for virtue, piety, and courage. In 1236, Córdoba fell, followed by Jaén in 1246 and Seville in 1248, leaving only the small kingdom of Granada as the last surviving Muslim realm on the peninsula.

Ferdinand's impact extended beyond the battlefield. He oversaw the early stages of colonization of his new lands, which would eventually result in a large population shift in Castile from north to south. His marriage to Beatrice of Swabia also had significant repercussions, as it gave their son, Alfonso X (*r.* 1252–1284), a claim to the Holy Roman Empire—which he would diligently pursue, much to the consternation of his countrymen. Ferdinand died on 30 May 1252, in the midst of planning an invasion of North Africa. He was buried in the cathedral of Seville in the habit of a Franciscan tertiary. Seville, which had developed a special relationship with her onetime conqueror, led the efforts for his canonization in the seventeenth century. In 1671, Clement X responded with several privileges, which fell just short of canonization but which many supporters considered to be enough to justify Ferdinand's cult.

BIBLIOGRAPHY

Lomax, Derek W. *The Reconquest of Spain.* London and New York: Longman, 1978.

Martínez Díez, Gonzalo. *Fernando III: 1217–1252.* Palencia, Spain: Editorial La Olmeda, 1993.

O'Callaghan, Joseph F. *A History of Medieval Spain.* Ithaca, N.Y.: Cornell University Press, 1957.

Wunder, Amanda J. "Search for Sanctity in Baroque Seville: The Canonization of San Fernando and the Making of Golden-Age Culture, 1624–1729." Ph.D. Diss., Princeton University, 2002.

JARBEL RODRIGUEZ

[See also **DMA:** Alfonso X (the Learned); Almohads; Castile; Seville; Spain, Christian-Muslim Relations; **Supp:** Las Navas de Tolosa.]

FINNSBURH FRAGMENT. The *Finnsburh Fragment* and the associated *Finnsburh Episode* are among the most cryptic and debated pieces of Old English literature. The *Fragment* survives only in a transcription made in 1705. The original was written in a late West Saxon dialect, although the poem itself likely dates from the early eighth century. The *Episode,* for its part, consists of lines 1063 to 1160 of the epic poem *Beowulf.* Together, they comprise 145 lines of text.

The background story to the events depicted in the *Fragment* and the *Episode* has been lost, but much can be reconstructed. After a war between the Frisians and the Danes, the warring sides reach a peace agreement that they seal with the marriage of Finn, king of the Frisians, and Hildeburh, sister of Hnæf, leader of the Danes. Some years after the truce, a band of Danish warriors accompanies Hnæf on a visit to Finn and Hildeburh at Finnsburh. During the visit, however, a fight breaks out between the Danes and the Frisians—it is here that the *Fragment* begins—with the Frisians attacking their guests in their hall one night. Although the Danes are outnumbered, they hold out heroically, killing many of the Frisians. The *Fragment* is essentially a description of the battle, filled with allusions to the beasts of battle (carrion birds, wolf, and raven), details of the bloody fighting, and praises for the bravery of the participants. It ends abruptly in the middle of the conflict.

Luckily, the *Episode* from *Beowulf* picks up the action not long after. However, several important events transpire in the interim, notably the deaths of Hnæf and Finn's son. When the *Episode* begins, the fighting has settled into a stalemate with the Frisians too weak to dislodge the entrenched Danes. Finn offers the Danes and their new leader, Hengest, a truce to which the Danes agree, and the Frisian king takes them into his service after an exchange of oaths. Hnæf and Finn's son are laid to rest in a funeral pyre as Hildeburh mourns the death of her son and her brother. The Danes spend the rest of the winter with the Frisians while they wait for spring and the chance to sail home. When spring arrives, however, it is not departure that the Danes seek but revenge for their slain leader and companions. Goaded by his

men, Hengest, who had been inactive through the winter—perhaps conflicted by the double oaths he has taken to Hnæf and Finn—finally decides to act (some scholars have suggested that Hengest had stayed with the Frisians through the winter to exact revenge when the right time came). The Danes attack the Frisians and kill Finn and his troops. After plundering the hall, the Danes depart, taking Hildeburh with them.

Modern scholars have focused significant attention on both of these works, raising questions concerning the background of the story, the reasons for the Frisian attack, Hengest's winter of indecision, the correct meaning of several ambiguous passages, and the placement of the *Episode* within the larger framework of the *Beowulf* narrative. Many of these questions remain. In spite of this, the *Fragment* and *Episode* are valuable and intriguing sources providing us with a suggestive view into the uncertainties, violence, and complexities of early medieval Germanic society.

BIBLIOGRAPHY

Bjork, Robert E. "Digressions and Episodes." In *A Beowulf Handbook.* Edited by Robert E. Bjork and John D. Niles. Lincoln: University of Nebraska Press, 1997.

Chickering, Howell D., Jr., trans. and ed. *Beowulf: A Dual-Language Edition.* Garden City, N.Y.: Anchor Books, 1977. See especially the commentary on pp. 322–331.

Fry, Donald K. *Finnsburh Fragment and Episode.* London: Methuen, 1974. An excellent discussion on both of these texts. Also includes both edited texts in Old English.

Klaeber, Friedrich, ed. *Beowulf and the Fight at Finnsburh.* 3d ed. Boston: Heath, 1950.

JARBEL RODRIGUEZ

[See also **DMA:** Anglo-Saxon Literature; *Beowulf;* Sutton Hoo.]

FIREARMS. Perhaps the greatest and certainly the most enduring invention in medieval military technology was gunpowder weaponry. Gunpowder was probably discovered in China during the eighth or ninth century A.D. Shortly thereafter the Chinese recognized its military potential, using it in bombs, grenades, rockets, and fireworks during the tenth to twelfth centuries; they did not develop cannons until later.

By the middle of the thirteenth century, gunpowder had made its way to western Europe, although by a means not yet ascertained. By about 1267 recipes for gunpowder had appeared in Roger Bacon's *Epistola de secretis operibus artis et naturae et de nullitate magiae* (Letter on the secret workings of art and nature, and on the vanity of magic), and these were followed by similar recipes written around 1275 by Albertus Magnus and around 1300 by "Marcus Graecus." These recipes varied slightly, but all combined saltpeter, sulphur, and charcoal in a mixture that, when lit, combusted with a forceful explosion. Still, none of these authors described a weapon that could use their gunpowder mixture. When this weapon was invented in Europe, it was a tube-shaped weapon that used gunpowder to discharge a missile from it; it was commonly called a "cannon," from the French *canon,* or a "gun," from the English *gynne* or *gonne.* It is difficult to determine when the first cannon was made in Europe. Written evidence from the early fourteenth century is scarce and often disputed. Less controversial are two artistic sources, an illumination found in Walter de Milemete's *De nobilitatibus, sapientiis et prudentiis regum* (Concerning the majesty, wisdom, and prudence of kings), produced in London about 1326, and a second illumination found in a companion volume to the Walter de Milemete treatise known as *De secretis secretorum Aristotelis* (The secrets of secrets of Aristotle), also produced in London at the same time. Each of these depicts a large vase-shaped cannon lying on its side.

The beginnings of gunpowder weaponry were thus quite modest, but its evolutionary progress was spectacular. Over the next 150 years guns were made both larger and smaller. Eventually they became handheld. The methods of manufacture also changed, as guns became less frequently made on the forge and more frequently at the foundry. Transportation methods, metallurgy, and powder chemistry were subjected to experiment and eventually improved. More important, gunpowder weaponry led to changes on the battlefield, at sieges, and in naval engagements.

USES IN WARFARE

The first and most enduring impact of gunpowder weapons was on siege warfare. Early gunpowder artillery pieces could be heavy cannons with large calibers that fired heavy projectiles, ideal for sieges, as the walls of castles were easily damaged by the ballistic force of gunshot, and by the middle of the fourteenth century nearly every siege was accompanied by gunpowder artillery bombardment. By the end of the century, cannons were even breaching fortification walls. Gunpowder weaponry continued to be significant in the siege warfare of the fifteenth century. Sometimes a long and heavy bombardment was required to defeat a besieged fortification. At the siege of Maastricht from 24 November 1407 to

7 January 1408, the town received 1,514 large bombard balls, an average of 30 per day; at the siege of Lagny in 1431, 412 stone cannonballs were fired into the town in a single day; at Dinant in 1466, 502 large and 1,200 smaller cannonballs were fired; at the siege of Rhodes in 1480 over 3,500 balls were shot into the town. At other times, simply the presence of large gunpowder weapons among the besieging army intimidated the inhabitants of a town or castle. At the siege of Bourg in 1451, which Charles VII captured in just six days after his heavy artillery was brought up to the walls of the castle, they never fired a shot. At other times gunpowder siege artillery was unsuccessful, especially since these early gunpowder weapons frequently exploded. Many commanders also did not recognize the capabilities of these new weapons and were thus unable to use them effectively, while misuse of the guns by inexperienced operators constantly caused problems.

Gunpowder weapons had less impact on late medieval battlefield warfare. Fourteenth-century battlefield uses of gunpowder weaponry were infrequent, and even then they rarely played a role in the outcome of the battle. It may in fact have been only at the Battle of Bevershoutsveld, fought outside the walls of the town of Bruges in 1382, where guns decided the outcome. With the adoption of smaller cannons in the early fifteenth century, as well as improved accuracy, these weapons began to appear more frequently on the battlefield. As in siege warfare, sometimes these guns were quite effective. More often, however, battlefield gunfire was ineffective. Smaller weapons that could be easily transported and maneuvered on the battlefield were needed. The solution was handheld gunpowder weapons. These were brought into use in the late fourteenth century; after this, uses of handheld gunpowder weapons, initially called *coulovrines à main* and later *haquebusses,* increased.

During the later Middle Ages, gunpowder weaponry also began appearing on ships. After the beginning of the fifteenth century, it seems that few ships left port without carrying a complement of cannons. Naval guns also seem to have been different from those used in land engagements. They were smaller, more standardized in barrel length, caliber, and chamber size, and capable of being loaded with both powder and ball from the rear. Handheld gunpowder weapons also frequently appeared on naval vessels.

VARIETIES OF GUNPOWDER WEAPONS

The earliest medieval gunpowder weapons were known simply as cannons, or *ribaudequins,* and it is uncertain what they looked like or how they were made.

But as the technology became better known and more common, gunpowder weapons began to be made in many different sizes and a few different shapes. The largest, best known, and most impressive of all of these weapons were the bombards. They measured as much as 17 feet (5.2 meters) in length, weighed as much as 36,000 pounds (16,400 kilograms), and had calibers as large as 28 inches (71 centimeters). At sieges, the presence of one or more bombards was significant, for they fired stone cannonballs weighing as much as 851 pounds (386 kilograms). However, bombards were expensive to make, and their use in nonsiege encounters was limited. In western Europe by the fifteenth century, bombards began to be supplemented by smaller weapons, as cannoneers discovered that at a siege a larger number of more easily maneuverable smaller guns could provide the same, and sometimes more, offensive power as a single large bombard and without the possibility of defensive fire easily destroying their firepower.

Measurements for medium-sized gunpowder weapons, known by a variety of terms, including *veuglaires, crapadeaux, bombardelles, courtaux,* mortars, falcons, and serpentines, vary greatly. Weights as small as 106 pounds (48 kilograms) are reported but so are weights of 7,900 pounds (3,584 kilograms). Lengths and calibers are more standard, with lengths averaging between 4 and 6 feet (1.22 and 1.83 meters) and calibers between 3 and 7 inches (7.6 and 17.8 centimeters). Stone cannonballs fired from these weapons weighed between 2 and 32 pounds (1 and 14.5 kilograms). They were used both at sieges and on the battlefield and would eventually become the most common type of nonhandheld gunpowder weaponry in the early modern army.

The smallest gunpowder weapons of the late Middle Ages were known most often by the name *coulovrine,* and their use was almost strictly limited to the battlefield, where they were sometimes employed in great numbers. Weights for these guns, averaging between 13 and 51 pounds (6 and 23 kilograms), were often very small in comparison with other gunpowder weapons. Lengths too were small, averaging between 6 and 48 inches (15 and 122 centimeters). Calibers are never recorded, but they must have been quite small, as many *coulovrines* fired lead instead of stone cannonballs—it was easier and ultimately cheaper to found small lead cannonballs than to carve stone ones. The origin of handheld guns may be seen in the *coulovrines,* as many of the smallest of these were capable of and often depicted as being attached to a stock, wooden or metal, and were transported and operated by hand.

Three types of metal were used for gunpowder weapons in the fourteenth and fifteenth centuries: bronze, forged iron, and cast iron. Bronze was the most highly prized metal for constructing cannons, but its high cost limited its use in most armies. Iron was a more plentiful and less expensive metal for the making of gunpowder weapons. However, it was also far more difficult to cast, especially since methods of iron founding in the late Middle Ages were expensive and primitive. Still, a few cast-iron cannons were made during this period. Most iron cannons were not made at the foundry but on the forge. They were constructed by welding several iron bars together to form a tube, adding a strong, solid piece of metal to the rear of the tube, and reinforcing the whole weapon with a number of iron rings welded around it. Forged gunpowder weapons were able to be repaired on the siege or battlefield site, and late medieval artillery trains always contained a number of forges, smiths, and prefashioned rings and bars for this purpose.

Most cannons in the late Middle Ages had removable chambers to hold the gunpowder, which fitted in an opening near the breech. These chambers were fixed solidly in place with a wedge of iron or wood, and several chambers accompanied each artillery piece, allowing for a fairly rapid rate of fire.

While gunpowder weapons themselves varied in weight, length, and caliber, what went inside them—projectiles and gunpowder—varied little. Although there was some experimentation with amounts, the three main ingredients of gunpowder remained the same. The ideal proportions of these substances—74.64 percent saltpeter, 11.85 percent sulphur, and 13.51 percent charcoal—were rarely achieved; however, most gunpowder recipes did approximate these ideal percentages, resulting in a combustion sufficient to propel a projectile to its target. The projectiles of gunpowder weapons also varied little in substance. The first projectiles may have been large bolts, although these seem to have disappeared before the fifteenth century. Most gunpowder-propelled projectiles were round balls made of stone or cast metal. Stone projectiles were fashioned by masons either in a central masonry or on site. Metal balls could be made of either lead or iron, although probably because of the poor quality of cast iron in the late Middle Ages, lead was the preferred metal.

In the fourteenth and early fifteenth centuries gunpowder artillery was transported to the site of a siege or battle by water or on carts. The guns were then placed on mounts especially constructed there by carpenters who always accompanied artillery trains. By the middle of the fifteenth century, however, cannons began to be mounted permanently on wheeled carriages, which also carried their ammunition and gunpowder. Sometimes these mounts featured protection for the guns and their operators by way of mantles, shields, palisades, and so on. Also at this time, cushions were added to the back of these guns to absorb the recoil of the weapon. The mount set the aim of a cannon, which could be accomplished in a number of ways: first, by placing a fixed mount on terrain angled to provide the correct aim; second, by mounting the cannon on a fixed axle to provide its aim; third, by using the terrain and axle together to aim the weapon; fourth, by using a wall or rock under the carriage to move the aiming angle; and last, by adding a calibrated aiming device to the mount to change the aiming angle. Although these methods seem simple in comparison with modern techniques, medieval cannoneers do seem to have been quite adept at aiming their weapons.

By the end of the fifteenth century and the beginning of the early modern era, gunpowder weaponry had become a feature of everyday life. Guns had become so conventional that they began to be used in celebrations, in fashion, and in crime. A musical instrument took the name "bombard" because of its shape and sound, both of which resembled the gunpowder weapon of that name. New surgical techniques were developed to heal the new wounds created by gunshot. And early in the history of gunpowder weapons, the church even furnished cannoneers with their own patron saint, St. Barbara. She was a fitting patron for those who operated gunpowder artillery, for at her martyrdom, her father, who had denounced her Christianity, was struck down by a clap of thunder and a lighting bolt.

BIBLIOGRAPHY

DeVries, Kelly. *Medieval Military Technology.* Peterborough, Canada: Broadview, 1992.

———. *Guns and Men in Medieval Europe, 1200–1500: Studies in Military History and Technology.* Aldershot, U.K.: Variorum, 2002.

Hall, Bert S. *Weapons and Warfare in Renaissance Europe: Gunpowder, Technology, and Tactics.* Baltimore: Johns Hopkins University Press, 1997.

Smith, Robert D., and Kelly DeVries. *The Gunpowder Artillery of the Dukes of Burgundy.* Woodbridge, U.K.: Boydell Press, 2004.

Smith, Robert D., and Ruth Rhynas Brown. *Bombards: Mons Meg and Her Sisters.* London: Royal Armouries, 1989.

KELLY DEVRIES

[See also **DMA:** Arms and Armor; Cannon; Metallurgy; Warfare, Western European.]

FITZRALPH, RICHARD (*ca.* 1300–1360), Oxford theologian and archbishop of Armagh. Richard Fitzralph was born in Dundalk, Ireland, and came from a well-to-do family. He received a master of arts degree from Oxford University and was a doctor of theology by 1331. Fitzralph's commentary on Peter Lombard's *Sentences* is the one complete work that survives from his university years. From 1332 to 1334 he served as chancellor of Oxford University, during a turbulent time when masters and students from the north seceded and founded an alternative university in Stamford, Lincolnshire. The "Stamford Schism" gave Fitzralph occasion to visit the papal curia in Avignon, where he made contacts that would be significant for his later career. In 1335 Fitzralph was made dean of the Lichfield cathedral, but he was absent during much of his deanship, engaged in litigation and other business at Avignon. He was elected archbishop of Armagh in 1346, but of the fourteen years of his archiepiscopate he spent only about six in Ireland, spending much of the rest of the time at the papal curia.

During his stays at Avignon, Fitzralph became known as an unusually talented preacher. A great deal about Fitzralph's preaching activity is known thanks to the detailed sermon diary he kept. The diary contains ninety-two items, including the full texts of Latin sermons, Latin summaries of sermons he preached in the vernacular, anti-mendicant sermons he delivered at Saint Paul's Cross in London, and the *Proposicio* preached in Avignon. The sermons are deeply pastoral and show that despite his frequent absences from his archdiocese, Fitzralph was engaged in a number of local issues: he worked to battle fraud and corruption; he rejected those who made the conflict between the English and the Irish clergy a pretext for violence; and he defended the rights of the church's weakest members, such as widows and orphans. His *Summa de quaestionibus Armenorum,* a dialogue in nineteen books, grew out of debates that Fitzralph witnessed in Avignon between representatives of the Greek and Armenian churches who were seeking papal support against the threat of Islam.

Armagh's active Gaelic Franciscan community, centered around the local Franciscan *studium,* enjoyed wide religious support among the lay people of the city. Finding it difficult to compete with the pastoral involvement of the friars, Fitzralph became increasingly hostile toward the Franciscans. He spent much of his time at the papal curia attacking the mendicant orders. He lashed out, for instance, against their alleged leniency in confessional. In his dialogue *De pauperie Salvatoris,* which appeared in 1356, he criticized the Franciscans' strict understanding of the obligation to communal property.

Discussing the problems of dominion, possession, use, and property in relation to creation and divine grace, Fitzralph argued that there was no biblical justification for the mendicant ideal of poverty.

John Wyclif was indebted to Fitzralph for his ideas on dominion and jurisdiction, and the Lollards also used the Irish archbishop's ideas for their doctrine of *sola scriptura*. These attempts to adapt some of Fitzralph's ideas tarnished his image, and efforts to canonize him in the later fourteenth century were met with opposition and ultimately failed.

BIBLIOGRAPHY

Dawson, J. D. "Richard FitzRalph and the Fourteenth-Century Poverty Controversies." *Journal of Ecclesiastical History* 34 (1983): 315–344.

Leff, Gordon. *Richard Fitzralph, Commentator of the Sentences: A Study in Theological Orthodoxy.* Manchester, U.K.: Manchester University Press, 1963. A study of Fitzralph's theology.

Trevisa, John. *Richard Fitzralph's Sermon: "Defensio curatorum," and Methodius: "De bygynnyng of de world and de ende of worldes."* Edited by Aaron J. Perry. London: Early English Text Society, 1925. (Translation of *Dialogus inter militem et clericum.*) Middle English translation of Fitzralph's "Defensio curatorum," a sermon preached in 1357 in Avignon against the friars.

Walsh, Katherine. *Richard Fitzralph in Oxford, Avignon, and Armagh: A Fourteenth-Century Scholar and Primate.* Oxford: Oxford University Press, 1981. The best full-length biography of Fitzralph.

ADAM JEFFREY DAVIS

[See also **DMA:** Franciscans; Lollards; Oxford University; Peter Lombard; Wyclif, John; **Supp:** Poverty.]

FRANKS. Roman historians first used the term "Frank" to describe the Germanic tribes who raided Rome's northwest frontier in the fourth century. By the sixth century, a substantial kingdom had been established by Clovis, who, under the title of "king of the Franks," led Germanic warriors and Gallo-Roman aristocrats to conquer much of Roman Gaul. By the eighth century, the name had been applied to their territory, transforming Gaul into France. In the late eleventh century, however, the term came to have a new, though related meaning. European chroniclers of the First Crusade referred to the achievements of the crusaders as the "gesta dei per Francos," that is, "the deeds of God achieved through the Franks," although the participants came from Flanders, England, and Italy as well as from northern France. The crusaders adopted this broadened use of "Frank" (*Frankoi* in Greek, *al-Ifranj* in Arabic) from Byzantines and Muslims, who considered any inhabitant of western Europe to be a Frank. Only Slavs, Vikings, and Christians living in Muslim Spain were not included within this capacious category.

This meaning probably first developed among the Byzantines, whose contact with western Europe was largely through the Frankish empire of Charlemagne and his successors. The Muslims subsequently absorbed the term from their Byzantine neighbors. Lack of contact with other European polities led "Frank" to suffice for all westerners. Following increased contact between western Europeans and Byzantines and Muslims during the First Crusade, those from the West started to adopt the nomenclature for themselves. The term "Frank" thus came to have two meanings. The early medieval sense of the word still survived; the king of France continued to be known in official documents by the same title as Clovis had been *(rex francorum)* into the thirteenth century. The adoption of the word by Europeans who settled in the Middle East following the First Crusade gave the term its second meaning. Yet the use of the term by western Europeans did not mean a pan-European identity overrode regional, linguistic, and ethnic identities. It was only in contrast to Byzantines, Muslims, and others outside of western Europe that they became "Frank," for in reference to individuals or groups within Frankish society western European writers still spoke of Normans, Catalans, and Englishmen. Afonso I of Portugal in negotiations with the crusaders who helped him capture Lisbon in 1147 spoke of the agreement between "the Franks and me," yet his Burgundian father had received the same designation when he arrived in Spain from France some forty years earlier. The term thus has the unusual distinction of being an ethnic identity that only applied to a group of people when they were immigrants, traveling, or otherwise away from their native lands.

Western Europeans were aware of the eastern origins of the name. Ekkehard of Aura, one of the chroniclers of the First Crusade, noted that "the barbarians are accustomed to call all westerners Franks." With the establishment of the crusader principalities of Edessa, Antioch, Tripoli, and Jerusalem, the name became particularly attached to settlers in the crusader kingdoms of the Levant and the Aegean. However, European writers sometimes used the term "Frank" in an ethnic sense, speaking of the *gens francorum,* a term that suggests the Franks shared common descent, language, and customs. Yet they were clearly aware that Franks included a diverse group of peoples who spoke a variety of languages and were divided by different cultural norms. The First Crusade became in some ways the origin myth for a new people, who were an army who settled the land given to them by God, as the Hebrews and the barbarian tribes of late antiquity had done before them. It was perhaps only in the crusader kingdoms that the new meaning of "Frank" became a significant term to describe a self-identifying ethnic community.

"Frank" also carried a religious meaning. William of Tyre, the only native-born historian of the crusader East, preferred the term "Latins" to refer to European settlers in the Holy Land, making clear that at the heart of this identity was adherence to Western Christian liturgy and religious traditions. The religious element was recognized by others as well. Armenians and Jacobite Christians often used "Frank" interchangeably with "Latin." Byzantines who opposed the union between the Orthodox and Catholic churches achieved at the Council of Lyons in 1274 accused unionist Greeks of becoming Franks.

Among Byzantines, Muslims, and other inhabitants of the Middle East the label "Frank" came with a set of associations. Franks were notably courageous in war but not considered particularly intelligent. They valued gold above all else and would do anything to get it.

The term began to die out in the later Middle Ages as the Latin settlements in the eastern Mediterranean fell to Mamluk and Ottoman conquests. By the sixteenth century, the term had lost its relevance for western Europeans. Those western merchants who still traded in cities such as Constantinople, Alexandria, and Aleppo lived there in trading colonies for temporary periods, and their identities remained rooted in their homelands of France, Venice, and England. Muslims, however, continued to refer to western Europeans as Franks into the nineteenth century, and their use of the term spread throughout Asia, so that when western Europeans arrived in China in the sixteenth century, they were referred to by the familiar name of "Fo-lang-ki," derived from the Arabic.

BIBLIOGRAPHY

Bartlett, Robert. *The Making of Europe: Conquest, Colonization, and Cultural Change, 950–1350.* Princeton, N.J.: Princeton University Press, 1993.

Epp, Verena. "Die Entstehung eines 'Nationalbewusstseins' in den Kreuzfahrerstaaten." *Deutsches Archiv für Erforschung des Mittelalters* 45 (1989): 596–604.

Lewis, Bernard. *The Muslim Discovery of Europe.* New York: Norton, 1982.

Murray, Alan V. "Ethnic Identity in the Crusader States: The Frankish Race and the Settlement of Outremer." In *Concepts of National Identity in the Middle Ages.* Edited by Simon Forde, Lesley Johnson, and Alan V. Murray. Leeds, U.K.: Leeds Studies in English, 1995.

CHRISTOPHER HATCH MACEVITT

[See also **DMA:** Clovis; Crusades and Crusader States: Near East; Crusades and Crusader States: To 1192.]

FRAXINETUM. For most of the tenth century, Muslim brigands used a citadel at Fraxinetum (modern La Garde-Freinet, near Saint-Tropez) as a base for their forays throughout Provence and the Alpine passes. The Muslim settlement at Fraxinetum was an autonomous, entrepreneurial community. It was not formally recognized as a polity or colony of the Islamic Empire, and its inhabitants produced no documents describing their political goals or internal organization. Muslim geographers of the thirteenth century make brief reference to the settlement, but contemporary reports of the activities and range of operation of its inhabitants come primarily from Latin Christian sources like saints' lives, chronicles, and monastic charters.

The riches of the fertile coast of Provence had been the target of foreign predation since the early ninth century, when Greek and Northman raiders threatened the cities of Marseille and Arles. According to the tenth-century German historian Liutprand of Cremona, however, Muslim pirates were the worst perpetrators of violence in the region. The exact date of their arrival in Provence is unknown, but it probably coincided with the marked increase in reports of Muslim raiders between 880 and 890. Liutprand described in detail how a small party of them murdered the Christian inhabitants of Fraxinetum and established a fortified base there (Antapodosis 1.2–4).

The Muslims of Fraxinetum profited from the political turmoil that gripped Provence in the tenth century. They served as mercenaries in regional feuds between Christian lords and plundered towns and monasteries throughout the region. They also made predatory forays into the Alpine passes to tap the rich vein of traffic that flowed between northern Europe and the city of Rome. Pilgrim and merchant caravans were particularly vulnerable to robbery because they usually traveled without an armed retinue and often carried considerable amounts of currency and supplies with them on their long journeys.

The forte of the brigands was kidnapping. They were able to exact a heavy toll in ransom from the families of their captives. In July 972, raiders from Fraxinetum abducted Abbot Maiolus of Cluny and his entourage as they traveled north across the Great Saint

Bernard Pass. The monks of Cluny ransacked the ornaments of their church to gather the sum necessary to ransom their spiritual father—1,000 pounds of silver, according to Radulphus Glaber (Historiae Quinque Libri 1.4.9). Abbot Maiolus and his followers eventually went free, but the audacity of the brigands outraged Christian leaders and galvanized the will of local lords. Within a year of the incident, Count William of Arles marshaled an army and laid waste to the fortress at Fraxinetum. The destruction of the citadel did not completely remove the threat of pirate raids along the coast of Provence, but it did effectively erase the Muslim presence from Fraxinetum and the Alpine passes.

BIBLIOGRAPHY

Février, Paul-Albert, et al. *La Provence des origines à l'an mil: Histoire et archéologie.* Rennes: Editions Ouest-France, 1989.

Poly, Jean-Pierre. *La Provence et la société féodale (879–1166): Contribution à l'étude des structures dites féodales dans le Midi.* Paris: Bordas, 1976.

Sénac, Philippe. *Provence et piraterie sarrasine.* Paris: Maisonneuve and Larose, 1982.

Zerner, Monique. "La capture de Maïeul et la guerre de libération de Provence: Le départ des sarrasins à travers les cartulaires provençaux." In *Saint Mayeul et son temps.* Dignes-les-Bains, France: Société scientifique et littéraire des Alpes de Haute-Provence, 1997.

SCOTT G. BRUCE

[See also **DMA:** Liutprand of Cremona; Provence; Radulphus Glaber; **Supp:** Maiolus.]

FREDEGUNDA (*ca.* 543–597) was the most famous wife of Chilperic I, who ruled the kingdom of Soissons from 561 to 584. Her humble origins were not unusual among wives of Merovingian rulers, who mostly married either lowborn Franks or foreign nobility. Indeed, prior to Fredegunda, Chilperic had married a Visigothic princess named Galswintha, at which time Fredegunda was probably no more than a concubine. Historians still debate whether Merovingians should be considered polygamists or serial monogamists, but clearly only one partner at a time could enjoy the status of queen. In any case, Gregory of Tours wrote that Chilperic had Galswintha killed. Although later commentators sometimes see the hand of Fredegunda in this murder, Gregory doubtlessly would have implicated her if there had been cause, for he did not spare her on many other occasions. Nevertheless, Galswintha's demise plays an important part in a notorious blood feud between Fredegunda and Brunhild, the deceased's sister and wife to King Sigibert I of Austrasia. Gregory juxtaposed his portrait of Fredegunda, vile and deadly, with that of her pious counterpart, and while other, less flattering sources balance out his depiction of Brunhild, nothing survives to redeem Fredegunda.

Although Gregory did not blame her for the death of Galswintha, Fredegunda bears the credit for plenty of other murders and plots. She was successful in eliminating her children's potential competitors, namely, the children of Chilperic's first wife, Audovera. One of these, Merovich, anticipated her hostility and sought shelter by marrying Brunhild, widowed since Fredegunda arranged her husband's assassination in 575. Praetextatus, the bishop who had sheltered the newlyweds at Rouen, was exiled and murdered, and Merovich committed suicide. Yet for all her efforts to ensure their success, Fredegunda's own children fared poorly, at least three of them dying of disease. Gregory reported that their mother suspected witchcraft in one case and interpreted the rest as demonstrations of divine displeasure. But her fourth son survived, and fifteen years after Fredegunda's death this son, Chlothar II, would execute the aged Brunhild along with most of her surviving progeny and unite all the Frankish kingdoms. In 584, however, when Chilperic was assassinated, Chlothar was only a child. The eighth-century *Liber Historiae Francorum* suggests that the murderer was Fredegunda, reacting after Chilperic had discovered her in an adulterous affair, but the seventh-century *Chronicle* of Fredegarius blames Brunhild for the deed.

Like other royal widows, Fredegunda retained a large personal treasure, including movable wealth, property, and possibly cities; Galswintha had received at least five cities as a wedding gift. Whatever its value, this wealth allowed Fredegunda not only to stay alive but also to maintain political influence during Chlothar's minority. When King Guntram of Burgundy called her son a bastard, she had three bishops and several hundred prominent laymen swear to the contrary. To deal with other opponents, she reputedly hired assassins. Unlike Brunhild, Fredegunda died naturally. She inspired a five-act tragedy by Louise-Jean Népomucène Lemercier (1771–1840), *Frédégonde et Brunehaut,* and several graphic twentieth-century novels.

BIBLIOGRAPHY

Nelson, Janet L. "Queens as Jezebels: The Careers of Brunhilde and Balthild in Merovingian History." In *Medieval Women.* Edited by Derek Baker. Oxford: Published for the Ecclesiastical Society by B. Blackwell, 1978.

Stafford, Pauline. *Queens, Concubines, and Dowagers: The King's Wife in the Early Middle Ages.* Athens: University of Georgia Press, 1983.

Wood, Ian. *The Merovingian Kingdoms, 450–751.* London and New York: Longman, 1993. See especially chapter 8.

KEVIN UHALDE

[See also **DMA:** Gregory of Tours, St.; Merovingians; **Supp:** Brunhild; Queens and Queenship.]

FRISIAN LITERATURE. The founders of comparative linguistics once took considerable interest in Old Frisian; nowadays, however, this medieval Germanic language seems to attract less scholarly attention. A similar claim can be made for medieval Frisian literature, although here a modest reputation is less surprising, since only a few truly literary texts have been preserved in medieval Frisian. In fact, the character of Old Frisian literature, as it has come down to us, is overwhelmingly legal instead of literary. Nonetheless, the Old Frisian laws have acquired a certain fame on account of their poetic qualities, although they were, of course, texts with a practical purpose only and were never intended as belles-lettres.

During the later Middle Ages, Frisian was spoken along the North Sea coast from the Zuider Zee in the west to the upper reaches of the river Weser in the east. In the early modern era, however, Frisian as a spoken language continued only in its westernmost part, the current Dutch province of Friesland. The lack of a literature proper, even from the latter area, is largely due to Friesland's distinct political and social structure. This may require some elucidation.

In the seventh century a Frisian tribal kingdom emerged, where paganism still throve. During the next century, however, it was subjugated by the Franks, who, with the exception of its law, eradicated every trace of the culture and identity of the vanquished tribe. The ensuing Christianization of the Frisians took place in close connection with this Frankish conquest. Later, new distinctive features began to develop in Frisian society, culminating in the establishment of the so-called Frisian freedom, an essentially republican form of government. As a result, the area between the Zuider Zee and the Weser fragmented into a large number of self-governing territories, called in Latin *terrae.* Peculiar characteristics of this era are the absence of feudalism and a class of knights and a belated development of cities. In addition, the rise of monasteries was exceptional in its density. Within this idiosyncratic society a basically archaic social structure remained in place until virtually the end of the Middle Ages.

It will hardly come as a surprise that the transition from an oral society to one dominated by the written word took place relatively late here. A few lengthy monastic chronicles, written in Latin and originating in the thirteenth century, are therefore all the more impressive. When the vernacular slowly replaced Latin as a written language, legal texts, which had been handed down orally till then, were the first to be written down. As a charter language, Frisian superseded Latin from about 1370, but, with very few exceptions, in the western territories only. In the east Low German made its appearance as a competing vernacular. Frisian as a written language was completely pushed aside here, even in legal texts, from approximately 1400.

The smaller western region initially showed a different development. In this area Frisian even was put to new uses, as it developed into the language of administration in the vast majority of the emerging cities. However, some cities adopted for this purpose the neighboring vernacular, Dutch, which also began to compete with Frisian as a charter language. Moreover, even here Frisian hardly penetrated into the remaining domains of writing: religion, education, and belles-lettres. Old Frisian literature thus never moved beyond its initial phase, failing to develop into a "complete" literature. This situation can be attributed to the fact that Frisian society lacked a court culture and a class of educated citizens and was therefore unable to provide patrons to commission a proper literature or an audience to consume it.

It should be added that in the sixteenth century Frisian as a written language completely vanished in the western territories as well. Yet it was here that the first literary author to choose Frisian as his medium of writing made his appearance a century later, whereas, during the same period, it faded away in the east.

LEGAL PROSE

The bulk of Old Frisian literature consists of legal texts, which have come down to us in sixteen manuscript codices and, most surprisingly, one incunabulum. With two exceptions, these manuscripts and even the incunabulum are not law books. Rather, they constitute private law compilations, consisting of a combination of "pan-Frisian" and local laws, most of which are much older than the actual manuscripts. The exceptions are the two so-called Brokmer Manuscripts, containing two recensions of the law book of an eastern territory, Brokmerland. One of them is the oldest Old Frisian codex, which probably dates from the end of the thirteenth century. The second oldest (*ca.* 1300) originates from another eastern *terra,* Riustringen. This work, now known as the

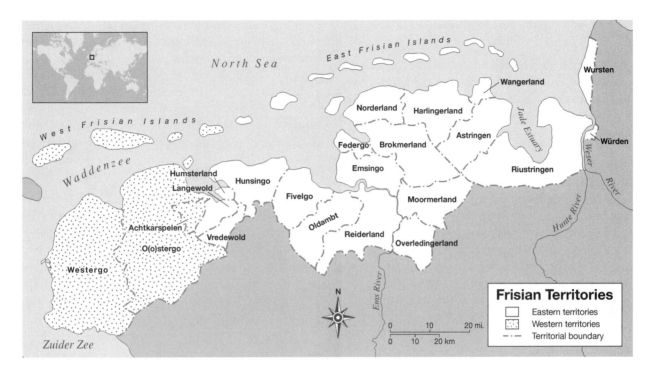

North Sea

East Frisian Islands

Wursten

West Frisian Islands

Waddenzee

Wangerland

Norderland   Harlingerland

Astringen

Jade Estuary

Würden

Federgo   Brokmerland

Emsingo

Riustringen

Weser River

Humsterland
Langewold   Hunsingo

Fivelgo

Moormerland

Hunte River

Achtkarspelen
Vredewold

O(o)stergo

Oldambt

Reiderland

Overledingerland

Ems River

Westergo

N

Zuider Zee

Frisian Territories

☐	Eastern territories
⬚	Western territories
–·–·–	Territorial boundary

0   10   20 mi.
0   10   20 km

XNR PRODUCTIONS/THE GALE GROUP.

First Riustring Codex, used to be referred to as the *asega-buch,* literally, "book of the *asega* (law-sayer)." The incunabulum, which bears a clearly western stamp, must have been printed somewhere in the Low Countries between 1484 and 1486, but it is unknown who commissioned it.

The nineteenth-century German scholar Jacob Grimm was the first to draw attention to the relationship between law and poetry, maintaining that both had "risen from one and the same bed." Quite a few of his examples of poetical elements in Old Germanic law were taken from the Old Frisian *asegabuch.* The theme was elaborated by Conrad Borchling in a now rather outdated work, published in 1908. Borchling likewise stressed the beauty of the writing of the Riustring laws, the dyke law in particular, but also drew attention to the oldest law texts from the western territories, such as the *Skeltana Riucht.* It is generally acknowledged that the shining example of Old Frisian legal poetry is the passage on the three needs of the fatherless child, describing the conditions under which a mother may sell her child's inheritance. It is recorded as an appendage to the second of the Twenty-Four Statutes, one of the most important of the pan-Frisian laws. The rich and vivid detail of this text can be regarded as artistic embellishment, included to suggest the spirit of the law. The numerous, mostly alliterative descriptions of infinity in time found in many of the Old Frisian legal texts have also acquired fame.

Among the poetic devices in the older Frisian laws are alliteration, formulaic phrasing, metonymy, kenning (the shortest form of metaphor), and aphorism; rhyme also occurs but is much less frequent. It is often assumed that these devices were originally intended to facilitate memorizing of the texts for oral recitation by the *asegas.* Even if there is no definite proof, they are certainly indicative of a transition from oral to written form.

In an important article, published in 1984, Eric Stanley rejects the much cherished idea that any passage of medieval legal prose adorned with alliteration is likely to be ancient. He advances the convincing thesis that alliteration remained in use in quite late prose compositions, especially the laws, but he also adopts the older view that alliterative verse once existed in Old Frisian, even though no such verses have survived.

POETRY AND NONLEGAL PROSE

Not a single line of epic poetry in Old Frisian has been preserved. Still, there are indications that the Frisians once had an oral tradition of heroic poetry. Of great importance here is an entry in the *Vita Liudgeri,* a saint's life, in which it is stated that during a missionary trip, which must have taken place around 780, the future saint Liudger cured a blind Frisian called Bernlef, who sang "the deeds of the elders and the wars of the kings." A few scholars have tried to ascribe the Old Saxon biblical epic *Heliand* to this Frisian bard, who supposedly followed Liudger to the Saxon monastery of Werden, but this thesis has met with skepticism.

A limited number of rhyming poems have been preserved from the last two centuries of the Middle Ages. It is remarkable that all are characterized by outspoken ideological themes, which can roughly be reduced to two motifs: the sanctioning of the Frisian freedom and of the Frisian legal system. From a historical point of view the most interesting poem, known as *Fon alra Fresena fridome* (About the freedom of all Frisians), describes how Charlemagne bestowed freedom on all Frisians. Presumably, it is an adaptation in rhyming verse of the most significant document of Frisian freedom ideology, the spurious privilege Charlemagne was supposed to have granted to the Frisians. Another rhyming poem, of which there are two recensions, one called *Hoe dae Fresen toe fridom koemen* (How the Frisians came to freedom) and the other *Hoe dae Friesen Roem wonnen* (How the Frisians won Rome), extols the alleged exploits of the Frisians in their conquest of Rome, a task assigned to them by Charlemagne. The most voluminous rhyming poem (1671 lines) bears the rather obvious title *Thet Freske Riim* (The Frisian rhyme) and deals with the same imaginative history as well as with law. Alistair Campbell, the editor of this text, considers it to be an elaboration of the story about the liberation of the Frisians, as told in the so-called Book of Rudolf, a rather confusing legal text, part of which also consists of rhyming verse. In addition, there are some minor rhyming texts of comparable content. In all of these poems the rhyme is of a most primitive kind.

Special attention must be given to a prose narrative entitled *Fan dae koningen Kaerle ende Redbad* (About the kings Charles and Redbad). In the first part Charlemagne's claim to the conquered Frisian territories is explained as the outcome of a trial by ordeal with the Frisian king Redbad. Of particular interest is the second part, which contains an account of how law came to the Frisians. "King Charles" summons twelve *asegas* as representatives of the Frisians to tell him their laws. When they have declared themselves unable to do so, they are placed in a rudderless ship out of sight of land. Then a mysterious thirteenth *asega,* Christ himself, teaches them law, after which he leads them ashore using a golden axe as a rudder. Some scholars have interpreted this highly interesting account of the divine origin of Frisian law as pre-Christian, albeit in a Christianized form.

A fragment of a glossed psalter, thought to date from the twelfth century, ranks as the oldest specimen of Old Frisian literature. Like comparable glosses, the ones in this psalter were in all probability meant as a help for a monk in memorizing the Latin psalm texts. Although religious literature in Old Frisian is scarce, some short texts can yet be found in legal manuscripts, including a redaction of the decalogue, the fifteen signs of doomsday, Adam's creation, the seven things hateful to God, the five keys to wisdom, the seven fruits of the Mass, and the profit of confession. For the rest, special mention must be made of three wedding speeches, one of which shows characteristics of a sermon. Conspicuously absent in this domain are catechisms in the vernacular, translations of saints' lives, and Marian legends.

A few chronicles in Frisian, invariably short, have been preserved. Even though it is known that some others were lost, it is highly improbable that a rich vernacular chronicle tradition ever developed among the Frisians.

We do not know of any vernacular drama from medieval Friesland.

Finally, a song, known as *Buhske di Remmer* (Buhske the shepherd), deserves to be mentioned, even though it was recorded as late as 1691, remarkably enough in Harlingerland, one of the eastern territories, where the Frisian language was rapidly disappearing at the time. It is written in archaic language and most probably originates from the Middle Ages. Of this ballad, which was apparently sung accompanying a ring dance, eight out of the presumably twelve original stanzas have been preserved for posterity.

BIBLIOGRAPHY

GENERAL WORKS

Bremmer, Rolf H., Jr. *A Bibliographical Guide to Old Frisian Studies.* North-Western European Language Evolution, Supplement vol. 6. Odense, Denmark: Odense University Press, 1992.

Markey, Thomas L. *Frisian.* Trends in Linguistics 20. The Hague, Netherlands; New York: Mouton, 1981.

Munske, Horst Haider, et al., eds. *Handbuch des Friesischen/Handbook of Frisian Studies.* Tübingen, Germany: Max Niemeyer, 2001.

SOURCES

Buma, Wybren Jan, and Wilhelm Ebel, eds. *Altfriesische Rechtsquellen. Texte und Übersetzungen.* 6 vols. Göttingen, Germany: Musterschmidt, Vandenhoeck and Ruprecht, 1963–1977. This is a series, containing text editions with full translations in German.

Campbell, Alistair. *Thet Freske Riim [and] Tractatus Alvini.* The Hague, Netherlands: Martinus Nijhoff, 1952. Text edition without translation.

Fairbanks, Sydney, ed. *The Old West Frisian* Skeltana Riucht. Cambridge, Mass.: Harvard University Press, 1939. Text edition with full translation in English.

STUDIES

Borchling, Conrad. *Poesie und Humor im friesischen Recht.* Aurich, Germany: D. Friemann, 1908.

Krogmann, Willy. "Altfriesische Literatur." In *Kurzer Grundriß der germanischen Philologie bis 1500.* Edited by Ludwig Erich Schmitt. Volume 2: *Literaturgeschichte.* Berlin: de Gruyter and Co., 1971.

O'Donnell, Daniel. "The Spirit and the Letter: Literary Embellishment in Old Frisian Legal Texts." In *Approaches to Old Frisian Philology.* Edited by Rolf H. Bremmer Jr., Thomas S. B. Johnston, and Oebele Vries. Amsterdamer Beiträge zur älteren Germanistik, no. 49. Amsterdam; Atlanta, Ga.: Rodopi, 1998, 245–246.

Schwartz, Stephen P. *Poetry and Law in Germanic Myth.* Folklore Studies, no. 27. Berkeley: University of California Press, 1973.

Stanley, Eric G. "Alliterative Ornament and Alliterative Rhythmical Discourse in Old High German and Old Frisian Compared with Similar Manifestations in Old English." *Beiträge zur Geschichte der deutschen Sprache und Literatur* 106 (1984), 184–217.

Wearinga, Juw fon. "The Heliand and Bernlef." *Michigan Germanic Studies,* 12 (1986), 21–33.

OEBELE VRIES

[See also **DMA:** German Language; *Heliand;* Old High German Literature; **Supp:** Alliterative Literature.]

GENDER, THEORIES OF. Much scholarship in the late twentieth and early twenty-first centuries distinguishes between gender and sex as categories of analysis. Sex is a biological category (for example, the fact that females give birth and men do not is a sex difference), and gender is a cultural category (for example, the fact that women in many societies have closer relationships with their children than men do is a gender difference). The distinction between these two kinds of categories can be blurry. Some people would argue that nurturing behavior in women is hardwired in the brain, biological rather than cultural; on the other side, others would claim that our use of biology as a category of difference is itself cultural and that sex difference only has meaning within a given culture.

Medieval people sometimes located the difference between male and female or masculine and feminine in biology, sometimes in culture, but for the most part they did not concern themselves with distinguishing between the two. They wrote much more about the nature of difference than its origin. They most often discussed the nature of gender difference in the context of discussions of women. There was no need to explain why male human beings were the way they were because discussions of human beings generally were about males unless specified otherwise.

ORIGINS OF GENDER DIFFERENCE

When medieval authors did write about the origins of gender difference, they usually located it in God's act of creation. While woman's subordination because of her secondary creation was probably the most widespread explanation of the origins of gender difference, many authors—some of them women—claimed a special privilege for Eve because she was created from Adam's rib rather than from mud as he was. This did not outweigh the idea that woman was derivative of man but helped balance it to some degree. The leading thirteenth-century theologian Thomas Aquinas taught complementarity—that woman was not created from man's head to rule over him, nor from his foot to be his slave, but from his side to be his companion. This explanation of the creation was not original to Aquinas—it goes back at least to Hugh of St. Victor in the twelfth century and would have been familiar to all theologians because Peter Lombard used it in his theology textbook, *Sentences* (1155–1157). Aquinas adopted it despite his belief that woman was inferior to man and meant to be subordinate, which indicates that theological views were more complex than they sometimes seem.

The creation of Eve from Adam also led to the argument that because they were the same flesh, there was a fundamental unity in their natures. In the view of many authors, Eve's responsibility for the fall breached any unity, and women's subordination was also a punishment for sin. As the Vulgate (Latin Bible) translated Genesis 3:16, "You shall be under the power of the man, and he shall dominate you." Theologians explained the domination of women by men as a preventive as well as a punitive measure. Eve's temptation and transgression showed that women were weak and easily turned to evil; therefore men needed to control them. Eve was not the only model theologians used to speak of women, but she did represent for them the origin of gender difference.

Medieval medicine had different explanations for the origins of gender difference. Like exegetes, medical writers assumed that women were weaker and sought ways to explain this weakness. Also like exegetes, they did not always agree and have left us a great range of opinion. Many relied on Aristotle, who, adopting Hippocrates's doctrine of the four qualities (hot, cold, moist, and dry), considered warmth better than cold and women cooler than men. Women's coolness made them inferior and passive. Medical explanations of difference could also rely on the Adam and Eve story: according to the twelfth-century nun Hildegard of Bingen, men were strong and hard because they are made from the earth, women softer and weaker because they are made from man's flesh. The gender division of labor, too, she derived anatomically from the creation: man tills the earth because he is made from earth, woman bears children because her substance is lighter. In the thirteenth century Albertus Magnus argued that women's biological make-up was more humid than men's, and this led to women's inconstancy.

Aristotle and medieval authors who followed him held that men provided the seed in conception, and when that seed was weak, it produced female offspring. Other authors believed both male and female produced formative seed, and the sex of the fetus depended upon whether the seeds came together in a warm or a cold part of the uterus.

THE CRITIQUE OF WOMEN

Theologians discussed the nature of gender difference as well as its causes. A number of different strands ran through these writings, but they all relied on the idea that woman was weaker than man. They also agreed, however, that woman's soul was equal to man's and that men and women were both made in God's image. Augustine drew the distinction that men's bodies were made in the physical image of God, whereas women's souls, but not their bodies, were in God's image; the soul, however, was what really mattered. One Frankish church council in 585 did discuss the question of whether the Latin term "homo" (human being) included women but concluded that in fact it did.

Despite gender equality in the soul, belief in women's weaker nature led theologians and other medieval writers to a number of arguments about gender difference. Women were weaker morally and therefore prone to sin; they were weaker intellectually and therefore could not hold positions of leadership or trust. Women's weakness of will meant that they had to be under the control of men to prevent sin; their weakness of reason meant that they had to be under the control of men who could make decisions for them. As Aquinas explained, woman was to be subordinate not as a slave but as a child.

Justifications for masculine dominance did not always proceed logically from the premise that women were particularly prone to certain vices. For example, women were understood as seducers of men, both inadvertently and deliberately, and this was one reason why they could not be permitted to preach: they would arouse lustful thoughts in the men to whom they spoke. Yet, although women were considered more lustful than men, no one made an argument that men should not preach to women because they risked arousing the lust of their listeners.

While theological authors and medical authors discussed gender difference explicitly, many other genres of medieval writing assumed fundamental gender difference but kept it implicit. For example, exempla (stories collected for use in sermons) and other didactic texts depicted women as inconstant, idle, and lustful. They also criticized men, but not usually in their capacity as men: either men stood for the vices of all human beings or their vices were specific to their status or occupational group, as with avarice for merchants or pride for the aristocracy.

These didactic texts, in marking women as wicked or vicious in particular ways, drew on a set of misogynistic commonplaces from ancient and patristic sources. These commonplaces also found their way into literary works like Jean de Meun's *Roman de la Rose* (1275/1280) and Geoffrey Chaucer's *Canterbury Tales* (1387–1400). There they did not, however, go unchallenged. In the Wife of Bath's Prologue in the *Canterbury Tales,* the Wife challenges her husband's use of stories derogatory to women, charging that they were all written by men:

> By God, if women had written stories
> As clerks have in their oratories
> They would have written of men more
>   wickedness
> Than all the mark of Adam may redress.

It is not clear how seriously Chaucer meant this challenge to be taken: scholars have debated whether his audience would have accorded any validity to the Wife's viewpoint or whether she would have seemed merely ridiculous. In either case, Chaucer at least presented an interpretation of gender difference that argued that it was a deliberate creation of a masculine establishment. A variety of other medieval literary texts also challenged the dominant theories about gender roles through their depictions of complex female and male characters.

GENDER AND SANCTITY

Medieval writers did not consider all feminine traits negative. The Virgin Mary, the prime example of virtuous womanhood, embodied the positive feminine qualities of nurture (as the ubiquitous images of her nursing the Christ child and also less common images of her feeding others with her milk indicate), humility and obedience, and emotionality. Other holy women also presented these qualities. But so did holy men. Paintings showed Christ himself feeding people from the wound in his side just as Mary fed them from her breast; texts from the Cistercian order in particular referred to Jesus as a mother and also to the abbots within the order as mothers caring for their monks. Humility before God was the hallmark of all saints. One of the greatest holy men of the Middle Ages, Francis of Assisi, was known for his affective piety similar to that of many devout women.

Though holy men might display positive feminine traits, it was more common for holy women to be considered masculine, not by usurping men's prerogatives but by rejecting feminine vices. Indeed, since women were considered weaker, for a woman to behave virtuously might actually be more commendable than for a strong man to do so (and, some writers suggested, woman's sin might be more excusable because women were weaker and could not help it as much as men could).

In one sense, saints had no gender. Female saints lost the feminine qualities of a lustful body and a willful and inconstant mind; male saints lost the masculine qualities of pride and aggressiveness. Some scholars have suggested that monks in general—not only those who were saints—were a third gender within medieval culture because their vows of obedience put them in a subordinate position that was not part of the masculine gender norm. They have also made similar arguments about other groups who did not fit normative gender models: if it was a norm for women to be married, were single women a different gender? Medieval people, even if they spoke metaphorically of holy men and women transcending their sex, would have had little trouble classifying monks as men and nuns and other single women as women, even if they did not adhere to all the norms of their gender.

To a certain extent, then, medieval religion could elide gender difference or at least make that difference less hierarchical (masculine was not always necessarily better). Most of the time, however, the hierarchical evaluation of gender difference remained in place—perhaps inevitably in a culture that described God as a father and a son. The hierarchical evaluation remained present in other aspects of culture as well as the religious, with men's work more important than women's and men's legal rights more extensive than women's.

GENDER THEORY AND SOCIAL PRACTICE

As in other medieval discourses, the theory of gender underlying medieval law was implicit, but it was nevertheless ubiquitous. A fundamental principle of most medieval systems of law, surviving well into the twentieth century in Anglo-American legal systems, was that the law applied differentially by gender. In some regions women had more property rights than in others, but ev-

erywhere their property rights were different from (and less than) those of men. The law punished women and men differently for crimes, both those particularly related to their gender (like sexual offenses) and those that were not. That lands and titles were inherited preferentially through the male line in most places, for a number of ideological reasons—ancient tradition, the connection of land with military service, the idea that the father is the shaper of the child and the woman only the vessel—reveals the assumptions held in medieval society.

Even those who defended women—like Christine de Pizan (1363/64–ca. 1430), who argued that women's incapacity was due to a lack of education rather than a natural inability to do many of the tasks men did—still accepted the theory that because men and women were fundamentally different, it was permissible to treat them differently, and men more favorably. She defended historical or mythological queens like Semiramis but did not challenge the assumptions that allowed women to rule as queens only during the minority of their sons or (for a king's daughter) in the absence of brothers. She argued that women could be prudent and wise and could be trusted with estate management when their husbands were off at war, but she did not argue that women should control things equally with the men when the men were at home. Despite many challenges to negative depictions of femininity, medieval authors all accepted that there were fundamental differences between men and women and that, whatever the origins of these differences, they led inexorably to men's leadership in the family, the polity, and the church.

Theories of gender, of course, were only stories that people told in order to explain the way things were or should be. They were not strict definitions of roles into which society forced everyone to fit. Men who violated gender norms might be ridiculed and women sanctioned, but not always. Some women wielded power effectively and managed to maintain popularity and influence despite (or even because of) lack of conformity to theories about normal feminine behavior.

Norms about masculine and feminine roles did change over time during the course of the Middle Ages. The changes were not simple and linear because at any given time people held varying views on gender issues. A definitive change appears from the twelfth century on, however, when the critique of women received more emphasis. One reason is the enforcement of clerical celibacy, which entailed the writing of elaborate critiques of women and marriage aimed at the clergy but reaching a wider audience as well. The enforcement of clerical celibacy was part of a larger church reform movement in the eleventh and early twelfth centuries, which attempted to emphasize the power of the church and its independence from secular authority. With the church as a power center, lay kinship networks became less crucial, so women as links in the chain of inheritance were no longer so important. Furthermore, since churchmen did not derive their power and authority from military supremacy, they had to define themselves as masculine in other ways, which involved drawing stricter lines between masculine and feminine. The twelfth century also saw the beginnings of the movement of the locus of intellectual life out of the monastery and into the university. Earlier, monastic life was available to both men and women. Now women monastics came under stricter rules of enclosure, while at the same time the exclusively masculine universities deprived women of what opportunity they had to be intellectual leaders. The universities promulgated the teachings of Aristotle that reduced women to incomplete males with little role in reproduction. The institutional context for the discussion of theories of gender, implicit or explicit, became more and more a masculine space, and the theories that disadvantaged women became more prominent.

DEFENSES OF WOMEN

Especially during the later Middle Ages, theories of gender that made women inferior did not go unchallenged. Poems and other works in praise of women became more common in the thirteenth century, as did those that criticized women. In the fifteenth century, Christine de Pizan may have accepted the basic social hierarchy with men at the top, but she nevertheless argued that women were by no means men's inferiors morally and intellectually. If women are so fickle and inconstant, she asked, then why is it that men have to resort to such trickery to seduce them? Christine even defended Eve from the charge of deceit, claiming that she had no malice but was fooled by the serpent. At least some members of heretical groups like the Lollards in England and Hussites in Bohemia argued that women, being made as much in the image of God as men, had the same rights to preach.

All the defenses of women, all the challenges to misogynist critiques, still rested upon a substratum of concepts about gender difference that some scholars have called "structural antifeminism" and that most medieval people saw as the natural condition of things: that masculine and feminine were binary opposites, associated, respectively, with strength and weakness, reason and emotion, order and disorder. Even most of those who praised women valued them for their motherhood, their humility, and their peaceableness, rather than on the basis that they were just as capable as men.

BIBLIOGRAPHY

PRIMARY WORKS

Blamires, Alcuin, ed. *Woman Defamed and Woman Defended: An Anthology of Medieval Texts.* Oxford: Oxford University Press, 1992.

Chaucer, Geoffrey. *The Riverside Chaucer.* Edited by Larry D. Benson. 3d ed. Boston: Houghton Mifflin, 1987.

Christine de Pizan. *The Book of the City of Ladies.* Translated by Earl Jeffrey Richards. Rev. ed. New York: Persea Books, 1998.

SECONDARY WORKS

Beidler, Peter G., ed. *Geoffrey Chaucer: The Wife of Bath.* Boston: Bedford, 1996.

Blamires, Alcuin. *The Case for Women in Medieval Culture.* Oxford: Clarendon Press, 1997.

Børresen, Kari Elizabeth. *Subordination and Equivalence: The Nature and Role of Woman in Augustine and Thomas Aquinas.* Kampen, Netherlands: Kok Pharos, 1995.

Bynum, Caroline Walker. *Jesus as Mother: Studies in the Spirituality of the High Middle Ages.* Berkeley: University of California Press, 1982.

Cadden, Joan. *Meanings of Sex Difference in the Middle Ages: Medicine, Science, and Culture.* Cambridge, U.K.: Cambridge University Press, 1993.

Fenster, Thelma S., and Clare A. Lees, eds. *Gender and Debate from the Early Middle Ages to the Renaissance.* New York: Palgrave, 2002.

McNamara, JoAnn. "The 'Herrenfrage': The Restructuring of the Gender System, 1050–1150." In *Medieval Masculinities: Regarding Men in the Middle Ages.* Edited by Clare A. Lees, with Thelma Fenster and Jo Ann McNamara. Minneapolis: University of Minnesota Press, 1994.

Scott, Joan Wallach. *Gender and the Politics of History.* Rev. ed. New York: Columbia University Press, 1999.

Swanson, R. N. "Angels Incarnate: Clergy and Masculinity from Gregorian Reform to Reformation." In *Masculinity in Medieval Europe.* Edited by D. M. Hadley. New York: Longmans, 1999.

RUTH MAZO KARRAS

[See also **DMA:** Antifeminism; Aristotle in the Middle Ages; Celibacy; Christine de Pizan; **Supp:** Sexuality; Sexuality, Medical; Women.]

GENIUS is derived from the Latin *gignere,* to engender. Indeed, many words with the Indo-European root *gen* suggest engendering and begetting. In the ancient world, the concept of genius was associated with the worship of household spirits. Each individual person was thought to have a distinctive genius or spirit, as was each household and each state. Ancient cults surrounding rulers involved public worship of an emperor's genius or numen. Altars were dedicated to the genius of a ruler like Augustus. It was also believed that places of significance, like Rome, possessed a perpetual and sempiternal genius. In early Christian art, cities and provinces were sometimes depicted adorned with a nimbus or halo, representative of the place's seminal power.

The pagan genius or daemon did not entirely disappear during the Middle Ages. Neoplatonists perpetuated the classical notion that an individual's genius was his spiritual double, or higher self, whether good or bad, a concept that appears in the poetry of Spenser. The classical belief in genii survived in the popular medieval belief in angels and demons as well as in the allegorized and moralized figure of Genius in medieval literature. Medieval writers such as Bernard Silvester, Alan of Lille, Jean de Meun, and John Gower appropriated the allegorical figure of Genius from a wide range of classical and early Christian authors. In *De mundi universitate* (*ca.* 1145–1153), Bernard Silvester listed four orders of genii found in the cosmos: the genius that governs the fixed stars and planets, the genius that presides over the lower moist air, the intermediary genii that reside in the upper air, and the twin sexual genii found in the human genitalia. Synthesizing an array of classical concepts of genius, Bernard depicts every sphere of the universe as being inhabited by genii, all of which are somehow involved in the genesis and regeneration of human life.

Bernard's slightly later contemporary, Alan of Lille, suggested a close connection between genius and nature. Indeed, he labeled genius nature's priest and its "other self." In his poem *De planctu Naturae* (1160–1175), genius is personified by both a scribe and a priest. The roles of scribe and priest reflect the two principal ways in which the allegorical figure of Genius was understood during the Middle Ages. Like the scribe whose task it is to reproduce copies of manuscripts, genius was thought to be the spirit responsible for generation, just as Genius was considered in ancient Rome to be the god of generation. There is also a strong creative element in Genius the scribe, portrayed by Alan as an *artifex,* who creates both men and the *figurae* of art. Genius employs Venus, concupiscence, as his agent. Genius was symbolized as a priest because it was thought to be a tutelary spirit that acted as the intermediary between nature and man, just as a priest served as an intermediary between humans and God. According to Alan, genius was the agent of the natural descent of the soul into the underworld. As the priest of nature, Genius condemned and excommunicated all unnatural and immoral men who refused to obey nature's laws. Thus, genius represented a rational and moral authority for mankind.

A range of scholarly interpretations of the role of genius in Jean de Meun's (*ca.* 1240–1305) *Roman de la Rose* have been offered. According to some, Jean depicts genius as a false priest. Reason, not genius, was man's innate tutelary spirit. As a result of man's Fall, a schism had developed between genius and reason, meaning that genius no longer had jurisdiction over man's reason. Genius was unable to make moral distinctions and therefore held no moral authority. Indeed, after the Fall, genius represented man's natural and inherent concupiscence. In genius's eyes, everything desirable appeared good. In the eyes of other scholars, however, Jean de Meun portrays genius both as the cosmic priest of nature, responsible for men's souls, and the earthly bishop of God, responsible for men's bodies. In his capacity as the cosmic priest of nature, Genius directs generation in the chapel of forms. As the earthly bishop of God, he urges men to use their genii to reproduce and condemns the Christian virtue of chastity. Yet he also serves as a guide to the spiritual life and works to ensure that human reason controls the appetites.

In the fourteenth century, John Gower assimilated elements from both Alan of Lille and Jean de Meun in his poem *Confessio Amantis.* Gower described genius both as Venus's priest, who instructs Amans, the courtly lover, on how to temper his love, and as an orthodox priest, who instructs the lover on the seven deadly sins and serves as a teacher of virtue. In his capacity as priest, Genius repairs and renews the fallen Amans, reconciling his soul to his body. Thus, like in the *Roman de la Rose,* genius could be natural concupiscence, but it could also be reason and morality. Gower largely ignored Genius's traditional role as god of generation and instead focused on his tutelary role.

In addition to medieval literary uses of the allegorical figure of Genius, the terms *genius* and *ingenium* also began to denote something closer to the modern usage of the word. Peter Abelard, for instance, in *Historia calamitatum,* repeatedly referred to his own genius, or innate ability and intelligence. "Through genius," he wrote, "I grew up with a facility for literary discipline." Abelard recognized that he had been born with extraordinary mental abilities that could not be developed with practice. He admitted that his abilities in theology and philosophy were due to the sheer power of his natural intelligence, or genius, not to any training or hard work. It was the display of these extraordinary natural abilities that in the twelfth century made him the most famous man in world.

BIBLIOGRAPHY

Baker, Denise N. "The Priesthood of Genius: A Study of the Medieval Tradition." *Speculum* 51, no. 2 (April 1976): 277–291.

Chance, Jane. *The Genius Figure in Antiquity and the Middle Ages.* New York: Columbia University Press, 1975.

Economou, George D. "The Character Genius in Alan de Lille, Jean de Meun, and John Gower." *The Chaucer Review* 4, no. 3 (1970): 203–210.

———. *The Goddess Natura in Medieval Literature.* Notre Dame, Ind.: University of Notre Dame Press, 2002.

Fleming, John V. *The* Roman de la Rose: *A Study in Allegory and Iconography.* Princeton, N.J.: Princeton University Press, 1969.

Wetherbee, Winthrop. "The Theme of Imagination in Medieval Poetry and the Allegorical Figure 'Genius.'" *Medievalia et Humanistica,* n.s., 7 (1976): 45–64.

ADAM JEFFREY DAVIS

[See also **DMA:** Abelard, Peter; Alan of Lille; Bernard Silvester; Gower, John; *Roman de la Rose.*]

GHOSTS. "People who move their arms and hands from their sides when they walk about do great harm," Mengart de Pomiès repeated for Jacques Fournier, the bishop-inquisitor of Pamiers, in 1320, as a heretic had once warned her, "because by moving their arms about in such a way," thoughtless men and women "bump many souls of the dead [*animas deffunctorum*] to the ground." Neither Mengart de Pomiès nor Jacques Fournier thought it odd to believe that they lived in a world where the living and the dead, the visible and the invisible, overlapped and intersected. It is this question of the relationship between dead and living people, an intimacy often fluctuating between the demonic and the divine, the lucidity of dreams and the fog of waking, that can be defined as the realm of ghosts and ghostliness in the Middle Ages. Admittedly, ghostly phenomena went by a variety of terms; soul *(anima)* or spirit *(spiritus)* were the most common, but a ghost might also be a sensory illusion *(sensibili illusione),* a deadly thing *(funestus),* a shadow *(umbra),* a dead person with the "image of a body" *(effigiem corporis),* or a deceased relative who only "appeared in voice." Nevertheless, there was great precision (often sensual rather than spiritual) among the living about what they meant when they spoke of the wandering dead. What is intriguing about medieval ghosts is that while there are almost no references in the early Middle Ages, between the twelfth and fourteenth centuries there was an extraordinary cascade of ghostly stories, a veritable supernatural invasion of itinerant souls, so much so that a peasant woman and a Cistercian bishop-inquisitor could easily believe that a careless swing of the arm might knock one over.

Augustine of Hippo in the early fifth century intellectually framed the problem of ghosts in his treatises on the soul *(De quantitate animae)* and on free will *(De libero arbitrio),* and especially in a letter to Paulinus of Nola concerning the care to be given to the dead *(De cura pro mortuis gerenda; ca.* 421–424). Augustine argued that the spirits of the dead *(spiritus defunctorum)* had no reason to involve themselves with the living and that what might appear to be a dead friend or relative was merely the "semblance of the man" *(similitudo hominis).* It was neither a body nor a soul visiting a family member but the "image of a body" *(effigiem corporis)* seen "imaginarily" in the mind, and, crucially to Augustine, during dreaming. Yet with his usual subtlety Augustine added that he did not think it impossible for the dead to contact the living in dreams; in fact, he thought it quite likely. What worried him was that the dead were equally unaware that they were nothing more than images perceived in the dreams of the living. It was this remarkable quality of dreaming, with its ability to confuse persons alive and dead, to make each one think he was awake bodily and spiritually when they communicated, that made Augustine and his medieval successors wary of dreaming and concerned that what seemed vividly real to the living and dead was actually the false fantasy of a demon.

Alcher of Clairvaux, writing seven hundred years later in his *Liber de spiritu et anima,* was still thinking within the Augustinian intellectual framework concerning ghosts, but a great change had occurred. Apparitions were still the "semblances of things" *(similitudes rerum),* not bodies or souls themselves, and such visions still took place during dreaming. Yet, fascinatingly, the dead now for the first time were thought to dream about those they left behind and to be concerned about their lives. The dead themselves could not perceive what the living did, and in this sense life had become a remembered (ghostly) image for them, but they asked the newly deceased about the world, learning "what some have permission to reveal and what others need to hear." There was an infusion of physical sensation into the dead from the twelfth century onward, including a need to ask and hear, and an unraveling of the timelessness of dreaming to allow the ebb and flow of time from the world of life into the world of death, and vice versa. The problem of resemblances, images, and effigies remained, as did the fear of demonic corruption or possession, but ghosts were no longer just imaginative gossamer in dreams; they seem to have acquired, if not bodies, then a curious spiritual materiality.

In July 1211, a young man named William, who had died some days earlier in a street brawl, started visiting his eleven-year-old cousin at Beaucaire. At first the little girl was afraid, as her cousin appeared naked and covered in rags, but then she relaxed, and they started to talk. The girl's parents in the next room heard only their daughter's voice, and when they rushed to see what was happening, the lad disappeared. William returned seven days later (accompanied by a tiny horned demon that the girl quickly chased away), and, the girl's parents now convinced that a ghost was visiting their daughter, he made repeated apparitions. All of Beaucaire soon started to believe in the dead youth's return, and everyone was eager to talk to him. Only his virginal cousin could see or hear him, however, so all questions and answers went through her. Gervase of Tilbury recorded William's ghostly afterlife and many of the lad's answers in his *Otia imperialia* (Recreation for an emperor, *ca.* 1211). Gervase described William as an "image of a body" *(effigiem corporis),* but the dead youth unquestionably had a sensuality and physicality that interacted with the world—at one point the prior of Tarascon almost trod on his ghostly foot—and was outside the realm of dreaming. William talked about the horror of his death, the importance of purgatory for souls, guardian angels, the virtue of saints (St. Michael accompanied him once), the evil of Albigensian heretics, and many other things. Once he confessed his sins, he eventually entered purgatory, after stressing that all souls were briefly nomadic in this world.

The tale of William, so very orthodox in its narrative, helps illustrate why spirits began to populate the medieval landscape from the thirteenth century onward. Ghosts were proof of the continuity of life into death, evidence that what one did on earth completely affected one's future spiritual existence and that this sharp sense of linear identity, that the boy of ten was not only the man of thirty but also the soul in purgatory (or hell), was absolutely unbreakable. This profound awareness of how actions and thoughts made a life, so vital in the confessional culture developing from the late twelfth century onward, meant that all men and women would be, for however short a time, ghosts in the world.

BIBLIOGRAPHY

Caciola, Nancy. "Wraiths, Revenants and Ritual in Medieval Culture." *Past and Present* 152 (1996): 3–45.

Joynes, Andrew. *Medieval Ghost Stories.* Woodbridge, U.K.: Boydell and Brewer, 2003.

Lecouteux, Claude. *Fantômes et revenants au Moyen Âge.* Paris: Imago, 1986.

Schmitt, Jean-Claude. *Ghosts in the Middle Ages: The Living and the Dead in Medieval Society.* Translated by Teresa Lavender Fagan. Chicago: University of Chicago Press, 1998.

MARK GREGORY PEGG

[See also **DMA:** Augustine of Hippo, St.; Death and Burial, in Europe; Purgatory, Western Concept of; Visions; **Supp:** Demons; Hell, Concepts of; Soul and Body.]

GIOVANNI DA LEGNANO. See **See Johannes de Lignano.**

GNOSTICISM, deriving from Greek *gnosis,* meaning spiritual insight and knowledge, is a term embracing a variety of religious and philosophical ideas that developed among Christian and Jewish thinkers throughout the Mediterranean world during the second century A.D. Despite a diversity in doctrine, or rather a splintering of ideas among various teachers and their schools, the fundamental Gnostic assumption was that salvation could be achieved through techniques of spiritual introspection or by the radiant gift of esoteric revelation (from either Jesus or Paul and, occasionally, from Adam or his son Seth). The early-second-century Christian Gnostic teacher Valentinus taught that there were three categories of persons: spiritual, psychic, and fleshly. Those with *gnosis* were spiritual and so able to receive the revelation of marvelous knowledge that allowed for redemption. Psychic persons, such as Christians, possessed souls and could (through the exercise of free will) choose to rise higher and become spiritual. Fleshly and material individuals were those who moved down into corruption and were therefore unable to receive knowledge or salvation. All created matter was, in consequence, inherently evil and not made by the one true God. Valentinus argued that Jesus and Paul had revealed this cosmic dualism in the New Testament. Theodotus, a disciple of Valentinus, amplified this vision by observing, according to an extract collected by Clement of Alexandria in his *Stromateis* (Miscellanies), that *gnosis* gave insight into "who we were, and what we have become; where we were; . . . where we hasten; from what we are being released; what is birth; what is rebirth." In understanding all the relationships that made an individual life, in knowing the causes and effects that linked body and soul, in perceiving the divine harmony of masculine and feminine energy, a person was able to understand all relationships that had ever been and that ever would be and so, through such insight, achieve salvation. It is this dualistic emphasis on revealed knowledge to a redeemed elect and the fact that some medieval Catholic intellectuals saw the origins of twelfth- and thirteenth-century heresy in the Gnostic doctrines attacked by ancient Christian polemicists that have caused some scholars to mistakenly assume Gnostic continuities into the heresies of the Middle Ages.

Intriguingly, very few groups actually called themselves "Gnostics" in the ancient world, and despite the apparent adoption of the term by a handful of individuals (or so wrote Hippolytus of Rome and Clement of Alexandria), it was largely a sobriquet of contempt used by Roman intellectuals and Christian apologists. For instance, the third-century Neoplatonic philosopher Plotinus, according to his disciple and editor Porphyry of Tyre, composed a polemic attacking the Gnostics in which he dismissed their beliefs as deeply immoral, pompously superstitious, and irritatingly melodramatic. Christian apologists and theologians like Justin Martyr, Irenaeus of Lyons, and Tertullian viciously denounced any Christian in search of *gnosis* as a heretic. Irenaeus, in his five-volume *Adversus haereses* (Against heresies) from about 180 (also known as *The Refutation and Overthrow of Falsely So-Called Knowledge*) condemned all Gnostic thought as a corrupt exegesis on the Scriptures and a perversion of Christian teaching. In particular he argued against Valentinus and, while noting that this Gnostic teacher initially meant well, castigated all disciples of Valentinus as falling into "an abyss of madness and blasphemy against Christ."

Almost all modern scholarly knowledge of Gnosticism came from Irenaeus and to a lesser extent other ancient heresiologists until a remarkable discovery was made in 1945 near Nag Hammadi in Upper Egypt. A six-foot ceramic jar containing thirteen papyrus codices of Christian Gnostic manuscripts in Coptic was unearthed in a cemetery below Egypt's oldest monastery. One of the more fascinating codices from this Gnostic library is the Jung Codex (named for the psychoanalyst Carl Jung because it was bought by the Jung Foundation), which, in addition to four other treatises, includes the *Gospel of Truth,* a reassessment of the creation narrative of Genesis in light of Christ's arrival in the world that possesses the same name as a text attributed to Valentinus by Irenaeus. This Gnostic rethinking of the Genesis story, in which an impure God who created the universe was a lesser being than the pure God that Christ revealed, meant that the Hebrew Bible was unavoidably tainted with the decaying weight of fleshly ignorance. Such an intellectual vision has caused some scholars to wonder whether Gnosticism arose as a debate within Judaism. Certainly, for upright Jews, a terrible cosmic du-

alism overshadowed the daily conflict of flesh and spirit, in that body and soul, as his creation, both faced God together and would be judged accordingly. Salvation only came to the faithful not through the soul discarding the corrupting clay of the body but when a reluctance to accept the will of the Creator had finally melted away in the "heart," that is, when the hidden core of the self embraced the will of God. An evil inclination permeated the entire human person, "the yeast in the dough of our nature" according to the *Babylonian Talmud,* and this pervasive tendency to resist the will of God was not simply in the body alone. In this sense, some Jewish Gnostics were undoubtedly reacting to this "singleness of heart" through a radicalization of body and soul, through the entrapment of all evil tendencies in the weak flesh. Nevertheless, one should be wary of reducing an elaborate and diverse philosophical and religious teaching into idealist origins, and though well worth considering, such searches are as misleading as the hunt for precise influences from Persian, Greek, or Egyptian thought in Gnostic writings. This methodological tendency falsely presupposes that religions have an intellectual purity and theological coherence in which it is possible to neatly sift out other less coherent ideas.

This scholarly method, in the end, effectively ignores historical specificity and so makes an original religion or heresy, no matter how many different societies rose and fell through the decades, no matter how great the geographical and cultural differences, stay recognizably the same. It is this detection of what appear to be homologous ideas through time and space that has caused some historians to see Gnostic influences in medieval heresies from the late eleventh century until the sixteenth century. Admittedly, the Cistercian Hélinand of Froidmont in a sermon from around 1229, probably delivered at Toulouse, in which he argued against the rejection of Christ and Mary's humanity by contemporary Manichaean heretics, did, at one point, trace such a belief all the way back to Valentinus in the second century and then through Mani and finally to Mohammed. This past effort at explanation should not persuade modern scholars to adopt identical approaches. The most famous example of this idealist methodology can be found in scholarly discussions about the twelfth- and thirteenth-century Cathars—the heretics that Hélinand is usually assumed to be attacking and yet, like ancient Gnostics, a diverse heretical group that never seems to have used this name. The influence of Gnosticism upon the Middle Ages can, at best, only be discerned in Catholic intellectuals of the twelfth and thirteenth centuries reading early Christian authors in an effort at tracing the genealogy of heresy and, crucially, establishing that heretics were forever threatening and had ancient pasts.

BIBLIOGRAPHY

PRIMARY WORKS

Robinson, James M. *The Coptic Gnostic Library: A Complete Edition of the Nag Hammadi Codices.* 5 vols. Leiden: Brill, 2000. Edition of the codices with English translation, introduction, and notes.

SECONDARY WORKS

Lambert, Malcolm. *Medieval Heresy: Popular Movements from the Gregorian Reform to the Reformation.* 3rd ed. Oxford: Blackwell, 2002.

Pagels, Elaine. *The Gnostic Gospels.* New York: Random House, 1979.

Williams, Michael A. *Rethinking "Gnosticism": An Argument for Dismantling a Dubious Category.* Princeton, N.J.: Princeton University Press, 1996.

MARK GREGORY PEGG

[See also **DMA:** Cathars; Dualism; Heresies, Western European; Philosophy and Theology; **Supp:** Fall, The; Matter; Soul and Body.]

GODFREY OF BOUILLON (*ca.* 1058–1100), prominent crusader, ruler of Jerusalem. The second son of Eustace II of Boulogne and Ida of Bouillon, Godfrey inherited the county of Verdun and territory of Bouillon, as well as other lands, from his maternal uncle, Godfrey III, in 1076. Other claimants to the lands contested his rights, and Emperor Henry IV of Germany refused him the title of duke of Lorraine, held by his uncle, until 1087. Joining the First Crusade in 1096, Godfrey sold most of his lands to raise the money for the journey. He set out in August 1096, accompanied by his brother Baldwin. Like most crusaders, Godfrey took the land route through Hungary and the Byzantine Empire, arriving in Constantinople in December 1096, where the various crusader armies joined forces. He participated in the siege of Nicaea and the long march across Anatolia to Antioch. Godfrey was among the most prominent leaders; his wealth particularly allowed him to serve as patron to other crusaders. Godfrey gave his brother Baldwin troops to conquer Tarsus and then to conquer parts of northern Syria in 1097; when Baldwin subsequently became count of Edessa, he was then able to support Godfrey at Antioch.

Godfrey was among the leaders of the march to Jerusalem in June 1099, and after the six-week siege his troops were the first to enter the city on 15 July. A week later, the crusader leaders gathered to choose a new ruler for the city and elected Godfrey over Raymond IV, count of Toulouse. Godfrey was not crowned king, as it was thought by some to be sacrilegious to wear a crown of gold where Jesus wore a crown of thorns. He took instead the title of "advocate of the Holy Sepulcher," which in northern Europe signified a lay defender of a church.

After defending Jerusalem against a Fatimid invasion on 12 August 1099, the majority of crusaders returned home, leaving Godfrey with approximately 300 knights and 2,000 foot soldiers to defend Jerusalem, Bethlehem, and Jaffa. The arrival of the papal legate Daimbert of Pisa with a large fleet in the fall of 1099 was both a curse and a blessing. The aid of the Pisan fleet would allow Godfrey to conquer more of the important coastal cities, such as Caesarea, but Daimbert's help came at a price. Backed by Bohemond of Antioch, Daimbert demanded to be elected patriarch of Jerusalem. Godfrey acceded, and the following Easter (1100) he and Daimbert came to an agreement that Jerusalem and Jaffa belonged to the patriarchate but that Godfrey would rule the two cities until he conquered two others, with Daimbert's help, to replace them. Godfrey died on 18 July 1100 before conquering any further cities, and his followers held Jerusalem against Daimbert for Godfrey's brother, Baldwin of Edessa.

Although he ruled the Holy Land for only a year, Godfrey was quickly remembered as the crusader par excellence. He figured prominently in the Old French Crusade Cycle and was considered one of the Nine Worthies (chivalric heroes from pagan, Old Testament, and Chistian times).

BIBLIOGRAPHY

Andressohn, John C. *The Ancestry and Life of Godfrey of Bouillon.* Bloomington: Indiana University Publications, 1947.

Aubé, Pierre. *Godefroy de Bouillon.* Paris: Fayard, 1985.

Murray, Alan V. "The Army of Godfrey of Bouillon, 1096–1099: Structure and Dynamics of a Contigent on the First Crusade." *Revue belge de philologie et d'histoire* 70 (1992): 301–329.

Waeger, Gerhart. *Gottfried von Bouillon in der Historiographie.* Zurich: Fretz und Wasmuth, 1969.

CHRISTOPHER HATCH MACEVITT

[See also **DMA:** Baldwin I of Jerusalem; Crusade, Concept of; Crusades and Crusader States.]

GODRIC OF FINCHALE, ST. (*ca.* 1070–1170), the English holy man, was born to a poor family in an undetermined village in Norfolk or Lincolnshire. After many years of trading, sailing, and pilgrimage, he turned to the ascetic life, settling eventually as a hermit at Finchale, (pronounced "finkle") near Durham. According to Reginald, the monk of Durham Cathedral Priory who wrote Godric's *Vita,* when Godric died, he had been a hermit at Finchale for sixty years and was over a hundred years old. Reginald's chronology may be exaggerated, but even the most conservative calculation gives Godric a life span in the nineties. Reginald's descriptions of Godric's life as a merchant have been regularly used by twentieth-century historians describing the twelfth-century economy. For Reginald the labor and danger of the seafaring mercantile life went some way toward redeeming Godric's profession. The hagiographer nonetheless makes it clear that the exchange of luxury goods was far inferior to the exchange of penitence and grace between God and Godric in his life as a hermit.

Like many other ascetics of the eleventh and twelfth centuries, Godric embarked on a life as a hermit without any of the traditional training as a Benedictine monk. From around 1110 he lived as a hermit for short periods in various places in northern England and visited ascetics in the Holy Land, until he secured the permission of Bishop Ranulf Flambard (*r.* 1099–1128) to live at Finchale. Reginald describes Godric's asceticism as extreme in some periods of his life. At Finchale he was known for wearing a hair shirt and a suit of chain mail, a combination that was common among many other twelfth-century ascetics.

Godric's connection with Durham Cathedral Priory began between 1138 and 1149 and was formalized after 1149. Thus Godric was over sixty years old and had been at Finchale for at least twenty years before he was brought within the confines of traditional monastic authority. He was visited by many people, including local peasants, devout laymen and women, monks from Durham Priory, and also Cistercians, such as Ailred of Rievaulx. His mother, brother, and sister also visited him at Finchale, and Burchwine, his sister, lived with him as an ascetic for some time before her death.

Although Godric remained a layman, Reginald says he preached "with the erudition of a cleric" to the many poor people who came to speak to him. Probably during his time as a merchant, Godric learned French, and later, perhaps while serving in a church at Durham before becoming a hermit, he acquired some understanding of Latin. As a hermit, Godric wrote and sang his own lyrics in English in praise of the Virgin Mary. These, with a score, are an integral part of Reginald's manuscript of the *Vita Godrici.* Godric was also known for his stories of wild men and other mythical creatures of the forest. Like many twelfth-century holy men, he straddled the divide between the world of rural folklore and the scriptural culture of educated monks. Godric's miraculous conjunction of the holy and the rustic is a recurring theme in Reginald's *Life.* Among the many miracles attributed to Godric during his lifetime, there are an unusual number that concern his control over and protection of animals. Other miracles involve his healing and feeding of local people and monastic friends. The cult that developed around Finchale after his death was local in character and based mainly on healing miracles.

BIBLIOGRAPHY

Lawrence, Clifford Hugh. *Medieval Monasticism: Forms of Religious Life in Western Europe in the Middle Ages.* London: Longman, 1984. A standard work.

Reginald of Durham. *Libellus de Vita et Miraculis S. Godrici, Heremitae de Finchale.* Edited by Joseph Stephenson. Surtees Society, 20. London: Nichols, 1845.

DOMINIC D. ALEXANDER

[See also **DMA:** Monasticism.]

GOMES EANES DE ZURARA. See **Zurara, Gomes Eanes de.**

GOSCELIN OF ST. BERTIN (*ca.* 1040–after 1114) was a prolific hagiographer, celebrated by William of Malmesbury as "second only to Bede in the celebration of England's saints." He wrote a work of spiritual guidance, *Liber confortatorius* (The book of encouragement), produced more than thirty hagiographical works covering the lives, miracles, and translations of some twenty-five English saints, and composed music and liturgical texts for the offices of several of these saints.

Educated at the monastery of St. Bertin at St. Omer, Flanders, he came to England a few years before the Norman Conquest to take up a post in the household of Herman, bishop of Sherborne (1058–1078). He probably served the bishop as a secretary, but he is also thought to have been a chaplain to the nuns of the nearby convent of Wilton. But with the appointment of Osmund, the first Norman bishop of the diocese, in 1078, Goscelin found that his skills were no longer in demand. Compelled to leave the diocese by what he called "viperous jealousy and stepfatherly barbarity," he became an itinerant hagiographer. In the 1080s and 1090s, he was often to be found writing in defense of ecclesiastics and religious communities threatened by the actions of the foreign elite that was then taking control of the English church. In his works for the nuns of Barking, for example, he defended the English abbess Ælfgyva, who was in conflict with Maurice, the first Norman bishop of London (1086–1107). It was during this phase of his career that Goscelin wrote *Liber confortatorius.* Constructed as a letter and addressed to Eve, a former nun of Wilton Abbey who had left England and become a recluse living on the Île de Chalonnes near Angers, this literary tour de force sets out a spiritual program for religious women founded on a belief in their spiritual fortitude, while also exploring the subjects of exile and loss.

It is often suggested that Goscelin was given a permanent refuge at St. Augustine's Abbey, Canterbury, around 1091 when the abbey's saints were translated to the new church that Abbots Scolland and Wido had built. An account of these translations, *Historia translationis S. Augustini* (History of the translation of St. Augustine), forms the centerpiece of the monumental cycle of hagiographical and liturgical texts that he produced for the monastery, a cycle that is aptly seen as the culmination of a lifetime's training in the art of hagiography. But *Historia translationis* cannot have been completed until after 1099, as it mentions the foundation of the Kingdom of Jerusalem. It was certainly finished by 1109, but Goscelin was still at work on the cycle in 1114, for he mentions Ralph, archbishop of Canterbury from that year, in one of its unprinted components, *Libellus de adventu beati Adriani abbatis in Angliam* (A book about the coming of the blessed abbot Adrian to England; Goscelin of St. Bertin, 248v.). It seems likely that St. Augustine's recruited the jobbing hagiographer during the long vacancy that preceded the appointment of Abbot Hugh de Flori (Hugh of Fleury, 1108/1109–1126), during which, with royal support, the monks brought a case contesting the archbishop's right to consecrate their abbot-elect before the altar of his cathedral. Significantly, the cycle gives considerable support both to the abbey's purported rights of exemption and to King Henry I's position in the English round of the investiture dispute, a conflict that reached its peak in the period from 1103 to 1107.

BIBLIOGRAPHY

Barlow, Frank, ed. and trans. *The Life of King Edward Who Rests in Westminster / Attributed to a Monk of St. Bertin.* 2d ed. Oxford: Clarendon Press; New York: Oxford University Press, 1992. Appendix C sets out the standard biography.

Colker, M. L. "Texts of Jocelyn of Canterbury Which Relate to the History of Barking Abbey." *Studia Monastica* 7 (1965): 383–460.

Goscelin of St. Bertin. *Libellus de adventu beati Adriani abbatis in Angliam.* London: British Library, MS Cotton Vespasian B.XX, fol. 233r–248v.

Hayward, Paul A. "Translation-Narratives in Post-Conquest Hagiography and English Resistance to the Norman Conquest." *Anglo-Norman Studies* 21 (1999): 67–93.

———. "An Absent Father: Eadmer, Goscelin, and the Cult of St. Peter, the First Abbot of St. Augustine's Abbey, Canterbury." *The Journal of Medieval History* 29 (2003).

Sharpe, Richard. "Words and Music by Goscelin of Canterbury." *Early Music* 19, no. 1 (1991): 94–97.

———. *A Handlist of the Latin Writers of Great Britain and Ireland before 1540.* Turnhout, Belgium: Brepols, 1997. Lists the canon of Goscelin's works on page 395.

Talbot, C. H. "The *Liber confortatorius* of Goscelin of St. Bertin." *Studia Anselmiana* 37 (1955): 1–117. Edits this key text.

Wilmart, André. "Eve et Goscelin." *Revue Bénédictine* 46 (1934): 414–438, and 50 (1938): 42–83.

PAUL ANTONY HAYWARD

[See also **DMA:** Anglo-Norman Literature; Canterbury; Hagiography, Middle English; Investiture and Investiture Conflict.]

GOTHIC ARCHITECTURE

PROBLEMS OF CLASSIFICATION

In telling the story of medieval architecture, historians have divided the one-thousand-year period into manageable chapters, or phases. The epithets applied to the first chapters are historically generated: Early Christian, Byzantine, Early Medieval, Merovingian, Carolingian, Ottonian. The last two epithets, however, are problematic: "Romanesque" and "Gothic." "Romanesque," coined in the early nineteenth century and associated, by general consensus, with the revival of monumental architecture between the eleventh and mid-twelfth centuries, paradoxically assigns a historicizing agenda based upon similitude (round arches look "Roman") to what was seen at the time as radical newness—the transfiguration of the landscape through a white cloak of churches, signifying a powerful program of Christian regeneration (Bizzarro, 1992; Nichols, 1983).

Richly paradoxical, also, is the term assigned to the following period, from the mid-twelfth to the fifteenth century and later: "Gothic." Recent scholarship (see Rowland, 1998; also, Frankl, 1959) has documented the disapproval of Northern culture fostered around 1500 by Italian humanists for whom "Gothic" or "Germanic" was synonymous with rustic, or barbaric. Raphael, in his famous 1519 letter to Pope Leo X, derided the kind of architecture that, he claimed, resulted from the tying together of branches from forest trees to create forms akin to pointed arches—but admitted that it could not be altogether bad, since it was derived from Nature, the only legitimate inspiration for all art.

Students may be troubled by the apparent absurdity of naming a twelfth-to-fifteenth-century architectural phenomenon after fifth-century Germanic invaders (Goths) of the Roman Empire—invaders who had fostered no stone architecture. Yet despite attempts to find an alternative ("Saracenic," "Ogival," "Pointed," "French," "German") "Gothic" has stuck. Indeed, with its power to collapse time, linking form with alleged function and ethnic roots, this epithet powerfully (if allegorically) conveys essential aspects of the phenomenon described. Mid-twelfth-century buildings featured elements of the classical order that pointed emphatically to the past. The construction of such buildings was powered by a renewal and extension of the mission of the Catholic church accompanied by intense interest in the agency of the saints (Denis, Nicasius, Remigius, and so on) who in the period of the late Roman Empire and Migrations had first brought Christianity to the North.

Disregarding, for the moment, the art historian's tiresome habit of first imposing, then bickering over a system of classification (see Gombrich, 1966), it can be argued that the term "Gothic" should be retained for its usefulness in conveying a recognizable (although variable) set of forms—pointed arches, rib vaults, and intensely linear articulation, together with (but not always) flying buttresses and skeletal system—developed under a definable set of historical circumstances in the North. Recent scholarship, however, has emphasized the astonishing variety of edifices (barns, halls, civic buildings, and so on) erected in the period under discussion (see Coldstream, 2002). Even among ecclesiastical buildings, regional variations led to very different outcomes; in France, for example, thin supports and vertical elongation contrasted with the thick walls and horizontality characteristic of England.

Rather than insisting, then, upon a unified product, it is useful to emphasize aspects of process. This process involved intensified communications between builders in the contiguous countries of western Europe, where Italy provided critical elements of a historicizing architectural language and where France, England, and Germany provided a vital transformative creative forum. What we call "style" can thus be understood as human interaction within a kind of architectural supraregionalism (Warnke, 1976). The process was powered not just by the search for beauty, appropriateness, structural efficacy, and sheer size but by overlapping agendas that were

potentially in conflict: the reassertion of the centralized power of the Catholic church and the stirrings of national, local, or urban identity (particularly in France and England). Localized traditionalism or revivals complicated the situation; in some of the great churches of twelfth-century "Germany," for example, builders continued to draw upon the largely unarticulated interior forms and complex massing of Ottonian architecture.

The architectural language of Italy provided the classical orders (columns with their bases and foliate capitals); the great basilica, with its (sometimes double) aisles and transept; and the annular crypt. Such forms conveyed the authority of the Roman church and at the same time referred to the great churches (like St.-Étienne in Paris) built under the Merovingian dynasty—the first firmly established political entity in the post-Roman Gothic North (Krautheimer, 1942; Clark, 1992). Such forms might also be employed in heavy buildings with no aspirations to the structural revolution associated with "Gothic."

The structural speculations of mid-twelfth-century French builders provided a central theme in the interactions described above. In the Île-de-France and surrounding areas the use of the cylindrical column in "Early Gothic" (see St.-Denis; Notre Dame of Paris; Laon, and so on) created a distinctly historicizing flavor but also brought potential problems. Such columns (particularly monoliths) were hard to obtain or manufacture and imposed sharp limitations upon structural developments. The combination in a building of slender columns and a tall upper elevation with the masonry (ribbed) vaulting fashionable in the North was risky: the vault might push the thin envelope outward. The most compelling narrative of "Gothic" represents the phenomenon as a solution to the dangerous combination of the masonry vault with slender supports (see Bony, 1983).

The solution involved the extension of the external buttresses as lateral struts set transverse-wise to the body of the basilica. Projected vertically these pylons supported exposed arches springing over the aisle(s) or gallery to support high-level vaults.

This was a radical break with the past: a kind of modernism or paradigm shift (Kuhn, 1970; Trachtenberg, 1991). Freed from the real business of supporting the superstructure, internal elements of the classical orders could become more slender, denying any fixed relationship between diameter and height. Columns could be transformed into colonnettes: not one, but many, in an infinite variety of configurations, extended from floor to high vaults in a coherent bay system. The resultant architecture of illusionism was in sharp contrast to the blocky functional "modernism" of the exterior. And it was modernism that triumphed, as direct reference to the classical orders progressively weakened and a linear grid became established, free from structural demands and thus subject to endless modification.

Thirteenth-century masons drew freely upon Nature in their creation of the foliate capitals and stringcourses that sprout from cathedrals like Amiens or, in England, Southwell (Murray, 1996; Pevsner, 1945). The freedom to attenuate and extend the classical orders that had, in theory, originally been derived from Nature allowed Northern builders to push their language back to its natural origins: a process accelerated in the fifteenth century as the sinuous forms of Late Gothic sprouted into branches, twigs, and leaves. In this way Gothic buildings projected the illusion of a growth or development that was based upon principles seemingly drawn from Nature (Crossley, 1992; Bechmann, 1981; Chenu, 1968).

THE MEANS OF PRODUCTION

While a great variety of economic circumstances lay behind the production of the tens of thousands of Gothic buildings—barns, halls, and urban structures, as well as churches and castles—there are important common factors. The sheer number of edifices, coupled with their considerable size, testifies to the substantial resources of the builders, while the forms of those edifices bear witness to continuing refinement in the business of working the principal raw materials, stone and wood (Kimpel and Suckale, 1985).

Mid-twelfth-century ecclesiastical administrators realized more fully the potential of their holdings of lands and rights to produce a revenue surplus. New methods of centralized administration and techniques of agrarian exploitation increased the flow of agrarian products necessary to sustain growing urban populations engaged in industrial or commercial activities (Duby, 1962). The economic muscle that powered the building boom resulted in part from the rapid increase in the price of grain. And towns with their fiscal, mercantile, and industrial activities provided revenues through whatever urban rights a bishop or abbot might possess. These funds might be supplemented by gifts from local seigneurial families or even the king. Rural folk of the diocese also played a substantial role in providing funds for cathedral construction (Murray, 1987).

Thus, from the mid-twelfth to the mid-thirteenth centuries cathedrals and abbeys were in receipt of an unprecedented flow of cash. Yet they simultaneously faced growing resentment on the part of the secular aristocracy, as well as the townsfolk or bourgeois, whose communal liberties might enjoy the protection of the king. The arrival of the mendicants in the early thirteenth century further undermined the power of the secular clergy. But it was, above all, the growing power of the king that ended the period of economic surpluses in the hands of the clergy. By the 1240s the king of France, driven by his crusading ambitions, was able to levy heavy taxation upon the northern cities and dioceses that had produced cathedrals like the ones in Soissons, Rheims, Amiens, and Beauvais (Jordan, 1979). If a northern French cathedral had not been completed by the later thirteenth century, it was likely that it would remain incomplete until the late fifteenth or beyond—this is not a stylistic issue, but an economic one.

Secular lords, rather than funding religious buildings, might translate their wealth into lavish accommodations or military activities, including the construction of castles (Mesqui, 1991–1993). Historians have sought stylistic linkages between ecclesiastical and secular architectural production. It is certainly true that a twin-towered church façade might resemble a castle gateway or the ribbed vaulting or foliate capitals of a castle chapel or that a great hall might appear "Gothic." But more important than this, we can associate the process of producing castles (or barns, halls, or civic buildings, for that matter) with the construction of Gothic churches. In each case we are dealing with the visible expression of dominion through the dissemination of (relatively) look-alike structures over the land. The success of the Norman Conquest of England resulted both from the reshaping of the English church through the construction of mighty urban cathedrals and from the rapid construction of hundreds of castles to secure the land. The process of construction, coupled with newly gained wealth from the land, facilitated technological advancements that allowed the earth-and-timber motte-and-bailey castle to be replaced by the formidable stone *donjon*. Continuing antagonism between Capetians and Anglo-Normans as well as a mass of local tensions resulted in a revolution in castle design that preceded and accompanied the "Gothic" revolution in church building. Innovations included changes in the overall shape of the castle, which increasingly incorporated curved shapes; the integration of concentric walls with towers; and projecting passages at the top of the wall (machicolations). And the need to construct ashlar walls at the increased height necessary to resist assault through escalation or missiles projected by siege machines like the trebuchet promoted a new concern with the stiffening of tall masonry structures through the application of deeper buttresses or curved

Fig. 1. Château Gaillard. *This Norman castle of the 1190s shows traces of the new techniques that would lead to the full Gothic.* THE CONWAY LIBRARY, COURTAULD INSTITUTE OF ART. REPRODUCED BY PERMISSION.

surfaces. The resultant army of well-trained masons was able to produce huge quantities of precisely cut ashlar masonry and to work closely with a patron whose ideas about an unbuilt edifice might be unconventional. Such was the case with the military engineer who worked with King Richard I (the Lionhearted) of England (*r.* 1189–1199) in the creation of the unusual forms of Château Gaillard, Normandy, (fig. 1) in the 1190s, just as the Gothic cathedral of Chartres was getting under way. The new creativity was based upon a combination of invention and standardization. Standardization was inherent in the castle-building program of King Philip II Augustus of France (*r.* 1179–1223), whose administration developed a template for the form of the edifice as well as the financial and logistical infrastructure (Baldwin, 1986). Such standardization of form was equally inherent in the massive building program of the Cistercian Order in the twelfth and thirteenth centuries (Kinder, 2002).

The construction of city walls in northern France in the 1180s and 1190s fostered huge numbers of qualified masons. Basic manual work was performed by local men, while elite masters with their companions moved from city to city, escaping the regulation of professional guilds (plasterers, carpenters, and so on). They mystified their métier and even in some instances, it seems, cloaked their identities as "Saracens" (Bechmann, 1991). By the later Middle Ages, especially in Germany, well-defined professional organizations both fostered and stymied creativity.

THE MEANS OF REPRESENTATION

The complexity of the program of meaning of the Gothic cathedral extended well beyond that of the castle. Forms and meanings may be "explained," to some extent, through reference to liturgical requirements. While the sacraments and the divine office can be celebrated in almost any kind of space, the aisled basilica expressed the distinction between corporate liturgy (performed in the choir's central vessel) and the private devotional use of altars and chapels (placed in the aisles), between laity (gathered in the nave) and clergy (whose space was the liturgical choir, often extending west of the crossing and surrounded by screens). The role of the church as a mediator between living and dead and increased attention to purgatory brought the assignment of chantry chapels, typically adjoining the nave or functioning as shrines incorporated into the main space (Le Goff, 1981).

Emphasis upon the cult of saints led to the standardization of a type of church (already found in Romanesque) that featured a complex east end, in which a curved ambulatory encircling the hemicycle allowed access to the shrines of the saints. The principal saint's shrine was often set in the choir's main vessel behind the main altar contiguous with the ambulatory. One of the most stunning achievements of French Gothic was the spatial integration of choir, ambulatory, and chapels to form a unified crown of light in which the rectangular body of the church gives way to radial geometry with a center pointing to the principal altar or saint's shrine (fig. 2). Bells and towers, often named after saints, projected the presence of the local church, as well as an urban identity, outward into the surrounding countryside.

Our search for meaning should be extended to the very substance of the edifice. Stone signifies Christ's role as the cornerstone and Peter's as the rock upon which the church was built. Just as the Eucharistic wine and bread bear physical resemblance to blood and flesh, so the role of the cathedral as a vehicle of salvation is conveyed by its physical resemblance to the boat—Noah's Ark—in which Noah and his family were delivered from the Flood. The cathedral, with its rounded choir (*chevet; coiffe:* "head") and its transept and nave, resembles the body of Christ (Neagley, 1997). The somatic quality of the envelope is reflected by the designation "rib" vaults. Columns (and to a lesser extent, piers) have an anthropomorphic character: the multiple elements of the cathedral represent the community of the Apostles, prophets,

Fig. 2. St.-Denis Retrochoir. *The columns, symbolizing the twelve apostles, and the unprecedented windows helped transform the old shrine into an entirely new architectural form.* THE CONWAY LIBRARY, COURTAULD INSTITUTE OF ART. REPRODUCED BY PERMISSION.

and saints upon whom the church/Church is built (Onians, 1988). But the most powerful mimetic metaphor was the image of the Celestial City. The arcades and lateral walls may be considered as the street façades; the twin-towered entrance as the fortified city gate (Sedlmayr, 1950). Such thoughts are buttressed not only by St. Augustine of Hippo's *City of God* but also by the specific references made in cathedral design to the image

of the celestial city seen by St. John the Evangelist—a vision described in Revelation 21, a chapter often used as a reading during consecration (Stookey, 1969). Thus, as Heaven was seen to be perfectly square, square schematism is a most important part of design in medieval architecture.

Other meanings were not generated mimetically. Although one may sense that the edifice results from an overall forming matrix, the geometric codes are only available to the intelligence through systematic measurement and analysis (Wu, 2002; Davis et al., 2000). The underlying ratio of the cathedral's elements allowed it to provide an image of the cosmos (Chenu, 1968). That the cathedral, as container of the sacramental body of Christ, is a type of Virgin Mary, is an insight available to the intelligence and the heart but not through the observance of similitude.

Attempts to explain the Gothic cathedral as an image of the transcendent have fared badly recently as Simson (1956) and Panofsky (1946) have come under energetic attack (see Kidson, 1987). Both authors tended to simplify and perhaps exaggerate the extent to which the forms of the Gothic cathedral should be understood in relation to Neoplatonic theories of the emanation of light, which pictured light as descending through orders of archangels and angels and understood it as a palpable sign of the beneficence of God. Panofsky saw Abbot Suger of St.-Denis (1081–1151), with his preoccupation with brightness, as one who funneled the light theories of the Pseudo-Dionysius into the forms of his church—this conception seemed to make particular sense owing to Suger's mistaken identification of the Pseudo-Dionysius with St. Denis, the Apostle of the Gauls and patron of Suger's church.

The notion of transcendence provides only partial understanding of the meaning of the Gothic cathedral, which was a physical and institutional entity rooted in local soil and dependent upon the material means of production (Erlande-Brandenburg, 1989). Construction was deeply embroiled in local politics. Critics like Peter the Chanter (d. 1197) of Notre Dame of Paris believed that such massive undertakings should not be entertained at all (Baldwin, 1970). Indeed, in what was intended as a transcendent sign, local people might have found oppression. The upper bourgeois of Beauvais, in revolt against a bishop who was bankrupt after seven years of cathedral construction, accused that bishop of taxing them excessively and wrongly (Murray, 1989). A citizen of Amiens in the 1230s might have viewed the Gothic cathedral, then under construction, as a symbol of local pride and collaboration between clergy and townsfolk. His counterpart in Rheims, however, might see that city's cathedral as a sign of the oppressive power of the archbishop with whom the townsfolk were locked in violent conflict (Branner, 1961).

Meanings can be appropriated and may shift over time. While Gothic architecture was invented within a framework dominated by agents of the Catholic church, within a century the power of Gothic had been appropri-ated by kings like Louis IX of France (r. 1226–1270) and Henry III of England (1207–1272) and was associated with the image of the city (Paris or London) and, by extension, the nation. Thus Burkard of Hall, the first writer to provide a descriptive epithet, called Gothic style "French Work" (see Mortet and Deschamps). This association between Gothic style and national identity endured, as can be seen in the restoration of Gothic edifices and the emergence of the neo-Gothic in nineteenth-century England, Germany, and (to a lesser extent) France.

TIMES AND PLACES

We should first recognize the limits inherent in any attempt to represent or explain the construction of thousands of complex edifices, where multiple interactions might take place, where local circumstances continued to change, and where multiple levels of meaning were susceptible to shifting over time (Grodecki, 1976; Bony, 1983; Wilson, 1990; Toman, 1999; Binding, 1999; and Coldstream, 2002, all provide recent surveys). Such limits lead to various simplistic tropes. "Gothic" style is defined through the characteristics of a "mature" specimen (the Amiens nave or Soissons choir) and then its "development" or "evolution" is tracked, creating the myth of inevitability, or entelechy. One is left with the uncanny image of Gothic as preexistent in the mind of a transcendent creator in the spirit of Plato's *Timaeus* or one of the twelfth-century commentaries on that text (Chenu, 1968). Regional variations are then assessed in relation to that "transcendent" (French) prototype—the trope has hardened thanks to the deeply ingrained art historical use of juxtaposed slides to define what a thing is through contrast with what it is not. Then, "Gothic" is sometimes represented geographically with a flight of arrows emanating from cities in and around the Île-de-France, purporting to depict the "spread" or "triumph" of Gothic. It is as if buildings could move over the land like armies or as if "style" spread like a contagious disease. Such metaphors have outlived their usefulness, and the story of Gothic should be retold with language that conceptualizes the forces behind Gothic in terms of human interactions and agency.

The extraordinary productivity and creativity of twelfth-century builders from the Loire to the Rhine has achieved universal recognition. It was not just the beauty of the forms of the new buildings and the facility of their production but their ability to project levels of meaning or ideological agendas that rendered them compelling. The attention of builders in the countries surrounding France (now recognized in the form of the modern states

Spain, Italy, Germany, and so on) turned inward, reversing the direction of the conventional arrows on the map. In some cases a mason experienced in the new architecture might be hired in Germany or England precisely for his ability to deliver the shock of the new to those accustomed to older or local forms—this can be seen, for example, with William of Sens (*fl.* late twelfth century) at Canterbury. In other cases masons from peripheral areas might travel and work in sites in France to gain understanding of the new architecture. Patrons also traveled—although Henry III, king of England, wanted to move the Ste.-Chapelle physically from Paris to London, he desired the French royal chapel for what it signified as much as for the thing itself. The force behind whatever unity we find in Gothic should be understood as multiple human interactions, bringing a process of continuing mnemonic contraction and expansion as existing buildings were compressed into ideas and images brought to the table in the debates among patron, mason, and logistical agent; as these images were tested through graphic renderings; and, finally, as the image of the unbuilt edifice was realized through the means of production (Bucher, 1976; Carruthers, 1990; 1998). A bishop might say: "I want my church to look like Rheims Cathedral . . . but I don't like the darkness of the middle level: find a way of making it brighter." Such critical response provided the force of "change" that powered the "modernism" of Gothic.

We may now stop apologizing for the creative role played by French builders in this period and rescind the victim status commonly claimed for the builders of the surrounding areas, who did not passively "receive" French Gothic forms but who were themselves actively engaged in appropriating and transforming to serve local agendas. On the other hand, it must also be recognized that the forms of Gothic could be exploited by French conquerors to signify their new domination: for example, in southern France and southern Italy (Bruzelius, 1991). Nonetheless, in the supraregional exchanges of "Gothic," French architectural solutions were in later periods supplemented and overwhelmed by images generated elsewhere—particularly in England and the countries of central Europe.

France. It is principally to the economic and political circumstances sketched above that one should turn in order to understand the significance of the architectural creativity of the area in and around the Île-de-France. Had the Plantagenets created an Atlantic empire with its cultural heart in the west of France, would we have seen the standardization, mass production, and dominance of a very different type of building—one

with domed square bays like the nave of Fontevrault? Compared with Burgundy, Normandy, and the Auvergne, the Île-de-France and the immediately surrounding areas were not home to a great Romanesque architectural tradition. The creative forum resulted from the ambition of ecclesiastical leaders (Abbot Suger of St.-Denis provides a perfectly appropriate illustration) to link the fortunes of their monastery or cathedral with the newly energized Catholic church and the growing power of France's Capetian monarchy. Coupled with these ambitions was the economic muscle resulting from the church's newly profitable estates and from commercial and industrial activities aimed at subsidizing its building program.

It has often been suggested that the early deployment of ribbed vaults in this area supplied the technological and visual catalyst to stimulate the invention of the "new style." Critics from the French rational tradition (e.g., Viollet-le-Duc, 1858–1870) considered the development to be structurally driven; Frankl, on the other hand, emphasized the aesthetic integration of rib and interior articulation (see Frankl, 1959). However, ribbed vaults may be found at earlier dates in Romanesque Durham, in northern Italy, or in the Rhineland, as well as in distant Islamic and Roman prototypes—yet their presence in these other environments did not stimulate a dynamic series of architectural speculations. Ribbed vaults were certainly an essential element of the new architecture. The reduced amount of precisely constructed wooden formwork needed for these thin canopies of stone rendered ribbed vaults desirable within the rationalized and accelerated production processes described above. The projecting ribs relieved the visual monotony of the concave interior surfaces of the vaults, allowing them to be pulled into closer visual relationships with the moldings and colonnettes that provided the illusionistic articulation of the elevation (fig. 2). But it was, above all, the reduction of the physical weight of the stone canopy (compared with older, thicker barrel or groin vaults) that made the units attractive to builders who wanted to work with thin supporting walls and supports (Bony, 1983).

The mid-twelfth-century reconstruction of the abbey church of St.-Denis has traditional pride of place in the story of Gothic. Abbot Suger was an indefatigable storyteller—the tales of St. Denis he told his fellow monks served as a preparation for his two written accounts on the new church in the books on the Consecration and Administration. These accounts provide more information on a "Gothic" construction program than does any contemporary written work with the exception of the *Chronicle* written by Gervase of Canterbury, who served as the cathedral's official historian from 1163 to 1210 (Panofsky, 1946). Suger recognized that words could lend authority and fix the meaning of visual forms intended to project the centrality of his monastery in the identity of France—these words included the inscriptions placed at strategic points in his church. Beyond the realm of myth, however, the architectural forms of the new construction suggest that this was, indeed, a place where critical architectural solutions were reached in the middle years of the twelfth century: solutions that led to radical change in the way churches were conceived and built (see Kuhn, 1970, for a discussion of this "paradigm shift").

The twin-towered western frontispiece (fig. 3; mid-1130s to 1140) of the abbey church of St.-Denis announced the importance of interactions with churches in Normandy (see, for example, St.-Étienne in Caen). New, however, were the syncopated horizontality, the emphasis upon triplets in major and minor forms (echoing the Trinity), and the concentration of figurative sculpture on three portals to create a systematic program glorifying the Last Judgment (a new subject), the Apostles of Gaul, and (probably) the Virgin Mary. The frontispiece included upstairs chapels—the one behind the central rose window dedicated to the Virgin Mary, St. Michael, and other saints—in a semi-independent western block connected with the extended nave of the older church. Windows to the lowest level lit a narthex whose newfangled rib vaults were awkwardly integrated with elaborately articulated interior supports.

The builders of St.-Denis then constructed a new retrochoir (1140–1144) beyond the old liturgical choir to glorify the shrine of the Apostles of Gaul—St. Denis (Dionysius), St. Rusticus, and St. Eleutherius (fig. 2). What appears to us as the striking novelty of the work may have resulted, to some extent, from the experiments of Parisian churches with the combination of lightweight structure and ribbed vaults, seen also in the choirs of St.-Martin-des-Champs and St.-Pierre-de-Montmartre. Suger's construction project was also, of course, the renovation of an older church and must be understood in relation to that older church—a precious relic from the reign of King Dagobert (r. 629–639), consecrated through a miraculous appearance of Christ himself. Both old and new were brightly illuminated: the old nave with light-reflective surfaces and painted walls and the new with light penetrating through colored glass in windows of unprecedented size. The use of columns in the new church made reference to the great basilicas of early Christian Rome as well as to the early medieval nave. The anthropomorphic associations of the column al-

lowed the central shrine of the Apostles of Gaul to be symbolically surrounded by the Twelve Apostles and by the Minor Prophets represented by the columns of the choir arcade and the intermediary supports of the double ambulatory. Despite its modest 33-foot (ten-meter) span, the new retrochoir had an expansive double ambulatory (this was a pilgrimage church) supported upon slender columns opening widely into a continuous crown of radiating chapels. Between the chapels are deeply projecting buttresses carrying the uprights of flying buttresses supporting the upper choir built a century later (1231). The existence of these externalized supports, coupled with the abbot's story of a violent windstorm that threatened to shake down certain high-level arches that had been decentered and left exposed to the weather, suggests that this was one of the very first combinations of externalized support (pylons from which flying buttresses sprang over the double ambulatory), lightweight stone canopies, and slender internal articulation featuring the classical column. That this was a dangerously experimental edifice where the builders advanced into an unknown architectural domain is confirmed by the fact that it failed and was rebuilt (after 1231).

Gothic did not "develop" because of transcendent visions whose elements were revealed bit-by-bit until the final, perfect product was realized. Rather, pressing local problems, an abundance of resources, and close collaboration between ambitious patrons and resourceful masons produced a sudden paradigm shift. We might privilege St.-Denis excessively in telling the story—but this is because it has survived relatively intact, together with its written records, providing the raw material for the critical illustrative case study. In the retrochoir of St.-Denis (fig. 2), then, the new paradigm led to an elevated and brilliantly lit central vessel surrounded by elegant columns freed, to some extent, from their supporting role by the astonishing new feature of the composition—slender arches springing from pylons neatly integrated between the chapels and overarching the double ambulatory to support a high rib vault of lightweight construction.

The shrine of the saints was thus elevated in an innovative architectural envelope that was essentially an inverted lantern and backlit by light entering through the faceted windows of the crown of radiating chapels (Grant, 1992). Backlighting enhanced the illusionistic effect of a dematerialization or flattening out of substance.

The circumstances surrounding such a breakthrough might involve not only collaboration but also rivalry. Suger, a showman, delighted in the many dignitaries who attended his flashy consecration ceremonies —among them the king himself, who assisted in the ceremonial laying of the foundation of the new retrochoir. While Suger sought universal recognition of the preeminence of St. Denis the man as patron of France and of St.-Denis the building as the premier monastery of the realm, his posturing likely produced resentment and competitiveness. The gathered prelates did not take blueprints of St.-Denis back to their monasteries and cathedrals, but they did take a desire not just to emulate but also to do better.

Perhaps the most intriguing edifice at the threshold of Gothic is Sens Cathedral, which was rebuilt (starting around 1140) under Archbishop Henri de Sanglier. The forms of Sens Cathedral are sometimes represented in terms of a dialogue with St.-Denis— though this should be understood more in terms of our *representation* of the problem rather than actual interactions. Sens Cathedral began with a premise in the heavy forms of Burgundian Romanesque (as in the north lateral chapel, and early work on the ambulatory): St.-Denis with its lightweight nave and cylindrical columns that imposed themselves upon the new work. The former embodies a plan with no transept and a wide (fifty-two-foot/sixteen-meter) central span; the central span of the latter was limited (thirty-three feet/ten meters), with a transept inherited from the original building. The former incorporated a monumental support system with a main arcade composed of ponderous compound piers deeply projecting into the interior space and alternating with substantial double columns. The almost-square double bays of Sens Cathedral are crowned with sexpartite rib vaulting, while at St.-Denis slender columns and thin walls were topped with (presumably) quadripartite vaults. In each case, however, the builders looked to the Roman past, and each combined lightweight rib vaults with the new structural system with exposed flyers; each had a three-story elevation with a small triforium in the middle. Each was rebuilt a century or so after completion: at Sens, the clerestory windows were enlarged and the high vaults modified.

Certain subsequent buildings stand in undeniably close relationship with the abbey church of St.-Denis— as can be seen especially with the frontispiece and shallow choir chapels of the new Notre Dame Cathedral in Senlis (begun *ca.* 1150). The Senlis elevation, however, is firmly "Romanesque," with references to Norman prototypes. The new choir of the Parisian abbey of St.-Germain-des-Prés (*ca.* 1145–1163), with its three-story elevation, cylindrical columns, and (probably) flying buttresses, clearly belongs to the same community.

Fig. 3. Abbey Church of St.-Denis, Paris. *The facade, dating from the 1130s, is the earliest instance of many Gothic characteristics.* THE CONWAY LIBRARY, COURTAULD INSTITUTE OF ART. REPRODUCED BY PERMISSION.

Some of the new construction projects initiated in the mid-twelfth century may actually have had chronological precedence over St.-Denis—the dates of the choirs of Noyon Cathedral and the Benedictine abbey church of St.-Germer-de-Fly, each with a crown of shallow chapels, have proved elusive. Similar features in such buildings, particularly rib vaults and a four-story elevation, reflect the existence of a community of builders, including both clerics and master masons who moved easily from site to site.

Notre Dame of Paris, begun around 1160, occupies a pivotal position in the history of Gothic architecture (Murray, 1989). With its sexpartite ribbed vaults more than a hundred feet above the pavement, Notre Dame brought dramatic upscaling. Such an ambitious project should be understood in part as an architectural manifesto intended to counter challenges to the metropolitan cathedral inherent both in the growing power of the monarchy and in the pretensions of the great abbey churches in Paris and the immediate surroundings—St.-Martin-des-Champs, St.-Germain-des-Prés, and, above all, St.-Denis, with its claim to be the premier monastery of

France. The builders of Notre Dame resolved the problem of supporting high-level vaults over a double-aisled basilica (like the St.-Denis retrochoir) through the disposition of deeply projecting pylons throwing long-reach flyers (about thirty-six feet/eleven meters) clear over double aisles and gallery to support the tall central vessel without charging the slender intermediary aisle piers. In the thirteenth century the four-story elevation (arcade, gallery, triforium, small clerestory) was changed to three stories with the extension of the clerestory window to occupy the upper two levels of the elevation.

The original four-storied elevation of the Cathedral of Notre Dame allowed this great cathedral to find its place in a group of structures of similar design, including the Tournai nave (1110), St.-Germer-de-Fly (1130/60), Noyon (1130/50), Laon (begun *ca.* 1160), the Soissons south transept (*ca.* 1176), the nave of Rouen (*ca.* 1200), and Meaux (*ca.* 1200), as well as the destroyed abbey of Notre-Dame-la-Grande in Valenciennes (1170s), Notre-Dame-en-Vaux in Châlons-sur-Marne (1150s–1180), and the choirs of St.-Remi of Rheims (1178–1180) and Montier-en-Der (*ca.* 1190–1200). The idea of the galleried elevation could have been derived from Norman prototypes, from the so-called pilgrimage churches or from Germany (i.e., Essen Minster or the Palatine Chapel in Aachen), which had itself borrowed the concept from Italo-Byzantine sources. Whether there was a common agenda behind the galleried elevation remains open to question. In some cases particular liturgical functions can be associated with the existence of a gallery: antiphonal singing of the Divine Office, special veneration for particular saints, or Easter liturgy, for example. In some cases (Durham; St.-Germer-de-Fly; Laon), a masonry spur hidden under the gallery roof may have provided extra stiffening for the upper wall, facilitating the construction of a taller edifice (Gardner, 1982). The comments of the *Pilgrim's Guide* about Santiago de Compostela provide the best explanation—the existence of a gallery lent additional beauty and prestige to the edifice and enhanced its affect upon the visitor (Gerson, 1998). The four-storied type certainly brought forth an astonishing variety of plans (from Laon, with its expansive transept and stubby original choir, to Paris, with its nonprojecting transept and generous choir, to Noyon, with its round-ended transept arms), and to consider such constructions as a kind of tightly unified "family" dependent upon a single "progenitor" would be a mistake. We are dealing, rather, with a community of patrons and masons in which ideas found easy circulation but multiple options remained available.

It is too easy to represent a procession of buildings in which the four-story galleried elevation is "replaced" by the "new" three-story structure. Chartres Cathedral (1194–*ca.* 1230) has traditionally had pride of place in this kind of simplification. Three-story designs were, of course, common in Romanesque (e.g., La Trinité at Caen, Cluny III, Paray-le-Monial) and continued to be built in the second half of the twelfth century (see the choir of St.-Germain-des-Prés in Paris, Sens Cathedral, St.-Yved-de-Braine, and the abbey church at Orbais). But it is certainly true that in the 1190s the builders in two great cathedral projects initiated construction of a new kind of structure with no gallery and a lofty superstructure supported on sturdy flying buttresses leaving substantial structural equipment outside. Because of the stunning beauty of Chartres, as well as its state of (near) completion, its extensive programs of sculpture and glass, the availability of a firm starting point (the 1194 fire), and the excellent press generated by admiring art historians, the cathedral has been represented by some as the fulfillment of all the promise inherent in the first generation of Gothic construction and the fountainhead of all that was to come (see Bony, 1983).

The study of Notre Dame, Cathedral of Soissons, provides a useful antidote to this misconceived scenario (Sandron, 1998). The four-story south transept had been under construction from the 1170s. It now seems that work began on the three-story choir earlier than had been thought, by the 1190s. Soissons is in the heartland of Gothic, and its stonework bears witness to a high level of rationalization. Chartres, on the other hand, in the wheat fields of the Beauce, where there was little industrial and only local commercial activity, was located well outside the area where the great early experiments had taken place. Its masonry, while beautiful to look at, does not conform to the new level of rationalization associated with edifices in the Île-de-France and Picardy (Kimpel and Suckale, 1985).

Yet the monumental three-story elevation of Chartres, featuring enormous clerestory windows matching the height of the arcade; the cathedral's beautiful piers, which combine a central columnar core with four colonnettes placed on the cardinal axes (*piliers cantonnés*) and subtle alternation of round and octagonal; and the wonderfully ponderous external structural equipment, with its wagon-wheel flying buttresses—all this has exercised an inordinate seductive power over the modern public (but perhaps to a lesser extent over twelfth-to-thirteenth-century contemporaries). The idea of a series of edifices (Rheims, Amiens, Beauvais, and so on) as "classic" cathedrals built in the image of Chartres can no longer be sustained (Jantzen, 1962).

Bourges Cathedral, on the other hand, nearly contemporaneous with Chartres but less well known to the general public, has fascinated the specialized world of architectural historians. Chartres is conservatively overbuilt; the five-aisled pyramidal structure of Bourges, however, pushes the Gothic structural envelope to its limits. Chartres conveys impressive spaciousness through its enormous clerestory; the designers of Bourges, on the other hand, realized that the visitor could be overwhelmed more effectively through greater spaciousness at arcade level. Bourges thus has slender, widely spaced piers and a tall main arcade with relatively small clerestories. Lateral vistas allow the beholder to sense the ambiguity of an envelope that can be read as a three- or five-story composition. Spatial elision is also achieved by the sexpartite vaulting that creates double-bay units and by the supports whose rounded contour continues from the floor all the way to the high vaults. The Gothic reconstruction of Bourges may actually have begun well before the 1195 date traditionally assigned for the start of work. The unusual forms resulted from a creative partnership between masons familiar with recent developments to the north (the Soissonais) and clerical organizers who were interested in Notre Dame of Paris (as reflected in the double aisles and smooth external mass), as well as in the pyramidal massing of Cluny III and Old St. Peters in Rome. The contrast between Chartres and Bourges provides a powerful reminder that the forms of the great Gothic cathedral were not bound by the need to emulate some canonic prototype or by functional or iconographic requirements.

With Soissons, Chartres, and Bourges (1190s) we reach the crescendo of French cathedral construction sometimes called "High Gothic." Gothic reconstruction of Rheims Cathedral began after a fire in 1210; in Amiens work began after a fire in 1220, while in Beauvais, home to the tallest French cathedral, it commenced in 1225. We tend now to emphasize the wide range of sources drawn upon by the builders of these great cathedrals, while also recognizing references to Soissons in the designs of Rheims and Amiens. Cistercian churches (e.g., Longpont, Royaumont) played an important role in the background of Amiens and Beauvais. These years also saw very important construction in the west of France (Angers, Poitiers, and so on) and in Normandy (Le Mans, Coutances, Bayeux, and so on)

In the following phase (beginning in the 1230s) interior articulation became thinner, and the linear forms of window tracery (first used in a large-scale context with the Rheims choir, *ca.* 1211) give a phase of design often termed "Rayonnant"—after the radiating spokes of the giant rose window characteristic of this period (see, for example, St.-Denis and the transept of Notre Dame of Paris). Major monuments include the abbey church of St.-Nicaise of Rheims (*ca.* 1231); the upper choir, transept, and nave of St.-Denis (1231); the upper choir of Troyes Cathedral (after 1228); the transept of Notre Dame (1240s–1260s); the upper choir of Beauvais (1250–1260s); the choir of Amiens (1250s); the Ste.-Chapelle in Paris (*ca.* 1241–1248); and, a little later, the collegiate church of St.-Urbain, Troyes (1260s). We begin to know some of our masons by name (e.g., Jean de Chelles, Pierre de Montreuil, Renault de Cormont, Jean des Champs).

The forms of "Rayonnant" exercised an enormous power of attraction in the surrounding areas. The small-scale, linear elements of this phase of Gothic production—cusped arches surmounted by gables, together with the elements of window tracery design (trefoils, quatrefoils, quinquefoils, and so on)—were very easily rendered in graphic form on paper and parchment: in other words, they traveled easily, creating a common language, or *koine*. It is from this period (the 1230s) that we have the remarkable images drawn by Villard de Honnecourt and the drawings of the so-called Rheims Palimpsest (see Bechmann, 1991). Such sketches, probably derived from project drawings, provided the means by which the ambition of King Henry III could be achieved and the Ste.-Chapelle could be brought from Paris to London—not as an actual building, but as a mnemonic entity supplemented by graphic images.

This is the framework by which we should understand the production of Gothic edifices in central and southern France, among them those churches associated with Jean des Champs: Clermont-Ferrand (1248–1280), St.-Just in Narbonne (begun in 1272), St.-Nazaire in Carcassone (begun in 1269), and St.-Étienne in Limoges (begun in 1273) (Freigang, 1992). The triumph of orthodoxy over the Albigensian heretics led to the rapid expansion of the power of the North over the South. In this situation we find not only the direct importing of ideas that owed their origins to the so-called Rayonnant architecture of the North but also the generation of a quite different kind of edifice with a higher degree of interior spatial unity. The church of the Jacobins in Toulouse (1240–1260s) features a unified interior with a central line of tall cylindrical supports culminating in the spectacular fan of ribs generated by the easternmost column at the base of the apse. In the cathedral of Ste.-Cécile at Albi (under way by the 1270s), the lateral struts necessary to support the high rib vaults were internalized, creating a succession of discrete pockets of space.

Ste.-Cécile belongs to a group of southern buildings (St.-Bertrand-de-Comminges, Béziers, Perpignan, and Mirepoix) whose enhanced spatial unity seems to indicate links with some of the extraordinary buildings of Catalonian Spain (e.g., the cathedrals of Barcelona and Gerona, discussed below).

England. The economic and social infrastructure of England was different from that of France: the dynamic link between agrarian productivity and urban growth, with its concomitant commercial and industrial activities, was less developed and the total population (especially urban) was smaller. The English church had been reorganized after the Norman Conquest through the creation of urban diocesan centers, often centered on a massive late-eleventh- or early-twelfth-century cathedral (sometimes combined with a Benedictine monastery). Whereas France saw an increasing concentration of power in the hands of the king, the twelfth and thirteenth centuries saw a succession of threats to the English monarchy.

English bishops led the way in the more efficient administration of estates and, like their counterparts in France, saw an increasing flow of cash from their more-efficiently worked land. The textile cities of northern France and Flanders consumed increasing quantities of English wool.

If "Gothic" is defined principally in terms of the early exploitation of rib vaults and the intensely articulated interior, then twelfth-century England was at the fore. Durham Cathedral (begun 1093) has the first datable rib vaults in the North. The massive walls of cathedrals like Ely or Norwich stimulated a rich play upon the elements of articulation: compound piers with multiple colonnettes, the torus, or roll molding, marking the edge of the multiple orders of the arcade, the diaphanous effects to be achieved by passageways running in the thickness of the wall. In the context of secular cathedrals articulated with a wealth of forms that might appear almost riotous, the arrival of the Cistercians and the construction of great abbey churches like Kirkstall, Furness, Roche, and Byland contributed some of the purposeful, structural look of Gothic. Important also was mid-twelfth-century work at York Minster and Ripon.

It was at Canterbury that the story of English Gothic, understood as enhanced communication with France, really begins. The cathedral/monastery church had been rebuilt at the end of the eleventh century under Archbishop Lanfranc of Bec (*d.* 1089), and the choir rebuilt in the early twelfth century. This was the choir that burned in 1174, four years after the martyrdom of St. Thomas Becket (1118–1170). Thanks to the chronicle of Gervase of Canterbury we have an extraordinarily complete account of the fire and the subsequent reconstruction. Masons from different regions had offered their services, yet a Frenchman, William of Sens, was chosen. Was this cultural imperialism on the part of the French—the "spread" of Gothic across the Channel? No, the choice of William of Sens allowed the clergy of Canterbury to achieve their own objectives. Above all, William offered them a kind of edifice that was different from other English churches—this was, after all, the principal church in England, established by St. Augustine.

William of Sens was able to take charge of the logistical requirements of the new project, procuring the necessary stone from Caen, in Normandy, and designing appropriate equipment. Despite pointing in certain respects to Sens, the construction of Canterbury Cathedral drew upon a wide range of prototypes, from the churches of northeast France to Rheims, tempering this "otherness" with the use of English Purbeck marble for the colonnettes. The clerestory passage allows us to link Canterbury with Geneva and Lausanne. It is intriguing to note that the Frenchness of the developing edifice was maintained even after William of Sens fell from the scaffolding and was replaced by William the Englishman, who deployed low-slung flying buttresses and the double columns of Sens Cathedral. St.-Denis provided a prototype for Canterbury's retro-choir, which featured a lantern shrine for the tomb of the local saint.

We can track the subsequent development of English Gothic partly in terms of the influence of Canterbury Cathedral (as with, for example, Lincoln Cathedral, where the early work after 1192 draws directly upon the structural and decorative forms of Canterbury but introduces some spectacular new features such as the Y-shaped rib vault) and partly in terms of the general popularity of the colonnette detached from the body of the wall (the so-called *en délit* shaft) and of the use of Purbeck marble. Another group of cathedrals (e.g., Wells or Salisbury; see fig. 4) is considered more emphatically "English," in its emphasis on horizontality and relatively thick, richly articulated walls. Although English masons did not pursue the vertical emphasis favored by their French colleagues, they were quick to exploit the decorative potential of the rib vault (e.g., the lierne vaults in the Lincoln nave) and window tracery.

The term "Episcopal Style" has been proposed to describe English Gothic of the early thirteenth century (see Brieger, 1957). This is a useful expression since it conveys interaction within a group of prelates who shared common goals, particularly increased efficiency in

Fig. 4. Salisbury Cathedral. *The English style gradually diverged from French models. Note the thick, richly articulated walls and horizontal extension.* THE CONWAY LIBRARY, COURTAULD INSTITUTE OF ART. REPRODUCED BY PERMISSION.

the exploitation of their estates and opposition to the foreign advisers of Kings John and Henry III. Episcopal style projected Englishness, even as it paradoxically drew from the common stock of French forms.

It is therefore not surprising that King Henry III—seeking to counter the growing popularity of Thomas Becket through the promotion of a cult of the sainted king Edward the Confessor (*r.* 1005–1066)—should favor a master mason familiar with French prototypes, particularly those buildings that conveyed the divinely

ordained power of French monarchy (Binski, 1995). The Frenchness of Westminster Abbey (from 1245) was not the result of some haphazard chemistry of regional "influences" but draws quite deliberately upon Rheims Cathedral (the coronation church), Amiens (a royal favorite), the Ste.-Chapelle (Louis IX's personal chapel), and Royaumont (the king's favorite Cistercian monastery). With its ambulatory and radiating chapels, its enhanced verticality and bristling flying buttresses, Westminster Abbey must have seemed to contemporary

Englishmen aggressively—even offensively—French. The royal abbey introduced a new lavishness of surface decoration as well as window tracery—elements that English masons elaborated within the framework of the sumptuous architecture of the second part of the thirteenth century, built in what is often called the "Decorated Style." Key monuments of this phase include the choir of Old St. Paul's Cathedral (begun in 1258) and the Angel Choir of Lincoln Cathedral (1256–1280).

Germany. Twelfth-century ecclesiastical architecture in Germany, or more correctly, the Holy Roman Empire, continued to be dominated by an imperial tradition that looked back to Carolingian and Ottonian sources and typically featured thick walls, unarticulated frontal surfaces, and complex exterior massing, often with multiple towers. Close contact with Lombardy led to the appearance of ribbed vaults in the twelfth century (e.g., Mainz Cathedral, *ca.* 1137), but their deployment failed to provoke an energetic structural reappraisal, and German builders continued to favor the frank expression of structure with large expanses of flat wall and unmolded arcades.

Rhenish churches demonstrated a range of contacts with Switzerland and Burgundy as well as France. Elevations were often three-storied, with a gallery (as in Basel) or triforium (as in Bonn) and alternating systems of support featuring bay systems arranged in squarish modules—which could be covered with domed-up vaults, as we find in Münster Cathedral (*ca.* 1225–1264; perhaps inspired by models in the west of France); sexpartite vaults, as in St. Apostolen in Cologne; or quadripartite ribbed vaults, as at Bamberg (after 1211, completed 1237). It is clear that whereas the builders of French Gothic initiated a continuing and dynamic series of structural speculations, their colleagues in Germany returned to favored prototypes: Laon Cathedral exercised a particular attraction—as can be seen with the western towers of Bamberg and the four-story elevation of Limbourg an der Lahn (*ca.* 1190–1200).

In the 1230s a more direct set of interactions with France began as German builders started to seek the kind of lightness and intense linear play that typified the work of their French colleagues. The Liebfraukirche in Trier (1236/1237–1274) is a centralized structure whose designers had studied the east end of the church of St.-Yved-de-Braine, with its diagonal chapels. The supports at Trier are derived from the *piliers cantonnés* of Rheims. The nave of Strasbourg Cathedral (*ca.* 1240–1275) is a speculation on the forms of the nave of St.-Denis. The Strasbourg façade, known not only from the actual building but also from the project drawings in the Musée

de l'Oeuvre, takes to an extreme the metallic brittleness of the Rayonnant design of works like the Notre Dame of Paris transept or the transept of St.-Urbain, Troyes. The two-story elevation of the nave of Freiburg Münster (begun *ca.* 1250) also responds directly to French prototypes.

This trend reached a crescendo in the design of Cologne Cathedral, begun in 1248 by Archbishop Konrad von Hochstaden. The plan of the choir with its seven shallow, radiating chapels is astonishingly close to Beauvais, and it is hard to see the height of the finished choir (156 feet/47.5 meters) as expressing anything other than the desire to surpass the tallest French cathedral. In the forms of the choir we find a combination of elements that could have been derived directly from the project drawings of Amiens, Beauvais, or St.-Denis. The Cistercian church of Altenberg, close to Cologne, also drew upon the French Cistercian abbey of Royaumont.

As far as the future of German Gothic architecture was concerned, the most significant monument of this period may perhaps be the church of St. Elisabeth at Marburg (fig. 5; begun 1235). While the form of the supports and other elements of the design were derived from French prototypes, the envelope is formed of three vessels the same height, producing a laterally expansive interior quite different from the east-west channeling of space that results from a tall clerestory with flying buttresses. The so-called hall church, not particularly popular in France (except in the west), was to give German designers the characteristic form that would dominate architectural production in the later Middle Ages.

German builders placed more emphasis upon massive towers than their colleagues in France. In some cases (e.g., Strasbourg, mid-to-late fourteenth century), tower construction may reflect the direct control of the municipality. The beautiful openwork west tower of Freiburg-im-Breisgau, added to the nave around 1280, initiated a sequence of such constructions, including the plan of the Cologne west towers (*ca.* 1300), Vienna (*ca.* 1370–1433), and the mighty Ulm (begun in 1392).

Italy. Italy was home to powerful architectural traditions resulting from the continuing attraction of Early Christian basilicas like Old St. Peter's in Rome, the presence of the Italo-Byzantine churches of Ravenna and elsewhere, and the sumptuous Romanesque edifices that continued the wooden-roof tradition (e.g., Pisa Cathedral) and included early square-bayed rib vaults (e.g., S. Ambrogio, Milan). Italian prosperity in the twelfth century was due to the growth of semi-independent cities that flourished as a result of industrial and commercial activities aimed at the wider Mediterranean world. Ital-

Fig. 5. St. Elisabeth, Marburg. *Note the equal-sized apse windows in two stories, characteristic of the so-called hall church.* ÖTERREICHISCHE NATIONALBIBLIOTHEK, VIENNA. REPRODUCED BY PERMISSION.

ian patrons, with such a range of resources at their disposal, found French prototypes less compelling than their counterparts in England or Germany.

The arrival of the Cistercian Order in Italy provided a framework for the construction of churches with linkages to their counterparts in France, particularly at Fossanova (1187–1208), Chiaravalle Milanese (1196), and Casamari (1203–1217).

The greatest transformative influence upon Italian architecture of the thirteenth century came from the mendicant orders, whose spacious churches generally featured thin walls, pointed arches, and ribbed vaults and were often laid out to plans whose flat east end and square schematism conformed to Cistercian norms.

The two-level basilica of S. Francesco at Assisi (1228–1253), intended for the display of the tomb of the founder, was a special case, paradoxically recalling the tradition of bishop's chapels, while making specific French references through its tracery windows and Burgundian-looking wall passage. In its rather low proportions and its emphasis upon the narrative cycle of paintings that encircle the interior, the composition is, however, anything but French.

A list of the most beautifully original architectural achievements of Italian Gothic of this period would perhaps include Franciscan urban churches like S. Maria Novella in Florence (fig. 6; begun 1279) and S. Maria sopra Minerva in Rome (*ca.* 1279), where thin walls and

Fig. 6. S. Maria Novella, Florence. The thin walls and articulated space are characteristic of Italian Gothic. THE CONWAY LIBRARY, COURTAULD INSTITUTE OF ART. REPRODUCED BY PERMISSION.

supports are linked by squarish ribbed vaults and taut articulation to provide a space that is bright and uplifting.

In southern Italy we can find clear instances of Gothic churches built under the direct inspiration of northern prototypes, particularly in the case of Naples's S. Lorenzo, which was built under the patronage of the Angevin court (Bruzelius, 1991). S. Fortunato in Todi, begun in 1292, is a vaulted hall church that refers to prototypes in Germany and in the west of France.

Spain. Spanish Gothic may be understood in relation to two principal currents, the first involving direct

references to French prototypes and the second bringing forth some of the most profoundly original and unforgettable monuments of Gothic.

Spanish Cistercian churches (e.g., Santes Creus, *ca.* 1174, and Poblet, 1170) perpetuated formulae that had been developed in the motherhouses (particularly Clairvaux III in Burgundy). But it was the triumph of the Christian armies at the battle of Las Navas de Tolosa in 1212 and the direct and continuing links between the royal house of Castile and the Capetian monarchy (Princess Blanche of Castile was the wife of Louis VIII of

France and the mother of the sainted Louis IX) that created the circumstances that led to the construction of three cathedrals based on French prototypes in almost all aspects of design. Toledo's cathedral was begun around 1220 and shows signs of direct links with Notre Dame of Paris in its peculiar Y-shaped buttresses, while its three-story elevation with an oculus reflects the form of many of the smaller churches around Paris, as well as the Beauvais Cathedral transept. The builders of Burgos Cathedral (1221) looked particularly to Bourges with its pyramidal elevation, while their colleagues at Léon (begun 1255) looked to the gridded elevation of the nave of St.-Denis, with its glazed triforium. The facade designs of Léon are particularly interesting, featuring towers set one bay beyond the main vessel like the transept of St.-Denis.

This string of references to the North was broken, however, with the construction of the great Catalan churches like Barcelona's mid-thirteenth-century mendicant churches and its cathedral (begun in 1298); or S. María del Mar (1328–1383), also in Barcelona; or, above all, Palma Cathedral in Mallorca (begun 1306, revised *ca.* 1350) and the cathedral in Gerona (1312–1347). These buildings exploited wide-span central vessels, enhanced spaciousness, deemphasized clerestories, and (in the case of Gerona) enormous height. The local tradition of ceramic tile vaulting enabled builders to produce lightweight wide-span vaults.

Late Gothic. We cannot hope here to provide an adequate exploration of this enormously rich topic. Suffice it to say that as we attempt to refine our systems of classification, it is convenient to mark a break in the years around 1300. The general scenario sketched above continued to apply: the use of a rationalized external structural frame facilitated continuing creativity in the treatment of the interior. Smaller-scale structures tended to assume greater importance, and the complex plan types associated with French cathedrals like Rheims and Amiens, with their systems of ambulatory and radiating chapels, found less popularity. Of course, any generalization of this kind finds its exceptions, and a great building like Notre Dame of Paris still had the power to inspire the fifteenth-century masons of the choir of St.-Séverin, Paris, with its double ambulatory.

Plans in Late Gothic are generally stripped down and streamlined and often reveal a high level of angularity. Builders favored elevations with two levels (arcade and clerestory) or just one (as with the hall church, particularly dominant in Germany). The rigid geometric matrix of window tracery is loosened to allow the elements of the window to assume sinuous double-curved shapes (hence the epithet, "Flamboyant"). This process matured first in England with the height of the "Decorated Style," as examples of fully mature curvilinear windows can be found beginning around 1300.

The Hundred Years War brought to an end the propitious circumstances in France that had promoted the astonishing achievements of French builders in the twelfth and thirteenth centuries, and as a result English, German, Italian, and Spanish builders contributed some of the most spectacular churches of the period. However, the late fifteenth century brought economic recovery following the end of the war and allowed France to participate in some of the most spectacular achievements of Late Gothic design: the Beauvais Cathedral transept in France, King's College Chapel in England, the Wenceslas Hall in Prague, the choir of St.-Séverin in Paris, the completion of the cathedral of Seville in Spain. In all of these cases designers were able to achieve spectacular effects through the application of sharply linear articulation that binds the interior of the edifice into a unified illusionistic space.

When did Gothic come to an end? While French builders shifted to Italianate forms in the third decade of the sixteenth century, their colleagues in other northern countries were more conservative. The nineteenth century saw an intense revival of interest in Gothic that continues to thrive to the present period on many an American university campus.

BIBLIOGRAPHY

Baldwin, John W. *Masters, Princes, and Merchants: The Social Views of Peter the Chanter and His Circle.* 2 vols. Princeton, N.J.: Princeton University Press, 1970.

————. *The Government of Philip Augustus: Foundations of French Royal Power in the Middle Ages.* Berkeley: University of California Press, 1986.

Bechmann, Roland. *Les racines des cathédrals: L'architecture gothique, expression des conditions du milieu.* Paris: Payot, 1981.

————. *Villard de Honnecourt: La pensée technique au XIIIe. siècle et sa communication.* Paris: Picard, 1991.

Binding, Gunther. *High Gothic: The Age of the Great Cathedrals.* Cologne, Germany: Taschen, 1999.

Binski, Paul. *Westminster Abbey and the Plantagenets: Kingship and the Representation of Power, 1200–1400.* New Haven, Conn.: Yale University Press, 1995.

Bizzarro, Tina. *Romanesque Architectural Criticism: A Prehistory.* Cambridge, U.K.: Cambridge University Press, 1992.

Bony, Jean. *French Gothic Architecture of the Twelfth and Thirteenth Centuries.* Berkeley: University of California Press, 1983.

Branner, Robert. "Historical Aspects of the Reconstruction of Reims Cathedral, 1210–1241." *Speculum* 36 (1961): 23–37.

Brieger, Peter H. *English Art, 1216–1307.* Oxford History of Art. Oxford: Clarendon, 1957.

Bruzelius, Caroline A. "*Ad Modum Franciae:* Charles of Anjou and Gothic Architecture in the Kingdom of Sicily." *Journal of the Society of Architectural Historians* 50 (1991): 402–420.

Bucher, François. "Micro-Architecture as the 'Idea' of Gothic Theory and Style." *Gesta* 15 (1976): 71–89.

Carruthers, Mary J. *The Book of Memory: A Study of Memory in Medieval Culture.* Cambridge, U.K.: Cambridge University Press, 1990.

———. *The Craft of Thought: Meditation, Rhetoric, and the Making of Images, 400–1200.* Cambridge, U.K.: Cambridge University Press, 1998.

Chenu, Marie-Dominique. *Nature, Man, and Society in the Twelfth Century: Essays on New Theological Perspectives in the Latin West.* Edited and translated by Jerome Taylor and Lester K. Little. Chicago: University of Chicago Press, 1968.

Clark, William. "Capetians in Merovingian Paris: Architecture and Its Audience at the Beginning of the Gothic Period." In *Artistic Integration in Early Gothic Churches.* Edited by K. Brush and P. Draper. Toronto: University of Toronto Press, 1992.

Coldstream, Nicola. *Medieval Architecture.* Oxford History of Art. Oxford and New York: Oxford University Press, 2002.

Conant, Kenneth John. *Carolingian and Romanesque Architecture, 800–1200.* Harmondsworth, U.K.: Penguin, 1959.

Crossley, Paul. "The Return to the Forest: Natural Architecture and the German Past in the Age of Dürer." In *Künstlerischer Austausch. Akten des XXVIII. Internationalen Kongress für Kunstgeschichte.* Edited by Thomas W. Gaehtgens. 3 vols. Berlin: Akademie Verlag, 1992.

Davis, Michael T., et al. "Mechanics and Meaning: Plan Design at Saint-Urbain, Troyes, and Saint-Ouen, Rouen." *Gesta* 39 (2000): 161–182.

Duby, Georges. *L'économie rurale et la vie des campagnes dans l'Occident médiéval.* Paris: Aubier, 1962.

Erlande-Brandenburg, Alain. *La cathédrale.* Paris: Fayard, 1989.

Frankl, Paul. *The Gothic: Literary Sources and Interpretations through Eight Centuries.* Princeton, N.J.: Princeton University Press, 1959.

———. *Gothic Architecture.* Translated by Dieter Pevsner. Harmondsworth, U.K.: Penguin, 1962. Revised edition, edited by Paul Crossley. New Haven, Conn.: Yale University Press, 2000.

Freigang, Christian. *Imitare Ecclesias Nobiles: Die Kathedrale von Narbonne, Toulouse, und Rodez und die nordfranzösische Rayonnantgotik im Languedoc.* Worms, Germany: Christian Freigang, 1992.

Frisch, Teresa G. *Gothic Art, 1140–c. 1450: Sources and Documents.* Englewood Cliffs, N.J.: Prentice-Hall, 1971.

Gardner, Stephen. "Nave Galleries at Durham Cathedral." *Art Bulletin* 64 (1982): 564–579.

Gerson, Paula, et al. *The Pilgrims' Guide to Santiago de Compostela: The Pilgrim's Guide: A Critical Edition.* London: Miller, 1998.

Gombrich, Ernst Hans. *Norm and Form.* London: Phaidon, 1966.

Grant, Lindy. *Abbot Suger of Saint-Denis: Church and State in Early Twelfth-Century France.* London: Longman, 1992.

Grodecki, Louis. *Gothic Architecture.* Translated by I. Mark Paris. New York: Rizzoli, 1976.

Jantzen, Hans. *High Gothic: The Classic Cathedrals of Chartres, Reims, Amiens.* Translated by James Palmes. New York: Pantheon, 1962.

Jordan, William C. *Louis IX and the Challenge of the Crusade: A Study in Rulership.* Princeton, N.J.: Princeton University Press, 1979.

Karge, Henrik. *Die Kathedrale von Burgos und die spanische Architektur des 13. Jahrhunderts.* Berlin: Gebrüder Mann, 1989.

Kidson, Peter. "Panofsky, Suger, and Saint-Denis." *Journal of the Warburg and Courtauld Institutes* 50 (1987): 1–17.

———. "Bourges after Branner" *Gesta* 39 (2000): 147–156.

Kimpel, Dieter, and Robert Suckale. *Die gotische Architektur in Frankreich, 1130–1270.* Munich: Hirmer, 1985.

Kinder, Terryl. *Cistercian Europe: Architecture of Contemplation.* Grand Rapids, Mich.: Eerdmans, 2002.

Krautheimer, Richard. "The Iconography of Medieval Architecture." *Journal of the Warburg and Courtauld Institutes* 5 (1942): 1–33.

Kuhn, Thomas S. *The Structure of Scientific Revolutions.* Chicago: University of Chicago Press, 1970.

Le Goff, Jacques. *La naissance du purgatoire.* Paris: Gallimard, 1981.

Mesqui, Jean. *Châteaux et enceintes de la France médiévale.* 2 vols. Paris: Picard, 1991–1993.

Mortet, Victor, and Paul Deschamps. *Recueil de textes relatifs à l'histoire de l'architecture et à la condition des architectes en France au moyen âge, XIe–XIIe siècles.* Paris: A. Pickard, 1911.

Murray, Stephen. *Building Troyes Cathedral: The Late Gothic Campaigns.* Bloomington: Indiana University Press, 1987.

———. *Beauvais Cathedral: Architecture of Transcendence.* Princeton, N.J.: Princeton University Press, 1989.

———. *Notre-Dame, Cathedral of Amiens: The Power of Change in Gothic.* Cambridge, U.K.: Cambridge University Press, 1996.

———. "Notre-Dame of Paris and the Anticipation of Gothic." *Art Bulletin* 80 (1998): 229–253.

Neagley, Linda. "Architecture and the Body of Christ." In *The Body of Christ in the Art of Europe and New Spain, 1150–1800.* Exhibition catalog. Munich and New York: Prestel, 1997.

Nichols, Stephen G. *Romanesque Signs: Early Medieval Narrative and Iconography.* New Haven, Conn.: Yale University Press, 1983.

Nussbaum, Norbert. *German Gothic Church Architecture.* Translated by Scott Kleager. New Haven, Conn., and London: Yale University Press, 2000.

Onians, John. *Bearers of Meaning: The Classical Orders in Antiquity, the Middle Ages, and the Renaissance.* Princeton, N.J.: Princeton University Press, 1988.

Panofsky, Erwin. *Abbot Suger on the Abbey Church of St.-Denis and Its Art Treasures.* Princeton, N.J.: Princeton University Press, 1946.

Pevsner, Nikolaus. *The Leaves of Southwell.* London and New York: Penguin, 1945.

Rowland, Ingrid D. *The Culture of the High Renaissance: Ancients and Moderns in Sixteenth-Century Rome.* Cambridge, U.K.: Cambridge University Press, 1998.

Sandron, Dany. *La cathédrale de Soissons: Architecture du pouvoir.* Paris: Picard, 1998.

Schröder, Jochen. *Gervasius von Canterbury, Richard von Saint-Victor, und die Methodik der Bauerfassung im 12ten Jahrhundert.* Cologne, Germany: Universität zu Köln, 2000.

Sedlmayr, Hans. *Die Entstehung der Kathedrale.* Zurich: Atlantis, 1950.

Simson, Otto von. *The Gothic Cathedral: Origins of Gothic Architecture and the Medieval Concept of Order.* London: Routledge, 1956.

Stookey, Laurence H. "The Gothic Cathedral as the Heavenly Jerusalem: Liturgical and Theological Sources." *Gesta* 8 (1969): 35–41.

Toman, Rolf, ed. *The Art of Gothic: Architecture, Sculpture, Painting.* Cologne, Germany: Könemann, 1999.

Trachtenberg, Marvin. "Italian 'Gothic': Toward a Redefinition." *Journal of the Society of Architectural Historians* 50 (1991): 22–37.

Viollet-le-Duc, Eugène-Emmanuel. *Dictionnaire raisonné de l'architecture française du XIe au XVI siècle.* 10 vols. Paris: B. Bance, 1858–1868.

Warnke, Martin. *Bau und Überbau: Soziologie der mittelalterlichen Architektur nach den Schriftquellen.* Frankfurt am Main, Germany: Syndikat, 1976.

Wilson, Christopher. *The Gothic Cathedral: The Architecture of the Great Church.* London: Thames and Hudson, 1990.

Wu, Nancy. *Ad Quadratum: The Practical Application of Geometry in Medieval Architecture.* Aldershot, U.K.: Ashgate, 2002.

STEPHEN MURRAY

[See also **DMA:** Aachen, Palace Chapel; Ambulatory; Amiens Cathedral; Apse; Arch; Architect, Status of; Burghausen, Hanns von; Buttress; Canterbury Cathedral; Chapel; Chartres Cathedral; Chevet; Church, Types of; Ciborium; Clerestory; Construction: Building Materials; Construction: Engineering; Dijon, Chartreuse de Champmol; Durand, Guillaume; Durham Cathedral; Gargoyle; Gervase of Canterbury; Glass, Stained; Gloucester Cathedral; Gothic Architecture; Gothic, Decorated; Gothic, Flamboyant; Gothic, Manueline; Gothic, Perpendicular; Gothic, Rayonnant; Guilds and Métiers; Iconography; Intrados; Jean d'Orbais; Libergier, Hugues; Mandorla; Masons and Builders; Nave; Notre Dame de Paris, Cathedral of; Old St. Peter's, Rome; Parler Family; Pierre de Montreuil; Pre-Romanesque Architecture; Rheims Cathedral; Romanesque Architecture; Ste. Chapelle, Paris; St. Denis, Abbey Church; Salisbury Cathedral; Scholasticism, Scholastic Method; Sluter, Claus; Suger of St. Denis; Tracery; Transept; Tribune; Triforium; Urbanism, Western European; Vault; Villard de Honnecourt; Vincent of Beauvais; Westminster Abbey; William of Sens; **Supp:** Architecture, Domestic.]

GOTHIC ART. Like most works created in the Middle Ages, Gothic art was largely religious in subject and in use. Unlike the art of other medieval periods, it has been described primarily in terms of its architecture—so much so, that the phrase "Gothic Art" is often interchanged with "The Age of Cathedrals." Indeed, the universal reception throughout Europe of Gothic architecture, known in the Middle Ages as *Opus francigenum* (Frenchwork), speaks to its all-encompassing nature. And while this essay does not address the history of Gothic architecture as such, given the original location and function of most Gothic art, the intertwining of the two are inescapable.

The producers and consumers of art created in western and central Europe between the middle of the twelfth and the beginning of the sixteenth centuries did not refer to the art of their own time as "Gothic." If categorized at all, works might be given labels based on working methods associated with particular locales, such as *Opus anglicanum,* signaling the sumptuous embroidery of English workmanship, or *Opus lemovicense,* indicating the richly enameled metalwork produced in the French city of Limoges. It was not until the fifteenth and sixteenth centuries that the expression "Gothic" came into use, and then it was used disparagingly. Italian humanist writers, eager to differentiate the classically inspired architecture of their own age from buildings created after the fall of Rome, dismissed these older buildings as products of a barbarous age. The migrating tribes of northern Europe, including the Goths who ravaged Rome in the year 410, were blamed for the destruction of ancient Roman civilization. As the revival of classical forms in Italy sought to recast the ideals of antiquity within a modern age, art associated with these so-called barbarian marauders could be both reviled and disregarded. Thus, as a descriptive term, Gothic (literally "of the Goths"), became essentially synonymous with "nonclassical." And as such, it was equated with disorder, irrationality, and rusticity—notions perpetuated well into the nineteenth century.

A new appreciation for the decorative qualities of Gothic architecture at the end of the eighteenth century led in succeeding generations to the admiration of its spiritual associations and nationalistic identifications. By the late nineteenth century, this recognition developed into scholarly study. As the formal properties of Gothic architecture were differentiated from those of earlier medieval periods, its history came to embrace all of Gothic art, covering over 350 years of artistic production in northern Europe, from the portal sculpture of the Royal Abbey Church at St.-Denis (1140), just north of Paris, to the famed Unicorn Tapestries, designed in Paris around 1500 (New York, The Metropolitan Museum of Art, The Cloisters). From the nineteenth century onward, scholars have celebrated the technical wizardry of Gothic cathedrals and have attempted to decipher their meaning, conceiving of them as vast encyclopedias of symbols and theological references. Forms such as window tracery and drapery folds have been classified and traced along evolutionary routes of stylistic development. Frequently, this approach further defined Gothic art within individual national schools.

At the same time, Gothic art (as with other periods of medieval production) has been traditionally defined according to the hierarchical precepts of the Fine Arts tradition codified in the eighteenth century to comprise architecture, sculpture, and painting. Ivories, ceramics, metalwork, textiles, and stained glass were relegated to the category of "minor" and "decorative arts," or were frequently ignored altogether. Such classifications were, however, antithetical to the artistic spirit of the Middle Ages. Recognition of the fundamental role these so-called minor arts played within late medieval society has increasingly characterized the study of Gothic art, providing a broader and more inclusive perspective.

STYLE

Certain commonalities exist within the stylistic vocabulary of Gothic art, transversing period and location. Departing from the spiritual abstraction practiced in Romanesque art, works of this last epoch of the Middle Ages can be stylistically defined by the use of sinuous and elegant line. This new attitude can already be detected in certain works of the latter twelfth century. Whether the jamb sculptures of the west portal of Chartres Cathedral, the stained-glass windows of the new ambulatory built by Abbot Suger at St.-Denis, or the enameled ambo (a form of raised pulpit) by Nicholas of Verdun at Klosterneuburg, line still functioned to pattern surfaces, yet it was also keenly employed to shape and proportion the human figure. Artists of the thirteenth and fourteenth centuries were virtuosic in their use of supple line to render naturalistic figures with a new sense of tangibility and substance. Around 1400, a mannered elegance took hold. Disseminated by aristocratic patronage throughout Europe, this lyrical style (often called International Gothic for its ubiquity), gave line center stage. Figures often appear secondary in comparison with complex compositions of softly falling drapery folds, orthogonal movements, and exacting renderings of detail.

Indeed, line (with its corollary, outline) can be seen as the agent of a renewed focus on the physical world, which in turn fostered an increasingly naturalistic approach to the representation of flora—such as the grisaille windows from the German Cistercian monastery at Altenberg (ca. 1276–1287) or the Golden Rose Branch created by Minucchio da Siena for Pope John XXII (ca. 1330; Paris, Musée national du Moyen Âge)—and fauna, such as the lion reputedly sketched from life by Villard de Honnecourt (ca. 1235; Paris, Bibliothèque nationale) or the carefully delineated birds from the *Pepysian Model Book* (ca. 1370–1390; Cambridge, Magdalene College).

This kind of acute observation of nature is also reflected in the portrayal of the human figure. The silver-gilt and enamel reliquary statue of the Virgin and Child (fig. 1) presented in 1339 to the Abbey of St.-Denis by the French queen, Jeanne d'Évreux, epitomizes a fundamentally Gothic approach to the body. The Virgin's elongated figure is aligned in a graceful S-curve, with her shoulders back, her hips forward, and her weight supported by one leg. She holds her son in the crook of one arm, further supporting his weight by jutting out the hip of her weight-bearing leg. Arranged in sequences of deep cascading folds, drapery is pulled to reveal distinct body parts—the Virgin's shoulders, breasts, and back. Her perfectly ovoid face is a paragon of ideal femininity: elegant almond-shaped eyes, seamlessly arching eyebrows flowing into the bridge of the nose, and flawlessly arranged curls of hair that defy the vagaries of weather or gravity. Beguilingly, the Christ Child reaches up to touch her lips, and she tenderly tilts her head toward him in response.

This subtle display of interaction is equally an overarching feature of Gothic art. While dramatic displays of emotion often characterize Romanesque scenes of martyrdom or damnation, a new sense of personal communication pervades Gothic art. Sometimes quietly affecting, like the walnut sculpture depicting the meeting of Mary and her aged cousin Elizabeth (fig. 2), or painfully anguished, such as the Pietà (fig. 3) from St. Dorothy's Church in Wrocław in modern Poland, Gothic images embody an attention to the outward signs of human relationships never before so insistently emphasized in medieval art.

Artists of the Gothic era both embraced tradition and fostered dynamic change. Objects for use in time-honored contexts—whether church buildings, holy books, or liturgical settings—were recast within the new formal idiom. Innovative forms came into their own, such as elaborate portal sculptural ensembles, stained-glass windows, tomb effigies, and objects intended to promote personal devotion. Secular art, too, found a foothold within an increasingly pluralistic society. Rather than as providing a trajectory to the Renaissance, Gothic art should be perceived as a lateral force, functioning as a vast net of interlocking and intertwining facets that infused all aspects of visual culture.

THE HEAVENLY JERUSALEM

Our modern understanding of the profuse layering of art within a Gothic church has been irrevocably hampered as much by changes in taste and religious practice as by the ravages of war and political upheaval. The effect has been for the Gothic cathedral to be interpreted solely as the sum of its walls, while its medieval incarnation was replete with polychrome sculpture, gleaming stained-glass windows, textiles, reliquaries, and liturgical furnishings. Like the Heavenly Jerusalem described in the Apocalypse as a city resplendent in colored light and precious gems, the Gothic church was envisioned as a radiant construction of Heaven on Earth.

Stained-glass windows. Stained glass was the preeminent form of Gothic monumental painting. Both a barrier and a filter, the stained-glass window defined the Gothic church as the revelation of God on earth. As light was equated with the Divine, so the colored radiance streaming through stained-glass windows was interpreted as a mystical conduit for the illumination of the soul.

The painted narratives of stained-glass windows (accomplished with vitreous paint applied onto individual pieces of colored glass and joined into a composition with lead cames) ran the gamut of biblical and hagiographic subject matter. Many compositions presented straightforward histories, while others reflected oral exposition or contemporary sermons. Some windows, like the one at Chartres Cathedral dedicated to a sixth-century bishop of Chartres, St. Lubin (fig. 4; *ca.* 1205–1215), presented yet another type, concerned with local history and episcopal governance. The uppermost central roundel of the Chartres window shows what would have been a common sight in any medieval church: a priest stands before the altar blessing a chalice of wine, while the attending deacon holds a cruet (used to transport the wine to the altar) and a liturgical knife (used for the ceremonial cutting of the Host). Yet, this scene is also depicted in ways unique to Chartres. Celebrations in honor of St. Lubin were granted the rare privilege of two candles—a processional candle and a large floor candle—both of which are clearly depicted in the roundel. The borders further add to the site-specificity of the window. They are replete with the figures of merchants and criers, each of whom proffers a goblet presumably filled with the best vintage of local wine. Documents testify that wine criers loudly proclaimed their advantageous prices from inside the cathedral, even offering tastes to worshippers from jugs they carried about. Here sacred and profane present a twofold utopia: an ideal episcopal administration in which competing interests cohabitate without rancor.

Monumental sculpture. Medieval churches had long reflected the realization that exterior art functioned to prepare entering worshipers for proceedings taking place within the building. Isolated sculptural elements, such as carvings above doorways (lintel and tympanum) or figural supports (embrasures and trumeau), had long been employed to dramatic effect. But with the western portals of the Abbey Church of St.-Denis and Chartres Ca-

Fig. 1. Virgin and Child. *Statuette (French, 1324–1339) constructed from silver gilt, opaque and translucent enamels, precious stones, crystals, and pearls. Paris, Musée du Louvre, M. 342 and 419.* © RÉUNION DES MUSÉES NATIONAUX/ART RESOURCE, NY. REPRODUCED BY PERMISSION.

thedral, a new approach to the doorway as a sculptural ensemble was created. Standing figures seemingly independent of their supporting structures were employed to separate and flank the doors (trumeau and jamb sculptures). They were surmounted by densely carved friezes and capitals. The arch-shaped tympanum set above the door was framed by rows of sculpted figures (voussoirs and archivolts) contained within a kind of architectural hood. Socles, embrasures, and bas-reliefs were carved at eye level. All elements were originally brightly painted. The effect, as at the south portal of Cathedral of Notre-Dame at Lausanne (*ca.* 1220–1230), which maintains its original paint, was to create a magisterial impression, reflecting the theological foundations and liturgical life within the church while also presenting an idealized interface with the urban setting at its doorstep.

From the planar disposition at St.-Denis, where each portal ensemble is discretely contained within its re-

Fig. 2. The Visitation. German (Constance), ca. *1310–1320. Walnut with polychromy and gilt.* THE METROPOLITAN MUSEUM OF ART, GIFT OF J. PIERPONT MORGAN, 1917. (17.190.724) PHOTOGRAPH © 1982 THE METROPOLITAN MUSEUM OF ART, NEW YORK. REPRODUCED BY PERMISSION.

spective doorway sections, Gothic monumental sculpture evolved both laterally to form an undulating frieze over the entire front as well as vertically to articulate successive levels of the facade. Tympana became increasingly subdivided; porches massively projected out from the building, their interior hoods encrusted with sculptural embellishment. In other instances, figural sculpture inhabited all reaches of the building, from grotesque masques installed at the junctures of walls and windowsills, to gargoyles designed to channel water away from the building, and angels marking the summits of flying buttresses. Figures that in the twelfth century maintained an architectonic verticality took on a self-sustaining kind of three-dimensionality by the middle of the thirteenth century. By the turn of the fifteenth century, when Claus Sluter worked on Chartreuse de Champmol, the mortuary chapel of the dukes of Burgundy at Dijon (1389–1406), portal sculpture freely extended outside the confines of its architectural framework. The effect was to progressively ornament the surface of the wall, playing with perceptions of solid and void, structure and decoration.

While these ensembles frequently dealt with the end of the world—with thirteenth-century examples stretching as far afield as the cathedrals of Lincoln, Burgos, and Strasbourg—the most pioneering themes involved the Virgin Mary. She was the dedicatee of scores of churches and cathedrals throughout Europe, and as such, her story received lavish artistic treatment. Images in all media recounted both her early life from her miraculous conception at the embrace of her parents to the divine birth of her son, Jesus. Exterior portal sculpture proclaimed the centrality of the Virgin, portraying her enthroned in majesty or crowned as the Queen of Heaven. Nor were such monumental images passive signs announcing the dedication of a church; rather, they invoked the Virgin's protection and intercession on behalf of humankind. Indeed, liturgies, such as the Palm Sunday processions of the clergy at Chartres Cathedral, switched from Palm Sunday chant to plainsong honoring the Virgin Mary as they walked under her commanding presence carved over the door.

Such elaborate monumental programs existed inside the church as well, although they have been much reduced from their original number. In Paris the private chapel of King Louis IX (the Ste.-Chapelle, dedicated in 1248), built to house precious relics from the Passion of Christ, among them the Crown of Thorns, included life-sized figures of the Apostles placed directly above the king and his retinue. Perhaps in emulation, the west choir of the Cathedral of Naumburg (*ca.* 1245–1255) in northeast Germany was similarly installed with twelve standing figures of the eleventh-century sponsors of the church building. The eight men and four women, much of their original polychromy intact, display an extraordinary range of naturalism and detail in personal features and gestures alike. Uta, the wife of the margrave Ekkehard II of St. Gall, in an uneasy gesture, draws her fur-lined cloak to her cheek, while Count Dietmar appears to pull his sword from its sheath while hefting his shield in defense against an unseen foe. These are not portraits per se, as the subjects' features had long been lost from memory, but they constitute real and tangible presences nonetheless.

The remarkable choir screen at Naumburg (*ca.* 1250) has survived the widespread dismantling of such barriers between the laity and congregation that were so important in the Middle Ages but that fell increasingly out of favor following the Protestant Reformation. The exceptional artistry of the Naumburg choir screen demonstrates the pivotal role played by monumental sculpture in church interiors. Rather than lifting the Crucifixion to the top of the screen, as at Halberstadt Cathedral (*ca.* 1220) or the remarkable painted wood "wheel cross" (*ca.* 1279–1290) in the Öja Church in Gotland off the coast of Sweden, the crucified body of Jesus forms the trumeau between the paired doorway openings through which the clergy entered the choir. Christ's sagging body is quintessentially Gothic in approach. Departing from the upright stance of earlier interpretations that envisioned Jesus triumphant over death, his eyes open and alert, the bloodstained body of the Naumburg Christ literally hangs from the cross. Eyes closed in death, his head limply falls against his shoulder. The gentle undulation of his body position is enhanced by the use of a single nail to attach his overlapping feet to the Cross. In contrast to this quiet death, the flanking figures of Mary and the young John the Evangelist installed on the portal embrasures gesture to Jesus with pathos and grief. Their heartache is heightened by the voluminous bolts of drapery they pull and wrap around their bodies.

Tombs. In addition to such vast architectonic ensembles, the Gothic era witnessed the introduction of sculpted tomb effigies to church interiors. Twelfth-century memorial portraits, such as the enameled plaque of Geoffrey Plantagenet (*ca.* 1151; Le Mans, Musée de Tessé), were supplanted by a wide variety of large-scale tomb slabs and three-dimensional effigies honoring royalty, the hierarchy of the church, aristocratic patrons, and even architects, for example, the engraved slab of Hugues Libergier (*d.* 1263, Rheims Cathedral). Serene idealized portraits favored in the thirteenth century, such as the gilded bronze of Queen Eleanor of Castile (1291–1293; London, Westminster Abbey), increasingly gave way to portrayals of the ravages of nature—whether in the rendering of timeworn visages, the introduction of specialized tombs to hold royal entrails, or the portrayal of naked and rotting cadavers, exemplified by the effigy of Guillaume de Harcigny (after 1393; Laon, Musée municipale).

The framing canopy, as with the profusion of florid gables and spires caging the alabaster effigy of Edward II of England (1327–1331) at the Cathedral of Gloucester, remained an important component of Gothic monumental tombs, whether carved in stone or incised in brass. By the end of the Middle Ages, canopies had become architectural structures in and of themselves, particularly in English chantry chapels, with their independent screenwork and altars, such as the chapel of William of Wykeham (1394–1403) at Winchester Cathedral.

Fig. 3. Pietà. *Czech-Silesian,* ca. 1390. Gilded wood. From the Church of St. Dorothy in Wrocław, Poland. MUZEUM NARODOWE WE WROCLAWIU. REPRODUCED BY PERMISSION.

"The Table of God" Described as the "Table of God" by Abbot Suger of St.-Denis (*De Administratione,* XXIV A), the altar was the focus of medieval Christianity. It was there that the sacrifice of Jesus—his death on the Cross, with its promise of salvation—was reenacted in the Mass. The very centrality of the altar spurred elaborate artistic treatment of its liturgical furnishings. In the Gothic era, these could come as much in the form of international gifts, commissions, and purchases as in works of local manufacture. Enameled candlesticks made in Limoges were prized possessions of English churches; *Opus anglicanum* was coveted by Pope Innocent IV; Parisian goldsmith work safeguarded the tooth of St. James at his major pilgrimage site at Compostela in northern Spain. The elaborate treatment of Gothic altars is evidenced in contemporary paintings which show the altar covered by finely woven white cloth (corporal), rich brocades, and embroidered silks, like the one signed by the English nun Johanna Beverlai (fig. 5; late thirteenth/early fourteenth century; London, Victoria and Albert Museum). Draperies hanging on rods, sometimes topped with painted and gilded finial sculptures of angels, could be drawn on both sides, enclosing the altar within a private space.

Fig. 4. The Life of St. Lubin. *Stained glass from Chartres Cathedral (ca. 1210–1215) showing candles typical of the local rite.* CENTRE ANDRÉ CHASTEL, CNRS/UNIVERSITÉ DE PARIS IV-SORBONNE. REPRODUCED BY PERMISSION.

Whereas a Romanesque setting might give prominence to a life-size image of the crucified Christ hanging above the altar, the thirteenth century witnessed the introduction of the altarpiece. This provided a new focus for the celebrant of the Mass with the growing acceptance of the doctrine of Transubstantiation (the belief that the bread and wine consecrated during Mass became the body and blood of Christ) and the consequential devotion to the Eucharist. Resting at the back of the altar and facing the priest, the Gothic altarpiece could include both painted panels and sculpted figures. It could be modest in size or of colossal proportions and, as such, provided an expansive venue for narrative, as seen with the *Maestà* (1311) painted by Duccio di Buoninsegna for the Cathedral of Siena or the *Dormition of the Virgin* (1477–1489) by the German sculptor Veit Stoss in the Church of St. Mary, Kraków.

The ceremony of the Mass had long inspired the creation of elaborate liturgical furnishings. Observing God's directives to Moses, medieval artists looked to create objects to serve the Lord with the finest artistic quality out of "gold, and silver, and brass, of marble, and precious stones, and variety of wood" (Exodus 31: 4–5). While maintaining basic traditional forms, Gothic liturgical serviceware responded to the prevailing styles of the time as well as to changes in liturgical practice. The conical cups of Gothic chalices (used to hold the wine of the Mass) demonstrated a preference for greater angularity and elongation in design, while at the same time, their generally smaller size spoke to the general decrease in lay participation in the sacrament of Communion. Similarly, the adoption of hexagonal over spherical-shaped feet of chalices emphasized linearity over mass but also secured the vessel against rolling while it was turned on its side to drain the wine, a practice adopted in the thirteenth century. The new technique of *basse-taille* enamel, in which translucent enamel is applied over an engraved surface of gold or silver, became a favored form of embellishment for chalices, enhancing both their elegance and brilliant appearance.

The motif of the Gothic cathedral as an embracing tabernacle for the celebration of the Mass inspired the shaping of liturgical furnishings as Gothic structures in miniature. Arnolfo di Cambio's ciborium at S. Paolo fuori le Mura in Rome (1285) reenvisioned the traditional Italian altar canopy as a lofty Gothic edifice. Its crocketed gables, pinnacles, and niches incorporated a sculptural ensemble of relief narrative and freestanding figures to produce a veritable Gothic microcosm. Smaller-scale objects also took Gothic architectonic form. A silver censer from Ramsey Abbey used to burn incense (*ca.* 1325; London, Victoria and Albert Museum) mirrors the characteristically hexagonal plan of an English chapter house, the monks' daily gathering place. Reliquaries, made to hold and protect tangible evidence of miracles and the sacred body parts or personal possessions of saints, were also conceived as miniature Gothic buildings. The *Tabernacle of the Holy Corporal* (1338; Orvieto Cathedral) by the Sienese artist Ugolino di Vieri is an imposing architectural shrine crowned with ornate gables and soaring pinnacles, with walls of translucent enamels depicting the Eucharistic miracle of the blood-stained corporal held within. Similarly, "monstrances" (from the Latin, meaning "to show") were popularized in the Gothic period as architectonic vessels with crystal windows to display the Host, the consecrated bread of the Mass.

As the respective spaces given to clergy and lay worshippers became increasingly separate, works installed upon the altar could at times become the focus of devotions among the congregants. Reliquaries, whether in the more familiar sarcophagus shape or in the form of the body part they encased, were traditionally displayed upon an altar when they were being shown in procession. Similarly, altarpieces were created for secular groups in Italy called *Laudesi,* who gathered together for the singing of hymns of praise *(laude).* These devotions inspired prosperous confraternities to commission magnificent paintings, such as the *Madonna and Child* by Duccio (now called the *Rucellai Madonna, ca.* 1285; Florence, Galleria degli Uffizi), and profusely illuminated hymnals, such as *Laudario of the Compagnia di Sant'Agnese. The Apparition of St. Michael* (fig. 6; 1325–1350; London, British Library), a painting by the Florentine artist Pacino di Bonaguida, demonstrates the resources lavished on such works, which were intended to be used in worship but were also indicators of the patrons' wealth and status.

This kind of secular devotion prompted the development new themes and subjects, such as the Pietà, which found particular favor in Germanic regions. Portraying Mary holding the body of her dead son in her lap, the Pietà captures an isolated moment after Jesus's body has been removed from the Cross. Whether its portrayal emphasizes Mary's peaceful acceptance of her

Fig. 5. The Meeting of Joachim and Anna. *Velvet embroidered with silver and silver-gilt thread and colored silks in underside couching, split stitch and laid and couched work. From the Life of the Virgin Apparels, English, 1320–1340.* VICTORIA AND ALBERT MUSEUM, LONDON/ART RESOURCE, NY. REPRODUCED BY PERMISSION.

child's death or her visible outpouring of grief, as in the Wrocław example (fig. 3), the Pietà is one of the most powerful images developed in the Gothic era. As the Virgin looks up and gestures to her broken heart, she invites viewers to share her agony over the tortured body of her Son, which appears to bleed from every pore. Such exhortations to identify with holy pain and suffering led to the development of a new emphasis on individual devotion.

WORKS OF PERSONAL DEVOTION

The increased emphasis on the personal contemplation of the Divine and the community of saints led to an explosion of works of art intended to facilitate such practice, often outside the traditional confines of a

gible and a visual means for the individual believer to imagine his- or herself as part of the holy drama.

Works created both by and for monastic audiences sought to foster a similarly affective piety. Miniature baby cribs made of painted and gilded wood, such as the fifteenth-century example made in Brabant (New York, The Metropolitan Museum of Art), were outfitted with playful bells and sumptuous bedding for the baby Jesus. Often given as gifts to nuns, these cribs touchingly enabled their owners to care for the Christ child as the child they would never have. The gentle and affecting Visitation (*ca.* 1320; New York, The Metropolitan Museum of Art) from the Dominican convent of Sankt Katharinenthal on Lake Constance may have allowed the nuns to see images of the Christ child and John the Baptist still in their mothers' crystal-covered wombs. Instructional aids like the image of the Heart on the Cross (*ca.* 1500; Eichstätt, St. Walburg), with its ladder rungs of successive virtues, or the French vignettes illustrating the progressive stages of mystical experience (*ca.* 1300; London, British Library) used explicit visual means to encourage nuns to pursue mystical union with the Divine.

The imitation of monastic devotion informed the development of the most popular form of personal devotion—the book of hours, a type of prayer book designed for the laity that swept Europe during the Gothic period. The thousands of surviving examples provide some measure of its widespread significance. Indeed, contemporary descriptions suggest that some well-heeled purchasers saw them as much as fashionable accessories as indispensable religious equipment. Patterned after the daily sequence of prayers observed in the monastery, books of hours were made to be used as well as valued. They were often personalized for their owners. Calendars at the front of the book could include saints associated with a specific locale or to whom the reader was particularly devoted. Certain prayers or lessons could be given prominence over others. Occasionally, portraits of the owner were included. In the most famous example, the young French queen Jeanne d'Évreux is shown twice, book in hand and kneeling at her prayer bench (*ca.* 1325; New York, The Metropolitan Museum of Art, The Cloisters). Depending on their owners, books of hours could be simply made, or their lavish illuminations could be the work of the greatest painters of their day, including Jean Pucelle (*d.* 1334), believed responsible for Jeanne d'Évreux's tiny book of hours; Pol, Jean, and Herman Limbourg (active *ca.* 1386–1416), who created arguably the most sumptuous books of hours for the voracious collector Duke Jean of Berry (1340–1416); and

***Fig. 6.* The Apparition of St. Michael.** *In this 14th-century painting by Pacino di Bonaguida, the archangel miraculously prevents a farmer's arrow from hitting his runaway bull, turning it against the shooter.* THE BRITISH LIBRARY, MS 35, 254 B. REPRODUCED BY PERMISSION.

church building. Some were smaller versions of church objects, such as the "house altarpiece" depicting female saints, for example, the *Anna Selbdritt* (St. Anne holding infant figures of her daughter, Mary, and grandson, Jesus) from Swabia (*ca.* 1490–1495; New York, Metropolitan Museum of Art, The Cloisters). Precious diptychs and polyptychs made from ivory or translucent enamel were popular among the wealthy. Narrative or figural segments could be hinged, allowing these devotional plaques to be easily folded and transported. Like monumental sculpture, ivories were originally colored and gilded, enhancing their naturalism and immediacy as an aid to prayer, while translucent enamels recalled the radiance of stained-glass windows. Other works of personal devotion were unique in form. Boxwood Paternoster beads, which first appeared in the last quarter of the fifteenth century, were meant as much to be fondled as to be studied while praying the rosary (a practice introduced in the late Middle Ages). These golf ball–size beads were carved with astounding intricacy into scenes from Christ's Nativity or Passion, providing both a tan-

Fig. 7. The "Offering of the Heart." *This 14th-century ivory mirror case shows a suitor presenting his heart to his lady, who in turn prepares to crown him with a chaplet in recognition of her favor. (Compare p. 334.)* VICTORIA AND ALBERT MUSEUM, LONDON/ART RESOURCE, NY. REPRODUCED BY PERMISSION.

artists like the Master of the Boucicaut Hours, whose given name remains unknown but whose style is eminently recognizable and associated with a book of hours made for the marshal of Boucicaut (*ca.* 1405–1408; Paris, Musée Jacquemart-André).

Luxurious books of hours share certain common features: expansive illuminations, intricate foliate ornament highlighted in burnished gold, and curious visual asides positioned in the margins of the manuscript. Hybrid monsters, beggars, street performers, and workers in the fields, as well as various sexually and scatologically suggestive forms enliven Gothic margins, leading to the name "marginalia" for these distinctive images. Many still are not fully understood, while others clearly offer commentary on the text and its illustration. A woman holding a mirror, symbolizing the vice of vanity, contrasts with the humility of the sainted king Louis IX

washing the feet of the poor; a nun suckling an ape serves as an antitype for the Virgin Mary nursing the Christ child; snails and squirrels suggest sexual wordplay generated from words in the text. Other marginal scenes offer a second narrative within the confines of the page. In the *Apparition of St. Michael* (fig. 6), the theme of good victorious over evil depicted in the principal scene of the Archangel Michael battling the forces of Satan is expanded by the marginal narrative at the lower corner: the poison arrow shot by a farmer to punish a runaway bull is miraculously turned against the vindictive shooter by the archangel.

THE SECULAR REALM

The development of religious art to aid in the personal devotions of the laity was part of a wider phenomenon of secular ownership. Secular art emerged in the

Gothic period as a vibrant and significant force. Visible displays of ownership or donation signaled by heraldic coats of arms burgeoned at this time, from the arms of the French royal family supporting the stained-glass rose window (*ca.* 1220) of the north transept of Chartres Cathedral; to the emblems of Jean, duke of Berry, in his books of hours; to heraldry emblazoned on more mundane items such as drinking vessels, basins for hand washing (gemellions), and glazed earthenware platters. Indeed, objects made for the table could rival religious metalwork in both sumptuousness and artistry. Surviving works and courtly manuscripts from the fourteenth and early fifteenth centuries testify to the lavishness of aristocratic table settings, which included extravagant gilded silver ships for storing eating utensils and the prized commodity of salt, metal and glass beakers for drink, and ingeniously shaped aquamanilia, used to store water for the ritual washing of hands that began and ended every meal in noble households. Fabulous beasts, livestock from the barnyard, and armored warriors were all pressed into service as aquamanilia (literally meaning "water hands") intended to dazzle and entertain guests. Similarly, the opulent tapestries hanging on walls were signs of artistic discernment and often of learning, but above all, they signaled the deep pockets of their owners.

Intimate items, too, were significant objects. Carved ivory, for example, was a preferred medium for mirror covers, boxes, writing tablets, and combs. Leisure scenes from aristocratic life—hunting, playing chess, and jousting—or tales from romances—featuring Pyramus and Thisbe, Arthur and his Knights of the Round Table, or Tristan and Iseult—were popular subjects. Images of courting or allegories of love were especially favored. The "Offering of the Heart" depicted on a French mirror cover from the beginning of the fourteenth century (fig. 7; London, Victoria and Albert Museum) shows a suitor presenting his heart to his lady, who in turn, prepares to crown him with a chaplet in recognition of her favor. A groom stands nearby, beating back two horses—an antitype to the ideal of courtly love in its suggestion of animal passions.

CONCLUSION

In Gothic art, the past was ever present. Just as Abbot Suger constructed western and eastern additions to the venerable nave of the Carolingian church at St.-Denis, so he inset an ancient sardonyx cup between an elaborately gilded silver base and lip to create his renowned chalice (1137–1140; Washington, D.C., National Gallery of Art). Thus, revered works of earlier ages were given new settings; traditional formats were imbued with the new stylistic language of linear elegance. Yet, Gothic art also spoke with the voice of innovation. Novel subject matter, formats, audiences, and uses for art all define the prolific output of the period. As new churches were constructed, "rising up their heads in wonderful splendor," a concurrent new and profound awareness developed of the relationship between the individual and art and its ownership. Fueled by social forces like the development of cities, trade, and the growth of a prosperous merchant class, this awareness grasped the power of images to argue for political and social status or to facilitate spiritual well-being. Vibrant, expansive, and unafraid to explore human emotions of fear and misery, art at the end of the Middle Ages permeated the world of the living just as it provided a vehicle for spiritual union with the Divine.

BIBLIOGRAPHY

Alexander, Jonathan, and Paul Binski, eds. *The Age of Chivalry: Art in Plantagenet England, 1200–1400.* Exhibition catalog. London: Royal Academy of Arts, 1987.

Barnet, Peter, ed. *Images in Ivory: Precious Objects of the Gothic Age.* Exhibition catalog. Princeton, N.J.: Detroit Institute of Arts and Princeton University Press, 1997.

Binski, Paul. *Medieval Death: Ritual and Representation.* Ithaca, N.Y.: Cornell University Press, 1996.

Boehm, Barbara Drake. "Body-Part Reliquaries: The State of Research." *Gesta* 36, no. 1 (1997): 8–19.

Boehm, Barbara Drake, Abigail Quandt, and William D. Wixom. *The Hours of Jeanne d'Évreux.* Luzern: Faksimile Verlag, 2000.

Camille, Michael. *The Gothic Idol: Ideology and Image-Making in Medieval Art.* Cambridge, Mass., and New York: Cambridge University Press, 1989.

———. *Image on the Edge: The Margins of Medieval Art.* London: Reaktion, 1992.

———. *Gothic Art: Glorious Visions.* New York: Abrams, 1996.

De Hamel, Christopher. *A History of Illuminated Manuscripts.* 2d rev. ed. London and New York: Phaidon, 1994.

Enamels of Limoges, 1100–1350. Exhibition catalog. New York: Metropolitan Museum of Art, 1995.

Grodecki, Louis, and Catherine Brisac. *Gothic Stained Glass, 1200–1300.* Translated from the French by Barbara Drake Boehm. Ithaca, N.Y.: Cornell University Press, 1985.

Hamburger, Jeffrey F. *Nuns as Artists: The Visual Culture of a Medieval Convent.* Berkeley: University of California Press, 1997.

Husband, Timothy, with contributions by Julien Chapuis. *The Treasury of Basel Cathedral.* Exhibition catalog. New York and New Haven: Metropolitan Museum of Art and Yale University Press, 2001.

Husband, Timothy B., Jane Hayward, et al. *The Secular Spirit: Life and Art at the End of the Middle Ages.* Exhibition catalog. New York: Dutton and the Metropolitan Museum of Art, 1975.

Jung, Jacqueline E. "Beyond the Barrier: The Unifying Role of the Choir Screen in Gothic Churches." *The Art Bulletin* 82, no. 4 (2000): 622–657.

Kanter, Laurence B., et al. *Painting and Illumination in Early Renaissance Florence, 1300–1450*. Exhibition catalog. New York: Metropolitan Museum of Art, 1994.

Lane, Barbara G. *The Altar and the Altarpiece: Sacramental Themes in Early Netherlandish Painting*. New York: Harper and Row, 1984.

Medieval Craftsmen series. 9 vols. Toronto: University of Toronto Press, 1991–1992.

Os, Henk van, with Eugène Honée, Hans Nieuwdorp, and Bernhard Ridderbos. *The Art of Devotion in the Late Middle Ages in Europe, 1300–1500*. Translated from the Dutch by Michael Hoyle. Princeton, N.J.: Princeton University Press, 1994.

Raguin, Virginia Chieffo, Kathryn Brush, and Peter Draper, eds. *Artistic Integration in Gothic Buildings*. Toronto: University of Toronto Press, 1995.

Williamson, Paul. *Gothic Sculpture, 1140–1300*. New Haven and London: Yale University Press, 1995.

M. B. SHEPARD

[See also **DMA:** Altarpiece; Amiens Cathedral; Archivolt; Artist, Status of the; Bible Moralisée; Book of Hours; Byzantine Art; Chartres Cathedral; Column Figure; Dijon, Chartreuse de Champmol; Ecclesia and Synagoga; Flemish Painting; Fresco Painting; Gargoyle; Giovanni Pisano; Glass, Stained; Gothic Architecture; Gothic Art: Painting and Manuscript Illumination; Gothic Art: Sculpture; Gothic, International Style; Guilds of Artists; Iconography; Icons, Manufacture of; Manuscript Illumination: European; Moissac, St.-Pierre; Notre Dame de Paris, Cathedral of; Pisano, Nicola; Psalter; Rheims Cathedral; Romanesque Art; Ste.-Chapelle, Paris; Sluter, Claus; Strasbourg Cathedral; Tympanum; Westminster Abbey; **Supp:** Gothic Architecture; Patronage, Artistic.]

GRÁGÁS, the first written collection of Icelandic laws. Prior to the reign of the Norwegians, which began between 1262 and 1264, Iceland was a country ruled by chieftains associated in a general assembly, the Althing, which met once a year and was responsible for all judicial and legislative decisions. In a country without a king, accurate and precise laws became increasingly important. For the first century or so of settlement, the laws were under the guardianship of a law speaker whose primary role was to memorize and recite them. It was through a mandate of the Althing that met in 1117 that the laws were committed to writing. The laws were codified that winter and submitted the following year for approval at the Althing, which approved or rejected each law on a majority vote. The laws approved in 1118 are the basis (although not the totality) of a collection of Icelandic laws that existed before the submission of the Icelanders to the king of Norway and are collectively known as *Grágás*. The name literally means "gray goose" and is a six-

teenth-century misnomer, but lacking a better alternative, *Grágás* has stuck. *Grágás* has survived in two manuscripts, each with corresponding strengths and weaknesses, and additional scattered fragments.

The laws themselves cover the usual variety of subjects, including laws concerning Christianity, procedures for the general assembly, sections on homicides and other physical assaults, inheritance practices, family law, and a miscellany of additional situations. They are comprehensive in their scope and in many cases provide explanations and definitions of terms and ideas to limit possible misinterpretations or debatable points—what constitutes a wound or the definition of a household, for instance. Penalties for transgressions could range from three marks (for working on Sunday, for example) to full outlawry, which entailed a loss of all goods and status and the denial of all assistance and fellowship. Full outlawry was typically reserved for major offenses, such as murder or practicing witchcraft, and was the equivalent of capital punishment. In addition to the legal verdicts rendered against him, a guilty party or his family might also have to pay compensation—wergild—to the victim or his kin.

The process of reaching a judgment was complex. The legal process began by the formal announcement of an injury. It typically included the neighbors of those involved in any particular legal proceeding. Neighbors were asked to give verdicts as to the facts, motives, or character of a particular case or participant. Judgments were rendered by courts of up to thirty-six judges. Evidence could only be introduced according to accepted standards, and problems in procedures could disqualify a piece of evidence from inclusion in the trial.

Grágás was a considerable accomplishment, more so for a society that in its formative years was a loose commonwealth of farmers and fishermen and whose medieval population probably never exceeded 100,000 inhabitants. In its breadth, preciseness, and details, *Grágás* gives us a unique glance into this western outpost of medieval Europe.

BIBLIOGRAPHY

Dennis, Andrew, Peter Foote, and Richard Perkins, trans. *Laws of Early Iceland: Grágás, the Codex Regius of Grágás, with Material from Other Manuscripts*. 2 vols. Winnipeg, Canada: University of Manitoba Press, 1980–2000.

JARBEL RODRIGUEZ

[See also **DMA:** Iceland; Wergild.]

GRATIAN (*fl.* first half of twelfth century). Since the publication of the article on Gratian—a theologian about whom very little is known but whose writings had a major impact on medieval canon law—in the main volumes of this dictionary, Anders Winroth has discovered four manuscripts that contain an earlier recension or redaction of Gratian's principal work, the *Decretum*. The evidence of the four manuscripts has significantly changed or called into question our notions about Gratian and his *Decretum*. These manuscripts have also confirmed several earlier conjectures about the genesis of the *Decretum*. From poorly sewn seams in Gratian's text, legal historians had long known that he must have worked on his *Decretum* over a period of time. Scholars knew that parts, especially the last section, *De consecratione,* were most likely not Gratian's work. Some scholars had speculated that the first section, the 101 *distinctiones,* was also added, or at least organized, later. Winroth has conclusively established that four manuscripts (found in Admont, Barcelona, Florence, and Paris) are witnesses to a redaction of the *Decretum* that Gratian finished between *ca.* 1120 and 1140. Carlos Larrainzar found another manuscript in St. Gall and a fragment in Paris that confirmed the evidence of Winroth's manuscripts.

All of these manuscripts establish that the set of *causae* known as *De penitentia,* were part of Gratian's earliest version of his text. Not all contain the tract *De consecratione.* The St. Gall manuscript could lead one to conclude that the *distinctiones* were added later. It omits the 101 *distinctiones* but places some of the canons of that section in a first *causa.* The early redaction clearly demonstrates that Gratian's main purpose was to produce a textbook that could be used for teaching canon law. It indicates that he began working on the *Decretum ca.* 1110–1120 and continued to teach and refine his compilation for the next quarter century. The first redaction of the *Decretum* reveals that he did not know Roman law well. Gratian added most of the Roman law texts to the *Decretum* in his final recension. In his final redaction he doubled the size of the *Decretum* and added texts from canonical collections that he had not used in the first recension. Gratian may have finished the final recension of the *Decretum ca.* 1140–1145.

The St. Gall manuscript does not contain the most important and innovative part of Gratian's *Decretum*: the first twenty *distinctiones,* in which Gratian discusses the nature of law. These *distinctiones* on law were Gratian's most significant contribution to medieval jurisprudence. It was also Gratian's greatest intellectual challenge because there were no models for his tract in the Roman or canonical legal tradition. If Gratian had searched Jus-

Decretum. *St. Gall Stiftsbibliothek 673 is a very important newly discovered manuscript, here showing* Decretum *C.19.* ST. GALL STIFTSBIBLIOTHEK. REPRODUCED BY PERMISSION.

tinian's codification, he would have found definitions of the different types of law but not a discussion of a hierarchy of laws that is the centerpiece of Gratian's tract *De legibus.* The canonical tradition also had no precedents. *De legibus* stimulated later canonists to reflect upon law and its sources for centuries.

Scholars have long wondered about the relationship of the *causae* and the *distinctiones.* The *causae* are splendid instruments for teaching. The *distinctiones* are a series of "tracts" that are not organized in any recognizable way. They are repetitive and are not good teaching tools (except for the tract *De legibus*). The evidence of the St. Gall manuscript suggests that the *causae* were, early on, the core of Gratian's work. One of the early important Bolognese canonists, Rolandus, did not even comment on the *distinctiones.*

The evidence of the manuscripts discovered by Winroth has not yet been fully evaluated. St. Gall may not reflect an earlier stage of Gratian's *Decretum* without *distinctiones;* it may be an abbreviation or an adaptation of his first recension. The evidence uncovered to date, however, is contradictory. Winroth argues that there were two Gratians. Gratian I knew little Roman law, and Gratian II botched Gratian I's work when he doubled the size of the first redaction (*ca.* 1860 canons to *ca.* 3945). He maintains that the original form of the *Decretum* was much more coherent and elegant. When Gratian II added his material, he destroyed the logic of strings of canons found in the first recension. We knew that there were earlier stages of the text of the *Decretum* from the "untidy seams" left in the final redaction. Yet, despite the convincing evidence of these earlier stages, the arguments for two Gratians are not conclusive. We must do much more work on these manuscripts before we will have a clear idea about the textual history and chronology of Gratian's *Decretum.*

BIBLIOGRAPHY

PRIMARY WORKS

Gratian. *The Treatise on Laws (Decretum DD. 1–20) with the Ordinary Gloss.* Translated by Augustine Thompson and James Gordley, with an introduction by Katherine Christensen. Washington, D.C.: Catholic University of America Press, 1993.

SECONDARY WORKS

Larrainzar, Carlos. "El borrador del la 'Concordia' de Graziano: Sankt Gallen, Stiftsbibliothek MS 673 (=Sg)." *Ius ecclesiae: Rivista internazionale di diritto canonico* 9 (1999): 593–666.

Lenherr, Titus. "Zur Überlieferung des Kapitels 'Duae sunt.'" *Archiv für Katholisches Kirchenrecht* 168 (1999): 369–374.

Weigand, Rudolf. "Chanchen und Probleme einer baldigen kritischen Edition der ersten Redaktion des Dekrets Gratians." *Bulletin of Medieval Canon Law* 22 (1998): 53–75.

Winroth, Anders. *The Making of Gratian's Decretum.* Cambridge, U.K.: Cambridge University Press, 2000.

KENNETH PENNINGTON

[See also **DMA:** Gratian; Law, Canon: After Gratian.]

GREGORY X, POPE (1210–1276). Born in Piacenza, Tedaldo Visconti studied in Paris and then joined the service of Cardinal James of Palestrina. He became a canon and then archdeacon at Liège and traveled to the Holy Land. He was there when he was elected pope in 1271. His election ended the longest vacancy in papal history, following the death of Clement IV on 29 November 1268. The cardinals' unexplained unwillingness to elect a new pope was overcome only when St. Bonaventure and the *podestà*, or mayor, of Viterbo locked the cardinals in a palace on a diet of bread and water. Tedaldo's journey from the Levant to Rome delayed his coronation until 27 March 1272.

Gregory's recent experience in the Latin East put a crusade at the top of his priorities, as well as the reconciliation of the Catholic and Orthodox churches. Before he left the East to be crowned pope, Gregory wrote to the Byzantine emperor Michael VIII Palaiologos, indicating his eagerness for union. As Charles of Anjou had defeated the last Hohenstaufen, Conradin, at Tagliacozzo on 23 August 1268, Gregory was the first pope in half a century who did not inherit an overwhelming struggle with the Holy Roman Empire. Continuing discussions begun by Clement IV, Gregory summoned a council to discuss union with the Byzantine church, which opened on 7 May 1274 in Lyons, a location chosen because he hoped to recruit Frenchmen for the subsequent crusade. The emperor Michael VIII sent a Byzantine delegation to the council, authorized to accept papal supremacy as well as Catholic definitions of the procession of the Holy Spirit, purgatory, and other issues separating the churches. Gregory's requirements for union, while still galling to the Byzantines, were less demanding than those of his predecessors. Much of the Byzantine eagerness for union derived from the hope that the papacy would prevent further attacks on Byzantium if it were a Catholic state.

Gregory also wished to institute reforms of the church at the council, but these concerns were not fully addressed. Gregory did succeed in reforming papal elections so that the long interregnum that preceded his own papacy would not happen again. A new constitution, *Ubi periculum,* further defined the conditions under which papal elections were to take place, mandating a system whereby the cardinals were increasingly isolated until a pope was elected. The council also decreed that the number of mendicant orders would not exceed the four already established (Franciscan, Dominican, Carmelite, and Augustinian).

Gregory X reversed earlier papal support for Charles of Anjou, believing that the French prince's influence throughout Italy threatened the independence of the papacy. He encouraged the communes of northern Italy to reconcile their Guelph and Ghibelline factions, limiting Charles's ability to manipulate Guelph factions to his own ends. Gregory confirmed the election of Rudolf IV of Habsburg on 20 October 1273, filling the imperial throne left open by the death of the last Hohenstaufen in 1268. Gregory died on 10 January 1276 in Arezzo. His crusade never advanced past the planning stage, and the union with the Byzantines quickly fell apart, in part because his papal successors did not believe Byzantine protestations of conformity. His reformation of papal elections, however, had a lasting impact.

BIBLIOGRAPHY

Gatto, Ludovico. *Il pontificato di Gregorio X, 1271–1276*. Rome: Istituto storico italiano per il Medio Evo, 1959.

Gregorio X nel VII centenario della morte. Piacenza, Italy: La Deputazione, 1977.

Guiraud, Jean, and E. Cadier, eds. *Les registres de Grégoire X (1272–1276) et de Jean XXI (1276–1277): Recueil des bulles de ces papes*. Paris: Éditions de Boccard, 1960.

CHRISTOPHER HATCH MACEVITT

[See also **DMA:** Councils, Western (1215–1274); Michael VIII Palaiologos.]

GUESCLIN, BERTRAND DU (*ca.* 1320–1380). The Hundred Years War between France and England and civil wars in Spain offered a wealth of opportunities to the professional soldier in the fourteenth century. Bertrand du Guesclin exploited these opportunities to the fullest. Born probably in the second decade of the century or perhaps early in the third, he never seems to have been intended for anything but a military career and remained illiterate throughout life.

As an adolescent and young man he was known as a splendid horseman, and he excelled at the tournament. Though he might have chosen to limit his horizons to Brittany, given the fact that he was Breton by birth, his earliest military exploits (in 1341 and 1343), leading a privately raised troop, were largely in the service of France. Knighted not long before 1354, he became involved almost immediately in diplomatic relations to redeem French noble captives from the English and their allies. In his own career he was several times (for example, 1360, 1364, 1367) captured and released for very large ransoms.

Before 1365 the principal arena of his operations was France. He fought generally but not always successfully in Brittany against the duke of Lancaster in 1356, taking part in a famous single combat with Sir Thomas of Canterbury while relieving Rennes in 1357. Elsewhere he was also usually but not wholly successful in this first phase of his career. Notable are his exploits at the siege of Melun in 1359 and in the Battle of Cocherel, where he was victorious over the Navarrese in 1364. A general truce in the Hundred Years War closed this phase of his career. Bertrand had garnered the lordships of Pontorson and La Roche-Tesson as rewards for his good service, as well as the countship of Longueville, the lieutenancy of Normandy, and the royal dignity of chamberlain.

The second major phase of his career took place in Spain, but the occasion for the shift in venue was the truce between England and France, which left thousands of unemployed troops on French soil. A consortium of interests (including the French king and the pope) who wanted to restrain the power of Pedro I the Cruel, the king of Castile, commissioned Bertrand to accept command of these troops and join the civil war in Castile on the side of their ally Henry of Trastámara, who was engaged in a bitter succession struggle with his royal half-brother. In 1366 Bertrand's army helped place Trastámara on the throne. Although the situation was reversed soon thereafter, owing both to the intervention of Peter's ally Edward, the Black Prince, and to Bertrand's capture, the latter's release and his subsequent campaigns redeemed Henry's cause. After Bertrand's victory at the Battle of Montiel in 1369, Henry of Trastámara reascended the throne. In this phase of Bertrand's career, he again garnered titles and dignities: constable of Castile, count of Trastámara, duke of Molinas.

The third and final phase of Bertrand's military career began in 1370. King Charles V appointed him constable of France (essentially commander in chief), and Bertrand developed a strategy that eventuated in defeat after defeat for the English in the renewed war. He avoided spontaneous pitched battles, the bane of French arms. He was particularly adept at achieving logistical superiority before committing his troops and methodically over the course of a decade, he retook control of most of the southwest of the realm as well as Brittany and part of Languedoc. Although his relations with his suzerain were sometimes strained (a military commander of his ability and fame might pose a threat to the throne), Bertrand served Charles well right up until his death at the siege of Châteauneuf-de-Randon in southern France in 1380.

By the standard of the time, Bertrand was a repulsively ugly child and man, and even his parents were said to have disliked looking at him. Despite two marriages, he left no legitimate heirs.

BIBLIOGRAPHY

Jacob, Yves. *Bertrand du Guesclin: Connétable de France*. Paris: Tallandier, 1992.

Minois, Georges. *Du Guesclin*. Paris: Fayard, 1993.

WILLIAM CHESTER JORDAN

[See also **DMA:** Castile; Edward the Black Prince; Hundred Years War; **Supp:** Routiers.]

GUILLAUME PEYRAUT. See **Perault, William.**

GUNS AND GUNPOWDER. See **Firearms.**

GYNECOLOGY. Neither gynecology nor obstetrics was recognized in medieval Europe as a formal medical specialty. Nevertheless, "women's matters"—the literal translation of the Greek *gynaikeia* as well as its Latin derivatives, *gynaecia* and *genecia*—were the subject of more than 150 different medical writings and, in certain instances, formed the focus of practitioners' expertise. Writings about women's medicine (which was sometimes defined to include cosmetics) can, when supplemented by other kinds of evidence, offer at least a partial perspective on the ways the female body was perceived and cared for in the Middle Ages.

ANATOMY AND PHYSIOLOGY

Knowledge about the anatomical structure of the female body largely derived from ancient descriptions of female mammals. The uterus, it was believed, was divided into two separate "cells" (an observation perfectly in accord with ungulate anatomy), from which two "testicles" projected. What are now called the ovaries were understood to be analogous to the male testicles and were assumed to produce semen (with important consequences for women's health). An alternate view that the uterus had seven cells (three on the left producing females, three on the right producing males, and one in the middle producing hermaphrodites) entered Europe in the late eleventh century and can be found in a variety of sources. The external configuration of the female genitalia elicited little interest, the clitoris being almost completely ignored.

Physiologically, the female body was seen as cold and wet compared with the hot and dry complexion of the male. Scientific literature debated such contested issues as whether the hottest woman was colder than the coldest man, that is, whether male and female formed a continuum along a single spectrum of physiological states or were completely distinct beings. The distinction of male and female temperaments served as the principal explanation for the phenomenon of menstruation.

Disparaging views of menstruation deriving from the ancient and early medieval writers Pliny, Solinus, and Isidore of Seville have been assumed to be typical, yet the medical tradition was largely neutral on menstruation, seeing it as a normal and necessary purgative function. A vernacular tradition (which can be found across western Europe) of calling the menses "the flowers" was enshrined in the *Liber de sinthomatibus mulierum* (Book on the conditions of women; one of the so-called *Trotula*

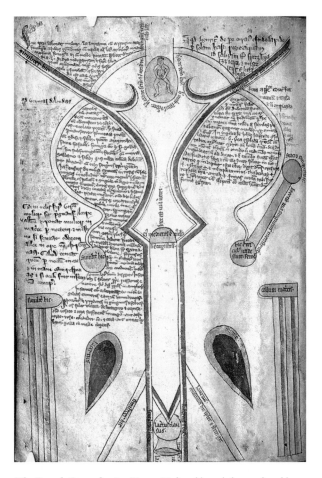

The Female Reproductive Tract. *Medieval knowledge was based largely on ancient descriptions of female mammals.* OXFORD, BODLEIAN LIBRARY, MS ASHMOLE 399, S. XIII EX., FOL. 13V. REPRODUCED BY PERMISSION.

treatises) in the twelfth century: "because just as trees without flowers do not bear fruit, so women without their 'flowers' are deprived of the function of conception." Women's cold bodies could not produce enough heat to sufficiently concoct (literally, cook) all the food they consumed, so nature granted them a special purgative process to rid them of the excess. When pregnant, this matter served to feed the fetus; after birth, it was transformed into milk. Later in life (estimates ranged from thirty-five all the way up to seventy, according to Hildegard of Bingen) as the female body dried out, the purgation ceased altogether, although certain later medieval authors theorized that the noxious substances continued to be produced in women's bodies and could emanate in the harmful effects of the evil eye.

PATHOLOGY

As a purgative process, menstruation needed to be regular in order to maintain health. It was also crucial to

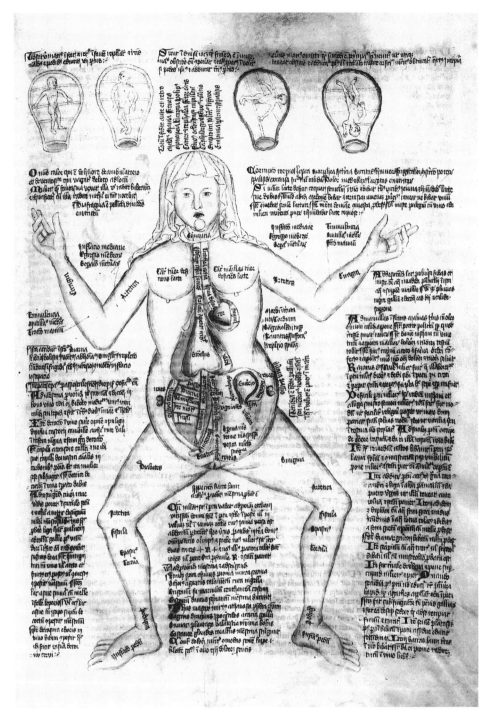

Ailments of Women. *This image from a medical manuscript is labeled with diseases that can afflict the various body parts.* WELLCOME LIBRARY, LONDON, MS 49, S. XV, FOL. 38R. REPRODUCED BY PERMISSION.

eliminate the menses from the uterus if the woman were to conceive. Thus we find that the most common gynecological treatments were mechanisms to induce menstruation if it was retained. Although certain historians have assumed that these emmenagogues (which are sometimes also said to be useful for expelling the fetus) were used as contraceptives and abortifacients, it is crucial to understand these remedies in their own context: if both female health and fertility are seen to revolve around a regularly cleansed womb, then emmenagogues will in fact be used for precisely the reasons stated. The very first remedy in the twelfth-century medical writer

Trota's *Practical Medicine* confirms this: "[A remedy] according to Trota to provoke the menses *because of whose retention the woman is unable to conceive.*"

Amenorrhea was only rarely seen as acceptable: the late antique writer Muscio (whose *Gynaecia* circulated widely until the *Trotula* texts superseded it in the thirteenth century) had recognized that physically active singers often did not menstruate. This view had little effect in the Middle Ages aside from two English writers who saw religious women (nuns) as subject to amenorrhea "because of rising at night and singing and occupation in their [divine] service, their blood wastes away." A fifteenth-century French writer, in contrast, classed religious women with noble and bourgeois women who drink wine and eat rich foods and who therefore must menstruate heavily in order to remain healthy. This same view that the body was regulating the amount of waste matter and menstruation also explains why alternate fluxes of blood—nosebleeds and even hemorrhoids—could be seen as salubrious if the woman was not otherwise menstruating.

Next to menstrual irregularities, the most commonly described gynecological condition was uterine suffocation (in Latin, *suffocatio matricis*). This derived from ancient Hippocratic views that the woman could literally be suffocated by a uterus roaming the body in search of moisture. The "wandering womb" theory had been recognized as an anatomical impossibility in antiquity, the disease explained now by the noxious effects of corrupting menstrual blood or female semen that affected the respiratory organs. Some medical practitioners used uterine suffocation as a "catch-all" diagnosis for abdominal or other conditions not readily categorized under other headings. Caesarius Coppula of Salerno wrote a *consilium* (a personalized diagnosis and regimen) for a certain lady who suffered from pains in the stomach as a result of the suffocation of her uterus. Thomas Fayreford, a rural practitioner in fifteenth-century England, notes in his casebook that he treated at least twelve different women for gynecological conditions, yet his only two diagnoses were menstrual retention and uterine suffocation.

CONCERNS WITH FERTILITY

Fertility seems to have been the focal point of most physicians' involvement with gynecology. Prior to the fourteenth century, male medical writers limited themselves to discussing the same narrow range of gynecological conditions that they found in the Arabic medical compendia that became available in the eleventh and twelfth centuries. From around 1300, however, brief in-

"Uterine Suffocation." The male physician and attendant are treating the afflicted woman with smells and fumigations. England, late 13th century. OXFORD, BODLEIAN LIBRARY, MS ASHMOLE 399, FOL. 33R. REPRODUCED BY PERMISSION.

dependent tracts "On Conception" *(De impregnatione)* or "On Sterility" *(De sterilitate)* were composed. By the fifteenth century, long Latin treatises addressed conditions of the male as well as female genitalia, while texts devoted strictly to women's conditions were composed in Dutch, English, French, German, and Italian. An anonymous text, written in French, discusses generation, the nature of the menses, and all manner of gynecological and obstetrical conditions; the author claims to have cured many women of the "white flux" in towns in Picardy, and he recounts at length the story of his cure of a young Parisian woman who suffered from uterine prolapse and hemorrhage.

CONTRACEPTION AND ABORTION

As noted above, concerns with provoking menstruation may have had more to do with pronatalist objectives than with deliberately interrupting the process of conception. Nevertheless, there were certain medical as well as social justifications for preventing or terminating pregnancy. The eleventh-century Benedictine monk Constantine the African, who was primarily responsible for the first wave of translations of Arabic medical texts into Latin, wrote that contraceptives were at times a necessity since not all women who were ill-suited for pregnancy (because of the narrowness of their vagina, for example) were able to abstain from intercourse. Around the middle of the twelfth century, the monastic chronicler Herman of Tournai accused Clemence of Burgundy, the countess of Flanders, of having employed "womanly arts" to avoid conceiving any more children beyond the three sons she had already borne so as to avoid further contestation of the patrimony. Women's knowledge of some kinds of contraceptive or abortifacient remedies is assumed by the writers of early medieval penitential manuals. Similarly, in the early fifteenth century, the preacher Bernardino of Siena openly condemned Florentine women for regularly practicing contraception, an accusation apparently supported by evidence that Florentine women's fertility began to taper off in their mid-thirties, several years before the natural fertility decline of the perimenopausal period. Information on contraceptives was systematically suppressed from translations made for women, and there is no mention of them at all in the one known gynecological text by a female author, Trota of Salerno's *De curis mulierum* (Treatments for women).

Although this omission seems odd in light of modern emphases on reproductive control as a centerpiece of women's health, in other respects Trota's work reflects a decidedly pragmatic character. Trota includes most of the common gynecological conditions—menstrual difficulties, uterine prolapse, and others—yet she also includes problems caused by forced or excessive heterosexual relations, cosmetic recipes, mechanisms to "restore" virginity, pediatric remedies, and even several prescriptions for men's urological disorders. A fourteenth-century Catalan treatise, written in this case by a male author for a queen or infanta, pushes the definition of "women's medicine" further in the direction of cosmetics, the one area of women's medicine that remained peripheral to male practitioners' expected expertise.

THE DISSEMINATION OF GYNECOLOGICAL KNOWLEDGE

When the first specialized gynecological texts were composed in the late antique period (most were translations directly from the Greek), Latin was the "vernacular" and literate midwives or female physicians (*obstetrices* or *medicae*) were often the targeted audience. There is no evidence, however, that this tradition of literate female practitioners continued beyond the sixth century, and aside from the anomalous twelfth-century female writers Trota of Salerno and Hildegard of Bingen, no written tradition of female-authored gynecological texts is known. Instead, male practitioners—monks and other clerics in the early Middle Ages, university-educated physicians and other healers on the boundaries of university culture in the high and late Middle Ages—readily adopted and adapted the written texts on women's medicine they found and, from the early fourteenth century on, started to write their own novel compositions. While most of these new gynecological writings were based on the collected wisdom of the traditional Greek and Arabic authorities (Hippocrates and Galen, Avicenna and Rhazes), new information was incorporated, too, drawn from the practitioners' own clinical experience and anecdotes they had heard from others. In late medieval Italy, postmortems were performed on women (often at the woman's own request), especially to determine the cause of death in disorders that might be hereditary. By the sixteenth century, gynecology became a regular feature of university medical lectures, the number of gynecological and obstetrical writings more than doubled, and the presence of male physicians and surgeons at difficult births was so normative as to be unworthy of special comment. Male practitioners' ability to examine directly the female genitalia remained problematic—southern Italy, for example, maintained a tradition of licensing female surgeons to treat female patients "in order to preserve matronly modesty" well into the fourteenth century—yet such difficulties were largely tolerated out of a sense that learned males were inherently best qualified to diagnose and prescribe for women's ailments.

Whether women's own medical views or practices differed substantially from those of male practitioners is nearly impossible to determine. Even when rendered into the vernacular, most gynecological texts were meant for much the same audiences that the texts had enjoyed in Latin: male physicians, surgeons, barbers, and apothecaries wishing to have a compendium of gynecological knowledge for their regular clinical practices or laymen interested in understanding the "secrets of women," that is, the processes of generation. One twelfth-century translator, for example, rendered at least three different gynecological texts into Hebrew; the only gesture toward a female audience is his fiction in couching one text as a dialogue between the biblical heroine Dinah (who plays the naïve here) and her father. Yet the earliest French translations of the *Trotula,* which date from around the mid-thirteenth century, claim women as (or among) their audience, a feature replicated in some later Dutch and English translations. Whether even these texts had much resonance with the lore transmitted orally among women themselves remains undetermined.

BIBLIOGRAPHY

PRIMARY WORKS

Barkaï, Ron, ed. and trans. *A History of Jewish Gynaecological Texts in the Middle Ages.* Leiden, Netherlands: Brill, 1998.

Barratt, Alexandra, ed. *The Knowing of Woman's Kind in Childing: A Middle English Version of Material Derived from the "Trotula" and Other Sources.* Turnhout, Belgium: Brepols, 2001.

Green, Monica H., ed. and trans. *The "Trotula": A Medieval Compendium of Women's Medicine.* Philadelphia: University of Pennsylvania Press, 2001.

SECONDARY WORKS

Green, Monica H. *Women's Healthcare in the Medieval West: Texts and Contexts.* Aldershot, U.K.: Ashgate, 2000. Includes a complete list of known medieval gynecological texts.

———. "From 'Diseases of Women' to 'Secrets of Women': The Transformation of Gynecological Literature in the Later Middle Ages." *Journal of Medieval and Early Modern Studies* 30 (2000): 5–39.

Hanson, Ann Ellis, and Monica H. Green. "Soranus of Ephesus: *Methodicorum princeps.*" In *Aufstieg und Niedergang der römischen Welt.* Edited by Wolfgang Haase and Hildegard Temporini. Berlin and New York: Walter de Gruyter, 1994.

Kruse, Britta-Juliane. *Verborgene Heilkünste: Geschichte der Frauenmedizin im Spätmittelalter.* Berlin: Walter de Gruyter, 1996.

Salmon, Fernando, and Montserrat Cabré i Pairet. "Fascinating Women: The Evil Eye in Medical Scholasticism." In *Medicine from the Black Death to the Great Pox.* Edited by Roger French et al. Aldershot, U.K.: Ashgate Press, 1998.

MONICA H. GREEN

[See also **DMA:** Hildegard of Bingen, St.; Medicine, History of; Trota and Trotula; **Supp:** Abortion; Childbirth and Infancy; Sexuality, Medical; Women.]

HAGIOGRAPHY, ISLAMIC.

The most recent research into Islamic hagiography has focused on the lives of the saints and pilgrimage sites, both of which represent fundamental aspects of a broad culture of *ziyāra* (visit, visitation) that encompassed pilgrimage or pious visitation to dead as well as living saints and the veneration and use of devotional and talismanic objects. No equivalent for the word "hagiography" exists within Islamic tradition or in modern scholarly discourse. Here it will be applied in the universal sense, divorced of its particular Christian connotation, to encompass the various classes of holy persons and the variety of works in which the lives and deeds of Muslim saints were recorded. As in various Christian traditions, where *vitae* were reproduced to perpetuate the memory of a saint, so too in Islamic tradition did writers seek to perpetuate the memory of saints among devotees, friends, family, and disciples, among whom were scholars, theologians, Sufis, and others. However, two important distinctions need to be made. First, hagiographical writings in Islamic context never assumed the liturgical significance they did in Christianity. Second, whereas Christians lived their lives in imitation of Christ, Muslims sought to emulate the *sunna,* the sayings, deeds, and silent affirmations of the prophet Muḥammad, and Shīʿa also relied on the traditions of the imams— Muḥammad's cousin and son-in-law ʿAlī ibn Abī Ṭālib and his descendants through the Prophet's daughter Fāṭima.

The best-known and one of the earliest examples of a hagiographical work, composed during the eighth and ninth centuries, is the biography of the prophet Muḥammad, which is generally regarded by Muslims as a testament to his exemplary piety and deeds. Traditions contained within the *Sīra* (Life) attribute to the Prophet the ability to work miracles, even though the Prophet himself maintained that he did not possess any extraordinary powers. However, Muslims universally acknowledge that the Koran, as it was revealed by God to the Prophet through the angel Gabriel, is his greatest prophetic miracle *(muʿjiza).* It may be said that the *Sīra* provided an impetus for Sunni Muslims to collect the traditions concerning the lives of the companions and followers of the Prophet and also for Shīʿa to collect those traditions concerning the imams. Muslim traditionists and historians also collected traditions pertaining to the martyrdom of those who died in battle during the early Islamic centuries (referred to as *shuhadāʾ*), such as the companion of the Prophet Abū Ayyūb al-Anṣārī, who died at Constantinople in 672 and whose tomb became a pilgrimage place for Muslims and Byzantines, particularly in time of drought. Also widely circulated were traditions concerning the companions and the followers, such as the companion Abū Dharr al-Ghifārī, who was among the first converts to Islam and was noted for his humility and asceticism.

DEFINING THE SAINT

No universal definition of what constitutes a saint (here referring to any holy person in the general sense) exists in Islam. Unlike various Christian traditions where saints received official recognition from the church, Muslim saints were almost always recognized through popular consensus, such as the acclamation of a town's residents based upon factors including the saint's exemplary piety and erudition, *baraka* (blessing), and the ability to produce miracles *(karamāt)* and effect cures. More controversial were the traits purportedly exhibited by some Sufi saints that were by no means universally recognized as signs of sainthood, such as the ability to fly or walk on water, to possess knowledge of the unseen, to assume different forms at will, and to appear in a location at the blink of an eye. The lack of centralized control over who was to be recognized as a saint and the spread of Sufism were both significant factors contributing to the great diversity in the types of saints that are attested to in the written sources.

The spread of Sufism, or Islamic mysticism, from the ninth century onward also contributed to the popularity of the veneration of saints, as did the establishment in the later Middle Ages of Sufi orders whose founders came to be venerated in their lifetimes and after their deaths. Similarly, shrines honoring various classes of saints proliferated during the eleventh and twelfth centuries in Cairo, Damascus, Aleppo, Baghdad, and other cities, towns, and villages.

The most common Arabic word for saint is *walī* (plural, *awliyā*), which in the Koranic context refers to the community of believers as "Friends of God," though not to any particular class of individuals. However, during the ninth and tenth centuries, writers appropriated the word and applied it to Sufi and non-Sufi saints. Other designations, which frequently occur in edificatory, literary, legal, theological, and historical works, include righteous individuals *(ṣāliḥūn)*, ascetics *(zuhhād)*, recluses *(nussāk)*, devout worshipers *('ubbād)*, and other classes of individuals that were not mutually exclusive. Another class of saint and a sort of anomaly existing at the margins of society was the *muwallah* (i.e., one enamored of God; a marginal holy man), who somewhat resembled in his bizarre behavior the "holy fool" of Christianity. The historical record attests to a number of male and female *muwallah*s who lived in Syria, Egypt, and elsewhere, whom common people regarded as possessing *baraka* (blessing) and spiritual illuminations yet who variously wallowed in their own filth, rambled incoherently, ignored the world around them, and disregarded the norms of religious propriety and social conventions. Per-

haps, owing to a lack of precision concerning the designations, a saint may be classified by his biographer, for instance, as an "ascetic devout worshiper." Finally, to the aforementioned categories of saints may be added the prophets *(anbiyā; singular, nabī)*. Although the prophets and patriarchs, with the sole exception of Muḥammad, are regarded not as "historical" saints who lived during the rise of Islam in the seventh century but rather as "traditional" saints, their tombs and shrines became objects of pilgrimage and devotion like those of other holy persons.

One of the greatest measures of the "sainthood" of an individual was the miracles produced at his or her tomb or shrine. Hagiographical texts, including pilgrimage works, pay particular attention to the miracles, divine blessings *(baraka)*, and other phenomena that manifested themselves at sacred places. Oral traditions, which are often referred to in the sources discussed below, constitute an essential element of *vitae* that also represented a means of legitimating the miracles and *baraka* associated with a particular place.

WOMEN SAINTS

Women saints were venerated throughout the Islamic world. Among them were the Virgin Mary, whose cult was widespread throughout Greater Syria and Egypt and whose shrine outside Damascus was a popular place of pilgrimage for Christians and Muslims; Fāṭima, the daughter of the Prophet; and Zaynab, the daughter of 'Alī ibn Abī Ṭālib, who had several shrines dedicated to her, including one in Cairo and another in Damascus. The sixteenth-century Syrian historian and preacher Ibn Ṭūlūn dedicated compositions to two women saints, both descendants of the Prophet—the aforementioned Sitt Zaynab and Sitt Nafīsa—and in a number of other works mentions women saints buried in and around Damascus.

Also prominent in biographical collections and pilgrimage guides were early mystics like Rābi'a al-Adawīya. Several individual compositions were devoted to women in addition to the hagiographical accounts found in biographical dictionaries, such as al-Sulamī's collection of eighty-two biographies of Sufi women saints who lived during the eighth through eleventh centuries and the works of al-Iṣfahānī and Farīd al-Dīn al-'Aṭṭār discussed below.

SOURCES

Descriptions of the pious and exemplary deeds, acts of intercession, charity, cures, and miracles *(karāmāt)* of holy persons are to be found in biographical accounts and obituary notices, hagiographical treatises devoted to the life of a person (referred to in Arabic as *manāqib*—qualities and characteristics), *faḍāʾil* literature, (i.e., excellences, merits, virtues), biographical entries (*tarājim;* singular, *tarjama*) and collections pertaining to a particular class or group of individuals (*ṭabaqāt*), historical works, pilgrimage guides (*kutub al-ziyārāt*), and incidentally in travel literature, which often contains brief accounts of a saint's pilgrimage site and anecdotes and descriptions of encounters with the saint. The vast majority of these works were composed in Arabic, though some, like the Persian mystical poet Farīd al-Dīn al-ʿAṭṭār's *Tadhkirat al-awliyāʾ* (Remembrance of the saints) in the thirteenth century, were composed in Persian.

Abū Nuʿaym al-Iṣfahānī's eleventh-century *Ḥilyat al-awliyāʾ* (Ornament of the saints) comprises 649 hagiographies, which contain often formulaic apothegms and pithy sayings concerning the Prophet's family, his companions and followers, and the earliest generations of righteous Muslims. The saints' lives are described in terms of mystical ideals. Scholars, preachers, theologians, scribes, and others composed individual compositions devoted to the life of a holy person or persons. These works include Ḍiyāʾ al-Dīn al-Maqdisī's thirteenth-century hagiographical biographies of his uncle Abū ʿUmar and of the other members of his family who settled outside Damascus after fleeing the crusader conquest of the Holy Land; works in praise of rulers, such as the thirteenth-century preacher Ibn al-Jawzī's *Manāqib ʿUmar ibn ʿAbd al-ʿAzīz* (Qualities and characteristics of ʿUmar ibn ʿAbd al-ʿAzīz), a biography of the Umayyad caliph, who was renowned for his exemplary piety; and works in praise of theologians, such as Ibn al-Jawzī's *Manāqib al-Imām Aḥmad ibn Ḥanbal* on the life of a founder of one of the four Sunni schools of jurisprudence. In addition to the aforementioned works of al-Iṣfahānī and al-ʿAṭṭār, other Sufi biographical dictionaries include the thirteenth-century ascetic Sufi Al-Ḥusayn ibn Jamāl al-Dīn al-Khazrajī's *Sīrat al-awliyāʾ fī-al-qarn al-sābiʿ al-Hijrī* (Biography of the saints in the seventh century of the Hijra), which describes some of the extraordinary acts of Sufi saints who lived primarily in Egypt during the thirteenth century. The sixteenth-century Egyptian historian and Sufi al-Shaʿrānī produced a collection concerning the lives and sayings of Sufis that was known as *al-Ṭabaqāt al-kubrā*. Later medieval writers, many of whom were Sufis, authored compositions concerning saints, their lives, and burial places, like the sixteenth-century Syrian Ibn Ṭūlūn, who is credited with twenty-three compositions on members of the Prophet's family, companions,

followers, and others. Such works were not entirely unique in their composition as they often relied upon older written and oral traditions.

Pilgrimage guides describe, though in less detail than other works, those characteristics for which a saint was renowned during his or her lifetime but do not usually present complete hagiographical biographies. Although some pilgrimage guides contained stories of the pious deeds and attributes of saints, their emphasis was largely on the pilgrimage sites, their efficaciousness, the miracles produced there, the legends and anecdotes associated with them, and proper pilgrimage etiquette. A common element of several of these guides is the night vision in which a saint or prophet appears, which attests to the site's sacredness as well as to the importance of venerating the saint associated with it. The following guides listed by region provide significant details of saints' lives: for Egypt, Ibn ʿUthmān's *Murshid al-zuwwār ilā qubūr al-abrār* (The pilgrims' guide to the tombs of the righteous); for Syria, Ibn al-Ḥawrānī's *al-Ishārāt ilā amākin al-ziyārāt* (Guide to pilgrimage places), which he composed for a fellow Sufi, intending "to guide [others] to righteousness so that it will serve as an aid to the one who sets out on pilgrimage." Similarly, al-Biqāʿī's *al-Nubdha al-laṭīfa,* which includes biographies of saints, was to be used during pilgrimage as an aid to remembering the saints who were buried in a particular location. For the Shiite pilgrimage sites of Iraq and elsewhere, Ibn Qūlūya's *Kāmil al-ziyārāt* (Complete pilgrimages) and the work of his disciple al-Shaykh al-Mufīd's *Kitāb al-Mazār* (The book of the pilgrimage site) contain traditions extolling the virtues of the Shiite imams and the efficaciousness of making pilgrimage to their tombs, in addition to the more important task of instructing devotees in the rites of the *ziyāra*.

BIBLIOGRAPHY

Arberry, A. J. *Sufism: An Account of the Mystics of Islam.* London: Allen and Unwin, 1950.

Bosworth, C. E. "Manāqib Literature." In *Encyclopedia of Arabic Literature.* Vol 2. London and New York: Routledge, 1998.

Brinner, W. M. "The Prophet and Saint: The Two Exemplars of Islam." In *Saints and Virtues.* Edited by John Stratton Hawley. Berkeley: University of California Press, 1987.

Denny, F. M. "'God's Friends': The Sanctity of Persons in Islam." In *Sainthood: Its Manifestations in World Religions.* Edited by Richard Kieckhefer and George D. Bond. Berkeley: University of California Press, 1988.

Goldziher, Ignác. "Veneration of Saints in Islam." In *Muslim Studies.* Edited by S. M. Stern. Translated by C. R. Barber and S. M. Stern. Vol. 2. London, 1967–1971.

Meri, Josef W. "Aspects of Baraka (Blessings) and Ritual Devotion among Medieval Muslims and Jews." *Medieval Encounters: Jewish, Christian, and Muslim Culture in Confluence and Dialogue* 5 (1999): 46–69.

———. "The Etiquette of Devotion in the Islamic Cult of Saints." In *The Cult of Saints in Late Antiquity and the Middle Ages: Essays on the Contribution of Peter Brown.* Edited by James Howard-Johnston and Paul Antony Hayward. Oxford: Oxford University Press, 1999.

———. "A Late Medieval Syrian Pilgrimage Guide: Ibn al-Hawrani's *Al-Ishārāt ilā amākin al-ziyārāt* (Guide to pilgrimage places)." *Medieval Encounters: Jewish, Christian, and Muslim Culture in Confluence and Dialogue* 7 (2001): 3–78.

———. *The Cult of Saints Among Muslims and Jews in Medieval Syria.* Oxford: Oxford University Press, 2002.

———. "Ziyāra." In *Encyclopaedia of Islam.* New ed. Vol. 11. Leiden, Netherlands: Brill, 1960–2002.

Pellat, Charles. "Manākib." In *Encyclopaedia of Islam.* New ed. Vol. 6. Leiden, Netherlands: Brill, 1960–2002.

Raven, W. "Sīra." In *Encyclopaedia of Islam.* New ed. Vol. 9. Leiden, Netherlands: Brill, 1960–2002.

Schimmel, Annemarie. *And Muhammad Is His Messenger.* Chapel Hill: University of North Carolina Press, 1985.

Smith, Margaret, and Charles Pellat. "Rābiʿa al-ʿAdawiyya al-Ḳaysiyya." In *Encyclopaedia of Islam.* New ed. Vol. 8. Leiden, Netherlands: Brill, 1960–2002.

Strothmann, R. "Nafīsa, al-Sayyida." In *Encyclopaedia of Islam.* New ed. Vol. 7. Leiden, Netherlands: Brill, 1960–2002.

Sulamī, Muḥammad ibn al-Ḥusayn. *Early Sufi Women.* Edited and translated by Rkia Elaroui Cornell. Louisville, Ky.: Fons Vitae, 1999. (Translation of *Dhikr an-Niswa al-Mutaʿabbidāt aṣ-Ṣūfiyyāt.*)

Taylor, Christopher S. *In the Vicinity of the Righteous: Ziyara and the Veneration of Muslim Saints in Late Medieval Egypt.* Leiden, Netherlands: Brill, 1999.

JOSEF W. MERI

[See also **DMA:** Hagiography, Byzantine; Hagiography, Western European; Islam, Religion; Muḥammad; Sects, Islamic; **Supp:** Hagiography, Jewish.]

HAGIOGRAPHY, JEWISH. The term "Jewish hagiography" has appeared only in recent decades. Its use acknowledges that the texts and ritual practices discussed here correspond in form and function to those traditionally called "hagiographical" in Western scholarship. In fact, there is no single term in Hebrew that describes the literature devoted to the depiction of "lives of heroic virtue," to borrow a generous definition of Christian hagiography coined by the historian Thomas Head. Scholars of Jewish texts have long referred to *sifrut ha-shevaḥ* (the "literature of praise") or *maʿase-tsaddiqim* (tales of the righteous), exempla and legends about the extraordinary piety and wisdom of the great rabbis of old. Tales of mar-

tyrdom, some set in the world of late antiquity and some in the medieval period, have also played an important role in Jewish religious identity and life.

Overall, the literature of Jewish "saints" (*tsaddiqim, ḥasidim,* or *qedoshim*) finds a place in a range of liturgical, polemical, didactic, homiletical, poetic, and popular genres. Most of this literature is in Hebrew, but oral and written vernacular stories circulated as well. Whether in Judeo-Arabic, Yiddish, or the Romance vernaculars, they provided access to the legends of sacred heroes to women and children as well as to the male audience for writing in Hebrew. Jewish hagiography thus served a variety of audiences throughout the medieval Jewish world. Significantly, Jewish hagiographic conventions deriving from Andalusia, the Maghreb (Morocco, Algeria, and Tunisia), and the Muslim East share features with Jewish hagiography produced in the Christian world, while in other ways the two literary traditions are distinct. Jewish hagiography also shares features with contemporary non-Jewish hagiography; in other respects, it consciously and unconsciously diverges from non-Jewish conventions. Following is a general description of the hagiographical literature and some remarks on its performance and use.

The exegetical and midrashic writing of late antiquity illustrates the early practice of "filling in" the lives of biblical and rabbinic heroes. In the medieval period, these traditions developed into literary treatments of the lives and deeds of contemporary holy men as well. Scholars describe an intermediate period between these two, focusing on the great rabbis of old but in parables or expanded narratives. Many of the "hagiographical" texts of this transitional period are really exempla embedded in longer exegetical, homiletical, midrashic, or legal works. The creative resources of liturgical poetry also rewove exegetical traditions into poetic memorials to biblical heroes, cultic priests, and rabbinic martyrs.

Several quasi-historical narratives appeared in the early medieval period that come close to full-blown hagiography. Among these, the tenth-century *Sefer Josippon,* based loosely on the works of Josephus, included many embellished narratives, as did the *Megillat Aḥimaʿats,* written by Aḥimaʿats ben Paltiel in the mid-eleventh century. Both of these works were produced in southern Italy, an important Jewish center in the early medieval period and the origin of many literary and religious traditions that took root in the Rhenish and French regions known as "Ashkenaz." Other works, such as Nissim ben Jacob ben Nissim ibn Shahin's *Ḥibbur yafeh min ha-yeshuʿa* (An elegant composition concerning relief after distress—originally written in Arabic), the *Alphabet of Ben Sira,* and the *Midrash on the "Ten Commandments,"* originated in the Holy Land and the Islamic east. Eventually, they made their way westward where they achieved great popularity with Jewish readers in Christian Europe. Still other legends, such as those collected in *Ma'aseh-Buch,* circulated in Yiddish. Two early sixteenth-century works integrated hagiographical material into historical chronicles. Solomon ibn Verga's *Shevet Yehudah* and Gedaliah ibn Yahya's *Shalshelet ha-Qabbala* were both produced by Spanish Jews who lived through the expulsion of 1492. Though composed relatively late, they preserve a wealth of medieval legends in accounts of the learning, piety, and miraculous powers of the rabbis.

Like the hagiographical ideal preserved in Christian prose and verse, the idealized figure of the Jewish "holy man" changed over time and place. Two types of heroic figures dominate the literature, one a learned scholar-rabbi and one a figure of extreme piety. Where the first type of "saint" is often pitted against Christian or Muslim adversaries, whom he defeats by a combination of wit and magical skill, the second type is revered less for learning than as an ascetic, healer, or miracle-worker. In addition to legends about such rabbinic figures as Akiba or Hananiah ben Teradion, *Ḥibbur yafeh min ha-yeshu'a* preserves a number of tales in which a pious Jew is astonished to learn that his future place in Paradise will be next to a local scoundrel. These stories require the respectable Jew to unearth the quiet and unpublicized deeds that have merited his future neighbor his eternal reward. In the more radical Pietist sources, the holy man was an ascetic devoted to uncovering the hidden Will of God.

In contrast, the scholar-heroes are historical figures such as Rashi (Solomon ben Isaac of Troyes, d.1105), Abraham ibn Ezra (*ca.* 1089–1164), Abraham ben Moses Maimonides (1135–1204), and Yehiel of Paris (*d. ca.* 1265). Legends featuring Maimonides refer to his skill as a doctor (in particular, his formidable knowledge of poisons and antidotes). Strikingly, the great philosopher, legal scholar, and man of medicine, who was a staunch rationalist, is also depicted as a master of "practical kabbalah" (magic). European Jewish legends about the great medieval rabbis frequently attribute them prophetic powers, along with the ability to transport themselves instantly from place to place (transvection), find lost objects, levitate, or disappear. These skills are exercised in confrontations with Christian bishops, lords, kings, sultans, or imams, emphasizing their polemical core. Muslim accounts of Maimonides's temporary conversion to Islam, such as the fourteenth-century version of *Salaḥ al-din al-Ṣafadi,* retain elements of "trickster"

tales found in Jewish legend and were probably imported from Jewish sources.

Some of these heroic legends recount a biographical "life," beginning with the hero's unusual birth and moving through adolescence, adulthood, and death. Of particular interest are the stories surrounding two great twelfth-century rabbis, the German Pietist Judah ben Samuel he-Hasid (Judah the Pious) and the Spanish-born exegete and poet Abraham ibn Ezra. Judah's life illustrates the motif of the "wild child" who by divine intervention achieves success in the schoolroom and beyond. Stories of Abraham ibn Ezra, in contrast, focus on his wanderings, a motif found elsewhere but richly supported in ibn Ezra's case by the historical record. In hagiographical accounts, the wandering scholar often travels in disguise as a rude beggar. His identity is concealed until he has unexpectedly completed a difficult poem or displayed some form of erudition.

Medieval Hebrew martyrology first appeared in the wake of the First Crusade (1096–1099). Rabbinic literature had preserved tales of martyrdom set in late antiquity, and some of the subjects of these tales—notably the "Ten Martyrs" of the Hadrianic persecutions—were honored in the liturgy for the Day of Atonement *(Yom Kippur).* Stories of the Maccabean martyrs reached medieval Jews indirectly, and the suicide-martyrs of Masada were described in *Sefer Josippon.* The brutal crusader attacks on the Rhineland Jewish communities in the spring of 1096 led to an outpouring of commemorative writing that drew on these and contemporary sources.

Some of the 1096 victims were slain by crusaders, while others slaughtered their families and themselves rather than wait for the crusaders and their ultimatum of conversion or death. Most of the literature that memorializes these holy "saints" *(qedoshim)* who died in the act of "sanctifying [God's] Name" *(qiddush ha-Shem)* is liturgical poetry; three prose chronicles appeared in the following decades. This literature breaks from the traditional conception of the "saint" as a figure of extreme learning or piety, stressing the demographic diversity of the victims (male and female, adult and child). Over the next two centuries martyrological writing flourished in northern European Jewish communities, which were battered not merely by crusader or mob attacks but increasingly by fiscal, legal, and social policies designed to marginalize, degrade, and ultimately convert them. The Jewish victims of judicial prosecutions in the wake of blood, murder, and host libels (charges that the Jews required Christian blood or a desecrated host for ritual purposes) found commemoration in verse and prose. In northern France, this "second-generation" martyrological literature reflects the powerful influence of the rabbinic dialecticians called Tosafists. The idealized martyr of Tosafist poetry reinforced the image of the scholar-rabbi as a religious, even prophetic, authority. Reflecting larger cultural tastes, Jewish martyrology from the late thirteenth century emphasized the physical suffering of the victims.

Women and children are poorly represented in medieval Jewish hagiographical writing, and a fuller reconstruction of the world of Jewish female piety and its textual representation awaits. The hagiographical literature reflects the values of a homosocial and textual community, marginalizing allusions to women and stressing obedience and passivity over female agency. When women do play a strong role (as in 1096 texts), it is to underline the unanimity of communal resistance. In liturgical poetry, allusions to women and children martyrs stress the willingness and haste with which they rush to the stake or to slaughter. The emphasis on learning as an attribute of holiness also inhibited the election of women (and children) to literary sainthood. Indeed, Jewish sacred books, especially the Torah, play an important role in hagiographical traditions and are depicted as having powers to ward off evil and also as "martyrs" who are desecrated and burned.

The Jewish communities under Islam, while generally better off, were subjected to periodic hostility. Yet they never developed the martyrological ideal to the same extent as the Jews in Christian Europe. Significantly, though, persecution in these communities, and later in Reconquista Spain, resulted in high rates of conversion (to Islam in the Maghreb and Yemen, to Christianity in Spain). Thus the "martyrocentric ideal" in northern Europe may have reinforced resistance to conversionary pressure. In fact, the stories of martyrdom from Arab-Jewish communities differ from the literature of France, England, and Germany. Even the technical expression *qiddush ha-Shem,* found ubiquitously in northern European Jewish texts, is absent, with a preference for the term *yiḥḥud ha-Shem* (unification of [God's] Name). Similarly, the language of pollution that surrounds representations of the Christian cult, particularly baptism, is gone; tales of forced conversion to Islam refer to "transgression" *(pesha')* not pollution.

Medieval Jewish literary traditions also include "antihagiographical" writing, such as the parodic "life of Jesus" *(Toldot Yeshu)* that circulated in Hebrew and Yiddish in the Rhineland. *Toldot Yeshu* depicts Jesus as a type of false messiah. The illegitimate child of Mary and her seducer, young Jesus steals "the Holy Name" of God, which he abuses (working "miracles"). A related genre circulated among Jewish communities in the Islamic East and described, sometimes sincerely, the exploits of contemporary "false messiahs" such as David Ro'ie in Yemen (active in the 1160s). The debunking of these figures (for instance, by Maimonides in his Epistles to the Jews of Yemen and Montpellier) testifies to the awareness of rabbinic authorities that spontaneous holiness posed a threat to the traditional, law-based, regulation of Jewish communal life.

Jewish "saints" were commemorated in a number of ways. Liturgical rites included the recitation of hymns or commemorative prayers during fast days such as the Day of Atonement, the Ninth of Av, the fast of Gedaliah, or local fast days or "Purims." Fast-day rituals also entailed the draping of the synagogue altar in white or black, the removal of the Torah scrolls for circumambulation of the synagogue, processionals to gravesites, and the wearing of mourning clothes. Sumptuary regulations describe the restrictions on communal acts of commemoration, including limits on celebrations or festive dress, the establishment of public fasts, and the like. In the Middle East and in North Africa, pilgrimages to the graves of "holy men" were a major feature of saint worship. Indeed, pilgrimages, songs in mixed Hebrew and Judeo-Arabic, and popular "miracle stories" constituted an important dimension of Maghrebi Jewish life. Curiously, in Morocco both Jews and Muslims frequently embraced saints from either faith.

Whether Sephardic, Oriental, or Ashkenazic, the individual hero of a Jewish hagiographical tale embodied, sometimes in exceptional form, the virtues of a communal ideal. Ultimately, the medieval narratives of sacred lives centered around the biography of a holy people, its trials and temptations, its fortitude in exile, and its unshattered faith in its God. From this vantage, the tokens of corporate affiliation—circumcision, mastery of shared textual traditions, the following of purity laws and regulations concerning food, and Sabbath observance—stamped the idealized individual as a quintessential Jew even as they ratified communal boundaries.

BIBLIOGRAPHY

PRIMARY WORKS

Gedaliah ibn Yahya. *Shalshelet haQabbalah.* Warsaw: Lebenson, 1877.

Nissim ben Cairouan. *Ḥibbur yafeh min ha-yeshu'a.* Edited by H. Hirschberg. Jerusalem: Mossad haRav Kook, 1954.

Sefer Ḥasidim of Judah the Pious. Edited by Reuven Margolies. Jerusalem: Mossad haRav Kook, 1957. Bologna text.

Sefer Ḥasidim of Judah the Pious. 1891. Reprint, edited by Judah Blau Wistinetzki, Berlin: Meqitsei-nirdamim, 1998. Parma text.

Solomon ibn Verga. *Shevet Yehudah.* Edited by A. Shoḥet. Jerusalem: Mossad Bialik, 1947.

Wertheimer, Abraham, ed. *Sefer Josippon.* Jerusalem: Hominer, 1955–1956. Falsely attributed to Joseph ben Gurion.

SECONDARY WORKS

Avishur, Isaac. "New Folktales from Egypt and Iraq about Abraham Ibn Ezra." In *Meḥqerim bitsirato shel Avraham Ibn Ezra, Teʿudah VIII.* Edited by Israel Levin. Tel Aviv, Israel: Universitat Tel-Aviv, 1992. In Hebrew.

Ben-Ami, Issachar. *Culte des saints et pèlerinages judéo-musulmans au Maroc.* Paris: Maisonneuve et Larose, 1990.

Berger, Isaiah. "The Rambam in Popular Legend." *Massad* 2 (1936): 216–238. In Hebrew.

Brüll, N. "Beiträge zur jüdischen Sagen- und Sprachkinde im Mittelater." *Jahrbücher für jüdische Geschichte und Literatur* 9 (1889): 1–85.

Einbinder, Susan. *Beautiful Death: Jewish Poetry and Martyrdom in Medieval France.* Princeton, N.J.: Princeton University Press, 2002.

Friedman, Mordechai Akiva. *HaRambam, haMashiah beTeman vehaShmad.* Jerusalem: Makhon Ben-tsvi and Hebrew University, 2001.

Gaster, Moses. *The Maʿaseh Book.* Philadelphia: Jewish Publication Society, 1934.

Habermann, Abraham. 1945. *Sefer Gezerot Ashkenaz veTsarfat.* Reprint, Jerusalem: Ophir, 1971.

Marcus, Ivan. "Une communauté pieuse et le doute: Mourir pour la Sanctification du Nom (Qiddouch ha-Chem) en Achkenaz (Europe du Nord), et l'histoire de rabbi Amnon de Mayence." *Annales* 5 (1994): 1031–1047.

Yassif, Eli. *The Hebrew Folktale: History, Genre, Meaning.* Translated by Jacqueline Teitelbaum. Bloomington: Indiana University Press, 1999.

SUSAN L. EINBINDER

[See also **DMA:** Hagiography, Western European.]

HEBREW LANGUAGE. Hebrew is a Northwest Semitic language of the Canaanite group, close to Phoenician, Moabite, Edomite, and Ammonite, documented in Syria Palaestina since the end of the second millennium B.C. The "classical" Hebrew language, that is, the language spoken by the ancient Israelites and in whose literary version the books of the Bible were written across several centuries, was no longer in use many years before Alexander the Great conquered the Near East (fourth century B.C.). The colloquial Hebrew employed by the rabbis for their teaching had also lost its living character by the end of the second century A.D. The exile and diaspora of most Jewish communities toward the east and west meant, for most of them, the adoption of local languages. At the beginning of the Middle Ages, under the Byzantine and Persian Empires, the use of Hebrew was confined almost solely to the synagogue for the reading of the Torah and the Prophets, for prayer, and for liturgical poems or midrashic homilies on the Bible. Only in a relatively small number of literary works was the old language still employed, though in a more or less artificial way.

In the early Middle Ages, Hebrew was not the main language spoken by the Jewish people. Most communities had adopted Aramaic first, and from the seventh century on, Arabic or the languages of the host countries were used for their daily life and cultural expressions. Hebrew as a spoken or literary tongue was very rare. It fully deserved the name *leshon ha-qodesh,* "the holy language," as the tongue of the sacred books reserved for religious activities.

As the Middle Ages progressed, the literary usage of Hebrew increased noticeably, due in part to the study of its grammar and lexicography. The language used by medieval writers was not a direct descendant of biblical or rabbinic Hebrew but the result of recovering the linguistic inheritance of these previous periods, transforming the senses of old words, and creating new ones by analogy or by adapting the morphology and the syntax to the new necessities of expression, under the influence of other Semitic or Romance languages.

TOWARD THE REVITALIZATION: THE FIRST MEDIEVAL STUDIES ON HEBREW

A new interest in biblical Hebrew and its grammar developed in the east region of the Islamic Empire during the ninth and tenth centuries. The origins of this tendency have been connected with the Karaites, a Jewish sect that, instead of accepting the legal authority of the post-biblical rabbis, devoted its energies to the interpretation of the biblical text through the text itself. Following the methods used by Arabic linguists in their exegesis of the Koran, the Karaites saw in the grammatical and lexicographical study of the language of the Bible the best way to elucidate its meaning. Some lists of grammatical terms, vocabularies, and philological observations to Arabic translations of the Bible, probably from the ninth century, have been preserved. Although the first large work on Hebrew grammar of Karaite origin seems to be Abū Yaʿqūb Yūsuf ibn Nuḥ's *al-Diqduq,* written in Jerusalem in the second half of the tenth century, the grammatical tradition that it reflects had probably a much earlier origin in Iraq and Iran. Some of these writings were in Hebrew, but most were in Judeo-Arabic (usually transliterated in Hebrew characters).

The Masoretes of Tiberias (in particular the Ben-Asher family at the end of the ninth and beginning of the tenth century), who studied the minute details of the reading tradition of the Bible and the written transmission of its text, contributed a deeper knowledge of very subtle aspects of the biblical language; and its grammar was attained. The grammatical and lexicographical works of Saadiah Gaon also contributed to the quick development of Hebrew linguistic studies. He wrote *Kitāb faṣīḥ lughat al-ʿibrāniyyīn* (The book of elegance of the language of the Hebrews; in Judeo-Arabic), the first normative and systematic grammar of biblical and rabbinical Hebrew, probably between 910 and 921 in Palestine, and later revised it in Babylon. Saadiah also wrote the first important Hebrew dictionary, the *Sefer ha-agron* (collection). Thanks to other philologists from north Africa (such as Ibn Quraysh or the Karaite David ben Abraham Alfasi), the basis of comparative Semitic studies consolidated, and Hebrew lexicography was therefore improved.

HEBREW REVIVED IN AL-ANDALUS AND THE ISLAMIC EMPIRE

From the middle of the tenth century on, Jewish intellectuals of al-Andalus, in the western end of the Islamic Empire, not only continued the linguistic study, but also decided to use Hebrew as a living language in their writings and especially in their new poetry, inspired by the techniques of Arabic poets. Hebrew was for the Jews of Sepharad (the Iberian Peninsula) a sign of identity and an instrument of cultural expression not only in the traditional biblical and rabbinic fields of study but also in new cultural forms that paralleled the best achievements of the dominant language, Arabic. The Bible served Jewish writers as a stylistic and linguistic model; however, it caused a confrontation with Arabic. This dispute involved national and religious pride, and it challenged Jewish writers to prove that Hebrew could also be a culturally significant language.

This revitalization of Hebrew language and culture was possible thanks to the new atmosphere in the court of Córdoba and the significant social change in the Jewish community. Trying to breed an autonomous cultural life in al-Andalus, in the tenth century the caliph ʿAbd al-Raḥmān III found an excellent collaborator in the Jewish court officer Ḥasdai ibn Shaprūṭ, whose secretary Menaḥem ibn Sārūq wrote the *Maḥberet,* a biblical dictionary in Hebrew—not in Arabic, like most previous linguistic works. Another linguist, Dunash ben Labrat, replied to Menaḥem in the same language. The poetry written by both scholars, dealing with nonliturgical topics, was also in Hebrew, imitating the language of the Bible with many literal expressions taken from the biblical books and adapted into completely new contexts.

The Sephardic Hebrew renaissance was related to a broader cultural phenomenon that first appeared in al-Andalus in the tenth century: the reaction of the *shuʿūbiyya,* which stressed the value of the national cultures, to ʿarabiyya with its pan-Arabistic perspective. Jewish authors, despite their admiration for Arabic culture, could contrast their historical Holy Land to Arabia, their Torah to the Koran, and Hebrew to Arabic.

From the tenth century on, the Jews under Islamic rule used Hebrew not only for their prayers but also for composing secular poetry. The genres in prose could be written in the same tongue, but for dealing with technical subjects, such as science, medicine, or philosophy, and even in many cases for philological studies, they preferred Judeo-Arabic. The everyday language of these Jews continued to be Arabic. Only in exceptional cases, for instance, when a Jewish traveler went from one community to another in far away regions, was Hebrew employed as a kind of lingua franca for mutual understanding.

The linguistic ideal for most Andalusian Jewish scholars was the "pure language," that is, the Hebrew of the Bible, used in the correct grammatical way and without any change or innovation; this excluded in particular the language of the rabbinical writings and the daring innovations of the synagogal poetry of the Byzantine epoch. The "puristic" trend, not yet apparent in earlier poets such as Samuel ha-Nagid and Solomon ben Judah ibn Gabirol, became particularly apparent in the secular poetry written at the end of the eleventh and the first half of the twelfth century, during the "golden age" of Hebrew poetry, by poets such as Moses and Abraham ibn Ezra, or Judah Halevi. In any case, Arabic culture had a deep influence in all spheres of the language of medieval Hebrew literature, including secular poetry, where quotations and expressions from the Bible were blended together with motifs, images, and technical words taken from Arabic.

One of the main problems found in Hebrew writing was that the number of words preserved in the biblical books was too limited when dealing with all possible fields of life and culture. Writers could choose to use a language with a larger vocabulary, like Arabic, for writing on technical matters or to enlarge the Hebrew vocabulary by creating new words. While some Jewish intellectuals thought that Arabic was much richer in possibilities than Hebrew, other philologists and poets regretted that the Jewish people had forgotten its own language and used that of other people. The need for introducing new words in the old language to make it more flexible was particularly felt when some Jews familiar with Islamic culture decided to translate scientific, philosophical, and philological works written in Arabic (by both Arabs and Jews) into Hebrew. These translators—above all, the Tibbonid family in the south of France in the twelfth and thirteenth centuries—enriched the language with many new words and lexical calques.

The medieval pronunciation of Hebrew in al-Andalus and other regions of the Islamic domain, as described by the grammarians of the time, conformed in general to the rules or usages collected in the Tiberian (Palestinian) studies on the traditional pronunciation of Hebrew and preservation of the biblical text (Masorah), with some peculiarities, such as the reduction from seven to five vowels. The influence of Arabic was especially clear in the pronunciation of the guttural and emphatic consonants and also in the syntax (particularly in the constructions of verbs and some sentences used in technical writings), while the morphology followed in general the biblical patterns.

HEBREW IN THE CHRISTIAN KINGDOMS OF EUROPE

The Jews that left al-Andalus in the time of the Almohads and established themselves in the northern kingdoms of the Iberian Peninsula remained familiar with Islamic culture, although they lived in a very different linguistic context, the recently formed Romance languages. Andalusian linguistic and literary traditions were preserved during several generations, especially among the most distinguished families. They continued writing poetry in biblical Hebrew (occasionally with some rabbinic additions), imitating the Andalusian masters in a different cultural atmosphere and reflecting the new trends in their works. At the same time, they developed a Hebrew literary prose almost unknown in the preceding period, and wrote in Hebrew their literary correspondence, ethical, exegetical, and philosophical treatises; polemics; books on history or travels; and scientific and medical writings. They also signed public documents and wrote notes on their commercial activities in Hebrew. The Jews of Provence and Italy shared many of these cultural and linguistic tendencies.

The Jewish communities of northern France in the Rhine valley (Ashkenaz) adopted the local language of this region, Middle High German, and blended it with Romance (French) and Hebrew elements to form Yiddish, which was written in the Hebrew alphabet. From the thirteenth century on, this language was spoken in eastern Europe, where it received a strong Slavic influence. Medieval Ashkenazi Jews used Hebrew mostly for prayer and for some juridical, ethical, and exegetical writings; it was not the pure biblical language but a rather miscellaneous language intermingled with rabbinic Hebrew and Aramaic, without well-defined grammatical rules, and with some influence from the vernacular languages. The Ashkenazi developed their own pronunciation of Hebrew, different from the usual one found in Palestine or Sepharad. One of the most representative scholars of Ashkenazi culture was Rashi (1040–1105), whose well-known commentaries on the Bible and the Talmud are written in an easy and intelligible Hebrew with many rabbinic and Aramaic words, calques from French, and a good number of neologisms.

During the Middle Ages, Hebrew left a clear trace in most Western languages. Many names of people and places, taken from the Bible, were incorporated into the vernacular; words and expressions from the biblical books and Jewish life were also adapted into Romance and German languages (mainly, but not exclusively, in the religious sphere). The Hebrew language not only received particular attention from the Jews, it also attracted the deep interest of some Christian theologians who found it helpful for understanding the Bible. At the same time, Hebrew became a very notable vehicle of culture in the process of transmission to Western intellectuals of many Hellenistic scientific works adapted by Arabic writers.

BIBLIOGRAPHY

Allony, Nehemya. *El resurgimiento de la lengua hebrea en al-Andalus.* Madrid, Spain: Aben Ezra Ediciones, 1995.

Dotan, A., ed. *Or rishon be-hokhmat ha-lashon: Sefer Tsahut leshon ha-'Ivrim / la-Rav Se'adyah Ga'on.* With introduction and critical edition. 2 vols. Jerusalem: World Union of Jewish Studies, The Rabbi David Moses and Amalia Rosen Foundation, 1997.

Glinert, Lewis, ed. *Hebrew in Ashkenaz: A Language in Exile.* New York: Oxford University Press, 1993.

Goldenberg, Esther. "Hebrew Language, Medieval." In *Encyclopaedia Judaica.* Vol. 16. Jerusalem: Keter Publishing House, 1971.

Halkin, A. S. "The Medieval Jewish Attitude toward Hebrew." In *Biblical and Other Studies.* Edited by Alexander Altmann. Cambridge, Mass.: Harvard University Press, 1963.

Kahn, Geoffrey. *The Early Karaite Tradition of Hebrew Grammatical Thought: Including a Critical Edition, Translation, and Analysis of the Diqduq of Abū Yaʿqūb Yūsuf ibn Nūh on the Hagiographa.* Leiden, Netherlands, and Boston: Brill, 2000.

Morag, S. "Hebrew in Medieval Spain: Aspects of Evolution and Transmission." *Miscelánea de estudios Árabes y Hebraicos* 44 (1995): 3–21.

Saenz-Badillos, Angel. *A History of the Hebrew Language.* Translated by John Elwolde. Cambridge, U.K., and New York: Cambridge University Press, 1993.

Saenz-Badillos, Angel, and Judith Targarona Borras. *Gramáticos hebreos de al-Andalus (siglos X–XIII): Filología y Biblia.* Córdoba, Spain: El Almendro, 1988.

Tene, David. "Linguistic Literature, Hebrew" (sections 1–4). In *Encyclopaedia Judaica.* Vol. 16. Jerusalem: Keter Publishing House, 1971.

ANGEL SÁENZ-BADILLOS

[See also **DMA:** Arabic Language; Hebrew Language, Jewish Study of; Hebrew Poetry; Jews in Christian Spain; Jews in Europe: After 900; Jews in Muslim Spain; Karaites; Saadiah Gaon; Sephardim; Translation and Translators, Jewish; **Supp:** Biblical Commentaries; Hagiography, Jewish.]

HELL, CONCEPTS OF. That hell should be a significant part of the worldview of a culture that resolutely believed in the enduring conflict between good and evil is not surprising. Just as God and his angels are in heaven, the ultimate goal of the righteous, so Satan and his demons must be in hell, the ultimate destiny of the reprobate. According to the major biblical source of the Last Judgment (Matt. 25:41), Christ as Judge will separate the saved on his right hand from those standing on his left, cursing the damned to be punished in the everlasting fire prepared for the devil. This fire is emphasized in the Apocalypse of John, which at the end of time expects the devil, the beast, and the false prophet—a trinity of evil—to be cast in a pool of fire burning with brimstone (Rev. 19:20). They will be tormented forever and ever (Rev. 20:10), so hell, like heaven, is understood to be eternal. Hell is also populated by the damned before doomsday. According to a popular parable (Luke 16), a rich man, named Dives in medieval accounts, upon death went immediately to hell, where in fiery torment he looked up to see the beggar Lazarus in the bosom of Abraham. When Dives cried for mercy, asking Abraham to send Lazarus to cool his tongue, Abraham explained that it is impossible to pass between heaven and hell.

Although the theological implications of hell were disputed during the early Christian period, their major features were established for the medieval church by Augustine, who devoted an entire book, titled *City of God* (410), to explaining the suffering of damned souls and examining the nature of eternal punishment. Augustine was particularly concerned to refute the argument of Origen in the third century, that punishment will not last forever, as well as the view that the intercession of saints will save the dead from damnation and that punishment after death primarily purified the soul in preparation for heaven.

During the Middle Ages, the question of what happens to the souls of most sinners between death and Judgment Day was answered by a middle—temporal rather than eternal—otherworld between hell and heaven. By the thirteenth century, the concept of purgatory was established in Western Christian theology, providing a place for the souls of the vast majority of sinners who, although not damned to hell, needed to experience purgative suffering after death to prepare for heaven. This third place had a profound influence on later medieval theological concepts of hell. Since another place was designed for purgation, hell was strictly for eternal punishment. This purpose was stressed by countless sermons and didactic works, such as treatises on the contempt of the world and on dying, which were designed to elicit fear of the Lord through contemplation of the horrors of hell.

TOURS OF HELL

The arguments of Augustine and later medieval theologians delineated a relatively abstract concept of hell: it is the locale of demons and a place of eternal punishment, but otherwise its features are remarkably unclear. Many of the more specific concepts of hell, therefore, are based less on biblical and theological works than on imaginative narratives, tours of hell, as Martha Himmelfarb calls them. Despite Abraham's reply to the rich man that there could be no commerce between heaven and hell, these apocryphal Jewish and Christian texts, which flourished from the second century A.D., describe otherworldly journeys in which visionaries, accompanied by guides, visit hell and sometimes heaven. Particularly influential during the Middle Ages, the *Apocalypse of Paul* (also known as the *Visio Pauli*) was translated from Greek to Latin by the sixth century and later into medieval vernaculars. Developing Paul's enigmatic allusion to his being taken up to the third heaven (2 Cor. 12:2–4), it describes paradise and then hell in great detail, focusing on specific punishments for types of sinners located in various pits, pools, and rivers of fire.

The *Apocalypse of Paul,* along with several popular medieval works such as *St. Patrick's Purgatory* and *Tundale's Vision,* outlined a hellish hierarchy of suffering based on the nature of the evil being punished. The population of hell now swelled. In addition to demons, the agents of punishment in these narratives include serpents, dragons, toads, worms, dogs, and lions who devour the damned with sharp teeth, wield iron hooks and axes, pierce with knives and needles, or turn wheels with hot nails to mutilate tongues, breasts, and genitals. Hellish tormentors squeeze out entrails, hang and stretch naked bodies, and baste sinners in cauldrons of liquid pitch and sulfur. The stench of hell and the shrieks and wails of its suffering inhabitants are also described in detail by these fascinating, if vividly gruesome, narratives.

The most famous literary tour of hell is Dante's *Inferno* (1306), the first part of his *Divine Comedy,* which has had the most enduring influence on Christian concepts of hell, even into modern times. This theological epic poem established in the popular imagination the notion of hell as a complex and crowded geography, mapped through an elaborate series of circles, terraces, and pockets where individual sinners—many Florentines known to Dante or famous from biblical, Roman, and medieval history and literature—are tormented for their besetting sins. Guided by the Roman poet Vergil, Dante the pilgrim enters the inferno through limbo and descends ever further to the frozen floor of hell located at the earth's central core, where he finally sees Satan chained. Although less famous, the *Pilgrimage of the Soul,* the second of three pilgrimage poems by Guillaume de Deguileville, describes a similar otherworldly journey. Although more allegorical than historical, it again focuses in excruciating detail on the suffering damned in hell. Composed in French in the 1350s, it was translated into other vernaculars in the fifteenth century and became a very popular work.

THEATRICAL HELL

Medieval drama is brimming with demons, many playing comic roles, and in the dramatic action they often pour out of the mouth of hell accompanied by sulfurous smoke and the din of banging pots and fireworks. In the cycles of biblical plays associated with the feast of Corpus Christi during the later Middle Ages, such as the mystery plays staged in the streets of York in the fifteenth and sixteenth centuries, the mouth of hell is the locale of much dramatic action. These plays span the full spectrum of salvation history, from the fall of the angels, in which Lucifer mourns his new "dungeon of dole," to doomsday, when demons relish receiving a large party of sinners to torment in endless pain. One of the most interesting plays, the *Harrowing of Hell,* stages a legend first fully developed in the apocryphal *Gospel of Nicodemus.* On the Saturday between the Crucifixion and Resurrection, Jesus descended to hell and released the righteous Hebrew patriarchs and prophets, from Adam and Eve to John the Baptist. When Jesus bangs on the gates of hell, quoting Psalm 24 and demanding "let my people pass," he is challenged by Satan, who disputes theological fine points of justice and mercy before finally sinking into the pit of hell.

In dramatic representations, hell is not only a place of suffering but also the capital of devils, from which

Dante and Vergil with the Condemned Souls in Eternal Ice. *From a 15th-century manuscript of Dante's* Inferno *(1306), the most famous medieval depiction of hell.* CORBIS-BETTMANN

they plot their schemes to govern human action and to manipulate salvation history. The *Jour du Jugement* (ca. 1330–1340), for example, a French play staging the life of Antichrist and the Last Judgment, represents an extensive parliament of devils in hell. Recognizing that the time of the end is at hand, Satan calls his companions Beelzebub, Pluto, Belial, and other demons together to prepare for the final assault on Christianity. They conspire to send two devils, Engignart and Agrappart, to Babylon to seduce a whore. She becomes the mother of Antichrist, whose birth is celebrated in hell by an elaborate devilish dance. Later, as doomsday approaches and the dead are resurrected, the devils prepare appropriate places for the damned.

VISUAL HELLS

Hell is a recurring scene in a wide range of medieval art. It is often represented as a gaping monstrous mouth with jagged teeth, an image recalling the Leviathan of Job. The fallen angels are shown tumbling into hell mouth in representations of the origins of evil; Christ releases the righteous dead through this hellish mouth in the harrowing of hell, as pictured in the *Winchester Psalter* (1140–1160); and Death exits hell mouth in many illustrations of the fourth horseman of the Apocalypse

Demons Tormenting the Damned Souls. *A 13th-century mosaic from a baptistery in Florence.*

(Rev. 6:7–8). Most often in manuscript and wall paintings picturing the Last Judgment, demons carry damned souls into this gaping mouth, which serves as an iconographic shorthand for hell, just as a gated city signals heaven. This visual tradition culminates in the full-page picture of hell in the *Hours of Catherine of Cleves* (*ca.* 1440), which imagines hell as a massive furnacelike castle complete with two giant mouths that devour naked sinners.

The interior landscape of hell is also detailed in a variety of medieval art, some focusing on sins of particular concern to their specific audience. For example, the *Silos Beatus Apocalypse* (1109), a manuscript created for a Spanish monastery, stresses the sins of greed and lechery, probably to recall monastic vows of poverty and chastity. It pictures Dives clutching moneybags at the center of hell and two upside-down lovers being tormented by a demon with huge genitals. A more public image is the dazzling thirteenth-century Last Judgment mosaic (1008) in the basilica of Torcello near Venice. It outlines the compartments of hell filled with skeletons and overs-

een by Satan, who, in an inversion of the parable of Lazarus in Abraham's bosom, holds Antichrist on his lap while seated on a double-headed serpent swallowing the damned. Manuscripts illustrating infernal journeys, such as *Tundale's Vision,* Dante's *Inferno,* and Guillaume's *Pilgrimage of the Soul,* provide yet more vivid details about hell's interior, its citizens, and the torments suffered by the damned.

Punishments are pictured with great relish and with exuberant creativity in many artistic media. Most typical is the *Holkham Bible Picture Book* (1320–1330), which shows demons carrying the damned on their shoulders or pushing them in carts into hell, where they are put into huge cauldrons boiling over flames. The 1391 fresco by Taddeo di Bartolo in the cathedral of San Gimignano shows how punishments are suited to the particular nature of the sin, so that, for example, a demon feeds coins into the mouth of a usurer. Other punishments are depicted in the stone sculpture often carved over the west entrances of Romanesque churches. For the Last Judgment (*ca.* 1125–1135) at Autun cathedral, Gislebertus sculpted a particularly disturbing image of huge disembodied hands reaching down to grasp a sinner's neck. The point of such imagery is made explicit by the accompanying inscription that invokes fear, reminding viewers that they witness horrors they are likely to suffer if they do not repent.

At the conclusion of the Middle Ages, several major painters, including Jan van Eyck and Rogier van der Weyden in the fifteenth century, pictured hell with a newly intense realism in altarpieces and panel paintings. Hieronymus Bosch, for example, portrayed hell in his Last Judgment triptych (1504) as a devastated burning landscape populated by hundreds of naked bodies suffering psychological as well as physical anguish at the hands of demons, insects, rodents, and unidentifiable monstrous creatures. His nightmarish vision and Dante's detailed elaborations of infernal topography are the most vivid cultural representations of the popular concept of hell.

BIBLIOGRAPHY

PRIMARY WORKS

Augustine. *Concerning the City of God against the Pagans.* Translated by Henry Bettenson. Harmondsworth, U.K.: Penguin, 1972.

Beadle, Richard. *The York Plays.* London: Arnold, 1982.

Dante Alighieri. *Inferno.* Translated by Charles S. Singleton. Princeton, N.J.: Princeton University Press, 1970.

Emmerson, Richard K., and David F. Hult. *Antichrist and Judgment Day: The Middle French Jour du Jugement.* Asheville, N.C.: Pegasus Press, 1998.

Gardiner, Eileen, ed. *Visions of Heaven and Hell before Dante.* New York: Italica Press, 1989.

SECONDARY WORKS

Bernstein, Alan E. *The Formation of Hell: Death and Retribution in the Ancient and Early Christian Worlds.* Ithaca, N.Y.: Cornell University Press, 1993.

Bevington, David, et al. *Homo, Memento Finis: The Iconography of Just Judgment in Medieval Art and Drama.* Kalamazoo, Mich.: Medieval Institute Publications, 1985.

Davidson, Clifford, and Thomas H. Seiler, eds. *The Iconography of Hell.* Kalamazoo, Mich.: Medieval Institute Publications, 1992.

Himmelfarb, Martha. *Tours of Hell: An Apocalyptic Form in Jewish and Christian Literature.* Philadelphia: University of Pennsylvania Press, 1983.

Hughes, Robert. *Heaven and Hell in Western Art.* New York: Stein and Day, 1968.

Vorgrimler, Herbert. *Geschichte der Hölle.* Munich: Wilhelm Fink, 1993.

RICHARD K. EMMERSON

[See also **DMA:** Augustine of Hippo, St.; Dante Alighieri; Mystery Plays; Origen; Purgatory, Western Concept of; **Supp:** Demons; Devil; Fall, The; Original Sin.]

HENRY I OF GERMANY, EMPEROR (*ca.* 876–936; *r.* 919–936). Also known as "the Fowler," Henry was the duke of Saxony and the most powerful of the German magnates when Conrad I (*r.* 911–918) chose him to be heir to the East Francian throne. The first of the Saxon dynasty, Henry I initiated the appropriation of the Carolingian imperial legacy and established the authority of the Saxon house in East Francia. Henry's political successes with the duchies, his military accomplishments, and his territorial consolidation made possible the subsequent achievements of his son, Otto I the Great (*r.* 936–973).

Henry's rule did not begin auspiciously. Although he had been designated heir by Conrad, not all duchies supported his election. As well, Henry refused consecration from the clergy during his coronation, claiming unworthiness, according to his biographer Widukind of Corvey. Yet Henry wielded his royal authority with confidence, continuing the tradition of royal participation in ecclesiastical synods and confirming the rights and privileges of the church. Most important for the future of the crown, Henry eradicated external and internal threats to royal power. Magyars had attacked Saxony and Bavaria from the early tenth century, and Slavs posed an immediate threat along the eastern frontier. In addition, during the chaos of late Carolingian rule the duchies had become increasingly independent, posing a growing threat to royal authority.

Henry dealt with external threats militarily. He negotiated a nine-year truce with the Magyars in 926, using the lull to construct fortifications in Saxony. Archeological finds have not substantiated contemporary description of these constructions, which may suggest that the military aspect of Henry's rule was exaggerated at the expense of his diplomatic achievements. Henry's forces defeated the Magyars in 933 at Riade, securing Saxony from further raids. The Magyar threat ended with their defeat in the Battle of Lechfeld in 955.

Henry also reestablished the Carolingian protectorate over Slavs east of the Elbe. Unlike Otto I, who sought to convert the Slavs, Henry's ambitions were primarily economic. In the winter of 928/929 he marched against the Elbian Slavs, building a fortress at Meissen in 929 from which to exact tribute. The territorial gains of Henry and Otto proved ephemeral, and the Slavs rebelled in 983. It was only with colonization in the twelfth century that the Slavic territories began to be incorporated into the German sphere of influence.

Although Henry has been credited with introducing military innovations, it is clear that he also exploited traditional Carolingian methods of diplomacy to strengthen royal power. This was particularly the case in his relations with the duchies that had initially resisted his suzerainty. Henry ingratiated himself with the aristocrats in Lotharingia by confirming their candidate as duke in 925. In 926 he appointed the cousin of Conrad I, Hermann I, to the dukedom of Swabia. Henry's success in discouraging the independence of the duchies created a base for royal authority upon which Otto I could build. Although factions in Bavaria continued to resist royal authority, its duke, along with those of Swabia and Lotharingia, attended and participated in the coronation of Henry's heir, Otto, in 936.

BIBLIOGRAPHY

Arnold, Benjamin. *Medieval Germany, 500–1300: A Political Interpretation.* Toronto: University of Toronto Press, 1997.

Barraclough, G. *The Origins of Modern Germany.* Translated by Bernard S. Smith. 2d ed. 1947. Reprint, New York: Paragon, 1979.

Fleckenstein, Josef. *Early Medieval Germany.* New York: Elsevier North-Holland, 1978.

Leyser, K. J. *Rule and Conflict in an Early Medieval Society: Ottonian Saxony.* Bloomington: Indiana University Press, 1980.

Reuter, Timothy. *Germany in the Early Middle Ages, c. 800–1056.* London and New York: Longman, 1991.

Elspeth Jane Carruthers

[See also **DMA:** Germany: 843–1137; Otto I the Great, Emperor.]

HENRY II OF GERMANY, EMPEROR

(*r.* 1002–1024). When Otto III died in 1002, he left no male Ottonian heir except for Henry IV, the Liudolfing duke of Bavaria. After eliminating his non-Ottonian rivals, the margrave of Meissen and the duke of Swabia, Henry was crowned king in June 1002.

Henry II retained the central features of the Ottonian imperial program while shifting its focus onto Germany itself, away from direct involvement in Italy and eastern Europe. Henry kept close control over Bavaria and Burgundy, controlling the appointment of the duke in the former and naming himself as heir to the latter. He further exerted and expanded royal control by settling regional disputes between lay and ecclesiastical authorities, particularly those in Lotharingia and Saxony, generally ending them in compromise.

Henry altered the political geography of Germany in ways that consolidated royal authority throughout. He continued the Ottonian practice of concentrating on central lands as the basis for royal authority, but he changed the patterns of itinerant rule by shortening the duration and increasing the frequency of visits by the royal court around a widening sphere of territories that now included Alsace, Bavaria, and Swabia at the expense of the independent ducal authority he himself had previously enjoyed. He established a new locus of central royal authority by creating the bishopric of Bamberg in 1007 and brought Saxony into the royal fold, holding frequent assemblies in Merseburg.

Like Otto III, Henry II stressed the sacral nature of royal office, and he intensified the imperial policy of alliance with the church. Bamberg and Würzburg formed a central nexus of Ottonian ecclesiastical control. Henry actively involved himself not only in making episcopal appointments but in furthering Gorze monastic reform, as well as participating in the synods he convoked.

Henry shifted the imperial focus away from Rome, reviving the formula *renovatio regni Francorum* to replace Otto III's program of *renovatio imperii Romanorum.* He revised the ideal of a revived Roman Empire but did not discard it; he confirmed the papal holdings described in the *Ottonianum,* something that not even Otto III had done. He made only three expeditions to Italy, the first to assert his claim to the Italian crown in 1004 against a rival; the second, in 1014, to be crowned emperor, taking advantage of the competition between Roman dynasties to enter Rome; and the third to battle Byzantium.

An important reason for Henry's near abandonment of Italy was the aggressive expansionism by the Polish ruler, a former imperial ally. After Bolesław I Chrobry withheld imperial homage for Bohemia, Henry shocked the Christian world by allying with the pagan Ljutizi against him in 1003, a pattern of warfare that ended only with the peace of Budziszyn in 1018, in which Henry confirmed Bolesław's possession of the Lausitz and Milzen lands.

Henry died childless in 1024, and a cult soon developed around his burial site in Bamberg Cathedral. In 1146 he became the only German king or emperor to be canonized, and in 1200 his wife Kunigunde was elevated to the same status.

BIBLIOGRAPHY

Arnold, Benjamin. *Medieval Germany, 500–1300: A Political Interpretation.* Basingstoke, U.K.: Macmillan, 1997.

Barraclough, Geoffrey. *The Origins of Modern Germany*. New York: Norton, 1984.

Bäuml, Franz H. *Medieval Civilization in Germany 800–1273*. London: Thames and Hudson, 1969.

Leyser, Karl. *Medieval Germany and Its Neighbours, 900–1250*. London: Hambledon, 1982.

Thietmar of Merseburg. *Die Chronik des Bischofs Thietmar von Merseburg und ihre Korveier Überarbeitung*. Edited by Robert Holtzmann. Monumenta Germaniae Historica, Scriptores rerum germanicarum, n.s., 9. Berlin: Weidmann, 1935.

ELSPETH JANE CARRUTHERS

[See also **DMA:** Bavaria; Gorze; Otto III, Emperor; Saxon Dynasty; **Supp:** Bolesław I Chrobry of Poland, King.]

HENRY V OF GERMANY, EMPEROR

(1086–1125). The reign of Henry V, the last Salian ruler, was shaped by the investiture contest between his father and the papacy over the right to appoint bishops. Henry was not his father's first choice as heir: his older brother Conrad was consecrated in 1087 but defected in 1093 to side with the reformers, who wished to limit Henry IV's intervention in ecclesiastical affairs. In 1098 Henry IV deposed Conrad and named Henry heir. In 1102 Paschal II renewed the excommunication of Henry IV first imposed by Pope Gregory VII, and as the German princes continued their agitations, Henry V, fearing for the future of Salian authority and his succession, turned against his father, siding with the princes. In 1105 he tricked and captured his father, forcing Henry IV to resign. Henry died in 1106, preparing to battle his son.

As sole ruler of Germany, Henry V reopened negotiations with the papacy concerning investiture, all the while aggressively exercising his right to appoint bishops. In 1110 Henry journeyed to Rome with an army. Paschal II responded by offering to give up claims to imperial regalia in return for Henry's promise to renounce investiture. When their agreement was read aloud at Henry's imperial coronation in 1111, the bishops, fearing the loss of much of their holdings, halted the ceremony with protest. Henry then kidnapped the pope and forced him to complete the coronation and recognize Henry's right to investiture. Reformers revoked this agreement in 1112 and excommunicated Henry.

Henry's fragile relationship with the princes shattered after a series of high-handed moves that culminated in his plan to introduce a general tax. Henry alienated an early ally, Archbishop Adalbert of Mainz, who then led the princes in opposition. Having appointed Lothar of Supplinburg to the duchy of Saxony in defiance of rival claims, Henry then tried to recover Saxon fiefs, whereupon Lothar led the Saxons in rebellion, defeating Henry in battle at Welfesholz in early 1115.

Henry's fortunes were soon improved by the death of the mercurial Matilda of Tuscany, to whom he was heir. Henry departed for Italy to settle her estate and to reconsolidate imperial influence; returning to Germany in 1118, he met increased opposition from the princes. Matters worsened with the papal election of Calixtus II, who as archbishop of Vienne had excommunicated Henry. Henry and the German princes negotiated a peace at Würzburg in 1121. With the princes acting as a third party, Henry convoked a general meeting in 1122 that produced the Concordat of Worms, settling the issue of investiture at last. By this time both sides were ready to compromise: Henry agreed to no longer invest bishops with the symbols of spiritual authority, and Calixtus agreed that Henry could be present at the elections of bishops and abbots of Germany and could still confer the regalia through investiture with the scepter before consecration.

The Concordat signaled the end not just of the contest but also of the imperial church of the Ottonians and Salians and the beginning of a new system whereby the German king exerted control through feudal ties. Henry V died in 1125, leaving no legitimate male heirs.

BIBLIOGRAPHY

Blumenthal, Uta-Renate. *The Investiture Controversy: Church and Monarchy from the Ninth to the Twelfth Century*. Philadelphia: University of Pennsylvania Press, 1988.

Fuhrmann, Horst. *Germany in the High Middle Ages, c. 1050–1200*. Translated by Timothy Reuter. Cambridge, U.K.: Cambridge University Press, 1986.

Hampe, Karl. *Germany under the Salian and Hohenstaufen Emperors*. Translated by Ralph Bennett. Oxford: Blackwell, 1973.

Haverkamp, Alfred. *Medieval Germany 1056–1273*. Translated by Helga Braun and Richard Mortimer. 2d ed. Oxford: Oxford University Press, 1992.

Leyser, Karl. *Medieval Germany and Its Neighbours, 900–1250*. London: Hambledon, 1982.

Weinfurter, Stefan. *The Salian Century: Main Currents in an Age of Transition*. Translated by Barbara M. Bowlus. Philadelphia: University of Pennsylvania Press, 1999.

ELSPETH JANE CARRUTHERS

[See also **DMA:** Germany: 843–1137; Henry IV of Germany; Investiture and Investiture Conflict; Paschal II, Pope; Worms, Concordat of.]

HENRY VI OF GERMANY, EMPEROR

HENRY VI OF GERMANY, EMPEROR (1165–1197), was the son of Frederick I Barbarossa, who revitalized and reconfigured imperial and royal authority after the crises of the investiture contest. By making Henry king of the Romans in 1169, Frederick secured the Hohenstaufen succession, and the marriage he arranged between Henry and Constance, the aunt of William II of Sicily, in 1184 would prove crucial to future imperial strategy. Henry succeeded to the throne in 1190 after Frederick died on crusade.

Prior to his departure for the crusade, Frederick stabilized his kingdom by making Henry regent and forcing the rebellious Henry the Lion into exile. Nonetheless, the early phase of Henry VI's reign was precarious. In 1191, Henry made his first expedition to Italy to claim the Sicilian crown and the title of emperor, with mixed results. William II had died without legitimate heir in 1189, and anti-imperialists had put the illegitimate Tancred of Lecce on the Sicilian throne, ignoring Constance's claim. After making last-minute concessions to Celestine III, Henry was crowned emperor, but illness forced him to defer his Sicilian claims and return to Germany, where Henry the Lion, having returned prematurely from exile, was conspiring against him.

Unfounded rumors that Henry VI was dead or had murdered a bishop fed growing opposition among the princes. Revolt was averted only by the fortunate capture of Richard I the Lionhearted, brother-in-law to Henry the Lion. Henry VI received an exorbitant ransom for Richard and, before his release in 1194, forced him to put his kingdom in fief from the emperor for annual tribute. After Henry the Lion died in 1195, Henry VI was sufficiently free of encumbrances at home to return to matters in Italy.

Now well funded, Henry easily captured the throne of Sicily in 1194. He arranged a marriage between his brother Philip and the daughter of the Byzantine emperor in 1195 as a pretext for interfering in Byzantine politics. Many historians speculate that Henry's declared crusade was an overture to more grandiose plans for expansion throughout the eastern Mediterranean, including the conquest of Constantinople.

Henry took the cross in 1195, and in 1196 he offered to recognize the heritability of the German magnates' imperial fiefs in return for their recognition of the heritability of Hohenstaufen claims to the crown, an act that would have altered the imperial constitution and possibly the course of German history. The papacy, already nervous about Henry's expanded Italian power, was vehemently opposed to this measure, which would have reduced the Roman see to the status of a mere imperial bishopric. Reluctant to part with their electoral rights, the princes also ultimately objected. Henry had to settle for the traditional election of his son, Frederick, as king of the Romans in December 1196.

Poised to embark on crusade, Henry was obliged to quell an uprising in Sicily. He then died of fever in Messina in 1197. Although his larger ambitions were unrealized, he succeeded in expanding the territorial base of imperial power in Italy, thus transforming the imperial ideal. The tragedy of his early death was compounded by the fact that he left only one young son as heir, circumstances that led to the immediate collapse of the Hohenstaufen empire.

BIBLIOGRAPHY

Arnold, Benjamin. *Medieval Germany, 500–1300: A Political Interpretation.* Basingstoke, U.K.: Macmillan, 1997.

Barraclough, Geoffrey. *The Origins of Modern Germany.* New York: Norton, 1984.

Fuhrmann, Horst. *Germany in the High Middle Ages, c. 1050–1200.* Translated by Timothy Reuter. Cambridge, U.K., and New York: Cambridge University Press, 1986.

Haverkamp, Alfred. *Medieval Germany, 1056–1273.* Translated by Helga Braun and Richard Mortimer. 2nd ed. Oxford: Oxford University Press, 1992.

Schmandt, Raymond H. "The Election and Assassination of Albert of Louvain, Bishop of Liège." *Speculum* 42 (1967): 639–660.

ELSPETH JANE CARRUTHERS

[See also **DMA:** Frederick I Barbarossa; Henry the Lion; Hohenstaufen Dynasty; Richard I the Lionhearted; **Supp:** William II of Sicily, King.]

HENRY VII OF GERMANY, KING

HENRY VII OF GERMANY, KING (1211–1242), was the eldest son of the Holy Roman Emperor Frederick II and Constance of Aragon. In 1220 Frederick had him elected king of the Germans before departing for Rome to receive the imperial crown from the hands of the pope. The emperor hoped that the kingdom of Germany would remain quiet and untroubled while he pursued his political ambitions in Italy and the Holy Land. Throughout the 1220s, Frederick ruled Germany from afar through regents such as Archbishop Engelbert of Cologne and Duke Louis I of Bavaria. During this time, he shored up his relationship with the German nobility by arranging the marriage of Henry to Margaret, a daughter of the duke of Austria. His diplomacy was quickly undone when Henry reached the age of majority and began to alienate lay and ecclesiastical princes alike by diminishing their power over German cities in favor of ministerials and burghers. In 1231 the princes rebelled against his policies and demanded a restoration of their rights, compelling Henry to issue the Statute in Favor of the Princes, which returned significant territorial power to their hands. Frederick reluctantly confirmed the statute. In 1232, at the Diet of Aquileia, he made his son swear an oath to desist from his disruptive policies under the threat of deposition.

Shortly thereafter, Henry returned north and plotted a rebellion. Many ministerials and several bishops rallied to his side against the absent emperor and the princes loyal to him. Henry also entered into an alliance with the Lombard League. By 1235 the situation had become so threatening that Frederick decided to travel in haste to Germany. He came without an army. His young son Conrad IV accompanied him on the journey. The emperor's return to Germany eroded the loyalty of Henry's followers and dissolved the rebellion. Henry was stripped of his royal title in favor of his half brother Conrad. The rebel king was made a prisoner and sent to Sicily to live out the rest of his life in captivity.

In 1242 Frederick summoned his son to the royal court, perhaps with the intention of pardoning him. Henry thought otherwise. Believing that his father was planning to kill him, he tried to escape his guards on a narrow mountain pass in southern Italy and died when his horse plunged down a steep embankment. Despite their troubled history, Frederick seems to have been deeply saddened by the death of his firstborn son. In a letter to the nobles of Sicily, the emperor likened himself to King David when he mourned the rebellion and loss of his son Absalom. His choice to depose and punish his son was never called into question, however. Frederick was well aware that any show of mercy toward a rebel like Henry would have undermined his authority as a dispenser of justice and threatened the stability of his empire.

BIBLIOGRAPHY

Abulafia, David. *Frederick II: A Medieval Emperor.* London: Allan Lane, 1988.

Borchardt, Karl. "Der sogenannte Aufstand Heinrichs (VII.) in Franken 1234/35." In *Forschungen zur bayerischen und fränkischen Geschichte: Peter Herde zum 65. Geburtstag von Freunden, Schülern und Kollegen dargebracht.* Edited by Karl Borchardt and Emmo Bünz. Würzburg, Germany: Kommissionsverlag Ferdinand Schöningh., 1998.

Der Staufer Heinrich (VII.): Ein König im Schatten seines kaiserlichen Vaters. Göppingen, Germany: Gesellschaft der Freunde Staufischer Geschichte, 2001.

Hillen, Christian. *Curia Regis: Untersuchungen zur Hofstruktur Heinrichs (VII.) 1220–1235 nach den Zeugen seiner Urkunden.* Frankfurt am Main: Peter Land, 1999.

———. "Tutor et privisor: Minority Government for German Kings: The Case of Henry (VII) (1220–1235)." *Medieval History,* new ser., 1 (2002): 30–48.

SCOTT G. BRUCE

[See also **DMA:** Frederick II of the Holy Roman Empire, King of Sicily; Germany: 1138–1254; Hohenstaufen Dynasty; Holy Roman Empire; Lombard League; **Supp:** Conrad IV of Germany, Emperor.]

HENRY THE NAVIGATOR OF PORTUGAL, PRINCE

HENRY THE NAVIGATOR OF PORTUGAL, PRINCE (duke of Viseu, 1394–1460), was born in the coastal city of Porto on 4 March 1394, the third surviving son of João I (*r.* 1385–1433) and Philippa of Lancaster. Due to his own propaganda efforts—carried out mostly by the Portuguese chronicler Gomes Eanes de Zurara—and those of later writers, Henry has achieved semi-legendary status as a patron of scholars and explorers, and he has received the bulk of the credit for launching Portuguese exploration of the West African coast and the Atlantic Ocean. The real man fell somewhat short of these lofty praises. During his own lifetime he was overshadowed by the literary accomplishments of his own brothers—Henry's own strength was in astrology—and his "navigating" was limited to coastal voyages and some brief expeditions to North Africa. The credit he deserves comes mostly as a result of his unquenchable thirst for riches, curiosity for the unexplored, and the support and encouragement he gave his captains.

Henry's first foray into the international scene came in 1415 with the Portuguese conquest of the Moroccan city of Ceuta, an expedition that Henry had played a leading role in planning and in which he displayed foolhardy bravery during the fighting. Upon returning from North Africa, his father made him duke of Viseu, the first duke in Portugal's history, and entrusted him with the administration of the new conquest. In 1420, he was appointed to lead the military Order of Christ.

In 1424, Henry took the first tentative steps into the Atlantic when he sent a large force of soldiers to capture the Canary Islands. The enterprise was a disaster. He would, however, remain committed to the islands' conquest for the rest of his life—a commitment that came to naught. Undeterred by his failure, Henry turned his attention to colonizing other Atlantic islands, the Madeira Archipelago and the Azores. Although less attractive than the Canaries, the islands, especially the Madeira group and its prized sugarcane fields, proved to be valuable additions to the growing Portuguese empire. While this was going on, Henry's mariners continued their long-running efforts to round the Saharan Cape Bojador, the physical and psychological gateway to additional exploration of the African coast. They succeeded in 1434.

Henry followed this success with a crusade against Morocco. Launched in the summer of 1437 and led by Henry and his brother Ferdinand, the crusade came dangerously close to unraveling much of the work the Portuguese had done in the previous quarter century. Not only were they defeated, largely due to Henry's ineptness, but Henry had to hand Ferdinand over to the Muslims as surety for the return of Ceuta. The Portuguese did not return Ceuta, and Ferdinand died in captivity in 1443. Further trouble followed with the death of Henry's brother, King Duarte (r. 1433–1438), and the succession by his six-year-old son, Afonso V. When the political situation stabilized again, Henry's captains continued their voyages down the African coast. In 1441 they captured the first of what would eventually be millions of African slaves. Henry, delighted by the profit the slaves brought, wholeheartedly encouraged their capture.

In the following years, Henry continued to press his captains to additional discoveries and even participated in another crusade against Morocco in 1458. Two years later he died. He never married and left no children.

BIBLIOGRAPHY

Fernández-Armesto, Felipe. *Before Columbus: Exploration and Colonization from the Mediterranean to the Atlantic, 1229–1492.* Philadelphia: University of Pennsylvania Press, 1987.

Parry, J. H. *The Age of Reconnaissance.* Cleveland, Ohio: The World Publishing Company, 1963.

Russell, Peter. *Prince Henry "the Navigator": A Life.* New Haven, Conn.: Yale University Press, 2000. Excellent new biography.

Zurara, Gomes Eanes de. *The Chronicle of the Discovery and Conquest of Guinea.* Edited and translated by Charles Raymond Beazley and Edgar Prestage. 2 vols. New York: B. Franklin, 1963.

JARBEL RODRIGUEZ

[See also **DMA**: Azores; Canary Islands and Béthencourt; Exploration by Western Europeans; Madeira Islands; Portugal: 1279–1481; Slavery, Slave Trade; **Supp**: Zurara, Gomes Eanes de.]

HERMANN OF SALZA, grand master of the Teutonic Order (*ca.* 1180–1239). A member of a Thuringian family of ministeriales, non-nobles in knightly service to a lord, little is known about Hermann until he became the fourth grand master of the Teutonic Order in 1210,

succeeding Hermann Bart. Under his leadership, the Teutonic Order grew from a relatively small military order with few lands to one of the most powerful religious groups in Western Christendom, and Hermann himself grew influential in many courts of Europe.

When Hermann became grand master, the Teutonic Order was a small group of German knights with their headquarters in Acre. The older military orders, the Hospitallers and Templars, overshadowed the new German foundation in both wealth and prestige. A year after Hermann's election, King András II of Hungary, perhaps inspired by Count Hermann of Thuringia, overlord of the grand master's family, requested the dispatch of a group of Teutonic knights to southeastern Transylvania to protect Hungary from the attacks of the Cumans. András soon awarded the knights with a grant of land along the Burza River, but the hostility of local Hungarian aristocrats forced the knights to leave in 1225. Their effective protection and settlement of the Slavic frontier did not go unnoticed. Bishop Christian of Prussia and Duke Conrad of Masovia invited the knights to protect Christian settlements in Prussia from local pagan attacks. This offer was supported by the emperor Frederick II, who confirmed the offer in March 1226 in what is known as the "Golden Bull of Rimini," granting to the order full sovereignty over any lands they might conquer from the native Prussians. This grant was the foundation of a territorial state the Teutonic Order controlled until 1525, and Hermann's friendship with Frederick was essential in its promulgation. Indeed, the grand master was more often serving the emperor on diplomatic missions than ruling his order in Acre or Prussia. Hermann negotiated a resolution to the empire's conflicts with Waldemar II of Denmark in 1223. In this endeavor, he may also have been seeking to limit Denmark's access to the lands he hoped the Teutonic Order would occupy.

Despite the order's new interest in the Baltic, Hermann remained committed to the defense of the Holy Land. He joined the Fifth Crusade (1218–1221) and encouraged Frederick II to fulfill his own crusade vows. In 1222 he was instrumental in arranging the marriage of Frederick to Isabelle II, the young queen of Jerusalem, particularly in winning the agreement of Isabelle's father, Jean de Brienne. Hermann's persuasive abilities convinced Louis of Thuringia and Walram of Limburg to contribute seven hundred knights to Frederick's crusade. In 1226, he helped reconcile the Lombard cities with Frederick II, which produced more crusaders, and accompanied the excommunicated emperor on his Crusade to Jerusalem in 1228. He returned to Italy with Frederick and helped to negotiate the Treaty of San Germano, reconciling the pope and emperor and reconstituting the Papal States. He remained in Italy until he died on 19 March 1239 in Barletta.

BIBLIOGRAPHY

Kluger, Helmuth. *Hochmeister Hermann von Salza und Kaiser Friedrich II: Ein Beitrag zur Frühgeschichte des Deutschen Ordens.* Marburg, Germany: N. G. Elwert, 1987.

CHRISTOPHER HATCH MACEVITT

[See also **DMA:** Chivalry, Orders of; Crusades and Crusader States: 1212 to 1272; Frederick II of the Holy Roman Empire, King of Sicily; Knights and Knight Service; **Supp:** Hospitallers; Templars; Teutonic Knights.]

HILĀL, BANŪ (SĪRAT BANŪ HILĀL). A nomadic tribe whose epic episodes about their battles during their emigration from the Arabian peninsula to North Africa are recounted in the *Sīrat Banū Hilāl,* also known as the *Taghrībat Banī Hilāl.* Like the *Sīrat ʿAntar,* the stories of the Banū Hilāl form an oral tradition and were not written down until the nineteenth century. The Hilālī poems should be considered a collection of heroic episodes composed by a number of oral poets rather than a single poem with one author. As such, they are still recited orally throughout Egypt and North Africa. While it is difficult to date the poems because of their oral nature, many of the episodes were likely composed between the twelfth and fourteenth centuries. The emphasis on individual and familial honor, the glorification of battle, the themes of revenge and feud, and the poetic use of epithets show that the Hilālī epic has much in common with Western chivalric epics, such as the *Song of Roland.*

The poems have at their core historical events. The Banū Hilāl were nomads from the area of Najd in Arabia who immigrated to Egypt in the eighth century. The Fatimids banished the tribe in the tenth century to Upper Egypt because of their destructive raiding, but the caliph al-Mustanṣir encouraged the tribe to invade Ifrīqiya (roughly modern Tunisia and parts of Algeria and Libya), whose governor, al-Muʿizz, had rejected Fatimid authority. Al-Muʿizz lost a decisive battle to the tribe in 1051. The Banū Hilāl captured the important city of Qayrawān on 1 November 1057 and continued to dominate the area for at least the next century. The Norman Conquest of parts of the North African coast in 1148 only strengthened the tribe's hold on the hinterlands.

The stories of the Banū Hilāl can be grouped into three cycles. The first cycle focuses on the origins of the tribe in the area of al-Sarw in Arabia and on the birth of the hero Barakāt, also known as Abū Zayd. Like the Arab hero ʿAntar, Abū Zayd is abandoned by his father at birth because he is born with black skin, a result of his mother's seeing a black bird on the day of his conception. Eventually his strength, courage, and cunning lead to acceptance by his father and a place of honor within the tribe.

The second cycle describes the tribe's flight from famine to Najd in northern Arabia. There they ally themselves with Dhiʾāb, a distant relative, and together defeat the rulers of Najd. Although the two clans work together to gain dominance over the area, they are also divided by feuds. The marriage of the leader of the Hilālīs, Ḥasan, to Dhiʾāb's sister does not prevent Dhiʾāb from killing two of his brothers-in-law.

The third cycle recounts the conquest of the province of Ifrīqiya by the Banū Hilāl, again forced to move by famine. The tribe first makes a foray to Persia, fighting the "king of the Kurds" as well as al-Bardawīl b. Rāshid, better known as Baldwin I of Jerusalem. In Ifrīqiya, they defeat al-Zanātī, the ruler of the area. After victory, conflict again breaks out within the tribe when Dhiʾāb kills Ḥasan and Abū Zayd. Buraykiʿ, son of Ḥasan, and al-Jāziya, Ḥasan's sister, avenge his death by killing Dhiʾāb. Buraykiʿ becomes emir but in turn is killed by Naṣr al-Dīn, son of Dhiʾāb.

BIBLIOGRAPHY

ʿAbd al-Hamid, Yunus. *Al-Hilālīya fī al-tārīkh wa-al-adab al-shaʿbī.* Cairo, Egypt: Dār al-Maʿrifah, 1968.

Abnoudy, Abderrahman. *La geste hilalienne: Impressions et extraits par Abderrahman Abnoudy.* Translated by Tahar Guiga. Cairo, Egypt: Organisation egyptienne générale du livre, 1978.

Ayyoub, A. "The Hilali Epic: Material and Memory." *Revue d'histoire maghrébine* 35–36 (1984): 189–217.

Berque, J. "Du nouveau sur les Banî Hilâl." *Studia Islamica* 36 (1972): 99–111.

Connelly, Bridget. *Arab Folk Epic and Identity.* Berkeley: University of California Press, 1986.

Lyons, M. C. *The Arabian Epic: Heroic and Epic Story-telling.* 3 vols. Cambridge, U.K., and New York: Cambridge University Press, 1995.

CHRISTOPHER HATCH MACEVITT

[See also **DMA:** Arabia: Pre-Islamic Arabia; Arabic Poetry; Fatimids; Ifrīqiya; Najd; Qayrawān, Al-; **Supp:** ʿAntar; Epic Genre.]

HILARY OF ORLÉANS (Hilarius Aurelianensis, *fl.* first half of twelfth century) was a Latin writer who was born in the last quarter of the eleventh century and died around the mid-twelfth century. Until recently he was often misdesignated as Hilary the Englishman, but that name was discarded for want of evidence that he was born or ever lived in England. All the attestations of Hilary in manuscripts of his works and in cartularies point toward France, especially the Loire Valley. At least one of his poems and possibly another suggest that Hilary studied with Peter Abelard at the Paraclete, and the first indicates Hilary's awareness of tensions between Abelard and his students in 1125 or within a couple of years afterward. In his own teaching career, Hilary was a grammar master, probably first in Angers (where he was a canon of Le Ronceray from about 1116), then in Orléans, and later back in Angers. In Orléans his most famous student was likely to have been Arnulf of Orléans. Toward the end of his life Hilary has been placed in Paris from around 1145, when William of Tyre studied with him.

The canon of Hilary's works has not been determined definitively, but the main constituents have been recognized for a long time: twelve rhythmic poems with dissyllabic rhyme and three plays (on the raising of Lazarus, on a miracle worked by St. Nicholas, and on the prophet Daniel), all preserved in a single manuscript now in Paris, and a letter collection, extant in manuscripts in Paris and Brussels. The letter collection was assembled from 1115 to 1140. The rhythmic poems apparently influenced the *Carmina burana,* in which two poems (nos. 95 and 117) may be the work of Hilary. In the main group of Hilary's poems, three homoerotic poems—one addressed to a boy of Angers and two to an angelic English boy—have attracted attention in the context of gay literary history. The five poems in the same manuscript in praise of women—one woman being unnamed and the others identified as Eve, Bona, Superba, and Rosea (the first- and last-mentioned both Englishwomen)—combine flattery, double entendre, and appeals for gifts and good will. The one for Eve eulogizes her after her death. The poetry, interesting in both form and content, holds significance for our understanding of how Latin lyric poetry developed in the late eleventh and twelfth centuries. The last of the plays may have inspired the anonymous *Play of Daniel* (from the cathedral school of Beauvais), for which musical notation has been preserved; Hilary's own poetry has unfortunately not come down to us with notation. Both the rhythmic poems and the plays contain occasional Old French refrains, a fact that has earned them a niche in the history of macaronic verse (verse that mixes two or more languages, in this case Latin and Old French).

Hilary's activity as a grammarian may have left traces in a gloss on a verse of Statius's *Thebaid.* It is also possible, but far from certain, that he was the author of a much-copied hymn commentary. Finally, he has been credited with a poem that provides an eyewitness account of a trial by ordeal in connection with a land dispute.

BIBLIOGRAPHY

PRIMARY WORKS

Astey V., Luis, ed. and trans. *Los tres dramas de Hilario y otros tres dramas temáticamente afines.* Publicaciones Medievalia 11. Ciudad Universitaria, Mexico: Universidad Nacional Autónoma de México, 1995. Although difficult to locate, this edition offers the best text of the three plays.

Boswell, John. *Christianity, Social Tolerance, and Homosexuality: Gay People in Western Europe from the Beginning of the Christian Era to the Fourteenth Century.* Chicago: University of Chicago Press, 1980. Contains translations of three poems.

Bulst, Walther, and Marie Luise Bulst-Thiele, eds. *Hilarii Aurelianensis versus et ludi, epistolae, ludus Danielis Belouacensis.* Mittellateinische Studien und Texte 16. Leiden, Netherlands: Brill, 1989. As close to a standard edition as exists.

Häring, Nikolaus M. "Hilary of Orleans and His Letter Collection." *Studi Medievali,* 3d ser., 14, no. 2 (1973): 1069–1122.

———. "Die Gedichte und Mysterienspiele des Hilarius von Orléans." *Studi Medievali,* 3d ser., 17, no. 2 (1976): 915–968. This and the following offer editions not entirely supplanted by the preceding.

SECONDARY WORKS

De Angelis, Violetta. "I commenti medievali alla *Tebaide* di Stazio: Anselmo di Laon, Goffredo Babione, Ilario d'Orléans." In *Medieval and Renaissance Scholarship: Proceedings of the Second European Science Foundation Workshop on the Classical Tradition in the Middle Ages and the Renaissance (London, the Warburg Institute, 27–28 November 1992).* Edited by Nicholas Mann and Birger Munk Olsen. Leiden, Netherlands: Brill, 1997.

Roy, Bruno, and Hugues Shooner. "Querelles des maîtres au XIIe siècles: Arnoul d'Orléans et son milieu." *Sandalion* 8–9 (1985–1986): 315–341. See pp. 325–326 for references to Hilary of Orléans by Arnulf and William of Tyre.

Szövérffy, Josef. *Die Annalen der lateinischen Hymnendichtung: Ein Handbuch.* 2 vols. Berlin: Erich Schmit, 1964–1965. See vol. 2, p. 76, for a discussion of the *Liber Hymnorum* with commentary that has sometimes been ascribed to Hilary.

JAN M. ZIOLKOWSKI

[See also **DMA:** Abelard, Peter; Arnulf; *Carmina Burana; Play of Daniel;* William of Tyre.]

HOMOSEXUALITY. See **Sexuality.**

HONORIUS III, POPE (**Cencius Savelli,** *d.* 1227).
Born in Rome to a noble family that gained prominence

through his papacy, Cencius Savelli had extensive experience in the Roman church before becoming pope. He was a canon of Santa Maria Maggiore, and under Pope Celestine III (1191–1198), Cencius's earliest patron, he was both papal chamberlain and chancellor. He compiled in 1192 the *Liber censuum,* a list of papal revenues, donations, and treaties. He also wrote a life of Celestine III and of Pope Gregory VII, as well as an "Ordo Romanus," detailing various rituals of the Roman church. He became cardinal-deacon of Santa Lucia in Orthea (a section of Rome) in 1193 and then the cardinal-priest of Santi Giovanni e Paolo in 1200. The bronze doors of the cloister of St. John Lateran, inscribed with his name and title, are a physical testament to Cencius's influence even before he became pope.

Cencius was elected pope on 18 July 1216 in Perugia two days after the death of Innocent III, despite having lost much of his influence after the death of Celestine. The work of the Fourth Lateran Council (1215) and Innocent's own ambitious policies left Honorius with several major papal commitments. The Albigensian crusade had faltered; many of Simon de Montfort's initial successes were being overturned by Count Raymond VII of Toulouse. Honorius vainly ordered towns to submit to Simon and urged the recruitment of fresh crusaders in northern France. His appeals had little impact; the pope accepted Louis VIII's claim to Languedoc in 1223, hoping the French monarchy would succeed where the papal crusade had failed.

King John of England at his death in 1216 left Honorius as the protector of his kingdom and his child heir, Henry III. Honorius granted to his legate Guala Bicchieri full papal power to protect both Henry III and the kingdom itself. Through his legate, Honorius wielded unparalleled papal authority in England. His support of Henry III helped crush the rebellion that aimed to replace the young king with Louis of France (later King Louis VIII), son of King Philip II Augustus of France.

Innocent III had authorized a fresh crusade at the Fourth Lateran Council to accomplish what the Fourth Crusade had not—the conquest of Egypt and the recapture of Jerusalem. Preparations were well underway when Honorius became pope. He was eager to complete what Innocent began, and he wrote to Jean de Brienne, king of Jerusalem, only two days after his election, to inform him of its continuing preparation. The Crusade set out in 1218 under the authority of the king of Jerusalem, but once it reached Egypt, the papal legate Cardinal Pelagius took charge, with Honorius's support. The pope hoped that papal leadership would prevent the hijacking of the Crusade by secular needs, as had happened with the Fourth Crusade. To Honorius's great disappointment, the Crusade failed, largely due to poor leadership.

Much of Honorius's papacy was devoted to maintaining a working relationship with the young Frederick II of Germany. Conflict arose despite his efforts, generated by Frederick's refusal to go on crusade, as he had pledged he would at his coronation as German king in 1215. Some historians suggest, however, that Honorius initially discouraged Frederick from joining the Fifth Crusade, fearing that Frederick's leadership would divert authority away from the pope. Honorius did not entirely trust the young king, and Frederick's actions in Tuscany undermining papal authority there further incited mistrust.

Honorius, however, changed his attitude at the end of 1218. Whether as the result of the death of Frederick's rival for the German throne, the Welf (or Guelph) Otto IV, or from worry over the troubled Fifth Crusade, Honorius came to realize that Frederick was the only leader who could lead the Crusade to victory. Frederick offered to lead a crusade departing 24 June 1219 but then requested various delays, first until 29 September, then until 21 March 1220, and again until 1 May 1220. To each request for a delay Honorius wearily complied, postponing complicated plans. Despite Frederick's procrastination, the pope crowned him Holy Roman Emperor in Rome on 22 November 1220. Frederick renewed his vow to go on crusade, agreeing to send reinforcements for the Fifth Crusade in March of 1221 and to depart himself in August of that same year. In June the emperor sent forty ships with funds for the crusaders, but he did not depart himself in August as planned, finding that conditions in his southern realm of Sicily required his attention. By 30 August, however, the Fifth Crusade had been defeated and an eight-year truce had been signed with the sultan of Egypt. Honorius, rightly or wrongly, placed much of the blame for its defeat on Frederick.

Despite Honorius's disappointment, he did not excommunicate Frederick but continued to work with him on planning another crusade. The pope and emperor met in Veroli, and again preparations were under way. Frederick's marriage in 1225 to Isabelle of Jerusalem gave the emperor further incentive to go on crusade, and debate over the departure date commenced again, with Frederick promising to leave on 24 June 1225. Frederick, however, then sent three crusade leaders to ask for a postponement; eventually he agreed to leave on 15 August 1227, promising to spend at least two years on crusade. At the time of Honorius's death in Rome on 18 March 1227, Frederick had not yet departed.

Honorius also crowned Peter of Courtenay as the third Latin emperor of Constantinople. This coronation, which took place in April of 1217, was held at the church of San Lorenzo, outside the walls of Rome, in order that it not imply authority over the Western empire.

Honorius had an uneasy relationship with the city of Rome. He was forced to leave the city briefly in 1219 and 1220, returning for the coronation of Frederick II, by whose mediation the citizens of Rome accepted Honorius back into the city. Honorius fled again to Rieti in 1225, after the establishment of an antipapal government. This government was overthrown after only several months, allowing Honorius to return in February of 1226. Despite these episodes, he had as good a relationship with the city as a thirteenth-century pope could hope for.

Honorius was a great patron of the mendicant orders, approving the creation of the Dominicans in 1216 and the Carmelites in 1226 and supporting the creation of a new rule for the Franciscans in 1223. Honorius supported the efforts of Hugolino of Ostia (the future Pope Gregory IX), whom he appointed cardinal-protector of the order, to introduce a rule that gave the order greater definition at the expense of Francis's distinctive spirituality.

BIBLIOGRAPHY

PRIMARY WORKS

Savelli, Cencius. *Le Liber censuum de l'église romaine.* 3 vols. Edited by L. Duchesne and Paul Fabre. Paris: Fontemoing, 1905.

SECONDARY WORKS

Clausen, J. *Papst Honorius III, 1216–1227: Eine Monographie.* Bonn, Germany: Hauptmann, 1895. Though inaccurate and out of date, this is the only book devoted to the pope.

Sayers, Jane E. *Papal Government and England during the Pontificate of Honorius III (1216–1227).* Cambridge, U.K.: Cambridge University Press, 1984.

Vernet, Félix. *Étude sur les sermons d'Honorius III.* Lyon, France: Vitte et Perrussel, 1888.

CHRISTOPHER HATCH MACEVITT

[See also **DMA:** Crusades and Crusader States: 1212 to 1272; Frederick II of the Holy Roman Empire, King of Sicily; Henry III of England.]

HORSES AND HORSEMANSHIP. The written documentation on medieval horses consists of scattered references in a wide variety of sources; treatises are practically nonexistent. The absence of pedigree records in the medieval West compounds the difficulty of tracing the breeds of medieval horses. References to such breeds as the Arabian, Barb, Andalusian, and Frisian appeared in various sources. Moreover, evidence of equine physical remains in warrior graves largely disappeared with the conversion of Europe to Christianity. Historians have assumed the existence of a standard European heavy horse with a physical appearance ranging from the build of a draft horse to a heavy hunter. The iconography of the Bayeux Tapestry, as corroborated by other contemporary depictions of horsemen, provides a reasonably accurate guide for the correct proportion of horse to rider. These comparisons suggest a horse standing about fifteen hands (five feet). A more accurate approach involves taking measurements from the sets of equine plate armor to determine the height and conformation of late medieval warhorses. The horse that could wear this armor resembled a heavyweight cob of 15 to 15.2 hands.

Arguing against an earlier thesis that heavy shock cavalry assumed an important role in the eighth century, Carolingian military historians have arrived at a consensus on the predominance of logistics and siege warfare, placing cavalry in the more supportive role of reconnaissance and raiding. During the early medieval period, small groups of special strike forces *(scarae)* engaged in strategic scorched-earth operations. Raiding expeditions *(chevauchées)* into enemy territory continued throughout the Middle Ages and served as an important adjunct to siege operations.

Traditional scholarship has associated medieval warfare with victories of heavy cavalry in set battles, but more recently, closer scrutiny has demonstrated the infrequency of set battles and has undercut the tactical decisiveness of heavy cavalry. In the battles that did involve cavalry, medieval knights displayed a sophisticated level of expertise. Their repertoire of skills included fighting in tactical units *(conrois)* that enabled them to execute feigned retreats and coordinating with infantry in a combined-arms mode. Groups of knights engaged in melee tournaments, as distinct from single combats or jousts, that ranged over the entire countryside for several days at a time on a regular basis during the summer season. As simulated battles that sometimes turned into the real thing, these encounters provided physical conditioning for the knights and their horses as well as combat training for set battles.

The distinctive style of medieval cavalry warfare, mounted shock combat, consisting of the couched lance, the high-backed saddle, and the lateral support provided by the stirrup, is now thought to have been in place by the end of the eleventh or the early twelfth century. The most important consideration about this riding style and the cavalry modes of antiquity as well is that the rider's arms were preoccupied with wielding offensive and defensive weaponry. The right arm wielded the lance or sword, while the left arm held the shield in a position to protect the left side of the knight's body. These conditions of battle placed a premium on the use of leg aids or cues to direct the horse with minimal use of the already occupied arms to manipulate the reins and bit. Bits aided the rider in controlling the horse, especially in emergencies. In the Merovingian and Carolingian eras, the snaffle bit, having a mouthpiece joined at the center, was considerably less severe than the curb bit. Relying on a solid mouthpiece and the leverage of elongated cheek pieces, the curb strap or chain, resting in the groove just behind the horse's chin, exerted pressure on the bars (symmetrical spaces on both jaws containing no teeth) or the horse's mouth. The curb bit came into widespread use as armor developed from chain mail to plate. In the style of medieval shock cavalry, the stirrup assisted the rider in maintaining balance by centering the weight of the rider on the horse's back. The lateral support provided by the stirrup stabilized the seat of the rider.

Precision equestrian maneuvers would be required in feigned retreats and tournaments. The training of horses in combat techniques eventually evolved into modern dressage, a riding style having the goal of achieving perfect harmony between horse and rider. For the trained warhorse, as for the modern dressage horse, the actual center of activity is the hindquarters. In order to perform, the horse must be in a state of collection, a dressage term that denotes a shortening of the outline of the horse with the hindquarters positioned well underneath the body to achieve the substantial thrust of energy known as impulsion. This state of collection is necessary to perform correct lead changes and execute 180-degree turns. For example, at a canter, the foreleg that extends ahead of the other is called the leading leg. A horse will have pushed off the left hind in order to canter on the right lead. Leads are indispensable for balance and turning. A horse on the right lead can turn more easily to the right; similarly, a left lead facilitates turning to the left. In military games the right lead was necessary so that the horse could more easily absorb the shock of the lance blow, as the lance was positioned to the left of the horse's head. Half turns could be performed as a turn on the haunches, a pivotal turn around the inside hind leg while the outside hind leg stepped around the turn, or as a canter pirouette, a turn that maintained the rhythm of the canter with the horse driving on both hind legs. This action of fully engaged hindquarters imparted a fluidity of motion in executing the turn and retained flexibility in either direction when facing an opponent.

Tracing its earliest beginnings in the West to the treatise of Xenophon on horsemanship and continuing with Arrian's work on the Roman cavalry, dressage did not surface again in a formal treatise until the *Ordini del cavalcare* of Federico Grisone in 1550. For the Middle Ages the history of dressage has to be pieced together from patchy evidence so as to ascertain how the horses must have been trained, instead of reasoning backward from the movements of dressage as a perfected art form to explain what must have happened in battle. The development of dressage lends support to Malcolm Vale's widely accepted view that knights fought in disciplined groups capable of executing complicated maneuvers.

BIBLIOGRAPHY

Ayton, Andrew. "Arms, Armour, and Horses." In *Medieval Warfare: A History*. Edited by Maurice Keen. Oxford: Oxford University Press, 1999.

Bachrach, Bernard S. "*Caballus et Caballarius* in Medieval Warfare." In *Warfare and Military Organization in Pre-Crusade Europe*. Aldershot, U.K.: Ashgate, 2002.

Bennett, Matthew. "The Medieval Warhorse Reconsidered." In *Medieval Knighthood*. Edited by Stephen Church and Ruth Harvey. Rochester, N.Y.: Boydell, 1995.

———. "The Myth of the Military Supremacy of Knightly Cavalry." In *Armies, Chivalry, and Warfare in Medieval Britain and France*. Edited by Matthew Strickland. Stamford, U.K.: Paul Watkins, 1998. A reevaluation of the one-dimensional performance of heavy shock cavalry.

Chibnall, Marjorie. "Aspects of Knighthood: The Knight and His Horse." In *Chivalry, Knighthood, and War in the Middle Ages*. Edited by Susan J. Ridyard. Sewanee, Tenn.: University of the South Press, 1999.

Gillmor, C. M. "Practical Chivalry: The Training of Horses for Tournaments and Warfare." *Studies in Medieval and Renaissance History* 13 (1992): 7–29.

Hyland, Ann. *The Medieval Warhorse: From Byzantium to the Crusades*. Conshohocken, Pa.: Combined Books, 1994.

———. *The Horse in the Middle Ages*. Stroud, U.K.: Sutton, 1999.

Morillo, Stephen. "The 'Age of Cavalry' Revisited." In *The Circle of War in the Middle Ages: Essays on Medieval Military and Naval History*. Edited by Donald J. Kagay and L. J. Andrew Villalon. Woodbridge, U.K.: Boydell 1999.

Vale, Malcolm. *War and Chivalry: Warfare and Aristocratic Culture in England, France, and Burgundy at the End of the Middle Ages*. London: Duckworth, 1981.

C. M. GILLMOR

[See also **DMA:** Arms and Armor; Games and Pastimes; Lance; Warfare, Western European.]

HOSPITALLERS, a military religious order that had its origins in a Jerusalem hospital founded by merchants from Amalfi sometime in the middle of the eleventh century. The hospital, which was attached to the monastery of St. Mary of the Latins, was dedicated to St. John the Almoner (a sixth-century patriarch of Alexandria) but changed its name to the more familiar St. John the Baptist after the crusader capture of the city, when the hospital began receiving donations separately from St. Mary's. By the time it was recognized as an order by Pope Paschal II in 1113, the hospital had established hospices at St. Gilles, Asti, Pisa, Bari, Taranto, and Messina. The original purpose of the hospital was the care of the poor as well as of sick pilgrims. The Hospitaller rule (that is, the set of regulations which governed the order's members) was based on the rule of St. Augustine and approved by Eugenius III (1145–1151). The order was originally divided into two groups, priests and lay brothers, who took the traditional monastic oaths of poverty, chastity, and obedience. Although the rule made no comment on military duties, by the early 1130s the Hospitallers had already taken on a military role. King Fulk of Jerusalem (*r.* 1131–1143) was impressed with their military abilities and in 1136 assigned them the castle and town of Bethgibelin (Beit Guvrin), an important stronghold facing Fatimid Ascalon. Some historians have suggested that in this early period members of the hospital remained dedicated to care of the poor and hired mercenaries to defend the order's extensive lands and many castles. Alternatively, the role of the knight-brothers may have evolved from contact with secular knights who had attached themselves to the hospital for a short period as part of their crusader vows. In either case, by 1144, when the Hospitallers received the castle of Krak des Chevaliers, they must have had a substantial and well-organized military wing. The militarization of the order has been seen as a reaction to a similar move by the Templars, but recent work suggests that the two military orders developed in parallel, responding to similar demands. Nevertheless, the papacy in the 1170s was still reminding the order that its first duty was to the poor. It is not until 1182 that their statutes reflected their military role.

Even after the militarization of the order, most Hospitallers had nonmilitary functions; during the twelfth and thirteenth centuries, the order had at most three hundred knight-brothers, who provided most of the leadership for the order. The rest of the order was devoted to managing the Hospitallers' many estates in western Europe, although members also had a military role in Aragon. With so few knight-brothers, the Hospitallers still depended on mercenaries and local troops to garrison their castles—Marqab, for example, in the county of Tripoli, may have held as many as a thousand men, and in the thirteenth century Krak des Chevaliers was reported to have as many as two thousand, only sixty of which were knight-brothers.

The Hospitallers were subject only to the pope himself and were otherwise unlimited by political boundaries. The order had both male and female adherents, often living together in the same convent, though with separate living quarters. The sisters probably did not serve as nurses but were devoted to prayer. By the thirteenth century, however, many Hospitaller sisters were placed in separate convents, though the commandery in Genoa still contained members of both sexes in the fourteenth century.

The organization of the Hospitallers was based on the commandery, which was the center for the management of a group of estates in a given area, which might be as small as a diocese or as large as a kingdom. The commandery often had a conventual building and a chapel. Ideally, the commanders sent the profits of these estates to their prior and attended his annual meetings. The priors in turn controlled priories, which were the larger administrative groupings of the order, usually encompassing a large area such as England. The prior was expected to attend general chapter meetings at the order's headquarters and to transmit the profits of his priory there. By 1295 the Hospitallers were further divided into seven "langues," each organized by language and containing one or more priories, with certain offices reserved for each.

The order's headquarters was in Jerusalem until the city's capture by Saladin in 1187, when it moved to Acre. Following the fall of that city to the Mamluks in 1291, the order moved again to Limassol on Cyprus. In 1306 the Hospitallers mounted an attack on the island of Rhodes in an attempt to seize it from the Turks. After nearly four years of fighting, they had consolidated their control over the island, where in 1309 they had established their new headquarters. Although the Holy Land had been lost, by winning Rhodes the Hospitallers showed themselves to be active in the fight against Islam and thus did not suffer the same fate as their brother order, the Templars, who were suppressed in 1312. The battle for Rhodes, however, had been an enormously expensive campaign for the order, and it took decades for it to recover financially. In Rhodes, the order established a state ruled theocratically by knight-brothers, although full sovereignty was not claimed until 1607.

As a result of establishing themselves on Rhodes, the Hospitallers were forced to become a naval power, abandoning their earlier role as mounted knights. They attacked Turkish military targets, raided Turkish ships and ports for booty and profit, and also licensed piracy, with 10 percent of the catch being paid to the hospital. They continued to participate in crusades and received the city of Smyrna (Izmir) as a result of the Crusade of 1344, holding it from 1374 until its capture by the Turks in 1402. The consolidation of Ottoman power left Rhodes vulnerable. The Turkish attack of 1480 nearly succeeded in capturing the island. In 1522 another Ottoman siege forced the knights to surrender; the Turkish sultan allowed the knights to withdraw on 1 January 1523. They were homeless until 23 March 1530, when Emperor Charles V granted them the islands of Malta and Gozo and the North African city of Tripoli. Here the Hospitallers remained until the island was captured by Napoleon in 1798. In modern times they are still sometimes referred to as the Knights of Malta and remain a sovereign order with their headquarters in Rome.

BIBLIOGRAPHY

PRIMARY WORKS

Delaville le Roulx, J. "Inventaire de pièces de Terre Sainte de l'ordre de l'Hopital." *Revue de l'Orient latin* 3 (1895): 36–106.

———, ed. *Les archives, la bibliothèque, et le trésor de l'ordre de Saint-Jean de Jérusalem à Malte, fasc. 32.* Bibliothèque des Ècoles françaises d'Athènes et de Rome. Paris: Thorin, 1883.

———. 4 vols. *Cartulaire général de l'Ordre des Hospitaliers de S. Jean de Jérusalem.* Paris: Leroux, 1894.

SECONDARY WORKS

Barber, Malcolm, ed. *The Military Orders.* 2 vols. Aldershot, U.K.: Ashgate, 1994–1998.

Luttrell, Anthony. "The Earliest Hospitallers." In *Montjoie: Studies in Crusade History in Honour of Hans Eberhard Mayer.* Edited by Benjamin Z. Kedar, Jonathan Riley-Smith, and Rudolf Hiestand. Aldershot, U.K.: Ashgate, 1997.

———. *The Hospitaller State on Rhodes and Its Western Provinces, 1306–1462.* Aldershot, U.K.: Ashgate, 1999.

Nicholson, Helen. *The Knights Hospitaller.* Woodbridge, U.K.: Boydell, 2001.

Riley-Smith, Jonathan. *The Knights of St. John in Jerusalem and Cyprus, 1050–1310.* London: Macmillian, 1967.

CHRISTOPHER HATCH MACEVITT

[See also **DMA:** Chivalry, Orders of; Rhodes; **Supp:** Templars.]

HUBERT DE BURGH (*ca.* 1175–1243), English royal administrator, soldier, justiciar, earl of Kent. History has been kind to Hubert de Burgh, seeing him as a military hero and last of a line of great Angevin justiciars. The praise may be deserved, but it requires nuance.

Hubert was born to modest landholders in Norfolk, the younger brother of a William de Burgh who served with John in Ireland. By late 1197 or early 1198 Hubert entered service with John, who was still count of Mortain, and soon was described as the count's chamberlain. When John became king in May 1199, Hubert became royal chamberlain. Like many courtiers, Hubert did not follow the king full-time but rather was entrusted with administrative and diplomatic tasks, including a mission in 1200 to the Portuguese court to negotiate a wife for John, who had renounced his previous wife, Isabella of Gloucester. As a trusted aide, Hubert began to assemble offices and lands, becoming sheriff of five counties, castellan of Dover, Wallingford, and other strongholds, and custodian of castles and fiefs in Wales.

John's need to control England while fighting in France led him to give Hubert his first military appointment, guarding the Welsh marches in 1201 and then commanding Dover. After the victory at Mirabeau, Hubert was given custody at Falaise of high-ranking captives, including the Lusignans and John's nephew Arthur of Brittany. The chronicler Ralph of Coggeshall wrote that Hubert refused John's orders to blind and mutilate Arthur, and Shakespeare used the story in *King John*; the tale is unverifiable, but it burnished Hubert's reputation. Hubert was assigned the defense of Chinon, which he held for a year after the English position collapsed elsewhere in Anjou and Normandy in 1204. When Chinon's fall was imminent, Hubert came out fighting; severely wounded, he was captured and held for two years until ransomed. John did little to help ransom Hubert, who returned to find that John had also rescinded his lucrative offices and grants. John soon resumed using Hubert, however, as sheriff of Lincolnshire (1208–1212), deputy seneschal (1213) and seneschal of Poitou (1214), and regent (1214). Hubert was appointed justiciar at Runneymede in June 1215, replacing his former deputy, Peter des Roches, now bishop of Winchester.

Two battles set Hubert on the final path to power. In 1216 and 1217, he held Dover Castle against the intermittent siege of Prince Louis (VIII) of France. And on 24 August 1217, near Sandwich, Hubert led an English flotilla that defeated the larger French fleet dispatched by Louis's energetic wife, Blanche of Castille. Within weeks of the victory Hubert and William Marshal, earl of Pembroke, negotiated generous terms for French withdrawal from England.

With the end of civil war between John and the barons came a gradual resumption of normal governance. Authority rested in a triumvirate consisting of Peter des Roches, the papal legate Gualo, and William Marshal, who as regent held supreme executive power. Hubert was a senior counselor and an administrator subordinate to Peter. When the aged William resigned in April 1219, a new triumvirate emerged, consisting of Hubert, Peter, and Gualo's successor, Pandulf. This time, Hubert had day-to-day control and began to exercise the functions of the justiciarship, supervising the exchequer and bench and witnessing charters. In 1221 Hubert accused Peter and his allies of a treasonous plot, and Peter's ally Peter de Maulay had to relinquish Corfe Castle. Later that year, the king was deemed to be no longer in legal pupilage and was transferred from the custody of Peter to Hubert, now the unchallenged chief minister to the teen-aged king.

Hubert had reinforced his position with a series of remarkable upwardly mobile marriages. After marriages to Beatrice, heiress of Wormegay, and to Isabella of Gloucester, the repudiated wife of King John, in 1221 he wed Margaret of Scotland, the daughter and sister of Scottish kings, who had once been intended as Henry's queen and whose guardian Hubert had been.

Hubert accepted the central goal urged by the pope, Pandulf, and the late William Marshal of "resuming" control over the royal castles, lands, and offices in the custody of others, which meant forcing even loyal allies to relinquish wealth, patronage, and power. The policy was resisted by dilatory tactics and sometimes force. Angry barons staged an armed rally in November 1223, but a truce was arranged on Hubert's terms. On a separate occasion, when Fawkes de Bréauté, one of "the great free-wheeling castellans who had won the war and gone on to dominate the peace" (Carpenter, *The Minority of Henry III,* p. 343) was lured into rebellion at Bedford, Hubert crushed him.

Hubert now had no rivals, but he soon began to alienate his friends. His dilemma was that he could either rule by managing a political consensus, in which case radical administrative reforms were impossible, or restore the bankrupt royal finances, which could only be done by alienating the magnates. There was much to praise about his rule. He reestablished regular government and royal rights while conciliating former rebels. When vigor was necessary against foes, he largely punished them within the law, attacking not their hereditary lands but only the lands and offices they held at royal pleasure. His reissue of Magna Carta (1225) became a basis of constitutional law. But by 1230 his position was

in danger, for he offended lay and ecclesiastical barons with tough but erratic measures for the restoration of the king's rights, finances, and lost foreign provinces, and he offended the king with the inadequacy of those measures.

Critics noted that Hubert had grown vastly rich. He was given the earldom of Kent in 1227. He aggressively sought land, including the Welsh castles that John had withdrawn twenty years before, and in some cases prevailed with irregular legal maneuvers. He also received gifts from suitors who saw that "he had the realm of England in his hand," and even admirers have termed Hubert greedy. But unlike some earlier justiciars who had been highly regarded but notoriously corrupt, Hubert tended to receive short-term grants, even after the king assumed legal majority and could issue perpetual charters. The courts that Hubert supervised also accepted fewer, smaller "proffers" for favorable resolution than in John's reign or Henry's later years.

The perceived failure of Hubert's foreign policy was also widely criticized. While he was resuming English castles in 1224, the French were conquering the English province of Poitou. Even Pope Honorius questioned English priorities. In Wales, Hubert enjoyed modest success in 1223, but that soon changed. His marcher allies were no match for the Welsh prince Llywelyn, who repeatedly played English factions against one another. In battle, by relying on defensive tactics and lumbering, the hero of Chinon, Dover, Sandwich, and Bedford lost castles, territory, and vassals to the Welsh.

Tension was inevitable after the king's decision in 1227 that he was ready to rule. In response to his chief minister's justified skepticism about the desirability of an expedition in 1229 to France, the enraged king accused him of treason. Meanwhile, Llywelyn's campaigns in 1228 and 1231 consolidated a generation of Welsh gains. Rivals worried that Hubert's lands made him overmighty, and his failures abroad cost the support of the barons, who declined to grant revenues in 1231 and 1232. The last of the old magnates were dying; their heirs had no interest in the crown's agenda of Aquitaine instead of Normandy and owed little to Hubert. When Peter des Roches returned from crusade and diplomatic triumph in 1231, Hubert was "isolated in his greatness" (Powicke, *King Henry III,* p. 47), unable to muster the coalition of barons and bishops that had allowed him to best Peter in 1223–1224 or to rely on the favor of the king.

From 1219 to 1232, said the Waverley annalist, Hubert "lacked nothing of royal power, save the dignity of a royal diadem." But his vast power unraveled in late

July 1232. Why the king finally jettisoned Hubert can only be surmised. Perhaps the cause was the king's penury; by now, even the crown jewels had been pledged to the duke of Brittany. Peter des Roches was crucial, for he had spent months telling the king of reforms that would restore wealth and glory and placing his allies back into government. By June 1232, Peter used a papal commission to investigate the molestations of Italian clerks in England and produced findings of Hubert's purported complicity; this became the official reason for the dismissal. Hubert was accused not only of malfeasance and corruption but of murder and sorcery. When he refused to submit to judgment, a hostile but deadlocked council compromised by restoring his hereditary lands but imprisoning him indefinitely at Devizes. Only after intervention by his kinsman Alexander of Scotland and Pope Gregory was Hubert released from chains. The unpopular Hubert became a rallying point for dissenters. He feared that des Roches intended to have him killed, and in October 1233 two Marshal allies whisked him to safety in Wales. Centuries after, lawyers held that the circumstances of Hubert's flight stood for the proposition that neither a fugitive nor a rescuer could be outlawed at common law if he was not appealed or indicted, even if he broke prison or waged war against the king.

Vindication came in May 1234, when Henry and the senior judge William of Raleigh publicly acknowledged that Hubert had been mistreated. He was not returned to office, but he and his allies were permitted to reclaim the lands they had lost. In 1236 he was again in disfavor when the king learned that Hubert or his wife arranged or allowed the marriage of their daughter Megotta to Richard, heir of the earldom of Gloucester, a former ward of Hubert's for whom the king had other plans. The marriage was disregarded, and Megotta died young. In 1237 he and Peter were among the surviving witnesses of the original Magna Carta whom the king used to witness a reconfirmation of the charter. Hubert was briefly charged with treason in 1239, and to regain the king's favor he again surrendered his Welsh castles. At his death in 1243, the dynasty he sought to found did not endure, for with his daughter's early death, his earldom lapsed.

BIBLIOGRAPHY

Carpenter, David A. *The Minority of Henry III.* London: Methuen, 1990.

———. *The Reign of Henry III.* London: Hambledon Press, 1996.

Ellis, Clarence. *Hubert de Burgh: A Study in Constancy.* London: Phoenix House, 1952. Based exclusively on secondary sources.

Johnston, S. H. F. "The Lands of Hubert de Burgh." *English Historical Review* 50 (1935): 418–432.

Powicke, F. M. *King Henry III and the Lord Edward: The Community of the Realm in the Thirteenth Century.* 2 vols. Oxford: Clarendon Press, 1947. The classic account, though superseded by Carpenter and Stacey.

Stacey, Robert C. *Politics, Policy, and Finance under Henry III, 1216–1245.* Oxford: Clarendon Press, 1987.

Walker, R. F. "Hubert de Burgh and Wales, 1218–1232." *English Historical Review* 87 (1972): 465–494.

Weiss, Michael. "The Castellan: The Early Career of Hubert de Burgh." *Viator* 5 (1974): 235–252.

West, Francis. *The Justiciarship in England, 1066–1232.* Cambridge, U.K.: Cambridge University Press, 1966.

JONATHAN A. BUSH

[See also **DMA:** England: Norman-Angevin; England: 1216–1485; Henry III of England; John, King of England; Magna Carta; William Marshal; **Supp:** Peter des Roches.]

HUMANISM. Depending on one's definition, medieval humanism is either a very small or a very large topic. It is a very small topic if one adopts the definition of humanism proposed by Paul Oskar Kristeller, as the recovery and close stylistic imitation of works of classical antiquity by Italian scholars whose range of expertise lay in grammar, rhetoric, history, and moral philosophy. It is a very large topic if one adopts the definition of R. W. Southern, as an intellectual practice grounded on convictions about both the dignity of humanity and the cosmic order and intelligibility of the natural world. If one adopts the Kristellan definition, then medieval humanism pales by comparison with the breadth, depth, and technical accomplishment of its Renaissance counterpart. If one adopts the definition of Southern, medieval humanism perhaps outscales its Renaissance counterpart in variety and vigor.

FIFTEENTH-CENTURY HUMANISM

The word "humanism" is an early-nineteenth-century coinage, but it does point to a distinctive fifteenth-century Italian phenomenon, when the term "umanista" was used to designate a teacher or student of classical literature. Such scholars, so the argument normally runs, developed practices first attempted in the mid-thirteenth century but first pursued with system, resources, and learning by Petrarch in the fourteenth. Prime among such practices was the recovery and philological reconstruction of ancient texts, including, crucially, the recovery and understanding of the original texts of Greek learning and literature, beginning in the very late fourteenth century in Italy. Almost as important was the close stylistic imitation of classical, especially Ciceronian, Latin. The movement was not, in origin, characterized by new philosophical ideas or new political theory, however much these two areas of study were eventually refreshed by the recovery of a broader range of classical texts. The introduction of printing in the second half of the fifteenth century gave enormous impetus to this scholarly movement, providing as it did common texts as the basis for critical argument and judgment. The institutions that framed such studies were principally schools (such as that of Guarino da Verona in Ferrara) and the courts of powerful patrons, who needed expert rhetoricians for the conduct of diplomatic business. The genres practiced by serving humanists were diplomatic letters, above all, and biographies that stressed the glory that can accrue for patrons and poets by mutual support. The movement began in Italy but spread north of the Alps at differing rates, establishing itself as a powerful practice throughout western Europe in the sixteenth century, when vernacular translations of classical works were produced in quantity.

New paradigms of study need to legitimate themselves. Fifteenth-century humanism did so by attacking (and in some ways creating) the large middle period (the "Middle Ages") that obscured access to the glory of classical antiquity. That "dark" period was attacked for not having attempted to recreate a historical sense of classical antiquity through the recuperation of pristine texts. The very project of "recovery" must imply a period of loss, a period designated as *media aetas* (a "middle period"). Recovery of classical norms of Latin style for imitation also involved hostile confrontation with the Latin developed for use in medieval universities, which was described by fifteenth-century humanists as barbaric. A powerful emphasis on rhetorical persuasion as far superior to the unadorned statement of philosophical truth led to the scornful dismissal of medieval Scholastic philosophy as equally barbaric. Such an attack amounted to an attack on the university practice by scholars concerned to shape new forms and new loci of scholarly authority. In a powerful sense, then, these humanists succeeded in transforming an educational movement into a periodic description, identifying philosophical, university Latin and textual practice with an immobile "Middle Ages."

In its own self-definition, then, this narrower but very significant definition of humanism repudiated the "Middle Ages," giving rise to the conviction that the medieval period had little to show in the way of "humanistic" activity. With this narrower definition of humanism the wider definition (concerning a belief in human dig-

nity and confidence in the powers of reason) came to be associated. Precisely because fifteenth-century humanists respected the works of classical antiquity, they implicitly and often explicitly appealed to a notion of universal reason and human nature. This association of the revival of classical letters with a revival of reason itself reached its apogee in the eighteenth century, when "humanist" activity came to be associated with the repudiation of superstitious "medieval" religious practice and belief.

By the time scholarship of the medieval period began in earnest in the later decades of the nineteenth century, then, scholars of the Middle Ages confronted two related prejudices about the absence of medieval humanism: the Middle Ages were innocent of the historical sense necessary to provoke the project of historical recovery; and the intellectual culture of medieval centuries was in any case profoundly religious, relying on biblical revelation and assigning a low place to reason. How did scholars respond to this challenge?

MEDIEVAL HUMANISMS

One response was to work within the narrower, philological, Kristellan definition, asking whether any medieval scholars conformed to that set of practices. This approach isolated small groups of scholars who did express a sense of historical regret at the loss of ancient civilization and/or who practiced stylistic imitation of classical models before (just before) the arrival of full-scale humanist textual practice in a given country. The twelfth-century Hildebert of Lavardin may be cited as an example of the first case, expressing as he did a sense of Rome as fallen from its former glory. The studies of Giuseppe Billanovich for late-thirteenth- and fourteenth-century Italy and of Roberto Weiss for fifteenth-century England exemplify the second case (of protohumanistic textual activity).

Another response was to be less restrictive in the definition of humanism and to look instead to the medieval centuries for cultural movements in which scholarly effort was in one way or another inspired by classical models and expressed a confidence in human reason in so doing. The tendency of this research has been to define pre-Renaissance renaissances. The "Carolingian renaissance" of the late eighth and early ninth centuries (whose most celebrated representative was Alcuin) and the "twelfth-century renaissance" thus came into focus as objects of scholarly attention. What these movements had in common was an educational movement designed to nourish bureaucratic needs. The twelfth century in France especially has been seen as the crucial century, in which a "humanistic" movement in the large sense gained momentum and force. The characteristics of this period were a widespread set of cathedral schools, especially in northern France (e.g., Chartres, Orléans); the study of classical authors, especially Ovid and Vergil; a Ciceronian rhetorical culture; the promotion of classical ethics, drawn especially from Cicero's *De officiis*; and a focus on the structure of the natural world, under the especial influence of the one genuinely Platonic text that had in large part been transmitted to the Latin West, *Timaeus*. In addition to the classical authors who inspired it, twelfth-century school culture was informed by late antique Neoplatonic texts, such as Calcidius's commentary on *Timaeus*, Martianus Capella's *Marriage of Philology and Mercury*, Macrobius's commentary on book 6 of Cicero's *De re publica*, and Boethius's *Consolation of Philosophy*. Some of the great scholars and poets associated with this movement are Bernard of Chartres, Peter Abelard, William of Conches, Bernard Silvester, John of Salisbury, and Alan of Lille.

Twelfth-century scholars and poets working in this matrix had a profound respect for natural human capacities, including a much sharper attention to psychological interiority, whereby the different functions of the psyche themselves mirrored larger structures in the universe. This respect for nature also entailed a corresponding confidence in the writings of non-Christian authors, both poets and philosophers, and a profound sense of the rationally intelligible order of the natural universe. For these scholars self-knowledge did not consist, as it did in some monastic traditions, of self-abasement in the knowledge of nature's fallen status. On the contrary, full self-knowledge could be achieved only by understanding the structure of the universe and, ultimately, by experiencing the divine source of being itself, which humans are capable of intuiting by virtue of their own divine intelligence. For this tradition, God is the God of an ordered cosmos, the God of the philosophers, the source and archetype of being itself, rather than the God of Abraham manifesting himself progressively through salvation history to a fallen humanity. One achieves perfection in this broadly humanist tradition not by penitence but by intellectual effort and educational perfection. At its most coherent, in such works as Alan of Lille's *Anticlaudianus* (*ca.* 1181–1183), these scholarly dispositions united a psychology, a politics, a cosmology, and a theology. Not least, poetics itself was a key mode of knowledge, as poetic structures alone were capable of enacting the complex, ecological structures of the universe and human being, macrocosm and microcosm. This philosophico-poetic, elitist enterprise expressed a profound optimism for the possibilities of perfection through education for a very select few.

Alongside this philosophic poetry in Latin, the last four decades of the twelfth century witnessed the rise of a classicizing vernacular poetry, which addressed itself to and challenged chivalric readers. The *Roman de Thèbes, Enéas,* and the *Roman de Troie* all promote the practical value of prudence above all, and they enact the rhetorical skill with which scholars must persuade powerful militarist patrons.

What became of this powerful, deeply conceived, broadly humanist cultural movement? One of its effects was none other than to lay the foundations in Italy for the development of schools that produced humanism in the narrower, Kristellan sense. Within the main lines of educational and scholarly history, however, this Platonizing culture was almost entirely displaced by the recovery of Aristotelian texts (translated into Latin via Arabic intermediaries) in the later twelfth century. With the absorption of that Greek learning into the theological programs of thirteenth-century universities, such as those of Paris and Oxford, a new and highly technical educational program had displaced the program of centers such as Chartres. A broadly "grammatical" culture lost out to dialectic. This university culture was the especial object of attack by fifteenth-century humanists for its deployment of "barbarous" Latin and relentlessly philosophical, antirhetorical presentation of truth. Within the broader definition of humanism, however, thirteenth-century Scholasticism, whose greatest name is that of Thomas Aquinas, is possibly the most powerful humanist movement under consideration in this article. It had a profound confidence in nature and natural powers, especially reason, and a correspondingly profound confidence in classical philosophy, especially Aristotle. Its God, too, was the God of the philosophers. Its purview was the entirety of earthly existence, from psychology and ethics to politics, natural science, and the newly formulated science of theology. Its textual methods were rigorously logical and rational, weighing all contributions (derived from both reason and authority) to a given question before arriving at a fresh resolution.

The deep-seated perception of Scholasticism as antihumanistic has, then, from the perspective of the larger definition of humanism, serious shortcomings. By the larger definition, thirteenth-century Scholasticism is one of European history's greatest and most sustained moments of philosophical confidence and investigation.

Although Scholastic theologians developed subtle ways of discussing poetic procedures, such scholars rigorously eschewed the poetic mode in their own writing. Did this mean that the poetico-philosophic humanist culture of twelfth-century France was entirely overtaken and lost to view? Not at all. The cultural constellation of that culture survived in deeply modified form in poetic practice throughout the thirteenth, fourteenth, and fifteenth centuries. Certainly many aspects of that elitist, Platonic culture were put to severe pressure under new influences: the Platonic psychology that stressed the perfection of the intellect in wholly disembodied form was, for example, questioned by an Aristotelian emphasis on *embodied* perfection. And the supremacy of Vergil as the governing poetic presence of twelfth-century culture was subject to extreme pressure from a massive, later medieval commitment to the poet of the passions and the body, Ovid. Correlatively, the restricted, often mannered Latin of twelfth-century poetic texts was challenged by vernacular practice in a limpid, accessible style. The theocratic politics of some twelfth-century texts was subjected to pressure from a conception of the ruler as embodied in and dependent on the body politic. Dante in Italy, Jean de Meun in France, and Chaucer in England: these are only the greatest names among later medieval vernacular poets whose enterprise would have been inconceivable without the twelfth-century precedent. In their work an exceptionally rich humanist tradition continued to present poetry as a critical mode of philosophical investigation.

BIBLIOGRAPHY

Benson, Robert L., Giles Constable, and Carol D. Lanham, eds. *Renaissance and Renewal in the Twelfth Century.* Oxford: Clarendon Press, 1982. For conspectus of twelfth-century renaissance.

Billanovich, Giuseppe. *I primi umanisti e le tradizioni dei classici latini.* Freiburg, Switzerland: Edizioni Universitarie, 1953. Example of "micro" history of prehumanist practice.

Chenu, Marie-Dominique. *La théologie comme science au XIIIe siècle.* 3d ed. Paris: Vrin, 1969. For presuppositions and procedures of thirteenth-century scholasticism.

Ferguson, Wallace K. *The Renaissance in Historical Thought: Five Centuries of Interpretation.* Cambridge, Mass.: Houghton Mifflin, 1948. For ways in which humanism provoked periodic definitions.

Kraye, Jill, ed. *The Cambridge Companion to Renaissance Humanism.* Cambridge, U.K.: Cambridge University Press, 1996. Chapters by Davies, Hankins, Jensen Kraye, Mann, and Reeve; very useful for Renaissance recovery of classical learning and its application.

Kristeller, Paul Oskar. *Renaissance Thought and Its Sources.* Edited by Michael Mooney. New York: Columbia University Press, 1979. Chapter 1 for definition of fifteenth-century Italian humanism.

Simpson, James. *Sciences and the Self in Medieval Poetry: Alan of Lille's "Anticlaudianus" and John Gower's "Confessio amantis."* Cambridge, U.K.: Cambridge University Press, 1995. For account of the transmission of twelfth-century humanism into later medieval vernacular poetry.

Skinner, Quentin. *The Foundations of Modern Political Thought.* 2 vols. Cambridge, U.K.: Cambridge University Press, 1970. For humanist political thought from twelfth century.

Southern, R. W. *Scholastic Humanism and the Unification of Europe.* Cambridge, Mass.: Blackwell, 1995. For definition of medieval humanism and twelfth-century school culture.

Weiss, Roberto. *Humanism in England during the Fifteenth Century.* 3d ed. Oxford: Blackwell, 1967. Example of micro history of "proto"-humanist practice.

Wetherbee, Winthrop. "Philosophy, Cosmology, and the Twelfth-Century Renaissance." In *A History of Twelfth-Century Philosophy.* Edited by Peter Dronke. Cambridge, U.K.: Cambridge University Press, 1988. For aspects of twelfth-century "renaissance."

JAMES SIMPSON

[See also **DMA:** Aristotle in the Middle Ages; Classical Literary Studies; Latin Language; Latin Literature; Petrarch; Scholasticism, Scholastic Method; Universities; **Supp:** Middle Ages.]

HUMBERT OF ROMANS (*ca.* 1194–1277), fifth master general of the Dominican order. Born in Romans, a small town in the Dauphiné region of southeastern France, Humbert earned a master of arts degree at Paris and stayed on to study theology and canon law. On 30 November 1224 he entered the Order of Friars Preachers. Around 1226 he moved from Paris to Lyons, where he served first as lector and then as prior of the Dominican convent. In 1240 he was chosen as provincial of the order's Roman province, and in 1244 he became provincial of the French province. At the general chapter held at Buda in 1254, Humbert was elected master general of his order, a position he held until his voluntary resignation nine years later.

During his years as master general, Humbert did much to strengthen the prestige of the Dominican order. He defended the Dominicans against attacks both by secular university masters and by diocesan secular clergy, but he did so in such a way as not to further alienate the seculars. Indeed, one of Humbert's most striking attributes was his skill as a mediator. In addition to working to resolve conflicts between the Dominicans and the secular clergy, Humbert also strove to foster a spirit of cooperation with the Franciscans. At a time when the two mendicant orders viewed each other with increasing distrust and envy, Humbert worked closely with the Franciscan minister general John of Parma to bring the two orders closer together so that they could realize their common objectives.

One of Humbert's achievements was his reform of the Dominican liturgy. The need to unify and simplify the rite had become more pressing as the Dominican order expanded and became more international. Humbert also sought to advance the language training of friars, particularly those engaged in missionary work. He recognized that a knowledge of foreign languages could aid the Dominicans' proselytization efforts in non-Christian lands. Perhaps not surprisingly, given his own university education, Humbert advocated a more rigorous education for Dominicans and defended the inclusion of philosophy in the university curriculum. At the same time, however, he opposed learning for learning's sake, arguing that a friar's education should always be oriented toward making him a better preacher. Learning was merely a tool to be applied toward the larger project of caring for others' souls.

During his career, Humbert wrote a number of treatises, including a massive *expositio,* or commentary, on the Augustinian Rule. He also composed a *summa* on the art of preaching, the *De eruditione praedicatorum,* in which he detailed the qualities that a preacher should possess and sketched dozens of model sermons for different occasions. In response to Pope Gregory X's request of 1272 that religious leaders submit reports on what they considered in need of reform, Humbert composed an influential treatise, the *Opusculum tripartitum,* in which he addressed the issues that would be raised at the Second Council of Lyons (1274): the need for a new crusade, a plan for reuniting the Greek and Roman churches, and clerical reform.

BIBLIOGRAPHY

Brett, Edward Tracy. *Humbert of Romans: His Life and Views of Thirteenth-Century Society.* Toronto: Pontifical Institute of Mediaeval Studies, 1984.

Humbert of Romans. *Treatise on Preaching.* Edited by Walter M. Conlon. Translated by the Dominican Students, Province of St. Joseph. Westminster, Md.: Newman Press, 1951.

———. *Opera de vita regulari.* 2 vols. Edited by Joachim Joseph Berthier, Torino, Italy: Marietti, 1956.

Tugwell, Simon, O.P. "Christ as Model of Sanctity in Humbert of Romans." In *Christ among the Medieval Dominicans: Representations of Christ in the Texts and Images of the Order of Preachers.* Edited by Kent Emery Jr. and Joseph Wawrykow. Notre Dame: University of Notre Dame Press, 1998.

ADAM JEFFREY DAVIS

[See also **DMA:** Councils, Western (1311–1449); Dominican Rite; Dominicans; Preaching and Sermon Literature, Western European.]

HYGIENE, PERSONAL. An elaborate doctrine of personal hygiene began to develop in thirteenth-century Europe as the medical writings of Greco-Arabic authors were translated and assimilated into Latin culture. In the ninth-century *Isagoge* of Johannitius (Ḥunayn ibn Isḥāq

Bathers. *From Petrus de Ebulo,* Nomina et virtutes balneorum; seu, De balneis Pureolorum et Baiarum *(13th century). Codice Angelico 1474.* THE NEW YORK PUBLIC LIBRARY. REPRODUCED BY PERMISSION.

al-Ibādī), translated by Constantine the African shortly before 1100, Latin readers found the basic idea that the content of medicine could be divided into naturals, nonnaturals, and contranaturals—that is, the things that make up life, those external agents that shape it, and those that are opposed to it. That second group, the nonnaturals, provided an ideal framework for future considerations, and Johannitius's outline fixed for centuries its six constituents, the factors that could be adjusted so as to keep one in health: air, motion and rest, food and drink, sleeping and waking, excretion and repletion, and the emotions. All these factors can be found mentioned in antiquity as helping individually to determine health, but they are not presented there in so structured a form; the systematization of the nonnaturals (under that name) occurred in the Byzantine schools of late antiquity. In addition to the *Isagoge,* Constantine also translated, under the title *Pantegni,* the encyclopedic *Kitāb Kāmil as-sinā' at at-tibbiya* (The complete book of the medical art) of 'Ali ibn al-'Abbās (Haly Abbas), and here, in book

5 of its first, theoretical, part, Latin readers would have found an extended explanation and elaboration of the nonnaturals and their relation to health.

Three other works of Greco-Arabic medicine rendered into Latin in the twelfth century contributed further to the growing medieval concept of hygiene as depending on a conscious regulation of the six nonnaturals. One was Burgundio of Pisa's translation from Greek of Galen's *Peri hygieion*, which circulated in medieval Europe under the title *De regimine sanitatis*. Here Galen had discussed the impact on the body's health of all those factors that would later be organized as the nonnaturals, which confirmed their authoritativeness for the Middle Ages. He added a refinement to the conceptualization of health by insisting that these factors could not be applied universally and mechanically but had to be adapted to the age and status of the patient: thus, for example, more exercise is needed to maintain a young man in health than an old one or a baby. This emphasis on the individuality of health and of a healthy regimen was carried further in the two great medical encyclopedias translated from Arabic by Gerard of Cremona and his circle in the later twelfth century, *Liber almansoris* of Rhazes (Abū al-Rāzī) and the *Canon* of Avicenna (Ibn Sīnā). Each dealt with hygiene as a discrete subject within medicine, and each structured its discussion of hygiene around the six nonnaturals, but, like Galen, they stressed the individuality of regimen in various ways. In book 4 of *Liber almansoris* Rhazes discussed the health not only of various age groups but of travelers and pregnant women and also explained how proper hygiene varied with the season of the year. And in book 1 fen 3 of the *Canon*, Avicenna provided a synthesis and exhaustive exploration of these earlier themes—the six nonnaturals, the individuality of regimen—but rooted it systematically in considerations of individual complexion: as Avicenna explained it, it was the qualitative balance appropriate to the individual at that particular stage in his life that needed to be maintained by adjusting the nonnaturals and the qualitative changes they were recognized as effecting.

This originally Greco-Arabic construction of what it meant to be healthy and how one's health should be maintained spread gradually in Europe, impelled by the growing esteem for the learned medicine coming to be taught at places like Paris and Montpellier, where by 1250 Avicenna's *Canon* had become the authoritative basis for medical education. From this point we begin to see the origins of a new genre of Latin medical literature, the *regimen sanitatis*—regimes of health sometimes constructed for a particular individual, sometimes addressed to a general readership, and usually structured more or less carefully around the six nonnaturals. This had been an Arabic medical genre as well, and it may not be coincidental that a number of these Arabic *regimina* were first translated into Latin in the later thirteenth century, as though to provide models for the new Latin works: these include, for example, Ibn Buṭlān's *Tacuinum sanitatis,* arranged (remarkably) in tabular form, for a general audience; and Moses Maimonides's *regimen sanitatis* composed for the son of Saladin.

REGULATION OF THE NONNATURALS

The system that was passed on with broad consistency by these Latin writers naturally shared many details with its Arabic models. Although the nonnaturals include many constituents that we now would subsume under hygiene, the details of what was comprised under each of the nonnaturals and what effects they were understood to have on the human body are sometimes a little unexpected. Under air *(aer),* for example, falls not just atmospheric air but all the body's surroundings that are capable of affecting its complexion—one's clothes, for example, which can help maintain the body in a temperate environment, or one's house, whose newly plastered walls can be unhealthy. Certainly, however, atmospheric air is the most important thing included here because of its direct connection with the basis of physiological life, cooling the natural heat of respiration: to seek pure air, neither too hot nor too cold, untainted by the strong odors that imply its putridity, is the ideal. Corrupt air can, however, be purified by aromatic substances; cold air can be heated by fires; hot and dry air can be made less unhealthy by sprinkling water on the walls and floors.

Exercise and rest *(motus et quies)* correspond closely to our understanding of these terms, though the explanation for their healthfulness does not. Physical activity increases the inner heat of the body, strengthens it, and improves digestion; it should be carried out before a meal, not afterward. Latin writers universally approved of walking as a means of exercise, but other forms were endorsed when appropriate to the individual's status—knights might be encouraged to go riding, for example.

Food and drink *(cibus et potus)* is a particularly important subject, since what is ingested will be incorporated into the nature of the body in a series of three digestions, and the wide range of foodstuffs available means that it is an unusually intricate one. The effects of a food vary according to whether it is gross or subtle, as well as according to its qualitative complexion, and more or less traditional judgments were established about each: beans are somewhat suspect; vegetables are healthiest when cooked; fruits should be consumed only as medicine, not as food; chicken is good, especially for the delicate; eggs are excellent, but milk less so; and so on. The foods thought to be best tended to be relatively costly; a peasant's normal diet would not have been judged a healthy one for the elite. The *regimina* maintained the Greco-Arabic tradition of endorsing a relative abstinence, recommending small meals spaced far apart: one meal a day or, more often, two (morning and evening); food should be chewed slowly, so as not to rush the digestion.

Sleep and waking *(somnum et vigilia)* affect health because in sleep the animal heat moves inward from the body's periphery as the senses shut down, and this encourages digestion in the inner members, the stomach and liver. One should sleep on a bed slightly raised at the head from eight to ten hours daily—and at night, not in a midday siesta.

Excretion and repletion *(inanitio et repletio)* refer to the need to ensure that the body is cleansed of the waste products of the three digestions, all of which should be removed regularly. The coarse residues of the first digestion are carried off in the feces; regular defecation every morning is thus important, and purges were often advised to make sure it took place. The second digestion's wastes are carried off in the urine. The third, concluding digestion, which takes place in the individual members, leaves a different character of waste to be removed: its products are things like hairs, tears, earwax, sweat, nasal mucous, and so forth. In the methods used to remove these materials we perhaps come closest to our own acculturated notions of hygiene: the face is to be washed thoroughly in the morning, the hands before and after meals, the teeth brushed daily, the face and sometimes the body shaved.

The *accidentia anime,* the emotions, may seem foreign to modern notions of health until we remember the role of tension or worry in precipitating heart attacks. The medieval physician thought of these passions as arising in the soul and leading immediately to physiological consequences. Joy, anger, sadness, worry, each had its own somatic consequences for the heart and body; conditions that induced joy were good for physical health, sadness obviously injurious—so these too were part of the circumstances of the external world that the individual or his physician had to control or regulate in order to remain entirely healthy.

Two aspects of the *Isagoge*'s list of nonnaturals left Latin medical writers in some perplexity. Baths *(balnea)* Johannitius had attached to the end of exercise and rest, the second nonnatural; should they not rather come under the fifth, the removal of the body's wastes? In any case, everyone acknowledged the close association of baths with exercise, since what they cleansed were the wastes, the sweat, produced by exercise. Bathing could be in water or in steam, and besides removing waste it had the power to heat the body and promote digestion. Spending a long time in a hot bath was considered dangerous, however, since this weakened the body; and one should not bathe immediately after eating, or drink anything cold while in the bath or when emerging from it. Similarly, Latin authorities wavered on the nature of coitus, sexual intercourse—does it fall under excretion, as Johannitius said, or under the *accidentia anime?* In general they favored the former answer: coitus is necessary to the maintenance of health because it expels one of the superfluities of the third digestion, the semen. The best moment for intercourse is therefore in the morning, after the process of digestion is complete. Certain individuals—the melancholic, those of a dry complexion, the thin—should indulge sparingly, however, for evacuating a hot, moist matter like semen too frequently can cool and dry the body unhealthily.

A REGIMEN FOR A KING

This general account must not lead us to forget that most regimens were probably composed for a particular person and that consequently our texts often display a marked individuality. The regimen that Arnald of Villanova drew up (1305–1308) for his royal patron, James II of Aragon, illustrates well not just this originality but the client's involvement in the process and his acceptance of the terms in which the discourse was cast, for while not highly technical, it certainly presumed the king's understanding of the principles of health: of complexion, of natural heat, of digestion, of the production and expulsion of superfluities, and of the interrelationship among these things. The first part of the regimen examines the nonnaturals sequentially as they may affect the king—Arnald chooses to present bathing following exercise and coitus following sleep. Then he turns back to take up *cibus et potus* in itemized detail, with chapters on different classes of foods—vegetables, bread, fruits, roots, animals, and fish and their benefits and disadvantages to health—as though diet were the aspect of regimen that Arnald (or the king) felt most important. The individuality of the work comes through here in part in Arnald's apparent concern to explain how changes in foodstuffs affect someone (presumably like King James) whose normal bodily complexion ranges between temperate and hot: rose syrup is good for such a person to drink, for example; fresh almonds and walnuts are harmful. But the individuality is even more obvious in the regimen's concluding chapter. King James suffered from chronic hemorrhoids, and that chapter explains how they are to be managed. Moreover, the discussion of the individual nonnaturals sometimes explains how they affect such a sufferer: he should not have intercourse when hungry or right after a meal; he should not eat spicy or oversweet foods but instead mild things like barley cooked with almond milk. Yet despite its individuality, Arnald's regimen for the king had a very wide circulation: almost eighty manuscripts of the Latin text are known, and it was translated into Catalan and at least twice into Hebrew. There is thus every reason to think that by the fourteenth century not only the elite recipients of these *regimina* but also the wider literate public understood and accepted the principles of the medical theory of health and felt competent to adapt the recommendations they found there to their own use.

BIBLIOGRAPHY

PRIMARY WORKS

Arano, Luisa Cogliati, ed. *"Tacuinum sanitatis": The Medieval Health Handbook.* Translated by Oscar Ratti and Adele Westbrook. New York: G. Braziller, 1976.

Garcia Ballester, Louis, Michael R. McVaugh, Pedro Gil-Sotres, and Juan A Penigua, eds. *Regimen sanitatis ad regem Aragonum.* Volume 10, part 1, of *Arnaldi de Villanova opera medica omnia.* Edited by Michael R. McVaugh and Garcia Ballester. Barcelona: Universitat de Barcelona, 1996.

Green, Robert Montraville. *A Translation of Galen's Hygiene ("De sanitate tuenda").* Springfield, Ill.: Charles C. Thomas, 1951.

Maimonides, Moses. *Moses Maimonides' Two Treatises on the Regimen of Health: "Fī tadbīr al-sihhah" and "Maqālah fi bayān baʿd al-aʿrād wa-al-jawāb ʿanhā."* Translated from the Arabic and edited in accordance with the Hebrew and Latin versions by Ariel Bar-Sela, Hebbel E. Hoff, and Elias Faris. Philadelphia: American Philosophical Society, 1964.

The School of Salernum: "Regimen sanitatis salernitanum." Translated by Sir John Harington, with a history of the school of Salernum by Francis R. Packard, M.D., and a note on the prehistory of the *Regimen sanitatis* by Fielding H. Garrison, M.D. New York: P. B. Hoeber, 1920.

SECONDARY WORKS

Ariès, Philippe, and Georges Duby, gen. eds. *A History of Private Life.* Volume 2: *Revelations of the Medieval World.* Cambridge, Mass.: Belknap Press, 1988. See pages 584–610.

García-Ballester, Luis. "Changes in the *Regimina sanitatis:* The Role of the Jewish Physicians." In *Health, Disease, and Healing in Medieval Culture.* Edited by Sheila Campbell, Bert Hall, and David Klausner. New York: St. Martin's, 1992.

———."On the Origin of the 'Six Non-Natural Things' in Galen." In *Galen und das hellenistische Erbe.* Edited by Diethard Nickel and Jutta Kollesch. Stuttgart, Germany: Franz Steiner, 1993.

Gil-Sotres, Pedro. "The Regimens of Health." In *Western Medical Thought from Antiquity to the Middle Ages.* Edited by Mirko D.

Grmek. Translated by Anton Shugaar. Cambridge, Mass.: Harvard University Press, 1998.

Jacquart, Danielle, and Claude Thomasset. *Sexuality and Medicine in the Middle Ages.* Translated by Matthew Adamson. Princeton, N.J.: Princeton University Press, 1988.

Siraisi, Nancy G. *Medieval and Early Renaissance Medicine: An Introduction to Knowledge and Practice.* Chicago and London: University of Chicago Press, 1990. See especially chapter 5.

MICHAEL MCVAUGH

[See also **DMA:** Arnald of Villanova; Medicine, Schools of; Rāzī, Abū Bakr Muḥammad ibn Zakarīya al- (Rhazes); Sīnā, Ibn; **Supp:** Baths and Bathing: Disease.]

HYPATIA was well known in the Middle Ages not only as the preeminent female philosopher of late antiquity, but also for her grisly death. Born sometime between 355 and 370, she was the daughter of Theon, a mathematician and member of the Alexandrian Museum. Father and daughter appear to have spent their entire lives in Alexandria and to have collaborated on at least one written project, a commentary on Ptolemy's *Almagest.* According to information in the tenth-century Byzantine *Suda,* Hypatia was also the author of a work on astronomy and a commentary on Apollonius's *The Conics.* Other than these mere titles, however, none of her work survives. Interestingly, there is no indication that she wrote philosophical treatises or commentaries, although it is in this area that she was most distinguished, according to contemporary evidence. Since at least the 390s, Hypatia attracted students from around the Eastern Roman Empire from distinguished backgrounds who went on to successful careers and maintained contact with their former teacher. Among these the best known to us, thanks to his surviving letters, is Synesius of Cyrene (*ca.* 365–415). As were many, if not most, of Hypatia's students, Synesius was Christian and later became bishop of Ptolemais (in modern Libya). From his letters to Hypatia and to fellow alumni, we know that Hypatia's philosophy was firmly grounded in Neoplatonism, specifically in the traditions of Plotinus (204–270) and Iamblichus (early fourth century). Synesius's sometimes elusive allusions to the secrets Hypatia imparted to her students, combined with circumstantial evidence that Neoplatonism sometimes involved magical practices (theurgy), have contributed to ancient and modern suspicions that there was a religious, cultic element to this circle. For example, John of Nikiu, the seventh-century Christian bishop and chronicler, charged that Hypatia led many Christians astray by "her satanic wiles" and thereby aroused the righteous anger of church authorities. The accusation is unlikely, however. Hypatia's popularity extended beyond a small circle of select students; she lectured publicly and was widely renowned for her philosophical demeanor and lifelong chastity. Like other late antique philosophers, she was an asset to her city; her public support could be influential in municipal politics and was therefore desirable. It was this political power, more than her religious identity, that was the most likely cause of Hypatia's demise. Beginning around 413, she was involved in a conflict between the imperial prefect of Egypt, named Orestes, and Cyril, the recently elected patriarch of Alexandria. Finally, in 415, a mob attacked Hypatia on the street, beat her to death, and mutilated her body. Several accounts, including the most reliable one, by Socrates Scholasticus (*ca.* 379–450), associated the mob with Cyril. For centuries afterward, numerous writers, including the modern English novelist Charles Kingsley, romanticized both Hypatia's physical beauty and the grotesque violence of her demise. At the same time, whether in Nicephorus Gregoras's fourteenth-century ecclesiastical history or in the titles of modern feminist journals, Hypatia's name has always epitomized the female intellectual.

BIBLIOGRAPHY

PRIMARY WORKS

John, Bishop of Nikiu. *The Chronicle of John, Bishop of Nikiu.* Translated by R. H. Charles. Oxford: Williams and Norgate, 1916.

Socrates Scholasticus. *Ecclesiastical History.* Select Library of Nicene and Post-Nicene Fathers. Second Series, Vol. 2. Grand Rapids, Mich.: Eerdmans, 1952.

Synesius of Cyrene. *The Letters of Synesius of Cyrene.* Translated by Augustine FitzGerald. London: Oxford University Press, 1926.

SECONDARY WORKS

Dzielska, Maria. *Hypatia of Alexandria.* Translated by F. Lyra. Cambridge, Mass.: Harvard University Press, 1995. An engaging and thorough biographical study, including a good discussion of Hypatia's *Nachleben* and of all the primary sources.

Knorr, Wilbur Richard. *Textual Studies in Ancient and Medieval Geometry.* Boston: Birkhäuser, 1989.

Roques, Denis. "La famille d'Hypatie." *Revue des études grecques* 108 (1995): 128–149.

Rougé, Jean. "La politique de Cyrille d'Alexandrie et la meurtre d'Hypatie." *Cristianesimo nella storia* 11 (1990): 485–504.

KEVIN UHALDE

[See also **DMA:** Alexandria; Cyril of Alexandria, St.; Neoplatonism.]

IDUNG OF PRÜFENING was an idiosyncratic twelfth-century author who wrote two treatises on monastic life in an age of religious reform. The dates of his birth and death are unknown. He was a cathedral schoolmaster in Regensburg until 1144, when a grave illness compelled him to enter the Cluniac abbey of Prüfening. Deathbed professions of this kind *(professio ad succurendum)* were common in the Middle Ages because consecration as a monk cleansed the individual of past sins and forestalled purgatorial punishments in the afterlife. Idung recovered from his illness, however, and for the next decade he wrestled with questions about the definition and meaning of his religious vocation. During this time, he composed a treatise, entitled *Argumentum super quatuor questionibus* (An argument concerning four questions), addressing some of the most pressing concerns of the twelfth-century reform of monastic life. He argued in favor of the following assertions about the social and pastoral role of monks: a person can be both a monk and a priest; ordination and not personal intention makes a person a priest; strict claustration is necessary for cloistered women but not for monks; and monk-priests can preach in church with the permission of their abbot. He based his arguments primarily on scriptural and patristic authority, but his work also displays an impressive knowledge of classical literature, church councils, and canon law.

Around 1154, after long deliberation, Idung abandoned the Cluniac abbey of Prüfening to join the Cistercian order. He took up residence at an unidentified Cistercian community, probably in Austria, where he wrote his second treatise, *Dialogus duorum monachorum* (A dialogue between two monks). Presented as a conversation between a Cluniac and a Cistercian, this treatise was first and foremost a personal defense against the charge that Idung had broken his vow of monastic stability by forsaking the community in which he had made his profession. Relying heavily on Bernard of Clairvaux, Idung contended that the concept of monastic stability had more to do with the integrity of a monk's adherence to Christ and the letter of the Rule of Benedict than with his place of residence. He also assailed the Cluniacs for presuming to follow customs that contradicted the mandates of the Rule of Benedict, which he argued had the authority of divine law. His attacks on the rashness and novelty of Cluniac customs were largely derived from statements made three decades earlier in an epistolary exchange between Peter the Venerable and Bernard of Clairvaux. Some of his charges were substantial, but most involved relatively minor details in observance and comportment.

Idung of Prüfening's treatises were so personal, particularly the *Dialogus,* that they were not widely copied and read in the later Middle Ages. They do, however, provide fascinating insight into the mind of a twelfth-century individual seeking to understand the social boundaries and religious obligations of his monastic vocation.

BIBLIOGRAPHY

Bredero, Adriaan H. "Le *Dialogus duorum monachorum:* Un rebondissement de la polémique entre Cisterciens et Clunisiens." *Studi Medievali* 22 (1981): 501–585.

Huygens, R. B. C. "Le moine Idung et ses deux ouvrages: *Argumentum super quatuor questionibus* et *Dialogus duorum monachorum.* " *Studi Medievali* 13 (1972): 291–470.

O'Sullivan, Jeremiah F., Joseph Leahey, and Grace Perrigo, trans. *Cistercians and Cluniacs: The Case for Cîteaux.* Kalamazoo, Mich.: Cistercian Publications, 1977.

Schmitz, Hans-Georg. *Kloster Prüfening im 12. Jahrhundert.* Munich: Kommissionsbuchhandlung R. Wölfe, 1975.

SCOTT G. BRUCE

[See also **DMA**: Benedictine Rule; Bernard of Clairvaux, St.; Cistercian Order; Cluny, Order of.]

IMMACULATE CONCEPTION OF THE VIRGIN.

In 1854 Pope Pius IX made belief in the Immaculate Conception an official doctrine of the Catholic Church. Despite its late acceptance, the evolution of this belief that from the Virgin Mary's conception in her mother's womb she was free from the original sin inherited by all other human beings began in the Middle Ages.

Mary's spiritual and physical fitness to bear the Son of God was central to medieval arguments surrounding the Immaculate Conception. Sin would render Mary unfit spiritually even as menstruation and afterbirth would render her impure according to Leviticus 12, 15: 19–32. That Jesus himself was without sin or impurity was a given to Christians. Yet this assumption immediately posed a problem: how could Jesus or the Holy Spirit enter someone who was corrupted by sin, as Mary must have been as a descendent from Adam and Eve, conceived through sexual intercourse? This conundrum was made more acute in the West because later Latin writers adopted Augustine of Hippo's (354–430) emphasis on the causal relationship between sexual desire on the part of parents and original sin in the child. Furthermore, in both the eastern Mediterranean and western Europe, Christians accepted the Aristotelian view that the physical body of a child was formed from the mother's blood. If Mary's body and blood were as impure as any other woman's, how could the Son of God be formed from it?

Early texts such as the *Protoevangelium of James* and texts that drew from it, like *Pseudo-Matthew* and *Liber de infantia Salvatoris et de Maria* (Book of the infancy of the Savoir and of Mary), implied or stated outright that Mary was free from pain, blood, or broken hymen in childbirth, indicating that many Christians saw Mary's body as fundamentally different from that of other women. Depicting her as free of pain suggested that she was exempt from the curse of Eve (Gen. 3:16) and therefore Eve's sin.

Eastern Christians, and eventually Latin ones, made the theology implied by the *Protoevangelium* explicit by frequently contrasting the sinful Eve with the stainless Virgin Mary. Most Greek writers from the sixth century onward accepted that Mary was free from sin. What is less clear is when they thought this cleansing occurred. In *De fide orthodoxa,* John of Damascus (*ca.* 675–ca. 750) argued that the Holy Spirit cleansed Mary both spiritually and physically in the process of Jesus's conception. Many other Byzantine thinkers seem to have believed that the purification took place before Mary's birth or that she had always been spared association with original sin. Certainly by the fourteenth and fifteenth centuries, when there was considerable exchange between Byzantine and Latin theologians, one of the few areas for which Byzantine polemicists did not condemn the Latins was their position on Mary's sinlessness.

John of Damascus's view was widely adopted by Western theologians because Peter Lombard (*ca.* 1095–1160), whose *Sententiae* was widely read by later Scholastics, quoted John of Damascus regarding Mary's purification. Byzantine views also influenced Western Marian theology through liturgy. The feast of Mary's conception had long been part of the Byzantine liturgical calendar, and by the twelfth century it was celebrated in many regions of Europe. The popularity of the feast in the West became an argument for the truth of the Immaculate Conception: If so many of the faithful accepted it, how could belief in Mary's sinless conception be wrong?

Unconvinced, Bernard of Clairvaux (1090–1153) worked to persuade his fellow believers of the inappropriateness of the feast and the beliefs that it celebrated. Yet even he, along with many of the other opponents of the Immaculate Conception, thought that Mary was purified from original sin before her birth but that this purification took place some time after conception. Most maintained that this sanctification occurred between her conception and her animation, or "ensoulment," following Aristotle's theory that a fetus was imbued with a rational soul after conception. Bernard and theologians

The Immaculate Conception. *This Flemish miniature (14th–15th century) is one of the earliest visual renderings of the subject, which would become a staple of later Catholic religious art.* THE BRITISH MUSEUM, ADD. MS 29434, FOL. 9V.

after him, such as Albertus Magnus, Thomas Aquinas, and Bonaventure in the thirteenth century, argued that Mary had to have been subject to original sin, if only briefly, in order for Jesus to redeem her. Otherwise Mary would have had no need of her son and his redemptive mission and would lack a grace that the most basic of believers possessed, namely, forgiveness and salvation through Jesus's death.

The earliest systematic presentation in favor of Mary's sinless status in Latin may have come from Paschasius Radbertus's *De partu Virginis* (On the virgin birth, *ca.* 850). Some scholars, however, have argued that the relevant passage is a twelfth-century addition. Interpolation or not, this passage and the tractate are important because of their popularity and influence during the twelfth century. More certain are the writings of Anselm of Canterbury, his secretary Eadmer, and Osbert of Clare in the eleventh and twefth centuries, Ramon Lull in the thirteenth and fourteenth, plus a series of anonymous or pseudepigraphical tracts defending the Immaculate Con-

ception. Explanations of the Immaculate Conception were not consistent. Some authors maintained that a seed free from sin had been preserved within the first couple and passed down until its fulfillment in Mary. Others suggested that Mary was predestined to be without sin or that since God was capable of creating someone without sin, he did so in Mary's case. Certain theologians maintained that since Mary's flesh was also Jesus's flesh, Mary's body and soul could not have been subjected to anything inappropriate for Jesus, such as decay or uncleanness, all of which were products of original sin. Most important were the arguments of William of Ware and his student John Duns Scotus in the thirteenth and early fourteenth centuries, which became standard for late medieval and early modern adherents to the Immaculate Conception. Duns Scotus countered objections by maintaining that preservation from sin was better than redemption from it and that Mary's preservation came through Jesus, making her even more dependent on Jesus's grace than the rest of humanity.

In the fourteenth and fifteenth centuries, loyalties were divided between the maculists, who championed the Dominican Thomas Aquinas, and the immaculists, who followed the teachings of the Franciscan Duns Scotus. The controversy created a major rift between the Dominicans and Franciscans. Popes and universities attempted to remain neutral, but John of Montesono brought the issue to a head in 1387–1389 when he insisted on the right to take a maculist position for his doctorate at the University of Paris. When the university opposed him, he pleaded his case first to Pope Clement VII in Avignon and then, fearing a bad outcome, switched loyalties to the Roman pope Urban VI. Between 1431 and 1449 theologians were asked to gather arguments for both sides, to be presented at the Council of Basel. John of Segovia wrote a number of documents presenting arguments for the Immaculate Conception, while the Dominican Juan de Torquemada (1388–1468) outlined the counterargument. Although the council came to naught, the texts produced for it were very influential. Responding to Vincent Bandelli, who viciously condemned any who taught the doctrine of the Immaculate Conception, in 1482 and again in 1483 Pope Sixtus IV issued bulls, both entitled *Grave nimis,* threatening to excommunicate any who accused either side of being heretics. Bandelli was silenced, but Sixtus's efforts to keep the peace met with mixed success. The controversy continued to divide theologians until 1854, and it has divided Christians since the Reformation.

BIBLIOGRAPHY

Boss, Sarah Jane. *Empress and Handmaid: On Nature and Gender in the Cult of the Virgin Mary.* London and New York: Cassell, 2000.

Delius, Walter. *Geschichte der Marienverehrung.* Munich: E. Reinhardt, 1963.

Jugie, Martin. *L'Immaculée Conception dans l'Écriture Sainte et dans la tradition orientale.* Rome: Acadamia Mariana, 1952.

Lamy, Marielle. *L'Immaculée Conception: Étapes et enjeux d'une controverse au Moyen-Âge (XIIe–XVe siècles).* Paris. Institut d'Études Augustiniennes, 2000.

Levi D'Ancona, Mirella. *The Iconography of the Immaculate Conception in the Middle Ages and Early Renaissance.* New York: College Art Association, 1957.

O'Conner, Edward D., ed. *The Dogma of the Immaculate Conception: History and Significance.* Notre Dame, Ind.: University of Notre Dame Press, 1958.

Pelikan, Jaroslav. *Mary through the Centuries: Her Place in the History of Culture.* New Haven, Conn., and London: Yale University Press, 1996.

Warner, Marina. *Alone of All Her Sex: The Myth and Cult of the Virgin Mary.* New York: Knopf, 1976.

Zavalloni, Roberto, and Eliodoro Mariani, eds. *La Dottrina Mariologica di Giovanni Duns Scoto.* Rome: Edizioni Antonianum, 1987.

ALEXANDRA CUFFEL

[See also **DMA:** Aquinas, St. Thomas; Bernard of Clairvaux, St.; Councils, Western (1311–1449); Duns Scotus, John; Virgin Mary in Theology and Popular Devotion; **Supp:** Fall, The; Original Sin.]

INFANTICIDE. See **Abortion; Childbirth and Infancy.**

INSURANCE. Strategies to remedy or circumvent risk in conducting business are as old as recorded history and probably older. This is particularly true in trade at the point of transport, as the perils of road and sea could wipe out the unlucky or unwary trader. Age-old practices to minimize risk of loss included dividing cargoes among two or more vessels, banding together in caravans or fleets to increase security, and seeking a sovereign's safe passage and personal guarantee of safety, to name just a few. What was completely lacking until roughly 1300 in Europe, however, was the intellectual breakthrough that grasped risk of loss as a quantifiable part of a business transaction. Once this was achieved medieval businessmen began to experiment with insurance instruments that resemble modern insurance policies.

To a considerable degree, insurance marked a stage in the triumph of calculation over all other forms of preventing or indemnifying loss. The development of insurance thus properly belongs to the broad cultural and intellectual changes of the thirteenth and fourteenth century associated with the rise of markets and more-or-less thorough monetization of economic life. It is not surprising then that the laboratories for the development of insurance were the teeming marketplaces of the towns of southern France and northern Italy, the most precocious and sophisticated financial centers of the era. And among these locales, Genoa and Venice emerged as insurance centers even before the end of the Middle Ages.

The intersection of obsessive calculation and the problem of risk was most prototypically found in maritime trade. Merchants, such as the late-fourteenth-century Florentine Francesco Datini, kept exhaustive records of trading routes, current conditions on those routes, types of cargo, and types of ships used in shipments. From this matrix of variables, a merchant had to arrive at an estimation of risk that was both number and approximation. This was more than a gamble, though it was not without elements common to wagering. But it allowed the partners of the Medici company of the fifteenth century to insure the value of goods carried in Venetian state galleys for the trip from England to Venice at a premium rate of 3 percent of estimated value. The same voyage in less secure ships or ships in smaller convoys would have required twice the amount of premium. This form of maritime insurance was already widely practiced by the late fourteenth century, with Genoa as the acknowledged leader. Maritime insurance was the most important and widespread of all medieval forms of insurance instruments, as the insuring of overland trade, individual lives, or real estate and other immovables remained rare.

This is not to say that risk management had become thoroughly rationalized and monetized by 1500. Underwriting was still in its infancy and concentrated in the hands of a few practitioners, as most merchants traded in insurance contracts as a sideline only. Most significant insurance contracts involved a consortium of merchants as underwriters, a group whose existence might begin and end with a single deal. More traditional forms of preventing loss also continued to be practiced. Datini, for example, not only used maritime insurance but also made sure he directed cargoes along safe routes, stayed out of politics, and exercised great patience in shepherding his wares. In one case, he purchased wool in Majorca for shipment to Florence and manufacture into finished cloth. The cloth was then reshipped and marketed in Spain and Majorca. Because of the threat of piracy and other troubles, the completion of this straightforward operation required three and a half years. Caution was the watchword of the late-medieval merchant.

Insurance as a practice did not develop without theological and practical difficulties, however. Some theologians objected to the concept and practice because they saw it as gambling on the will of God. This seemed to them a violation of the second commandment, that of tempting or putting God to the test. As such, this critique of insurance practices is an interesting analogue to the church's ban on usury, which also seemed to moralists as a sale of God's possession—time—for the purpose of monetary gain. Eventually, however, the more flexible thinking of later scholastics, particularly the mendicant Peter John Olivi (1247/1248–1298) and the Parisian masters Jean Buridan (*ca.* 1295–*ca.* 1358) and Nicole Oresme (*ca.* 1320–1382), removed this obstacle. Yet insurance as an industry was never successfully launched in the Middle Ages. At best it remained a sideline of merchants, similar to banking and money changing. And like banks, insurance companies as large, well-capitalized enterprises of considerable specialization are a development of the seventeenth and not the fifteenth century.

Nonetheless, the conceptual breakthrough was achieved in the late Middle Ages, and even a modern company like Lloyd's of London can trace a direct line to the coffee-shop consortia of merchants who deepened and elaborated medieval business ideas and practices in the great merchant cities of Europe.

BIBLIOGRAPHY

Hunt, Edwin S., and Murray, James M. *A History of Business in Medieval Europe, 1200–1550.* Cambridge, U.K.: Cambridge University Press, 1999.

Kaye, Joel. *Economy and Nature in the Fourteenth Century: Money, Market Exchange, and the Emergence of Scientific Thought.* Cambridge, U.K.: Cambridge University Press, 1998.

Tenenti, Alberto. "Versicherung." In *Lexikon des Mittelalters.* Vol. 8. Munich: Lexma, 1997.

JAMES M. MURRAY

[See also **DMA:** Travel and Transport, Western European.]

JACQUES DE RÉVIGNY (Jacobus de Ravanis, 1230/1240–1296), French teacher of Roman law. Very little is known about Révigny's life. He was born in the Lotharingian village of Révigny and studied law at Orléans, where his teachers included Jean de Monchy, Guichard de Langres, and Simon de Paris. He taught at Orléans from around 1260 until no later than 1280, and then all traces of him are lost for nearly a decade. In 1289 he reappeared as archdeacon of Toul, and in that year he was one of two candidates chosen by the canons of Verdun to be their bishop. Révigny and the other bishop-elect, Jean d'Aspremont, went to Rome, where in December 1289 Pope Nicholas IV chose Révigny and in March 1290 consecrated him. In the interim it is possible that he served briefly as a judge on the Roman Rota, but there is little definitive evidence. Révigny's tenure as bishop was neither calm nor long. The see of Verdun had been vacant for three years before he was elected, and he spent much of his episcopacy struggling to regain its property from the secular rulers who had seized the goods. He was also in conflict with the citizens of Verdun, who sided with the English when war broke out between England and France in 1294. The bishop placed the town under interdict, but he still had to flee to Rome. He died on the way in Ferentino in 1296.

Although the details of his life are sketchy, he left a large number of works behind. Révigny is said to have written the first dictionary of legal terms, but it is no longer extant. What remains of his scholarship are transcriptions of his lectures on Roman law taken down by designated senior students known as reporters. Révigny lectured on the whole corpus of Roman law. These year-long courses were often cursory discussions that attempted to get through as much as possible of a designated book of the law. At the end of each semester, professors also gave "repetitions" or lectures devoted to certain laws in the Roman law corpus that were used as jumping-off points for discussions of specific legal issues. We possess Révigny's regular lectures on the medieval books of the Roman law (the Digest, the Code, the Novels, and the Institutes) as well as many of his repetitions. In the tradition of Orléans, Révigny was not slavishly devoted to either a strict interpretation of the Roman law canon or to the accepted gloss of Accursius that accompanied it. He was willing to challenge the wisdom of the laws and encouraged his students to look for the reason behind the law.

Unfortunately, Révigny's works remain difficult to access. Many of the lectures have yet to be edited, and the fact that the texts consist of transcriptions means that they are often difficult to follow. In addition, those of Révigny's lectures on the Code that were printed in 1519 were incorrectly attributed to Pierre de Belleperche, Révigny's successor at Orléans, and a lecture on the Institutes that may be by Révigny is found in the opera of Bartolus de Saxoferrato.

BIBLIOGRAPHY

PRIMARY WORKS

Bezemer, C. H. "A Repetitio by Jacques de Révigny on the Creations of the Ius Gentium." *Tijdschrift voor Rechtsgeschiedenis* 49 (1981): 287–321.

———. *Les répétitions de Jacques de Révigny: Recherches sur la répétition comme forme d'enseignement juridique et comme genre littéraires.* Leiden, Netherlands: Brill, 1987.

Feenstra, Robert. "'Quaestiones de materia feudorum' de Jacques de Révigny." *Studi Sensi* 84 (1972): 379–401. Discusses the incorrect attribution to Révigny of a commentary on the *Libri feudorum* and edits his lecture on feudal law from the Institutes.

Gordon, W. M. "Going to the Fair: Jacques de Révigny on Possession." In *The Roman Law Tradition.* Edited by A. D. E. Lewis and D. J. Ibbetson. Cambridge, U.K.: Cambridge University Press, 1994.

Soest-Zuurdeeg, L.J. van, ed. *La lectura sur le titre De actionibus (Inst. 4,6) de Jacques de Révign: Edition du texte, précédée de prolégomènes.* Leiden, Netherlands: Brill, 1989.

Waelkens, Laurent. *La théorie de la coutume chez Jacques de Révigny: Éditions et analyse de sa repetition sur la loi De quibus (D. 1, 3, 32).* Leiden, Netherlands: Brill, 1984. Contains an edition and lengthy analysis of three of Révigny's lectures as well as an extensive bibliography.

SECONDARY WORKS

Bezemer, Kees. *What Jacques Saw: Thirteenth-Century France through the Eyes of Jacques de Révigny, Professor of Law at Orleans.* Frankfurt: Vittorio Klostermann, 1997. With a thorough bibliographical essay.

Feenstra, Robert. *Le droit savant au moyen âge et sa vulgarization.* London: Variorum, 1986. Pages 13–29 update Meijers on the school of law at Orleans.

Meijers, E. M. "L'Université d'Orléans au XIIIe siècle." In vol. 3. of *Études d'histoire du droit.* Leiden, Netherlands: Leiden University Press, 1959. Still the basic biography of Révigny and his work.

MISATTRIBUTED EARLY MODERN EDITIONS

Révigny's commentary on the Code appeared under the title *Petri de Bella Perthica, Lectura insignis et fecunda super prima [secunda] parte Codicis domini Justiniani.* Paris: Jehan Petit, 1519, repr. under the title *Lectura super Codice.* Opera iuridica rariora, 1. Bologna: Forni, 1967.

Printed editions of Bartolus de Saxoferrato's *Opera* contain Révigny's lecture on the Institutes.

EMILY KADENS

[See also **Supp:** Accursius; Peter of Belleperche.]

JAMES I OF ARAGON, KING (the Conqueror, 1208–1276).

James I came to the throne under unusually difficult circumstances in 1213. His father, Pedro II, had fallen fighting against Simon de Montfort and his northern French forces in the field of Muret during the Albigensian Crusade. James became king at the age of five while he was a hostage in Simon de Montfort's custody. Adding to his difficulties was the pitifully weak state of the crown's finances and the prospect of regents and aspirants to the throne muddling the royal succession.

With the help of papal mediation James gained his freedom in 1214, but the early years were troubled ones for the boy king, and James later recalled in his autobiography, the *Libre des feyts*, a day in the royal castle of Monzón when there was nothing to eat. By 1228, however, he had put most of these difficulties behind him, subdued unruly nobles, and was preparing to embark on the first expedition that would later earn him the sobriquet "the Conqueror."

The conquest of Majorca from the Muslims, who had ruled over the Balearics since the early tenth century, began in earnest in early September 1229. Although some minor pockets of resistance still held out, by the end of the year the island was under Christian control. James quickly installed Catalan law and began the process of colonizing the island.

In the meantime, James and his nobles were setting their eyes on an even bigger prize: the kingdom of Valencia. The operation, which took two years, ended with the capitulation of the city of Valencia in 1238 and the relatively peaceful departure of many of its Muslim residents. Many, however, remained and James confirmed their right to use Islamic law and continue their religious practices. The following year, he recognized Valencia as a separate realm and granted it many of the rights and privileges enjoyed by his two other realms, Aragon and Catalonia. As with Majorca, James encouraged the Christian colonization of his new conquest, but it would be many years before Christians became the majority.

These conquests of Muslim territory were mirrored by reverses James suffered against the Capetians north of the Pyrenees. One by one, he saw regions that had been in the Aragonese sphere of influence pass to scions of the French royal house. In 1258, these losses were formally recognized in a treaty between James and Louis IX of France.

Aragonese society and government also made important strides during James's lengthy reign. Barcelona, in particular, seems to have benefited from the substantial privileges that the king granted it, and it is during James's reign that we may begin to date its ascendancy as a Mediterranean commercial power. The importance of the representative assemblies of Aragon and Catalonia also came to the fore during his tenure as the king realized the political advantages in convening them.

By virtue of his successes against the Muslims, his longevity, and his piety, James must be considered among the most successful kings of the Middle Ages—the *Libre des feyts,* which James may have personally written or, at the very least, commissioned, ensured that he played a role in crafting his own historical image. His ability to recover from an unenviable position early in his reign and the notable territorial additions he made gave the Crown of Aragon much of the vitality it displayed in the years after his reign.

BIBLIOGRAPHY

Burns, Robert Ignatius. *Islam under the Crusaders: Colonial Survival in the Thirteenth-century Kingdom of Valencia.* Princeton, N.J.: Princeton University Press, 1973.

James I. *Cronica o llibre dels feits.* Edited by Ferran Soldevila. Barcelona: Edicions 62, 1982.

Soldevila, Ferran. *Vida de Jaume I, el conqueridor.* 2d ed. Barcelona: Editorial Aedos, 1969.

JARBEL RODRIGUEZ

[See also **DMA:** Aragon, Crown of (1137–1479); Reconquest; Spain, Christian-Muslim Relations.]

JEAN RENART (*fl.* 1200–1222), French author of two romances and a poem in the early thirteenth century. Virtually nothing is known about the life of Jean Renart, whose name was probably a pen name that alluded to the crafty literary figure Renard the Fox. His works were written in Francien, the dialect of the region surrounding Paris.

His poem *Le lai de l'ombre* tells the story of a young knight who tries to convince a married lady to become his lover. When she rejects the knight's gift of a ring, he drops it into a well in which he sees her reflection, finally persuading her of his devotion. *L'escoufle* recounts the story of two young lovers, Guillaume and Aelis, who elope to Normandy after facing family opposition. Accidentally separated, they spend most of the romance searching for each other and at the end are finally reunited, married, and crowned emperor and empress. Renart's most famous work is *Le Roman de la Rose,* also sometimes called *Guillaume de Dôle,* the name of one of its protagonists. The romance describes how Conrad, the young emperor of the Germans, is uninterested in finding a wife until one of his court jongleurs tells him the story of Jean Renart's own *Le lai de l'ombre.* Intrigued by the *conte*'s description of the married lady, Conrad asks the jongleur where he might find such a beautiful woman. The jongleur then describes Lïenor and her chivalrous brother, Guillaume, a lowly knight from Dôle. Without ever having seen Lïenor, Conrad publicly announces his intention to marry her. An unnamed seneschal, however, who is jealous of the Dôle family's influence, seeks to destroy the marriage plans. Having learned from Lïenor's mother about a birthmark in the shape of a rose on the maiden's inner thigh, the seneschal uses the information to make it appear that he has seduced Lïenor. But Lïenor devises a counterplot in which she plants incriminating evidence on the seneschal and accuses him of raping her. In the end, both accusations are shown to be false, the seneschal is punished, and Conrad and Lïenor marry.

Jean Renart's works are littered with allusions to contemporary lyric poetry, the Tristan and Iseut legend, and the romances of Chrétien de Troyes. Perhaps intending to provide a sense of realism and thereby make his works more believable in the eyes of his aristocratic audience, Renart also includes an array of details such as recognizable places, events, and contemporary personages. One of the most striking features of *Le Roman de la Rose* is the way it incorporates forty-eight quotations from the lyric repertory, including sixteen quotations from the chansons of troubadours and trouvères, into the narrative. Renart was by no means modest about his innovation, asserting in the prologue that he had created something new ("une novele chose") that surpassed all others. At several points in the narrative, he makes clear that he intended for his romance to be both read and sung. It is impossible to know how it was performed, since the one extant manuscript of the romance contains no musical notation. Although there is little record of how Renart's work was received in the Middle Ages, scholars now view Jean Renart as having played a significant role in the development of the romance as a literary genre. Renart's innovation, combining narrative and song in *Guillaume de Dôle*, helped create the new literary genre of the lyric anthology, which was further popularized by his close contemporary Gerbert de Montreuil.

BIBLIOGRAPHY

Baldwin, John W. *Aristocratic Life in Medieval France: The Romances of Jean Renart and Gerbert de Montreuil, 1190–1230.* Baltimore: Johns Hopkins University Press, 2000.

Durling, Nancy Vine, ed. *Jean Renart and the Art of Romance: Essays on Guillaume de Dole.* Gainesville: University Press of Florida, 1997.

ADAM JEFFREY DAVIS

[See also **DMA:** French Literature; Picard Literature; *Roman de la Rose.*]

JEROME OF PRAGUE (*ca.* 1370–1416) was a university-trained religious reformer and Czech nationalist closely associated with John Hus in Bohemia. He was a tireless activist but wrote very little. Nothing is known about his family background or upbringing. Most of the information about his life and activities comes from the proceedings of heresy trials that condemned his teachings, especially the Council of Constance (1415–1416), and from the posthumous account of his martyrdom in John Foxe's *Acts and Monuments of Matters Most Special and Memorable Happening in the Church, Especially in the Realm of England.*

Jerome's academic career began at King Wenceslas College of Prague University, where he studied with John Hus and was promoted to bachelor of arts in 1398. Around 1399 he traveled to Oxford and discovered the condemned writings of John Wyclif, whose criticisms of the church resonated with the young Czech scholar. Jerome was instrumental in the transmission of Wyclif's work from England to Bohemia. After a visit to the Holy Land in 1403 he promoted the doctrine of Wyclif's philosophy of realism as a university master in Paris, Heidelberg, and Cologne from 1404 until 1406, but his views always met with resistance from ecclesiastical authorities. After several narrow escapes from prosecution for heresy, Jerome returned to Prague, where he remained an outspoken advocate of Wyclif's teachings. With John Hus he opposed the German control of Prague University at the expense of Bohemian academics and developed a Christian political theory in support of Czech nationalism based on the doctrines of Wyclif. A popular preacher, he fulminated continuously against the pretensions of the papacy, particularly the marketing of indulgences in Prague by the antipope John XXIII and the emperor Wenceslaus IV for a crusade against King Ladislas of Naples.

Jerome spent his final years in the shadow of John Hus and ultimately shared his fate. When Hus left Bohemia in 1414 to defend his views at the Council of Constance, Jerome followed him at a distance. The great peril to his own life became clear when the leaders of the council imprisoned Hus on the accusation that he was a Wycliffite and condemned him to death as a heretic in the summer of 1415. After the death of his friend, Jerome attempted to flee, but he was soon captured and imprisoned. He recanted his heretical views under the duress of torture, but his enemies doubted his sincerity and sentenced him to be burned at the stake. He died on 30 May 1416.

BIBLIOGRAPHY

Bernard, Paul P. "Jerome of Prague, Austria, and the Hussites." *Church History* 27 (1958): 3–22.

Betts, Reginald. *Essays in Czech History.* London: Athlone Press, 1969.

Walsh, Katherine. "Wyclif's Legacy in Central Europe in the Late Fourteenth and Early Fifteenth Centuries." In *From Ockham to Wyclif.* Edited by Anne Hudson and Michael Wilks. Oxford: Blackwell, 1987.

Watkins, Renee Neu. "The Death of Jerome of Prague: Divergent Views." *Speculum* 42 (1967): 104–129.

SCOTT G. BRUCE

[See also **DMA:** Bohemia-Moravia; Councils, Western (1311–1449); Heresies, Western European; Hus, John (Jan); Hussites; Wyclif, John; **Supp:** John XXIII, Antipope.]

JOAN, POPE. It appears that in 1255 a story first began to be told about a ninth-century German woman of Mainz, but of English lineage, who was in love with a professional schoolman. Desiring to join him in the pursuit of knowledge, she wore men's clothes, afterward traveled to Rome, and became well known for her intellectual accomplishments. After service (as a man) in the papal curia, she was elevated to the papal throne. During a papal procession the pope, who had gotten pregnant, went into labor and gave birth. Voilà, the pope proved to the prelates in the entourage and the onlookers to be a woman.

The story, in the hands of thirteenth-century and later commentators, served an etiological purpose; that is, it explained the origins of certain ceremonial curiosities and rumors about the initiation and processional rites of the supreme pontiffs: Did they avoid a certain location when they processed because "Pope Joan," as she was known, gave birth there? Were preconsecrated popes checked out to confirm their maleness before installation?

How did this story arise and remain popular? It has been suggested that the ever more powerful papacy of the twelfth and thirteenth centuries generated criticism in many forms—satirical poems, such as the one titled "Gospel according to the Mark of Silver," and perhaps stories like Pope Joan's. In the fourteenth century, to refer to the impurity of Pope Joan (Latin, Johanna) was a way, too, of mocking the hated Pope John XXII (Latin, Johannes), the fierce and deadly opponent of the Franciscan radicals. Protestant and Enlightenment figures later used the story, ostensibly regarding it as true, to denigrate the office of the papacy and the Roman Catholic Church in general. In fact, there is absolutely no trustworthy evidence that such a person ever existed, although a few small and ephemeral heretical movements are known to have recognized women as their leaders. Occasionally such a woman might designate herself or a female disciple or be designated by her followers as pope and participate in ceremonies and exercise powers over those followers that mirrored the ceremonies and authorities of the Catholic pontiffs. One such sect with an entirely female hierarchy existed in Italy from about 1260 to 1300 before it was suppressed.

BIBLIOGRAPHY

Boureau, Alain. *The Myth of Pope Joan.* Translated by Lydia Cochrane. Chicago: University of Chicago Press, 2001.

WILLIAM CHESTER JORDAN

[See also **DMA:** Biography, Secular; Boccaccio, Giovanni.]

JOHANNES BASSIANUS

JOHANNES BASSIANUS (*d.* after 1190) was born in Cremona (Cremonensis). He was an important twelfth-century jurist. Most scholars since the sixteenth-century biographer Thomas Diplovatatius have distinguished the civilian Johannes Bassianus from the canonist Bazianus. Recently, Annalisa Belloni and Domenico Maffei have argued that the two jurists were identical. Rudolf Weigand and André Gouron, however, have rejected the conflation of the two jurists. On the basis of glosses in manuscripts Weigand observed that the sigla "Io. Cre." or "Io. b." were uniform when referring to the civilian, and that "magister basianus," "b.," "ba.," "baz.," and "bar." were the standard abbreviations for the canonist. These are, most likely, two different jurists.

Johannes Bassianus taught Roman law at Bologna from around 1160 to 1187. He studied with Bulgarus and taught Azo. He lectured on the Institutes, Digest, and Code, but his glosses on these works are scattered in the margins of manuscripts. He also wrote *consilia*, short tracts on procedure, in which he seems to have had a special interest, and an influential commentary, *De regulis iuris* (Dig. 50.17). His opinions were among the most respected among the jurists, and he was cited regularly in their works. His influence stretched to England, where he may have taught after 1190. An English summa on the Institutes was heavily influenced by his work.

Bazianus (Basianus) taught canon law at Bologna in the 1180s. Like Johannes Bassianus his glosses on Gratian's *Decretum* are preserved in manuscripts or in the works of other canonists, such as Gratian's *Apparatus "Ordinaturus magister."* He does not seem to have composed a coherent work of his own, but there are several contemporary summae that closely follow his teachings. His influence on the *Summa casinensis* (*Continuatio prima* to Huggucio of Pisa's *Summa decretorum*), for example, was very strong; he may even be the author. Little is known about his life, but if we believe the information given on a tombstone in the cathedral of Bologna, Bazianus was a native of Bologna and died there in 1197.

BIBLIOGRAPHY

PRIMARY WORKS

Caprioli, Severino, and Ferdinando Treggiari, eds. *De regulis iuris.* Rimini, Italy: Maggioli, 1983.

De Zulueta, Francis, and Peter Stein, eds. *The Teaching of Roman Law in England around 1200.* London: Selden Society, 1990.

Gaudenzi, Augusto, ed. *Bibliotheca iuridica medii aevi.* Vol. 2. 1892. Reprint, Torino, Italy: Bottega d'Erasmo, 1962. Contains Bassianus's tracts *Summae De iudiciis, Quicumque vult actionem suam,* and *De accusationibus.*

SECONDARY WORKS

Belloni, Annalisa. "Baziano, cioé Giovanni Bassiano, legista e cano-nista del secolo XII." *Tijdschrift voor Rechtsgeschiedenis* 57 (1989): 69–85.

Gouron, André. "A la convergence des deux droits: Jean Bassien, Bazi-anus et maître Jean." *Tijdschrift voor Rechtsgeschiedenis* 59 (1991): 319–332.

Müller, Wolfgang P. *Huguccio: The Life, Works, and Thought of a Twelfth-Century Jurist.* Washington, D.C.: Catholic University of America Press, 1994.

Weimar, Peter. "Johannes Bassianus." In *Lexikon des Mittelalters.* Vol. 5. Munich: Artemis, 1991.

KENNETH PENNINGTON

[See also **DMA**: Law, Canon: After Gratian.]

JOHANNES DE LIGNANO (*ca.* 1320–1383), pro-fessor of canon law at Bologna. Born into a minor noble family outside Milan, Johannes pursued the liberal arts and philosophy before turning to the study of law. By 1350 he was teaching law at Bologna, later becoming professor of civil and then canon law. His most famous student was Cardinal Francesco Zabarella. In addition to teaching law at the university, Johannes applied his legal training on behalf of the church and various city-states, particularly his beloved Bologna. In 1358 he worked as a lawyer for the Franciscan convent in Venice. In a *quaes-tio disputata* (disputed question) he defended the morali-ty of Genoa's public debt, arguing that the city's borrow-ing money from the citizenry at interest did not technically constitute usury and was necessary for the city's self-maintenance. Johannes was viewed favorably by a succession of popes and secular leaders, including Pope Urban V, who rewarded him with lands and reve-nues, and Emperor Charles IV, who made him Count Palatine in 1368. After the city of Bologna rebelled against the papal legate in 1376, Johannes proved him-self to be a skillful mediator in repairing the frayed rela-tions between the pope and the city. In 1377 Pope Greg-ory XI made Johannes his vicar-general in Bologna.

Johannes was a prolific writer whose works spanned the spheres of canon and civil law, political and moral philosophy, theology, and astrology. In the tradition of Cicero, he wrote a treatise on friendship, *De amicitia;* he also wrote a commentary on the first two books of Aris-totle's *Politics.* In *De bello,* which he dedicated to Cardi-nal Gil Albornoz in 1360, and the unfinished *De pace,* he confronted the many legal issues related to war and peace. His most famous work, *Somnium,* was written in the form of a dialogue and claimed to report a dream that Johannes had experienced. In it, Johannes respond-ed to contemporaries who criticized legal learning. In de-fending the study of the law, he took a decidedly philo-sophical approach, applying the intellectual virtues that Aristotle had laid out in the *Nicomachean Ethics.* In con-trast to some of his contemporaries, who argued that civil and secular law should have an authority indepen-dent of canon law, Johannes maintained that the two legal spheres were necessarily interdependent. In his eyes, canon law was superior to civil law in having the pope, God's vicar, as its author.

Johannes enjoyed wide renown during his lifetime, as is evidenced by Geoffrey Chaucer's comparison of the Bolognese lawyer's fame as both lawyer and philosopher to Petrarch's fame as a poet. In his last years of life, which were marked by the onset of the Great Schism, Johannes served as a defender of Urban VI's election in 1378. In *De fletu ecclesiae,* he defended the Italian pope's legitima-cy and responded to the objections of the partisans of Clement VII. Johannes died on 16 February 1383, most likely from the plague, and was buried in the Church of S. Domenico in Bologna.

BIBLIOGRAPHY

Donovan, G. M., and M. H. Keen. "The 'Somnium' of John of Leg-nano." *Traditio* 37 (1981): 325–345.

Kirshner, Julius. "Conscience and Public Finance: A Questio Dis-putata of John of Legnano on the Public Debt of Genoa." In *Philoso-phy and Humanism: Renaissance Essays in Honor of Paul Oskar Kristel-ler.* Edited by Edward P. Mahoney. Leiden: E. J. Brill, 1976.

McCall, John P. "The Writings of John of Legnano with a List of Manuscripts." *Traditio* 23 (1967): 415–437.

ADAM JEFFREY DAVIS

[See also **DMA**: Bologna, University of; Law, Canon: After Gratian; Schism, Great; Zabarella, Francesco.]

JOHN OF SACROBOSCO (**John of Holywood,** *d.* 1244 or 1256), astronomer and mathematician. Little is known about Sacrobosco's life. The place of his birth, for instance, remains in dispute. Some medieval sources refer to Sacrobosco as an Englishman, and some scholars have surmised that he came from Halifax, the Yorkshire center of the wool trade. But others have argued in favor of Irish origins since there were and are several places in Ireland called Holywood. Still other scholars maintain that Sacrobosco hailed from Scotland, perhaps Niths-dale.

Around 1220, Sacrobosco composed his famous as-tronomy textbook, *Tractatus de sphaera,* which was first

Tomb of Johannes de Lignano (**detail**). *Marble bas relief by Jacobello and Pierpaolo Dalle Masegne (ca. 1383) showing students of Johannes* (biography, opposite page) *in a lecture hall. Now in Museo Civico, Bologna.* SCALA/ART RESOURCE, NY. REPRODUCED BY PERMISSION.

used in classrooms at the University of Paris and then at other universities. Most remarkable about this textbook was the way in which Sacrobosco combined the early medieval school of literary astronomy, citing classical authors such as Vergil, Ovid, and Lucan, with twelfth-century scientific astronomy based on Latin translations of Arabic texts. While on some points Sacrobosco closely followed the work of the second-century Greek astronomer Ptolemy, as well as his medieval Arabic commentators, such as Muḥammad ibn Kathīr al-Farghānī and al-Battānī, in other areas Sacrobosco made significant departures.

De sphaera is divided into four chapters. The first chapter deals with the fundamentals of astronomical theory, including the definition of a sphere, the structure of the universe, and the shape, position, and size of the earth. Chapter 2 describes the various circles of the celestial sphere. The third chapter treats the phenomena caused by the daily rotation of the heavens as seen from the various climates of the inhabitable world. The planetary orbits and causes of eclipses are the subject of chapter 4. By the fifteenth century, there were at least twenty-five manuscript versions of *De sphaera,* and more than forty printed editions had appeared by 1547. First printed at Ferrara in 1472, *De sphaera* was the first astronomical work to be printed.

Taking up only twenty-four pages in a modern translated edition, *De sphaera* is a remarkably short text, covering the bare essentials of astronomy in a clear and concise style. Although a few thirteenth-century scholastics wrote treatises on the spheres that were similar to Sacrobosco's (notably Robert Grosseteste and John

Peckham), Sacrobosco's textbook quickly became the standard rudimentary account of planetary motion and the subject of many longer and more technical commentaries. The earliest of such commentaries has been attributed to Michael Scot. But commentaries on Sacrobosco's text continued to be written and used in universities well into the seventeenth century, despite the scientific advances brought about by the Copernican revolution. Except for Euclid, no elementary textbook on astronomy has ever had a more lasting influence than Sacrobosco's.

In addition to *De sphaera,* Sacrobosco is known to have authored two other important works: *Tractatus de algorismo,* which was the most widely used manual of arithmetic during the Middle Ages, and *Tractatus de computo,* a treatise on time reckoning that included a proposal for reforming the Julian calendar.

Sacrobosco died in Paris, probably either in 1244 or 1256 and was buried in the cloisters of the monastery of St. Mathurin, which was closely connected to the University of Paris. His tombstone, long since destroyed, was said to have been adorned with an astrolabe and an engraved Latin epitaph commemorating Sacrobosco's achievement in *De computo*: "he divided time."

BIBLIOGRAPHY

Moreton, Jennifer. "John of Sacrobosco and the Calendar." *Viator* 25 (1994): 229–244.

Pedersen, Olaf. "In Quest of Sacrobosco." *Journal for the History of Astronomy* 16 (1985): 175–221.

Thorndike, Lynn. *The Sphere of Sacrobosco and Its Commentators.* Chicago: University of Chicago Press, 1949. (Includes a translation of *De sphaera.*)

ADAM JEFFREY DAVIS

[See also **DMA:** Astrology/Astronomy, Islamic; Astronomy; Grosseteste, Robert; Mathematics; Peckham, John.]

JOHN XXIII, ANTIPOPE (*ca.* 1360–1419), Neapolitan churchman and antipope (1410–1415). Born Baldassare Cossa from a noble Neapolitan family, the future Pope John XXIII received a doctor's degree in law from the University of Bologna. In 1392, Pope Boniface IX, himself a Neapolitan, named Cossa archdeacon of Bologna, a post that involved serving as the chief administrator of the university. Four years later Cossa became the pope's private chamberlain. In 1402 the pope made Cossa cardinal of Saint-Eustachius and, a year later, papal legate of Bologna. As legate, Cossa succeeded in recovering Bologna from the Milanese. Indeed, it was later said that he was more skilled in war and arms than in religion. For nine years Cossa ruled the papal territory with a firm hand and proved himself to be a talented financial administrator. Due to his imposition of heavy taxes, however, he was unpopular, and there were even several failed plots to assassinate him.

In 1408 Cossa was one of several cardinals to desert Gregory XII. In 1409, at the Council of Pisa, representatives of the Roman and Avignonese lines of claimants to the papacy were deposed and a third, Alexander V, was elected. When this new pope died just a year later, Cossa was elected (17 May 1410), taking the name John XXIII. Of the three papal claimants—Roman, Avignonese, and Pisan—John possessed the largest obedience. He appointed several reforming cardinals during his pontificate, including Francesco Zabarella, the French theologian Pierre d'Ailly, and the canonist and dean of Rheims, Guillaume Fillastre. In 1412–1413 John convened what turned out to be an ineffective council at Rome, whose only accomplishment was the condemnation of the heretical writings attributed to John Wyclif.

John allied himself with Louis II of Anjou, and in 1411 their armies defeated those of King Ladislas of Naples, who controlled Rome and was allied with Gregory XII, the Roman papal claimant. The victory did not eradicate the threat posed by Ladislas, however, and soon John turned to Emperor Sigismund of Germany for protection. The emperor, who wished to see the Schism finally come to an end, put pressure on John to summon a council at Constance (convened November 1414). Aware that his position was in jeopardy, John was reluctant to attend the council, but his cardinals persuaded him to do so. It soon became apparent that the only hope for ending the Schism would be for all three popes to either abdicate or be deposed. After being pressured to formally promise that he would voluntarily abdicate the papacy, John secretly fled to the lands of his newest ally, Duke Frederick of Austria. He was soon forced to return to Constance, however, and on 29 May 1415, he was formally deposed and was once again referred to as Baldassare Cossa. The council accused him of the gravest offenses, including simony and perjury. Although Cossa had had a reputation for ambition and unscrupulousness throughout much of his career, many of the accusations levied against him by the council appear to have been untrue or highly exaggerated. Cossa was imprisoned in Germany until 1418, when he was released by the newly elected Martin V, to whom he paid homage. On 23 June 1419 the pope appointed him cardinal-bishop of Tusculum, but Cossa died in Florence on 27 December and was buried in the Florentine baptistery.

BIBLIOGRAPHY

Brandmuller, Walter. "Infeliciter electus fuit in Papam: Zur Wahl Johannes XXIII." In *Ecclesia et regnum: Beiträge zur Geschichte von Kirche, Recht und Staat im Mittelalter: Festschrift für Franz-Josef Schmale zu seinem 65. Geburtstag.* Bochum, Germany: Winkler, 1989.

Girgensohn, Dieter. "Antonio Loschi und Baldassare cossa vor dem pisaner Konzil von 1409." *Italia medioevale e umanistica* 30 (1987): 1–93.

Guillemain, Bernard. "Les sermons des papes d'Avignon." In *La prediction en pays d'oc.* Edited by Jean-Louis Biget. (Cahiers de fanjeaux, 32). Toulouse, France: Privat, 1997.

Kitts, Eustace J. *In the Days of the Councils: A Sketch of the Life and Times of Baldassare Cossa, afterward Pope John the Twenty-Third.* London: Constable, 1908. Treats the period up to the Council of Pisa.

———. *Pope John the Twenty-Third and Master John Hus of Bohemia.* London: Constable, 1910. Covers John XXIII's career beginning with his election as pope.

ADAM JEFFREY DAVIS

[See also **DMA:** Ailly, Pierre d'; Antipope; Babylonian Captivity; Councils, Western (1311–1449); Schism, Great; Zabarella, Francesco.]

JOSEPH OF VOLOKOLAMSK, ST. (1439/
1440–1515). The future monastic reformer and theologian was born as Ivan Sanin in the village of Yazvishche in 1439/1440. In 1460 he became a monk under the direction of Pafnuty of Borovsk (1394–1477) and received the name Joseph. He lived eighteen years in the Borovsk monastery and eventually succeeded Pafnuty as hegumen (abbot). Frustrated by his fellow monks' opposition to his reforms of their way of life, Joseph and seven supporters left Borovsk for Volokolamsk, where he and the local prince Boris Vasilievich (1449–1494) founded the Dormition monastery in 1479. His foundation developed into an influential religious and cultural center, producing numerous bishops and housing a rich library.

In his *Monastic Rule,* Joseph combined cenobitic (common life) and eremitic (solitary, desert-style) forms of monasticism. Although the hegumen had final responsibility for the governance of the monastery, Joseph also imposed a council of elders who assisted in the daily operation of the community and guarded against possible abuses of office. The monks owed obedience to the hegumen but also to their elder, who regulated their spiritual life. While respecting the customs and norms of early Christian and Byzantine monasticism, Joseph incorporated adaptations made by Slavic ascetics such as Antoni and Theodosius of the Caves, the eleventh-century cofounders of the Kievan Pecherskaya Lavra (Monastery of the Caves); Sergius of Radonezh

(1314–1392); and Cyril of Belozero (1337–1427). Richly decorated churches and sumptuous liturgies, balanced by extravagant almsgiving to the needy, characterized Joseph's monastic philanthropy.

Controversy dogged Joseph throughout his life. Conflicts with local princes forced him frequently to change his political allegiance, and in 1507 he placed his monastery under the protection of Grand Prince Vasilii III Ivanovich (1479–1533) of Muscovy. This decision embroiled Joseph in a dispute with the popular Archbishop Serapion of Novgorod that ended in 1509 with the deposition and two-year imprisonment of Serapion by order of Vasilii III. By 1511 Joseph had fallen out of favor, partly because of his defense of monastic landholdings. Vilified for his treatment of Serapion, Joseph never regained his footing with the grand prince. He was quickly identified as a spokesperson for the Possessors, who resented the grand prince's expropriation of church properties. The Nonpossessors, favoring a materially poor church, flourished for a time under grand-princely patronage.

Between 1492 and 1505 Joseph composed the *Prosvetitel'* (Enlightener), a type of summa of the fundamental tenets of the Orthodox faith unique in medieval Russian letters. Appreciation of the work has been hampered by its association with the campaign against the so-called "Judaizing heresy," an ill-defined religious and political protest of the second half of the fifteenth century.

In most accounts, Joseph compares unfavorably with his contemporary, the Nonpossessor sympathizer Nil Sorsky (d. 1508). Nil emphasized solitude and spiritual interiority, while Joseph promoted community, liturgical prayer, and social involvement. Both fostered a reform of monastic life, a return to the sources.

Besides his *Monastic Rule, Prosvetitel',* thirty-two letters and numerous treatises, two *Lives,* a *Funeral Oration,* a *Paterikon* (collection of anecdotes), and a liturgical service survive. Joseph was canonized for general veneration in 1591.

BIBLIOGRAPHY

Goldfrank, David M., ed. *The Monastic Rule of Iosif Volotsky.* Revised Edition. Kalamazoo, Mich.: Cistercian Publications, 2000.

Pitrim, Archbishop, ed. "Volokolamskii Paterik." *Bogoslovskie Trudy* 10 (1973): 177–222.

Poslaniia Iosifa Volotskogo. Texts prepared by A. A. Zimin and Ia. S. Lur'e. Moscow and Leningrad: Akademiia Nauk SSSR, 1959.

Smith, Thomas Allan. "The Volokolamskiy Paterik. A Study, Translation, and Commentary." Th.D. diss., Friedrich-Alexander-Universitaet Erlangen, 1988.

T. ALLAN SMITH

JUGLARÍA

[See also **DMA:** Hesychasm; Nil Sorsky, St.; Pecherskaya Lavra; Russian Orthodox Church; Sergius of Radonezh, St.; Theodosius of the Caves, St.]

JUGLARÍA. Juglars were medieval entertainers whose activities included being musicians, mimes, jugglers, buffoons, acrobats, and singers and writing songs and poems. They thrived mostly in the Spanish kingdoms and southern France, but ranged as far as England, Flanders, and other parts of northern Europe. Their job, according to several sources, was to bring joy to those who engaged their services, and many juglars adopted names that reflected their cheerful disposition, such as Alegret (Joyful) or Graciosa Alegre (Graceful Joy.) Others adopted romantic names—Corazón (the Heart)—or, like the Goliards of northern Europe, names that slyly mocked the clerical and chivalric values of the day: "Archpriest of Hita" or the "Master of Santiago."

The juglars date back to at least the sixth century A.D., when the term "joculator" was used to refer to court or public entertainers. These may have been the early medieval heirs of Roman mimes and entertainers. The juglars that emerged in Spain around the eleventh century were also influenced by Muslim poets and performers. They also shared many characteristics with German minnesingers and especially with their cousins from across the Pyrenees, the troubadours, with whom they were often associated. The juglars, however, were often grouped as a separate class of entertainer, although, at times, the distinctions between the two are hard to discern. As a general rule, troubadours were mostly creative artists and juglars were primarily performers, yet juglars also wrote and adapted many of the works they interpreted, while troubadours performed many of their works. It was also not uncommon for juglars to accompany troubadours and provide musical or comedic accompaniment. The juglar often served as the foil to the troubadour, becoming the target of his jokes and puns in a performance.

Juglars performed not only for kings and their courts but also for the common people, as almost every significant social gathering provided them with a stage. Some juglars were kept on retainer in royal and ecclesiastical courts, receiving large stipends, properties, and even titles from thankful and, we may assume, amused patrons. Others lived an errant lifestyle, traveling from court to court and from town to town, taking on work as they found it. They were a staple in coronation festivities, weddings, feasts, and jousts and even traveled with their patrons. They also performed in municipal ceremonies ranging from Feast Days to funerals. Juglars also

served important military duties as they performed for troops before battles, encouraging and inspiring the combatants with their tales of past heroic deeds. In naval warfare, they played an even more important role; they became the de facto signal corps of fleets, using their drums and trumpets to pass messages between ships.

Native Iberian juglar poetry and literature began to thrive in the late thirteenth century, coinciding with the decline of Provençal lyric after the Albigensian Crusade. Strongly influenced by Portuguese and Galician folk songs, juglar verse represents some of the earliest examples of works in the vernacular. Juglar poetry was also instrumental in preserving historical knowledge and became an important source for some of the chronicles of the thirteenth and fourteenth century. The *Song of Roland* and *El Cid* were but two of the works in the juglar's repertoire that were later committed to writing.

BIBLIOGRAPHY

Akehurst, F. R. P., and Judith M. Davis. *A Handbook of the Troubadours.* Berkeley: University of California Press, 1995.

Criado de Val, Manuel, ed. *La Juglaresca: Actas del 1 Congreso Internacional sobre la Juglaresca.* Madrid: Edi-6, 1986.

Menéndez Pidal, Ramon. *Poesía Juglaresca y Juglares.* 1924. Reprint, Madrid: Colección Austral, 1962.

———. *Poesía Juglaresca y origenes de las literaturas romanicas.* Madrid: Instituto de Estudios Politicos, 1957.

JARBEL RODRIGUEZ

[See also **DMA:** Goliards; Minnesingers; Troubadour, Trouvère.]

JUS PRIMAE NOCTAE. See **Droit du Seigneur.**

JUST PRICE. Until the middle of the twentieth century the prevalent historical view of the just price *(iustum pretium),* so often mentioned by medieval lawyers, moralists, and theologians, was that it was an ideal price, determined primarily by the labor and expenses involved in a good's production, while allowing producers a modest surplus that would befit their social position and permit them to maintain it. The just price thus conceived would necessarily be more or less fixed, independent of individual calculation and the fluctuations of supply and demand. The problem with this neat vision of the just price, which conforms to an image of the medieval period as one innocent of economic calculation and deficient in economic understanding, is that the textual evidence contradicts it in every point. John Baldwin and Raymond De Roover were two of the first scholars (in the late 1950s) to directly challenge the old, idealized view of the just price, questioning whether it ever existed, in fact or in theory, as a normative determination detached from the mechanisms of price formation in the marketplace.

The debate over just price hinges on larger questions. To what degree did those who used the term "just price" recognize the place of calculated self-interest in economic exchanges? To what degree did they understand the process of price formation and the role of factors such as common need and scarcity in the determination of price? To what degree were they conscious of the marketplace as a suprapersonal system within which prices were determined in some sense independently of individual needs and decisions? And if medieval writers on just price did recognize the existence of market prices and individual economic calculation, did they then seek to deny the rough give and take of economic exchange in the name of corporatist or religious ideals, as was characteristic of medieval writing on usury?

DETERMINING JUST PRICE

The roots of medieval legal thinking on market price and just price are found in Roman law. In the official collection of Roman law, the *Corpus iuris civilis,* compiled under the Christian emperor Justinian in the sixth century, the establishment of an equality between buyer and seller was recognized, without exception, as a dynamic and sometimes messy process—a product of the conflicting desires of the buyer to pay as little as possible and the seller to charge as much as possible. With the exception of outright fraud (selling at a greatly elevated price to someone incapable of good judgment), buyer and seller were permitted to outwit each other in order to obtain a price advantage. As it is written in the portion of the *Corpus iuris civilis* known as the *Digest,* "In sales and purchases it is naturally allowed to buy a thing of greater value for a smaller price; and to sell a thing of lesser value for a greater price." Despite the deception permitted in Roman law, there is no discussion there of a distinction between selling price and just value. A legally sufficient equivalence between cost and value was assumed to exist in all sale agreements entered into freely, an assumption expressed in the often repeated legal principle "a thing is worth what it can be sold for."

Roman law contained one small exception to this rule, in the case of real estate sold by a minor (someone, presumably, who was not fully informed) for less than half of its "just price." Although minor, this exception implied that agreed prices can, in certain situations, be unjust. Medieval lawyers greatly expanded this limited exception to the rule of free bargaining in Roman law under the heading *laesio enormis* (extreme damage). In twelfth-century legal commentaries, the new, expanded principle allowed that any sale price exceeding one-half above or one-half below the "just" price provided either buyer or seller grounds to rescind the sale.

The question still remained: How, precisely, is the "just price" to be determined? The answer was never made explicit within Roman law, but the prevalent current historical view is that the just price of Roman law was essentially the common, or market, price; in John Baldwin's words, "a normal and customary price . . . determined in commerce of free exchange which is regular and orderly." The identification of just price with market price is conveyed in two nearly identical texts from the *Digest* that state: "The prices of things are determined not by their value and utility to individuals, but by their value determined commonly."

Since both medieval Roman (civil) lawyers and canon (church) lawyers regularly cited and agreed with this opinion in their writings, we can say that in essence, medieval legists recognized that prices freely and commonly arrived at in the marketplace were the best guide to the determination of economic value—the best guide to the determination of a "just price." Indeed, in medieval legal writings, common (market) price often came to be seen not in opposition to an ideal, "just" price but rather as a corrective guide to the estimation of value, acting to prevent particular buyers or sellers from taking advantage of the particular needs of individuals.

From the mid-thirteenth century, with the translation into Latin of the complete text of Aristotle's *Nicomachean Ethics,* medieval thinkers received a second authoritative source for the analysis of economic exchange to add to the inheritance from Roman law. Perhaps the most important contribution contained in Aristotle's detailed and perceptive analysis of money and exchange in book 5 is his insight that human need *(indigentia)* is the unifying measure of everything in exchange—the prime determinant of economic value. In their many comments on this discussion over succeeding centuries, scholastic philosophers expanded and refined Aristotle's economic analysis, reaching a high point in the commentary of the fourteenth-century Parisian master Jean Buridan. Buridan offered detailed examples to show that economic value is essentially relational value, determined by the shifting estimation and measurement of goods and services relative to ever shifting need, both personal and within larger markets. He showed, moreover, that economic need is itself relative, varying in relation to real and perceived scarcity. Because of his essential relativization of all aspects of buying and selling, Buridan held that any price arrived at between two knowledgeable exchangers is valid and falls within the bounds of commutative justice.

THEOLOGIANS AND PRICE

What did the theologians, concerned primarily with the religious ethics of exchange, make of this identification of the just price with the agreed or market (common) price? The answer here is more complicated than it was in the case of the lawyers, since there were theological problems associated with a view in which economic justice was seen to result from an impersonal process of price formation rather than from a conscious ethical decision on the part of the individual exchangers. In the earliest theological discussions of just price in the late twelfth century, we see a clear distinction being made between a market price that met the legal requirements of justice and an agreed price that conformed to the stricter moral requirements of divine law.

Theologians were well aware that civil and canon law allowed deception in economic exchange within limits. They knew that, legally, all sales in which the price fell within the broad bounds of *laesio enormis* (one-half above and below the normal market price) were considered final and just. Most insisted, however, that divine law, the *lex divina,* made no such broad allowances. They therefore thought it quite possible for someone to knowingly buy for less than the just price or to sell for more. In their opinion, such sales violated the strict requirement for equality between buyer and seller that was the essence of economic exchange, and as such they were illicit.

In the mid-thirteenth century Thomas Aquinas expressed this requirement in these words in the *Summa theologiae:* "Considered in itself, the transaction of buying and selling is seen to have been introduced for the common utility of both buyer and seller. . . . Therefore if the price exceeds the quantity of the value of a thing or, conversely, if the value of the thing exceeds the price, the equality that justice demands is destroyed. And therefore, to buy a thing for less or to sell a thing for more than it is worth is in itself unjust and illicit." Historians still disagree about what St. Thomas actually means here. As much as he and other theologians implied a distinction between just price and sale price, nowhere did they ever determine or even discuss how the just price was to be defined. St. Thomas recognizes that the labor and expenses involved in a good's production are involved as well in the formation of its price, but in a number of places he reveals that his concept of "just price" was not solely determined by "fixed" factors such as cost of production. Rather, he recognizes that scarcity and need play a role in its determination. His reluctance to accept the simple link between just price and market price (shared by a number of other moralists and theologians who followed him) resulted from his recognition that such a linkage brought with it disturbing implications. If the just price is identified with the common, or market, price and is divorced from individual judgment and direction, then the individual's responsibility in economic activity is effectively eliminated, as is the Christian requirement for charity in dealing with others. Furthermore, the recognition that ideal economic ends (equality and justice) could follow from the base motive of deception and the base desire to buy cheap and sell dear (as Roman law has it) severs the link between economic order and the moral order—a link that medieval theologians often sought to strengthen.

St. Thomas does not deny that current market price provides a legally sufficient guide to value (he clearly recognized that it did) nor that in certain cases current price might conform to the highest standards of justice and virtue nor that, even if it is too lax, common estimation might at all times serve as a useful indicator or benchmark by which to determine just price. But for Thomas and for a number of other theologians writing from the thirteenth century through the end of the medieval period, market price based on common estimation, without conscious human choice and direction, cannot in itself guarantee an equality sufficient to merit the word "just."

A generation after St. Thomas, the Franciscan theologian Peter John Olivi wrote an exceptionally detailed and perceptive treatment of price formation in the marketplace. Olivi recognized that the prices of goods and services were determined primarily by the relationship between supply *(raritas)* and human need *(indigentia)* and that economic need varies in relation to the difficulty of obtaining certain goods at certain times. Since the formation of price in the marketplace depends on constantly shifting factors and the human judgment of value is itself based in conjecture and estimation, Olivi fully accepted that the "just price" can never be either fixed or determined with absolute precision. Rather, he introduced the technical term "latitude of just price" to signal the range in which sale prices could vary and still remain "just." And despite his standing as a rigorous moralist, he drew no moral distinction (as St. Thomas had) between sale price (or market price) and just price, provided that it resulted from the free agreement of the exchanging parties and fell within the latitude established by law.

Olivi's insightful analysis of price formation and his allowance of a wide latitude of just price were followed by a number of influential theologians and moralists over the following centuries, from John Duns Scotus in the early fourteenth century to St. Antoninus of Florence and San Bernardino of Siena in the mid-fifteenth century. The close, almost word-for-word, repetition of Olivi's insights on price in the sermons of San Bernardino is particularly instructive for illustrating the profound differences between medieval thinking on usury and medieval thinking on the just price. In the thought of San Bernardino, clear-sighted perception and acceptance of the dynamics of economic exchange in the determination of just price in buying and selling exists side by side with the most ferocious condemnation of usury and the most determined attempt to impose the ideal of charity and biblical injunction on the real conditions of lending in his society.

In pointed contrast to the standard treatment of usury in the medieval period, the history of writing on just price through the fifteenth century demonstrates that legal thinkers, philosophers, and theologians looked carefully and insightfully into the complex dynamic of economic exchange (buying and selling), understood its primary underlying principles, and to a large degree (with exceptions noted above) accepted the process on its own terms.

BIBLIOGRAPHY

Baldwin, John. *The Medieval Theories of the Just Price: Romanists, Canonists, and Theologians in the Twelfth and Thirteenth Centuries.* Volume 49, part 4, of *Transactions of the American Philosophical Society.* Philadelphia: American Philosophical Society, 1959.

De Roover, Raymond. "The Concept of the Just Price: Theory and Practice." *Journal of Economic History* 18 (1958): 418–434.

———. *San Bernardino of Siena and Sant' Antonino of Florence: The Two Great Economic Thinkers of the Middle Ages.* Boston: Harvard Graduate School of Business Administration, 1967.

Ibanès, Jean. *La doctrine de l'église et les réalités économiques au XIIIe siècle.* Paris: Presses Universitaires de France, 1967.

Kaye, Joel. *Economy and Nature in the Fourteenth Century: Money, Market Exchange, and the Emergence of Scientific Thought.* New York: Cambridge University Press, 1998.

Langholm, Odd. *Economics in the Medieval Schools: Wealth, Exchange, Value, Money, and Usury According to the Paris Theological Tradition, 1200–1350.* Leiden, Netherlands: E. J. Brill, 1992.

Sapori, Armando. "Il giusto prezzo nella dottrina di San Tommaso e nella pratica del suo tempo." *Archivo storico italiano,* 7th ser., no. 18 (1932): 3–56.

Spicciani, Amleto. *La mercatura e la formazione del prezzo nella riflessione teologica medioevale.* Rome: Accademia Nazionale dei Lincei, 1977.

Todeschini, Giacomo. "Oeconomica Franciscana II: Pietro di Giovanni Olivi come fonte per la storia dell'etica economica medievale." *Rivista di storia e letteratura religiosa* 13 (1977): 461–494.

JOEL KAYE

[See also **DMA:** Aquinas, St. Thomas; Fairs; Law, Civil; Markets, European; Peter John Olivi; Trade.]

KALĪLA WA-DIMNA. A Sanskrit collection of fables that became widely known throughout the Islamic and Christian Middle East. An anonymous Brahmanic author probably composed the text in the fourth century in Kashmir. It is preserved in Sanskrit under the title of the *Panchatantra* (Five parts), while medieval versions of the text can be found in Arabic, Greek, Hebrew, Syriac, and Persian. The text first came to the Middle East through a now lost sixth-century translation into Pahlavi, which, according to a story preserved with the fables, was accomplished by Burzōe, physician to King Khusraw Anusharwan (531–579). This text, which also contained stories from the *Mahābhārata,* was translated into Arabic by Abd Allāh ibn al-Muqaffa, an eighth-century Muslim of Persian ancestry, who added an introduction and "The trial of Dimna," an epilogue that provided a moral conclusion to the fables. It is from al-Muqaffa's text that all subsequent translations were made. In the eleventh century Symeon Seth made a Greek translation under the title *Stephanites and Ischnelates,* and in the thirteenth century John Capua, a converted Jew, translated the fables into Latin from a Hebrew edition in his *Directorium vitae humanae.* From Latin the work was translated into French, Spanish, Italian and German, influencing fabulists up to the seventeenth century. Perhaps the most influential version was a prose version by the sixteenth-century Persian author Husayn Wā'iz Kāshifī. Although far more complex in form and grammar than its predecessors, this text was eventually used as part of the examination for English officials studying Persian in India. An English edition of the text was published in 1699 as *Fables of Bidpai.*

The fables are a series of stories, many of them nested within each other. Following an introduction and an account of the life and adventures of the first translator, Burzōe, the fables begin with an Indian king, Dabshalim, asking advice from a philosopher named Bidpai. Bidpai, who is sometimes identified as the author of the text, launches into the story "The Lion and the Ox," which tells of two jackals named Karataka and Damanaka, who are courtiers at the animal court, ruled over by the lion. The Arabic title, *Kalīla wa-Dimna,* by which the fables are best known, is derived from the names of the two jackals. Different characters at the court tell stories illustrating the dangers of greed, trusting your enemies, and engaging in conspiracies and pointing out the importance of good advice, wisdom, and truth. The story of the ambitious jackal Dimna's schemes to gain influence over the king provides a framework for many of the shorter fables and illustrates the dangers ambitious courtiers can pose. The text was thus intended as a "mirror for princes," perhaps even for young rulers, so that they might be prepared to govern justly and wisely.

BIBLIOGRAPHY

SOURCES

Bothmer, Hans-Caspar, Graf von. *Kalila und Dimna: Ibn al-Muqaffa's Fabelbuch in einer mittelalterlichen Bilderhandschrift: Cod. arab. 616 der Bayerischen Staatsbibliothek München.* Wiesbaden: Reichert, 1981. Arabic text.

Geissler, Friedmar. *Beispiele der alten Weisen des Johann von Capua. Übersetzung der hebräischen Bearbeitung des indischen Pañcatantra ins Lateinische.* Berlin: Akademie Verlag, 1960. Latin text.

Irving, Thomas Ballantine. *Kalilah and Dimnah: An English Version of Bidpai's Fables Based upon Ancient Arabic and Spanish Manuscripts.* Newark, Del.: Juan de la Cuesta, 1980.

Schulthess, Friedrich. *Kalila und Dimna.* Berlin: G. Reimer, 1911. Syriac text.

STUDIES

Atil, Esin, ed. *Kalila wa Dimna: Fables from a Fourteenth-Century Arabic Manuscript.* Washington, D.C.: Smithsonian Institution Press, 1981. Beautiful illustrations.

Cowen, Jill Sanchia. *Kalila wa-Dimna: An Animal Allegory of the Mongol Court: The Istanbul University Album.* New York: Oxford University Press, 1989.

O'Kane, Bernard. *Early Persian Painting: Kalila wa Dimna Manuscripts of the Late Fourteenth Century.* London: I. B. Tauris, 2003.

CHRISTOPHER HATCH MACEVITT

[See also **DMA:** Arabic Literature, Prose; Muqaffa, Abd Allāh ibn al-.]

KALISZ, STATUTES OF (1264). Jewish migration into Poland became fairly substantial in the thirteenth century. Some Jews, with no other wish than to benefit from the opportunities of commerce and agriculture, accompanied the settlement of Germans in the movement known as the *Drang nach Osten* ('drive to the East'). Others were motivated by violence directed at Jews per se—or by the generally violent tenor of the times accompanying the Mongol invasions—to seek refuge in Poland, although the disruptions reached that kingdom, too.

Typical of ethnically distinct immigrant communities, Jewish settlers sought guarantees of their privileges to dwell, trade, and settle their internal disputes without the interference of outsiders. They drew, too, on a particular strain in this tradition, the stereotypical "charter to the Jews" that explicitly or implicitly categorized Jews as the property of the prince on whose lands they resided (a phrase like *servi camerae,* denoting serfs or slaves of the princely fisc, implied this). In the case of the relatively recently settled Jews of Kalisz in medieval western Poland, a document was already available that could serve as a model for the charter they sought from their prince: the charter granted by Duke Frederick II Babenberg of Austria (1244). This model was already influential, having been used as the basis of similar princely charters for the Jews of Bohemia and Hungary.

The prince or duke of Kalisz who issued the charter, or set of statutes, for the Jews of his domains in 1264 was Bolesław V the Pious, whose power extended to much of western Poland. The charter he issued, very much like Frederick of Austria's original, became in turn the model for many other local Polish lords' charters for Jews. More important, perhaps, King Casimir III the Great applied the Kalisz charter in 1334 to the Jews of Poland who lived under his lordship. Thereafter it was intermittently confirmed both by the crown and regionally, although sometimes with local variants.

The provisions of the 1264 charter put the Jews under the special protection of the prince; they included permission for the Jews to practice their religion, to engage in trade, and to practice moneylending at interest. The charter also regulated the adjudication of disputes between Jews and Christians—compurgation was the common mode of proof; one side had to "outswear" *(superjurare)* the other. Yet despite the enthusiasm that has sometimes attended discussion of the Kalisz charter, it hardly constitutes a more generous normative set of expectations about Jewish life than was expressed in other contemporary charters (after all, it borrowed most of its so-called statutes directly from existing normative texts). It is more favorable than somewhat earlier western European charters, like that of Louis X of France, issued in 1315. Alone, however, it scarcely testifies to a strong and positive affective dimension to Jewish-Christian relations in Poland. And, finally, the church's ambivalence about the privileges hardly documents a peculiar rift between the Polish church and a more "tolerant" Polish lay population, princely or otherwise. The church frequently condemned privileges that other princes granted to Jews to practice moneylending in western Europe, and this is rarely taken to mean that religious tolerance was a value prized among western rulers. Yet the allegedly generous impulses of the Kalisz charter and the Polish princes who promulgated it and its imitations have led many modern writers to place the charter at the root of Poland's vibrant early modern and modern Jewish culture and to see it as an expression of the often symbiotic and friendly relations—despite some dramatic and ugly episodes—between Jews and Christian Poles before the horrors of the mid-twentieth century.

BIBLIOGRAPHY

Pogonowski, Iwo. *Jews in Poland: A Documentary History.* New York: Hippocrene Books, 1993. Includes the Latin charter, along with an English translation, and the subsequent royal writs confirming it.

WILLIAM CHESTER JORDAN

[See also **Supp:** Casimir III the Great of Poland, King.]

KRAKÓW. There is strong evidence of the continuous Slavic occupation of the present site of Kraków (Cracow) on the Upper Vistula, probably as a fortified hilltop emplacement and perhaps from as early as the seventh century. Popular tales have Kraków take its name from a legendary Duke Krak; the tales also include references to his daughter Wanda and the dragon of Wawel Hill. But Mieszko I, the first Christian ruler of Poland (962–992), was in many ways the primary influence on the development of the town. He incorporated it into the geographically expansive principality he assembled in the late tenth century. Bolesław I Chrobry (the Brave), king from 992 to 1025, seems to have persuaded the pope to elevate the city to a bishopric, although the first lists of the bishops (written much later) are not trustworthy with regard to the early history of the see. The relics of St. Stanisław, bishop of Kraków and martyr (*d.* 1079), are venerated at the cathedral (Wawel), which also served as the royal necropolis. In the late Middle Ages (from 1443 until the partitions of Poland in the late eighteenth century) the bishop of Kraków was also duke of Severia, a congeries of lands that lay between Kraków and Silesia.

Kraków, besides being a major see, was a major trading entrepôt. Despite the havoc wreaked by the Tatar inroads into Poland in the early thirteenth century and the sack of Kraków itself in 1241, the city survived and soon after began a spectacular rise, partly because its merchants, many of whom were German, enjoyed the privileges of Magdeburg law by charter (1257) and the commercial rights associated with it. Formal craft guilds further regulated production and commerce. In 1430 Kraków became a member of the Hanseatic League.

Periodic crises in Polish history caused the kingdom to variously shrink and grow in size. Kraków's role tended to be more important in periods of territorial consolidation. In 1320, during one of these periods, King Władysław I Łokietek (the Short; *r.* 1306–1333, as king from 1320) made Kraków his capital and the coronation city, which it continued to be thereafter. Later in the century, in 1364, King Casimir III the Great founded the Academy of Kraków, the forerunner of the Jagiellonian University, one of the most important centers of higher studies in central and eastern Europe.

Many physical traces of Kraków's medieval past grace its cityscape. Significant parts of St. Mary's Church and of the cathedral, though restored, are essentially medieval. St. Mary's possesses a wooden altarpiece (1447–1489) depicting scenes from the life and death of the Virgin Mary, considered the masterwork of Veit Stoss (Wit Stwosz). The remnants of the so-called Florian Gate, which abuts the historic city's Barbican, or thick brick walls, are like the walls themselves also medieval. The Florian Gate dates from the thirteenth century, the Barbican from the fifteenth.

BIBLIOGRAPHY

Carter, F. W. *Trade and Urban Development in Poland: An Economic Geography of Cracow from Its Origins to 1795.* New York: Cambridge University Press, 1994. A detailed study.

Zygulski, Zdzisław, Jr. *Cracow: An Illustrated History.* New York: Hippocrene Books, 2001. A lighter but well-informed romp.

WILLIAM CHESTER JORDAN

[See also **DMA:** Hanseatic League; Poland; Stoss, Veit; **Supp:** Bolesław I Chrobry of Poland, King; Casimir III the Great of Poland, King; Mieszko I of Poland, King; Stanisław, St.]

LAS NAVAS DE TOLOSA, BATTLE OF. On 16 July 1212, Muslim and Christian forces fought the most decisive battle of the Spanish *Reconquista* at Las Navas de Tolosa, north of Jaén. The confrontation had been brewing for a number of years as the Christian forces, having recovered from the disastrous Battle of Alarcos in 1195, again began to challenge the Muslim Almohads for control of the Iberian Peninsula. Renewed calls to resume hostilities against the Almohads were being raised from Castile and León to Aragon. As Christians began to raid Muslim defenses, the Almohad caliph Muḥammad al-Nāṣir responded by launching a punitive campaign against Castile in 1211.

His first stop was the castle of Salvatierra belonging to the Military Order of Calatrava. Although the castle fell, its siege had consumed most of the summer campaigning season, forcing Muḥammad to postpone any additional attacks. The Castilians spent the winter months preparing for the onslaught that was coming and appealing to the rest of Christendom for aid. The response came in a variety of forms. Pope Innocent III granted a plenary indulgence to those who went to help; the kings of Aragon and Navarre promised their assistance; and a substantial number of French crusaders began to arrive in Toledo in the spring.

The Christian army departed from Toledo in late June, led by Alfonso VIII of Castile, Pedro II of Aragon, and Rodrigo Jiménez de Rada, the archbishop of Toledo. As they marched south, many of the French knights abandoned the army, complaining about the heat and lack of booty, but they were replaced by the timely arrival of Sancho VII and his forces from Navarre. Muḥammad meanwhile had set out with his own army, composed of Arabs, Berbers, and Andalusians from Córdoba, intent on engaging the Christian forces. The Christian forces numbered between 60,000 and 80,000 men, while the Muslim armies exceeded 100,000 troops.

On 16 July, the opposing armies met on the plains of Navas de Tolosa. The battle began as the Castilian forces in the center of the Christian lines began to push against the Muslim center. The outcome hung in the balance until Alfonso led his reserves into the fray, shattering the Almohad main body. The wings of the Christian line under the command of the kings of Aragon and Navarre met with similar success, and the battle turned into a rout. One group of soldiers, possibly under Sancho of Navarre, broke into the rear of the Muslim lines, where after defeating the chained Negro slaves who guarded Muḥammad, they captured the caliph's tent and his battle standard. Muḥammad was able to flee, however, and made it safely to Jaén.

The long-term effects of the battle, although not immediately evident, were decisive. The Christian victory had broken the power of the Almohads and shifted the balance of power to the Christian kingdoms. Over the next forty years, Ferdinand III of Castile and James I of Aragon were able to turn this advantage into substantial conquests as they captured Majorca, Córdoba, Valencia, Jaén, and Seville, among others, leaving only Granada as the last surviving Muslim kingdom in the Iberian Peninsula.

BIBLIOGRAPHY

Huici Miranda, Ambrosio. *Las grandes batallas de la Reconquista durante las invasiones Africanas (Almoravides, Almohades y Benimerines).* Madrid: Consejo Superior de Investigaciones Científicas, 1956.

Lomax, Derek. *The Reconquest of Spain.* London: Longman, 1978.

JARBEL RODRIGUEZ

[See also **DMA:** Almohads; Calatrava, Order of; Castile; Reconquest; Spain, Christian-Muslim Relations.]

LATIFUNDIA. Latifundia are large agricultural estates organized for commercial profit. A manager oversees the labor, and the labor—provided by slaves or tenant farmers or a mixture of both—is cheap. It was not a technical term in antiquity: there are just over a dozen occurrences in classical sources, none of them in legal or agricultural texts; medieval usage is rarer still. A lament by Pliny the Elder (23/24–79) looms over the early history of latifundia: "latifundia perdidere Italiam, iam vero et provincias" ("latifundia have ruined Italy, and now the provinces," *Natural History,* 18.35). Wealthy landowners pieced them together from smaller parcels at the expense of peasant farmers. Pliny mentioned six proprietors whose estates jointly comprised half of Africa, reminiscent of vast estates in Gaul surveyed at more than 2,000 hectares. Elsewhere, however, he implies that latifundia could be considerably smaller, perhaps 300 hectares. It is the style of management and mode of production, therefore, that distinguished latifundia from other estates, not their size. The predominance of free over slave labor, the subdivision of estates into land tenures, and increasingly long contracts all played a part in the emergence of the medieval agrarian economy. It is unlikely, however, that latifundia were in any meaningful way the direct antecedent of feudal manors.

In the western Mediterranean, latifundia lasted longest wherever either the church or Byzantine government retained direct control of the land, although the coincidence of surviving evidence from these same regions doubtless affects our impression. Gregory I's letters from the end of the sixth century, for example, provide the most detailed picture of working latifundia in Sicily: partially divided into multifamily farms, overseen by contracted managers, and responsible to a regional director. Throughout southern Italy, the basic management structure of latifundia and their organization for commercial profit closely resemble later medieval latifundia; even their excavated buildings sometimes occupy the same physical location. Nevertheless, latifundia did not enjoy a continuous history. Those in Sicily seem to have declined between roughly the ninth and thirteenth centuries due to both social disruption and agricultural experimentation under Muslim rulers.

Agricultural experimentation was abandoned with the resurgence of latifundia in southern Italy at the end of the thirteenth century, and production was once again limited almost exclusively to cereal crops. Landowners preferred to reside in cultural and political centers like Naples, while their estate managers worked on-site on short-term contracts. Debt likely tied many peasant farmers to the land, and the incentive for technological innovation and improvement was low. As a result, it has long been believed, medieval latifundia ruined Italy once again. In terms of agricultural yields, however, Sicily at least appears to have been roughly as productive as anywhere else in late medieval Europe. Furthermore, although latifundia were inarguably based on gross social inequality, special moral depravity was attributed to them only in hindsight by Enlightenment commentators. Land reform legislation finally broke up the Italian latifundia in 1950. By that time, along with the latifundia of Spain, they seem to have inspired the tea, rubber, and cocoa plantations of Latin America, the famous haciendas.

BIBLIOGRAPHY

Bresc, Henri. *Un monde méditerranéen: Économie et société en Sicile, 1300–1450.* 2 vols. Rome: École Française de Rome, Palais Farnèse, 1986. The most thorough and influential case for the debilitating effects of latifundia.

Du latifundium au latifondo: Un héritage de Rome, une création médiévale ou moderne? Publications du Centre Pierre Paris 25. Paris: Boccard, 1995. Papers and discussions from an important symposium.

Epstein, Stephan R. *An Island for Itself: Economic Development and Social Change in Late Medieval Sicily.* Cambridge, U.K.: Cambridge University Press, 1992. Formidable attack on Bresc and the notion of latifundial decline prior to the eighteenth century.

Whittaker, C. R., and P. Garnsey. "Rural Life in the Later Roman Empire." In *Cambridge Ancient History.* 2d ed. Vol. 13. Cambridge, U.K.: Cambridge University Press, 1998. Concise overview and bibliography.

KEVIN UHALDE

[See also **DMA:** Agriculture and Nutrition: The Mediterranean Region; Grain Crops, Western European.]

LATIN LITERATURE: SECULAR LYRICS.

Defining lyric is a challenge. On the one hand, as applied to medieval Latin literature, lyric is never restricted solely to songs performed to instrumental accompaniment. On the other hand, the term "lyric" cannot be regarded merely as a synonym for any short poem written in Latin in the Middle Ages, on analogy with its usage in reference to modern English poetry. For instance, categories such as proverb and riddles are generally admitted to be distinct from lyric. More important, the designation

***Manuscript Page from the* Carmina Burana.** *Page from the 13th-century manuscript of the largest collection of secular medieval Latin lyrics. From the Abbey of Benediktbeuern, Clm 4660, fol. 107r. Now in the Bayerische Staatsbibliothek, Munich.*

"lyric," especially when qualified by the adjective "secular," excludes hymns and other types of poetry set to music for performance in churches. Differentiating between secular and ecclesiastic can be difficult in an era in which the church dominated as it did in the Middle Ages, but this very distinction provided the basis of much twentieth-century scholarship on medieval Latin lyrics.

In form secular Latin lyrics from the Middle Ages encompass an extraordinary range. Virtually all of the meters known from classical Latin quantitative poetry were imitated at one time or another. The so-called lyric meters were familiar from Horace and from the metrical portions of prosimetra (combinations of prose and verse) by Boethius, Martianus Capella, and others. Additionally, medieval Latin lyrics made heavy use of dactylic hexameters and pentameters, frequently incorporating elaborate (and utterly unclassical) schemes of internal and/or end rhyme. Rhyme was also a pronounced feature of rhythmic, or accentual, poetry—poetry that was based on syllable count and word accent but that in many cases had roots in earlier quantitative meters. Finally, secular Latin lyric is sometimes encountered in the sequence form, in which a text accompanied a complex melisma that was originally an extension of the final vowel *a* in the word "alleluia."

Countless secular Latin lyrics are preserved in medieval anthologies. One of the earliest and most important is the so-called *Cambridge Songs* (also called the *Carmina Cantabrigiensia*). This extraordinarily rich and varied collection includes praise poems and dirges for both secular and ecclesiastic leaders, occasional poems, political poems, comic tales, admonitory poetry, didactic poems, spring poems, and love poems, as well as samplings from the verse of Horace, Vergil, Statius, and Boethius. Although the manuscript was produced in England, a significant constituent was songs that emanated from the Rhineland. Beyond the few anthologies that have earned a special place in literary history because of their early date or size, many others remain less known. No two of these codices come close to being identical in their contents, and most of them contain a sizable fraction of lyrics unique to them alone.

Although the authorship of many medieval Latin lyrics is certain, vast numbers of poems circulated anonymously or pseudonymously in anthologies. A few lyric poets acquired legendary stature and nicknames; examples would be Hugh Primas, the Archpoet, and Golias. The last mentioned is associated with the Goliards, an alternative term to *vagantes,* or "wandering poets," that describes clerics who traveled among the nascent universities and courts of western Europe in search of education and employment. In the past these students and scholars were routinely cast as having been footloose and fancy free, rebelling against the oppressive moralities and social structures of the Middle Ages. But more recent study of their poetry has dispelled any lingering illusions that these were prototypes of later absinthe-drinking boulevardiers, scribbling verses on scraps of paper. Their lyric poems often have an intensely personal aura, and the pointed requests for patronage clearly reflect real need on the part of the poets, but it would be a mistake to accept the voices within the poems as being unmediated expressions of the poets themselves. On the contrary, the personas evident in the lyrics appear to have been conditioned—and controlled—by the grammatico-rhetorical training upon which Latin literacy rested. Men such as Walter of Châtillon, Peter of Blois, and Philip the Chancellor may not have satisfied all their ambitions in their careers, but they were far from being disenfranchised outsiders.

The Latin lyric tradition of the Middle Ages embraces many topics. Poems of friendship, between men and men or boys as well as between men and women, are one genre found in the latter half of the eleventh century among the so-called Loire Valley poets, who include Marbod of Rennes, Baudri of Bourgueil, Hildebert of Lavardin, Radulfus Tortarius, and others less well known. Friendship poetry had been cultivated long before, particularly among poets of the Carolingian renaissance, and even earlier Venantius Fortunatus had written poems of friendship to women. The poems of friendship often contain erotic undercurrents that have led to widely divergent interpretations by modern readers.

From the late eleventh century, love becomes an ever more frequent theme, often in conjunction with panegyric descriptions of spring, attractive places, and beautiful women. In both style and content Ovid projects a strong influence, but the vivid yearning of the Song of Songs also exerts a powerful force on the self-expression of poets. Since love is sometimes interrupted or postponed and often unhappy, the repertoire of love lyric included subgenres such as the lament over a lost or even dead lover *(planctus),* the dawn song to express sorrow at parting *(alba),* and the dialogue between young women of humble social class who were wooed or attacked by knights or clerics *(pastourelle).*

In the *Carmina Burana*—the largest collection of secular medieval Latin lyric—love poems are the second and most numerous group of poems. The love lyrics are flanked on one side by songs devoted to drinking, eating, and gambling, as well as a miscellany of poems about courts, clerics, and the like. Preceding the love lyrics is a group of moral and satirical poems; these lyrics point out the mutability of fortune, attack moral failure in general and avarice and simony in particular, and deal with topical events, such as the Crusades. Although exceptional in the degree to which they remain in popular awareness in the twenty-first century, the *Carmina Burana* is representative of many other anthologies in the diversity and appeal of their lyrics in both form and content.

Most of the poems named thus far have been from the eleventh, twelfth, and early thirteenth centuries. Even within this span many important collections of secular lyrics, such as those composed and translated in Ripoll and Arundel and those of such poets as Henry of Huntingdon and Hilary of Orléans have not even been mentioned, because they are too numerous.

Hilary's poems include one that has an Old French refrain, "Tort a vers nos li mestre." Whether or not Hilary's master Peter Abelard was in the wrong toward him and his fellow students (as the refrain asserts), the poem is worth noting for its macaronic form: it combines Latin and Old French. Such macaronic forms are found occasionally in earlier medieval secular lyric, but they become considerably more frequent in the twelfth century.

The increase in macaronic poetry corresponds to a growth in the self-assurance and appeal of the vernacular lyric traditions in Occitan, French, German, and other spoken languages. The secular Latin lyric—perhaps especially satiric poems—continued to be written even after the early thirteenth century, which saw both the great anthologizing embodied in the *Carmina Burana* manuscript and the vast output of poetry by Philip the Chancellor. But it is fair to say that the strengths and attractions of the vernacular literary traditions diverted poets from creating new Latin lyrics. Dante Alighieri wrote treatises, letters, and eclogues in Latin, and Petrarch also composed eclogues, as well as verse letters and an incomplete epic in Latin, but their lyrics are in Italian. In England, John Gower demonstrated an ability to write in Latin as prolifically as in English and French, but little of his Latin comes in the form of lyrics. Throughout Europe new Latin hymns continued to be produced, but most poets who wished to write of love other than for God used the spoken languages.

BIBLIOGRAPHY

EDITIONS AND TRANSLATIONS

Adcock, Fleur, ed. and trans. *Hugh Primas and the Archpoet.* Cambridge, U.K.: Cambridge University Press, 1994.

Godman, Peter. *Poetry of the Carolingian Renaissance.* London: Duckworth, 1985.

Walsh, P. G., ed. and trans. *Love Lyrics from the Carmina Burana.* Chapel Hill, N.C: University of North Carolina Press, 1993.

Ziolkowski, Jan M., ed. and trans. *The Cambridge Songs (Carmina Cantabrigiensia).* New York: Garland, 1994.

STUDIES

Dronke, Peter. *Medieval Latin and the Rise of the European Love-Lyric.* 2d ed. 2 vols. Oxford: Clarendon Press, 1968. The first volume offers a fundamental study of the development of the medieval Latin love lyric in relation to the vernaculars; the second constitutes an important anthology of texts.

———. *The Medieval Lyric.* 3d ed. Cambridge, U.K.: D. S. Brewer, 1996. An introduction to the medieval lyric in a number of languages, with consideration of the religious as well as secular lyric.

Norberg, Dag. *An Introduction to the Study of Medieval Latin Versification.* Edited by Jan M. Ziolkowski. Translated by Grant C. Roti and Jacqueline de La Chapelle Skubly. Washington, D.C.: Catholic University of America Press, 2003. The fundamental starting point for information about medieval Latin metrics.

Raby, F. J. E. *A History of Secular Latin Poetry in the Middle Ages.* 2d ed. 2 vols. Oxford: Clarendon Press, 1957. Volume 1 makes much incidental mention of lyric; volume 2 includes two chapters explicitly on the Latin lyric.

Rigg, A. G. *A History of Anglo-Latin Literature, 1066–1422.* Cambridge, U.K.: Cambridge University Press, 1992. Contains the best and most detailed information on anthologies that has ever been compiled.

Szövérffy, Joseph. *Secular Latin Lyrics and Minor Poetic Forms of the Middle Ages: A Historical Survey and Literary Repertory.* 4 vols. Concord, N.H.: Classical Folia Editions, 1992–1995. From the tenth through the thirteenth centuries.

JAN M. ZIOLKOWSKI

[See also **DMA:** Alba; Anthologies; Baudri of Bourgueil; Cambridge Songs; *Carmina Burana;* Carolingian Latin Poetry; Goliards; Hildebert of Lavardin; Hymns, Latin; Latin Meter; Marbod of Rennes; Pastourelle; Peter of Blois; Philip the Chancellor; Planctus; Proverbs and Sententiae; Radulfus Tortarius; Sequence; Venantius Fortunatus; Walter of Châtillon.]

LAW, CRIMINAL PROCEDURE. Late-antique Roman law shaped the definition of criminal law for jurists in the Middle Ages and established many of the norms of its procedure. Roman law defined criminal offenses by individual statutes, not by the categories of civil and criminal wrongs. In the late empire, trials for criminal offenses were conducted using many of the same procedural norms that were used to try civil cases. The Roman court procedure was called a *cognitio* (judicial examination) and in the late empire was known as the *cognitio extraordinaria* or *extra ordinem.* Roman magistrates sat as judges, the testimony presented to the court was written, and the norms governing the procedure were extensive. Although Roman rules of procedure did not distinguish between civil and criminal offenses, Roman statutes dictated that special procedural rules could be used for certain crimes. For example, torture could be used in particularly heinous crimes like treason against the emperor. Although citizens and children below the age of twelve could not normally be tortured, slaves could be tortured for a variety of reasons. Persons of humble status seem to have been tortured with some regularity in the later empire. Torture could not normally be used to extract testimony from witnesses in civil offenses.

In the period before the revival of Roman law in Italy during the late eleventh and twelfth centuries, there was no procedure that was specifically criminal. In the early Middle Ages the Germanic procedure of the ordeal (*iudicium Dei,* judgment of God) was used throughout Europe. The ordeal did not distinguish between criminal and civil offenses because Germanic custom did not distinguish between these two categories. Furthermore, legal procedures in the early Middle Ages varied greatly from place to place. Roman procedural norms persevered in southern Europe much more than in northern Europe. Some Germanic customary codes included some Roman procedural practices.

We can glean information about early medieval procedure from these Germanic codes. The Burgundian Code regulated the behavior of judges and listed the persons who could exercise judicial authority in the Burgundian kingdom. There were rules for presenting testimony in court. When plaintiffs and defendants attempted to prove their cases, they called witnesses who would swear oaths that attested to the truth or justice of each side. This oath was called compurgation and was taken on a sacred object. Sometimes the compurgators (oath takers) and the defendant would place their hands on the same object at the same time. Procedural rules established how many compurgators were necessary to establish someone's innocence from a particular accusation. The Burgundian Code dictated that if an oath taker perjured or was suspected of perjury, the parties would then resort to judicial combat (a type of ordeal) in order to settle the matter. If combat determined that the witnesses on one side had perjured themselves, all the witnesses were fined. If the compurgators failed for some other reason, the ordeal was used to decide a case. Salic law ordained that oath takers could be summoned to court even if they were unwilling and stipulated that if a defendant had no oath takers he would be subjected to an ordeal.

Oaths of purgation remained an important part of medieval criminal procedure even after the age of the ordeal. Although capital punishment was ordained for some very serious crimes like treason, the punishments for crimes in the Germanic codes were often monetary fines, even for very serious crimes like murder. There is, unfortunately, only incomplete evidence about the procedure of the ordeal and its use. This lack of evidence has not prevented scholars from vigorously debating its effectiveness.

When the emperor Justinian codified Roman law in the sixth century, his jurists collected all the statutes governing criminal law in book 9 of the *Codex* and the jurists' commentaries on criminal law in books 47–49 of the *Digest*. After the revival of Roman law in the twelfth century, sixth-century Roman classifications and jurisprudence provided the foundations of the distinction between criminal and civil law in European law from then until the present time. The Roman jurists defined criminal trials as public, in contrast to private judicial proceedings. The main offenses that they classified as criminal were treason, adultery, sodomy (criminalized and condemned only after the empire became Christian), murder, patricide, embezzlement, violence and violent acts, counterfeiting, arson, perjury, sacrilege, kidnapping, and extortion. They also defined criminal procedure as capital and noncapital. Capital proceedings were those in which the penalties could be death or exile; noncapital trials levied fines or corporal punishments. A person who had been convicted in a criminal trial became "infamous" *(infamis),* a legal status *(infamia)* that rendered the person unable to bring accusations against others or to testify in court (except in special circumstances).

THE REVOLUTION OF PROCEDURE DURING THE TWELFTH CENTURY

Medieval conceptions of authority and power were intimately connected with judicial procedure. In the early Middle Ages, customary usages regulated court procedure, not written jurisprudential norms. In this age without jurists, without lawyers, and without judges who were trained in law, the rules of procedure were often uncertain and tentative, especially in difficult cases. Literary sources give us some evidence that before the thirteenth century, the prince or judge did not exercise his public authority in the courtroom. Rather, the community under his lordship gathered around him in court. They dictated the course of a trial and determined its outcome. With the revival of Roman law and the emergence of canon law as a legal system at the beginning of the twelfth century, the role of public authority in medieval courts changed dramatically. Princes and magistrates left the periphery of the judicial system and took their place at the center of it. Justice in the early Middle Ages had been a community affair, but as ecclesiastical and secular courts adopted new rules that the jurists called the *ordo iudiciarius,* princes in both spheres discovered a new and powerful instrument of governance when they exercised their authority as judges.

***The* ordo iudiciarius.** In the first of two revolutions of procedure during the twelfth century, the Romano-canonical legal process, *ordo iudiciarius,* replaced ordeal, with oral and written evidence presented in a court taking the place of the hot iron or judicial combat. The *ordo iudiciarius* became the model for the secular and ecclesiastical courts on the European continent. Only the secular courts of England remained outside this development.

This revolution of procedure or modes of proof for civil and criminal cases began long before the Fourth Lateran Council forbade clerical participation in the ordeal in 1215. From at least 1150 on, when the evidence becomes plentiful, church courts all over Europe had almost completely abandoned the ordeal as a mode of proof for deciding ecclesiastical cases. This fact is attested by the vast number of twelfth-century papal decretals that describe implicitly and sometimes explicitly the procedures of the *ordo iudiciarius*. At the same time, the jurists who commented on the texts of canon law unanimously condemned the ordeal as a legitimate form of procedure. It was, as one jurist concluded, tempting God to ask him to judge human guilt.

The centralization of papal legislative and judicial power in the eleventh century had introduced far-reaching changes in how ecclesiastical justice functioned. The *Dictatus papae* of Pope Gregory VII stipulated that "no one shall dare to condemn one who appeals to the apostolic chair." Under the old system of the ordeal, in which the outcome embodied the judgment not of man but of God, appeal from that decision was logically and theologically impossible. The inexorable logic of the pope's dictum demanded that the old systems of proof not be used in church courts. As the papal court became the court of appeal for all the courts in Christendom, ecclesiastical procedure had to adapt to a system of proof that was based on evidence. The jurists helped to clarify the principles of the new procedure. Sometime before 1141, Bulgarus, the famous doctor of Roman law, wrote a short *ordo* that summarized the rules of procedure for Haimeric, the papal chancellor. Within a few years other jurists were writing tracts on criminal law. In a *Tractatus criminum* that an unknown jurist wrote around 1160 for secular judges, the author treats at some length the rules of procedure by which a plaintiff could bring a suit. These tracts provide good evidence of the revolution that was taking place in European continental courts. Many of the procedural norms that the jurists established were taken from ancient Roman legal texts culled from Justinian's codification of Roman law.

Papal letters also provide evidence of the change. Litigants and institutions obtained letters from the papacy guaranteeing that their cases would be heard according to the *ordo iudiciarius,* a clear indication that they wished to protect themselves from other forms of proof, the ordeal or other forms of procedure that violated the principles of the *ordo iudiciarius.*

The new procedure took root slowly in some parts of Europe. Although twelfth-century jurists produced scores of treatises describing the *ordo iudiciarius,* local customs were resistant to change. The accusatorial procedure of the *ordo* was dangerous to local interests, usurping the authority of the community to render justice. By taking procedure out of the hands of the community and placing it squarely under the power of the ecclesiastical prince, the *ordo* centralized judicial authority. Only in England did the community preserve its role and voice in court through the jury. The new procedure would not have been victorious if it had not offered better justice than the ordeals. By the second half of the twelfth century, criticism of the ordeal was prevalent and persuasive.

As the *ordo* was established as the sole, legitimate mode of proof in ecclesiastical tribunals, the jurists in the schools needed to justify its substitution for other modes of proof. Although they might have pointed to its use by the ancient Romans, they preferred to cite biblical examples. Their reliance on the Bible is another example of its importance for the legal culture and jurisprudence of the *ius commune,* or common law. The jurists found their inspiration in the Old Testament and ingeniously traced the origins of the *ordo iudiciarius* to God's judgment of Adam and Eve in paradise. By doing so, they created a powerful myth justifying the *ordo* that retained its explanatory force until the sixteenth century.

Around 1150 Paucapalea was the first canonist to connect the form of procedure used in ecclesiastical courts with a biblical model. He noted that the *ordo* originated in paradise when Adam pleaded innocent to the Lord's accusation in Genesis 3:12. When Adam complained to God that "My wife, whom You gave to me, gave [the apple] to me, and I ate it," he responded to God's summons, "Adam ubi es?" (Adam, where are you?). Although Paucapalea may not have been aware of the implications of Adam's cheeky reply to God, Adam came dangerously close to accusing the Lord of entrapment, a term in Anglo-American law used to describe a situation in which a government agent induces a person to commit a crime.

Paucapalea's main point was subtle and was not lost on later jurists: even though God is omniscient, he too must summon defendants and hear their pleas. Besides the text from Genesis, Paucapalea cited a passage from Deuteronomy in which Moses decreed that the truth could be found in the testimony of two or three witnesses. Since the rules of the accusatorial procedure also required two or more witnesses, Deuteronomy was further proof of the procedure's antiquity. Two principles emerge from Paucapalea's gloss of these biblical texts that do not enter English common law until centuries later. The first is that every accusation requires witnesses testifying in open court; the second that defendants have the right to testify in their own defense.

A few years later (*ca.* 1165) Stephen of Tournai further dissected the "trial" of Adam and Eve, finding even more evidence that this event marked the beginning of the new procedure. He pointed out that each part of the story conformed to the stages of a trial and labeled each part with the appropriate technical term. He noted that Adam raised, as it were, a formal objection (*exceptio*) to the Lord God's complaint (*actio*) and shifted the blame to his wife or to the serpent. *Exceptio* and *actio* were technical terms taken from Roman law that had already become essential parts of the *ordo iudiciarius*. Stephen was the first jurist to define the new procedure:

> The defendant shall be summoned before his own judge and be legitimately called by three edicts or one peremptory edict. He must be permitted to have legitimate delays. The accusation must be formally presented in writing. Legitimate witnesses must be produced. A decision may be rendered only after someone has been convicted or confessed. The decision must be in writing.

The story of Adam and Eve's trial in Genesis provided a historical, theological, and judicial justification for Romano-canonical accusatorial procedure.

Inquisitorial procedure. The second revolution in procedure in the twelfth century was the change from an accusatorial to an inquisitorial mode of proof. Although "inquisition" and "inquisitorial" have taken on very negative connotations in English, the word as used in this context only means "investigation" by an appropriate magistrate. The twelfth century saw a pervasive change in the perception of a prince's or judge's duty to prosecute crimes. This change is more difficult to track than the disappearance of the ordeal. Under the rules of the *ordo iudiciarius* a private plaintiff had to make his accusation to the court in writing. He had to include the name of the defendant, the crime of which he had been accused, the place, and the date. The plaintiff had to present sureties (*fideiussores*) to the court who would vouch for him. The defendant was also required to present sureties. The main point is that a plaintiff could not depend on a prince, a judge, or a magistrate to bring someone to justice. The injured party bore that responsibility. Unlike the modern world, there were no public officials whose duty it was to seek out criminals and prosecute them for their crimes. Only after the plaintiff had presented his accusation to the court could the defendant be summoned and coerced to present evidence and witnesses in his defense.

Under inquisitorial procedure the reputation of a criminal could be a cause for a judge to summon a defendant to clear his name. The mode of proof that had been used for centuries to restore the reputation of the accused was the oath of compurgation. The church courts adapt-

ed the oath of compurgation and used it as a device to examine clerics who were accused of crimes. They called this procedure canonical purgation (*canonica purgatio*). They named the procedure through which a cleric could restore his good name an "inquisition" (*inquisitio*). An ecclesiastical judge could summon a cleric accused of crimes to undergo canonical purgation. The development of this procedure probably led to the adoption of a more general investigation of criminal accusations by a judge.

Scholars have debated about when the doctrine and practice of inquisitorial procedure was established, and most have concluded that Pope Innocent III (1198–1216) brought this procedure into existence. The lack of sources make it difficult to know exactly when this significant change occurred in European courts, but it is more likely that Innocent was responsible for shaping the rules governing this procedure than for inventing it. Lotte Kéry has demonstrated that prelates had been ordered to investigate (*inquisitio veritatis*) since the pontificate of Alexander III (1159–1181). No one, however, denies that by the end of the pontificate of Innocent III the obligation of bishops to prosecute clerical crimes had become firmly established as an important part of ecclesiastical procedure.

A signpost of this development is the birth of an important maxim of criminal law, *publicae utilitatis interest ne crimina remaneant impunita* (It is in the interest of the public good that crimes do not remain unpunished). *Ne crimina remaneant impunita* became a standard maxim of the *ius commune* in the later Middle Ages. It was used by the jurists to signal the duty that princes and judges had to prosecute crime. Like many of the rules of law that became part of medieval jurisprudence, elements of the maxim had its origins in Roman law, but its final form was shaped by the medieval jurists of the *ius commune*.

The maxim was born in the Roman chancellery during the first years of Innocent III's pontificate. In a letter to the king of Hungary, Innocent demanded that the king take action against the criminals who had committed crimes against the church, using *ne crimina remaneant impunita* to urge the king to act. A few years later the pope used the maxim again in a decretal to the archbishop of Lund in 1203. The bishop had asked Innocent two questions: first, whether he could imprison incorrigible clerics who persistently committed crimes; second, if he could give judicial orders to laymen instructing them to seize criminal clerics, even violently, without suffering the penalty of automatic excommunication that was normally imposed on laymen who perpetrated violence on clerics. In the name of law and order, Innocent permitted prelates in Sweden to jail clerics who persistently committed violence. They could also delegate the task of forcibly apprehending these criminals to laymen because *publice utilitatis intersit, ne crimina remaneant impunita.* The jurists quickly adopted the maxim as a fundamental principle of medieval criminal law. By 1210 Tancred of Bologna began his important tract on criminal law with the words *Quoniam rei publice interest ut crimina non remaneant impunita,* and the maxim's career was established. More importantly, the maxim signaled that the church would no longer depend upon the accusatorial procedure to bring criminal clerics to justice. Prelates had a duty to prosecute crimes for the public good.

At the end of his pontificate Innocent III promulgated a decree at the Fourth Lateran Council (1215) that laid down extensive rules about how and when an ecclesiastical judge could prosecute criminals under his jurisdiction. This conciliar canon, *Qualiter et quando,* established basic rules for ecclesiastical judges to investigate and punish criminal clerics. Its provisions were based on a number of earlier decretal letters that Innocent's curia had sent in answer to questions that judges had posed about the rules governing court procedure. The rules for the accusatorial procedure had been well established. When one party brought suit against another and the judges sat as arbiters in the proceedings, the judges were disinterested parties when they applied the rules governing and protecting the rights of each litigant. However, when judges had initiated a prosecution, their role and their relationship to the defendant changed significantly. From the first year of Innocent's pontificate, judges from various parts of Christendom asked the Roman curia for guidance about these issues. Their questions and Innocent's responses to them were not, most likely, the creation of a new procedure but the gradual resolution of procedural questions raised by ecclesiastical judges who were beginning to play a more active role in prosecuting crime.

Consequently at the end of his pontificate Innocent issued *Qualiter et quando,* in which he summed up the rules that were scattered among his decretals. The first and most important point that Innocent made was that prelates had the right and the duty to prosecute criminal clerics. Just as jurists had used the biblical story of Adam and Eve to justify the accusatorial procedure a half century earlier, Innocent cited the Bible and quoted two passages, one from Genesis (18:21) and the other from the Gospel of Luke (16:2). The first quoted God's words to Abraham before he rendered judgment on Sodom and Gomorrah: "I must go down to see for myself whether they have merited their reputation." The second was a proverb of the rich man who had heard that his steward had mismanaged his affairs. "What do I hear about you? Either you must explain your actions or you can no longer exercise your office." Innocent had first used these biblical passages years earlier in a previous decretal letter. These biblical passages became powerful justifications for inquisitorial procedure.

The Fourth Lateran canon instructed judges to investigate and prosecute clerics whose crimes were well known. Innocent noted that the accusatorial procedure was not being replaced but that ecclesiastical judges should not have any scruples when they opened an investigation of clerical misdeeds. The pope insisted that all the procedural protections that were granted to defendants in accusatorial procedure were also given in this procedure. Defendants had the right to defend themselves with testimony, witnesses, and exceptions as well as replications (judicial replies to specific charges). The defendant should also be present at the trial.

The jurists defined the jurisdiction of a judge who investigated a criminal as being based on his office *(ex officio suo).* The judge would summon witnesses and make defendants swear that they would respond to questions but not, as is often asserted, that they must tell the truth. If the witnesses produced incomplete proofs, then the defendant could clear his name by taking the oath of canonical purgation. If oath takers declared the defendant innocent, he was freed without any penalty or infamy. The jurists who first commented on the conciliar canon thought that the only new element in the procedure was that the defendant had to be present at the hearing. The question arose because in the accusatorial procedure litigants were often represented in courts by proctors. Later jurists and legislation concluded that defendants could be represented by proctors when the accusation was not serious.

The inquisitorial procedure got its infamous reputation as the procedure used to prosecute heretics during the Middle Ages. It has been often asserted in popular and even in scholarly literature that the inquisitorial procedure was invented to combat heresy. As we have seen, it was a procedure that developed slowly, and it evolved primarily with the purpose of giving judges new authority and jurisdiction to prosecute public crimes. Nonetheless, it was adopted to combat heresy. In fact the procedure was in some ways not suitable for prosecuting secret crimes.

Heresy had long been a crime in Christendom and was a criminal offense in ancient Christian Roman law.

During the early Middle Ages in the West, heresy was not a crime that seems to have been prosecuted with regularity, but that changed in the eleventh and twelfth centuries. Secular and ecclesiastical rulers began to view religious dissent as a serious threat to society. Popes began to issue new legislation that dealt with the problem. Pope Alexander III (1159–1181) promulgated a decree at the Third Lateran Council *(Sicut ait beatus Leo)* that listed the penalties for convicted heretics. Shortly after, in 1184, Pope Lucius III issued a decretal *(Ad abolendam)* in which he described the procedure that bishops should use in the trials of heretics. He mandated that bishops actively root out heretics by summoning persons who had been accused by reliable witnesses to their courts. Secular rulers were required to assist episcopal judges. It stipulated that those lay rulers who refused to help the bishops would be punished. Lucius declared that he acted with the consent of the emperor Frederick I and with the advice of his bishops. At the same time Frederick issued statutes that subjected convicted heretics to the confiscation of their property and exile. If they did not go into exile, they were executed.

Pope Gregory IX (1227–1241) established the first inquisitors. He sent especially appointed judges to seek out and prosecute heretics. These "inquisitors of heretical depravity" *(inquisitores hereticae pravitatis),* as they came to be called, established courts whose sole competence was the crime of heresy. They used the inquisitorial procedure. Although historians have pointed out that these judges often broke the rules that governed inquisitorial procedures, other scholars have misidentified the misconduct of judges as being the norms of the procedure rather than departures from legal rules. The most common misconceptions about inquisitorial courts that prosecuted heresy were that torture was regularly employed, that defendants had no rights to counsel, and that the sentences of the inquisitors could not be appealed.

The rules governing the inquisitorial courts prosecuting heresy did depart from normal due process. Innocent III had declared that heresy was equivalent to treason against the emperor. Consequently inquisitorial courts employed the procedural rules for treason. These norms were, particularly when misused by overenthusiastic judges, violations of due process. Under certain conditions torture could be used, and the names of witnesses could be suppressed when the judges thought that their lives might be threatened by the defendants.

The most important development in the procedural rules for the inquisitorial procedure was the development of "summary procedure" during the thirteenth century.

The clause that mandated this procedure for cases that should be expedited in the interests of the litigants read "simpliciter et de plano et absque strepitu et figura" (simply and plainly without clamor and the normal forms of procedure). Canonical procedure recognized that certain serious matters should be handled swiftly and without delay.

At first this procedure caused confusion. Judges were not sure what could be omitted. Inquisitors sometimes used the procedure to expedite trials and to deny defendants their rights. Pope Clement V promulgated a decretal, *Saepe contingit,* in 1314 that was incorporated into canon law. In *Saepe* Clement specified where the judge could take shortcuts during inquisitorial procedure: the book that detailed the case was not required, holidays must not be observed, and objections *(replicationes),* appeals, and witnesses could be limited but not omitted. The pope insisted, however, that a judge may not omit necessary proofs, the summons, or legitimate defenses from the proceedings. The norms governing the criminal inquisitorial trial conform almost exactly to the doctrine of due process that is found in modern legal systems. During the rest of the Middle Ages inquisitorial procedure was used in secular and ecclesiastical courts on the European continent and in the ecclesiastical courts of England. It established the foundation of procedure used in civil law courts today.

The operation of the inquisitorial procedure can be clearly seen from the abundant court records in the Italian city-states. In December 1299 Vecto, the criminal judge of the podesta of Bologna, began an investigation of Mengho, son of Ugolino, who had been accused of robbing the store of a silk merchant. Vecto ordered a knight *(miles)* named Lazario to conduct an investigation. On 5 December Lazario supervised the testimony of nine witnesses and had their testimony recorded. Some of them reported that Mengho was a robber and had a bad reputation, while others claimed that they thought that Mengho was good or that they did not know him. Several testified that Mengho was suspected of the crime. On the same day Lazario and a notary searched Mengho's house, where they found four skeins of silk. It was identified as the stolen goods. Mengho was brought before Vecto at the bench for criminal offenses next to the new city hall in Bologna. Vecto questioned him about the evidence and the crime. The testimony of the witnesses was read to Mengho in Italian. He denied everything. On 7 December, Mengho was tortured under the supervision of four magistrates and a notary. He confessed, and the notary recorded it. More goods were recovered. Once he had admitted to stealing the silk, Mengho confessed to numerous other crimes over the past few years. On the same day, he confirmed his confessions before the court and Judge Vecto. His confession "added or subtracted nothing" to the written report submitted by the notary who had heard his confession. Mengho "persisted and persevered" in his confession when he repeated it before the court. The stolen goods were returned to their owner. Mengho was condemned to the gallows and hanged.

This case illustrates many of the norms of inquisitorial criminal procedure in secular courts. The judge could order investigations on the authority of his office. He had the power to conduct searches and to summon witnesses for interrogation. If there were a grave presumption of guilt and if a defendant refused to confess, the defendant could be tortured. Torture, however, should be used only as a last resort and only when the defendant had a bad reputation. The Bolognese statutes of 1288 stated that no person who lived in Bologna and belonged to a guild could be tortured without legitimate proofs. The lord captain must examine each case and approve the use of torture in the presence of the defendant and six officials of the city. Four officials of the commune and a notary should hear the confession of the man being tortured. As Johannes Andreae noted several decades later, the statutes of the Italian cities prohibited torture unless there was a grave presumption of guilt. In this case the conflicting testimony of the witnesses was probably not sufficient for torture, but the discovery of the silk in Mengho's home created the required grave presumption of guilt. In addition to prohibiting indiscriminate and arbitrary torture, the jurists agreed that a confession extracted by torture must be repeated in court when the defendant was under no coercion. The Bolognese statute mandated that if torture was used in violation of the norms, the podesta would be condemned to a fine of 1,000 Bolognese pounds and excluded from the governance of the city. By the end of the thirteenth century, the rules of inquisitorial procedure promulgated by Pope Innocent III had become part of the criminal justice system on the European continent.

THE DEVELOPMENT OF CRIMINAL PROCEDURE IN ENGLAND

Criminal procedure in England developed different modes of proof from those of the *ius commune* on the Continent. English criminal law in the Middle Ages centered on the word "felony." The Latin words *felo* (felon) and *felonia* (felony) were coined in the twelfth century and were not unique to English law. At first the word was applied to the feudal relationship in continental feudal law and meant a man who betrayed the trust of his lord. A *felo* was a traitor. The punishment was the loss of his fiefs and the disinheritance of his heirs.

In medieval English law, at a very early time, a *felonia* meant a serious crime, not necessarily treasonous, for which the defendant was threatened with loss of property or body parts. The crime had nothing to do with the feudal relationship, but it has been suggested that calling a crime a felony enabled judges to apply the penalty of confiscation of property (escheat), to which feudal vassals were subject, to nonfeudal crimes. The convicted defendant lost his real property to his lord and his chattels to the king. By the middle of the thirteenth century, the great English jurist whom we refer to as Bracton discussed felony in several sections of his treatise on the laws of England. Bracton mixes the meaning of felony in feudal law with the English meaning, denoting some sort of a serious crime, such as robbery, theft, rape, or murder. Courts, judges, and lawyers imposed the terminology and the logic of penalties taken from continental feudal law on English society. The development did have long consequences. The dead hand of feudal law cast a shadow over English law until the Abolition of Forfeitures for Treason and Felony Act of 1870 abolished confiscation of a defendant's goods for felonies.

A defendant could be indicted and brought to trial in two ways: through an indictment by a jury or through an "appeal of felony" by the victims or their kin. The indictment, presentment, or accusation of a jury was a twelfth-century procedure that appears for the first time in the Assize of Clarendon (1166). The Assize ordered that 12 lawful men of the 104 of the township should inform royal judges if there were any persons who had committed or were suspected of serious crimes. Those accused by the jury should be arrested and brought before visiting (itinerant) justices. If the justices found that the accusations had merit, the accused were subject to the ordeal of water. If the accused were not convicted by the ordeal but had bad reputations, they were sent into exile. This procedure is the ultimate origin of the jury trial in common law. It is noteworthy that the English king Henry II (1154–1189) began the public prosecution of criminals at the same time that the inquisitorial procedure was evolving in ecclesiastical courts.

When the Fourth Lateran Council forbade clergy to participate in ordeals, English courts had to find some other mode of proof. At first there seems to have been chaos. The Statute of Westminster of 1219 instructed justices to imprison those accused of serious crimes, exile those accused of less serious crimes, and take security from those who had committed minor offenses to ensure their good behavior. No trials were possible because there was not, it seems, an appropriate procedure.

Another jury of neighbors, the petty jury, evolved to replace the ordeal. It was the petty jury that decided on the guilt or innocence of the accused. We cannot follow its development precisely, but it was fully in place by the second half of the thirteenth century. Since the defendant would quite naturally believe that his neighbors might be prejudiced against him, he had to consent to be subject to the judgment of the jury. If he did not consent, he could be imprisoned until he consented, or he could be subject to *peine forte et dure* (severe and hard punishment). This procedure used a form of torture to coerce the defendant into submitting to a jury trial. If a defendant died while being tortured, his property was not confiscated because he had not been convicted as a felon. Only in 1772 was this barbarous rule abolished and a refusal to submit to a jury trial became a conviction. In the early juries sometimes the same persons would serve on the jury of indictment and the petty jury. In 1352 a defendant was granted the right to challenge a juror who had served on the panel that accused him.

An appeal of felony was a form of self-help that began early. Bracton had already mentioned it as a remedy, but the procedure seems to have been formalized around 1300. Victims of a felony crime or their kin would submit a written appeal to a court. This procedure bears some resemblance to the accusatorial procedure on the Continent. By the fourteenth century English court records also show traces of the *ius commune*. Royal commissions to investigate crimes resemble inquisitorial mandates on the Continent and include the formula that "we do not wish that crimes remain unpunished" *(si perpetrata fuerit relinquere noluimus impunitam)*, which echoes the maxim that crimes should not be left unpunished for the public good. Even though a felony conviction meant the confiscation of the defendant's goods, victims had little hope of recovering their chattels until 1529. In a statute of Henry VIII, victims who had brought a defendant to trial on appeal and had provided evidence bringing about a conviction might have their goods restored to them.

The felonies of murder, manslaughter, theft (larceny), and robbery accounted for most of the criminal trials in the Middle Ages. Less frequent felonies in the records were arson, forgery, counterfeiting, rape, false prophecy, breaking out of jail, and witchcraft. Grand larceny was distinguished from petty larceny by the value of the object. A crime of twelve pence or more was grand larceny, which carried a penalty of death. King Edward III and his judges in the 1340s decided that counterfeit-ing was even worse than a felony: it was treason. This change in English criminal law was probably influenced by the jurists of the *ius commune*, who had long connected counterfeiting money with treason.

English law in the Middle Ages evolved due process for defendants much more slowly than did continental law. It is sometimes asserted that article 39 of Magna Carta reflects a precocious anticipation of due process in English law. But when the barons demanded that any freeman could not be tried without "the lawful judgment of his peers," they did not have a jury trial in mind. They simply meant that a baron could not be convicted by the king alone without the consent of his barons. English due process took centuries to develop. If English courts did permit defendants to have witnesses testify for them before the sixteenth century (and we are not sure if they could), the accused had no powers to summon them. The courts did not permit witnesses to testify for defendants in crimes of felony or treason until the sixteenth century. The accused could not have the benefit of counsel until 1696 in cases of treason and until 1836 in felony cases. In contrast, the rules of procedure of the continental *ius commune* gave the defendant an absolute right to defend himself in court and to present witnesses on his behalf since the end of the thirteenth century.

THE PROCEDURAL NORMS OF CRIMINAL TRIALS

The most common misconception that emerges from the pages of books dealing with crime and procedure in the medieval and early modern periods is that inquisitorial procedure had rules that violate modern conceptions of fairness and justice. At the very core of the modern conception of the right to due process is the idea that litigants have a right to have their case heard in court and that this right cannot be taken away (under normal circumstances). From the point of view of persons living in the twelfth century, the most disconcerting and distressing issue about the dramatic changes in procedure that occurred during their lifetimes was uncertainty about their rights. The community participated in and controlled the ordeal. A litigant could exercise self-help and bring his claim to the attention of a judge in the accusatorial procedure. But how did a wronged litigant gain the ear of a judge in an inquisitorial court? These changes occurred as the system of justice became the preserve of magistrates and professional jurists. The result was that most of the local community was excluded from the courts.

A key issue became whether a person had a right to a trial. Twelfth-century jurists inherited a vague sense of a right to a trial from Roman law. The term *actio* could mean the particular formulary of Roman procedure by which the plaintiff brought suit, the whole judicial proceedings, or, as a passage in Justinian's *Institutes* puts it, "the right of an individual to sue in a trial for what is due to him." In this last sense *actio* meant *ius* or right. At first the medieval jurists wavered about whether a litigant had a right to receive justice and to have his case heard in court.

The jurists tentatively raised the issue in various ways. Linda Fowler-Magerl has described what she sees as a significant shift of emphasis in the judicial procedure of the twelfth century. In classical Roman law, litigants had very few rights to intervene in or to alter the pace of proceedings. The Romans considered procedure as an indispensable extension of public authority. Medieval jurists saw it as a right of the litigants. In Roman law, the litigants could not object to a judge whom they considered partial, nor could they delay proceedings easily. In contrast, medieval rules of procedure granted litigants a range of devices with which they could control the tempo of a case. They could raise objections to the plaintiff, the judge, and the witnesses and thereby delay or stop the course of a trial.

Most legal systems of any sophistication have some conception of "due process" in their procedure as well as at least the germ of the idea that a defendant has the right to be heard. The strictures of the Old Testament and Roman law required that a defendant be given an opportunity to defend himself in court. Even in the world of the ordeal the right to a trial can be seen. A man (or a woman) had the right to prove his innocence. In the *Roman de Tristan,* after King Mark condemns Tristan and Isolt to death without a trial when they are caught "flagrante delicto," the people of the kingdom cry out: "King, you would do them too great a wrong if they were not first brought to trial. Afterwards put them to death." Although the people's plea might seem to be a simple cry for fair play, the jurists were faced with great difficulty when they confronted notorious crimes like Tristan's. They did not find it easy to justify a right to a trial for a defendant who had been caught in the act of committing the crime.

We know almost nothing about the norms governing judicial process in the early Middle Ages, but from the ninth century on there is substantial evidence that a defendant's right to a trial was an accepted norm. In the twelfth century Gratian collected a number of texts in his *Decretum,* where he treated the question of whether someone may be accused in absentia. A Pseudo-Isidorian text attributed to Pope Calixtus II expressed the general

idea most precisely: "No one may sentence and no law may condemn someone who is absent." This chapter, included in a large number of collections from the eleventh and twelfth centuries, repeatedly reminded canonists that a defendant must be canonically summoned and publicly convicted. In his famous decretal *Venerabilem* (1202), Pope Innocent III stated that if a defendant had not been cited, witnesses could not present testimony against him. Consequently, the general principle that defendants must be summoned to court and given an opportunity to defend themselves was well established in the *ius commune.*

Defendants did not, however, have an absolute right to a trial before the thirteenth century. The jurists attempted to draw distinctions between those crimes that required a trial and those that did not. For the canonists the locus classicus for this question was *Causa* 2, *questio* 1 of Gratian's *Decretum.* Gratian included texts that permitted a judge to condemn someone without a trial if his crime was "manifest" or "notorious." Later canonists refined and altered these concepts. In the end, however, the jurists commonly agreed that under certain circumstances, usually when a crime was heinous and notorious, a judge could render a decision against a defendant without a trial.

The question was not just theoretical. It had already surfaced during the great conflict between Pope Gregory VII and the emperor Henry IV. In 1076 at a Lenten synod in Rome, Gregory VII excommunicated the German bishops who had taken part in the synod at Worms. Gregory's summary action led to an exchange of letters between Bernoldus and Adelbertus of Constance and Bernhardus of Hildesheim. Bernhardus insisted that Gregory had no right to excommunicate the bishops without a trial. He conceded that if the bishops had been summoned but refused to appear, their condemnation would have been justified. Bernoldus insisted, however, that the pope could excommunicate criminals without a trial if their crimes were public and they were contumacious. Petrus Crassus raised the same issue when he defended Henry IV in 1084. Citing texts from Roman and canon law, Petrus insisted that since Gregory had refused to hear the king's advocates and had condemned him in absentia, his sentence was not just.

In spite of objections, the pope's right to render a sentence without granting due process became well established. The thirteenth-century jurist Hostiensis effortlessly defended Pope Innocent IV's deposition of the emperor Frederick II at the First Council of Lyons in 1245. Notorious crimes, he concluded, particularly those committed against the church, need no examination.

A primary reason why the jurists accepted the right of the prince to subvert the judicial process was that they considered legal procedure *(actiones)* to be a part of the civil law, which was considered positive law, or law established by the authority of the prince; legal procedure was therefore completely under that authority. Since the early twelfth century, the jurists had difficulty limiting the prerogatives of the prince that were established by the rules of positive law. For procedure a further difficulty lay in the mythological history of law that every law student read at the beginning of Justinian's *Digest.* Two texts provided authoritative proof that *actiones* were a part of positive law. In one the Roman jurisconsult Papinianus had declared that the praetorian law, the Roman law governing procedure, was a part of civil law. In the other Pomponius described the origins of the *actiones* in the early history of Rome at the time of the Twelve Tables: "the three laws were born, the laws of the Twelve Tables, and from these tables arose the civil law, and from them actions of law were composed." Consequently, by the early thirteenth century, the jurists unanimously agreed that the *actiones* were a part of the civil law. Accursius summed up their thought when he wrote in his *Glossa ordinaria* to the *Digest* that in contrast to contracts, *actiones* are derived from the civil law, as Pomponius had noted.

In the second half of the thirteenth century, the jurists reconsidered the idea that the norms of procedure were a part of man-made, positive law. Paradoxically, at a time when some historians have seen medieval conceptions of due process rapidly being eroded by the introduction of torture and by a fierce determination of ecclesiastical and secular magistrates to eradicate crime, the jurists rethought the origins of the judicial process. As they did, defendants' rights became a central issue.

A small intellectual revolution had to take place, however, before the jurists could create a coherent argument that asserted the absolute right of litigants to a trial. They had to take the fundamental procedural norms out of the realm of positive law and place them in a system of law over which the human prince had no authority. Consequently, in the second half of the thirteenth century, the jurists gradually removed *actiones* from civil law and placed them under the law of nature. Paucapalea's inspired argument that Genesis 3:12 proved that the *ordo iudiciarius* could be traced back to Eden must have prepared the jurists to think of it as a universal institution rather than solely the product of civil law. Finding the *ordo iudiciarius* in the Bible enabled jurists to attach

divine sanction to it. Slowly, they began to argue that the judicial process was not established only by civil law but by natural law or the law of nations as well. And, following the inexorable logic that flowed from that conclusion, they perceived that since the *ordo* was sanctioned by the law of nature, the prince could not violate its basic rules. After a century of dialogue in commentaries, glosses, and *consilia,* the jurists established an inviolable right to due process.

The most sophisticated and complete summing-up of juristic thinking about due process in the late thirteenth and early fourteenth centuries is found in the work of Johannes Monachus, a French canonist who studied in Paris and became bishop of Meaux and an adviser to Philip the Fair. While glossing a *decretalis extravagans* of Boniface VIII *(Rem non novam),* he commented extensively on the rights of a defendant. He began by asking, Could the pope, on the basis of this decretal, proceed against a person if he had not cited him? Johannes concluded that the pope was only above positive law, not natural law. Since a summons had been established by natural law, the pope could not omit it. He argued that no judge, even the pope, could come to a just decision unless the defendant was present in court. When a crime is notorious, the judge may proceed in a summary fashion in some parts of the process, but the summons and judgment must be preserved. A summons to court *(citatio)* and a judgment *(sententia)* were integral parts of the judicial process because Genesis 3:12 proved that both were necessary. Johannes referred to the history of the judicial process first told by Paucapalea and Stephen of Tournai and given final form by Guillaume Durand in the prologue of his *Speculum iudiciale.* Even God was bound to summon Adam to render a defense. Johannes took medieval conceptions of due process one step further: everyone is presumed innocent unless they are proven culpable *(Item quilibet presumitur innocens nisi probetur nocens);* the law is more inclined to absolve than to condemn. Johannes Monachus was the first jurist to formulate that maxim, which is a benchmark for due process, justice, and fairness in modern jurisprudence. Guillaume Durand stretched this norm to its ultimate extreme: even the devil should have his case heard in court. An argument might be made that the pope or some other judge could know the truth about a case from secret sources, but Johannes did not think that this objection was valid. A judge is not a private person and does not judge as one. He is a public person, and he should learn the truth publicly. Johannes's gloss established the rules of due process in the *ius commune.* These rules governed inquisitorial and accusatorial trials throughout the Middle Ages and beyond.

Many standard accounts of criminal procedure in the late Middle Ages and the early modern period question that principles of due process were deeply embedded in the jurisprudence of the *ius commune*. Nonetheless, the sources reveal that these norms were respected even under difficult political circumstances. For example, when judges and jurists had to decide whether Jews were protected by the same procedural rights of due process in criminal trials, their answer was always the same: Jews had the same rights of due process as Christians. And if proofs failed, Jewish defendants, even those accused of heinous crimes, were presumed innocent. To be sure, the theory did not always find its way into the courtroom, but the rules were repeated again and again in papal mandates sent to local judges in secular courts of the Papal States and to courts of the Inquisition. In 1469 Pope Paul II confirmed the petition of the emperor Frederick III that absolved Christian judges, notaries, and scribes who participated in cases involving Jews from any wrongdoing. Some Christian priests had refused to absolve the Christian advocates from their sins unless they did penance for their work of aiding Jews in court. "Justice," Pope Paul wrote, "ought to be common to all, Christian or Jew." Later popes issued decretals that specified in great detail the procedural protections that Jews must be given. A letter of Pope Sixtus IV in 1482 mandated that Jews should receive the names of their accusers and should be able to present legitimate exceptions, proofs, and defenses to the court. If their rights were violated, Jews could appeal to Rome. From the number of times the Roman curia repeated these admonitions over the next fifty years, theory and practice may not have always coincided. Several sixteenth-century letters emphasized a Jew's right to a defense, to have an advocate, and to receive money from supporters for a defense in heresy and apostasy trials. As Pope Paul III declared in 1535, "no one should be deprived of a defense, which is established by the law of nature." The right to a defense, a lawyer, and the means to conduct a defense were deeply held principles of justice in medieval continental jurisprudence. By contrast, English common law did not recognize the right of a criminal defendant to counsel in treason trials until 1696.

In the jurisprudence of the *ius commune,* the rights of a defendant were protected regardless of his or her status, religion, or citizenship. Defendants were protected from being coerced to give testimony and to incriminate themselves. They were granted the absolute right to be summoned, to have their case heard in an open court, to have legal counsel, to have their sentence pronounced publicly, and to present evidence in their defense. These norms governed the criminal courts on the European continent until the early modern period.

BIBLIOGRAPHY

SOURCES

Albertus Gandinus und das Strafrecht der Scholastik. Edited by Hermann U. Kantorowicz. 2 vols. Berlin: J. Guttentag, 1907.

Fowler-Magerl, Linda. *Ordo iudiciorum vel ordo iudiciarius.* Frankfurt: V. Klostermann, 1984.

Tractatus criminum saeculi 12. Edited by Giovanni Minnucci. Bologna, Italy: Monduzzi, 1997.

LITERATURE

Baldwin, John. "The Intellectual Preparation for the Canon of 1215 against Ordeals." *Speculum* 36 (1961): 613–636.

Bartlett, Robert. *Trial by Fire and Water: The Medieval Judicial Ordeal.* Oxford: Oxford University Press, 1986.

Bellamy, J. G. *The Criminal Trial in Later Medieval England: Felony before the Courts from Edward I to the Sixteenth Century.* Toronto: University of Toronto Press, 1998.

Blanshei, Sarah Rubin. "Crime and Law Enforcement in Medieval Bologna." *Journal of Social History* 16 (1982): 121–138.

———. "Criminal Justice in Medieval Perugia and Bologna." *Law and History Review* 1 (1983): 251–275.

Brundage, James A. "Proof in Canonical Criminal Law." *Continuity and Change* 11 (1996): 329–339.

Caenegem, R. C. van. *The Birth of English Common Law.* Cambridge, U.K.: Cambridge University Press, 1973.

———. "Public Prosecution of Crime in Twelfth-century England." In *Church and Government in the Middle Ages: Essays Presented to C. R. Cheney on His Seventieth Birthday.* Edited by C. N. L. Brooke et al. Cambridge, U.K.: Cambridge University Press, 1976.

Dean, Trevor. "Criminal Justice in Mid Fifteenth-Century Bologna." In *Crime, Society, and the Law in Renaissance Italy.* Edited by Trevor Dean and K. J. P. Lowe. Cambridge, U.K.: Cambridge University Press, 1994.

Diehl, Peter. "*Ad abolendam* (X 5.7.9) and Imperial Legislation against Heresy." *Bulletin of Medieval Canon Law* 19 (1989): 1–11.

Fraher, Richard M. "The Theoretical Justification for the New Criminal Law of the High Middle Ages. 'Rei publicae interest, ne crimina remaneant impunita.'" *University of Illinois Law Review* (1984): 577–595.

———. "Preventing Crime in the High Middle Ages: The Medieval Lawyers' Search for Deterrence." In *Popes, Teachers, and the Canon Law in the Middle Ages.* Edited by Stanley Chodorow and James R. Sweeney. Ithaca, N.Y.: Cornell University Press, 1989.

———. "IV Lateran's Revolution in Criminal Procedure: The Birth of the Inquisitio, the End of Ordeals, and Innocent III's Vision of Ecclesiastical Politics." In *Studia in honorem Eminentissimi Cardinalis Alphonsi M. Stickler.* Edited by Rosalio Iosepho Castillo Lara. Rome: LAS, 1992.

Fried, Johannes. "Wille, Freiwilligkeit und Geständnis um 1300: Zur Beurteilung des letzten Templergrossmeisters Jacques de Molay." *Historisches Jahrbuch* 105 (1985): 388–425.

Groot, Roger D. "The Early Thirteenth-Century Criminal Jury." In *Twelve Good Men and True: The Criminal Trial Jury in England, 1200–1800.* Edited by J. S. Cockburn and Thomas A. Green. Princeton, N.J.: Princeton University Press, 1988.

Hageneder, Othmar. *Die geistliche Gerichtsbarkeit in Ober- und Niederösterreich von den Anfängen bis zum Beginn des 15. Jahrhunderts.* Graz, Germany: H. Böhaus Nachf, 1967.

Hartmann, Wilfried. "Il vescovo come giudice: La giurisdizione ecclesiastica su crimini di laici nell'Alto Medioevo (secoli VI–XI)." *Rivista di storia della Chiesa in Italia* 40 (1986): 320–341.

———. "Probleme des geistlichen Gerichts im 10. und 11. Jahrhundert: Bischöfe und Synoden als Richter im ostfränkisch-deutschen Reich." In *La giustizia nella'alto Medioevo (secoli IX–XI).* 2 vols. Spoleto, Italy: Presso la Sede de Centro, 1997.

Kelly, Henry Ansgar. *Inquisitions and Other Trial Procedures in the Medieval West.* Aldershot, U.K.: Ashgate, 2001.

Kéry, Lotte. "Inquisitio—denunciatio—exceptio: Möglichkeiten der Verhahrenseinleitung im Dekretalenrecht." *Zeitschrift der Savigny-Stiftung für Rechtsgeschichte: Kanonistische Abteilung* 87 (2001): 226–268.

Langbein, John H. *Torture and the Law of Proof: Europe and England in the Ancien Régime.* Chicago: University of Chicago Press, 1977.

Lepsius, Susanne. *Die Richter und die Zeugen: Eine Untersuchung anhand des Tractatus testimoniorum des Bartolus von Sassoferrato: Mit Edition.* Frankfurt: V. Klostermann, 2003. Contains a discussion of procedure and the norms governing witnesses.

Pennington, Kenneth. *The Prince and the Law, 1200–1600: Sovereignty and Rights in the Western Legal Tradition.* Berkeley: University of California Press, 1993.

———. "Due Process, Community, and the Prince in the Evolution of the *Ordo iudiciarius.* " *Rivista internazionale di diritto comune* 9 (1998): 9–47.

———. "Innocent III and the Ius commune." In *Grundlagen des Rechts: Festschrift für Peter Landau zum 65. Geburtstag.* Edited by Richard H. Helmholz et al. Paderborn, Germany: F. Schöningh, 2000.

———. "Innocent Until Proven Guilty: The Origins of a Legal Maxim." In *A Ennio Cortese.* Edited by Domenico Maffei et al. Vol. 3. Rome: Il Cigno Galileo Galilei Edizioni, 2001.

Peters, Edward. "The Prosecution of Heresy and Theories of Criminal Justice in the Twelfth and Thirteenth Centuries." In *Vorträge zur Justizforschung.* Edited by Heinz Mohnhaupt and Dieter Simon. Frankfurt: V. Klostermann, 1993.

Pollock, Frederick, and Frederic William Maitland. *The History of English Law before the Time of Edward I.* 2d ed. 2 vols. London: Cambridge University Press, 1968.

Robinson, O. F. *The Criminal Law of Ancient Rome.* London: Duckworth, 1995.

Schmoeckel, Mathias. "Ein sonderbares Wunderwerk Gottes: Bemerkungen zum langsamen Rückgang der Ordale nach 1215." *Ius commune* 26 (1999): 123–164.

Shoemaker, Karl Blaine. "Criminal Procedure in Medieval European Law: A Comparison between English and Roman-Canonical Developments after the Fourth Lateran Council." *Zeitschrift der Savigny-Stiftung für Rechtsgeschichte. Kanonistische Abteilung* 85 (1999): 174–202.

Simon, Dieter. *Untersuchungen zum Justinianischen Zivilprozess.* Munich: Beck, 1969.

Stern, Laura Ikins. "Inquisition Procedure and Crime in Early Fifteenth-Century Florence." *Law and History Review* 8 (1990): 297–308.

———. *The Criminal Law System of Medieval and Renaissance Florence.* Baltimore: Johns Hopkins University Press, 1994.

Trusen, Winfried. "Der Inquisitionsprozeß: Seine historischen Grundlagen und frühen Formen." *Zeitschrift der Savigny-Stiftung für Rechtsgeschichte: Kanonistische Abteilung* 74 (1988): 168–230.

———. "Das Verbot der Gottesurteile und der Inquisitionsprozeß: Zum Wandel des Strafverfahrens unter dem Einfluß des gelehrten Rechts im Spätmittelalter." In *Sozialer Wandel im Mittelalter. Wahrnehmungsformen, Erklärungsmuster, Regelungsmechanismen.* Edited by Jürgen Miethke and Klaus Schreiner. Sigmaringen, Germany: Monumenta Germaniae Historica, 1994.

Ullmann, Walter. "Some Medieval Principles of Criminal Procedure." *Juridical Review* 59 (1947): 1–28. Reprinted in Walter Ullmann, *Jurisprudence in the Middle Ages.* London: Variorum Reprints, 1980.

Kenneth Pennington

[See also **DMA:** Johannes Monachus; Law, Canon: After Gratian; Law, Civil—Corpus Iuris, Revival and Spread; Law, English Common; Law, German; Law, Procedure of, 1000–1500; Ordeals; **Supp:** Capital Punishment; Natural Law.]

LAW, FEUDAL. The law regulating the relationships of lords and vassals in the period before about A.D. 1000 was primarily based upon unwritten customary usages. The sources from the period from 800 to 1000 contain terms like "lord" (*dominus*), "vassal" (*vassalus*), "fief" (*beneficium* or *feudum*) that later jurists would carefully analyze and define. Historians have learned that when they find these words in early medieval sources, they cannot simply assume that the words describe the lord-and-vassal relationship found in later feudal law, in which a lord bestowed a fief upon a vassal in return for military service and the vassal swore homage and fealty to the lord.

In the period from 800 to 1150, the word that described a fief (sometimes, but not always, a piece of land) was generally *beneficium.* Although the word *feudum*, from which the English word feudal is derived, is found in early sources, it replaced *beneficium* as the standard word to describe a fief only during the twelfth and thirteenth centuries. At the same time the law governing the bestowal of fiefs, the rights of lords and vassals, and the complicated property rights of fiefs emerge from unwritten, ill-defined, customary chaos in which rules and principles were fluid. For political relationships the feudal contract had several advantages over a contract in Roman law. The feudal contract could be inherited and broken for political reasons. When a feudal contract passed from one generation to another, the bonds that the contract cemented were renewed in public ceremonies that reminded each party of its obligations and duties.

EARLY TEXTS

Law can exist without jurisprudence, but law without jurisprudence is uncertain. Unless there are jurists to interpret the law, the rights of persons cannot be secure. Before about 1100 Europe was a land without jurists and without jurisprudence. In the first half of the twelfth century the study of law in schools began in north central Italy, especially in the city of Bologna. A professional class of jurists began to teach, practice, and participate in the exercise of power in the courts of the nobility and the governmental institutions of the Italian towns. They used Justinian's great codification of the sixth-century *Corpus iuris civilis* (Collection of civil law) as the text upon which they commented and with which they taught. A man named Gratian produced a book of canon law upon which the jurists based the study of ecclesiastical (canon) law. These books became the standard *libri legales* (law books) for the study of law, the *ius commune*, in the schools and for the practice of law in the courts.

There were no books for feudal law. Because secular and ecclesiastical institutions were involved in legal relationships that were feudal, there was a need for written law and a jurisprudence that would provide an interpretive tool to understand it. Monasteries had feudal ties with persons and institutions. Bishops had feudal relationships with men and towns. Towns had feudal contracts with other towns and persons. The nobility had traditional feudal contracts with vassals but also with towns. Feudalism had become much more than a contract that regulated and defined a relationship between a lord and a vassal. Lawyers who studied the new *ius commune* at Bologna and other schools quickly realized that texts were needed. Mid-twelfth-century jurists began to organize the study of feudal law around a diverse set of texts. The most unusual was the central role that a letter of Fulbert, the bishop of Chartres in the early eleventh century, played in the development of feudal law.

William V, the count of Poitou and duke of Aquitaine, had asked Fulbert for advice about the obligations and duties that a vassal owed to a lord. William had troubled relationships with his vassals. In his reply (*ca.* 1020) Fulbert wrote a short treatise on feudal relationships that circulated fairly widely. Its future as a fundamental legal text was assured when Bishop Ivo of Chartres (1091–1115/1116) placed it in his canonical collections.

Around 1120 Gratian placed it in his *Decretum* where it became a locus classicus for canonistic discussions of the feudal contract and the relationship of lord and vassal. Fulbert told William that when a vassal took an oath to his lord, six things were understood to be contained in it whether explicitly expressed or not: to keep his lord safe, to protect him from harm, to safeguard his secrets, to preserve the lord's justice, to prevent damage to his possessions, and not to prevent the lord from carrying out his duties. Fulbert alleged that he got this list from written authorities, but his exact source, if there was one, has never been discovered. For the next four centuries jurists cited Fulbert's list of obligations and duties as being central to the feudal oath of fealty.

The canonists' discussion of this text illustrates why feudal law became so important in the later Middle Ages. They applied Fulbert's principles to the relationship between popes and bishops, between the emperor and the pope, and between bishops and the clerics under them. The greatest canonist of the twelfth century, Huguccio of Pisa, noted that these principles applied to the oath that the emperor and bishops made to the pope and that clerics sometimes made to their bishops. Huguccio and later canonists concluded that if a cleric gave legal assistance to litigants in a case against the church or bishop to whom he had sworn an oath, he could be deprived of his benefice just as a vassal could be deprived of his fief for the same offense. Principles of feudal law were extended into relationships that had little to do with the traditional bond between a lord and vassal. Canonistic commentaries also seem to have shaped the ethical and moral standards that a vassal had to maintain. Although they certainly drew upon unwritten customary practices, the canonists laid down the rules in their commentaries on Fulbert's letter that forbade vassals from violating the sanctity of their lords' women (wives, daughters, and other members of the household) and from injuring their lords' interests in court by testifying against them.

LIBRI FEUDORUM

The basic books of feudal law were formed in the second half of the twelfth century. In the middle of that century Obertus de Orto, a judge in Milan, sent his son Anselm to study law in Bologna. When Anselm reported to his father that no one in Bologna was teaching feudal law, Obertus wrote two letters to his son ("letters" may be rhetorical conceits) in which he described the law of fiefs in the courts of Milan. Those letters became the core of a set of texts for the study of feudal law. Obertus put his letters together with other writings on feudal law, especially from Lombard law, to create the first of three "recensions" of the *Libri feudorum* (in the manuscripts the book was also named *Liber feudorum, Liber usus feudorum, Consuetudines feudorum,* and *Constitutiones feudorum*). The manuscripts of the first two recensions reveal that there was no standard text. Some of them included eleventh- and twelfth-century imperial statutes of the emperors Conrad II, Lothair II, and Frederick I. Manuscripts of the second recension often contained the letter of Fulbert of Chartres and additional imperial statutes. Typical of legal works in the second half of the twelfth century, the jurists and scribes added texts of various types *(extravagantes)* to this recension. There are almost no two manuscripts that contain exactly the same text. The text's entry into the schools must have been slow because the jurists did not immediately comment on it. The first jurist to write a commentary on the *Libri* was Pillius de Medicina, a jurist of Roman law. He wrote his commentary on the second recension around 1200, probably while he was a judge in Modena. He did not comment on all parts of the *Libri,* leaving the interpretation of Fulbert's letter to the canonists. This illustrates an important point about feudal law in the twelfth century: its jurisprudence was not the product of one area of law but of the *ius commune.*

The final, or vulgate, recension of the *Libri feudorum* added constitutions of the emperor Frederick II, the letter of Fulbert, and other texts that had circulated in the twelfth-century manuscripts. Accursius, the most important jurist of Roman law in the thirteenth century, wrote a commentary based on Pilius's in the 1220s. It may have gone through several recensions, not all by Accursius. Accursius also wrote the *Glossa ordinaria* on the rest of Roman law at about the same time. His authority and the importance of feudal law combined to give *Libri feudorum* along with Accursius's *Glossa ordinaria* a permanent place in the *ius commune.* From the 1230s on, the *Libri* was included in the standard manuscripts of Roman law that the stationers at the law schools produced for jurists, students, and practitioners. They placed it immediately after the *Authenticum* (legislation of Justinian). In the fourteenth century Johannes Andreae questioned whether the *Libri feudorum* had been legitimately included in the *libri legales* since no public official had mandated its inclusion in the body of law. Johannes presented both sides of the question, but most jurists decided that it was a legitimate text because it had been accepted by custom and the schools.

AFTER THE TWELFTH CENTURY

Canon law continued to contribute to the jurisprudence of feudal law after the twelfth century but did not produce any legislation as central as Fulbert's letter. Pope Innocent III (1198–1216) touched upon feudal matters in many of his letters, two of which entered the official collections of canon law under the title *De feudis.* One of these letters shaped feudal law in an important area: the right of a lord to bestow a fief when he had taken an oath not to bestow the fief on someone else. Feudal law in the later Middle Ages found its jurisprudential roots in Roman law, canon law, and in secular legal systems. This cross-fertilization accounts for the vigor of feudal law until the end of the sixteenth century.

The first penetration of feudal law into secular law can be found at the beginning of the thirteenth century. When the commune of Milan published its statutes in 1216, the titles that dealt with feudal law were taken primarily from the *Libri feudorum.* The statutes contain an oath that a vassal took to his lord: "I swear that I will be henceforward a faithful man and vassal to my lord. I will not lay open to another to [my lord's] injury what he has entrusted to me in the name of fealty." When Emperor Frederick II promulgated a law code for the Kingdom of Sicily in 1231, the Constitutions of Melfi, he carefully regulated the succession of fiefs and the rules governing the nobility in bestowing fiefs. The jurists commented on Frederick's legislation and incorporated it into the jurisprudence of the *ius commune.* After the early thirteenth century many secular legal codes dealt with feudal customs in their jurisdictions. They acknowledge a wide range of different practices. In Spain the *Siete partidas* and in France the *Établissements de St. Louis* dealt extensively with the customary law of lords and vassals.

Feudal relationships generated legal problems and court cases in the later Middle Ages. The earliest reports of court cases involving feudal disputes and using feudal law date to the late twelfth century, and their numbers proliferate during the thirteenth and fourteenth centuries. As the number of these cases increased, jurists were called upon to write *consilia* (legal briefs) to solve them. The jurist who best illustrates this development is Baldus (Baldo degli Ubaldi). He had taught for many years in the republican city of Perugia when, in 1390, Gian Galeazzo Visconti called him to the University of Pavia. Baldus became Gian Galeazzo's court lawyer and devoted much of his time to struggling with Visconti's legal problems and those of his vassals. Gian Galeazzo was trying to assert feudal rights over his vassals, and to support his lord, Baldus became enmeshed in the intricacies of feudal law. He finished a commentary on the *Libri feudorum* in 1393. It became the most important exposition of feudal law in the late Middle Ages. Baldus also wrote a number of long *consilia* in which he tried to give legal justification to the state based on feudal privileges, rights, and obligations that Gian Galeazzo wanted to create. Baldus found it difficult to justify Gian Galeazzo's claims when they violated deeply embedded norms of feudal law and the *ius commune*. The result was a series of tortuous and convoluted *consilia* whose composition betrays Baldus's ambivalence about his task.

Feudal law remained an important part of European jurisprudence until the seventeenth century. Jurists regularly treated feudal problems in their *consilia*. They also continued to write commentaries on the *Libri feudorum*. The last two great commentators on feudal law were Johannes Antonius de Sancto Georgio and Mattheus de Afflictis in the sixteenth century, who wrote extensive and widely circulated commentaries on the *Libri*.

BIBLIOGRAPHY

SOURCES

Consuetudines feudorum. Edited by Karl Lehmann, revised by Karl August Eckhardt. 1892. Reprint, Aalen, Germany: Scientia Verlag, 1971.

Montorzi, Mario, ed. *Diritto feudale nel basso medioevo: Materiali di lavoro e strumenti critici per l'esegesi della glossa ordinaria ai Libri feudorum: Con la ristampa anastatica dei Libri feudorum e della loro glossa ordinaria.* Torino, Italy: G. Giappichelli, 1991. Reprints the *Liber* and the "ordinary gloss," with commentary.

LITERATURE

Caravale, Mario. *La monarchia meridionale: Istituzioni e dottrina giuridica dai Normanni ai Borboni.* Rome: Laterza, 1998. On feudal law in southern Italy.

Cortese, Ennio. *Il diritto nella storia medievale.* Volume 2: *Il basso medioevo.* Rome: Il cogno Galileo Galilei, 1995. Places feudal law in the larger context of legal developments.

Danusso, Cristina. *Ricerche sulla "Lectura feudorum" di Baldo degli Ubaldi.* Milan: Giuffrè, 1991. Discusses later commentaries on the *Libri feudorom* and the later jurists' views about its authenticity.

Giordanengo, Gérard. *Le droit féodal dans les pays de droit écrit: L'exemple de la Provence et du Dauphiné, XIIe–début XIVe siècle.* Rome: École Française, 1988. Giordanengo has done the best work on French feudal law.

———."Epistula Philiberti." In *Féodalités et droits savants dans le Midi médiéval.* Hampshire, U.K.: Variorum, 1992.

———. "Consilia feudalia." In *Legal Consulting in the Civil Law Tradition.* Edited by Mario Ascheri, Ingrid Baumgärtner, and Julius Kirshner. Berkeley, Calif.: Robbins Collection, 1999.

Lexikon des Mittelalters. Vol. 5. Munich: Artemis Verlag, 1991. Articles by various authors on feudal law and institutions in France, Germany, England, Kingdom of Sicily, Scandinavia, Poland and Bohemia, Hungary, Iberian Peninsula, and the Latin East can be found on pages 1807–1825.

Pennington, Kenneth. "The Authority of the Prince in a Consilium of Baldus de Ubaldis." In *Popes, Canonists, and Texts, 1150–1550.* Aldershot, U.K.: Variorum, 1993. Contains an example of the *consilia* that the jurists wrote on feudal problems of sovereignty.

———. "Allegationes, Solutiones, and Dubitationes: Baldus de Ubaldi's Revisions of his *Consilia.*" In *Die Kunst der Disputation: Probleme der Rechtsauslegung und Rechtsanwendung im 13. und 14. Jahrhundert.* Edited by Manlio Bellomo. Munich: R. Oldenbourg, 1997.

Reynolds, Susan. *Fiefs and Vassals: The Medieval Evidence Reinterpreted.* New York: Oxford University Press, 1994. A broad, interpretive work covering more of Europe than any other single text.

Vallone, Giancarlo. *Iurisdictio domini: Introduzione a Matteo d'Afflitto ed alla cultura giuridica meridionale tra Quattro e Cinquecento.* Lecce, Italy: Milella, 1985.

———. *Istituzioni feudali dell'Italia meridionale: Tra Medioevo ed antico regime: L'area salentina.* Rome: Viella, 1999. On feudal law in southern Italy.

Villata di Renzo, Gigliola. "La formazione dei 'Libri feudorum.'" In *Il feudalesimo nell'alto medioevo.* Spoleto, Italy: Centro Italiano di Studi sull'Alto Medioevo, 2000.

Weimar, Peter. "Die Handschriften des 'Liber feudorum' und seiner Glossen." *Rivista internazionale di diritto comune* 1 (1990): 31–98. An examination of the development of the *Libri feudorum.*

———. "Liber feudorum." In *Lexikon des Mittelalters.* Vol. 5. Munich: Artemis Verlag, 1991.

KENNETH PENNINGTON

[See also **DMA:** Baldus; Feudalism; Fief; Fulbert of Chartres; Gratian; Law, Canon: After Gratian; Law, Civil—Corpus Iuris, Revival and Spread; **Supp:** Accursius; *Libri Feudorum.*]

LE FRANC, MARTIN (*ca.* 1410–1461), was born in Aumale in Normandy. He studied in Paris and had a distinguished career as a priest, writer, diplomat, and papal secretary, participating in some of the more significant events of the fifteenth century. He is best remembered, however, for writing the allegorical poem *Le champion des dames* (The champion of ladies).

In 1435 Martin participated in the Congress of Arras, which secured peace between Philip III the Good, duke of Burgundy, and the king of France, bringing an end to that theater of the Hundred Years War. After Arras, he moved into the service of Amadeus VIII, duke of Savoy. In 1439 the Council of Basel tried to depose Pope Eugenius IV (1431–1447) and selected Amadeus to replace him as Pope Felix V (1439–1449)—or rather antipope Felix V—as Eugenius fought a determined battle to stay on the throne of St. Peter. The new antipope quickly installed Martin in the Council and made him papal secretary. The favors from Felix continued as he named Martin canon and later *prévôt* of Lausanne. Additional benefices followed, as he became canon of Turin in 1444 and of Geneva in 1447. Martin's constant travel as papal legate, however, caused a minor revolt among the priests who served under him in Lausanne and grew disgruntled over his chronic absenteeism from his duties there. By 1449 the struggle between Felix V and Nicholas V (1447–1455), Eugenius's successor, was drawing to a close in favor of the latter. That year Felix resigned and returned to his court in Savoy. Martin, however, remained as papal secretary, helping Nicholas in local matters in Lausanne. In 1459 he was placed in charge of the old Benedictine abbey of Novalesa near Turin. Two years later, on 8 November 1461, he died in Rome.

In 1442 Martin completed *Le champion des dames,* which he dedicated to Philip the Good. This poem of over 24,000 lines has survived in nine manuscripts. It was, in many ways, a revolutionary work in its passionate defense of women and a direct response to their negative portrayal in the *Romance of the Rose* (written between 1237 and 1280). The work revolves around a debate between the forces of Malebouche—who are laying siege to the "Castle of Love" and the ladies within—and Franc Vouloir, the "Champion of Ladies." In the course of the debate, Vouloir successfully defends the ladies by countering the arguments of Malebouche's lieutenants using historical and mythological examples, including Joan of Arc and the Virgin Mary, Vouloir not only defends women, but also argues that they are the equals of men. *Le champion* also offers some insightful comments on fifteenth-century music, especially the impact of English music on the continent. Finally, one of the manuscripts contains the first pictorial image of a witch flying on a broomstick.

Le Franc's other significant work was the *L'estrif de fortune et vertu* (The conflict of Fortune and Virtue, 1447–1448). Like *Le champion, L'estrif* was also dedicated to the duke of Burgundy and was likewise set up as a debate, this time between "Fortune" and "Virtue," to determine which of the two ought to guide the actions of man.

BIBLIOGRAPHY

PRIMARY WORKS

Le Franc, Martin. *Le champion des dames.* 5 vols. Edited by Robert Deschaux. Paris: Honoré Champion, 1999. This is the first complete edition of the poem.

———. *L'estrif de fortune et vertu.* Edited by Peter Dembowski. Geneva: Droz, 1999.

SECONDARY WORKS

Barbey, Léon. *Martin le Franc: Prévôt de Lausanne, avocat de l'amour et de la femme au XVe siècle.* Fribourg, Switzerland: Editions Universitaire, 1985.

France, Peter. *The New Oxford Companion to Literature in French.* Oxford: Clarendon, 1995.

JARBEL RODRIGUEZ

[See also **DMA:** Councils, Western (1311–1449); *Roman de la Rose; Savoy, County of.]*

LIBRI FEUDORUM (Books of fiefs) is a private compilation of laws relating to feudal property holding that was put together gradually in northern Italy between the mid-twelfth and the mid-thirteenth centuries. According to legend, when Anselm de Orto, son of the prominent Milanese judge Obertus de Orto, arrived in Bologna to study law in the mid-twelfth century, he was astonished to discover that the feudal law with which his father occupied his time was completely ignored. In response, Obertus wrote Anselm two letters laying out the fundamentals of Milanese customary feudal law. This experience, so the legend goes, motivated Obertus to compile the *Libri feudorum,* though this attribution to Obertus is probably unjustified.

While perhaps apocryphal, the story does contain a grain of truth. The lawyers of Bologna were concerned with the Roman civil law—the law of the emperor Justinian—and its close relation, the canon law. But Justinian's law had been written for a very different society, one in which personal and property relationships did not function as they did in the High Middle Ages. It is not surprising that the civilians (scholars of the civil law) recognized the lacuna in the corpus of civil law. It is also not entirely incredible that a legal community as taken with systematization of the law as that of the twelfth century should see fit to write down and organize the customary law. What is astonishing, however, is that the feudal law should have become a subject of great academic concern at the very moment when feudal relations were rapidly being replaced by a money economy.

The *Libri feudorum* evolved in four stages. By 1150, a compilation had been made by combining five or six short treatises, or perhaps excerpts of treatises, on the feudal law by Lombard lawyers with the two letters of Obertus de Orto. This is known as the *Compilatio antiqua* (Old compilation) or the Obertian recension. (This part comprises book 1, title 1, to book 2, title 24, minus titles 6 and 7 of book 2 in the final version and includes the short treatise by Hugh of Gambolo that was excluded from the final version.) The *Compilatio antiqua* was not a scholarly product. It had no clear organization, lacked division into titles and books, and did not display a profound knowledge of the learned law, though the treatise authors and certainly Obertus were familiar with Roman legal terminology. It also apparently did not immediately become the important academic text it would later be once it had made its way from its birthplace in Lombardy to the school of Bologna. We know of no twelfth-century Bolognese commentators on feudal law referring to it.

Toward the end of the twelfth century, the *Compilatio antiqua* was divided into two books, each separated into titles, and over twenty-five additional titles were added. This text is known as the Ardizone recension, after Jacob de Ardizone, who assembled an appendix of extracts from the *Decretum* of Gratian, papal decretals, legislation of the recent Holy Roman emperors, and the *Lombarda,* an eleventh-century compilation of Lombard, Frankish, and Carolingian legislation. This version began to attract the attention of civilians. Pillius de Medicina, a professor of Roman law in Bologna from 1169 to 1182, began a gloss on the Ardizone recension toward the end of his life, shortly after 1200, when he was living in Modena. He also wrote a summa on the *Libri.* Pillius never finished the gloss, and it was reworked and completed by Jacobus Columbi. Shortly after 1220, the great glossator Hugolinus appended the Ardizone recension to the end of the corpus of Roman law, making the *Libri feudorum* part of the standard corpus of civil law taught and used throughout Europe. The final version, known as the vulgate or Accursian version and completed around 1250, included a few additional titles as well as the standard gloss by Accursius, who had also glossed the whole of the Roman law.

The *Libri feudorum* deals with the acquisition and loss of fiefs. It considers who can hold a fief and under what circumstances it is forfeit, what constitutes proper investiture, who can inherit, how a fief can be alienated, the duties of a vassal, and the relationship between lord and vassal. The text derives mainly from northern Italian custom and imperial legislation. Its many repetitions betray its convoluted origin as a private collection assembled by numerous hands over a long span of time.

Although a private collection, the *Libri feudorum* had a remarkable popularity, and this presents a historical puzzle for two reasons. First, by the thirteenth and perhaps as early as the twelfth century, the system of personal and property relationships that historians have denominated feudalism was distinctly on the wane. Medieval society was no longer structured around warrior vassals holding fiefs in return for military and other services. Mercenary armies and professional civil servants were instead the new key pieces of a changing economic and administrative world. Second, what feudal custom did remain in use varied from place to place. The Lombard customs in the *Libri feudorum* had no necessary similarity to the customs anywhere else in Europe. Yet not only was the *Libri feudorum* the second most popular private law collection after the *Decretum* of Gratian, but it also continued to be published, consulted, and commented on by academics and practitioners throughout Europe well into the early modern period.

Two possible explanations for the unexpectedly long tenure of this distinctly early medieval legal creation can be offered. First, the written feudal law was largely an academic creation, and once it became part of the Roman law corpus taught in law schools, it was perpetuated by inertia and tradition. Second, the *Libri feudorum,* though built around Lombard law, was essentially a work of generalities. For example, nowhere did it attempt to give a narrow definition of "fief." It might describe what did and did not constitute a true fief according to Lombard custom, but it also made allowances that other customs might vary. What the text provided, rather than a strict set of categories and rules such as were present in the Roman law, was a checklist of criteria and possible variations to look for in trying to decide whether a particular landholding constituted a fief, and it offered lawyers throughout Europe a common vocabulary with which to discuss similar landholding patterns. Consequently, as long as medieval property rights maintained their legal standing, the *Libri feudorum* remained a useful manual for Western lawyers.

BIBLIOGRAPHY

STUDIES

Danusso, Cristina. *Richerche sulla "Lectura feudorum" di Baldo degli Ubaldi.* Milan: Giuffre, 1991.

Laspeyres, Ernst Adolf. *Über die Entstehung und älteste Bearbeitung der Libri feudorum.* 1830. Reprint, Aalen, Germany: Scientia Verlag, 1969. Still the main secondary work on the *Libri feudorum.*

Reynolds, Susan. *Fiefs and Vassals: The Medieval Evidence Reinterpreted.* Oxford: Oxford University Press, 1994. Considers how the *Libri feudorum* shaped later historians' views of the Middle Ages.

Ryan, Magnus. "*Ius Commune Feudorum* in the Thirteenth Century." In *"Colendo iustitiam et iura condendo:" Federico II legislatore del regno di Sicilia nell'Europa del duecento.* Edited by Andrea Romano. Rome: Edizioni de Luca, 1995. An important discussion of the role played by the *Libri feudorum* in European law.

Weimar, Peter. "Die Handschriften des Liber feudorum und seiner Glossen." *Rivista Internazionale di Diritto Commune* 1 (1990): 31–98.

SOURCES

Belviso, Jacobus de. *Commentarii in authenticum et consuetudines feudorum.* 1511. Reprint, Bologna, Italy: Forni, 1971.

Lehmann, Karl. *Consuetudines feudorum.* 1892. Reprinted, Aalen, Germany: Scientia Verlag, 1971. Study and critical edition of the *Compilatio antiqua* and comparison with the vulgate version.

Montorzi, Mario. *Diritto feudale nel basso medioevo: Materiali di lavoro e strumenti critici per l'esegesi della glossa ordinaria ai Libri feudorum.* Torino, Italy: G. Giappichelli, 1991. Discussion of the gloss and reprint of the Venice 1574 edition.

EMILY KADENS

[See also **DMA**: Feudalism; Fief; Law, Civil—Corpus Iuris, Revival and Spread; Law, Schools of; **Supp**: Accursius; Law, Feudal.]

LISBON. According to some sixteenth-century writers, Ulysses, the Homeric hero, founded the city of Lisbon as he tried to make his way home after the Trojan War. In reality, the Phoenicians were probably first to settle the area, establishing a trading colony called Olisipo. They chose a site at the mouth of the Tagus River, which gave the city a fertile and healthy hinterland and an excellent harbor. Olisipo remained under Phoenician and then Carthaginian dominion until the end of the Second Punic War in 201 B.C., when the Romans annexed most of the Iberian Peninsula. The Romans controlled Lisbon for the next six centuries, and it became the center of Roman administration in the region, thanks in part to Julius Caesar, who granted it Roman rights. The city grew and prospered, enjoying many of the civic benefits that befitted a Roman city—baths, temples, markets, and a theater. By the fourth century, the city was an active participant in the Roman and Christian world, as her bishops and churchmen engaged in dialogues with some of the greatest names in Christendom.

THE BARBARIAN INVASIONS

The city's fortunes changed, however, as the Roman Empire began to fall apart under pressure from barbarian tribes at its borders and its own internal problems. Successive waves of Germanic invaders, notably Sueves and Vandals as well as Alani from the Caucasus penetrated the Pyrenees and made their way into the heart of Hispania and eventually into Portugal, with the Sueves sacking Lisbon in 469. The region also became a haven for Priscillianists (who believed in the absolute renunciation of all sensory pleasures). But the Visigoths, recent arrivals to Iberia, were first to establish firm control over the whole peninsula in the late sixth century. Lisbon fared badly under their rule, as they reduced most of its population to servitude and put them to work cultivating the fields for their new Visigothic masters. The Visigoths were also responsible for changing the name of the city to Ulixbone, whence the modern name, Lisbon, comes.

LISBON UNDER THE MUSLIMS

Visigothic control lasted for more than a century. Then, in 711, a large Muslim raiding party crossed the straits of Gibraltar into Iberia and crushed the Visigoths, opening a new age in the history of the peninsula. Lisbon did well under Muslim domination, at least in the early years. The population, happy to be rid of the Visigothic yoke, seems to have welcomed the new masters, and a substantial number converted to Islam. They coexisted with the recent Muslim arrivals and with the Mozarabs, Christians who adopted Arabic language and culture while clinging to their faith.

After recovering from the initial shock of the conquest, the Christian forces, now relegated mostly to the mountainous northern regions of Iberia, began a slow counteroffensive against the Muslims. In 798 Alfonso II of Asturias (*r.* 791–842) reached Lisbon and sacked the city but lost it again soon thereafter. This pattern continued over the next two and half centuries, as Christian invaders captured the city only to see the Muslims recover it. In the 840s the Vikings also sacked Lisbon, in the course of a particularly destructive raid down the Iberian coast.

The Christian effort to recover the city began in earnest in the late eleventh century, as northern Europeans, filled with crusading zeal, trekked across the Pyrenees to do battle with the Muslims. Preeminent among them was Henry of Burgundy, whose descendants founded the kingdom of Portugal, after detaching the County of Portugal from León-Castile. The new Portuguese dynasty, led by Henry's energetic son Afonso Henriques (*r.* 1139–1185), began to advance against the now fragmented Islamic kingdoms on the peninsula. By 1137 he was able to strike at Lisbon, but continued attempts over the next decade to capture the city proved ineffective. In 1147, a large fleet of northern European crusaders, on their way to the Second Crusade, appeared at the mouth of the Tagus. Afonso offered them the lion's share of the spoils if they agreed to help him conquer Lisbon. The siege, which lasted more than four months, ended with the capitulation of the city in October 1147. Three years later, the ancient see of Lisbon was restored when Gilbert of Hastings, an English crusader, was appointed its new bishop.

CHRISTIAN LISBON

The Lisbon that Afonso Henriques captured was not a great city, even by medieval European standards, but its magnificent harbor and location on the Atlantic proved to be valuable assets. By the late twelfth century ships from the city were becoming a common sight in northern European waters, as the Portuguese developed important trade networks with England and Flanders. Capitalizing on its maritime success, Lisbon built its first shipyards in the mid-thirteenth century; a few years later, in 1256, Afonso III made the city the capital of the kingdom of Portugal. He also installed the royal chancery in the city's *Torre do Tombo*. A royal palace was built soon thereafter, and in 1290 a university was established in the city, although it would be moved to Coimbra in 1308. The university would relocate several times between Lisbon and Coimbra before finally settling in the latter in 1537. By the end of the thirteenth century, Lisbon probably had a population of between twenty and thirty thousand people.

The fourteenth century would not be as kind. Earthquakes rocked the city several times; a massive one in 1344 devastated the palace and the *Sé,* the cathedral. The city had barely gotten over this disaster when the Black Death struck in 1348. In 1383 a political crisis shook Lisbon, after a dynastic marriage had brought Portugal perilously close to becoming part of Castile. A rebellion led by John, master of the military order of Aviz, and merchants from Lisbon, among others, exploded in late 1383, and numerous Castilians and their supporters were killed in the city. Although Castilian troops laid siege to Lisbon, the Portuguese were successful in their revolt, and John I (*r.* 1385–1433) was proclaimed king, inaugurating the House of Aviz.

The city maintained its identity as a maritime community, with its neighborhoods of sailors, dockworkers, fishermen, and merchants, including notable colonies of Italians. There was also a sizable Jewish community and a smaller Muslim quarter. Lisbon was also becoming increasingly wealthy, generating more than 40,000 *dobras* in customs revenue alone by the end of the fourteenth century. The discoveries and expansion of the fifteenth century ensured that this prosperity continued, as Lisbon became a gateway for the goods—slaves, spices, sugarcane, and gold—that the new colonies provided. By the end of the fifteenth century, Lisbon was not only the capital of Portugal but also the center of a rapidly expanding and increasingly powerful Portuguese empire.

BIBLIOGRAPHY

Couto, Dejanirah. *Histoire de Lisbonne.* Paris: Fayard, 2000.

Livermore, H. V. *A New History of Portugal.* 2d ed. Cambridge, U.K., and New York: Cambridge University Press, 1976.

Santana, Francisco, and Eduardo Sucena, eds. *Dicionário da história de Lisboa.* Lisbon: C. Quintas, 1994.

JARBEL RODRIGUEZ

[See also **DMA:** Alani; Aviz, Order of; Barbarians, Invasions of; Mozarabic Rite; Portugal; Spain, Muslim Kingdoms of; Vandals; Visigoths.]

LITURGICAL YEAR, EASTERN. The liturgical year of the East is the cycle of feasts and fasts identified and celebrated by the Eastern churches over the course of one solar year, as calculated by the Julian calendar. The liturgical year operates on two calendars (movable and fixed) and three cycles (daily, weekly, and yearly). By the end of the fourth century, the basic framework of the liturgical year was in place, though many of its constituent elements continued to evolve until at least the eleventh century.

THE TWO CALENDARS

The *Kanonarion* is the lunar calendar that chronicles the Paschal season. According to the Council of Nicea (A.D. 325), Pascha (the Orthodox term for Easter) is the first Sunday after the first full moon after the vernal equinox. In its developed form, the *Kanonarion* comprises a seventeen-week period: a three-week pre-Lenten period (known as the *Triodion*), a forty-day Lent, Holy Week, Pascha, Ascension, and Pentecost. Because Pascha was the focus of the liturgical year, the starting point for the Sunday lectionary (a book containing the weekly Gospel readings) was the first Sunday following Pentecost. Consequently, Gospel passages were arranged from one Paschal celebration to another.

For most of the Middle Ages, Eastern and Western Christians celebrated Easter on the same day. By the later period, the Julian calendar's reckoning fell behind the astronomical equinox. In the sixteenth century, the West amended its calendar to correct this error, but the East retained the Julian dating, in part to maintain the link to the Jewish Passover (it is possible, according to the Gregorian calendar, to celebrate Easter before Passover). The two calendars can have the same date for Easter, but more often the Eastern reckoning is one, two, or as many as five weeks later than the Western.

The *Synaxarion* is the fixed calendar linked to the solar year. This calendar records the fixed feasts and saints' days of the liturgical year, such as Christmas, the Annunciation, and the beheading of John the Baptist. Unlike the *Kanonarian,* the *Synaxarion* continued to evolve throughout the Byzantine era and beyond, reflecting the canonization of new saints. Contrary to Western practice, the *Synaxarion* includes Old Testament figures (patriarchs, prophets, and kings) as Christian saints, identifying specific days for their veneration.

From 313 to 462, the liturgical year began with 23 September, the feast of the conception of John the Baptist, most likely because it was the first event detailed in the Gospels. Beginning in 462, the liturgical year conformed to the Byzantine civil year and thus began on 1 September. By the late Byzantine period, 1 September had developed its own liturgical significance as the first day of the religious calendar. In most of the West, the civil new year was either 25 March or Easter, and the beginning of the liturgical year was the first day of Advent.

THE DAILY AND WEEKLY CYCLES

Through monastic influence, the liturgical day revolved around a cycle of eight services: vespers, compline, midnight office, matins, and the first, third, sixth, and ninth hours. Each included psalmody, readings, prayers, and hymns. Following the Jewish tradition, and departing from the ancient Greek and Roman, Eastern Christians marked the beginning of the day at sunset and commemorated the event with the service of vespers. In turn, matins occurred just before sunrise. By the middle Byzantine period, many monastic communities offered the Eucharist (a ninth service) nearly every day of the year.

One of the earliest Christian uses of liturgical time was the Jewish week. As early as the first century, Christians celebrated Christ's resurrection on Sunday, the day after the Jewish Sabbath. According to the *Epistle of Barnabas,* the "Lord's Day" was a day of festivity, not a day of rest like the Sabbath. The second-century text *Didache* documents the reception of the Eucharist on Sundays and details the ancient Eucharistic rite. The same text identifies Wednesday and Friday as days of fasting—the recommended practice for Eastern Christians to this day.

CODIFYING WORSHIP

Each of the eight services included a group of psalms, prayers, and hymns that were repeated throughout the year. These fixed elements were known as the Ordinary. The majority of each service, however, changed according to the date, the day of the week, a cycle of eight weeks, and the liturgical season; these elements were known as the Proper. The *Menaion* (book of months) contained the hymns and prayers specific to the matins and vespers of every day, as regulated by the *Synaxarion* calendar. Though the commemoration of saints' days is certainly older, the first complete manuscript of the *Menaion* dates to the eleventh or twelfth century. A separate book known as the *Oktoechos* (eight modes) organized a series of hymns, according to day, in an eight-week cycle. Each of the weeks in the cycle oper-

ated under a distinct musical mode, or *echos.* Like the Sunday lectionary, the *Oktoechos* begins with the Sunday after Pentecost and ends with the beginning of the Paschal season (initially it included the Lenten period as well). John of Damascus likely authored many of the hymns that constitute the *Oktoechos* in the early eighth century, but the book was completed after his death.

During the seventh and eighth centuries, Palestinian monks developed the *Triodion,* a liturgical book that incorporated the distinct hymns of the Paschal season. This book was subsequently expanded and diffused through Byzantium by the Studite monks of Constantinople. The oldest manuscripts of the *Triodion* date to the tenth century. During the fourteenth century, this material was divided into two books: the *Triodion* contained the hymns for the pre-Lenten period, Lent, and Holy Week (up to the midnight office of Holy Saturday), and the *Pentekostarion* contained the services between Pascha and the Sunday after Pentecost (All Saints' Day).

The liturgical *Typikon* brought order to the multiple calendars and cycles. Originating in the ninth or tenth century, the *Typikon* identified those elements that trumped others on days in which there was a potential for conflict. For example, if the feast of St. John Chrysostom falls on a Sunday, the *Typikon* determines, among other things, the proper Gospel reading (in this case, the one that corresponds to the Sunday lectionary rather than the one assigned to the saint's feast).

FEASTING AND FASTING

An important component of the liturgical year in the East is the regulation of feasting and fasting. Following the dual calendar system, some feasts and fasts were fixed, others were movable. The Eastern liturgical year includes twelve major feast days, in addition to Pascha, associated with the Virgin Mary (known in the East as the Theotokos, literally, "God-bearer") and Jesus Christ: Nativity of the Theotokos (8 September), Entrance of the Theotokos into the Temple (21 November), Annunciation (25 March), Dormition of the Theotokos (15 August), Christmas (25 December), Epiphany (6 January), Presentation of Christ into the Temple (2 February), Transfiguration (6 August), Elevation of the Holy Cross (14 September), Palm Sunday (Sunday before Pascha), Ascension (forty days after Pascha), and Pentecost (fifty days after Pascha). Though the classification of twelve major feast days is a later development, most of the individual feasts were in place by the end of the sixth century.

Each of the twelve is accompanied by a liturgical fore-feast *(proeortia)* and an after-feast *(metheorta),* most easily identified in the vesper and matins services. The final day of the *metheorta* was known as the *apodosis*. For example, the Dormition of the Theotokos is anticipated through hymnography on 14 August, one day before the actual feast. Reciprocally, the theme of the Dormition continues for a nine-day after-feast, with the *apodosis* falling on 23 August. The length of these fore- and after-feasts varies, depending on the commemoration (Christmas has the longest *proeortia*, Pascha the longest *metheorta*).

Fasting regulations varied, but healthy Orthodox Christians were generally expected to abstain from meat, dairy, eggs, wine, oil, and sexual activity. Preparatory fasting accompanied four festal seasons (Pascha, Christmas, the Dormition of the Theotokos, and the feast of Sts. Peter and Paul). In the case of Pascha and Christmas, these commemorations were followed by extended feasting periods that negated the Wednesday and Friday fasts. The commemoration of these feasts and especially the fasting periods that precede them are a product of liturgical development. Evidence of fasting in preparation for Pascha is quite old (an early-third-century text, *Didascalia apostolorum,* prescribes fasting during Holy Week). In the ancient church, Pascha was the customary date for baptismal initiation. Most scholars believe that the Lenten fast originated with pious Christians who, in a show of solidarity, fasted along with the catechumens who were preparing for baptism. By the fourth century, Christians were expanding that seven-day fast to forty or more. In 336, St. Athanasius of Alexandria issued a Paschal letter that prescribed a forty-day fast before the fast of Holy Week. Unlike the West, where Lent began on a Wednesday, the fully developed form of the "Great Fast" in the East began on a Monday and ran for forty consecutive days through the Friday before Palm Sunday. The intervening Saturday commemorated the raising of Lazarus; Holy Week began with vespers after sundown on Palm Sunday. Between Pascha and Pentecost, the Wednesday and Friday fast was dropped.

As in the West, 6 January was often identified with Jesus's birth. According to the Julian calendar, 25 December was the date of the winter solstice, and there appears to have been some reluctance among Christians to mark the birth of Christ on a day of pagan festivity. In the East, 25 December was first identified as the Nativity of Jesus during the late fourth century (recorded by John Chrysostom). For some easterners, the "birthday" of Christ was the beginning of his earthly ministry (i.e., his baptism by John the Baptist). By the sixth century, the Nativity and Baptism (Epiphany) were firmly established on 25 December and 6 January, respectively (the Church of Jerusalem was the last to adopt this dating). Advent developed later in the East than it did in the West. By the eleventh century, it comprised a forty-day fast in preparation for Christmas. Between Christmas and Epiphany, the Wednesday and Friday fast was negated, but 5 January, regardless of the day of the week, was a day of fasting.

As the feasts of the Dormition and Sts. Peter and Paul (29 June) grew in importance, the Eastern church developed additional fasting periods. The fortnight 1–14 August served as the preparation for the Dormition, while the duration of the apostles' fast changed according to the Paschal cycle (it began on the second Monday following Pentecost). Certain lesser feasts included a single day of strict fasting on the actual day of commemoration: the Beheading of John the Baptist (29 August) and the Elevation of the Holy Cross. Other days, such as the Annunciation and Palm Sunday, partially relaxed the typically rigorous fast of Great Lent.

Though the laity may not have understood the finer points of Orthodox theology, they would have noticed the change between liturgical seasons. In addition to the church's proscription against certain foods and sexual activity during the Lenten periods, the liturgical cycles had many other consequences. For example, the laity knelt or prostrated periodically during services. On Sundays and between Pascha and Pentecost, however, there was no kneeling. Moreover, the festal liturgy of St. John Chrysostom was not served on weekdays during Lent (a liturgy of presanctified gifts was offered instead). During the same period, the clergy wore dark vestments and the hymnography followed a more somber tone, in deference to the Passion of Christ. This would have been a sharp contrast to the bright lights, colors, and festive chanting of the Sunday services (commemorating, even during Lent, the Resurrection of Jesus Christ).

The liturgical year of the non-Chalcedonian churches was similar to that of the Byzantine with a few notable exceptions. The Armenian church celebrated both the Nativity and Epiphany on 6 January and expanded the Advent fast to fifty days. Instead of twelve major feasts, the Coptic church celebrated seven major (Annunciation, Nativity, Epiphany, Palm Sunday, Pascha, Ascension, and Pentecost), seven minor, and seven Marian. And the Jacobite church saw still greater variation. There, the liturgical year began in December and was composed of seven liturgical seasons of seven or eight Sundays (Annunciation, Nativity-Epiphany, Lent, Resurrection, Apostles, Transfiguration, and Cross).

BIBLIOGRAPHY

Carr, Ephrem, "The Liturgical Year in the Syriac Churches." *L'adattamento culturae della liturgia.* Rome: Pontificio Ateneo S. Anselmo, 1993.

Dix, Gregory. *The Shape of the Liturgy.* London: Adam and Charles Black, 1945.

Salaville, Sévérien. "La formation du calendrier liturgique byzantin d'après les recherches critiques de Mgr Ehrhard." *Ephemerides Liturgicae* 50 (1936): 312–323.

————. *An Introduction to the Study of Eastern Liturgies.* Translated by John M. T. Barton. London: Sands, 1938.

Schulz, Hans-Joachim. *The Byzantine Liturgy.* Translated by Matthew J. O'Connell. New York: Pueblo, 1986.

Taft, Robert F. *The Liturgy of the Hours in East and West: The Origins of the Divine Office and Its Meaning for Today.* Collegeville, Minn.: Liturgical Press, 1986.

————. *Liturgy in Byzantium and Beyond.* London: Variorum, 1995.

Talley, Thomas J. *The Origins of the Liturgical Year.* New York: Pueblo, 1986.

GEORGE E. DEMACOPOULOS

[See also **DMA:** Advent; Byzantine Church; Calendars and Reckoning of Time; Christmas; Easter; Feasts and Festivals, European; Holy Week; John of Damascus, St.; Lent; Liturgy, Byzantine Church; Synaxary; **Supp:** Liturgical Year, Western.]

LITURGICAL YEAR, WESTERN.

Long before conscious awareness of it existed, a Christian liturgical year is recognizable. From the earliest witnesses on, it is clear that Christians celebrated the paschal feast (in the later anglophone term, Easter) each year, with a lesser commemoration each Sunday. These celebrations provided two of the three basic elements in what was to become the liturgical year: the annual and the weekly.

ANNUAL, WEEKLY, AND FIXED COMMEMORATIONS

This apparently simple structure was complicated, however, by the fact that Easter can be calculated in several ways, none of which place it on the same calendar day each year. By the time the formula based on the calculations of Dionysius Exiguus was widely accepted—in the West, mainly by the eighth century—a whole rhythm of observances had evolved around an Easter that itself varied over a period of some five weeks. Chief among these observances was Pentecost, on the fiftieth day of Eastertide (with the Ascension coming to be commemorated on the fortieth day, always a Thursday), and the season of penitential preparation for the paschal celebration called in English Lent (in Latin, *quadragesima,* "forty," derived from the number of days the season

came to have). So as Easter can fall anywhere from 22 March (but very rarely: only eight times between 500 and 1500) to 25 April (seven times in the same period), Ash Wednesday at the beginning of Lent ranges between 5 February and 10 March, Pentecost between 10 May and 13 June. (This is the case in the Western church, not necessarily in the Eastern churches, which cannot be considered in the present article.) The week before Easter came to be seen, at least by the fourth century, as following a chronology roughly derived from the gospel accounts of Jesus's Passion: triumphal entry into Jerusalem on what was eventually called (from the detail of the children waving palm branches) Palm Sunday; the Passover meal or "Last Supper" on Thursday (widely known as Maundy Thursday, from the foot-washing ceremony by which the "new commandment," *mandatum novum,* that the disciples should love one another is expressed); and the crucifixion on Good Friday.

The third principle underlying the fully articulated liturgical year, first evident in the third century and developing rapidly by the late fourth, is commemoration on fixed days: first of martyrs, both the locally and the generally known, then of signal events in the early life of Jesus, and finally of Christian worthies venerated for a perceived holiness that seemed to qualify them as "saints" regardless of whether they had been martyred. These commemorative days developed centuries before the establishment of anything like formal rites of canonization, predominant in the West only from the second half of the twelfth century.

Individual communities kept in remembrance the dates on which members of their own faithful had been martyred and often added to these names those of more broadly known heroes, mostly having some connection with Rome, whose death days (in Christian Latin, *dies natales,* birthdays into heaven) seem to have been celebrated widely: preeminently, such figures as Peter and Paul on 29 June, John the Baptist on 24 June, the deacon Lawrence on 10 August, and Agnes on 21 January. A mid-fourth-century compilation by the anonymous Chronographer of 354 contains a list of roughly fifty martyrs with their death days; it is headed by the birthday of Christ, placed on 25 December.

From the second half of the fourth century that day came increasingly to be observed in the West (but not the East) as the feast of the Nativity of Jesus, possibly complementing a somewhat earlier observance on 6 January of several initiatory aspects of his life: his baptism, his first miracle at the wedding of Cana, and the visit of the Magi to the infant Christ—the latter becoming the primary Western focus of the feast known as Epiphany ("appearance" or "manifestation"). There also developed, in the fifth and sixth centuries, a season of expectation and reflection before the feast of Christ's "coming" *(adventus),* and therefore called Advent; this period in some places could be as long as nine weeks, but eventually it came to be standardized at roughly four—"roughly" because it was measured in Sundays before Christmas rather than as a fixed number of days. (That local saints had been venerated before the widespread adoption of the great general feasts helps to explain why many medieval calendars and service books include a *memoria,* or brief commemoration, of an obscure figure like Anastasia on Christmas day or Sabina on the feast of the Beheading of John the Baptist, 29 August.)

COMMEMORATIONS OF SAINTS AND THE VIRGIN MARY

The greatest stimulus to the proliferation of fixed saints' days that seems to be such a major feature of medieval religious life is the element referred to above, the veneration of holy persons not necessarily martyrs. Whereas opportunities for martyrdom diminished drastically after Christians ceased to be persecuted within the Roman Empire from about 312 on (save in missionary contexts like that of St. Boniface, killed by pagan Frisians on 5 June 754), there could be an open-ended number of men and women whose intercessions and, often, capacity to work miracles seemed as efficacious as those of the early Christian martyrs. The first of these "confessors" (as men of this sort came to be called as a primary omnibus category; women tended to be subsumed under the category "virgins," even if martyred) to have a widespread cultus was Martin of Tours, who died in 397 and whose death day, 11 November, soon became an important feast in many places. Others who died peaceful deaths but came to be widely commemorated include figures like Geneviève of Paris (died *ca.* 500; feast day 3 January), Gall the Irish hermit and monastic pioneer (died *ca.* 630; feast day 16 October), Pope Gregory I (died 12 March 604), and the Anglo-Saxon hermit-bishop Cuthbert (died 20 March 687). The cases of Gregory and Cuthbert show the difficulty caused by the clash of principles based on a variable Easter and fixed days; both saints' days would always fall during Lent, and Cuthbert's not infrequently during Holy Week. This overlap helps to explain a further proliferation of observances related to saints, that of secondary feasts, most often connected with translations of their bodies or at least of major relics. Thus there came to be a translation feast for Cuthbert on 4 September and one (ostensibly) for the anniversary of Gregory's ordination on the previous day.

Commemorations focused on the Virgin Mary became a significant part of the liturgical year in the late seventh century, mainly introduced into the West by popes of Eastern origin. Although a couple of strands of devotion centering on Mary at the birth of Jesus received some earlier liturgical expression—the octave day of Christmas, 1 January, was one obvious time (later kept as the Circumcision), the awaiting of his imminent birth another (there was apparently an early Spanish Marian feast on 18 December)—her main feasts are those of her Nativity (8 September), Annunciation (25 March; the announcement by the angel Gabriel that she is to become the mother of Jesus), Purification (2 February; alias the meeting with Simeon and Anna in the Temple, hence the alternative Latin title, Hypapanti, taken over directly from the Greek, *hypapante,* "meeting"), and above all her Assumption, or (earlier, and still in the East) Falling Asleep, on 15 August. From the eleventh century on there was pressure, fully successful only in the fifteenth century, for a feast of her Conception on, logically, 8 December. Other feasts of the Virgin, like those of the Visitation (2 July), Presentation (21 November), and Dolors, or Compassion (various days), reflect the expansion of Marian devotion in the later Middle Ages.

THE CIRCLE OF THE YEAR

A conscious sense of what we call the liturgical year is evident in a phrase in the headings of the oldest Roman sacramentary manuscripts that have survived, the Old Gelasian (mid-eighth century; its nucleus is probably a good deal older) and the Gregorian (early ninth century, again with older antecedents): *circulus anni,* the circle of the year. In the early Gelasian book the Mass forms for the majority of the (fixed) saints' days are in a separate section from those for most of the Sunday/Easter cycle, and this division comes to prevail in most Western service books of the High and later Middle Ages. The terms that reflect this structure are Proper of Saints (or *sanctorale*) for the saints' days and Proper of Time (or *temporale*) for the Sunday/Easter cycle, eventually standardized as beginning with the first Sunday in Advent. The development of liturgical forms specific to the Sundays after Pentecost (twenty-three to twenty-eight, depending on when Easter falls and how many Advent Sundays there are) took somewhat longer, becoming virtually universal only around the turn of the millennium; in any case, awareness of the distinct identity of, say, the fifteenth Sunday as opposed to the twenty-first was never strong. In northern Europe the popularity of Trinity Sunday, which emerged in roughly the twelfth century from being a votive occasion (i.e., of special devotion) on the octave day of Pentecost to become a full-blown feast, caused the numbering of these Sundays to be after Trinity—as in many of the cantatas of J. S. Bach in the early eighteenth century—rather than, as it remained in southern Europe, after Pentecost.

While the sanctoral cycle of the liturgical year was continually enriched by the addition of new saints (especially after papal control of canonization became the rule)—indeed, swollen to such an extent that the problem of overbalancing the liturgical year with such observances became acute in the later Middle Ages—the temporal (Sunday/Easter) cycle gained only one major celebration: the feast of Corpus Christi, on the Thursday after Trinity Sunday, which from its mid-thirteenth-century origins in Liège spread throughout Europe as a greatly popular early summer occasion. Another popular feature of the temporal cycle, much older, is that of the three weekdays before the feast of the Ascension, called Rogation Days because of the prayers ("rogations"), especially for crops, uttered then, along with other practices like "beating the bounds" of the parish. A regular punctuation of the temporal cycle was provided by the ember days (originally "Quatember" from *quattuor temporum*, "four times"): sets of Wednesdays, Fridays, and Saturdays falling within Advent, within Lent, just after Pentecost/Trinity Sunday, and in the early autumn; these were connected mainly with ordinations.

In its fullest form, the liturgical year as observed in western Europe was so complex that systems of grading became necessary to determine which observance was to be celebrated on any particular day. The tension latent in any effort to integrate an irregular Easter and all the Sundays and other occasions (like ember days) dependent on that with an ever expanding number of fixed feast days became so obvious that it was often necessary to produce an entire small book, sometimes called an ordinal or pie, to sort out the complications. One aid in this process was the grading of feasts. By the time of the printed Sarum Use missals (i.e., the usage of Salisbury cathedral, which had spread widely throughout southern England by the fifteenth century), for example, distinction was made among principal, double, minor double, inferior double, nine-lesson, and three-lesson feasts, and the permutations and combinations dictating which took precedence in cases of conflict between a temporal and a sanctoral occasion would have to be worked out afresh each year.

In sum, although the period offers no single pattern or model officially recognized as fixing *the* liturgical year, the structuring of liturgical time throughout the *circulus anni* (as distinct from the division of the day into "hours" of prayer or the distribution of psalms within a week in the daily office), in its ever increasing magnitude and complexity, plays a central part in the rhythm of life and in the dynamics of religion throughout the Western Middle Ages.

BIBLIOGRAPHY

Adam, Adolf. *The Liturgical Year: Its History and Its Meaning after the Reform of the Liturgy.* Translated by Matthew J. O'Connell. New York: Pueblo, 1981. Comprehensive but, as the title indicates, based on the post–Vatican II Roman Catholic liturgy.

Cheney, C. R. *A Handbook of Dates for Students of British History.* Revised by Michael Jones. Cambridge, U.K.: Cambridge University Press, 2000. Includes tables showing how the liturgical year is laid out for each date on which Easter can fall.

Dalmais, Irénée Henri, Pierre Jounel, and Aimé Georges Martimort. *The Liturgy and Time.* Translated by Matthew J. O'Connell. Volume 4: *The Church at Prayer: An Introduction to the Liturgy,* edited by A. G. Martimort et al. Collegeville, Minn.: Liturgical Press, 1986. Highly scholarly but, like Adam (above), post–Vatican II in approach.

Dix, Gregory. *The Shape of the Liturgy.* 2d ed. London: Dacre Press, Adam and Charles Black, 1945. Pages 303–396 of this older classic are devoted to "The Sanctification of Time," mostly premedieval.

Kellner, K. A. Heinrich. *Heortology: A History of Christian Festivals from Their Origin to the Present Day.* Translated by a priest of the diocese of Westminster. London: Kegan Paul, 1908. Packed with well-organized, though sometimes outdated, information about individual feasts.

Pfaff, Richard W. *New Liturgical Feasts in Later Medieval England.* Oxford: Clarendon Press, 1970. On feasts of Christ and Mary, not of individual saints.

———. "Telling Liturgical Times in the Middle Ages." In *Procession, Performance, Liturgy and Ritual.* Edited by Nancy van Deusen. Leiden, Netherlands: Brill. Forthcoming.

Talley, Thomas J. *The Origins of the Liturgical Year.* 2d ed. Collegeville, Minn.: Liturgical Press, 1991. The best treatment through about the fifth century.

RICHARD W. PFAFF

[See also **DMA:** Calendars and Reckoning of Time; Christmas; Corpus Christi, Feast of; Easter; Holy Week; Lent; Marian Feasts; Pentecost; Sacramentary; **Supp:** Liturgical Year, Eastern.]

LOUIS IV THE BAVARIAN, EMPEROR

(1282–1347), was the son of Louis II of Upper Bavaria and Mechthild of Habsburg. He was raised and educated in the Habsburg court, but little else is known about his childhood. When Emperor Henry VII died in 1314, the Luxembourg party elected Louis as his successor, but civil war erupted when the supporters of Frederick the Fair, the ruler of Austria, contested his claim to the throne. The struggle lasted until 1322, when Louis won a decisive victory at the Battle of Mühldorf.

Louis spent most of his reign in conflict with the papacy. The Avignon pope John XXII feared that the king had political ambitions in Italy and used every means at his disposal to undermine his authority. He refused to acknowledge Louis's royal title, scornfully dubbed him "the Bavarian," and finally excommunicated him in 1324, stripping him of his dukedom and placing the entire German nation under interdict. Louis responded by charging the pope with heresy, which earned him the support of the Franciscan spirituals, whose doctrine of poverty made them enemies of what they considered the decadent Avignon papacy. He aroused the pope's wrath by receiving at his court Marsilius of Padua, whose treatise *Defensor pacis* (Defender of the peace) denied papal claims of authority over temporal rulers and argued that the papacy should be subject to the will of the people and the secular representatives who act on their authority.

Louis then marched on Rome, where he was crowned emperor in January 1328 by an antipapal faction. John XXII, remaining in Avignon, did not take part in the ceremony and later nullified the coronation. In response, Louis declared the pope deposed and elected in his place the Franciscan Peter of Corvaro as Pope Nicholas V, but the king and his antipope were soon expelled from the city. In 1330 Louis returned to Germany with little to show for the efforts of his Italian campaign. John XXII resumed his struggle against the excommunicated king but found little support among the clergy and towns of Germany.

In 1338 the German electors convened at Rhens in a bid for political stability and autonomy after two decades of papal interference. They declared that a duly elected king had sovereign rights without the need for papal confirmation. Their proclamation severely limited the power of the popes to intervene in German politics. The same electors who sought to strengthen the legal autonomy of the king also played a role in his downfall. Disaffection for Louis's policies was on the rise in Germany. The Luxembourgs pressed the claim of Charles IV of Bohemia, who had the support of Pope Clement VI. In 1346 the electors removed Louis from the throne and duly elected Charles king of the Germans. Shortly thereafter, Charles sided with the French king Philip VI against the invading English, who defeated them at Crécy, wounding Charles and killing his father, John of Bohemia. Louis was unable to take advantage of his rival's weakness to reclaim his crown. He died the following summer from a heart attack.

BIBLIOGRAPHY

Benker, Gertrud. *Ludwig der Bayer: Ein Wittelbacher auf dem Kaiserthron, 1282–1347.* Munich: Verlag Callway, 1980.

Huber, Alexander. *Das Verhältnis Ludwigs des Bayern zu den Erzkanzlern von Mainz, Köln und Trier (1314–1347).* Kallmünz über Regensburg, Germany: Verlag Michael Lassleben, 1983.

Stengel, Edmund E. *Avignon und Rhens: Forschungen zur Geschichte des Kampfes um das Recht am Reich in der ersten Hälfte des 14. Jahrhunderts.* Weimar, Germany: Hermann Böhlaus Nachfolger, 1930.

SCOTT G. BRUCE

[See also **DMA:** *Defensor Pacis;* Germany: 1254–1493; Germany: Electors; Habsburg Dynasty; John XXII, Pope.]

LOVE AND COURTSHIP. To speak of love and courtship in the Middle Ages is, in many cases, to describe at least two separate sets of necessities, experiential and textual. For the experience of love and courtship there is a certain amount of anecdotal evidence that, inevitably, must be contextualized. For the literary emergence and use of the language of desire there is a literature that came to define the very nature of the courtly self.

THE EXPERIENCE OF LOVE AND COURTSHIP

Unmarried love. People in the Middle Ages certainly fell in love and grew to love each other, but romantic love was more often seen as dangerously irrational and thus as personally and socially disruptive. Near the end of book 6 of his *Confessions,* St. Augustine recounts his grief when his concubine of many years, who had borne him a son, was torn from him. At that time, Augustine was a man of thirty and living and teaching in Italy. His mother, Monica, came to him from their home in Africa and, wishing to arrange a marriage for him with a young and suitable girl, asked that his concubine be sent away. Speaking of this woman, he writes, "My heart, to which she adhered, was violently dragged away, cut and wounded and bloody." The passage is, however, more than a statement of past sorrow; it is also a deeply ambivalent account of feelings that Augustine links to irrationality. After describing his grief, Augustine suggests its sexual origin by saying that, while waiting for his fiancée to grow to marriageable age, he took another concubine to satisfy his lust. Moreover, his use of *vulneratum* (wounded) to describe his heart echoes Vergil's use of *vulnus* (wound) as a sign for Dido's fatal passion for Aeneas in the *Aeneid,* a text Augustine describes himself as reading with great pleasure as a schoolboy. Even as he admits his emotional attachment to this unnamed woman with whom he had enjoyed a stable relationship for fourteen years, he establishes a link between his wounded and bleeding heart and his ignoble lust, which impelled

Courtship. *This ivory mirror case, a seemingly innocent account of courtly petition, offers both a witty take on medieval social convention (note the ladies feigning reluctance and the rabbit about to jump upon another rabbit) and a sophisticated reading of love in the world. (Compare p. 244.)* VICTORIA AND ALBERT MUSEUM, LONDON/ART RESOURCE, NY. REPRODUCED BY PERMISSION.

him to find her replacement. His expectation that Monica will "court" for him, will provide for him a Christian bride, separates his experience of sexual desire and emotional attachment from the communal experience of legal marriage.

In the second decade of the twelfth century, Abelard, the famous and controversial teacher and logician in the cloister school of Notre Dame in Paris, became passionately involved with Heloise, the young niece of Fulbert, one of the canons of the cathedral. In his *Historia calamitatum* (History of my calamities), he describes himself as setting out to seduce her. He arranged to live in Fulbert's house and to tutor Heloise, who was already accomplished and learned beyond her sex. According to Abelard's account, the two of them abandoned themselves to love: "Her studies allowed us to withdraw in private, as love desired, and then with our books open before us, more words of love than of our reading passed between us, and more kissing than teaching." Heloise's pregnancy, her refusal to ruin his career as a philosopher by accepting his offer of an open marriage, their secret marriage, and his subsequent castration by Fulbert's men Abelard describes as the results of this irrational passion. Heloise, however, was more than literate; she was eloquent, and the letters they exchanged over fifteen years after taking monastic vows testify to Heloise's continuing passionate love for Abelard. In her first letter to Abelard, she writes, "God knows I never sought anything in you except yourself; I wanted simply you, nothing of yours." After her third letter, the erotic intimacy of this address disappears, and their subsequent letters concern the monastic and devotional life. Nonetheless, to the end, their correspondence maintains a regard for their mutual sense of intellectual and personal integrity. When Abelard died, Peter the Venerable, the abbot of Cluny, wrote Heloise a personal letter, comforting her by telling her that God now cherished Abelard, saving him so that he could be restored to her at the Last Day.

In canto 5 of the *Inferno,* in the second circle, the realm of the lustful, Dante allows Francesca da Rimini to tell the story of her adulterous affair with her brother-in-law Paolo:

> Love, which is quickly kindled in a gentle heart, seized this one for the fair form that was taken from me. . . . Love, which absolves no loved one from loving, seized me so strongly with delight in him, that, as you see, it does not leave me even now. Love brought us to one death.

Like that of Abelard and Heloise, their "courtship" is furthered by their literacy. Francesca describes them as reading together the romance of Lancelot; in her account, the book serves as their go-between.

Courtship and marriage. The marital affairs of the fourteenth-century Joan of Kent, the so-called Fair Maid, also provide a window into the processes of late medieval love and courtship. Famous for her beauty and stylishness, Joan, who had spent most of her childhood under the guardianship of Edward III's queen, Philippa, was expected to be married off appropriately. However, in 1340, when she was twelve, she was wooed secretly by Thomas Holland, who was some years older and already a devoted soldier to the crown. Privately but before witnesses, the two exchanged vows in which they took one another as man and wife, and they apparently consummated the marriage. In the eyes of the church, the clandestine procedure was frowned upon but common and certainly valid. Holland then went off to war, and in that same year Joan was married off to William Montague, son and heir to the earl of Salisbury, who, like Joan, was twelve. Some seven years later, Thomas Holland, who had grown wealthy from his success in war, reclaimed his wife, presenting his case before the papal curia. Joan, sequestered by the earl of Salisbury, was prevented from testifying. Despite delays, in late 1349 Joan was restored to Holland; she thereafter bore him six children. Sir Thomas died in 1360, when Joan was thirty-two. A year later, without consulting Edward III, Edward the Black Prince and Joan, who had become the countess of Kent in 1352 after both of her brothers had died, exchanged private vows of marriage. This second clandestine marriage necessitated more petitions to the curia, since the two were cousins. The prince would not give up Joan, and the king negotiated with the pope for a dispensation, ending in a public wedding. Joan died in 1385 and, in her will, directed that her body be laid by that of her first husband, Thomas Holland.

In the last half of the fifteenth century, the letters of the East Anglian Paston family record some of the hazards and strategies of love and courtship. In March 1467, John II advised his younger brother John III in the techniques of wooing, telling him to show good will to the girl, "byndyng hyr to kepe it secret . . . thys ye kannot do with owt som comfort of hyr in no wyse; and ber yor selfe as lowly to the moder as ye lyst, but to the mayde not to lowly, ner that ye be to gladde to spede nor to sory to fayle." Though this suit failed, ten years later John III found success in courtship with Margery Brews, whose kinswoman wrote him that he had "made hyr suche advokett for yowe, that I may never hafe rest nyght ner day, for callyng and cryeing upon to brynge the saide mater to effecte." After "the matter" was brought to effect, Margery Brews wrote to John III, "Ryght reverent and wurschypfull, and my ryght wele-beloved Voluntyne, I recomande me unto yowe, ffull hertely, desyryng to here of yowr welefare." Shortly thereafter, she again wrote him, telling him that her father would part with no more than "Cli. and 1 marke, whech is ryght far fro the acomplyshment of yowr desire. Wherfore, yf that ye cowde be content with that good, and my por persone, I wold be the meryest mayden on grounde," going on to tell him that he was more than free to choose. He did, and they seem to have had a happy and companionate marriage.

Love and courtship did not run as smoothly for another Margery, the sister of John II and John III. In 1468 she formed an attachment with Richard Calle, who was employed by the family as its agent and was thus beneath her in status. Her mother, Margaret, kept her away from Calle, but that did not prevent a letter from reaching her. Calle wrote, "Myn owne lady and mastres, and be for God very trewe wyff, I with herte full sorowefull recomaunde me unto you . . . consederyng the gret bonde of matrymonye that is made be twix us, and also the greete love that hath be, and as I truste yet is, be twix us, and as on my parte never gretter." Despite the pressure to renounce her marriage, Margery persisted, testifying before the bishop that she considered herself "bound." Her mother was adamant, writing John II, "wan I hard sey what her demenyng was, I schargyd my servaunts that sche xuld not be reseyved in my hows."

Marriage contracts. Though the above examples suggest that love or passion could play a part in courtship, which might or might not result in marriage, such a progression—inspired by personal attraction—was certainly not the norm. The language to be found in medieval contracts of betrothal is not the language of love but the language of exchange or the language of consanguinity. Love was not normally the basis for marriage but a quality of affection that might develop after marriage. In the early Middle Ages, endogamy was common and accepted; thus children were frequently betrothed to cousins. If not, marriages that broadened family connections were made for young people. When men chose for themselves they more often looked for advantageous connections or wealth or, as did Francesco di Marco Datini, for a bride whose youth and large family augured fruitfulness.

Although the church was increasingly concerned with insisting on the permanence and exclusivity of marriage, there were no carefully worked-out canon laws on the formation of marriage until the 1150s, when Gratian's *Decretum* and Peter Lombard's *Sententiae in IV libris distinctae* became available. Where previously marriage had been the provenance of family custom and was only moderately regulated by the church, now the church began to scrutinize marriage, beginning with the issue of the consent of both parties. As Michael M. Sheehan argues, this scrutiny was the beginning of a long and slow shift in power: in *Causa* 31, *questio* 2 of the *Decretum,* Gratian wrote, "A woman may not be compelled to marry a man," later saying, "A father's oath cannot compel a girl to marry one to whom she has never assented," and "Where there is to be union of bodies there ought to be union of spirits and therefore no unwilling person is to be joined to another." In the late twelfth century, Pope Alexander III synthesized the canon law of the formation of marriage for church courts, which, all over Europe, had jurisdiction over suits pertaining to marriage and betrothal. Each of these rules emphasized the consent of both parties, who must be over the minimum age of consent and not too closely related to one another. About 1200, confessors' manuals that incorporated these new views began to appear, specifying the questions the priest should ask of the couple before the marriage was celebrated. By its efforts to bring marriage rituals within the sphere of the clergy, the church slowly effected a shift in control from family and lord to society and, equally slowly, granted western European women the beginnings of control in the rights of refusal they might exercise.

The above account certainly does not describe all conditions and countries. In remote areas of Europe, the church's teachings about marriage seem not to have made any difference, and women had no say over their disposal. For Jewish girls, the situation was different: at twelve and a half they were considered legally independent and theoretically could negotiate their own marriage contracts, although a girl of that age would likely be guided by her family's choice, especially since she would not have moved much beyond a circle of family members and close friends. In Islam, a woman could not dispose of herself. There is some evidence that women in Anglo-Saxon England had some say in marriage partners. One marriage contract, cited by Christine Fell, reads, "Here is declared in this document the agreement which Godewine made with Brihtric when he wooed his daughter. In the first place he gave her a pound's weight of gold, to induce her to accept his suit, and he granted her the estate at Street with all that belongs to it, and 150 acres at Burmarsh and in addition 30 oxen and 20 cows and 10 horses and 10 slaves" (*Women in Anglo-Saxon England,* p. 58). Brihtric's daughter may well have been wooed with goods, but her consent seems to have been necessary.

This is not, however, to say that young girls were free to move about society or to engage in behavior that might entice a courting lover. Both women and girls lived existences regulated by domestic duties, by social and religious codes, and by the walls, doors, and grilles of contemporary architecture. As a Genoan poet, quoted by Georges Duby in *A History of Private Life,* notes, they stood, framed by windows and porches, looking upon the festive ceremonies their worlds provided. If they were also there to be seen, the chaperoned objects of admiring gazes, their husbands would be found for them by their families. Though young people in the Middle Ages had many social, familial, and religious restrictions upon their behavior and at no time would have conceived of themselves as autonomous, the gradual process by which women acquired power and wealth inevitably affected the power they perceived themselves to have in matters of love and courtship. Moreover, in the business of marriage women of upper and middling degrees were trained in the gentle arts. In the later Middle Ages, part of that training involved literacy, even for merchants' daughters. As we have seen, letters can afford private space and occasionally give evidence of private life.

THE LITERATURE OF LOVE

Love as a literary language. To speak of love and courtship is also to speak of literary texts, of the language that the men and women of the Middle Ages used to describe and analyze key aspects of individual and social experience. For reasons that cannot be ascertained—perhaps because of the church's insistence upon consent as a prerequisite for marriage, or because of the increasing importance of courts as centers of power and civilization, or because of a growing interest in the psychology of ethical behavior, or because of the growing importance of Platonic thought and Latin humanism in the schools, or because of the influence of Islamic culture, with its well-developed traditions of love poetry, in southern Mediterranean countries—during the twelfth century medieval writers of all sorts began to focus upon love. More important, they used the language of love as a discourse that enabled them to explore issues of identity, cognition, subjectivity, and status, as well as to seek to understand the psychology of desire. Love poetry does not begin in the twelfth century, but about this time love and courtship became far more than increasingly popular literary subjects.

The language of desire provided both courtiers and churchmen with a lexicon that could be used with remarkable flexibility, despite its many rhetorical flourishes and formal requirements. The last half of the twelfth century saw the emergence of troubadour lyric poetry in Occitania (or Languedoc; the region of southern France between the Pyrenees and the Rhône) and of the chivalric romance in northern France. The twelfth century was also the period when Bernard of Clairvaux, Richard of St. Victor, Alan of Lille, and Philip of Harvengt produced treatments of the Song of Solomon, reading its accounts of erotic pursuit and satisfaction as allegorical depictions of the love between God and the soul or between Christ and Mary. The Song of Solomon had been allegorized previously, and these twelfth-century exegetes followed the steps of both St. Augustine and St. Gregory the Great, who had drawn upon the work of earlier Christian and Jewish interpreters in their treatments of the book. Nonetheless, their scrutiny of the very nature of love, which can also be described as a scrutiny of the psychology of love, employed a set of terms that was likewise used by vernacular writers to describe more mundane tactics of pursuit. Though a strong lyric tradition in medieval Latin literature played with the stances and topoi of love and courtship, the power to shape increasingly belonged to the vernacular, the language of women and men—and of the princely patrons of literature.

Whereas in the late nineteenth and early twentieth centuries scholars too often accepted the language of the medieval troubadours as literal and personal, more recently scholars have focused on its formality and sophistication and upon the ways in which love poems can be seen as elaborately finished social gestures. Both formal and cultural approaches are grounded in the recognition that the lyrics Occitania bequeathed to the West reflect a cultural world stretching from Catalonia to Provence, a world where feudal ties were not as strictly formulated as in northern France, a world where there were women of great political power, and a world where there was a good deal of cross-fertilization between Christian and Hispano-Arabic courts. Moreover, the troubadours of the Midi, like the lords of the Midi, traveled, visiting courts in northern France and Italy and maintaining ties with the Christian courts in the Middle East that had been established during the early Crusades. Love, as it was articulated by the men and women who wrote the poems of urban and urbane Occitania, cannot be separated from its social milieu, where these poems would have been experienced as songs that echoed and built upon the poems of other "makers." It is a poetry grounded in a system of patronage, a social relationship between "lover" or poet and a lady or a lord who is distinct from him in degree.

The language of love in the Middle Ages was not a static lexicon but was expanded and reformulated from the twelfth to the fifteenth centuries in ways that suggest changing social and political conditions. Medieval lyric poetry, much of which was focused upon the subject of love and courtship, at once suggests the shifting hierarchical relationships within medieval courts at various times and places and the shifts in focus to be found in centers of learning throughout Europe. For example, relatively early Latin poets like Alan of Lille in the philosophical *De planctu naturae* (The complaint of nature; 1160–1175) are also interested in the language used by courtly poets, who explored issues of learning, class, and gender by using the language of amorous petition. When it was translated into thirteenth-century Italy, the formal language of courtly desire employed by the troubadours and the trobairitz (women troubadours) was augmented by intellectual changes like the rediscovery of Aristotle, by spiritual trends like mendicant spirituality, and by social factors like the aspirations of an emerging bourgeoisie. The Italian poetry of desire, which includes, by then, conventional play with language and subject positions, was further shaped by later writers like Dante, Petrarch, and Boccaccio into spiritual autobiographies for which frustrated earthly love served as the beginning of a longer, spiritual journey. A passion originally limited by the strictures of carnality became limitless and beneficent once transformed into spiritual love. The idea that love could ennoble the lover is also apparent in the German minnesong, which imitated its French models thematically, formally, and musically. In the West, the poetry of love was thus firmly linked to a courtly ideal, which was also a social ideal, to forms of entertainment associated with the aristocracy, and hence to the ideals of the noble life as they were worked out in each time and place.

The subject of love was not confined to the lyric but was also fundamental to the romance, which, like troubadour poetry, began to appear in the twelfth century in France. Both the *romans antiques* (the *Enéas,* the *Roman de Troie,* and the *Roman de Thèbes*) and the Arthurian romances of Chrétien de Troyes, associated with the courts of Marie of Champagne and Philip, count of Flanders, belong to the twelfth century. The *romans antiques* and possibly Chrétien's *Érec and Énide* can be linked to the court of Henry II of England, as can the *lais* of Marie de France, who also scrutinized the courtly life through the lens of love. All of these writers explore issues of identity—nobility, chivalry, spirituality, gender—by means of sexuality and love and their pursuits. The romances, in general, do not give women the voicing that can be found in the poems of the trobairitz, the twelfth-century women who engaged with the technicalities and play of the Provençal *canso* and *tenso,* the love poem and the debate poem. However, Marie de France in her *lais* not only explores courtliness, as expressed through the contradictions and restrictions of love, but also uses women as subjects as often as she uses men. As these writers also make clear, though love can ennoble, it can also destroy. What is therefore explored is the relationship between passion and behavior, the threatened abandonment of selfhood in passion, and the relationship between the self and the bounds set by community. As a literary phenomenon, the literature of love and courtship provides occasion for debate about self-consciousness and about the tensions between rational and irrational faculties that are highlighted by love.

The classical source for such scrutinies of love was Ovid, who wrote for a sophisticated Roman audience willing to follow his elegant and frequently obscene forays into the vagaries of human motivation and rationalization, but whose work became the mainstay of medieval grammar schooling, where it was taught for its rhetorical and ethical lessons. The Ovidian language of desire, in all its worldly formalism, play, and ambiguity, became the language of the medieval schools and of monastic culture. It also became the dominant voice in the discourse of love to which belong works like Andreas Capellanus's *De amore,* Guillaume de Lorris and Jean de Meun's *Roman de la Rose,* and Juan Ruiz's *Libro de buen amor,* and it informed the works of fourteenth-century poets like Geoffrey Chaucer, John Gower, Guillaume de Machaut, Eustache Deschamps, and, at the end of the

medieval period, François Villon. By situating the lover within a set of social codes or a philosophical frame of reference, these authors explored the nature of desire as the occasion for a broader inquiry into individual psychology, contemporary mores, or social institutions. The provocative appeal of medieval Ovidianism came to a point in Paris in the period 1401–1403, when Jean de Meun's *Roman* became the subject of intense debate between Jean Gerson and Christine de Pizan, on the one hand, and Pierre and Gontier Col and Jean de Montreuil, on the other. Again, the subject of love and courtship was the occasion for a broader debate, for at stake were texts themselves and the methodology of textual interpretation. This is a debate that continues today, as witnessed by the work of scholars like John V. Fleming and A. J. Minnis. Throughout her participation in this debate, Christine de Pizan insisted upon linking interpretation to gender, a position that is central to her discussion of love and courtship throughout her works.

The language of love in court and church. The classical discourse of erotic desire and petition, combined with the Ciceronian language of friendship, also became the language of medieval courtship, a language used by both churchmen and courtiers to express commitment and nobility. The classical learning protected and nurtured in the cathedral schools of France and Germany during the early Middle Ages was used as a means of transmitting the necessities of the noble life—the literacy, the manners, and the eloquence—that were considered fundamental for those who would determine the shape of the intertwined institutions of state and church. Letters between churchmen and descriptions of early education employ or emphasize the language of love, for love was seen as corrective and ennobling, as drawing men or boys away from boorishness and toward virtue and virtuous behavior. The language used is erotic, but it is also deliberately classical and elegantly ambiguous. While John Boswell argued that what appear passionate letters and poems of friendship between men and from masters to students are evidence for a homoerotic culture during the eleventh century, Stephen Jaeger and Michael Clanchy have insisted that these texts use what are formal tropes to describe the pleasurable connections between love and virtue. The language of love was also used to construct relations of patronage. Peter the Venerable and Bernard of Clairvaux both employed the language of spiritual friendship in addressing those to whom they were bound. As Heloise's spiritual adviser after the death of Abelard, Peter the Venerable wrote to her, "I have saved a place especially for you in the innermost recesses of my heart." Clanchy quotes a portion of one of Bernard's letters to Countess Ermengard of Brittany, a benefactor of Clairvaux and, like Heloise, an aristocratic nun: "I wish I could find words to express what I feel towards you." Similarly, the language of feudal relations of all sorts was conventionally the language of lovers. The rhetoric of a love that conferred honor upon its practitioners was used to describe hierarchically conceived relationships between teacher and schoolboy, confessor and nun, patron and monk, prince and vassal, God and soul, lady and lover.

Because virtue is ennobling, virtuous love was perceived as having a social function, a function likewise integral to the courtly romance, which makes the terms of classical nobility, or courtesy, available to the lay nobility. The connections between courtly literature and courtly culture are less reflective than active, for authors like Chrétien, Gottfried von Strassburg, Wolfram von Eschenbach, Hartmann von Aue, and Marie de France, as well as rulers such as Otto I and Otto III of Germany and Henry II of England, were actively engaged in creating worlds whose systems of social and pedagogic control translated into the common tongue classical ideals of authority and order. As with the songs of the troubadours, some of the pleasure of the courtly chivalric romance was social and performative. Moreover, all of these works prompt questions about social codes, individual morality, order, and intent and thus suggest the degree of communal self-consciousness in which they are grounded. Poets may have "belonged" to courts and to noble patrons, but they were nonetheless capable of quizzing the very feudal hierarchies that also defined the love relationships about which they wrote. Chrétien's description of Lancelot's ignoble behavior in Guenevere's service or Érec's difficulties in reconciling his love with his chivalric identity cannot but also raise issues of power and abjection all too pertinent to a courtier's service of a haughty lord. Marie de France's *lai Laüstic* juxtaposes the feminine and private to the masculine and public and juxtaposes sentiment to a brutal disregard for emotion. Marie, like other courtly authors, contextualizes love and courtship within a world of exigencies, thus creating a text whose social effect is a part of its function. Love gave her the language she needed to pose problems relating to the courtly and feudal life.

In the mystic love poetry of the thirteenth-century Beguines—women who pursued lives of chastity, poverty, and religious devotion outside of an approved religious order—the courtly language of ennobling desire was joined with the monastic language of the search for God through love. Hadewijch of Brabant, Mechthild von Magdeburg, and Marguerite Porete, in particular, adapted and expanded the performative subjectivity of

the courtly, loving self, the sexual fantasy and frequently daring language of amorous address, and the role-playing and sometimes violent, passionate longing of the loving subject. Barbara Newman's juxtaposition of Tristan, the secular lover, to Hadewijch, the spiritual lover, points up the use of a common tongue to express a preoccupation with the effects of love upon the desiring self. Gottfried von Strassburg's Tristan can avow, "Another world I have in mind, which together in one heart bears its bittersweet, its joyous grief; its heart's joy, its longing's woe, its joyous life, its painful death, its joyous death, its painful life. To this life let my life be given: this world I will make my world, to be lost or blessed with it." Tristan's description of love as self-annihilating is matched by Hadewijch's account of how the loving soul is subsumed into Christ: "She is nailed so fast to the cross with the hammer of mighty love that all creatures cannot call her back. . . . Her body is killed in living love, while her spirit is exalted above all human senses . . . She hangs high in the sweet air of the holy Spirit, in the everlasting sun of the living Godhead, on the cross of high love, until all that is earthly has withered away in her."

The discourse of passionate love—whether it describes erotic desire, affection between men, political relationships between vassal and lord, patronal bonds between poet and lord or lady, or love between the soul and Christ—concerns power and powerlessness, the death of one self and the creation of another, the willed willlessness that, for good or ill, is transformative.

BIBLIOGRAPHY

PRIMARY WORKS

Augustine. *Confessions.* Commentary by James J. O'Donnell. Oxford: Oxford University Press, 1992.

Bruckner, Matilda Tomaryn, Laurie Shepard, and Sarah White. *Songs of the Women Troubadours.* New York: Garland, 1995.

Dante Alighieri. *The Divine Comedy.* Translated with commentary by Charles S. Singleton. 6 vols. Princeton, N.J.: Princeton University Press, 1970.

Gairdner, J., ed. *The Paston Letters, 1422–1509.* 6 vols. 1904. Reprint, New York: AMS, 1965.

Origo, Iris. *The Merchant of Prato, Francesco di Marco Datini.* New York: Knopf, 1957.

Radice, Betty, trans. *The Letters of Abelard and Heloise.* Harmondsworth, U.K.: Penguin, 1981.

SECONDARY WORKS

Ashtiany, Julia, T. M. Johnstone, J. D. Latham, R. B. Serjeant, and G. R. Smith. *Abbasid Belles-Lettres.* Cambridge, U.K.: Cambridge University Press, 1990.

Bond, Gerald A. *The Loving Subject: Desire, Eloquence, and Power in Romanesque France.* Philadelphia: University of Pennsylvania Press, 1995.

Boswell, John. *Christianity, Social Tolerance, and Homosexuality: Gay People in Western Europe from the Beginning of the Christian Era to the Fourteenth Century.* Chicago: University of Chicago Press, 1980.

Bumke, Joachim. *Courtly Culture: Literature and High Society in the High Middle Ages.* Translated by Thomas Dunlap. Berkeley: University of California Press, 1991.

Cheyette, Fredric L. *Ermengard of Narbonne and the World of the Troubadours.* Ithaca, N.Y.: Cornell University Press, 2001.

Clanchy, M. T. *Abelard, a Medieval Life.* Oxford: Blackwell, 1999.

Donahue, Charles, Jr. "The Canon Law on the Formation of Marriage and Social Practice in the Later Middle Ages." *Journal of Family History* 8 (1983): 144–158.

Dronke, Peter. *Medieval Latin and the Rise of European Love-Lyric.* 2d ed. 2 vols. Oxford: Clarendon Press, 1968.

Duby, Georges. *Love and Marriage in the Middle Ages.* Translated by Jane Dunnett. Chicago: University of Chicago Press, 1994.

———, ed. *Revelations of the Medieval World.* Translated by Arthur Goldhammer. Volume 2 of *A History of Private Life.* Edited by Philippe Ariès and Georges Duby. Cambridge, Mass.: Belknap Press, 1988.

Fell, Christine E., Cecily Clark, and Elizabeth Williams. *Women in Anglo-Saxon England and the Impact of 1066.* Bloomington: Indiana University Press, 1984.

Fleming, John V. *Reason and the Lover.* Princeton, N.J.: Princeton University Press, 1984.

Frank, Roberta. "Marriage in Twelfth- and Thirteenth-Century Iceland." *Viator* 4 (1973): 473–484.

Gaunt, Simon. *Gender and Genre in Medieval French Literature.* Cambridge, U.K.: Cambridge University Press, 1995.

Goitein, S. D. *Mediterranean Society: The Jewish Communities of the Arab World as Portrayed in the Documents of Cairo Geniza.* 6 vols. Berkeley: University of California Press, 1967–1993.

Harvey, Ruth. "Courtly Culture in Medieval Occitania." In *The Troubadours.* Edited by Simon Gaunt and Sarah Kay. Cambridge, U.K.: Cambridge University Press, 1999.

Jaeger, C. Stephen. *The Origins of Courtliness: Civilizing Trends and the Formation of Courtly Ideals, 939–1210.* Philadelphia: University of Pennsylvania Press, 1985.

———. *Ennobling Love: In Search of a Lost Sensibility.* Philadelphia: University of Pennsylvania Press, 1999.

Kelly, Henry Ansgar. *Love and Marriage in the Age of Chaucer.* Ithaca, N.Y.: Cornell University Press, 1975.

Kolve, V. A. "Ganymede/*Son of Getron*: Medieval Monasticism and the Drama of Same-Sex Desire." *Speculum* 73 (1998): 1014–1067.

Krueger, Roberta L., ed. *The Cambridge Companion to Medieval Romance.* Cambridge, U.K.: Cambridge University Press, 2000.

Mersami, Julie Scott. *Medieval Persian Court Poetry.* Princeton, N.J.: Princeton University Press, 1987.

Minnis, A. J. *Magister Amoris: The "Roman de la Rose" and Vernacular Hermeneutics.* Oxford: Oxford University Press, 2001.

Newman, Barbara. *From Virile Woman to WomanChrist.* Philadelphia: University of Pennsylvania Press, 1995.

Paden, William D., ed. *Medieval Lyric.* Urbana: University of Illinois Press, 2000.

Scaglione, Aldo D. *Knights at Court: Courtliness, Chivalry, and Courtesy from Ottonian Germany to the Italian Renaissance.* Berkeley: University of California Press, 1991.

Sheehan, Michael M. "Choice of Marriage Partner in the Middle Ages: Development and Mode of Application of a Theory of Marriage." *Studies in Medieval and Renaissance History* 1 (1978): 1–34.

Van Deusen, Nancy, ed. *The Cultural Milieu of the Troubadours and Trouvères.* Ottawa: Institute of Mediaeval Music, 1994.

Veyne, Paul, ed. *From Pagan Rome to Byzantium.* Translated by Arthur Goldhammer. Volume 1 of *A History of Private Life.* Edited by Philippe Ariès and Georges Duby. Cambridge, Mass.: Belknap Press, 1987.

Wentersdorf, Karl P. "The Clandestine Marriages of the Fair Maid of Kent." *Journal of Medieval Studies* 5 (1979): 203–231.

LYNN STALEY

[See also **DMA:** Capellanus, Andreas; Chrétien de Troyes; Christine de Pizan; Courtly Love; Family, Western European; Marie de France; Minnesingers; Ovid in the Middle Ages; Paston Letters; Provençal Literature; *Roman de la Rose;* Troubadour, Trouvère; **Supp:** Sexuality.]

LUND. The present-day city of Lund is located in southern Sweden, in the province of Skåne and northeast of Malmö. The medieval limits of Denmark and Sweden do not conform to the modern boundaries, and medieval Lund was in the lands of the Danish crown. Lund itself was founded about 1020 by the Danish king, Cnut I the Great. About 1060, a quarter century after Cnut's death, the city became a bishopric. The year 1103 was the occasion of the elevation of the see to an archbishopric. Its metropolitan status was also established that year over the whole Danish church *(metropolis Daniae),* and considering the size of the Danish empire about this time, the common scholarly designation of Lund as the primatial see of "all Scandinavia" is accurate, even if the language is anachronistic.

A cathedral church must have existed before the present cathedral was built, and it is possible that a building campaign as early as 1080 should be considered the initial phase of the present-day structure. But most architectural historians prefer a later date for the commencement of the existing basilica—1104 or even 1123. Archbishop Eskil, who was consecrated in 1137 and who served in Lund to a great age (until 1178; he died in 1181), dedicated the church in 1145. In touch with powerful and influential figures like Pope Alexander III and Bernard of Clairvaux, Eskil and his successor Ab-

Lund Cathedral. *This Romanesque cathedral, built in what is sometimes called the Italian style, for its four-corned towers, was one of the few churches in Lund to survive the Lutheran Reformation in the 16th century.* ANTHONY SCIBILIA/ART RESOURCE, NY. REPRODUCED BY PERMISSION.

salon (to 1201) helped make Lund and Denmark in general an integral part of Christendom. The archbishop's cathedral church occasionally served as the Danish coronation church, and in 1387 Margaret I was proclaimed queen of Denmark in the basilica.

The city grew extensively in the twelfth and thirteenth centuries, becoming a major center of international trade and of religious life. According to the best estimate, at the height of its population in the early fourteenth century there were twenty-two churches and four abbeys in and around Lund (by another count, twenty-one churches and six abbeys). Of these, almost none, except the three-aisled Romanesque cathedral in what is sometimes called the Italian (or Italian-Byzantine) style, with its four-cornered towers, substantially survived the Lutheran Reformation, and even it was extensively restored and altered in the sixteenth century and again in the nineteenth. The identity of its Italian (Lombard) builders is known: the masters Comacini, who worked under the supervision of Master Donatus of Fiesole. Other medieval artifacts associated with the basilica are

a fourteenth-century astronomical clock and a Gothic choir stall and reliquary. Parts of two other churches in the city incorporate significant medieval elements.

The Swedish king Charles VIII sacked Lund in 1452, but despite Swedish interest in the city, it remained under the Danish crown throughout the Middle Ages—indeed until the Swedish conquest of Denmark in 1658—although it never again had the prominence it enjoyed in the twelfth and thirteenth centuries.

BIBLIOGRAPHY

McGuire, Brian. *A Guide to Medieval Denmark.* Copenhagen: C. A. Reitzel, 1994.

Mediaeval Scandinavia. 13 vols. Odense, Denmark: Odense University Press, 1968–. The most comprehensive study of medieval Scandinavia in English; full of useful information.

WILLIAM CHESTER JORDAN

[See also **DMA:** Cnut the Great; Donatus of Fiesole; Denmark.]

MAIOLUS (Mayeul, after 909–994) was the fourth abbot of Cluny (954–994). Born in Avignon to a prominent family of the Provençal aristocracy, he enjoyed the advantages of a privileged upbringing and studied the liberal arts at the cathedral school at Mâcon in preparation for an ecclesiastical career. Maiolus was eventually ordained a deacon, but in 948 he turned down the archbishopric of Besançon and donned the monastic habit at Cluny. Abbot Aymard immediately recognized his abilities and appointed him to be the treasurer of the abbey *(apocrisiarius).* In 954 the ailing abbot was so impressed with his performance in that office that he designated Maiolus his assistant and successor.

The personal character of Maiolus is ultimately elusive. He was a well-educated man, but unlike other early abbots of Cluny he did not leave a written corpus of sermons, treatises, or letters that would provide valuable insight into the development of his thoughts and ideals. There is no doubt, however, that Maiolus was a man of considerable energy. His itinerary shows that he was a tireless advocate of political concord and religious reform. As abbot, he traveled extensively in Italy and Provence. A persuasive and powerful arbiter of peace, he was instrumental in reconciling the German empress Adelaide with her son Otto II and also assisted in the latter's marriage with the future empress Theophano. At the invitation of secular patrons, Maiolus played a role in the founding and restoration of many monastic communities, including S. Apollinare in Classe; S. Pietro Cielo d'Oro, S. Salvatore, and S. Maria in Pavia; and S. Paolo fuori le Mura in Rome.

Maiolus's frequent voyages exposed him to considerable peril. In July 972, Muslim brigands from Fraxinetum captured the abbot and his entourage as they crossed the Great St. Bernard Pass through the Alps on their return from Rome to Cluny. From captivity, he sent a desperate ransom note to his brethren in Burgundy: "Brother Maiolus, a captive and in misery, sends greetings to his lords and brothers, the monks of Cluny. The hordes of Belial have encircled me, the snares of death have seized me. Please send a ransom for me and those held captive with me" (Radulphus Glaber, *Historiae Quinque Libri* 1.4.9). Maiolus and his followers were soon released, but the news of his kidnapping so outraged Count William of Arles and other Christian lords that they raised an army and destroyed the Muslim enclave at Fraxinetum.

After Maiolus's death in 994, monks at Cluny and Pavia quickly assembled an impressive hagiographical dossier detailing the virtues of his life and the miracles he performed. By 1040 elements of these stories had made their way into the divine office at Cluny. A church dedicated to Maiolus outside the walls of the abbey became the focus of regular processions. The posthumous fame of Maiolus endured well into the twelfth century in both Cluniac and Cistercian circles. Peter the Venerable maintained that more tales were told about the holiness of Maiolus than any other Christian saint in Europe. His feast day is celebrated on 11 May.

BIBLIOGRAPHY

Bourdon, Léon. "Les voyages de Saint Mayeul en Italie: Itinéraires et chronologie." *Mélanges d'archéologie et d'histoire* 43 (1926): 63–89.

Iogna-Prat, Dominique. *Agni immaculati: Recherches sur les sources hagiographiques relatives à Saint Maieul de Cluny (954–994).* Paris: Cerf, 1988.

Saint Mayeul et son temps: Actes du congrès international de Valensole, 12–14 Mai 1994. Dignes-les-Bains, France: Société scientifique et littéraire des Alpes de Haute-Provence, 1997.

SCOTT G. BRUCE

[See also **DMA:** Cluny, Order of; Radulphus Glaber; **Supp:** Fraxinetum.]

MANDAEANS. See **Sabians.**

MANFRED OF SICILY, KING (*ca.* 1230–1266), was the illegitimate son of the emperor Frederick II Hohen-

staufen and Bianca Lancia d'Agliano. Frederick had Manfred legitimized and for a time intended that he would inherit the kingdom of Arles. Contemporary chroniclers depict Manfred as the true son of Frederick—intellectual, handsome, a falconer like his father, and comfortable in the cosmopolitan world of Sicily. Manfred was at his father's side when he died in 1250 and was appointed regent of Sicily until Frederick's only legitimate living son, Conrad IV, could come south to claim the kingdom. Frederick furthermore created Manfred prince of Taranto.

Manfred fought to preserve his brother's authority against papal opposition until his brother's death in 1254. For a time, Pope Innocent IV was willing to cooperate with him, believing that Manfred's ambitions were limited to Sicily. Innocent confirmed Manfred as prince of Taranto and named him papal vicar for the mainland portion of the kingdom, with the exception of Calabria and the Abruzzi. Innocent IV led an army to Naples to assert papal overlordship, but Manfred resisted, defeating the papal armies. Innocent died shortly thereafter in Naples, and his successor, Alexander IV, excommunicated Manfred the following Easter. With the support of an assembly of the nobility in Barletta, Manfred again became regent in 1256, nominally for Conrad's infant son, Conradin, but in fact seeking to claim the kingdom for himself. Two years later Manfred was elected king and was crowned in Palermo, in contravention of his nephew's claims. Manfred married Helena, the daughter of Michael, the despot of Epirus, and received Corfu and the southern coast of Albania as dowry.

Manfred increasingly filled the role of Ghibelline champion in northern Italy against the papacy, as his father had before him. He aided the Ghibellines of Siena against their Guelph enemies at the battle of Montaperti, alarming the papacy, who saw in Manfred the specter of his father, desiring to dominate all of Italy, including Rome. The papacy actively sought a replacement for Manfred, first giving the rights to the kingdom to Edmund of Lancaster, the son of Henry III of England, and then granting them to Charles of Anjou, the younger brother of Louis IX of France. To help finance Charles's invasion and to attract further support, the pope declared a crusade against Manfred. Charles of Anjou defeated and killed Manfred on the battlefield at Benevento on 26 February 1266, allowing the French prince to conquer the rest of the kingdom. Manfred's wife and three sons died soon after in prison. Manfred also left behind a daughter from a previous marriage, Constance, married to Peter III of Aragon, who later came to rule Sicily following the revolt of the Sicilian vespers in 1282. Manfred's death marked the end of the Hohenstaufen dynasty, with the exception of Conradin's brief attempt to conquer Sicily in 1268. Manfred maintained the efficient Norman government of Sicily, which continued with some changes into the reign of his successor.

BIBLIOGRAPHY

Matthew, Donald. *The Norman Kingdom of Sicily,* Cambridge, U.K.: Cambridge University Press, 1992.

Morghen, Raffaelo. *L'età degli sveva in Italia.* Palermo, Italy: Palumbo, 1974.

Pipisa, Enrico. *Il regno di Manfredi: Proposte di interpretazione,* Messina, Italy: Sicania, 1991.

Runciman, Steven. *The Sicilian Vespers,* Cambridge, U.K.: Cambridge University Press, 1958.

CHRISTOPHER HATCH MACEVITT

[See also **DMA:** Frederick II of the Holy Roman Empire, King of Sicily; Hohenstaufen Dynasty; Innocent IV, Pope; Sicily, Kingdom of.]

MANNERS. See **Etiquette and Manners.**

MANOR AND MANORIALISM. Scholars conventionally regard the manor as the basic juridical unit of medieval rural society and therefore call the economic, social, legal, and administrative system in which it was embedded manorialism (or seigneurialism, from the French word for "lord"). This convention generalizes to Europe as a whole a form of organization that was common in the English Midlands and on the great north European plain but was not characteristic of many other parts of the British Isles, Scandinavia, and large parts of southern Europe, particularly mountainous regions. Manors were also less common in regions where allodial tenure (outright ownership) prevailed among peasants, population densities were low, the hamlet or farmstead rather than the village was the dominant form of settlement, and traditions of rural independence were particularly vigorous. Strictly speaking a manor, like an estate, is a bundle of rights over land, people, and the transactions in which they are involved, not the land itself or the people on it. The content of such bundles of rights varied from manor to manor, although some generalizations are possible.

A simplified view reifies the manor and conceives of it as coextensive with a village and its lands. The villagers then fall under the manorial system, administered by the lord of the village through his delegate (steward, reeve, provost, mayor), who presided, with the community elders, at the manorial court. (In fact many manors included extensive rights in multiple villages.) It is also common to think of the lord as resident in a big manor house in each village or manor. But, of course, individual lords often held many manors, and they did not necessarily maintain a major residence in every one. Each lord, however, in this simplified picture would have agricultural lands in every village that fell under his direct control, the so-called demesne (from the French for "lordly portion"), although he might rent them out rather than exploit them directly. The other lands of the manor were either used in common or exploited by individual peasant families who had dwellings in the village. (Again, however, this simplifies the reality; peasant families often held property in other villages and manors.) Such phrases as "common of waste" and "common of pasture" describe the kind of usages that all the village or manor households shared in particular lands.

The manorial court, presided over by the lord's delegate, who was a member of the village community, issued bylaws regulating access to the various commons, such as the number of pigs that a household could pasture in the woods, and formulated decisions about the exploitation of the plantable acreage, such as when and how much gleaning was permitted. Manorial courts also registered in the collective memory the conveyance of property from peasant tenants to their heirs (although heirship is a problematic concept, as will be shown). The manorial court disciplined those in the community who violated its norms. The court's jurisdiction was typically limited to relatively minor matters, at least in England. Serious crimes—felonies—were usually reserved for adjudication under the princely authority, unless jurisdiction had been granted to the manorial lord. Manorial courts adjudicated questions like the following: Did the villagers send the proper number of men to wash the lord's sheep? Did those who were obliged by "custom" to help plow the lord's land do a creditable job? Were there out-of-wedlock pregnancies in the village? All the infractions, if proved, were liable to fines that were carefully calibrated according to the nature of the offense. The modes of proof in such cases varied according to the nature and seriousness of the alleged offense. Witnesses to an infraction might be required, or, where circumstantial evidence predominated, the accused might have to bring in oath helpers (compurgators) to swear to the "cleanness" of his oath—that is, that his oath could be believed.

The use of the word "custom" raises another issue. There was an implicit contractual relationship between the lord of the manor and his tenants. Their holdings were protected from infringement as long as they fulfilled their obligations, which were redacted in books of customs, often called custumals. Obligations included annual rent and perhaps other monetary and labor services. The nature of the services and other restrictions on particular members of the village community and the various parcels of lands were the basis of the distinction between free and unfree (*nativus, servus, villanus;* the last word certainly carried with it overtones of unfreedom in England and France by the thirteenth century). An unfree person, in a typical scenario, could not marry someone outside the manor, could not marry a free person, was barred from becoming a priest, monk, or nun, had no formal inheritance rights, and so on. All of these restrictions were mitigated in practice by the lord's willingness to manumit his serf or to accept money or goods for a particular privilege. Two examples can stand for many. On many manors, for example, a serf "inherited" upon giving the lord the best beast of the inheritance. As another example, a servile man might marry a servile woman of another manor upon both the payment of a fine and the arrangement between the two lords about the disposition of the children, that is, as to which lord they would owe the inherited obligations of servility.

Theoretically a free tenant holding a free tenement could defend his possession, if challenged, by recourse to the appropriate royal or princely court, whereas a servile tenant, or perhaps anyone possessing a servile tenement, was obliged to defend his holding in the manorial court. The uncertainty here—what if a servile villager managed to become the tenant and exploiter of a free tenement?—gave rise to attempts at simplification among thirteenth-century jurists. Occasionally they articulated rather draconian principles in this regard, ruling, for example, that the occupation of a servile tenement for a year and a day reduced a free man to servile status. How systematically these principles were enforced in court remains unclear.

Nor was the situation unchanging. Late medieval and early modern courts in England began to rule that the so-called common lands in fact belonged to the lords. Lords could therefore legitimately bar tenants from their use. Given the relatively low margin of profit that most villagers enjoyed, even rigorous enforcement of customary restrictions on access to the commons could put families at risk. Absolute denial of access could be catastrophic. Concern over this and the enclosure of common lands that sometimes accompanied it underlay a great many violent disputes between lords and tenants in the late Middle Ages and early modern period. But the same judicial-administrative system that was confirming lords' ownership of the commons concurrently gave tenants on manors access to royal courts to defend their lands. The development of so-called copyhold tenure is too complex to go into here, but suffice it to say that property that had been conveyed traditionally at meetings of the manorial court from one tenant to another, the record (copy) of which was registered on the court roll, came to be considered copyhold property whose title could be defended by suing out a writ of trespass in a royal court.

Much of the detail in what has been written above is based on English experience, despite the fact that manors existed in France, Germany (where one word for them is *Höfe*), and elsewhere. Moreover, most of the description pertains to the period from the thirteenth century until the end of the Middle Ages, even though it would be possible to argue that the much earlier pre-Carolingian and Carolingian polyptychs describe a manorial system. The reason for the skewing of the discussion is the peculiar fact that some of the most important evidence on the legal, administrative, tenurial, and disciplinary characteristics of manors comes from manorial court rolls. While some fiscal records and *libri consuetudinum* survive from many regions and for many periods, manorial court records began to be kept and preserved in England—and virtually only in England—in the thirteenth century. Historians contend that the sorts of matters being addressed in English manorial courts were being addressed in very similar ways elsewhere, but the rich and fully satisfactory evidence to document this contention in detail does not exist.

For royal and princely administrators the manor often served as a unit on which they authorized the levy of taxes. This usage gave rise to a conventional reckoning of the size (and, implicitly, the tax liability) of a manor. Groups of manors also were constituent elements of fiefs, the property (rights) held by lords from superior lords in return for particular services, especially military service. Consequently, the seigneurial exploitation of manors has given rise in the historiography to another meaning of manorialism. Non-Marxist scholars in particular have sometimes used the word as a synonym for what Marxists call feudalism—the exploitation of a dependent peasantry by a seigneurial upper class.

BIBLIOGRAPHY

Bloch, Marc. *Seigneurie française et manoir anglais.* 2d ed. Paris: A. Colin, 1967.

Brunner, Otto. *Land and Lordship: Structures of Governance in Medieval Austria.* Translated by Howard Kaminsky and James van Horn Melton. 4th ed. Philadelphia: University of Pennsylvania Press, 1984.

Duby, Georges. *Rural Economy and Country Life in the Medieval West.* Translated by Cynthia Postan. Columbia: University of South Carolina Press, 1968.

Duby, Georges, and Armand Wallon, eds. *Histoire de la France rurale.* 4 vols. Paris: Seuil, 1975–1976.

Finberg, H. P. R., gen. ed. *The Agrarian History of England and Wales.* 8 vols. London: Cambridge University Press, 1967–.

Razi, Zvi, and Richard Smith. *Medieval Society and the Manor Court.* New York: Clarendon Press, 1996.

Rösener, Werner. *Peasants in the Middle Ages.* Translated by Alexander Stützer. Cambridge, U.K.: Polity Press, 1992.

WILLIAM CHESTER JORDAN

[See also **DMA:** Feudalism; Tenure of Land, Western European; **Supp:** Law, Feudal.]

MANUFACTURING AND INDUSTRY.

MANUFACTURING AND INDUSTRY. The modern "industrial revolution," beginning in mid-eighteenth-century Great Britain, was essentially based upon technological innovations in two key industries, textiles and metallurgy, involving in particular the application of mechanical power to these and then to other industries. That industrial "prime mover" was, as is so well known, steam power. But medieval Europe, from as early as the fifth century, had also experienced a similar application of mechanical power with the widespread diffusion of the water mill; and from at least the twelfth century, its application in these two industries, along with other major innovations, had consequences that were just as profoundly revolutionary for this era. Indeed, the industrial revolution in both textiles and metallurgy actually began with waterpower, and the nineteenth-century transition to steam power was far slower than is commonly realized.

INDUSTRIAL WATERPOWER IN THE EARLY MEDIEVAL ECONOMY

The importance of medieval Europe's resort to this industrial "prime mover" cannot be exaggerated; as Terry Reynolds has contended, "if there was a single key element distinguishing western European technology from the technologies of Islam, Byzantium, India, or even China after around 1200, it was the West's extensive commitment to and use of water power." There were two types of vertical waterwheels: the undershot and the overshot. As the name indicates, the former was driven directly by the flow of the water underneath the wheel, acting on paddles or flat radial blades fixed to its circumference, and its power was derived from two elements: the volume or weight of the water flowing against the wheel's blade per minute and the speed or impulse of the water acting against the blades. Conversely, the overshot wheel was driven by a water flow that was delivered to the top of the wheel and poured into inclined buckets or other receptacles fixed into the rim of the wheel, which ejected the water at the bottom of the revolution. Thus the wheel's rotation resulted from the weight of the water contained in these buckets rather than from the speed of the flowing water. The medieval overshot wheel was potentially twice as powerful as the undershot wheel, with an efficiency ranging from 50 to 70 percent of the potential force of the water, while requiring only about one-quarter as much water as undershot wheels. Thus it was especially useful in those areas with smaller, slower moving streams and rivers. But such water mills were far more costly to build than those with undershot wheels, especially since they usually required the construction of storage ponds, often with hydropower dams, millraces, and aqueducts to deliver the water to the top of the wheel with a sufficiently forceful "head" or "fall."

The first water mills with effective hydraulic machinery whose use can be documented were those using undershot wheels: in Roman Syria, Asia Minor, and southern Italy (at Venafro, near Pompei) in the first century B.C. From then until the twelfth century the virtually sole use of such wheels was in grinding grain between two millstones. To operate them, the waterwheel used a tapered horizontal axle that was attached to two sets of gears, vertical and horizontal. The vertical gear, revolving with the wheel as it rotated with the water flow, drove the horizontal gear, which in turn rotated the upper of two millstones. The latter's gearwheel was made smaller than the vertical, so that this millstone would rotate more rapidly than the wheel itself, grinding the kernels of grain poured through a hole in the center of the upper stone. These early undershot waterwheels produced from one to three horsepower, and they liberated between thirty and sixty persons—women more likely than men—from the laborious task of producing flour. Subsequently, in the Renaissance era, an Italian mining engineer named Vannoccio Biringuccio contended that the power of the waterwheel "is much stronger and more certain than that of a hundred men."

Possibly he was referring to the now widespread overshot wheels, for which the earliest documented evidence comes from Christian wall paintings in Roman catacombs of the third century. Almost a millennium would pass before it would reappear in Europe—in England, where it was accurately depicted in the famous Luttrell Psalter of 1338 and also about this same time (*ca.* 1350) in Germany as a crude drawing in the *Dres-*

dener Bilderhandschrift des Sachsenspiegels. Nevertheless, after examining all of the available iconographical evidence, both A. P. Usher and Terry Reynolds have concluded that overshot wheels were far less common than undershot wheels until the sixteenth century. Certainly their diffusion depended upon the costly construction of the aforementioned hydropower dams, storage ponds, and aqueducts.

Even though the undershot wheels were far less costly to construct and operate, their early medieval diffusion was surprisingly slow, with a marked increase across western Europe only from the fifth and sixth centuries. Perhaps cultural factors were partly responsible, with the erosion and then virtual disappearance of a Greco-Roman cultural heritage that had been hostile to interference with the Aristotelian "natural order" and long influenced by a partly slave-based economy. Possibly more important were purely economic factors, with not only the disappearance of the once abundant supply of cheap slaves but a genuine labor scarcity from almost continuous depopulation since the second century A.D., reducing the number of Europe's inhabitants (less than 40 million) by the tenth century to less than half of its Roman peak. The subsequent population growth, more than doubling by the early fourteenth century, was also marked by a rapid increase in the number of European water mills. Thus, in England, their number grew from the 6,082 mills recorded in the Domesday Book (1086) to slightly more than 10,000 (with an additional 2,000 windmills) in 1300, their medieval maximum (thereafter declining with the fall in population of the later Middle Ages). The earlier medieval diffusion of water mills may also have been due to the peculiar role of monastic, episcopal, and secular feudal landowners, who had the capital to build seigniorial mills and the desire to augment incomes by compelling their servile tenants to pay for their use *(banalités).* That may also help to explain, along with obvious geographic advantages, why water mills became so much more widely used in Christian Europe than in the Muslim and Byzantine worlds, or even in China—where, moreover, an agrarian economy based on rice was far less likely to require such power than one based on wheat, rye, and barley.

THE EARLIER INDUSTRIAL USES OF WATERPOWER: ROTARY POWER

Indeed, in western Europe, the second recorded use for waterpower, utilizing exactly the same technology as in flour milling, was in pulverizing barley malt into beer mash, documented in Picardy, in northern France, from at least 861. By at least the eleventh century, similar mills were used in Italy to produce olive oil; but since seeds had to be crushed rather than ground, the mills employed an edge roller that used an axle to connect the mill's driveshaft to vertically placed crushing stones, which were directed to follow a circular path by the wheel's rotation. Such edge roller mills were soon used for similar tasks: in crushing mustard and poppy seeds (to extract oils), sugar (Norman Sicily, 1176), and subsequently various dye plants. Perhaps the most important use of these mills was in extracting the tannin required for converting hides into leather by crushing oak bark into small pieces for the leaching process. First documented at Charment (near Paris) in 1138, tanning mills had become widespread by the thirteenth century.

The medieval industry that gained by far the greatest benefit and the greatest stimulus to technological innovation from the application of rotary waterpower was metallurgy. Simple rotary water mills were being widely used by this era for various tasks in metalworking, using carborundum (carbon-silicon) grindstones rather than millstones for polishing and sharpening cutlery, swords, and other blades. The earliest known cutlery mill (1204) was again located in northern France, at Évreux (Normandy). Subsequently, from the fifteenth century, rotary water mills were also being used in northern France (Raveau, 1443) for cutting metals by forcing the metal through a pair or revolving cylinders to produce sheets, rods, or bars.

LATER INDUSTRIAL USES OF WATERPOWER

Reciprocally powered machines in iron manufacturing. But the far more important applications of waterpower in metallurgical (and other) industries depended upon a radical innovation in the water mill's own hydraulic machinery: to convert its natural rotary power into reciprocal power by using first the cam and then the crankshaft. The cam, whose basic principles were known to Alexandrian Greeks, was simply a small projection fixed to the axle of the waterwheel that was designed to lift mallets or pounders, in the form of vertical triphammers. As the waterwheel rotated, the cams came into contact with similar cam projections on the heavy hammer's vertical shaft, thus lifting it and allowing it, by the simple force of gravity, to fall on the object to be pounded or hammered. The more efficient alternative to the cam in producing reciprocal power was the crankshaft, part of the axle or driving shaft bent into a right angle. Possibly known in ancient China, it was not effectively employed in the West until the later Middle Ages, when many cam-operated systems were replaced with crankshafts.

By far the most important application of cam- and then crankshaft-equipped watermills was again in metallurgy, from the eleventh or early twelfth century in Germany, Scandinavia, and France—specifically in producing iron, certainly the most important industrial metal in the medieval economy. Prior to the applications of this hydraulic machinery, the traditional method of "iron winning" involved the use of charcoal-fired "bloomery" furnaces to extract usable iron from its ferric oxide ore: the carbon in the charcoal fuel—an absolutely pure form of fuel, unlike highly contaminated coal—combined with the oxygen in the ore to liberate the iron, releasing carbon dioxide and leaving a viscous or sponge-like mass of carbonized iron known as a "bloom." The next stage in producing purified iron required extensive hammering or pounding of the "bloom" in another charcoal-fired forgery, with large amounts of both fuel and labor, to burn off or oxidize the carbon, sulfur, silicon, and other impurities. Thus the application of hydraulic trip-hammers greatly reduced the costs of labor and even fuel in iron refining, permitting larger outputs of bar iron with a given quantity of fuel. But even greater fuel economies were achieved with the application of reciprocally powered water mills to operate bellows that were designed to fan the charcoal-based fires in the forge to much higher temperatures. The first evidence for such hydraulic bellows can be found at a monastic iron foundry at Trent, in northern Italy, in 1214.

Even more momentous was the subsequent application of such waterpowered bellows for operating brick-kiln furnaces of a radically new design, almost thirty feet (nine meters) high, known as blast furnaces. The far higher temperatures, reaching about 1,800 degrees Fahrenheit (1,000 degrees Celsius), and combustion achieved with the air blast from the waterpowered bellows rapidly liberated the iron from its ferric oxide ore, while also forcing the iron itself to absorb some carbon (about 3 percent) from the charcoal fuel. The absorption of carbon in turn reduced the melting point to this temperature (while pure iron becomes molten only at the much higher temperature of 2,795 degrees Farenheit—1535 degrees Celsius), allowing the iron product to be poured or "cast" into molds, providing the name for what was a new form of iron, cast iron. The earliest documented evidence for the construction of a waterpowered blast furnace is for Liège, in the eastern Low Countries, in 1384; by the later fifteenth century these blast furnaces had become fairly widespread in France, Germany, and finally England (by 1496, in the Weald district). Certainly one of the major objectives, especially with state influence, in establishing these blast furnaces

was military: to produce cast-iron artillery, as a supplement, if not a substitute, for cast-bronze (copper and tin, in a ratio of 8 to 1) and wrought-iron artillery, whose origins date from the early to mid-fourteenth century. (The techniques for producing bronze cannon were evidently derived from casting bronze church bells.)

The introduction of the blast furnace marked a veritable late medieval "industrial revolution," particularly in establishing a genuine capitalist form of industrial organization. While the very small-scale bloomery forges, producing only about twenty tons of iron a year, were relatively cheap—cheap enough to be built and operated by a typical handicraft blacksmith—the blast furnaces were constructed on a vastly larger scale. Even the earliest models produced ten times as much iron a year, at least 200 tons; and by the seventeenth century they had grown in scale to more than 300 or 350 tons. Such giant kilns, combined with their complex and large-scale hydraulic machinery, were far too costly for any blacksmith, requiring substantial investments by wealthy mercantile or industrial "capitalists," often through partnerships (and subsequently joint-stock companies). In this fashion, the ownership of the means of production came to be divorced from the labor of the artisans who actually fashioned the metal and who were thus required to work for their capitalist employers for wages, usually piecework wages, with no access to industrial profits.

This veritable industrial revolution in iron manufacturing necessarily introduced a two-stage process for making fully refined or malleable iron, involving both furnaces and finery forges, often owned by the same group or company of capitalists. Cast iron, having a very high carbon content, was as hard as steel and, as such, was useful for preshaped pans, pipes, and machinery parts, as well as for some artillery. But it was also very brittle, subject to cracking or shattering under stress, and thus cast-iron cannons were inferior and more dangerous to use than were cast-bronze cannons (and thus also cheaper). Most of the iron demanded in early modern Europe was in fact still in the form of completely purified and much softer metal known as malleable or wrought iron. When used for this purpose, the product of the blast furnace, known from its shape as "pig iron," was taken to the refinery forge, or chafery (whose scale was increasing in the early modern era), which also used a charcoal fuel and waterpowered tilt-hammers to subject the pig to successive pounding, at red-hot but not molten heat, in order to decarbonize and purify the iron.

Mining and silver-copper metallurgy. An equally important application of such waterpowered machinery occurred in the fifteenth century in the related field of metal and mineral mining, especially silver and copper, with the use of hydraulic drainage pumps. After several centuries of intensive silver mining, with no technological advances beyond those devised by the Romans, the most accessible seams had become depleted by the later fourteenth century, and some newly discovered ore bodies were similarly becoming depleted during the fifteenth century. In still operating mines, diminishing returns had severely raised marginal costs. Furthermore, since the best or potentially the richest silver lodes were found in mountainous regions with high water flows, the problem that had brought so much European silver mining to a virtual halt by the 1440s, preventing access to deeper-lying seams, was flooding. By the 1450s, much of western Europe was suffering from a true bullion "famine," a relative scarcity of both gold and silver for coinage. Evidence for such a scarcity can be seen, first, in the very low mint outputs, or even closures of mints, in England, the Low Countries, France, and Germany. But even more impressive proof can be found in a sharp deflation that reached its nadir in the 1460s, in falling money-of-account prices based on the local silver penny. Those lower silver-based prices meant a correspondingly higher purchasing power (and thus value) of silver, and such a rise in the metal's purchasing power clearly provided the economic incentive to seek out the technological innovations that produced a veritable silver-mining boom in south Germany and central Europe from the 1460s.

The first of those highly successful innovations, from just before this decade, was the waterpowered suction piston pump. The reciprocally powered hydraulic machinery forced piston rods to rise and descend within tightly fitting iron cylinders (piston chambers), thereby expelling the air in order to create a vacuum within the pumps, which were placed at various levels of the mine shaft. Such a vacuum permitted the atmospheric pressure outside the piston chamber to force the water up through the pump to the next level of the mine shaft, where the next piston pump pumped the water to the higher levels. The famous 1556 treatise *De re metallica* by the German engineer Georg Bauer (better known as Agricola) depicts a triple-action piston pump, operated by an overshot wheel. Added to these pumps were adits drilled into the mountainsides (sloping downward) to drain off excess water; together they permitted far deeper shafts to be constructed to reach previously inaccessible but often rich ore seams. Such hydraulically operated mines were also normally capitalist enterprises. Indeed, in south Germany and Slovakia, many were operated by the famous merchant banking firm of the Fuggers.

The complementary and necessary part of this technological revolution in metallurgy was in chemical engineering: the so-called Saiger smelting process, which utilized lead in separating and extracting silver and copper in argentiferous cupric ores. Previously, by far the largest silver lodes to be found in medieval central Europe were those intermixed with copper to a degree that made them inseparable and thus impossible to extract. During the early to mid-fifteenth century, however, metallurgical engineers in Nuremberg found that when lead was added to the well-heated ore within the furnace, it combined with the silver and allowed the copper to be extracted as a precipitate. The well-known principles of lead-silver extraction, with a far lower melting point for lead, were then applied to extract the silver. As with iron manufacturing, these silver-copper furnaces required hydraulic machinery to operate the bellows (in the first licensed furnace, in Saxony, dated 1450).

From the 1460s until its peak and then decline in the 1540s, the silver-copper mining boom—in Saxony, the Austrian Tyrol, Thuringia, Bohemia, Hungary—increased Europe's silver supplies at least fivefold, which meant that Europe was receiving far more new silver than it would gain from the Spanish Americas before the 1560s. Indeed, this mining boom provided the fundamental origins for the sixteenth-century European "price revolution," even though sustained inflation did not really commence until the new silver stocks had become sufficiently augmented, about 1515.

THE LATE MEDIEVAL REVOLUTION IN SHIPBUILDING

European overseas expansion, beginning with the Portuguese in the 1430s, would not have been possible without another industrial revolution, this one in shipbuilding. The Portuguese had evidently made the first advance in developing the caravel ship (so called because of its carvel structure, with the hull planks nailed flush together, on a framework, and not overlapped, as with the earlier clinker-built ships). It was actually modeled on the Arabic dhow, in having triangular lateen sails, but three of them, on a vastly larger-scaled ship, beginning with 40 tons capacity in the 1430s and reaching 200 tons by the 1480s. This lateen rigging permitted the Portuguese caravels to sail much closer to the wind, successfully navigating the treacherous trade winds south of Cape Bojador (twenty-six degrees north latitude), a problem that had thwarted all square-rigged ships. But by far the most important achievement, dating from about the 1450s, was the production of the so-called Atlantic or full-rigged ship, also known as the carrack (originating in some unknown shipyards of Portugal, Spain, or

France), which, especially when armed with banks of cannons, would decisively dominate the world's oceanic trade routes until the 1860s. Indeed, it would serve as the key instrument of European imperialism over those five centuries. It was actually a combination of the caravel, having lateen sails fore and aft for maneuverability, with the northern (or Hanseatic) cargo boat, known as the cog *(kogge),* which had one or more very large square sails in the center of the ship, to provide power and speed. They were also built on a much larger scale than the caravels: from 600 tons in the later fifteenth century to more than 1600 tons by the later sixteenth (especially in the form of armed galleons).

The shipyards that built these giant ships were also operated by capitalistic enterprises (and virtually all private from the early 1330s, as opposed to the state-run Venetian Arsenal that produced oared galleys). They were also at least partly mechanized, with cranes and especially cam-fitted hydraulic sawmills, which date from the very early thirteenth century (Normandy, 1204; with a well-known drawing by Villard de Honnecourt, dated *ca.* 1235). Such sawmills used the rotary power of the wheel itself to feed the log or timber into the saw and then reciprocal power, with cams and later crankshafts, to drive the saw itself, in cutting back and forth.

TEXTILE MANUFACTURING AND ITS MEDIEVAL "INDUSTRIAL REVOLUTION"

Carding and spinning. Two other medieval manufacturing industries used similar cam-fitted hydraulic machinery: paper manufacturing and textiles. The former requires only a very brief mention. The first well-documented paper mills, using trip-hammers to pound and crush linen rags into pulp, were those of Xativa, near Valencia (Spain), in 1238, and in Italy, at Fabriano, in 1268. By the fourteenth century, waterpowered paper mills had become widespread in France and the Low Countries, and then in Germany by the fifteenth century.

The textile industry was by far the most important in the medieval and early modern economies, in terms of industrial employment, the value of manufactured output, and especially its value as the major industrial commodity entering both regional and international trade. Obviously the demand for textiles was universal— for warmth and protection from the elements, for manifesting social status, and for satisfying personal tastes in adornment. If many or even most people in medieval society wore locally produced homespun textiles, many others chose to buy more costly apparel from specialized regional producers; and their often highly favorable

value-to-weight ratio helps explain their predominance, above all other manufactures, in international trade. Of all these textiles, the two most important were wool-based: woolens and worsteds (and mixtures of the two). In general, woolens were made from very fine, scaly, curly, and delicate wool fibers, whose superior quality commanded a high price and produced cloth of a far greater density, weight, and durability. Worsteds, conversely, were generally made from much cheaper, coarser, straighter, but much stronger wool fibers; they were not only generally far cheaper but also much lighter and far less durable textiles. Following them were the various products of linen, fustian, and silk manufacturing. Of these, only two, and the two more luxurious—woolen and silk manufacturing—came to employ waterpower, whose importance, albeit a limited one in woolens, can be appreciated only with some understanding of the basic processes of textile manufacturing, including the other very important technological innovations that they experienced during the medieval era.

By the later Middle Ages, woolen cloth manufacturing had superseded worsteds as the most important wool-based and indeed the most important of all the textiles manufactured in western Europe, chiefly because the widespread, chronic, and often horrendous disruptions of international trade created by warfare and then plagues, from the 1290s to the 1460s, had raised transport and transactions costs to often prohibitive levels for long-distance commerce in low-valued textiles.

The typical industrial organization of most medieval and early modern commercially oriented textile crafts (except silk manufacturing), whether urban or rural in location, exemplified one form or another of the precapitalist "putting-out" system of production, which was a combination of artisan handicraft production and mercantile finance. Merchants engaged in regional or long-distance trade exercised the predominant role in textile manufacturing, supplying the necessary textile fibers, dyestuffs, and other raw materials and marketing the final products, though often doing both by the agency of brokers. They also generally supplied credit to finance some, or even all, of the working-capital needs of the artisans, though much less commonly the fixed capital. Indeed, most of the artisans themselves bore those capital costs, in acquiring the machinery or tools of production with which they worked, and they usually worked in their own homes or dwellings—giving rise to the alternative term, the "domestic" system. In the woolen cloth industry, the direction of the actual industrial processes was usually (if not always) delegated to an intermediary commonly known, in northern Europe, as the draper (*drapier*) or clothier, who was often a master weaver (or sometimes a fuller, dyer, or cloth finisher, though his Italian counterpart, the *lanaiuolo,* was often more purely mercantile). Typically, therefore, the cloth merchant or the broker intermediary would sell the inputs, on credit, to the draper or clothier (or *lanaiuolo*), who would then "put out" the textile fibers and other materials to various artisans, largely female in the preparatory processes, and often largely rural, to be "worked up" into the yarns required for weaving. Since such artisans, working in their own homes scattered across town and the adjacent countryside, could not be effectively monitored, they received piecework wages—they were paid for the amount produced and not for the time expended.

The first stage in cloth production, after the wools had been shorn from their fleeces (usually by the wool sellers or merchants), was preparation of the wools by a sequence of sorting, beating, cleansing, souring, and then greasing. Since wool fleeces (woolfells) usually contained wools that varied in staple length and fineness, the first task (usually assigned to men) was to sort them, allocating them by the type and grade of cloth to be produced. The wool sorters then beat the segregated fibers to complete the sorting and remove dirt and other extraneous matter, and thoroughly cleaned them. Those destined for higher-grade woolen cloth production were also scoured with hot alkaline water, lye, and stale urine to remove not just the remaining dirt and grease but also the natural lanolin; those wools were then thoroughly regreased with butter or olive oil. Such lubrication was necessary to protect these fine, curly wools from any damage or entanglement in the ensuing production processes of combing, carding, spinning, warping, and weaving. For this reason, the woolen draperies on the Continent were typically called *draperies ointes* (greased), while the worsted were *draperies sèches* (dry).

The wools so prepared were then "put out" to combers and (in later medieval Europe) carders, who prepared them to be spun into the warp and weft yarns on the weaver's loom, respectively. The distinction is most important because the warp yarns, in serving as the tautly stretched foundation yarns on the loom, necessarily had to be stronger than the weft yarns, which were woven between alternate warps.

Medieval spinning was a tripartite process by which combed or carded wool fibers were converted into yarns through drafting, twisting, and winding on. For several millennia, the almost universal method was handspinning using a distaff and a spindle whorl, or "drop spindle." The former was a forked or cleft stick, hooked to the spinster's belt, containing the mass of raw wool

fibers; the latter was a tapered rod that was inserted through a disk-shaped whorl commonly made from stone—hence the term "rock spinning." The spinster first "drafted" or drew out wool fibers from the distaff and attached them to the tip of the spindle. Spinning the spindle's top between thumb and forefinger, she dropped the spindle; as it descended, its whorl acted as a flywheel, rotating rapidly in one direction, to impart twist to the yarn. Finally, she removed the yarn from the spindle and wound it on to a bobbin (for its subsequent use on the loom). That yarn had a high degree of fineness, strength, and uniformity that was determined by the spinster's manual dexterity, the weight of the whorl, its rotation speed, and the extent of the spindle's drop.

During the thirteenth century, western European spinning underwent a revolutionary change with the introduction of the spinning wheel, probably from the cotton industries in adjacent Muslim lands, with both significant benefits and costs. In this new device, the spindle was mounted horizontally as an axle between two slotted uprights and inserted through the disk whorl, which was now grooved to serve as a pulley, connected to the wheel with a looped leather band or cord. The band was thus driven by the hand-rotated wheel, mounted on an axle—in a figure-eight loop to produce S-twist yarns, for linen, cotton, and woolen wefts, or, with a tauter, stronger yarn, in an open loop to make Z-twist yarns, for stronger worsted yarns and combed woolen warps. The larger the wheel, the faster the belt transmission of power; and with the "great wheel" (45 inches in diameter), the one favored by the woolen industry, a skilled spinner could rotate the wheel 100 times per minute to produce 3,600 rpm in the spindle, thus effecting at least a threefold increase in productivity over the drop spindle (about 380 yards of yarn per hour versus 120 for the drop spindle).

Evidently the new spinning wheel, better suited for carded wools, was quite inferior to the traditional drop spindle for warp yarns because of its vastly greater speed and the spinner's inability to control drafting and twisting together. Indeed, according to the *Livre des mestiers* (Book of trades), composed at Bruges around 1349, the wheel-spun warps were generally much too weak and, especially, too uneven, with insufficient twist and "too many knots," to withstand the considerable stress imposed upon them when stretched on the weaving loom. Such defects were not so serious with the inserted weft yarns. Thus the spinning wheel, with its obvious superiority in productivity, soon gained supremacy in spinning both cotton and carded weft yarns. The *Livre des mestiers* explicitly confirms that wheel-spun yarns cost much less to produce than "rock"-spun yarns.

In the later fifteenth century, however, the introduction of the so-called Saxony wheel may have remedied these deficiencies of the now traditional great wheel in producing woolen warp yarns by permitting the simultaneous drafting, twisting, and winding on of the yarns. Evidently the Saxony wheel had at least double the productivity of the standard spinning wheel, but far more important was its ability to produce uniformly strong yet very high quality warp yarns (a use demonstrated by Dutch paintings of the era) for the woolen, worsted, and linen industries. Quite possibly, therefore, its recent introduction into the Low Countries explains why documents from both the Mechelen and Brussels draperies (1435–1467) confirm that very high quality woolens were now being made, in both weft and warp, from wheel-spun carded wools, whose use can also be documented in the English woolen industry, by parliamentary legislation of 1464.

Weaving. The next and most central process of textile manufacturing was weaving these two yarns into cloth. In the late eleventh or early twelfth century European weaving underwent a truly revolutionary change with the adoption of the horizontal foot-treadle loom, possibly imported from the Byzantine silk industry (with ultimately Chinese origins). The original European version of the new loom had a narrow, boxlike construction with two gear-ratcheted beams that were rotated by hand levers. From the warp beam in the rear, the warp yarns were tautly stretched and wound onto the cloth beam in the front. Heddle harnesses were suspended from pulleys hooked to the loom's upper cross beam and operated by foot-powered treadles underneath the loom. Each harness was a rod to which were attached numerous heddles—linen cords with looped ends through which individual groups of warp yarns were passed. Similarly suspended from the upper cross beam and placed between the heddle rods and the front of the loom was the combination of the laysword and the reed attached to its front. Attached between the two narrow wooden laths of the reed was a multitude of parallel wire teeth, which were designed to keep the warp yarns passing through them evenly spaced, to ensure that the cloth had an even width. The laysword itself was a movable frame with a grooved wooden channel for the passage, through the alternating warp yarns, of the shuttle containing the weft yarns.

In commencing the weave, the single weaver (for the original, simple loom) depressed the left treadle, thus raising the right heddle harness to open the "natural shed" of even-numbered warps; then he (or she) slung the shuttle through the grooved laysword with his right hand, grasping it at the other side with the left, and pulled it through the shed, thus unwinding and inserting the weft. After so inserting the first weft, he pulled the laysword with its reed to the front of the loom, in order to beat the weft up into the fell of the cloth. By next depressing the right foot-treadle, he raised the left heddle harness to lock the first interlacing of warp and weft, while also opening the countershed of odd-numbered warps for the next passage of the shuttle. In repeating these processes, the weaver periodically used the appropriate beam levers to feed out more warps from the rear beam and to wind up the woven cloth on the front beam.

This horizontal loom provided a number of significant advantages over the older vertical warp-weighted loom. First, by stretching the warps much more tautly on the two beams, with more even tension, and by beating up the wefts much more firmly and evenly, it produced a uniformly better-quality, more densely woven woolen (or other fabric), with proportionately more weft than warp. Second, the weaver vastly increased control over the weaving sheds for all types of cloth with the treadle-operated heddle harnesses, further improving the quality and uniformity of the cloth. Third, by using two separate revolving beams, for winding on the warps and winding up the cloth, this new loom could produce cloths of far longer lengths: twenty-five to thirty yards or more, compared to cloths of only a little more than three yards woven on the warp-weighted loom. Fourth, the horizontal loom permitted a large increase in productivity, eventually a more than threefold increase (up to 425 yards of weft per hour, compared to about 130 yards with warp-weighted loom). Even greater gains in productivity, quality, and especially size, in doubling the width of the cloth (up to three meters), were achieved with the subsequent evolution, by the later twelfth or thirteenth century, of the two-weaver broadloom, which allowed the first weaver to sling the shuttle with his right hand along the laysword toward the outstretched left hand of his partner. They repeated these movements in a constant rhythm, without alternating arms, thereby permitting a much more rapid weft insertion per unit of width. By the time the broadloom became predominant, weaving had also become almost exclusively a male occupation, with indeterminate effects on productivity.

Nevertheless, those productivity gains, impressive though they undoubtedly were, must be placed in historic perspective. In late medieval Flanders, weaving a standard broadcloth of 42 ells by 3.5 ells (32 yards by 2.75 yards), containing about 84 pounds of wool (36 pounds of warp and 48 pounds of weft), typically required about two working weeks. Another dozen days were expended in wool beating, wool greasing, carding, combing, spinning, reeling, and warping the yarns for the same cloth, involving about twenty-six to thirty artisans and helpers. To this we must add one or more weeks expended on the cloth-finishing processes. A weaver-draper with one broadloom could produce only about twenty or twenty-five such broadcloths per work year (with typically 220 to 240 days). Productivity in weaving itself did not appreciably change again before the modern industrial revolution era.

More important in the medieval textile revolution was the vast improvement in both density of weaving and quality to permit the true emergence of the very fine, heavy, luxury woolen cloth that came to displace most worsted textiles in late medieval international trade. That density, weight, and luxury quality depended, however, upon the successful completion of the next and thus equally vital stage in cloth production: fulling. Indeed, fulling was necessary simply to ensure that the cloth, if woven from yarns that were composed of the very fine, scaly, and short-fibered wools, did not quickly fall apart with normal wear.

Fulling and industrial organization. Traditionally the fulling process had depended entirely on human labor, in the form of foot power, unaided by tools or machinery. The master fuller, on receiving the raw woolen cloth from the weaver-draper (his employer), had it placed in a large stone or wooden vat filled with an emulsion of warm water, urine, and "fuller's earth" (a chemical mixture composed of various hydrous aluminum silicates). Two of his journeymen, sometimes accompanied by the master, then trod upon the cloth for three or more days to achieve three objectives. The initial objective was to remove all the grease and cleanse the cloth, and for this purpose the ammonia in the urine enhanced the scouring and bleaching properties of fuller's earth and combined with the grease to form a cleansing soap. Second, the process forced the short, scaly, curly wool fibers to interlace, mat, and felt together, thus providing the fabric's requisite cohesion and durability. Third, it shrank the cloth by more than 50 percent, thus largely accounting for the cloth's very heavy weight. Indeed the best-quality woolens weighed about three times as much as did worsted fabrics (which were not fulled, though hybrid woolen-worsted fabrics did receive some cursory fulling). The fullers then hung the fulled cloth by hooks on a tentering frame to remove all the wrinkles and to ensure even dimensions throughout its length. While the cloth was still on the frame, they engaged in a preliminary raising of the cloth's nap (loose fibers), using teasels, a type of thistle. The woolen cloth was then returned to

the draper, who usually sold it to a cloth merchant or commercial broker. The merchant in turn commissioned professional dyers and shearers to "finish" the cloth in accordance with current perceptions of market demand, in terms of colors and styles. The shearers, also using teasels, along with razor-sharp steel shears, subjected the cloth to repeated teaseling or "napping" and then shearing of the nap fibers so raised. As a consequence of both fulling and shearing, the weave pattern was totally obliterated and the texture of the woolen became as soft and as fine as silk.

In the industrial organization of the northern medieval cloth industry, those engaged in most of the preparatory processes (combing, carding, spinning, warp winding) were predominantly female, while the last four groups of artisans were almost exclusively male and were the only ones to enjoy guild protection. The most independent and usually the most prosperous were the dyers and shearers, professional craftsmen who worked on commission for various merchants, and some drapers, for fees set by the guild (and town governments). The weaver-drapers who dominated the weavers' guild were, as noted, industrial subcontractors and entrepreneurs who earned neither fees nor wages (as did their journeymen) but profits: the difference between their raw material, labor, and other production costs and the sales income received from the cloth merchants. The foot fullers, masters and journeymen alike, were employees of the weaver-drapers (though usually working for several and not just one), and they were the only guild artisans who worked for wages—a combination of piecework and time wages, since they were required to full a cloth within a prescribed time, usually three days. In the Low Countries, industrial strife between weavers and fullers, principally over wages, led to periodic disruptions of the woolen cloth industry from the later thirteenth through the sixteenth centuries.

Drapers and fullers in the medieval Low Countries formed an exception to other European cloth manufacturers by eschewing one of this industry's most important technological innovations, indeed the only one that involved the use of mechanical power before the modern industrial revolution: the waterpowered fulling mill. The fulling mill evidently represents the first European use of waterpower in industrial manufacturing (i.e., after its initial uses in flour milling and brewing). The earliest fulling mills to be documented were in tenth-century Italy: in Abruzzo (962), Parma (973), and Verona (985). In northern Europe, the first known fulling mill was established at Argentan, Normandy, in 1086, and it was not introduced into England until the late twelfth century.

Although the renowned historian E. M. Carus-Wilson undoubtedly exaggerated in calling the subsequent diffusion of English fulling mills "an industrial revolution of the thirteenth century," her numerous critics were misguided in dismissing their significance. This innovation reduced the immensely laborious and time-consuming task of foot fulling to just a matter of hours, generally a day for most cloths, with just one man to operate the mill. In what was also the first application of reciprocal power, the waterwheel used cams on its axle to operate two large and heavy oaken trip-hammers, which pounded the cloth up to forty times a minute. Reliable comparative output and cost data for fifteenth-century Italy and the Low Countries show that fulling mills increased productivity in fulling by at least 3.5 times. While foot fulling was responsible for about 20 percent of the weaver-draper's value-added labor costs, mechanical fulling accounted for less than 5 percent of those costs.

The refusal of woolen cloth industries in the medieval Low Countries (and parts of northern France) to adopt fulling mills certainly was not due to any supposed lack of waterpower, for grain and paper mills were in widespread use. Nor was it due to any supposed guild opposition, for guild records are silent on the issue. Indeed, in the aforementioned industrial strife, the more powerful weaver-drapers (and mercantile drapers in Holland) virtually always prevailed, and had fulling mills actually offered a distinct advantage, the weaver-drapers or mercantile drapers ought to have resorted to them, especially to avoid continual strife with foot-fullers over wages. In fact, with the strong reorientation of cloth production to ultra-high priced luxury woolens during the fourteenth and fifteenth centuries, which also meant that fine English wools and costly dyestuffs accounted for 80 to 90 percent of full production costs, the use of fulling mills would have reduced wholesale cloth prices by no more than 3 percent, but at the major cost of losing many customers. The comparative advantage of these woolen industries lay in their unrivalled reputation for luxury quality, one that justified the very high prices for these cloths. Mechanical fulling posed a severe threat to that reputation because of the widespread belief that the rapidly pounding heavy oaken trip-hammers damaged the very fine, delicate English wool fibers. Evidently this was not so much a problem for cheaper-grade woolens; indeed, when draperies in the southern Low Countries reverted to such woolens and to hybrid woolen-worsteds in the sixteenth century, they did resort to waterpowered fulling mills. Subsequently, the quality problem was resolved by encasing the hammer's head in fine wrought iron. Even stronger resistance however, prevented any widespread use of an ancillary device: the waterpowered gig mill (attached to the fulling mill) for raising the woolen nap in cloth finishing, a process that most observers deemed to be seriously injurious to the finished fabric's quality.

SILK MANUFACTURING AND ITS MEDIEVAL "INDUSTRIAL REVOLUTION"

Yet, in striking contrast, the application of waterpower in the medieval silk industry evidently improved quality while vastly increasing productivity. Indeed, the early European silk-manufacturing industry, in thirteenth-century Italy, which sought to displace at least some imported silks from the Byzantine Empire and China, was evidently based on the adoption (or perhaps invention) of the waterpowered silk-throwing machine, documented at Bologna from 1272. In its fully developed form, this machine had two concentric wooden structures housed in a veritable "capitalist" factory: an inner one that revolved on the axle of the waterwheel and an outer fixed, stationary framework, which supported two rows of twelve horizontal reels (swifts), each of which was fed by ten revolving spindles below, for a total of 240 spindles. Spokes or blades that were attached to the revolving inner framework made intermittent contact with drum gears on the outer framework, thereby rotating the spindles and then the reels at different speeds. Contained within each spindle was a rotating bobbin onto which the silk filaments (reeled from the boiled silkworm cocoons) were wound; from the bobbin they were then fed to the swift-reels above through S-shaped wire "flyers." The silk-throwing machine provided a continuous process of drafting, twisting, and winding on to produce very strong yet very fine and homogenous silk yarns.

The later medieval silk-throwing mills in Florence and Venice, with up to 480 powered spindles, permitted from two to four operatives to replace several hundred hand-throwsters in producing yarns of evidently better quality. By the fifteenth century, silk manufacturing (throwing and weaving, using traditional textile looms and then the Asian drawloom for pattern weaving) had spread to France, beginning with factories established at Tours in 1470 and subsequently at Lyons. Much later, in 1717, Thomas Lombe established England's first waterpowered silk-throwing factory, with basically the same technology. But waterpowered silk manufacturing did not, of course, provide one of the roads to the modern industrial revolution, since such costly fabrics, even when intermixed with cheaper fibers, could never become articles of mass consumption in the way that cotton textiles did.

Such a survey cannot possibly cover all medieval manufacturing industries; other important industries, in terms of both mass consumption, if only in local markets, and employment, included brewing, baking, leather goods, brick making, and glassblowing. Their histories, however, do not offer similar examples of technological changes and the more complex forms of industrial organization that have been examined in the metallurgical, textile, shipbuilding, and other major industries considered here.

BIBLIOGRAPHY

Agricola, Georg. *De re metallica*. Translated from the 1556 Latin edition by Herbert Hoover and Lou Henry Hoover. New York: Dover, 1950.

Boone, Marc, and Walter Prevenier, eds. *La draperie ancienne des Pays Bas: Débouchés et stratégies de survie (XIVe–XVIe siècles)* (Drapery production in the late medieval Low Countries: Markets and strategies for survival [fourteenth to sixteenth centuries]). Louvain, Belgium: Garant, 1993.

Braunstein, Philippe. "Innovations in Mining and Metal Production in Europe in the Late Middle Ages." *Journal of European Economic History* 12 (1983): 573–591.

Cardon, Dominique. *La draperie au Moyen Âge: Essor d'une grande industrie européenne*. Paris: CNRS Éditions, 1999.

Carus-Wilson, E. M. "An Industrial Revolution of the Thirteenth Century." *Economic History Review*, 1st ser., 11 (1941): 39–60. Reprinted in E. M. Carus-Wilson, *Medieval Merchant Venturers: Collected Studies*, 2d ed. (London: Methuen, 1967).

———. "The Woollen Industry." In *Cambridge Economic History of Europe*. Edited by M. M. Postan and H. J. Habakkuk. 2d ed. Volume 2: *Trade and Industry in the Middle Ages*, edited by Edward Miller, Cynthis Postan, and M. M. Postan. Cambridge, U.K.: Cambridge University Press, 1987.

Chorley, Patrick. "The Evolution of the Woollen, 1300–1700." In *The New Draperies in the Low Countries and England, 1300–1800*. Edited by N. B. Harte. Oxford: Oxford University Press, 1997.

Cipolla, Carlo M. *Guns, Sails, and Empires: Technological Innovation and the Early Phases of European Expansion, 1400–1700*. 1965. Reprint, Manhattan, Kans.: Sunflower University Press, 1985.

Cleere, Henry, and David Crossley. *The Iron Industry of the Weald*. Cardiff, U.K.: Merton Priory Press, 1995.

Coleman, D. C. "An Innovation and Its Diffusion: The 'New Draperies.'" *Economic History Review*, 2d ser., 22 (1969): 417–429.

Coornaert, Emile. "Draperies rurales, draperies urbaines: L'évolution de l'industrie flamande au moyen âge et au XVI siècle." *Revue belge de philologie et d'histoire* 28 (1950): 59–96.

Endrei, Walter. *L'évolution des techniques du filage et du tissage: Du Moyen Âge à la révolution industrielle*. Translated by Joseph Takacs and Jean Pilisi. Paris and The Hague: Mouton, 1968.

Forbes, R. J. *Studies in Ancient Technology*. 2 vols. Leiden, Netherlands: E. J. Brill, 1955.

Harte, N. B., ed. *The New Draperies in the Low Countries and England, 1300–1800*. Oxford: Oxford University Press, 1997.

Harte, N. B., and Kenneth G. Ponting, eds. *Cloth and Clothing in Medieval Europe: Essays in Memory of Professor E. M. Carus-Wilson*. London: Heinemann Educational Books, 1983.

Hatcher, John. *The History of the British Coal Industry*. Vol. 1: *Before 1700: Towards the Age of Coal*. Oxford: Clarendon Press, 1993.

Hoffmann, Martha. *The Warp-Weighted Loom: Studies in the History and Technology of an Ancient Implement*. Oslo: Universitetsforlaget, 1964.

Holt, Richard. *The Mills of Medieval England*. Oxford: Basil Blackwell, 1988.

Hoshino, Hidetoshi. *L'arte della lana in Firenze nel basso Medioevo: Il commercio della lana e il mercato dei panni fiorentini nei secoli XIII–XV*. Florence: L. S. Olschki, 1980.

Langdon, John. "Water-mills and Windmills in the West Midlands, 1086–1500." *Economic History Review*, 2d ser., 44 (August 1991): 424–444.

Malanima, Paolo. "The First European Textile Machine." *Textile History* 17 (1986): 115–127.

Mazzaoui, Maureen Fennell. *The Italian Cotton Industry in the Later Middle Ages, 1100–1600*. Cambridge, U.K.: Cambridge University Press, 1981.

Munro, John H. "Medieval Woollens: Textiles, Textile Technology, and Industrial Organisation, c. 800–1500." In *The Cambridge History of Western Textiles*. Edited by David Jenkins. Volume 1. Cambridge, U.K., and New York: Cambridge University Press, 2003.

———. "Medieval Woollens: The Western European Woollen Industries and Their Struggles for International Markets, c. 1000–1500." In *The Cambridge History of Western Textiles*. Edited by David Jenkins. Vol. 1. Cambridge, U.K., and New York: Cambridge University Press, 2003.

———. "The Monetary Origins of the 'Price Revolution': South German Silver Mining, Merchant-Banking, and Venetian Commerce, 1470–1540." In *Global Connections and Monetary History, 1470–1800*. Edited by Dennis O. Flynn, Arturo Giráldez, and Richard von Glahn. Aldershot, U.K., and Brookfield, Vt: Ashgate, 2003.

Nef, John U. "Mining and Metallurgy in Medieval Civilization." In *Cambridge Economic History of Europe*. Edited by M. M. Postan and H. J. Habakkuk. 2d ed. Volume 2: *Trade and Industry in the Middle Ages*. Edited by Edward Miller, Cynthis Postan, and M. M. Postan. Cambridge, U.K.: Cambridge University Press, 1987.

Pariset, Ernest. *Les industries de la soie*. Lyon: Pitrat, 1890.

Poerck, Guy de. *La draperie médiévale en Flandre et en Artois: Technique et terminologie*. 3 vols. Bruges, Belgium: De Tempel, 1951.

Reynolds, Terry S. *Stronger Than a Hundred Men: A History of the Vertical Water Wheel*. Baltimore and London: Johns Hopkins University Press, 1983.

Spallanzani, Marco, ed. *Produzione: Commercio e consumo dei panni di lana (nei secoli XII–XVIII)*. Florence: L. S. Olschki, 1976.

Swanson, Heather. *Medieval Artisans: An Urban Class in Late Medieval England*. Oxford: Basil Blackwell, 1989.

Thrupp, Sylvia L. "Medieval Industry, 1000–1500." In *Fontana Economic History of Europe*. Edited by Carlo M. Cipolla. Volume 1: *The Middle Ages*. London: Collins/Fontana, 1972.

Unger, Richard W. *The Ship in the Medieval Economy, 600–1600.* London: Croom Helm, 1980.

Usher, Abbott Payson. *A History of Mechanical Inventions.* 2d ed. Cambridge, Mass.: Harvard University Press, 1954.

Uytven, Raymond van. "Technique, productivité, et production au Moyen Âge: Le cas de la draperie urbaine aux Pays-Bas." In *Produttività e tecnologia nei secoli XII–XVII.* Edited by Sara Mariotti. Florence: F. Le Monnier, 1981.

Van der Wee, Herman. "Structural Changes and Specialization in the Industry of the Southern Netherlands, 1100–1600." *Economic History Review,* 2d ser., 28 (1975): 203–221.

JOHN H. MUNRO

[See also **DMA:** Cotton; Linen; Metallurgy; Metalworkers; Mills; Mining; Ships and Shipbuilding; Silk; Technology; Textile Technology; Textile Workers; Trade; Wool; **Supp:** Merchants; Textiles, Byzantine.]

MANUSCRIPT COLLECTIONS.

MANUSCRIPT COLLECTIONS. There are several hundred thousand extant medieval manuscripts in European and North American libraries, museums, and other repositories, offering one of the largest and most comprehensive bodies of original documentation for the study of history and culture during the Middle Ages. As used here, the word "manuscripts" refers to handwritten texts, most commonly in codex format and kept in libraries, rather than handwritten administrative and legal records in files and registers, preserved for their enduring value in public archives. The manuscripts were originally dispersed among long-established libraries of monasteries, cathedrals, and other ecclesiastical institutions, as well as in university libraries and private collections of more recent origin. Monastic libraries varied widely in size but rarely contained more than a few hundred volumes, enough to serve the devotional, educational, and reference needs of cloistered communities and their schools. Such holdings obviously pale by comparison with modern research libraries, each with holdings measured in millions of bibliographic items. Medieval monasteries such as St. Gall (Switzerland), Lambach (Austria), and St. Catherine (Mount Sinai) still maintain functioning manuscript libraries, as do a larger number of medieval cathedrals. But most ecclesiastical libraries were broken up at various times between the sixteenth and early twentieth centuries.

Private collections of manuscripts multiplied in the fourteenth and fifteenth centuries, from small scholarly libraries of professional texts to great princely libraries of luxury manuscripts. The English cleric and scholar Richard de Bury (Richard Aungerville; 1287–1345), bishop of Durham, receives special honor as a medieval collector because of *Philobiblon,* his treatise on collecting and preserving books. But there were more significant private collections of medieval manuscripts, some of which became the kernel of manuscript collections in research libraries. King Henry VIII of England's suppression of more than four hundred religious houses in the British Isles (1536–1540) resulted in the disbanding of most monastic libraries and promoted the rapid growth of private collections of medieval manuscripts. Over the next four centuries, these manuscripts changed hands through inheritance and were sold with the assistance of a robust antiquarian book trade. Among private collections, the library of Humphrey, duke of Gloucester (1391–1447), became part of the University of Oxford's Bodleian Library, founded in 1602; and Archbishop Matthew Parker (1504–1575) built the fine manuscript collection at Corpus Christi College, University of Cambridge. Sir Thomas Phillipps (1792–1872) was the most successful British private collector, amassing more than 23,000 manuscripts and thousands of documents, chiefly medieval. For more than a century after his death, the Phillipps manuscripts were gradually sold off to other private collectors and libraries.

On the Continent, there were many notable manuscript collectors, including King Charles V of France 1337–1380), who amassed a substantial royal library, including important illuminated manuscripts that are preserved at the Bibliothèque nationale de France and the British Library; and Duke Philip II (the Bold) of Burgundy (1342–1404) and his successors, who assembled a ducal library of illuminated manuscripts and vernacular texts, housed in Brussels since 1559 and now part of the Bibliothèque royale Albert Ier. Duke Julius (r. 1568–1589) of Braunschweig-Wolfenbüttel and his successors developed a fine princely library with several thousand manuscripts. In 1644 Duke August II (r. 1635–1666) reestablished the library in Wolfenbüttel. The Herzog August Bibliothek came under public control after World War II. In Renaissance Italy, humanistic focus on the ancient world led to the creation of research libraries with manuscripts and printed editions of classical texts. The private library of Pope Nicholas V (1397–1455) was the beginning of the Vatican Library (Biblioteca Apostolica Vaticana), which grew significantly under several Renaissance popes. In the course of more than five centuries, it has acquired more than 60,000 manuscripts. Among major private collectors in Italy were Niccolò III d'Este, duke of Ferrara (1383–1441), who began to develop the Biblioteca Estense, which was later moved to Modena, by acquiring manuscripts of classical and vernacular texts; Cosimo de' Medici (1389–1464), who began collecting the thousands of manuscripts that have been in Florence's Laurentian Library (Biblioteca Laurenziana) since its foundation in 1571; Cardinal Johannes Bessarion (*ca.* 1403–1472), the learned Byzantine émigré, who in 1468 bequeathed his substantial collection of Greek manuscripts to the Republic of Venice, where they remain in the Biblioteca Marciana; and Cardinal Federico Borromeo (1564–1631), who founded the Biblioteca Ambrosiana, Milan, with a donation of 12,000 manuscripts in 1609. King Matthias I Corvinus of Hungary (1440–1490) created the Corvinian Library (Bibliotheca Corviniana), with more than 2,000 codices; Ottoman Turks carted many of its manuscripts off to Constantinople, though some manuscripts survive in the National Library of Hungary and other libraries in Budapest.

The establishment of national libraries, which began in the second half of the eighteenth century and reached its peak in the nineteenth century, resulted in the formation of manuscripts departments with large medieval holdings. Founded in 1753, the British Museum Library (now British Library) initially brought together large private libraries with thousands of medieval manuscripts amassed by Sir Robert Bruce Cotton (1571–1631); Robert Harley (1661–1724) and Edward Harley (1689–1741), earls of Oxford; and Sir Hans Sloane (1660–1753). Its manuscript collections continued to grow under the leadership of Antonio Panizzi (1797–1879) and subsequent directors. Royal collections were added between 1757 and 1823; other series include the Arundel, Egerton, Hargrave, Lansdowne, Stowe, and Additional manuscripts. The British Library holds more than 60,000 manuscripts today. On the Continent, the French Revolution and Napoléon Bonaparte's armies provided major impetus to collection formation by spreading the principle of public ownership and custody of original research materials that had hitherto been held privately in royal, aristocratic, and ecclesiastical collections. Publicly accessible manuscript collections and archives came to be seen as essential to the preservation of national heritage, cultural patrimony, and the rights of citizens.

The Bibliothèque nationale de France was the successor to a royal library that had existed from the fifteenth century until its nationalization in 1789. Large-scale secularization of French church property (including monastic libraries), decreed in the same year, also contributed to the Bibliothèque nationale's growing holdings, which have grown to more than 180,000 medieval and other manuscripts. Complementing its holdings are substantial collections in three other Paris libraries (Arsenal, Mazarine, and Ste. Geneviève) and many municipal

or public libraries in the French *départements*. National libraries were established in Germany, Austria, Italy, the Netherlands, Belgium, Spain, and other countries. They were beneficiaries of the secularization of monastic libraries, and their manuscript collections continued to grow by gift and purchase. Among the most sizable collections of medieval manuscripts are those at the Österreichische Nationalbibliothek (Vienna), with more than 54,000 manuscripts; the Bayerische Staatsbibliothek (Munich), with more than 50,000 manuscripts; and the Biblioteca Nacional (Madrid), with some 35,000 manuscripts. At the same time, hundreds of European municipal libraries, universities, and museums acquired solid, if less sizable, collections of medieval manuscripts, often focusing on monastic manuscripts from the immediate area.

North American institutions have relatively modest medieval holdings, perhaps 20,000 manuscripts in all. Significant private collecting of medieval manuscripts did not begin in the United States until the second half of the nineteenth century, when American collectors began to acquire manuscripts from private collections in Europe through the antiquarian book trade and auction sales. Some of the most successful American collectors of medieval manuscripts later established independent libraries and museums or donated their collections to particular academic and research universities. The Pierpont Morgan Library (New York), which opened to the public in 1924 with collections from John Pierpont Morgan (1837–1913) and John Pierpont Morgan Jr. (1867–1943), has the largest collection (more than 1,300 manuscripts), with an emphasis on illuminated manuscripts. Other American institutions have some hundreds of manuscripts each. There are art museums such as the Walters Art Museum (Baltimore) and J. Paul Getty Center (Los Angeles); independent research libraries such as the Huntington Library (San Marino, California) and Newberry Library (Chicago); academic libraries such as the Beinecke Library (Yale University), Houghton Library (Harvard University), Princeton University Library (which also houses the private Scheide Library), and Columbia University Library; large public libraries such as the Free Public Library of Philadelphia and the New York Public Library; and the Library of Congress. Smaller collections of medieval manuscripts can be found in a host of libraries and museums, and there are three large microfilm libraries offering copies of manuscripts in major European collections: the Hill Monastic Manuscript Library, Collegeville, Minnesota; Vatican Film Library, St. Louis University; and Biblioteca Ambrosiana Microfilm Archives, University of Notre Dame.

Manuscripts researchers must use a wide array of reference tools, including published repository-level catalogs and handlists; union lists of manuscript collections; specialized guides by subject, variety of text, region, language, time period, or religious order; illustrated guides to illuminated manuscripts, studies of particular scriptoria, scribes, and workshops; checklists of incipits, explicits, and colophons; catalogs of dated and datable manuscripts; editions of medieval library catalogs and reconstructions that locate extant manuscripts; antiquarian dealers' and auction catalogs; and unpublished in-house inventories.

Repository-level manuscript catalogs are very numerous. Selected titles are listed in the bibliography that follows. In addition, there are published catalogs for the Huntington Library, Beinecke Library, Newberry Library, and Walters Art Museum, as well as ongoing manuscripts cataloging projects at Harvard, Princeton, and Columbia. Complementing these are electronic resources, including on-line manuscript catalogs, descriptions in bibliographic utilities, virtual collections of digitized manuscripts and miniatures, full-text databases, and on-line exhibitions.

BIBLIOGRAPHY

HISTORICAL, INSTITUTIONAL, AND BIBLIOGRAPHIC OVERVIEWS

Boyle, Leonard E. *Medieval Latin Palaeography: A Bibliographical Introduction.* Toronto: University of Toronto Press, 1984.

Kristeller, Paul Oskar. *Latin Manuscript Books before 1600: A List of the Printed Catalogues and Unpublished Inventories of Extant Collections.* 4th ed. Munich, Germany: Monumenta Germaniae Historica, 1993.

Olivier, Jean Marie. *Répertoire des bibliothèques et des catalogues de manuscrits grecs de Marcel Richard.* 3d edition. Turnhout, Belgium: Brepols, 1995.

Van Caenegem, R. C., with F. L. Ganshof. *Guide to the Sources of Medieval History.* Amsterdam: North-Holland Publishing Company, 1978.

ENGLAND

British Library. Home page at http://www.bl.uk. Provides on-line manuscripts catalog.

Cambridge University Library. *A Catalogue of the Manuscripts Preserved in the Library of the University of Cambridge.* 5 vols. Cambridge, U.K.: Cambridge University Press, 1856–1867.

Ker, Neil Ripley. *Medieval Manuscripts in British Libraries.* 4 vols. Oxford: Clarendon, 1969–.

Madan, Falconer, et al. *A Summary Catalogue of Western Manuscripts in the Bodleian Library at Oxford.* 7 vols. Oxford: Clarendon, 1895–1953.

Nickson, M. A. E. *The British Library: Guide to the Catalogues and Indexes of the Department of Manuscripts.* 2d ed. London: British Library, 1982.

CONTINENTAL EUROPE

Bayerische Staatsbibliothek. *Catalogus codicum manu scriptorum Bibliothecae Monacensis.* Munich, Germany: Palm'schen, 1866–.

Bibliothèque Nationale de France. *Catalogue général des manuscrits latins.* 7 vols. Paris: Bibliothèque Nationale, 1939–.

France. Ministère de l'Éducation Nationale. *Catalogue général des manuscrits des bibliothèques publiques des départements.* Quarto Series. 7 vols. Paris: Imprimerie nationale, 1849–1885.

————. Ministère de l'Instruction Publique. *Catalogue général des manuscrits des bibliothèques publiques de France.* Octavo Series. 51 vols. Paris: Plon-Nourri, 1886–.

Kristeller, Paul Oskar. *Iter italicum: A Finding List of Uncatalogued or Incompletely Catalogued Humanistic Manuscripts of the Renaissance in Italian and Other Libraries.* 6 vols. London: Warburg Institute, 1963–1993.

Mazzatinti, Guiseppe, Albano Sorbelli, et al. *Inventari dei manoscritti delle biblioteche d'Italia.* 111 vols. Turin, Forli, and Florence: L. S. Olschki et al., 1890–.

NORTH AMERICA

De Ricci, Seymour, and W. J. Wilson. *Census of Medieval and Renaissance Manuscripts in the United States and Canada.* 3 vols. New York: Wilson, 1935–1940.

Faye, Christopher, and William H. Bond. *Supplement to the Census of Medieval and Renaissance Manuscripts in the United States and Canada.* New York: Wilson, 1962.

DON C. SKEMER

[See also **DMA:** Codicology, Western European; Libraries; Manuscript Books, Binding of: European; Manuscript Books, Production of; Manuscript Illumination, European; Manuscript Illumination: Hebrew; Manuscripts, Celtic Liturgical; Manuscripts, Hebrew; **Supp:** Manuscript Illumination, Byzantine.]

MANUSCRIPT ILLUMINATION, BYZANTINE.

This article discusses the illumination of manuscripts written in Greek and of non-Greek books worked on by Greek-speaking artists.

ILLUMINATION AND TEXT

Both nonrepresentational ornament and images are found in Byzantine books. In medical, geographic, and other works illustrations were often essential for making a point and thus integral to the text itself. Elsewhere, above all in biblical manuscripts, images accompanied specific passages, showing what the text recounted or clarifying its implicit meaning. It was also felt that a portrait of the writer certified a work's authorship and in this way guaranteed the validity of its contents. Religious as well as secular texts could be introduced by such portraits. Thus, Gospels often contained images of the four evangelists.

Placed immediately before their associated texts, author portraits also marked the start of a new section in a volume. Smaller divisions within the text were correspondingly signaled by less elaborate pieces of illumination. Titles were surrounded by headpieces (ornamented frames). Individual chapters could be preceded by similarly decorated but narrower headbands. Paragraphs would open with decorated initial letters that on occasion also contained minute animal or human figures.

Large figural pictures could accompany or replace author portraits. Like them, they both served as the ultimate punctuation marks and introduced the text that followed.

CONTEXT

The impetus for having Byzantine manuscripts illuminated was a common conviction that a book's contents are important and must therefore be presented in an appropriately decorous form. Even canon tables in Gospels and Paschal tables in Psalters would receive ornate decorative frames. Among surviving volumes, relatively few contain pictures (though many that originally did have since lost them), but many more have painted ornament, and almost all have some simple form of decoration by the scribe's pen.

Certain manuscripts feature dedicatory images showing the person who commissioned the book presenting it to God, through the intermediacy of a saint or of the Virgin. They symbolically indicate that the volume was given to a church or monastery, as an act of piety and a token for the remission of the donor's sins. Many illuminated Byzantine manuscripts contain texts used in the liturgy: priestly prayers (written on long scrolls), readings from the Gospels (collected in the lectionary), sermons (especially those of St. Gregory of Nazianzus, from which a special selection was made for liturgical use), and lives of saints (which were publicly read on their respective feast days from the Menologion). However, few such books show signs of regular use. They were obviously prized possessions rather than liturgical furnishings, and their value was symbolic, not practical.

Several illuminated volumes are identified by inscriptions as imperial belongings. Their size and contents are generally the same as those of liturgical manuscripts, their decoration is equally lavish, and their state of preservation just as fine. In the palace, such books betokened royal devoutness, munificence, and in the case of secular works, love of learning.

There are also illuminated manuscripts made for actual reading rather than display. Edifying texts like Olympiodorus's commentary on the Book of Job, the *Heavenly Ladder* of John Klimakos, or the *Romance of Barlaam and Josaphat* were sometimes accompanied by illustrations. The Gospels and the Psalter were often copied in small, decorated volumes for personal use. Some books of this kind belonged to members of the imperial family—for example, the Praxapostolos (Acts and epistles of the apostles) Moscow, University Library, Cod. 2280 (dated 1072); the Psalter St. Petersburg, National Library of Russia, Cod. gr. 214 (datable 1074); or the Klimakos Milan, Biblioteca Ambrosiana, Cod. B 80 sup. (datable 1071–1078). The original owners of most are, however, unknown.

PRODUCTION

Illuminated manuscripts in Byzantium were accessible only to a small upper-class minority. The price of books, even without illumination, was significant, and a large volume certainly entailed no small cost. The preferred book material was parchment. Paper first came into use, mostly in the imperial chancery but also for books, in the eleventh century. In the twelfth, some artists found it better to use paper for painting, and single paper leaves with pictures are found in parchment manuscripts like Milan, Ambrosiana, Cod. M 54 sup. (datable *ca.* 1100–1150).

Such experiments must have been prompted by the difficulty of making pigments adhere to the parchment's surface. For the same reason, it was preferable to place miniatures on the slightly coarser flesh side of a sheet, rather than on the smoother hair side. For full-page pictures, painters often used single leaves inserted among the regular sixteen-page gatherings of a volume. In spite of this, flaking remained a problem. To remedy it, some Byzantine miniatures were partially overpainted already in medieval times.

Little research has been done on the composition of pigments. In places where they have fallen off or in miniatures left unfinished, vague outline underdrawings are seen. Stencils and compasses were sometimes used for the outlines of ornamental motifs. It is not known whether model books of any sort existed. Artists could evidently paint the more common biblical scenes from memory or improvise on the basis of known compositional schemes: the person who around 1360 illustrated the Bulgarian Tomich Psalter (Moscow, State Historical Museum, Cod. 2752) was guided by short Greek instructions written in the outer edges of the book's margins. In other instances, painters copied the illustrations from an older book.

Because they worked in different materials, ink on the one hand, colored pigments on the other, scribe and illuminator were often not the same person. However, there are also cases of a single individual both copying and illuminating a book. Scribes sometimes signed their work (painters practically never did) and individual handwritings can be recognized with a fair amount of certainty. Personal traits can be distinguished also in miniature painting, and clusters of stylistically related works identified. Broader period styles are recognizable, though at times of increased productivity different manners of painting coexisted.

NINTH CENTURY

It is unknown whether the early Christian style of miniature painting continued through the politically troubled seventh and eighth centuries, but it is seen again in the early ninth, in the illuminated astronomical tables of the Vatican Ptolemy, Cod. gr. 1291 (datable *ca.* 828–835). Other styles were practiced as well. Manuscripts supposedly produced in Egypt/Palestine (the Dioscorides Paris, Bibliothèque nationale, Ms. gr. 2179) or Rome (the Milan Gregory, Ambrosiana, Cod. E 49–50 inf.; the Paris Sacra Parallela, BN, Ms. gr. 923) have illustrations with thick lines and unnuanced patches of color or gold. In three Psalters that must have been made in Constantinople soon after the end of Iconoclasm (most importantly the "Chludov Psalter," Moscow, SHM, Cod. 129D), the text is "glossed" in the margins with stocky figures of expressive, sometimes grotesque faces and gestures. A Gregory copied under the emperor Basil I (*r.* 867–886) (Paris, BN, Ms. gr. 510) has a large number of full-page miniatures densely filled with biblical and hagiographic scenes.

TENTH CENTURY

The Paris Gregory also provides the earliest Byzantine example of initial letters decorated with animal or human motifs. Other, increasingly elaborate ones appear in the first half of the tenth century, in particular in the work of a scribe (the "Chrysostom Initialer") who copied and decorated three volumes: Paris, BN, Ms. gr. 654; Venice, Biblioteca Marciana, Cod. gr. II.179; and Vatican Library, Cod. Ottob. gr. 14. These are drawn and colored in wash, as are the illustrations of the Chrysostom manuscript Athens, National Library, Cod. 211.

Unlike such drawings, which interlock with the manuscripts' text, most painted miniatures of the tenth century are framed as independent pictures upon an entire page and are most likely based on sixth-century or earlier prototypes. Examples include the illustrations of

The Heavenly Ladder. *From the famous scribe Joasaph's 14th-century copy of the* Climax (Heavenly Ladder *or* Scala Paradisi) *of John Klimakos* (d. *649*). SPECIAL COLLECTIONS LIBRARY, UNIVERSITY OF MICHIGAN, MS 134, FOL. 13V. REPRODUCED BY PERMISSION.

the Bible commissioned by a certain Leo, a castrated court dignitary (Vatican, Cod. Reg. gr. 1), of the Paris Psalter (BN, Ms. gr. 139), and of the Gospels Mount Athos, Stavronikita Monastery, Cod. 43. In the last manuscript, the text is in the hand of the scribe Ephraem, who also copied works of classical literature. Indeed, it has often been suggested that the retrospective style of some tenth-century Byzantine miniature painting was inspired by the contemporary interest in ancient Greek learning.

The tenth century also saw the rise of the first truly calligraphic Greek minuscules (types of writing with ligatures between some letters, upstrokes, and downstrokes): the *bouletée* and the *Perlschrift*. Parallel to this and at first quite independent of figural miniature painting, a rich repertory of book ornament (known as "flower-petal") developed. It remained largely in use throughout the subsequent history of Byzantine illumination. Its first dated specimens are found in two manuscripts on Mount Athos: Iviron Monastery, Cod. 70 (dated 954), and Dionysiou Monastery, Cod. 70 (dated 955). A Psalter in Paris (BN, Ms. suppl. gr. 610), datable to the late

---

TRANSLATION OF AN EXCERPT FROM THE
HOMILIES OF ST. GREGORY OF NAZIANZUS

Ms. Mount Athos, Iviron Monastery, Cod. 27, a tenth-century copy of the Homilies of St. Gregory of Nazianzus, fol. 87 verso.

Iambic Verses as if Spoken by the Book:

I was
By Gregory's divine mind engendered,
And through Ignatius' zeal beautified.
My words' sanctity is from my father,
And my delightful pages, from the scribe.
So I was splendidly adorned by both of
    them,
Most excellent and God-inspired men.
Now you, lover of words divinely spoken,
Rejoice in my beautiful appearance,
Rejoice in our Lord's heavenly doctrines,
That you take in through your ears and
    eyes!

SOURCE: Greek text in P. Sōtēroudēs, *Hiera Monē* Ivērōn: Katalogos hellēnikōn cheirographōn, Vol. 1. Mount Athos, Greece: Hiera Mone Iveron, 1998, pp. 44–45.

---

tenth century, is among the earliest examples of integrating nonrepresentational with figural illustration.

ELEVENTH CENTURY

The trend toward coordinating script, ornament, and illustration marks books made during this century. After around 1060 small pictures often came to be embedded in or around the text, making for a virtually simultaneous reading of script and images. The "renaissance" style practiced in the tenth century was gradually abandoned in favor of less illusionistic ways of painting.

A few illustrated volumes were commissioned by aristocrats in cities like Adrianople (the Armenian Gospels Venice, San Lazzaro, Cod. 887/116, dated 1007) or Antioch (the Lectionary Athos, Koutloumousiou, Cod. 61, datable *ca.* 1070). The quality of their miniatures is however markedly inferior to works from the capital Constantinople, where the imperial palace formed a powerful and steady source of patronage. Two large illustrated books, a Psalter in Venice (Marciana, Cod. gr. 17)

and a collection of short saints' lives in the Vatican (Cod. gr. 1613), contain dedicatory poems praising the emperor Basil II (*r.* 976–1025). Volumes from a similarly illustrated hagiographic collection commissioned by the emperor Michael IV (*r.* 1034–1041) survive in Baltimore (Walters Art Museum, W. 521) and in Moscow (SHM, Cod. Synod. gr. 183). The Chrysostom Paris, BN, Ms. Coilsin 79, and perhaps the Menologion London, British Library, Add. ms. 11870, were made for the emperor Michael VII Doukas (*r.* 1071–1078) or for his successor, Nikephoros III Botaneiates (*r.* 1078–1081).

The organization of the workshops that produced luxury books is unclear. The miniatures of Vatican gr. 1613 are by several painters who evidently joined forces specifically for illustrating it. Other manuscripts were made by monks in the capital. At the Stoudiou Monastery, the scribe Theodore copied in the century's third quarter a number of richly illustrated books: a Gospels in Paris (BN, Ms. gr. 74), two Psalters (Vatican, Cod. Barber. gr. 372; and London, British Library, Add. ms. 19352, dated 1066), and the now-destroyed Smyrna Physiologus (Evangelical School, Cod. B8). Constantine, active toward the end of century at the small convent of Louphadion, copied and illustrated a *Heavenly Ladder* (Vatican, Cod. gr. 394) and a Gregory (Athos, Dionysiou, Cod. 61).

TWELFTH CENTURY

Three practically identical illustrated Octateuchs—Vatican, Cod. gr. 746; İstanbul, Topkapi Sarāy Cod. gr. 8; and the destroyed Smyrna, Evangelical School, Cod. A.1—are all datable to between 1125 and 1150. The style of one of the illustrators of the İstanbul and Smyrna volumes (the "Kokkinobaphos Master") is recognizable in the miniatures of several other manuscripts, including the New Testament Codex Ebnerianus (Oxford, Bodleian Library, Auct. T. inf. 1.10); the Gospels Vatican, Cod. Urbin. gr. 2; the Georgian Lapskaldi Gospels (Mestia, Museum of Svanetia, no. 482); and two copies of the homilies of James the Monk (James of Kokkinobaphos) in Paris (BN, Ms. gr. 1208) and in the Vatican (Cod. gr. 1162). This painter must have been patronized by the court, since the Vatican Gospels open with a portrait of the emperor John II Komnenos (*r.* 1118–1143) and his son Alexios (coruler 1122–1142). The century's second quarter also saw the increased popularity of initial letters decorated with images of wild animals and of hunting, a favorite imperial sport.

Constantinopolitan monasteries, too, remained important as centers of patronage and production. A richly illustrated Gregory (Mount Sinai, Cod. gr. 339, datable

Medicinal Plant in a Manuscript of Dioscorides. *The text areas and illustration are highlighted in gold.* BIBLIO-THÈQUE NATIONALE DE FRANCE, MS GREC 2179, FOL. 4V. REPRODUCED BY PERMISSION.

ca. 1142) was presented by the abbot of the imperial Pantokrator Monastery to another convent near the capital. The Georgian Vani Gospels (Tbilisi, Kekelidze Institute, Cod. A-1335) was copied in the Sokhasteri Monastery near Constantinople and illuminated by the Greek Michael Koreses.

The making of multiple copies of an illuminated volume, as exemplified by the Octateuchs and Kokkinobaphos's homilies, became common practice in the second half of the century. The vast majority of illuminated books dated to this period are small Gospels and Psalters for personal use. The best-known representatives of this large group, subsumed under the name "decorative style," are two volumes with similar cycles of narrative miniatures, the Rockefeller McCormick New Testament (University of Chicago Library, Ms. 965) and the Karahissar Gospels (St. Petersburg, NLR, Cod. gr. 105). Whenever the commissioner or scribe of a late-twelfth-century illuminated book is known, he can be located in either Cyprus or Palestine. The importance of imperial and Constantinopolitan book patronage seems to have declined sharply after around 1150. Based in the provinces, the "decorative style" continued after 1204, when the Byzantine capital was conquered by the Fourth Crusade.

Gospel of Matthew. Title page from an 11th-century lectionary. Athens, Bibliotheke tes Boules (Library of Parliament), MS 7, fol. 107r. ILLUMINATION FROM *GOSPEL BOOK*, W.7, FOLIO 107. THE WALTERS ART MUSEUM, BALTIMORE. REPRODUCED BY PERMISSION.

LATE THIRTEENTH TO MID-FIFTEENTH CENTURY

The Byzantine reconquest of Constantinople in 1261 was followed by a revival of the old traditions of luxury bookmaking. The calligraphic *Perlschrift* that had fallen into disuse after around 1100 and tenth-to-twelfth-century miniature painting provided models to follow. The illustrated Gospels Athos, Iviron, Cod. 5, exemplify these retrospective tendencies, apparently without imitating an actual earlier manuscript. The Octateuch Athos, Vatopedi, Cod. 602, is a direct late-thirteenth-century copy of Vatican gr. 746. Its contemporary the Palatina Psalter (Vatican, Cod. Palat. gr. 381) is based upon the tenth-century Paris Psalter.

After 1261 Constantinople regained its foremost position in the production of illuminated books. The script of the illustrated Job Jerusalem, Greek Patriarchate, Cod. Taphou 5, can be attributed to a notary working at the imperial chancery in the early fourteenth century. Other scribes were employees of the patriarchal office; for example, George Galesiotes, who in 1346 copied for Prince Isaac Palaiologos Asan the illustrated Gospels Sinai, Cod. gr. 152. A characteristic calligraphic script was cultivated at the Constantinopolitan monastery of Hodegon. Its two foremost practitioners were Chariton (*fl.* 1319–1346) and Joasaph (*fl.* 1360–1406). Only recently did illustrated manuscripts copied by Chariton come to light: the Gospels Athos, Iviron, Cod. 2110 (dated 1323), and a lectionary (dated 1341) presented by the emperor John VI Kantakouzenos (*d.* 1383) to the Monastery of Vatopedi and still kept in its sacristy (Cod. 16). Illustrated books made by Joasaph include the Akathistos Hymn Moscow, SHM, Cod. Synod. gr. 429 (probably owned by Patriarch Philotheos Kokkinos, *d. ca.* 1377), and a copy of Kantakouzenos's writings (Paris, BN, Ms. gr. 1242, completed 1375).

Thessaloniki emerged as center of book illumination as well. It was probably there that the scribe Theodore Hagiopetrites (*fl.* 1278–1308), one of the foremost imitators of the old *Perlschrift*, worked in collaboration with different painters. Demetrios Palaiologos, who ruled the city from 1322 to around 1340, commissioned the Oxford "Menologion" (Bodleian Library, Cod. gr. th. f. 1), a picture book with various saints' images and scenes from Christ's life.

Contacts with the West played a significant role in the late Byzantine period. Two early-fourteenth-century books illustrated in Byzantine style—the Gospels Paris, BN, Ms. gr. 54, and the Hamilton Psalter (Berlin, Kupferstichkabinett, Ms. 78 A.9)—have parallel texts in both Greek and Latin. The remarkably lifelike portraits of the emperor John VIII Palaiologos (*r.* 1425–1448) in the Psalter and New Testament Sinai, Cod. gr. 2123, and of his brother Demetrios (*d.* 1470) in the Gospels St. Petersburg, NLR, Cod. gr. 118, both show the strong influence of Italian painting. Demetrios is depicted in black monastic habit rather than princely attire: In 1460, his residence, Mistra, had fallen to the Ottomans.

BIBLIOGRAPHY

INTRODUCTORY WORKS

De Gregorio, Giuseppe. "Scriba: Area bizantina." In *Enciclopedia dell'arte medievale.* Vol. 10. Rome: Istituto della Enciclopedia Italiana, 1999. With bibliography.

Lowden, John. "Early Christian and Byzantine Art, § V, 2: Manuscripts, Greek." In *The Dictionary of Art.* Edited by Jane Turner. Vol. 9. New York: Grove, 1996. With bibliography.

———. *Early Christian and Byzantine Art.* London: Phaidon, 1997. Accessibly written and excellently illustrated; lots of attention given to manuscripts.

Ševčenko, Nancy Patterson. "Illuminating the Liturgy: Illustrated Service Books in Byzantium." In *Heaven on Earth: Art and the Church in Byzantium.* Edited by Linda Safran. University Park: Pennsylvania State University Press, 1998.

REFERENCE WORKS

Canart, Paul. *Paleografia e codicologia greca: Una rassegna bibliografica.* Vatican City: Scuola vaticana di paleografia, diplomatica, e archivistica, 1991.

Spatharakis, Ioannis. *Corpus of Dated Illuminated Greek Manuscripts to the Year 1453.* 2 vols. Leiden, Netherlands: Brill, 1981.

Voicu, Sever, and Serenella D'Alisera. *I.MA.G.E.S.: Index in Manuscriptorum graecorum edita Specimina.* Rome: Borla, 1981.

SELECT STUDIES

Carr, Annemarie W. "Thoughts on the Production of Provincial Illuminated Books in the Twelfth and Thirteenth Centuries." In *Scritture, libri, e testi nelle aree provinciali di Bisanzio.* Edited by Guglielmo Cavallo et al. Vol. 2. Spoleto, Italy: Centro per il collegamento degli studi medievali e umanistici nell'Università di Perugia, 1991.

D'Aiuto, Francesco. "Su alcuni copisti di codici miniati mediobizantini. 2." *Bollettino della Badia Greca di Grottaferrata,* n.s. 53 (1999): 119–150.

Hutter, Irmgard. "*Le Copiste du Métaphraste.* On a Center for Manuscript Production in Eleventh Century Constantinople." In *I Manoscritti greci tra riflessione e dibattito: Atti del V Colloquio Internazionale di Paleografia Greca.* Edited by Giancarlo Prato. Florence: Gonnelli, 2000.

Iacobini, Antonio, and Lidia Perria. "Un Vangelo della Rinascenza macedona al Monte Athos. Nuove ipotesi sullo Stavronikita 43 e il suo scriba." *Rivista di studi bizantini e neoellenici,* n.s. 37 (2000): 73–97.

Mokretsova, I. P., M. M. Naumova, V. N. Kireeva, E. N. Dobrynina, and B. L. Fonkich. *Materialy i tekhnika vizantiiskoi rukopisnoi knigi.* Moscow: Indrik, 2003.

GEORGI PARPULOV

[See also **DMA:** Byzantine Art (843–1453); Canon Table; Codicology, Western European; Donor Portrait; Early Christian Art; Evangeliary; Gospelbook; Joshua Roll; Macedonian Renaissance; Manuscript Books, Binding of: European; Manuscript Illumination, European; Menologion; Octateuch; Palmette; Parchment; Paris Psalter; Quire; Renaissances and Revivals in Medieval Art; Scriptorium; Synaxary; **Supp:** Manuscript Collections.]

MAPS AND MAPMAKING. See **Cartography.**

MARRIAGE, CHRISTIAN.

Christian religious beliefs combined with Roman institutions to furnish the fundamental premises that shaped medieval ideas and practices concerning marriage, separation, and divorce. Medieval authorities, both civil and ecclesiastical, adapted and elaborated those ideas and practices to produce a new and distinctive matrimonial system whose basic premises remain visible in Western family law down to the present day.

ROMAN AND EARLY CHRISTIAN CONCEPTS AND PRACTICES

The basic elements of the early church's doctrines on these matters are scattered through the documents that make up the New Testament. Christians from the outset defined marriage as a monogamous union that, save under exceptional circumstances, they expected to endure through the lifetimes of the spouses (Mark 1:2–16; Matt. 5:32, 19:9; 1 Cor. 7:10–11). Early Christian teachings about the proper relationship between man and wife were ambivalent. Men and women, they believed, were equals in the eyes of God (Gal. 3:28; 1 Pet. 3:7), but in this life husbands should have charge over their wives. Early Christians expected married women to remain modest, veiled from the sight of other men, submissive to their husbands' wishes within the family, and silent in the churches (1 Cor. 11:3–16; Eph. 5: 22–24; 1 Tim. 2:11–15; 1 Pet. 3:1–6). A man, to be sure, should love his wife as he loved himself, while she in return was bound to show him respect in all things (Eph. 5:28–33). These prescriptions about female behavior reflected common expectations in the Palestinian Jewish communities where Christianity originated.

As Christianity slowly spread through the Roman Empire, the church's members not surprisingly adopted many of the marriage customs in the surrounding society. Christian authorities shared with pagan Romans the belief that marriage ought to be monogamous. That premise was so basic to Roman ideas about marriage that jurists apparently found it inconceivable that a Roman citizen might contract more than one marriage at a time, and classical Roman law had no provisions to deal with bigamy.

Free consent of the spouses and their families to a proposed marital union became a basic element of Christian marriage, as it was in Roman matrimonial law. In Roman practice, heads of households typically negotiated marriages between their children. Once they reached agreement upon the terms, they laid these out in a formal betrothal contract, to which the prospective bride and groom were then expected to assent. This practice also became the usual way that early Christians arranged their marriages. Marriage ceremonies in early Christian communities largely followed traditional Roman patterns as well. Weddings among Christians, like those among their pagan neighbors, were basically private household affairs that centered on the ritual delivery of the bride and her possessions to the groom's household, followed by a celebratory banquet. Christian authorities only began to insist on formal, public wedding ceremonies that incorporated specifically religious rituals much later.

Christian practice differed, however, from both Jewish and Roman practices when it came to divorce followed by remarriage. Jewish law had always allowed married men to repudiate their wives (Deut. 24:1–3), but wives could not repudiate their husbands, although some evidence suggests that by the first century A.D. this had begun to change, at least in a few Hellenized Jewish communities. Despite the fact that ancient Romans, like Christians, believed that marriage should ideally be a lifelong partnership, they had come to tolerate divorce and subsequent remarriage. By the second century A.D. divorce had become both easy and common in Roman society. Christian teachers, by contrast, from the time of St. Augustine (354–430) sharply rejected the institution of divorce. Augustine insisted that the references to divorce that appear in the New Testament (Matt. 5:32, 19:9; Mark 10:2–16; 1 Cor. 7:10–11) simply authorized unhappy married couples to separate under certain circumstances. Despite separation, however, their marriage remained intact and neither party could remarry until the other had died. Even then, moreover, Christian authorities strongly discouraged remarriage of the surviving spouse. It was far better, they taught, for the survivor to remain single and chaste. While this view was consistent with St. Paul's belief that celibacy was spiritually superior to marriage (1 Cor. 7:1–2, 6–7), it was foreign to mainstream Roman and Jewish traditions.

Once the emperor Constantine the Great (r. 311–337) had publicly embraced Christianity, many inhabitants of the empire deemed it not merely safe but advantageous as well to adopt the Christian faith. In consequence imperial authorities gradually began to incorporate Christian beliefs about marriage and divorce into Roman law and public policy. Canons adopted by church councils also came to have the force of public law. The administration of the new laws on these matters, moreover, fell increasingly under the jurisdiction of religious courts presided over by Christian bishops. Among other things, the marriage laws of the Christian empire for the first time defined bigamy as a crime and prohibited married men from keeping concubines. The Christian emperors also introduced laws that enabled slaves to contract legal marriages, restricted the right of individuals to marry close blood relatives, and began to encourage formal wedding ceremonies that included a blessing of the couple by a priest. Property settlements at the time of marriage, especially a dowry provided by the bride's family, likewise became more formal and more expensive under the Christian emperors. For a time a dowry was even mandatory for legal marriages, with the result that young men began to marry earlier and young women to marry later than had previously been customary.

The Christian emperors, guided by religious authorities, likewise introduced changes in divorce law. Constantine severely restricted the grounds on which a man could divorce his wife, while at the same time he made it slightly easier for a wife to free herself from an abusive husband. His legislation imposed no restrictions on remarriage following divorce. It was later generations of religious authorities that insisted that no validly contracted marriage could legally be terminated in such a way that the parties became free to contract another marriage during the lifetime of the former spouse.

THE EARLY MIDDLE AGES

While Roman civil law had begun to incorporate substantial elements of Christian marriage doctrine by the late fourth century, barbarian invaders, who were by that time beginning to undermine the stability and integrity of the Western Roman imperial government, brought with them very different ideas about marriage than those held by the great majority of the empire's Christian inhabitants. Two contrasting marriage traditions thus came to coexist in western Europe through much of the early Middle Ages.

The great majority of the Roman or romanized population of the empire survived the invasions reasonably intact and continued for many generations to conduct their private business and personal relationships in much the same ways that they had done under Roman rule. German settlers comprised only a minority of the population in most regions of the former Western Roman Empire and were far outnumbered by the indigenous peoples of Roman heritage among whom they dwelled. Although the descendants of the German invaders ultimately accepted the Roman form of Christianity, differences between their customary marriage practices and those approved by the church bred persisting tensions between the new rulers and church authorities.

Germanic peoples traditionally treated marriage as a social, economic, and political union. The parents of the prospective bride and groom negotiated the terms of their marriage and entered into a betrothal contract. A wedding ceremony subsequently symbolized the completion of the union, which the newlyweds then sealed by sexual consummation in the marriage bed. Germanic rulers and other wealthy and powerful men frequently found it useful to enter into more than one such alliance and often presided over households that contained multiple wives and sometimes second-class wives, or concubines, as well. Powerful men frequently deemed it advantageous to ally themselves with closely related kindred groups in marriages that ecclesiastical law disallowed. Germanic practice, moreover, permitted men to dissolve their marriages for cause and to remarry if and when this suited the interests of the husband or his family. Adultery furnished the grounds for divorce mentioned most frequently in written Germanic laws, but other antisocial activities, such as witchcraft or grave robbery, also appear in some codes. A husband had the further option of dismissing his wife without invoking any of the accepted grounds for divorce provided that he was prepared to furnish her and her family with appropriate compensation. It was far more difficult for a wife to initiate a divorce. The Burgundian laws, for example, decreed a particularly shameful form of the death penalty—smothering in mire—for a woman who attempted to divorce her husband. Still, women with influential family connections sometimes succeeded in ridding themselves legally of disagreeable husbands. Accounts of couples who divorced by mutual consent also appear occasionally in sources from seventh- and eighth-century Gaul.

Although churchmen repeatedly deplored these practices, efforts to discourage them met dogged resistance. During the seventh and eighth centuries both religious writers and secular rulers become increasingly uneasy about conflicts between the church rules concerning marriage and the ways that families of Germanic heritage actually conducted their marital strategies. Rulings from ecclesiastical authorities, moreover, often widened the existing gap between ecclesiastical prescriptions and the marriage practices of the laity. Bede (672/73–735), for example, reproduced in his *Ecclesiastical History of the English People* a series of pronouncements attributed to Pope Gregory the Great (r. 590–604) that not only reiterated earlier prohibitions on marriage between close kin but also extended them further. The pope, according to Bede, had declared that marriages between blood kin within seven degrees of relationship were contrary to canon law and demanded that couples so related separate. This seven-degree rule, which could easily rule out thousands of possible marriage partners, gradually became accepted as the canonical norm, although enforcement of it remained problematical. The rulings attributed to Gregory further limited an individual's choice of marriage partners by banning marriages in which one party had had sexual intercourse, marital or nonmarital, with any of the blood kin of the other party. The Merovingian kings also adopted a similar rule. Church leaders complicated matters still more by insisting that baptismal sponsorship created a spiritual relationship between godparents and their godchildren, which gave rise to still another impediment to marriage.

The eighth century witnessed efforts to narrow the gap between church teachings and lay practice concerning marriage and divorce. Around 860 Archbishop Hincmar of Reims (*ca.* 806–882) proposed a novel theory of marriage that combined the church's traditional emphasis on consent with the Germanic principle that consummation was what made a marriage binding. Hincmar argued that dowry, parental consent, a public wedding, free consent of the parties, and consummation were all necessary to create a valid marriage. A union that lacked any of these five requirements was not legally binding. Hincmar's formulation borrowed elements from earlier authorities, notably Pope Gregory II (r. 715–731), who had implied that sexual union was a basic component of marriage when he allowed a man whose wife was unable to have sexual relations with him to divorce her and marry a sexually compatible partner. The pope had noted, however, that the husband's obligation to support his first wife continued even after the termination of their marriage. Some penitential writers in this period, too, were less censorious than the canons in their treatment of remarriage following a separation on grounds approved by the church.

Marriage and divorce doctrine continued in flux throughout the ninth and tenth centuries. Some authorities in this period, both ecclesiastical and secular, reiterated earlier views that forbade remarriage following separation until after the first spouse had died. Charlemagne (r. 768–814), who had four wives as well as a number of concubines, adopted this restrictive policy on divorce as imperial law and extended it throughout his empire. His son, Louis the Pious (r. 814–840), renewed Charlemagne's action in 829, and several of his successors did likewise. Yet a Roman synod under Pope Eugenius II (824–827) not only allowed divorce on grounds of adultery but also permitted the innocent party to remarry.

Jurisdiction over disputed marriages raised further problems. Few writers during the ninth and tenth centuries were prepared to claim that the church had an exclusive right to adjudicate matrimonial issues. Yet bishops and other church authorities could, and often did, make judgments about whether or not particular marriages met the standards that the canons laid down. The church had not yet developed a uniform procedure for handling these matters, however, and efforts to secure compliance with the rules about Christian marriage were more hortatory than juridical.

THE HIGH AND LATER MIDDLE AGES

This situation began to change once leaders of the eleventh-century church reform movement secured control of the papacy. Pope Leo IX (*r.* 1048–1054) and his successors sought, among other things, to establish a working system of church courts, to expand ecclesiastical jurisdiction over many facets of everyday life, including marriage and divorce, and to make that jurisdiction more effective than it previously had been. These efforts were hampered by uncertainty about just what the law of the church concerning marriage, among other vital matters, really was. Bishops and others in the mid-eleventh century had no single source to which they could turn when they needed to find what church law said. Collections of the canons abounded, and reformers compiled still more of them, but none of these secured general recognition as authoritative. Even worse, the authorities cited in these collections differed among themselves over such basic issues as how a valid marriage was contracted, at what point an agreement to marry became binding, and how, under what circumstances, and by whom a marriage could be annulled or indeed whether it could be annulled at all. Leading figures in the reform movement strongly disputed Hincmar's opinion that consummation was essential for a valid marriage but agreed with his contention that secret marriages were improper, although most of them stopped short of claiming that they were invalid. With few exceptions, members of the reform party rejected the venerable tradition that permitted divorce on the grounds of adultery, yet some were prepared to countenance it as grounds for separation without the right of remarriage. They commonly taught that a married person who wished to make a vow of chastity and enter a monastery could be allowed to do so, provided that his or her spouse did likewise. Many canonists of the late eleventh century regarded consanguinity, affinity, or impotence as an adequate basis for holding a marriage invalid and were prepared, although reluctantly, to permit subsequent remarriage in these situations.

The appearance around 1150 of the vulgate version of the *Decretum* of Gratian supplied the authoritative compendium of canon law that had been lacking for so long. Gratian not only assembled a huge body of opinions and rulings about the organization of the church and the conduct of its members but, even more important, tried to make sense out of the contradictions in the legal sources that had bedeviled earlier generations of ecclesiastical lawyers, judges, and administrators. Gratian's analysis of earlier pronouncements about marriage, divorce, and separation attempted, sometimes successfully, to resolve the uncertainties found in the legal sources. While his book failed to solve all of the problems, it at least made them more manageable. Gratian's treatment of conflicting authorities also helped to clarify which old problems still needed new solutions.

Gratian confronted a welter of unresolved issues concerning marriage. Some pronouncements held that marriage came into existence when a couple agreed to live together for the remainder of their lives, and a few went so far as to claim that such a marriage was binding even if no one else knew about it. Other authorities vehemently denied both of these propositions. The consent of the parties' parents was essential, they claimed, and moreover a marriage had to be contracted in public. Still others said there was no real marriage until the couple consummated their union. Some thought that a dowry was essential to constitute a true marriage, rather than some less formal union, but others denied this. It was far from clear whether or not a Christian marriage must involve any sort of church ceremony or a nuptial blessing from a clergyman. Nor was there any general agreement as to whether marriage was or was not a sacrament and thus subject to exclusive ecclesiastical control.

Gratian sought to reconcile the view that marriage was essentially a consensual contract with the competing claim that consummation was the critical factor in marriage formation by establishing a two-step process. Consent between the parties, according to Gratian, initiated a marriage, while sexual consummation completed it. Both steps were necessary to create a fully binding marriage *(matrimonium ratum)*. Gratian thus saw marriage as both a spiritual union, signified by the exchange of consent, and a physical union, achieved through sexual intercourse. Once marital consent had been ratified by coitus, the marriage was binding and could not be dissolved so long as both parties lived.

Gratian's theory of marriage formation, sometimes known as "the Italian model," faced vigorous competition from an alternative theory known as "the French model." The most influential champion of this view was the Paris theologian Peter Lombard (*ca.* 1095–1160), who wrote his vastly influential theological textbook, *The Four Books of Sentences,* at just about the same time that Gratian completed the final version of his own work. Lombard and other Paris theologians argued that consent and consent alone created the marriage bond that held a couple together. The essence of marriage, according to Peter Lombard and his followers, lay in the intention of the parties to commit themselves to a life-long union. Since intent lay at the core of marriage, the precise way in which the parties expressed their consent was vitally important. If a man and woman who were eligible to marry one another exchanged marriage vows in the present tense, regardless of the circumstances in which they did so, they instantly created an indissoluble marriage that bound them together for the remainder of their natural lives. If, however, they used the future tense when they exchanged those promises, they were not married. The exchange of future consent merely created a betrothal contract, which was revocable. Subsequent sexual intercourse between the betrothed couple, however, automatically transformed their betrothal into an irrevocable marriage.

Pope Alexander III (1159–1181) found Gratian's model of marriage formation unsatisfactory and took steps to recast the church's domestic relations law in ways that would make marriages easier to contract yet more difficult to dissolve than they were in current law. In a series of decretals Alexander adopted the main points of the French model of marriage formation, which made it extremely easy to contract marriage. Under the rules that he adopted, free consent of the man and woman themselves became the only essential requirement for marriage, provided, of course, that they were otherwise eligible to marry each other. Pope Alexander at the same time promoted the freedom of couples to choose marriage partners of whom families and parents might not approve. Under the terms of Alexander III's decretals, even couples who exchanged marital consent before they reached the minimum legal age for marriage (which, following Justinian, he set at twelve for girls, fourteen for boys) became married the instant they subsequently had sexual relations. In a series of further decretals, Alexander III defined what he meant by free consent when he insisted that it must be given without fear of consequence. The pope instructed ecclesiastical judges to nullify any exchanges of marital consent made under coercion. He borrowed again from Roman law when he defined the level of pressure that nullified matrimonial consent as a degree of force or fear that would be "sufficient to sway an intrepid man" *(metu coactus qui posset in virum constantem cadere).*

Alexander III was aware that promoting freedom of choice entailed the less desirable consequence that couples could, if they wished, marry surreptitiously, informally, without witnesses and that under the terms of his decretals these covert marriages would be perfectly valid. In one decretal, to be sure, he made it clear that he thoroughly disapproved of such goings-on—but he still refrained from requiring parental approval, witnesses, sacred ceremonies, or public disclosure as conditions for a valid marriage. On the contrary, he expressly ruled in other decretals that a secret exchange of marital consent, without a priest or solemnity, produced a fully binding marriage. Alexander III was determined that persons should be able to marry freely, unconstrained by considerations such as poverty, social disapproval, or the opposition of family, friends, or feudal lords.

The clandestine marriages that Alexander III's decretals permitted, however, had the potential to undercut marital stability and family relationships. A wife might find herself ejected from her marital home if her husband successfully challenged the validity of their marriage on the grounds that before their wedding he had exchanged words of present consent with some former flame. Nor could any husband be sure that a long-forgotten suitor might not turn up some day to claim his wife on similar grounds. Indeed, the problems that clandestine marriage could produce under the rules adopted by Alexander III were not merely hypothetical: more than 70 percent of the matrimonial cases in some jurisdictions involved couples who claimed that they had exchanged consent privately, not in a church, but instead at home, in a garden, an open field, under a tree, in a tavern, or, not infrequently, in bed.

Alexander III's successors, especially Pope Innocent III (r. 1198–1216), made vigorous efforts to deal with the problem. Pope Innocent III directed the bishops at the Fourth Lateran Council (1215) to adopt a constitution that forbade clandestine marriages and admonished priests that they must not give their blessing to such unions under pain of suspension from office and forfeiture of income for three years. The council further required parish priests to announce forthcoming weddings publicly during Mass and to do so far enough in advance so that anyone who knew of a reason why a couple should not be joined in matrimony could raise timely objections. Couples who defied the council's decree were warned that any children they might have would be deemed illegitimate. The council fathers nevertheless stopped short of holding clandestine marriages invalid. Clandestine marriages, with all the problems they entailed, continued to bedevil the church and its members throughout the later Middle Ages. The Latin church was so strongly committed to the principle that free consent of the parties was the central element of Christian marriage that it failed to take decisive action to deal with this issue until 1563, when the canon *Tametsi* of the Council of Trent at last declared clandestine marriages invalid. Even so, the practice lingered on in many regions, among Protestants as well as Roman Catholics. In England, for example, clandestine marriages continued to be recognized by law until the Marriage Act of 1753.

Another important constitution of the Fourth Lateran Council reduced the degrees of blood relationship within which marriage was forbidden from seven to four and also drastically diminished the scope of marriage impediments that arose from affinity. These actions greatly enlarged the number of eligible marriage partners that an individual might legally marry. In consequence, fewer unions after 1215 were open to attack on grounds of consanguinity or affinity, and divorce cases brought on these grounds became relatively uncommon in later court records. The emergence of consent as the central element in creating marriage meant that defects of consent (such as fraud, deceit, coercion, or incapacity to consent arising from insanity) also tended to become central issues in much marriage litigation during the High and later Middle Ages.

By the thirteenth century the church had secured virtually unchallenged jurisdiction over most disputed matters that involved marriage, including alimony and child support, although the courts of civil authorities jealously guarded control over the dowry and property issues associated with marital breakup, as well as with disputes concerning legitimacy and wardship of minor children. Prior to the late twelfth century bishops routinely handled marital disputes themselves, although they sometimes referred hotly contested cases to a diocesan or provincial synod, especially if the parties were prominent and powerful. Proceedings tended to be relatively flexible and informal, so that ordinary people could present their claims or denials orally, in the hope that whatever evidence and eloquence they could muster might persuade the bishop or synod to grant what they desired.

Beginning in the 1170s, however, bishops in many regions started to delegate all but the most sensitive of their judicial duties to clerics with formal legal training. These "bishop's officials," as they were usually called, became the chief judges of a permanent court, often styled the bishop's consistory, which dealt with the vast majority of marital and other disputes that came within the bishop's jurisdiction. Exceptionally important or sensitive marriage cases might be appealed to the pope. He, too, began during this period to delegate the disposition of most marriage cases to a group of legally trained judges who made up what later came to be called (and is still known as) the Roman Rota. Proceedings in consistory courts and especially at the rota and other appeals courts often demanded substantial knowledge of the law and familiarity with complex procedures, which litigants without formal legal training were not likely to possess. Although parties continued to appear in court by themselves, they increasingly needed professional advice and counsel to do so successfully, while those who could afford it employed proctors or advocates to represent them. This naturally meant that bringing or defending a marriage case grew more costly. Despite this, medieval church courts never became the exclusive preserve of the rich and well-born. Peasants and fishermen, carpenters and peddlers, blacksmiths and tailors, regularly appeared in court records as parties to marriage cases. They did so for the most part at their own expense, although judges occasionally provided legal aid for impoverished litigants by ordering one of the court's lawyers to assist them without charge.

Despite persistent complaints about the length of legal proceedings, church courts handled routine marriage cases with remarkable speed and efficiency, especially after summary procedures came into common use around the beginning of the fourteenth century. Simple uncontested cases were often closed after a single hearing, but even contested cases, at least in English church courts, seldom went on for more than six or seven months.

Marriage and separation among the wealthy and powerful naturally left more abundant traces in the surviving records than did those among their more humble contemporaries. Royal and noble marriages were elaborately negotiated political alliances that often involved the contribution of substantial properties by the families to support the new couple in a style appropriate to the status of their ancestors. When marriages at this exalted social level broke down, those involved often scrambled furiously to discover plausible grounds so that they could persuade church authorities to grant an annulment, which would permit each party to enter into a second marriage with some new and, perhaps, more desirable partner. The multiple marriages of Louis VII of France (r. 1137–1180), Henry II of England (r. 1154–1189), and Eleanor of Aquitaine (ca. 1122–1204) or those of Philip II of France (r. 1180–1223) (with Ingeborg of Denmark in 1193 and Agnes of Meran in 1200) offer well-known examples, to which the marital adventures of less prominent magnates furnish countless parallels.

While such schemes and calculations are most visibly documented among those in the higher ranks of society, families further down the social hierarchy commonly practiced similar, if less lavish, stratagems. Parents engaged in elaborate calculations to determine the level of dowry or bridegift they would need to attract acceptable suitors for their children, and some late medieval Italian cities even set up special funds, such as the *Monte delle doti* at Florence, to enable families to arrange the marriages of their children, especially their daughters. Some charitable associations specialized in raising money for the same purpose. Municipalities, alarmed that the competition was getting out of hand, attempted to impose limits on the value of marriage gifts and the lavishness of weddings.

When a marriage failed and a couple went their separate ways, the couple and their families, often with the assistance of legal advisers, had to devise an agreement concerning the division of marital property, which might well involve even more difficult bargaining than did the original marriage settlement. The terms of separation settlements were almost always negotiated out of court. They frequently took the form of a private contract drawn up by a notary. Judges rarely tried to impose property settlements on couples, although they sometimes took notice of the terms of an out-of-court agreement when they closed a case.

The settlements themselves sought, at least in principle, to divide the marital property in such a way that each party received an equitable share, while also providing appropriate support for any children of the marriage. Although customary practices varied considerably from one region to the next, marital property arrangements fell into two basic types. One widespread type was the separate property system, which became characteristic of English common law. Variations on this pattern also appear in many other parts of Western Christendom. Under a separate property system, each party remained the owner of any property brought into the marriage and retained ownership when the marriage ended. Should the husband under this system predecease his wife, she was also entitled to claim part of his property—generally one-third of it in English common law—but otherwise their property remained distinct. Likewise, if the parties separated, each party kept its own property, including any profits that may have accrued to it during the term of their marriage.

The other widespread arrangement was the community property system, characteristic of northern France but also found elsewhere. In community property jurisdictions, just as in separate property systems, partners in a marriage normally expected to retain at the end of their marriage whatever they had owned when it began. Any acquests, or additional property acquired during the term of the marriage, constituted community property, which, at least in principle, was divided equally between the parties when the marriage ended. In practice, however, the division of acquest property at the termination of a marriage was not always so simple. Regional custom, the circumstances under which it was acquired, and especially arrangements for the custody of any minor children of the marriage might introduce variations into the basic pattern.

BIBLIOGRAPHY

PRIMARY WORKS

Corpus iuris canonici. Edited by Emil Friedberg. 2 vols. Graz: Akademische Druck- u. Verlagsanstalt, 1959.

Decrees of the Ecumenical Councils. Edited by G. Alberigo et al. Translated by Norman P. Tanner et al. 2 vols. London: Sheed and Ward, 1990.

Medieval Handbooks of Penance. Edited and translated by John T. McNeill and Helena M. Gamer. Records of Western Civilization, no. 29. New York: Columbia University Press, 1990.

Select Cases from the Ecclesiastical Courts of the Province of Canterbury, c. 1200–1301. Edited by Norma Adams and Charles Donahue Jr. Selden Society Publications, 95. London: Selden Society, 1981.

SECONDARY WORKS

Aznar Gil, Federico R. *La institución matrimonial en la Hispania cristiana bajo-medieval (1215–1563).* Bibliotheca Salmanticensis, Estudios, vol. 23. Salamanca: Universidad Pontificia Salamanca, 1989.

Brooke, Christopher N. L. *The Medieval Idea of Marriage.* Oxford: Clarendon Press,1989.

Brundage, James A. *Law, Sex, and Christian Society in Medieval Europe.* Chicago: University of Chicago Press,1987.

Dauvillier, Jean. *Le mariage dans le droit classique de l'église, depuis le Décret de Gratien (1140) jusqu'à mort de Clément V (1314).* Paris: Sirey Recueil, 1933.

Donahue, Charles, Jr. "What Causes Fundamental Legal Ideas? Marital Property in England and France in the Thirteenth Century." *Michigan Law Review* 78 (1979) 59–88.

———. "The Canon Law on the Formation of Marriage and Social Practice in the Later Middle Ages." *Journal of Family History* 8 (1983) 144–158.

Duby, Georges. *The Knight, The Lady, and the Priest: The Making of Modern Marriage in Medieval France.* New York: Pantheon, 1983.

Epstein, Louis M. *Marriage Laws in the Bible and the Talmud.* Harvard Semitic Studies, 12. Cambridge, Mass.: Harvard University Press, 1942.

Gaudemet, Jean. *Le mariage en Occident: Les mœurs et le droit.* Paris: Éditions du Cerf, 1987.

Helmholz, Richard H. *Marriage Litigation in Medieval England.* Cambridge, U.K.: Cambridge University Press, 1974.

———. *Canon Law and the Law of England.* London: Hambledon, 1987.

Herlihy, David. *Medieval Households.* Cambridge, Mass.: Harvard University Press, 1985.

McNamara, Jo Ann, and Suzanne F. Wemple. "Marriage and Divorce in the Frankish Kingdom." In *Women in Medieval Society.* Edited by Susan Mosher Stuard. Philadelphia: University of Pennsylvania Press, 1976, pp. 95–124.

Noonan, John T., Jr. *Power to Dissolve: Lawyers and Marriages in the Courts of the Roman Curia.* Cambridge, Mass.: Belknap Press, 1972.

Pedersen, Frederik. *Marriage Disputes in Medieval England.* London: Hambledon Press, 2000.

Phillips, Roderick. *Putting Asunder: A History of Divorce in Western Society.* Cambridge, U.K.: Cambridge University Press, 1988.

Reynolds, Philip Lyndon. *Marriage in the Western Church: The Christianization of Marriage during the Patristic and Early Medieval Periods.* Leiden: E. J. Brill, 1994.

Sheehan, Michael M. *Marriage, Family, and Law in Medieval Europe: Collected Studies.* Edited by James K. Farge. Toronto: University of Toronto Press, 1996.

Treggiari, Susan. *Roman Marriage:* Iusti coniuges *from the Time of Cicero to the Time of Ulpian.* Oxford: Clarendon Press, 1991.

JAMES A. BRUNDAGE

[See also **DMA:** Annulment of Marriage; Barbarians, Invasions of; Betrothal; Church, Early; Church, Latin: 1054 to 1305; Concubinage, Western; Consanguinity; Family, Western European; Family and Marriage, Western European; Gratian; Law, Canon; Law, German: Early Germanic Codes; Penance and Penitentials; Peter Lombard; **Supp:** Love and Courtship]

MARTIN LE FRANC. See **Le Franc, Martin.**

MARTIN OF TOURS, ST. (*ca.* 316–397), was born in Pannonia (in modern Hungary); he was the son of a Roman army officer and became a soldier himself from age fifteen. While stationed in Amiens, he encountered a beggar, tore his cloak in two, and gave half to the destitute man. Christ then visited him in a dream and, when he awoke, Martin found his cloak intact. He abandoned the military and was baptized. This became the most celebrated moment in the saint's life during the Middle Ages, but it was only one among many indications that Martin did not adhere to social conventions. He subsequently traveled through Italy and lived alone on an island, refining the ascetic devotions that would make him famous. When Hilary, bishop of Poitiers, returned home from political exile around 360, Martin went with him. He purportedly founded the first monastic community in Gaul at Ligugé and, in any case, generated enough recognition for the people of Tours to acclaim him their first bishop in 371. They discovered that Martin was not like other bishops. Prone to confrontation with pagan tree shrines and Roman emperors, Martin annoyed his colleagues with his ongoing ascetic zeal. He founded a monastery across the river at Marmoutier and preferred to live there rather than in the usual urban quarters.

After Martin's death in 397 (or possibly 399/400), there was a contest over the rights to his body, and Tours beat out Poitiers. Martin had no apparent scholarly interests and left no written records of his own, but the best Latin authors of late antiquity wrote his life stories: the dossier on St. Martin is thick and complex. In Martin's own lifetime, Sulpicius Severus wrote a biography, which he revised and added to shortly after his subject's death. The poet Paulinus of Périgueux versified this biography around 470, enlarging it with more recent miracles performed at Martin's tomb. His own recovery there from an eye problem might have motivated Paulinus, but probably a commission was involved as well. Between 461 and 470, Bishop Perpetuus of Tours was occupied in rebuilding and expanding a church for the tomb. He improved the architectural elements and added a series of murals and verse inscriptions. Paulinus contributed an original poem to this project, as did Sidonius Apollinaris, although scholars still disagree over whether the poems we read today were ever actually written on the walls. The shrine was destroyed by fire in 994, so we will never know for certain. It hardly matters, because the cult, church, and St. Martin himself had already undergone dramatic transformations centuries before that. A fire around 558 severely damaged St. Martin Cathedral. Gregory of Tours, who had been a pilgrim there in 563, a decade before becoming bishop, directed the next great reconstruction. Following Perpetuus's example, he enlarged the church building and decorated its interior with murals depicting scenes from Martin's life, either restorations of the originals or new works. These were described by the poet Venantius Fortunatus, who in 576 had also composed a new verse rendition of Sulpicius's life of Martin. Gregory wrote up his own collection of miracle stories into an independent life of the saint, which he later revised into a second version. Martin remained a target for pilgrims, the focus of a religious community, and a subject of religious art and literature throughout the Middle Ages. A relic of his cloak was preserved at Tours, and he was frequently portrayed either as an armored soldier or as a bishop showing compassion to a beggar. Martin became the patron saint of France.

BIBLIOGRAPHY

Brennan, Brian. "'Being Martin': Saint and Successor in Sixth-Century Tours." *Journal of Religious History* 21, no. 2 (1997): 121–135.

Farmer, Sharon A. *Communities of Saint Martin: Legend and Ritual in Medieval Tours.* Ithaca, N.Y.: Cornell University Press, 1991.

Van Dam, Raymond. "Images of Saint Martin in Late Roman and Early Merovingian Gaul." *Viator* 19 (1988): 1–27.

———. *Saints and Their Miracles in Late Antique Gaul.* Princeton, N.J.: Princeton University Press, 1993. See pages 199–318. Translations of the verse inscriptions and Gregory of Tours's life of St. Martin append this excellent study.

KEVIN UHALDE

[See also **DMA:** Gregory of Tours, St.; Hilary of Poitiers, St.; Paulinus of Périgueux; Sidonius Apollinaris; Venantius Fortunatus.]

MATHEMATICS, ISLAMIC.

Islamic mathematics designates, in this article, mathematics done in Islamic lands from about 750 to 1450. Its practitioners—Arabs, Persians, Uzbeks, Turks, Afghanis, and others—wrote most of its literature in Arabic and were mostly Muslims. But adherents of other faiths in the Islamic lands—predominantly Christians and Jews—also made important contributions.

HISTORICAL ORIGINS

The historical origins of Islamic mathematics lie in the learned cultures bordering Islam. From Arabic translations of Greek texts, mathematicians of ninth- and tenth-century Islam learned the rigorous geometry of Euclid, Archimedes, and Apollonius, the number theory of Euclid and Diophantus of Alexandria, and the mathematical astronomy of Ptolemy. From India came a decimal system with a zero (which we use today), the sine function of trigonometry, and techniques in mathematical astronomy.

Beginning in about 750 Islamic elites supported and participated in the appropriation of this ancient cultural heritage. For example, during the reign of Caliph Abū Jaʿfar ʿAbd Allāh ibn Muḥammad al-Manṣūr (r. 754–775) a delegation of Indian scholars visited Baghdad, and al-Manṣūr used the occasion to order the composition of an astronomical work known as the *Sindhind,* which incorporated material by the Indian writer Brahmagupta (*ca.* 598–*ca.* 665), with some Iranian material. When al-Fazārī completed this task in 770, medieval Islam had its first major astronomical work.

EARLY MEDIEVAL ISLAMIC MATHEMATICS

The earliest extant Arabic mathematical works are three treatises that date from the first half of the ninth century. Of these, two are by Muḥammad ibn Mūsā al-Khwārizmī—one on what he called "Hindu reckoning" and the other on algebra—and the third, on algebra, is by Abū al-Faḍl ibn Turk. One of these two authors (just which is a contested issue) also wrote the first extant textbook on algebra. In any case, both were explaining matters already known to those interested in such things.

(Bishop Severus Sebokht, for example, writing on the upper Euphrates River in the mid-seventh century, refers to the Indians' numerals and their ingenious way of writing numbers with only 9 digits—the "0" being only a placeholder.)

Al-Khwārizmī explains in his work on arithmetic the base-10 positional system for representing whole numbers, such as 2056, and how to do the usual operations of arithmetic, including finding square roots. He also explains how to use a base-60 positional system to represent fractions of numbers.

In his *Algebra,* which he dedicated to Caliph al-Maʾmūn (r. 813–833), al-Khwārizmī uses the words "roots" and "assets" to refer to what we call "unknowns" and "squares." He explains how to solve equations involving these quantities, such as "assets and two roots equal ten," and he gives geometric arguments for the validity of his solutions. His work contains no algebraic symbolism, however, and even the numbers are expressed by words. Al-Khwārizmī's works were so popular they spread throughout medieval Islam, from Andalusia to Afghanistan, although no Arabic version of his *Arithmetic* survives today and we are not even sure of its exact title.

Like calculation, geometry, too, received a royal impetus when Caliph Hārūn al-Rashīd (r. 786–809), whose reign has been immortalized in the *Thousand and One Nights,* ordered al-Ḥajjāj ibn Maṭar to translate Euclid's *Elements.* (Scholars disagree on whether al-Ḥajjāj worked from a Greek text or from an earlier translation into Syriac, the language of many of the learned Christians the Muslims used as translators.) Of course, translation of such a highly technical work, into a language whose technical vocabulary had yet to develop, was no light task. And it was only when Thābit ibn Qurra (836–901) revised a new translation by Isḥāq ibn Ḥunayn (d. 910) that a fully satisfactory Arabic translation of Euclid's classic work was available.

Similar accounts of successive polishings could be given for the works of Archimedes and Apollonius, both of whose writings began important traditions in Islamic geometry. In the case of Archimedes, it was investigations of areas and volumes of figures with curved boundaries, such as Thābit's on the area of a parabola and Ḥasan ibn al-Haytham's (*ca.* 1000) on the areas of solids obtained by rotating parabolas around certain lines. In the case of Apollonius, it was tools for performing advanced geometrical constructions by means of conic sections (ellipse, parabola, and hyperbola).

Although al-Khwārizmī's *Algebra* contained some basic mensurational geometry, three brothers known as

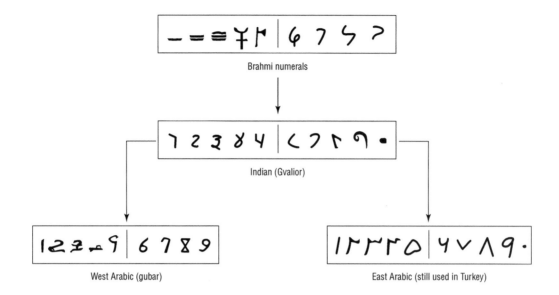

Brahmi numerals

Indian (Gvalior)

West Arabic (gubar)

East Arabic (still used in Turkey)

Family Tree of Hindu-Arabic Numerals.

the Banū Mūsā wrote the earliest sophisticated Arabic treatise on geometry. (The oldest brother, Muḥammad, died in 873.) Their highly influential *On Knowledge of the Measurement of Plane and Spherical Figures* not only gave results about areas and volumes of circular and spherical figures but also proved them, a feature indicative of medieval Islamic respect for rigorous mathematics. The Banū Mūsā's inclusion of solutions to other famous problems, such as trisecting the angle, also stimulated fruitful efforts to improve on Greek solutions to these problems.

The Banū Mūsā were also patrons of the abovementioned Thābit ibn Qurra, whom they met in Harran on a trip to Byzantium to buy manuscripts. Thābit wrote independent works in such areas as algebra, number theory, and trigonometry, and rose to the position of court astrologer under Caliph al-Muʿtaḍid.

ALGEBRA FROM THE TENTH TO THE THIRTEENTH CENTURY

Algebraists such as Abū Kāmil the Egyptian (*d. ca.* 930), Abū Bakr ibn Muḥammad ibn al-Ḥusayn al-Karajī (one of whose works is dated to 1016), and al-Samawʾal (*fl.* mid-twelfth century) carried forward the tradition of al-Khwārizmī and developed techniques for manipulating algebraic expressions with the same ease that the decimal system allowed the arithmeticians to manipulate numbers. Al-Karajī also discovered what is

now called Pascal's triangle, used to easily calculate the expansion of expressions like $(a + b)^5$.

ʿUmar Khayyām (1048–1131) followed up on these developments by finding a method of extracting arbitrary roots of any given number N, that is, of solving the equation $x^r = N$, where r may be any whole number 2, 3, 4. . . . Also, ʿUmar, and after him Sharaf al-Dīn al-Ṭūsī (*d.* 1213), worked on solving equations in a single unknown having exponent no greater than three, such as $x^3 + 5x = 7x^2 + 12$. ʿUmar tells us he tried but failed to find an algebraic procedure for solving these equations, although he expressed the hope—realized in the Renaissance—that a later worker would succeed. But working under the patronage of the chief judge of Samarkand in 1070, he showed how to use the geometry of conic sections to find a solution to cubic equations as line segments, when such solutions exist. Sharaf al-Dīn completed ʿUmar's discussion and explained a method of successive approximation to find numerical solutions to cubic equations.

NUMBER THEORY

Scholars from the ninth century onward, such as Thābit ibn Qurra, Ḥasan ibn al-Haytham (965–1040), and Kamāl al-Dīn al-Fārisī (*d.* 1320), studied problems in number theory. Some of these problems generalized questions the ancient Greeks had asked about sums of divisors of a given number. Others investigated the sums

SEXIGESIMAL FRACTIONS

JUST AS IT CAN BE SAID THAT MINUTES ARE SIXTI-
ETHS OF AN HOUR AND SECONDS ARE SIXTIETHS
OF A MINUTE (SO THERE ARE 3,600 SECONDS IN AN
HOUR), SO TOO ONE CAN CONTINUE AND ARRIVE
at a consistent way of representing any fraction. For
example, 1/2 = 30/60 and 5/8 = 37/60 + 30/3600, so
one could say that 1/2 is 30 minutes and 5/8 is 37
minutes and 30 seconds. Although this system originated in ancient Babylon and was well known to the
Greeks from at least 150 B.C. onward, al-Khwārizmī
attributes his knowledge of it to the Indians. It was
very much a part of astronomy, though the polymath
Muḥammad ibn Aḥmad Abū 'l-Rayḥān al-Bīrūnī
(973–ca. 1050) tells us that astronomers often converted sexagesimal fractions into decimal whole-
number multiples of the lowest unit ("seconds," or
whatever) in the fraction. They did the calculations
with those whole numbers and then converted the
result back to sexagesimal fractions. The Indian decimal, positional system was beginning to show its convenience for serious computations.

of powers of consecutive whole numbers, up to the
fourth power. Another important topic was the so-called
"Chinese remainder" problem. This probably originated
in astronomy and asks for a number that leaves given re-
mainders (say, 2, 3, and 4) when divided by given numbers (say, 5, 7, and 13).

APPLIED MATHEMATICS

Geometry found important uses in optics, the study
of vision. And, although Ibn al-Haytham in his *Optics
(Kitāb al-manāzir)* also dealt with the physics, physiology, and psychology of vision, he used geometry to show
how vision occurred based on his assumption that from
each point on an illuminated body light rays spread out
in all directions. He also posed and solved, in the closely
allied science of mirrors, the difficult problem of where,
on the surface of a convex spherical mirror, an observer
would see the image of a given object.

Muslim scientists also applied geometry to the science of mechanical equilibrium. And the tenth-century
geometer Abū Sahl al-Kūhī was aware, as Archimedes

was, of a relationship between calculating the volumes of
figures and finding the position of their centers of gravity. However, his overly hasty extrapolation of a numerical pattern he had discovered in locating centers of gravity of some plane and solid figures led him to believe that
the value of the constant pi was 3 1/9.

Computational mathematics was applied to problems of astronomy that gave rise to equations that could
not be expressed only in terms of algebraic unknowns
but involved trigonometric functions as well. These were
solved by methods of successive approximation, and a
particularly elegant method was described by Ḥabash
al-Ḥāsib (fl. 890), who worked in Baghdad and Damascus. Although some of these methods originated in India
or the Hellenistic world, others were original to medieval
Islam.

A common problem for astronomers was that of interpolating values between two entries in an astronomical table. Thus one might have tabular values for the position of Jupiter on noon of two consecutive days and
might have to compute its position at the midnight between the two noons. Here again medieval Islamic scholars used older methods and developed new ones, including methods for interpolating in tables where the values
depend not on one but on two arguments.

Stimulated by problems in astronomy and cartography, scholars such as Abū Ḥāmid al-Ṣāghānī (active in
the late tenth century) and the previously mentioned
al-Bīrūnī developed new geometrical projections of the
surface of the sphere onto the flat surface of the astrolabe
or world map. Among the results of this activity are maps
of a hemisphere of the globe (rendered onto flat disks),
which are centered at Mecca and allow the user to find
the direction and distance of Mecca relative to a given
locality in the hemisphere. There is much that is still not
known about these maps, but it has been persuasively argued that they go back at least to the eleventh century.

TRIGONOMETRY

During the late tenth century scholars such as Abū
al-Wafāʾ al-Būzjānī and Abū Naṣr Manṣūr ibn ʿIrāq,
teacher of al-Bīrūnī, discovered beautiful new theorems
in trigonometry. Work at that time took both the theory
of the subject and the precision of its tables well beyond
what was found in Ptolemy's *Almagest*. This made astronomical and geodetic calculations much simpler and
stimulated the production of numerical tables. Among
such tables are those of Ibn Yūnus (d. 1009) of Cairo,
used for astronomical timekeeping, and Shams al-Dīn
al-Khalīlī, a timekeeper at the Umayyad Mosque in
fourteenth-century Damascus, used for finding the direction of Mecca and calculating times of prayer.

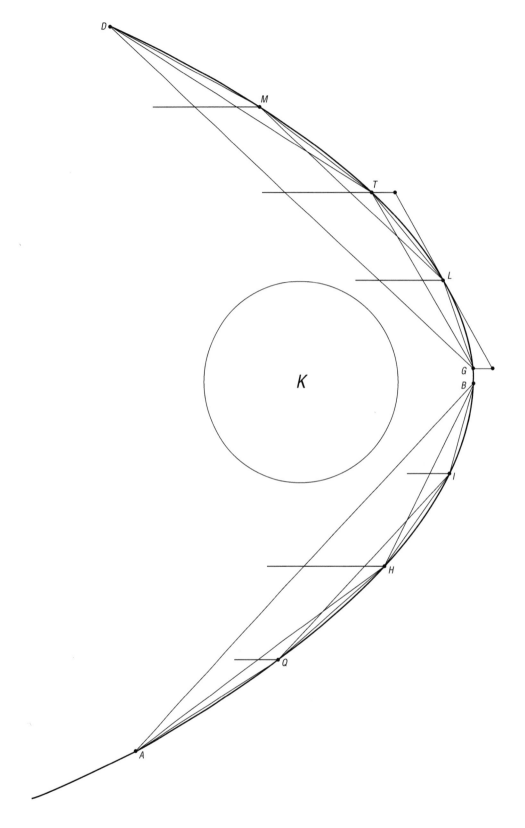

Conic Section. *An expert rendering of a parabola after a manuscript by al-Qūhi (10th century) dealing with the area of that figure.*

RAINBOWS

GEOMETRIC EXPLANATIONS OF THE APPEARANCE OF A RAINBOW DATE BACK AT LEAST TO ARISTOTLE IN THE FOURTH CENTURY B.C., BUT GREEK AUTHORS FAILED TO EXPLAIN THE phenomenon satisfactorily. Ibn al-Haytham, in his *Optics,* went well beyond Greek treatises in his understanding of refraction, the basic principle underlying the rainbow, but the idea of analyzing the primary (and secondary) rainbow as the cumulative effects of a double refraction and one (or two) reflections in myriads of individual spherical droplets of water eluded him. However, a successful qualitative treatment of the phenomenon of the rainbow was given in the first decade of the fourteenth century, after experimental studies of light passing through a glass sphere filled with water were carried out by Kamāl al-Dīn al-Fārisī, who then published a correct qualitative analysis of both the single and double rainbow in his commentary on the *Optics.* (In one of many examples of simultaneous discovery in the history of science, Theodoric of Freiberg [*d. ca.* 1310] also gave a correct analysis of these natural phenomena in his *De iride,* composed around the same time.)

Such advances also resulted, in the mid-thirteenth century, in the foundation of plane and spherical trigonometry as mathematical studies independent of astronomy. This was achieved by Naṣīr al-Dīn al-Ṭūsī (*d.* 1272) at Maragha in his *Transversal Figure.* At the same time, he assembled a group of astronomers who jointly worked out mathematical solutions to long-standing problems in Ptolemaic astronomy, solutions that, although still geocentric, are mathematically identical to some of the methods of Copernicus.

DEVELOPMENTS IN WESTERN ISLAM

Stimulated by problems derived from linguistics and poetry, Muslim scientists in western Islam—such as the Maghribi mathematicians Ibn Munʿim (*d.* 1228) and, later, Ibn al-Bannāʾ—solved new problems in the study of permutations and combinations. Ibn Munʿim, for example, solved the problem of finding the number of possible Arabic words. In the course of his work he discov-

Formulas for Trinomial Equations

$x^2 + 10x = 56$; $x^2 = 8x + 20$;

$x^2 + 20 = 12x$; $x^2 + 16 = 8x$;

$6x^2 + 12x = 90$; $4x^2 + 48 = 32x$;

$3x^2 = 12x + 63$; $\frac{1}{2}x^2 + x = 7\frac{1}{2}$;

Proportions

$7 : 12 = 84 : x$ ......

$11 : 20 = 66 : x$ ......

Maghribi Mathematical Notation.

ered and applied the same pattern of numbers that al-Karajī had found in his algebraic studies.

Maghribi scholars from the fourteenth century onward also began to use algebraic symbolism, which Ibn Qunfudh (*d.* 1406), for example, used in teaching the subject.

The last significant figure in medieval Islamic mathematics was Jamshīd ibn Masʿūd al-Kāshī (*fl. ca.* 1410), whose computational achievements still inspire admiration. One is his use of an iterative method to compute the basic value for trigonometric tables, the value of the sine of 1°. This allowed his patron and collaborator, the Sultan Ulugh-Beg of Samarkand, to publish the most accurate trigonometric tables up to that time. Another is his computation of a value of the mathematical constant pi, which is correct to sixteen decimal places. Also striking is his computation of the volumes and surface areas of features of Muslim architecture such as domes (*qubbas*) and stalactite-like structures known as *muqarnas.*

The medieval Islamic mathematical tradition, the creative phase of which ended with the death of al-Kāshī, contributed importantly to late medieval Latin and Renaissance traditions of arithmetic, geometry, and mathematical astronomy. It was superseded by non-

Islamic advances in the sixteenth century but continued in Islamic lands into the nineteenth century.

BIBLIOGRAPHY

PRIMARY WORKS

Berggren, J. L. "Medieval Islam." In *A Source Book in Non-Western Science.* Edited by Victor Katz. Princeton, N.J.: Princeton University Press, 2003. A collection of pieces by Muslim mathematicians, many of them mentioned in this article, representative of the diversity of medieval Islamic mathematics.

Crossley, John N., and Alan S. Henry. "Thus Spake al-Khwārizmī: A Translation of the Text of Cambridge University Library Ms. Ii.vi.5." *Historia Mathematica* 17, no. 2 (1990): 103–131.

Mohammad ben Musa. *The Algebra of Mohammad ben Musa.* Edited and translated by Frederic Rosen. Reprint, Hildesheim, Germany: Olms, 1986. A classic introduction to algebra in medieval Islam.

SECONDARY WORKS

Berggren, J. L. *Episodes in the Mathematics of Medieval Islam.* New York: Springer, 1986.

———. "Mathematics and Her Sisters in Medieval Islam: A Selective Review of Work Done from 1985–1995." *Historia Mathematica* 24 (1997): 407–440. Updates both Berggren's *Episodes* and Yuschkevitch's *Les mathématiques arabes* (cited below).

Gillispie, C. C., ed. *Dictionary of Scientific Biography.* 16 vols. New York: Scribners, 1970–1980. A standard source for biographies of scientists from all ages and civilizations.

King, David A. *World Maps for Finding the Direction and Distance to Mecca: Innovation and Tradition in Islamic Science.* London and Leiden, Netherlands: Al-Furqan Islamic Heritage Foundation and Brill, 1999.

King, David A., and Mary Helen Kennedy, eds. *Studies in the Islamic Exact Sciences.* Beirut, Lebanon: American University in Beirut, 1983. A collection of papers, mostly by E. S. Kennedy—the leading living scholar of mathematical sciences in medieval Islam—but with others by colleagues and former students. Many are accessible to a nonspecialist reader.

Sabra, A. I. "The Exact Sciences." In *The Genius of Arab Civilization: Source of Renaissance.* Edited by John R. Hayes. 1975. Reprint, Cambridge, Mass.: MIT Press, 1978.

———. "'Ilm al-Hisab." In *The Encyclopaedia of Islam.* 2d ed. Vol. 3. Leiden, Netherlands: Brill, 1986. A good introduction to the development of various kinds of arithmetic in medieval Islam. The whole encyclopedia is a major scholarly source for information about all aspects of Islamic science and Islam in general.

Youschkevitch, A. P. *Les mathématiques arabes (VIIIe–Xve siècles).* Paris: Vrin, 1976. A French translation of a good account of the history of the subject, originally published in Russian in 1961.

J. L. BERGGREN

[See also **DMA:** Astrology/Astronomy, Islamic; Mathematics; Optics, Islamic.]

MATILDA, EMPRESS

MATILDA, EMPRESS (1102–1167). Matilda was the elder child of King Henry I of England and his first queen, Matilda of Scotland. Betrothed early to the German emperor Henry V, Matilda left England at the age of eight to be educated in Germany. She married the emperor in Worms in 1114. When Henry V died in 1125, Matilda returned to England, where she found herself the only surviving legitimate child of her father. In 1127, Henry I had the magnates of England swear to accept Matilda as his heir should he die without a legitimate son. The next year Matilda married Geoffrey Plantagenet, who soon became count of Anjou. This marriage was unpopular among Henry's baronage, particularly among the Norman barons, who disliked this promotion of Angevin interests. At the time of Henry's death in 1135, Matilda and Geoffrey were together in rebellion against Henry, which helped allow Matilda's cousin Stephen to seize the English throne. When challenged for their acceptance of Stephen, nobles who had participated in the 1127 oath taking claimed either that they had been forced to take the oath or that Matilda's marriage to Geoffrey was against their interests, and by acting against the interests of sworn vassals, Henry had broken the bonds of good lordship and made the oaths invalid.

It took Matilda until 1139 to formally challenge Stephen's accession. At first, she appealed the legality of Stephen's accession to the English throne to the pope; she then mounted an invasion into England. By that time, several of the nobles who had supported Stephen were ready to switch their allegiance to Matilda. Her half brother Robert of Gloucester and King David of Scotland were among the leaders of those who supported her cause. Matilda almost gained the English throne when Stephen was captured in 1141, but she never gained the support of the Londoners and was denied access to the capital. She lost her most valuable captive when Stephen's forces captured Robert of Gloucester and she was forced to release the king in return for Robert. Matilda continued to claim the throne and attempted to exercise some of the prerogatives of sovereignty, as "Lady of the English," but never very successfully.

Matilda and Geoffrey did manage to hold Normandy for most of Stephen's reign. Finally, in 1153, after the death of Stephen's wife and son, Stephen and Matilda sealed the Treaty of Winchester, allowing Stephen to hold the throne until his death, after which it would go to Henry, the oldest of Matilda and Geoffrey's three sons.

Although she is best remembered for her failed attempt to gain the English throne, Matilda was a successful queen consort in Germany and a patron of reformed monasteries, particularly the house of Le Bec in Normandy. She is buried in Rouen Cathedral, where her tomb inscription proclaims that she was "great by birth, greater by marriage, and greatest of all in her offspring."

BIBLIOGRAPHY

Chibnall, Marjorie. *The Empress Matilda: Queen Consort, Queen Mother, and Lady of the English.* Oxford: Blackwell Press, 1991.

———. "The Empress Matilda and Her Sons." In *Medieval Mothering.* Edited by John Carmi Parsons and Bonnie Wheeler. New York: Garland, 1996.

Huneycutt, Lois L. "Female Succession and the Language of Power in the Writings of Twelfth-Century Churchmen." In *Medieval Queenship.* Edited by John Carmi Parsons. New York: St. Martin's, 1993.

Truax, Jean A. "Winning Over the Londoners: King Stephen, the Empress Matilda, and the Politics of Personality." *The Haskins Society Journal: Studies in Medieval History* 8 (1996): 43–61.

LOIS L. HUNEYCUTT

[See also **DMA:** Henry I of England; Henry II of England; Plantagenets; **Supp:** Henry V of Germany, Emperor; Stephen of England, King.]

MATTER. Medieval philosophical theories of matter mainly derive from an intensive interpretation of Plato's *Timaeus* and Aristotle's *Physics* and *Metaphysics,* often in confrontation with the biblical narrative of the creation of the world. Although Plato does not have a particular notion corresponding to "matter," he posits *chôra* ("space") as that in which the eternal forms are received. Moreover, he represents all bodies as consisting of elements, which have a three-dimensional mathematical structure. Criticizing Plato's notion of matter as the receptacle of forms, Aristotle conceives *hylê* (matter) as the subject of change, which does not exist by itself but is always united to a determinate *morphê* (form) or *eidos* (species); matter and form are related to one another as potency and actuality. Like form, matter is *ousia* (substance) and one of the principles or causes in the natural world, but it is less existent than form. "First" or "ultimate matter"—a Peripatetic concept not developed in Aristotle's own writings—is the purely potential substrate underlying all generation and corruption, as well as all qualitative and quantitative changes. In reality, matter is always qualified by one or more of the four basic qualities (warm and cold, moist and dry). United with "first matter," these elementary forms constitute the four elements (fire: warm-dry; air: warm-moist; water: cold-moist; earth: cold-dry), out of which all sublunary bodies are composed. The heavenly bodies, however, consist of ether, the "fifth substance." Through Galen, the doctrine of the four elements also became very influential in the medical and psychological theories of the temperaments.

NEOPLATONIC AND ARABIC VIEWS

In the early Middle Ages, Neoplatonic views of matter were predominant. Augustine argues that God created "formless matter," which was able to receive the forms of heaven and earth. Following the Neoplatonic tradition, he claims that, owing to its mutability, matter in itself is "almost nothing" and cannot be perceived or understood. Still, matter is, insofar as it is created by God from nothing, fundamentally good. Whereas Augustine reflects on the nature of matter from a theological (anti-Manichaean) perspective and establishes the principles for all later Christian-theological speculations on matter, Calcidius and Boethius look upon matter from a philosophical point of view. In his translation of and commentary on *Timaeus,* Calcidius renders *hyle* as *silva* (wood) and, combining Platonic and Aristotelian notions, interprets it not only as a space in which material forms come into existence but also as a passive nature out of which all sensible things are produced. Boethius stresses the "flowing," ever changing nature of matter and shows that "nothing is said to be because of its matter, but because of its proper form"; material forms are not truly forms but rather mere images of divine ideas. One finds Neoplatonic metaphysical doctrines wherein matter is depreciated as something near to nothing, though not considered a source of evil, also in Greek Christian thinkers, such as Gregory of Nyssa and Pseudo-Dionysius, who influenced John Scottus Eriugena. In his *Periphyseon* (On the division of nature), Eriugena defines formless matter as "the changeability of material things, capable of receiving all forms." Since every corporeal creature is composed of matter and form, matter itself is incorporeal; in the last analysis, it is a "primordial cause," a paradigmatic idea in God's mind. During the twelfth century, the doctrines of Plato, Calcidius, and Boethius were integrated by various authors (especially Bernard of Chartres, Thierry of Chartres, and William of Conches) into a relatively new worldview. Their rediscovery of nature opened the way for the introduction in the Latin West of the natural philosophy of Aristotle and his Arabic commentators.

Arabic culture produced several notions of matter, which were essential in the creationism of the *mutakallimūn* (theologians), the atomism of natural philosophers and physicians (such as al-Rāzī), and alchemy. For Western Scholasticism, however, three Peripatetic thinkers were much more important: Ibn Gabirol (Avicebron), Ibn Sīnā (Avicenna), and Ibn Rushd (Averroës). According to Avicebron, God created both a "universal matter" and a "universal form," which constitute all finite substances, including spiritual substances. Avicebron's universal hylomorphism became quite influential among thirteenth-century Scholastics, especially Franciscan theologians. In his *Shifā'* (*Sufficientia* or Book of the cure), Avicenna criticizes the identification of corporeity with three-dimensionality and rejects the atomistic conception of the body as something composed of indivisible particles. Instead, he defines a body as a continuous though divisible "substance in which it is possible to posit any of the dimensions." Insofar as a body is capable of receiving anything, it is potential; this potentiality is the body's prime matter. Matter is never really devoid of form, since it owes its existence to form. As such, matter does not have quantity; its measures and space derive from its form, its accidents, or an extrinsic cause.

In his *De substantia orbis* (On the substance of the celestial sphere), Averroës introduces the notion of "indeterminate dimensions" with a view to explaining the multiplication of material substances. Since matter in itself is one and undifferentiated, it needs a formal principle, namely quantitative extension, in order to be multiplied. While Avicenna regards this extension as something accidental to matter, Averroës argues in agreement with Philoponus and other Neoplatonic Aristotelians that the three-dimensional extension is the basic formal determination of matter, which prepares the reception of a substantial form. This extension does not consist in concrete dimensions but rather in indeterminate dimensions—corporeity as such. Averroës's concise observations gave rise to the scholastic discussions concerning the ontological status of prime matter and the indeterminate dimensions, the divisibility of matter, and individuation.

THE HIGH AND LATER MIDDLE AGES

David of Dinant, a thirteenth-century natural scientist and translator of some of Aristotle's works, is one of the very few medieval authors who espoused a materialistic pantheism. Interpreting Aristotle in a Platonic perspective, he equates the physical world with God and *hyle* (matter) with the divine *mens* (mind) and regards earth and fire respectively as the material and formal principles of the universe. His doctrines were sharply criticized by Albertus Magnus, who defended, as did Aquinas after him, a Christianized interpretation of Aristotle's hylomorphism.

In Aquinas's view, matter somehow exists, insofar as it is "con-created" and participates through its form in being. Prime matter is a principle that underlies all substantial changes. In contrast with some Franciscan contemporaries (e.g., John Peckham), who believed that God could keep prime matter in some kind of actual existence without any substantial form, Aquinas argued that although God has an idea of prime matter insofar as it has (potential) being, it is nothing but pure potentiality and can be known only by analogy. Designated matter *(materia signata),* however, is matter endowed with a form and determinate dimensions; it serves as the principle of individuation in material substances.

Though indebted to Averroës and Aquinas, Giles of Rome (Egidius Colonna) unfolds a fairly original theory of matter. He understands the indeterminate dimensions of matter as the quantity that makes prime matter, which is purely potential, into a physical substrate (i.e., matter that is subject to change); these indeterminate dimensions are distinguished from the determinate dimensions, which are understood as the quantity whereby matter occupies a place with a particular extension. The indeterminate dimensions are identified with the (undetermined) *quantum* or *multitudo materie* (multitude of matter). The density of a body, which in the Aristotelian view belongs to the category of quality, is defined by Giles in quantitative terms, as a function of the multitude of matter contained within certain dimensions: if there is much matter within small dimensions, the body is dense; if a small quantity of matter is contained within large dimensions, the body is rare. The small or large dimensions in this definition of density and rarity are the determinate extension or the volume of the body, which varies in the process of condensation or rarefaction. The multitude of matter in the same definition refers to a certain quantity that remains unchanged in the process of condensation or rarefaction. Like Averroës's indeterminate dimensions, this multitude of matter precedes the substantial form: it endows matter with the potency of occupying a certain space but does not determine a body's space until it has received the determinate dimensions of a concrete body.

Giles's innovative view of matter was criticized not only by theologians, such as Thomas Sutton, Godfrey of Fontaines, and James of Viterbo but also by philosophers such as Henry Bate of Malines, who maintains in his *Speculum divinorum* that even though the essence of matter may remain the same in the process of condensation or rarefaction, its quantity can increase or decrease. However, quantitative approaches to matter, similar to that of Giles, are to be found in English late-thirteenth-century commentators on Aristotle's *Physics* and also in the works of the so-called Oxford Calculators. As Richard Swineshead points out in his *Calculations,* rarity and density depend upon the proportion between the volume of a body and its *massa elementaris,* the quantity of matter that remains constant in the process of condensation or rarefaction. The notions of "quantity of matter" and "elementary mass," as they were defined by Giles and the Oxonians, in some sense foreshadow the concept of "mass" developed in classical physics.

Following a more metaphysical line of thought, John Duns Scotus argues against Aquinas that matter, though being potential, is actual if "act" is understood as everything which exists outside its cause; as a cause of being, matter has the lowest degree of actuality. Moreover, Scotus rejects matter as the principle of individuation; its quantity as such is not individual but is individualized by the individual thing to which it accidentally belongs, more precisely by its *haecceitas* ("this-ness").

In his nominalist criticism of the traditional Aristotelian picture of nature, William of Ockham attacks the idea that matter and form are real principles of extramental things, arguing that they are merely "common names." Likewise, "quantity" denotes not a thing but rather the extension of a concrete thing having parts between which spatial motion is possible. Since things are individual, the only matter that really exists is individual matter. Although agreeing that prime matter is something that exists in potency in respect of all forms, Ockham denies that matter contains an active potency toward form and dismisses the notion of an *inchoatio forme* (beginning of the form), which according to many scholastic philosophers inheres in matter. Furthermore, he defends the un-Aristotelian thesis that celestial bodies are composed of the same matter as sublunary beings; their incorruptibility depends solely on God's will. Ockham's critique of the "old" theory of matter was further elaborated by Jean Buridan, Marsilius of Inghen, and other nominalists.

In his *De docta ignorantia* (On learned ignorance) Nicholas of Cusa questions the Peripatetic and Platonic doctrines of matter, especially the notion of pure potentiality, with which prime matter was traditionally identified. In Nicholas's dialectical view, God is both the form of all forms and absolute possibility, whereas all other beings are "contracted"—determined and rendered finite by a particular actuality. Hence creation is interpreted at the same time as the introduction of forms into matter (according to Avicenna's model) and as the eduction of forms out of the potency of matter (according to Averroës's model).

BIBLIOGRAPHY

Adams, Marilyn McCord. *William Ockham.* Vol. 2. Notre Dame, Ind.: University of Notre Dame Press, 1987.

Bormann, Claus von, Winifried Franzen, and Ludger Oeing-Hanhoff. "Form und Materie." In *Historisches Wörterbuch der Philosophie.* Edited by Joachim Ritter and Karlfried Gründer. Vol. 2. Basel: Schwabe, 1972.

Cross, Richard. *The Physics of Duns Scotus: The Scientific Context of a Theological Vision.* Oxford: Clarendon Press, 1998.

Detel, W., and M. Schramm. "Materie." In *Historisches Wörterbuch der Philosophie.* Edited by Joachim Ritter and Karlfried Gründer. Vol. 5. Basel: Schwabe, 1980.

Donati, Silvia. "La dottrina delle dimensioni indeterminate in Egidio Romano." *Medioevo* 14 (1988): 149–233.

———. "Materie und räumliche Ausdehnung in einigen ungedruckten Physikkommentaren aus der Zeit von etwa 1250–1270." In *Raum und Raumvorstellungen im Mittelalter.* Edited by Jan A. Aertsen and Andreas Speer. Berlin and New York: Walter de Gruyter, 1998.

Haas, Frans A. J. de. *John Philoponus' New Definition of Prime Matter: Aspects of Its Background in Neoplatonism and the Ancient Commentary Tradition.* Leiden, Netherlands: Brill, 1997.

McMullin, Ernan, ed. *The Concept of Matter in Greek and Medieval Philosophy.* Notre Dame, Ind.: University of Notre Dame Press, 1965.

Pines, Shlomo. *Studies in Islamic Atomism.* Edited by Tzvi Langermann. Translated by Michael Schwarz. Jerusalem: Magnes Press, 1997.

Sorabji, Richard. *Matter, Space, and Motion: Theories in Antiquity and Their Sequel.* London: Duckworth, 1988.

Speer, Andreas. "Von Plato zu Aristoteles. Zur Prinzipienlehre bei David von Dinant." In *Freiburger Zeitschrift für Philosophie und Theologie* 47 (2000): 307–341.

Steel, Carlos. "Introduction." In *Henricus Bate: Speculum divinorum et quorundam naturalium.* Edited by Carlos Steel. Louvain, Belgium: Louvain University Press, 1993.

Verbeke, Gerard. "Le statut de la métaphysique." In *Avicenna Latinus: Liber de philosophia prima sive scientia divina.* Edited by S. van Riet. Vol. 1. Louvain, Belgium: Peeters, 1977.

Winden, J. C. M. van. *Calcidius on Matter, His Doctrine and Sources; A Chapter in the History of Platonism.* Leiden, Netherlands: Brill, 1965.

Wippel, John F. *The Metaphysical Thought of Thomas Aquinas: From Finite Being to Uncreated Being.* Washington, D.C.: Catholic University of America Press, 2000.

GUY GULDENTOPS AND CARLOS STEEL

[See also **DMA:** Aquinas, St. Thomas; Aristotle in the Middle Ages; Augustine of Hippo, St.; Boethius, Anicius Manlius Severinus; Duns Scotus, John; Egidius Colonna; John Scottus Eriugena; Neoplatonism; Ockham, William of; Philosophy and Theology; Rushd, Ibn (Averroës); Sīnā, Ibn; Solomon ben Judah ibn Gabirol.]

MAYEUL. See **Maiolus.**

MEDICINE, ISLAMIC. The phrases "Islamic medicine" and "Arabic medicine" refer to learned medical works written in Arabic in the medieval Islamic world. These terms neither imply that the authors who contributed to this medicine were all Muslims, as their numbers included Christians and Jews, nor that they were native Arabic speakers, as some were Syrian or Persian. This learned medical tradition defined itself as a continuation of ancient Greek Hippocratic and Galenic medicine, and displays few characteristics that one would define as specifically "Islamic." As a reaction against this foreign, non-Islamic medical science, a distinct "medicine of the Prophet" was also developed.

THE EASTERN ISLAMIC WORLD (EIGHTH–THIRTEENTH CENTURY)

The Arabic language was little used in medical writing before the ninth century. The two medical encyclopedias (the lesser and the greater *Kunnāsh*) compiled at the beginning of the Abbasid dynasty by the Nestorian physician Yūḥannā ibn Sarābiyūn were originally written in Syriac; the extant sections in Arabic are tenth-century translations. In 850 a medical compendium, this time in Arabic, was dedicated to the caliph al-Mutawakkil by ʿAlī ibn Sahl Rabbān al-Ṭabarī, under the title *Paradise of Wisdom (Firdaws al-Ḥikmah)*. It blended moral concerns with praise of the medical art and a comparative overview of theories and practices derived from the Greek and Indian traditions. More in line with the tradition of ancient Greek learning was Yūḥannā ibn Māsawayh, who was born in Baghdad during the caliphate of Hārūn al-Rashīd (786–809) to a Nestorian Christian family from Jundīshāpūr and died in Samarra in 857. He is believed to have written around forty works, of which thirty (still little known) survive. As well as works on diet, a book of anatomy, and an ophthalmological treatise integrating Indian sources, Ibn Māsawayh produced a collection of *Aphorisms (Kitāb al-Nawādir al-ṭibbīya)*, in the Hippocratic tradition. From this collection of 124 precepts there emerges a conception of medicine as centered on matching the treatment to the nature of the individual patient and on respecting the numerical relations governing the constitution of the human body and the substances ingested.

A decisive turning point was marked in Baghdad with translations from the ancient Greek, often with a Syriac intermediate version, by Ḥunayn ibn Isḥāq al-Ibādī, also of Christian origin, and by his son Isḥāq ibn Ḥunain and his nephew Ḥubaish, thanks to which the majority of the works of Galen were transmitted. Ḥunain and his nephew Ḥubaish were also the authors of a set of "Questions on Medicine" *(al-Masā ʿil fī l-ṭibb)*, which in later centuries were to be the starting point of medical teaching. The "Questions" are firmly

within the tradition of late Alexandrian teaching, with a few innovations such as the addition of a seventh subject to the study of physiology: the "spirits," or pneumata *(al-arwāḥ)*. On these foundations, tenth-century physicians built up a corpus of doctrines and practices. Three authors, all of Persian extraction, stand out for the importance and wide diffusion of their works. Abū Bakr Muḥammad ibn Zakarīyaʾ al-Rāzī *(ca. 865–ca. 925)* practiced for part of his life in Baghdad and is notable for his great knowledge of the available medical texts in Arabic and for the acuity of his observations of patients. Among his numerous works the best known were *Kitāb al-ṭibb al-Manṣūrī* (The book of medicine of al-Manṣūr), the compendium he dedicated to a Samanid prince and governor of Rayy; a treatise on eruptive diseases such as smallpox and measles *(Kitāb fī l-jadarī wa l-ḥaṣba)*; and the immense *al-Ḥāwī*, compiled posthumously by his disciples from his notes. ʿAlī ibn al-ʿAbbās al-Majūsī left a single work, *al-Kitāb al-Malakī*, dedicated shortly before 978 to the Buyid prince ʿAḍud al-Dawla. An encyclopedia aiming to gather all medical knowledge in a single book, *al-kitāb al-Malakī* is divided in two parts ("theory," *ʿilm*, and "practice," *ʿamal*); it is still very much influenced by the late Alexandrian and Byzantine medical traditions. Next came the central figure of Ibn Sīnā (Avicenna) (980–1037), whose medical works were as influential as his contribution to philosophy. His *Canon of Medicine (Qānūn fī l-ṭibb)*, drawn up over the course of several years amid great trials and tribulations, shows a desire to break with Alexandrian tradition as represented by Ḥunain's "Questions." Ibn Sīnā's intention is to found medical science on principles entirely aimed at fulfilling its therapeutic purposes, even if they differ from the principles of natural philosophy. The five books of the *Canon*, his greatest work, reconstruct the whole of medical knowledge according to a structure based on a hierarchy of general and particular rules, or "canons."

Ibn Sīnā's desire for systematization is absent in later authors from the eastern Islamic world. The writings of ʿAlī ibn Riḍwān *(d. 1068)*, who practiced in Cairo, consist of commentaries on Galen (including the "Art of Medicine"), a treatise on the conditions of pathology in Egypt in the tradition of Hippocrates's "Airs, waters, and places," and an essay on medical instruction providing evidence of the late Alexandrian curriculum. Ibn Riḍwān is also famous for the controversy that brought him into conflict with Ibn Buṭlān, the Christian physician, philosopher, and theologian, during the latter's visit to Cairo around 1040. Buṭlān's most popular work was his *Tacuini sanitatis (Taqwīm al-ṣiḥḥa*, or "Almanac of health"), which supplied rules for healthy living in the form of tables. Under the Ayyubid dynasty and later under Mamluk rule in the thirteenth century, the cities of Cairo and Damascus were important centers of medical activity, which led to the desire to produce a carefully written history of medicine from its origins. Whereas the bio-bibliographical dictionary of scholars since antiquity compiled by Ibn al-Qifṭī (1172–1248) addressed the different branches of learning, the entries in the *Kitāb ʿuyūn al-anbāʾ fī ṭabaqāt al-aṭibbāʾ* (Sources of information on the categories of physicians) of Ibn Abī Uṣaybiʿa (*d.* 1270), an oculist at the Nūrī hospital in Damascus, were devoted entirely to medicine. Still too little studied, the work of his contemporary Ibn al-Nafīs (*d.* 1288), who was born near Damascus but spent most of his life in Cairo, is of great breadth. Most useful to medical historians is his commentary on the anatomical sections of Ibn Sīnā's *Canon (Sharḥ tashrīḥ al-Qānūn)*, which gives the first description of pulmonary circulation, refuting Galen's notion of a passage between the two ventricles of the heart. In this fertile period for medicine in Syria and Egypt we should also mention Ibn al-Quff al-Karakī (1233–1286), who was Christian in origin and is recalled above all for his manual on surgery. These were the most prominent figures of the medieval East in the history of Arabic medicine, which remains largely to be written.

THE WESTERN ISLAMIC WORLD (TENTH–FOURTEENTH CENTURY)

In the westernmost part of the Islamic world, the tenth century marks the significant beginnings of medical writing in Arabic. Born and trained in Baghdad, Isḥāq ibn Imrān was called between 903 and 909 to al-Qayrawān (Kairouan) to serve in the court of Ziyādat Allāh III, the last representative of the Aghlabid period. As well as an opuscule (or short work) on melancholy, he composed a work on the preservation of health and another on medicines, now known only through citations by various other authors, including al-Rāzī in *al-Ḥāwī*. His disciple Isḥāq al-Isrāʾīlī, who wrote works about urine, fever, and diet, was of Jewish origin and came from Egypt. Ibn al-Jazzār, a native of al-Qayrawān, is the third medical author who should be mentioned in connection with the al-Qayrawān circle of the second half of the tenth century; his best-known work is *Zād al-musāfir* (The traveler's provisions), a manual of pathology.

From the tenth century onward, Muslim Spain as well saw the development of medical writing in Arabic. At first the emphasis was on an attempt to achieve a synthesis between indigenous knowledge derived from the Latin tradition and the knowledge imported from the Is-

lamic East. In his work *Ṭabaqāt al-aṭibbāʾ wa l-ḥukamāʾ* (Generations of the physicians and the wise), completed in 987, Ibn Juljul (943–*ca.* 994) situated the medicine of al-Andalus within a general history covering the different civilizations since antiquity. Straddling medicine and botany, the pharmacopoeia was an Andalusian specialty, represented by numerous authors—from Ibn Juljul, who took Dioscorides as a starting point, to Ibn al-Baiṭār (*d.* 1248), who, born and trained in Málaga, then traveled to the East. Ibn al-Baiṭār's compilations on simple medicines were a reference for later centuries.

A contemporary of Ibn Juljul, Abū ʾl Qāsim al-Zahrāwī (*d.* shortly after 1009) was born in the caliphal town of Madīnat al-Zahrāʾ (near Córdoba). His work on surgery, in the tradition of Paul of Aegina but also providing information about contemporary practices and drawings of the principal surgical instruments, ensured his fame. The Zuhr family, established first in Marrakech and then in Seville, were remembered as experts in medical practices in the eleventh and twelfth centuries. The principal work of Abū Marwān ʿAbd al-Mālik ibn Zuhr (1092–1162), the *Kitāb al-Taisīr fī l-mudāwāt wa l-tadbīr* (Book facilitating treatment and regimen), was recommended as a practical manual by Ibn Rushd (1126–1198) in his *Kulliyāt fī l-ṭibb* (Generalities of medicine). Ibn Rushd's medical theory as presented in this work is inspired by a critique of Galen, appearing also in his commentaries on the latter's works. Contrary to Ibn Sīnā, Ibn Rushd believes that medicine should strictly apply the principles of natural philosophy, namely those represented by the Aristotelian corpus. Twelfth-century Córdoba, where Ibn Rushd distinguished himself, also calls to mind his contemporary Moses Maimonides, who died in Cairo in 1204. Maimonides was the author of several medical works in Arabic, including some *Aphorisms* and a *Regimen of Health* dedicated to Saladin's eldest son in 1198. At a time when Muslim Spain consisted only of the Nasrid kingdom of Granada, the epidemic of 1348 led Ibn al-Haṭīb and Ibn Hātima to write treatises on the plague, in which they each suggested the possibility of transmission by contagion. Ibn al-Haṭīb was also the author of a long treatise on the preservation of health.

MEDICINE BETWEEN PRACTICE AND PHILOSOPHY

It is difficult to assess the place of medical theory described in the surviving texts in medical practice. Rulers, court circles, and scholars were the most natural patients for such a medicine. For the rest of the population medical care varied widely according to the time and place. There no doubt existed a crowd of medical charlatans whom their learned competitors do not fail to describe in an unflattering light. The *adab* literature (devoted to the rules of social living) assigns no little importance to the medical code of ethics. An attack on learned medicine more explicit than popular medicine or fraud originated in religious quarters, from which emerged a condemnation of learning foreign to the revelations of the Prophet. Attested from the tenth century, the genre usually referred to as "medicine of the Prophet" *(al-ṭibb al-nabawī)* mixed together passages of the Koran, ḥadīths, popular and even magical practices, and sometimes elements drawn from Hippocratic-Galenic medicine.

The most innovative achievement in the practice of Islamic medicine—even taking into account links with Byzantine practices—was the institution of the hospital, or *bīmāristān* ("sick person's place"; from a word of Persian origin). The oldest hospital attested by documentary evidence was built in Baghdad during the reign of Hārūn al-Rashīd, between 786 and 809. The construction of further hospitals in Baghdad, Syria, and Egypt is attested in the following centuries. Among the most active and well organized of the thirteenth and fourteenth centuries, the Manṣūrī hospital in Cairo and the Nūrī hospital in Damascus deserve mention. Despite the novelty of these initiatives, they bear little resemblance to modern hospitals. Even if sources attest that the *bīmāristān* was genuinely a place for medical care, it was primarily frequented by patients who were poor or concerned about piety; in better-off circles the sick were mainly cared for at home. Nevertheless the treatment of the mentally ill appears to have been an innovation without precedent. The importance of teaching at the patient's bedside in a hospital environment is difficult to assess. It is mentioned in al-Majūsī from the tenth century; Rāzī likewise alludes to the patients he observed in the hospital. The presence of medical students seems to have been expected in the hospitals of Cairo and Damascus in the twelfth and thirteenth centuries.

Whatever the part played by the *bīmāristān,* the attention to the observation of patients, the description of diseases and their classification according to their causes and symptoms, and the abundance of writings both on the preservation of health and on pharmacology demonstrate a deliberate practical orientation in the Arabic-language medicine of the medieval period. (It is worth noting, however, that there was little development in anatomy in comparison to the level it had reached with Galen, barring the work of Ibn al-Nafīs.) This practical orientation was solidly anchored in theoretical considerations that aimed to locate medical science within rational knowledge as a whole; medicine came under the heading of natural philosophy along hierarchies of subordination that varied from author to author. Apart from advances made in the description of diseases, the principal contribution of medieval Islamic medicine lay in the intimate combination of theoretical principles and everyday practice.

BIBLIOGRAPHY

Dols, Michael W. *The Black Death in the Middle East.* Princeton, N.J.: Princeton University Press, 1977.

———. *Majnūn: The Madman in Medieval Islamic Society.* Oxford: Oxford University Press, 1992.

Hau, F. R. "Die Bildung des Arztes im islamischen Mittelalter." *Clio Medica* 23 (1978): 95–124 and 175–200; 24 (1979): 7–33.

Institut du Monde Arabe. *À l'ombre d'Avicenne: La médecine au temps des califes.* Exhibition catalog. Paris: Institut du Monde Arabe, 1996.

Jacquart, Danielle, and Françoise Micheau. *La médecine arabe et l'Occident médiéval.* 2d. ed. Paris: Maisonneuve-et-Larose, 1996.

Klein-Franke, Felix. *Vorlesungen über die Medizin im Islam.* Wiesbaden, Germany: Steiner, 1982.

Leiser, Gary. "Medical Education in Islamic Lands from the Seventh to the Fourteenth Century." *Journal of the History of Medicine and Allied Sciences* 38 (1983): 48–75.

Meyerhof, Max. *Studies in Medieval Arabic Medicine: Theory and Practice.* Edited by Penelope Johnstone. London: Variorum Reprints, 1984.

Morales, Camilo Alvarez de, and Emilio Molina, eds. *La medicina en al-Andalus.* Granada: Junta de Andalucía, 1999.

Romana Romani, F. "Sull'origine del modello islamico di ospedale." *Medicina nei secoli* 14 (2002): 69–99.

Rosenthal, Franz. "The Physician in Medieval Muslim Society." *Bulletin of the History of Medicine* 52 (1978): 475–491.

Savage-Smith, Emilie. "Medicine." In *Encyclopedia of the History of Arabic Science.* Edited by Roshdi Rashed. Volume 3: *Technology, Alchemy, and Life Sciences.* London and New York: Routledge, 1996.

Selin, Helaine, ed. *Encyclopaedia of the History of Science, Technology, and Medicine in Non-Western Cultures.* Dordrecht, Netherlands; Boston; and London: Kluwer, 1977.

Sezgin, Fuat. *Geschichte des arabischen Schrifttums.* Volume 3: *Medizin-Pharmazie-Zoologie-Tierheilkunde, bis. ca. 430.* Leiden, Netherlands: E. J. Brill, 1970.

Ullmann, Manfred. *Die Medizin im Islam.* Leiden, Netherlands: E. J. Brill, 1970.

———. *Islamic Medicine.* Translated by Jean Watt. Edinburgh: University of Edinburgh Press, 1974.

Weisser, Ursula. "Ibn Sina und die Medizin des arabisch-islamischen Mittelalters, Alte und neue Urteile und Vorurteile." *Medizinhistorisches Journal* 18 (1983): 283–305.

DANIELLE JACQUART

[See also **DMA:** Medicine, Byzantine; Medicine, History of; Sīnā, Ibn.]

MEDIEVAL STUDIES

MEDIEVAL STUDIES. Broadly defined, medieval studies is the interdisciplinary approach to understanding the Middle Ages. Medievalists in fields such as literature, music, art history, history, philosophy, history of science, religion, and law often feel intellectually closer to each other than to members of their academic departments whose interests tend to be focused on the present or the recent past. More narrowly defined, medieval studies is also a specific effort within colleges and universities to integrate the approaches of various disciplines based on a wide range of medieval sources, genres, and methods.

THE INSTITUTIONAL CONTEXT

Medieval studies as a term has been used since the early twentieth century in implicit contrast to the specialized treatment of the Middle Ages within the limitations imposed by modern academic divisions. Thus when David Knowles delivered an inaugural lecture at the University of Cambridge in 1947 entitled *The Prospects of Medieval Studies,* he evoked (and at the same time distinguished his own outlook from) the inaugural lecture given only three years earlier by his predecessor Z. N. Brooke entitled *The Prospects of Medieval History.* Medieval studies programs fitting the narrow definition mentioned above—institutionalized interdisciplinary affiliations of medievalists—are more common in North America than in Europe. While there are important European centers (notably the Medieval Studies Department of the Central European University in Budapest) and conferences (at Leeds, Poitiers, and Spoleto, for example), medieval studies has had a particular strength in North America. Even in the United States and Canada, however, there are only a few actual doctoral programs in a specific field called medieval studies (as at Notre Dame, Toronto, Wisconsin, and Yale).

The relatively close relations between medievalists in different disciplines in North America is to some extent an apparent virtue created by necessity. The medieval period occupies only a modest place within large departments such as English, in contrast to the situation in European universities that might have, for example, an entire department of medieval history or in which the Middle Ages enjoys a more privileged position with numerous faculty members concentrated in each academic division. The United States and Canada have nothing resembling European governmental support for research through such institutions as the French Centre National de la Recherche Scientifique and École des Chartes or the German Max-Planck Institutes and Monumenta Germaniae Historica, to say nothing of the myriad local

subsidies to archives, conferences, journals, or archaeology. The Middle Ages is significant enough to attract a large number of scholars and students, but research in the New World remains individual, artisanal, rather than an undertaking of large, ongoing work groups of students dedicated to long-term projects. There are important collections of medieval documents and artifacts in North America (the Morgan Library, the Newberry Library, the Cloisters in New York, and the Walters Art Gallery in Baltimore). There are also repositories of copies of European medieval manuscripts, such as the Hill Monastic Manuscript project in Collegeville, Minnesota, and the Vatican Library manuscripts at Saint Louis University, and magnificent reference resources such as the Index of Christian Art at Princeton. But with very few exceptions there are no long-term, externally funded, or institutional group projects of medieval research.

Although the nature of what is called medieval studies thus depends to some extent on academic organization and other external influences, some degree of interdisciplinary collaboration is essential to comprehending the medieval period. From the seventeenth century onward such great undertakings as the medieval Latin dictionary of Charles du Cange, the Bollandist project of describing the lives of the saints, or Jean Mabillon's *De re diplomatica* have required an immense range of sources. The importance of literary, numismatic, and philological evidence was recognized early on, as was the peculiar way in which the Middle Ages has left more written records than the classical era but in a more disorganized fashion. The significance of religious controversy in forwarding pursuit of medieval texts and interpretations also meant that, from the beginning, fields, methods, and the use of sources could not be narrowly limited.

Tastes and approaches would change, and thus the nineteenth and early twentieth centuries would see great strides in both the accurate reconstruction of texts and the combination of literature and history in works by such scholars as Gaston Paris (on courtly love) and Joseph Bédier (on *Tristan and Isolde* and *The Song of Roland*). The so-called *Annales* school that dominated the field of history for most of the late twentieth century rejected this literary humanist tradition, advocating a different kind of interdisciplinary study based on a "total history" that depicted historical settings and long-term conditions of life ("structures") in terms of geography, environment, demography, and other natural- and social-science categories. The *Annaliste* approach investigated the mental outlook of the population of a past era according to a more anthropological than intellectual-historical sensibility, one that emphasized the complexity of ordinary people rather than the insights of unique individuals.

Within the field of literature, the nineteenth century witnessed the flowering of historical criticism but also a great emphasis on philology in Germany and the Anglo-American world, a way of understanding the relation between language and literature that waned throughout most of the twentieth century in favor of a more aesthetic and symbolic analysis of medieval literature. More recently, a "new philology" concerned with language and textuality rather than linguistic origins has broadened the definition of what is considered literature and the ways in which it is shaped.

The study of the Middle Ages to some extent, therefore, inevitably involves work across disciplinary boundaries. Methodology particular to an academic department assumes less importance than skills required for examining sources (such as mastery of languages or paleography). The proper investigation of medieval art or music, for example, requires knowledge of religious ceremonial, institutions, iconography, and liturgy. But beyond such connections, the way in which the Middle Ages is approached in North America has been influenced by the dispersion of academic institutions, how departments are organized, and the fact that the Middle Ages is not part of U.S. or Canadian history and yet is of sufficient interest or apparent relevance to liberal arts programs that thousands of people have been able to find employment teaching aspects of the period in institutions of higher education.

The founding of the Medieval Academy of America in 1925 was a landmark in the development of something that could be called "medieval studies." The academy brought together members of various academic departments who shared an interest in the medieval period; as E. K. Rand wrote in the first issue of *Speculum* (whose subtitle was "A Journal of Mediaeval Studies"), it was to serve as a "rallying point" from which the study of all aspects of medieval civilization could be encouraged and pursued. *Speculum* has always included articles on varied aspects of the Middle Ages drawn from scholars in all traditional humanities departments, and this interdisciplinary approach is followed by many other North American journals *(Traditio, Mediaeval Studies, Viator)*. European journals tend to be more strictly organized by discipline as well as period. The Italian journal *Studi medievali* is the oldest European periodical with an interdisciplinary conception of the Middle Ages and has been joined by newer journals such as *Médiévales, Micrologus,* and *Medievistik* that treat particular concepts or themes (heresy,

frontiers) or objects (rivers, food, alchemy). The notion of "medieval studies," however, is often used as only a minor expansion of an outlook centered primarily on one discipline—the Spanish periodical *Anuario de estudios medievales,* despite its name, is essentially a journal of medieval history.

In North America, the word "interdisciplinary" dates from the 1920s, but it became a fashionable (if not usually realized) part of educational planning only with the postwar era. The Medieval Academy's founders were less interested in breaking down methodological or bureaucratic barriers than in finding an alternative to the indifference of professional organizations, such as the Modern Language Association, or of departments and organizations of classicists. In the minds of those who established the Medieval Academy and its journal, what particularly united its members was devotion to the study of medieval Latin. Preliminary plans in 1921 for what would become the Medieval Academy proposed to call the body the "Academy of Mediaeval Latin Culture." Ironically, scholars of medieval Latin in North America are now deprived of a consistent departmental base, and the study of Latin philology takes place at the margins of modern literature and classics departments.

At about the same time that the Medieval Academy of America was founded, the Catholic division of the University of Toronto, St. Michael's College, established a center for the study of the Middle Ages. The Institute of Mediaeval Studies, founded in 1929, received a papal charter ten years later and was henceforth the Pontifical Institute of Mediaeval Studies. As with the Medieval Academy, its original emphasis was heavily weighted toward the pursuit of research in medieval Latin but in this instance accompanied by courses in philosophy, theology, patristics, and church history. Only in 1935 were vernacular literature and history added to its offerings. Étienne Gilson, the eminent historian of scholastic philosophy, was attracted to Toronto while keeping his position at the Collège de France and was one of the institute's founders. Gilson succeeded in placing the study of medieval theology and philosophy in a more historical context than had previously prevailed in both Europe and North America. At the same time, the Toronto institute brought the history of institutions, law, and society into closer contact with the legacy of medieval thought. Partly because of confessional differences and in part because of different interpretations of the relationship between the medieval and the modern, scholars pursuing topics related to religious thought had often been set apart from those interested in such things as parliaments or commerce. In 1963, the University of Toronto established a Centre for Medieval Studies that operated in co-operation with the Pontifical Institute. The Centre offered advanced degrees, established a magnificent independent library, and has become the leading North American medieval studies program.

THE NINETEENTH AND EARLY TWENTIETH CENTURY

Although the creation of an institutional structure for medieval studies was first accomplished in the 1920s, the attraction of the Middle Ages to American intellectuals has a considerable earlier history. Not only did North America lack a medieval past of its own, but the United States in particular saw itself in the eighteenth and nineteenth centuries as originating in opposition to such practices as feudalism or the merging of church and state that characterized the Middle Ages. By the late nineteenth century the vogue for the neomedieval style emanating from the romantic aesthetic found expression not only in the Gothic architecture of American and Canadian colleges and churches but in railroad stations, museums, office buildings, and private houses, challenging and often supplanting the classical tradition. As in Britain, the medieval style in North America gestured at escape from the drab uniformity of industrial civilization even as it lent itself to a mass-produced appropriation by that civilization. A certain ambiguity resulted from a tendency to regard the medieval past on the one hand as America's past as well ("our European heritage") and, on the other hand, as antimodern, radically different from the industrial and mass culture perfected by the New World. Henry Adams, the first scholar to have an academic appointment in the United States as a medievalist, taught classes at Harvard between 1870 and 1877 on such topics as the Anglo-Saxon basis of American law and institutions, but later he would write an idiosyncratic but widely read description (or vision) of the organic society of the Middle Ages, *Mont Saint-Michel and Chartres,* contrasting medieval spiritual ideals with the soulless materialism of modernity. Thus in his happier earlier years Adams upheld a view of the Middle Ages as the foundation of modern institutions and ideas, but by 1900, as a more passionate antimodernist, he attempted to free himself of a crass and conformist world through a meditation on what he considered to be the civilized society most unlike modern America in its ethos and outlook.

Before Henry Adams and the beginnings of the professional study of the Middle Ages, the passion for Dante in nineteenth-century America led to the formation of what might be considered the first scholarly association for medieval studies in America, the Dante Club (now known as the Dante Society of America). The arrival of Lorenzo da Ponte, enduringly famous as the librettist for three of Mozart's operas, at Columbia University in 1825 marked the hesitant beginning of study of Dante in the New World (the appointment did not include an actual salary). Henry Wadsworth Longfellow's blank-verse translation of the *Divine Comedy* was published in 1867, and its popularity, along with the efforts of Charles Eliot Norton and James Russell Lowell, led to the establishment of the Dante Club at Harvard in 1880. Norton composed a prose translation that was printed in 1891–1892.

This oscillation between the medieval as beautiful and distant, on the one hand, and as vigorously relevant, on the other, has affected the practice of medieval studies to the present day. What might be called the optimistic or foundational tendency to see the medieval as intimately related to the contemporary had its most memorable exemplar in Charles Homer Haskins. As a professor at Harvard beginning in 1902, he was the founder of the scientific study of medieval history in America. Haskins was also an important man of affairs, an adviser to President Wilson who was involved in the negotiations leading up to the Treaty of Versailles. Although an academic historian and author of studies of institutional and legal history, Haskins worked extensively on intellectual history and the history of science as well. His most enduring work, *The Renaissance of the Twelfth Century,* is a great contribution to the history of ideas and culture and is considered a landmark of medieval studies, not simply a work of historical research.

For Haskins the twelfth century was not a world separated from ours by its possession of a universal, harmonious, and confident faith but rather the true beginning of the modern spirit of inquiry and the modern forms of individualism and the state. In pushing back the supposed innovations of the Italian fifteenth century to what he regarded as their true beginning in the Middle Ages, Haskins emphasized the significance of medieval to modern European and by extension American history, not as a contrasting era of premodernity but as the foundation of both our institutions and outlook. The Middle Ages, Haskins argued in an article published in 1923, "is of profound importance to Americans." The histories of Europe and America, he continued, are ultimately one. This view of the connections between America and a medieval European past would be repeated in its basic form as late as 1963 in S. Harrison Thomson's survey of medieval studies, in which he remarked: "the Middle Ages are early American history and they should be so presented." For the American student, Thomson asserted, "all Europe is his *sedes patrum*." Few scholars would advocate this notion quite so firmly today, but the evolution of the field of medieval studies remains conditioned by efforts to prevent it from succumbing to antiquarianism or obscurity and a conviction that in both admirable and unfortunate ways, the distant past exerts a hold on the present.

GERMAN ÉMIGRÉ SCHOLARS AND POSTWAR MEDIEVAL STUDIES

The evolution of North American medieval studies was greatly influenced by one of the great historical tragedies of recent times, the rise of fascism and the Nazi regime in Europe in the 1930s and the consequent emigration of intellectuals. Entire medieval fields, such as art history and canon law, were either completely changed in America by scholars from German-speaking lands or essentially established by them. The only major area of research in which their impact was minimal was, not surprisingly, Middle English literature.

It is impossible to generalize about their overall contribution aside from remarking on the vast growth in the sophistication of research methods and questions and the impact of this generation on the training of medievalists from the 1940s until the 1980s. In many respects the German scholars broke down some of the provincialism of North American medieval studies and its preoccupation with the origins of American institutions, but the spectacle of the destruction of Western traditions of civility and individualism also reinforced the sense of a connection between the medieval and the contemporary. Hans Baron's interpretation of the link between humanism and the struggles of Renaissance Florence against despotic Milan offered a confident assessment of democracy's encouragement of high culture. On the other hand, Paul Oskar Kristeller's gloomy meditations on the decline of learning before a new barbarian tide (see the prologues to his multivolume *Iter italicum,* for example) were explicitly based on the experience of Germany and his reaction to American student radicalism of the 1960s and to popular culture.

Without advocating a program of interdisciplinary studies as such, the German émigrés encouraged the breakdown of disciplinary barriers. By training and conviction they saw the Middle Ages as part of a continuous Western tradition, so that classical culture was regarded not simply as a species of learning revived in the twelfth (or perhaps ninth) century but rather as a set of themes, styles, and topoi endlessly reworked in medieval Christian society and after. These themes appeared in texts, architecture, liturgy, propaganda, and coins, forming a

language and tradition apart from modern academic categories. Art and latinity owed their medieval elaboration to the classical and late Roman world, but the understanding of medieval secular and religious institutions also required a deep knowledge of the earlier background. The complex nature of state institutions, literary forms, and ecclesiastical ideology was revealed by the iconographic approach of Ernst Kantorowicz, by the literary and philological themes traced from antiquity to modernity by Erich Auerbach, and by the philosophical and art historical studies of Gerhard Ladner. Perhaps most dramatically, German scholars such as Erwin Panofsky and Ernst Kitzinger made the study of art history something more than stylistic influences and antecedents, tying it to the heritage of Christian and classical images and ideas.

The period from the mid-1950s to the early 1970s saw both the zenith of the influence of the German émigré generation and the establishment of medieval studies programs throughout the United States and Canada. This efflorescence was of course part of the overall expansion of universities and research programs resulting from demographic growth, the democratization of higher education, and the vast investments in research by governments that, although primarily benefiting applied and social sciences, provided what seem in retrospect extraordinary opportunities simply in terms of the number of people employed in teaching some aspect of the Middle Ages. Three features of this expansion deserve to be underscored: the establishment and growth of the International Medieval Congress at Western Michigan University in Kalamazoo (1966), the founding of regional associations of medievalists, and the organization of campus programs in medieval studies.

The Kalamazoo meeting began as something of an alternative (or perhaps supplement) to the annual meetings of the Medieval Academy of America. The latter organization brought together medievalists at its annual meetings, but the conferences were perceived as dominated by a few elite universities, and the opportunity to present research was by invitation issued within a rather small circle. Kalamazoo functioned less as a select "academy" and more as a fair or bazaar. The administrative supervision of the conference organizers was relatively slight, focused on providing a venue for what proved to be an ever-increasing variety of associations and exhibitors. For individuals, often isolated in their interests by the size of the continent or the indifference of their departmental colleagues, Kalamazoo afforded an opportunity to find each other and to participate more actively than was possible at the Medieval Academy. Many of the associations of specialists congregating at Kalamazoo simply reflected subdivisions of traditional academic disciplines, such as the Richard III Society or the *Pearl*-Poet Society, but others represented interdisciplinary activities, such as the Society for Medieval Feminist Scholarship or the International Boethius Society. That the Kalamazoo congress eventually would involve more than 3,000 participants and nearly 600 sessions, producing approximately 1,800 communications, demonstrates both the level of activity in medieval studies in North America and its interdisciplinary nature. The fragmentation of interests reflected in the multiplicity of small "societies" and affinity groups occurs, nevertheless, in the context of something of an open market or borderless intellectual world, so that although large fields such as English and history have often remained rather firmly apart, the congress has inevitably encouraged the exchange of ideas across disciplinary boundaries even as it has expanded the program beyond what properly constitutes medieval studies as envisaged by the founders of the Medieval Academy.

Regional associations such as the Medieval Association of the Pacific and the Midwest Medieval Conference were another outgrowth of the decentralization and proliferation of academic research in medieval studies beginning in the 1960s and early 1970s. Like Kalamazoo but on a smaller scale, these associations sponsored conferences that countered the isolation within universities of Chaucerians, manuscript scholars, and students of polyphony. The regional associations did not spring from a particular master plan. Their distribution reflects the relative density of institutions (the Rocky Mountain Medieval and Renaissance Association versus the Delaware Valley Medieval Association) and particular circumstances (the existence of two Midwest associations, one primarily historical, the other more literary).

Finally, individual campuses established various kinds of associations across disciplinary boundaries to further collaboration or at least interaction among medievalists. These ranged from informal groups to hear occasional papers to ambitious institutes such as those at Notre Dame, Arizona, and UCLA that sponsored conferences or journals. The Medieval Academy's Committee on Centers and Regional Associations counts more than seventy-five such campus groups that express, with varying degrees of success, the desire to unify academic medievalists around a common interest.

DEVELOPMENTS SINCE 1980

Since about 1980 medieval studies has been influenced by changes in subjects of research and to some ex-

tent by controversies affecting the humanities that are sometimes grouped together under the heading of postmodernism. The impact of feminism and a growing sophistication in investigating voices not readily transmitted through official sources have strongly affected how medieval piety, family economy, and codes of behavior were studied. The waning popularity of quantitative methods of analysis, which had seemed at one time destined to transform the field of medieval history, has been accompanied by an eclipse of many other social science approaches and a greater concern with mentalities and the formation of popular ideas and outlooks. If history has thereby become more humanistic, literature has rediscovered the historical context of the text in what is often referred to as the "new historicism." The late 1980s and much of the 1990s were a time of both excitement and apprehension in medieval studies. At the time of *Speculum*'s special issue on "the new philology" in 1990 it was widely understood that medieval studies was being transformed by approaches and methodologies that would contest the claims of erudition to impartiality, question the transparent nature of the sources, and replace the assumption of a connection between text and the reality of the past with an appreciation of contingency, partiality, and opacity. While it is too soon to assess the long-term impact of postmodernism, it would appear from our current vantage point that medieval studies has changed less in its methodologies than might have been expected. Nevertheless, the relationship of present to past and the distortions of understanding imposed by historical distance, the accidental nature of what survives and the accretion of tradition, remain problems that confront researchers of all theoretical persuasions.

In many respects the question of whether to regard the Middle Ages as a coherent but vanished civilization or as a progressive era that saw the foundation of modern institutions and ideas persists but in a new key. There is much less confidence than at the mid-twentieth century that the rule of law or the rights of the individual have their origins in an unbroken line that begins with the twelfth or thirteenth century. This is not so much the result of a consciously new approach to the Middle Ages but of a revised attitude toward the nature of modernity. Some scholars have tried to see the Middle Ages from within, as contemporaries experienced the world, without the teleological impulses that attempted to separate the forward-looking (Abelard, John of Salisbury, Marsilius of Padua) from the reactionary (St. Bernard, Bernard of Gui, Boniface VIII). Conversely, others have tried to orient medieval studies toward recent or contemporary problems such as colonialism, slavery, racism, religious intolerance, "patriarchy," and even environmental irresponsibility. Ironically, after many years of trying to point to the significance of the Middle Ages as an era when such innovations as universities, wind and water power, parliaments, and individualism were developed, medievalists have made a better case recently for the connections between their period and modernity in terms of more negative impulses of European culture. Scholars in other fields and the educated public have become interested in such topics as the history of Christian-Muslim relations, the expansion of Europe, the growth of anti-Semitism, and other aspects of cultural conflict and oppression.

The field of medieval studies has avoided some of the apocalyptic scenarios sketched out for it at various times in the recent past. Medieval subjects have not been abolished in colleges and universities as irrelevant; students have not abandoned the humanities or completely shut themselves off from the past; Latin is still being learned; theses are being written on difficult subjects. The future of the medieval fields will be affected in Europe by what is likely to be a declining interest among political leaders in supporting high culture in general and research that has a limited public in particular. The decline of the teaching of classical languages in the schools affects the skills of students in European universities, as does the simultaneous depopulation and suburbanization of the rural countryside and the consequent changes in familiarity with agriculture or the cohesion of local historical understanding. The end of Soviet hegemony in eastern Europe has brought great benefits in terms of freedom of research (especially into religious topics), preservation of monuments, and vastly better intellectual interchange across Europe. At the same time the economic and social dislocations following the collapse of European communism have adversely affected many aspects of government support of education. The greatest damage to the European medieval and early modern patrimony in the years since the Second World War occurred relatively recently in Bosnia and Herzegovina.

Within North America the institutional structure for the pursuit of medieval studies (college and university programs, conferences, associations) will probably undergo incremental but not dramatic changes in the near future. What is widely regarded as the most unpredictable and usually assumed to be the most massive transformation to come is new technology. While exaggerated claims of immediate revolutionary shifts in knowledge and information have been rightly discredited, it is obvious that such developments as electronic mail and the Internet have affected the humanities, medieval studies in particular. Probably nothing has done more than electronic mail and list-serves to alleviate some of the geographical and intellectual isolation imposed by the decentralization of North American education. Although the Internet does not yet come anywhere near to serving as a substitute for traditional library and archival resources, access to information about such collections is greatly facilitated by recent developments, and one can anticipate a time when large numbers of manuscripts and archival documents will be readily available for research at a distance. It would seem at this moment less likely that entire archives and libraries will soon become available in this way or that it will become unnecessary to contemplate actual visits to these collections. Already, however, changes in the availability and diffusion of images has substantially changed the practice of art history, both increasing accessibility to reproductions and limiting the ability to examine original works. It is not particularly original to caution that the increased velocity of communication and dissemination of information do not in themselves mean an increase in knowledge.

BIBLIOGRAPHY

Biddick, Kathleen. *The Shock of Medievalism.* Durham, N.C.: Duke University Press, 1998.

Bloch, R. Howard, and Stephen G. Nichols, eds. *Medievalism and the Modernist Temper.* Baltimore: Johns Hopkins University Press, 1996. Includes biographical studies of founders and "continuators" of medieval studies, including Migne, G. Paris, Bédier, Auerbach, Curtius, and Kantorowicz.

Brownlee, Kevin, Marina S. Brownlee, and Stephen G. Nichols, eds. *The New Medievalism.* Baltimore: John Hopkins University Press, 1991.

Cantor, Norman F. *Inventing the Middle Ages: The Lives, Works, and Ideas of the Great Medievalists of the Twentieth Century.* New York: William Morrow, 1991. Strangely fascinating but eccentric and unreliable.

Coffman, George R. "The Mediaeval Academy of America: Historical Background and Prospect." *Speculum* 1 (1926): 5–8.

Cohen, Jeffrey Jerome, ed. *The Postcolonial Middle Ages.* New York: St. Martin's, 2000. Medieval scholarship, its assumptions, implicit prejudices, and exclusions.

Damico, Helen, ed. *Medieval Scholarship: Biographical Studies on the Formation of a Discipline.* 3 vols. New York and London: Garland, 1995–1998. The lives and work of distinguished medievalists from the sixteenth to twentieth centuries. Volume 1 deals with figures in history, 2 with literature and philology, and 3 with philosophy and the arts.

Frantzen, Allen J., ed. *Speaking Two Languages: Traditional Disciplines and Contemporary Theory in Medieval Studies.* Albany: State University of New York Press, 1991. "Traditional" medieval studies and (or versus) contemporary critical methods and theory.

Freedman, Paul, and Gabrielle Spiegel. "Medievalisms Old and New: The Rediscovery of Alterity in North American Medieval Studies." *American Historical Review* 103 (1998): 667–704.

Gentry, Francis G., and Christopher Kleinhenz, eds. *Medieval Studies in North America, Past, Present, and Future.* Kalamazoo, Mich.: Medieval Institute Publications, 1982. Somewhat dated now, but the article by William Courtenay on medieval studies from 1870 to 1930 is of particular significance.

Hamesse, Jacqueline, ed. *Bilan et perspectives des études médiévales en Europe.* Louvain-la-Neuve, Belgium: Presse Universitaire de Louvain-la-Neuve, 1995.

Journal of Medieval and Early Modern Studies 27, no. 3 (fall 1997). Special issue edited by Helen Solterer devoted to "European Medieval Studies under Fire, 1919–1945."

Morrison, Karl F. "Fragmentation and Unity in American Medievalism." In *The Past before Us: Contemporary Historical Writing in the United States.* Edited by Michael Kammen. Ithaca, N.Y.: Cornell University Press, 1980. A perceptive estimation of optimistic claims versus reality for interdisciplinary medieval studies in America.

Paden, William D., ed. *The Future of the Middle Ages: Medieval Literature in the 1990s.* Gainesville: University of Florida Press, 1994.

Speculum 65, no. 1 (January 1990). A group of articles edited by Stephen G. Nichols devoted to "The New Philology."

Speculum 68, no. 2 (April 1993). Articles edited by Nancy Partner on sex, gender, and feminism in relation to medieval studies.

Spiegel, Gabrielle M. *The Past as Text: The Theory and Practice of Medieval Historiography.* Baltimore: John Hopkins University Press, 1997.

Studies in Medievalism. A journal devoted to modern ideas about the Middle Ages. Thematic issues include medievalism in Europe, England, Germany, and North America.

Thomson, S. Harrison. "The Growth of a Discipline: Medieval Studies in America." In *Perspectives in Medieval History.* Edited by K. F. Drew and F. S. Lear. Chicago: University of Chicago Press, 1963.

Van Engen, John, ed. *The Past and Future of Medieval Studies.* Notre Dame, Ind.: University of Notre Dame Press, 1994. Varied and comprehensive essays covering most medieval fields.

PAUL FREEDMAN

[See also **Supp:** Medievalism; Middle Ages.]

MEDIEVALISM. John Ruskin apparently coined this word in his lecture on Pre-Raphaelitism (1853) to distinguish three periods in European history: "Classicalism, extending to the fall of the Roman empire; Mediaevalism, extending from that fall to the close of the fifteenth century; and Modernism thenceforward to our days." The *Oxford English Dictionary* similarly identifies "mediaevalism, medievalism" as "the system of belief and practice characteristic of the Middle Ages" but adds a second acceptation, "the adoption of or devotion to me-

diaeval ideals." Yet the phrase "Middle Ages" *(medium aevum)* was tendentious from the outset, a label imposed by scholars of the Renaissance to disparage the thousand years between themselves and the presumably superior civilization of Greece and Rome. Medievalism may therefore be viewed as a multifaceted and ever changing idea of the Middle Ages in Western culture, extending its influence to art, architecture, literature, religion, economics, popular culture, and scholarship. In both popular and academic discourse the word still sometimes blurs with "the Middle Ages" or continues to imply intentional revival of medieval models (perhaps better described as "neomedievalism"); further confusion results from occasional mistranslation of the French *médiévisme* or the German *Mediävistik* (medieval studies) as "medievalism." But current scholarly practice adheres to the definition proposed in 1996 by Leslie J. Workman: "Medievalism is the continuing process of creating the Middle Ages." The institutionalization of medievalism as a formal academic subject dates from a session organized by Workman at the International Congress on Medieval Studies at Western Michigan University in 1976. In 1979 Workman founded the journal *Studies in Medievalism,* calling in the first issue for "the interdisciplinary study of medievalism as a comprehensive cultural phenomenon, analogous to classicism or romanticism."

THE SIXTEENTH AND SEVENTEENTH CENTURIES

The Renaissance humanist Giorgio Vasari dismissed "Gothic" (i.e., medieval) architecture as barbaric, and the Protestant Reformation likewise deplored what John Calvin termed the "depraved superstitions" of medieval Catholicism. A signal event was Henry VIII's dissolution of the English monasteries in 1539, precipitating the decay of hundreds of abandoned structures into objects of solemn contemplation. However, Protestant apologists such as Matthew Parker, John Bale, and John Foxe looked to Anglo-Saxon ecclesiastical history for precedent, which led in turn to revived study of Old English. On the Continent, the debates of the Counter-Reformation instigated editions of medieval texts by Jean Bolland, Charles Dufresne, Seigneur du Cange, Jean Mabillon, and Ludovico Muratori, with the consequent development of paleography (the study of ancient writing) and diplomatic (the science of deciphering and authenticating documents).

The Tudor dynasty appealed to Geoffrey of Monmouth's *Historia regum britanniae* (History of the kings of Britain, *ca.* 1136) to assert descent from King Arthur, though the Italian-born Polydore Vergil discredited

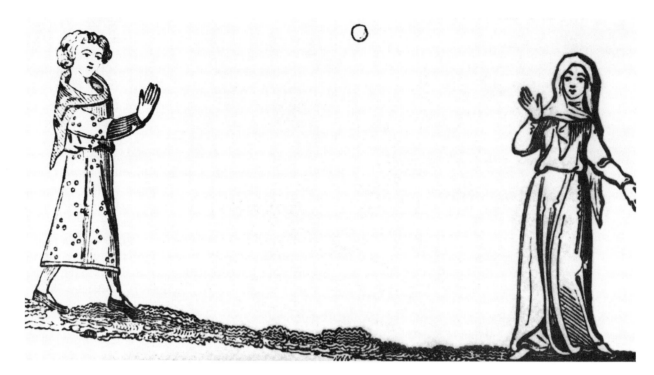

An Early Ball Game. Illustration from Joseph Strutt's Sports and Pastimes of the People of England *(1801), one of the earliest attempts at accurate depiction of medieval costume.*

Geoffrey in his *Anglica historia* (History of England, 1534). Edmund Spenser's *Faerie Queene* (1590, 1596), intentionally archaic in form and diction (as had been Spenser's Italian models, the romantic epics of Tasso, Ariosto, and Boiardo), coincided with the equally anachronistic revival of tilts and tournaments at Elizabeth's court. John Leland undertook to prove Arthur's historicity through a new form of archaic recovery, the topographical survey describing the features of a region, and in 1586 William Camden published his landmark *Britannia,* a comprehensive account of antique roads, trenches, inscriptions, and coins. The Society of Antiquaries, founded the same year, represents the first institutional sponsorship in England for the preservation and study of early artifacts; a prominent member was Sir Robert Cotton, who acquired an enormous library of manuscripts, including *Beowulf* and *Sir Gawain and the Green Knight.* With the English Civil War (1642–1648), the heroic antiquarian endeavor of the seventeenth century gave way to political exigency and marshaled antiroyalist arguments around the Magna Carta (1215), now hallowed as a founding document of liberty. Treatises of legal and constitutional history, with reference to Tacitus's *Germania* (A.D. 98), traced representative government and trial by jury to the tribal councils of the German forests ("Gothicism") or cast the Norman conquerors as foreign oppressors (the "Norman yoke").

In Europe, Miguel de Cervantes burlesqued medieval romance in his *Don Quixote* (Part 1, 1605), but his treatment attests to the genre's popularity. As in England, medieval stories were disseminated in chapbooks such as the French *Bibliothèque bleue* (founded *ca.* 1600); François Rabelais drew on this tradition with his tales of Gargantua and Pantagruel (1532–1552). Ole Worm's *Danica literatura antiquissima* (Danish antiquities, 1636) marks the beginning of antiquarian research in Scandinavia. Research into French history and language was undertaken by Estienne Pasquier and Claude Fauchet, a tireless collector of manuscripts. In 1616 the letters of Abelard and Heloise were printed in Paris, initiating a romantic cult. Dramas of chivalry entered the French classical theater, and Pierre Le Moyne's epic poem *Saint Louis* (1658), drawn from new editions of the thirteenth-century chronicles of Jean de Joinville, extolled the crusader king.

THE EIGHTEENTH CENTURY

Although the arch-neoclassicist Voltaire disdained the Middle Ages, Charles-Louis de Montesquieu's *L'esprit des lois* (The spirit of laws, 1748) and Sir William Blackstone's mighty *Commentaries on the Laws of England* (1765–1769) continued to honor Gothic antiquity. But Horace Walpole, with his intentionally medievalized villa at Strawberry Hill and invention of the Gothic

Abbotsford. *Home of 19th-century writer Sir Walter Scott. Scott embraced medieval architecturalism, transforming a farm on the right bank of the River Tweed in Edinburgh, Scotland, into a Gothic-style baronial mansion.* MARY EVANS PICTURE LIBRARY. REPRODUCED BY PERMISSION.

novel in *The Castle of Otranto* (1764), marks a cultural turn toward romantic effect. Literary and historical scholarship proliferated in the so-called medieval revival: Richard Hurd's *Letters on Chivalry and Romance* (1762), appearing the same year as Thomas Warton's revised edition of *Observations on the Faerie Queene* and inspired by the *Mémoire sur l'ancienne chevalerie* (Memoir of ancient chivalry, 1759) by the French antiquarian Jean-Baptiste de La Curne de Sainte-Palaye; the *Reliques of Antient English Poetry* (1765) by Thomas Percy, a collection of "ballads, songs, and metrical romances" from the folio manuscript Percy professed to have snatched from a household fire; Thomas Tyrwhitt's edition of Chaucer in 1775; Joseph Ritson's edition of Robin Hood ballads in 1795 and his *Ancient English Metrical Romances* in 1802; George Ellis's *Specimens of Early English Metrical Romances* in 1805. Patronage by the Danish crown supported research by Paul-Henri Mallet, translated by Percy in 1770 as *Northern Antiquities,* and the earliest edition of *Beowulf,* by Grimur Thorkelin, in 1815. The aura surrounding the Middle Ages created conditions for literary hoaxes such as James Macpherson's wildly popular *Poems of Ossian* (1765) and Thomas Chatterton's "Rowley Poems" (1777–1778). What medieval people

had actually worn burst upon the public with *Dress and Habits of the People of England* (1796) by Joseph Strutt, permitting in turn more accurate representations of the Middle Ages on stage and canvas. In the German-speaking countries, interest in the Middle Ages was stimulated by the literary works of Johann Jakob Bodmer, Friedrich Gottlieb Klopstock, and Gottfried August Bürger, whose "Lenore" (1773) exerted influence all the way to Edgar Allan Poe, as well as by Friedrich von Schiller's historical dramas (*Die Jungfrau von Orleans,* 1801; *Wilhelm Tell,* 1804) and Johann Wolfgang von Goethe's *Faust,* Part 1 (1808).

Scholarly, artistic, and architectural medievalism united in Sir Walter Scott. Scott followed the example of Percy with his *Minstrelsy of the Scottish Border* (1802–1803); his long poems *The Lay of the Last Minstrel* (1805) and *The Lady of the Lake* (1810) catapulted him into international fame, and he is recognized as father of the historical novel. Scott's fiction emerged in tandem with the growing historiographical enterprise stimulated by Edward Gibbon (significant titles include Sharon Turner's *History of the Anglo-Saxons,* 1799–1805, and Henry Hallam's *View of the State of Europe in the*

The Lady of the Lake Telleth Arthur of the Sword Excalibur. *From J. M. Dent's* Birth Life and Acts of King Arthur *(1893–1894), an edition of Malory's* Le Morte d'Arthur *based on Caxton's 1485 printing but with illustrations by Aubrey Beardsley.* THE ART ARCHIVE. REPRODUCED BY PERMISSION.

Middle Ages, 1818). François Guizot and Leopold von Ranke were among nineteenth-century European historians to acknowledge Scott's salutary influence on historical narration.

VICTORIAN MEDIEVALISM

Despite Edmund Burke's lament in 1790 that "the age of chivalry is gone," chivalry—in Scott's words, "the stay of the oppressed, the redresser of grievances, the curb of the tyrant"—became a hallmark of Victorian society through publications like Robert Southey's edition of Malory in 1817, Scott's *Ivanhoe* (1819), and *The Broad Stone of Honour* (1822) by Kenelm Digby. The proverbial knight in shining armor pervades the paintings of George Frederick Watts, John Everett Millais, and Frank Dicksee. The Arthurian poems *The Idylls of the King* (first version published in 1859) by Alfred, Lord Tennyson, gave chivalry its definitive poetic expression. Through "muscular Christianity," a union of chastity, piety, and strenuous athletics endorsed by Charles Kingsley and Thomas Hughes, chivalry invaded the En-

glish public schools and led to Lord Baden-Powell's Boy Scouts, founded in 1907. With the outbreak of the Great War in 1914, chivalric images on recruitment posters seduced young men on both sides of the Channel to sacrifice their lives.

English historians sympathetic to Catholicism—among them Alban Butler, John Milner, and John Lingard—anticipated the Gothic revival in church architecture espoused by A. W. N. Pugin, who in 1836 published his series of engravings, *Contrasts.* The Oxford movement and John Henry (later Cardinal) Newman's *Tracts for the Times* (1833–1841) urged reforms in the Anglican church in keeping with medieval ritual; the Camden Society promoted stained glass and restoration of Gothic churches; Henry Milman's influential *History of Latin Christianity* appeared in the mid-1850s. These developments created a receptive climate for the medievalism of Ruskin, crystallized in his essay "The Nature of Gothic" (from *The Stones of Venice,* 1851–1853). Gothic architecture (and the values presumed to inform it) was now inseparable from the Victorian establishment, as evidenced in approval of a Gothic style (with Pugin among the designers) for the new Houses of Parliament in 1834. In 1857 the British government initiated publication of historical documents through the Rolls series, a project joined by William Stubbs, who published his magisterial *Constitutional History of England* between 1874 and 1878. John Mitchell Kemble's *The Saxons in England* (1849) and Edward A. Freeman's *History of the Norman Conquest* (1870) continued to address the nation's origins. A cult of the ninth-century Anglo-Saxon king Alfred joined popular enthusiasm for Vikings, and new racial theories sent the "knights of the Empire" on their way assured that the northern races were bred to rule.

If medievalism upheld conservatism, it also authorized counterstatements. The Pre-Raphaelite painters Dante Gabriel Rossetti, William Morris, and Edward Burne-Jones eroticized King Arthur and Dante; Thomas Carlyle inveighed in *Past and Present* (1843) against industrialism; Ruskin attempted a quixotic revival of medieval guilds. Morris, repelled by the removal of material creation from home to factory, reformed the domestic arts by designing fabric, wallpaper, tapestries, furniture, and fine books inspired by the Middle Ages; in 1884 he formed the Socialist League and began writing medievalist utopian novels (among them *News from Nowhere,* 1891), works that invite comparison with the economic medievalism discoverable in Karl Marx and later in G. K. Chesterton. Morris was a chief shaper of the Arts and Crafts movement, which also fed a turn-of-the-century enthusiasm for mummers' plays, maypole dancing, and historical pageants. Sir Henry Irving's 1896 production of J. Comyns Carr's play *King Arthur,* with music by Arthur Sullivan and sets by Burne-Jones, consummated Arthur's installation as national symbol, but illustrations for the *Morte d'Arthur* designed in 1893 and 1894 by Aubrey Beardsley, their sinuous borders stylistically presaging the art nouveau *(Jugendstil)* movement, recast the king for the fin de siècle.

NINETEENTH-CENTURY EUROPE

Medievalism in postrevolutionary France was instigated primarily by the foundation of the Musée des Monuments Français in 1795 by Alexandre Lenoir and the publication in 1802 of *Le génie du Christianisme* (The genius of Christianity) by François-Auguste-René de Chateaubriand. A campaign for preservation of medieval architecture was carried on by Charles Nodier and Prosper Mérimée; the "cult of ruins" culminated with restoration of French cathedrals and extensive rebuilding of medieval Carcassonne by Eugène Viollet-le-Duc. Chateaubriand's romantic Catholicism informs French historiography of the period, especially that of Antoine-Frédéric Ozanam, Joseph-François Michaud, Augustin Thierry, Charles de Montalembert, and Jules Michelet. In Victor Hugo, the mysticism of Chateaubriand united with the historical fiction of Scott to produce Hugo's masterpiece *Notre-Dame de Paris* (1831).

Romantic enthusiasm for the German Middle Ages was stimulated in the first decades of the century by the lectures of the Schlegels, August and Friedrich; the publication by Germaine de Staël of *De l'Allemagne* (Germany, written 1810); and the immensely popular work of "Novalis" (Friedrich von Hardenberg), E. T. A. Hoffmann, Friedrich de La Motte Fouqué, and Ludwig Tieck. In art, the Middle Ages inspired the quasi-monastic "Nazarenes" and studies of ruins by Caspar David Friedrich. But the century's political turmoil enlisted medievalism in the service of an increasingly aggressive nationalism. Collections of folksong like Johann Gottfried von Herder's *Stimmen der Völker* (Voices of the people, 1778–1779) and *Des Knaben Wunderhorn* (The boy's magic horn, 1808) by Clemens Brentano and Achim von Arnim located the springs of national identity in the German "folk"—as did, more notably, the *Kinder- und Hausmärchen* (fairy tales) published from 1812 to 1815 by Jacob and Wilhelm Grimm. The Monumenta Germaniae Historica, founded in 1819 for the publication of historical documents, attracted the talents of Georg Waitz, Germany's greatest constitutional historian, and affirmed the mandate of von Ranke, in his

Geschichte der romanischen und germanischen Völker von 1494 bis 1514 (History of the Romanic and Germanic peoples from 1494 to 1514; 1824), for depiction of history "wie es eigentlich gewesen" ("as it really was"). But across Europe the new academic discipline of philology (the study of texts as documents of linguistic and cultural history) led the quest for national origins. Herder's location of the spirit of a people in their language impelled Jacob Grimm to construct a distinctly German identity in his *Deutsche Grammatik* (German grammar, 1819–1837), *Geschichte der Deutschen Sprache* (History of the German language, 1848), and *Deutsche Mythologie* (German mythology, 1835). In Scandinavia, the Royal Danish Society of Antiquaries was founded in 1825 by the philologists Carl Christian Rafn and Rasmus Rask; N. S. F. Grundtvig made Nordic cultural history accessible in his collections of folksong and *Nordens Mytologi* (Norse mythology; 1808, revised 1832)—as did the tales of Hans Christian Andersen.

Romantic enthusiasm and philological investigation combined in the identification of medieval literary texts as repositories of national genius: the cult of Dante, crucial to the Italian *Risorgimento,* mirrors Spanish interest in *El Cid,* elevation of the *Nibelungenlied* in Germany, and canonization of the *Chanson de Roland* by the French philologists Paulin Paris, his son Gaston, and Gaston's student Joseph Bédier. Philological research and romantic art united also in Richard Wagner, who delved into Grimm's *Deutsche Mythologie* and Norse saga to produce his operas *Tannhäuser* (1845), *Lohengrin* (1850), the *Ring of the Nibelung* cycle (1853–1874), *Tristan und Isolde* (1865), and *Parsifal* (1882). Wagner's anti-Semitism (itself a form of medievalism) and absorption of Germanic myths of origin tragically foreshadowed the Nazi regime. In France, religious medievalism deriving from Chateaubriand was bolstered by editions of the church fathers by Jacques-Paul Migne; the visions of Marie-Bernarde Soubirous (later St. Bernadette) at Lourdes in 1858, soon the site of religious pilgrimage; and Pope Leo XIII's establishment of a chair of Scholasticism at the University of Louvain in 1879. Gustave Flaubert's *La tentation de Saint Antoine* (The temptation of St. Anthony, 1874) and *La legénde de Saint Julien l'Hospitalier* (1877) reflect a contemporary interest in hagiography. Medieval spirituality is evident in paintings by Gustave Moreau, in plays such as Paul Claudel's *L'annonce faite à Marie* (The tidings brought to Mary, begun 1892), and in Paul Sabatier's biography of St. Francis of Assisi (1893). Joan of Arc—subject of poems, plays, and operas since the end of the sixteenth century and prominent in patriotic iconography during the Great War—was canonized in 1920.

The Arrival of Lohengrin at Antwerp. *King Ludwig II of Bavaria designed an entire "swan castle" (Neuschwanstein) around the medieval imagery of Richard Wagner's* Lohengrin *and other operas.* THE ART ARCHIVE/ NEUSCHWANSTEIN CASTLE, GERMANY. REPRODUCED BY PERMISSION.

MEDIEVALISM IN AMERICA, 1500–1900

Medievalism has pervaded American history since the Jamestown colonist Captain John Smith aligned his autobiography with chivalrous romance and the Plymouth governor William Bradford decried the "Maypole of Merrymount" as a pagan idol. The founding fathers defended American independence from Britain by appeal to a common heritage: Thomas Jefferson urged the study of Anglo-Saxon, and in the 1760s John Adams produced the journalism collected as his *Dissertation on Canon and Feudal Law.* Plays of Robin Hood were performed in American theaters, chapbooks perpetuated medieval adventures, and the Gothic novel soon took root in American soil.

In the nineteenth century, Washington Irving invoked popular Rhine legends in his tales of the Hudson, and contemporary medievalism pervades the "romantic" historians William Hickling Prescott and John Lothrop Motley. Like Irving's Sunnyside, the mansions of the American wealthy frequently imitated medieval castles as architects like Andrew Jackson Downing and Alexander Jackson Davis adapted the taste for Gothic to the American landscape. Henry Hobson Richardson, Bertram Goodhue, and Ralph Adams Cram designed Gothic

churches and university buildings, complementing the decorative artistry and stained glass of John La Farge and Louis Comfort Tiffany. Henry Wadsworth Longfellow introduced readers to medieval literature through *The Poets and Poetry of Europe* (1845) and his translation of Dante's *Divine Comedy* (1867). In the South, "chivalry" became so much a watchword that Mark Twain, in *Life on the Mississippi* (1883), blamed Walter Scott for the Civil War. In the Gilded Age, *The Boy's King Arthur* (1880) and other books by Sidney Lanier promulgated chivalry to children, as did the illustrated tales of King Arthur and Robin Hood by Howard Pyle. Twain, notoriously, challenged Arthurian chivalry in *A Connecticut Yankee at King Arthur's Court* (1889), but the murals painted by Edwin Austin Abbey for the Boston Public Library in 1895 proclaimed the social status of Arthurian myth. More insidiously, the Ku Klux Klan dignified its racism with images of mounted knights.

Studies of medieval witchcraft and the Inquisition were published by the publisher Henry C. Lea, but in America as in Europe medieval studies were gradually absorbed by the academy. At Harvard, Henry Adams was appointed professor of medieval history in 1870; Charles Eliot Norton, professor of fine arts since 1874,

The Quest of the Holy Grail *(Panel 15). Edwin Austin Abbey's series of murals for the Boston Public Library (1895) proclaimed the social status of Arthurian myth.* COURTESY OF THE BOSTON PUBLIC LIBRARY. REPRODUCED BY PERMISSION.

became the leading American Dantist of his time; Francis J. Child, professor of English literature, published *English and Scottish Popular Ballads* (1883–1898). But it is difficult to extricate the founders of American medieval studies from romantic medievalism. Adams, in his *Mont-Saint-Michel and Chartres* (1904, 1913) and *Education of Henry Adams* (1907, 1918), betrays a mystical sensibility, and the architect Cram, among the founders of the Medieval Academy in 1925, had produced in 1892 a short-lived periodical titled *The Knight Errant.*

THE TWENTIETH CENTURY

If chivalry sustained a serious wound in the Great War, it survived in the simultaneous romancing of the air war and resurfaced in military leaders like General George S. Patton; even Adolf Hitler was piously depicted in medieval armor. Religious medievalism traceable to Pugin and Chateaubriand stimulated a "Catholic renaissance" represented in England by Chesterton, Hilaire Belloc, Eric Gill, and the poetry of Geoffrey Hill; in France by Charles Péguy, Léon Bloy, and the Thomist

Jacques Maritain. *The Golden Bough* (1890) by Sir James George Frazer linked the emerging discipline of anthropology with earlier philological research, leading to Jessie Weston's synthesis of pre-Christian fertility religion and Arthurian legend in *From Ritual to Romance* (1920), acknowledged inspiration of T. S. Eliot's modernist poem *The Waste Land* (1922). The Celtic past pervades the poetry of William Butler Yeats and David Jones, and the Nordic traditions popularized by Grundtvig found fictional expression in the trilogy *Kristin Lavransdatter* (1920–1922) by Sigrid Undset.

The century witnessed also a "realization" of the Middle Ages in the performing arts. In 1901 William Poel revived the fifteenth-century play *Everyman* in London; in 1911 Hugo von Hoffmannsthal staged a similar production, *Jedermann,* complementing tourism to the decennial passion play at Oberammergau. The Religious Drama Society, founded at Canterbury in 1929, sponsored T. S. Eliot's *Murder in the Cathedral* in 1935—the same year that Gustave Cohen mounted a production at the Sorbonne of the thirteenth-century *Miracle de*

Orc Warriors from **The Lord of the Rings: The Fellowship of the Ring.** *The 2001 film version of J. R. R. Tolkien's heroic romance draws upon medieval demon imagery. (Compare demon images on pp. 151–153.)* THE KOBAL COLLECTION/NEW LINE/SAUL ZAENTZ/WING NUT/VINET, PIERRE. REPRODUCED BY PERMISSION.

Théophile. In 1951 the cities of York, Coventry, and Chester celebrated the postwar Festival of Britain by staging their mystery cycles. The medieval *Play of Daniel* at the Cloisters in New York was a major theatrical event in 1953. Medieval music became at last performable, thanks to pioneering efforts by Charles Bordes and Arnold Schering and the formation in the 1950s and 1960s of early music societies, such as Noah Greenberg's New York Pro Musica.

Finally, the twentieth century saw a pronounced medieval presence in popular culture. Advertisers appropriated King Arthur, Robin Hood, and St. Joan, and Hollywood subjected the same figures to seemingly endless reincarnation (the iconic cowboy exchanging easily with mounted knights of the Round Table); the comic strip *Prince Valiant* first appeared in 1937; Disney films introduced a new generation to the tales of the Grimms. Indeed, successful instances of medievalism have come from writers and artists willing to reach the larger public: the interplanetary Arthurian trilogy (1938–1945) of C. S. Lewis outpaces sales of his scholarly work, and the

philologist J. R. R. Tolkien created a cult classic in his trilogy *The Lord of the Rings* (1954–1955), heralding an explosion of medievalist fantasy and science fiction in the 1960s. Notable in the cinema have been Carl Theodor Dreyer's *The Passion of Joan of Arc* (1928), Ingmar Bergman's *The Seventh Seal* (1956) and *The Virgin Spring* (1959), Eric Rohmer's *Perceval le Gallois* (1978), John Boorman's *Excalibur* (1981), and the comedic *Monty Python and the Holy Grail* (1975). In the 1960s, Alan Jay Lerner and Frederick Loewe's musical *Camelot*—inspired by T. H. White's tetralogy *The Once and Future King* (1939–1958)—lent its name to the Kennedy administration, anticipating the widespread Arthurian revival represented by, among numerous others, Susan Cooper's juvenile series *The Dark Is Rising* (1967–1977), Marion Zimmer Bradley's feminist classic *The Mists of Avalon* (1982), and, in the German-speaking countries, Tankred Dorst's *Merlin oder Das Wüste Land* (Merlin, or the waste land, 1981), Christoph Hein's *Die Ritter der Tafelrunde* (The knights of the Round Table, 1989), and Adolf Muschg's *Der rote Ritter* (The red knight, 1993).

Medieval mystery fiction, practiced in English by Ellis Peters and Candace Robb, reached an apotheosis in *The Name of the Rose* (translated 1983) by Umberto Eco. Since the last decades of the twentieth century, a robust industry of medieval scholarship has existed in reciprocal relation with the fairs and jousts of the Society for Creative Anachronism, the rituals of Wicca and neo-Druidism, commercialized simulacra, and a thriving market for museum reproduction.

BIBLIOGRAPHY

Bloch, R. Howard, and Stephen G. Nichols, eds. *Medievalism and the Modernist Temper.* Baltimore: Johns Hopkins University Press, 1996.

Cantor, Norman F. *Inventing the Middle Ages: The Lives, Works, and Ideas of the Great Medievalists of the Twentieth Century.* New York: William Morrow, 1991.

Chandler, Alice. *A Dream of Order: The Medieval Ideal in Nineteenth-Century English Literature.* Lincoln: University of Nebraska Press, 1970.

Dakyns, Janine R. *The Middle Ages in French Literature, 1851–1900.* Oxford: Oxford University Press, 1973.

Damico, Helen, and Joseph B. Zavadil, eds. *Medieval Scholarship: Biographical Studies in the Formation of a Discipline.* 3 vols. New York: Garland, 1995–1999.

Dellheim, Charles. *The Face of the Past: The Preservation of the Medieval Inheritance in Victorian England.* Cambridge, U.K.: Cambridge University Press, 1982.

Eco, Umberto. "Dreaming of the Middle Ages." In *Travels in Hyperreality.* Translated by William Weaver. San Diego: Harcourt Brace Jovanovich, 1986.

Emery, Elizabeth, and Laura Morowitz. *Consuming the Past: The Medieval Revival in Fin-de-Siècle France.* London: Ashgate Press, 2003.

Frantzen, Allen J. *Desire for Origins: New Language, Old English, and Teaching the Tradition.* New Brunswick, N.J.: Rutgers University Press, 1990.

Fraser, John. *America and the Patterns of Chivalry.* Cambridge, U.K.: Cambridge University Press, 1982.

Gentrup, William F., ed. *Reinventing the Middle Ages and the Renaissance: Constructions of the Medieval and Early Modern Periods.* Turnhout, Belgium: Brepols, 1998.

Girourard, Mark. *The Return to Camelot: Chivalry and the English Gentleman.* New Haven, Conn.: Yale University Press, 1981.

Glencross, Michael. *Reconstructing Camelot: French Romantic Medievalism and the Arthurian Tradition.* Cambridge, U.K.: D. S. Brewer, 1995.

Gossman, Lionel. *Medievalism and the Ideologies of the Enlightenment: The World and Work of La Curne de Sainte-Palaye.* Baltimore: Johns Hopkins University Press, 1968.

Harty, Kevin J., ed. *Cinema Arthuriana: Twenty Essays.* Rev. ed. Jefferson, N.C.: McFarland, 2002.

Lears, T. J. Jackson. *No Place of Grace: Antimodernism and the Transformation of American Culture, 1880–1920.* New York: Pantheon, 1981.

Lupack, Alan, and Barbara Tepa Lupack. *King Arthur in America.* Cambridge, U.K.: D. S. Brewer, 1999.

Mancoff, Debra N. *The Arthurian Revival in Victorian Art.* New York: Garland, 1990.

Matthews, David. *The Making of Middle English, 1765–1910.* Minneapolis: University of Minnesota Press, 1999.

Moreland, Kim. *The Medievalist Impulse in American Literature: Twain, Adams, Fitzgerald, and Hemingway.* Charlottesville: University Press of Virginia, 1996.

Parry, Graham. *The Trophies of Time: English Antiquarians of the Seventeenth Century.* Oxford: Oxford University Press, 1995.

Shippey, T. A. *The Road to Middle-Earth: How J. R. R. Tolkien Created a New Mythology.* London: HarperCollins, 1992.

Simmons, Clare A. *Reversing the Conquest: History and Myth in Nineteenth-Century British Literature.* New Brunswick, N.J.: Rutgers University Press, 1990.

Smith, R. J. *The Gothic Bequest: Medieval Institutions in British Thought, 1688–1863.* Cambridge, U.K.: Cambridge University Press, 1987.

Szarmach, Paul, and Bernard Rosenthal, eds. *Medievalism in American Culture.* Binghamton, N.Y.: State University of New York, 1989.

Utz, Richard. *Chaucer and the Discourse of German Philology: A History of Reception and an Annotated Bibliography of Studies, 1793–1948.* Turnhout, Belgium: Brepols, 2002.

Utz, Richard, and Tom Shippey, eds. *Medievalism in the Modern World: Essays in Honour of Leslie J. Workman.* Turnhout, Belgium: Brepols, 1998.

Wawn, Andrew. *The Vikings and the Victorians: Inventing the Old North in Nineteenth-Century Britain.* Cambridge, U.K.: D. S. Brewer, 2000.

Workman, Leslie J., ed. "Medievalism and Romanticism, 1750–1850." *Poetica* 39–40 (1994).

KATHLEEN VERDUIN

[See also **DMA:** Gothic Architecture; Middle Ages; **Supp:** Medieval Studies; Middle Ages.]

MERCEDARIANS. The Mercedarian order was established in Catalonia in the Crown of Aragon sometime before 1230 by the Provençal lay brother Pere Nolasc for the purpose of ransoming Christian captives from the hands of Muslims. James I, the king of Aragon, gave Nolasc his support, and his successors continued the close association between the crown and the order.

The Mercedarians began as an organization of lay associates but its quick growth and charitable mission brought it under the protection of the church, and on 17 January 1235 Pope Gregory IX recognized the order in a bull *(Devotionis vestrae)* and placed it under the Augustinian Rule. The order quickly added new houses and properties in Majorca, Gerona, Languedoc, Valencia, and Aragon to complement the first Mercedarian house in Barcelona. In the second half of the century, the order began to spread into Castile, but its growth there was limited by direct competition with the Trinitarians and the Order of Santiago, which shared a similar mission and had a dominant presence in Castile.

Throughout the thirteenth century, lay brothers ran the Mercedarians. This practice began to change in 1301 when a disputed election for a new master led to a schism, as two new masters were elected, one lay and the other a cleric. By 1317, the clerics had assumed control of the order, which they never relinquished. The Black Death and disagreements with the crown further weakened the order, as did the continuing competition with the Trinitarians, to the point that by 1357 a plan was presented to merge the Mercedarians into the Trinitarians. Although the Mercedarians survived, charges of immorality and abuses plagued the brethren in the second half of the fourteenth century, limiting their effectiveness in fulfilling their ransoming activities. The Catalan part of the order never fully recovered, and by the mid-fifteenth century another split was threatening to tear the Mercedarians apart as the Castilian houses sought to gain autonomy from their Catalan masters. In 1467, the order officially divided, and from that point on it was the Castilians who dominated and who would lead the order to the expansion, power, and effectiveness that it enjoyed during Spain's golden age.

The Mercedarian mission was dependent on substantial influxes of money needed for ransoms. To this end, the order depended on alms, testamentary bequests, and funds generated by their properties and even by goods, which they sold in Granada and North Africa during their ransoming expeditions. The ransomers, usually two or three of the most experienced brethren, enjoyed a certain amount of freedom granted to them by Muslim rulers as they negotiated for the release of captives. A successful mission could free scores of captives, but more modest results were more common. Captives did not have to repay their ransom to the Mercedarians, but they pledged to serve the order for up to a year and help its fund-raising efforts. In so doing, they arguably became among the order's most prized assets, not only heralding Mercedarian successes but also helping to secure the financial resources for future ransoming expeditions.

BIBLIOGRAPHY

Brodman, James. *Ransoming Captives in Crusader Spain*. Philadelphia: University of Pennsylvania Press, 1986.

Sáinz de la Maza Lasoli, Regina. "Los Mercedarios en la Corona de Aragón durante la segunda mitad del siglo XIV." *Miscel·lània de textos medievales* 4 (1988): 221–299.

Taylor, Bruce. *Structures of Reform: The Mercedarian Order in the Spanish Golden Age*. Leiden, Netherlands: Brill, 2000.

JARBEL RODRIGUEZ

[See also **DMA:** Spain, Christian-Muslim Relations; **Supp:** James I of Aragon, King.]

MERCHANTS are best defined by their activities: they were in the business of buying and selling. In the Middle Ages merchants were suspect because they were not producers but rather relied on someone else's labor to derive their profits. The motto "Buy cheap and sell dear" was a commonplace within merchant circles, though merchant acquisitiveness, in keeping with the deadly vice of avarice, was officially denounced by the church. Nonetheless, the profit motive and the love of risk and adventure attracted some merchants to the very dangerous business of long-distance trade. Merchants themselves existed from time immemorial, but the Middle Ages represents one era when merchant influence and wealth increased greatly. As towns multiplied in the eleventh through fourteenth centuries, merchant elites came to dominate urban society. Most merchants in long-distance trade were men, although women often functioned as local merchants, as hawkers, and as wives of merchants, sometimes rising to prominence, as did the Englishwoman Alice Claver in silks. Myriad local, small-scale merchants had much in common with artisans of the craft industry. The itinerant trader or peddler was also a feature of medieval Europe. Merchants operating more ambitiously often traveled in a group or Hansa for protection.

Maritime merchants who traveled to foreign lands are the most glamorous and best known of medieval merchants. Twentieth-century scholarship focused largely on these long-distance merchants, and they will be prominently featured in the present discussion. It was in these merchant circles that innovations in business technology were most marked. It was here, too, for the most part, that the greatest fortunes could be made and the greatest risks taken. International merchants were bankers and purveyors to kings and popes and the dominant political forces in their home cities. The operations of international merchants have left the greatest documentary trace and thus can be the most easily studied.

The medieval market environment varied over time, but markets were a constant of life in Europe throughout the Middle Ages. Village markets attracted primarily local and part-time merchants. Urban sites might attract regional and long-distance trade as well as much local commerce associated with everyday life, since people in towns and cities were specialized economically and generally purchased food and other necessities of life from producers or merchants. There were two large trading areas in the Middle Ages, the Mediterranean world and the North Sea–Baltic zone, which connected at various points over the whole medieval period, but nowhere more dramatically than at the Champagne Fairs, the great commercial meeting place of Europe in the late twelfth through early fourteenth centuries.

MERCHANTS AND SOCIETY

The traditional tripartite division of medieval society counted those who fought (the nobility), those who prayed (the church), and those who worked (the peasantry). The merchant and the urban dweller were nowhere to be seen in this classification. Moreover, the Middle Ages inherited a disdain for mercantile activities from the late antique era, particularly from churchmen, although certain ecclesiastical writers such as Bede did not condemn merchants so much as dishonest and unjust commercial dealings. Gratian in the *Decretum* (*ca.* 1140) characterized the merchant as one who could not please God easily. In the thirteenth century St. Thomas Aquinas viewed trade with some suspicion. The church frowned on the desire for profit, which Thomas, following Aristotle, saw as essentially boundless and thus dangerous. In many ways the church had difficulty adapting to the emergence of a profit economy in western Europe.

However, the growth of cities provided the locus for the increasing importance of merchants in Europe, stimulating economic expansion, the emergence of new urban and commercial law, and a society based on contacts and exchange between urban and rural worlds. Merchants who made fortunes often bought large estates from impoverished nobles. Some rose high on the social scale, becoming ennobled. William de la Pole of Hull, for example, flourished in the English wool trade, acquired great landed wealth, and was elevated to a peerage in the early fourteenth century.

Medieval merchants frequently were viewed as outsiders as they, initially at least, lacked the network of kin- and client-based connections that conferred membership in the medieval community. This was all the more true of merchants who traveled far afield in European and non-European cultures of the Mediterranean world and the north, and there were advantages and disadvantages to this position. Merchant foreigners often entered the sphere of international trade and banking and the wholesale trade more easily than local business and retail trade. The Hanseatic League (*ca.* 1160–1669), a federation of German merchants of the North Sea and Baltic areas, restricted foreigners to the import-export trade. It was often necessary for the foreigner to belong to a local guild to do business, as in the case of the fifteenth-century French royal official and merchant Jacques Coeur, who joined the Arte della Seta guild in Florence. Towns feared the departure of capital to foreign parts and sometimes prohibited the export of funds. By the same token, Tuscan towns sent many merchants and artisans into political exile, forcing them to make new lives far from home. The protectionism of medieval industry and business is well known. Hanging over the foreign merchant was the possibility of expulsion and confiscation of goods, not an uncommon experience for the Italians in France. On the other hand, as an outlier the merchant was free to be responsive to change, amenable to adaptation, and open to innovation. Enterprise may have come easier, and risks were perhaps more readily assumed. Merchants developed means of coping with their stranger status. Networks of intermediate commercial personnel at home and abroad—brokers, innkeepers, notaries, and others—helped merchants respond to demand with supply and find buyers when they had something to sell. Staples, *fondachi*, and caravanserai stretched across Europe and the Mediterranean world, creating additional connections and providing physical bases that offered compensation for the anomie of the merchant in territories beyond his native soil. Merchants could tap into these networks and operate with greater focus and efficiency, it could be argued, than would have been possible if traditional local networks of kinship and clientage had been the only connections available.

Merchant diasporas contributed to the networks of kin, clientage, and the trade infrastructure. In the earlier medieval period, the Radhanite Jews were beneficiaries of the Jewish diaspora in the Mediterranean world. Later the Genizah community of Cairo enjoyed commercial connections with the Indian Ocean, enhanced by the establishment of Jews in southern India. In the twelfth century Benjamin of Tudela visited Jewish communities throughout the Mediterranean world. Continuities in language and religion within the Arab world created a common cultural zone from North Africa to Asia for Arab merchants, scholars, and geographers such as the fourteenth-century traveler Ibn Baṭṭūṭa (1304–1368). The Italians and, to a lesser degree, the southern French and the Catalans established colonies in the Levant and North Africa, and some few intrepid merchant explorers, such as the Genoese in the thirteenth century, went as far as China, settling there for a time, as did the Venetian Marco Polo and his father and uncle. The spread of merchants across Asia was greatly facilitated by the Mongol peace from the mid-thirteenth century to the 1330s, at which point the great Mongol empire began to fragment.

Merchants relied heavily on credit in their business dealings, but the church condemned usury, which, in the Middle Ages, represented any interest on a loan or other transaction. The Third Lateran Council (1179) linked usurers and heretics, and the Second Council of Lyons (1274) pursued a strong stance against usury. The Middle Ages witnessed an extension of the definition of usury to certain contracts in *fraudem usurarum,* such as loans based on collateral that was remunerative, fictive sales, purchases and sales on credit, and dry money exchange—with the result that many mercantile activities were rendered illegitimate. Historians differ in their interpretations of the effects of the church's usury prohibition on the medieval banking and finance that underpinned mercantile activity, though it seems clear that businessmen proceeded in an ad hoc fashion that required their use of credit. Kings and towns authorized relatively high rates of interest. Gradually, canonists came to defend interest and profits through pretexts such as *damnum emergens* (damage meriting recompense), *lucrum cessans* (compensation for less-well-remunerated investment), and *periculum sortis* (indemnification for the assumption of risk). The canonist Hostiensis (*d.* 1270) defended all contracts but the loan itself from condemnation. With the establishment of the friars in towns and the discussion of market-related issues, particularly by Franciscans such as Peter John Olivi, whose understanding of the operations of the market were strikingly modern, there was increasing justification offered for mercantile vocation. Later Bernardino of Siena (1380–1440) and St. Antoninus of Florence (1389–1459) adopted the theories of Olivi that the value of merchandise justified the profits of commerce and permitted loans in certain circumstances, for example, *damnum emergens.* The profit economy of the new merchants found its most eloquent defenders among the mendicant orders.

TRAINING AND TECHNIQUES

From the early Middle Ages, education had been in the hands of the church, and monastic schools generally trained those becoming ecclesiastics. But even before the emergence of secular schools, merchants, by virtue of their business affairs and their travel, at times over long distances and within very diverse cultures, had need of certain basic skills: reading, writing, arithmetic, geographical knowledge, and foreign languages. Merchants were among the first products of lay schools run by municipalities in Italy and in cities such as Ghent by the later twelfth century. Merchants also required hands-on training in their craft. Apprenticeships were common. For long-distance merchants in the Mediterranean world, many years might be spent in travel before returning to a more stable existence in Europe.

The "commercial revolution," to use a phrase popularized by the economic historian Robert Lopez, involved the revival of trade and the development of new business tools and commercial techniques during the eleventh through thirteenth centuries. The mercantile economy was based on trust. A merchant's reliability and connections made trade possible. Modern distinctions between wholesale and retail trade were not sharply drawn, and merchants could operate on several levels. A host of contractual agreements emerged to further commercial and financial interests. Many of these contracts have roots in Roman law; others are of medieval invention. They include a variety of partnership arrangements such as the *commenda,* delegations of authority in agency or procuration, transport contracts for the shipment of goods, the hiring of services, and the apprenticeship of young workers. Merchant-bankers engaged in traditional business loans, transfer and deposit banking, money exchange transactions, and sea loans, the latter only to be repaid if the merchandise arrived safely. While the Hanseatic world of the north developed partnerships and credit techniques, it was in the Mediterranean that technical advances were the most pronounced.

By the late Middle Ages surviving merchant accounts begin to appear. The earliest example of the use of the Italian language (rather than Latin) was from a Sienese account of 1211. Italian accounts, such as those of the Bardi, Peruzzi, and Medici are well known, but accounts of small shopkeepers and trade intermediaries, such as brokers of Prato, are also extant. Southern French merchants also kept accounts, a few of which have been preserved: those of the Bonis brothers of Montauban, of Ugo Teralh of Forcalquier, and of Jacme Olivier of Narbonne, for example.

Merchant manuals such as *La pratica della mercatura* by Francesco di Balduccio Pegolotti, a factor of the Bardi company, or that of Zibaldone da Canal, and arithmetic manuals such as those of the Pisan Leonardo Fibonacci (1202), Paolo dell'Abaco (1340), and Luca Pacioli (1494) are a testimony to the importance of technical expertise for merchants. Merchant letters were most numerous in Italy and are best illustrated by the extraordinary collection of Francesco Datini of Prato, who corresponded with his associates throughout the Mediterranean world of the later fourteenth century.

Facilitating the long-distance commerce of merchants was a well-developed system of overland transport within Europe and maritime shipping in the North Sea–Baltic area, where the large cogs (flat-bottomed boats) of the Hanseatic cities carried bulky cargo, and in the Mediterranean, where round ships rigged with lateen sails conveyed luxury goods and grain. These great cargo carriers were supplemented by smaller vessels, such as the galley in the Mediterranean and the hulk in the North Sea. Merchants often combined maritime knowledge with business expertise. They owned or chartered ships to move their goods. Merchants contracted with transporters, muleteers, or carters to send goods overland; innkeepers were close collaborators of both merchants and transporters in the movement of items of trade across Europe.

MERCHANTS AND TRADE

The Belgian historian Henri Pirenne focused on long-distance trade and international merchants in his work on the economic development of the Low Countries and northern France, while Italians Gino Luzzatto, Armando Sapori, and Robert Lopez, among others, had a similar focus in their studies of the Mediterranean world from the perspective of Italy. In general, twentieth-century study of merchant activity concentrated on the High and late Middle Ages, simply because most surviving documents dated from those periods. It is only recently, with the work of scholars such as Stéphane Lebecq, Richard Hodges, David Whitehouse, and Michael McCormick, that serious knowledge of merchants of the earlier medieval period is coming to the fore. McCormick, in addition to his archaeological finds, particularly in northern Europe, has created a database of travelers that further enables the study of trade from the standpoint of travel and communications.

Disruption of mercantile activity and depopulation of some of the larger Roman towns occurred during the period of Germanic invasions, but commercial life reestablished itself quickly. Merchant activity in the early Middle Ages in Anglo-Saxon Britain, Scandinavia, and the Low Countries has left considerable archeological evidence. There were laws to protect and to tax merchants. The minting of gold coins continued for upward of one hundred years after the Roman presence had disappeared in Britain and on the Continent. St. Gregory of Tours mentioned the existence of merchant houses in Merovingian towns. The Merovingians of Gaul established contacts with the Mediterranean world that preserved some earlier commercial connections. Syrians, Greeks, and Jews came to dominate long-distance mercantile activities between western Europe and parts of the Mediterranean world. Even in the seventh and eighth centuries when Islam spread around the southern periphery of the Mediterranean Sea, the flow of luxury products to the West and the drainage of gold to the East did not entirely cease. In exchange for expensive spices and fabrics, Europeans could offer raw materials such as iron for military purposes, wool cloth, wood, and slaves. To supplement these exports, they also used precious metals in financing their purchases.

New information has also affected our perception of the Carolingian period. The idea of a closed or domestic economy in a Carolingian world dominated by large estates has been laid to rest. The large estates themselves belonged to a market economy in which surpluses were sold. Palace merchants supplied a royal court that was frequently itinerant; dependent merchants were in the employ of large religious establishments. There is mention at Aachen of merchant residences under the emperor Louis I (the Pious). Radhanite Jews were the main operatives in international trade in the Mediterranean world. The Carolingian economy sustained the growth of markets and merchants operating in local agricultural trade, but also over considerable geographic distance.

Connected to the Carolingian world on the north was the North Sea–Baltic trading sphere. Here the Frisians were prominent traders in a commercial network that stretched from England to Russia, with merchant emporia at sites such as Quentovic near the mouth of the Canche River and Duurstede in the Rhine delta, Hedeby on the Jutland peninsula, Visby on Gotland, Birka on Lake Mälar in Sweden, and Staraya Lagoda and Novgorod in Russian lands. During the second wave of invasions, destruction by the Vikings caused a decline in this network, but the Vikings overall distinguished themselves by trading as well as raiding and marauding. In all, they may have stimulated mercantile activities in the local populations of those areas of continental Europe into which they penetrated, releasing back into the economy the hoarded precious metal objects of church treasuries. Invasions by Magyars or Hungarians from eastern Europe also took their toll on merchant activity in the ninth and tenth centuries, and urban sites were targeted in eastern and southern France, Italy, and Germany while Saracens raided the western Mediterranean coasts of Europe. A new era was signaled, however, by the Magyar defeat at Lechfeld in Germany in 955 and that of the Saracens at La Garde-Freinet in Provence in 972.

Foremost among medieval merchants throughout the Middle Ages were the Italians, whose Mediterranean operations connected the eastern and western basins of the inland sea. From as early as the ninth century, merchants of the Italo-Byzantine towns of Bari, Amalfi, Gaeta, and Naples in southern Italy and Venice in the north, favored by the continuity of their contacts with the Byzantine Empire, were the first to initiate an important commerce with the Levant. Italo-Byzantine merchants established a triangular trade linking Italy with North Africa and the Levant. Merchants sold southern agricultural products in North Africa for gold that they then used to trade for luxury goods—silks, spices, drugs, dyestuffs, nuts, and fruits, among them—in the Levant. The advent of the Normans as conquerors of Sicily and southern Italy in the mid- and later-eleventh century signaled the end of the dramatically successful exploits of Amalfitan merchants and others of southern Italy. Merchants of Genoa and Pisa rose to prominence, boosted by their role in transport services and supply in support of the armies of the First Crusade (1096–1099); they then catered to the needs of the newly established crusader principalities and soon were competing with Venice. The Byzantine Empire was simultaneously a center of consumption of luxury goods and an assembly point for purchases. Western merchants were also attracted to Alexandria in search of eastern luxury products. Colonies in the crusader principalities of the Syrian coast and farther east in the Black Sea area (Caffa) and the Sea of Azov (Tana) provided merchants with additional entrepots for trade routes from south and east Asia. The Near East and, by extrapolation, South Asia and the Orient continued to furnish those spices, apothecary products, silks, and ornate fabrics so coveted by Europeans. Agricultural commodities figured, as well, in long-distance trade.

Pirenne linked the revival of long-distance trade and traders to the growth of towns from the eleventh century. Godric of Finchal was Pirenne's archetypal itinerant merchant of peasant origin who began as a peddler of shipwreck goods, ultimately trading among England, Scotland, Denmark, and the Low Countries. He made a great fortune that, toward the end of his life, he gave to the poor, becoming a hermit and a saint. Scholars such as Jean Lestoquoy and Georges Espinas focused on merchant recruits from rural and seigneurial administrative background in towns like Arras. Demographic growth in Europe, sustained by agricultural expansion and technological strides, supplied candidates for a mercantile vocation. But merchant numbers would always remain a small, albeit significant proportion of town population in a Europe that was perhaps 10 percent urbanized overall, with heavier concentrations of urbanization, as high as 30 percent, in some areas of the Low Countries and Tuscany.

In the North Sea–Baltic area, trade revived quickly after the end of the Viking invasions. By the twelfth century, German merchants of prominent towns such as Cologne and Lübeck in the west and Riga and Rostock in the east had begun the creation of a mercantile network for their mutual protection and profit. Merchants established "factories" at prime commercial sites such as the Steelyard in London and St. Peter's Yard in Novgorod. The Hanseatic League of German merchants, formalized by the fourteenth century, would endure until the seventeenth century. At its base was an east-west exchange: raw materials of the east for finished goods of the west. The Baltic area in the north was traditionally a source of grain for northern Europe. Tar, pitch, potash, and furs also figured among products traded by merchants in the North Sea–Baltic sphere. The Rus of Novgorod procured huge quantities of furs for export to the west from their network of contacts with Finno-Ugrians and other peoples of the far north.

Beginning in the twelfth century, the cycle of the Champagne fairs—with six annual gatherings, spread out across the whole year, in the towns of Troyes, Provins, Bar-sur-Aube, and Lagny—represented the apogee of an economy based on traveling merchants. They linked the world of the north with that of the Mediterranean. Having started as agricultural fairs, by the later twelfth century the Champagne fairs were attracting Italian merchants in search of high-quality wool cloth of Flemish and northern French confection that might be finished in the cloth-finishing industry of Tuscany, particularly under the auspices of the Arte di Calimala of Florence. Northern merchants, such as members of the Hansa of seventeen towns, frequented the fairs to sell cloth and to obtain the luxury products of the eastern Mediterranean markets, as well as the saffron and leather of the Iberian Peninsula. By the late thirteenth-century the fairs had shifted from a focus on cloth to become a financial clearinghouse for merchant bankers. The opening of an Atlantic sea route in the 1270s by the Genoese and Majorcans and the increasing use of Alpine passes such as the St. Gothard to bypass Champagne en route to Bruges contributed to the decline of the fairs, by giving merchants several choices of north-south routes. The development of a total cloth industry in Italy, led by the Arte della Lana in Florence, eliminated the need for Italian merchants to travel to Champagne to obtain wool cloth. The way merchants did business also changed.

The historian Robert L. Reynolds has identified a sedentarization of trade by the end of the thirteenth century. The age of the traveling merchant made way for a more complex commercial organization. The large merchant companies of Italy developed the practice of establishing branch offices in important business sites such as Bruges, Paris, and London. Though directors of these companies no longer peddled their merchandise along the roads and seaways, they still traveled at times. Yet the management of the great merchant companies was carried out on site through branch managers and factors.

In the late thirteenth and fourteenth centuries the great merchants in Tuscany and northern Italy forged large partnerships of merchant bankers, such as the Ricciardi of Lucca; the Salimbeni and Tolomei of Siena; and the Bardi, Acciaiuoli, and Peruzzi of Florence. Later, in the fifteenth century, the Medici of Florence operated on a reduced scale. Between 1310 and 1345 the Bardi employed 346 agents at more than 25 branch offices in Italy, France, England, Spain, the Low Countries, Tunis in North Africa, and the Levant. In any given year more than 100 agents may have been on the Bardi payroll. The Peruzzi had 133 factors in their employ in the years 1331 to 1343. The Bardi closed their books in 1318 at about 875,000 florins, a huge fortune when cities such as Avignon and Montpellier could be bought for a fraction of this sum. Economic changes in the fourteenth century, combined with political turmoil and bad loans, led to bankruptcies. For the Bardi and Peruzzi, operating under a system of unlimited liability, the financial difficulties of one branch were assumed by the company as a whole, and a disaster could and did bring down the entire structure in the 1340s. By the fifteenth century, the size of the Italian company had declined, and the Medici of Florence controlled assets of about 75,000 florins in 1451, with about one quarter of this sum invested in two wool shops and one silk shop in Florence. The Medici had learned from earlier mistakes and ran branches independently, avoiding unlimited liability. Elsewhere in Europe over the High and late Middle Ages partnerships were also common, though the size of their capitalization and the number of partners never rivaled the scope of the Italian companies.

Individual merchant fortunes were at times staggering, but many merchants—such as the Venetian Romano Mairano—not only made but also lost fortunes. Their activities were incredibly diverse. The Genoese Benedetto Zaccaria was both admiral and merchant, operating for the French king at times and for the Castilian king at others, inserting himself in societies as far afield as Andalusia. His most successful endeavor lay in the alum industry on Phocaea, an eastern Mediterranean island that he controlled, with production valued at as much as 50,000 Genoese lire per annum. Zaccaria also ran mastic plantations, controlled ships, and traded in other merchandise with additional investments in such areas as public debt and real estate. The immensely wealthy merchant Salimbene Salimbeni of Siena, a member of the Salimbeni company, blessed Siena with his philanthropy through a gift of 118,999 Sienese lire (slightly less than the same value in Florentine florins) in 1260, when Siena was at war with Florence. The fifteenth-century Venetian merchant Andrea Barbarigo, who left surviving books of accounts, could, because of earlier losses, boast only a modest fortune when he died in 1449. Barbarigo dealt in traditional trade goods: cotton, wool, spices, copper, and cloth. He used the official Venetian fleet with the aid of brokers. He kept his accounts in double entry and speculated in letters of exchange. After a stint as a traveling merchant, he conducted his business from the great center of Venetian affairs at Rialto. Jacques Coeur, born in central France at Bourges, stands out as a remarkable operator in mid-fifteenth century France, exercising the roles of royal bursar, financier, and Mediterranean merchant, trading with Muslim lands, especially for spices. Coeur established a role for the French king in Mediterranean trade, foreshadowing later mercantilist endeavors, all the while expanding his own fortune only to fall victim, ultimately, to royal envy and political factions. The size of Coeur's fortune is difficult to calculate, but when Coeur was condemned for treason and other crimes by royal decree in 1453, he was ordered to pay 400,000 écus in debts and fines to the king. For the ransom of King John II after his capture at the battle of Poitiers in 1356, all of France could only muster the equivalent of 375,000 écus.

POLITICS

Towns were the primary locus of merchant politics, and towns, at least the Italian communes, were aptly described by Robert Lopez as republics of the merchants, by the merchants, and for the merchants. The great Italian merchants formed no guilds but rather trafficked through a commission called the Mercanzia in Florence or in Genoa and Venice through the communes, which were essentially the corporations of the great merchants. In contrast, in England the guild merchant was an important political force in towns. Merchants dominated the early phases of development of autonomous municipal governments as they emerged in Italy as communes, in France as communes in the north and consulates in the south, in Germany and the Low Countries as independent cities, in Spain as *fueros,* and in England as chartered boroughs. With the economic difficulties of the later thirteenth and fourteenth centuries, tensions between the dominant mercantile factions split the Florentines into an array of Guelph and Ghibelline parties and divided merchant guilds and craft guilds in Tuscany, the Low Countries, and Germany. In Florence the period from 1343 to 1378 witnessed the triumph of the middle and lower guilds over merchant patricians, the *popolo grasso,* who themselves had bested the older traditional noble and mercantile government in 1293. The Low Countries were particularly hard hit by urban social unrest, mixing hostility between mercantile and craft interests with royal and comitial politics that were part of the struggle between England and France. The Low Countries economy was based on the import of English wool and the production of wool cloth for export throughout Europe. Grain had to be imported from northern France to feed the cities. In the fourteenth century the entrepreneurs of the cloth industry—merchant patricians sympathetic to the French—succumbed to weaver interests, leading to the ascension of the demagogic van Arteveldes of Ghent; Jacob van Artevelde's power was concentrated in the years 1338–1345, while that of Philip van Artevelde climaxed in 1381–1382.

As mercantile populations of towns grew in wealth, monarchs at work constructing their kingdoms took greater notice and increasingly involved merchants in governance. In the late Middle Ages, English merchants and gentry were of interest to the English king, who in an earlier time relied heavily on foreign merchants, such as the Ricciardi of Lucca, for wool export and banking functions. Aragonese merchants played a significant role in the Mediterranean political ambitions of their sovereigns. In France royal and urban politics were linked in a growing alliance between the kings and the bourgeoisie of essentially mercantile background. Some merchants acquired rentier status, ennoblement, and membership in the king's council. Charles VII relied on merchants such as Jacques Coeur to rationalize royal finance, a strategy that contributed to French victory in the Hundred Years War.

CONCLUSION

The willingness of some merchants to take risks was somewhat dampened by the unforgiving series of crises—social, demographic, economic, and war-related—that characterized the fourteenth and fifteenth centuries in Europe. But change was on the horizon. The age of European expansion, beginning with the discovery and exploitation of the Atlantic Mediterranean, would create a new stage upon which European merchants could operate. However, the world formed in the Middle Ages by merchants set in place the economic foundations of the early modern and modern eras.

BIBLIOGRAPHY

Bautier, Robert-Henri. *The Economic Development of Medieval Europe.* Translated by Heather Karolyi. London: Thames and Hudson, 1971.

Constable, Olivia Remie. *Trade and Traders in Muslim Spain: The Commercial Realignment of the Iberian Peninsula, 900–1500.* Cambridge, U.K.: Cambridge University Press, 1994.

Dollinger, Philippe. *The German Hansa.* Translated and edited by D. S. Ault and S. H. Steinberg. Stanford, Calif.: Stanford University Press, 1970.

Favier, Jean. *Gold and Spices: The Rise of Commerce in the Middle Ages.* Translated by Caroline Higgitt. New York: Holmes and Meier, 1998.

Hodges, Richard, and David Whitehouse. *Mohammed, Charlemagne, and the Origins of Europe.* Ithaca, N.Y.: Cornell University Press, 1983.

Kedar, Benjamin Z. *Merchants in Crisis: Genoese and Venetian Men of Affairs and the Fourteenth-Century Depression.* New Haven, Conn., and London: Yale University Press, 1976.

Kermode, Jenny. *Medieval Merchants: York, Beverley, and Hull in the Later Middle Ages.* Cambridge, U.K.: Cambridge University Press, 1998.

Kowaleski, Maryanne. *Local Markets and Regional Trade in Medieval Exeter.* Cambridge, U.K.: Cambridge University Press, 1995.

Lane, Frederic C. *Andrea Barbarigo, Merchant of Venice, 1418–1449.* 1944. Reprint, New York: Octagon, 1967.

Lebecq, Stéphane. *Marchands et navigateurs frisons du haut moyen âge.* Lille, France: Presses Universitaires de Lille, 1983.

Le Goff, Jacques. *Marchands et banquiers du moyen-âge.* Paris: Presses Universitaires de France, 1956.

Lopez, Robert S. *Genova marinara nel Duecento: Benedetto Zaccaria ammiraglio et mercante.* Messina-Milan: Principato, 1933.

———. *The Commercial Revolution of the Middle Ages, 950–1350.* Englewood Cliffs, N.J.: Prentice-Hall, 1971.

Lopez, Robert S., and Irving W. Raymond, eds. and trans. *Medieval Trade in the Mediterranean World: Illustrative Documents.* 1955. Reprint, with a foreword and bibliography by Olivia Remie Constable, New York: Columbia University Press, 2001.

Luzzatto, Gino. *An Economic History of Italy from the Fall of the Roman Empire to the Beginning of the 16th Century.* Translated by Philip Jones. London: Routledge and Kegan Paul, 1961.

Masschaele, James. *Peasants, Merchants, and Markets: Inland Trade in Medieval England, 1150–1350.* New York: St. Martin's, 1997.

McCormick, Michael. *Origins of the European Economy: Communications and Commerce, A.D. 300–900.* Cambridge, U.K.: Cambridge University Press, 2001.

Miskimin, Harry A. *The Economy of Early Renaissance Europe, 1300–1460.* Englewood Cliffs, N.J.: Prentice-Hall, 1969.

Mollat, Michel. *Jacques Coeur ou l'esprit d'entreprise au XVe siècle.* Paris: Aubier, 1988.

Murray, James M., and Edwin S. Hunt. *A History of Business in Medieval Europe, 1220–1550.* Cambridge, U.K.: Cambridge University Press, 1999.

Nicholas, David. *The van Arteveldes of Ghent: The Varieties of Vendetta and the Hero in History.* Ithaca, N.Y.: Cornell University Press, 1988.

Noonan, John Thomas. *The Scholastic Analysis of Usury.* Cambridge, Mass.: Harvard University Press, 1957.

Pirenne, Henri. *Medieval Cities: Their Origins and the Revival of Trade.* Translated by Frank D. Halsey. Princeton, N.J.: Princeton University Press, 1925.

Pirenne, Henri, et al. *Mahomet and Charlemagne: Byzance, Islam, et Occident dans le haut moyen âge.* Milan: Jaca, 1987.

Renouard, Yves. *Les hommes d'affaires italiens du moyen âge.* Paris: Colin, 1968.

Reyerson, Kathryn L. *Business, Banking, and Finance in Medieval Montpellier.* Toronto: Pontifical Institute of Mediaeval Studies, 1985.

Reynolds, Robert L. "Origins of Modern Business Enterprise: Medieval Italy." *Journal of Economic History* 12 (1952): 350–365.

Roover, Raymond de. *Money Banking and Credit in Medieval Bruges.* Cambridge, Mass.: Medieval Academy of America, 1948.

———. *The Rise and Decline of the Medici Bank, 1397–1494.* New York: Norton, 1966.

Sapori, Armando. *The Italian Merchant in the Middle Ages.* Translated by Patricia Ann Kennen. New York: Norton, 1970.

Unger, Richard W. *The Ship in the Medieval Economy, 600–1600.* London: Croom Helm, 1980.

KATHRYN L. REYERSON

[See also **DMA:** Commenda; Fairs; Fairs of Champagne; Hanseatic League; Inns and Taverns; Markets, European; Trade; Usury.]

MERTON CALCULATORS.

"Merton Calculators" is a label given to a group of authors at Oxford in the mid-fourteenth century who introduced quantification into logical and natural philosophical disputations. Their work culminated in the *Liber calculationum* (*Book of Calculations, ca.* 1350). Its author, often referred to in later centuries simply as "Calculator," is now thought to have been Richard Swineshead (*fl.* 1340–1355), who is known to have been a fellow of Merton College in 1344 and in 1355. Others whose work may be associated with the *Liber calculationum* were also Merton College fellows, notably Walter Burley (*ca.* 1275–after June 1344), Thomas Bradwardine (*ca.* 1300–1349), William Heytesbury (*ca.* 1313–1372), and John Dumbleton (*d. ca.* 1349). This has resulted in associating calculatory work with Merton College, Oxford, although not all "Calculators" at Oxford were Mertonians and not all fourteenth-century Mertonians who contributed to science were calculators in the sense meant here: some contemporary Mertonians, such as Simon Bredon (Merton fellow 1330; *d.* 1372) and William Rede (*d.* 1375), were more interested in astronomical than physical calculations.

"Calculations" of the sort to be found in the *Book of Calculations* seem to have arisen in connection with the disputations required of all Oxford undergraduates at this period. Undergraduates studied logic, mathematics, and natural philosophy. To cement their facility with logical argument, students were expected to take part in disputations that followed a prescribed format. In disputations *de sophismatibus* (on sophismata), students disputed the truth or falsity of propositions purposely formulated to be ambiguous or peculiar sounding. So the proposition "All the disciples were twelve" was taken as a sophism sentence partly because, although there were never more than twelve disciples at any one time, one might suppose that there were thirteen disciples in all since, after his betrayal of Jesus, Judas was replaced by Matthias. So there is a problem in determining the time period to which the proposition applies. More importantly "All the disciples are twelve" posed a problem for those trying to formalize logic, because from most propositions of the form "All A are B" it follows that "This A is B," whereas no individual disciple is twelve.

Calculationes entered disputations on sophismata when solutions of logical puzzles were proposed that involved measures or quantifications of various sorts. William Heytesbury's *Regulae solvendi sopismata* (Rules for solving sophismata, 1335) and his *Sophismata* provide many examples of *calculationes* along with other rules and solutions to sophismata that are purely logical. The standard toolbox of approaches that the Calculators used to solve problems have been called "analytical languages" and include the language of ratios and of operations on ratios; the language of the suppositions of terms in propositions; the theory of the intension and remission of forms; theories of infinity and continuity; the theory of beginning and ceasing or of first and last instants; the theory of maxima and minima; and questions of the measures of motions, whether of local motion, alteration, or augmentation and diminution. In the application of many or most of these languages, the authors took a second-intentional, or metalinguistic, point of view and assumed that most nouns or other so-called categorematic terms in propositions stand for things in the world. So, for example, in the proposition "All humans are mortal," the term "humans" stands, or "supposits," for all (and only) humans, and the term "mortal" supposits for all (and only) those beings destined to die.

If all humans fall within the group of all beings destined to die, then the proposition will be true. Through supposition theory, especially as deployed by nominalists, language was linked rigorously to the world, and logic and physics were made to cast light on each other.

An example of the sort of analysis a Merton Calculator might do is the following. Heytesbury and most of the other Merton Calculators argued that motions of rotation should be measured by the motion of the fastest moved point of the body. Then if one had a rotating disk that continued to move with constant angular velocity while the disk expanded (for instance by being heated) and the outside edge of the disk was removed, it could happen that the motion of the disk as a whole became slower and slower (because the removal of the fastest moved points of the disk means that the greatest velocity becomes less and less), while, at the same time, each point that continued to be part of the disk moved faster and faster as it moved away from the axis of rotation as a result of the disk's expansion. On the basis of this case, a calculator might assert the truth of the sophism sentence, "a body moves at a steadily decreasing speed during an hour, while the speed of every point of the body continually increases during the same hour." While this proposition seems, at first sight, to be self-contradictory, the student-calculator could show that it is true in the hypothetical or imaginary case described.

The introduction of questions of physics and mathematics into disputations connected to the teaching of logic seems to have been encouraged by the notable success of Thomas Bradwardine's 1328 *De proportionibus velocitatum in motibus* (On the ratios of velocities in motions). In this work, Bradwardine developed a single mathematical relationship explaining how velocities vary with ratios of force to resistance, which had clear advantages over what had previously been thought to be Aristotle's view. But if, intellectually, it was the success of Bradwardine's *De proportionibus velocitatum in motibus* that encouraged contemporary Mertonians to apply mathematics to physics more widely, institutionally it was the undergraduate curriculum with its required disputations exercising students in logic that fed the development of *calculationes*. Contemporary with Bradwardine, Richard Kilvington (*ca.* 1305–1361), who was not a Mertonian, was already applying calculatory approaches in his *Sophismata,* as well as in his commentaries on Aristotle. Also before the works of Heytesbury and Swineshead, Walter Burley developed calculatory approaches in his work *De primo ultimo instanti* (On first and last instants), *Tractatus primus* (First treatise), and *De intensione et remissione formarum* (On the intension and remission of forms).

Although there is little evidence of calculatory work at Oxford after 1350, the work of the Merton Calculators influenced Nicole Oresme (*ca.* 1320–1382) and Albert of Saxony (*ca.* 1316–1390) at Paris and later scholars in Italy, Portugal, and Spain, notably Alvarus Thomas of Lisbon, who published what amounted to a commentary on the work of Heytesbury and Swineshead in 1509. In the late seventeenth century, Gottfried Wilhelm Leibniz, cocreator of the calculus, praised Swineshead for what he did to introduce mathematics into physics.

BIBLIOGRAPHY

PRIMARY WORKS

Bradwardine, Thomas. *On the Ratios of Velocities in Motions.* In *Thomas of Bradwardine: His Tractatus de proportionibus, Its Significance for the Development of Mathematical Physics.* Edited and translated by H. Lamar Crosby Jr. Madison: University of Wisconsin Press, 1959.

Clagett, Marshall. *The Science of Mechanics in the Middle Ages.* Madison: University of Wisconsin Press, 1959. Clagett's book is useful in providing translated excerpts relevant especially to the history of physics.

Kilvington, Richard. *The Sophismata of Richard Kilvington.* Edited and translated by Norman Kretzmann and Barbara Ensign Kretzmann. Cambridge, U.K.: Cambridge University Press, 1990.

SECONDARY WORKS

Clagett, Marshall. "Richard Swineshead and Late Medieval Physics." *Osiris* 9 (1950): 131–161.

———. *The Science of Mechanics in the Middle Ages.* Madison: University of Wisconsin Press, 1959. Best single source for a survey of the Merton Calculators' ideas in mechanics.

Hoskin, Michael, and A. G. Molland. "Swineshead on Falling Bodies: An Example of Fourteenth-Century Physics." *British Journal for the History of Science* 3 (1966): 150–182. Includes one treatise of the *Book of Calculations.*

Murdoch, John. "From Social into Intellectual Factors: An Aspect of the Unitary Character of Late Medieval Learning." In *The Cultural Context of Medieval Learning.* Edited by John Murdoch and Edith Sylla. Dordrecht, Netherlands: Reidel, 1975.

Murdoch, John, and Edith Sylla, "Swineshead, Richard." In *Dictionary of Scientific Biography.* Vol. 13. Edited by C. C. Gillispie. New York: Scribners, 1976. Describes the *Book of Calculations* in detail.

Sylla, Edith. "The Oxford Calculators." In *The Cambridge History of Later Medieval Philosophy.* Edited by Norman Kretzmann, Anthony Kenny, and Jan Pinborg. Cambridge, U.K.: Cambridge University Press, 1982. Argues for the relation of the work of the Calculators to disputations on sophismata.

———. "Alvarus Thomas and the Role of Logic and Calculations in Sixteenth Century Natural Philosophy." In *Studies in Medieval Natural Philosophy.* Edited by Stefano Caroti. Florence: Olschki, 1989, 257–298.

———. *The Oxford Calculators and the Mathematics of Motion, 1320–1350: Physics and Measurement by Latitudes.* Harvard University dissertation, 1970. Reprint, New York and London: Garland Press, 1991. Contains outlines in Latin of several of the works of the Calculators.

Wallace, William A. "The 'Calculatores' in Early Sixteenth-Century Physics." *British Journal for the History of Science* 4 (1969): 221–232.

Wilson, Curtis. *William Heytesbury: Medieval Logic and the Rise of Mathematical Physics.* Madison: University of Wisconsin Press, 1956. Good place to start for the logical side of the Calculators' work.

EDITH DUDLEY SYLLA

[See also **DMA:** Bradwardine, Thomas; Burley, Walter; Oxford University; Physics; Swineshead.]

MIDDLE AGES. Although Petrarch is often credited with creating the concept of a dark middle age between the shining glories of Rome and the resurgent culture of modernity, he neither coined the term nor did he envision himself as living in a new era. For Petrarch, the history of the West divided neatly into the golden age of antiquity, ending when Christianity made official inroads into the governance of the empire, and the long modern dark age of decline, in which he was unfortunate enough to live. He did, however, see a glimmer of hope that a rebirth of classical culture in a Christian context would soon occur that would put an end to the decline and return Rome, at least, to her former, pre-Christian heights.

Petrarch's humanist followers further developed the idea of a distinction between themselves and the thousand years of ignorance and barbarity that they believed preceded them, but their perspective was limited to arts, literature, and learning. While they assumed that they lived in a new era, free from what they took to be the ignorance that marked the preceding era, they did not develop this into a new historiographical schema that eliminated the one inherited from the early church and cultivated throughout the Middle Ages. Under this scheme six ages and four empires had to pass before the end of the world and the Second Coming of Christ would occur. Thus the age preceding them was not a *middle* age at all. Furthermore, although the Italian humanists of the fifteenth century disdained the period between them and classical antiquity as one of limited cultural worth, they also admitted that the roots of their present flowering lay in the work of the likes of Dante and Giotto in the thirteenth and fourteenth centuries.

The humanists were not the only ones to look back disdainfully to the period after the Christianization of the Roman Empire. For Protestants during the Reformation, the era between Constantine's turning Christianity into a state religion and thus corrupting its evangelical purity and the coming of Luther represented a period of decadence during which the church turned its back on the heavenly city and became concerned only with things of the world. The Reformation thus was a return not to classical but to early Christian antiquity.

It was only in the second half of the seventeenth century, however, that the humanist and Protestant ideals of antique or early Christian culture and a new secular, tripartite historical scheme that discarded the traditional Christian historiography crystallized into strictly defined ancient, medieval, and modern periods. The writer of popular textbooks and professor at Halle, Christoph Cellarius, is believed to have coined the term "medium aevum" or "middle age" in 1688 to describe the period between the emperor Constantine in the fourth century and the fall of Constantinople to the Turks in 1453. The eighteenth-century philosophies of the Enlightenment especially delighted in denigrating the ignorance, superstition, and clericalism of this middle age in order to demonstrate their own cultural superiority.

Yet, in the nineteenth century, a romantic notion of the Middle Ages as a period of order, faith, and purity of emotion took hold. Gothic architecture, rather than being reviled as the uncivilized creation of the barbarian Goths, was celebrated as an achievement of the Germanic spirit and of an age of faith whose spirituality was in marked contrast to the materialism of the present. Modernity came to be seen as a decline from medieval greatness.

Viewed as a golden age or as an era of decay, the concept of the Middle Ages suffers from at least two serious flaws. First, historians have found it difficult to determine when the middle age begins and ends. Second, however one dates it, medieval Europe was not a monolithic, unchanging whole, as it was too often treated by both its partisans and its denigrators. Understanding that the middle age was in fact a series of "ages" was the insight of twentieth-century historians, and it is a historiographical problem with which contemporary scholars continue to struggle.

On the one hand, some manner of periodization is necessary to permit historians to make sense of the past. On the other hand, scholars encounter a great deal of difficulty when trying to decide what characteristics of a society should be taken into account when dividing periods. To the Renaissance humanists, it was obvious that their age was different from the one that preceded it because they believed themselves to be experiencing a new approach to the world of art and letters. Yet the so-called renaissance of the twelfth century was perhaps even more revolutionary than that of the fifteenth century because it included not only a sea change in learning due to the introduction of entirely new philosophical, legal, and literary ideas but also a tremendous demographic shift—a population explosion and a growth of cities and commerce unlike anything that had been seen since the heyday of the Roman Empire. Indeed the social, political, and commercial structures that were born in the twelfth and thirteenth centuries were often discarded only in the eighteenth. From this perspective, then, the Renaissance looks like nothing more than yet another cultural upsurge similar to that of the Carolingian age and the twelfth century, while the period from roughly 1100 to 1800 seems like a coherent whole. In addition, periodization can be horizontal as well as vertical. The ages of agricultural history do not coincide quite with those of the history of learning, nor does the history of the northern Italian cities with that of the Flemish cities. For that matter, a periodization of the Flemish cities would differ from that of the neighboring cities of Brabant and Holland. In a time during which communication was slow and travel difficult, homogeneity of development is not to be expected, rendering the concept of an "age" with definable characteristics somewhat tenuous.

Current scholarship on pre–industrial revolution Europe has tended to divide the period in one of two ways. One school, represented by Jacques Le Goff, sees antiquity extending until about 1000, when social and economic changes conspired to create something quite different from the Roman-barbarian world. The next period extends until about 1800, at which point industrialization and the French Revolution signal the beginning of modernity. The second school is less concerned with dating the beginning and end of the middle age than with defining the various middle ages. Following the lead of Henri Pirenne and Peter Brown, they see the Roman world giving way to a Roman-barbarian late antiquity extending until the late ninth or tenth centuries. The so-called High Middle Ages, or the long twelfth century, encompasses the centuries *ca.* 1000–*ca.* 1300, a period of cultural flowering and tremendous demographic and socioeconomic change. The late Middle Ages, an era described by Johan Huizinga as the fading away of a culture, then extends from around 1300 into the sixteenth or mid-seventeenth centuries before giving way to an early modern age.

BIBLIOGRAPHY

Barraclough, Geoffrey. "*Medium Aevum*: Some Reflections on Mediaeval History and on the Term 'The Middle Ages.'" In *History in a Changing World*. Norman: University of Oklahoma Press, 1956.

Ferguson, Wallace K. *The Renaissance in Historical Thought: Five Centuries of Interpretation*. Boston: Houghton Mifflin, 1948. Still the basic work on interpretations of the Renaissance and of the Middle Ages by the humanists.

Huizinga, Johan. "The Problem of the Renaissance." In *Men and Ideas: History, the Middle Ages, the Renaissance*. Translated by James S. Holmes and Hans van Marle. Princeton, N.J.: Princeton University Press, 1959.

Knowles, David. *Great Historical Enterprises and Problems in Monastic History*. London: Thomas Nelson and Sons, *ca.* 1962. A wonderful collection of essays on the making of such critical collections of medieval texts as the Acta Sanctorum and the Monumenta Germaniae Historica.

Le Goff, Jacques. "Pour un long moyen âge." In *L'imaginaire médiéval: Essais*. Paris: Gallimard, 1985.

Mertens, Dieter. "Mittelalterbilder in der Frühen Neuzeit." In *Die Deutschen und ihr Mittelalter: Themen und Funktionen moderner Geschichtsbilder vom Mittelalter*. Edited by Gerd Althoff. Darmstadt: Wissenschaftliche Buchgesellschaft, 1992, pp. 29–54.

Mommsen, Theodore E. "Petrarch's Conception of the 'Dark Ages.'" *Speculum* 17 (April 1942): 226–242.

Neddermeyer, Uwe. *Das Mittelalter in der Deutschen Historiographie vom 15. bis zum 18. Jahrhundert*. Cologne: Böhlau Verlag, 1988.

Ridé, Jacques. "Les humanistes allemands et le Moyen Âge." In *L'histoire au temps de la renaissance*. Edited by M. T. Jones-Davies. Paris: Klincksieck, 1995.

Van Engen, John. "The Christian Middle Ages as an Historiographical Problem." *The American Historical Review* 91 (June 1986): 519–552.

EMILY KADENS

[See also **Supp:** Humanism; Medieval Studies; Medievalism.]

MIESZKO I OF POLAND, KING (*ca.* 930–992; r. *ca.* 963–992). The Piast duke Mieszko I consolidated the territory that would become the core of medieval Poland. With Ottonian Germany to the west and Kievan Rus to the east and situated amidst competing states emerging in central Europe, Mieszko managed to fend off incursions while expanding his realm through a combination of strategic alliances, opportune religious conversion, and military expansion.

That Mieszko was already a ruler of consequence in central Europe by the 960s is conveyed in the earliest sources in which he is mentioned. The contemporary account by Widukind of Corvey describes an agreement in 963 between Mieszko and the Saxon count Gero to subdue the nearby Veleti tribe. The merchant Ibrāhīm ibn Ya'qūb wrote in 966 that Mieszko's territory was larger than that of the Obodrites, the Bulgarians, or the Bohemians. By the time of Ibrāhīm's account Mieszko had already confirmed his alliance with Bohemia and married Dubravka, daughter of the Přemyslid duke. It is impossible to divine Mieszko's precise motives for conversion, but political calculation was a significant factor. His defeat by the Veleti, led by a Saxon noble named Wichmann, occurred around this time.

The ramifications of Mieszko's conversion and marriage for the political future of Poland cannot be overstated. Not only did the Bohemian alliance free Mieszko to concentrate on northern expansion, but by voluntarily converting to Latin Christianity Mieszko preempted the threat of forced conversion, occupation, and the end of political autonomy. Imperial expansion either militarily or by means of ecclesiastical administration was a real concern since Otto I's defeat in 955 of the Veleti and Obodrites and his plans to expand the mission eastward. The one document extant from Mieszko's reign, the eleventh-century transcription of the *Dagome iudex,* is a deed placing his state under the direct protection of the papacy, thereby ensuring that the German church would not make incursions on the administrative independence of the church in Poland.

The benefits of conversion were almost immediate. After Mieszko and his court were baptized in 966, he entered into diplomatic relations with Otto I. As Otto's *amicus,* Mieszko gained control over the area around the lower Oder in 967, the year he defeated a renewed attack by Wichmann. By 972 he had defeated incursions by the German margrave Hodo and secured his gains. In 979 Mieszko defended this same region against Otto II, who had been provoked by Mieszko's support for his rival, Duke of Bavaria Henry the Wrangler; the conflict ended in truce. This insured Piast control over the important Baltic ports and direct access to the Baltic trade. After the death of Otto II in 983 Mieszko again supported a rival claim to the throne, but by 985 he had come to support Otto III, possibly inspired by further problems with the Veleti, Lutici, and Obodrites. With his imperial alliance secure, Mieszko was able to devote the last years of his reign to territorial expansion in the south, wresting part of Little Poland from his former allies the Bohemians. Mieszko died on 25 May 992, leaving a greatly expanded state for his oldest son, Bolesław I Chrobry (the Brave).

BIBLIOGRAPHY

PRIMARY SOURCES

Thietmar of Merseburg. *Die Chronik des Bischofs Thietmar von Merseburg und ihre Korveier Überarbeitung.* Edited by Robert Holtzmann. Monumenta Germaniae Historica, Scriptores rerum Germanicarum, new ser., vol. 9. Berlin, 1935.

SECONDARY SOURCES

Braun, Jerzy, ed. *Poland in Christian Civilization.* London: Veritas Foundation, 1985. A useful collection of essays by Polish scholars in translation.

Dvornik, Francis. *The Slavs in European History and Civilization.* New Brunswick, N.J.: Rutgers University, 1962.

Halecki, Oskar. *A History of Poland.* 9th ed. New York: D. McKay, 1976.

Kürbisówna, Brygida. "Dagome iudex—studium krytyczne." In *Początki państwa polskiego: Księga tysiąclecia.* Edited by Kazimierz Tymieniecki. 2 vols. Poznań, Poland, 1962.

Łowmiański, Henryk. "Imię chrzestne Mieszka I." *Slavia Occidentalis* 19 (1948): 203–308.

Vlasto, A. P. *The Entry of the Slavs into Christendom: An Introduction to the Medieval History of the Slavs.* Cambridge, U.K.: Cambridge University Press, 1970.

ELSPETH JANE CARRUTHERS

[See also **DMA:** Piast Dynasty; Poland; Widukind of Corvey; **Supp:** Bolesław I Chrobry of Poland, King.]

MONSTERS AND THE MONSTROUS. The word *monstruositas* first appears in the *Enchiridion* of St. Augustine in a discussion of deformed humans who will be restored to normal human shape at the resurrection. For classical authors the more common word had been *monstrum;* its primary sense was that of a divine omen or portent—most usually a human or animal birth—presaging misfortunes. There was also the contrary belief, associated with the Greek philosopher Aristotle, that a monstrosity in human or animal birth had no divine significance and was purely a result of embryological excess or defect. The third and more modern sense of *monstrum,* which developed in the classical period with the *Historia naturalis* of the Roman encyclopedist Pliny the Elder, was that prodigious births and unusual human and animal species revealed God's continuous involvement with human affairs and his omnipotence in being able to change his plan for the creation at will and revitalize man's sense of the marvelous. Pliny, moreover, widened the meaning of *monstrum* to include not only individual prodigious births but also whole races of men and exotic animals as monstrosities, speaking of men and animals of unusual appearance and habits ("huius monstri") who have lived in Italy or India or Africa. With this foundation, by the end of the Middle Ages the word *monstrum* had acquired a complex range of emotional overtones involving fear of God's wrath, curiosity, and the pleasure derived from the contemplation of monstrosity for its own sake.

An important early medieval work for the developing concept of monstrosity was the *Liber monstrorum* of

Plinean Creatures. *An English bestiary's characteristic rendering of some creatures described in Pliny the Elder's* Historia naturalis. OXFORD, BODLEIAN LIBRARY, MS DOUCE 88, FOL. 70R. REPRODUCED BY PERMISSION.

English seventh-century authorship. This compilation of human, animal, and serpent monsters in three books makes a correlation between abnormal size and monstrosity. The author had a strongly rhetorical cast of mind and was especially fond of the words "monster" and "monstrous" to induce fear, wonder, and excitement in the reader. In book 1 of the *Liber,* on human wonders, fifteen of its fifty-six creatures are marvelous with respect to size, and a typical comment by the author of the *Liber* concerns "monstra mirae magnitudinis" (monsters of an amazing size) like the Geatish king Hygelac, so large that from the age of twelve no horse could carry him. Clearly, the word *monstrum* and the idea of something to be marveled at go naturally together in the writer's mind.

By the thirteenth century the Plinean wonder-inducing and titillating sense of *monstrum* had come to be very important in the *De natura rerum* (*ca.* 1245) of Thomas of Cantimpré and the *Speculum naturale* (*ca.* 1245–*ca.* 1260) of his fellow Dominican Vincent of Beauvais, as well as in various abridgments and popularizing adaptations of their works. Thomas of Cantimpré, especially, was familiar with the thirteenth-century *Hi-*

storia orientalis of Jacques de Vitry, with its accounts of human and animal wonders in the lands visited by the crusaders, and Vincent of Beauvais was acquainted with the thirteenth-century narrative of travel to Mongol lands by John of Plano Carpini. Vincent observed that "if God had chosen to set the nature of each creature at the first moment of its creation so that it would persist unchangeably in its order, Nature would have come to direct herself, and the works and power of God would be forgotten by man. That Nature often turns from her usual order, however, continually reminds men that God is the artisan of all natures and that he acted not once only, but does so each day."

COLLECTIONS OF MARVELS

Their interest in such matters reflects the view of monstrosity as entertainment in the *Otia imperialia* of Gervase of Tilbury, an English courtier living in Arles who composed a compendium of knowledge and anecdote for Emperor Otto IV between 1209 and 1218. *Otia imperialia* is perhaps the first collection of wonders since those made by the marvel writers of Greek antiquity that give the marvelous and monstrous the value of "news" for entertainment. Gervase offered Otto 129 such marvels, some derived from classical and biblical sources and some popular, among them natural phenomena such as the magnet; sacred wonders such as the Veronica, or cloth imprinted with Christ's likeness in St. Peter's at Rome; and some personally experienced or folkloric wonders such as reports of recent encounters with werewolves. Gervase's prologue to his third *decisio,* or division, of the *Otia,* containing an account of human and animal wonders in India and Africa, speaks of the relation of marvels, largely topographical in character, to the human desire for entertainment:

And since the appetite of the human mind is always keen to hear and lap up novelties, the oldest things will have to be presented as new, natural things as miraculous, and things familiar to us all as strange. For . . . things are adjudged novelties on four criteria: . . . originality, . . . recentness, . . . rarity, or . . . strangeness. Now we generally call those things miracles which, being preternatural, we ascribe to divine power, as when a virgin gives birth . . . while we call those things marvels which are beyond our comprehension, even though they are natural.

This passage is one of the few medieval analyses of wonder, a feeling understood to arise from the sudden encounter with the novel (like the phoenix) and at the same moment the inability to understand or explain the cause of the unexpected phenomenon (like magnetism). Gervase recognizes that each person may have a different response or threshold for a wonderful event, but he sees in all people the same emotional fascination with novelty.

Vernacular collections of wonders in the fourteenth and fifteenth centuries sometimes used an organizational structure such as a pilgrimage narrative, as in the case of John Mandeville's *Travels* (*ca.* 1360) or the fourteenth-century *Itinerarius* of Johannes Witte of Hese, or were sometimes simply collections of miscellaneous marvels, such as the strange animals, monstrous races of men, and topographical features appearing with detailed texts on the Ebstorf and Hereford world maps (*ca.* 1230 and *ca.* 1290). Among the most interesting of these collections was the work called *Secretz de la nature,* or *Merveilles du monde* (*ca.* 1370), alphabetically arranged and heavily illustrated, treating fifty-six real and imagined countries or islands. The work is largely a translation into French of Pierre Bersuire's *Reductorium morale,* book 14 (*ca.* 1360). The compiler talks of the unusual peoples of Europe and Asia (Frisians are of exceptionally large stature; on the island of Taprobane people live in houses made from snail shells) and in his prologue combines religion and wonder in equal measure as a reason for writing the work: "I translated this little book from Latin into French so that those reading it could experience the marvels and diversity of the world and by this knowledge know the creator in the created and so love Him."

NATURALISTIC EXPLANATIONS

While these vernacular works were developing—often with the aid of the Dominican encyclopedias—the recovery and popularization of Aristotle's works through Arabic and then Latin and French translations introduced a more naturalistic line of thought. Perhaps the most important of the many Western commentaries written on Aristotle's *Libri naturales* was by the thirteenth-century Dominican Albertus Magnus, whose *De animalibus* offers clear statements of the Greek philosopher's opinions on abnormalities in nature: "monstrosities . . . do not represent nature's intent, but rather such things occur due to the flaw of some error of the natural principles." Albertus, like Aristotle, does not tie these failings in the natural process to divine intervention or give them any theological dimension.

Albertus was, however, intensely interested in human psychological responses to monstrosities and recognized their fear-inducing potential. Besides commenting on Aristotle's *De animalibus,* he also wrote on that author's *Metaphysics.* In an important rationalization of the wonder and fear people feel in the presence of monstrosity, Albertus noted that wonder was an *agoniam,* a kind of struggle or shock of surprise and a momentary heart stoppage or systolic response *(stupore).* Thus the response that beholding monstrosity creates in us is both physiological, a heart-stopping fear, and psychological, a mental struggle to explain rationally this wonder.

Associated with Albertus's name in the Middle Ages but of late-thirteenth- or early-fourteenth-century date, the *Secrets of Women* is an important text for the development of the concept of monstrosity, adding the idea of astrological causation and clarifying the divine aesthetic purpose in monstrosity and its contemplation. In a chapter devoted to monstrosities in nature, it is noted:

> You might ask why monsters are brought into being. Philosophers answer to this that they are created for the adornment of the universe. For if different colors on a wall decorate that wall, so different monsters embellish the whole world. Monsters are caused especially by celestial influences, for whenever a special constellation reigns, different forms are influenced by it.

This material on astrological causation, though attributed to Albertus, most probably comes from the twelfth-century Latin translation of the *De radiis* of Ya'qūb al-Kindi (*b.* 830), a work which developed a theory of reciprocal causality. The terrestrial world has a "similarity" to the sidereal one and can accordingly affect it and be affected by it through invisible rays rather than some form of physical contact.

The astrological or celestial explanation for monstrosity was quickly popularized, moving from a learned monastic or university context to a vernacular one, especially in Germany. The romance *Reinfried von Braunschweig* (*ca.* 1300) notes that since human beings are organized according to the motions of the heavens, it can happen that their birthdays place them under the sign of a planet that gives them a deformity. Konrad von Megenberg in his *Buch von der Natur,* a German version (*ca.* 1348–1350) of Thomas of Cantimpré's *De natura rerum,* adds his own view that individual monstrosities result from celestial influence on the mother's body.

Sometimes celestial influence was combined with climatic explanations for monsters and marvels, based on Aristotelian beliefs in extreme and median parts of the world. From antiquity through the late Middle Ages, the median and ideal climate was generally that of the country or region in which a map was made or a travel book was written. In such a place, planetary influence was most benign. Some medieval thinkers held that their ideal or Edenic clime was not only divinely favored and superior to others but also free from the monstrosity natural to the extremes. Guy de Bazoches in his *Apologia,* for example, claims that "France alone has no monsters."

In his *Tetrabiblos,* a work widely cited in the Middle Ages, the second-century Alexandrian astronomical and geographic writer Claudius Ptolemy tied temperament and physical appearance to climate and celestial influence, observing that "the extreme lands of India and adjacent regions are connected with Capricorn and Saturn, and so their inhabitants are dirty, and ugly in build, having the character of wild beasts." Following Ptolemy's reasoning, Andreas Walsperger, the author of an important map with extensive texts made in Constanz in 1448, saw extreme northern climate as the source of wild cannibal peoples "of such frightful shapes that one can scarcely discern whether they are human beings or animals." The Dominican missionary Ricold of Monte Croce (*d.* 1320) saw extreme low temperatures as the source of monstrous defects in his account of a voyage to inner Asia: "The cold is such there that we saw many mutilated people, some lacking one foot or both, others one hand."

As if in reaction to the growth of collections of monstrosities and *mirabilia* of all types, by the late fourteenth century a number of writers attempted to reassert "natural" Aristotelian explanations for such phenomena. Among those was Nicole Oresme, an important translator of Aristotle for Charles V of France in the 1360s. His *De causis mirabilium* proposes to show the causes for certain effects which seem to be marvels and to show that such effects occur naturally. He goes on to say that there is no reason to seek explanation for marvels in celestial causality, demons, and even God's direct intervention, claiming instead that monsters "arise by reason of a deficiency [of the sperm]." Oresme is particularly interested in separating such births from consequences—if a monster occurs in some village or country, it does not signify that evil will come to pass there—and he argues against the power of celestial influence suggested as a cause of monstrosity by the author of the *Secrets of Women,* ridiculing the notion "that there is in heaven one constellation which produces in this . . . woman such a monster and yet does not [do the same] in the next one."

By the end of Middle Ages, then, *monstrum* had become a very complex term attracting the attention of a number of thinkers. Scholastic speculation on the human condition raised specific questions about whether monstrous beings had souls. The old Greek and Roman terror of monstrous forms had become a "safe" fear, and

"histories" of prodigious births and portents as a form of "news" were amassed and disseminated as the intermingled horror of and curiosity about unusual births and races of men gave rise to the notion of monstrosity as a form of spectacle or entertainment in the later Middle Ages. Thus, the gradual widening of the term *monstrum* to convey its contemporary meaning of monstrosity was a long, slow process with much of the development occurring from the thirteenth century onward in conjunction with the recovery and dissemination of Aristotle's works on natural history and the widening range of missionary and mercantile travel encounters with non-European peoples.

BIBLIOGRAPHY

PRIMARY WORKS

Albertus Magnus. *Metaphysica libros quinque priores.* Volume 16 of *Opera omnia ad fidem codicum manuscriptorum edenda . . . Alberti Magni Coloniense.* Edited by Bernhard Geyer et al. Monasterii Westfalorum, Germany: Aschendorff, 1960.

———. *On Animals: A Medieval Summa Zoologica.* Translated by Kenneth F. Kitchell Jr. and Irven M. Resnick. 2 vols. Baltimore and London: Johns Hopkins University Press, 1999. (Translation of *De animalibus.*)

Gervase de Tilbury. *Otia Imperialia: Recreation for an Emperor.* Edited and translated by S. E. Banks and J. W. Binns. Oxford: Clarendon Press, 2002.

Konrad von Megenberg. *Das Buch der Natur.* Edited by Franz Pfeiffer. Hildesheim, N.Y.: G. Olms, 1994.

Lemay, Helen Rodnite. *Women's Secrets: A Translation of Pseudo-Albertus Magnus's De Secretis Mulierum with Commentaries.* Albany: State University of New York Press, 1992.

Orchard, Andy. *Pride and Prodigies: Studies in the Monsters of the Beowulf Manuscript.* Cambridge, U.K.: D. S. Brewer, 1995. *(Liber monstrorum.)*

Oresme, Nicole. *Nicole Oresme and the Marvels of Nature: A Study of His De Causis Mirabilium with Critical Edition, Translation, and Commentary.* Edited by Bert Hansen. Toronto: Pontifical Institute of Medieval Studies, 1985.

Ricold of Monte Croce. *Perégrination en Terre Sainte et en Proche Orient: Texte latin et traduction.* Edited by René Kappler. Paris: Honoré Champion, 1997.

Vincent of Beauvais. *Speculum naturale.* Volume 1 of *Speculum quadruplex sive speculum maius.* Graz, Austria: Akademische Druck u. Verlagsanstalt, 1964–1965.

SECONDARY WORKS

Bologna, Corrado. "La tératologie comme science de la classification, en Italie, du moyen âge à la Renaissance." In *Monstres et prodiges au temps de la Renaissance.* Edited by Marie Thérèse Jones-Davies. Paris: Diffusion J. Touzot, 1980.

Céard, Jean. *La nature et les prodiges.* Geneva: Droz, 1977.

Daston, Lorraine, and Katharine Park. *Wonders and the Order of Nature, 1150–1750.* New York: Zone, 1998.

Friedman, John Block. *The Monstrous Races in Medieval Art and Thought.* 1981. Reprint, Syracuse University Press, 2000.

———. "Secretz de la Nature." In *Trade, Travel, and Exploration in the Middle Ages: An Encyclopedia.* Edited by John Block Friedman, Kristen Mossler Figg, et al. New York: Garland, 2000.

Westrem, Scott D. *The Hereford Map: A Transcription and Translation of the Legend with Commentary.* Turnhout, Belgium: Brepols, 2001.

JOHN BLOCK FRIEDMAN

[See also **DMA:** Albertus Magnus, St.; Aristotle in the Middle Ages; Encyclopedias and Dictionaries, Western European; Vincent of Beauvais; **Supp:** Nature.]

MORISCOS. The Moriscos were the baptized Muslims of sixteenth-century Spain. Their coerced conversion (1499–1526) and expulsion (1609–1614) marked the final dissolution of the religiously plural society that had characterized Spain during the Middle Ages.

CONVERSION AND DEMOGRAPHY

The surrender of the Nasrid sultan of Granada, the last Muslim state on Iberian soil, to Queen Isabella I of Castile and King Ferdinand II of Aragon (Ferdinand V of Castile) on 2 January 1492 brought a new Muslim population under the jurisdiction of the Castilian monarchy. Like the long-established Mudejar (protected Muslim) communities of Castile and the Crown of Aragon (which included Aragon, Valencia, and Catalonia), the Granadan Muslims were granted the freedom to practice Islam, protection of their persons and property, the right to choose communal officials and judges for Islamic courts, and other privileges stipulated in the capitulations of surrender. The Granadans, however, did not long enjoy their Mudejar status. Pressure from grasping Christian colonists, new taxes, and, especially, the forced baptism of Muslims in Granada by Cardinal Francisco Ximénez de Cisneros moved them to rebel, first in Granada in December 1499, then in other parts of the former sultanate in 1500–1501. The monarchs felt that the Muslim revolt had, in effect, voided the treaty between them and the Muslims. As royal armies suppressed the revolts, they offered the subdued rebels baptism as a condition of pardon.

Isabella and Ferdinand now worried about the threat to the Spanish church posed by the inevitable mingling of the newly converted Moriscos with unbaptized Muslims. The monarchs had already seen Jews corrupt the Catholic faith of baptized Jews *(conversos),* fostering a judaizing heresy inside the Spanish church. They had therefore established the Spanish Inquisition to eradicate the judaizing *conversos* (1478–1483) and ex-

pelled the Jews who had influenced them (1492). In order to prevent the Muslims remaining in Isabella's realms—Castile and Granada—from contaminating the new converts with Islamic heresies, the monarchs decided to compel them all to accept baptism. They completed the Christianization of Granada by July 1501. In February 1502 they offered the Mudejars of Castile the choice of baptism or exile under difficult conditions; most converted. Now all of Isabella's Muslim subjects were Moriscos. The monarchs hoped that without non-baptized Muslims to influence them they would over time become sincere Christians. Furthermore, because few had chosen exile, the royal officials and nobles governing the new kingdom of Granada retained a crucial source of labor and revenue.

Ferdinand, however, did not seek the baptism of the many Muslims in his own Crown of Aragon. He preferred not to antagonize the Aragonese and Valencian nobles on whose lands most Mudejars lived or to cause serious economic problems by provoking Mudejar flight or rebellion. The conversion of the Mudejars of the Crown of Aragon occurred during the reign of his successor, the Holy Roman Emperor Charles V. In 1521–1522 rebel artisans in the kingdom of Valencia, the *Germanías,* forcibly baptized thousands of Muslims as a means of damaging their enemies, the Muslims' lords. After a commission headed by an inquisitor declared the baptisms valid, Charles, pursuing the logic of his royal predecessors, issued edicts in the fall of 1525 ordering the expulsion of all Muslims from Valencia who would not convert by 8 December and from Aragon and Catalonia by 31 January 1526. A few Valencian Muslim communities rebelled unsuccessfully, but most received baptism quietly in order to remain in the lands where they had lived for centuries. Emigration to North Africa was a forbidding and economically impractical option for Mudejar communities composed largely of peasants and artisans.

Though all were Christian (at least in name) after 1526, the Morisco populations in the different kingdoms varied in size, residential pattern, and degree of familiarity with Old Christians (Christians without Muslim or Jewish background) and their culture. Granada had the largest Morisco population—some 150,000 by midcentury, over half of the total population, most residing in rural areas. The last to be conquered, the Granadan Moriscos were the least acculturated and were primarily Arabic speaking. Valencian Moriscos, the descendants of Mudejars conquered in the thirteenth century, constituted roughly a third of their kingdom's population. Withdrawing from urban areas after their conversion, most lived in rural villages, many of which were wholly Morisco. They were usually bilingual, speaking Arabic and Catalan. Coming under Christian rule a century before the Valencians, Aragonese Moriscos, who formed a fifth of their kingdom's population, were more acculturated and had largely lost the ability to speak Arabic. Though the majority dwelt in rural areas, their villages often had mixed populations; a good number also lived in urban centers. Catalan Moriscos were few in number and could not speak Arabic. Castilian Moriscos, living mainly in towns, formed a small population—some 20,000 altogether at the end of the fifteenth century—and, like the Aragonese, were highly acculturated Romance-language speakers.

REPRESSION AND REBELLION

Royal and ecclesiastical authorities recognized that the hastily converted Moriscos required a thorough education in Christian doctrine while their Islamic practices were suppressed. Hence parishes were established in Morisco areas, schools were set up for the indoctrination of Morisco children, and evangelizing campaigns were launched. Success, however, was limited. Many Morisco villages were left without rectories; rectors assigned to Morisco parishes were often underpaid and unsuited to their delicate task; and the lords of Moriscos resisted clerical interference in the affairs of their vassals. Furthermore, the crown and Inquisition did not make a thorough effort to eradicate the Moriscos' crypto-Islam. The large subsidies the Moriscos paid to the king stayed the implementation of repressive legislation, while nobles often impeded inquisitorial action. Only egregious displays of Islamic heresy were prosecuted. In rural areas especially, Moriscos who did not flaunt their adherence to Islam continued to live much as they had before conversion. Assimilation occurred mainly among elite city-dwelling Moriscos who had the most to gain from accommodation with Old Christian society.

This state of affairs persisted until the reign of Philip II, when royal and clerical attitudes toward the Moriscos hardened. A more militant Counter-Reformation church was not about to let the Moriscos' Islamic heresy fester. Moreover, Spain's growing conflict with the Ottoman Empire and North African corsairs heightened Old Christian fears of the Moriscos as a threat to national security, particularly in Granada and Valencia. Spanish authorities therefore assaulted Morisco crypto-Islam more aggressively, attacking not only their Islamic beliefs and practices but all aspects of Morisco culture regarded as "Moorish" and ethnically distinctive. Typical of the new approach was the legislation passed in 1567 in the king-

dom of Granada. It required Moriscos to abandon the Arabic language, Arabic names, traditional marriage celebrations, Muslim hygienic practices (baths), and Muslim-style clothing, such as veils for women. The Inquisition also increased its surveillance and prosecution of Moriscos.

For the Granadan Moriscos, who, unlike Moriscos elsewhere, had not had centuries in which to adjust gradually to Christian culture, the new legislation represented the destruction of their whole way of life. They were already pinched by economic difficulties caused by the deterioration of the silk industry and by the crown's arbitrary and prejudicial alteration of the proprietary regime. Between 1559 and 1568 crown officials conducted a review of property boundaries and titles. If Moriscos did not possess a formal title or deed to their property—as was frequently the case—they were fined. If they could not pay the fine, the authorities confiscated and auctioned off their property. In this manner, some 100,000 hectares of land changed hands. On Christmas Eve 1568 a Morisco revolt began in the city of Granada and quickly spread to the Alpujarras mountains. The insurgents received some assistance from the Turks in Algiers and North African Berbers, but it was their knowledge of the terrain and their deep resentment that enabled them to resist royal armies until the autumn of 1570. Before the revolt was crushed, both sides committed atrocities, indicative of the mutual hatred that had been developing in the region for decades. In order to eliminate the danger to Spanish security that the Granadan Moriscos presented, Philip II ordered their expulsion on 1 November 1570. Perhaps as many as 80,000 were deported to Castile. Their dispersion among the Old Christian population was meant to facilitate assimilation. It did not achieve the desired result.

The rebellion in Granada increased the authorities' suspicions of the Moriscos in other parts of Spain, especially Valencia and Aragon, even though the Moriscos there had not risen in support of their Granadan brethren. In Valencia, efforts were made to disarm the Moriscos and to distance them from coastal areas whence they could communicate with North African corsairs. The Inquisition prosecuted Morisco religious leaders (*alfaquís*) and arrested Old Christian nobles who permitted their Morisco vassals to practice Islam. In the mid-1570s the inquisitors lessened their prosecution of Moriscos in return for sizable subsidies, but in the mid-1580s they resumed their activities and condemned many Moriscos to the galleys. In Aragon, inquisitorial prosecution and punishment of Moriscos for Islamic practices was more severe. Because there were many more mixed communities in this kingdom, the authorities were more concerned about the exposure of Old Christians to the Moriscos' Islamic heresies. There were also more opportunities for Old Christians to witness the Moriscos' Islamic observances and denounce them to the Inquisition.

Inquisitorial harassment was complemented by redoubled efforts to educate the Moriscos in the Catholic faith. Jesuit preachers and teachers stepped up their activities, while bishops attempted to improve the quality of the clergy working in Morisco parishes. Still, they did not have a great deal of success in overcoming Morisco obduracy.

MORISCO RELIGION AND CULTURE

After 1526 Catholicism was the only legitimate religion in Spain; Islam was driven underground. Its survival among the Moriscos depended on the transmission of fundamental Islamic beliefs among family members, the teaching of Morisco religious leaders, the circulation of texts in Arabic and *aljamiado* (Romance written in Arabic characters), and the perpetuation of cultural practices (e.g., certain dances or public baths) that could not be easily disentangled from religion per se and that, in the Moriscos' unusual circumstances, acquired religious significance. The extent to which any Morisco family maintained an Islamic lifestyle was contingent on a number of factors—the size of the Morisco community to which it belonged, the density of the local Old Christian population, the attitudes and actions of lay and ecclesiastical authorities, and Arabic and/or *aljamiado* literacy. Since all Moriscos had to practice Christianity to some extent, their Islamic culture was inevitably eroded. In the relatively few cases of Morisco–Old Christian intermarriage, the Muslim identity of the Morisco spouse and that of his or her children were put more at risk.

Morisco anxieties about whether, as baptized crypto-Muslims in the lands of unbelievers, they could be regarded as true Muslims in terms of Islamic law were assuaged by the ruling of a mufti (jurisconsult) of Oran in 1504. He asserted, in accordance with the Islamic concept of *taqīya* (dispensation), that Muslims under duress could be released from Islamic requirements and feign allegiance to another religion as long as they adhered to Islam in their hearts.

Many Moriscos did much more than this. Inquisition trial records reveal that Moriscos recited Islamic prayers, gathered together on Fridays for prayer meetings, performed ritual ablutions, circumcised their sons, observed Islamic marriage and burial ceremonies, slaughtered their animals as Islamic law required while avoid-

ing the consumption of pork and wine, and observed the fast of Ramadan. Some Moriscos possessed copies of the Koran and other Islamic religious and legal texts written in Arabic. The *alfaquís* (from Arabic *faqīh*, or jurist) were most likely to have such texts. They interpreted them to illiterate and uneducated Moriscos and preached to the latter on the essentials of Islamic belief and practice.

The more acculturated Moriscos of Aragon and Castile produced a substantial body of *aljamiado* literature. (The earliest *aljamiado* texts date from the Mudejar period; most extant texts are of Aragonese provenance.) The contents of this literature provide some insight into Morisco concerns. Among the texts were commentaries on the Koran, summaries of Islamic law, accounts of the prophet Muḥammad and his companions, tales set in Muslim Spain, medical and magical treatises, prophecies of the Moriscos' liberation by the Ottoman Turks, and polemics against Christianity. This underground Morisco literature expressed a vital and tenacious popular Islamic culture.

The Moriscos' Muslim identity was further strengthened through their perpetuation of a traditional family life. The Moriscos for the most part married among themselves. Such endogamy enhanced the solidarity of the Morisco community and limited Old Christian intrusion and knowledge of its inner life. Morisco families tended to be organized along patrilineal lines and to have a high degree of lineage consciousness and solidarity. Marriage between paternal first cousins was often preferred. The Moriscos' clandestine religious observance nonetheless placed women in an unusually prominent position. Because Islamic practice was confined largely to the home, Morisco women assumed a crucial role in transmitting the tenets of the faith and social customs to their children and to others outside the family. While Morisco men interacted more with Old Christian society and made the inevitable compromises, the women tended to cling more fiercely to the traditional culture.

The remarkable endurance of Morisco crypto-Islam was partly due to the Moriscos' identification with the wider Muslim world. They never felt alone. They communicated with North African Muslims and with the Ottomans, took pride in the military exploits of Muslim princes, and fostered memories of Muslim Spain's brilliant past. Moriscos were sustained by the hope that one day the Ottoman Turks or some other Muslim power would deliver them from their Christian oppressors.

EXPULSION

The Moriscos ultimately were delivered in a way most of them would not have preferred: they were expelled from Spain. Some Spaniards began arguing for such a radical solution at the time of the Granadan revolt. In 1581 Philip II appointed a special committee to discuss the matter, and in 1582 the Council of State formally proposed a general expulsion. Those who supported the measure noted the Moriscos' persistent rejection of Christianity, their rapidly expanding population, and their threat to the security of Catholic Spain. The staunchest opponents were the nobles of Aragon and Valencia, who warned of the economic disaster an expulsion would cause. Others asserted that it would be wrong to send baptized people abroad where they would openly return to Islam. They believed that the Moriscos could be made into sincere Catholics through preaching and instruction. Indeed, there was a small minority of assimilated Moriscos that lent support to this argument. The issue was put aside for two decades, but Philip III and his chief minister, the duke of Lerma, revisited it in 1602. Finally, on 30 January 1608 the Council of State voted unanimously for expulsion, and on 9 April 1609 it issued the formal decree.

The expulsion took place in several stages between 1609 and 1614, although most Moriscos were expelled during the first two years. Approximately 300,000 Moriscos were forced to leave Spain. Perhaps 20,000 remained, some because they were notably faithful Catholics, others at the special request of their lords, and still others secretly. Of the expelled Moriscos, the majority settled in North Africa (Morocco, Algeria, Tunisia), some in Ottoman lands (Syria, Egypt, the Balkans), and a few in France, through which many had traveled en route to Muslim countries.

BIBLIOGRAPHY

Cardaillac, Louis. *Morisques et Chrétiens: Un affrontement polémique, 1492–1640.* Paris: Klincksieck, 1977. A study of religious controversies between Moriscos and Old Christians, drawing on *aljamiado* and other texts.

Caro Baroja, Julio. *Ciclos y temas de la historia de España: Los moriscos del reino de Granada: Ensayo de historia social.* 2d ed. Madrid, Spain: ISTMO, 1976.

Chejne, Anwar G. *Islam and the West: The Moriscos: A Cultural and Social History.* Albany: State University of New York Press, 1983. A useful overview of Morisco history in English.

Domínguez Ortiz, Antonio, and Bernard Vincent. *Historia de los moriscos: Vida y tragedia de una minoría.* Madrid, Spain: Revista de Occidente, 1978. The most useful general history of the Moriscos.

García Arenal, Mercedes. *Los moriscos.* Madrid, Spain: Editora Nacional, 1975. A useful collection of edited primary sources.

Halperín Donghi, Tulio. *Un conflicto nacional: Moriscos y cristianos viejos en Valencia.* Valencia, Spain: Institución Alfonso el Magnánimo, 1980.

Harvey, L. P. "The Political, Social and Cultural History of the Moriscos." In *The Legacy of Muslim Spain.* Edited by Salma Khadra Jayyusi. Leiden: E. J. Brill, 1992. Thoughtful overview by a leading scholar of the Moriscos.

Monter, William. *Frontiers of Heresy: The Spanish Inquisition from the Basque Lands to Sicily.* Cambridge, U.K.: Cambridge University Press, 1990. A wide-ranging work with insightful chapters on Aragonese and Valencian Moriscos and their treatment by the Inquisition.

Vincent, Bernard. *Minorías y marginados en la España del siglo XVI.* Translated by Marina Guillén. Granada, Spain: Diputación Provincial de Granada, 1987. Important collection of Vincent's essays on the social history of the Moriscos, including family life, encounters with the Spanish Inquisition and the Jesuits, and banditry.

MARK D. MEYERSON

[See also **DMA:** Granada; Inquisition; Jews in Christian Spain; Mudéjar Art; Spain, Christian-Muslim Relations; Spain, Muslim Kingdoms of.]

MUSICUS. In the ancient and medieval worlds, the definition of the true musician was closely tied to broader ideas about the nature of music. Music as an area of study formed part of the quadrivium, the four-part educational course consisting of arithmetic, geometry, astronomy, and music, and was therefore a mathematical art more about harmonics than practical music making. In Boethius's scheme, sounding music (*musica instrumentis constituta*) stood in a distant third place to the inaudible *musica mundana* (cosmic music) and *musica humana* (human music). For modern people this broader definition may perhaps be best understood by considering common-language meanings of words such as "harmony" or "consonance." The presumed connection of sounding music to inaudible harmonies was seen as the source of music's power, as testified by the story of Orpheus and other descriptions from the ancient world.

Because music was about more than sound, the musician was necessarily more than a mere creator of sound. Boethius's formulation in *De institutione musica* is best known: "every art and also every discipline considers reason inherently more honorable than a skill which is practiced by the hand and the labor of an artisan. . . . [A] musician is one who has gained knowledge of making music by weighing with the reason, not through the servitude of work, but through the sovereignty of speculation. . . . That person is a musician who exhibits the faculty of forming judgments according to speculation or reason." Here the *musicus* is contrasted to the cantor (singer) and to players of instruments, who are named by their instrument (e.g., a kitharist, the player of a kithara) and not given the name of "musician." This idea further reflects an Aristotelian ambivalence toward performance: some knowledge of practical music making is necessary to enable one to judge music, but too much is vulgar and dangerous. It is worth remembering that both Aristotle and Boethius are speaking of the education of men of a relatively high social class and that in their times professional performers, especially players of instruments, were usually drawn from lower classes.

The distinction between *musicus* and cantor, however, is not always as absolute as it might appear at first glance. Boethius does not explicitly exclude the performer from the status of musician so much as argue that the ability to create sound is insufficient without the ability to understand and judge. This tacit inclusion of the performer may be one reason why speculative music theory, focused on Boethius's *De musica,* continued to be transmitted throughout the Middle Ages and beyond, even though a parallel thread of theoretical treatises focused on more practical matters, such as the notation and categorization by mode of chant, began to flourish, especially from the time of Guido d'Arezzo in the eleventh century. The coexistence of both theoretical traditions, sometimes in the same treatise, suggests the possibility that musician and singer could be combined in a single person: as the authors of the thirteenth-century *Summa musice* tell us, "every musicus is a cantor, but the reverse is not the case."

BIBLIOGRAPHY

Boethius. *Fundamentals of Music.* Translated by Calvin M. Bower. New Haven, Conn.: Yale University Press, 1989. (Translation of *De institutione musica.*)

Page, Christopher. "Musicus and Cantor." In *Companion to Medieval and Renaissance Music.* Edited by Tess Knight and David Fallows. New York: Schirmer Books, 1992.

———, ed. and trans. *The "Summa musice": A Thirteenth-Century Manual for Singers.* Cambridge, U.K.: Cambridge University Press, 1991.

Reimer, Erich. "Musicus—cantor." In *Handwörterbuch der musikalischen Terminologie.* Edited by Heinz Heinrich Eggebrecht. Vol. 4. Wiesbaden, Germany: Franz Steiner Verlag, 1978.

Santosuosso, Alma Colk. "A Musicus versus Cantor Debate in an Early Eleventh-Century Norman Poem." In *Essays on Music and Culture in Honor of Herbert Kellman.* Edited by Barbara Haggh. Paris and Tours, France: Minerve, 2001.

ALICE V. CLARK

[See also **DMA:** Boethius, Anicius Manlius Severinus; Music, Western European; Musical Treatises; Quadrivium.]

NATURAL LAW. The origins of natural law lie in the thought of the philosophers and jurists of the ancient world, who were convinced that there were rules for human behavior based upon objective, eternal norms. They conceived of these norms as having been established by nature and reason. The Romans were the first to coin the term "natural law" *(ius naturale).* Medieval jurists and theologians found the idea of natural law attractive. It was congruent with their conception of the universe and with their notions of human psychology. Expanding upon and developing further the definitions of natural law they found in the ancient sources, medieval jurists and theologians placed natural law at the pinnacle of a hierarchy of laws that regulated and guided human behavior. Their paradigm held sway in western jurisprudence until the nineteenth century.

The Roman orator Cicero (106–43 B.C.) summed up an important strand of ancient thought when he argued in his *De re publica* that "true law was right reason that was congruent with nature." He concluded that "there was one eternal, immutable, and unchangeable law" and that God had established it as the Emperor and Master of all humankind. Later Christian thinkers incorporated Cicero's conception of law into their own thought. The ancient Roman jurists dealt with two types of law that transcended the law of the Roman Empire: the law of peoples (or nations) *(ius gentium)* and natural law *(ius naturale).* In the second century A.D. the Roman jurist Gaius in his *Institutes* was the first to define the *ius gentium* as having been established by the natural reason of all humankind. Later jurists did not always distinguish carefully between natural law and the *ius gentium.* This conceptual ambiguity would long remain a problem of jurisprudential and theological thought. In the third century the jurist Ulpian defined natural law as what "nature teaches all animals," including human beings. He distinguished natural law from the *ius gentium* that was common only to human beings and established by their customary usages. He cited marriage and the procreation of children as examples of natural law. Ulpian's definition was later included in the emperor Justinian's comprehensive codification (*ca.* 533–536) of Roman law. Justinian's codification also included an introductory textbook for the study of law called the *Institutes.* The definition of natural law in the *Institutes* moved the source of natural law from the behavior of creatures to God: "Natural laws are established by divine providence and always remain firm and immutable." A little later the authors of the *Institutes* asserted that the *ius gentium* is identical with natural law. In every European law school from the eleventh to the seventeenth century, professors and students pondered Ulpian's and the *Institute*'s definitions—and their contradictions.

Although some late antique Christian theologians mentioned natural law in their writings, they did so infrequently. Natural law never became an important concept in the theological thought of the early church fathers. When St. Isidore of Seville composed (*ca.* 620) his encyclopedic *Etymologies* he combined the two traditions that had circulated in the ancient world. He defined "natural law" as the law common to all nations that was established by the instigation *(instinctus)* of nature, not by human legislation. Examples of natural law were marriage and the procreation of children, "one liberty of all human beings *(omnium una libertas)*," and the acquisition of property taken from the heavens, earth, and sea.

From Isidore to the jurist Gratian in the twelfth century there was virtually no discussion of natural law as a norm for human society. As part of his plan to bring order to the chaotic state of church law, Gratian compiled (*ca.* 1130/1140) a legal collection of ecclesiastical norms. At the beginning of his canonical collection, called the *Decretum*, he discussed the various types of laws that regulated and guided the behavior of human beings. In the opening sentence of his collection Gratian brought natural law to the forefront of all future discussions about the structure of human law: "The human race is ruled by two things, namely, natural law and customary usages. Natural law is what is contained in the law and Gospels." Gratian concluded that natural law dictated that "Each person is commanded to do to others what he wants done to himself," connecting natural law with the biblical injunction to do unto others what you would have them do unto you (Matt 7:12). By defining natural law as the duty to treat other human beings with care and dignity, Gratian stimulated jurists to reflect upon central values of natural law: the rendering of justice and the administering of equity in the legal system. To define the contents of natural law he placed Isidore's definition of natural law on the first page of his *Decretum*. Together with the texts of Roman law in Justinian's compilation, Gratian's *Decretum* became one of the standard introductory texts for the study of law (the *ius commune*) in European law schools, and Isidore's definition became one of the most important starting points for all medieval discussions of natural law.

Medieval jurists and theologians found several natural laws in their sources. During the twelfth century, when the jurists subjected these definitions of natural law to careful analysis, they identified various contradictions. They pointed out that natural law could be the natural instinctive behavior of all God's creatures. It could be the rules and norms of behavior that governed primitive human beings before human societies established their own particular laws. It could be the common sense of justice and equity that one could find in all human laws. They also argued that human reason might be a source of knowledge about the norms of natural law. On the other hand, natural law could be divine law. It could also be the *ius gentium,* the law of nations.

The jurists discussed all these possible types of natural law and did not, at first, give primacy of place to one. They distinguished between a natural law that was established by nature and one that was established by the natural order of the world. If nature can be said to create natural law, some jurists concluded, then "nature is God" *(natura, id est Deus)*. They did not embrace a juristic pantheism but simply acknowledged that the word "nature" in this sense could be used for the creator. The jurists who commented on Gratian's *Decretum* developed the most elaborate analysis of natural law. The most important of the twelfth-century jurists, Huguccio, located (*ca.* 1190) the origin of natural law in human beings. Natural law is reason, and that reason is a natural power of the soul *(naturalis vis animi)* that permits the soul to distinguish good from evil. This reason is called "law" *(ius)* because it commands and "law" *(lex)* because it binds. Huguccio also summed up twelfth-century juristic opinion on the force of natural law in human affairs. Natural law, he observed, consists of three levels of authority: commands, prohibitions, and indications or declarations *(demonstrationes)*. An example of a command was the precept to "love your Lord God." A prohibition of natural law may be taken from the Ten Commandments, "Thou shalt not steal." The third level of natural law leads human beings to choose what is licit and good over what is bad and evil. For example, in Gratian's excerpt from Isidore of Seville, liberty is a state that should be granted to all human beings. Huguccio noted, however, that all men are not free. Natural law leads men to liberty but does not command it. Huguccio explained that although liberty has its roots in natural law, God introduced slavery into the world because of human sins. Although medieval thinkers had to confront Isidore's elegant and stirring maxim that expressed the basic norm of human freedom *(omnium una libertas)* constantly, they could not overturn the institution of slavery that was endemic in their world or undermine the rights of slave owners.

Medieval ideas about natural law were transmitted to the modern world primarily through the vehicle of theology, especially the theology of St. Thomas Aquinas (*ca.* 1225–1274), who treated natural law comprehensively in his *Summa theologica.* Aquinas's conclusions drew heavily on the thought of the jurists: Natural law has its origins in human nature. This nature is the same in all human beings. Reason is the foundation upon which all natural law is based. The primary goal of natural law is to direct human beings toward the good. Men follow the dictates of natural law in three ways: by following the order that exists in nature, by obeying what nature has taught all animals, and, finally, by pursuing the inclinations and tendencies of human reason. When Aquinas asked the question "Can natural law be changed?" he augmented the thought of the jurists by explaining why some elements of natural law are immutable and some are not. Natural law consisted of first principles that cannot be changed and secondary principles that can be. Aquinas explained how slavery could be justified by noting that it did not arise from nature but from human reason for the benefit of human life.

Natural law became an integral part of medieval legal and theological thought. In private law the jurists used natural law in creative ways to justify and regulate particular legal institutions. Twelfth- and thirteenth-century jurists of the *ius commune* argued that property rights were protected by natural law because when God forbade stealing, he sanctioned private property. Since natural law protected private property, they concluded that even the emperor, king, or prince could not deprive a person of his or her property except for just and necessary reasons. By the end of the twelfth century, the jurists included contractual rights under the provisions of natural law. Consequently, they even concluded that the emperor was bound by the contracts that he might make with his subjects. The prince was not exempt from the precepts of natural law. In the fourteenth century the jurists argued that the norms that governed judicial procedure were also derived from natural law. Consequently every person had an absolute right to be summoned, present witnesses, and have a public trial. In an ingenious use of the story of God's condemnation of Adam and Eve in Genesis 3:9–12, the jurists decided that God had established the norms of procedure when he conducted the first trial in the Garden of Eden. By the end of the Middle Ages the Spanish theologian and jurist Francisco de Vitoria (1492–1546) put forward the remarkable argument that the right of the majority of people to render their consent in political matters was also a norm of natural law.

In this short and far from complete catalog of rights that theologians and jurists grounded in the norms of natural law, an important point must be emphasized. In some cases, like the norms of procedure, they found justifications for their arguments in Sacred Scripture. In others, like the inviolability of contracts, they could discover no precedents in Scripture. Instead they relied on norms that had evolved in the *ius commune.* These norms conformed to reason, reason so compelling that it expressed eternal truths; they were based on what Huguccio and Aquinas called "the reason of natural law."

By the end of the Middle Ages jurists and theologians had reached general agreement about the structure and content of natural law. Gradually these ideas about natural law migrated from the *ius commune* into the customary, local legal systems of Europe, and jurists incorporated natural law into their discussions of local customary law. The thirteenth-century commentary on English law that circulated under the name of "Bracton" borrowed word for word the definitions of natural law from the jurists of the *ius commune. Bracton's* discussion of natural law did not bear fruit in English legal thought until the fifteenth and sixteenth centuries, but the seeds of a natural law tradition in the common law were planted early.

The Iberian legal compilation *Las siete partidas,* published during the reign of Alfonso X the Learned (1221–1284), devoted the second title of book one to natural law and the *ius gentium.* This summary of natural law and its handmaiden, the *ius gentium,* also reflected the thought of the jurists: Natural law governs all men and animals. Its precepts regulate the institutions of marriage and the raising of children. The *ius gentium* is law that is common for all men but not animals. Its two fundamental principles are the rights of property and self-defense. Gregorio López de Tovar wrote an extensive commentary on *Las siete partidas* in the sixteenth century. He emphasized that Aquinas's natural reason was fundamental for knowing and understanding the contents of natural law: "Natural reason 'inclines' human beings to marry." Marriage is, therefore, founded on natural law. Even the natives in the new world have a true marriage because natural reason instigates them to form this bond. By the end of the Middle Ages the support, education, and inheritance of children were generally considered to be precepts of natural law, and López made the point that a child's right of inheritance could not be taken away by contract or custom. Spanish thinkers in the sixteenth and seventeenth centuries made significant contributions to the development of natural law thought.

Medieval natural law provided the basis of all discussions of natural law in early modern juristic and philosophical thought. When Thomas Jefferson wrote in the Declaration of Independence that "We hold these truths to be self-evident, that all men are created equal, that they are endowed by their Creator with certain unalienable rights, that among these are life, liberty, and the pursuit of happiness," the ultimate origins of his ideas lay in medieval juristic and theological thought.

BIBLIOGRAPHY

Cortese, Ennio. *La norma giuridica: Spunti teorici nel diritto comune classico*. 2 vols. Milan: Giuffrè, 1962.

Greene, Robert A. "Instinct of Nature: Natural Law, Synderesis, and the Moral Sense." *Journal of the History of Ideas* 58 (1997): 173–198.

Lisska, Anthony J. *Aquinas's Theory of Natural Law: An Analytic Reconstruction*. Oxford: Clarendon Press, 1996.

Oakley, Francis. *Natural Law, Conciliarism, and Consent in the Late Middle Ages: Studies in Ecclesiastical and Intellectual History*. London: Variorum, 1984.

O'Connor, Daniel John. *Aquinas and Natural Law*. London: Macmillan, 1968.

Tierney, Brian. "*Natura id est Deus*: A Case of Juristic Pantheism?" *Journal of the History of Ideas* 24 (1963): 307–322. Reprinted in his *Church Law and Constitutional Thought in the Middle Ages*, London: Variorum, 1979.

———. *The Idea of Natural Rights: Studies on Natural Rights, Natural Law, and Church Law 1150–1625*. Atlanta, Ga.: Scholar's Press, 1997.

Weigand, Rudolf. *Die Naturrechtslehre der Legisten und Dekretisten von Irnerius bis Accursius und von Gratian bis Johannes Teutonicus*. Munich: Max Hueber, 1967.

KENNETH PENNINGTON

[See also **DMA:** Law, Canon: After Gratian; Law, Canon: To Gratian; Law, Civil—Corpus Iuris, Revival and Spread; Law Codes: 1000–1500.]

NATURE. As an ontological category, the universe as a whole, or the latter's set of regulating principles, the concept of Nature permeates medieval thought and culture.

Until the modern decline in interest in metaphysics, the primary ontological questions were central to both Eastern and Western philosophy. In Plato, "nature" (Greek: *physis* or *ousia*; Latin: *natura* or *substantia*) can mean "essence," "goal," or "an inherent quality," and is identifiable at times with the Platonic Form (*Philebus* 64e, 66a; *Cratylus* 389c; *Republic* 597b; *Republic* 409d; *Parmenides* 132b). Aristotle employed it variously as the raw matter of any natural or artificial thing (*Physics* 193a 28–29; *Metaphysics* 1014b 16–1015a 1); an immanent cause of self-realization (*Physics* 199a 12ff; *Metaphysics* 1014b 18); and a permanent, inherent quality (*Physics*

192b 35–36). In both philosophers the term also denotes Nature, the entirety of created matter (*Metaphysics* 1074b 3–4; Plato's *Lysis*, 214b). This range of meanings, mostly indirectly transmitted, informs the varieties of medieval theology, natural philosophy, and the arts.

The Christological debates of early Christianity operated as a vortex of traditional ontological questions. Philosophical conservatism shaped an often heated discussion on whether Christ was of divine or human nature or a combination, and debate resulted over the status of the Virgin Mary. At the Council of Chalcedon in 451 the boundaries of orthodoxy on the matter were tentatively set: Christ was of two natures united in one "hypostasis," wholly human and wholly divine. Christology continued to occupy Eastern Church councils, but with the exception of Arianism and, to a lesser extent, Spanish Adoptionism, it did not trouble Western theologians after Boethius's *Contra Eutychen et Nestorium* (512?). Henceforth, speculation concerning the divine nature shifted to the Eucharistic sacrament in the Mass.

"Nature" also denotes the whole of the created world as governed by certain regularities. Ostensible deviations from it ("miracles") were central to medieval Christianity. The belief that the Eucharistic sacraments, once properly consecrated, turned into the flesh and blood of Christ by direct divine intervention was accepted by the fourth century and was unchallenged at first. Increasing heterodoxy on the matter, however, created a need for a canonical statement concerning Christ's Real Presence. This challenge was met by the doctrine of Transubstantiation in the Fourth Lateran Council (1215). Thomas Aquinas grounded the doctrine in Aristotelian natural philosophy by arguing that a change in the nature, or substance, of the sacraments left their "accidents" (here, their external appearance) unaltered. The transmission of the Aristotelian corpus into Latin Christendom over the twelfth and thirteenth centuries and the consequent establishment of Aristotle's writing at the center of the university curriculum profoundly influenced the formation of a rationalized image of Nature and its regularities that was open to philosophical investigation.

Aquinas's intellectual endeavor is emblematic of an age of synthesis that was in progress. Many thinkers were concerned with reconciling the existence of a creating, all-powerful God with an ordered, knowable Nature. This effort signaled an emerging affirmative view of a Nature "striving toward truth," which contrasted sharply with the Augustinian view of Nature as synonymous with a corrupt, stagnant, postlapsarian existence. This new outlook required the abandonment of rigid, self-enclosed Neoplatonic hierarchies (such as those espoused by John Scottus Eriugena) in favor of flexible continuums as characteristic of natural structures and the reestablishment of scientific knowledge based on observation rather than pure logic. The dynamic view of Nature was implicit in the empiricism of William of Ockham. A Nature in flux later became the premise of natural philosophers such as Thomas Bradwardine and the Merton Calculators in their seminal quantitative treatment of qualitative change. Although their calculations, like much of medieval natural philosophy, were hypothetical, the Mertonians' fundamentally revised view of Nature and the methodologies they devised for its investigation satisfied a major precondition for the emergence of empirical, computational science.

This is not to say that Nature did not enthrall medieval people well before the thirteenth century. Isidore of Seville, Bede, and Virgilius of Salzburg were all avid students of natural phenomena, and during the twelfth century there was a veritable explosion of interest in Nature. Moved by a new sensitivity to the human condition as a microcosm of Nature, in its turn a microcosm of God, Platonic humanists investigated the modus operandi of a plethora of psychological, social, physiological, and celestial phenomena. Ethelred of Rievaulx studied the nature of Christian friendship *(On Spiritual Friendship);* William of St. Thierry composed a treatise examining *The Nature of Body and Soul;* Adelard of Bath addressed twenty-four *Quaestiones naturales;* and Bernard Silvester authored a *Cosmographia* and *De mundi universitate* (On the entirety of the world). Similarly, political philosophers such as John of Salisbury rendered the state and positive law as part of a divinely ordered Creation, rather than as requisite necessities of a fallen humanity. In literature, offsetting an early-Christian image of the defeated pagan Goddess Natura (see, for example, Prudentius, *Against Symmachus* [402]), contemporary Latin and vernacular authors crafted illustrious personifications, notably in Alan of Lille's *De planctu Naturae* (Nature's plaint), Jean de Meun's *Roman de la Rose* (1275–1280), and Chaucer's *Parliament of Fowls* (1380?), all of which reflected contemporary trends in natural philosophy.

Medieval people's attitudes toward wondrous objects, creatures, and events also shed light on contemporary conceptions of Nature. Paradoxography, whether independent or woven into bestiaries, herbals, and lapidaries, was not a medieval invention, yet the genre flourished throughout this period. It was accompanied at times by a Eurocentric understanding of Nature (such as in Ranulf Higden's *Historia Polychronica*): histories, travel accounts, and vision literature reported how "unnatu-

ral" occurrences multiplied beyond the borders of Christendom, whether in India, Africa, or Ireland. Scholastic efforts to expose a stricter regularity operative in Nature, however, curbed recourse to such interventionalism. Gradually, an erratic natural diversity was transformed into a manifestation of divine genius, though chroniclers continued to interpret or exploit events such as comets as divinely ordained interference precipitating future trials.

A further medieval understanding of Nature emerges from its juxtaposition with culture. Social elites, perceiving themselves as "cultured" and thus at the positive end of the human scale, associated peasants with the natural and therefore bestial world.

Conceptually, then, Nature is present in medieval thought as (1) an inborn (as opposed to acquired and artificial) characteristic; (2) a defining operational cause of anyone or anything; (3) a condition examined vis-à-vis divine grace; and (4) the total state of affairs in Creation, tangible and not.

BIBLIOGRAPHY

Armstrong, A. H. *The Cambridge History of Later Greek and Early Medieval Philosophy.* London: Cambridge University Press, 1967.

Boas, George. "Nature." In *Dictionary of the History of Ideas.* Edited by Philip P. Wiener. New York: Scribners, 1973.

Chenu, M.-D. *Nature, Man, and Society in the Twelfth Century: Essays on New Theological Perspectives in the Latin West.* Edited and translated by Jerome Taylor and Lester K. Little. Chicago and London: University of Chicago Press, 1968.

Daston, Lorraine, and Katherine Park. *Wonders and the Order of Nature, 1150–1750.* New York: Zone Books, 1998.

Freedman, Paul. *Images of the Medieval Peasant.* Stanford, Calif.: Stanford University Press, 1999. Illustrates how social elites mostly perceived medieval peasants as part of the natural landscape or as inferior elements of humanity.

Gilson, Étienne. *History of Christian Philosophy in the Middle Ages.* New York: Random House, 1955. With extensive bibliography.

Grant, Edward. *The Foundations of Modern Science in the Middle Ages: Their Religious, Institutional, and Intellectual Contexts.* Cambridge, U.K., and New York: Cambridge University Press, 1996. An accessible discussion of natural philosophy.

Gurevich, A. J. *Categories of Medieval Culture.* Translated by G. L. Campbell. London and Boston: Routledge and Kegan Paul, 1985.

Haskins, Charles Homer. *The Renaissance of the Twelfth Century.* Cambridge, Mass.: Harvard University Press, 1927. Still a formidable statement of Latin learning in the period.

Kaye, Joel. *Economy and Nature in the Fourteenth Century: Money, Market Exchange, and the Emergence of Scientific Thought.* New York: Cambridge University Press, 1998. Stresses the ties between social and intellectual environments.

Maier, Anneliese. "The Achievements of Late Scholastic Science [1964]." In *On the Threshold of Exact Science.* Edited and translated by Steven D. Sargent. Philadelphia: University of Pennsylvania Press, 1982.

Panofsky, Erwin. *Renaissance and Renascences in Western Art.* Stockholm: Almqvist and Wiksell, 1960. A famous treatment of a pertinent aspect not explored here, namely, the place of naturalism in Western medieval plastic arts.

Post, Gaines. *Studies in Medieval Legal Thought: Public Law and the State, 1100–1322.* Princeton, N.J.: Princeton University Press, 1964. See especially "The Naturalness of Society and the State," pp. 494–561.

Salisbury, Joyce E. *The Medieval World of Nature: A Book of Essays.* New York: Garland, 1993. A wide-ranging collection, chronologically and geographically.

GUY GELTNER

[See also **DMA:** Arianism; Aristotle in the Middle Ages; Christology; Church Fathers; Philosophy and Theology; Scientific Instruments; **Supp:** Humanism; Matter; Transubstantiation.]

NICHOLAS II, POPE

NICHOLAS II, POPE (*ca.* 1010–1061). We know little of Gerard of Burgundy's background. Perhaps a native of Lorraine, he was first a canon at Liège, and he became bishop of Florence in 1045, where he reformed the cathedral clergy. The death of Pope Stephen IX (or X) in Florence in 1058 sparked a crisis in the church. An aristocratic faction in Rome elected John Minicius, bishop of Velletri, as Benedict X, despite Stephen's injunction that no election should take place until Hildebrand (the future Gregory VII), the leader of the reform party in Rome, returned from his mission to Germany. When he returned, Hildebrand, supported by Godfrey of Lorraine and Tuscany, assembled the cardinals in Siena, who elected Gerard in December 1058. Godfrey accompanied Nicholas to Rome, driving Benedict X out of the city in January 1059.

Nicholas was an advocate of church reform, and the Lateran Council he summoned in April 1059 discussed clerical celibacy and simony, but reform of papal elections was perhaps the most important product of the council. Nicholas established that cardinal-bishops should elect the pope at Rome, if possible, and that the emperor should have the undefined right to "confirm" this election. These changes lessened secular influence over the election process. Although the decree was soon amended to include other cardinals, the essential principles of the pronouncement became a fundamental part of papal elections. The emperor refused to accept these conditions and assembled a synod to annul them. At the Lateran Council, Nicholas also condemned Berengar of Tours, whose Eucharistic theology denied the Real Presence of Christ in the Eucharistic bread.

In further synods, Nicholas inveighed against clerical marriage and simony. As he had as bishop in Florence, he encouraged clergy to live a regular communal life. Nicholas cautiously supported the Patarine movement in Milan, which sought to purify the clergy, and sent Peter Damian and Anselm of Lucca (the future Pope Alexander II) to reform the Milanese clergy and reconcile Archbishop Guido to the reformers. While these efforts temporarily brought peace to the city, by 1066 Guido and the Patarines were again at loggerheads. In 1059 Nicholas formed an alliance with the Normans of southern Italy, who conquered Praeneste, Tusculum, and Numentanum for the papacy and captured the antipope Benedict X. Nicholas formalized the alliance at the Council of Melfi in August, where he invested Robert Guiscard with Apulia, Calabria, and Sicily, should he conquer it from the Muslims. Guiscard, in return, promised to pay tribute and defend the papacy. The Normans were thus intended to be the guarantors of the papal independence Nicholas sought to establish with his election reforms earlier that year. This alliance, however, reversed his predecessors' policies toward the Normans and in so doing created a legacy of conflict that was resolved only in the late thirteenth century. Nicholas died in July 1061 at Florence, where he had remained bishop even while he reigned as pope. His reign laid the groundwork for the Gregorian reforms of Hildebrand later in the century.

BIBLIOGRAPHY

PRIMARY SOURCES

Jasper, Detlev. *Das Papstwahldekret um 1059: Überlieferung und Text gesalt.* Sigmaringen: J. Thorbecke, 1986.

SECONDARY SOURCES

Brand, Placide. *Un pape savoyard: Gérald de Chevron, évêque de Florence (1044–1059) et pape (1059–1061) sous le nom de Nicolas II: Étude biographique.* Paris: Gabalda, 1925.

Cowdrey, H. E. J. *The Age of Abbot Desiderius: Montecassino, the Papacy, and the Normans in the Eleventh and Twelfth Centuries.* Oxford: Clarendon Press, 1983.

Laudage, Johannes. *Priesterbild und Reformpapsttum im 11. Jahrhundert.* Cologne: Böhlau, 1984.

CHRISTOPHER HATCH MACEVITT

[See also **DMA:** Berengar of Tours; Councils, Western (869–1179); Gregory VII, Pope; Robert Guiscard.]

NICHOLAS III, POPE

NICHOLAS III, POPE (1210/1220–1280). Born to one of the most powerful families of Rome, Giovanni

Gaetano Orsini was at a young age marked out for an ecclesiastical career. His father was Matteo Rossi Orsini, the notorious Guelph senator who had ruled Rome with a strong hand. Innocent IV made Giovanni cardinal-deacon of St. Nicholas in Carcere Tulliano on 28 May 1244 at the approximate age of twenty-eight, likely in gratitude to Giovanni's father, who had preserved Rome and the papacy against the attacks of the emperor Frederick II. A month after his elevation, the young cardinal fled Rome with Innocent to escape the clutches of Frederick II; from Lyons he was sent on a number of papal missions. In 1252 he unsuccessfully attempted to end the civil war between Guelphs and Ghibellines in Florence, and in 1258 he ratified the peace treaty between Louis IX of France and Henry III of England. In 1261 he supported the election of Urban IV, who subsequently named him protector of the Franciscans, continuing Orsini support for that order. Giovanni was one of the four cardinals who in 1266 crowned Charles of Anjou, whose ambitions he would later struggle against as pope, king of Sicily. He placed the tiara on the head of Gregory X and was a counselor to John XXI, whom he succeeded as pope on 25 November 1277 at Viterbo.

Continuing to further the goals of Gregory X, Nicholas sought to maintain Rome's independence. He encouraged Rudolf of Hapsburg to renounce his claim to the Romagna in 1279, then speedily subjected it to papal authority. He further stipulated that the office of senator could only be held by Romans, thus preventing foreign princes such as Charles of Anjou from gaining authority in the papal city. He also encouraged the Guelph and Ghibelline factions in Florence and elsewhere to reconcile, lessening Charles's ability to manipulate the factions to his own benefit. Nicholas unsuccessfully promoted peace between Castile and France, and he encouraged Christianity in Hungary, which was threatened by the pagan Cumans. He increased the demands on the Greek clergy following the union of the churches at the Second Council of Lyons in 1274, insisting on a renewal of the oath sworn at the council. Those clergy opposed to the union were required to obtain absolution from papal envoys, thus further alienating Byzantine churchmen. Nicholas also helped to further define the Rule of St. Francis, encouraging a stricter interpretation of poverty in the bull *Exiit qui seminat,* issued in 1279. He enlarged the Vatican palace, making it a more suitable papal residence. Unsurprisingly, the Orsini flourished under his papacy. His nephew Berthold became count of Romagna, while another nephew, Latino, he made cardinal. He conferred many civil and ecclesiastical offices on other Orsini relatives as well. Nicholas died on 22 August 1280 at Soriano near Viterbo. He was included in the eighth circle of hell in Dante's *Inferno* (canto XIX), condemned for simony.

BIBLIOGRAPHY

Davis, Charles T. "Roman Patriotism and Republican Propaganda: Ptolemy of Lucca and Pope Nicholas III." *Speculum* 50, no. 3 (July 1975): 411–433.

Demski, Augustin. *Papst Nikolaus III: Eine Monographie.* Münster: H. Schöningh, 1903.

Gay, Jules, ed. *Les registres de Nicolas III (1277–1280): Recueil des bulles de ce pape publiées ou analysées d'après les manuscrits originaux des archives du Vatican.* Paris: A. Fontemoing, 1938.

CHRISTOPHER HATCH MACEVITT

[See also **DMA:** Councils, Western (1215–1274); Franciscans; Frederick II; Guelphs and Ghibellines; **Supp:** Orsini Family.]

NICHOLAS IV, POPE (1227–1292). The first Franciscan pope, Girolamo Masci was born to a humble family at Lisciano (near Ascoli Piceno), Italy, on 30 September 1227, and early in his life he joined the Franciscans. He studied at Assisi and Perugia and in 1272 became the Franciscan provincial of Dalmatia. Gregory X included him that same year among the delegates sent to Constantinople to invite the emperor and patriarch to the Second Council of Lyons, and in 1274 Girolamo succeeded St. Bonaventure as the minister-general of the Franciscan Order. He was sent to negotiate peace between Castile and France in 1278 and was made cardinal-priest of S. Pudenziana the same year. He continued to climb in papal service, becoming cardinal-bishop of Palestrina in 1281. It was perhaps at this time that Girolamo allied himself with the Colonna family, who ruled the town.

The death of Honorius IV on 3 April 1287 left the College of Cardinals divided into pro- and anti-Angevin factions that could not agree on the next pope. After an eleven-month interregnum, Girolamo was the compromise candidate, elected at a second conclave on 15 February 1288. He at first refused to be pope but relented after a second election confirmed him as the cardinals' choice. He took the name Nicholas in memory of Nicholas III, who had been a lifelong advocate of the Franciscans.

Nicholas attempted to resolve the continuing crisis in Sicily, refusing to recognize James of Aragon's right to rule Sicily despite the latter's control of the island after the massacre of the Angevin garrisons in the Sicilian Vespers of 1282. Insisting on the papacy's authority over Sicily, Nicholas crowned Charles II of Anjou king of Naples and Sicily and made him a papal vassal. Nicholas continued to keep the imperial throne vacant, for although Rudolf of Habsburg had been elected king of Germany at papal insistence, he refused to crown Rudolf emperor. Nor did he accept Rudolf's son Albert as king of Hungary, appointing instead Charles Martel, son of Charles II of Anjou.

Nicholas sought a new crusade to the Latin east, a desire strengthened by the fall of Acre, the last Frankish outpost in the Middle East, in 1291. He contemplated uniting the Hospitallers and the Templars into one order. Political conflicts within Europe, however, left few sovereigns willing to lead a crusade. Continuing Franciscan interest in conversion of the Middle East and Asia, Nicholas sent missionaries, including John of Monte Corvino (later the first archbishop of Beijing), to Ethiopia, the land of the Tartars, Bulgaria, and China. In Rome, Nicholas depended on the Ghibelline Colonna family to maintain authority, but he sought to spur interest among the cardinals in the administration of the Papal States. On 18 June 1289 he issued the decree *Celestis altitudo potentie,* stating that the cardinals should receive half of the income of the Holy See and share in the financial administration of the church. Despite the possible benefits, his plan was never implemented. Nicholas died in Rome on 4 April 1292 and was buried in the Basilica of S. Maria Maggiore, close to which he had earlier built a palace.

BIBLIOGRAPHY

Franchi, Antonino. *Nicolaus Papa IV: 1288–1292 (Girolamo d'Ascoli).* Assisi, Italy: Edizioni Porziuncola, 1990.

Langlois, Ernest, ed. *Les registres de Nicolas IV: Recueil des bulles de ce pape, publiées ou analysées d'après les manuscrits originaux des archives du Vatican.* Paris: E. Thorin, 1886–1893.

Menestò, Enrico, ed. *Niccolò IV: Un pontificato tra Oriente ed Occidente.* Spoleto, Italy: Centro italiano di studi sull'alto medioevo, 1991.

CHRISTOPHER HATCH MACEVITT

[See also **DMA:** Taxation, Church; **Supp:** Colonna Family.]

NOTARIES. The notary was vital to social, economic, and legal life in the High and late Middle Ages. He served a diverse clientele from all walks of life, both Christians and Jews, as record keeper, intermediary in information exchange, stationer, and at times legal representative. Notaries might record documents in the absence of the principals to a contract. The notary set up shop in a medieval marketplace where potential clients existed. Sometimes notaries were called to private homes or places of business to record contracts. Notaries wrote a variety of acts *(instrumenta),* cash and credit sales, rentals, loans, money exchanges, partnerships, apprenticeships, emancipations, dowry and marriage contracts, and last wills and testaments. The notarial minute provided legal proof of a contractual engagement, and the notary's register functioned much as a registry of public deeds does today. The operations of the notary were integral to the growth of the medieval economy.

Notaries of northern Europe functioned most often as scribes in administrative contexts associated with bishops, counts, and other officials, but in the thirteenth century some northern notaries, particularly in the Low Countries, came to resemble more closely the public notaries of southern Europe. The presence of Italian merchants, trading in the north with their own notarial practices, influenced the development of the northern notariate. However, only in the early modern era does a public notariate akin to that of the south emerge in northern Europe.

The notarial culture associated with medieval Europe was concentrated primarily in the Mediterranean world. Medieval notaries in southern Europe practiced as public scribes, licensed by political authorities, both lay and ecclesiastical. They were educated in the Roman law tradition, as the medieval notariate owes its inspiration to three Roman offices—the *tabellio, notarius,* and *tabularius*—that fused by the eleventh century into the medieval office of notary. Access to the notarial profession was often regulated by laws and statutes. Notaries were to be laymen with upstanding reputations, often adults of at least thirty years of age, and long-term inhabitants of their communities. They were literate in Latin and in vernacular languages. Notarial training was relatively uniform across southern Europe, and notarial practice, despite minor local variations, provided consistency over a broad geographical range, making it possible for merchants and travelers to operate with some ease at considerable distance from their homes.

Notaries were present in large numbers in Italian towns. Over two hundred were operating in Pisa in the late thirteenth century and the same number in Genoa in 1303; six hundred were said to practice in Florence in the years 1336–1338, and as many as fifteen hundred in Milan in 1288. Evidence from elsewhere in Europe is less complete, but fourteenth-century Montpellier may have had seventy or more notaries in practice.

Most notarial acts survive in the form of registers in towns of Mediterranean Europe, although individual acts are also extant. Genoa has the richest and earliest surviving notarial archive. The first register preserved there, covering the years (1154–1166), is that of Giovanni Scriba. Additional registers from the later twelfth century remain, while those from the thirteenth century number in the hundreds and those from the fourteenth in the thousands. Other Italian cities, such as Venice, Pisa, and Lucca, also have impressive collections of notarial registers. Towns of southern France, such as Marseille, Manosque, Perpignan, and Montpellier, have some registers surviving from the thirteenth century on. Barcelona and Valencia have early series of registers as well. There are Italian registers remaining from sites of colonization in the Near East, such as Pera, a Genoese suburb of Constantinople. Italians also brought their notarial culture to northern Europe, as noted above, where they often established themselves and traded, and there are survivals at major market sites, such as Bruges.

The drafts of acts recorded in notarial registers are termed minutes and contain specific information relating to a particular transaction. Notarial acts also exist in the form of brief notes *(breve)* with a few contractual details, often jotted down on a scrap of paper, and in the extended form of the transaction *(grossus)*, which the notary might produce for the personal use of one or more participants in the contract. Fewer brief notes and extended contracts survive because they were held in private hands. Among registers preserved are both public registers, recording the transactions of clients who sporadically needed to obtain a legal record of their engagements, and private registers, maintained long-term for individual clients or families. Notarial fees were usually determined by the type of contract drafted and the word length of the document.

Notarial contracts consisted of three parts: the protocol, the corpus, and the eschatocol. Within the protocol, which begins the act, one finds the date of the transaction and a reference to the political authority under which it was written, taking the form, for example, of the regnal year of a king. The corpus presented the body of the contract. Participants in the transaction were identified here, usually by their place of origin and their occupation. The nature of and reason for the contract were then indicated; thus indebtedness might be by reason of a credit purchase. Also present in the corpus of the act were specific circumstances governing the contract, that is, dates of payment of debt, descriptions of real property, the specific obligations of parties to the contract, and the means of enforcement of the contractual agreement. Contingencies, such as weather, pirates, and coinage devaluations, could affect the way a contract would play out. Legal provisions involving oaths, promises to pay, and Roman law renunciations were also mentioned in the corpus. Women renounced the legal protection of the *Senatusconsultum Velleianum* in order to be free to contract obligations for themselves and on behalf of others. The eschatocol concluded the contract with a mention of the site where the document was written, a list of witnesses to the transaction, and the notary's sign or signature. Witnesses could either have been called specially by the parties to the contract or could simply be other notarial clients, milling around the notarial atelier after having had their own contracts recorded or while waiting to do the same. The formulaic provisions of the notarial contract were often abbreviated but would be written out if the notary produced an extended form of the document. If he did produce a fully drafted version, the notary usually signaled this at the end of the act with a clause stating that the instrument had been extracted. In a paragraph after the original act, the notary might later add a statement to the effect that the contract had been cancelled or that the obligation had been acquitted. An X or parallel lines drawn through the act might also indicate cancellation.

Notaries operated without a specific agenda as they gained their livelihoods from writing down other people's obligations. The records left by notaries do not lend themselves easily to quantification or to a study of the economy overall, but they provide insight into social and economic trends and preserve a slice of life at a particular moment in time. The notary was an important intermediary and record keeper in the business and everyday lives of people of Europe in the Middle Ages.

BIBLIOGRAPHY

Burns, Robert I. *Jews in the Notarial Culture: Latinate Wills in Mediterranean Spain, 1250–1350.* Berkeley and Los Angeles: University of California Press, 1996.

Clanchy, M. T. *From Memory to Written Record, England 1066–1307.* 2d ed. Oxford and Cambridge, Mass.: Blackwell, 1993).

Emery, Richard W. *The Jews of Perpignan in the Thirteenth Century: An Economic Study Based on Notarial Records.* New York: Columbia University Press, 1959.

Herlihy, David. *Pisa in the Early Renaissance: A Study of Urban Growth.* New Haven, Conn.: Yale University Press, 1958.

Lopez, Robert S. "The Unexplored Wealth of the Notarial Archives in Pisa and Lucca." In *Mélanges d'histoire du Moyen Age, dédiés à la mémoire de Louis Halphen.* Paris: Presses universitaires de France, 1951.

Lopez, Robert S., and Irving W. Raymond. *Medieval Trade in the Mediterranean World: Illustrative Documents Translated with Introductions and Notes.* New York and London: Columbia University Press, 1955.

Murray, James M. *Notarial Instruments in Flanders between 1280 and 1452.* Brussels: Commission royale d'histoire and Koninklijke Commissie voor Geschiedenis, 1995.

Pryor, John. *Business Contracts of Medieval Provence: Selected Notulae from the Cartulary of Giraud Amalric of Marseille (1248).* Toronto: Pontifical Institute of Mediaeval Studies, 1981.

Reyerson, Kathryn L., and Debra Salata. *Medieval Notaries and Their Acts: The 1327–1328 Register of Jean Holanie.* Kalamazoo, Mich.: Medieval Institute, TEAMS Documents of Practice, Forthcoming.

KATHRYN L. REYERSON

[See also **DMA:** Seals and Sigillography, Western European; **Supp:** Signs, Theories of.]

NOVEL (BYZANTINE LAW) (*neara;* Latin, *novella*). In the legal tradition of the Byzantine Empire a novel was a work of new legislation, promulgated by the emperor and intended as an addition to the corpus of Roman law. Novels could be addressed by the emperor to a particular imperial official or judge, and a single novel could cover a variety of topics. The term "novel" did not need to appear in the title of an imperial pronouncement for it to have the force of law.

The term "novel" was used to refer to legislation promulgated after the compilation of Roman law in the *Codex Theodosianus,* issued in 438. The *Codex Theodosianus* was intended as an assembly of all valid Roman law issued since Constantine I (324–337). A more thorough law compilation, the *Codex Justinianus,* was issued by Justinian I (527–565). This *Codex Justinianus,* along with the *Digest* (also known as the *Digesta* or *Pandectae*), which contained legal precedents, and the *Institutes* (or *Institutiones*), a legal textbook, has been known as the *Corpus iuris civilis* (CIC) since the sixteenth century. The laws issued by Justinian after the completion of his *Codex* were called novels and added separately to the CIC. Unlike the rest of the CIC, Justinian's novels were issued in Greek.

With the CIC, the system of Roman law was theoretically complete. Most legislative activity undertaken by emperors therefore consisted in "cleansing" or "renewing" the Justinianic legislation. Novels were to be issued only to deal with new situations arising in Byzantine society. Roman law was considered a complete system in which judgments must be based on existing legislation. Contrary to the English system of common law, judges were not able to declare law through decisions but were supposed to rely exclusively on the statutes promulgated by the emperors.

While Justinian's *Corpus* was theoretically always the law of the empire, from the seventh to ninth century it was not commonly used because it required more training in legal theory and Latin than most judges had. The emperors Leo III and Constantine V therefore issued a "selection of laws," *Ecloga ton nomon,* in 741. This collection, known as the *Ecloga,* is a brief handbook to a small selection of laws dealing with commonly occurring topics. Christian ideas of justice and biblical law exerted a strong influence on the *Ecloga.*

The revival of Roman law in ninth-century Byzantium is now seen as a process somewhat like the reception of Roman law in western Europe in the twelfth century. In the sixth century, when Latin was the common language of legal training, bilingual legal scholars made Greek translations and commentaries on the CIC for teaching purposes. Latin technical legal terms were not translated into Greek but merely transliterated. By the ninth century so few people in Byzantium knew Latin that the sixth-century Greek "translations" of the Justinianic corpus were unintelligible. Numerous ninth-century glossaries and commentaries on the meaning of Latin legal terminology attest to the new efforts to understand Roman law. In addition to these works of commentary, several new law books were issued that had the goal of reviving Roman law. The *Eisagoge* (or *Eisagoge tou nomou,* or "Introduction to law," also known as the *Epanagoge*) was issued most probably between 880 and 883. It called for a revival of Roman law, but it also outlined a political theory for the proper interaction between the patriarch, the emperor, and the law. The *Eisagoge* may have been partially composed by the famous Patriarch Photios (858–867 and 877–886). The dating of another handbook, the *Procheiron,* (or *procheiros nomos,* "Law at hand"), is now disputed. Andreas Schminck's argument that it was issued in 907 and that its polemic was directed against *Eisagoge* has been widely accepted. More recently, however, Thomas Ernst van Bochove has argued persuasively for a return to the traditional interpretation that it was issued between 870 and 879. The CIC became fully accessible to Greek legal scholars with the publication of the *Basilics* in 888. The *Basilics* (also called the *Hexabiblos* or the *Basilica*) is a Greek translation and reorganization of the CIC, with commentary. In the era of legal humanism of the sixteenth century, scholars were able to complete or correct deficiencies in the Latin manuscripts of the *Corpus* through reference to the Byzantine *Basilics.*

As part of the ninth-century legal revival, the emperor Leo VI (886–912) issued 113 novels. This is the largest collection of novels issued by a Byzantine emperor after Justinian. These new laws worked to reconcile discrepancies between contemporary custom and the CIC.

They may have been issued while the work on the *Basilics* was in progress, in response to queries arising from the study of Roman law. A series of novels about land ownership issued in the tenth century have been important for our understanding Byzantine social history. These novels are sometimes called the Macedonian legislation after the name of the dynasty then in power.

Subsequent emperors continued to issue novels as they felt new situations in the empire warranted new legislation. The term "novel" was used fairly frequently in the ninth through eleventh centuries. Manuel Komnenos (1143–1180), for instance, issued legislation as novels. An imperial solution *(lysis)* to a question posed by a judge also had the force of law. In the late eleventh century, new laws were frequently issued as solutions to particular cases brought to the attention of the emperor by judges in Constantinople. Legislation could also be promulgated through a *chrysobull,* a solemn document signed by the emperor in red ink and sealed with a gold seal. *Chrysobulls* were usually used for treaties and grants of privileges. The terms *horismos,* "decree," and *prostagma,* "ordinance," became more common for new legislation in the twelfth through fifteenth centuries. Scholars sometimes loosely refer to new laws made through any of these methods as "novels."

BIBLIOGRAPHY

Burgmann, Ludwig. "Lawyers and Legislators: Aspects of Law-Making in the Time of Alexios I." In *Alexios I Komnenos.* Edited by Margaret Mullett and Dion Smythe. Belfast, Northern Ireland: Belfast Byzantine Enterprises, School of Greek and Latin, the Queen's University of Belfast,1996.

Fögen, Marie Theres. "Reanimation of Roman Law in the Ninth Century: Remarks on Reasons and Results." In *Byzantium in the Ninth Century: Dead or Alive? Papers from the Thirtieth Spring Symposium of Byzantine Studies, Birmingham, March 1996.* Edited by Leslie Brubaker. Aldershot, U.K., and Brookfield, Vt.: Ashgate, 1998.

Laiou, Angeliki E., Dieter Simon, eds. *Law and Society in Byzantium: Ninth–Twelfth Centuries.* Washington, D.C.: Dumbarton Oaks Research Library and Collection, distributed by Harvard University Press, 1994. An important collection of essays by leading scholars.

Macrides, R. J. *Kinship and Justice in Byzantium, Eleventh–Fifteenth Centuries.* Aldershot, U.K., and Brookfield, Vt.: Ashgate, 1999.

Schminck, Andreas. *Studien zu mittelbyzantinischen Rechtsbüchern.* Frankfurt am Main, Germany: Löwenklau Gesellschaft, 1986.

Stolte, Bernard. "Not New but Novel. Notes on the Historiography of Byzantine Law." *Byzantine and Modern Greek Studies* 22 (1998): 264–279.

Svoronos, Nicolas, and P. Gounaridis, eds. *Les novelles des empereurs Macédoniens.* Athens: Centre de recherches Byzantines, 1994.

van Bochove, T. E. *To Date and Not to Date: On the Date and Status of Byzantine Law Books.* Groningen: E. Forsten, 1996.

LEONORA NEVILLE

[See also **DMA:** Basilics; Byzantine Empire; Codex Theodosianus; *Corpus Iuris Civilis;* Law, Byzantine.]

NUMEROLOGY, "the semantics of number," as the Swedish scholar Gunnar Qvarnström puts it, appears very early among the essential structures implemented by mankind to interpret and organize their world. In Western thought, the most comprehensive theory of numbers, as related to "cosmos," has been the Pythagorean, but the Platonic and Judaic traditions have also developed the use of numeric concepts as an integral part of their semiosis. The church fathers adopted a large proportion of ideas stemming from these approaches while working to adapt them to the principles of Christian faith.

St. Augustine, inspired by a classical culture grounded in part on Neoplatonic theories, established the basic equivalence between God as Unity and the monad as a philosophical notion. Furthermore, he not only exposed the complexities of the Trinity in regard to this divine unity but also proposed many specific applications of numerology to the tenets of Christianity. Augustine's status as "author" in the Middle Ages would authorize medieval thinkers to pursue the subject of numerology. In the seventh century, Isidore of Seville systematized Augustine's approach and officially opened the door to an extensive use of numerology by stating that all numbers to be found in the Holy Scripture are endowed with a metaphysical or allegorical meaning. This meant that virtually everything could be read according to the laws of numerology.

Many theologians elaborated on these theories. Numbers were perceived as the underlying foundation of the quadrivium, the four (out of seven) liberal arts related to science and the material world. Since the universal course of study throughout the Middle Ages was based on the seven liberal arts, numbers and their relationships came to occupy a dominant position in the medieval worldview. Among the four parts of the quadrivium, *arithmetica* was the science of numbers, while *geometria* considered primarily their translation in terms of physical measurements of space. *Musica,* on the other hand, was perceived as the science of the relationships between notes and their intervals; the musical art was consequently the closest to the perfect purity of the ideal world and the most appropriate to deal with "divine things," as many writers, from Boethius to the composers of the *Ars nova,* insisted. *Astronomia,* finally, which comprehended astrology as well as what we call astronomy, was the science of numeric relationships between the various planets, which could be used to measure and in-

427

terpret planetary influences. Music and astronomy were two aspects of a single mode of epistemological handling of the world.

The first numbers are naturally the most meaningful. Unity, the one God, of course represents perfection, and so does the Trinity; one and three are the numbers of God. As opposed to them, two is seen as imperfect and is associated with man. The binary rhythm is also perceived as imperfect and lacking, contrary to the perfect ternary rhythm. Two, in effect, renounces the completion of one and appears as the sign of corruption. Four (two by two, but also one plus three) symbolizes the spatial world; it is very much present in the mental structures of the medieval man: as there are four rivers flowing from the earthly paradise or four Gospels, there are four seasons, four virtues, four letters composing the name of Adam, and so on. Five (two plus three) signifies the double nature of man, born of imperfection (two) but redeemed by God (three), and from there comes to mean the whole universe. Seven is the magical number par excellence: the sum of three (the number of God) and four (the physical world), it also assumes the values of a very rich proto-Christian tradition: it especially expresses the fullness of time, as seen in the seven days of Genesis. Ten is a figure of perfection but less so than twelve: the product of three by four, twelve is in many respects the absolute number, coalescing antique and Christian symbolism. Twelve has an overwhelming presence in the medieval system (as, indeed, in ours): there are twelve months, twelve signs of the zodiac, twelve apostles, and twelve tribes of Israel. There were also a few special numbers, gifted with their own meanings: according to Revelation, for instance, 666 is the number of the beast (Antichrist).

This basic reading of numbers is omnipresent in all medieval productions; it is a fair assumption that everybody, at least, who was part of the clerical element of society was familiar with it. But this material also had considerably more sophisticated uses. Theologians, like Thierry of Chartres, made extensive use of numerology in their sometimes cryptic commentaries on the Holy Scripture. Pseudo-Dionysius the Areopagite's "theology of Light" is also anchored in his seminal mastery of numerology. A further stage is reached when the numeric interpretation is applied to secular works. Although many literary works—allegorical ones especially—were constructed in accordance with elaborate numeric patterns, modern scholars sometimes go too far in their quest for numeric structures in the texts. If there is little doubt that Dante's *Divine Comedy* is built around series of mystical numbers, some analyses stretch the credulity of the average reader: for instance, it is difficult to argue, as Joan Helm did, that Chrétien de Troyes's *Érec and Énide* is written entirely on the basis of scrupulous numeric measurements, mirroring the cosmic order down to the last line of the romance. Numerology is certainly an invaluable tool when dealing with the Middle Ages, but it is by no means the only one, and it must be handled with some prudence.

BIBLIOGRAPHY

Davy, M.-M. *Initiation à la symbolique romane.* 1964. Reprint, Paris: Flammarion, 1977.

Hopper, Vincent Foster. *Medieval Number Symbolism: Its Sources, Meaning, and Influence on Thought and Expression.* New York: Columbia University Press, 1938.

Ifrah, Georges. *Universal History of Numbers: From Prehistory to the Invention of the Computer.* Translated by David Bellos. London: John Wiley, 2000.

Meyer, Heinz. *Die Zahlenallegorese in Mittelalter.* Munich: Wilhelm Fink Verlag, 1975.

Murray, Alexander. *Reason and Society in the Middle Ages.* Oxford: Clarendon Press, 1978.

Schimmel, Annemarie. *The Mystery of Numbers.* Oxford: Oxford University Press, 1993.

Surles, R. L., ed. *Medieval Numerology: A Book of Essays.* New York: Garland, 1993.

ANNE BERTHELOT

[See also **DMA:** Augustine of Hippo, St.; Mathematics; Musical Treatises; Pseudo-Dionysius the Areopagite; Quadrivium; Trinitarian Doctrine.]

OBLATES AND OBLATION. Oblation, the act of consecrating a child to God's service in a monastery, was a common practice in early medieval society. Young children (male and female) were offered at the altar by their parents or guardians as living sacrifices to God. The parental vow on behalf of their child was irrevocable. Children who entered monastic communities in this way were obliged to remain monks for the rest of their lives. Oblation was not a form of child abandonment driven by economic necessity, as some scholars have maintained. Rather, it is better understood in social terms as the gift of a child made by its parents in the hope of initiating and sustaining a personal lifelong relationship with a monastic community, whose prayers interceded with God on behalf of humankind.

The Old Testament story of Samuel was the most influential biblical model for child oblation in the Middle Ages. Samuel's mother, Hannah, was unable to bear children until she promised God to consecrate her first-born to divine service. She soon conceived a son. When Samuel was still a little boy *(infantulum)*, Hannah offered him at the temple in the presence of the priest, together with gifts of flour and wine, with the intention that the boy would serve God for his entire life (1 Sam. 1:1–28). In imitation of the Samuel story, the sixth-century Rule of Benedict placed the ritual of child oblation firmly in a eucharistic setting. The parents of the oblate drew up a written oath *(petitio)* confirming the monastic vow on behalf of their offspring and pledging that they would never provide the child with the means to leave the cloistered life. The oblate's hands were wrapped in an altar cloth, along with the petition and an offering of bread and wine. The parents then led the child to the altar, where they offered him or her as a living sacrifice to God. Witnesses were present to validate the oath.

Between the eighth and eleventh centuries, child oblation was the primary means of recruitment for many large monastic communities, including Corvey, St. Gall, Reichenau, and Cluny. Children raised in the abbey from infancy *(nutriti)* were considered to be more pure than adult converts to the monastic life *(conversi).* In the early Middle Ages, adults entered monasteries for a number of reasons: voluntary religious conversion, the performance of public penance, even forcible political exile. Irrespective of their motives for becoming monks, adult novices were considered to be tainted with worldly knowledge and sexual experience. Many abbeys required a period of indoctrination up to a year in length to prepare them for the ceremony of profession that marked their formal entry into the community. In contrast, the ritual of oblation was immediate and irrevocable. Children became full participants in the cloistered life from the moment their parent or guardian handed them over to the abbot at the altar. Their schooling in Latin and the liturgical customs of the community began immediately. The sexual continence of oblates made them the most effective mediators between God and humankind because they maintained the constant state of personal purity necessary to touch the sacraments and celebrate the Mass.

Monastic customaries from the tenth and eleventh centuries contain detailed prescriptions of daily practice that emphasize the pivotal role played by oblates in the celebration of the liturgy. At Cluny and other abbeys, children were entrusted with a number of specific singing and reading assignments. They were also instrumental in the organization of the divine office. In particular,

the oblates were often responsible for preparing the *brevis,* a written outline of the specific chants assigned to individual monks that was read aloud every day in the chapter meeting. By the time they reached adulthood, oblates had acquired an unparalleled fluency in Latin and an intimate knowledge of liturgical customs. These skills made them the most valuable members of the monastic community.

The legality of child oblation was contested, even at the height of its popularity. The most famous dispute occurred in 829. Gottschalk of Orbais, a monk of Fulda, attacked the legitimacy of his oblation on the grounds that it was performed against his will. A synod held at Mainz that same year confirmed his liberty from the monastic vow and recommended the restoration of his inheritance. Abbot Hrabanus Maurus of Fulda contested this decision and appealed to Emperor Louis the Pious. He composed a detailed treatise on the rationales and biblical models for child oblation *(Liber de oblatione puerorum)* in defense of his position. A compromise was mediated by the emperor, whereby Gottschalk was permitted to leave the abbey of Fulda without his inheritance, but he remained a monk for the rest of his turbulent career.

Several factors contributed to the waning of child oblation in the High Middle Ages. First, the twelfth century presented a new world of secular and religious career alternatives for promising young men, so parents were less inclined to offer their children for a lifetime of service in an abbey. Instead, they often put forward male offspring who were considered to be ill suited for public careers because of physical or mental deficiencies. This tendency evoked harsh complaints from monastic authors because unfit monks contributed to the erosion of the integrity of their communal life. Second, new educational opportunities produced literate adult priests who could fill the liturgical roles traditionally played by monks raised in an abbey from childhood. This development effectively undermined the central role of oblates in monastic communities. Lastly, personal consent reemerged as a central issue in twelfth-century canon law. New monastic orders like the Carthusians and the Cistercians set minimum age limits on new recruits as a way to ensure the sincerity of their vow. At the close of the century, Popes Clement III and Celestine III required oblates to make a statement of consent when they reached the age of puberty (twelve years of age for girls and fourteen for boys). These rulings effectively ended the practice of child oblation as it was understood in the early Middle Ages.

BIBLIOGRAPHY

Boswell, John. *The Kindness of Strangers: The Abandonment of Children in Western Europe from Late Antiquity to the Renaissance.* New York: Pantheon, 1988.

Boynton, Susan. "The Liturgical Role of Children in Monastic Customaries from the Central Middle Ages." *Studia Liturgica* 28 (1998): 194–209.

De Jong, Mayke. *In Samuel's Image: Child Oblation in the Early Medieval West.* Leiden, Netherlands, New York, and Cologne, Germany: E. J. Brill, 1996.

SCOTT G. BRUCE

[See also **DMA:** Gottschalk of Orbais; Hrabanus Maurus; **Supp:** Corvey, Abbey of.]

OLD AGE and the elderly were constant and regular features of medieval society. While this does not deny the overwhelming weight of all the available data about high mortality rates, the prevalence and ubiquity of infant mortality, and the limited duration of the "average" life span, it is a serious factor—and a warning against complacent generalization—in assessing the medieval understanding of the life cycle and the realities of family, social, and political life and interaction.

Medieval theories about the life cycle were largely based upon the idea that a full life consisted of a number of discrete stages or segments and that life as a whole could be seen either as a linear progression (from starting line to finish) or as a cyclical process (as the wheel revolved full circle). Those who contributed to this dialogue accorded the various later stages of the cycle—that of "eld" (or *senectus,* or the age of Saturn and melancholy, or of *gravitas*)—a full, though not necessarily a revered, role. Different authors opted for a varying number of stages, ranging from a mere three or four to a complex division of the full complement of years into as many as ten or twelve segments, as they sought to explain the process or life line that snaked its way from helpless infancy through the years of power and potency and then beyond, on the way to the canonical threescore years and ten. Likewise, the actual presence of aged men and women was encountered at virtually all social levels and in all social settings. The response of their world to their existence and their role ranged from contempt and impatience to charity, retirement provisions and pensions, veneration and respect, and sometimes even an acceptance that the turnover of power in patriarchal society was a measured march whereby generation eventually succeeded generation.

THE STAGES OF LIFE

From the early Middle Ages onward the presentation of human life as a number of segments, moving from cradle to grave, proved to be an attractive and intriguing concept. Influential theologians and creative writers, in a search for the key to God's plan for the human race, saw both practical wisdom and symbolic significance in such divisions. Though there was never a consensus on the number of segments, the positions of Augustine of Hippo (six stages) and Isidore of Seville (seven stages) carried considerable weight with later thinkers. Depending on the scheme adopted, the divisions of life could be thought of as a reflection or counterpart of the seasons, the humors and elements, the days of the week or the months of the year, or the positions of the zodiac, among the numerous possibilities. Augustine's six stages corresponded to the days of creation and the ages of human history, though Shakespeare was later to make the seven-part division the most famous paradigm of them all. Though there was a powerful logic in favor of a simple scheme, just as artists came to depict the three magi as representing youth, maturity, and age (and as representing the races of humanity, divided between Europe, Asia, and Africa), this kind of theoretical demography always remained an open issue. And within and between the segments of the life cycle, the question of the exact point(s) when youth became maturity and when that in turn passed into old age also remained a field for debate.

The value assigned to old age, as such, in either the spiritual or the social hierarchy, was also a variable. One line of thought went back to the Old Testament patriarchs and to such pagan wisdom as Cicero's *De senectute* (On old age); this is what we can think of as the positive assessment. It emphasized the pleasures of old age (among which was a release from the passions and responsibilities of youth and maturity), and it accorded the elderly a venerated niche in the social fabric. A less sanguine line, heavily reinforced by Innocent III's *De miseria humanae conditionis* (On the misery of the human condition, 1195), seemed almost to take pleasure in emphasizing the physical and mental deterioration that invariably accompanied old age—for those so unlucky as to live that long. Nor was this negative view confined to social theorists and theologians, there also being a very considerable body of literary ridicule directed at such activities as May-December marriages (as in Chaucer's "Miller's Tale" or as a theme in such paintings as those of Lucas Cranach). Old men and women might be dignified and worthy of respect, but they were just as likely to be lecherous and waspish as they descended into their "envyous and angrye" years. That Caxton published Cicero's treatise indicates that he thought its sympathetic views would find a ready market, but he himself remarked, while in his fifties, that "age crepeth on me dayly and febleth all the bodye."

THE PHENOMENON OF LONGEVITY

It is hardly to be wondered at that medieval society was too complex, over its thousand years and vast geographical and cultural span, to give us a single view of or policy toward the aged. That old age was an arresting social phenomenon is clear. Obviously, by the standards of industrialized society the proportion of the aged (whether we begin marking old age at fifty or sixty or even somewhere beyond) to all live births was painfully small. Current demographic thinking holds that about one in three live births succumbed within the first year, and of those who did survive to adulthood a high incidence of early mortality, for both men and women, was always to be expected. But despite the dangers of childbirth, battle, plague, malnutrition, and the medical thinking of the time (though there were treatises outlining routines to prolong life), many did survive into what, even by current standards, would be old age. Where data exist (for elite groups, such as the late medieval English peerage) we see that the "universe" of those who reached age twenty might well see about half its number survive to fifty or fifty-five, and of those survivors some fair proportion could count on at least another decade or two. Studies of upper- and middle-class groups bear this out across much of late medieval Europe; it is possible that those who survived the famines and plagues of the fourteenth century found themselves in a world where a lower population meant better living conditions and perhaps a longer life. In offering these comments, however, it is necessary to distinguish between the impressive longevity of the few and what was still, by the standards of the modern world, a grim story of aggregate mortality and demographic patterns of the many. Instances of prominent individuals who lived to a very ripe age are not hard to find. That they were unusual in their longevity was apt to make them memorable, and if we skim a list of such survivors from the social classes about whom records were kept we find long lists of the aged. Such material is hardly systematic; a particular family here, a group of bishops or abbots there, some writers or counselors or urban officials in other instances. Though a king who reigned for 45 or 50 years (as did English kings Henry III, 1216–1272, and Edward III, 1327–1377) pretty surely acceded to the throne while a young man or even a child, five decades on top still gives us an old man at the end. If Edward III's decline into senility

might tilt contemporary thought about old age toward Innocent III's view rather than Cicero's, Edward was at least a hardy champion of survival (dying at age 64). For some examples from the secular world we can turn to the Carolingians in the ninth century; Charlemagne lived to at least 71, Louis II the German to at least 70, Louis I the Pious to 62, Lothar I to 60, and even Charles the Bald made it to 54, while among twelfth-century figures Henry the Lion of Bavaria and Saxony (1129/30–1195) barely outlasted his imperial rival, Frederick I Barbarossa of Germany (*ca.* 1122–1190). And in the ecclesiastical sphere, we note that the power and repute of the Abbey of Cluny rested to an appreciable extent on the longevity—and thereby the continuity—provided by some of its abbots: Maiolus (964–994), Odilo (994–1049), Hugh of Semur (1049–1109), and Peter the Venerable (1122–1156).

These exalted or noteworthy examples tell us about longevity at the far end of the spectrum but not about self-perception regarding age and the life course. In various judicial and administrative (or inquisitorial) proceedings jurors, witnesses, or deponents were asked to begin their testimony with some vital statistics: name, occupation, residence, and age. In such records we have countless instances of men giving such an age as "60 and more" or specifying an even higher number. While this stab at precision raises questions about memory, the reliability of the oral or written record, and the consonance of literacy and numeracy, the frequent inclusion of such a datum offers an insight into how credibility and rank was established among one's contemporaries. A man who claimed to be 65 may not have been all of that, but that he so testified in the presence of his peers argues for a relative or comparative grid on an age scale; he presumably looked older, to the eye and to social memory, than those around him, and his memories went farther back. An analysis of the self-stated ages of those testifying in the fourteenth century at the proceedings against the Templars shows that 144 of 372 deponents (or 40 percent of the total) were over 50, and of these 17 were in the 55 to 59 range, 37 were 60 to 64, and 17 were 65 or beyond.

COPING WITH OLD AGE

In the many depictions of old age found in wall paintings and manuscript illuminations, usually inserted to illustrate the theme of the Wheel of Life or the Ages of Man, the aged are generally depicted as being well short of patriarchal grandeur. In the medallion in the De Lisle Psalter that shows man in his last days, the figure says he is now "given over to decrepitude [and] death will be my condition." But medieval society did, at times, recognize a responsibility regarding the failing powers and special needs of its aged survivors. Records testifying to this are found, early and late, in secular and in ecclesiastical records. In the sixth century Benedictine Rule, the basic guidelines of western monasticism, provision was made to exempt the elderly from the full rigors of monastic routine and discipline. While kings did not resign from or abdicate their high office, as Diocletian had done in the fourth century or Charles V would do in the sixteenth, it was accepted that some provision might have to be made for those who could no longer cope with the burdens of their years. In peasant society, among those close to the poverty line—if not starvation—agreements could be hammered out whereby parents turned over their holding to a child, or even a tenant, in return for support in their last years; food, clothing, shelter, and prayers after death, perhaps, in return for immediate occupancy of twenty acres of arable. Among both clergy and laity we find comparable provisions: a pension for a priest "now suffering from old age and madness," a petition from a bishop or nobleman to be excused from Parliament, a dispensation to an aged couple to commute a vow to go on pilgrimage, permission for an old man to eat meat on fast days, exemption to Londoners at age seventy from service on the watch and ward, and the like.

Though the progression from infancy to maturity to age might be presented with great reverence in a depiction of the Christ child, the Virgin, and St. Anne, no single model covers all the cases. If an English lord begged indulgence because he was a "septuagenarian and a valetudinarian," this can be countered with the majestic portrayal of the 200-year-old Charlemagne of the *Song of Roland*. In sum, it is a tale of alternatives, conflicting anecdotes, and a mixed moral. Though caring for the aged was never by itself one of the Acts of Mercy, on a par with visiting the sick or prisoners, Nicholas of Cusa in the fifteenth century established a hospice with a special mandate to care for thirty-three of the aged and enfeebled (the number thirty-three equaling the years of Christ's life). In surveying medieval society we see a world ruled by numerous men (and occasionally women such as Eleanor of Aquitaine [*ca.* 1122–1204], Henry II's wife, or his mother, the empress Maud [1102–1165], or Hildegard of Bingen [1098–1179]), on secular and ecclesiastical thrones, who were in their sixties or beyond. The problem of their survival, their treatment, and their grip on their place in society is a universal one; the responses of medieval society to these issues reflect the same levels of ambivalence, denial, and concern that we find in the ancient and in the modern world.

BIBLIOGRAPHY

Burrow, John A. *The Ages of Man: A Study in Medieval Writing and Thought.* Oxford: Clarendon Press, 1986.

Chew, Samuel. *The Pilgrimage of Life.* New Haven, Conn.: Yale University Press, 1962.

Clark, Elaine. "Some Aspects of Social Security in Medieval England." *Journal of Family History* 7 (1982): 307–320.

Coffman, George R. "Old Age from Horace to Chaucer: Some Literary Affinities and Adventures of an Idea." *Speculum* 9, no. 3 (1934): 249–277.

Dove, Mary. *The Perfect Age of Man's Life.* Cambridge, U.K., and New York: Cambridge University Press, 1986.

Gilbert, Creighton. "When Did Man in the Renaissance Grow Old?" *Studies in the Renaissance* 14 (1967): 7–32.

Harvey, Barbara F. *Living and Dying in England, 1100–1540: The Monastic Experience.* Oxford: Clarendon Press, 1993.

Hollingsworth, T. W. *The Demography of the British Peerage.* Supplement to *Population Studies* 18, no. 2 (1964).

Jones, J. W. "Observations on the Origins of the Division of Man's Life in Stages." *Archaeologia* 35 (1853): 167–89.

Laslett, Peter. *Family Life and Illicit Love in Earlier Generations: Essays in Historical Sociology.* Cambridge, U.K.: Cambridge University Press, 1977. See especially "The History of Aging and the Aged," pages 174–213.

Minois, Georges. *History of Old Age: From Antiquity to the Renaissance.* Translated by Sarah Hanbury Tenison. Cambridge, U.K.: Polity, 1989.

Rosenthal, Joel T. *Old Age in Late Medieval England.* Philadelphia: University of Pennsylvania Press, 1996.

Russell, Josiah Cox. *British Medieval Population.* Albuquerque: University of New Mexico Press, 1948.

———. *The Control of Late Ancient and Medieval Population.* Philadelphia: American Philosophical Society, 1985.

Sears, Elizabeth. *The Ages of Man: Medieval Interpretations of the Life Cycle.* Princeton, N.J.: Princeton University Press, 1986.

Shahar, Shulamith. *Growing Old in the Middle Ages: "Winter Clothes Us in Shadow and Pain."* Translated by Yael Lotan. London and New York: Routledge, 1997.

Sheehan, Michael M., ed. *Aging and the Aged in Medieval Europe: Selected Papers from the Annual Conference of the Centre for Medieval Studies, University of Toronto, Held 25–26 February and 11–12 November 1983.* Toronto: Pontifical Institute of Mediaeval Studies, 1990.

Simmons, Leo W. *The Role of the Aged in Primitive Society.* 1945. Reprint, Hamden, Conn.: Archon Books, 1970.

Tristram, Philippa. *Figures of Life and Death in Medieval English Literature.* London: P. Elek, 1976.

JOEL T. ROSENTHAL

[See also **DMA:** Benedictine Rule; Innocent III, Pope; Nicholas of Cusa; Roland, Song of; **Supp:** Childbirth and Infancy; Childhood and Adolescence.]

OLDRADUS DE PONTE (*d.* after 1337). Oldradus de Ponte (his family name) or de Laude (Lodi), the name that he most often used when he signed documents, was a professor of law and advocate in the Roman curia in Avignon. He was born in Lodi and died sometime after 1337, probably in Avignon. Oldradus studied law at Bologna at the end of the thirteenth century. He was a layman (lay canonists were not unusual in the fourteenth century), married with three sons, one of whom became a jurist. He entered the entourage of Cardinal Pietro Colonna for a short time in 1297 and later taught law at the University of Padua until around 1310. Oldradus left Padua for Avignon, where he served as an auditor and judge in the Rota (papal judicial court). He may have also taught in the Avignon court's law school. From the evidence of his *consilia* (legal briefs), Oldradus was the most important jurist at the papal court from around 1311 until about 1337. He met Petrarch at Avignon, and the poet called him the most famous jurist of the age.

Oldradus wrote many minor works and a significant number of *consilia*. He composed *additiones* (supplementary comments) to Justinian's *Corpus iuris civilis* (to the *Code, Digest,* and *Institutes*) and to the *Liber feudorum*. Oldradus's importance lies in the several hundred *quaestiones* and *consilia* that he wrote during his career. He was one of the first jurists to write a large number of *consilia* on actual legal problems. He was also one of the first to collect and publish a collection of *quaestiones* and *consilia*. *Consilia* became one of the most important legal genres of the fourteenth and fifteenth centuries. His collection stands at the very beginning of "the age of *consilia.*"

It is important to distinguish between *quaestiones (disputatae)* and *consilia*. The jurists had composed *quaestiones* since the twelfth century. Their origins lay in the classroom. A problem would be posed, and a jurist would then propose a solution to it. Professors would hold special classes in which these "disputed questions" would be debated. In the early thirteenth century, judges or litigants began to request legal opinions from jurists. These briefs were called *consilia*. When Oldradus worked the two genres had not yet separated. Some *consilia* were turned into *quaestiones,* and some *quaestiones* looked very much like *consilia*. During the fourteenth century jurists began to write *consilia* for two reasons: judges and litigants turned to jurists for legal opinions as a part of the legal process, and jurists were paid very well for them.

Oldradus wrote *consilia* on some very important political questions, and they were cited for centuries by other jurists. When the Holy Roman Emperor Henry VI condemned the king of Sicily, Robert of Naples, for treason, Oldradus wrote two *consilia* defending Robert, who was a vassal of the pope. Some of the key points that Oldradus made in these *consilia* were later incorporated into Pope Clement V's legislation dealing with the emperor's jurisdiction. Oldradus's *consilia* also touched upon many other legal issues: the legal status of infidels, Jews, and Moslems, as well as issues of church governance and private law. Oldradus's collection of *consilia* as found in the manuscripts differs considerably from what is found in most printed editions of the late fifteenth and sixteenth centuries. Three different redactions of his *consilia* collection can be found in the manuscripts. One tradition contains 220 *consilia,* and another 264. Other manuscripts have his *consilia* arranged in various ways. No manuscript contains the redaction of 333 *consilia* that printers published for the first time in Rome in 1478 and that became the standard edition of his work in every later printing. Since they are not contained in any manuscript, *consilia* 265 to 333 in this edition must be treated with caution, as they may not be Oldradus's work.

BIBLIOGRAPHY

PRIMARY WORKS

Oldradus de Ponte. *Jews and Saracens in the Consilia of Oldradus de Ponte.* Edited and translated by Norman Zacour. Toronto: Pontifical Institute of Mediaeval Studies, 1990.

SECONDARY WORKS

McManus, Brendan. "The Consilia and Quaestiones of Oldradus de Ponte." *Bulletin of Medieval Canon Law* 23 (1999): 85–113.

Migliorino, Francesco. "Alchimia lecita e illecita nel trecento: Oldrado da Ponte." *Quaderni Medievali* 11 (1981): 6–41.

Schmidt, Tilmann. "Die Konsilien des Oldrado da Ponte als Geschichtsquelle." *Consilia im späten Mittelalter: Zum historischen Aussagewert einer Quellengattung* (1995): 53–64.

Will, Eduard. *Die Gutachten des Oldradus de Ponte zum Prozess Heinrichs VII. gegen Robert von Neapel: Nebst der Biographie des Oldradus.* Abhandlungen zur mittleren und neueren Geschichte 65. Berlin and Leipzig: Rothschild, 1917.

KENNETH PENNINGTON

[See also **DMA:** Law, Canon: After Gratian; Law, Canon: To Gratian; Law Codes: 1000–1500.]

OLEŚNICKI, ZBIGNIEW (1389–1455), bishop of Kraków, cardinal, and statesman. A descendant of the Dębno family of Little Poland, Oleśnicki studied at the University of Kraków. Following his studies, he worked in the royal chancellery for twelve years, where he exerted great influence with the king, Władysław II Jagiełło, who had only converted to Christianity in 1386. It was reported that during the battle at Grunwald in 1410, Oleśnicki saved the king's life. From 1420, Oleśnicki held the benefice of the Church of St. Florian in Kraków. That same year, he participated in negotiations with Sigismund of Luxembourg on the continuing territorial battles between the Poles and the Teutonic Orders, which neither the Peace of Toruń nor the Council of Constance had been able to resolve.

In 1423, Oleśnicki was appointed to the episcopal see in Kraków. In this capacity, he played a significant role in state affairs. Oleśnicki was head of a royal council that ruled during the minority of King Władysław III (1434–1444), who was elected king of Poland at the age of ten. The Polish bishop also helped arrange Władysław's acquisition of the Hungarian crown, thereby enabling the Polish royal council to rule in the young king's absence. Oleśnicki's opponents played on Hussite arguments in trying to liberate the Polish royal court from the influence of the episcopal curia, but Oleśnicki was largely successful at maintaining his influence with the king.

After the death of King Władysław III in 1444, Oleśnicki promoted the candidacy of Władysław's brother, Casimir Jagiellończyk (the Jagiellonian). After Casimir's election (as Casimir IV) in 1447, however, Oleśnicki found that working with the new king was much more difficult than he had expected. Indeed, the new king restricted the powers of the bishop and his supporters among the nobles, who had held such sway under the reign of the previous two kings. Despite these restrictions, Oleśnicki continued to exert some power, and whenever the new king was absent in Lithuania, where he ruled as grand duke, the bishop ruled with the help of the royal council.

In 1439 Pope Eugenius IV nominated Oleśnicki to the cardinalate, but because of his conciliarist views, the Polish churchman did not accept the nomination. By 1447, however, Oleśnicki and a group of Polish conciliarists had decided to approve of the pope (who was then Nicholas V), and in 1449 the pope made Oleśnicki a cardinal.

There is no question but that Oleśnicki had his share of enemies, who frequently accused him of nepotism. From almost a dozen fifteenth-century accounts of the bishop's career, however, including one by the Italian humanist Phillip Buonaccorsi, who spent twenty-five years serving the Polish monarchy, it is clear that Oleśnicki did much to augment the temporalities of the bishopric, improve the discipline of the Polish clergy, and promote the cult of national saints. During his thirty-two years as bishop, Oleśnicki oversaw the building of many churches, hospitals, and castles. He also lent significant support to the development of the Kraków university, where he had studied as a young man. He built up an impressive library of his own, as well. Moreover, it was largely due to Oleśnicki's encouragement that Jan Długosz, a canon of the Kraków cathedral, became the greatest medieval Polish historian.

BIBLIOGRAPHY

Buonaccorsi, Filippo. *Vita et mores Sbignei cardinalis.* Edited by Irmina Lichońska. Warsaw: Państwowe Wydawnictwo Naukowe, 1962. Buonaccorsi's portrait of Oleśnicki.

Walczak, Marek. "Działalność Fundacyjna Biskupa Krakówskiego, Kardynała Zbigniewa Oleśnickiego." *Folia Historiae Artium* 28 (1992): 57–73; 30 (1994): 63–85. A study of Oleśnicki's patronage of art and architecture.

Wünsch, Thomas. "'Ne pestifera doctrina corrumpat gregem dominicum': Zur Konfrontation zwischen Wyclifismus und Konziliarismus im Umkreis der Universität Krakau in der ersten Hälfte des 15. Jahrhunderts." *Zeitschrift für Ostmitteleuropa Forschung* 44, no. 1 (1995): 5–26.

ADAM JEFFREY DAVIS

[See also **DMA:** Jagiełło Dynasty; Poland; **Supp:** Casimir the Jagiellonian of Poland, King.]

ORIGINAL SIN. The medieval debate over original sin traces back to an incorrect translation of Scripture, a heated controversy that ended with the triumph of a minority view and centuries of subsequent attempts to make sense of the outcome. The position developed by Augustine of Hippo, according to which humans inherited the guilt of original sin through the lust that accompanied their parents' sexual intercourse, maintained adherents throughout the Middle Ages and later influenced Martin Luther and John Calvin. There was a range of alternative interpretations, and one associated with Thomas Aquinas prevailed within Roman Catholic doctrine at the Council of Trent (1545–1563). In the Eastern church, theologians had long ago backed away from the Augustinian position they officially shared with the Latins. Meanwhile, the concept of original sin was all but absent within Judaism and Islam.

INTERPRETATIONS OF THE FALL

To most ancient and medieval commentators on Genesis, the experience of Adam and Eve in the Garden of Eden demonstrated a sobering fact about humanity, that "every inclination of his heart is evil from childhood" (Gen. 8:21). From earliest history, human beings were weak, and their weakness compelled Adam and Eve to violate the will of God. As a result, they and all humans after them suffered disease, mortality, and—worst of all—the propensity to sin again. In rabbinical literature, the source of this moral weakness was none other than God, and it was one of the rare acts God regretted. According to most medieval Jewish theologians, however, although humans were weak like Adam and Eve and suffered disease and death like them, the connection ended there. After God made a covenant with Moses, the people of Israel were free even from the lust to which Adam and Eve had succumbed. Children were born without sin and remained in that state until, as adults, their weakness impelled them toward sins of their own. Muslim theologians, too, affirmed that Adam and Eve's failure inflicted mortality on the human race but that people entered the world without inherent guilt or the need for absolution. Moreover, they did not consider actions that resulted from moral weakness to be anywhere near as offensive to God as willful acts of transgression: the original offense was not even a sin in the gravest sense. It remained for other commentators to identify humanity's direct implication in the Fall.

GREEK THEOLOGY

By the end of the fourth century, generations of Christian authorities had shown little consensus on the nature and effects of original sin. In fact, the earliest writers demonstrated scant interest in the matter. Greek and Latin theologians alike had usually interpreted the small number of relevant scriptural passages as evidence that people shared in Adam and Eve's punishment but not in their offense. Part of this unfortunate inheritance included the same weakness that confounded the first humans, and this weakness continued to result in sinful behavior. Some theologians, such as Irenaeus of Lyon in the second century, emphasized humanity's distance from divine grace since the Fall, a spiritual isolation they mapped in opposition to contemporary, dualist notions of sin. For the most part, however, disagreements over original sin were matters of degree: despite their implication in the trespass of Adam and Eve and their need for divine grace to gain salvation, all humans remained capable of taking the first step toward meriting that grace. The question was the extent to which humans were debilitated and thus how difficult that initial voluntary step would be. As for guilt, each person's sin was his or her own, including Adam and Eve's. Every sin was a result of a voluntary exercise, a product of free will. Most East-

ern theologians, furthermore, rejected any suggestion that infants were born tainted with sin and in need of absolution, as some Western theologians contended, most notably among them Tertullian and Cyprian of Carthage in the third century. Although from the fifth century onward the medieval Greek church tacitly accepted the Western doctrine of original sin, most of its theologians maintained that humans were capable of cooperating with the divine gift of grace in their own progress toward salvation.

PELAGIANISM

The key text for the Christian doctrine of original sin was Paul's letter to the Romans, where he described how sin entered the world through Adam (Rom. 5:12). In the original Greek, the crucial phrase in this passage reads literally, "death came to all humans because [*eph hô*] all sinned." In the Latin translation some theologians used, the same text was rendered, "death came to all humans in whom [*in quo*—that is, in Adam] all humans sinned." This unlikely reading implicated all humanity in the actual, historical commission of Adam's sin. Theologians also faced the logical problem of how guilt was transmitted generation to generation. By the end of the fourth century, "traducianism" was condemned: most condemned the view that parents "handed on" (Latin *tradere*) their corruption into the soul of their offspring because it diminished the soul's spiritual nature and God's exclusive role as creator. Instead, God created each soul fresh at the first moment of a human's existence; the affiliation of that brand new soul with the ancient guilt of original sin was mysterious and inexplicable but nonetheless real. Despite the questions it left unanswered, this explanation satisfied many theologians. For others, it did not move far enough away from traducianism.

Pelagius, a Briton famous at Rome in the fourth and early fifth centuries for his piety, denied that humans were in any way corrupt at birth or incapable of good works. Instead, he contended that humans were completely responsible for their own sins or merits and could attribute neither their salvation nor their failure to anyone but themselves, not even to divine grace. Pelagius won support despite formidable opponents, yet his insistence on the soul's purity—effectively a denial of original sin—ran counter to the inclinations of most theologians. Moreover, it opened a debate over the role of grace toward which his contemporary Augustine of Hippo directed the full force of his argumentative ability and political clout. Pelagius's views were condemned in two North African councils and by Pope Innocent I between the years 416 and 418 and again at Ephesus in 431.

Some Latin theologians, for more than a century afterward, argued that humans retained the capacity for good works, at least enough to make the first step toward meriting further grace. These views, which later ecclesiastical historians would categorize as semi-Pelagianism, were closest to those maintained among most Eastern theologians. Nevertheless, they were condemned in 529 by a council at Orange, which reiterated the judgment against Pelagius.

AUGUSTINE

During the wide-flung debates that framed the first condemnations of Pelagianism, Augustine of Hippo sharpened both his rhetoric and his philosophy, ultimately honing the edge on a precise doctrine of original sin. Even before those debates, Augustine emphasized the sinfulness of humans rather their capacity for good. He was certain that humans were incapable of attaining salvation on their own, but his written debates with Pelagius and the formidable Julian of Eclanum clarified for him—and all subsequent Latin theologians—what exactly was at stake in the question of original sin. Although God created each soul at the beginning of a human's existence, the parents' concupiscence—the lust accompanying their sexual intercourse—physically transmitted original sin at the moment of conception. The precise mechanics of this formative process remained obscure and provided an attractive target for Augustine's critics. But its consequences were perfectly lucid. In Augustine's memorable phrase, humans were born as "one lump of sin" *(una massa peccati)* without redeeming qualities. While many Christians viewed baptism as the positive infusion of grace, Augustine stressed its remedial function: to cleanse the stain of original sin. Even then, humans remained so far removed from divine justice that they had no hope of meriting its mercy. Augustine was directly opposed to Pelagian prospects for human potential. Grace accomplished everything, human will nothing. He also opposed all compromises, which included traditional views of original sin most of his contemporaries accepted. Original sin was all-consuming. Grace was never awarded on the basis of merit. There were no small steps toward salvation, only the gift of grace or its absence. Those people received grace whom God willed. By implication, those who were no more or less a lump of sin but did not receive grace were doomed from their conception. These included unbaptized infants, although Augustine suggested that their torments would be less severe than those who had sinned after baptism. According to Augustine original sin alone was sufficient to result in eternal separation from God.

SCHOLASTICS

Augustine's reputation all but sanctioned a doctrine of original sin that was a minority view in its own day and for centuries afterward, as subsequent conflicts revealed. Among the corollaries of Augustine's position on original sin, the condemnation of unbaptized infants was the most troubling on an emotional level. Predestination, meanwhile, upset people on a theological level; in Francia in the ninth century it pitched Hincmar of Rheims and John Scottus Eriugena against Gottschalk of Orbais. According to a strict Augustinian like Gottschalk, original sin completely undid human beings and their potential for salvation. God bestowed grace on those whom he mysteriously elected, singling them out for eternal life and condemning all others to damnation. Any notion of free will that suggested humans could choose whether or not to attain salvation diminished the importance of grace, the omnipotence of God, and the true extent of human depravity. Against this bleak anthropology, Hincmar and Eriugena struggled to give room for voluntary behavior within the narrow confines of Augustine's logic. They contended that God moved outside of time, knew what people would do, and predestined the consequences for their actions, but not their actions. After a series of conflicting councils, there was no meaningful resolution.

When debates over original sin resurfaced in the twelfth and thirteenth centuries, the issues and poles of contention were essentially the same even if the vocabulary changed. Anselm of Canterbury focused on the transmission of original sin, denying the role of concupiscence and instead positing universal generation within Adam. If some later theologians such as Albertus Magnus shared his discomfort over concupiscence, others like Peter Lombard adhered closely to Augustine's explanation. In many ways, Thomas Aquinas also followed Augustine in his stance on original sin. Like Gottschalk, Aquinas contended that God bestowed grace on people selected according to divine will, not because God knew they would prove themselves worthy of grace by their merits. Without grace, as Augustine had concluded, humans were hopelessly depraved. Aquinas also believed, however, that all humans including Adam and Eve retained a pure nature upon which grace worked in order to attain salvation—they were not only lumps of sin. Original sin bound humanity together at a distance from the joy of divine grace, and Christians must conduct their lives without the guarantee of ever achieving that joy. On the other hand, Aquinas denied that original sin alone condemned those who did not enjoy the gifts of grace to suffer eternal punishment. Infants, for example, who died with the taint of original sin would never know divine joy, but they would also not be able to comprehend or even perceive their loss—one of the rare proposals made earlier by Peter Abelard that the council of Sens had not condemned in 1140. The pure nature of unbaptized infants, therefore, would enjoy the happiest existence possible outside of God's presence. Not all theologians agreed with every aspect of Aquinas's reasoning on original sin, but his relative optimism appealed to many Christians over the bleak prospects of Augustinianism. Against promoters of the latter tendency, particularly Martin Luther and John Calvin in the sixteenth century, Dominic Soto supported the views of Aquinas, tempered with a notion of generation similar to that which Anselm had proposed. This was the doctrine that the Roman Catholic church promulgated at the fifth session of the Council of Trent in 1546.

BIBLIOGRAPHY

Bonner, Gerald. *Church and Faith in the Patristic Tradition.* Brookfield, Vt.: Variorum, 1996. On the development and impact of the Pelagian controversy.

Ferguson, Everett, ed. *Doctrines of Human Nature, Sin, and Salvation in the Early Church.* New York and London: Garland, 1993.

Gaudel, A., and M. Jugie. "Péché originel." In *Dictionnaire de théologie catholique.* Edited by A. Vacant and E. Mangenot. Vol. 12. Paris: Letouzey et Ané, 1933. An excellent and detailed presentation.

Gross, Julius. *Geschichte des Erbsündendogmas.* 4 vols. Munich: Reinhardt, 1960–1972. The standard work.

Köster, Heinrich. *Urstand, Fall und Erbsünde in der Scholastik.* Freiburg, Germany: Herder, 1979.

Rondet, Henri. *Original Sin: The Patristic and Theological Background.* Translated by Gajetan Finegan. Shannon, Ireland: Ecclesia Press, 1972. Particularly strong on theological traditions before Augustine but also covers later developments and topical issues.

Weaver, David. "The Exegesis of Romans 5:12 among the Greek Fathers and Its Implications for the Doctrine of Original Sin: The Fifth to Twelfth Centuries." *St. Vladimir's Theological Quarterly* 29 (1985): 133–159, 231–257.

KEVIN UHALDE

[See also **DMA:** Anselm of Canterbury, St.; Aquinas, St. Thomas; Augustine of Hippo, St.; Baptism; Gottschalk of Orbais; Hincmar of Rheims; John Scottus Eriugena; Pelagius; **Supp:** Fall, The.]

ORIGINALITY IN ARTS AND LETTERS.

In the nineteenth and much of the twentieth century, a preeminent theme in histories of medieval culture, particularly of the early Middle Ages but to some extent the later period, was that writers, artists, and artisans of this epoch

Hrabanus Maurus before the Cross. This miniature from In honorem sanctae crucis *is a fine example of the medieval willingness to combine an expression of humility with a "signature" announcing the producer's pride in his work.* ÖSTERREICHISCHE NATIONALBIBLIOTHEK, VIENNA, MS 652, FOL. 33V. REPRODUCED BY PERMISSION.

were principally motivated by a desire to preserve more ancient traditions and achievements. The culture's character was largely defined by reference to features that seemed to link it to the past: images, architecture, and letters evoking older styles and forms, incorporating older materials, or echoing older expressions of thought; texts announcing the writers' intention to record the teachings of earlier authorities or mainly consisting of abbreviations of, paraphrases of, or excerpts from those sources; commentaries on the same authorities; and innumerable manuscript copies of older writings, sometimes with their illustrations.

In particular, scholarly attention centered on the seemingly episodic ebb and flow of medieval interest in Greco-Roman antiquity, most notably the Christian Roman Empire. The classical Mediterranean provided the criteria by which historians often assessed medieval productions, and preference was for study of regions and periods before the Italian Renaissance that they held to have experienced "renaissances" because of the classicizing literary, artistic, and architectural works extant from them, above all the ninth-century Carolingian territories (France, western Germany, northern Italy) and twelfth-century western Europe. Generally speaking, two related concerns were to map out the "descent" of traditions and to search for archetypes and sources, especially antique, many no longer surviving but implicitly viewed as of superior quality and greater originality than the medieval objects at hand. Artistic images, especially from the early Middle Ages, were treated as windows into older eras and tools for reconstructing lost models. The language of medieval Latin writings was evaluated according to classical rules of grammar, style, and orthography. Medieval authors, especially of the earlier centuries, were regarded as chiefly passive mediators of classical and patristic learning, their success determined by how accurately they seemed to transmit that material; discussions of hagiography (saints' lives) stressed the commonalities of structure linking these texts with one another, traceable back to the earliest Christian lives and the Bible. With writings as with visual productions, adherence to precedent was typically deemed the norm, and departures were frequently dismissed as the consequence of misunderstanding, inadequate materials or skills, or other circumstances interfering with fidelity to the presumed exemplar.

This outlook has roots in the Renaissance concept of medieval Europe as dominated by a unified intellectual elite espousing a shared set of doctrines and a supposedly profound otherworldliness. The inclination toward the spiritual and eternal over the temporal, it was believed, meant a lack of interest in individual distinction or earthly accomplishment. In the last two decades of the twentieth century, however, a growing volume of scholarship focused on the considerable evidence of cultural diversity, experimentation, and innovation in the early as well as later Middle Ages. The impetus has partly come from new research concerning the margins of medieval Europe, primarily the central and eastern territories; also significant are materials recently made available through archaeological excavations, archival searches, and new editions and facsimiles. In other cases, though, attention is directed to writings, art, and architecture known beforehand but never examined from this perspective or, sometimes, never carefully examined at all because they were thought to be of little scholarly interest. A telling example is the treatise *In honorem sanctae crucis* (In honor of the holy cross) written by the Carolingian theologian Hrabanus Maurus in 813/814; the work's main component is twenty-eight of the most sophisticated *carmina figurata* (poetry integrated with decorative forms) surviving in Western literature. The genre already existed in antiquity, yet no classical author produced figure poems approaching the complexity of Hrabanus's or as thematically unified a collection of them.

THE ROLE OF THE SCRIBE

IN THE ACT OF COPYING A TEXT, THE SCRIBE SUPPLANTS THE ORIGINAL POET, OFTEN CHANGING WORDS OR NARRATIVE ORDER, SUPPRESSING OR SHORTENING SOME SECTIONS, WHILE INTERPOLATing new material in others. As with the visual interpolations, the scribal reworkings may be the result of changing aesthetic tastes in the period between the original text production and the copying. Even in such cases, however, the scribe's "improvements" imply a sense of superior judgment or understanding vis-à-vis the original poet. . . .If we accept the multiple forms in which our artifacts have been transmitted, we may recognize that medieval culture did not simply live with diversity, it cultivated it.

SOURCE: Nichols, Stephen. "Introduction: Philology in a Manuscript Culture." *Speculum* 65 (1990), pp. 8–9.

Nevertheless, the nineteenth-century scholar Ernst Dümmler omitted the treatise from his edition of Carolingian poetry because he considered it too tedious, and for decades thereafter it sank virtually into oblivion. Recent analyses have reversed Dümmler's judgment, stressing Rabanus's unique skill and creativity, the influence of ninth-century intellectual and literary concerns on his work, and the admiration it gained from later writers, including possibly Dante.

Other new studies of medieval culture, too, are sensitive to the continuities with previous traditions and recognize that differences between a medieval "copy" and its "prototype" are often the result of accidental errors, yet they demonstrate greater interest in how certain writers, artists, and artisans seem to have deliberately broken with their cultural heritage. There is more reluctance now to take at face value medieval claims of humility; even early medieval artists recorded their names more frequently than used to be realized, in inscriptions implying pride in their creations and a conviction they were new and exciting. Since the last decades of the twentieth century, historians have been more likely to treat these and other medieval productions as autonomous works shedding light on and elucidated by contemporary contexts of production. Correspondingly, the concern with identifying models and defining some peri-

ORIGINALITY ROOTED IN TRADITION

THE EARLY MEDIEVAL ARTISTIC TRADITION NOT ONLY RECEIVES AND TRANSFORMS, IT LITERALLY INVENTS A TRADITION UPON WHICH IT FOUNDS ITSELF. UNLIKE TODAY, WHEN THE MOST hackneyed images and conceptions are commonly presented as novel or "original," in the early Middle Ages, the most novel and original images and conceptions were often presented as if continuing an ancient tradition.

SOURCE: Nees, Lawrence. *Early Medieval Art*. Oxford History of Art. Oxford: Oxford University Press, 2002, p. 15.

ods as renaissances has declined, both for this reason and because of increased understanding of the complexity of the interpenetration of barbarian with classical influences under the Roman Empire and in subsequent centuries. The issue of what constitutes classicizing traits in medieval arts and letters and their relation to other features is known to be more problematic than previously thought; at no point in the Middle Ages was there a universal consensus on which aspects of the antique were compatible with Christian values or on a single mode of its reception. Even where debts to older influences, classical or other, are detected in medieval works, modern scholarship reveals a new interest in ways that those borrowings, sometimes from multiple sources, may have been selected, organized, adapted, and otherwise transformed into expressions of the medieval producers' own identities. Indeed, historians now appreciate better how much medieval authors, artists, and artisans were responsible for forming the "traditions" they passed on to subsequent generations.

Stephen Nichols has remarked that the manuscript culture of the Middle Ages allowed for a degree of diversity and change far exceeding anything possible with print. Each manuscript is effectively an original deserving study as such, whether or not it is the copy of an earlier document, since the copyist had the ability to choose to reformat, emend, add to, or subtract from text or decoration. This observation can be extended to other facets of medieval textual and visual production. Insofar as there was no perfect copy before the discovery of print,

every medieval creation testifies to a culture in which originality was a fundamental, defining characteristic.

BIBLIOGRAPHY

Aers, David. "Rewriting the Middle Ages: Some Suggestions." *Journal of Medieval and Renaissance Studies* 18 (1988): 221–240

Brenk, Beat. "Originalità e innovazione nell'arte medievale." In *Arti e storia nel Medioevo*. Edited by Enrico Castelnuovo and Giuseppe Sergi. Volume 1: *Tempi spazi istituzione*. Turin, Italy: Giulio Einaudi, 2002.

Chazelle, Celia M., ed. *Literacy, Politics, and Artistic Innovation in the Early Medieval West*. Lanham, Md.: University Press of America, 1992.

Ferrari, Michele Camillo. Il *"Liber sanctae crucis" di Rabano Mauro: Testo, immagine, contesto*. Bern: Peter Lang, 1999.

Nees, Lawrence, ed. "Approaches to Early Medieval Art." *Speculum* 72 (1997). A special issue on new methodologies.

New Cambridge Medieval History. Cambridge, U.K.: Cambridge University Press, 1995–. Each volume contains survey articles outlining recent trends in the study of medieval arts and letters, with bibliographies.

Nichols, Stephen. "The New Philology." *Speculum* 65 (1990). A special issue of the journal offering an overview of new research in the field.

CELIA CHAZELLE

[See also **DMA:** Hrabanus Maurus.]

ORSINI FAMILY. Among the most powerful Roman aristocratic families, the Orsini were, with rare exemption, Guelphs; that is, supporters of the papacy in its struggles with the empire. Throughout the High Middle Ages and Renaissance, the Orsini supplied the papacy with a steady stream of administrators, soldiers, bishops, and cardinals; they even furnished the church with two medieval popes (Celestine III and Nicholas III) and an eighteenth-century pope (Benedict XIII).

The Orsini, together with their inveterate enemies, the Colonna family, have been held responsible for the ruin of medieval Rome through feuding, pillaging, and constant warfare. The feuding and the devastation it caused have been overestimated. The Orsini and Colonna intermarried and often cooperated in ruling both the city and the church. The Orsini were lords of Mugnano, Marino, Monterotundo, Galeria, Castel Sant'Angelo, and Licenza, and by the early Renaissance, branches of the family held the titles of count of Nola, Pitigliano, Soana, and Manopello, as well as duke of Bracciano and Gravina. In Rome itself the Orsini controlled the fortified Theater of Pompey, Monte Giordano, and the area around the Campo dei Fiori.

The Orsini first gained significant power in Rome at the end of the twelfth century through the support of Giacinto Bobone, who became Pope Celestine III. He established his nephew, Orso di Bobone, as an influential magnate in the city, but it was Orso's grandson Matteo Rosso Orsini who established the family as one of the most powerful in Rome. Gregory IX made him sole senator in 1241 so that he might defend Rome against the emperor Frederick II of Germany, and he was responsible for the disastrous conclave following the death of Gregory IX; he locked the cardinals in the Septizonium palace and denied them food or water until they elected a pope. At least one cardinal died, and the Sacred College was understandably reluctant to hold papal elections in the city after that. His three sons inherited his power. One son, Giovanni Gaetano, became Pope Nicholas III, while another, Napoleone, served as senator; a third, Giordano, was a cardinal.

Nicholas III attempted to consolidate the hold of the Roman aristocracy over Rome and the papacy itself. He limited the term in office of the senator (a political institution that fluctuated from having more than fifty members to being the single ruler of the city) to one year and ruled that only native Romans could hold it, thus preventing foreign princes such as Charles I of Anjou from gaining official power in the city and assuring that Roman families such as the Orsini would dominate the city. Nicholas created the title count of Romagna for his nephew Bertoldo Orsini and established other Orsini in prominent civil and ecclesiastical positions. But his patronage did not benefit the Orsini alone; he made one of his Colonna cousins cardinal and another one senator. After Nicholas's death in 1280, other Orsini continued to oppose foreign influence in Rome. His brother, Cardinal Giordano, and his nephew Matteo Rosso (son of Rainaldo, cardinal under Urban IV in 1262), opposed the election of the Frenchman Simon de Brie as pope following the death of Nicholas III. The two Orsini cardinals were arrested, leaving the remaining cardinals to elect Simon as Martin IV, and Orsini power suffered a serious setback in consequence. The family was, however, among the supporters of the tempestuous Pope Boniface VIII and in league with him against the Colonna. Boniface gave much of the property he confiscated from the Colonna to the Orsini.

The death of Boniface VIII in 1303 engendered a split within the family. Cardinal Matteo Orsini supported the followers of Boniface, while his brother Cardinal Napoleone allied himself with the French opponents of Boniface, later supporting the imperial ambitions of Louis IV of Germany and the Franciscan Spirituals against Pope John XXII. When the French faction at the papal court secured the election of Clement V in 1305, the papacy abandoned Rome and retreated to Avignon under the protection of the French king, Philip IV. This effectively left Rome in the control of the local aristocracy, led by the Colonna. Several Orsini cardinals, such as Napoleone from 1306 to 1309 and Gian Gaetano from 1326 to 1334, were sent to the Papal States from Avignon to maintain papal authority there but were unsuccessful. Gian Gaetano placed the city under interdict in 1328 after the crowning of Louis IV the Bavarian by Senator Sciarra Colonna in the name of the Roman people on 17 January but subsequently accepted the people's oath of allegiance to the papacy following the entry of the armies of Robert of Anjou into Rome. The brief populist government of Cola di Rienzo in 1347 united the Orsini and Colonna against his campaign against aristocratic power, and the two families subsequently shared power in the city for some years, but by 1377 they were again at odds.

The Orsini remained closely linked to the papacy through the late fifteenth and early sixteenth centuries, being particularly favored by Sixtus IV, Innocent VIII, and Leo X, but suffered at the hands of Alexander VI's illegitimate son Cesare Borgia, who had three Orsini killed. Perhaps the family's final moment of papal loyalty came when Lorenzo Orsini valiantly defended Rome, though unsuccessfully, against Holy Roman Emperor Charles V in 1527 at the request of Clement VII. The independent power of the Roman aristocracy, including the Orsini, faded as the Renaissance popes consolidated their rule over Rome, but the Orsini did later supply another pope, Benedict XIII, and the family continued to be prominent both within the church and in secular government to the present day.

BIBLIOGRAPHY

Allegrezza, Franca. *Organizzazione del potere e dinamiche familiari: Gli Orsini dal Duecento agli inizi del Quattrocento*. Rome: Istituto storico italiano per il Medioevo, 1998.

Bretano, Robert. *Rome before Avignon: A Social History of Thirteenth-Century Rome*. New York: Basic Books, 1974.

Celenza, Christopher S. "The Will of Cardinal Giordano Orsini (ob. 1438)." *Traditio* 51 (1996): 257–286.

Morghen, Rafaello. *Tradizione religiosa nella civiltà dell'Occidente cristiano: Saggi di storia e di storiografia*. Rome: Istituto storico italiano per il medioevo, 1979. See especially pages 109–142 on Matteo Rosso Orsini.

Shaw, Christine. "Alexander VI, Cesare Borgia, and the Orsini." *European Studies Review* 11 (1981): 1–23.

CHRISTOPHER HATCH MACEVITT

[See also **DMA:** Boniface VIII, Pope; Cola di Rienzo; Guelphs and Ghibellines; Papal States; Rome; **Supp:** Colonna Family; Louis IV the Bavarian, King; Nicholas III, Pope.]

OTTO II OF GERMANY, EMPEROR

(*r.* 973–983). The son of Otto I, Otto II was made co-emperor in 967, the last German ruler to be crowned by the pope while his father still lived. Although Otto II pursued many of the same policies that had worked so well for Otto I, his reign as emperor was beset by crises exacerbated if not precipitated by his unbridled and expensive military ambitions in Italy.

Otto I did as much as he could to secure the succession and subsequent reign of his son. Otto II's marriage in 972 to Theophano, the niece of the Byzantine ruler John I Tzimiskes, was the product of prolonged diplomatic efforts by Otto I with the goal of finally garnering Byzantine recognition of the Ottonian imperial dynasty. Theophano became a trusted adviser to her husband, contributing frequently to his *diplomata,* and not only influenced his imperial aspirations but afterward ruled as regent during their son Otto III's minority.

Otto II continued the Ottonian policy of using control over the church to keep the German magnates in line, granting the church immunities and relying on ecclesiastics as advisers. He was less successful in sustaining his father's hold over the duchies, with problems in Bavaria and Lorraine in particular. For years Otto fought his cantankerous cousin, Henry the Wrangler, the duke of Bavaria, who started a rebellion that came to include Lorraine, Swabia, Bohemia, and Poland. In 976 Otto separated Carinthia from Bavaria and made it into another duchy and granted Bavaria to his nephew Otto of Swabia. The west Frankish ruler Lothar's attempt to recover Lorraine ended in a stalemate, and Otto II and Lothar signed a treaty in 980.

Otto's domestic accomplishments thus were mixed, but his foreign endeavors were disastrous. He seemed at first to be simply continuing his father's Italian policies when he set forth to help the pope in 980. He then detoured into the south, however, and tried to claim Byzantine holdings for the imperial crown under the guise of defending them against Muslim attack. This plan went horribly awry on 15 July 982, when Muslims devastated Otto's forces at Cape Colonne, and Otto barely escaped on a passing Greek ship.

When news of this catastrophic defeat traveled east of the Elbe River, the Redarii, Ljutizi, and Wilzi tribes joined with the Abodrites to throw off the imperial yoke. The Slavs destroyed Brandenburg, Zeitz, and Havelburg and burned Hamburg. All the gains of previous Ottonian rulers east of the Elbe were lost, except for the area near Denmark, and would remain so until the colonization of the twelfth century.

Just months before the disaster at Cape Colonne an imperial diet at Verona had agreed to elect Otto II's three-year-old son king. In the same month that Otto died of malaria at the age of twenty-eight, Otto III was crowned king at Aachen. Although Otto II's ambitions had weakened the imperial position in Italy, some small part of them was fulfilled at his burial: he would be the only German emperor interred in Old St. Peter's.

BIBLIOGRAPHY

PRIMARY WORKS

Thietmar of Merseburg. *Die Chronik des Bischofs Thietmar von Merseburg und ihre Korveier Überarbeitung.* Edited by Robert Holtzmann. Monumenta Germaniae Historica, Scriptores rerum germanicarum, n.s., 9. Berlin: Weidmann, 1935.

SECONDARY WORKS

Arnold, Benjamin. *Medieval Germany 500–1300: A Political Interpretation.* Basingstoke, U.K.: Macmillan, 1997.

Fleckenstein, Josef. *Early Medieval Germany.* Translated by Bernard S. Smith. Amsterdam: North-Holland, 1978.

Leyser, Karl. *Medieval Germany and Its Neighbours 900–1250.* London: Hambledon, 1982.

———. *Communications and Power in Medieval Europe: The Carolingian and Ottonian Centuries.* Edited by Timothy Reuter. London and Rio Grande, Ohio: Hambledon, 1994.

Reuter, Timothy. *Germany in the Early Middle Ages, c. 800–1056.* London and New York: Longman, 1991.

ELSPETH JANE CARRUTHERS

[See also **DMA:** Otto I the Great, Emperor; Otto III, Emperor; Saxon Dynasty.]

OTTO IV OF GERMANY, EMPEROR

(1182–1218). The Hohenstaufen emperor Henry VI died in 1197, leaving one young heir, Frederick II. The subsequent disputed election and troubled reign of Otto IV inaugurated a pattern of external intervention in German politics that would continue for centuries. In an attempt to quell the agitations of anti-Hohenstaufen princes, Henry VI's brother Philip, duke of Swabia, was elected king in 1198. In response, the rebellious princes eventually selected Otto of Brunswick (younger son of Henry the Lion, the Welf former duke of Saxony and enemy of the Hohenstaufen) as their antiking. Otto was crowned in Aachen in July; Philip was crowned in September.

There was foreign involvement in the double election from the start: Richard I of England promoted and financed Otto, who had been raised in the English court and, as count of Poitou, was Richard's vassal. Pope Innocent III was also deeply interested. After the death of Henry VI's widow, Constance, in 1198, Innocent became guardian of Frederick II, the young Hohenstaufen heir to the German and Sicilian crowns. Overcoming initial military opposition from the imperial ministerial, Innocent ruled Sicily as regent.

Philip of Swabia had the backing of some German princes, but Otto's support was initially greater. Who would determine which claim was more legitimate? Innocent III took advantage of the confusion, asserting the supremacy of ecclesiastical over secular authority to an unprecedented degree. He eventually supported Otto IV in 1201, on the grounds that Otto would defend the interests of the church more vigorously than would Philip. But the collapse of English financing following the death of Richard I in 1199 and the subsequent decline in Plantagenet fortunes impelled Otto to recognize papal territorial acquisitions in Italy and to adapt imperial policy in France and Italy to suit Innocent.

But as Otto began to lose ground and his German supporters (including his brother) defected, Innocent began to rethink his position. He was on the verge of publicly endorsing Philip when the latter was murdered in a private feud, ending the immediate crisis in 1208. Otto further healed the rift by marrying Philip's daughter, and in 1209 he was crowned emperor.

Once emperor, however, Otto ignored his promises and embarked on an imperial program nearly identical to that of Henry VI, threatening Innocent's determination to keep Sicily separate from the empire. When Otto invaded Sicily in 1210, Innocent excommunicated him and with French support began to undermine his position in Germany by arranging the election of Frederick II. Otto returned to Germany at once, followed promptly by Frederick, who was elected king (again) in 1213 after making concessions to the papacy similar to those reneged on by Otto. Although Frederick had Capetian and Bohemian support, his territorial gains were slow, and the civil war ended only with the French king Philip Augustus's defeat of Otto IV's forces at Bouvines in 1214. Representatives from each side continued the dispute until the Fourth Lateran Council extinguished Otto's imperial ambitions. Thereafter Otto faded from prominence, although Frederick feared reprisal until Otto died excommunicated in 1218.

BIBLIOGRAPHY

Arnold, Benjamin. *Medieval Germany, 500–1300: A Political Interpretation.* Toronto: University of Toronto, 1997.

Barraclough, Geoffrey. *The Origins of Modern Germany.* New York: Paragon Books, 1979.

Hucker, Bernd Ulrich. *Kaiser Otto IV.* Hannover: Hahnsche, 1990.

Leuschner, Joachim. *Germany in the Late Middle Ages.* Translated by Sabine MacCormack. Amsterdam: North-Holland, 1980.

Winkelmann, E. "Philipp von Schwaben und Otto IV von Braunschweig," 1–2, *Jahrbuch der deutschen Geschichte.* 1873–1878. Reprint 1968.

ELSPETH JANE CARRUTHERS

[See also **DMA:** Hohenstaufen Dynasty; Holy Roman Empire; Innocent III, Pope; Richard I the Lionhearted.]

OTTOMAN ART AND ARCHITECTURE

OTTOMAN ART AND ARCHITECTURE. The history of Ottoman art is the history of the Ottoman Empire. The distinctive features of Ottoman art emerged during the formative phase of the state, and art became an imperial industry, reaching its zenith between the conquest of Constantinople and the late sixteenth century. It then witnessed a long decline, save for a brief renaissance in the first half of the eighteenth century. The material and aesthetic aspects of this art were directly influenced by court patronage.

ARCHITECTURE

From its beginnings in the centers of Iznik, Bursa, and Edirne, Ottoman architecture experimented with new forms, most notably the dome over a cubic space. In the large halls of the Friday Mosque *(Ulu Cami)* of Bursa (1396–1399) and the Old Mosque *(Eski Cami)* of Edirne (1402–1413), square bays are surmounted, for the first time, by hemispheric domes on pendentives and heavy pillars. This innovative use of a simple unit gave the archaic ground plan enhanced monumentality. In the absence of an open courtyard, the ablution is performed in one of the bays on the longitudinal axis, close to the entrance. An oculus in the dome above the ablution pool turns this bay into a covered courtyard.

A cubical space under a dome, a covered internal courtyard, and an entrance porch characterize another category of mosque, exemplified by the mosques of Bāyāzid I, Mehmed I, and Murad II. Such small mosques with attached complexes *(külliyye)* were an Ottoman innovation, closely connected with the sultans' policy of urban development, which drew in the traditional corporations and dervish orders. The mosque and its complex—including the founder's tomb *(turba)*, a school of Muslim law *(madrasa),* a public bath, a soup kitchen *('imaret),* and sometimes a caravanserai or hospital—became the nucleus of a new populated quarter.

The typical plan of such a mosque, which combines the traditions of Seljuk *madrasas* and dervish lodges *(zāwīya)* with those of multi-space Byzantine churches, resembles an inverted T. The entrance porch opens into small rooms on one or two floors reserved for the sultan and his retinue and leads to a central hall with an ablution pool under a high dome with an oculus. Surrounding the central hall, two *eyvāns* (halls with openings to the inner courtyard) and occasionally two side rooms with fireplaces were used for study, meditation, or hospitality. On the longitudinal axis, the central hall leads to a slightly raised prayer hall with a *miḥrāb* (a niche showing the direction of Mecca) at the far end. All the units are square and topped by domes. The mosques are usually of stone and incorporate a variety of reused Byzantine materials; the interiors are richly decorated with frescoes and ceramic tiles. The entire exterior of the Green *(Yesil)* Tomb in Bursa (1421) has a turquoise tile revetment. The other buildings of the mosque complex, following the Byzantine tradition, are constructed in alternative courses of stone and brick, with brick decoration.

Already before the conquest of Constantinople the Ottomans experimented with a big central dome over a larger prayer hall in the Mosque of Three Galleries *(Üç Şerefili)* in Edirne (1437–1447). Its open forecourt, surrounded by domed galleries, and the integrated placement of its minarets were innovations. Following the conquest, with the church of Hagia Sophia in close sight, the central domes grew larger and higher and covered a more unified internal space. This process started in the huge, strictly symmetrical complex of Mehmed II, the Conqueror, in the center of the new capital. The tall mosque (1470) is covered by a central dome, accompanied by a half-dome over the side of the *miḥrāb.* The two side aisles, enlarging the space, are under smaller domes. Twelve *madrasas* arranged in two blocks around the mosque reflect the growing importance of orthodox religious functionaries *('ulamā'),* who came to supplant the dervish orders.

The design of the central dome, a symbol of heaven and of the sultan, was subject to further experimentation, appearing as a single dome in the complex of Beyazid II in Edirne (1484–1488), as two half-domes in the mosque of Beyazid II in İstanbul (1501–1506), as three half-domes in the mosque of Mihrimāh in Üsküdar (1548), and as four half-domes in the mosque of Şehzade Mehmed (1545–1548). The two latter monuments were built by Sinān, the great Ottoman architect who, having

The Green Tomb. *Ceramic* miḥrāb *of the Green Tomb in Bursa (1421).* COURTESY RACHEL MILSTEIN. REPRODUCED BY PERMISSION.

served as a janissary, was appointed chief court architect of Süleyman the Magnificent in 1538. Sinān is responsible for 476 buildings: religious complexes with royal tombs, living quarters (such as the kitchens in the Topkapi palace), bathhouses (the *hammām* of Khasseki Khürem, wife of Süleyman), public and commercial institutions, and military works and bridges. He worked for three sultans (Süleyman, Selīm II, and Murad III); their families, including the women; and the highest echelons of the Ottoman administration. His plans were executed in many parts of the empire (e.g., the Süleymaniye complex in Damascus).

The elevations of Sinān's monuments show a rhythmic line descending from the dome to the façade without an apparent juncture. All the architectural elements, from the low-roofed forecourt through the arches of various heights, graded buttresses, domed counterweight towers, and series of domes of varying sizes and heights up to the central dome, follow a hierarchical ascent. The reduction of the vertical supports better integrates the space of the one large hall.

The classical features of Ottoman architecture are finely exemplified in the splendid mosque built by Sinān for Sultan Süleyman in 1550–1557. The longitudinal

Süleymaniye Complex in İstanbul (1550–1557). *The mosque complex* (külliye) *was a distinctively Ottoman contribution to the urban landscape.* PHOTOGRAPH BY ARA GÜLER. REPRODUCED BY PERMISSION.

hall, under a central dome and two half-domes, between two aisles, recalls the sixth-century Hagia Sophia, but the superstructure and aesthetics are very different. The central dome of the Süleymaniye is supported by four giant pillars and twelve buttresses. This system of support, completely hidden by balconies in the side façades, relieves the walls of the mass of the dome, enabling them to open in seven tiers of windows. Five small domes alternating in size top the side aisles, which are practically integrated into the central hall. With an open forecourt and a tomb garden in the back, the mosque is planned on a longitudinal axis, passing from the high ceremonial portal through the forecourt fountain, the sultan's lodge above the entrance, the *miḥrāb,* and the sultan's tomb to the small Koranic school at the other end. The octagonal mausoleum recalls, in plan and decorations, the Dome of the Rock in Jerusalem, where Sultan Süleyman carried out major reconstruction work.

Every detail in the mosque symbolizes the role of the sultan as caliph, protector of the holy places and orthodox Islam, and his place in a dynasty heir to the great civilizations of the world. Koranic calligraphy and the restrained ornamentation of expensive building materials,

colored glass windows, and ceramic tiles decorate the three-dimensional architectural forms. The mosque and its garden stand on a large artificial terrace, surrounded by an asymmetrical complex. The *madrasa*s, hospital and medical school, hospitality and service buildings, and rows of shops are built on staggered elevations so as not to obscure the pyramidal silhouette of the mosque. Of the four minarets in the corners of the courtyard the two adjoining the prayer hall are taller than the others, thus suggesting an undulating line from the *miḥrāb* wall to the main portal through which the sultan entered in ceremonial procession.

Sinān's greatest work is the Selīmiye mosque in Edirne (1569–1575), whose single dome rests on eight elegant pillars, placed close to the walls. The support system is hidden between the open balconies of the façades, and both the interior and the external silhouette of the mosque appear hemispheric. In the absence of a symmetrical axis, the protruding niche of the *miḥrāb* gives a sense of direction, and a tribune above a small fountain in the center of the hall corresponds in a vertical line to the peak of the dome. The flowers painted on the tribune, the floral Iznik ceramic tiles, and the floral-

The Selīmiye Mosque Complex in Edirne. *This late-16th-century design is the masterpiece of Sinān.* PHOTOGRAPH BY ARA GÜLER. REPRODUCED BY PERMISSION.

patterned communal prayer rugs turn this house of prayer into a paradisiacal garden. Four slender minarets at the outer corners of the hall create a transparent cubic frame around the dome and together with the eight encircling pointed counterweight towers seem to push the dome up.

Sinān's style endured into the seventeenth century. In the eighteenth century the increasing influence of European taste introduced baroque elements into the traditional forms, as exemplified in the mosques of Nuruosmaniye (completed in 1755) and Laleli (1759–1763). Outside İstanbul, from the fifteenth century onward, cosmopolitan styles were echoed throughout the empire, modified and reflected in nineteenth-century Ottoman palaces, the most important of which was the Dolmabahçe, where the royal court moved from the classical Topkapi *sarāy.*

The construction of the Topkapi palace, in the most beautiful and symbolically charged part of the city, close to Hagia Sophia and the royal Byzantine palace, began at the time of the Conqueror (mid-fifteenth century).

Further developed in the following centuries, mainly under Sultan Süleyman, the palace consists of pavilions in various styles, grouped in four consecutive courtyards according to function. Gates with symbolic names and meanings represent an ascending hierarchy from the public sphere of the town to the secluded, semi-sacred private court of the sultan. Besides functioning as a habitation for the sultan's household and as the administrative center of the empire, the palace was the major center of artistic production and consumption. Annexed to the court, workshops of all the known arts and crafts and the mint, armory, and architect's office provided for the material and aesthetic needs of the palace and the empire.

PAINTING

Sultan Mehmed II, who established the court workshops as part of the new state patronage of the arts, was interested in the Italian Renaissance. Italian painters worked in his court at the same time as Iranian artists. Painted and carved portraits of the sultan by the Italians encouraged experiments by local Ottoman painters, such

Mehmed II the Conqueror. *Portrait ca. 1475–1481. İstanbul, Topkapi Museum Library.* THE GRANGER COLLECTION, NEW YORK. REPRODUCED BY PERMISSION.

as the hybrid but striking portrait of the Conqueror, modeled in light and shade to create a feeling of volume and realistic facial features.

After the domination of the linear and lyrical Iranian style at the court of Selīm I, a new generation of native artists under Sultan Süleyman laid the foundations of distinctively Ottoman painting. Their realistic renderings of court life and state events were set against actual contemporary architecture. Towns and camps painted in a documentary style, based on careful observation, illustrate the account by Nasuh Matraqi of Sultan Süleyman's Iraqi campaign (1534). An image of İstanbul, showing major monuments and their urban setting, makes up the double frontispiece. Topographical painting also illustrated charts or maps of port cities and sailing books with harbor descriptions, such as those by Pīrī Re'is.

The main subject of fully developed Ottoman painting is the history of the sultans; written accounts are illustrated with accurately depicted accessions, receptions of ambassadors, and military enterprises. A first move in this direction, the *Süleymanname,* by the court historian ʿĀrif Čelebi (1558), presents the sultan as the scion of a long dynasty and the head of an imperial system. Characterized by a certain expressiveness in feature and gesture, the illustrations in the *Süleymanname* also reflect the hierarchical order of the state through tight, orderly groupings and the excessive size of the sultan's representation. The illustrations in later imperial histories, written for Selīm II and Murad III by the court historian Loqmān, use rigid lines and simple compositions, with little expressiveness or decoration. Besides administrative and diplomatic life and military campaigns, the miniatures depict architectural structures, such as the courtyards of the Topkapi palace, in a map-like perspective. The *Sūr-nāme,* the book of the celebration of the crown prince's circumcision (*ca.* 1582–1583), illustrates the social and economic life of İstanbul, depicting all the guilds of craftsmen and stage-artists who exhibited their skills in a public parade at the hippodrome.

In addition to the portrayals of the sultans and eminent personalities in the historical illustrations, an independent series of dynastic portraits is seen in Loqmān's *Shemāʾil-nāme* (Book of descriptions, 1579). This work was followed by the monumental *Hüner-nāme* (Book of accomplishments, 1584–1588) and other series, notably the *Silsilnâme* (Genealogy), containing portraits, presented within medallions, of important mythical and historical figures, from Adam to the ruling sultan. Facial features and bodily characteristics were thought to express the qualities of the individual and his family; thus the schematic and ideal portraits combine personal traits with conventions that characterize the entire dynasty. These portrait series persisted until the end of the Ottoman empire, even after the disappearance of historical and religious painting.

Illustrations of religious subjects were popular in the late sixteenth and early seventeenth centuries, when historical court painting was approaching its end. Royal manuscripts, such as copies of *Zübdetüʾt-tewārikh* (The quintessence of history, 1583), depict biblical prophets and heroes as precursors of the Ottoman sultans, the defenders of justice and orthodoxy. Other manuscripts, with moralistic overtones (like *Tales of the Prophets*) or Sufi inclinations, were produced in commercial workshops and in provincial towns like Baghdad. Images of saints and their pilgrimage sites were exhibited in the bazaars as instruments of divination, while schematic images of the *ḥajj* route in pilgrims' guides were sold as souvenirs, mainly in Mecca.

THE DECORATIVE ARTS

Besides luxurious manuscripts, richly bound, illuminated, and illustrated, the court painters provided designs for other media. The participation of these designers in various crafts produced a unified taste and a common repertory of motifs, which appeared simultaneously in manuscript illumination and bindings, textiles and metalwork, rugs and ceramics. The Ottoman art that resulted was based on a limited number of floral or abstract motifs, with hardly any human or animal figures. Two generic motifs, the *rūmī* ("Anatolian")—a geometric arabesque of Mediterranean origin—and the *hatayi* ("Chinese")—a floral scroll of Chinese origin—appear in typical combinations in all the crafts. The *saz* ("reed") motif—an energetically winding serrated leaf, Iranian in origin—spread from the art of the book to other media and was combined with rosettes and occasionally with animated figures. Bouquets of naturalistic flowers became prominent in the classical age of Ottoman art, probably under the influence of Italian herbalist albums.

CERAMICS

Royal patronage turned traditional pottery production for private consumption, centered in Iznik, into a large-scale industry that produced mainly tiles for the imperial buildings. Already in the early fifteenth century, Iranian artists decorated the sultans' complexes in Bursa and Edirne in the Timurid style of tile-cutting and *cuerda seca* (in which glazes of different colors are outlined by thin contours of greasy pigment to prevent the smelted colors from fusing). After the conquest these artists moved to İstanbul and then to İznik, while another group of Iranian tile-cutters decorated the Tiled Pavilion (*Çinili Köşk,* 1473), which Mehmed II built in the new Topkapi palace.

At that time, in order to satisfy elite demand, the potters of Iznik took a revolutionary step, launching the new technique of frit-ware (a composite of silica and while clay), painted under a transparent, colorless glaze. The decoration of blue and white *rūmī* and *hatayi* motifs reflects a taste for Chinese porcelains and also the manner of Baba Naqqāsh (Old Master Designer), a leading artist in the manuscript atelier of Mehmed II. A later subdivision of this style, with tiny floral motifs on spiral stems, closely resembles the illuminated background of the imperial monogram *(ṭughra)* of Sultan Süleyman.

Stencils prepared by the court painters were often used for ceramic decoration, as is demonstrated by four panels of incomparable quality in the Circumcision Room *(Sünnet Odası)* of the Topkapi palace. These giant

Selīmiye Mosque, Edirne. *Note the floral İznik tiles in the sultan's loggia.* PHOTOGRAPH BY ARA GÜLER. REPRODUCED BY PERMISSION.

tiles were made in 1527–1528 in the then-current *saz* style of the court painter Şahkulu. Applying the decoration using stencils resulted in rapid and less costly production and made İznik pottery accessible to a wider clientele, even beyond the borders of the Ottoman empire. These new markets encouraged the potters to vary their product with new colors and motifs like the floral scrolls on Chinese blue and white porcelains, the favorite vessels of the imperial court. Experiments in new colors reached a peak in the second part of the sixteenth century, when coral red and emerald green gave brilliance to a new style of naturalistic flowers intertwined with imaginary plants. From the Süleymaniye mosque to the later imperial monuments of the sixteenth century, tiles with underglazed decoration replaced the earlier *cuerda seca* technique, thus encouraging large-scale tile production in İznik and smaller centers like Kütahya. The combination of naturalistic flowers with imaginary foliage gradually gave way to a new vogue for naturalistic flower wreaths or growing plants, such as decorate the Selīmiye mosque in Edirne. In the late sixteenth century the ceramic industry declined in quantity and quality, due to irregular court commissions and restrictive price controls. The workshops of İznik, which began to look for other markets, were finally closed in the eighteenth century. Secondary centers, like Kütahya, continued to work, but on a negligible scale.

RUGS

In the fourteenth and fifteenth centuries, centers of weaving in western Anatolia continued the famous Seljuk tradition of woolen pile rugs, made with the typical Turkish "Gördes" knot. Abstract animal figures gave way to combinations of geometric and *rūmī* motifs, in alter-

Selīmiye Mosque, Edirne. *The masterpiece of the great architect Sinān. The eight pillars uphold an immense dome whose supporting system is concealed between the external balconies.* PHOTOGRAPH BY ARA GÜLER. REPRODUCED BY PERMISSION.

nating compartments or in groupings of small units around a bigger one. Study of these rugs is based on depictions by contemporary European painters whose names, (Hans) Holbein or (Lorenzo) Lotto, are associated with the various stylistic categories.

Two new groups of rugs, differing in technique and design, developed under the imperial patronage of the Conqueror and his descendants. The first, originating in the late fifteenth century, is known collectively as "Uşak," although a few other towns produced the same type of rug. These large rugs, destined for big mosques or for commerce, including European markets, fall into two categories, the medallion and the star. The first is patterned in a linear series of central medallions and side half-medallions, composed of palmettes and pairs of *rūmī* motifs. The field is decorated with flowers and florettes on stems. In the "Uşak star" the field is covered with an unending alternating pattern of eight-pointed stars and lozenge motifs. The two subdivisions are in contrasting blue and red. Some rugs made to European order contain coats of arms of European royal and noble houses.

The other group, that of Ottoman court rugs, was a result of the encounter with Iranian and Mamluk styles, following Ottoman victories in the sixteenth century. These rugs, produced in Cairo, Bursa, and İstanbul, used the Persian "Senna" knot, which was better suited to the complex and delicate designs of the court artists. The multicolored compositions contain curved, pointed *saz* leaves, palmettes, and naturalistic flowers intertwined on a curved stem. Toward the end of the century Chinese clouds and blossoming branches were added, along with royal symbols like *chintamani* (groups of three dots) and leopard or tiger marks. Royal court rugs greatly influenced the European carpet industry, which copied their designs.

BIBLIOGRAPHY

Aslanapa, Oktay. *Turkish Art and Architecture.* New York: Praeger, 1971.

Atıl, Esin. *Turkish Art.* Washington, D.C.: Smithsonian Institution Press, 1980.

———. *The Age of Sultan Süleyman the Magnificent.* Washington, D.C.: National Gallery of Art; New York: H. Abrams, 1987.

ARCHITECTURE

Cezar, Mustafa. *Typical Commercial Buildings of the Ottoman Classical Period and the Ottoman Construction System.* Ankara: Türkiye Iş Bankasi Cultural Publications, 1983.

Goodwin, Godfrey. *A History of Ottoman Architecture.* Baltimore, Md.: Johns Hopkins Press, 1971.

Kuban, Doğan. *Sinan's Art and Selimiye.* Beşiktaş, Turkey, and Istanbul: Economic and Social History Foundation, 1997.

Kuran, Aptullah. *The Mosque in Early Ottoman Architecture.* Chicago: University of Chicago Press, 1968.

———. *Sinan: The Grand Old Master of Ottoman Architecture.* Washington, D.C.: Institute of Turkish Studies; İstanbul: Ada Press Publishers, 1987.

Necipoğlu-Kafador, Gülrü. "The Süleymaniye Complex in Istanbul: An Interpretation." *Muqarnas* 3 (1985): 92–117.

———. *Architecture, Ceremonial, and Power: The Topkapi Palace in the Fifteenth and Sixteenth Centuries.* New York: Architectural History Foundation; Cambridge, Mass.: MIT Press, 1991.

Vogt-Göknil, Ulya. *Living Architecture: Ottoman.* New York: Grosset and Dunlap, 1966.

Yenişehirlioğlu, Filiz (Çalişar), ed. *Ottoman Architectural Works outside Turkey.* Ankara: T. C. Dişişleri Bakanligi, Kültür Işleri Genel Müdürlügü, 1989.

PAINTING

Atasoy, Nurhan, and Filiz Çağman. *Turkish Miniature Painting.* Translated by Esın Atıl. İstanbul: R. C. D. Cultural Institute, 1974.

Atıl, Esın. *Süleymanname: The Illustrated History of Süleyman the Magnificent.* Washington, D.C.: National Gallery of Art; New York: H. Abrams, 1986.

Çağman, Filiz, and Zeren Tanındı. *The Topkapı Saray Museum: The Albums and Illustrated Manuscripts.* Edited and translated by J. M. Rogers. London: Thames and Hudson, 1986.

Milstein, Rachel. *Miniature Painting in Ottoman Baghdad.* Costa Mesa, Calif.: Mazdâ, 1990.

Renda, Günsel, et al. *A History of Turkish Painting.* Geneva: Palasar; Seattle: University of Washington Press, 1988.

Topkapı Saray Museum. *The Sultan's Portrait: Picturing the House of Osman.* İstanbul: Işbank, 2000.

CERAMICS

Atasoy, Nurhan, and Julian Raby. *Iznik: The Pottery of Ottoman Turkey.* Edited by Yanni Petsopoulos. London: Alexandria Press in association with Thames and Hudson, 1989.

RUGS AND TEXTILES

Mackie, Louise W. *The Splendor of Turkish Weaving: An Exhibition of Silks and Carpets of the Thirteenth–Eighteenth Centuries, November 9, 1973 through March 24, 1974.* Washington, D.C.: Textile Museum, 1973.

Yetkin, Şerare. *Historical Turkish Carpets.* Translated by Maggie Quigley. Ankara: Türkiye Iş Bankasi Cultural Publications, 1981.

RACHEL MILSTEIN

[See also **DMA:** Bāyāzid I, Yildirim; Bāyāzid II; Ceramics, Islamic; Eyvān; Ḥammām; Islamic Art and Architecture; Madrasa; Manuscript Illumination, Islamic; Mehmed (Muḥammad) I; Mehmed (Muḥammad) II; Miḥrāb; Mosque; Murad II; Ottomans; Rugs and Carpets; Selim I; Seljuks; Sultan; Zāwīya.]

OVENS. Unlike open hearths, most ovens had a superstructure enclosing the heat source, which permitted higher temperatures and required less fuel. It was possible, however, not only to cook food and bake bread in open hearths but also to fire pottery in pits. A rich Latin and vernacular vocabulary described ovens in medieval texts. The Latin term *fornax* generally meant a kiln used especially for manufacturing pottery or metals, while the Middle English *furnus* referred to a cooking oven. Definitions were not absolute, and terminology was fluid: the Old English *ofen* or *ofn* (Old High German *ovan*) originally referred to a furnace but by around 1000 also meant cook oven. Moreover, ovens likely served multiple functions. Cook ovens doubled as heat sources in virtually all homes that had them until the late Middle Ages and in most homes thereafter. In moderately well-to-do homes, plain or tiled heat ovens became a fixture of private social culture from the fifteenth century. Ovens might serve dual functions on a larger scale: excavations at Jaffa, for example, have revealed a Crusader bake oven that shared its heat source with the neighboring bathhouse.

Physical remains of kilns survive from most historical periods and regions. Slag heaps from metalworking, piles of potsherds, and occasionally material from superstructures reveal major production sites—for example, the late Roman kilns excavated at the port of Quentovic south of Calais or the new kilns that appeared in the Rhineland near Bonn from Carolingian times. On the other hand, in some areas famous for producing and exporting pottery only isolated kilns have been discovered: in Ipswich (East Anglia), where Anglo-Saxon fineware circulated widely, just one kiln has been properly identified.

Most medieval kilns, however, supplied local markets. Although its furnaces have not surfaced, a distinctive pottery produced near Nîmes in Languedoc supplied an area roughly nine kilometers in circumference. From the thirteenth century, ceramic tile or brick kilns equipped some rural monasteries or cathedral construction sites, as at Uppsala. When building was completed, the kilns were abandoned.

Legal sources provide a different perspective, especially on bake ovens. Since at least the eleventh century, a monopoly over mills, winepresses, and ovens was one of the banal (or compulsory feudal) rights many lords claimed. Peasants were required to bake their bread in the lord's ovens and pay a share of their loaves in return. In an agrarian economy with fixed rents of limited profit potential, oven monopolies tapped numerous possibilities for financial growth: population growth, increased crop yields, and greater numbers of ovens. As long as it was possible, therefore, lords retained their banal rights; at Daroca in the province of Saragossa, furnaces and bake ovens were monopolized into the fifteenth century.

One other oven type merits attention. Around 1050, "oast," or *ast,* had the same meaning as *cyln* (kiln). Later, however, "oast" referred to ovens for drying grain, and in particular hops. Stalks were laid on a floor above the furnace room, provided good draught, and thus dried to prevent rot. By the sixteenth century oasthouses with their conical roofs appeared throughout hop-producing areas like Kent.

BIBLIOGRAPHY

Boas, Adrian J. *Crusader Archaeology: The Material Culture of the Latin East.* London: Routledge, 1999.

Duby, Georges. *Rural Economy and Country Life in the Medieval West.* Translated by Cynthia Postan. Philadelphia: University of Pennsylvania Press, 1998. Classic study of banal rights.

Henkel, Matthias. "Der Kachelofen, ein Gegenstand der Wohnkultur im Wandel: Kulturgeschichtliche Aspekte anhand historischer Bildquellen." In *Material Culture in Medieval Europe.* Edited by Guy de Boe and Frans Verhaeghe. Zellik, Belgium: I. A. P. Reports, 1997.

Kaufmann, E. R. "Ofen und Wohnkultur." In *Material Culture in Medieval Europe.* Edited by Guy de Boe and Frans Verhaeghe. Zellik, Belgium: I. A. P. Reports, 1997. Extensive bibliography.

Mateos Royo, J. A. "Monopolio señorial frente al control público: Hornos y panaderías en la Daroca del siglo XV." In *El poder real en la Corona de Aragón (siglos XIV–XVI).* Vol. 5. Zaragoza, Spain: Gobierno de Aragón, Departamento de Educación y Cultura, 1994.

McCarthy, Michael R., and Catherine M. Brooks. *Medieval Pottery in Britain, A.D. 900–1600.* Leicester, U.K.: Leicester University Press, 1988.

McCormick, Michael. *Origins of the European Economy: Communications and Commerce, A.D. 300–900.* Cambridge, U.K.: Cambridge University Press, 2001. Covers ceramic production and trade, with references to archaeological reports.

Medieval Archaeology: An Encyclopedia. Edited by Pam J. Crabtree. New York and London: Garland, 2001. Contains general bibliography and descriptions of important sites, including Ipswich, Quentovic, and Uppsala.

KEVIN UHALDE

[See also **DMA:** Feudalism; Heating.]

PAGANISM AND PAGAN GODS, SURVIVAL OF

RELIGIOUS LIFE

Once Christianity became the official faith of the Roman state in the fourth century, other religions were handled in two main ways—either by demonization and abolishment or by reinterpretation, *interpretatio Christiana.* Since the laws of the Christian emperors (and, later, of the diverse realms) imposed the baptism of all children and forbade apostasy, a theoretically watertight system, enforced through heavy punishments, excluded medieval Europeans from any religious practices but those of Catholicism. The gods of the classical pantheon and of the other pagan religions were either declared to be bad demons or construed as erroneously deified mortals. In several cases, however, they also were replaced by Christian saints who kept more or less of the old divinity's character. Nevertheless, beliefs and practices of the old religions continued to exist among the people, though they were condemned as superstitions and eradicated by church and state when detected.

From the early nineteenth until the middle of the twentieth century, scholars tended to construe medieval and modern folklore traditions and superstitions as Teutonic relics—the still indispensable *Teutonic Mythology* of Jakob Grimm being the most famous example of that tendency. However, after the end of the Third Reich, during which these concepts had been used to build a nationalistic ideology, many scholars refused all evidence for religious continuities from pagan times. They preferred to explain the phenomena in question as rather recent innovations within medieval and modern Catholicism, though deviant from the official faith. For example, are we to understand the use of masks during Shrovetide as a relic of pre-Christian customs or as a derivative from the religious plays of the late Middle Ages?

As the many well-documented cases of Christianization in modern times indicate, the changing of a religion does not simply replace one system of beliefs and practices with another one but also involves an amalgamation of elements of the old faith. Among the medieval beliefs dating back to pagan times (both Germanic and Celtic), many texts from the eleventh century onward refer to a "wild hunt" consisting of a "family" of souls of deceased people led by a psychopomp (Wodan, or Odin; Hellequin, the King of the Fairies) and roving restlessly through the air. According to the *interpretatio Christiana,* these are poor souls being punished for their sins by this kind of purgatory, although Christian eschatology gives no warrant for this explanation. Another instance of syncretism is the world described in the vision of the Holstein peasant Gottschalk in 1189, which blends elements congruent with Christian dogma and German conceptions such as the need of the souls to receive shoes in order to cross the thorn-studded field of purgatory like the Old Norse *helskor* or the rivers full of cutting instruments like the Slithr and similar streams in the Eddas.

Many place-names still show the presence of pagan holy places. Montmartre in Paris got its name from "mons Martis" because here the god of war possessed a temple. But the name was reinterpreted as "mons martyrum," and St. Denis and his companions were said to have been executed on this hill. Among many similar examples, Odense, Denmark's third-largest town, received its name as a cult center of the god Odin. Many of the wells, trees, hills, and other places where a saint is venerated have been holy places of the old religion, "baptized" in the Middle Ages. In Chartres, for example, a Celto-Roman goddess of the fountain was replaced by the Virgin. Many buildings, churches not excluded, were protected by crossed horse heads, an apotropaic (evil-averting) symbol hinting at a pair of helpful German deities.

While the beings of the so-called nether mythology like goblins, brownies, fairies, and elves appear rather often in medieval sources, an undisguised survival of the main pre-Christian gods can be proved only seldom. In one such instance, the Old High German Second Merseburg Charm (written down in a tenth-century manuscript) evokes the healing of an ill horse by Odin. Place names like Wudinsberg clearly embody a memory from the pagan epoch. When, as in Ille-et-Vilaine, an *ecclesia sancti Veneris* is mentioned in church documents in 838 and modern excavations have unearthed two Gallo-Roman sculptures of Venus at this place, there can be no doubt about cultic continuity. The same is true concerning several female triads of saints (three Marys: Ainbet, Wilbet, Walbet), who are the successors of the Celto-Roman *tres matres* or the Teutonic three Norns. In medieval Antwerp, Priapus seems to have been venerated, mostly by women, under the name Ters. A French manuscript from 1317 contains a prayer to Ste. Avonde, who, being otherwise completely unknown, might well be a reminiscence of a pagan goddess called Abundia or Habundia, whose veneration several authors condemn. However, the speculations of Margaret Murray on the persistence of a witch god and pre-Christian fertility rites as elements of the Sabbath practiced by underground covens lack sound evidence. Only occasionally, in times of crisis, a revival of pagan rites is described in medieval

Statua Solis. Mosaic, showing a stele with the image of the sun's chariot, from S. Marco, Venice (13th century). According to Christian teaching, the statues of the heathen deities were inhabited by demons. By the victory of the Christian God, these were driven out, and the sculptures broke down—a topos found in many lives of missionary saints. Print provided by The Library of Congress. © NOBERTO GRAMACCINI. REPRODUCED BY PERMISSION.

sources: in England, an outbreak of rinderpest in 1268 was fought by a kind of priapic worship, though we cannot tell whether this was a survival or a new invention.

The survival of the old gods in the form of demons is such a well known and uncontested fact that a very few examples will suffice. In several churches, sculptures of an antique god were preserved in order to be used as mock images: at Trier, in St. Matthias, a statue of Venus was kept in chains and ritually hit with stones; at Vienna, in St. Stephan, the image of an unknown godhead was shown near an inscription confirming his or her confinement in hell. The devil in a Carolingian Psalter shows the very same exterior with antlers that we know from representations of the Celtic god Cerunnus. Several French Romanesque churches contain reliefs of the personified *luxuria* (sexual sin), whose appearance is identical with that of the Roman Terra Mater, keeping snakes at her breasts. A Silesian spell of the fourteenth century

Cerunnus as Personification of Hades. *Pre-Christian gods were commonly represented as demons, as with the Celtic Cerunnus in this illustration from a medieval hymnbook.* WÜRTTEMBERGISCHE LANDESBIBLIOTHEK, STUTTGARTER PSALTER, FOL. 16. REPRODUCED BY PERMISSION.

claims to give protection against Odin, his army, and all his men, who obviously were interpreted as bad spirits. And when Martin Luther said that everywhere the swamps were inhabited by devils, he did not quote from the Bible but transformed the lesser aquatic divinities of the local folk belief into the fiends of Christian demonology.

LITERATURE

In literature and art, one could deal with the old gods in a more relaxed way. Notwithstanding the continuous references to them in the works of the classical Roman poets, their texts continued to be transcribed as indispensable devices for mastering the Latin tongue. For that reason even mythographic handbooks were written, culminating in Giovanni Boccaccio's *Genealogia deorum gentilium* (Genealogy of the pagan gods). During the renaissance of the twelfth century, some of the Roman epics were adapted into the vernacular languages (e.g., the Old French romance of Troy; the Middle High German *Eneide* of Heinrich von Veldeke), thereby constituting a lay tradition of ancient mythology. Its figures

and stories were regularly interpreted *per allegoriam* and considered useful because they taught moral lessons compatible with Christian truth. The mythological fable or divine person was understood as such a lesson's "integument," or outer skin, concealing the meaning within. For example, when a poet of the early fourteenth century rendered Ovid's widely read *Metamorphoses* into French *(Ovide moralisé),* he either moralized all fables and persons or declared them to be precursors of the New Testament. As mere allegories, unconnected with religious practice, the gods were completely acceptable; in late medieval lyrics, Amor as personification of love's power is nearly omnipresent.

The other method that permitted the survival of the gods, also coming from antiquity and frequent already with the early theologians, was euhemerism: the gods are declared to have been mortals, usually sinful ones, who were idolized by the pagans and venerated in temples (their burial places). When Jupiter appears in an antic romance, he is considered a famous adulterer; Neptune in reality must have been a pirate or sorcerer. In addition, many antique divinities, especially Apollo, were held to be gods of the Muslims, whom the Christians generally suspected to be polytheists.

The Teutonic and Celtic divinities do not figure in medieval literature, as there was no written tradition telling about them. Some scholars have speculated that heroes of the Arthurian romances originally stemmed from Celtic supernatural beings, or figures of the German heroic poems from Teutonic ones, but such esoteric hypotheses have remained unprovable.

FINE ARTS

A great number of iconographical contexts offered the opportunity to make an image of the ancient gods. In polemical situations, such as when a saint destroys heathen statues or the Holy Family passes by, the gods are represented as little idols, usually breaking and falling down. Often small devils—the demons who inhabited the statues—are shown taking flight. Like poetry, ecclesiastic art did not hesitate to present the gods of classical antiquity as mere allegories, especially for natural phenomena: they represented sun and moon (often accompanying the Crucifixion), rivers and the sea, or, as Janus, the beginning of a new year. A special tradition existed for astronomical manuscripts, which often include drawings of the planetary gods, who figured also in connection with the ages of man and the character types.

Interpretations of certain Romanesque sculptures on churches as representing a Teutonic or Celtic god, fixed into the stone by the power of the Christian God, are questionable. However, a Romanesque capital at Trucy-en-Laonnais shows the Celtic divinities Succellus and Nantosvelta grasping their apotropaic hammer, and some Anglo-Saxon crosses depict stories from the pre-Christian Scandinavian mythology dealing with Odin. These examples are some of the clearest demonstrations of the syncretism that shaped the religion of the newly converted Christians.

Some ancient gods maintain a vivid presence in the profane painting of the Gothic period. Many romances with themes from classical antiquity were illuminated, as were medieval poems on love and fortune. Numerous manuscripts of the *Roman de la Rose* have images of winged Venus and Amor, and many carved ivories representing the siege of the castle of love also show this god. In a few blasphemous pictures, the lover is even depicted in the position of adoring Amor like a saint, as are the lovers on the famous Florentine *desco da parto* (birthing plate, *ca.* 1400), whose center of interest is, however, the genitals of a naked Venus.

The Gosforth Cross. *Decorations on this Celtic Christian cross from Cumberland seem to depict the struggle of Thor and the Midgard serpent.* © WERNER FORMAN/ART RESOURCE, NY. REPRODUCED BY PERMISSION.

BIBLIOGRAPHY

Adhémar, Jean. *Influences antiques dans l'art du Moyen Âge français.* Paris: Editions du C.T.H.S., 1996.

Camille, Michael. *The Gothic Idol.* Cambridge, U.K.: Cambridge University Press, 1989.

Chance, Jane. *Medieval Mythography.* Gainesville: University of Florida Press, 1994.

Crosas López, Francisco. *De diis gentium: Tradición clásica y cultura medieval.* New York: P. Lang, 1998.

Dinzelbacher, Peter, ed. *Handbuch der Religionsgeschichte im deutschsprachigen Raum.* Volume 2: *Hoch- und Spätmittelalter.* Paderborn, Germany: F. Schönigh, 2000.

Gramaccini, Norberto. *Mirabilia: Das Nachleben antiker Statuen vor der Renaissance.* Mainz, Germany: P. von Zabern, 1996.

Kemp, Wolfgang. "Götter, heidnische." In *Lexikon der christlichen Ikonographie.* Edited by Engelbert Kirschbaum. Vol. 2. Rome: Herder, 1970.

Kern, Manfred, and Alfred Ebenbauer, eds. *Lexikon der antiken Gestalten in den deutschen Texten des Mittelalters.* Berlin: de Gruyter, 2003.

Senec, Jean. *The Survival of the Pagan Gods.* Translated by Barbara F. Sessions. 1940. Reprint, Princeton, N.J.: Princeton University Press, 1972.

PETER DINZELBACHER

[See also **DMA**: Eddic Poetry; Heinrich von Veldeke; Irish Literature; *Nibelungenlied;* Norns; Odin; Ovid in the Middle Ages; Scandinavian Mythology; Vergil in the Middle Ages.]

PATRONAGE, ARTISTIC. The term "patronage" is usually reserved for arrangements made between an artist and a client to produce a work of art for private use or for the benefit of a community. Until the late Middle Ages, works of fine art were produced at the direction of a specific patron rather than on speculation, an arrangement that allowed the purchaser a great degree of potential control over the work's content and style. For every sophisticated medieval patron involved in the fine points of producing a work of art, however, there were many more who left the artistic decisions to the professionals.

We are limited in the search for evidence by what was written down and what has survived, but art historians tend to assume with some reason that the practices current in the better-documented centuries reflect earlier conventions. The interpretation of the terms and attitudes expressed in the documents we do have has shifted over the years, from a tendency to see the patron as superfluous to individual artistic genius, to a view of the artist as the unthinking servant of a visionary patron or a learned adviser, to a more moderate consideration of individual cases.

CHURCH PATRONAGE

The very idea of artistic patronage was a charged issue in the early Christian church, and one that resurfaced during periods of religious reform. Imperial patronage was a mixed blessing for the early church, for it brought with it a tradition of luxurious representational artworks out of joint with the asceticism and mistrust of idols that characterized much of early Christian writings. Simple, abstract Chi-Rho monograms scratched into the walls of early Christian tombs would have pleased some theologians better than Constantine's lavish church foundations and church furnishings. His gifts included hundreds of pounds of gold and silver ornaments to decorate St. Peter's and the Lateran basilica (donations made between 313 and 337), among them life-size silver statues of Christ enthroned with the apostles.

The equivocal power of art to dazzle the viewer was a perennial if not a constant concern in the patronage of objects for use in the churches. The concerns expressed by iconoclasts, who objected to religious art on theological grounds, were bolstered by more practical objections to art in the monastery, where glittering images might divert attention from prayer. At the very least, art would consume money that might better serve the church else-where. In a letter to William of St. Thierry (*ca.* 1120s), St. Bernard of Clairvaux laid out objections to the commissioning of art for monastic environments. The grotesque animal carvings he describes, in order to warn against their distracting allure, are still visible in the carved capitals that support many Romanesque cloisters—proof that not all monasteries shared his mistrust of such decoration. His remarks about the ability of a church richly decorated with gilt reliquaries, polychrome saints, and gem-studded chandeliers to draw donations from the bemused visitor provide a glimpse inside a Romanesque church. His characterization also suggests that churchmen whose establishments depended on impressing a lay audience knew the power of art to capture the public interest and that even Bernard acknowledged that the needs of a monastic setting were far different from a church that hosted pilgrims and served the laity.

Abbot Suger of St. Denis, one of art history's most remarkable patrons, commissioned just such a church as we see described in Bernard's critical letter, and the two men's disagreement over the function of art in a religious setting has provided us with eloquent apologies for both views of church patronage. Suger's three treatises on his intentions and achievements for the abbey of St. Denis reveal the practical and spiritual concerns that led to the decision to rebuild the abbey church and detail his involvement in creating what is acknowledged as the first example of true Gothic architecture. The church at St. Denis testifies to the power of a patron not only to sponsor an important building project but even to affect the stylistic development of medieval art in a way few individual artists have.

Chief among Suger's projects after he became abbot in 1122 was enlarging and redecorating the abbey's venerable but cramped Carolingian church, which was too small to accommodate the crowds of pilgrims who would come on feast days to see the relics of St. Denis. Rebuilding began at the west end and proceeded so rapidly that the altars in the choir were consecrated with great ceremony in 1144. It is in the chevet (the apse, ambulatory, and radiating chapels at the east end of a church) that the Gothic combination of decorative, pared-down stone columns rising into rib vaults and tall pointed arches framing expanses of stained glass first appeared.

Suger did not work out the technical improvements necessary to sustain such an effect without sacrificing stability, and it is unlikely that he devised the decorative patterns or set the stones in mortar, though his enthusiasm for the glory of St. Denis did lead him to scour the forests for suitable timber. His architectural contribution emerges from his writings, which celebrate the role of colored light to transport the viewer to a higher world, and from his requirement that the choir in particular be open to the traffic of pilgrims. The means for achieving a continuous luminous ring of chapels at St. Denis would have been left to professionals, but Suger's vision was unusually vivid, his patronage unusually ambitious, and his record of the building unusually self-conscious.

THE MECHANISM OF PATRONAGE

The rise of guilds for urban artisans, beginning as early as the eleventh century, affected the uniformity of the work produced, the prices charged by artisans, and instruction for the next generation. The guild rules of the masons of Paris, for example (submitted in 1258 but thought to reflect earlier practices), cover working hours and the training period for apprentices, but they also give investigative and disciplinary procedures for controlling the standard of work. Plasterers who habitually cheated their patrons by cutting the quality of the plaster or giving short measure, for example, would be subject to fines; if obdurate, to expulsion from the craft. Artists in the larger cities formed their own guilds—painters under the name of St. Luke, whose legend records a portrait he painted of the Virgin—and protected their members by excluding those with insufficient mastery of the craft (or insufficient funds to pay the guild dues) from practicing within the city.

Guild regulations were often irrelevant to the dealings of artist and patron at the highest level, however, since artists who found favor at court could gain exemption from guild rules. Prosperous cities also often appointed a painter, who was paid a small annual sum and awarded commissions to decorate civic buildings. In 1498 Gerard David finished painting two cautionary scenes of historic arrest and punishment (the *Judgment of Cambyses*) for the justice chambers of Bruges. Progress on the panels may have been delayed by the need to accommodate portraits of the members of the judicial body, who can be seen in contemporary late-fifteenth-century dress behind the flayed body of the miscreant Sisamnes.

By the later Middle Ages, contracts between artists and patrons typically spelled out the expectations on both sides, detailing the size of the work, its high quality and perhaps the artist's exclusive labor during the project, and a schedule for completion and payment. The contract might specify that the artist use a higher-priced material such as lapis lazuli, or gold leaf, presumably because an artist would otherwise use the cheaper blue pigment, azurite, or substitute tin leaf glazed with yellow.

Details about setting, gestures, or the attributes a figure is to hold, however—elements that often preoccupy art historians in search of meaning—are notably absent from these contracts. In most cases, the patron seems to have left decisions about expression and iconography to the discretion of the artist, who might simply be instructed to portray a subject as it is usually done, with no specifications beyond the title.

INTERMEDIARIES

We usually think of the commissioning of a work of art as a transaction between the artist and the patron, in more or less direct communication, perhaps with a lawyer to draw up the contract. There were a number of variations on this relationship, however, and several kinds of intermediaries who might have a say in the process.

Noble patrons often employed an agent to handle the financial arrangements with an artist and perhaps keep an eye on the progress of the work, particularly if artist and patron were separated by distance. The presence of an intermediary in various commissions has been fortunate for historians as it moves the principals to commit to writing things that might otherwise have been settled orally and hence lost. When Piero de' Medici had criticisms about the Magi frescos that Benozzo Gozzoli had recently painted for him in the family chapel (in the Palazzo Medici-Riccardi in Florence), he and the painter communicated by letter through the patron's agent, Roberto Martelli. Benozzo's letter of 1459 addresses the criticism (two angels in the corners, nearly obscured by clouds) and politely offers to paint them out if Piero insists; his remark that he will leave the scaffolding up until Piero has seen the work suggests both that artists could be flexible, at least on minor points, and that the patron in this case was following the project fairly closely.

For an artistic project with a complicated or unusual iconography, the patron might call on a learned consultant. The contract (1464) for the altarpiece painted by Dirk Bouts for four members of the Brotherhood of the Holy Sacrament of St. Peter's church in Leuven (Louvain), where it can still be seen, specified that a pair of theology professors would prescribe the subjects to be represented and would answer for their "order and truth." The contract's specifications are familiar from much older contracts, except for the presence of academic advisors, a provision that may spring less from widespread practice than from Leuven's status as a university town. There was evidently more communication between patrons and painter than the logistical points written into the contract: the four men in fifteenth-century clothing, included as witnesses to the Last Supper, are thought to represent the four members of the brotherhood who paid for the altarpiece.

The sheer size and expense of architectural projects brought their own complications, but only rarely have they been documented. Milan Cathedral, begun in 1386 under Duke Gian Galeazzo Visconti, underwent many modifications over the years. The Gothic design of the church was nudged into place by a group of local architects under the influence of contradictory theories during years of debate, detailed in the records of the committee responsible for the project. When technical difficulties arose, the committee invited the opinions of French and German experts schooled in the soaring northern Gothic style, although they ultimately rejected foreign expertise. In any case, there was no single designer and no single architectural or structural proposal, and the architects themselves determined the form of the building gradually. The survival of the committee's records is unusual in the view it provides of many sides of the process of constructing a church, from the building's symbolism to the masons' rules of thumb to the latitude accorded the architects, but the building is probably not extraordinary in its rather diffuse process of design and execution.

THE IMPACT OF PATRONAGE

Occasionally a patron's aims and taste are so powerful that they define the course of art for generations. When Charlemagne initiated his *renovatio Romani imperii*, looking to the achievements of the golden age of Christian emperors, his reverence for their art and practices infused his patronage and that of his court and descendents. We know almost nothing of Charlemagne's dealings with artists, but his preference for authentic Roman forms in architecture, liturgy, script, and "minor" arts such as ivory carving and manuscript illumination, imitated in the court workshops in the late eighth and early ninth centuries, produced works that rivaled their antique models.

Medieval patrons had the potential to control more than the scale, materials, content, and (occasionally) style of the art they commissioned, however. Since goldsmiths, illuminators, and tapestry weavers, among other makers of luxury goods, often depended on the patronage of the wealthy, the attention of a powerful patron could make an enormous difference not just to the reputation of an individual workshop but to the survival of the craft. Paris led the production of tapestries until about 1400, but the enthusiastic patronage of the wealthy dukes of Burgundy, who commissioned tapes-

tries increasingly from the textile cities under their control in the southern Low Countries, bolstered the production of luxury textiles, first in Arras and then in Tournai and Brussels. Patronage at its most expansive level conferred the ability to foster an industry, even to make the fortune of an entire town. The majority of those who undertook to sponsor a project apparently gave the artist few restrictions and fewer guidelines, but medieval art also bears evidence of patrons with extraordinary vision, whose impact on the history of art sometimes exceeded that of the artists who served them.

BIBLIOGRAPHY

Ackerman, James. "'Ars sine scientia nihil est': Gothic Theory of Architecture at the Cathedral of Milan." *The Art Bulletin* 31 (1949): 84–111.

Ainsworth, Maryan W. "The Business of Art: Patrons, Clients, and Art Markets." In *From Van Eyck to Bruegel: Early Netherlandish Painting in the Metropolitan Museum of Art*. Edited by Maryan W. Ainsworth and Keith Christiansen. New York: Metropolitan Museum of Art, 1998.

Baxandall, Michael. "Conditions of Trade." In *Painting and Experience in Fifteenth-Century Italy: A Primer in the Social History of Pictorial Style*. Oxford: Oxford University Press, 1988.

Davis-Weyer, Caecilia. *Early Medieval Art, 300–1150*. Englewood Cliffs, N.J.: Prentice-Hall, 1971.

Frisch, Teresa. *Gothic Art, 1140–c. 1450*. Englewood Cliffs, N.J.: Prentice-Hall, 1971.

Gilbert, Creighton E. *Italian Art, 1400–1500*. Englewood Cliffs, N.J.: Prentice-Hall, 1980.

Stechow, Wolfgang. *Northern Renaissance Art, 1400–1600*. Englewood Cliffs, N.J.: Prentice-Hall, 1966.

Suger, Abbot of Saint Denis. *Abbot Suger on the Abbey Church of St.-Denis and Its Art Treasures*. Edited and translated by Erwin Panofsky. Princeton, N.J.: Princeton University Press, 1979.

ELIZABETH J. MOODEY

[See also **DMA**: Bernard of Clairvaux, St.; Early Christian Art; Gothic Architecture; Gothic Art; Guilds of Artists; Suger of St. Denis; **Supp**: Patronage, Literary.]

PATRONAGE, LITERARY. Literary patronage, through which the powerful give protection to writers and supply the means for them to pursue their literary activities, was common in the Middle Ages. At the time, intellectuals rarely enjoyed any kind of professional or institutional status, and the search for a patron was essential for their creative efforts. There is considerable evidence for such patronage at the courts of the kings and territorial princes, who attracted to their entourage men who could write, recruiting them primarily for the bureaucratic and administrative services they could provide. In some cases these intellectuals were used to prepare propaganda, writing speeches, poems, or treaties that extolled the glory of their patron. Indirectly, however, patronage itself had a positive effect on the patron's image, for even when the resulting work was not political in the strict sense it often carried a laudatory dedication. Moreover, the manuscripts themselves were things of beauty. Rare and precious objects that were frequently illuminated and often displayed, they enhanced the prestige of the court at which they were kept.

EARLY GERMANIC AND CAROLINGIAN PATRONAGE

In the Germanic kingdoms the fascination with imperial Rome and its authors resulted in patronage designed to perpetuate classical culture. Scholars of the time developed the notion of the *translatio studii,* the transfer of knowledge from Athens to Rome and then to the courts of the petty barbarian kings in the West. The history of Boethius (*ca.* 480–524), a tireless translator of Greek mathematical and philosophical texts at the court of Theodoric, king of the Ostrogoths, who had recently occupied Italy, is characteristic of a relatively demanding patronage arrangement: Boethius fell into disgrace and was condemned to death by his patron. In Toledo the seventh-century Visigoth king Sisebut, himself the author of a life of St. Didier in Latin and a poem in hexameter verse on lunar eclipses, attracted a number of intellectuals to his court. Isidore of Seville dedicated his *Etymologies,* the most frequently consulted encyclopedia in the Middle Ages, as well as a *Treaty on Natural History,* to the king. During this same period, the Merovingian kings Clothar II and Dagobert I played a similar role, even though the works of the authors in their entourage were less accomplished.

When their rule was supplanted by the Carolingians, the consequences for literature were considerable. The emperor Charlemagne (768–814) carried out an early form of "brain drain," attracting to Aix-la-Chapelle the most prominent intellectuals of his time. According to his biographer Eginhard, he learned to read late in life but "possessed books in great number." His principal advisor was Alcuin of York, who was the intellectual successor of the cultural tradition of the monasteries of the British Isles and the work of the Venerable Bede. Through his writing Alcuin reinforced the imperial ideology. The same was true of Theodulf of Orléans, the likely author of the *Libri Carolini,* which defended the emperor's position in the Iconoclastic Controversy. The use of pseudonyms by the intellectuals at the court of

Aix-la-Chapelle reflects this desire to create a literary circle modeled on the antique: Charlemagne was David the king at his harp; Alcuin was Horace; Theodulf, Pindar; Anglibert, Homer; Modoin, Ovid; and so on. This patronage continued at the ninth-century court of Louis I the Pious and his wife, Judith of Bavaria, both passionate lovers of poetry. Hrabanus Maurus, in his *Louanges de la sainte croix* (In praise of the holy cross), included a glowing dedication to the emperor, whom he referred to as the "warrior of Christ." Dedications to Louis's successor, Charles II the Bald, appeared in more than fifty works, and the king himself helped prepare works of propaganda, ordering his cousin Nithard to set down in writing the "story of the events of his time." His contemporary Alfred the Great, king of Wessex, with the help of his Welsh counselor Asser, translated into Anglo-Saxon the work of Augustine, Boethius, and Gregory the Great. This courtly culture, specific to the Carolingian empire and Anglo-Saxon kingdoms, was perpetuated in the tenth century by Otto I the Great of Germany and his brother Bruno, archbishop of Cologne. Its political goal was not simply to promote forms of propaganda and ideology favorable to the emperor but to civilize the aristocracy, who were often called to take up residence in the palace, a strategy designed to inhibit the impulse to revolt and increase their attachment to the king.

TWELFTH AND THIRTEENTH CENTURIES

The collapse of the Carolingian empire coincided with the dispersion of literary patronage, which was now exercised in the palaces of the territorial princes and in the chateaus of the noblemen. However, in the tenth and eleventh centuries literary culture barely existed outside of monasteries and cathedral schools. The twelfth-century "renaissance" changed the situation, though, introducing a new interest in literature to the princes and lay aristocracy. For example, in England, Robert of Gloucester, the illegitimate son of Henry I, was a generous patron who protected William of Malmesbury, Geoffrey of Monmouth, and Geffrei Gaimar and created a true literary circle with the Anglo-Norman nobles, who were themselves amateurs of literature. Around 1225 the son of William Marshal, regent of England, asked the trouvère Jean d'Erlée to compose a long poem in his honor; in Erlée's poem, Marshal's fidelity to his king and his loyalty to his subjects were used to justify his political decisions. In Flanders in 1203, Lambert, curé (parson) of Ardres, completed a Latin genealogy to the glory of Comte Baudoin de Guînes and his ancestors, the local lords; from him we learn that Baudoin had the books of the Old Testament and various scientific works translated by the clerics of his court. These examples illustrate the role that was now played by the nobility, even the minor nobility, in the literary life of the period.

At this time patronage became increasingly focused on works in the vernacular, which were easier to diffuse in a society where literature was transmitted orally. Henry II, the king of England, thus obtained a benefice for Wace, a cleric born into the Jersey aristocracy, so he would write, in French, the *Roman de Rou,* recording the noble deeds of his Norman ancestors. However, the king soon tired of his poet because of his support for Church liberties and his attachment to the party associated with Thomas Becket. He replaced him with Benoît de Sainte-Maure, an intellectual from Touraine who demonstrated even greater obsequiousness toward the king, even as he extolled the sacred nature of the English royal houses and the sanctity of the dukes of Normandy. This example shows the increased polarization in the relations between the writer and his patron, which continued to increase along with the genesis of the modern state.

In the countries of the Mediterranean, the thirteenth century saw the birth of the sirventes, a partisan song of narrowly political intent. The etymology of this poetic genre reflects the "service" performed in the interests of the lord, for whom the songs served as propaganda—the majority of the time by denigrating his enemies through some form of invective. Their success was largely based on their characteristic humor, produced in particular by means of the contrafactum, which joined a political text to the melody of a popular love song. Composed at the court of a nobleman who wished to affect public opinion, the sirventes was initially sung by a jongleur but then repeated from person to person among his listeners. Around 1200, Peire Duran, a troubadour from Carpentras, demonstrated his awareness of the sirventes's mobility and range of activity when he wrote of one of his own compositions, "Ma vile chanson engagée, facile et vulgaire, tient le pied à l'étrier, sur le point de partir" (My poor song begun, simple and common, puts foot to stirrup, on the point of departure). At the start of the thirteenth century, a number of sirventes were circulating in Occitan; at the time, the Albigensian Crusade was at its peak, and the poems often encouraged the subjects of the count of Toulouse to fight against Simon de Montfort and the king of France. But there were other songs as well, written in languages other than Occitan. One of the most celebrated is attributed to the twelfth-century English king Richard the Lionhearted, who composed the song in Anglo-Norman during his captivity in Germany to encourage his subjects to raise the necessary ransom and obtain his freedom.

Politics played an important role in other literary genres employed at court. This was true of correspondence throughout a period when letters, often polemical or moral in tone, were rarely private but widely distributed. The letters of Peter of Blois, an outstanding Latinist, and Gilbert Foliot, the bishop of London, were collected into volumes and frequently copied to defend the interests of King Henry II of England, especially during his struggle with Thomas Becket and the partisans of ecclesiastical freedoms. The patrons monitored the literary quality of the Latin compositions favorable to them, for polished rhetoric and flowery eloquence were more effective in transmitting propaganda. The thirteenth-century emperor Frederick II brought to his court Pietro della Vigna, one of the best representatives of the *ars dictaminis* school at Capua, to write his edicts, letters, and speeches, knowing that Vigna's style would compete directly with that of the chancellery of the pope, his sworn enemy. However, the papal curia, whose bureaucratic precocity and effectiveness are unique in the West, did a great deal to cultivate literary style in its effort to promote orthodoxy in the face of other religions and the prevailing heresies. In Italy the renewal of the classical culture of the early humanists, encouraged by the papacy, was part of this movement. However, it was also made use of by the territorial princes. In 1341 Petrarch traveled to Naples to offer Robert of Anjou his *Africa,* with its florid dedication; he also promised to write an epic poem celebrating his deeds. This king took every opportunity to encourage the promotion of letters as part of his efforts to ensure the success of the Guelphs, whose spokesman he was.

Other works were used to provide advice on good government to the princes. This was the case with the *Policraticus* (1159) of John of Salisbury, who attempted to win the good graces of Henry II through his chancellor Thomas Becket by means of this ambiguous work—a scathing satire of the vices of the courtesans as well as a manual of diplomacy for the king, whom he hoped to encourage to pay greater attention to the advice of his churchmen. *Policraticus,* which was frequently copied and translated, contains the celebrated maxim, "an illiterate king is like an ass with a crown," encouraging the powerful to embrace learning. In many ways this book resembled the "mirror of princes," in which moral advice and guidelines for behavior were offered to the future king so that, by exercising virtue and eschewing vice, he would ensure the happiness of his subjects. In 1279 Egidius Colonna, a member of the order of the Hermits of St. Augustine, wrote *De regimine principum,* which was to have considerable future success, for the young

Philip IV, king of France. During this same period, the poem *The Tyrolean King,* written in Thuringia, portrays a prince who introduces his son to the duties of administering his kingdom, hoping to initiate him into the responsibilities of government.

THE LATER MIDDLE AGES

Clearly, literary patronage has often had a narrowly political aspect as propaganda, criticism of an adversary, and even ideological commentary. But it did not remain within these confines and underwent considerable diversification toward the end of the Middle Ages. The pontifical curia, for example, favored the production of medical works on physiognomy and ways of extending life through the use of elixirs. In the thirteenth century Alfonso X the Wise, king of Castile and Léon, who claims to have taken Solomon as his model, had a number of legal texts compiled (*Espéculo, Fuero real,* and *Siete partidas*) but also encouraged translation from the Arabic and the writing of poems *(Cantigas de Santa María),* historical, astronomical, and mathematical works, even treatises on hunting and chess. In fourteenth-century France Charles V (the Wise) surrounded himself with a number of intellectuals, including lawyers and philosophers such as Nicole Oresme, Raoul de Presles, and Philippe de Mézières. He founded the royal library of the Louvre and commissioned French translations of Aristotle's ethical and political works as well as St. Augustine's *City of God.* His patronage was the origin of the *Songe du vergier* (Dream of the orchard), an encyclopedia vaunting the superiority of royal power, and a richly illuminated version of the *Grandes chroniques de France,* which glorified his dynasty. King Matthias I Corvinus played a similar role in Hungary in the fifteenth century; he was supported by the humanist chancellors Johannes Vitéz and Péter Váradi, who had studied at the University of Vienna and the University of Bologna, respectively. The list of "wise" kings in the thirteenth to fifteenth centuries could be extended. It demonstrates that, at the dawn of the Renaissance, many princes understood the personal benefit of literary patronage, at a time when knowledge had, more than ever, become power.

BIBLIOGRAPHY

Abels, Richard. *Alfred the Great: War, Kingship, and Culture in Anglo-Saxon England.* London and New York: Longman, 1998. Biography of a protector of literature.

Aurell, Martin. *La vielle et l'épée : Troubadours et politique en Provence au XIIIe siècle.* Paris: Aubier, 1989. Study of the sirventes and the courts of southern France.

———. *L'empire des Plantagenêt, 1154–1224.* Paris: Perrin, 2003. Political culture and the patronage of Henry II and his sons.

Autrand, Françoise. *Charles V: Le Sage,* Paris: Fayard, 1994. Another biography of a "wise" king.

Bezzola, Reto. *Les origines et la formation de la littérature courtoise en Occident (500–1200).* 3 vols. Paris: Honoré Champion, 1958–1967. A rich source of information on church culture.

Bumke, Joachim. *Courtly Culture: Literature and Society in the High Middle Ages.* Berkeley: University of California Press, 1991

Fontaine, Jacques. *Isidore de Séville: Genèse et originalité de la culture hispanique au temps des Wisigoths.* Turnhout, Belgium: Brepols, 2000. Vital source of information on the Visigoth kings and their literature.

Hanna, Ralph. "Sir Thomas Berkeley and His Patronage." *Speculum* 64 (1989): 878–916.

Heullant-Donat, Isabelle, ed. *Cultures italiennes (XIIe–XVe siècles).* Paris: Cerf, 2000. Several articles on the relation between writing and politics at the time of the early humanists.

Jaeger, C. Stephen. *The Origins of Courtliness: Civilizing Trends and the Formation of Courtly Ideals.* Philadelphia: University of Pennsylvania Press, 1985. Examines the influence of knowledge on the growth of courtly behavior.

Klein, Karen Wilk. *The Partisan Voice: A Study of the Political Lyric in France and Germany, 1180–1230.* Paris: Mouton, 1971. Study on the partisan lyric.

McKitterick, Rosamond, ed. *Carolingian Culture: Emulation and Innovation.* Cambridge, U.K.: Cambridge University Press, 1994.

Nelson, Janet L. *Charles the Bald.* London: Longman, 1992. Biography of an important patron.

Riché, Pierre. *Education and Culture in the Barbarian West, Sixth through Eighth Centuries.* Translated by John J. Contreni. Columbia: University of South Carolina Press, 1976. A classic work with an abundance of information on patronage among the German kings.

Sherman, Clair Richter. *Imaging Aristotle: Verbal and Visual Representation in Fourteenth–Century France.* Berkeley: University of California Press, 1995.

Vale, M. G. A. *The Princely Court: Medieval Courts and Culture in North-West Europe, 1270–1380.* Oxford: Oxford University Press, 2001.

Willard, Charity Cannon. *Christine de Pizan: Her Life and Works.* New York: Persea Books, 1984.

MARTIN AURELL
TRANSLATED FROM THE FRENCH BY ROBERT BONONNO

[See also **DMA:** Carolingian Latin Poetry; Charlemagne; Charles V of France; Contrafactum; John of Salisbury; Mirror of Princes; Sirventes; Troubadour, Trouvère.]

PEACEMAKING. In the modern Western world, peace tends to be thought of as a general state of affairs, defined negatively simply by the absence of war between societies or the absence of strife within a society. The two main conceptions of peace in the Middle Ages were entirely different.

THE BILATERAL PEACE

The first of these conceptions envisioned peace as a state of balanced, reciprocal relations among individuals, families, or political entities embodied by individuals such as kings. The hallmark of this kind of peace was that two individuals willingly agreed on the terms that ended a dispute between them; thus the term for "peace" (*pax*) came easily to shade into terms denoting "treaty" or "agreement" (such as *pactio/pactus, amicitia, fraternitas, foedus, concordia, convenientia*). One therefore spoke not of peace but of *a* peace, habitually treated as a voluntary relationship publicly manifested through formal signs of friendship.

In the nineteenth and early twentieth centuries, when medieval history was the ground on which German nationalisms were built, it was assumed that this kind of reciprocal, bilateral peace was a legacy of Germanic legal culture, quite different from Roman in both form and values. Since the 1950s, it has been recognized that much of what had been thought "Germanic" was, in fact, Roman or late Roman. This is true for the bilateral peace as well. It was already prominent in Roman law and later taken for granted by Isidore of Seville (*d.* 636); and when one finds Merovingian kings settling their feuds, regulating their interactions, and organizing their successions with pacts, it is a Gallo-Roman episcopacy that is teaching them the language of such bilateral peace.

The importance of this background for understanding peacemaking is that both the ritual forms of peacemaking and the politics underlying them reflect this assumption that peace was an ongoing relationship of trust and support between individuals of honorable status. In this sense, it was the opposite of feud. Of course, not since the time of the Germanic law codes, and perhaps not even then, did the Middle Ages have a strong notion of feud as popularly understood: revenge fighting passed on from generation to generation, implicating and obligating even distant kin and conducted according to strict rules of retaliation and escalation. However, medieval aristocracies—and free persons generally—did have a visceral and durable notion of feud in a looser sense, where injuries and affronts to honor required avenging by the victim and his or her immediate kin. The "feud" (*faida*) or "war" (*bellum*) that resulted was conceived of as a state of hostile social relations—*inimicitia,* in a common Latin formulation. Feud was therefore literally the opposite of "friendship" (*amicitia*). It was conceptually the opposite as well. Both, for example, were possible only between equals or men of honor (open disagreement by the unfree or half-free being interpreted not as feud but

as rebellion). The implications for peacemaking are important. If honor, friendship, and feud could exist only between equals, then the essential act of peacemaking was to have two parties engage each other in a relationship of equality (or at least honor) structured in terms of "friendship." Peacemaking therefore emphasized supportive reciprocities, made public by exchanges between the parties of items high in the scale of honor, most frequently gifts, oaths, hostages, and embraces or kisses. Indeed, defining the nature and value of these exchanges often required much hard bargaining and formed the larger part of the terms of a peace. Most important, since *inimicitia* was the opposite of *amicitia* and since *amicitia* was most essentially expressed by marriage (*amici* frequently referring to close affines), the best, most honorable kind of peace involved the exchange of women, through one or more marriages that united the parties by making *amici* out of *inimici* and turning the sons of enemies into brothers.

Since conflict among nobles and free persons was waged by individuals within specific localities or associational groupings, conflict was ended by mobilizing social relations that were specific to those individuals and their groupings. Usually the peacemakers would be neighbors, shared kin, or common lords and patrons, all acting as third-party mediators or "go-betweens" (*intercurrentes*—"those who run in between"—was a frequent term for mediators of all sorts). Since peace required both parties to be treated with honor and since peace both presumed and confirmed a stance of equality, in many cases, especially those involving property, the peace negotiated often simply required an equal division of the rights in dispute, regardless of "right" or "law." The settlement of Icelandic feuds, particularly when melees involved numerous fighters and multiple woundings and slayings, typically balanced out the injuries and killings according to a commonsense calculus of blame, severity, status, and power called "man-evening" (*mannjafnaðr*). Marriage alliances between disputants and their families were common. Because they were more adaptable, fictive kinship ties were even more so—these included fosterage, especially in Iceland, with one party ceding a son to the other to be raised within that family, and hostage giving, in England and on the Continent, with one party sending a son to the court of the other to be raised. Spiritual kinship ties were more pervasive still. In the ninth and early-tenth centuries, pacts between a Christian king and a non-Christian chieftain often stipulated the baptism of the latter together with all his family and household, uniting both sides by ties of spiritual kinship. Here again, the fundamental principles of equality and honor are revealed by the fact that such treaties often provide our very first evidence for the pagan chieftain being accepted as a "king" and by the carefully maintained parallelism between the baptized and their baptismal sponsors: father and father, wife and wife, sons and sons, nobles and nobles, all members of a single spiritual "family."

With the foundation, reform, and endowment of monasteries in the ninth and tenth centuries and the consequent development of complex networks of monastic patronage linking local aristocracies, disputants would usually share a patronage relationship with some nearby monastery. Monasteries therefore became prized go-betweens in peacemaking. And when monks managed to negotiate an end to the dispute, the resolution required the parties to formalize the spiritual kinship that bound them within the shared monastic nexus—through joint gifts of land to the monastery, oblations of children, or rights of spiritual "brotherhood" (fraternitas) that gave the parties privileges of burial or commemoration within the monastery.

Even in the later Middle Ages, with the appearance of formal courts and court procedures under the aegis of more centralized governments, the above characteristics often remained the cultural norm hidden behind formal legal language. For example, thirteenth-century English county and manorial courts regularly gave litigants a "love day" on which they could try to settle a case without formal judgment, by agreement, to become "at one with each other" (une genz, "one family")—and the negotiations proceeded and ended much like they would have two hundred years earlier, right down to an even division of the rights in dispute. In the twelfth and thirteenth centuries, when ecclesiastical disputes were increasingly brought to the papal audientia to be settled through a learned, Romanized procedure, the papacy's procedure of choice was to have the dispute tried locally by judges-delegate nominated by the parties. The judges were usually their neighbors, shared superiors, or common associates; their preferred settlement technique was to get the parties to agree to mediators (chosen from the same common network of superiors and friends), who would settle the dispute as old-fashioned intercurrentes, fashioning a concordia that restored amicitia to the parties. Even in the last century of the Middle Ages, apparently new "international" treaties between rulers were still written according to the centuries-old forms that represented peace as an agreement between those who were brothers by marriage.

PEACEMAKING TO RESTORE ORDER

One of the most important things on which peacemakers had to get parties to agree was how to categorize a dispute: honorable feud, unwarranted injury, or faithless rebellion. If it were one of the latter two, ending the conflict would require the loser to perform some humiliating act of satisfaction, such as the early medieval harmscara, in which he might have to approach the offended lord to ask forgiveness by carrying a saddle on his back or a dead dog around his neck. Given their sense of atoning a wrong against an authority, such rituals were readily integrated into a discourse of sin that permeated a second way of imagining peace that required correspondingly different forms of peacemaking. This essentially Augustinian conception imagined peace as social harmony founded on the respect inferiors owed superiors and the protection superiors owed inferiors, where such asymmetrical obligations reflected a set of embedded hierarchical relationships (human/animal, man/woman, spirit/body) culminating in that between God and his creation. This kind of peace tended to be most readily imaginable in social groupings that were well bounded physically or conceptually: monasteries and churches throughout the Middle Ages; the king's court in the early Middle Ages; cities and kingdoms in the later Middle Ages. Disputes perceived by elites as violating this standard of peace were judged not according to an ethos of mutual honor but as rebellion, as the pollution of a social body, as the overthrow of a divinely ordained order by inferiors who had stepped above their place or rejected the authority of their natural superiors. In such situations, the restoration of peace required the restoration of order through acts of atonement and satisfaction borrowed largely from the language of public penance.

Prominent within monastic communities as far back as the sixth-century Rule of St. Benedict, this conceptualization of peace was taken over by royal courts in the ninth and tenth centuries and by towns in the eleventh century. Monastic and ecclesiastical rites of penitential atonement and satisfaction were taken over with them, so that the rebel came to be assimilated to a sinner against a sacramental body. When required to capitulate or compromise, offenders prostrated themselves, begged pardon, received corporal punishment, or performed humiliating public rituals. Adulterers, for example, were paraded through town half-naked and bound by cords, and criminals performed amendes honorables by walking barefoot through streets to churches, where they would kneel and be publicly beaten. Visible from the eleventh century in the Peace of God and gathering force and frequency in the later Middle Ages are similar but more explosive peacemaking rites intended to restore broken relations between God and humankind (more precisely, where droughts, famines, and epidemics suggested that such relations had been violated). Here, masses of individuals in a town or village would engage in collective penitential rites, often set off by touring preachers or bands of penitents, who told the crowds around them that disasters indicated God's displeasure with humanity and required acts of atonement and satisfaction. Invariably, feuds were the fundamental ill thought to have set off all the others.

Thus medieval Europe's dilemma: peace was a collective good that could only be established by individuals. In the end, the right of individuals won out every time. Even the most frenzied collective penitential revivals assumed that making peace in a feud was the responsibility and decision of the individuals dishonored. And no matter how much political theorists favored the hierarchical, Augustinian idea of peace, ordinary political rhetoric usually described social peace as a generalized, highly Christianized bilateral peace. Thus the centerpiece of Carolingian *admonitiones generales* was a ringing demand "that there be peace, concord, and unanimity among all the Christian people between bishops, abbots, counts, judges, and all persons everywhere whether greater or lesser." Three centuries later, a reformed monastic order like the Cistercians saw itself as a society regulated not by coercive law imposed by superiors but as a brotherhood of equals agreeing to end disputes in love through pacts and concords. Even the urban "commune" was at first essentially a "peace" among elites of a city that determined how they would avoid and settle conflicts among themselves, and it was this understanding of peace that motivated later penitential movements within cities: even while preaching that a city as a whole had been possessed by demons who fractured the unity of the community by fostering feuds, they could still restore unity only by convincing specific enemies to make a specific peace with each other. Despite its importance, the Augustinian ideal of peace as social order therefore never challenged an even more fundamental assumption enshrined in the bilateral peace: whatever the value of the collectivity, peace required the willing agreement of individuals, seen here, even at the most critical social conjunctures, as autonomous and sovereign.

BIBLIOGRAPHY

Althoff, Gerd. *Spielregeln der Politik im Mittelalter: Kommunikation in Frieden und Fehde.* Darmstadt, Germany: Primus Verlag, 1997.

Cheyette, Frederick L. "Suum cuique tribuere." *French Historical Studies* 6 (1970): 287–299.

Clanchy, Michael. "Law and Love in the Middle Ages." In *Disputes and Settlements: Law and Human Relations in the West.* Edited by John Bossy. Cambridge, U.K.: Cambridge University Press, 1983.

Kosto, Adam J. *Making Agreements in Medieval Catalonia: Power, Order, and the Written Word, 1000–1200.* Cambridge, U.K.: Cambridge University Press, 2001.

Koziol, Geoffrey. *Begging Pardon and Favor: Ritual and Political Order in Early Medieval France.* Ithaca, N.Y.: Cornell University Press, 1992.

———. "Monks, Feuds, and the Making of Peace in Eleventh-Century Flanders." In *The Peace of God: Social Violence and Religious Response in France around the Year 1000.* Edited by Thomas Head and Richard Landes. Ithaca, N.Y.: Cornell University Press, 1992.

Le Jan, Régine. *Famille et pouvoir dans le monde franc (VIIe–Xe siècle): Essai d'anthropologie sociale.* Paris: Publications de la Sorbonne, 1995.

Miller, William Ian. *Bloodtaking and Peacemaking: Feud, Law, and Society in Saga Iceland.* Chicago: University of Chicago Press, 1990.

Schneider, Reinhard. *Brüdergemeine und Schwurfreundschaft: Der Auflösungsprozess des Karlingerreiches im Spiegel der Karitas-Terminologie in den Verträgen der karlingischen Teilkönige des 9. Jahrhunderts.* Lübeck, Germany: Matthiesen, 1964.

Tardif, Joseph. "Un abrégé juridique des Etymologies d'Isidore de Séville." In *Mélanges Julien Havet.* Paris: E. Leroux, 1895. The text of Isidore of Seville's *Interrogationes seu interpretationes de legibus divinis et humanis.*

Wallace-Hadrill, J. M. "War and Peace in the Early Middle Ages." In *Early Medieval History.* Oxford: Basil Blackwell, 1975.

White, Stephen D. "*Pactum Legem Vincit et Amor Judicium:* The Settlement of Disputes by Compromise in Eleventh-Century Western France." *American Journal of Legal History* 22 (1978): 281–308.

———. "Feuding and Peace-Making in the Touraine around the Year 1100." *Traditio* 42 (1986): 195–263.

GEOFFREY KOZIOL

[See also **DMA:** Benedictine Rule; Law, Civil—Corpus Iuris, Revival and Spread; Law, German: Early Germanic Codes; Peace of God, Truce of God.]

PEDRO III "THE GREAT" OF ARAGON, KING (Pere II in Catalonia, 1240–1285).

Pedro was the son of James I of Aragon and Iolanda of Hungary. His rise to prominence began in 1257, when his father appointed him procurator of Catalonia. Of greater significance during these early years was his marriage in 1262 to Constance, the daughter of Manfred Hohenstaufen and the heiress of Naples and Sicily.

Pedro succeeded James I after the latter's death in July 1276. According to traditional Aragonese policy of splitting the kingdom among surviving sons, Pedro inherited Aragon, Catalonia, and Valencia, while his younger brother James received Majorca, Rousillon, and Cerdanya. At the time of Pedro's succession, the crown was threatened by two rebellions: one led by Catalan nobles who had grown increasingly rebellious to royal demands and a second by the Muslim population of Valencia. By

1280, Pedro had succeeded in quelling both revolts, and he prepared to make good his wife's claim to Sicily, which Charles of Anjou had wrested from the Hohenstaufens in the mid-1260s.

In March 1282, the Sicilians revolted against Angevin rule—perhaps with Pedro's help and almost certainly with his knowledge—and called on the protection of Pedro and Constance. The annexation of the island to the Crown of Aragon proceeded swiftly, but then the real problems began. The pope, the Frenchman Martin IV, quickly condemned the rebels and placed Sicily under an interdict. He punished Pedro by excommunicating him and then formally deposing him in March 1283. Martin then named Charles of Valois, the son of Philip III of France, as king of Aragon, and the French began plans for an invasion. In spite of the forces arrayed against him, by the late spring of 1283 Pedro had subdued most of the Angevin forces in Sicily, at which point he returned to Iberia.

The situation in Spain was not much better, as the nobles of Aragon, unhappy with Pedro's Sicilian venture, were threatening to depose him. The Catalans and Valencians also had grievous complaints against their monarch. In order to pacify them and urgently needing their help against the coming French army, Pedro agreed to a number of demands that essentially changed the relationship between the crown and its subjects. Among the more notable concessions, Pedro consented to convene the *corts,* or *cortes* (the representative assemblies of his kingdoms), on a regular basis and agreed that new laws or special taxes needed the agreement of his people.

The French army finally materialized in the spring of 1285 under the leadership of Philip III himself and in the form of a crusade officially sanctioned by the papacy. After some initial successes the crusade fell apart as Pedro's navy disrupted its lines of communications and supplies and pestilence attacked its ranks. As the army returned to France, Philip fell ill and died in Perpignan. Pedro's ability not only to survive but also to emerge victorious against the enormous forces against him afterwards earned him the sobriquet "the Great."

Pedro immediately turned his attention to those who had betrayed him, especially his brother James, who had allied himself with the French. However, as Pedro was preparing his invasion of Majorca, he fell ill and died on 11 November 1285.

BIBLIOGRAPHY

Bisson, Thomas N. *The Medieval Crown of Aragon: A Short History.* Oxford: Oxford University Press, 1986.

Desclot, Bernat. *Chronicle of the Reign of King Pedro III of Aragon by Bernat Desclot.* Translated by F. L. Critchlow. 2 vols. Princeton, N.J.: Princeton University Press, 1928–1934.

Hillgarth, J. N. *The Spanish Kingdoms, 1250–1516.* Oxford: Oxford University Press, 1976. The works by Bisson and Hillgarth provide useful and complementary introductions to Pedro's reign.

Runciman, Stephen. *The Sicilian Vespers: A History of the Mediterranean World in the Later Thirteenth Century.* Cambridge, U.K.: Cambridge University Press, 1958.

Soldevila, Ferran. *Pere el Gran.* Barcelona: Institut d'Estudis Catalans, 1995. Cut short by the death of the author but still the best biography.

JARBEL RODRIGUEZ

[See also **DMA:** Angevins: France, England, Sicily; Aragon, Crown of (1137–1479); Crusades, Political; Hohenstaufen Dynasty; Sicilian Vespers; Sicily, Kingdom of; **Supp:** James I of Aragon, King.]

PERAULT, WILLIAM (**Guillaume Peyraut, William Peraldus,** *ca.* 1200–*ca.* 1271).

William Perault's *Summa de vitiis et virtutibus* (The sum of vices and virtues, *ca.* 1260) was one of the most influential medieval treatises on the topic of the Seven Deadly Sins. Perault was probably born around 1200 in Peyraut in the modern French department of Ardèche. He joined the Dominican order in Lyons sometime in the 1230s. In 1249, he was the order's official preacher in that city, and in 1261 he was elected prior of the local Dominican house. He would live ten more years, dying in 1271. At some point he may have studied at the University of Paris, but this fact, along with many others about his life, is obscured by missing and erroneous information.

Perault wrote the *Summa* in two parts, completing the first around 1236 and the second in 1248. The first part, dealing with the vices, is divided into nine books. Book 1 offers a general introduction to the vices. Books 2 through 8 deal with each of the Seven Deadly Sins, while the last book examines the sin of the tongue, the *peccatum linguae,* and is one of the earliest to deal with this type of sin. All of the books but the first are ordered along similar lines. They begin by explaining why the sin in question is evil or offensive to God. This is followed by a more in-depth analysis of the sin as well as related transgressions. Finally, Perault offers a remedy for each sin. The part dealing with the virtues does not share the same organized structure; it is more a collection of information on the virtues, and it includes a book on the Holy Spirit and one on the Beatitudes.

Perault wrote the *Summa* to aid his Dominican brethren with their preaching duties. The work was filled with *exempla,* as the author used stories to depict some of the vices. He also quoted extensively from the Fathers and from Gregory the Great, whose *Moralia on Job* served as the basis for much of the later work on the Seven Deadly Sins. The author, however, did not intend the *Summa* to be a work of high theology or canon law. Instead, it was aimed at making the vices and the virtues understandable to the masses of Christendom. It was a preaching tool. The Dominican Master General Humbert of Romans (*ca.* 1194–1277) considered it one of the texts that every Dominican priory should have. Consequently, the *Summa* became one of the most widely transmitted books of the medieval period—it has survived in hundreds of manuscripts. However, its fame and usefulness went beyond the Dominicans, as it was also widely circulated among the Franciscans and other orders.

The *Summa*'s greatest contribution may be its impact on later writers. We find its influence in a variety of genres, including encyclopedias, penitentials, and other works on the virtues and the vices. The most famous borrower of Perault was probably Geoffrey Chaucer, whose "Parson's Tale" owes a considerable debt to the *Summa de vitiis* for its material.

BIBLIOGRAPHY

Bloomfield, Morton W. *The Seven Deadly Sins: An Introduction to the History of a Religious Concept, with Special Reference to Medieval English Literature.* East Lansing: Michigan State College Press, 1952. Good introduction to the topic, with useful comments on Perault.

Dondaine, Antoine. "Guillaume Peyraut: Vie et oeuvres." *Archivum Fratrum Praedicatorum* 18 (1948) 162–236. Biography and analysis of Perault's works; also includes an incomplete, though extensive, list of surviving *Summa* manuscripts.

Newhauser, Richard. *The Treatise on Vices and Virtues in Latin and the Vernacular.* Turnhout, Belgium: Brepols, 1993. Perhaps the best English introduction.

Petersen, Kate Oelzner. *The Sources of the Parson's Tale.* New York: AMS Press, 1973.

Jarbel Rodriguez

[See also **DMA:** Chaucer, Geoffrey; Dominicans; Middle English Literature; Seven Deadly Sins; **Supp:** Humbert of Romans; Virtues and Vices.]

PERCY FAMILY. The house of Percy, which was to become one of the greatest families in northern England during the later Middle Ages, originated from Percy-en-Auge in Normandy. William (I) de Percy, who came to England in 1067, probably aided William the Conqueror in the brutal suppression of Anglo-Saxon resistance in the northern counties, and by 1070 he was established in Yorkshire, where he built the castle of Topcliffe and refounded the derelict abbey of Whitby. The twelfth century saw the family consolidating its position, particularly in the Yorkshire district of Craven, though it possessed estates in other counties. By 1166, William's grandson William (II) Percy, who in 1138 played an important role in the Anglo-Norman victory over the Scots at the Battle of the Standard (at Northallerton, Yorkshire), held over forty knight's fees. Though still only of comparatively modest ranking within the English aristocracy, Richard Percy was among the discontent northern nobles who opposed King John and in 1215 was named in Magna Carta as one of the committee of twenty-five lords appointed to ensure John kept its provisions. By contrast, his grandson Henry (II) Percy was captured at the Battle of Lewes in 1264, fighting for Henry III against Simon de Montfort. An important step toward the extension of Percy influence into Northumberland came in 1309 when Henry (III) Percy, who had been created a baron in 1296 and had played a prominent role in the Scottish campaigns of Edward I, purchased the great castle of Alnwick, which was to become to be one of the family's principal seats. As one of the Ordainers, he opposed the misrule of Edward II and took part in the capture, but not the execution, of Piers Gaveston. In 1346, his son Henry, second baron Percy, fought with distinction at the Battle of Neville's Cross, outside Durham, where the Scottish king David II was captured.

The establishment of the family as the dominant power in the north was the achievement of Henry Percy (1341–1408), first earl of Northumberland, an accomplished soldier, diplomat, and administrator. Rising to prominence in the service of the dukes of Lancaster, Percy was created sheriff of Northumberland for life in 1372, then earl at Richard II's coronation in 1377. He undertook diplomatic missions to Scotland and France and in 1389 was made governor of Calais. Through his second marriage to the heiress of Thomas Lucy, Percy gained the castle and honor of Cockermouth and later obtained the lordship of Egremont, thereby extending his influence into Cumberland, while in Northumberland he was lord of the castles of Alnwick, Warkworth, Langley, and Prudhoe and custodian of the great royal fortresses of Newcastle and Bamburgh. Briefly granted the sole wardenship of both the West and East March in 1384, Percy enjoyed virtual autonomy in the governance of the north and, as E. F. Jacob observed, "frequently behaved with all the freedom of a sixteenth-century elector of Saxony." By 1399, Percy's mounting resentment at Richard II's misgovernment led to his re-

Alnwick Castle. *Henry (III) Percy's purchase of the great castle of Alnwick in 1309 was an important step toward the extension of Percy influence into Northumberland.* ERICH LESSING/ART RESOURCE, NY. REPRODUCED BY PERMISSION.

fusal to join the king in Ireland, resulting in a sentence of banishment. Accordingly, he and his son Henry became leading supporters of Henry of Bolingbroke's coup d'état against Richard later that year, following which they were richly rewarded. Though also famed for his courtliness, the younger Henry Percy (1364–1403), immortalized in Shakespeare's *Henry IV, Part One,* earned his sobriquet "Hotspur" from his impetuousness as a commander, well demonstrated at Otterburn on 19 August 1388, when he launched a night attack on a Scottish raiding force. In the confused battle (made famous in the "Ballad of Chevy Chase"), the Scots commander James, earl of Douglas, was slain but Percy himself was captured. Quickly ransomed, Percy served as governor of Bordeaux in 1393, commanded the royal forces sent to crush rebellion in Wales in 1401, and the following year assisted his father in the notable victory at Homildon Hill, where the English longbowmen routed the Scottish army. Yet, although the Percys were at the apogee of their power, Henry IV's failure to reimburse their heavy campaign expenses and his refusal to allow them to offset this debt with the ransoms from prisoners taken at Homildon led to their increasing alienation. In 1403, they plotted to ally with Owain Glyn Dwr and place Edmund Mortimer, earl of March and the nephew of Hotspur's wife, on the throne, now claiming that Henry IV had broken a promise made to them in 1399 that his aim was not to depose Richard but only to recover his inheri-

tance. Hotspur's premature insurrection, however, allowed Henry IV to intercept his army before he could join forces with the Welsh or receive reinforcements from Northumberland. At Shrewsbury on 21 July 1403, Hotspur was slain and his uncle Thomas Percy, earl of Worcester, was executed soon after. Though Hotspur's father was pardoned, he could never be truly reconciled with Henry IV. In 1405 he incited the rebellion of Richard Scrope, archbishop of York, but after failing to provide military support, he fled to Scotland. While making a new incursion in 1408, he was slain by royalist troops at Bramham Moor, near Tadcaster.

Despite these disasters, the family remained powerful, and during the Wars of the Roses their political affinities reflected the bitter feud with their long-standing rivals, the Nevilles. The second earl of Northumberland fell in the first battle at St. Albans in 1455 against the Yorkists, while his son, Henry, third earl, took part in the Lancastrian victories at Wakefield, 1460, and at the second battle at St. Albans in 1461, only to be slain himself later that year at the bloody Battle of Towton. Though Percy's forfeited estates and earldom were granted to John Neville in 1464, Edward IV's distrust of Neville's power led him to reinstate his son Henry Percy as the fourth earl of Northumberland in 1470. Percy backed Richard III's usurpation in 1483 but at the Battle of Bosworth failed to support Richard and subsequently found favor with Henry VII before being killed in a tax riot in 1489. The Percy family continued to play a leading role in the politics of the north throughout the sixteenth century, supporting the Pilgrimage of Grace in 1536 and, as one of the leading Catholic families, the northern rebellion against Elizabeth I in 1569.

BIBLIOGRAPHY

Bean, J. M. W. *The Estates of the Percy Family, 1416–1537.* Oxford: Oxford University Press, 1958.

———. "Henry IV and the Percies." *History* 44 (1959): 212–227.

Hicks, M. A. "Dynastic Change and Northern Society: The Career of the Fourth Earl of Northumberland, 1470–1489." *Northern History* 14 (1978): 78–107.

Jacob, E. F. *The Fifteenth Century, 1399–1485.* Oxford: Clarendon Press, 1961.

Rose, Alexander. *Kings in the North: The House of Percy in British History.* London: Weidenfeld and Nicolson, 2002.

Storey, R. L. "Wardens of the Marches of England toward Scotland, 1377–1489." *English Historical Review* 72 (1957): 593–615.

Weiss, Michael. "A Power in the North? The Percies in the Fifteenth Century." *Historical Journal* 19 (1976): 501–509.

MATTHEW STRICKLAND

[See also **DMA:** England: Norman-Angevin; England: 1216–1485; Henry IV of England; Richard II; Wars of the Roses.]

PERSIAN LANGUAGE. New Persian, the language of medieval Iran, evolved from Old Persian, the language of the Achaemenid era (*ca.* 550–330 B.C.), and from its more immediate predecessor, Middle Persian, of the Sasanian period (A.D. 226–636) In the Middle Ages, New Persian was the written and literary language of many Iranian and non-Iranian ethnic groups that spread well beyond the present borders of Iran, into parts of present-day Iraq, Afghanistan, Central Asia, and the Caucasus. Distinct Iranian dialects continue to flourish in these regions. This article will discuss the development and characteristics of New Persian, including issues of script, and the principal Iranian dialects that have survived into the present.

Iranian languages in general belong to the Indo-European family of languages, that is, to languages whose speakers identify themselves as "Aryans," a linguistic term by which the ancient peoples of India and Iran designated their distinct Indo-European branch. While there is now much debate about the original areas of Indo-European languages, there is some consensus among Iranologists that these lands of origin were probably the steppes of Central Asia, between the Caspian and Aral Seas, and northward. A branch of this group moved southward sometime during the second millennium B.C., toward Afghanistan and, later, India. The people now called "Iranians," and sometimes "Irano-Aryans," eventually expanded toward the west and the east. The move of one of their groups onto the Iranian plateau set in motion the beginnings of vast empires made up of many ethnic groups and languages.

The three stages of the Persian language, Old, Middle (also known as *pahlavī*), and New (or *darī*), derive from the language of the people of the province of Fārs (the "true" Persia, historically speaking), located in southwestern Iran, in empires inhabited by other groups, such as Medes, Parthians, and Sogdians. The Persians, inhabitants of Fārs, became politically predominant under the Achaemenid and Sasanian dynasties and through them Persian was slowly imposed upon a huge empire. New Persian spread eastward in pre-Islamic times through the activities of Sasanian merchants. After the Muslim conquest of Iran (A.D. 637–644), New Persian was firmly established on the Iranian plateau, and it is likely that Muslim armies helped it to spread north and northeast. It is interesting to note that the first surviving records of New Persian literature originate from these eastern regions, from the cities of Ṭūs, Herat, Merv, and Gurganj, located at a considerable distance from the southwestern cradle of the language.

According to linguists, the differences between Old and Middle Persian are substantial both phonetically and grammatically, similar to differences between Latin and French. Most of the surviving traces of Old Persian come from two types of sources: epigraphic, such as the monument inscriptions of Darius I (*d.* 486 B.C.) and Xerxes I (*d.* 465 B.C.) of the Achaemenid period; and textual, represented by the Avesta, the collection of texts that comprises the scripture of Zoroastrianism, the pre-Islamic religion of Iran. Only a few inscriptions and a number of texts in Parthian (mostly on Manichaeism), written after the fall of the Parthians, survive from the Parthian era (247 B.C.–A.D. 225). Middle Persian appears with the Sasanians and is well represented by Zoroastrian literature.

NEW PERSIAN *(DARĪ)*

New Persian, the language of medieval as well as present-day Iran, remains close to Middle Persian, especially phonetically. The relationship between these three stages is clearly demonstrated, for example, by the word for "king": Old Persian *khshāyathiya*; both Middle and New Persian, *shāh*. Similarly, the syntax and morphology of Middle and New Persian are closely related. However, the vocabulary of New Persian expanded considerably with the absorption of words from other Iranian dialects, such as Parthian and Sogdian. After the Muslim conquest, New Persian incorporated a large Arabic vocabulary.

Arabic literary texts attest to the fact that New Persian was called *darī*, or, sometimes, *pārsī* (from "Fārs") in the tenth century and probably much earlier. *Darī* derives from *dar* ("court"; literally, "gate"), which suggests that it was the language of the court in the Sasanian capital at Ctesiphon. However, *darī* was also in use in Khorāsān in the eastern province of the empire. The tenth-century Arab geographer al-Muqaddasī (*b. ca.* A.D. 946) claims in his famous book *Aḥsān al-Taqā sīm fī ma ʿrifat al-aqālīm* (The best divisions for knowledge of the regions) that *darī* was just one of the Iranian dialects that, together, were called *pārsī,* a form of Persian that we may assume was the common spoken language of the Persian empire. Some scholars believe that *darī* may have been from the beginning a kind of formal, perhaps chancery language of the Sasanian court and gradually spread eastward, although the official language of the Sasanian court was Middle Persian *(pahlavī).* According to Ibn al-Muqaffaʿ, a Manichaean or Zoroastrian convert to Islam in the eighth century, Middle Persian was spoken in Media, *fārsī* was the language of the province of Fārs, and *darī* was the language of the eastern parts of the empire centering around Balkh. *Darī* was also the first written New Persian language just prior to the adoption of the Arabic script.

Darī is unlike the Persian languages spoken in the northwestern and southeastern regions of the Persian empire. Although it gradually absorbed many dialectal features, it was clearly distinct from Middle Persian and quite adequate as a literary vehicle. By the tenth century *darī* and Persian literature were also firmly established in the western provinces and throughout Iran. While it cannot be maintained that *darī* is the direct continuation of any particular form of Middle Persian, linguists agree that it is a more evolved form of that language whose basic aspects originated in the southwestern parts of the empire and were subsequently enriched by a strong admixture of dialectal features from the northern, western, and eastern provinces and by a considerable influx of foreign vocabulary. *Darī* continues to be the designation of literary Persian to the present day.

The influence of Arabic. The literary language of Iran has not changed morphologically from its earliest stage to the present. Its vocabulary, however, has expanded considerably, primarily through contact with the Arabic language beginning in the middle of the seventh century. Many Persian words and expressions fell into disuse in the new, increasingly Islamized Iranian world, and many more new words and concepts entered the Persian language in order to express the political, religious, and social changes of becoming a province of the Muslim caliphate. The tremendous flexibility of Arabic presented a ready supply of words which penetrated New Persian and led to a mixed language accepted by the educated elite but resented by many purists. Some Mongol and Turkic words also entered the language through waves of Mongol and Turkic conquests of the Persianate (a term coined by the historian Marshall G. Hodgson in *The Venture of Islam* to indicate the spread of the Persian language and Iranian culture beyond the borders of present-day Iran) world.

Scripts. The Old Persian system of writing (archaic and in limited use, primarily in royal inscriptions) was a type of cuneiform that consisted primarily of a syllabary and some logograms of Akkadian symbols. Middle Persian, with its great paucity of letters to represent sounds, was no less complicated and cumbersome; it employed Aramaic heterograms and masks for the spoken language, a graphic system known as "Huzvāresh" (*Zuvārishn*). This script was known and used almost exclusively by priests and scribes who had a vested interest in limiting access to it. It is interesting to note, therefore, that the earliest written traces of New Persian uncovered thus far are in the Hebrew alphabet. Iranian Jews, whose sojourn in Iran is traditionally dated to 587 B.C. (Nebuchadnezzar's exile of the Judeans to Babylonia), have left behind epigraphic and documentary evidence to this effect dating from the second half of the eighth century. As in the case of other "Jewish" languages, the Hebrew alphabet proved itself adequate to record the common language *(darī)* of Iran, not incidentally marking the beginning of what was to develop into Judeo-Persian literature. Interestingly, other minorities, such as the Christians of Turkistan, also experimented with writing New Persian in a different script, in their case Syriac.

Given the difficulties in using the script of Middle Persian, it is not surprising that the Arabic script, easier both to write and to learn, spread quickly through the Persianate world with only minor changes, such as omitting the Arabic emphatic consonants and adopting the Arabic approximate consonants *b, j,* and *k* for the Persian sounds *p, ch,* and *g* that were absent in Arabic. Although Persian has many more long vowels than Arabic, the latter script can accommodate these as well. One major deficiency was the inability of the Arabic script to indicate the genitive case and adjectival connection of the Persian language, known by its Arabic term, *iḍāfat*. The new alphabet also caused, to some extent, the mispronunciation of some archaic Persian words as well as of newly integrated Arabic vocabulary. Perhaps these shortcomings were amply compensated for by the highly ornamental quality of the Arabic script. Calligraphy developed into a distinct field of Islamic art throughout the Muslim world and especially in Iran.

IRANIAN DIALECTS

As a field of linguistics, dialectology is comparatively new, having begun in the nineteenth century with the effort to better define the historical features of Indo-European peoples. Pre-Islamic Iranian texts as well as living Iranian languages began to be studied in depth only in the second half of that century. While there is no general agreement as to what truly differentiates the concept of language from that of dialect, most linguists agree that a systematic phonology, grammar, and lexicon, in general use in a given geographic area by a specific group of people, constitutes a language. Therefore the concept of dialect is best described as the encroachment of any type of variation on the three elements just mentioned; it is not always easy to distinguish between languages that are closely related and dialects. Thus, of necessity, the study of dialects is comparative in nature.

The diversity of languages and dialects in the Persianate world is particularly rich. Early Muslim geographers took ample notice of this diversity and were the first to record geographic variants that were in existence side by side with the development of *darī*. The dialects of early Iranian languages have been reconstructed to some extent based on names of persons and places preserved in early records from Mesopotamia.

Both Iranian languages and dialects have been divided into two major categories, western and eastern, a classification that persists into the present, although some linguists dispute its validity, preferring a division into northern and southern Iranian and even into southwestern, northwestern, southeastern, and northeastern; all these divisions correspond only roughly to the geographic distribution of Iranian dialects. The earliest forms of the western branch are Old Persian and Avestan. They remained distinct from eastern languages and dialects, such as Sogdian, Saka (Khotanese and Tumshuqese), and Chorasmian, throughout the Parthian era. Basic Persian prevails in the entire western branch in Iran, Afghanistan, Tajikistan, and Tātī-Persian (in the southern Caucasus). The major dialects of the western branch are Kurdish and Baluchi; lesser dialects are Zāzā, Gōrānī, various Tātī and Tāleŝī dialects, Gīlakī, and Lorī, each in distinct geographic areas.

Eastern Iranian languages are spoken mostly in lands to the east of present-day Iran. The most important eastern Iranian language is Pashto; Parāčī and Ōrmurī, the Pamir region languages (with numerous subdivisions of their own), Yaḡnōbī, and Ossetic also fall into this category.

New Persian and the numerous Iranian dialects still in existence cover an enormous geographic area and are spoken by a large number of peoples whose kinship, at least in the linguistic realm, has endured over the millennia.

BIBLIOGRAPHY

PRIMARY WORKS

Muqaddasī, Muḥammad ibn Aḥmad. *The Best Divisions for Knowledge of the Regions.* Translated by Basil Anthony Collins. Reading, U.K.: Garnet Publishing, 1994.

SECONDARY WORKS

Bailey, Harold W. "Persian: II. Language and Dialects." In *Encyclopaedia of Islam.* Leiden, Netherlands: E. J. Brill, 1936. Reprint 1987.

Darmesteter, James. *Études iraniennes, par James Darmesteter.* Paris: F. Vieweg, 1883.

Emmerick, Ronald E. "Indo-Iranian Languages: The Iranian Languages." In *The New Encyclopedia Britannica.* Vol. 22. Chicago: Encyclopaedia Britannica, 2002.

Geiger, Wilhelm, and Ernst Kuhn, eds. *Grundriss der iranischen Philologie.* Vol. 1. 1895–1904. Reprint, Berlin and New York: De Gruyter, 1974.

Henning, Walter B. "Mitteliranisch." In *Handbuch der Orientalistik.* Vol. 1. Edited by B. Spuler. Leiden, Netherlands: E. J. Brill, 1958.

Khānlarī, Parvīz Nātil. *Zabān shināsī va zabān-i Fārsī.* Tehran: Amīr-i kabīr, 1964.

———. *Tārīkh-i zabān-i fārsī.* 3 vols. Tehran: Nashr-i Naw, 1990.

Lazard, Gilbert. "Dialectologie de la langue persane d'après les textes des Xe–XIe siècles ap. J.-C." *Revue de la Faculté des Lettres de Tabriz* 13, no. 2 (1961): 1–18.

———. *La langue des plus anciens monuments de la prose persane.* Paris: C. Klincksieck, 1963.

———. "Pahlavi, Pârsi, Dari: Les langues de l'Iran d'après Ibn al-Muqaffaʿ." In *Iran and Islam: In Memory of the Late Vladimir Minorsky.* Edinburgh: Edinburgh University Press, 1971.

———. "The Rise of the New Persian Language." In *The Cambridge History of Iran.* Vol. 4. Edited by R. N. Frye. Cambridge, U.K.: Cambridge University Press, 1975.

———. "Le judéo-persan ancien entre le pehlevi et le persan." In *Transition Periods in Iranian History.* Louvain, Belgium: L'Association pour l'avancement des Études Iraniennes, 1987.

———. "Lumières nouvelles sur la formation de la langue persane: Une traduction du Coran en persan dialectal et ses affinités avec le judéo-persan." In *Irano-Judaica II: Studies Relating to Jewish Contacts with Persian Culture throughout the Ages.* Edited by Shaul Shaked and A. Netzer. Jerusalem, Israel: Ben-Zvi Institute, 1990.

——. "Pârsi et dari: Nouvelles remarques." *Bulletin of the Asia Institute* 4 (1990): 239–242.

——. "Reconstructing the Development of New Persian." *Al-ʿUṣur al-Wuṣṭā* 5 (1993).

——. "Rīšahā-yi zabānī-i fārsī-i adabī." *Irān-nāma* 11 (1993).

——. "Darī." In *Encyclopaedia Iranica*. Edited by Ehsan Yarshater. Costa Mesa, Calif.: Mazda Publishers, 1996.

Sims-Williams, Nicholas. "Eastern Iranian Languages." In *Encyclopaedia Iranica*. Edited by Ehsan Yarshater. Costa Mesa, Calif.: Mazda Publishers, 1996.

Windfuhr, Gernot L. "Dialectology." In *Encyclopaedia Iranica*. Edited by Ehsan Yarshater. Costa Mesa, Calif.: Mazda Publishers, 1996.

VERA B. MOREEN

[See also **DMA:** Arabic Language; Avesta; Calligraphy, Islamic; Fārs; Iran, History: After 650; Iranian Languages; Judeo-Persian; Muqaddasī, Al-; Pahlavi Literature; Sasanian History; Zoroastrianism; **Supp:** Hebrew Language.]

PETER DES ROCHES (*d.* 1238), English administrator and royal counselor, justiciar, royal guardian, bishop of Winchester, crusader, diplomat. Despite the widespread dislike Peter awakened in the baronage and his episcopal colleagues, Peter, who had been one of the senior councillors to King John, returned to the inner circles of government in 1217–1221 and 1232–1234. He was above all, a survivor and a "courtier of genius" (Vincent, p. 478).

Born in the 1160s or early 1170s in the county of Touraine, by April 1197 Peter had entered the service of Richard the Lionhearted as a clerk, moving within a year to the royal chamber and at Richard's death to King John's royal chamber. When Hubert de Burgh, his superior, was captured at Chinon, Peter assumed Hubert's responsibilities and then his title. A frequent witness to royal charters and participant in exchequer and judicial proceedings, he was also a trusted aide, for more than one royal letter instructs Peter, alone or with others, to resolve a claim by using discretion, for which some suitors paid handsomely. Peter also became John's personal friend, and he was rewarded with church offices and lands, culminating in his disputed election to the diocese of Winchester in 1204, which was only resolved when Innocent III personally consecrated him in St Peter's.

Peter was widely seen as a bishop more political than pious, but he took an interest in effectively managing his Winchester resources. Since he was a baron of the exchequer as well as a bishop, it is perhaps no coincidence that the earliest extant English manorial account books (1208) are from his estates. He also employed learned canonists and implemented various diocesan reform measures. As his biographer puts it, Peter also was a master builder and "a patron of the religious orders on a scale otherwise unprecedented at the courts of either King John or Henry III," giving lands and artifacts especially to the Cistercians and Premonstratensians. He was one of the first to bring Dominican friars into England (1221), and he established them in Winchester. In all, he endowed a dozen abbeys and hospitals in England, France, and the Holy Land. Peter was also known for his love of hunting and luxury, for which he was denounced by the chroniclers, and for his patronage of artists and foreign clerics.

However attentive Peter was to managing church assets and endowing abbeys, he was chiefly a royal counselor and financial administrator based at the court rather than the shires. Though best known for his financial expertise, his broad portfolio reached into diplomatic, military, and legal areas. He served as envoy to Philip Augustus in 1202, Archbishop Stephen Langton in 1208 and 1210, and the papal representatives in 1209, justiciar after Geoffrey fitz Peter died in October 1213, regent in 1213 and 1214, military captain in France in 1206 and Wales in 1209, and chief judge of the briefly reconstituted Bench at Westminster in 1214–1215. He was one of two bishops to stay with the king during his excommunication, the king having exempted Peter's property from sequestration, and it was in Winchester that John solemnized his reconciliation to the church (1213). For fifteen years, Peter was among the best-known associates of a king who used legal pretexts and harsh means to extract revenues for the reconquest of Normandy, Anjou, and Maine. When that goal collapsed at the Battle of Bouvines in 1214, John and his inner circle prepared for civil war.

Peter was replaced as justiciar by Hubert de Burgh at Runneymede in June 1215 but soon served as one of three loyalist commissioners reporting on English politics to the pope. The committee suspended the archbishop of Canterbury after it had convinced the pope to overrule the archbishop and repudiate Magna Carta, sparking civil war. When war came, Peter ensured that his tenantry stayed loyal to the king. With William Marshal, earl of Pembroke, Peter parleyed with Philip Augustus in April 1216 in a failed bid to avert French invasion. He attended John on his deathbed in October 1216 and, with Archbishop Langton in Rome, crowned John's young son Henry in the midst of civil war and invasion. It was a dangerous time for England's first experiment with a minor king, and John's counselors and loyal barons coalesced into a regency administration. William

Marshal was the consensus choice as regent, but Peter was named the king's guardian. Formally, that meant responsibility for the king's safety, upbringing, and education; informally, it guaranteed access to power. Peter solidified his claim by his diplomatic and military prominence and was one of the heroes of the "Fair of Lincoln" (May 1217), where French invaders and their English allies were routed, though rivals noted that Peter's men used crossbows, a canonically prohibited weapon. When William Marshal resigned as regent in 1219, Peter bid to succeed him, but William thwarted him by assigning Henry to the custody of the new papal legate, Pandulf, with Peter continuing as mere guardian in a new triumvirate with the legate and Hubert.

Peter still held a prominent role in government, but he had been passed over because William Marshal knew that broad sentiment among the baronage still distrusted the alien bishop. Nor was the distrust groundless; more than once, when Peter acted alone on significant matters, his actions were rash and overruled by Hubert or Pandulf. While Peter was on a pilgrimage to Compostela, rumors circulated about his real aims, and charges of treason with France were raised against him and two high-flying Poitevin allies. The charges were soon dropped, but Peter de Maulay had to relinquish Corfe Castle, and des Roches's faction was weakened.

Hubert forcefully pursued Pandulf's policy of resuming control of royal lands, castles, and sheriffdoms from even loyal barons to whose custody they had been entrusted during the civil war, a policy that directly threatened the power and profits of Peter and his allies. Another threat came in 1221, when the king was deemed to be no longer in legal pupilage and was moved from the care of Peter to Hubert. The showdown came in late 1223, when papal permission was sought to end the king's minority. Whether the initiative came from Peter, as recent scholars contend, or from his enemies, the results were devastating for Peter's faction, for Hubert used the king's new authority to justify further recalls of lands and castles. Peter and his allies may have considered rebellion but instead attended an armed rally at the Tower of London and a council meeting at which angry dissenters demanded Hubert's resignation. A temporary truce was arranged, but the dissidents had to surrender their castles, with Peter yielding custody of three castles in Hampshire and the sheriffdom in January 1224.

Ousted from national government for the first time since 1200, Peter busied himself with local politics and patronage. In 1227 Peter won permission to go on crusade with the emperor Frederick II. Illness forced the emperor to turn back, for which he was by prearrangement excommunicated, but Peter continued with the main party. After rejoining his army in September 1228, the emperor quickly negotiated a favorable but controversial treaty with Sultan al-Kamil that returned Jerusalem to the crusaders. Peter was one of the few churchmen willing to participate in the excommunicated emperor's entry into Jerusalem. On the way home, Peter stayed in Italy, winning the confidence of Pope Gregory IX and helping reconcile emperor and pope at Ceperano in August 1230. In 1231 he negotiated a three-year truce between the English and French kings. Only then did Peter, friend now of emperor, popes, and kings, return to his Winchester seat and then the English court.

Almost immediately he was engaged in court politics. For the first time in over a decade, Hubert was vulnerable, largely over the failures of his French and Welsh policies and the endemic crises in royal finance. Peter maneuvered his familiars back into office and enticed the king with the prospect of a wealthy and more powerful monarchy. Suddenly, in late July 1232, Hubert was dismissed from office and soon charged with grave crimes and imprisoned. After the coup Peter left daily rule to his longtime allies, but he was responsible for the new policy of enhanced royal power at home, in disregard of both magnates and Magna Carta, as well as the relentless persecution of Hubert and the brazen reversal of royal grants.

While others in the new administration sought to explain these reversals, Peter "did not hide behind such justifications. He relished the return to the days of John, ridiculed the concept of judgment by peers, and justified actions *per voluntatem* on the grounds that the king possessed *plenitudo potestatis*." (Carpenter, *The Reign of Henry III*, p. 39).

Initially the removal of Hubert was broadly popular, but over the next two years the Poitevins had few programmatic successes, chiefly because they were preoccupied with patronage. Also blocking progress was the larger challenge that defeated Hubert: either govern in coalition with baronial factions, in which case administrative reform was difficult, or forgo coalition, in which case one governed dangerously alone. Little was accomplished for royal finances aside from the adoption of harsher policies toward the beleaguered English Jewish community, which probably never recovered. Followers of Richard Marshal, the son of William, rose up, and Hubert's nephew Richard, a leading magnate in Ireland, was restless. Soon Richard Marshal and the Welsh prince Llywelyn were allied in open rebellion. The bishops opposed Peter and excommunicated him despite his claim to papal immunity. By early 1234 Henry saw that Peter's administration had no support. The intervention of the new archbishop of Canterbury led to the dismissal of Peter and his nephew in April, and the murder of Richard Marshal led to the arrest or flight of the other Poitevins in May.

After negotiating his nephew's safety, Peter left for Rome, where he helped Pope Gregory subdue the Romans at the Battle of Viterbo. In autumn 1236 Peter came home, an old man ready to make his will, which was confirmed in front of his protégés and Henry. His last years saw Peter concerned with monastic endowments more than politics, though he did serve, along with Hubert, as one of six participants from Magna Carta to witness Henry's confirmation of the charter in 1237. Peter's fall ushered in a period of twenty-five years in which a chastened Henry III attempted to rule largely unguided by a chief minister and came to grief on his own.

BIBLIOGRAPHY

Carpenter, David A. *The Minority of Henry III.* London: Methuen, 1990.

———. *The Reign of Henry III.* London: Hambledon Press, 1996.

Meekings, C. A. F. "The Early Years of Netley Abbey." *Studies in Thirteenth-Century Justice and Administration.* London: Hambledon Press, 1981. First published in *Journal of Ecclesiastical History* 30 (1979): 1–37. Close examination of one of Peter's major endowments.

Powicke, F. M. *King Henry III and the Lord Edward: The Community of the Realm in the Thirteenth Century.* 2 vols. Oxford: Clarendon Press, 1947. The classic account, though superseded by Carpenter, Stacey, and Vincent.

Stacey, Robert C. *Politics, Policy, and Finance under Henry III, 1216–1245.* Oxford: Clarendon Press, 1987.

Treharne, R. F. *Simon de Montfort and Baronial Reform: Thirteenth-Century Essays.* London: Hambledon Press, 1986. Traditional highly critical assessment of Poitevin government.

Vincent, Nicholas. *Peter des Roches: An Alien in English Politics, 1205–1238.* Cambridge, U.K.: Cambridge University Press, 1996. Superb biography, soundly researched.

West, Francis. *The Justiciarship in England, 1066–1232.* Cambridge, U.K.: Cambridge University Press, 1966.

JONATHAN A. BUSH

[See also **DMA:** Crusades and Crusader States: 1212 to 1272; England: Norman-Angevin; England: 1216–1485; Henry III of England; John, King of England; Magna Carta; Richard I the Lionhearted; William Marshal; **Supp:** Hubert de Burgh.]

PETRUS ALFONSI (known prior to conversion as Moisés [Mosé] Sefardi, *ca.* 1062–*ca.* 1140) was one of the most important polemicists of the twelfth century. Alfonsi was born a Jew, probably in Huesca while it was still under Muslim control. He was the beneficiary of an education in Muslim-controlled Andalusia, receiving training in medicine, astronomy, and philosophy as well as Hebrew and Arabic. In 1106 he decided to convert to Christianity and was baptized in Huesca, the capital of the kingdom of Aragon, with the king of Aragon, Alfonso I, serving as his sponsor and godfather.

By 1116 he had made his way to England, where he served in the court of Henry I, possibly as Henry's physician. In England he taught astronomy and translated a series of astronomical tables from Arabic into Latin. He also spent some time in France, where he continued teaching, writing, and translating. There is little information about the last years of his life or the place and time of his death, although 1140 has been suggested as a date.

In the years following his conversion (1108–1110), Alfonsi wrote his *Dialogus contra Judaeos.* The *Dialogus,* a highly influential work, consists of a series of conversations between Petrus and Moses, Alfonsi's Jewish alter ego. The two men discuss not only Judaism and Christianity but also Islam, as Alfonsi tries to prove that Christianity is the only religion that can withstand a thorough scrutiny based on reason and logic. Alfonsi introduced several new elements into Jewish-Christian polemics, including the use of reason and science, a good knowledge of Judaism and Islam (sorely missing from Christian works up to that point), and attacks on the Talmud. He was also the first anti-Jewish Christian writer to assert that Jews were guilty of willful deicide, accusing the rabbis of killing Christ out of a sense of envy while knowing that he was the Messiah. He also attacked Islam, but here the tone was slanderous and insulting as opposed to the rational and civil tenor of his charges against Judaism. Muḥammad, in particular, bears the brunt of many of his denunciations. The *Dialogus* was also novel in its extensive use of medicine, astronomy, physics, and other sciences as part of its arguments, showing not only Alfonsi's familiarity with these disciplines but also his determination to base his polemics on a rational and scientific basis.

Alfonsi's other major work was the *Disciplina clericalis,* a guide for scholars, as he claims in the prologue. The *Disciplina* is a collection of moral and didactic tales framed around fables, parables, and the sayings of wise men. The thirty-four short stories draw their content from a variety of (mostly Arabic) sources, including *Thousand and One Nights* and *The Book of Sinbad.*

Alfonsi's works were among the most widely read texts of the Middle Ages. The *Dialogus,* for example, survives in seventy-nine manuscripts, and the *Disciplina* in seventy-six. The influence of his works on later writers was also significant, as their imprint can be found in diverse works, including anti-Jewish treatises, scientific texts, and books of sermons.

BIBLIOGRAPHY

PRIMARY SOURCES

Petrus Alfonsi. *Dialogus.* In *Patrologia latina cursus completus.* Edited by Jacques-Paul Migne. Vol. 157, cols. 535–671.A. Paris: Garnier, 1844–1902. Also available as on-line database (*Patrologia Latina Database,* Alexandria, Va.: Chadwyck-Healey, 1995).

———. *The Scholar's Guide: A Translation of the Twelfth Century* Disciplina clericalis *of Pedro Alfonso.* Translated by Joseph Ramon Jones and John Esten Keller. Toronto: Pontifical Institute of Mediaeval Studies, 1969.

SECONDARY SOURCES

Cohen, Jeremy. "The Mentality of the Medieval Jewish Apostate: Peter Alfonsi, Hermann of Cologne, and Pablo Christiani." In *Jewish Apostasy in the Modern World.* Edited by Todd M. Endelman. New York: Holmes and Meier, 1987.

Septimus, Bernard. "Petrus Alfonsi on the Cult at Mecca." *Speculum* 56, no. 3 (July 1981): 517–533.

Tolan, John Victor. *Petrus Alfonsi and His Medieval Readers.* Gainesville: University Press of Florida, 1993.

JARBEL RODRIGUEZ

[See also **DMA:** Catalan Literature; *Disciplina Clericalis;* Exemplum; Polemics, Christian-Jewish; Spanish Latin Literature; **Supp:** Conversion.]

PETRUS DE BELLA PERTICA. See **Pierre de Belleperche.**

PHILOSOPHICAL GENRES. The separation of disciplines common in contemporary universities is a modern construct, and conceiving of philosophy as distinct from, and unrelated to, theology would have been impossible for medieval scholars. Philosophy as we understand it was ancillary to theology, and it is impossible to consider medieval philosophical literature without regard for the theological setting in which dialectical reasoning was practiced. One of late antiquity's bequests was the tradition of *disputatio,* Latin for dialexis, the process of reasoning in the question-and-answer format familiar to readers of Plato and Aristotle. From the time of St. Augustine, any thinker engaged in the explication or exegesis of Scripture or doctrine was said to be in *disputatio.* By the twelfth century, such dialectical reasoning became organized through the syllogistic exposition of premises leading to conclusions, and its formalization likely incorporated extant argument procedures in canon and civil law, perhaps even making use of Islamic juridical procedure. Once formalized, *disputatio* acquired a pedagogical utility and was incorporated into the evolving university curricula. Candidates for baccalaureate degrees had to display proficiency in the theory and practice of the dialectic of Aristotle's *Organon,* and by the end of the thirteenth century, theologians had to have mastered logical analysis at a level of complexity unrivaled before the twentieth century.

Disputatio had become formal academic exercises by the thirteenth century, providing public opportunities for young scholars to display their dialectical abilities by defending their masters' theological positions against any objection. Further, each year in Advent and Lent, the masters subjected themselves to a public *disputatio* called a quodlibet, in which they argued on any topic suggested by someone in attendance in an atmosphere suggestive of a medieval tournament. After the public *disputatio* the master would summarize his students' arguments, along with his own assessment of the position's strengths and weaknesses, in a *determinatio.* If the summary was only in the form of a simple transcript, it was called *reportatio,* and if edited and expanded by the master, an *ordinatio.*

Attention to Scripture was central to the evolving scholastic *disputatio* and gave rise to a formalized exegetical, speculative, and philosophical theological genus called *quaestiones.* St. Augustine, St. Jerome, St. Isidore of Seville, and the Venerable Bede had used this term to describe the subject matter of *disputatio,* and by the time of St. Anselm of Canterbury it had coalesced into the formal *quaestiones sacrae paginae,* the fundamental genre for most of what is considered to be medieval philosophical literature. By the 1150s *quaestiones* had become so popular, and the literature had become so voluminous, that a system of organizing was necessary, which became known as *sententiae,* the sentence literature, of which the best known is the *Sententiae* of Peter Lombard.

The most common genre of philosophical literature was the commentary, the theologian's analysis of ideas directly or indirectly associated with a given authoritative text. The point was not necessarily the introduction of the commentator's innovative or unique interpretations but the clearest and best understanding of the truths the text addressed. If the theologian chanced upon novel objections to established interpretation or ingenious arguments to support interpretations threatened by other theologians, he generally referred obliquely to them without attribution, complicating our understanding of the origin of ideas. Among the texts most frequently commented upon were Aristotle's works, the treatises of earlier theologians, and Lombard's *Sententiae*. Sentence commentaries were so popular as to form a genre to themselves, with more philosophically oriented commentaries typical of the thirteenth century and more theologically directed ones predominating in the fourteenth. Generally, commentaries would be structured according to questions arising from the text, with careful review of all possible answers, analysis of the most likely answers, and a resolution favored by the commentator. In many cases, the commentator refers to the arguments of predecessors and contemporaries as guideposts for expanding the question into intellectual territory that might have amazed the text's author. The number and range of these commentaries, as well as their suitability for the establishment of doctrinal truth, gave rise to theologically systematic summaries called *summae,* which were made up of treatises, or tractates, on given aspects of philosophical theology. These summaries, despite their appeal to beginning students, risked becoming outdated, given the rapidity with which innovations proceeded, leading at least one theologian to give them a shelf life of perhaps twenty years.

Especially valuable for students of medieval thought are treatises on formal logic, which contain theoretical and practical outlines of the varied genres through which the structures of reasoning underlying theology evolved. The logically oriented curriculum compelled theologians to recognize that their understanding of the relation of concepts, terms, propositions, and arguments to "Truth" defined the theological edifices on which they labored, much as architects' plans, masons' tools, and quarrymen's skill defined a cathedral's aesthetic unity and structural integrity. The later Middle Ages experienced a remarkable flowering of formal logic; indeed, until twentieth-century scholars trained in analytic methods examined them, these texts languished in obscurity, misinterpreted as exclusive games of an elite educated class.

The building block of any medieval philosophical text is the syllogistic argument, consisting of two premises and a conclusion, and the dialectical connection of the premises demanded a systematic approach to the logical relation of propositions. This was the basis for so-called "topics" literature, based in Aristotle, refined by Anicius Boethius and Alcuin of York, and adopted by early scholastics as the ideal means for understanding the mechanics of syllogistic reasoning. As appreciation for the complexity of the relation of argument structure to

ontological presuppositions increased, a more refined species of analyzing the ties between metaphysics and logic called *consequentia* arose. Consequences literature addresses implication, entailment, and inference, three distinct ways in which premises lead to a conclusion, as well as the relation holding between the truth of conditional propositions and an argument's validity. Peter Abelard, William of Ockham, Walter Burley, and Jean Buridan each contributed significantly to the development of the philosophy of logic in their treatment of consequences.

The constituents of any proposition are the terms that compose it, and medieval thinkers were absorbed in exploring how terms signify in writing, speech, and in the mind. They divided terms into categorematic ones, capable of standing alone, like "Socrates" or "runs," and syncategorematic terms, words like conjunctions or prepositions requiring categorematic terms to signify within propositions. Categorematic terms signify through supposition, a theory of reference that would underlie much medieval thought. A genre arising from this distinction called *sophismata* explored the reference of syncategorematic terms like "besides" or "all" through the analysis of *sophisma* like "Socrates twice sees every man besides Plato." This sentence's ambiguity lies in the confusion over how "twice" or "besides" refers to the categorematic terms. Thinkers struggled to find a rule or set of rules that would determine how two differently referring syncategorematic terms work together to function within a meaningful proposition. This attention to the basis of paradox within propositions was useful in metaphysics and natural philosophy, in which confusion in language might lead to serious mistakes about the scope of understanding or extramental reality. Paradox might also arise from the possibility that a proposition might only be true if it is false, as with the liar's paradox: "What I am now saying is false." *Insolubilia* literature addressed the problems arising from assuming that a sentence must be false if it does not correspond to reality, and thinkers like Thomas Bradwardine, Richard and Roger Swineshead, and William Heytesbury each contributed importantly to discussions of the limitations of semantic theory.

Interest in examining the relation of rule-governed dialectical reasoning to the boundaries of belief gave rise to *obligationes* literature in the mid-thirteenth century. This genre, grounded in the Aristotelian position that nothing impossible follows from the possible, analyzes the underpinnings of *disputatio* by examining its dialectical structure as well as its implications for consistency of belief. In an *obligatio,* a respondent must adopt a possible position and avoid being led by an opponent into holding something impossible. Complicating matters is the stipulation that the respondent is bound by agreed-upon rules limiting the scope of potentially viable responses to the opponent. The game-like structure of the exercise allowed the *obligatio* theorist to examine and categorize species of rational discourse in light of the structure and reference of the propositions wielded, as well as the necessary and possible connections holding between propositions. Unlike *consequentia,* which were concerned with how propositions followed from one another, *obligationes* focused on more philosophically complex issues, like the relation of dialectical rules to the reference of propositions and the relation of inference to epistemological issues of the consistency of belief. John Duns Scotus, Burley, Ockham, Richard Kilvington, and the Swinesheads figure among notable contributors to *obligationes* literature.

BIBLIOGRAPHY

Kretzmann, Norman, Anthony Kenny, and Jan Pinborg, eds. *Cambridge History of Later Medieval Philosophy: From the Rediscovery of Aristotle to the Disintegration of Scholasticism, 1100–1600.* Cambridge, U.K.: Cambridge University Press, 1982.

Kretzmann, Norman, and Eleonore Stump, eds. *Logic and Philosophy of Language.* Cambridge Translations of Medieval Philosophical Texts, Vol. 1. Cambridge, U.K.: Cambridge University Press, 1988.

Lubac, Henri de. *Medieval Exegesis.* Volume 1: *The Four Senses of Scripture.* Translated by Mark Sebanc. Grand Rapids, Mich.: Eerdmans, 1998.

Yrjönsuuri, Mikko, ed. *Medieval Formal Logic: Obligations, Insolubles, and Consequences.* Dordrecht, Netherlands: Kluwer, 2001.

STEPHEN LAHEY

[See also **DMA:** Proverbs and Sententiae; Quaestiones.]

PHYSICIANS. In today's English usage, "physician" is a relatively uncontested term and implies a medical healer who possesses professional credentials based on formal training and qualification: in many modern societies, such physicians have been given the social authority to control healing. In this sense of the word, however, "physicians" were only gradually coming into existence in the fourteenth century. For most of the earlier Middle Ages, a number of different lines of demarcation distinguished between the various kinds of individuals who might offer health care.

One distinction that was made very early set apart the healer who based his practice on his own experience from the one who based it on medical texts and learning.

Richer of Rheims (writing 996–998) tells the story of a medical competition between a French bishop grounded in the liberal arts and an empiric healer, a layman from Salerno in southern Italy—a competition in which the latter came off worse: each tried to poison the other, but only the bishop was skilled enough to counteract the poison. Ironically it was at Salerno, during the twelfth century, where healers first attempted to imitate the liberal arts and to study systematically, by gloss and commentary, the few translations of Greek and Arabic medical texts available to them, so as to present themselves as capable of understanding and explaining the reasons for their practice. It is in the course of that century that some newly learned healers first began to speak of their subject as *physica* and themselves as *physici* rather than mere *medici,* to set themselves apart from illiterate and unlearned empirics. This conception of the proper character of medicine became assimilated to the new European universities after 1200, where faculties of medicine can be found at Montpellier (by 1220) and Paris (by 1254); their masters began now to study and teach newly translated texts of Galenic medical theory, above all Avicenna's *Canon,* and they shared in the widening prestige of higher academic training enjoyed by theology and law. By the end of the thirteenth century there was a wide enough market for the products of such education to ensure that even bachelors of medicine could expect to find patrons who believed in the value of their training and would offer them employment, although not everyone was convinced that learned medicine was the best.

A second distinction is also embodied in Richer's story, overlapping but not identical, a distinction between a clerical and a lay healer. We know far less about the practice of the latter in the early Middle Ages than we do of the former: secular clerics like Bishop Fulbert of Chartres sought and gave medical advice and remedies; monasteries typically had an *infirmarius* who might care not only for his sick brethren but for laity who sought him out. Canonical regulation in the twelfth and thirteenth centuries began to restrict clerical involvement in medicine somewhat, though by no means completely: the Second Lateran Council in 1139 forbade monks and canons regular to practice medical care for fees, and Honorius III's *Super specula* (1219) prohibited the formal study of medicine to all beneficed clergy. While Honorius's rescript continued to leave it open to the secular clergy to practice medicine, the increasingly high valuation placed upon academic training meant that lay physicians educated in medical faculties gradually began to supplant clerical practitioners, although certainly the clerical practice of medicine had by no means disappeared in the fourteenth century and remained commonplace in England, for example.

One other distinction was already being drawn in Richer's day. The unfortunate man from Salerno lost his foot to the bishop's poison; it had to be cut off by a surgeon *(cirurgis)*. Surgery, though understood as a part of medicine (as Richer also tells us), was already practiced by a separate group of practitioners distinguished by their claims to manual skills, who passed on their craft by apprenticeship. The increasing status enjoyed by physicians in the course of the eleventh century, insofar as they could claim that their subject was a learned science that could be taught from texts in the schools, led some surgeons in the northern Italian cities to make similar claims for their own subject. Broadly speaking, a surgeon dealt with symptoms and complaints manifest on the body's surface, using not just his hands but the tools of his craft: knives, cauteries, caustic medicines. He set bones, reduced dislocations, sewed up wounds, and cauterized abscesses and ulcers; he treated diseases of the eyes and skin, too, which could be extended to the treatment of tumors, goiter, hernia, and so forth. The physician, in contrast, dealt with internal medicine, using diet and pharmacy to cure fevers and other humoral imbalances.

Beginning with Ruggiero Frugardi (Roger of Parma) about 1170, a series of such practitioners described their techniques in texts that imitated the texts emerging from the medical faculties: they glossed their predecessors' works, they incorporated the teachings of Galen and Avicenna. By the late thirteenth century, when this tradition was carried to Paris by Lanfranc of Milan, these writers were insisting that surgery was a part of medicine, that surgeons needed an understanding of medical science to practice competently, above all a scientific knowledge of anatomy. Perhaps in principle this argument weakened the distinction between physicians and surgeons, but in practice academic physicians proved unwilling to accept that surgery could be a truly learned subject. In fourteenth-century France a formal distinction was insisted upon, and surgery failed to become a university subject; in Italy, surgical training and a medico-surgical degree could be obtained in a number of medical faculties, but even there the surgeon did not enjoy the prestige of the physician, and his medical degree sometimes did not even entitle him to offer medical treatment.

All these developments discussed above, especially the growing prestige of academic medicine, led in time to a distinction among healers that would have been inconceivable in Richer's day, a distinction—in theory, at least—between licit and illicit practitioners. In its stat-

Surgeon Setting the Leg of an Apprehensive Patient. BIBLIOTECA APOSTOLICA VATICANA, MS VAT. LAT. 4804, FOL. 140V. REPRODUCED BY PERMISSION.

utes of 1271, the medical faculty at Paris claimed the right to supervise medical practice in the city, and in the fourteenth century it obtained ecclesiastical backing for the principle that a medical degree was necessary to practice there; several prosecutions for illegal practice are known. Elsewhere, in towns and communities where there was no university striving to protect its own interests, there was still often public concern to establish standards of qualification for practitioners. Emperor Frederick II had already laid it down in 1231 that no one could practice medicine in the Kingdom of Sicily without a license. In Catalonia, one or two small towns were requiring a mastery of medical science, confirmed by a formal examination, by the 1290s, and the number of such communities grew in subsequent decades. The legal code called the *Furs* of Valencia of 1329–1330 established this principle for the entire kingdom, and prosecutions for illegal practice there go back at least to 1334; a number of Valencian licenses surviving from the 1370s and 1380s show that not only physicians but also surgeons were being examined by the municipal authorities and that surgeons might receive licenses to carry out only specialized procedures, like the repair of hernias. Nevertheless, in most of Europe, for most of the Middle Ages, such a distinction had little practical effect. The number of academically trained physicians was so small and the pressure for medical services so great that even those communities with licensing laws rarely took action against "illegal" practitioners. Traditional patterns of practice were thus left largely unaffected.

All the distinctions that have been drawn in the preceding paragraphs should be understood as rough rather than sharp ones. Some academically oriented practitioners had master's or bachelor's degrees, others might have had only a year or so of schooling and never taken a degree. A university-trained practitioner might well have engaged a succession of apprentices who would have absorbed some medical learning from him and subsequently vaunted it in their own practice. Still other practitioners might possess medical books, for use or for show. Academics might complain about the ignorance of untrained empirics, but not all empirics were utterly unlearned. Similarly, the line between physicians and surgeons could not be entirely clear-cut: it was not easy to decide whether certain ailments were "medical" or "surgical," and both groups of practitioners were eager for patients and so might claim the ability to treat these intermediate conditions. And of course in smaller communities where specialization was impossible, the local healer might simply call himself a *medicus* and treat whatever kinds of ailments were presented to him.

Finally, one needs to recognize that people in other occupational roles were involved in healing in the Middle Ages and so might often function as physicians even without the name. Apothecaries dealt in more than drugs, to be sure, but they certainly offered medical advice and prescribed medicines to patients who sought them out, often independent of a physician's control; the assumption that they had some specialized medical knowledge might even lead towns to hire them as municipal medical officers, charged with offering diagnoses to citizens on the basis of uroscopic examinations. In like manner, barbers engaged in a wide variety of activities—cutting hair, pulling teeth, cupping, drawing blood—which encouraged people to come to them for surgical care when no other practitioner was available, and there are numerous instances of men who began as barbers and ended their careers as self-styled *chirurgici*.

Are women, too, to be found within the groups we have mentioned? The evidence for women's medical practice is very slim. Yet is clear that, all across Europe, they might occasionally function (under particular circumstances) as physicians, surgeons, apothecaries, or simply as unspecialized empiric healers, though various prosopographical studies rarely show them to have been

more than 1 percent of the practitioner population. The growing acknowledgment that medicine was a learned subject worked against the activity of women as physicians, since they were excluded from pursuing degrees in the medieval university, but because learning never became a formal prerequisite for surgical practice, women surgeons were not uncommon even in the fourteenth century.

BIBLIOGRAPHY

Amundsen, Darrel W. *Medicine, Society, and Faith in the Ancient and Medieval Worlds.* Baltimore: Johns Hopkins University Press, 1996.

Bullough, Vern L. *The Development of Medicine as a Profession: The Contribution of the Medieval University to Modern Medicine.* Basel and New York: Hafner, 1966.

García-Ballester, Luis, Roger French, Jon Arrizabalaga, and Andrew Cunningham, eds. *Practical Medicine from Salerno to the Black Death.* Cambridge, U.K.: Cambridge University Press, 1994.

Getz, Faye. *Medicine in the English Middle Ages.* Princeton, N.J.: Princeton University Press, 1998.

Green, Monica. "Women's Medical Practice and Health Care in Medieval Europe." *Signs* 14 (1989): 434–473.

Jacquart, Danielle. *Le milieu médical en France du XIIe au XVe siècle.* Geneva: Droz, 1981.

MacKinney, Loren C. *Early Medieval Medicine, with Special Reference to France and Chartres.* Baltimore: Johns Hopkins Press, 1937.

McVaugh, Michael R. *Medicine before the Plague: Practitioners and Their Patients in the Crown of Aragon, 1285–1345.* Cambridge, U.K.: Cambridge University Press, 1993.

MICHAEL MCVAUGH

[See also **DMA:** Barbers, Barber-Surgeons; Medicine, Schools of; **Supp:** Disease.]

PIERRE DE BELLEPERCHE (Petrus de Bella Pertica, *d.* 1308), the late-thirteenth-century jurist probably from southern France, is one of the earliest postglossators, or commentators, on Roman law. In the long aftermath of Accursius's standard interpretation, or gloss *(Glossa ordinaria),* postglossators wrote on the body of texts known as the *Corpus iuris civilis,* the collection of sources (judicial maxims, legal opinions, laws, and so on) brought together and published under the emperor Justinian's aegis beginning in 529. The *Glossa ordinaria* is usually dated to the 1230s, and the era of the postglossators is said to extend well into the Renaissance.

The law school of Orléans was the center of an impressive group of postglossators in the thirteenth century, including Jacques de Révigny (*d.* 1296), Pierre's somewhat older contemporary. Scholars have not securely attributed all of the works that appeared from the thirteenth-century Orléans postglossators. A commentary on the Code (part of the Justinianic corpus of texts), for example, long assigned to Pierre de Belleperche and published in a 1519 edition under his name (and reprinted in facsimile in the late twentieth century), was probably written by Jacques de Révigny. Similarly, the notion that Pierre taught at the nascent school of Avignon is not well founded.

Pierre de Belleperche was an eminent lawyer and jurisprudent. The phrase *pater peritorum* ("father of experts") has sometimes been applied to him. His commentaries constitute scholarship of the highest order, and his interpretations, though perhaps commonplace (such as his insistence that a "prince could, with sufficient cause, issue a rescript derogating natural law," such as the commandment not to kill), would not have been displeasing to a monarch. His distinguished reputation probably brought him to the attention of one such monarch, King Philip IV (the Fair) of France, in the 1290s. In this period Pierre served the king in various capacities—as a negotiator of peace settlements with England and Flanders; an ambassador to the pope and on lesser missions throughout France; a member of the high court (Parlement of Paris); keeper of the seals (the equivalent of chancellor, the highest office in the royal administration); and in more mundane roles as an assessor of taxes and supervisor of accounts. An indication of his value to the crown was that he was paid ten shillings of Paris money a day as a royal clerk, twice what other clerks were paid. A pious man and prelate, he finished his career as bishop of Auxerre from 1306 (until his death in 1308). He left an endowment for eight vicarages in Villeneuve-sur-Allier in the Auvergne.

BIBLIOGRAPHY
PRIMARY WORKS

Pierre de Belleperche. *Commentaria in digestum novum. Repetitiones variae. Opera iuridica rariora:* 10. Bologna: Forni, 1968.

———. *Super IX libros codicis.* Frankfurt: Minerva, 1968.

———. *Questiones vel distinctiones. Opera iuridica rariora:* 11. Bologna: Forni, 1970.

———. *Lectura institutionum. Opera iuridica rariora:* 7. Bologna: Forni, 1972.

SECONDARY WORKS

Pennington, Kenneth. *The Prince and the Law, 1200–1600: Sovereignty and Rights in the Western Legal Tradition.* Berkeley: University of California Press, 1993. Wider context for understanding the postglossators.

Strayer, Joseph R. *The Reign of Philip the Fair.* Princeton, N.J.: Princeton University Press, 1980.

WILLIAM CHESTER JORDAN

[See also **DMA:** Accursius; Glossators; Philip IV the Fair; Postglossators; **Supp:** Jacques de Révigny.]

PILGRIM SOUVENIRS. Medieval pilgrims always wanted to bring back some memento of their travels, even if few went to the lengths of the notorious Fulk, count of Anjou, who on one of his three visits to Jerusalem early in the eleventh century is supposed to have bitten a piece off the Holy Sepulchre. Such a fragment constituted not just a souvenir but a relic, for in the earlier medieval centuries, the word was applied not only to bodily remains but to dust or chippings from a shrine, snippets of cloth that had been in contact with the saint's body or tomb, or any object associated with him or her. Monks and clerics were assiduous in their collection of such relics: Wilfrid of York and Benedict Biscop of Wearmouth accumulated them on their visits to Rome in the late seventh century and distributed them to friends and churches at home. The value of these objects far surpassed that of the souvenir as we think of it. They brought with them a blessing, even a curative value, which derived from their holy origin. This was true of pilgrim souvenirs of all types, including naturally occurring objects such as the stones that pilgrims to Mont-St.-Michel in Normandy took away from the mount or the palm fronds, blessed in the Palm Sunday ceremonies at Jerusalem, that were brought back by returning Holy Land pilgrims.

Man-made souvenirs, however, have a long history. Ceramic ampullae, containing water from the river Jordan or oil from the Holy Sepulchre, were being sold in the sixth century, embossed with a variety of designs including the Adoration of the Magi, the first pilgrims to the infant Christ. It has been argued that, because the Magi got home safely, an ampulla bearing their image may have had a special talismanic value for the bearer. Similar ampullae were made at other eastern shrines, notably that of St. Menas near Alexandria, large numbers of which survive and are to be found in many museum collections; they have turned up as far afield as Norway and Chester.

That "manufactured" souvenirs should first appear in the west in the twelfth century seems to fit with the economic and demographic growth that doubtless stimulated the practice of pilgrimage itself. By the mid-twelfth century, according to the Pilgrim's Guide (*ca.*

Pilgrim Souvenirs. *The Canterbury shrine of Thomas Becket* (d. 1170) *was the first in England to market "souvenirs." Here, a variety of Becket trinkets, including ampullae* (bottom row) *and pilgrim badges.* ASHMOLEAN MUSEUM. REPRODUCED BY PERMISSION.

1140), scallop shells were being sold from stalls in the plaza in front of the church of Santiago de Compostela, our first evidence for the trade in such objects in the Latin west. These rapidly became the emblem of the Santiago pilgrim; sometimes a hole was pierced in the shell to make possible its attachment to a bag, hat, or other garment. Soon cheap metal reproductions were being marketed, and other shrines followed suit. According to a miracle story of around 1170, a badge from the newly prominent Marian shrine of Rocamadour in southern France cured a sick priest from Chartres. Badges of the Three Magi were being sold within a short time of the establishment of their cult in Cologne Cathedral, also around 1170, while at Rome Pope Innocent III in 1199 conceded the control of the manufacture and sale of badges of the apostles to the canons of St. Peter's.

Consistent with this chronology, the Canterbury shrine of Thomas Becket (*d.* 1170) was the first in England to market "souvenirs." An important element in the spread of the martyr's cult was water in which a minute quantity of his blood had supposedly been diluted. At first the water was distributed in wooden containers, but this was clearly unsatisfactory, and they were rapidly replaced by ampullae, little flasks that could be suspended around the neck and performed the additional function of identifying a Canterbury pilgrim. By the fourteenth century the ampullae were supplanted by badges made in a variety of forms. There were busts of the martyr, tiny replicas of the sword that killed him, and little representations of the murder and other motifs. Canterbury's example stimulated the appearance first of ampullae and then of badges at other English shrines.

The rights in a souvenir trade were normally owned by the proprietors of the shrine concerned, but they were sometimes vigorously disputed, for example at Rocamadour and at the shrine of St. Mary Magdalen near Aix-en-Provence in the fourteenth century. Badges might well be pirated. The actual production of the objects was frequently subcontracted to craftsmen who made other small metal items, including badges of secular character, and sometimes they were able to deal in them on their own account. Fast work might be necessary to establish a badge manufacture when a cult suddenly became popular, as at Regensburg in 1520 when pilgrims began to flock to an image of the Virgin and Child painted by Albrecht Altdorfer. With the development of paper and print technologies in the fifteenth century came souvenirs that were still more ephemeral, such as the little paper "reproductions" of the Veronica, the veil on which Christ's face was supposedly imprinted, which was venerated by pilgrims to St Peter's at Rome.

Badges helped to identify a pilgrim as such and might even serve as a kind of passport, for example in time of war. They might be produced as proof that a penitential pilgrimage had been fulfilled, but like other articles of pilgrim gear, badges were easy to obtain and to assume. A certificate issued at the shrine was regarded as more reliable and was often required by the authorities who imposed the pilgrimage. Mostly cheap, fragile, and easily lost, many have been discovered in the silt of rivers such as the Thames or the Seine; it has been suggested that returning pilgrims may in fact have thrown their badges into the water as a thank-offering for their safe homecoming. Sometimes pilgrim emblems, especially the Santiago scallop shell, were buried in graves. The distribution of all these finds, although obviously very much subject to chance, makes it possible to gain a rough idea of the catchment area of particular shrines. Occasionally, too, badges bear witness to the popularity of a cult that has left little written documentation: a good example is that of the English parish priest John Schorne

of North Marston in Buckinghamshire, greatly venerated there and at Windsor in the fifteenth century.

BIBLIOGRAPHY

Cohen, Esther. "*In haec signa:* Pilgrim-badge trade in Southern France." *Journal of Medieval History* 2:3 (September 1976), 193–214.

Ousterhout, Robert, ed. *The Blessings of Pilgrimage.* Illinois Byzantine Studies 1. Urbana: University of Illinois Press, 1990. Part Two includes several essays on pilgrim souvenirs in the Byzantine East.

Spencer, Brian. *Pilgrim Souvenirs and Secular Badges.* Museum of London, Medieval Finds from Excavations in London 7. London: Stationery Office, 1998. Fully documented and illustrated catalog of a rich collection of badges.

Webb, Diana. *Pilgrims and Pilgrimage in Medieval Europe.* London and New York: J. B. Tauris, 1999. Chapter 4, "Remembering Pilgrimage: Souvenirs," includes a short selection of translated sources.

———. *Medieval European Pilgrimage, c. 700–c. 1500.* Houndmills, U.K., and New York: Palgrave, 2002. Contains numerous references to souvenirs in the context of a general discussion of medieval pilgrimage.

DIANA WEBB

[See also **DMA:** Becket, Thomas, St.; Pilgrimage, Western European; Pilgrim's Guide; Relics; Santiago de Compostela.]

PILGRIMAGE, CELTIC, is normally taken to refer to pilgrimage as practiced by an elite of adepts among Irish monks whose activities spilled over into the rest of the British Isles and much of the European continent. This was pilgrimage (in Latin, *peregrinatio*) in a literal sense.

The practitioner made himself into a *peregrinus,* a foreigner or stranger, by cutting ties with home and kin and thus deliberately entering into a condition that in most early societies, whether Celtic, Roman, or Germanic, was regarded as uncomfortable and even dangerous. This *peregrinatio* led its most famous practitioners into missionary activity and the foundation of monasteries, and it prompted imitation by Anglo-Saxons and others. Its influence, although immense, waned with the gradual establishment of the Benedictine model of stable enclosed monasticism as the western European norm from the eighth century on. St. Benedict in the sixth century already expressed his strong disapproval of "wandering" monks.

The motivation for pilgrimage of the "Celtic" type was fundamentally penitential. It was not merely a response to the individual's need to make reparation for particular sins but more generally a remedy for the fallen human condition. The *peregrinus* embraced the homeless, friendless condition of Christ himself and thereby achieved a greater closeness to him. It was a form of self-exile, and it is significant that lengthy or even perpetual pilgrimages could be imposed on persons guilty of various heinous offences. It is uncertain whether the exile from Ulster on which St. Columba (*d.* 597) entered in 563, which led to his missionary and monastic activity in Scotland, was enforced or undertaken voluntarily after his involvement in a battle. Such penances or punishments (the distinction is a fine one) were prescribed in the early Irish penitentials and through them influenced later Anglo-Saxon law codes such as the early-eleventh-century Laws of Cnut.

The Irish practice of *peregrinatio* was akin to the flight from the world undertaken by the "Desert Fathers" of Egypt and may well have been intended to emulate it, although it was obviously located in a very different geographical environment. Like the Desert Fathers, the pilgrim was not by any means always committed to perpetual mobility. He might go to sit at the feet of a famous holy man or simply seek out a place of solitude in which to pray and do penance. Adamnan's *Life of Columba* has much to say about pilgrims, such as Cormac, who combined different modes of life at different times. A stream of such visitors sought out Columba on Iona, and he sometimes advised them on their future options and the forms of penance they should undertake. Pilgrimage of this kind was far from incompatible with the pursuit of scriptural learning for which the Irish were also famous, and it shaded easily into the foundation of new religious communities, which served as centers of learning and Christianization. This is well illustrated by the careers of such men as St. Columbanus (*d.* 615), founder of Luxeuil in Gaul and Bobbio in northern Italy, and St. Gall (*d. ca.* 650), who gave his name to one of the greatest of medieval monasteries (in what is now Switzerland). In a much-quoted observation, Gall's Carolingian biographer, Walafrid Strabo, said that custom had made *peregrinatio* second nature to the Irish.

Although *peregrinatio* was not necessarily or even usually directed to a particular shrine or holy place, it was by no means uncommon for individual pilgrims to visit such places (notably Rome) during their travels. Some Irish *peregrini*, however, thought it essential to place complete reliance on the Lord and to go where wind and tide took them. This tradition produced the famous story of the voyage of St. Brendan *(Navigatio sancti Brendani),* apparently first written down around 900 by an émigré Irish monk in the Netherlands or the Rhineland and immensely popular in the Middle Ages. According to this tale, Brendan (an Irish abbot who died *ca.* 575 and is mentioned by Adamnan) set sail with some companions in a small boat, hoping to find the Isles of the Blest. In 891, very near the date of composition of the *Navigatio,* three Irish monks, who had undertaken a similar voyage, were washed up on the shore of Cornwall and presented themselves to King Alfred.

Ireland attracted *peregrini* as well as exporting them. The Venerable Bede (*d.* 735) mentions several Englishmen who betook themselves to Ireland in quest of spiritual self-improvement; some of them then embarked on further journeys, which in some instances led to missionary activity. A little later, Boniface of Wessex (*d.* 754) struck an authentic note when he apologized to a correspondent in his homeland that they saw little of each other because of his love of "wandering." Women were not excluded from *peregrinatio,* but there were constraints on their freedom to indulge in full-blown holy "wandering." An Irish recluse, consulted by Columbanus before he entered the monastic life at Bangor, told him that she herself would have sought out a more fitting place of pilgrimage across the sea had it not been for "the fragility of my sex." *Peregrinatio* was as much a condition of life as it was a journey: Adamnan quotes Columba as recalling that he had been living for thirty years "in pilgrimage" in Britain.

It should perhaps be emphasized that pilgrimage as practiced by ordinary Irish men and women was similar to pilgrimage elsewhere in Christian Europe. It involved a journey to a holy place in order to venerate relics, which were usually in the custody of monks. Writing around 650, the monk Cogitosus described the church that had been built in honor of St. Brigid at Kildare and the people who assembled there on her feast day. Some of them had come in the hope of cures, some bearing offerings to the saint's annual festivity, some because of the abundance of foodstuffs available there, and some just to look at the crowds of people. Similar gatherings were to be seen at shrines everywhere.

BIBLIOGRAPHY

PRIMARY SOURCES

Adamnan of Iona. *Life of St Columba.* Translated by Richard Sharpe. London: Penguin Books, 1995. Translation with a long introduction and abundant annotation and reference to scholarly literature.

Bede, the Venerable. *Ecclesiastical History of the English People.* Edited by Bertram Colgrave and R. B. Mynors. Oxford: Clarendon Press, 1969. Parallel text and translation.

Farmer, D. H., ed. *The Age of Bede.* Rev. ed. Harmondsworth, U.K., and New York: Penguin Books, 1988. Contains translations by J. F. Webb of the *Navigatio sancti Brendani* and also of the *Life of St. Wilfrid* by Eddius Stephanus, which well illustrate a contrasting style of pilgrimage.

Navigatio sancti Brendani abbatis, from Early Latin Manuscripts. Edited by Carl Selmer. Notre Dame, Ind.: University of Notre Dame Press, 1959.

SECONDARY WORKS

Bitel, Lisa M. *Isle of the Saints: Monastic Settlement and Christian Community in Early Ireland.* Ithaca, N.Y.: Cornell University Press, 1990.

Charles-Edwards, T. M. "The Social Background to Irish *Peregrinatio.*" *Celtica* 11 (1976): 43–59.

Harbison, Peter. *Pilgrimage in Ireland: The Monuments and the People.* New York: Syracuse University Press, 1992.

Hughes, Kathleen. "The Changing Theory and Practice of Irish Pilgrimage." *Journal of Ecclesiastical History* 11 (1960): 143–151.

DIANA WEBB

[See also **DMA:** Adamnan, St.; Columba, St.; Columbanus, St.; Irish Literature: Voyage Tales; Pilgrimage, Western European.]

PIRATES AND PIRACY. "Piracy" is a protean term denoting a host of plundering activities in the medieval worlds, from impromptu raids on merchant river craft to sustained campaigns of privateering against commercial and political rival fleets on the high seas. Generalizations about medieval piracy remain especially risky, since the contexts in which it took place varied as widely as the practice itself, and many scholars (including this one) have drawn unwarranted conclusions about the nature, frequency, profitability, and ubiquity of piracy and of the number, motivation, background, and origin of the people engaged in it. It is best, before turning to specifics, to fix some working assumptions and definitions.

Medieval piracy was generally an extralegal, as opposed to an illegal, activity, so long as one is referring to the Mediterranean, North, Baltic, and Black Seas. These waterways, being outside the jurisdiction of any state, were by definition zones without law; consequently, customary norms of behavior rather than legal statutes per se governed engagements at sea. Piracy therefore became a legal concern only in those areas under law, namely in the coastal harbors. Riverine piracy was a different matter since the rivers themselves—or the pertinent segments of them—commonly formed part of the demesne of landed lords and the jurisdictions of towns. Legal rights over river systems were guarded as closely as was the trade that passed along them. Piracy formed the shadow of commerce: raids on merchant craft were endemic and provided an unlikely impetus to the development of a credit economy and advanced financial instruments, since to carry cash was to invite trouble. Fluctuations in trade paralleled the profitability and pop-

ularity of piracy so closely that the extent of pirate attacks is often one of our most reliable indices of commercial activity in an era when more mundane evidence is lacking.

CORSAIRS

As medieval law developed, it distinguished between piracy and corsairing, or privateering. Piracy was simply criminal theft, the opportunistic plundering of goods and cash from traveling merchants along a waterway. Corsairing, by contrast, was a licensed activity promoted and at least partially organized by states. Corsairs applied to their governments for official sanction—and usually paid a hefty licensing fee in the process—and aimed their attacks at declared enemies of their state; corsairs were in fact satellites of the military forces, ad hoc naval militias whose purpose was to open a commercial "front" in an otherwise conventional ongoing war. (The term "corsair" derived from the medieval Latin *cursus,* meaning an "incursion" in the hostile sense of that word; *cursus,* in fact, commonly meant a "front" in an explicitly military context.) Applicants for corsairing licenses identified the specific harbors they intended to attack, the ships they hoped to raid, and occasionally even the individual merchants they planned to target. They appointed their own crews and assigned them specific wages or set percentages of the booty. Merchants frequently invested in corsairing as entrepreneurial ventures, underwriting the costs of the campaigns in return for shares in the spoils; if an attack failed, the investors lost their capital but the sanctioning government lost only its anticipated portion of the rewards. The governments remained obliged to ransom any captured corsairs or to pay reparations for damages due to excessive violence. So long as corsairs limited themselves to sanctioned targets, engaged only in theft and kidnapping, and eschewed gratuitous assault, their activities were generally regarded as acceptable risks of maritime trade. By the fourteenth century corsairing licenses were widely known as letters of marque (from the Latin *marcare,* meaning "to seize as a pledge"), as evidenced by the Catalan Consulate of the Sea for Mediterranean privateering and by the statutes of Edward III for corsairing in the North Sea.

THE TARGETS

It sounds more civilized than it was. Attacks by pirates and privateers depended as much on violence as on surprise to succeed, and many pirate-adventurers enjoyed well-deserved reputations for cruelty and bloodshed. Viking raiders into Northumbria and East Anglia, along the Breton coast, or up the Seine and Loire Rivers paid little attention to the niceties of their supposed profession. Greek or Slavic seagoers readily slew their commercial hostages whenever it became inconvenient to treat them according to piratical norms. The single most successful and feared pirate of the Middle Ages—the Catalan admiral Roger de Lauria, who amassed an enormous fortune from robbery and extortion—was renowned for his gleeful and brutish ferocity. And Muslim pirates operating along the North African coasts seldom blanched at the thought of slitting the throats of the Christian merchant-captives in the holds of their ships.

Sea raiders showed clear preferences for certain types of vessels and cargoes to beset. The bulk commodities of medieval trade—grain, lumber, oil, salt, wine, and wool—were safe from pillage, for the most part, since transporting them on the black market would have been cumbersome. Slaves were valuable and plentiful but posed similar logistical problems and were likewise avoided. This left items like jewelry, fine metalwork, spices, and luxury cloths such as silk, commodities that had the highest cash value in relation to their bulk, in addition to cash itself. Since these commodities had year-round markets, there were no "seasons" to piratical attacks. Some scholars have posited a kind of negative-seasonal aspect to piracy, on the supposition that merchants in grain (to choose an example) would be likely to engage in piracy and corsairing during the growing seasons when their legitimate activities were at a lull, but such thinking is little more than guesswork. The most successful pirates and corsairs whom we can identify were more often drawn from the professional classes than from the mercantile: government officials, diplomats, judges, military leaders, engineers, managerial agents, and financiers outnumbered merchants, among pirates and corsairs whom we can name.

PREVALENCE OF PIRACY

How widespread were piracy and corsairing? Answers vary, depending on the locale and era. The Mediterranean remained relatively free of sea-bandits through the fourth century, until the appearance of the first Germanic maritime raiders (the Vandals) and the gradual relinquishing of control over the western Mediterranean by the Byzantine Greeks when sea-lanes were opened to adventurers of all sorts. Justinian's conquests in the sixth century briefly curtailed robbery on the sea, but it came back with a vengeance during the Islamic ascendancy in the seventh. Pirates were more frequently to be found in the eastern sea, where luxury trade still flourished; Cilicia (especially Tarsus) and Crete were renowned pirate bases. As the Isaurian emperors swept these sites clean,

pirates began to operate chiefly from Tunisian harbors (especially from the island of Djerba), Corfu, Cyprus, and Rhodes. The advent of the Crusades caused a temporary decrease in piracy, but from the mid-twelfth century onward sea robbers acted with near impunity; the Byzantine chronicler Niketas Choniates (ca. 1155/1157–ca. 1215/1216) famously described the eastern Mediterranean of his time as "a pirate thalassocracy." In the late Middle Ages the worst offenders in the eastern sea (including up into the Black Sea) were Genoese and Venetian pirates. Throughout the western Mediterranean the leading robbers operated out of Catalonia, the Balearic Islands, Tunisia, Sicily, Naples, and Pisa, although references exist to English, Flemish, German, and Slavic pirates and corsairs, too. Not surprisingly, piracy and privateering were exclusively male concerns: no medieval equivalents of a Grace O'Malley—the sixteenth-century Irish adventuress who harassed trade ships throughout the Irish Sea and English Channel—have yet been found.

The Arabs, who adapted so quickly to seafaring and maritime trade after extending their control to the Mediterranean, also took quickly to piracy. Records from the eighth to tenth centuries are full of references to pirates operating out of Muslim North Africa and the islands under Islamic rule. The ninth-century *Life of St. Gregory the Decapolite,* probably written by his disciple Joseph, who himself was captured and sold into slavery by Muslim pirates from Crete, is so filled with encounters with Arab pirates that one wonders if any other ships existed at sea.

Whether Christian or Muslim, whether Danish, Irish, Italian, or Slav, medieval pirates generally operated as close to shore as possible; the most successful raids beset ships at anchor or when venturing into estuaries to take on fresh water, instead of attacking them on the high sea. Tactical realities determined this. Most large trade ships sailed with smaller transit craft tied to their stern. These small vessels shuttled the goods and merchants to the docks and up the rivers. Once these craft had cut free and begun to shuttle their cargoes ashore, the large ship lay undermanned and vulnerable—which is when the raiders generally tried to attack.

Piracy and corsairing remains a promising area of research, with rich veins of evidence lying untapped in archival holdings. Sifting through this material will take considerable time but is necessary before our understanding of sea robbery progresses beyond formulaic reconstructions.

BIBLIOGRAPHY

Ahrweiler, Hélène. "Course et piraterie dans le Méditerranée orientale aux IVe–XVe siècles (Empire Byzantin)." In *Course et piraterie.* 2 vols. Paris: XVe Colloque internationale d'histoire maritime, 1975.

Backman, Clifford R. *The Decline and Fall of Medieval Sicily: Politics, Religion, and Economy in the Reign of Frederick III, 1296–1337.* Cambridge, U.K.: Cambridge University Press, 1995.

Bracewell, Catherine W. *The Uskoks of Senj: Piracy, Banditry, and Holy War in the Sixteenth-Century Adriatic.* Ithaca, N.Y: Cornell University Press, 1992.

Bresc, Henri. "Course et piraterie en Sicile, 1250–1450." *Anuario de estudios medievales* 10 (1980): 751–757.

Burns, Robert I. "Piracy as an Islamic-Christian Interface in the Thirteenth Century." *Viator* 11 (1980): 165–178.

Favreau, Marie-Louise. "Die italienische Levante-Piraterie und die Sicherheit der Seewege nach Syrien im 12. und 13. Jahrhundert." *Vierteljahrschrift für Sozial- und Wirtschaftsgeschichte* 65 (1978): 265–338.

Mollat, Michel. "Guerre de course et piraterie à la fin du moyen âge: Aspects économiques et sociaux: Position des problèmes." *Hansische Geschichtsblätter* 90 (1972): 1–14.

Morgan, G. "The Venetian Claims Commission of 1278." *Byzantinische Zeitschrift* 69 (1976): 411–438.

Pryor, John H. *Geography, Technology, and War: Studies in the Maritime History of the Mediterranean, 649–1571.* Cambridge, U.K.: Cambridge University Press, 1988.

Puhle, Matthias. *Die Vitalienbrüder: Klaus Störtebeker und die Seeräuber der Hansezeit.* Frankfurt, Germany: Campus Verlag, 1994.

Tenenti, Alberto. *Piracy and the Decline of Venice, 1580–1615.* Translated by Janet and Brian Pullan. Berkeley: University of California Press, 1967.

Trasselli, Carmelo. "Naufragi, pirateria e doppio giuoco." In *La gente del mare mediterraneo.* Edited by R. Ragosta. Naples, Italy, 1981.

Unali, Anna. *Marinai, pirati e corsari catalani nel basso Medioevo.* Bologna, Italy: Cappelli, 1983.

Wolf, John B. *The Barbary Coast: Algiers under the Turks, 1500–1830.* New York: Norton, 1979.

Clifford R. Backman

[See also **DMA**: Navies, Western; Navigation: Western European; Trade, Western European.]

PLANCTUS MARIAE *(Marienklagen),* a type of *planctus,* or lament, usually sung in the voice of the Virgin Mary at the foot of the cross. Like other forms of *planctus,* examples survive in Latin and many vernacular languages, especially German but also French, English, Occitan, Italian, Spanish, Catalan, and Portuguese. The earliest example is generally considered to be from the fourth century (in the Greek Acta Pilati), but Eduard Wechssler and others argue that the genre proper in the West dates only from the eleventh and twelfth centuries,

reflecting general developments in Marian devotion; Janthia Yearley cites examples from the twelfth through the sixteenth centuries. Sandro Sticca links the height of the genre with Franciscan piety in the thirteenth century, culminating in Jacopone da Todi's *Stabat mater dolorosa* (The sorrowful mother was standing), though Wechssler argues that work is in fact not a *Marienklage* because it is not in the Virgin's voice. Some *planctus Mariae* are transmitted as part of Passion plays, so there is reason to see a relationship between the genre and medieval drama, but it is debated whether, as was once thought, the *planctus Mariae* is in fact the source for the medieval Passion play; Sticca argues that it is not. There is also some evidence for public performance of a dramatic or semidramatic nature of free-standing examples. Though the *planctus* is not strictly speaking liturgical, the subject matter of the *planctus Mariae* and the formal relationship of many verse *planctus* to the sequence may suggest the possibility of paraliturgical use; indeed, Solange Corbin demonstrates that *planctus Mariae* were often sung during the Good Friday office, at the foot of the crucifix.

The length and complexity of individual *planctus Mariae* vary widely, the only thing often uniting examples of the genre being their focus on the sorrows of the Virgin at the foot of the cross. Two of the best-known examples are *Planctus ante nescia* (Once I did not know grief) by Geoffrey of St. Victor and *Flete fideles animae* (Weep, faithful souls), both of which use the paired-stanza principle characteristic of the Latin sequence and the vernacular *lai.*

No single comprehensive study of the genre exists (Sticca perhaps comes closest), and the unsettled state of the literature for the *planctus Mariae,* the *planctus* in general, and liturgical drama makes it difficult to draw conclusions, especially across centuries, languages, and performance settings. Moreover, while some texts have been edited, relatively few of the melodies are readily available. There is no single edition of *planctus Mariae* texts, with or without music; the best guide available to published versions of individual *planctus* is Yearley.

BIBLIOGRAPHY

Corbin, Solange. *La déposition liturgique du Christ au Vendredi saint: Sa place dans l'histoire des rites et du théâtre religieux.* Paris: Société d'éditions "Les belles lettres," 1960.

Sticca, Sandro. *The Planctus Mariae in the Dramatic Tradition of the Middle Ages.* Translated by Joseph R. Berrigan. Athens and London: University of Georgia Press, 1988.

Wechssler, Eduard. *Die romanischen Marienklagen: Ein Beitrag zur Geschichte des Dramas im Mittelalter.* Halle, Germany: Max Niemeyer, 1893.

Yearley, Janthia. "A Bibliography of 'Planctus' in Latin, Provençal, French, German, English, Italian, Catalan, and Galician-Portuguese from the Time of Bede to the Early Fifteenth Century." *Journal of the Plainsong and Mediaeval Music Society* 4 (1981): 12–52.

ALICE V. CLARK

[See also **DMA:** Drama, Liturgical; Passion Cycle; Passion Plays, French; Planctus; Virgin Mary in Theology and Popular Devotion.]

POLLUTION AND TABOO.

An eighth-century penitential banning coitus for a husband and wife during menstruation, an eleventh-century knight vowing not to fight on Sundays, the eighteenth canon of the Fourth Lateran Council in 1215 forbidding priests from participating in judicial ordeals, and a fourteenth-century woman mystic embracing virginity were all attempts at articulating the shifting relationship between humanity and divinity through the strict (and therefore stabilizing) power of pollution. Paradoxically, the danger and fear of pollution was at the same time exhilarating, in that the clear definition of what was profane and polluting in life was also the stark classification of what was pure and holy. Pollution in the Middle Ages exemplified an interweaving of the metaphoric and the material, so individually intimate, so collectively strengthening, that the pollution-related taboos (of a person or thing) in one realm determined the holiness (of a person or thing) in another. It was through this sharp awareness of what was most potentially polluting in daily existence that the holy came into being. The sacred existed wherever the effort at enforcing or accepting certain polluting categories was successful. Throughout the Middle Ages there was an astounding precision and a marvelous diversity in the definitions of what polluted and what did not. Pollution was never just a symbol of something else or even the balance by which ideas of virtue or sin were weighed; it was the basic condition of medieval reality. What was thought to be polluting was always changing with what constituted a person. This exactitude about pollution could be achieved because to understand pollution was, in a very real sense, to know precisely what it meant to be human.

Early medieval penitentials, cataloging with exquisite specificity the right penance for almost any polluting behavior, from fellatio to rain magic to swearing to bestiality to raping a neighbor's daughter, allowed men and women to defuse all conflict in their small communities. These communities had profoundly limited horizons; power did not reach very far, protection went no farther than the eye could see, and the face of one's protector and of the person protected were crucial. The world of the tenth and eleventh centuries, for instance, was basi-cally one of habitual violence, but this cultural brutality, or rather the terrible potential of injustice and injury, was for the most part localized. Men and women lived in universes hedged in by dark, thick forests with danger forever dwelling just past the line of sight. The "correctness" of the right penance functioned in communities as a desperately needed deterrent to conflict arising from "incorrect" (and possibly socially contagious) behavior. Penitentials, like detailed memoranda from God, little slide rules of the holy, used the circumstantial risk of pollution in day-to-day existence, and so the risk of cosmic calamity, as a way of coercing men and women into restraining their potential for violence and chaos. A particular polluting act, once the correct medicinal penance was performed (and seen to be done), disappeared from the life of the individual and the memory of the community. The laundry list of ordinary and extraordinary sin in a penitential allowed for the resolution of all spiritual and social abnormalities with no recriminations or lasting guilt, either here or in the hereafter.

It was when this vision of penitential precision began to encompass a wider cosmos, as it did by the middle of the eleventh century and certainly by the end of the twelfth, that we see a redefinition of individual pollution and redemption. In this cultural shift, in this search for the ability to generalize across time and space about the human experience with the divine, the need for the communally contingent exactitude of the penitential was eliminated. New shapes and contours of pollution were developing throughout the world. In these decades radical ecclesiastical reformers, exemplified by Pope Gregory VII and his followers, began to advocate a widespread renewal of the Christian world, led not by emperors but by popes. The morals of the clergy, especially, were to be redone on a much more universal basis, one in which the polluting stain of the small worlds in which priests lived was to be washed out of them and the corrupting taint of secular investiture was to be eliminated in the elevation of bishops. The idea that priests and monks should not be married was finally instituted. Gregory VII may have demanded a pristine pool where what was spiritual was never muddied by the secular, but in wanting such purity, in praising it, he made it into something to be desired by all. Significantly, what started to obsess the imaginations and lives of thousands of men, women, and children was the desire to imitate Christ, the desire to model ordinary lives on the actions and words of one life, at once holy and human.

This new concern with the life of Christ lasted from the end of the eleventh until the fifteenth century and involved not only extraordinary individuals like St. Francis of Assisi but also ordinary persons endeavoring to achieve a holy life in day-to-day existence. As Christ used his humanity, and thus all that was most potentially polluting within himself, to save the world, so men and women could use their humanity to capture the sacred and so save themselves. It was not so much that body and soul came together, although they did; rather, it was an acceptance, for the first time, that to be human and divine was possible. It was, remarkably, a realization that people combined within themselves the pure and the polluting, the sacred and the profane, and that the living of a life was an exercise in accurately knowing the boundary of each. By comparison with the earlier penitential culture, this was the time when the habit of constantly looking into one's past and searching for the possibility of wrongdoing became the defining quality of the individual's relation to God. What happened from the thirteenth century onward was the assumption that men and women lived lives that were linear in direction. This new confessional culture allowed for persons to be interrogated by themselves, their confessors, or an inquisitor, over and over again, because there was a sense that within the existence of a person lay infinite avenues of possible pollution and salvation, of potential dangers and purity. Intriguingly, women were more likely to experience the divine because they had within themselves more polluting qualities, and for the same reason they were also more likely to be seduced by the devil, to be possessed by demons. Similarly, the idea that some men and women possessed inherent residues of pollution that could not be erased caused the medieval world to become what has been called a "persecuting society" in that lepers, Jews, heretics, witches, and Muslims were considered so defiled that their ability to pollute Christendom necessitated their containment and exclusion.

Yet by the middle of the fifteenth century this notion that humanity and divinity were unified in a person had begun to fragment. The desire to grasp the divine through the very things that made a human polluted had started to wane—so much so that by the sixteenth century each was thought to be out of the reach of the other. The sensation that pollution possessed a tidal quality, always ebbing and flowing through a person, always defining and shaping the holy, had begun to dissipate. The human and the divine had drifted apart, each one becoming self-contained and immutable. New ways of classifying what was causing pollution did arise, as is most clearly seen in ideas about ethnicity and race, but the use of pollution as a precise way of grasping the holy, so characteristic of the Middle Ages, had come to an end.

BIBLIOGRAPHY

Brown, Peter. *The Body and Society: Men, Women, and Sexual Renunciation in Early Christianity.* New York: Columbia University Press, 1988.

Douglas, Mary. *Purity and Danger: An Analysis of Concepts of Pollution and Taboo.* London: Routledge and K. Paul, 1966.

Kieckhefer, Richard. "The Holy and the Unholy: Sainthood, Witchcraft, and Magic in Late Medieval Europe." In *Christendom and Its Discontents: Exclusion, Persecution, and Rebellion, 1000–1500.* Edited by Scott L. Waugh and Peter D. Diehl. Cambridge, U.K.: Cambridge University Press, 1996.

Meens, Rob. "Pollution in the Early Middle Ages: The Case of Food Regulations in Penitentials." *Early Medieval Europe* 4 (1995), 3–19.

Moore, R. I. *The Formation of a Persecuting Society: Power and Deviance in Western Europe, 950–1250.* Oxford and New York: Blackwell, 1987.

MARK GREGORY PEGG

[See also **DMA:** Celibacy; Confession; Gregory VII, Pope; Penance and Penitentials; **Supp:** Body, The; Original Sin; Sexuality; Soul and Body; Violence.]

POOR CLARES. Poor Clares or Clarisses are members of the female or Second Order of Friars Minor, more commonly known as the Franciscans. Those names, however, are not contemporaneous with the period of Clare of Assisi; during her lifetime her communities of sisters were known rather as Poor Ladies, Poor Sisters, Sisters Minor, Religious Women, Poor Enclosed Nuns, Poor Recluses of the Order of St. Damian, Damianites, and the Order of Poor Sisters, this last being the denomination ultimately preferred by Clare. It was not until 1263, ten years after Clare's death, that Pope Urban IV attempted to channel all the various Clarissan communities into the Order of St. Clare (O.S.C).

CLARE OF ASSISI (1194–1253)

The circumstances of Clare's first meeting with her spiritual mentor Francis are not known; but it is likely, since she lived in the shadow of the cathedral of San Rufino, that their initial encounter occurred when he was preaching there in 1210. A year or two later, when she was about eighteen, Clare slipped out of her house and made her way to the church of the Porziuncola, where Francis and his brethren were waiting to receive her. Francis himself cut Clare's hair, consecrating her into the religious life. Since social norms dictated that Clare could not remain with Francis and his brethren, she was relocated to San Damiano, a little church just outside the walls of Assisi, in which Francis had first undergone a conversion experience and where he prophesied a cele-

Poor Clares Grieving over the Body of St. Francis (detail). *Giotto's early-14th-century fresco cycle on the life of St. Francis is in the upper church of San Francesco, Assisi.* © ELIO CIOL/CORBIS-BETTMANN. REPRODUCED BY PERMISSION.

brated monastery of women would reside. Fittingly, then, Clare found her spiritual home at San Damiano, where she led a small community of women vowed strictly to poverty. These followers of Clare's were neither traditional monastics nor the semi-religious women known as penitents.

SPIRITUALITY: WORK AND EVANGELICAL POVERTY

The imitation of Christ and his apostles—the *vita apostolica*—which was characterized by a common life of prayer, manual labor, preaching, and voluntary poverty was the ideal to which most religious movements of the thirteenth century, including the Poor Ladies, adhered. Unlike many of her contemporaries, however, Clare and her companions endeavored to live out the precepts of the *vita apostolica* within the cloister. Throughout the medieval period and well beyond, female convents were

often wealthy foundations, the purviews of aristocratic women. But Clare's conception of the monastery was unlike any that had preceded her. Rooted firmly in the tenet of evangelical poverty, Clare aimed paradoxically to maintain an "open" monastic enclosure for women, but without the financial stability of endowments or possessions. Her community would instead survive solely upon alms and the fruit of the sisters' manual labor. Indeed, the very first written witness of the Poor Ladies confirms this vision. In a letter of 1216 Jacques de Vitry observed that the "Sisters Minor" lived "near cities in various hospices, as they are called. They accept nothing, but live by the labor of their own hands." Mindful that the Poor Ladies' new form of religious community diverged strikingly from older traditions, Jacques followed local usage and selected the word "hospice" rather than "monastery" to indicate the new institutional form. What also made the Sisters Minor distinct was their handiwork—textile labor, mainly spinning and weaving of silk, linen, and woolen cloth, along with embroidery and sewing. Although some sisters were "external sisters," those who did the community's business outside the cloister, all of the Poor Sisters were required to work with their hands, including Clare herself.

Work was central to Clare's monastic project because it provided the community with a measure of material support, which in turn released the sisters from the obligation of accepting property or possessions. Thus they could live according to the *Form of Life* Francis had given to the Poor Ladies; that is, in "holy poverty," which became the defining attribute of Clarissan spirituality.

INSTITUTIONALIZATION

Clare's community at San Damiano was but one of a multitude of forms of religious life that flourished in the early years of the thirteenth century. The profusion of new religious movements, however, became such a concern for the church that the Fourth Lateran Council (1215) forbade the foundation of new orders. Perhaps for this reason, in that same year Francis imposed on Clare the title of "abbess," a title strongly associated with the cenobitic traditions of St. Benedict. Not surprisingly, Clare at first vehemently rejected it, not only out of humility but because she feared that her new religious enterprise would be crushed under the weight of centuries of Benedictine practice, a form of life that she had rejected explicitly just a few years earlier.

One venerable line of Franciscan scholarship maintains that before accepting the office of abbess, Clare in 1216 won from Pope Innocent III a privilege that ensured that her Poor Ladies could continue to live according to their radical vision of poverty. A more recent body of scholarship, however, has revived an old debate about the authenticity of the *Privilege of Poverty* issued by Innocent III. The late-twentieth-century debate, however, turns on diplomatic criteria that show convincingly that the *formulae* used in the text are not concurrent with those used by Innocent III's chancery; therefore, the *Privilege* is a forgery. The argument furthermore maintains that it is a fifteenth-century forgery, most likely from an Observant Clarissan milieu. This important discovery, however, by no means vitiates or undercuts Clare's passionate commitment to holy poverty: indeed, thirteenth-century evidence attests that Clare spent her entire life battling a succession of popes for the Poor Ladies' right to live in absolute poverty.

By 1218 a network of Poor Ladies extended from Umbria into Tuscany, and the papal legate, Cardinal Hugolino of Ostia (the future Pope Gregory IX), was anxious both to protect their welfare and to impose juridical uniformity on them. For these reasons, in 1218–1219 he issued a set of constitutions based on the Benedictine *Rule,* the keystone of which prescribed strict claustration for the Poor Ladies. Although far from the spirit of her original monastic vision, Clare accepted the *Constitutions of Hugolino,* though to what extent they were ever implemented at San Damiano and its closest sister foundations remains unclear. Clare, it should be emphasized, made this concession without renouncing her fervid commitment to holy poverty. Indeed, to safeguard it in 1228, one year after Hugolino ascended the pontificate as Gregory IX, Clare solicited and received from him the *Privilege of Poverty,* which decreed, "no one can compel you to receive possessions." Initially, the privilege was granted only to San Damiano, but within a year it was conceded also to Monteluce in Perugia and Monticelli in Florence, two of the first Damianite convents closely associated with Clare herself.

In 1247, in yet another attempt to impose unity on the Damianites, Pope Innocent IV promulgated a new *Rule* for Clare's order which by now included houses throughout Italy, France, Spain, Bohemia, the Holy Roman Empire, and the Low Countries. The *Rule* had the merit of bringing the Poor Ladies juridically into the Franciscan family in two ways: first by authorizing them to profess the Franciscan *Rule* approved by papal bull in 1223, and second by assigning the Minorites the pastoral care of the sisters. Nevertheless, it struck a blow at the heart of Damianite monasticism as it formally authorized corporate possessions for the Poor Ladies, explicitly contravening Clare's fervid dedication to apostolic poverty.

In 1252, foreseeing her own demise and provoked by Innocent's new *Rule* for her sisters, Clare responded with her own *Rule,* or *Form of Life,* which drew on the entire corpus of documents and oral traditions by which her community had lived for over forty years. Enshrined in chapter 6 of Clare's *Rule* was the *Form of Life* that St. Francis himself had prescribed for the Poor Ladies at their inception. Clare's *Form of Life* placed adherence to holy poverty at the very core of her religious project by insisting on corporate poverty. On 9 August 1253, just two days before her death, Pope Innocent IV signed the bull *Solet annuere* approving Clare's *Rule* for the monastery of San Damiano, where thirteen sisters were then residing. Clare's *Form of Life,* it should be noted, was the first piece of religious legislation written by a woman to achieve papal approbation as a monastic *rule* for female religious.

Notwithstanding her deathbed victory, in 1263, only eight years after Clare had been canonized, in yet another attempt to regularize the observances of the Poor Ladies, Pope Urban IV gathered all the various Damianite foundations together under the rubric of the order of St. Clare and again authorized the use of possessions and property in a new *Rule* written for the Order. Significantly, the Urbanist *Rule* did not juridically abrogate Clare's *Form of Life;* nonetheless Clare's *Rule* increasingly fell into disuse during the later thirteenth and fourteenth centuries, although there were notable examples of its use prior to its revival during the reform period of the fifteenth century. In the fourteenth century, for example, Queen Sancia of Mallorca founded the convent of Santa Croce (1338) in Naples expressly to follow the *Rule* of St. Clare.

FOUNDATIONS AND GROWTH OF THE ORDER

The first Damianite foundations, those bound most closely to Clare, were made by 1219 and were established in the nearby Umbrian and Tuscan towns of Foligno, Perugia, Florence, Siena, and Lucca. By 1228 Cardinal Rinaldo, the Cardinal-Protector of the Poor Ladies (and later Pope Alexander IV), had 24 convents inscribed in his list of those that received Franciscan visitation, although by this date there were probably at least 12 others as well. Within a year or two, Clarissan foundations had moved beyond the Alps, and by the time of Clare's death in 1253, there were close to 170 convents throughout Europe following some form of Clarissan observance. By the end of the thirteenth century, over 400 foundations had been made, more than half of those located in Italy. Roughly estimated, thirteenth-century Clarissan foundations were distributed throughout Latin Christendom as follows: Italy, 210; Iberian Peninsula, 60; France, 51; Holy Roman Empire, 43; Bohemia and eastern Europe, 23; Low Countries, 7; Britain and Ireland, 4; Crusader Kingdoms and Holy Land, 7; and Scandinavia, 2. Despite the disasters of the fourteenth century, Clarissan monasticism expanded throughout Europe, increasing the number of convents by over 200 new foundations. A renewal of the Clarissan Order, owing to reforms undertaken separately by St. Colette of Corbie and the friars of the Franciscan Observance, aided in the establishment of more than 300 new houses in the fifteenth century. Thus, by the eve of the Reformation well over 1,000 Clarissan foundations had been made throughout Europe and the Mediterranean.

FOUNDERS AND REFORMERS

The founders of Clarissan convents came from all sectors of medieval society. In many cases convents were founded by groups of pious women already living together as penitents, tertiary Franciscans, or Humiliate who requested and ultimately received the *Rule* of St. Clare. Nor was it out of the ordinary, as was the case at Recanati in 1290, for a Benedictine convent to convert itself into a Clarissan monastery. Preaching campaigns by the Observant Franciscans were yet another occasion on which convents were sometimes founded as happened in Verona in 1425 or Milan in 1446, when the sermons of St. Bernardino of Siena inspired the foundation of Observant Clarissan houses.

The size of Clarissan communities varied enormously. Clare's original foundation at San Damiano, along with many others throughout the medieval period, housed no more than a few Poor Ladies, but even as early as the last quarter of the thirteenth century, the convent at Laguiche, for example, housed up to 100 sisters. Though some monasteries saw their ranks decimated by the vicissitudes of plague or warfare, other Clarissan populations flourished, as did that at Santa Chiara in Naples founded in 1310 by Sancia of Mallorca and Robert of Anjou, monarchs of the kingdom of Naples. By 1318 the convent had to apply for permission to have its number of sisters increased from 120 to 150. It was not unusual that limitations—papal or otherwise—were imposed on how many sisters a convent could maintain.

Sancia and Robert were by no means the only royal patrons of the Poor Ladies. Agnes of Bohemia, who with Clare's blessing made her profession at a Damianite monastery she had founded in Prague in 1234, was the first in a long line of royalty to patronize Clarissan convents. The lists also includes, among others, Isabel of France who made a foundation at Longchamp in Paris (1252); Iolanthe, queen of Castile, patron of a house at Allariz (1282); Sancia's mother in law, Maria Arpád, who rebuilt Santa Maria Donnaregina in Naples after the earthquake of 1297; Sancia of Mallorca herself, who in addition to Santa Chiara (1310) also founded Santa Croce in Naples (1338); Blanche of Savoy, founder of a house in Pavia (1380); Ferdinand and Isabella of Spain who founded a house (seized from the Jews) at Plasencia (1475); Margaret of York, duchess of Burgundy, patron of a house at Paris in 1483 and Lille in 1490; and Lucrezia Borgia d'Este, duchess of Ferrara, founder of a Clarissan monastery at Ferrara (1510) for her niece, Camilla.

The great age of reform for the Poor Clares came in the fifteenth century, particularly under the leadership of Colette of Corbie (1381–1477). During her lifetime she founded 17 monasteries in France and Flanders that practiced a strict observance of the *Rule* of St. Clare, which meant above all a return to austere poverty, both individual and corporate. Many Clarissan foundations followed suit; consequently, about 140 monasteries subject to the Conventual branch of the Franciscan Order observed the Colettine reform.

A separate reforming impulse not to be confused with the Colettine reform came from the Observant branch of the Franciscans associated with Bernardino of Siena and St. Giovanni of Capistrano, among others. Like Colette of Corbie, they too were interested in returning the order to strict observance of the Clarissan *Rule,* which privileged evangelical poverty. Communities of Observant Clares in Milan, Mantua, Verona, and L'Aquila were founded in association with some of the leading lights of the Observant Reform. Many more convents were reformed according to the Franciscan Observance. Blessed Eustochia Calafato tried to reform her convent in Messina according to this spirit; failing that, she departed with a few sisters, and by 1493 she was heading up a flourishing community of 53 sisters.

CULTURAL PRODUCTION

The Observant milieu fostered literary and artistic production among and for Clarissan communities. Clare herself established a literary tradition for the order with her letters and *Form of Life,* or *Rule,* although one school of scholarly thought has rejected Clare's authorship of the *Testament,* a text long attributed to her. Like the *Privilege of Poverty,* with which it shares a manuscript tradition, scholars have recently suggested that the *Testament* is also a fifteenth-century forgery, one that originated in an Observant Clarissan reform context, possibly at Monteluce.

The Observant environment also generated more conventional contributions to the Clarissan literary canon. Camilla Battista of Varano (1458–1524), abbess of an Observant convent in Camerino, wrote in both Latin and the vernacular, producing a devotional work, *I dolori mentali di Gesù* (The mental sorrows of Jesus, 1488), and her spiritual autobiography, *Vita spiritualis* (1491), written when she was just thirty-three. St. Catherine of Bologna (Caterina Vigri, 1413–1463), who began her religious life in the Third Order and concluded it as abbess of Corpus Domini in Bologna, was, notably, a gifted writer, musician, and painter. Her literary works include *laude,* or religious poetry, and sermons, which she often preached in chapter. Among her sermons is one honoring St. Clare, whom she lauds as a "humble and prudent mother." She is also the author of a treatise called *Le sette armi spirituali* (The seven spiritual weapons), an advice manual addressed to religious women, which she composed in Ferrara while serving as

novice mistress. And following in a long tradition of nuns who illuminated manuscripts (including the Clarisses at Monteluce), Caterina's visual works include a decorated breviary and a number of panel paintings depicting the Madonna and Child.

Finally, in addition to works produced by Clarissan sisters themselves, artistic memorials were frequently produced for them, including the *Santa Chiara Dossal,* the first known panel of a contemporary female saint, painted *ca.* 1280–1285, and Pacino di Bonaguida's *Tree of Life* panel, likely painted for the Poor Ladies at Monticelli in Florence. Also noteworthy was the architecture that was created for and commissioned by Clarissan communities. Two celebrated churches, both dedicated to St. Clare, one in Assisi (1265) and one in Naples (1310), are renowned for their elaborate decorative programs and innovative conventual architecture. They are monuments that remind us still of a great monastic enterprise, now almost eight centuries old, whose cornerstone was Clare of Favarone's fierce commitment to holy poverty.

BIBLIOGRAPHY

PRIMARY WORKS

Armstrong, Regis J., O.F.M. Cap., ed. and trans. *Clare of Assisi: Early Documents.* Rev. 2d. ed. St. Bonaventure, N.Y.: Franciscan Institute Publications, 1993.

Mueller, Joan, ed. *Clare's Letters to Agnes: Texts and Sources.* St. Bonaventure, N.Y.: Franciscan Institute Publications, 2001.

Omaechevarría, Ignacio, et al., eds. and trans. *Escritos de santa Clara y documentos contemporáneos.* 1970. Rev. 3d ed. Madrid: Biblioteca de Autores Cristianos, 1993. Bilingual.

Varano, Blessed Battista da. *Le opere spirituali.* Edited by Giacomo Boccanera. Iesi, Italy: Scuola Tipografica Francescana, 1958.

Vigri, Caterina de'. *I sermoni.* With an introduction and commentary by Gilberto Sgarbi and a critical essay by Enzo Lodi. Bologna, Italy: Barghigiani, 1999.

———. *Laudi, tratti, e lettere.* Edited by Silvia Serventi. Florence, Italy: SISMEL–Edizioni del Galluzzo, 2000.

———. *Le sette armi spirituali.* Edited by Antonella Degl'Innocenti. Florence, Italy: SISMEL–Edizioni del Galluzzo, 2000.

Vitry, Jacques de. *Lettres de Jacques de Vitry (1160/1170–1240), évêque de Saint-Jean-d'Acre.* Edited by R. B. C. Huygens. Leiden, Netherlands: Brill, 1960.

BIBLIOGRAPHICAL WORKS

De Villapadierna, Isidoro, and Pietro Maranesi, eds. *Bibliografia di Santa Chiara di Assisi: 1930–1993.* Rome: Istituto Storico dei Cappuccini, 1994.

Hone, Mary Francis, ed. *St. Clare of Assisi and Her Order: A Bibliographic Guide.* St. Bonaventure, N.Y.: Franciscan Institute Publications, 1995.

SECONDARY WORKS

Alberzoni, Maria Pia. *Chiara e il papato*. Milan: Biblioteca Francescana, 1995.

———. "'Nequaquam a Christi sequela in perpetuum absolvi desidero.' Chiara tra carisma e istituzione." In *Chiara d'Assisi e la memoria di Francesco*. Edited by Alfonso Marini and M. Beatrice Mistretta. Fara Sabina, Italy: Petruzzi, 1995. (Translated into English as "'Nequaquam a Christi sequela in perpetuum absolvi desidero' [I will never desire in any way to be absolved from the following of Christ]: Clare between Charisma and Institution." *Greyfriars Review* 12 [1998]: 81–122.)

———. "*Sorores Minores* e autorità ecclesiastica fino al pontificato di Urbano IV." In *Chiara e la diffusione delle Clarisse nel secolo XIII*. Edited by Giancarlo Andenna and Benedetto Vetere. Galatina, Italy: Congedo, 1998.

———. "San Damiano nel 1228: Contributo alla 'questione clariana'." *Collectanea Franciscana* 77 (1997): 459–476. (Translated into English as "San Damiano in 1228: A Contribution to the 'Clare Question'." *Greyfriars Review* 13 [1999].)

Andenna, Cristina. "Chiara di Assisi: Alcune considerazione su un problema." *Rivista di storia e letteratura religiosa* 34 (1998): 547–579.

Andenna, Giancarlo, and Benedetto Vetere, eds. *Chiara e il Secondo Ordine: Il fenomeno francescano femminile nel Salento*. Galatina, Italy: Congedo, 1997.

———. *Chiara e la diffusione delle Clarisse nel secolo XIII*. Galatina, Italy: Congedo, 1998.

Bartoli, Marco. *Clare of Assisi*. Translated by Frances Teresa, O.S.C. Quincy, Ill.: Franciscan Press, 1993.

Bruzelius, Caroline. "Hearing Is Believing: Clarissan Architecture, *ca.* 1213–1340." *Gesta* 31, vol. 2 (1992): 83–91.

Casagrande, Giovanna. "Le compagne di Chiara." In *Chiara di Assisi*. Edited by the Società internazionale di studi franciscana. Spoleto, Italy: Centro Italiano di Studi sull'Alto Medioevo, 1993.

Corsi, Pasquale, and Ferdinando L. Maggiore, eds. *Chiara d'Assisi e il movimento Clariano in Puglia*. Bari, Italy: Centro di Studi Francescani, 1996.

Grundmann, Herbert. *Religious Movements in the Middle Ages*. 1935. Translated by Steven Rowan. Reprint, Notre Dame, Ind.: University of Notre Dame Press, 1995.

Lainati, Chiara Augusta. *Temi spirituali dagli scritti del secondo ordine francescano*. 2 vols. Assisi, Italy: Tipografica Porziuncola, 1970.

Lopez, Élisabeth. *Culture et sainteté: Colette de Corbie (1381–1447)*. Saint-Etienne, France: Publications de l'Université de Saint-Etienne, 1994.

Maleczek, Werner. *Das "Privilegium paupertatis" Innocenz' III. und das Testament der Klara von Assisi: Überlegungen zur Frage ihrer Echtheit*. Rome: Istituto Storico dei Cappuccini, 1995. (Translated into English as "Questions about the Authenticity of the Privilege of Poverty of Innocent III and the Testament of Clare of Assisi." *Greyfriars Review* 12 [1998]: 1–80.)

Mooney, Catherine M. "*Imitatio Christi* or *Imitatio Mariae*? Clare of Assisi and Her Interpreters." In *Gendered Voices: Medieval Saints and Their Interpreters*. Edited by Catherine M. Mooney. Philadelphia: University of Pennsylvania Press, 1999.

Moorman, John R. H. *A History of the Franciscan Order from Its Origins to the Year 1517*. Oxford: Clarendon, 1968.

———. *Medieval Franciscan Houses*. St. Bonaventure, N.Y.: Franciscan Institute Publications, 1983.

Peterson, Ingrid J., O.S.F. *Clare of Assisi: A Biographical Study*. Quincy, Ill.: Franciscan Institute, 1993.

Rusconi, Roberto. "L'espansione del francescanesimo femminile nel secolo XIII." In *Movimento religioso femminile e francescanesimo nel secolo XIII*. Assisi, Italy: Società internazionale di studi franciscana, 1980. (Translated into English as "The Spread of Women's Franciscanism in the Thirteenth Century." *Greyfriars Review* 12 [1998]: 35–75.)

Società internazionale di studi franciscana, ed. *Chiara di Assisi*. Spoleto, Italy: Centro Italiano di Studi sull'Alto Medioevo, 1993.

Wood, Jeryldene M. *Women, Art, and Spirituality: The Poor Clares of Early Modern Italy*. New York: Cambridge University Press, 1996.

KATHERINE LUDWIG JANSEN

[See also **DMA:** Benedictine Rule; Benedictines; Bernardino of Siena, St.; Cloister; Francis of Assisi, St.; Franciscans; Monastery; **Supp:** Clare, St.]

POPULAR RELIGION. See **Religion, Popular.**

PORNOGRAPHY. The identification of pornography in the medieval period is a complex problem for several reasons. First, the word "pornography" itself is notoriously difficult to define. In its widest sense, pornography may be said to refer to cultural productions—literary, visual, and aural—that graphically depict human sexual organs and sexual practices. However, because its personal meaning, social reception, and moral value are assumed to be intrinsic to its nature as a cultural object, pornography is rarely defined in this neutral way. Accordingly, pornography is usually regarded not only as having a specific content but also as expressing forms of sexuality and gender that cannot be consumed with affective or aesthetic disinterest. Pornography in the Middle Ages is thus often defined in relation to the attitudes that church and other moral authorities held toward its effects on individuals. These erotic cultural products were almost invariably condemned as dangerous because of the sexual feelings they aroused or, more rarely, the antifeminist beliefs they engendered.

DEFINING MEDIEVAL PORNOGRAPHY

There was no word in the Middle Ages to designate the genre or aesthetic category that is now familiar to us simply as "porn," thanks largely to its mass distribution, starting with the spread of print culture beginning in the early modern period. The word "pornography," from the Greek *pornographoi* (*porno* and *graphoi*: "whore-painters"), was coined in the nineteenth century to describe the erotic frescoes of Pompeii dating from the first century A.D. that cover walls sacred to bacchanalian orgies. The term itself is thus a modern invention, and, for many scholars, pornography as an independent aesthetic category cannot be traced back further than sixteenth-century Italy or even seventeenth- and eighteenth-century France and England (albeit with important antecedents in ancient Greece and Rome). These scholars (e.g., Lynn Hunt and Ian Moulton) suggest that, because pornography is a historical and not an essential category, the term itself can only be applied anachronistically to the Middle Ages.

The second, and related, difficulty with specifying the pornography of the medieval period is the lack of any historical knowledge about its actual modes of consumption. Because modern mass-marketed and mass-consumed pornography based upon sexual stimulation has no direct analog in the Middle Ages, even the most explicit representations of sexuality in, for example, goliardic verse, the fabliaux, and the illustrations of some manuscripts of the *Roman de la Rose* leave us doubtful as to whether their sole, or even primary, aim was to arouse. Pornography provoking stimulating experiences seems to have been a luxury mainly reserved for a tiny elite in the Middle Ages and through the early modern period. The stories of the rich and doubtless idle classes for whom pornographic pleasures were a form of social diversion and amusement are well known: Pope Alexander VI (1431–1503), who, at the finale of a banquet on All Saints' Eve in 1501, watched as fifty naked courtesans crawled on all fours in search of chestnuts thrown to them; Francis II, duke of Alençon (1435–1488), who is said to have made his friends drink from a cup engraved with scenes of bestiality.

Such stories, by raising the issue of the relation of pornographic pleasure to social privilege, also call attention to another of the most striking differences between modern and medieval modes of erotic consumption. These differences concern the relation of sexuality to both privacy and literacy. Unlike contemporary pornography, that of the Middle Ages was very rarely consumed in the private scene of reading or viewing. The third obstacle we face, then, in defining medieval pornography is whether or not its public consumption undoes one of the fundamental assumptions concerning pornography as a genre, namely, that it is used for the purpose of private sexual gratification. The skill of reading silently (and the luxury of doing so in the solitude and quiet of one's own bedchamber) was possible in the medieval period for only a very privileged few. By the fifteenth century,

however, the practice of intimate solitary and silent reading had become a real possibility and pleasure in wealthy secular as well as clerical spheres. Such a revolution in literacy practices, while bringing readers into more intimate relations with God through the private contemplation of religious texts, was nevertheless regarded by the moralists as perilous. The church was fast beginning to regard the private world of sexual stimulation as a powerful threat to society. It was now possible to encounter, free from observation, the kinds of sexually stimulating material that could incite private desires and nourish fantasies. It is worth noting that, along with Luther's Bible, the largest early press runs (4,000 or more) included Aldus Manutius's early-sixteenth-century introduction to the erotic Latin poetry of Catullus.

It seems, then, there are three ways to specify pornography in the Middle Ages: one, in terms of its manifest content; two, in terms of its latent, obviously personal meanings, usually defined in psychological terms (such as fantasy and perversion); and three, in terms of its mode of consumption—that is, the social contexts in which it is read and preserved.

VARIETIES OF THE PORNOGRAPHIC

Despite these difficulties, it is still possible to suggest what pornography, or at least the pornographic, might have looked like in the Middle Ages. Medieval pornographic representations, though consistently held in low repute, were widespread, often finding literary expression in riddles (such as riddles number 12, 25, 44, 45, and 91 from the Old English Exeter Book), common jokes (a popular joke asked, What is the dirtiest word in the Psalter?—the answer was *conculcavit*, combining the words for cunt [*con*], ass [*cul*] and prick [*vit*]), doggerel, and satirical verses such as those of the goliards (e.g., the thirteenth-century collection known as the *Carmina Burana*). Pornographic moments are found among the highest literary achievements of the Middle Ages. Chaucer's "Miller's Tale" and "Reeve's Tale" from the *Canterbury Tales* and Boccaccio's *Decameron,* several of the 100 stories of which are licentious in nature, are commonly cited as evidence of their authors' interest in the vicissitudes of earthly sexuality. A principal theme associated with pornographic representations in the Middle Ages was the sexual license of monks and other churchmen, where displays of hypocrisy were the favorite material of satire. The Old French fabliau tradition—comic verse from around the thirteenth century—is especially noted for satirizing church strictures on sexual matters. Medieval pornography, like its later incarnations, is often linked to forms of freethinking and heresy, to natural philosophy and science, and to attacks on absolutist authority. The popular Middle High German mother-daughter advice poems display an openness to sexual matters and an irreverence consistent with the ideology of pornographic representation in the fabliaux.

The lyrics of the troubadours of southern France also provide evidence of an abiding interest in sexual matters. These songs, usually addressed to impossible love objects, tended to celebrate erotism and sex, couching more sexually explicit ideas in artistically veiled metaphors. Reading these lyrics, therefore, often amounts to an act of deciphering, where actual sex is expressed in a kind of code. Despite a very limited surviving corpus (eleven poems), William IX (1071–1126), the duke of Aquitane, the first noble troubadour, is renowned for the vulgarity of his lyrics, specifically his references to female genitalia. In a courtly milieu where noblewomen were idealized in song, the antifeminism of the troubadour, as well as of the trouvère and minnesinger, nevertheless flourished, with the twelfth-century poetry of Marcabru exemplary in this regard. The Old French *Roman de la Rose* of the thirteenth century, a long poem of erotic seduction, departs from the courtly tradition of feminine idealization in its aggressive display of virility. The theologian John Gerson found the poem scurrilous, while Christine de Pizan condemned its misogyny. Troubadour lyrics and the *Roman de la Rose* dramatize the extent to which some verbal images, while not inherently pornographic, can assume the status of pornography when they are seen as leading to the enjoyment of the humiliation of women. The depiction of women as irrepressibly sexual is not limited to European literature. The collection of stories known throughout the Arab world as the *Thousand and One Nights,* which reached its more or less definitive form in the sixteenth century, is notable for its decidedly adult tales of scandal and treachery, often involving faithless women. When aimed against women especially, the pornographic can also serve the purpose of political condemnation. Procopius of Caesarea, who is the most important source for information concerning the reign of the Byzantine emperor Justinian and his wife Theodora, wrote, in addition to a number of official histories, a scurrilous attack on the empress, published after his death as *Secret History (Anecdota).* Parts of this book (such as the ninth chapter) were so pornographic that for some time translations from Greek were only available into Latin. Gibbon, for example, wrote about Theodora that "her arts must be veiled in the obscurity of a learned language."

The drawings and sculpture of the Middle Ages at the margins of the page and of the church remind us that obscene or pornographic imagery was often found in proximity to the sacred and the serious. Sculptures and images haunting churches across Europe put before the parishioner exaggerated, sometimes horrific, visions of sexual practice: tongue-protruding gargoyles, *femmes aux serpents* (women as serpents), coital couples, megaphallic and priapic figures, exhibitionists such the *sheela-na-gig* (a female grotesque with disproportionately sized genitals), tress pullers, penis swallowers, and so on. Such images cautioned against certain behaviors by demonstrating the results of degradation through sin. Sexual images are often found in the margins of prayer books. A book of hours from the fourteenth century, for example, has as part of its playful marginalia an image of a nude couple engaged in what appears to be oral sex. Serious treatises were sometimes adorned with erotic illustrations. For example, a number of miniatures accompanying the balneological treatise of the popular German *Teutsch Kalender* (1481) portray scenes of mixed nude bathing, suggesting an uninhibitedness verging on pornography. Nudity in medieval writing was often considered a sign of shame, especially for women.

The moralists of the Middle Ages had nothing but suspicion toward erotic stimuli. As early as the fourth century, St. John Chrysostom, in a homily on the First Letter of Paul to the Thessalonians, castigated obscene spectacles in the theaters and images depicting nudity or, worse, sexual relations as leading to sin through the incitement of fantasy and taboo pleasures. The church's position on pleasure was clear: it was not to be the goal of sexual intercourse. Even as the by-product of procreative intention, pleasure was considered moderately sinful. Peter Lombard (*ca.* 1095–1160), in the *Sentences,* drew from St. Augustine the belief that there would have been little pleasure in the sexual act before the fall of man from paradise. The lack of pleasure in prelapsarian sexual acts, it was argued, signifies the control of deliberative reason over the "motions" of the sex organs. Theologians such as Robert Grosseteste, Albertus Magnus, and Thomas Aquinas in the twelfth and thirteenth centuries became deeply concerned with explaining the failure of the genitals to obey reason. Pornographic images, according to the logic of their arguments, could command movement toward what they termed concupiscence (desire or appetite pursuing its own object in disregard for the proper order of reason), as made visible in the erection and completed in the act of masturbation.

Masturbation was one among many sexual sins graphically described in the confessional manuals known as the penitentials. These texts, which first appeared in the sixth century and were in use through the twelfth, and their successive genre form, the *summae confessorum* (summas for confessors), condemned a panoply of sexual sins including homosexuality, fornication, bestiality, adultery, and nocturnal emissions. Burchard of Worms (*ca.* 965–1025) wrote a penitential castigating the use of dildos by women, a practice that carried a penance of five years. Pornographic imagery also circulated in other forms that are in principle directly opposed to it: medical and scientific treatises. Numerous treatises entitled *De coitu* (On intercourse) circulated throughout the Middle Ages, all of them more or less revised and expanded versions of a text of the same name ascribed to Constantine the African (*d.* 1087). A provocatively titled Catalan text of the fourteenth century, *Speculum al foderi* (literally, A mirror for fuckers), was discovered in the 1970s. This text is significant as being the only treatise prior to the early modern period describing an art of sexual positions. Medical treatises concerning the anatomy and care of women doubtless owed some of their popularity in the Middle Ages to their pornographic character. Gynecologic and cosmetic treatises, such as *De passionibus mulierum* (On the diseases of women, *ca.* 1100) by Trota of Salerno, enjoyed a popularity in the Middle Ages that cannot be explained solely in terms of their purported scientific value.

The question of how much sexuality we can impute to medieval cultural productions that are clearly not intended to be pornographic is a contentious one. The image of Christ's body with genitals revealed, as found in much fifteenth-century art and piety, became the topic of some debate when Leo Steinberg argued that this new genital emphasis was an imaginative attempt on the part of painters to reintegrate the sexual into the ideally human. Christ's body, he argued, became the site upon which was projected a sexuality that is without guilt. Other scholars refused to acknowledge the presence of the sexual. Caroline Bynum maintained that Christ's genital exposures were symbolic of a generative, as opposed to sexual, ideal. Her argument depended upon demonstrating that Christ's body was sometimes rendered as female in late medieval iconography.

BIBLIOGRAPHY

Bynum, Caroline Walker. *Fragmentation and Redemption: Essays on Gender and the Human Body in Medieval Religion.* New York: Zone Books, 1992.

Camille, Michael. *Image on the Edge: The Margins of Medieval Art.* Cambridge, Mass.: Harvard University Press, 1992.

Foxon, David. *Libertine Literature in England, 1660–1745.* New York: University Books, 1965.

Hunt, Lynn, ed. *The Invention of Pornography: Obscenity and the Origins of Modernity, 1500–1800.* New York: Zone Books, 1993.

Kendrick, Walter. *The Secret Museum: Pornography in Modern Culture.* Berkeley: University of California Press, 1996.

Michelson, Peter. *The Aesthetics of Pornography.* New York: Herder and Herder, 1971.

Moulton, Ian Frederick. *Before Pornography: Erotic Writing in Early Modern England.* Oxford: Oxford University Press, 2000.

Nelli, René. *L'érotique des troubadours.* 2 vols. Toulouse, France: Union générale d'éditions, 1963.

———. "Love's Rewards." In *Fragments for a History of the Human Body.* Vol. 2. Edited by Michel Feher with Ramona Naddaff and Nadia Tazzi. New York: Zone Books, 1989.

Sontag, Susan. "The Pornographic Imagination." In *Styles of Radical Will.* New York: Anchor, 1991.

Spearing, A. C. *The Medieval Poet as Voyeur: Looking and Listening in Medieval Love-Narratives.* Cambridge, U.K.: Cambridge University Press, 1993.

Steinberg, Leo. *The Sexuality of Christ in Renaissance Art and in Modern Oblivion.* 2d ed. Chicago: University of Chicago Press, 1996.

Turner, James Grantham. *Schooling Sex: Libertine Literature and Erotic Education in Italy, France, and England 1534–1685.* Oxford: Oxford University Press, 2003.

Weir, Anthony, and James Jerman, eds. *Images of Lust: Sexual Carvings on Medieval Churches.* New York: Routledge, 1999.

MICHAEL UEBEL

[See also **DMA:** Fabliau and Comic Tale; Trota and Trotula; Troubadour, Trouvère; William IX of Aquitaine; **Supp:** Body, The; Original Sin; Sexuality; Sexuality, Medical.]

PORTUGUESE LITERATURE. The lack of overlap between a political entity and recognizably national cultural-linguistic characteristics partially determines early Portuguese literary production. This is one reason why a large corpus of vernacular poetry is referred to as "Galician-Portuguese," since medieval Portugal shares its language and culture with Galicia, then belonging to the kingdom of León. Moreover, multilingualism marks literary production on the Iberian Peninsula until fairly late. Early on, Galicians and Castilians alike wrote poetry in Portuguese. In the late medieval period, it was the Portuguese who began to write in Castilian, particularly in their poetry. Thus, in the mid-fifteenth century, Pedro, constable of Portugal (1429–1466), briefly ruler of Catalonia (1463–1466), and recipient of the Marqués de Santillana's famous *Proemio e carta al condestable de Portugal* (Preface and a letter to the constable of Portugal, 1449), on the origins of Castilian poetry, is also the author of a fundamental Castilian text in the peninsular sentimental romance genre, the *Sátira de la infelice e* *felice vida.* This cultural complexity cannot be properly addressed in a short article such as this, which will focus exclusively on literary production in Portuguese.

POETRY

The Galician-Portuguese lyric form known as *cantigas* flourished from the late twelfth century, the date of the earliest known poem, to the mid-fourteenth century. The corpus—some 1680 extant texts composed by over 150 different poets—is preserved primarily in three great codices (or "songbooks"): *Cancioneiro da Ajuda* (hereafter referred to as A), *Cancioneiro da Biblioteca Nacional de Lisboa* (B; formerly called *Cancioneiro de Colocci-Brancuti*), and *Cancioneiro da Vaticana.* Of these, the oldest, but also the least complete, is A, containing only compositions prior to King Denis I (1279–1325), himself an outstanding poet, whose reign coincides with both the zenith and waning of this poetic mode.

These compositions were seemingly intended for performance, as evidenced by the musical notation found in two separate manuscripts, seven *cantigas* by Martim Codax *(Pergaminho Vindel)* and another set by Denis (the Sharrer manuscript). Poets and performers were designated either as *trovador* or *jogral,* according to both class and a division of artistic labor—the *trovador* being presumably of noble origin and a composer, while the lower-class *jogral* was the performer. This occasionally explicitly antagonistic classification (in *tenções,* for instance) was belied by actual practice: among its greatest exponents were kings, clerics, and men of humbler origins.

Though the Provençal *fin'amors* tradition found its way into the *cantigas,* in combination with elements from oral, popular literature, there is an evident affinity between the *cantigas de amigo,* the Hispano-Arab *kharjas* appended to *muwashshahs* (odes), and the vernacular women's songs thought to precede much of the early European medieval lyric. In a fragmentary *ars poetica* included in *Cancioneiro B,* known as *Arte de trovar,* the poems are divided into three types, according to the poetic subject; this categorization is still used today. In the *cantigas de amigo* a woman usually addresses either her mother or another female friend and speaks of her lover, or *amigo;* the *cantigas de amor,* the type with the clearest affinity to troubadour poetry, are often concerned with the casuistry of love or praise of the woman, and in them the poet-lover speaks to or of his *senhor;* in the third type, the *cantigas de escarnho e de maldizer,* poets give free reign to their satiric or parodic impulses, some reaching seldom paralleled heights of cheerful obscenity. Unmentioned in the fragmentary *Arte de trovar* and infrequently

found in the Portuguese *cancioneiros,* religious poetry is nevertheless represented by a large corpus, over 420 extant *cantigas de Santa María,* dedicated to the Virgin; these were cultivated and extensively compiled by Alfonso X the Learned (1252–1284) of Castile, in whose court *Cancioneiro* A may have been originally compiled.

A *cantiga* consists of a variable number of stanzas (*coblas* or *cobras*), enhanced by numerous devices: enjambment *(ateúdas),* a refrain or final abbreviated comment *(finda),* internal repetitions (*dobre* or *mordobre*), different rhyme schemes, and so forth. There are two aspects, known as *paralelismo* and *leixa-prem,* that specifically affect *cantigas de amigo,* making them vibrate with uncommon lyricism and emotional power. Parallelism designates the repetition of syntactic-semantic structures for rhythmic effect or to accentuate meaning. In this case a verse can be reproduced in its entirety (*paralelismo literal),* in consecutive stanzas, slight variations being introduced either through synonyms or chiasms. *Leixa-prem* designates the integral repetition of a verse, where the second verse of a *cobla* is the first verse of the third, and so on until the end of the *cantiga.*

Portuguese lyric waned in the second half of the fourteenth century, as other genres were privileged by the court and feudal nobility; the genre also became increasingly dependent on Castilian models. The sole *cancioneiro* reflecting poetic production in Portugal in the second half of the fifteenth century, the *Cancioneiro geral* (General songbook) of Garcia de Resende, was compiled much later (1516). It gathered together texts in Castilian and Portuguese and was directly inspired by Hernando del Castillo's *Cancionero general* (1511). From the early fourteenth century on, Galician-Portuguese, or Portuguese, became increasingly flexible as a vehicle of scientific, technical, and historiographical thinking, as well as an increasingly vigorous narrative tool. In this process, Denis again played a pivotal role, along with Pedro, count of Barcelos, his son and spiritual heir. Both promoted translations and in some instances are responsible for the composition of essential original texts.

PROSE

Epic and the matière de Bretagne. Interest in Arthurian legends was already evident in the five translated *lais* that open *Cancioneiro B,* which were probably drawn from the *jogral* repertoire. These five *lais* are thought to be from the time of Pedro of Barcelos, but there is earlier evidence of knowledge of the *ciclo bretão* (Breton cycle) or Arthurian legend in the Galician-Portuguese *cantigas* and the *cantigas de Santa María.* Of the three identifiable cycles known to have been at least partially translated into peninsular languages (the Vulgate or Pseudo-Map cycle, the Tristan cycle, and the Post-Vulgate or Pseudo-Boron cycle), two Portuguese texts, *Demanda do Santo Graal* and *José de Arimateia* (Joseph of Arimathea, internally dated 1314), are important elements for the study of the Post-Vulgate cycle, and at the same time they attest to the increasing narrative suppleness of the language. Recently two other fragments have come to light—a Galician-Portuguese Merlin fragment of the second branch of the Post-Vulgate cycle, as well as a noteworthy Tristan fragment. An unresolved bone of contention between some Portuguese and Spanish critics is the origin of the primitive *Amadís de Gaula* (Amadis of Gaul)—the first peninsular hero in the Arthurian mold and a contemporary of the early *cantigas*—recast in Castilian by Garci Rodríguez de Montalvo in the late fifteenth century.

From this period also date renderings into prose of Portuguese or Castilian oral epics, often in connection with historiography. It is likely that there was an epic cycle of narratives about the origins of the nation that has not survived, unlike that of Castile; we can gather this from the legendary material incorporated into the *Crónica geral de Espanha de 1344* (General chronicle of Spain of 1344) concerning Afonso Henriques (1139–1185), the first Portuguese king, and his entourage. This material—organized around six episodes of the king's life, from the death of his father until his defeat by Ferdinand of Castile and León—is endowed with tragic unity, and the young king himself appears as the homologue of the impetuous Cid of the Spanish ballad tradition.

Historiography. A common thread in the Latin annals (twelfth century) is the encomiastic narrative of the deeds of the founding king, Afonso Henriques, and of the local nobility. Noticeable is an often decidedly crusading spirit, invoked to legitimize Portuguese independence vis-à-vis Asturian claims. The earliest genealogies also date from this period, with both traditions converging into the first genealogy composed in the vernacular, the *Livro Velho de Linhagens* (*ca.* 1270), a text that reflects the tensions between the nobility and the centralizing ambitions of the monarchy. Prior to 1315 the *Crónica do Mouro Rasis* (by the tenth-century Cordobese historian Ahmed Arrazi) was translated and then, in parallel development to Alfonso X's practice of fusing Latin and Arabic sources, incorporated into the great chronicles of the fourteenth century, both in Castile and in Portugal. Chief among such works is Pedro of Barcelos's four-part *Livro de Linhagens,* which integrates genealogical history and chronicle, while expanding on the Latin tradition in

its overarching preoccupation with the logic of the totality of historical events. From Adam through Troy, Rome, and Britain, all threads were seen as leading to the genealogies of the various peninsular kingdoms, with the so-called *crónica universal* superseding the earlier *crónica régia* and *crónica particular.* Also unprecedented is the inclusion into these chronicles of contemporary events, like the battle of Río Salado (1340), which put a decisive end to Islamic ambitions of peninsular reconquest. Pedro's prologue is also notable for the enunciation of the author's concept of historiography and its sociopolitical role. Moreover, the *Livro* includes a number of literary narratives, some native, some translated: the Troy legend and Arthurian material appear side by side with Iberian legends and folklore. Pedro of Barcelos's legacy also includes the *Crónica geral de Espanha de 1344* (General chronicle of Spain of 1344), which recasts and amplifies the *Primera crónica general* (First general chronicle) begun by Alfonso X of Castile.

Portuguese historiography reached new heights in the fifteenth century under the Aviz dynasty. Duarte, son of the first Aviz king, John I, in 1418 appointed Fernão Lopes the *guarda-mor* (chief officer) of the *Torre do Tombo,* the national archives. Making full use of the archives, Fernão Lopes composed a series of superb chronicles covering the period from the middle of the fourteenth century to his own lifetime: *Crónica de Portugal de 1419, Crónica de D. Pedro I, Crónica de D. Fernando, Crónica de D. João I,* and *Crónica de D. Duarte.* His chronicles reveal a constant—and modern—preoccupation with historical accuracy and truth, while casting a critical eye toward the historiographical tradition. A man who benefited from the political upheavals of the last decades of the fourteenth century, Lopes, unlike his predecessors had a good understanding of social mobility and the forces at work in his sociopolitical environment. Favoring the insurgency of John against the claims of the Castilian crown to the Portuguese throne, he skillfully laid the arguments for legitimation of the new dynasty of Aviz and ardently supported the *arraia miuda,* the common folk—identified as the "true" Portuguese—who brought John I to power, in opposition to the nobility (whom Lopes castigates elsewhere). Lopes thus recast the event as a class conflict. Balancing sharp character portraits of individuals with accounts of the behavior of masses, he was a master of description, with a gift for organizing convergent threads to create a sweeping social and political panorama.

If not always endowed with the epic flair of their predecessor, but no less dexterous at their craft as historians and rhetoricians, the historians of the next generation were also the first chroniclers of Portugal's initial contact with other nations and peoples, first in North and then in West Africa, in the early stages of the formation of an overseas empire. Outstanding among these chroniclers are Rui de Pina (*Crónica de D. João II,* among others) and Gomes Eanes de Zurara, Fernão Lopes's successor, who presided over the restructuring of the archives. Best known for his *Crónica da Guiné* (Chronicle of Guinea) and aware of the pitfalls of writing contemporary history, Zurara was rigorous to the point of traveling to Morocco to see the region for himself and to gather information for the last of his three chronicles on the Portuguese presence there *(Crónica da Tomada de Ceuta* [Chronicle of the capture of Ceuta], *Crónica de D. Pedro,* and *Crónica do Conde D. Duarte de Meneses).*

The epic or chivalric spirit was also enlisted in the service of competing feudal interests, as in the *Crónica do condestabre* (mid-1430s), which updates the *crónica particular.* John I's constable, Nuno Álvares Pereira, is portrayed in light of chivalric codes as filtered through clerical ideology. Warrior-like and saint-like and, like the Cid, presented as father to future kings, the youthful Nuno Álvares is seen in this chronicle reading Arthurian romances, where he finds his model for lifelong imitation: Galahad.

Doctrinal, apologetic, and mystic prose; hagiography. Among the surviving doctrinal texts, *Orto do Esposo* (late fourteenth or early fifteenth century) stands out. An anonymous and seemingly original work, it is a finely structured compilation that draws on folk tales, biblical or patristic sources, moral *exempla,* miracles, and hagiography, with a strong allegorical intent. The third part, dedicated to human vanity, is by far the longest and also best reflects the verve of the popular turn of phrase, with its broad satire, social criticism, and sly barbs against useless scholasticism. Also unique among doctrinal prose, not least for the manner in which it assimilates Petrarch's prose and presence in the peninsula, is *Bosco deleitoso* (late fourteenth or early fifteenth century). Taking *De vita solitaria* as its primary, though not exclusive, point of departure, *Bosco deleitoso* is virtually a new text, seamlessly abbreviating or adding new sections and recasting the very nature of the Petrarchan source as it recounts the Soul's search for its Bridegroom, in which it leaves behind the *vida do segre* to attain the necessary solitude conducive to contemplation and spiritual plenitude.

Among the mystical texts, the Portuguese version of *Visão de Túndalo* displays a firm command of narrative technique as well as great visionary imagination, as does the beautiful tale of *Barlaão e Josafate,* a Christianized version of the life of Buddha. No less interesting in the

genre is the Portuguese *Navegação de São Brandão.* In the apologetic vein the most significant text is *Corte Imperial* (late fourteenth or early fifteenth century), an apology for the Christian religion and a diatribe against Muslims and Jews, whose communities and religious practices were tolerated in the peninsula until the late Middle Ages. The work also attacks pagans, Eastern Christians, and even atheists.

Vernacular hagiography also developed relatively early, but the first compilations, *Flos sanctorum em linguagê portugues*—to which are appended the lives of a number of Portuguese saints—and the *Livro e legenda dos santos martires* (both 1513), appear rather late. However, there are also hagiographic texts in Portuguese dispersed among several Alcobaça codices, some datable as early as the thirteenth century. Two legends in particular are interesting; "Conto de Amaro" and "Lenda de Santa Iria," known through texts dating from the fifteenth and early sixteenth century, respectively, both contain strong hagiographic elements.

As in other genres, the role and interests of the ruling dynasty are sometimes evident in hagiography. Worth mentioning in this regard are the *Vida e milagres de Dona Isabel, Rainha de Portugal* (Life and miracles of Dona Isabel, fourteenth century), a life of King Denis's wife, and *Vida do Infante D. Fernando* (Life of the Infante Dom Fernando, *ca.* 1460). Part historiography and part hagiography, the latter relates the story of Fernando, the hapless son of John I, who languished for years as a hostage and died in Morocco; the work obscures a less exemplary history of political interests. Like that of Queen Isabel's life, this *crónica* also has the particularity of having been written by the prince's confessor, João Alvares, who brings into it the "veracity" of the eyewitness account, a sense of proximity to the events that other examples of the genre inevitably lack.

Didactic prose and "mirror of princes" literature. Finally, to a technical tradition that already included, among others, the *Livro de Alveitaria* (from Denis's reign) and Pero Menino's *Livro de Falcoaria* (from Fernando's reign), the Aviz dynasty added four major works, one by John I (*Livro de Montaria* [Book of hunting]), two by his son, Duarte (*Livro da Ensinança de Bem Cavalgar Toda a Sela* and *Leal Conselheiro* [Loyal counselor]), and another by the Infante Pedro (*Livro da Virtuosa Bemfeitoria*). If John I's work is a paean to the charms of hunting and the outdoors, the two works by Duarte broaden the scope of the genre, *Ensinança* with its concern for moral discipline and *Leal Conselheiro* with its concern for domestic rectitude. The latter is in essence a spiritual and practical guide for marriage and family life, an unusual contribution to the so-called mirror of princes literature that astonishes not only for its inherent literary merits but also for its psychological depth. *Benfeitoria* takes the education of the prince into the sociopolitical sphere, in essence defining a social model in terms of a chain of mutual obligations binding the nobility and its subjects. Taken as a whole, while bearing in mind what was said above about historiography, these texts appear as the culmination of a new literary practice whose groundwork was laid in the fourteenth century, with lay people writing in the vernacular about politics, ethics, and the art of government—a shift signaling the emergence of Renaissance practices and mentality.

BIBLIOGRAPHY

EDITIONS AND ANTHOLOGIES

Cancioneiro Geral de Garcia de Resende. Edited by A. da Costa Pimpão and Aida Fernanda Dias. 2 vols. Coimbra: Centro de Estudos Românicos, 1973–1974.

Cancioneiro Geral de Garcia de Resende. 5 vols. Edited by Aida Fernanda Dias. Lisboa: Imprensa Nacional-Casa da Moeda, 1990–98. Final vol., vol. 6, in press.

Diogo, Américo A. Lindeza, ed. *Lírica Galego-Portuguesa. Antologia.* Braga: Angelus Novus, 1998.

Gonçalves, Elsa, and Ana Maria Ramos, eds. *A Lírica Galego-Portuguesa (Textos escolhidos).* Apres. crítica, sel., notas e sugestões para análise literária de E. Gonçalves. Transcrição, notas linguísticas e glossário de A. M. Ramos. Lisboa: Editorial Comunicação, 1985.

Lanciani, Giulia, and Giuseppe Tavani. *As Cantigas de Escarnio.* Vigo: Edicións Xerais, 1995.

Lapa, Manuel Rodrigues. *Cantigas d'Escarnho e de Mal Dizer dos cancioneiros medievais galego-portugueses.* Vigo: Galaxia, 1970.

Lírica Profana Galego-Portuguesa. Corpus Completo das cantigas medievais, com estudio bibliográfico, análise retórica e bibliografia específica. Edited by Mercedes Brea. 2 vols. Santiago de Compostela: Centro de Investigacións Lingüísticas e Literárias Ramón Piñeiro, 1996.

Nunes, José J. *Crestomatia arcaica. Excertos da Literatura Portuguesa desde o que mais antigo se conhece até ao século XVI.* Lisboa: Livraria Clássica Editora, 1981.

Simões, Manuel. *Il Canzoniere di D. Pedro, conte di Barcelos.* L'Aquila: Japadre, 1991.

STUDIES

Beltran, Vicenç. *Canción de mujer, cantiga de amigo.* Barcelona: PPU, 1987.

———. *A cantiga de amor.* Trad. Xela Arias. Vigo: Edicións Xerais de Galicia, 1995.

D'Heur, Jean-Maire. "L'art de Trouver du chansonnier Colocci-Brancutti." *Arquivos do Centro Cultural Português* 9 (1975): 321–398.

Dias, Aida Fernanda. *O Cancioneiro Geral e a poesia peninsular de quatrocentos—contactos e sobrevivências.* Coimbra: Almedina, 1978.

Dronke, Peter. *Latin and Vernacular Poets.* Variorum, 1991.

Ferrari, Anna. "Linguaggi lirici in contatto: Trobadors e trobadores." *Boletim de Filologia* 29 (1984). *Homenagem a Manuel Rodrigues Lapa.* II: 35–58.

Ferreira, Manuel Pedro. *O Som de Martim Codax: Sobre a dimensão musical da lírica Galego-Portuguesa.* Lisboa: Imprensa Nacional-Casa da Moeda; UNISYS, 1986.

Lorenzo Gradín, Pilar. *La canción de mujer en la lírica medieval.* Santiago de Compostela: Universidad de Santiago de Compostela, 1990.

Oliveira, António Resende de. *Depois do espetáculo trovadoresco. A estructura dos cancioneiros peninsulares dos sécs. XIII e XIV.* Lisboa: Colibri, 1994.

Rocha, Andrée Crabbé. *Garcia de Resende e o Cancioneiro Geral.* Lisboa: ICALP, 1987.

Sharrer, Harvey L. "Fragmentos de sete *Cantigas d'Amor* de D. Dinis, musicadas—uma descoberta". *Actas do IV Congresso da Associação Hispânica de Literatura Medieval.* Org Aires Augusto Nascimento. Lisboa: Edições Cosmos, 1991. Vol. 1: 13–29.

Stegagno Picchio, Luciana. *A lição do texto. Filologia e literatura. I. A idade média.* Lisboa: Edições 70, 1979.

———. *La méthode philologique. Écrits sur la littérature portugaise. I. La poésie.* Pref. Roman Jakobson. Paris: Fundação Calouste Gulbenkian-Centro Cultural Português, 1982.

Tavani, Giuseppe. *Repertorio metrico della lirica galego-portoghese.* Rome: Edizioni dell'Ateneo, 1967.

———. *Poesia del Ducento nella Penisola Iberica Problemi della lirica galego-portoghese.* Rome: Edizioni dell'Ateneo, 1969.

———. *Ensaios Portugueses. Filologia e Linguística.* Lisboa: Imprensa Nacional-Casa da Moeda, 1988.

———. "Il camino de Santiago nella genesi della poesia medievale galega." *Studi di iberistica in memoria di Alberto Boscolo.* Ed. Giuseppe Bellini. Roma: Bulzoni Editore, 1989. 233–239.

———. *A Poesia Lírica Galego-Portuguesa.* Lisboa: Editorial Comunicação, 1990.

ISABEL DE SENA

[See also **DMA:** Alfonso X (the Learned); *Amadís de Gaula;* Arthurian Literature, Spanish and Portuguese; Cancionero General; Cantiga; Dinis; Hagiography, Western European; Historiography, Western European; Lai; Lopes, Fenão; Portugal; Portuguese Language; Spanish Literature; **Supp:** Zurara, Gomes Eanes de.]

POVERTY. Christians throughout the Middle Ages found a divine source for the glorification of poverty and of the poor in the New Testament—above all, in the Gospels. Poverty, which the classical world understood as we do today—as a rank within a social and economic hierarchy—became deeply enmeshed in notions of sanctity, the imitation of Christ, and rewards in a life to come. Poverty and its attendant activity, charity (Christian charity), were deeply intertwined in the medieval imagination and in the normative texts of Christian civilization. In the Gospel according to John (12:7–8),

Jesus, responding to Judas Iscariot's demand that Mary of Bethany's costly perfumed oil (used to anoint Jesus's feet) be sold and its proceeds used to help the poor, answered: "Let her keep it till the day when she prepares for my burial; for you have the poor among you always, but you will not always have me." Thus, by setting up an equivalence between himself and the poor, Jesus transformed the poor from a despised social category to an eternal and immutable part of Christian society.

The link between Christianity and poverty reverberated over the long history of the Middle Ages and far beyond, into modernity. The apostolic privileging of poverty and the poor, reiterated in numerous canonical texts, sermons, and hagiographical examples, complicated the social and economic position of the poor within Christianity. Within the Christian framework of salvation, poverty could never be defined on purely economic grounds; and voluntary or otherwise, it acquired a meaning that transcended the parameters of the well-defined orders of medieval society.

Poverty, of course, is not immutable, and many would argue that it was not meant to be eternal. We do not need to have the poor "always with us." Nor do we need to see poverty as a concomitant to salvation. So what did Jesus mean by "the poor"? Did he mean the poor in spirit, as understood from the benediction: "Blessed are the poor in spirit, for theirs is the kingdom of heaven" (Matthew 5:3)? Will the humble, then, reap eternal rewards? Or did he mean the downtrodden, those at the bottom of society, as suggested in his statement "you have the poor among you always"? Or was he encompassing both definitions of poverty and the poor? In many respects, the history of poverty and the poor in the Middle Ages hinges on the uneasy relationship between the evangelical representation of the poor and the apostolic command to help them, on the one hand—think of Paul's injunctions in 1 Corinthians that Christians should love and help the poor—and the cold realities of everyday life, whereby the poor were harshly treated, often segregated from the rest of society, and, in a later age, confined to poorhouses or prisons. The idealized treatment of the poor was essentially that, an ideal, but even into the late Middle Ages, it could still cast a powerful spell on receptive ears. Think of Peter Waldes, Francis of Assisi, or the countless men and women who embraced a life of poverty for the love of Christ and the salvation of their souls. In truth, the church in its first two centuries defined itself by an aggressive embrace of the poor and the enslaved and by a tireless commitment to those in spiritual and material need. Its early successes in the ancient world can in fact be ascribed to the church's vigorous advocacy of the oppressed and the promise of their redemption.

THE CHRONOLOGY AND TOPOGRAPHY OF POVERTY

In discussing medieval poverty, chronology and topography must be carefully considered. The travails of the poor in the early Middle Ages differed sharply from those of the poor on the eve of the early modern period. Changes in social, economic, and political contexts and in mental outlook dramatically affected the representation of poverty as well as the actual status of the poor. Place also mattered a lot. Rural poverty had a very different feel from urban poverty. "National" or regional attitudes toward the poor also varied significantly. The way in which poor men and women endured their lot in fourteenth-century England, to give just one example, diverged sharply from the way they endured it in Iberia, Italy, or Poland during the same period. We are faced, therefore, with myriad, complex histories of poverty, and to reduce them to a single, lineal narrative may be to ignore the numerous perspectives from which this social, and often religious, phenomenon can be observed.

THE HISTORIOGRAPHY OF POVERTY

The growing historiography of poverty is already quite extensive. Michel Mollat's *The Poor in the Middle Ages: An Essay in Social History* has long been the standard treatment, though Mollat's work concerns the poor's resistance to their condition as well as poverty itself. Monographs and scholarly articles by Lester Little, Georges Duby, Sharon Farmer, Mollat himself, and many others have greatly expanded our understanding of poverty, shedding light on the place of the poor in Christian society and on changing social attitudes toward the poor. To summarize this vast literature here would be to trivialize this significant topic and slight its centrality in the overall development of medieval society and culture. Thus, rather than present a chronological narrative, this article focuses on specific themes, examining them over the thousand-year interval (but with emphasis on the later period) between the collapse of the ancient world and the onset of modernity. These topics are (1) taxonomies of the poor, or types of poverty as social and economic categories; (2) rural and urban poverty; (3) beggars and charity; (4) voluntary and involuntary poverty; (5) poverty and Christianity; and (6) the transition from the late Middle Ages to the early modern period in the treatment of the poor. Each of these themes deserves a separate study, and none of them exhausts the ways in which we may study the history of the poor in the Middle Ages. They are grouped here to provide us with diverse perspectives on the complex and troubling question of poverty.

POVERTY AS A SOCIAL AND ECONOMIC CATEGORY

Who the poor were and what poverty meant changed dramatically over time. As Mollat has shown, poverty is always relative and continually redefined by income level and geography. Its definition essentially depends on how much one has—or lacks—in relation to others. Medieval sources used the term *pauper,* or its vernacular equivalent, "poor," to describe individuals who, in reality, stood on a social and economic plane far above the real poor. In late medieval and early modern England, France, Italy, Germany, Spain, and elsewhere, literary and legal accounts made numerous references to poor nobles; similar reports can be found in other western European literary sources about poor clerics and the like. But these instances, of course, rarely reflected the unmitigated, harsh realities of poverty in that period. Poor noblemen, clerics, even scholars were not poor in the same way that those at the very bottom of society were poor. To pursue the myriad social, moral, and health-related meanings of the word "poor" would lead us into a fruitless linguistic quest. The focus here is not on the shifting semantic meanings of poverty (except for the idealized Christian concept of voluntary poverty), nor on those who may have been less well-off than others in their own social order, but on the plight of those who were truly at the bottom of society.

In the classical world, poverty as a social, economic, and, above all, political category was well understood and admitted no ambivalence. In the Roman Empire, especially in the cities throughout the empire, elaborate systems of assistance to the needy sought to keep social peace and secure political support for the ruling elites. Bound within complex networks of patronage, the Romans understood poverty and the poor in exacting income- and property-governed categories that were intimately linked to the maintenance of political control and social order. Christianity radically altered this relationship. Its initial message and preaching targeted the downtrodden, the enslaved, the infirm, and other marginal people, bringing the hope of eternal redemption to those who had lost any expectation of a better life. If every poor man or woman who came begging at the doorstep was, as the Gospels affirmed, Christ, then the relationship of every Christian to the dispossessed became a potential instrument of salvation and charity, enacting the believer's love of Christ. But these new, highly charged, and seldom fulfilled notions of charity and love for others did not succeed in eradicating the seldom contested social and economic differences between those who had and those who had not.

Throughout the Middle Ages, famine, plague, and warfare played a crucial role in swelling the ranks of the poor, as did ill health, gender, and old age. Food distribution, a Christian charitable practice meant to replace Roman philanthropy and patronage, could barely meet the real needs of the poor. The writings of Gregory the Great, Bede, and Gregory of Tours, as well as the extensive hagiographical literature of the early Middle Ages, addressed the issue of poverty in the period and illustrate the growing tide of poverty plaguing medieval society, the poor's disposition to violence in the face of want, and, most significant, the new taxonomies by which the poor were classified. Closely linked to the dramatic social and economic changes taking place over the long span of the Middle Ages, the stratification of the poor manifested itself in two ways: in a sharply defined hierarchy of poverty and in a clear distinction between rural and urban poverty.

Categories of poverty. Essentially, the poor became part of an elaborate classificatory scheme. This development had its origins in the early Middle Ages but acquired a new immediacy as the number of the poor grew apace in response to social and economic changes. By the later Middle Ages, the attempts to construct different types of poor men and women became enshrined in legal codes and in the new mental categories emerging in the West from the twelfth century onward. Rather than addressing poverty or the poor, the codes legitimizing the classification of the poor were mainly concerned with the question of who deserved charity or welfare support and how to rank the poor—that is, with determining who was truly needy, who was shirking, and who truly could not work.

Regardless of the legislative intent, legal codes provided a clearly spelled-out guide that identified the poor and who among them should be helped first. By the fourteenth century, English beggars needed permits to travel from one locality to another within the realm, and by 1350 those under sixty years of age or capable of working were forbidden to beg. Similar legislation could be found in France in the fourteenth and fifteenth centuries, but even earlier, in the thirteenth century, Louis IX, a king well known for his heroic efforts on behalf of the poor, commissioned a far-ranging investigation of the social and moral conditions of France. The *enquêteurs* conducting this task drew up a taxonomy of different types of poverty and of the gross abuses suffered by the poor. In Castile, the *Siete partidas,* a comprehensive Roman-based code of law written under the sponsorship

The Beggars. *Oil on canvas by Pieter Bruegel the Elder, 1568.* THE ART ARCHIVE. REPRODUCED BY PERMISSION.

of Alfonso X, reflected the new attitudes toward the poor in the medieval West, and in Castile in particular, in the late thirteenth century. The *Siete partidas* recommended guidelines for those unable to give to all of the needy: (1) help Christians before non-Christians; (2) help poor men held captive in Moorish lands next; (3) help those imprisoned because of debt next; (4) choose the appropriate time to give alms; (5) divide your alms among many—do not give excessively or to just one person; (6) be charitable to poor relatives before helping strangers; (7) give to the aged before the young; (8) help the sick or handicapped before the healthy; (9) give to noblemen or to those who were rich and had fallen on hard times before giving to those who had always been poor. Some of these recommendations sought a more rational distribution of almsgiving, but others reflected the martial and aristocratic character of Castilian society (save the captives), as well as its hierarchical distinctions (relieve the hardship of noblemen). While emphasizing the spiritual nature of charity—that is, that alms without love would not lead to salvation—the *Siete partidas* also commanded "that alms should not be given to those who were healthy and refused to work the land."

As coercive measures were being introduced in the medieval West to force the indigent to work and the definition of "deserving poor" was being restricted to the aged, the sick, the very young, and widows, begging itself came under attack. Beggars' movements and their soliciting of alms became restricted in England, France, Italy, and other parts of the West by the fourteenth century. In some cases, even religious orders had to obtain royal licenses to beg, and in 1338, when Alfonso XI of Castile granted such a permit to the monks of Silos, he did so because "many men go around the land [begging] with lies and tricks, and the simple men of the land receive much harm." In late-fifteenth-century France, royal legislation forced able-bodied beggars to work.

This social reshuffling of the poor replicated earlier distinctions based on age, health, and gender, but the wills, legal codes, and charitable donations of the late Middle Ages emphasized a new type of poverty that came to play an important role in transforming the social negotiations of charity and in positioning the poor within a well-defined hierarchy of need. Medieval sources drew sharp distinctions between the once wealthy or well-off and those who had always been poor. The former, the "ashamed poor," were often depicted as more deserving of charity and moral support in the pious donations and legislative edicts of the period. Too ashamed to beg after falling from a privileged station, they were ranked first among those meriting assistance. Those who had known poverty all their lives were relegated to a secondary and not too wholesome position.

Although such distinctions were not entirely new, the link between former wealth and entitlement to charity (and thus in helping restore the social standing of the newly impoverished) had dark implications indeed. The rejection or diminished expectations of those who had always been poor marked a hardening of the social and economic boundaries among Christians, boundaries that were now drawn in terms of wealth. Those who had wealth and lost it were to be pitied and helped. Those who had always been poor were to garner little or no compassion, if they were fit to work.

In tandem with these developments, the late Middle Ages witnessed a growing divide between the poor who were viewed as deserving and those were deemed undeserving. The idea that the poor collectively represented Christ is most vividly represented in an anecdote about John Chrysostom. In the story, a sly poor man kept joining the line of beggars, again and again, to collect far more alms than he needed or deserved. Alerted to what was taking place, Chrysostom's response was that he knew what was going on but it did not matter, because Christ could appear at the door begging for charity under many guises. By the thirteenth and fourteenth centuries, such scams received little sympathy. Clear distinctions were drawn between those who, because of age or illness, could not work and were thus deserving of charity, and those who were able-bodied and did not wish to or could not find work. The distinction between the deserving and the undeserving created a cleavage within the somewhat homogeneous category of the poor. Those who were deserving could hope to receive charity—a charity that, as shall be seen below, had become highly ritualized by the late Middle Ages—while the undeserving poor were to be highly monitored and often physically confined or punished.

RURAL AND URBAN POVERTY

Following the demise of the Roman Empire in the West, the main source of labor shifted from slaves to a vast servile and semi-servile peasant population. Although peasant life was for the most part synonymous with a life of poverty, the reality may have varied somewhat. The conditions of rural and urban poverty provide a useful lens for an inquiry into the complex nature of this topic in the late Middle Ages.

Rural poverty. The agricultural revolution of the central Middle Ages (from the ninth to the twelfth century) brought about an expansion of arable land, increased food production, and a marked improvement in the lives and diets of peasants. These developments, along with the rise of towns and the expansion of a money economy, also had a negative impact on peasant culture. In villages throughout the West, a widening social gap between rich peasants and bourgeois investors and those at the bottom began to disturb the precarious balance of village communal life. In the twelfth and thirteenth centuries, when conditions were still relatively good, life must have been bearable for most peasants in the core areas of medieval society. This is not to say that periods of dearth did not affect specific areas from time to time. Even in the more prosperous regions of medieval Europe, bad weather, plagues, and civil conflict produced dramatic spikes in the number of the poor. In 1095, harvests failed throughout most of western Europe, and chronicles report that ecclesiastical establishments in France, England, and elsewhere had no grain to help the plight of hungry peasants. Nonetheless, in spite of this and other reports (famines in the 1140s and in the late twelfth century), it may be assumed that there was less real poverty in the countryside than in urban centers. In the first place, the village was a traditional setting in which long-held communal ties fostered forms of aid and support that did not exist in urban environments. People who, from time immemorial, were used to either working together or perishing alone may have been well disposed toward contributing to networks of support for the needy in their midst. Moreover, in most villages in the twelfth and thirteenth centuries, almost all of the peasants had a stake in the rural economy, in the form of rights to the commons or some holdings, however minuscule. Those who had little land, few skills, or too many children or who were weakened by ailments may have had a hard time, but the village economy, which allowed for the gleaning of fields after the harvest and encompassed the resources of nearby woods and waste, offered more flexibility for escaping crushing poverty except in times of famine.

The custom of equating peasants with poverty notwithstanding, only some types of peasants in specific times and places conformed to the habitual image. There is no evidence of widespread poverty before 1300 in the European countryside, though there is evidence of dearth and famine during specific periods. With the noted exception of times of crisis, the social and economic manifestations of rural poverty contrasted sharply with the grim conditions the urban poor faced at the end of the Middle Ages.

That said, the crises in late medieval society (in the fourteenth and fifteenth centuries) threw a great deal of the rural world into despair. The widespread famines of the period 1315–1321, the recurring plagues, the devastation of the Hundred Years War, and successive peasant uprisings created distressful conditions. In addition to these catastrophes, the intrusion of urban capital into the countryside—due to the purchase of village lands by the bourgeois, who sometimes privatized parts of the commons—and the emergence of social differences within village society itself turned many peasants into landless journeymen. These changes set peasants wandering about the countryside in search of seasonal work or found them migrating to urban centers in the hope of securing employment in manufacturing or obtaining relief from charitable institutions.

Thomas More's *Utopia* (1516) describes in moving terms the plight of peasants thrown off their lands by enclosures. Joining huge armies of itinerant beggars, they traveled from town to town seeking work or assistance. Their treatment—the lash, imprisonment, denial of entry to towns and villages—bespeaks a dramatic rise in rural poverty and the breakdown of local systems of support. What took place in England at the end of the fifteenth century was replicated in other parts of the medieval West. Rural poverty became vividly evident during the successive crises of the fourteenth and fifteenth centuries. In the region of Frías in northern Castile, the town scribe Ferrán Pérez (who was probably a moneylender), included legacies in his will (1344) to feed and clothe three hundred poor men and women, just before the onslaught of the Black Death. What is remarkable about this will is the number of poor people supposedly in need of charitable support in a small town and surrounding villages lacking a sizable population. It is futile to attempt to calculate the actual percentage of poor people in any given locality, because the poor paid no taxes and their names and lives seldom made it to the written records, unless they committed a crime. The mention of such a large number of poor men and women in Frías and in similar rural locations throughout late medieval western Europe alerts us to the increased harshness of their lives. That they were often described as "hungry" or "lean" in the wills that established legacies for feeding the poor and in chronicles that report their violent resistance to the existing conditions illustrates how the very look of the poor (not to mention their sack or burlap vestments) differed from that of the well-to-do. Together with the growing rise in rural poverty, representations of the poor, both rural and urban, acquired a nasty turn. Peasants had long been the target of vitriolic depictions that often described them as animals or worse. Poor men and women from other walks of life shared in these pejorative representations. Poverty was seen as evil in the *Roman de la Rose* and in the works of Christine de Pizan.

Mollat quotes Agrippa d'Aubigné to the effect that poverty "makes men ridiculous."

Historians have also noted the expansion of charitable endeavors aimed at helping the poor in the countryside after 1300. Small village hospitals, housing usually fewer than ten poor or disabled men and women, began to sprout throughout most of the West as a clear sign of the rise in the number of the rural poor, following the social and economic dislocations of the late Middle Ages. In England, however, hospitals did not develop at such a fast pace as on the continent, and in Poland, Hungary, and other regions of eastern Europe, the establishment of hospitals for the poor lagged behind that of other areas in the West.

Villagers sought to combat the rising tide of the destitute. In some locations, those with no connections to the village were not welcome and were often driven away by threat or force. In others, special arrangements were made to rotate the burden of charity among all villagers. At the turn of the twentieth century, Ruth Behar described the survival of such distinctly medieval practices in a Leonese village. In Santa María del Monte, Behar noted that a staff was rotated among the village households to indicate where charity would be dispensed on given days. Beggars coming into the village were not to ask for food or alms from any household except the one where the staff had been placed. The communal safety net imbedded in custom and kinship, which had prevented the most abysmal kind of poverty in the countryside, was thus replaced by a "rational" way of organizing the giving of alms. This new method allowed villagers to claim the right of refusing to give charity without incurring guilt.

Urban poverty. The economic changes of the eleventh and twelfth centuries—the expansion of arable land, the increase in food production, demographic growth, the expansion of trade and of the monetary economy—led to the rise of towns throughout the medieval West. Although life in towns and cities (two distinct categories of urban settings) had nothing in common with life in the countryside, many towns were symbiotically linked to their hinterlands. In terms of jurisdiction, social fabric, and economic structure, towns were indeed different; after all, towns stood somewhat outside the feudal social order. Urban centers also served as a site for the emergence of a new system of values and of new mental outlooks that radically affected the definition of poverty and, with it, the treatment of the poor. Jacques Le Goff, in his deservedly famous article "Church's Time and Merchant's Time," draws attention to such changes in attitudes occurring in urban areas, focusing on how tradesmen in the cities stopped looking at time as something that belonged to God and began looking at it as a commodity. This desacralization of time is reflective of sharp contrasts between town and country in myriad ways and sheds light on the way in which attitudes about the poor were shifting in the cities.

Not all towns were commercial centers in the Middle Ages. Many were little more than overgrown villages, essentially agro-towns in which the boundary between the rural and the urban was vague. But in the paradigmatic towns, where trade and manufacturing became the sinews of economic life (as in the Flemish and northern French towns of Ghent, Bruges, Lille, and Arras and the Italian cities of Florence, Genoa, and Venice), two new social types emerged as an integral part of the new urban order: the low-paid workers who were often hired by the textile industry and the urban destitute or beggars. The first category, consisting of workers whose salaries were not high enough to support them, forcing them to seek charity to survive, could be found in such different towns as Marseilles, Bordeaux, Nantes, London, Bruges, and Lübeck. Towns became magnets, attracting a rural population to new employment opportunities and giving rise to a plethora of charitable and philanthropic institutions (most of them paid for or subsidized by municipal governments). The experience of the rural poor crammed within the narrow confines of the city walls must have been painfully different from what they were accustomed to. There were no easily accessible fields nearby to glean; there were no woods in which to keep a few pigs, gather some nuts, trap small animals, and collect brush for the hearth. There was no communal safety net to provide any bit of comfort from hunger, inclement weather, or inadequate shelter. Moreover, the poor were often segregated from the rest of the population by neighborhoods, as was the case in Antwerp, Lübeck, Nantes, and other places.

The poor and the sick—growing at an alarming rate in the late Middle Ages—came in two distinct and sometimes overlapping categories. The lowliest of the urban working class comprised those without permanent employment or with jobs so ill paid and wearying as to place them inescapably in the category of the poor. Owning no property, they were at the mercy of economic dislocation and downturns in business. They were the first victims of the plague and died in proportionally greater numbers than any other group in society. They suffered most from the disruptions caused by endemic warfare in the fourteenth and fifteenth centuries. We meet them as the *ongles bleu* (those whose nails had turned blue from working with dyes) in Michel Mollat and Philippe

Wolf's vivid account of urban (and rural) uprisings in the fourteenth century. In Flanders in the 1320s and in Florence in 1378, to give just two examples, the "blue nails" provided the core of the rebellions against urban oligarchs that occurred throughout the medieval West. In Florence, the Ciompi rose up in arms, demanding enfranchisement and a share in the city's governance. That they were crushed and their demands brushed aside was part of a pattern of resistance and swift repression that was common in the late Middle Ages and the early modern period. Not all low-paid and ill-treated workers rebelled, however. After all, their lot was infinitely better than that of those below them: the beggars and the marginalized. It is difficult for us even to imagine the high number of poor people, including low-paid workers, in medieval urban settings. In fifteenth-century Prague—not an industrial city—the number of the poor has been calculated at 40 percent of a population of around 35,000. Almost one of every two inhabitants lived in crushing poverty.

BEGGARS AND CHARITY

In cities, most of the poor found little or no employment. The sight of throngs of people milling about city gates, churches, monasteries, and the marketplace, in spite of legislation that forbade them to beg outside churches, was an unvarying feature of the urban landscape. Depending for survival on the spontaneous assistance of passersby, they begged, uttering ancient, formulaic entreaties intended to sacralize the act of begging: "a piece of bread (or alms) for the love of God." Although little is known about how the well-to-do behaved upon coming across beggars in the street, impromptu acts of charity formed part of the repertoire of ritual gestures that reinforced social status and rank; they came with the territory of being well fed next to someone who was hungry and were part of the accepted burdens of social distinction. In some instances, giving was prompted by compassion, fear, or merely the desire to get rid of a nagging beggar. An old, feeble woman or a mother with a child was more likely to trigger a charitable impulse than a young, able-bodied man. Some acts of informal charity were recorded in the early modern period. As children, high nobles kept diaries of the charitable donations they had given to beggars in the street, but there is no evidence that such record keeping was common in the Middle Ages. To keep a record of charitable gifts, as some do today for income tax purposes, would have invalidated the principle of charity. Nonetheless, informal charity must have gone a long way toward meeting the needs of the poor, even though we cannot calculate how much these contributions represented of their daily income.

After 1300, it became obvious that churches and monasteries were neither equipped nor always willing to tend to the growing pressure of the poor. Clearly, the bourgeois control of legacies and the wane of unrestricted gifts to the church created economic conditions that seriously limited the ecclesiastical ability to deal with the poor in the late Middle Ages. Moreover, a great deal of the church's formal charity had become exceedingly ritualized. Charity had become a symbolic act that did not always take account of emergencies or changes in the number and composition of the poor.

As the church faltered in its traditional mission of managing "the patrimony of the poor" (in theory if seldom in fact, the church held its property in trust for the poor), secular bodies jumped into the breach, invoking religion and political ideal to justify the control and surveillance of the poor in their midst. Hospitals, hospices, poorhouses, and other forms of structured assistance—one can call this social welfare, despite its pervasively Christian discourse of charity—were clearly aimed at keeping the poor in their place and preventing the violent outbursts that were so common in the late Middle Ages. But even the hospitals settled to help the poor or the disabled were not always safe from the encroachment of the powerful. Although Louis IX of France founded hospitals for the blind and even earlier hospitals can be found in Chartres or later in London, as well as institutions such as Bedlam aimed at taking care of the insane and numerous foundling houses, the rich took advantage of these institutions for their own benefit. While on the one hand, the growing number of hospitals founded in the late Middle Ages alert us to the rising number of the poor; on the other hand, the well-to-do often bought or appropriated beds in the hospitals as a guarantee for their old age or reverses in their fortunes. Mollat reports such occurrences in the Low Countries and other places throughout Europe.

Royal and municipal policies went beyond the standard distribution of food and shelter; through license grants, they resorted to such drastic measures as regulating the right to beg. Other enactments forced the able-bodied to work and forbade wandering beggars to come into the city or expelled them, as happened in Barcelona at the beginning of the fourteenth century. In many respects, the anti-poor legislation, so characteristic of the early modern period, was already in place in the late Middle Ages. These measures devalued the apostolic meaning of involuntary poverty and marginalized the poor.

Poverty, marginality, and charity. Although precedents can be found in an earlier age, in the late Middle Ages a broad-based move occurred to define who was poor and who was unworthy of charity. In turn, new representations of the poor appeared—specifically, representations that counteracted the idealized Christian vision of poverty. In literary works—Juan Ruiz's *Libro de buen amor* (Book of good love), Froissart's ferocious depictions of peasant uprisings in France, Chaucer's *Canterbury Tales,* and late medieval law codes—the poor became, as we have seen above, undesirable, ridiculous, or unworthy of heaven. As recipients of alms, the poor were often viewed as mere instruments for the salvation of the rich. In fact, the poor became marginalized in an entirely new way. Although the modern term "marginalization" may not fully reflect the social reality of medieval life—after all, every Christian was secured a place in the church's program of salvation—in reality, some came to play an uncontested role in the economics of salvation, while the vast majority was pushed to the fringes of society or excluded altogether from its spiritual and material benefits.

By the late Middle Ages, poverty had acquired a harsher face, and many of the poor became lumped with other marginal social characters. Bronislaw Geremek's influential study of marginality in late medieval Paris demonstrates how the boundaries between the poor *qua* poor and the criminal became blurred. Scam artists, prostitutes, pimps, and similar social types were often folded into the broader category of the poor. Surely, not all poor people were criminals and not all beggars were con men, but, increasingly, as the Middle Ages gave way to the early modern period, poor men and women came to be identified with those who, socially and legally, had been branded as outcasts. As a result, the medieval conception of poverty and forbearance toward the poor within Christian society was radically transformed. From the eleventh century onward, medieval men and women began to view poverty uncompromisingly, as either voluntary or involuntary.

VOLUNTARY AND INVOLUNTARY POVERTY

The early Middle Ages abounded in hagiographical narratives of Christians from Benedict of Nursia to Martin of Tours abandoning a life of wealth to embrace Christ. This well-known trope in Christian culture stood in sharp contrast to the story told in Matthew, a paradigmatic text in any discussion of poverty. In the Gospel, a rich young man approaches Jesus and asks how to gain entry into the kingdom of heaven. Told by Jesus that he must comply with the Mosaic law, the young man replies that he has done so. Jesus then commands him to leave everything he owns and follow him. When the young man proves unable to give up his material wealth, Jesus turns to his disciples and utters the oft-quoted saying that "it is easier for a camel to go through the eye of a needle than for a rich man to enter into the kingdom of God."

In many ways, this story was a terrifying one. On the one hand, it served as a model for all Christians: give up all earthly possessions and gain salvation in Christ. On the other hand, it became a permanent thorn in the side of the church, for it served as a reminder of ecclesiastical excesses and raised the specter of the sinfulness of property. The relationship between salvation and property was often debated in the early church; theologians and church fathers agreed more or less on the legal necessity of private property, so long as it was directed—through donations to the church, alms to the poor, charitable deeds—to Christian ends.

Thanks to the work of Jacques Le Goff, Lester Little, Sharon Farmer, and other scholars, we know the ways in which property could be placed at the service of salvation in the late Middle Ages. The notion of purgatory, an intermediary place between heaven and hell, provided the rising mercantile and artisanal groups with an opportunity "to have their cake and eat it too." Offering a means to avoid eternal damnation after a period of penance, it gave the better-off leave to accumulate wealth and make as much profit as possible; then, by bequeathing testamentary legacies for the saying of masses and endowments for candles, proper burial for those too poor to afford it, and other pious donations, they could escape the fires of hell. This solution, however, did not prove palatable to all. Those who led evangelical lives of poverty argued that only an outright rejection of worldly riches could lead to salvation.

It should come as no surprise that the emergence of a bourgeoisie in Europe and the early stages of capital accumulation coincided with a rise in the censure of ecclesiastical wealth and of the laity's pursuit of material possessions. This critique came in orthodox and heterodox forms, and the extremely thin line separating heresy from orthodoxy depended on whether the critic, like Francis of Assisi, accepted ecclesiastical authority without question or whether, like Peter Valdès, he did not. The Cathars, a heretical group that spread throughout southern France and areas of northern Italy in the twelfth century, belonged to the latter category and preached a rejection of the material world (which they associated with Satan). The Waldensians' embrace of evangelical poverty challenged the church's authority. Both heresies had a tremendous impact on European culture and religious sensibilities, but they were limited in their appeal because

their ideas were branded as heretical. Thus, they were unable to capture the interest of the great mass of Christians.

The powerful message of Francis of Assisi in the thirteenth century and of lesser-known saints advocating poverty as a way of life met with a very different outcome. The immediate and overwhelming success of their mendicant preaching bestowed upon voluntary poverty a spiritual cachet never associated with involuntary poverty. Francis's message, which in many respects was fairly similar to that of Valdès, ignited an extraordinary response during his lifetime and long afterward from many Christians throughout the West. After his order turned away from his strict views on a life of poverty, a faction of the Franciscans, the Fraticelli—many of them dissidents and heretics—kept alive Francis's credo of apostolic poverty. These radical interpretations of Francis's preaching and, by implication, the Gospels remained at the core of the revolutionary fervor and attacks on property of a series of millenarian movements into the modern age.

For the majority of Christians in the late Middle Ages, however, Francis's message offered a convenient path to salvation without demanding full renunciation of the world and its pleasures. Through membership in the Third Order of St. Francis (and similar mendicant secular offshoots) and charity—dispensed in wills in highly ritualized and symbolic language and in many ways antithetical to idealized Christian charity—the middle level of society, that is, the mercantile and artisanal elites, developed new forms of spirituality, relations to God, and visions of the afterlife. In the late twelfth century, urban wills began to make provisions for the feeding and clothing of the poor. These legacies usually specified a number of poor men or women, often twelve or some other symbolic number. Some wills enjoined executors to parcel out the bread of charity over the tomb of the donor; others stipulated that the poor accompany the body of the deceased to its last burial place or attend a funeral meal on the burial day or on the anniversary of the donor's death. Late medieval wills often insisted that food and garments given to the poor be of lesser quality than those assigned to ecclesiastical and lay executors of wills. Burlap and sackcloth, rough bread, and inferior wine reinforced the social distance between donors and the poor. But donations to feed and clothe the poor were minuscule when compared to legacies that were bequeathed to family and friends or provisions that were made for the saying of masses. Even in the bid for salvation, the poor came last.

We have seen how new concerns linking property, charity, and salvation operated in the late Middle Ages and how a new system of values led to the postulation of purgatory and to new definitions of poverty. The poor *qua* poor and the understanding of poverty had been sharply reconceptualized. On the one hand, poverty remained part of a complex Christian ideal (the poor as Christ, the poor as being close to Christ); on the other, poverty became nothing but a social and economic category in the newly configured hierarchies of wealth and power.

The redrawn landscape of Christian poverty and the clear distinction between voluntary and involuntary poverty did not produce salutary results. As Kenneth Wolf has argued, the stirring mendicant message of poverty for the love of Christ may in fact have had a negative impact. By privileging the voluntary aspect of poverty and deeming the renunciation of wealth essential for Christian life, Francis of Assisi and others who embraced a life of poverty unwittingly dispossessed the involuntarily poor of any social good will that might have helped assuage unequal social relations in earlier times. Poverty was thus desacralized and viewed as the end result of personal failure, immorality, dissoluteness, and unwillingness to work. In this light, the poor became a burden to society and required increased surveillance and disciplinary measures. Salvation, which had long been half understood as a poor person's reward for a life of penury, was now fairly erased from the equation. To be born poor was no longer a way into heaven, quite the reverse. The formerly well-off, no longer able to support themselves or their families, would now be designated as the "ashamed." For to be poor meant, essentially, to carry a stigma of shame. And in the new meritocracy of charity, the "ashamed poor," those who had fallen from grace, were awarded first place.

POVERTY, CHRISTIANITY, AND THE STATE

It would be extreme to argue that poverty, above all crushing urban poverty, was de-Christianized in the late Middle Ages. Numerous examples can be mustered to show the lasting power of Christian charity beyond the end of the Middle Ages and into the present. In truth, for every example of the new attitude toward the poor, a counterexample can be found illustrating the abiding power of Christian teachings on poverty. Nonetheless, literary, legal, and even theological sources provide a clear road map of the way the Christian church changed its posture toward the growing hosts of the poor in the fourteenth and fifteenth centuries. This new position

was not always charitable or efficient. On the other hand, the church did not always have the means or the will to deal with the new social, economic, and political aspects of poverty. Indeed, poverty and the pressing tide of the poor became important and disruptive problems, affecting governments and the social order across western Europe.

The widespread rebellions of the late Middle Ages—the rebellion of the "Karls" in 1320s Flanders, the Pastoreaux uprising around the same period, the Jacquerie, the Ciompi, the English peasants' rebellion of 1381, the civil war of late-fifteenth-century Catalonia, and the great German peasant uprising in the early sixteenth century—were grim reminders to those in power, secular and ecclesiastic, that the heady mix of radical evangelical Christianity, millenarian expectations, and social grievances posed a serious threat to the stability of late medieval society. The secularization of the status of the poor led to new ways of handling individual beggars and the impecunious hordes. Following intense debates, increasingly heavy-handed measures were employed to control the poor in the early modern period.

THE CAMPAIGN AGAINST THE POOR

Historians of poverty have long debated whether or not the transition from the late Middle Ages to the early modern period signaled a dramatic shift in the perception and treatment of the poor. The sixteenth century saw ferocious controversies over the issues of begging and almsgiving. Catholic and Protestant polemicists alike, men such as Joan Lluís Vives and Martin Luther, denounced beggars and sought to rationalize the social and religious meanings of charity. Catholic writers such as Domingo de Soto, Cristóbal Pérez de Herrera, and Thomas More advanced an impassioned defense of the poor, calling for a renewal of Christian charity and new social measures to address their plight. Focusing on the beginning of the sixteenth century, Soly, Gutton, Lis, Martz, and other historians have regarded the social, political, and economic transformations that the rise of the state and precapitalist economic structures ushered in as trigger mechanisms for the new definitions of poverty. By exploring this changing context, they sought to explain what they perceived as a dramatic shift in western European attitudes toward poverty and the poor.

One must be cautious about positing too sharp a break, however. Although recent students of poverty make allowances for geographical variation—Spain, a supposedly "aristocratic" (read, backward) country, was believed to be far more charitable than its northern (read, more developed) neighbors—their approach is questionable at best. For one thing, the debasement of poverty was rooted in the Middle Ages, in the twelfth-century urban and mercantile renewal that spawned new ways of thinking about property and salvation. And while attitudes toward the poor varied according to location and social and economic development, these differences were never so sharp as to allow us to posit two separate tracks. Moreover, the legal codes and social mores regulating behavior toward beggars and almsgiving in thirteenth- and fourteenth-century England, France, Italy, and Iberia were in fact no different from those of the rest of Europe in the early modern period.

But fundamental changes did occur in the early sixteenth century, in spite of the slow pace of events and the lack of sharp chronological boundaries between the late medieval and early modern periods. It could not have been otherwise. To begin with, the late fifteenth and early sixteenth centuries witnessed significant demographic growth. Throughout western Europe, the population replenished itself and often surpassed preplague levels. More people competing for ever-shrinking resources—the familiar Malthusian scenario of inelastic supplies that lasted until the agricultural revolution of the eighteenth century—proved a sure recipe for disaster. In addition, the village community, that great producer of manpower, was less able and less willing to accommodate surplus population. Enclosure, increased taxation, the widening gap between rich farmers and landless or semi-landless peasants, and the erosion of common lands forced rural folks out of their farms, onto the roads, and into the cities. As noted earlier, their plight was vividly depicted by Thomas More in the early pages of *Utopia*.

Governments were now in control, and solutions were often kingdomwide, not regional or piecemeal as in medieval feudal monarchies. The world had changed, and although the devaluation and desacralization of the poor had a firm medieval pedigree, the penalties exacted by early modern societies were markedly different. By finalizing the transition from charity to welfare and by sanctifying wealth, as the Puritans would do in a later period, western Europe moved forcefully into new ways of defining poverty. These new ways—poor laws, poorhouses, confinement, and punishment (though less exaggerated than Foucault may have wished us to believe)—turned the poor-as-Christ into a social quandary, a vexatious thorn in the side of the capital-driven, rational state.

BIBLIOGRAPHY

PRIMARY WORKS

de Soto, Domingo. *Deliberación en la causa de los pobres: Domingo de Soto y réplica de Juan de Robles.* Madrid, Spain: Instituto de estudios políticos, 1965.

Hervaeus Natalis. *The Poverty of Christ and the Apostles.* Translated by John D. Jones. Toronto: Pontifical Institute of Mediaeval Studies, 1999. (Translation, with introduction and notes, of *Liber de paupertate Christi et apostolorum.*)

Olivi, Pierre Jean, 1248/9–1298. *De usu paupere: The quaestio and the tractatus.* Edited by David Burr. Florence, Italy: L.S. Olschki, 1992.

Pérez de Herrera, Cristóbal. *Amparo de pobres.* Edited by Michel Cavillac. Madrid, Spain: Espasa-Calpe, 1975.

SECONDARY WORKS

A pobreza e a assistência aos pobres na península ibérica durante a idade média: Actas das primeiras Jornadas Luso-Espanholas de História Medieval, Lisboa, 25–30 de setembro de 1972. Lisbon, Portugal: Instituto de Alta Cultura, Centro de Estudios Históricos, 1973. The best treatment of poverty and charity in the Iberian Peninsula, with important methodological contributions by Michel Mollat and others.

August, Andrew. *Poor Women's Lives: Gender, Work, and Poverty in Late-Victorian London.* Madison, N.J.: Fairleigh Dickinson University Press; London: Associated University Presses, 1999.

Behar, Ruth. *Santa María del Monte. The Presence of the Past in a Spanish Village.* Princeton, N.J.: Princeton University Press, 1986.

Brodman, James William. *Charity and Welfare: Hospitals and the Poor in Medieval Catalonia.* Philadelphia: University of Pennsylvania Press, 1998. An excellent synthesis of charitable activities in medieval Catalonia set within a comparative framework. An up-to-date and thorough bibliography.

Burr, David. *Olivi and Franciscan Poverty: The Origins of usus pauper Controversy.* Philadelphia: University of Pennsylvania Press, 1989. A good discussion of the heterodox aspects of the Franciscan preaching on poverty.

Carroll, William C. *Fat King, Lean Beggar: Representations of Poverty in the Age of Shakespeare.* Ithaca, N.Y.: Cornell University Press, 1996.

Chiffoleau, Jacques. *La comptabilité de l'au-delà: Les hommes, la mort, et la religion dans la région d'Avignon à la fin du moyen âge, vers 1320–vers 1480.* Rome: Academie française de Rome, 1980.

Clopper, Lawrence M. *"Songes of Rechelesnesse": Langland and the Franciscans.* Ann Arbor: University of Michigan Press, 1997.

Davis, Natalie Z. "Poor Relief, Humanism, and Heresy: The Case of Lyon." *Studies in Medieval and Renaissance History* 5 (1968).

Eijnden, Jan G. J. van den. *Poverty on the Way to God: Thomas Aquinas on Evangelical Poverty.* Louvain, Belgium: Peeters, 1994.

Farmer, Sharon A. *Surviving Poverty in Medieval Paris: Gender, Ideology, and the Daily Lives of the Poor.* Ithaca, N.Y.: Cornell University Press, 2002. Following a series of insightful articles on the topic, this book is a formidable contribution to the study of poverty and its relation to gender issues.

Flood, David. ed. *Poverty in the Middle Ages.* Westphalia, Germany: D. Coelde, 1975.

Geremek, Bronislaw. *Les fils de Caïn: L'image des pauvres et des vagabonds dans la littérature européenne du XIVe et XVe siècle.* Paris: Flammarion, 1976.

————. *The Margins of Society in Late Medieval Paris.* Translated by Jean Birrell. Cambridge, U.K.: Cambridge University Press, 1987. The best introduction to the study of marginality in the late Middle Ages.

Grell, Ole Peter, and Andrew Cunningham, eds. *Health Care and Poor Relief in Protestant Europe, 1500–1700.* London and New York: Routledge, 1997.

————. *Health Care and Poor Relief in Counter-Reformation Europe.* With Jon Arrizabalaga. London and New York: Routledge, 1999.

Gutton, Jean Pierre. *La société et les pauvres en Europe, XVIe–XVIIIe siècles.* Paris: Presses universitaires de France, 1974.

Hanska, Jussi. *"And the Rich Man Also Died; and He Was Buried in Hell": The Social Ethos in Mendicant Sermons.* Helsinki, Finland: Suomen Historiallinen Seura, 1997.

Holman, Susan R. *The Hungry Are Dying: Beggars and Bishops in Roman Cappadocia.* Oxford and New York: Oxford University Press, 2001.

Larmat, Jean. *Les pauvres et la pauvreté dans la littérature française du moyen âge.* Nice, France: Centre d'études médiévales, Université de Nice Sophia Antipolis, 1994.

Little, Lester K. *Religious Poverty and the Profit Economy in Medieval Europe.* Ithaca, N.Y.: Cornell University Press, 1978.

Makinen, Virpi. *Property Rights in the Late Medieval Discussion on Franciscan Poverty.* Louvain, Belgium: Peeters, 2001.

Martínez García, Luis. *La asistencia a los pobres en Burgos en la baja Edad Media: El Hospital de Santa María la Real (1341–1500).* Burgos, Spain: Excma. Diputación Provincial de Burgos, 1981.

Martz, Linda. *Poverty and Welfare in Habsburg Spain: The Example of Toledo.* Cambridge, U.K., and New York: Cambridge University Press, 1983.

Mollat, Michel. *The Poor in the Middle Ages: An Essay in Social History.* Translated by Arthur Goldhammer. New Haven, Conn.: Yale University Press, 1986. The best comprehensive study of poverty in medieval Europe.

————, ed. *Études sur l'histoire de la pauvreté: Moyen âge–XVIe siècle.* 2 vols. Paris: Publications de la Sorbonne, 1974.

Mollat, Michel, and Philippe Wolff. *The Popular Revolutions of the Late Middle Ages.* Translated by A. L. Lytton-Sells. London: Allen and Unwin, 1973.

Newman, Lucile F., ed. *Hunger in History: Food Shortage, Poverty, and Deprivation.* Cambridge, Mass.: Blackwell, 1990.

Pelling, Margaret. *The Common Lot: Sickness, Medical Occupations, and the Urban Poor in Early Modern England: Essays.* London and New York: Longman, 1998.

Rotberg, Robert I., and Theodore K. Rabb, eds. *Hunger and History: The Impact of Changing Food Production and Consumption Patterns on Society.* Cambridge, U.K., and New York: Cambridge University Press, 1985.

Ruiz, Teofilo F. "The Business of Salvation: Property and Charity in Late Medieval Castile." In *On the Social Origins of Medieval Institutions: Essays in Honor of Joseph F. O'Callaghan.* Edited by Joseph F. O'Callaghan, Donald J. Kagay, and Theresa M. Vann. Leiden, Netherlands: Brill, 1998.

TEOFILO F. RUIZ

[See also **DMA:** Bede; Cathars; Famine in Western Europe; Francis of Assisi, St.; Franciscans; Froissart, Jehan; Gregory I the Great, Pope; Gregory of Tours, St.; Hospitals and Poor Relief, Western European; Peasants' Rebellion; Purgatory, Western Concept of; Urbanism, Western European; Waldensians; **Supp:** Charity; Ciompi, Revolt of the; Commercialization; Martin of Tours, St.; Poor Clares.]

PROBABILITY. The Latin adjective *probabilis* (probable) had a range of meanings in medieval philosophy and law. These meanings were related, on the one hand, to Aristotle's theories of proof and persuasion and, on the other, to legal standards of proof in court. The current view that law enforcement officers must have "probable cause" to obtain a search warrant descends from the earlier legal usage of probability in which, for instance, a court might be required to have a "half proof" of guilt (e.g., the testimony of one eyewitness, if the testimony of two eyewitnesses would be sufficient for conviction) before torture could be applied in the hopes of eliciting a confession (also considered a full proof of guilt).

For Aristotle, in a true science *(episteme)* it is possible to demonstrate true conclusions on the basis of principles known to be true and certain. Once scientists in any branch of knowledge know the principles of their science, they can demonstrate the conclusions of their science syllogistically, explaining effects by their causes. Aristotle's model of science in this sense was geometry, in which theorems are proved on the basis of definitions, axioms, and postulates. But whereas in geometry the axioms are better known to us than the theorems, in natural sciences like physics we know the effects, for instance, that all or some things move, before the causes. Aristotle was optimistic that humans could reason back (a posteriori) from observed effects to causes or from conclusions to principles (by so-called demonstration "that," or *quia*), and subsequently create a demonstrative science reasoning from causes to effects (reasoning a priori, using so-called *propter quid* demonstrations).

"Probability," on the other hand, was relevant to those areas of inquiry in which scientific demonstration was impossible either because the principles were unknown or uncertain or because the methods of argumentation were not demonstrative. Ethics was one such discipline, and, as a result, rhetoric rather than logic was taken to be the appropriate approach to ethical persuasion (see Aristotle, *Nicomachean Ethics,* Bk. I. Ch. 3, 1094^b 12–28). In ethics one reasons from premises that are generally accepted opinions (*endoxa*—see Aristotle, *Topics,* 100^b 21–23) but not known certainly to be true.

In medieval philosophy, then, a "probable opinion" was a respectable or plausible one, an opinion that was not claimed to be true or scientifically demonstrated but one for which one could make good arguments or one that was supported by respected individuals. A "topical syllogism" was one that reasoned from probable rather than known or certain premises. St. Thomas Aquinas (1224–1274) agreed with Aristotle that in human affairs one cannot have demonstration and infallible proof but only conjectural probability (see, for example, *Summa theologiae,* Iᵃ IIᵃᵉ, Q.105, art 2, reply obj. 8). For instance, although it is possible that two or three witnesses will agree to tell the same lie, it is not probable, so if the testimony of two or three witnesses is consistent, it is to be taken as true in a court of law.

But even in disciplines like physics or natural philosophy that Aristotle expected ultimately to achieve scientific certainty, medieval authors not infrequently acknowledged that they had not yet reached such certainty. In question commentaries on Aristotle's natural philosophical works, commentators might conclude that more than one alternative reply to a question was probable. Jean Buridan (*ca.* 1295–*ca.* 1358), commenting on a text of Peter of Spain (Pedro Juliano Rebolo, *ca.* 1205–1277), in his *Summulae de dialectica* (Treatise 8.4.1), states:

> We often have probable arguments in favor of either side concerning the same conclusion, so much so that while some great philosopher who carefully considers the arguments for both sides, because of the probability of the arguments for one side, believes this side; yet another, on account of the probability of the arguments for the other side, believes the other. Both arguments, therefore, are dialectical, and probable, if they are able to influence great philosophers in this way.

Some historians conclude that scholastics labeled their arguments in physics and cosmology as only "probable," just as they sometimes wrote that they proposed arguments only to exercise the minds of students, because they hoped thereby to avoid the ecclesiastical censure that might result from firm adherence to a view opposed by the authorities. Another interpretation, however, is that the authors honestly judged that certain philosophical issues were undecided. The latter interpretation fits, for instance, the normal usage of the term "probable" in the natural philosophical works of Buridan and Nicole Oresme (*ca.* 1320–1382).

In the later medieval approach, probability produced by dialectical arguments and scientific certainty produced by demonstrations were not necessarily correlated. Some propositions might be true but improbable,

while other propositions were probable but false. With regard to questions relevant to both theology and philosophy, some scholastics, for instance, John of Mirecourt (*fl.* 1345), argued that propositions contrary to the faith, and therefore false, might nevertheless be probable and even more probable than the articles of the faith. Others such as Pierre Ceffons countered that they would have been probable on the basis of reason and natural philosophy were it not for their opposition to articles of faith.

Thus in late medieval philosophy opinions came to be labeled probable because of the arguments and evidence in their favor or because they had been held by all or most of the wise or by experts in the field. Nearly no medieval philosophers considered probability in the modern sense of relative frequency. An exception was Nicole Oresme, who argued against astrology on the grounds that it is based on similar effects resulting when the planets jointly return to the same positions. But, he argued, most probably the relative velocities of the planets are incommensurable with each other. If so, it follows that if they are ever in conjunction at a given place, they will never again be in conjunction at that same place, undermining the method of astrological prediction. Although medieval Aristotelians believed that natural processes need not hold true all the time, but only for the most part *(ut in pluribus),* they did not think of stable statistical frequencies. In addition, God might cause miracles disrupting the normal course of nature.

Centuries later, in a decree of 8 April 1546, the Council of Trent declared that in matters of faith and morals it was not permitted for an individual to interpret the Bible in a sense contrary to what had been determined by the Catholic Church. In his trial in 1633 Galileo Galilei was found guilty not only for believing that the sun is in the center of the world and does not move but also for believing that "an opinion may be held and defended as probable after it has been declared and defined to be contrary to the Holy Scripture." In the period between the late Middle Ages and Galileo there had been a fierce argument between moralists called "probabilists," who believed it was allowed to take a course of action if at least one respected church father had sanctioned it, and a group labeled "probabiliorists," who said that this was too lax and that the correct approach was to follow the course of action that was safer, better advised, and supported by more authorities.

BIBLIOGRAPHY

PRIMARY WORKS

Buridan, Jean. *Summulae de dialectica.* Translated and with an introduction by Gyula Klima. New Haven and London: Yale University

Press, 2001. Treatise 8, "On demonstrations," describes and compares scientific demonstrations and probable or dialectical reasoning.

Grant, Edward, ed. and trans. *Nicole Oresme and the Kinematics of Circular Motion: Tractatus de commensurabilitate vel incommensurabilitate motuum celi.* Madison: University of Wisconsin Press, 1971. Contains Oresme's argument that any two celestial motions are probably incommensurable.

SECONDARY WORKS

Byrne, Edmund. *Probability and Opinion: A Study in the Medieval Presuppositions of Post-Medieval Theories of Probability.* The Hague, Netherlands: Nijhoff, 1968. The single best place to start for medieval concepts of probability, focusing on the work of Thomas Aquinas.

Franklin, James. *The Science of Conjecture: Evidence and Probability before Pascal.* Baltimore and London: Johns Hopkins University Press, 2001. Excellent synthesis of topics relevant to probability before Pascal.

EDITH DUDLEY SYLLA

[See also **DMA:** Buridan, Jean; Dialectic; Oresme, Nicole; Rhetoric: Western European.]

PRODROMIC POEMS. Constantinople in the twelfth century was home to more than one poet named Prodromos. Theodore Prodromos (*ca.* 1100–*ca.* 1170) was a prolific, versatile, and learned writer in both prose and verse who produced a wide range of texts, including theological commentaries and witty imitations of classical authors; he also wrote poems of praise for his patrons as well as verse petitions for benefactions to himself. He is not to be confused with a contemporary, whose family name was also Prodromos though his baptismal name is unknown. This other Prodromos is now conventionally known as Manganeios Prodromos since several of his poems concern attempts to be admitted to the hospice of the Mangana monastery in Constantinople. Manganeios Prodromos was in the employ of Irene, sister-in-law of the emperor Manuel I Komnenos, and most of his output, all in verse, deals with occasions in her life and that of her family. A third set of poems circulated under the name of Ptochoprodromos ("Penniless Prodromos"); scholarly opinion is divided over whether these are to be attributed to a third Prodromos or whether the skillful Theodore is their author. It is this third group that is commonly known as the Prodromic, or Ptochoprodromic, Poems.

Four in number, the poems of Penniless Prodromos present many problems. Culturally, they are written in a register of Greek that allows the use of nonclassical words and syntax. This breaks Byzantine linguistic and educational conventions; indeed, these are among the first texts to be composed in a language close to the spoken Greek of the time. Debate continues over the reasons for this innovation. The poems use the rhythmic fifteen-syllable line (the *politikos stichos*), which had no classical antecedents but came to be used in informal contexts. The Ptochoprodromic poems are preserved in seven manuscripts dating from the thirteenth to fifteenth centuries; these display divergent readings, making it difficult to reconstruct the author's original text. The variants may be a result of the poems' informal language level since the vocabulary would have been familiar to the copyists and may have encouraged recomposition.

Nevertheless, the poems were clearly composed during the middle years of the twelfth century. The first is dedicated to the emperor John II Komnenos, who reigned from 1118 until 1143, the second to his son Andronikos, and the third and fourth to his successor, the emperor Manuel I; only an introduction to the fourth poem, not included in all manuscripts, suggests a date in the 1170s. The poems' purpose is to request the dedicatee's support for the author. However, in the process they give a lightheartedly satirical view of Constantinopolitan society. They are written in the guise of a henpecked husband (poem 1), a starving father of a large family (poem 2), a poverty-stricken man of letters who wishes he had been taught a trade (poem 3), and a harassed junior monk in a large monastery (poem 4). They give many insights into life in Constantinople: thin partitions between dwellings, artisans' workshops, women weaving in the home, unruly children, cats stealing food. But above all the ostensibly starving poet is preoccupied with food: he lists spices, fish, vegetables, savory sausages, and so forth in mouthwatering detail. Although the genre of begging poems has other practitioners in Byzantine literature, the Ptochoprodromic poems are uniquely lively; they show many intriguing parallels with the slightly later Archpoet writing in Latin in Germany, raising the question of cultural interaction at this period between Latin West and Greek East.

BIBLIOGRAPHY

PRIMARY WORKS

Eideneier, Hans, ed. *Ptochoprodromus: Einführung, kritische Ausgabe, deutsche Übersetzung, Glossar.* Cologne: Romiosini, 1991. With German translation. Note that Eideneier's poems 3 and 4 are Hessling and Pernot's poems 4 and 3 and that the line numbering differs.

Hesseling, D.-C., and H. Pernot, eds. *Poèmes prodromiques en grec vulgaire.* Amsterdam: J. Müller, 1910.

Prodromos, Theodoros. *Historische Gedichte.* Edited by Wolfram Hörandner. Vienna: Österreichische Akademie der Wissenschaften, 1974. Contains extensive bibliography.

SECONDARY WORKS

Alexiou, Margaret. "The Poverty of Écriture and the Craft of Writing: Towards a Reappraisal of the Prodromic Poems." *Byzantine and Modern Greek Studies* 10 (1986): 1–40. Insightful on Hesseling and Pernot, poem 4 (Eideneier, poem 3).

Beaton, Roderick. "The Rhetoric of Poverty: The Lives and Opinions of Theodore Prodromos." *Byzantine and Modern Greek Studies* 11 (1987): 1–28. Interesting, but wrong on Manganeios Prodromos.

Kazhdan, Alexander, and Simon Franklin. *Studies on Byzantine Literature of the Eleventh and Twelfth Centuries.* Cambridge, U.K.: Cambridge University Press; Paris: Maison des Sciences de l'Homme, 1984. See especially pp. 87–114.

Magdalino, Paul. *The Empire of Manuel I Komnenos, 1143–1180.* Cambridge, U.K., and New York: Cambridge University Press, 1993.

ELIZABETH JEFFREYS

[See also **DMA:** Archpoet; Byzantine Literature; Greek Language, Byzantine; Komnenoi; Manuel I Komnenos; Theodore Prodromos; **Supp:** Latin Literature: Secular Latin.]

QUEENS AND QUEENSHIP.

In the Middle Ages, the term "queen," or *regina* in Latin, could have many meanings, because the medieval queen played many different roles. Most of the time, the term was applied to a woman who was the wife of a ruling king. In that case, she was serving as a queen consort. If he had died, she was the dowager queen or the queen mother if her son inherited the throne. If her son was underage and she ruled on his behalf, she held the title of queen regent. And in rare cases, a woman succeeded to the throne in her own right, in which case she was the ruling queen, or queen regnant. Understanding the queen's activities can be essential in reconstructing the dynamics of family structure, kingship, and statecraft during the medieval era. The queen's role changed over time and also differed depending on the area of Europe in which she lived. There were few formal or constitutional roles for a queen, and so much depended on her individual interests and abilities, her relationship to the king, the financial resources she had at her disposal, and perhaps most important, her ability to produce a suitable heir to the throne. In general, the early medieval queen enjoyed physical proximity to the court and the sources of political power, but her status was insecure and depended on her relationships with her male relatives as much as her own abilities. By the Carolingian era, Christian familial ideals had made her status somewhat more secure, although she usually could be replaced fairly easily if she proved infertile or otherwise unsuitable. The twelfth century represents a high point in the queen's independent authority and ability to control the power structures in place within her realm. But even after the rise of administrative kingship in the later twelfth and thirteenth centuries, individual queens managed to leave their marks on the political, cultural, and ecclesiastical life of their realms.

EARLY MIDDLE AGES (*CA.* 350–*CA.* 750)

Both in the later Roman world and in early Germanic society, succession to kingship or the imperial title was not straightforward. Usually, monarchs came from a designated bloodline, but smooth father-son succession was not the norm. Especially in Germanic society, which was based on war, the monarch usually needed to be an adult male with a record as a warrior and with a group of subordinates who supported him in his bid for the throne. If a king died young, leaving only minor sons, he was as likely to be succeeded by an adult brother as he was by a son. Kings and other powerful, wealthy males had sexual access to many women, and often, as long as a man chose to recognize the sons of any sexual partners, they were accepted as his and theoretically part of the succession pool. In practice, this meant that the death of a ruler was often followed by a violent succession crisis.

The women in early Germanic royal bloodlines knew that their status was secure only insofar as they remained in favor with their spouses and their sons. Kings' wives came from a variety of social backgrounds. Some were "treaty brides" from other royal bloodlines who married the king as a seal of a peace treaty between two warring groups. Some of the king's mistresses might have started life as slaves within his household, but if they bore sons whom the king recognized, these sons became part of the royal bloodline, and their mothers were sometimes treated with honor and rewarded with treasure. Because most Germanic kings fathered children by a number of women over the course of their lives, the mothers of these sons had to compete with each other for the king's favor. Such women were often gifted with treasure and large tracts of land from which they drew enormous revenues. They used these resources to form factions and attract supporters, and thus advance their sons' chances for succession. Early medieval chronicles are filled with colorful stories of women who managed to succeed in these trying circumstances.

One of these women was Galla Placidia (*d.* 450), daughter of the Roman emperor Theodosius I. Galla Placidia was captured by the Visigoths under their king Alaric I and taken to Spain. She married Alaric's brother Ataulf, who became king, and she prospered as queen of the Visigoths until his death. With no living son and deprived of a husband's protection, Galla Placidia had no secure place in Visigothic society, so she returned to Italy. At her brother's insistence, she then married a Roman general who became emperor. After he too died, Galla Placidia fled with her children to Constantinople, where her son's claim to imperial authority was recognized. She served as his regent for over twelve years and remained influential up until her death.

The stories of the Merovingian queens Brunhild (*d.* 613) and Fredegunda (*ca.* 543–597) tell us more about the positions of early-medieval queen consorts. Chilperic I, King of Neustria, married the Visigothic princess Galswintha, only to have her murdered, probably at the insistence of his slave mistress Fredegunda, who became Chilperic's queen. Meanwhile, Chilperic's brother Sigibert I, king of Austrasia, had married Galswintha's sister Brunhild. In revenge for her sister's murder, Brunhild arranged to have Chilperic murdered. The blood feud between the rival queens and their descendants drove the political history of both kingdoms for over forty years.

The patterns in these and other stories demonstrate how tenuous court life could be for the queen. Marriages were easily made and easily dissolved, so women needed money and support. A treaty bride usually came with rich treasures from her natal family. Some of her treasure was given to her husband's family as a gift, but most would be retained to support her during her lifetime and in case of her widowhood. The bridegroom was expected to add to his queen's wealth by gifts given at the time of the marriage. Sons, natal relatives, and retainers from her native area would form the nucleus of her support group, and she usually used her wealth to help her form alliances at court, often with influential churchmen or with members of powerful noble families. Women of less exalted status depended on the gifts and whatever they could extract from those for whom they did favors.

A queen who was known to have a good relationship with her husband often secured an important place at court. Those wishing royal favors would ask the queen to intercede with the king on their behalf. Literary portrayals, such as that of Waltheow in the poem *Beowulf,* depict the queen as a wise and trusted counselor whose ceremonial duties fostered and regularized relationships between the king and his attendant nobility. One of the poetic terms often applied to early medieval queens was "peaceweaver," a name paying tribute not only to her status as a treaty bride but also to her skill at creating and maintaining harmonious relationships at court. On the other hand, ignoring or insulting the queen could cause her to turn her husband against the one who had offended her. In *Egils saga Skallagrímssonar* (Egil's saga), Eiríkr

Bloodaxe's queen's animosity toward Egil leads to his losing his lands and going into exile.

Beginning with the story of the conversion of the Merovingian king Clovis (*d.* 511), medieval sources often portray queens as influential in a king's decision to adopt Christianity. This portrayal is so formulaic that some commentators have wondered whether the stories reflect more of a literary construction than historical reality. But Christian queens did correspond with popes and other churchmen and did often further the cause of Christianity. In Anglo-Saxon England and Ottonian Germany in particular, queens were often patrons of monasticism, reform movements, and ecclesiastical building programs. Many queens entered monasteries after their husbands' deaths, and many daughters of royalty entered into monastic life as consecrated virgins. Some of these women were recognized as saints and thus over time helped add an aura of holiness to further legitimate royal bloodlines.

CAROLINGIAN ERA (*CA.* 750–*CA.* 987)

By the eighth century, Christian teachings on marriage and the family had begun to permeate the upper ranks of society, and polygyny was replaced by serial monogamy. Over time, illegitimate children were generally excluded from full inheritance, and by around the year 1000, primogeniture had begun to replace partible inheritance among the medieval nobility. These changes had mixed effects on queenship. There was less opportunity for social mobility for the king's mistresses, but legitimate wives enjoyed a somewhat more secure position in society as the church insisted that marriages should be both monogamous and indissoluble. Theoretical writings on queenship stressed the necessity of choosing a queen wisely. Sedulius Scottus's ninth-century *De rectoribus christianis* (On Christian rulership) reminded rulers that they ought not to overlook the good counsel their wives offered. Carolingian sources confirm that the queen had charge over the royal palaces, including the treasury. One of Charlemagne's capitularies ordered his judges to carry out fully any order that came from his queen.

As the queen began to be seen as a unique individual within the realm, so also rose the need to formally mark her accession to queenship. Installation of the queen was not normally a ritual occasion before the ninth century, but under the Carolingians, Frankish queens and empresses were anointed, often along with their husbands. About the same time, the Anglo-Saxons developed an inauguration ceremony focused on the ritual enthronement of a new queen. But in ninth-century Wessex, after a negative experience with a too-powerful queen, it actually became illegal to raise a woman to queenly status. Asser, bishop of Sherborne and biographer of King Alfred the Great, tells us that the nobles swore that they would not permit any king to rule over them who allowed a queen to sit beside him on his throne. The royal consort could not be called "queen" *(regina)* but only "king's wife" *(regis coniunx)*. This situation changed when the Frankish king Charles II (the Bald) agreed to allow his daughter Judith to marry the king of Wessex but insisted that she be crowned and that he be given some sort of guarantee that her queenly status would be recognized. A few of the rituals from Frankish and Anglo-Saxon coronation ceremonies survive to provide clues to such early-medieval concepts of the queenly office. The earliest continental rituals stress the queen's fertility and recognize her potential influence over the king. By 973 the English coronation ritual named the queen as a protector of good religious practice in her realm.

CENTRAL MIDDLE AGES (CA. 987–CA. 1250)

In Capetian France, the consecration ceremony itself became an essential component to kingship. In a ceremony that became almost a religious ordination, the queen, king, and the heir to the French throne were given a special elevated status within human society. The last third of the eleventh century and the opening years of the twelfth saw the medieval queen consort at perhaps her highest level of power and influence. It was also during the twelfth century that several women in major European kingdoms claimed thrones in their own name. The Norman Conquest of England in 1066 practically necessitated a sharing of power since the monarch could not be on both sides of the channel at once. Both William I (the Conqueror) of England (r. 1066–1087) and his son Henry I of England (r. 1100–1135) had competent, trusted wives who became true partners in governing the realm. They judged cases at law, participated in the king's council, chaired it in his absence, issued charters and writs, and corresponded with popes and other leaders of European society. Later, Matilda of Boulogne (d. 1152), Stephen of England's queen, not only headed Stephen's government during his captivity but also organized a siege and pled his cause before an ecclesiastical council. French queenship also reached its apogee with the reign of Louis VI (the Fat) (r. 1108–1137) and his consort Adelaide of Maurienne (d. 1154). During Adelaide's tenure, royal charters were sometimes dated with her regnal year as well as that of the king's.

The papal reform movement that began in the mid-eleventh century brought the church into the marital lives of European Christians more fully than ever before. Kings discovered that they could no longer divorce or annul marriages that were not proving useful. Several monarchs during these centuries found that their attempts to discard their barren or otherwise problematic wives led to excommunications or interdicts for their entire kingdoms. There are several instances of queens using church law to their favor in this period, and alliances between the queen and the bishop often proved useful. But eventually, the church's stricter rules against consanguinity became useful to monarchs who could almost always get out of a marriage that proved to be within the prohibited degrees of relationship.

Three major kingdoms also saw queens regnant, or attempts to have queens regnant, during the middle part of the twelfth century. In England, Henry I had the nobles take an oath to support the claims of his daughter Matilda (d. 1167) should he die without a son. Her cousin Stephen won the English throne first, but Matilda's claim plunged England into nineteen years of civil war. In the end, Matilda renounced her own claim in return for Stephen's recognition of her son Henry (later Henry II of England, r. 1154–1189) as his heir. In the Latin kingdom of Jerusalem, Melisende (d. 1161), along with her husband Fulk of Anjou, inherited the throne from her father in 1131. Royal documents confirm that she considered herself a ruler and not just a consort. After Fulk's death she ruled another thirteen years, and although she is generally listed as a regent for her minor son, it seems clear that she considered herself at least a coruler and had to be forced to relinquish power when her son reached majority age. Finally, Urraca of Castile (d. 1126) is recognized as the first woman to rule a Spanish kingdom in her own right.

As royal bureaucracies grew and became more professional, it became less necessary for monarchs to depend on family members to participate directly in the business of ruling. Queen consorts gradually took on more ceremonial roles and tended to participate less in the day-to-day business of government. Eleanor of Aquitaine (d. 1204) was queen to both Louis VII of France (r. 1137–1180) and Henry II of England, but her role in governing either realm was limited until her widowhood. As queen mother, she occasionally assisted her sons, Richard I (the Lionhearted) of England (r. 1189–1199) and John of England (r. 1199–1216). Eleanor's granddaughter Blanche of Castile (d. 1252) married Louis VIII of France (r. 1223–1226) and ably served as regent for their son, Louis IX (St. Louis, d. 1270), both during his minority and while he was away from France on Crusade.

One effect of the rise of professional royal bureaucracies was that all of the royal finances were often subsumed into a treasury controlled, not by the queen, but by officials who were most likely not personally beholden to or appointed by the queen. After the mid-twelfth century it is rare to find a royal consort with direct control over her own income, and this loss of autonomy may have contributed to the decline in the actual power of the queen consort during the later medieval period.

LATER MIDDLE AGES (*CA.* 1250–1500)

During the thirteenth and fourteenth centuries bloodline remained important, and during several succession crises in Scotland, the Holy Roman Empire, and Sicily, women transmitted the right to rule to their sons. Even this ability was questioned in France, though, when the death of the last male descendant of Philip IV (the Fair) (*r.* 1285–1314) led to the "discovery" of the Salian (Salic) law that prohibited females from transmitting the right to rule to their descendants. During the fourteenth and fifteenth centuries, queenship became ever more social and ceremonial. Queens set the fashions at court, became extravagant consumers, and were known as patrons of art and literature. Literature such as the Arthurian legends portrays some of the social tension that could arise around issues such as a queen's fertility or sexual fidelity. Negative reactions to the marriage between Edward IV of England (*r.* 1461–1483) and the commoner Elizabeth Woodville show that queens were still supposed to come from exalted bloodlines. In the fifteenth century, queens could still be used as "peaceweavers," as evidenced by the marriage of Henry V of England (*r.* 1413–1422) and Catherine of Valois (1401–1437) under the terms of the Treaty of Troyes, which was supposed to end the Hundred Years War.

Even in a time when the queen exercised very little direct power, her potential influence over her husband and her realm should not be discounted. Eleanor of Castile (*d.* 1290), consort to Edward I of England (*r.* 1272–1307), helped to popularize the Dominicans in her new kingdom, and religious dissidents probably followed Anne of Bohemia (1366–1394) into England when she married Richard II. Finally, Anne pleaded the cause of Londoners with Richard, just as Philippa of Hainault (1311–1369) had interceded with Richard's grandfather Edward III and saved six burghers of Calais from execution.

Family dynamics in the medieval period are often described from a male perspective, in which women appear as pawns to be traded in arrangements between men. Examination of women's texts has shown that mothers were usually active in forming alliances for their sons and daughters and in negotiating the terms of those alliances, and that women maintained long-standing ties to their natal families even when they traveled great distances away from their birthplaces. Such women were trained to represent their natal family's interests in a new setting and often did so very effectively, making an understanding of the dynamics of queenship an essential part of understanding the political and cultural history of the medieval world.

BIBLIOGRAPHY

BIOGRAPHIES

Chibnall, Marjorie M. *The Empress Matilda: Queen Consort, Queen Mother, and Lady of the English.* Oxford: Blackwell, 1991.

Howell, Margaret. *Eleanor of Provence: Queenship in Thirteenth-Century England.* Oxford: Blackwell, 1998.

Huneycutt, Lois L. *Matilda of Scotland and the Development of Medieval Queenship.* Woodbridge, U.K.: Boydell, 2003.

Mayer, H. E. "Studies in the History of Queen Melisende of Jerusalem." *Dumbarton Oaks Papers* 26 (1972): 93–182.

Parsons, John Carmi. *Eleanor of Castile: Queen and Society in Thirteenth-Century England.* New York: St. Martin's, 1995.

Sivéry, Gérard. *Marguerite de Provence: Une reine au temps des cathédrals.* Paris: Fayard, 1987.

———. *Blanche de Castille.* Paris: Fayard, 1990.

Stafford, Pauline. *Queen Emma and Queen Edith: Queenship and Women's Power in Eleventh-Century England.* Oxford: Blackwell, 1997.

Strickland, Agnes. *Lives of the Queens of England from the Norman Conquest.* 16 vols. Philadelphia: G. Barrie, 1902–1903.

Trinidade, Ann. *Berengaria: In Search of Richard the Lionheart's Queen.* Dublin: Four Courts, 1999.

Turner, Ralph V. "Eleanor of Aquitaine and her Children: An Inquiry into Medieval Family Attachment." *Journal of Medieval History* 14 (1988): 321–335.

STUDIES

Baker, Derek, ed. *Medieval Women.* Oxford: Blackwell, for the Ecclesiastical History Society, 1978.

Carpenter, Jennifer, and Sally-Beth MacLean, eds. *Power of the Weak: Studies on Medieval Women.* Urbana: University of Illinois Press, 1995.

Crawford, Anne. "The Queen's Council in the Middle Ages." *The English Historical Review* 116, issue 469 (2001): 1193–1211.

Duggan, Anne J., ed. *Queens and Queenship in Medieval Europe.* Woodbridge, U.K.: Boydell, 1997.

Enright, Michael J. "Lady with a Mead-Cup: Ritual, Group Cohesion, and Hierarchy in the Germanic Warband." *Frühmittelalterliche Studien* 22 (1988): 170–203.

Parsons, John Carmi, ed. *Medieval Queenship*. New York: St. Martin's, 1993.

Stafford, Pauline. "The King's Wife in Wessex, 800–1066." *Past and Present* 91 (1981): 3–27.

Wemple, Suzanne. *Women in Frankish Society: Marriage and the Cloister, 500–900.* Philadelphia: University of Pennsylvania Press, 1981.

Wheeler, Bonnie, and John Carmi Parsons. *Eleanor of Aquitane: Lord and Lady.* New York: Palgrave Macmillan, 2003.

LOIS L. HUNEYCUTT

[See also **DMA:** *Beowulf;* Eleanor of Aquitaine **Supp:** Brunhild; Fredegunda; Matilda, Empress.]

RACE. Medieval notions of race are no more easily explicated than contemporary ones. In both cases we are faced with a composite category of identity which gathers together ambivalent, often contradictory elements. Because it has been so often invoked to disparage some groups while ennobling others, race can be best understood as emerging within a struggle for power both tangible (control of government, land, literacy) and intangible (prestige, social influence, the ability to narrate history effectively). Race, in other words, cannot be a neutral term.

THE COMPOSITION OF MEDIEVAL RACE

In a widely influential formulation, the historian Robert Bartlett has drawn upon the writings of the tenth-century canonist Regino of Prüm to argue that medieval races *(diversae nationes)* typically thought of themselves as distinct in descent, customs, language, and law. Arguing that biological forms of racism were rare during much of the Middle Ages, Bartlett downplays the importance of descent as a racial determinant. Because the remaining three categories are neither innate nor inalterable, the race of an individual or group could change over time. Customs like hairstyle and dress might be adopted. The English colonizers of Ireland were often accused of "going native" in their coiffure, costume, and even manner of horseback riding. So much power did Isidore of Seville ascribe to words that he argued that the dispersal of peoples at the destruction of the Tower of Babel had created not only the world's linguistic groups but also its distinct races. Yet a new tongue could be mastered in order to gain social advantage. The languages spoken by subordinate or conquered peoples might recede due to loss of prestige. Sometimes, like Arabic in Spain, Wendish in areas occupied by German speakers, or Pictish in Britain, a language would vanish entirely as its native speakers died out, were forced to leave, or were absorbed into other linguistic populations.

Law was no less protean. As a living, human institution, juridical power could be manipulated to constitute new communities, enfranchising some groups while excluding others. After William the Conqueror was crowned king of England, he instituted what became known as the *murdrum* fine, the sum of money to be paid by the English of any area in which a Frenchman was found dead by unknown hands. Such a penalty was necessary to ensure the safety of an alien minority among their new subjects, and its application was a potent reminder of how dramatically control of the land's governance had shifted. A century later, however, Richard fitz Nigel could argue that the *murdrum* fine now applied to any unsolved homicide since intermarriage had, he claimed, rendered the English and French indistinguishable, at least at social levels higher than the peasantry. William's desire to protect his imported cohort reinforced their separateness from the country over which they now had dominion, while Richard's generalization of the law's purview envisioned a newly unified community, capable of transcending the differences engendered by the Norman Conquest.

Other cultural components of medieval race could be added to Bartlett's list. Because race is intimately related to social status, economic class was demarcated along racial lines. Rural dwellers and the poor might be imagined as having descended exclusively from a subordinated group and might even be represented with darkened skin and other features that visually set them apart from elites. Race frequently had theological undertones. Although medieval Jews, Muslims, and Christians each experienced a great deal of internal heterogeneity in the practice of their faiths, all three groups were as a whole confident that they possessed the only true knowledge of the divine, and this difference, they held, set them apart. The imagined unity of each religion also offered a potent ideological tool. That all Christians could be supposed to constitute a single race was a sentiment that proved useful in promulgating support for the Crusades. According to this logic, Jews and Saracens were different not because they had darker skin or distinguishing facial features but because they practiced inferior ritual and held to an alien creed. In theory baptism could completely transform an unbeliever. In the romance *The King of Tars,* a Saracen's dark flesh is said to be whitened through the sacrament's transformative power.

The connection between race and religion, moreover, inevitably erased internal nuance from those imagined as inhabiting supposedly inferior categories. Latin Christians classified as Saracens a diverse array of Muslim and non-Muslim Arabs, Turks, Armenians, Kurds, and

Dark-Skinned Saracen Jousting with a Christian Knight. *During the crusading era, darkness came to be associated with the enemy as monstrous other. Miniature from the Luttrell Psalter, ca. 1340.* THE BRITISH LIBRARY, ADD. MS 42130, FOL. 82R. REPRODUCED BY PERMISSION.

non-Western Christians such as the Nestorians, Jacobites, and Maronites. The Arab chroniclers who recorded the invasion of their lands during the Crusades in turn typically referred to the polyglot and multiethnic invaders from Europe as the Franj, mainly because a majority of their leaders could converse in French. Medieval imaginings of race often invoked the species line. Disparaged races were either compared to animals or held to be bestial themselves, as in the unflattering portraits which Gerald of Wales painted of the Irish in his *History and Topography of Ireland.*

Finally, and more abstractly, race was also a matter of allegiance. Early in his life Gerald identified with the Anglo-Norman side of his family, but later he became (in recognition of his mixed blood) more sympathetic to the Welsh; William of Malmesbury and Henry of Huntingdon, both of mixed Norman and English descent, became in the course of their lives progressively more English-identified.

RACE OR ETHNICITY?

Given that a collective religious designation such as Christian could function like a racial category, it could be objected that the conceptualization of "race" that the Western Middle Ages inherited from the classical past is closer to what is today meant by the term "ethnicity." When the Romans described the Greeks, Germans, and Celts as races, for example, they were usually implying only that these peoples varied from them in language, customs, and geographic origin. Similarly, dissimilarities between the Welsh and the English, the Irish and the Vi-

kings, the Germans and the Slavs, and so on would appear to be exclusively ethnic differences, if ethnicity is the proper contemporary term to describe the cultural variations that distinguish peoples, and if race refers to the distribution of physical or biological differences throughout human populations.

Yet to differentiate between the two terms by asserting that one has mainly to do with culture and is therefore changeable while the other involves bodies and is essentially immutable generates immense difficulties. Contemporary science has made it clear that there is no genetic basis for racial classification (that is, race is not ultimately a matter of discernable variation in human biology), while classical and medieval theories of astrological influence, climatology, and physiology ensured that the differences that set one people apart from another were understood to be as corporeal as they were cultural. Galenic humoralism was especially influential in this respect. According to humoral theory, the temperateness or inclemency of a given geography and the position of the astral bodies in its skies profoundly influenced both the character and physiology of that land's inhabitants. Climate and celestial influence determined the distribution of the four bodily humors, the vital fluids that were thought to regulate health and hold sway over personality and emotion. Encyclopedists like Isidore of Seville and Bartholomaeus Anglicus therefore stated that the men of Africa suffered from an overheating of their blood, darkening their skin and rendering them spiritless cowards. In contrast, frigidity for Bartholomaeus engendered whiteness; the pale skin of northerners was for him the outward sign of their innate valiance. Christian polemicists declared that intense sun and the ascendancy of the planet Venus ensured that Saracens were forever bellicose and sensual. Like geographical location and climate, moreover, religion and law were thought to have immediate, bodily effects. When Englishmen like John of Salisbury stated that the Welsh were "rude and untamed," they based their assertions mainly on the fact the Welsh people so vigorously resisted assimilation into England. Inferior customs and religious ritual rendered the Welsh, it was thought, inferior beings. This supposed deficiency had intellectual, emotional, ethical, and physical components.

Differences between medieval races were clearly imagined in corporeal as well as cultural terms. Nonetheless, it has been argued by some medievalists that a period that did not live with the legacy of chattel slavery based upon skin color could not possibly have conceptualized race in the modern sense of the word. While there is undoubtedly truth to this observation, the issue becomes more complicated when investigating geographies in which slavery based upon dermal pigmentation did exist, such as late medieval Italy, or when the uneven relations among Latin Christians, Jews, and Muslims are examined. Even if these groups did not necessarily enslave each other or make judgments about identity based solely upon general differences in skin color, all became entangled in a circulation of mythologies that entwined cultural and bodily differences to deadly effect. That is, even if the contemporary terms race and ethnicity can often be used interchangeably in the study of medieval cultures, it could be reasonably asserted that when imbalances of power exist between groups, and especially when physical, mental, and ethical differences are held to differentiate a powerful group from those over whom a superiority is being actually or imaginatively asserted, race will be the preferred term.

RACE AND BLOOD

Race is a controversial term among medievalists in large part because the word has no exact medieval equivalent. *Natio, gens, genus, and stirps* (and to a lesser extent *populus, nomen, sanguis,* and *lingua*) are the most frequently encountered Latin nouns today translated as "race," but in many instances these terms could more accurately (or at least more neutrally) be rendered nation, people, ethnic identity, linguistic community, family, or kin group. Yet in a medieval context even a word as seemingly familiar as *natio* does not imply an ideological entity like the United States. A medieval *natio* need be nothing more than a group of people linked by their common descent: *natio* and its vernacular equivalents derive ultimately from the verb *nasci,* "to be born," and the word therefore carries with it implications that we would today describe as biological. Race, in other words, may be inseparable from culture, but it is almost always also involved in questions of blood.

Twelfth-century England provides a useful example of these complexities of medieval race. When William the Conqueror invaded England in 1066, the duke of Normandy ruptured the unity of a nation that, despite the ethnically diverse origins of its inhabitants, had long possessed a shared language, sense of history, governmental coherence, and powerful belief in its own community. In the years after the victory at Hastings, the French-speaking followers of William replaced the English at the highest levels of power. Racial tensions were endemic; even the monasteries witnessed deadly violence.

Although cities had been forcibly reconfigured, property seized, and lives lost and although English had suffered a complete loss of its prestige as a written language, in time the French began to feel at home enough in their country to begin calling themselves English. Within two or three generations they had almost completely assimilated, illustrating how malleable medieval race could be. Yet a group of French speakers whom the Normans had brought with them across the channel did not find it so easy to become part of this reconfigured nation. Ashkenazic Jews had emigrated from Normandy shortly after the conquest and by the middle of the twelfth century could be found inhabiting many English cities. Beginning in Norwich in 1144, accusations circulated that Jews were ritually murdering Christians. These stories, obsessed with the flow of blood and depicting Jews as innately hostile to Christians, raised as much skepticism as belief, but their effect could be powerful: in 1190 Jews were murdered on the streets of Lynn and incinerated in the wooden tower in which they had taken refuge in York. The Jews were permanently excluded from England's newly shared sense of community on account of their supposedly absolute otherness. To emphasize this racial separateness, Jews were eventually enjoined to wear distinguishing garb and forced to pay punishing taxes. In 1290 they were expelled completely from the island.

The assimilation of the Normans and English into a unified realm and the fate of the Jews suggests that medieval race was ultimately a process rather than a stable state of being. Just as the Frenchness of the Norman rulers would eventually vanish, allowing them to become as English as a family that traced its origin to the Germanic migrations, likewise the Jews—who initially were not met with any discernible hostility as they settled into English towns—were over time transformed into a bloody people whose persecution and exclusion would (it was imagined) allow England a triumphant sense of community. Perhaps the truest statement to make about medieval race is that it is always possessed most vividly by the excluded and the ostracized.

BIBLIOGRAPHY

Akbari, Suzanne Conklin. "From Due East to True North: Orientalism and Orientation." In *The Postcolonial Middle Ages.* Edited by Jeffrey Jerome Cohen. New York: St. Martin's, 2000. Explores the relations among climate, skin color, and medieval race.

Bartlett, Robert. *The Making of Europe: Conquest, Colonization, and Cultural Change, 950–1350.* Princeton, N.J.: Princeton University Press, 1993. A seminal discussion of the components of medieval race.

Foot, Sarah. "The Making of Angelcynn: English Identity before the Norman Conquest." *Transactions of the Royal Historical Society,* 6th ser., 6 (1996): 25–49. Details how Anglo-Saxon ethnic variation was overcome by a powerful myth of shared race.

Gillingham, John. *The English in the Twelfth-Century: Imperialism, National Identity, and Political Values.* Woodbridge, U.K.: Boydell, 2000. Argues in several essays that twelfth-century England saw a renewed sense of unity at the expense of the Welsh and Irish.

Heng, Geraldine. "The Romance of England: Richard Coer de Lyon, Saracens, Jews, and the Politics of Race and Nation." In *The Postcolonial Middle Ages.* Edited by Jeffrey Jerome Cohen. New York: St. Martin's, 2000. Examines the mutual dependency of racial categories of difference and their utility in creating national unity.

Kruger, Steven F. "The Bodies of Jews in the Late Middle Ages." *In The Idea of Medieval Literature: New Essays on Chaucer and Medieval Culture in Honor of Donald R. Howard.* Edited by James M. Dean and Christian K. Zacher. Newark: University of Delaware Press, 1992. Delineates the ways in Jewish bodies were thought to differ from Christian bodies.

———. "Conversion and Medieval Sexual, Religious, and Racial Categories." In *Constructing Medieval Sexuality.* Edited by Karma Lochrie, Peggy McCracken, and James A. Schultz. Minneapolis: University of Minnesota Press, 1997. Emphasizes the ambivalence of conversion in affecting medieval conceptions of race.

"Race and Ethnicity." *Journal of Medieval and Early Modern Studies* 31 (winter 2001). A special issue containing many articles debating the usefulness of "race" to the study of the Middle Ages.

Uebel, Michael. "Unthinking the Monster: Twelfth-Century Responses to Saracen Alterity." In *Monster Theory: Reading Culture.* Edited by Jeffrey Jerome Cohen. Minneapolis: University of Minnesota Press, 1996. Surveys medieval depictions of the Saracen as a monstrous figure.

Wormald, Patrick. "Engla Lond: The Making of an Allegiance." *Journal of Historical Sociology* 7 (1994): 1–24. Describes the process of identification that enabled the unity of "Anglo-Saxon" England.

JEFFREY J. COHEN

[See also **DMA:** Anti-Semitism; Jews in Europe: After 900; Jews in Muslim Spain; **Supp:** Monsters and the Monstrous.]

RADEGUNDA, ST. (*ca.* 518–587). Born in Thuringia (modern central Germany), Radegunda was the daughter of King Berthar. Following an unsuccessful conflict with the Franks in 531, she and her brother were taken away by Chlothar I (511–561). Radegunda was confined to the royal villa at Athies, where she was educated in letters and Christianity, until she became another wife of Chlothar. Her burgeoning religious zeal put off her husband, who, to the pious amusement of Gregory of Tours writing years later, found himself with "more a monk than a queen for a wife." After he arranged the assassination of her brother, Radegunda left Chlothar. Sharp rebukes and generous gifts persuaded the reluctant bishop Médard of Noyon to consecrate her as a deaconess. Residing at Tours, Candes, and her own villa at Saix, the queen occupied herself with prayer and charitable works. Finally, sometime in the 550s she established a female monastery just inside the city of Poitiers, where she would spend the last decades of her life.

Radegunda refused to serve as abbess, yet she also refused to withdraw completely from secular society as dictated by the monastic rule her community adopted. She was already an accomplished relic collector when in 569 she obtained a portion of the True Cross from the emperor Justin II and the empress Sophia of Constantinople. It became the namesake of the convent and a boon to her adopted city, but the relic also complicated what appears to have been a dangerously strained relationship between the royal nun and the local bishop Maroveus. The latter made himself scarce during the installation of this most esteemed of all relics, so that another bishop had to be brought in from outside to preside over the ceremony. He did the same on the occasion of Radegunda's funeral in 587, so that once again another bishop, this time Gregory of Tours, officiated.

Within Merovingian hagiography, the dossier on Radegunda is second only to that of the Gallic saint Martin of Tours. Martin in fact provided a model for Radegunda's biographers. Venantius Fortunatus had both a personal and professional relationship with Radegunda, composing hymns and poems at her request, writing her first biography, and serving as bishop of Poitiers after her death. Gregory of Tours, who included many details about her life and the subsequent, tumultuous happenings at Holy Cross in his historical and miracle writings, had a niece in the same convent. Another nun at Holy Cross, Baudonivia, wrote a second biography soon after 600, including incidents Fortunatus might necessarily have suppressed. Finally, we have Radegunda's own letters, although Fortunatus probably contributed a helping, if not total, hand, in some of them. Radegunda was buried in the funerary church she had built just outside the city walls. Pilgrims appeared soon after and continued to arrive throughout the Middle Ages, demonstrated by the creative efforts to win their devotion made by nuns on behalf of her former cell in Holy Cross and, in competition, by canons of the successive churches of Ste. Radegonde built above her tomb.

BIBLIOGRAPHY

Brennan, Brian. "St. Radegunda and the Early Development of Her Cult at Poitiers." *Journal of Religious History* 13, no. 4 (Dec. 1985): 340–354.

Carrasco, Magdalena. "Sanctity and Experience in Pictorial Hagiography: Two Illustrated Lives of Saints from Romanesque France." In *Images of Sainthood in Medieval Europe.* Edited by Renate Blumenfeld-Kosinski and Timea Szell. Ithaca, N.Y.: Cornell University Press, 1991.

Coates, S. "Regendering Radegunda?: Fortunatus, Baudonivia and the Problem of Female Sanctity in Merovingian Gaul." *Studies in Church History* 34 (1998): 37–50.

McNamara, Jo Ann, John E. Halborg, and E. Gordon Whatley, eds. and trans. *Sainted Women of the Dark Ages.* Durham, N.C.: Duke University Press, 1992. Includes translations of both lives; see pages 60–105.

KEVIN UHALDE

[See also **DMA:** Gregory of Tours, St.; Merovingians; Relics; Venantius Fortunatus; Women's Religious Orders; **Supp:** Queens and Queenship.]

RANSOMING ORDERS. See **Mercedarians; Trinitarians.**

RAPE. The words "ravish" and "rape" (Latin, *rapere, raptus*) mean "seizing," whether of things (e.g., movable goods, as in *The Rape of the Lock*) or of persons, for good or ill. St. Paul was "rapt" or "ravished" (*raptus*) to the third heaven (2 Cor. 12:2), and similar literal or metaphorical possessions or ecstasies are called "raptures" or "ravishments," including pathological trance conditions. As a crime, it can refer to forced sex (the rape of Lucrece) or abduction (the rape of Helen) or both.

Justinian's Code (A.D. 534) in the title *De raptu virginum* (On the rape of virgins) refers exclusively to sexual rape, with no suggestion of kidnapping or forced marriage. But later in the Middle Ages, rape more frequently had the latter meaning, and often the question of coitus was secondary. In his *Decretum* (*ca.* 1140), Gratian twice cites the definition of rape in Isidore of Seville's *Etymologies* (*ca.* 635) as "illicit coitus" (no mention of force) next to the statement of the fifth-century pope Gelasius that

rape refers to the abduction of a girl with no previous negotiation concerning her marriage. On his second citing, in the canon *Raptus quoque,* Gratian asserts that not every illicit coitus or deflowering is called rape; rape occurs when a girl is violently taken from her father's home, whether the violence is used against her or her father or both, so that, once "corrupted," she may be held as the abductor's wife. The crime carried a death penalty, but it could be commuted. He adds that there is no rape when there is no violence, but when a man forces a virgin without abducting her he commits rape because he has violently taken away *(eripuit)* the flower of her virginity.

The rape of the Sabine women was the classic example of marriage by kidnapping. Various law codes in the early Middle Ages prohibited and punished the practice. The Vikings were notorious practitioners of it, and after they introduced it into Normandy, it persisted for generations. But in spite of laws forbidding such rape (that is, abduction), Gratian concluded that once it was atoned for, a licit marriage could be arranged. His judgment was confirmed by Pope Innocent III in the decretal *Accedens* (1200), which stipulated that an abductor might marry a ravished girl who at first was unwilling but later changed her mind. The decretal *Cum causam* (1181–1185) of Lucius III authorized elopements: it stated that the abduction of a willing woman from unwilling parents or guardians did not deserve the name of rape, if the man married her before having sexual intercourse with her; and if she were to be subsequently "raped by force" from her husband and placed in a monastery, she must be restored to him. But sometimes a marriage might be forced upon a sex-rapist who did not intend marriage, in keeping with the biblical precedent of Deuteronomy: a man who finds a virgin and takes her and lies with her will be judged to pay a fine to her father, "and he shall have her to wife, because he hath humbled her" (Deut. 22:28–29).

Ecclesiastical laws dealt primarily with the validity of marriage, leaving secular laws to provide for the disposition of property and punishment of abductors, as can be seen in the various "statutes of rapes" in England. For instance, chapter 34 of the statutes of Westminster II (1285) provided the death penalty for ravishing a woman without her consent, even if she consented afterward. The law could be invoked even in the case of a husband who took his own wife back after she was abducted by her former guardian. A frequent use of the statute was for husbands to claim damages from an alleged abductor, even in cases where the wife had secured an ecclesiastical annulment. In such cases the charge of rape was often merely a way of getting the case into court, where the real grievance would come out. The term "rape" was also used of male heirs, even when they were taken away by their own mothers.

Unforced coitus (fornication, adultery) was prosecuted in England not by the royal courts but by church tribunals and sometimes municipal courts, but elsewhere, notably Italy, it was often not prosecuted at all. In England, as in Italy and elsewhere, violent crimes were prosecuted in the secular courts, but mere fornicators and adulterers, including the clergy, may have been indicted for rape in England, as a means of punishing them by humiliation and imprisonment before eventual acquittal.

When a rape involved forced sex, clarifying qualifications were often added: "he raped her of her pure virginity" or "he raped her and lay with her carnally against her will" were typical additions in England. In Venice, the term "rape" was left out—"he knew her carnally by force"—and the crime was punished relatively lightly, even when the victims were very young. In England, sexual rape was one of the two crimes for which a woman was allowed to bring a criminal appeal (accusation) in the king's courts (the other was the killing of her husband); but by the late thirteenth century, rapists could be indicted by a grand jury, and wronged women could make their complaint known by other means. A woman could continue to pursue her appeal even when the defendant secured a pardon for breaking the king's peace. Convictions, however, were relatively infrequent.

In contrast to the West, early Byzantine law, beginning with the *Ecloga* of Leo the Isaurian (741), was more concerned with sex-rape than abduction-rape, though abduction did receive more attention by the eleventh century. The penalty for forced sex with an unmarried girl was a slit nose, and eventually a fine was added of one-third of the rapist's property. Sex with a girl under the age of thirteen—the age of marriage—brought a punishment of half of the offender's property, in addition to the slitting of his nose, whether the girl consented or not. In Western law, the age of marriage for a girl was twelve but could be even younger, if "malice supplied the age"—that is, if it was demonstrated that she was capable of coitus. There was an equivalent of the Byzantine "statutory rape" in English practice, based on the statute of Westminster I (1275) against "raping" underage girls with or without their consent..

Literary depictions of rape in the Middle Ages are often heavily indebted to Ovid, whether directly or indirectly. In addition to the stories of Helen and Lucretia, Ovid's accounts of rape include Philomela (mutilated and repeatedly violated by her brother-in-law Tereus),

Medea (seduced and taken by Jason from her outraged father), and the victims of Jupiter and other gods, like Proserpina (taken by Pluto) and Daphne (pursued by Phoebus).

BIBLIOGRAPHY

Amsler, Mark. "Rape and Silence: Ovid's Mythography and Medieval Readers." In *Representing Rape in Medieval and Early Modern Literature.* Edited by Elizabeth Robertson and Christine M. Rose. New York: Palgrave, 2001. For a range of criticism, including feminist readings, see the editors' introduction and summaries of the essays in this volume.

Brundage, James A. *Law, Sex, and Christian Society in Medieval Europe.* Chicago: University of Chicago Press, 1987.

Gravdal, Kathryn. *Ravishing Maidens: Writing Rape in Medieval French Literature and Law.* Philadelphia: University of Pennsylvania Press, 1991.

Kelly, Henry Ansgar. *Inquisitions and Other Trial Procedures in the Medieval West.* Aldershot, U.K.: Ashgate, 2001. See chapters 9 and 10.

Kittel, Ruth, "Rape in Thirteenth-Century England: A Study of the Common-Law Courts." In *Women and the Law: The Social Historical Perspective.* Edited by D. Kelly Weisberg. Vol. 2. Cambridge, Mass.: Schenkman, 1982.

Laiou, Angeliki E., ed. *Consent and Coercion to Sex and Marriage in Ancient and Medieval Societies.* Washington, D.C.: Dumbarton Oaks, 1993.

Orr, Patricia. "Men's Theory and Women's Reality: Rape Prosecutions in the English Royal Courts of Justice, 1194–1222." In *The Rusted Hauberk: Feudal Ideals of Order and Their Decline.* Edited by Liam O. Purdon and Cindy L. Vitto. Gainesville: University Press of Florida, 1994.

Saunders, Corinne J. *Rape and Ravishment in the Literature of Medieval England.* Rochester, N.Y.: D. S. Brewer, 2001.

Wolfthal, Diane. *Images of Rape: The "Heroic" Tradition and Its Alternatives.* Cambridge, U.K.: Cambridge University Press, 1999.

HENRY ANSGAR KELLY

[See also **DMA:** Gratian; Law, Civil—Corpus Iuris, Revival and Spread; **Supp:** Sexuality.]

RELIGION, POPULAR

RELIGION, POPULAR. "Popular religion" is one term modern scholars use to describe the broad range of religious beliefs and practices cultivated by medieval Christians, whether they were approved or condemned by the institutional church's clerical leaders. Its synonyms include "popular Christianity," "popular piety," "lay piety," "popular devotion," and "traditional religion."

The modern study of medieval popular religion emerged in the middle of the twentieth century as scholars debated the question of how "Christian" medieval Christians were. One school of thought, noting the doctrinal misunderstandings to which many uneducated medieval believers seemed prone and the persistence of non-Christian magical and superstitious practices, argued that Christianity never deeply penetrated into the worldview of the medieval laity, especially those who lived in rural areas. Their rough-hewed religious beliefs and routines appeared to clash with the more refined Christianity practiced by educated members of the clergy, whose beliefs some scholars have characterized as "learned" or "elite" religion. Scholarship of the last several decades, however, suggests that, at least by the thirteenth century, in most parts of Europe lay people did have a rudimentary understanding of basic Christian doctrines, and they willingly incorporated the rituals of Christianity into their devotional life despite whatever non-Christian trappings they may have grafted onto them. Furthermore, lay people and clergy alike shared many of the hallmarks of popular religion, such as the veneration of saints and their relics, a fascination with miracles, an overawed respect for the consecrated host, a preoccupation with aiding the souls of the dead, and the use of magical amulets and charms. Although church officials vigorously condemned popular practices that seemed either overtly "pagan" or strayed into heresy, they were usually tolerant and even encouraging of customs that helped teach Christian doctrine or stimulated piety. To this degree, lay people were not simply passive recipients of the religious viewpoints of their clerical teachers; in many cases, their own religious instincts and inclinations influenced and inspired the clergy. This commerce of devotional ideas between the two groups is especially notable in lay people's advocacy of new saints and new religious feasts.

Like most religions, Christianity furnished its believers a body of doctrine to explain the relationship between the human and the divine, to express that relationship through ritual actions, and to embody it in daily life through an ethical system. But beyond the sense of the meaning of life and the spiritual satisfaction it offered, medieval people also turned to religion as a way to cope with the adversities of a precarious world. In an age of limited economic, technological, and medical resources, it was a powerful tool for weaving a safety net in the face of subsistence living and recurring hardship. Prayers and rituals could cure sickness, ward off spiritual and earthly danger and disaster, ensure good fortune, appease divine wrath or praise divine blessings, guarantee salvation, and care for the souls of the dead. To this extent, popular religion was practical minded: to deal with life's challenges people turned to whatever means were at hand, whether

Arma Christi. *The five wounds of Christ printed on a devotional card.* OXFORD, BODLEIAN LIBRARY. REPRODUCED BY PERMISSION.

they were Christian or the remnants of pre-Christian customs and folk wisdom. It was also literal minded; its most basic instinct was to make the spiritual physical. According to medieval Christian doctrine, faith was "the evidence of things unseen" (Heb. 11:1); but for ordinary people, seeing was believing. Concrete, physical evidence reinforced the mysteries of faith. Finally, popular religion was contractual, tending to deal with divine beings through reciprocation, an arrangement best seen in medieval people's relationship with the saints. (For example, people requesting favors of a saint often bent a coin or pledged a candle as a sort of promissory note to be offered at the saint's shrine when the favor was granted.)

Average Christians always showed an aptitude for absorbing basic Christian ideas and then embellishing them with their own religious imagination and inclinations. Since their beliefs typically came from the heart and addressed the pressing concerns of life, ordinary people were seldom interested in intellectual subtlety or abstractions. They wanted a religious system that was certain, concrete, and above all effective.

The cultural circumstances in which Christianity developed influenced much of the characteristics of what ordinary people understood about their faith. First, Christian doctrine was esoteric and complex, positing complicated ideas about the Trinity, the Incarnation, the sacraments, and the means of salvation. Well-educated theologians, not to speak of ordinary Christians, found these notions hard to grasp and explain clearly. Thus, there was always room for people to misunderstand or misinterpret aspects of Christian belief. Second, medieval Christianity's doctrines and rituals were preserved in Latin, which by the early Middle Ages was unintelligible to the vast majority of lay people. Its basic beliefs and stories, therefore, had to be passed on to unlettered Christians either through vernacular preaching or the visual arts, "the lessons and scriptures of the laity," as the thirteenth-century canonist William Durandus called them. Finally, despite the fact that Christendom was the one unifying cultural element across Europe by the High Middle Ages, the institutional church's power to impose universal standards of Christian belief and practice was always limited by its inability to provide uniform and universal religious education for its clergy—much less for ordinary Christians—or to provide routine oversight of what went on in the hundreds of dioceses and thousands of parishes scattered across Christendom. Consequently, Christian practice, though grounded in a common doctrine and liturgy, was always subject to regional variations depending on its era, its locale, the level of education of any particular parish's priests, the conscientiousness of the diocese's bishop, and the local customs of a place.

MISSIONARY STRATEGIES

It is important to recall that, through much of the early Middle Ages, Christianity was a missionary religion evangelizing the various tribes settled in central and northern Europe along and beyond the borders of the dilapidated Roman Empire. Systematic efforts to convert Europe's tribal people began only in the late sixth century. Christianity arrived even later along Europe's eastern and northern borders. Parts of Scandinavia and Lithuania embraced Christianity only in the late thirteenth and fourteenth centuries.

Since most tribes converted en masse following the example of their leaders, missionaries faced the challenge of evangelizing large groups of ill-educated people who already had their own local deities and religious customs. But in these early medieval centuries the church lacked

---

A METHOD OF DIVINATION

FROM THE COMMON PLACE BOOK COMPILED IN THE EARLY 1470S BY ROBERT RAYNES, THE REEVE OF THE VILLAGE OF ACLE IN ENGLAND.

(In English) Take a young child—that is, between 7 and 13 years old—and set him in the sun between your legs. And then wrap a red silk thread around his right thumb three times, and scrape his fingernail well and clean. And then write on the nail these letters with olive oil: O, N, E, L, I; while writing these letters have the child say the Our Father. And then say this prayer: (In Latin) "Lord Jesus Christ, King of Glory, send us three angels on your behalf, who may tell us the truth and nothing false about everything we shall ask them." (In English) And say this prayer three times with good heart and devoutly. And then three angels shall appear in the child's nail. And then have the child say this after you, either in Latin or English: (In Latin) "Lord Angels, I command you through the Lord Father Almighty who made you and us from nothing, and through the Blessed Virgin Mary, and the Blessed John the Evangelist, and through all virgins and the power of all of God's saints, show us the truth and nothing false about everything we shall ask you." (In English) And then have the child ask what he wishes and they shall show it to him.

SOURCE: From Medieval Popular Religion, 1000–1500: A Reader, ed. by John Shinners. Peterborough: Broadview Press, 1997, pp. 337–338.

---

the organization, the personnel, and the pastoral theology necessary to supplant all of its new converts' former beliefs. Accommodation and adaptation became the preferred strategy of pastoral care. Pope Gregory I (ca. 540–604) promoted this policy in his famous letter of 601 to the missionary Mellitus, who had written to him for guidance in dealing with newly converted Anglo-Saxons, who still offered animal sacrifices at their pre-Christian temples. Reasoning that people did not climb to a mountaintop in leaps and bounds but gradually, step-by-step, Gregory advised him not to tear down their temples; instead, he should remove the idols from them and consecrate them as Christian churches. This same policy was also applied in the cities of the old Roman Empire, where, for instance, Rome's Pantheon, originally dedicated to all the Roman gods, was rededicated in 609 to the Virgin Mary and all the martyrs—the first such Roman temple converted to Christian use.

Another strategy of evangelization Christianized the non-Christian year, superimposing Christian feasts on earlier festivals, which were geared to astronomical and agricultural cycles. Christmas, for instance, was fixed to correspond with the ancient Roman Saturnalia, a week-long celebration of the winter solstice. The Celtic festival of the dead called Samhain was replaced by the feast of All Saints ("holy ones" or "hallows" in Old English); the night before the feast became Hallows Eve or Halloween. As feasts in honor of God, the Virgin Mary, and the saints multiplied, eventually the whole year was marked with Christian milestones. Though this Christian veneer helped people reorient their sense of time according to Christian sacred time, pre-Christian elements were never far beneath the surface. Thus, across Europe on St. John's Eve, or Midsummer's Eve (June 23, the summer solstice) people gathered on hillsides where they lit bonfires, sometimes made of animal bones, which were meant to ward off dragons, and spun wheels to symbolize the declining course of the post-solstice sun. The Greater Rogation celebrated on St. Mark's day (April 25) was a Christian adaptation of the ancient Roman *Robigalia*, which venerated the agricultural deity Robigus. In both the Greater Rogation and the Lesser Rogation (held in early summer), priests and their parishioners circuited their parish carrying religious banners, ringing bells, and chanting a litany that beseeched God and his saints to expel demons from the parish, bless their crops, and protect them from bad weather. Parishioners often carried a large dragon stuffed with straw during the Lesser Rogation, a sign of the intermingling of this Christian festival with earlier pre-Christian customs.

Sources from the early Middle Ages record the efforts of missionaries to eradicate their new converts' pre-Christian beliefs. But in an age where the power of magic was taken for granted by both educated and uneducated Christians and non-Christians, it was hard even for theologians to draw distinct lines between what was orthodox belief and what was superstitious. Pastors faced deeply ingrained religious habits among their flocks, who turned to religion to cope with practical, daily problems such as ensuring fertile crops, curing sickness, protecting livestock, controlling the weather, predicting the future, and warding off malignant spirits. To its adherents, pre-Christian religion offered effective tools certified by long-standing custom: amulets and incantations offered protection against adversity; sacred stones, trees, and wells were portals to the spiritual world where people could seek the help of the gods. To counteract these beliefs the Christian church offered saints and their relics as more powerful miracle workers. But with some resignation they also adapted the trappings of pre-Christian religions to their own still-evolving rituals. Judaism and Roman and tribal religions, for example, all ascribed protective attributes to candles, water, salt, and bells; Christian leaders appropriated them to their own sacraments.

For their part, new converts were adept at blending Christian practices into their previous devotional lives. In fact it is always characteristic of popular religion, no matter the era, to hedge its bets by using any religious exercises that promise results no matter their source and despite their apparent incompatibility. A typical example of this religious syncretism is a mold surviving from tenth-century Denmark used to cast both ornamental Christian crosses and the Teutonic god Thor's hammer. When missionaries were too quick and uncompromising about erasing past beliefs and rituals, new Christians, hastily converted with little subsequent instruction, could become confused and resentful. In his life of the Anglo-Saxon saint Cuthbert of Lindisfarne (*ca.* 635–687), for instance, the historian Bede (672/ 673–735) related that, when Cuthbert urged local people to pray for his monks imperiled by a storm, at first they refused, claiming that the monks had banished their ancient customs and left them uncertain about how to practice the new ones.

THE CULT OF SAINTS

The veneration of saints and their relics was a pillar of popular religion, embodying most of its characteristic features, especially its urge to make intangible things tangible. By the end of the Middle Ages people throughout Europe venerated hundreds of saints, many of whom enjoyed merely local fame while others were universally acclaimed. They regarded saints as powerful patrons and intercessors between God and humanity. Saints pervaded the medieval religious mentality and were omnipresent. Every parish church was dedicated to a saint or saints. Every altar contained a saint's relic embedded in its altar stone. Statues and painted images of saints decorated even the humblest churches, where people offered candles before them. Every day of the year was dedicated to a saint; each profession had its patron saint. By the thirteenth century, saints' names even began to replace older ethnic given names in many places.

Though the clergy held up saints as models of Christian perfection whose virtues should be imitated, for most medieval Christians saints were primarily wonder

St. Christopher Bearing the Christ Child across a River. *According to legend, St. Christopher was a giant who once carried the infant Jesus across a river, as in this 15th-century German woodcut. The popular saint was known as the patron of all travelers.* THE J. PAUL GETTY MUSEUM. REPRODUCED BY PERMISSION.

workers, particularly healers. Saints gained reputations for the specialized favors they could perform, which people often associated with some aspect of their lives. Thus, St. Apollonia, whose teeth were broken during her martyrdom, was invoked for toothaches; St. Lucy, whose eyes, legend said, were plucked out during hers, was invoked for eye trouble; St. Elmo, said to have been disemboweled, aided those suffering from stomach complaints. Women in labor called on St. Margaret of Antioch, since, according to her legend, when she was swallowed whole by a dragon, she burst out through its belly. The legend of St. Christopher, one of the most popular medieval saints, said that he was a giant who once carried the infant Jesus across a river. He therefore became the patron of travelers. Pictures of him carrying the Christ child, painted on church walls or wooden tablets, or printed on small pieces of paper or parchment, were enormously popular, since people believed that

anyone seeing his image was protected from a sudden death for that day.

The tombs of noteworthy saints—enshrined in cathedrals, monasteries, and sometimes local churches—dotted the European landscape and became magnets for pilgrims as soon as rumors spread that miracles could be expected there. The enormous popularity of these shrines suggest both the importance that popular religion placed on tangible signs of divine power and the intermingling of lay and clerical interests as clerical custodians of shrines tried to attract pilgrims both for the pilgrims' spiritual and physical health and the shrine's financial gain. In fact, some churches took their relics on tour through their region to raise money for pious causes, as the monks of Laon did after their cathedral was damaged by fire in 1112.

Pilgrims seeking cures swamped shrines famed for healing. Records kept at shrines report scores of sick pilgrims clustered around each tomb seeking to touch it and thereby come into direct contact with the saint's relics interred within, which were a conduit to divine power. Some people even slept on the shrines hoping to absorb more saintly power.

People who received a saintly blessing, especially a cure, traveled to that saint's shrine to leave a payment of coins, candles, jewelry, or, most commonly, an "ex-voto" ("from a vow")—a small model, usually of wax or wood, of a healed limb or organ meant to be displayed at the shrine to advertise the saint's prowess. Sometimes sick people measured their height with a string and then used it as the wick for a slender candle. Coiled into a *rotula* ("trindle" in English), it was left at the shrine in thanksgiving and as payment. Conversely, if a saint failed to deliver on a promise, people might take revenge, occasionally even attacking the shrines of saints who failed to protect them. A popular thirteenth-century story told how a woman who unsuccessfully petitioned the Virgin Mary to release her imprisoned son from captivity stole the infant Jesus from a statue of the Virgin and Child and held it for ransom.

Like travelers in every age, medieval pilgrims collected souvenirs at saints' shrines to take back home. But often these souvenirs were meant to make a saint's power portable. At many shrines pilgrims could buy small lead ampullae filled with water mixed with dust from the saint's tomb meant to be used medicinally. But sometimes people sprinkled it on their fields and then buried the ampulla there to promote fertile crops. Some shrines offered small tin mirrors for sale. Pinned to pilgrims' hats, they were intended to catch and store the spiritual energy emanating from the relics so that it could be taken back home.

Saints were so vital to medieval religion and people could be so haphazard about whom they venerated that sainthood was as often an ascribed as an achieved status as people attributed holiness to local religious celebrities or to anyone who suffered some unusual or seemingly unjust death. Several popes from the late eleventh century onward tried to supervise the process of canonization, and finally in 1234 Pope Gregory IX made it strictly a papal prerogative. But official pronouncements could not stem the popular enthusiasm for making saints. In surely the strangest case of popular canonization, the Dominican inquisitor Stephen of Bourbon (or Étienne de Bourbon, *d. ca.* 1262), touring near Lyons, heard country people praise their local St. Guinefort, especially famed for healing sick children. On investigation, he was stunned to learn that Guinefort was actually a greyhound, popularly canonized after it had saved its master's infant son from a serpent. Though some scholars would point to this episode as an example of how thinly Christianity had penetrated the European countryside even at this late date, others see in it a sincere, if misinformed, attempt by ordinary people to accommodate what they knew about Christian doctrine to their local customs and folklore.

The case of the fictitious St. Wilgefortis, whose cult arose in the fifteenth century, suggests how the popular religious imagination generated saints from the slimmest evidence. Her name probably derives from the Old German "hilge Vartz" ("holy face"), itself a translation of "Volto Santo," the name of a statue of the crucified Christ venerated in the Italian city of Lucca. Her legend portrayed her as a Christian princess vowed to virginity whose father tried to force her to marry a pagan king. To thwart the wedding, she prayed to be made repulsive and consequently sprouted a beard. Her furious father then ordered her to be crucified. Known as St. Liberata in France, St. Librada in Spain, St. Kümmernis in German lands (where her name means "grief" or "anxiety"), and St. Uncumber in England, she was venerated by people seeking relief from their tribulations, especially by women seeking to "liberate" (or disencumber) themselves from their abusive husbands. But her cult seems to spring from a misinterpretation of Lucca's "Volto Santo," which is an early Byzantine crucifix, depicting a bearded but androgynous Christ crowned and dressed in a floor-length tunic instead of a loincloth. This unfamiliar iconography led westerners to create a narrative to explain the image.

Outranking all other saints in power and popularity, the Virgin Mary took such hold of the medieval imagination that she sometimes seemed to supplant even God; to some extent people perceived her as a goddess, the *fourth* person of the Trinity. The names by which she was known—Notre Dame or Our Lady, Madonna—were the reverent forms of address applied to noblewomen. She stood as the "Queen of Heaven," the ultimate, merciful, motherly mediatrix between her son—whose power to judge the living and the dead could be intimidating—and humanity. By the twelfth century her popularity was unrivaled among Christians as miracle stories spread that emphasized her mercy for even the greatest sinners if they held her in regard and prayed the Hail Mary.

Items of her clothing, strands of her hair, and even purported drops of her breast milk were widely venerated. Her house in Nazareth was believed to have been transported to Loreto in Italy, where it became a major site of pilgrimage. A replica of that house built at Walsingham made it a major center of pilgrimage in England. By the thirteenth century, lay people began praying to her through the rosary, a sequence of 150 Hail Marys (echoing the 150 psalms of the monastic Divine Office) interspersed with Our Fathers counted off on a circlet of beads—an item that frequently appeared as a bequest in lay people's last wills from the fourteenth century onward.

THE HOST

By the eleventh century, most theologians agreed that the bread (or host) and wine consecrated at mass were converted into the real body and blood of Christ, an idea confirmed by the doctrine of transubstantiation declared at the Fourth Lateran Council in 1215. Prompted by this idea of the real presence of Christ, church leaders grew wary of allowing lay people to take communion with both the consecrated bread and wine for fear that the sacrament could be desecrated, since the wine was more easily spilled. Consequently, by the early thirteenth century, almost all lay people received only the communion bread. Moreover, as regard for the real presence of Christ in the sacrament increased, theologians and canon lawyers argued that allowing lay people to receive communion regularly might diminish their respect for this principal Christian sacrament. By another decree of the Fourth Lateran Council, therefore, all Christians were legally obliged to take communion only once a year at Easter, though in some dioceses they also received it at Christmas and Pentecost. The effect of this restriction of communion was to magnify lay people's

Pilgrims at the Shrine of Edward the Confessor. *A 13th-century drawing of pilgrims at the shrine of Edward the Confessor. Holes cut into the sides of the shrine enable the devout to get closer to the relics.* THE J. PAUL GETTY MUSEUM. REPRODUCED BY PERMISSION.

reverence and awe for the host. Popular stories began circulating about people skeptical of the real presence who suddenly saw a miniature figure of Jesus in the host after it was consecrated, or who discovered real flesh and blood in their mouth when they received communion. In fact, lay people's growing devotion to the host helped to inspire a new ritual gesture in the mass. By the late twelfth century, priests, who prayed the mass with their backs to the congregation, began elevating the wafer of bread and chalice of wine above their heads while saying the words of consecration so that people could see them and partake in a "spiritual communion" that conveyed some degree of spiritual blessing. People's enthusiasm for seeing the consecrated host led them to endow money to purchase tall candles to be raised alongside the host at the elevation to spotlight it in dim churches. It also led some townspeople, always eager to multiply their spiritual capital, to rush from church to church on Sundays, hoping to see several elevations even if it meant abandoning one mass in midservice.

Pious fervor for the host ultimately led to creation of the very popular feast of Corpus Christi (the body of Christ), which was inspired by the laywoman Juliana of Liège (also known as Juliana of Cornillon, *ca.* 1193–1258). She claimed that Christ appeared to her and urged her to promote a new feast honoring the host.

When theologians offered no objection, the bishop of Liège allowed the first celebration of Corpus Christi in 1246. Pope Urban IV declared it to be a universal feast of the church in 1264, and by the fourteenth century, public processions of the host on the feast of Corpus Christi (the Thursday after Trinity Sunday) were held in towns and villages throughout Europe. It stands as one of the best examples of how popular religious impulses could affect church rituals.

In the Christian arsenal, there was no more powerful weapon against evil than the host. People believed that public processions of it could stave off plagues or put out fires. Prior to the thirteenth century, when the church outlawed it, one type of trial by ordeal required the accused to swallow a host, which people believed would stick in a guilty person's throat. But it could be put to more mundane uses. An early thirteenth-century miracle story told how a woman crumbled up a stolen host and scattered it on her cabbage patch to expel caterpillars. Another story recounted how a woman put a host in her beehive to cure her sick bees; out of instinctive reverence, the bees built a tiny wax chapel for it, complete with a belfry. People widely believed that evildoers stole hosts by holding them unswallowed in their mouths at communion and then used them to work harmful spells. Church leaders deemed this sort of defilement of the

A CURE FOR AN INTERMITTENT FEVER

FROM THE COMMON PLACE BOOK COMPILED IN THE EARLY 1470s BY ROBERT RAYNES, THE REEVE OF THE VILLAGE OF ACLE IN ENGLAND.

(In Latin) In the name of the Father, and of the Son, and of the Holy Spirit, amen. Peter was lying on a marble stone with a fever. Jesus came up and said to him, "Peter, why are you lying here?" He said to him, "Lord, I lie here from a bad fever." And Jesus said to him, "Get up and let it go." And he rose up from the fiery furnace and let it go. Peter said to him, "Lord, I ask you that whoever carries on himself in writing these words with my name, let no fevers harm him, neither with chills nor heat, neither diurnal, biduous, tertian, quartan, quintan, sextan, septan, octan, nor nonan." And Jesus said to him, "Peter, let it be as you have asked."

"Lord, by your will and power may this your servant, N., be defended without end from all evil fevers. In the name of Jesus, I sign myself with the [Greek] letter *tau* [i.e., τ]. Jesus of Nazareth, King of the Jews, Son of God, have mercy on me, amen. And let five Our Fathers and five Hail Marys and one Creed be said in honor of our Lord Jesus Christ, and an Our Father, Hail Mary, and Creed in honor of St. Peter the Apostle."

SOURCE: From *Medieval Popular Religion, 1000–1500: A Reader,* ed. by John Shinners. Peterborough: Broadview Press, 1997, pp. 337–338.

host as a particularly horrible crime. To prevent it the Fourth Lateran Council ordered churches to lock up their hosts and holy chrism (consecrated oil) so that no one could use them for sacrilegious ends.

MAGIC

Until the latter half of the twentieth century, many historians studying the religion of ordinary medieval people tended to regard it as little more than a patchwork of primitive magic and superstition. Profiting from insights of cultural anthropologists, nowadays scholars realize that the line between orthodox Christian belief and practice and what we would call magic is very thin, especially since the prescientific world view of the Mid-

dle Ages believed that magical power was real. In fact, no matter how devout Christians were, most people did not hesitate to use whatever religious techniques were available to them to cope with life's crises; popular religion is always and everywhere open-minded about alternatives to official religion.

For medieval people, the border between this world and the supernatural world was fragile and easily breached. Passing back and forth between these spheres, benign and malevolent spirits were at large in the everyday world. In particular, all sorts of demons infested the earth; St. Bonaventure (*ca.* 1217–1274) claimed that they were everywhere, "swarming like flies." Many other elemental spirits (elves, fairies, gnomes, and goblins), half-human monsters (werewolves, vampires, changelings), and ghosts roamed about, sometimes causing minor annoyances like souring milk or harassing livestock, sometimes bringing death and disasters such as fire, wilted crops, and plague. People, therefore, felt compelled to arm themselves with an arsenal of spiritual weapons both to tap the power of God and his saints to work on their behalf and to protect themselves from harassment by diabolical forces. The church encouraged the use of prayers, the sign of the cross, holy water, and blessed candles as effective agents against evil. But popular religion frequently turned to various kinds of ritual magic for added protection. Church leaders routinely compiled lists of forbidden charms, spells, and other prohibited practices such as predicting the future, enchanting lovers with potions, invoking evil spirits, ascertaining the state of the souls of the dead, and using incantations to heal the sick or to find lost objects. Bishops warned that baptismal fonts should have lockable covers to prevent people from stealing the blessed water and using it for magical purposes.

Although church officials cautioned lay people against superstitious practices, there was little they could practically do to curb all but the most flagrant abuses. In fact clergy did not discourage people's recourse to magical amulets and charms so long as they employed Christian formulas. Manuals for confessors, for example, often asked whether, when gathering medicinal herbs, people had said incantations other than the Our Father. Amulets for curing headaches, toothaches, bleeding, and other maladies were made by writing Christian prayers on parchment and wearing them. One popular amulet, written on a parchment strip supposedly as long as Jesus was tall, could be wrapped around the abdomen of women in labor. Finger rings made from pennies collected from churches on Good Friday and inscribed with the names of Jesus and the Three Kings could cure intestinal cramps. Most physicians' manuals included prayer charms and recommended writing the name of Jesus or a saint or making the sign of the cross on an afflicted part of the body.

A widely used book of blessings compiled at the end of the thirteenth century suggests how intricately ideas about spiritual power were interwoven through medieval culture. It contained blessings for food eaten at Easter feasts; for pilgrims and their gear; for the first fruits of the harvest; for bread and grapes; for a new house, boat, well, or field; for sick animals; for weapons and war banners; and an omnibus blessing "for anything you wish." Other manuals offered blessings against bad weather (it had long been the custom to toll church bells to ward off thunderstorms), to aid women in childbirth, to cure weak eyes, or to consecrate a new knight and his sword.

PURGATORY AND INDULGENCES

In the early centuries of Christianity, believers were faced with a stark fate at death: the good went to heaven; those with unforgiven mortal sins went to hell. But many theologians, speculating about the state of the souls of individuals between their deaths and the Last Judgment of all humanity, believed that prayers on behalf of the dead might benefit them. Driven in part by popular belief and practice, these conjectures led to the evolution in the twelfth and thirteenth centuries of the idea of purgatory, a way station between heaven and hell where the souls of those dying with less serious, venial sins or penance still left to perform for confessed sins could be purged of their guilt through suffering and then admitted to heaven. Since purgatory offered the hope of salvation to ordinary, imperfect Christians, as its theology developed and was spread through preaching, popular Christianity accumulated an array of techniques to lessen the time spent suffering there. In particular, Christians sought ways to accumulate indulgences, which erased some specified amount of time from their sentence in purgatory. When Boniface VIII offered a plenary (or full) indulgence to all who visited the major churches of Rome during the jubilee year of 1300, hundreds of thousands of pilgrims from across Europe swarmed to the city. The jubilee indulgence proved so popular that later popes were persuaded first to reduce the period between jubilees from one hundred to fifty years (in 1343) and then from fifty to twenty-five (in 1470). More common were partial indulgences, which deleted a shorter span of penance, usually forty days. These could be gained by a variety of prayers and charitable acts such as building or repairing churches and other religious buildings or roads and bridges, offering alms to the poor, and visiting saints' shrines.

The theology of indulgences required those receiving them to be contrite and confessed of their sins through the sacrament of penance before they took effect, but the popular understanding of them seldom bothered with this detail. Most people regarded them as instantly valid waivers, and many became obsessed about collecting them, seeking to stockpile as many as they could before death. Indulgences and the periods of time granted by them snowballed; by the fifteenth century they could be measured in thousand of years.

Pope Sixtus VI made the last step in the evolution of indulgences in 1476 when he officially ruled that they could be effectively applied by the living to souls already in purgatory, a practice that had been in use since the thirteenth century. In fact, when medieval people encountered ghosts, the latter were usually deemed to be unfortunate souls suffering in purgatory and seeking intercessory prayers and masses from the living. Often a certificate of indulgence was buried with the dead, guaranteeing them a sort of first-class ticket through purgatory.

The most powerful intercession that the living could perform on behalf of the souls in purgatory was to have masses celebrated for them. Wealthy nobility and merchants could hire chantry priests to pray a daily mass for their departed relatives in their private chapels or the side chapels of churches and cathedrals. But even people of limited means often left a few pennies in their last wills to have a priest say a least a few masses for their souls. One of the chief attractions of the religious guilds and fraternities that mushroomed across Europe from the fourteenth century onward was the ability of guild members to pool their resources to hire priests to offer masses on behalf of all their dead members.

LATER TRENDS

From the eleventh century onward, as social conditions stabilized across Europe and Christian doctrine was more widely disseminated, groups of lay people and dissident clergy sporadically joined in popular religious movements that challenged official doctrine. Many were fleeting, but from the twelfth century onward some were organized well enough that they endured as serious heresies in the church. Some of these, such as the Cathars (or Albigensians) of southern France, preached doctrines radically different from Christianity. Others, such as the Waldensians founded by Peter Valdès, a rich merchant of Lyons who renounced his wealth and embraced poverty as the highest Christian ideal, tapped into the same sort of spiritual yearnings that inspired St. Francis and the early Franciscans a generation later. In England in the late fourteenth and early fifteenth centuries, a movement called Lollardy formed among some members of the middling classes which attacked clerical privilege and promoted translating scripture into English so that lay people could read it for themselves.

All these movements were violently suppressed by the official church. But by the later Middle Ages, many thoroughly orthodox lay people were actively and devoutly plotting their own religious lives. Most parishes had religious guilds or confraternities, which sponsored masses for the souls of their dead members, paid for members' funerals, endowed candles in honor of the guilds' patron saints, sponsored religious processions, and performed other acts of charity. Lay people also became "tertiaries" or associate members of religious orders, especially the mendicant houses, which required a more rigorous spiritual regimen from them, but allowed them to live married lives and carry on with their secular occupations. Two movements centered in the Netherlands and Rhineland suggest the confidence lay people had in setting their own spiritual courses. The thirteenth-century beguines were laywomen living in community but without vows; the late fourteenth-century Brothers and Sisters of the Common Life likewise took no religious vows and lived by no religious rule. Expressing their spiritual aspirations through communal prayer and meditation, especially meditation on the life of Jesus, they created the movement known as the *Devotio Moderna,* or the New Devotion.

The growing merchant classes of the towns and the old feudal aristocracy were increasingly literate. The richest among them commissioned lavish books of hours, which were basic prayer books in Latin and the vernacular containing psalms and prayers extracted from the monastic Divine Office, litanies, and other popular prayers. These devotional books allowed literate lay people to cultivate a more interior devotional life, somewhat less obsessed with concrete signs and wonders.

Though saints and their relics and shrines never dimmed in popularity, devotion to Christ and the Blessed Virgin increased from the thirteenth century onward. By the fourteenth century, emotional meditation on Christ's passion became increasingly important in lay devotion. The Five Wounds of Christ, the Three Nails of the Crucifixion, the Instruments of the Passion, the image of Christ as the suffering Man of Sorrows, and his Seven Words on the cross were revered through votive masses, prayers, and verses, and depicted in art. People wore drawings of the Five Wounds as amulets against evil or to stanch wounds. Usually these new devotions had hundreds of years of indulgences attached to them.

Likewise, devotion to the Blessed Virgin became more emotionally affective as popular attention focused on her role as the *Mater dolorosa,* or Sorrowful Mother, of the crucified Christ, a motif represented through the emerging popularity of depictions of the *Pietà*—Mary cradling her dead son.

As the Protestant Reformation rolled across Europe in the first decades of the 1500s, the web of beliefs and practices that had been the unifying glue of Christendom dissolved; many Christians readily welcomed new ways to put their beliefs into practice. Relying on the words of scripture alone to sanction Christian belief and practice, radical Protestant reformers vigorously attacked most of the traditional elements of medieval popular religion, focusing particular scorn on the veneration of saints and the cult of Mary, which they deemed idolatrous. Many historians now argue that the Reformation succeeded so quickly not because ordinary people were lukewarm about their old beliefs and so were eagerly willing to abandon them for something new but because the Protestant emphasis on the individual reading of scripture and the priesthood of all believers appealed to Christians already deeply involved in charting their spiritual destinies.

BIBLIOGRAPHY

PRIMARY WORKS

Caesarius of Heisterbach. *The Dialogue on Miracles.* 2 vols. Translated by H. von E. Scott and C. C. Swinton Bland. London: Routledge, 1929. An early thirteenth-century digest of stories about all aspects of medieval belief.

Jacobus de Voragine. *The Golden Legend: Readings on the Saints.* 2 vols. Translated by William Granger Ryan. Princeton, N.J.: Princeton University Press, 1993. An essential mid-thirteenth-century collection of saints' lives and miracles and the popular customs associated with them.

The Malleus Maleficarum of Heinrich Kramer and James Sprenger. Translated by Montague Summers. 1928. Reprint, New York: Dover, 1971. Published in 1486 for inquisitors investigating alleged witches, the *Malleus Maleficarum* (Hammer of witches) summarizes medieval theologians' and canonists' ideas about demons and witchcraft and permissible ways to combat them.

Shinners, John, ed. *Medieval Popular Religion, 1000–1500: A Reader.* Peterborough, Canada: Broadview, 1997. An anthology of translated sources.

SECONDARY WORKS

Cuming, G. J., and Derek Baker, eds. *Popular Belief and Practice.* Studies in Church History, 8. Cambridge, U.K.: Cambridge University Press, 1972.

Duffy, Eamon. *The Stripping of the Altars: Traditional Religion in England, 1400–1580.* New Haven and London: Yale University Press, 1992. A groundbreaking study of late medieval piety: thorough, learned, and balanced.

Finucane, Ronald C. *Miracles and Pilgrims: Popular Beliefs in Medieval England.* London: Dent, 1977. A wide-ranging survey of the place of pilgrimage in medieval life.

Fletcher, Richard. *The Barbarian Conversion: From Paganism to Christianity.* New York: Holt, 1997. A comprehensive account of how Christianity spread throughout Europe's Middle Ages.

Flint, Valerie I. J. *The Rise of Magic in Early Medieval Europe.* Princeton, N.J.: Princeton University Press, 1991. A detailed, perceptive study; essential for understanding how the medieval church adopted popular non-Christian magical practices.

Gurevich, Aron. *Medieval Popular Culture: Problems of Belief and Perception.* Translated by János M. Bak and Paul A. Hollingsworth. Cambridge, U.K.: Cambridge University Press, 1988.

Jansen, Katherine Ludwig. *The Making of the Magdalen: Preaching and Popular Devotion in the Later Middle Ages.* Princeton, N.J.: Princeton University Press, 2000.

Le Goff, Jacques. *The Birth of Purgatory.* Translated by Arthur Goldhammer. Chicago: University of Chicago Press, 1984.

Os, Henk van, et al., eds. *The Art of Devotion in the Late Middle Ages in Europe, 1300–1500.* Translated by Michael Hoyle. Princeton, N.J.: Princeton University Press, 1994.

Rubin, Miri. *Corpus Christi: The Eucharist in Late Medieval Culture.* Cambridge, U.K.: Cambridge University Press, 1991.

Schmitt, Jean-Claude. *Ghosts in the Middle Ages: The Living and the Dead in Medieval Society.* Translated by Teresa Lavender Fagan. Chicago: University of Chicago Press, 1998.

Sumption, Jonathan. *Pilgrimage: An Image of Medieval Religion.* Totowa, N.J.: Rowman and Littlefield, 1975. A classic introduction to medieval saints and pilgrimage.

Swanson, R. N. *Religion and Devotion in Europe, c. 1215–c. 1515.* Cambridge, U.K.: Cambridge University Press, 1995. An approachable and informative survey of popular religion in the High and Later Middle Ages.

Thomas, Keith. *Religion and the Decline of Magic: Studies in Popular Beliefs in Sixteenth- and Seventeenth-Century England.* London: Weidenfeld and Nicolson, 1971.

Trinkhaus, Charles, and Heiko Oberman, eds. *The Pursuit of Holiness in Late Medieval and Renaissance Religion.* Studies in Medieval and Reformation Thought, vol. 10. Leiden, Netherlands: Brill, 1974.

Van Engen, John. "The Christian Middle Ages as an Historiographical Problem." *American Historical Review* 91 (1986): 519–552. An important overview of the twentieth-century historiography of popular religion.

Vauchez, André. *The Laity in the Middle Ages: Religious Beliefs and Devotional Practices.* Edited by Daniel E. Bornstein; translated by Margery J. Schneider. Notre Dame, Ind.: University of Notre Dame Press, 1993.

Webb, Diana. *Pilgrims and Pilgrimage in the Medieval West.* London: Tauris, 1999.

JOHN SHINNERS

[See also **DMA:** Beguines and Beghards; Book of Hours; Brethren of the Common Life; Cathars; Corpus Christi, Feast of; Feasts and Festivals, European; Heresies, Western European; Indulgences; Magic and Folklore, Western European; Mass, Liturgy of the; Missions and Missionaries, Christian; Pilgrimage, Western European; Purgatory, Western Concept of; Relics; Virgin Mary in Theology and Popular Devotion; Waldensians; **Supp:** Christopher, St.; Demons; Ghosts; Paganism and Pagan Gods, Survival of; Pilgrim Souvenirs.]

RIBĀṬ. Long considered an Islamic fortified monastery with both religious and military components, the widespread existence of such an institution has now been called into question. According to older historiography, a *ribāṭ* was essentially a fortress, found in frontier areas from Seville to Samarkand. Individuals, called *murābitīn,* volunteered to defend Islam and were housed in the *ribāṭ.* The majority stayed only for a short time, perhaps a period of months, but some may have vowed to remain for their lifetimes. It was considered a pious deed to found or support a *ribāṭ,* and in some areas being buried in or near the *ribāṭ* brought spiritual benefits. Some historians have seen a parallel between the development of Catholic military orders, such as the Templars and the Hospitallers, in this combination of war and religion, but no direct influences have been found.

Recent scholarship, however, has questioned the translation of the term *ribāṭ,* preferring to see it as a verbal noun rather than as an actual place or building; that is, *ribāṭ* is an act, not a building. The word signifies "strengthening" or "linking" and thus was associated with the gathering of mounted warriors for battle— "rebato" in Spanish, for example, means the actions of a group of horsemen. By the early Islamic period, it developed the meaning of "spending time at the frontier" and was often associated with jihad. Just as mujahideen are those who go on jihad, *murābitīn* are those who go on *ribāṭ.* Much of the evidence for the existence of *ribāṭ* buildings derives from later chronicles that recast the history of the conquest and Islamification of much of the outer Islamic world as achieved by pious volunteers fighting on the frontiers out of faith rather than by mercenaries and armies that likely did much of the fighting.

Buildings called *ribāṭ* did exist. Often, however, the term was used as a synonym for caravansary, an inn for caravans, such as the Ribāṭ-i-Sharif in northwest Iran, on the road between Bukhara and Samarkand, or it referred to hospices for visitors and resting places for messengers in government service. Indeed, there seems to be little discernable difference between the architectural plan for a caravansary and a *ribāṭ.* North Africa and the Magreb may be one area where *ribāṭs* did serve a military purpose. Fortified *ribāṭs* could be found along the Tunisian coast, such as at Sfax, Susa, Tripoli, and Monastir. The *ribāṭ* in the latter city is the oldest, founded around 796 to protect the coast against raiding. It also was said to be a link in a chain of signal towers along the North African coast, from Alexandria to Tangiers. Whether it was staffed by volunteers or not, service in the *ribāṭ* was considered particularly meritorious. The *ribāṭ* became the mausoleum for local aristocrats as well as the Zirid dynasty. An imam who visited it in the early twelfth century commented that the *murābitīn* did not live there but had become local landowners, yet they still received the charitable donations accorded to the *ribāṭ*. He may well have been displeased by their abandonment of their ascetic duties rather than any military ones. In the later Islamic period, the term was used to refer to Sufi monasteries, particularly in Seljuk Turkish areas.

BIBLIOGRAPHY

Bosworth, C. Edmund. "The City of Tarsus and the Arab-Byzantine Frontier." *Oriens* 33 (1992): 268–286.

Chaabi, Jacqueline. "La fonction du ribat à Baghdad du Ve siècle au début du VIIe siècle." *Revue des études islamiques* 43 (1974): 101–121.

Lézine, Alexandre. *Le Ribat de Sousse, suivi de notes sur le ribat de Monastir.* Tunis: La Rapide, 1956.

CHRISTOPHER HATCH MACEVITT

[See also **DMA:** Jihad.]

RICARDUS ANGLICUS (*ca.* 1160–1242) was the first Englishman to become a professor of canon law at Bologna. His identity was for a long time in doubt, since numerous twelfth- and thirteenth-century Englishmen would have been called Magister Ricardus, but research has demonstrated that the canonist was Richard de Mores (or de Morins), prior of Dunstable from 1202 to 1242. Born in Lincolnshire, Richard seems to have studied and taught canon law in Paris. He published his first work, *Quaestiones decretales,* there about 1186–1187. This work consists of the text of special lectures given on Fridays in which the master raised and answered questions of canonistic doctrine brought up by the *Decretum* of Gratian. After leaving Paris, Richard may have returned to England to teach, but it is unknown where. About 1191 he reappeared in Bologna as a professor of canon law, and he remained there until about 1198. It was during these years that Richard completed his oeuvre of legal scholarship.

After Bologna he returned to England, perhaps to become a canon of the Augustinian priory of Merton. He was a Merton canon in 1202 when he was elected prior of the canons of Dunstable, a position he was to hold for the rest of his life. Only a deacon when he was elected, he was ordained a priest soon after. If we are not well informed about the first half of Richard's life, we are abundantly informed about the second half because it was Richard himself who kept the Dunstable Annals. They tell us about a prior and lawyer actively involved in the practice of law, both as a litigant and as a judge. He went to court to protect the priory's property, but often he was there as an ecclesiastical judge-delegate. Research has found mention of him as judge in forty-eight cases, nearly half of which he managed to bring to a conclusion through settlement and arbitration rather than judgment. In 1203, Richard also went on a diplomatic mission to Rome on behalf of the English king John. He returned to Rome again to take part in the Fourth Lateran Council in 1215. On the way back in 1216, Richard spent a year in Paris studying theology.

In the few years that Richard was in Bologna, he wrote or revised seven of his eight known works. The *Ordo iudiciarius,* or manual of civil procedure, was written in Paris or England before 1190. It shows the influence of the Anglo-Norman canonists who surrounded Richard before he went to Bologna. However, while in Italy, he revised the work, adding references to the new *Compilatio prima* of Bernard of Pavia, which was becoming a standard textbook in Bologna. Another important work, written about 1196–1198, was *Distinctiones decretorum,* part original observations, part collation and summary of works of earlier scholars concerning significant legal issues raised by the *Decretum* of Gratian. His other works were the *Summa brevis,* written about 1196–1198, an introductory summary of the *Decretum* marked by frequent use of verse, perhaps as a mnemonic device; two works on legal commonplaces, the no longer extant *Argumenta* or *Notabilia decretorum* and the more extensive *Generalia* or *Brocarda;* and two works on the *Compilatio prima,* the *Casus decretalium,* a case by case summary of the decretals, and a gloss, written toward the end of Richard's time in Bologna.

BIBLIOGRAPHY

STUDIES

Figueira, Robert C. "Ricardus de Mores and His *Casus decretalium:* The Birth of a Canonistic Genre." In *Proceedings of the Eighth International Congress of Medieval Canon Law.* Vatican City: Biblioteca Apostolica Vaticana, 1992.

Fowler-Magerl, Linda. *Ordo iudiciorum vel ordo iudiciarius: Begriff und Literaturgattung.* Frankfurt: V. Klostermann, 1984. Discusses Richard's procedural work.

Kuttner, Stephan. "Richardus Anglicus (Richard de Mores ou De Morins)." In *Dictionnaire du droit canonique.* Vol. 7. Paris: Librarie Letouzey, 1965.

Kuttner, Stephan, and Eleanor Rathbone. "Anglo-Norman Canonists of the Twelfth Century." *Traditio* 7 (1949–1951): 279–358.

Sayers, Jane E. *Papal Judges Delegate in the Province of Canterbury, 1198–1254: A Study in Ecclesiastical Jurisdiction and Administration.* London: Oxford University Press, 1971.

EDITIONS

"Die summa de ordine iudiciario des Ricardus Anglicus." In *Quellen zur Geschichte des römischen-kanonischen Prozesses im Mittelalter.* Edited by Ludwig Wahrmund. Vol. 2. Innsbruck: Wagner, 1915.

Luard, Henry Richards, ed. *Annales prioratus de Dunstaplia (A.D. 1–1297).* Volume 3 of *Annales monastici.* 1866. Reprint, Wiesbaden, Germany: Kraus Reprint, 1965.

Silano, Giulio. "The 'Distinctiones Decretorum' of Richardus Anglicus." Ph.D. diss., University of Toronto, 1982.

EMILY KADENS

[See also **DMA:** Decretals; Decretists; Gratian; Law, Canon: After Gratian.]

RITUAL, CIVIC. The historical study of ritual has drawn upon the fields of sociology, anthropology, and ethnography. At key times, a fertile dialogue has occurred between creative historians and social scientists.

THE CONCEPT

The study of ritual is intimately tied to the historical sociology of religion. In *Elementary Forms of Religious Life* (1912) Émile Durkheim interprets ritual as the scaffolding of any society's collective consciousness and cultural system: rites make social roles and beliefs concrete. In *The Forest of Symbols* (1967) Victor Turner defines ritual as "formal behavior for occasions not given over to technological routine, having reference to beliefs in mystical beings or powers." Clifford Geertz focuses equally on religious content in *The Interpretation of Cultures* (1973), interpreting ritual as "consecrated behavior" and as a performance that represents a set of cultural symbols. Turner and Geertz were fascinated primarily by the anthropology of religious symbols. This fundamental interest in the sacred explains their "mystical" approach and their disengagement with secular rites.

Those interested in a broader application of ritual theory might find the conceptualization of Bradd Shore more useful. In *Culture in Mind* (1996) Shore defines rituals as a highly complex set of stylized actions and includes daily gestures as well as solemn coronations. David Kertzer likewise casts the net widely in *Ritual, Politics, and Power* (1988) by identifying ritual as action wrapped in a web of symbolism. In *Ritual Theory, Ritual Practice* (1992) Catherine Bell argues that ritual is essentially social action and faults early anthropologists for creating an arbitrary dichotomy between belief and ritual, with ritual as action derived from belief. In *Public Life in Renaissance Florence* (1980) Richard Trexler studies the efficacy of rituals as an instrument to shape social and political life.

For the study of medieval ritual, however, it is essential to distinguish between social scientific theories of ritual and how medieval people developed and understood ritualization. Theories of ritual cover a broad range of formal behavior, including repeated sequences of collective and individual actions for expressing respect, sympathy, identity, jubilation, and mourning. These solemnities elicit a significant response both from the actors (the couple of a royal marriage, for example) and from audience (the cheering subjects). But medieval contemporaries had their own ways of framing and understanding ritual action. In *The Dangers of Ritual* (2001) Philippe Buc provides an elegant synthesis of the medieval classifications of ritual and its implicit anthropology: ritual is "a plurality of solemnities," a "native classification," fitting within a "wider set of characteristics." Medieval ceremonialists used the term "rite" to characterize ritual's role in securing right conduct, pomp, and tradition.

Using recent anthropological theory alone to decode medieval rituals would be a methodological error. Buc, with a nod to Geertz's "thick description," rightly warns against the unsophisticated use of social scientific models in the absence of sensitivity to indigenous conceptualizations. Anthropological theory, on the other hand, offers useful frameworks of analysis, particularly when contemporaries fail to explain the meaning of their rites and gestures. But historians should be careful not to mix freely medieval and twentieth-century science categories, not to force medieval documents and discourses inside heuristic categories contemporaries never had. The best approach should ferret out the local intentions behind the behaviors displayed in medieval ceremony, recognizing the ambiguity and pluralism of much medieval ritual, meticulously respecting the contextuality of medieval narratives of ritual, and using, where appropriate, the insights of contemporary theory to extend the possible meaning of the ritual acts under study.

Buc highlights the intentions of actors in medieval ritual according their own vocabulary. He also discusses what medieval writers thought happened in the minds of performers when ceremonies and ordinary events occurred that they themselves failed to define as ritualized behavior. The vast majority of these solemnities had liturgical elements and served either explicitly religious or political purposes. They evince strong commitment to ideals of old traditions and of right conduct. Such a medieval conceptualization of ritual as the barometer of tradition can be found in a range of documents: juridical regulations, instructions for medieval princes, informal catalogs of writers and philosophers on politically significant rituals. It can also be detected in orally transmitted sets of rules of behavior, to which medieval chronicles refer. The frequency and repetition of these statements show that unwritten habits and customs follow strong prescriptions regulated by long-standing ideals considered normalized. Historians gain much by reading ritual through the lens and vocabulary of medieval writers and participants, but anthropology and sociology can extend our understanding of these rites so long as medieval texts are respected on their own terms.

Conceptualizations of ritual have changed much over time. In the Middle Ages theology dominated, with ritual conceived as the acts prescribed by prior beliefs. Traditional Catholic rituals were largely repudiated by sixteenth-century Protestant theologians, who argued that rites had superseded their theological referents, thereby becoming empty. Luther and other Protestant theologians introduced a radical conceptual disjunction between sacramental and religious rites, on the one side, and civic and political solemnities, on the other side. In Protestant theory, ritual had a mystical dimension, while ceremony had a political and pragmatic character. Having made as firm a distinction between religious ritual and secular ceremony as they desired, early modern Protestants freely mixed religion and politics and enacted rituals even as they criticized Catholic attachment to their rites. While Protestants might rail against Catholic processions, they themselves would parade about clutching Bibles and psalm books in tightly sequenced ritual acts.

ORIGINS OF THE STUDY OF RITUALS IN HISTORIOGRAPHY

One of the first historians interested in this topic, Numa-Denys Fustel de Coulanges, borrowed a sizable amount of the methodology of his work *La cité antique* (1864) from contemporary sociologists. Fustel de Coulanges discovered links between ritual and power and was interested in the question of how civic rites foster identity and freedom.

In 1912 the sociologist Émile Durkheim identified in religious rituals several of the crucial characteristics that much later were understood as typical for civic rituals and social networks: the reinforcement of group solidarity, the reaffirmation of common bonds, and the imposition of self-discipline. In 1909 Arnold van Gennep published *Rites de passage,* and in 1922 Lucien Lévy-Brühl published *La mentalité primitive.* The impact of these two classic works can be discerned from 1929 onward, most noticeably in the French journal *Annales,* with its interdisciplinary approach. The cofounder Lucien Febvre was a fervent champion of the history of ideas and mentalities, paying keen interest to ritual. Marc Bloch extended these perspectives in the seminal *Les rois thaumaturges* (1924), a study of the medieval royal touch. However remarkable Febvre and Bloch's attraction to anthropological theory, their contemporaries, positivist historians, largely ignored it. Similar disregard and disrespect by the then-dominating historiography afflicted two other works published between the world wars, dealing with medieval civic rituals: *Waning of the Middle Ages* (1919) by Johan Huizinga and *The Civilizing Process* (1939) by Norbert Elias. Huizinga explored the role of court rituals in the fifteenth century, while Elias analyzed especially quotidian rituals, such as eating and bodily manners.

The great upswing in studies of ritual occurred in the 1970s among historians such as Natalie Davis, Robert Muchembled, Richard Trexler, and Edward P. Thompson. These social historians were more attracted to Turner and van Gennep in formulating their ritual theory. But it was Clifford Geertz's book on the "theater state" in Bali in 1980 that represented a breakthrough in attention among historians to the study of ritual. To his already celebrated "thick description" model, popularized by Robert Darnton among European historians, Geertz added an explicit demand that ritual be no longer regarded in social scientific theory as a mere epiphenomenon of ideas. Ritual, Geertz argued, was not secondary propaganda of society's power brokers but reality itself. Geertz also popularized a semiotic dimension to the study of ritual, which dovetailed nicely with medievalists' concern with the primacy of original documents and native vocabularies.

Throughout the 1990s, medievalists revealed the same powerful role for ritual that Geertz found in traditional Bali—Geoffrey Koziol (1992) for the pardoning function of the French king in the tenth and eleventh centuries, Peter Arnade (1996) for the ceremonies in fifteenth-century Ghent.

FORMS AND TYPES OF RITUALS

The oldest form of ritual is body language, or corporal gestures. Begging pardon is a gesture of submission, the physical expression of the inferiority of a subject and the superiority of a ruler. Physical movements may also be collective in events such as processions, festivities, and warfare. A variant of nonverbal communication is the use of specific clothing to codify social distinction (scarlet costumes for nobles and wealthy burghers) or to structure a mass event (uniforms in a battle).

Rituals can also be expressed in oral and written communication. Codes of conduct for noblemen are prescribed in countless late medieval textbooks of chivalry. Rituals differ significantly depending on whether a society is dominated by either oral or written forms of communication: before 1050, communal rituals dominated, while in the period between 1050 and 1200 individual behavior and consciousness received more emphasis.

Rituals as images of power. Since Clifford Geertz compared the exercise of power in nineteenth-century Bali to a semiotics, or grammar, of theatrical spectacle, several historians, following the earlier but less explicitly theorized examples of Marc Bloch and Ernst Kantorowicz, focused on medieval state ceremony as rites of political legitimation. In *Sacred Void* (1991) David Parkin argues that political rituals serve as representations of power but also negotiate and transform power relations as much as they reify them.

The ultimate visualization of power is the ceremony of crowning and oath taking, which involves symbols, dialogues, and gestures that can be easily linked to the royal function. Coronation had a high degree of familiarity for the audience as it may have followed a pattern similar to initiation rituals of ordinary individuals. If a royal wedding was a spectacular celebration, the birth of a new prince produced a politically even more significant ritual: the public exhibition of the genitals of the newborn, essential since gender could be a crucial factor for the political stability of the country and the dynasty.

Funerals are another occasion for homages to the dynasty. In the early Middle Ages ritual gifts in graves aspired to transmit power across time. Burial rituals, like saints' lives, are as much cultural constructions of identities as they are mirrors of the deceased persons. In the late Middle Ages the death of a ruler caused insecurity since succession was never absolutely guaranteed. The funeral ceremony helped stabilize political power and soothe anxieties about changes in that power. The royal family and the political elites took measures to ensure that the representation of the emotions surrounding loss and continuity was not restricted to a short-term event with its symbolic black velvet decoration of the church and the black clothes of all the members of the prince's household. The funeral's procession of mourners was often transformed into a stone monument, a permanent meta-event. Sometimes twenty or more statuettes recreated a constant guard around the corpse and tomb of

the deceased prince, as in the mausoleum of the Burgundian duke Philip the Bold by Claus Sluter in Champmol (near Dijon), with its funeral procession in stone. A second device for turning a momentary into an eternal ritual was the foundation of a long-standing and prepaid series of prayers. Originally limited to princes and high society, this ritual became more widely popular as a consequence of massive urbanization and the increased insecurity resulting from the failure of protection networks for new immigrants in cities around 1300. Jacques Chiffoleau has called this mass psychological attitude the "comptabilité de l'au-delà" (an accounting of the hereafter) and explained the need for continued existence in an afterlife by the growth of enforced loneliness in real life. The panic caused by the Black Death beginning in 1348 stimulated the success of rituals like flagellation in order to implore forgiveness for a former life of sin and to prevent the risk of death.

Perhaps the event most beloved by medieval princes to champion and negotiate authority was the "joyous entry" ceremony. This entry was in essential ways a repetition of the crowning ceremony but with a fundamental shift in quality and meaning. While the crowning expressed the intimate connection between supernatural and earthly power, the entry was a constitutional necessity, expressing the recognition of the ruler by his subjects and idealizing the harmony between both. But the event had more than a legal significance. Direct contact with his subjects enabled the prince to assert authority and to involve a great part of the citizens emotionally by the pleasure of participatory processions and endless banquets. After a conflict the visit could turn into a ritual of the humiliation of the submissive city and eventually into one of reconciliation. As a last resort, princes used the entry ceremony to restore otherwise frayed relations with a town. In such delicate entries, citizens could strategically deploy sensitive symbolic elements to nourish rapport. The entry in Ghent in 1458 of the duke of Burgundy, Philip the Good, after he defeated the city in 1453 was brightened up by "tableaux vivants" (living pictures). The burghers staged a representation of Hubert and Jan van Eyck's *Adoration of the Lamb.* The use of this theme symbolized the court's Order of the Golden Fleece, in which the lamb is the central symbol of the chain. The Ghent entry illustrates how an ephemeral show could, with help of smart communication, become a functional dialogue between prince, urban elites, and masses. For ordinary people such an event was a unique chance for a real encounter with a normally distant ruler. This physical presence also provoked concrete expectations. Many entries became the theater of pardon granting and of the presentation of claims and protests. Such

Mourning. *The famous* pleurants *from tomb of Philip the Bold, completed in 1410 by Claus de Werve from the design of Claus Sluter. Now in the Musée des beaux arts, Dijon.* ART RESOURCE, NY. REPRODUCED BY PERMISSION.

rituals often turned into opportunities to realign political life. The claim of medieval burghers that their princes should regularly honor the urban space by visits could be interpreted as a need of urban populations to add a human face to the structures of political power.

From the ruler's vantage point, entries turned abstract political ideas into real moments, especially when they concerned unusual events. By contrast, representative institutions like the estates of counties and duchies, the Estates General, or the English Parliament were channels for permanent conversation about routine political affairs. Both the ritual of the entry and the daily grind of bargaining in representative institutions demonstrate the function of ritual to stimulate communication. In the estates the language of political ritual was that of diplomacy over taxes and law. Princes conferred trade privileges to foreign merchants that favored the regional economy. In return burghers rendered taxes to the ruler's treasury. The entry rituals put a higher premium upon the charisma of the prince because of their highly performative nature and their personalized agenda, with themes such as ransom for the imprisonment of the king's son or the planning of a crusade. The manifold

rituals were supposed to charm various audiences. Common people were wooed by extravagant distribution of drinks in public places, by music, and by theatrical performances and dances. Elites were pampered with fabulous banquets, like the Feast of the Pheasant of 1454 in Lille, at which Philip the Good solemnly vowed to undertake a crusade against the Turks after the fall of Constantinople.

Analysis of the medieval theater state and its ritual components profited much from Clifford Geertz. Two elements from his Balinese model are at work in the medieval context. The first is the identification of the ceremonial forms in the ritualized events and the institutional forms of the real decision making. The second is the functioning of the ritual as an archetypal event. The king acting in the entry is not only an individual of flesh and blood but also an icon, an image of an abstract notion, kingship.

Rituals in criminal prosecution and pardoning. Criminal investigations, convictions of offenders, executions of the condemned, and pardoning after conviction are routine procedures in medieval public justice that carry strong ritual elements, especially in the earlier Mid-

Humiliation. *Burghers kneel before the ducal couple Thomas of Savoy and Joanna of Constantinople, depicting the ritual of humiliation (of a defeated city) in this manuscript painting from* Privileges of Ghent and Flanders *(1453).* ÖSTERREICHISCHE NATIONALBIBLIOTHEK, VIENNA, MS 2583, FOL. 13R, 1241. REPRODUCED BY PERMISSION.

dle Ages. This was particularly true for the formal proofs of the ordeals, which were based on the belief that men needed supernatural intervention to establish the guilt of suspects. The ordeal originated in Germanic tribal law, brought to western Europe with the invaders in the sixth century. But as with so much of Germanic life, the ordeal was soon Christianized and largely accepted by secular and ecclesiastical rulers. In the course of the twelfth century, rulers, urban aldermen, and learned lawyers began to display distrust in these appeals to God to establish guilt or innocence. The cleric Galbert of Bruges was one of the first to register skepticism, referring in 1127 to contemporaries who harbored doubts about the rationality of ordeals. Finally the Fourth Lateran Council prohibited ordeals in 1215. Irrational and formalist procedures may have been more frequent in the early Middle Ages, but it would be a mistake to consider the contrast between the earlier and later phases of jurisprudence

as a pure dichotomy between irrational and rational forms of evidence. The two impulses in fact coexisted until the twelfth century. In Carolingian law, testimonies, written proofs, and inquests were generally used together with ordeals and judicial duels. But after 1200 the evolution toward more rational views in science, law, and custom left less space for irrationality in jurisprudence and gave more opportunities to hard evidence and the critical evaluation of facts. One should not overestimate, however, the degree of rational legal procedure in the later Middle Ages, with its frequent use of questionable testimonies and confessions after torture.

In the twelfth to fifteenth centuries rituals were not absent in the investigations of crime, but they assumed a totally different quality. The regulation most redolent of imagination is public penance and public humiliation for criminals and sinners, such as forced walks in the local streets. In fifteenth-century London customary law provided several public penances for prostitutes, such as cutting their hair before conducting them to a pillory. Prostitutes were also required to wear distinctive clothing for easy identification, with every city using specific signs—a yellow token in Hamburg, yellow shirts for pimps in Venice. The goal of such practices was stigmatization, the use of public shame and the discouraging of "deviant" social behavior. Executions also became a stage for ritual representation of exemplary punishment: horrifying spectacles of quartered men, women drowned in rivers. Punishments were also given visual representation, as in the diptych by Gerard David (1498), presenting in an extremely gruesome manner how Judge Cambyses was tortured and flayed alive after an unjust judgment. The painting was displayed in the courtroom where the aldermen of Bruges conducted their daily business of judgments. One step further is the materialization of the penance, a formula in which the accused could buy off the punishment by producing, in 1551 in the Flemish city of Furnes, a bronze replica of his fist, to be put on public display together with a text explaining the crime and sentence. An even more popular ritual to avoid imprisonment and banishment was to undertake a pilgrimage abroad, though by the late Middle Ages this option was allowed to be bought off, corrupting its original purpose as legal-cum-religious penance.

A second territory of late medieval juridical rituals was the settlement of disputes through reconciliation between two parties in a conflict, originally without a formal procedure. The idea had its origins in the Peace of God movement of the late tenth and eleventh centuries but was employed soon thereafter in order to prevent private wars in noble families and feuds between urban patricians, extremely frequent in the cities of northern Italy and the Low Countries in the thirteenth and fourteenth centuries. Medieval princes put great effort into this collective policy of prevention, but they also tried to settle individual conflicts by systems of formal compromise *(compositio)*. By a formal agreement before a representative of the ruler, the two parties promised to stop whatever conflict they were involved in, while the offender paid a fine to the offended.

The third variant of judicial ritual was the pardon procedure. Geoffrey Koziol, studying the system for tenth- and eleventh-century France, argued that the ruler's authority to grant pardon was based on his position as intercessor between God and his subjects. It is difficult to decide if the medieval king was acting in the name of God or as an ambitious politician. From the viewpoint of the subject, the supplication of pardon was

Pardon. *A French miniature (1524) representing the ritual of pardon just before the execution of the sire de Saint-Vallier. Paris, Bibliothèque nationale, MS français 17527, fol. 54r.* BIBLIOTHÈQUE NATIONALE DE FRANCE. REPRODUCED BY PERMISSION.

originally an act of religious devotion, but it was also a mark of self-humiliation toward a political leader. Koziol's analysis is valuable for the period he discusses, but the model is less applicable for the late Middle Ages. From 1300 on, references to divine authority in the pardons of secular rulers became meaningless. The new political culture was based on power politics and clientelism. New rituals replaced the traditional rules of the game. The legitimation for a remission letter mostly pays lip service to unconvincing formalist arguments, such as inexperience of young people, unaccountability of older men, and former services rendered to the crown. An effective argument, at least for male murderers, was hot anger (*chaude colle*) since it introduced the role of emotions into the procedure. Gender was indeed a determining factor: women were expected to be motivated by other emotions, such as jealousy and affection. Natalie Davis and Barbara Rosenwein have characterized the pardon technique as the ritualization of favoritism, while other historians have presumed a more shameless underlying discourse: the promotion of a protection system, as an escape route from normal administration of justice.

Urban ritual and identity. A city is a "lieu de mémoire" (realm of memory). The medieval city was well defined as a symbolic space protected by walls, inside which burghers enjoyed common rights. The citizenry considered itself part of a unique social, economic, and cultural unit. As a space of identity formation, the city was rife with symbols. Town fathers consciously employed public places to mount rituals to affirm urban consensus, but such rituals often failed to paper over social differences and conflict in general, as Richard Trexler noted for Florence and Peter Arnade for Ghent. In parades local and foreign merchants, craftsmen and workers, marched in hierarchical order, an effective way to confirm one's place in the community. However, constant collisions occurred between rich and poor, family and collective interests. Rituals could capture this tension or try to conceal it beneath a veneer of harmony. But no city succeeded in burying conflict through ceremony. Yet even the most hotly divided cities managed to create a sense of overall urban identity. Local boosterism often vied with cosmopolitan yearnings in such cities as Florence or Bruges. Locals at once celebrated their civic idioms and aped courtly or royal manners.

The built environment, both space and architecture, embodied urban identity. The practical function meshed with the symbolic valences and purposes. Tournai's town bell gave rhythm to working time, but it was also so symbolic of urban autonomy that it was destroyed after the 1332 revolt against the prince. Town gates re-

flected the symbolic contrast between outsiders and insiders: the ritual of coming in through the gate was a metaphor for admission into the urban community. The medieval Place de Grève on the Seine riverside in Paris was originally the site of the city's harbor, at the time also the main marketplace and the location for the town hall. Alongside these primary functions was its symbolic one as a location for execution of prominent convicts, for the mobilization of urban armed forces, for festivities and banquets, and for strikes and revolts.

Virgilio Titone and Lauro Martines have explored the function of medieval urban streets as a living theater, commissioned and controlled by aldermen, guilds, and cultural societies. In the cramped streets these authorities mounted music and drama, May tree dances, saint-day festivities, and civic processions for visiting foreign rulers and merchants. Most spectacular was the public ritual of the tournament: formally it was theater and romance full of literary allusions, while functionally it was practice for future battles and simulation of real war. Costumes and movements had symbolic meanings, well understood by those watching. In all these social actions individuals and groups used specific clothing and typical speech and gestures, with immense impact on identity formation. For Susan Crane these performances make a self and precede the social identity, not vice versa.

Daily rituals. Daily rituals range from rare life-changing events to regular outbursts of protest. Best known are the rites of passage of the human life cycle, transitions from one status in society or position in the life cycle to another. Historians of these rituals can draw upon a rich body of ethnography. According to Susan Crane, these life-cycle rites secure and develop personal identity from the cradle to the grave. Childbirth, for example, is followed by the ritual of purification of the mother—a real passage, as she first leaves the house with her child before being reintegrated into the community.

The medieval matrimonial rite of passage was crucial because it accompanied a fundamental shift for individuals, leaving their clans to create new social solidarities. The successive ceremonies of betrothal and marriage, with consent of the partners and benediction of a priest, were ecclesiastical rituals regulated by canon law, and public events such as the bans were published at the church door. But these ceremonies jockeyed regularly with profane rituals such as "créantailles" (prenuptial relations), which included gifts and promises, and clandestine marriages, both in absence of a priest.

Among other rituals, the formal emancipation from parents was crucial for young adults. Dancing ceremonies helped to identify marriage partners. Young men enjoyed rituals of knighting and introduction to hunting, essential in defining their male identity, which sometimes included a powerful allusion to King Arthur's glorious decapitation of giants. At the end of the life cycle the ritual of mourning accompanied death and helped the survivors to readapt to normal daily life.

A second series of rituals was linked to individual recreation and private festivities. Games often transcended pure leisure, turning into fertility rites during Lent and around Christmas. Johan Huizinga's *Homo Ludens* (1938) argues that civilization is in essence a game, with freely accepted rules, all rooted in rituals. For Huizinga chivalry was less a social concept than a game, thrilling for those playing and those observing.

A third category covers rites of violence, misrule, and conflict. The ritual of carnival was centered on the individual level on food. The contrast between the fasting of Lent and the excesses of carnival is represented in a painting by Pieter Bruegel as a comic tournament. Food and drink mark the passage into or out of a ritual state. On the collective level carnival was a festival that included reversal of social order, suspension of hierarchical rank, parody of officialdom, and raunchy folk humor. In *Rabelais and His World* (1968) Mikhail Bakhtin offered the safety-valve model of misrule. In his opinion carnival was a critical utopia that, by turning the city upside down socially, could be used as a force for change and progression. He developed a theory of carnival as resistance, as freedom from all domination, as a promise of a shift to a more egalitarian society. Carnival gave space for two lives: the official life of ordered disorder, respecting strict, hierarchical order, and the unrestricted life of the carnival square, in which mockery may turn into violent street action.

Charivari were gangs of youth, mainly boys, disrupting celebrations and privacy, their activities varying from innocent aubades to vandalism, from humiliation of the cuckold to mockery of remarrying widows, from spontaneous displays of virility and bravado to ritualized social criticism and censure. They may be viewed as another rite of passage, a youth's quest for admission in an adult world that is excessively hierarchical and closed off.

Natalie Davis popularized the notion of rites of violence, also explored for a later period in England by E. P. Thompson. For the crowd the riot becomes a ritual, and in lieu of wanton destruction the historian finds meaningful patterns of ritualized action that vary depending upon the social actors fomenting the discord.

INTERACTIONS BETWEEN SYSTEMS OF RITUAL

The general notion that rituals are linked to social class, are ethnically specific, and are functional tools for the construction of group and class identity has great value if refined. In medieval cities social and ethnic groups may as often have lived apart as in close proximity. In public, they constantly met, impressed, and imitated each other. Encounters between ethnic and religious cultures, like those of Christian, Islamic, and Jewish scientists and writers in twelfth-century Toledo, Perpignan, and Andalusia, produced interaction, acculturation, and the mutual recuperation of ritualized traditions.

Ivan Marcus (1996) demonstrated how easily medieval Jews could borrow innumerable elements of rituals, stories as well as gestures, from the dominant Christian culture because Christianity was celebrated in public ceremonies and therefore open to all contemporaries. This fusion happened partly deliberately, partly accidentally. In some contexts the interaction was intensified when similar Jewish and Christian cults existed, like the transition rituals at the beginning of formal education at age five or six. The Jewish spring festival of Shavuot was strongly influenced in the twelfth century by the Christian Pentecost feast. The Jewish representation of a child learning the alphabet on a teacher's lap could well have been inspired by the Christian icon of Mary holding Jesus.

More fusions unsurprisingly appear in the frequent references in civic rituals to scripture and in the use of religious symbolism and heraldic allegories. Visual and literary connections with heroes from antiquity (Alexander the Great) and later (King Arthur) were constantly used to embellish rulers. "Joyous entries" have roots in long-standing ecclesiastical and chivalric traditions, such as processions for new bishops and noble tournaments. A reconciliation entry can be compared with the coming of the Messiah, as the seminal work of Ernst Kantorowicz proved. The messages in joyous entries are often an ideological mixture because courts and cities collaborated to design and stage the event.

BIBLIOGRAPHY

Arnade, Peter. *Realms of Ritual: Burgundian Ceremony and Civic Life in Late Medieval Ghent.* Ithaca, N.Y.: Cornell University Press, 1996.

Arnade, Peter, Martha Howell, and Walter Simons, eds. "The Productivity of Urban Space in Northern Europe." *Journal of Interdisciplinary History* 32 (spring 2002): 515–704.

Bell, Catherine M. *Ritual Theory, Ritual Practice.* Oxford and New York: Oxford University Press, 1992.

Bertelli, Sergio. *The King's Body: Sacred Rituals of Power in Medieval and Early Modern Europe.* University Park: Pennsylvania State University Press, 2001.

Blockmans, Wim, and Janse Antheun, eds. *Showing Status: Representations of Social Positions in the Late Middle Ages.* Turnhout, Belgium: Brepols, 1999.

Buc, Philippe. *The Dangers of Ritual: Between Early Medieval Texts and Social Scientific Theory.* Princeton, N.J.: Princeton University Press, 2001.

Bucknell, Peter A. *Entertainment and Ritual 600–1600.* London: Stainer and Bell, 1979.

Burke, Peter. "The Repudiation of Ritual in Early Modern Europe." In *The Historical Anthropology of Early Modern Italy.* Cambridge, U.K.: Cambridge University Press, 1987.

Cohn, Samuel K., Jr. *The Cult of Remembrance and the Black Death: Six Renaissance Cities in Central Italy.* Baltimore: The Johns Hopkins University Press, 1997.

Crane, Susan. *The Performance of Self: Ritual, Clothing, and Identity during the Hundred Years War.* Philadelphia: University of Pennsylvania Press, 2002.

Kertzer, David I. *Ritual, Politics, and Power.* New Haven, Conn.: Yale University Press, 1988.

Klapisch-Zuber, Christiane. *Women, Family, and Ritual in Renaissance Italy.* Chicago: University of Chicago Press, 1985.

Koziol, Geoffrey G. *Begging Pardon and Favor: Ritual and Political Order in Early Medieval France.* Ithaca, N.Y.: Cornell University Press, 1992.

Le Goff, Jacques, and Jean-Claude Schmitt, eds. *Le Charivari.* Paris and New York: Mouton, 1981.

Mansfield, Mary C. *The Humiliation of Sinners: Public Penance in Thirteenth-Century France.* Ithaca, N.Y.: Cornell University Press, 1995.

Marcus, Ivan G. *Rituals of Childhood: Jewish Acculturation in Medieval Europe.* New Haven, Conn.: Yale University Press, 1996.

Prevenier, Walter, and Wim Blockmans. "Propaganda and the Legitimation of Power." In *The Burgundian Netherlands.* Cambridge, U.K.: Cambridge University Press, 1986.

Rosenwein, Barbara, ed. *Anger's Past: The Social Uses of an Emotion in the Middle Ages.* Ithaca, N.Y.: Cornell University Press, 1998.

Shore, Bradd. *Culture in Mind.* Oxford: Oxford University Press, 1996.

Trexler, Richard. *Public Life in Renaissance Florence.* New York: Academic Press, 1980.

Turner, Victor. *The Forest of Symbols.* Ithaca, N.Y.: Cornell University Press, 1967.

WALTER PREVENIER

[See also **DMA:** Carnival; Kingship, Rituals of: Coronation; Ordeals; Ritual; **Supp:** Liturgical Year, Eastern; Liturgical Year, Western.]

ROLANDINUS DE PASSAGERIS (ca. 1217–1300) was a Bolognese notary and an important figure in the city's political life. The city memorialized him with a re-

Tomb of Rolandinus de Passageris. *Rolandinus's tomb in Bologna.*
COURTESY OF KENNETH PENNINGTON.

markable funeral monument near the church of San Domenico that attests to his fame and influence. The son of an innkeeper, whose profession bestowed his surname on him, he studied the notarial arts (undoubtedly in Bologna) and in 1234 was enrolled as a Bolognese notary (Comunis Bononie notarius). Notaries were important figures in medieval society. They were responsible for drafting wills, contracts, and other legal documents. Their guilds were powerful forces in all the Italian city-states. During the twelfth century Bologna became a center for educating notaries. By the 1220s notaries were producing *formularia* (formulary books) that contained models for drafting many kinds of legal documents. Rolandinus's treatises surpassed other notarial works in the number of formulaic documents and in clarity of his explanations. Consequently, he became the medieval notary who exemplified his craft.

In 1255 Rolandinus published his principal work, the *Summa artis notariae,* to which he added two shorter works, "De notulis" and "Flos ultimarum voluntatum." In his prologue he noted that the models notaries used for legal documents were often inadequate and full of errors. Guilielmus Durantis later incorporated almost all of Rolandinus's *Summa* into his great work on procedure, the *Speculum iudiciale* (1574), while Petrus de Unzola eventually completed a commentary on Rolandinus's *Summa* that Rolandinus himself had begun. In addition to his *Summa,* Rolandinus also wrote a short tract on a notary's duties in the countryside, "De officio tabellionatus in villis vel castris." These two works usually circulated together and became the standard notarial text for centuries.

Some of Rolandinus's comments give important information about Bologna in the thirteenth century. In his tract "De notulis" he observed that the *podestà* (the highest magistrate of the city) judged the criminal cases in which students were accused, even though the rector of the university had exercised this power over students. He was also no armchair intellectual. From 1274 he exercised the offices of consul and rector in Bologna. He taught notarial arts in Bologna, if briefly. (In the 1280s he was called a professor of the "ars notaria.") He also played a role in driving the Lambertazzi family out of Bologna and opposed the city's subjection to the papacy in 1278.

BIBLIOGRAPHY

PRIMARY WORKS

Flos vltimarum uoluntatum. 1503. Also in *Tractatus universi iuris,* 1584.

Orlandini Rodulphini Bononiensis Doctoris in vtroque iure consumatissimi in artem notariae ordinatissimae summulae, una cum insigni Notularum tractatu, necnon Tabellionatus officio in castris vel villis. 1549.

Rolandini Passagerii Contractus. Edited by Roberto Ferrara. Rome: Consiglio nazionale del notariato, 1983.

Summa totius artis notariae Rolandini. 1546. Reprint, Bologna, Italy: Consiglio nazionale del notariato, 1977.

SECONDARY WORKS

Era, A. "Di Rolandino Passagerii e della sue 'Summa artis notariae'." *Rivista di storia del diritto italiano* 7 (1934): 388–407.

Giansante, Massimo. *Retorica e politica nel Duecento: I notai bolognesi e l'ideologia comunale.* Rome: Istituto storico italiano per il Medio Evo, 1999.

Intersimone, G. "Rolandino di Passaggeri uomo politico e maestro di arte notarile." *Rivista del notariato* 16 (1962): 570–587.

Racine, Pierre, ed. *Il notariato italiano del periodo comunale.* Piacenza, Italy: Fondazione di Piacenza e Vigevano, Edizioni Tip.Le.Co., 1999.

Tamba, Giorgio, ed. *Rolandino e l'ars notaria da Bologna all'Europa: Atti del Convegno Nazionale di Studi Storici sulla figura e l'opera di Rolandino,* Milan: Giuffrè Editore, 2002).

Weimar, Peter. "Rolandinus (Rodulphini) Passagerii." In *Lexikon des Mittelalters.* Edited by Robert Auty et al. Vol. 7. Munich: Artemis, 1995.

KENNETH PENNINGTON

ROUTIERS. Volume 28 of the massive nineteenth-century *Grande Encyclopédie* offers both a wide and a narrow definition of the term "routiers." Unlike more modern scholarly definitions that usually limit the activities of routiers to the period of the Hundred Years War (1337–1453), the author of the entry in the *Grande Encyclopédie* asserts that the routiers came into prominence as early as the reign of Philip II Augustus (1180–1223), and they continued committing their despicable acts down through the fifteenth century. Even though the saintly Louis IX (1226–1270) tried to suppress them, whatever success he had was, our author implies, ephemeral. The author narrowed his vision when he came to describe the social composition of the routiers. Acknowledging that they were organized into military companies and led by knights, even by the bastard sons of great noble houses, he nevertheless asserted that the routiers were predominantly peasants with a taste for plunder.

More recent authors are less simplistic as to the motives of the routiers, many of whom were assuredly peasants, but many others of whom were downwardly mobile small landholders whose tenancies were being ravaged during the Hundred Years War. Young and youngish men, even men in clerical orders, from small and mid-sized towns joined the bands as well—for adventure and plunder and also because the routier bands appeared to be carrying out a particularly rough but deserved kind of retributive justice against hoarders and political opportunists. Many, moreover, came from the lower nobility of poor knights who saw their affiliation with one side or another in the civil strife of the fourteenth and fifteenth century as the logical continuation of their traditional political affiliation with the great noble houses, like the Armagnacs, and their causes. Often enough, companies of routiers served for or with French and English royal forces or those of their noble allies. In the periods of truce that punctuated the Hundred Years War, a great many demobilized soldiers affiliated with the routiers companies.

That the routiers were often savage in their attacks, killed innocent civilians, engaged in extortion, and committed unspeakable acts of rape and arson is not in doubt. Medieval armies were not always well disciplined, and medieval contingents like those of the routiers, with deep personal grievances and living off the land, were probably worse in this respect than regular armies. Regions were ravaged over and over again. Although the routiers probably justified a great deal of this behavior to their own satisfaction, there is also no doubt about the long-term negative impact of their actions on the productive resources of the French economy and on social and political life. Creative but stopgap measures to divert demobilized troops to other regions, like Bertrand du Guesclin's expedition to Castile in the late 1360s to join the Trastámara side in the civil war there, did not conclusively solve the problem. Only peace—the end of the Hundred Years War—allowed the state the breathing spell needed to marshal its resources with sufficient effect to suppress the routiers. By the time this was accomplished, however, the French kingdom had endured an intensity of personal violence and devastation of property unparalleled except during the Wars of Religion and the Revolution.

BIBLIOGRAPHY

Faugeras, Jacques. *Perrinet Gressart: Redoutable "routier" au service des Anglais et des Bourguignons.* Sury-en-Vaux, France: Terroir, 1999. A study of the career of the routier captian Gressart, who was active in the time of Joan of Arc.

La Grande Encyclopédie: Inventaire raisonné des sciences, des lettres et des arts, par une société de savants et de gens de lettres. Edited by André Berthelot et al. 31 vols. Paris: H. Lamirault, 1886–1902.

Sumption, Jonathan. *The Hundred Years' War.* Volume 1: *Trial by Battle,* Volume 2: *Trial by Fire.* London and Boston: Faber and Faber, 1990–1999. The best way to map the activities of the routiers is through studies of the Hundred Years War, of which this is an excellent example.

WILLIAM CHESTER JORDAN

[See also **DMA:** Hundred Years War; **Supp:** Guesclin, Bertrand du.]

RUDOLF OF HABSBURG

RUDOLF OF HABSBURG (1218–1291). For two decades after the death of Conrad IV in 1254 and the collapse of the Hohenstaufen dynasty, the territories of Germany had no emperor. After a double election in 1257, Richard of Cornwall and Alfonso X of Castile had competing claims for the throne, but neither of them was able to consolidate the loyalties of the German towns. During this so-called interregnum period (1257–1273), the rule of the kingdom fell to the ecclesiastical and lay princes who composed the electoral college: the archbishops of Mainz, Trier, and Cologne; the count-palatine of the Rhine; the duke of Saxony; the margrave of Brandenburg; and the king of Bohemia. After the death of Richard in 1272, the electors were free to choose a new king. Alfonso X of Castile was no longer considered to be a legitimate claimant because domestic troubles had prevented him from traveling to Germany for the coronation. From a crowd of contenders, the electors chose Rudolf I of Habsburg, the son of Count Albrecht IV of Habsburg and Hedwig of Kiburg.

The first ruler of the Habsburg dynasty, Rudolf was very successful at consolidating his family's new grip on imperial power. He secured the loyalty of towns by rewarding those that supported his candidacy with charters that granted them considerable freedom and autonomy from taxes and external control. He forged alliances with German princes by strategically marrying his four daughters to the sons of powerful lords. His conquest of the duchies under the control of Ottokar II of Bohemia extended his authority over a vast new territory. Ottokar had unlawfully seized the duchy of Austria and other holdings of the Babenbergs in 1251 after the death of the last male heir of that ancient family. He refused to recognize Rudolf as king because he would then have to relinquish control of his duchies, which were in fact vacant imperial fiefs. In 1275 Rudolf outlawed the duke for his disloyalty. Three years later, his forces defeated the Bohemian army at the Battle of Drünkrut, where Ottokar was killed in combat. The rebel's death allowed Rudolf to assume control of the duchies of Austria, Styria, Carniola, and Carinthia, which he gave to his sons Albert and Rudolf II. These territories became the hereditary power base of the Habsburg dynasty, which survived until the collapse of the Austro-Hungarian Empire in 1918.

Rudolf accumulated territories and wealth during his reign as king, but he was unable to find an opportunity to travel to Italy for an imperial coronation. He died on 15 July 1291. His wish to be laid to rest in the cathedral at Speyer shows that he felt a strong affinity for the Salian and Hohenstaufen emperors buried there. His failure to be crowned emperor himself made the issue of succession difficult for his eldest son, Albert. Wary of the growing power of the Habsburgs and their desire to establish a dynasty, the electors chose Count Adolf of Nassau as Rudolf's successor. Adolf was a minor noble with no dynastic pretensions. He soon fell before a coalition of forces led by Albert, who was elected king in 1298. His tumultuous reign lasted a decade before he was murdered.

BIBLIOGRAPHY

Boshof, Egon, and Franz-Reiner Erkens, eds. *Rudolf von Habsburg, 1273–1291: Eine Königsherrschaft zwischen Tradition und Wandel.* Cologne: Böhlau Verlag, 1993.

Habsburg, Otto. *Rudolf von Habsburg*. 2d ed. Vienna: Verlag Herold, 1977.

Kunze, Ulrike. *Rudolf von Habsburg: Königliche Landfriedenspolitik im Spiegel zeitgenössischer Chronisten.* Frankfurt am Main: Peter Lang, 2001.

SCOTT G. BRUCE

[See also **DMA:** Austria; Babenberg Family; Germany: 1254–1493; Germany: Electors; Habsburg Dynasty; **Supp:** Conrad IV of Germany, Emperor.]

SABAEANS. See **Sabians.**

SABIANS.

Although it had a variety of meanings in the medieval Islamic world, the term "Sabian" principally referred to two religious groups—the polytheists of Ḥarrān and the monotheist Mandaeans of Iraq and Iran. Despite a long-standing confusion, neither of these groups is related to the inhabitants of Saba (biblical Sheba) on the Arab peninsula.

THE SABIANS OF ḤARRĀN

The Sabians of Ḥarrān (a town of medieval Syria, now in southern Turkey) contributed to the development of Islamic math and science as well as Islamic mysticism but left behind no religious writings of their own. Historians have therefore relied on Muslim and Christian accounts, which impute to them a variety of religious beliefs. It is difficult, however, to use these often contradictory sources to outline a consistent religious tradition in medieval Ḥarrān. What Christian and Islamic sources primarily reveal are changing attitudes on the part of Christians and Moslems toward the ancient religious and philosophic traditions of the Middle East. Late antique Syriac Christian sources, such as the late-fifth-century *Homily on the Fall of Idols* by Jacob of Serugh (451–521), depict the Ḥarrānians as worshiping a traditional Near Eastern pantheon including the moon god Sin, Ba'alshamen, and Bath Nikkal, a Syrian version of Ishtar. The emphasis on paganism reflects Christian fears that lingering pagan traditions and belief undermined the faith of the Christian community.

The name "Sabian," however, derives from Islamic sources. The tenth-century writer Ibn al-Nadīm recorded that in A.D. 830 the Ḥarrānians first claimed to be the *ṣābiʾūn,* a mysterious group mentioned in the Koran alongside Jews and Christians as "people of the book" whose religion should be tolerated. Although apocryphal (earlier references to the Ḥarrānians as Sabians exist), this story may nonetheless reflect a possible

survival strategy on the part of the Ḥarrānians. Other explanations of Islamic toleration of the Ḥarrānians may be rooted in biblical traditions about Ḥarrān as a city in which the patriarch Abraham lived. In the Islamic tradition Abraham was the first Muslim; thus some Muslims believed that the Ḥarrānians practiced a form of Abrahamic religion. Indeed, some esoteric and gnostic Islamic groups, such as the Ismaiʿlī "Brethren of Purity" *(Ikhwān al-Ṣafā),* developed doctrinal beliefs influenced by the Sabians of Ḥarrān.

While Islamic writers sometimes ascribed to the Sabians of Ḥarrān religious traditions similar to those ascribed by Christian sources, more often they described them as star worshippers and Neoplatonists. Where Christian authors saw the remnants of ancient paganism, Islamic authors saw transmitters of classical physical and mystical sciences, probably as a result of the influence of Ḥarrānian mathematicians and astronomers. The historian Michel Tardieu has argued that the Platonic Academy was reconstituted in Ḥarrān following its closure in Athens in 529 (and a short sojourn in Persia). Among the best known of the Ḥarrānian scientists was Thābit ibn Qurra (born *ca.* 826 in Ḥarrān), a mathematician and theoretical astronomer who lived in Baghdad. Working in Syriac, Greek, and Arabic, he both translated Greek texts, such as Archimedes's treatise *Sphere and Cylinder,* and composed his own works. Thabit left behind a dynasty of scholars, scientists, and poets in Baghdad. Although his son Sinān, a physician to the Abbasid caliphs, was forced to convert to Islam, his grandsons apparently remained Sabians. Thabit's great-great-grandson, Abū ʿAli al-Muhassin (also known as Ṣāḥib al-Shama), a poet, was still practicing his ancestral religion in the beginning of the eleventh century.

It is difficult to determine how long the Ḥarrānians resisted conversion. Islamic and Christian sources mention a number of temples in Ḥarrān and the surrounding area, yet no structure has been identified by archaeologists. According to the thirteenth-century chronicler Ibn-Shaddād of Aleppo, the main mosque of Ḥarrān, the ruins of which survive today, was built over the temple of the Sabians shortly after the Muslim conquest. Ibn-Shaddād further recorded, however, that the Ḥarrānians were allowed to build a replacement elsewhere. It is possible that temples survived in the surrounding villages, where some texts suggest Sabian rites were performed. All trace of the Sabians disappeared when the Mongols transported the population of Ḥarrān to Mardin and Mosul and left the city abandoned in 1271.

THE MANDAEANS

The Arabic term *ṣabi'ūn* was also used to describe the Mandaeans, a gnostic dualistic religious group that still survives today in southern Iraq and Iran. They call themselves *Ṣubba* or, more formally, *Mandai*, but to medieval Islamic writers they were known as *as-sabi'at al-bata'ih*, or the Sabians of the marshes. Europeans of the early modern and colonial periods called them "St. John's Christians," inaccurately believing them to be followers of St. John the Baptist. The tenets of their religion are difficult to uncover; in medieval accounts they were frequently confused with the Ḥarrānians, and their teachings are still kept secret from outsiders. What we do know suggests that their beliefs draw on several sources—including Zoroastrianism, Judaism, and early Christianity—and perhaps arose somewhere in Palestine, although some traditions link them to Ḥarrān. Their religious texts, written in the Mandaic language (a dialect of eastern Aramaic) and edited sometime in the fifth to seventh centuries, include the "Treasury" (the *Ginza*, also known as the *Sidra rba*, "the great book,"), a collection of disparate fragments of creation stories, prayers, and prescriptions for treatment of the dead. Important too are the "Book of the Zodiac" *(Sfar Malwasha)* and the "Thousand and Twelve Questions" *(Alf Trisar Shiala),* as well as many others.

Medieval Islamic writers also called the Mandaeans the *Mughtasila*, a name that means "the washing ones," reflecting the community's emphasis on baptism. Among the modern community, baptism and ablutions are an essential part of ritual, for Mandaeans believe that flowing or "living" water descends from heavenly rivers in the world of light. In Mandaean cosmography, the divine world of light is opposed to an equally powerful world of darkness. A demiurge, Pthahil, created the flawed physical universe, assisted by powers from the dark world. He also created the body of the first man, Adam, who remained lifeless until inhabited by a soul from the world of light. The descent of the soul created a link between the earthly Adam and the heavenly Adam (also known as Adakas, the secret Adam). Baptism and ablution help to return the soul to the realm of light after death. The Mandaeans believe that such religious practices directly parallel those practiced in the "realm of light."

The term *ṣabi'ūn* thus referred to at least two particular communities in the medieval Islamic world. Other uses of the word suggest that it could at times also have a generalized meaning of "pagan" and not have a direct connection with either of these two communities. It is in this sense that Maimonides used the term.

BIBLIOGRAPHY

PRIMARY WORKS

Drower, E. S., trans. *The Book of the Zodiac (Sfar Malwasia)*. London: Royal Asiatic Society, 1949.

———, trans. *The Canonical Prayerbook of the Mandaeans*. Leiden, Netherlands: Brill, 1959.

———, ed. and trans. *The Thousand and Twelve Questions (Alf Trisar Šuialia)*. Berlin: Akademie-Verlag, 1960.

Lidzbarski, Mark, trans. *Der Ginza oder das grosse Buch der Mandäer*. Göttingen, Germany: Vandenhoeck und Ruprecht, 1925.

SECONDARY WORKS

Buck, Christopher. "The Identity of the Sabi'un: An Historical Quest." *Muslim World* 74 (1984): 172–186.

Carmody, Francis. J. *The Astronomical Works of Thabit b. Qurra*. Berkeley: University of California Press, 1960.

Chwolsohn [Khvol'son], Daniil Avraamovich. *Die Ssabier und der Ssabismus*. 1856. 2 vols. Reprint, New York: Johnson Reprint, 1965.

De Blois, François. "The 'Sabians' (Sabi'un) in Pre-Islamic Arabia." *Acta Orientalia* 56 (1995): 39–61.

Lloyd, Seton, and William Brice. "Ḥarrān." *Anatolian Studies* 1 (1951): 77–111.

Morelon, R. "Tabit b. Qurra and Arab Astronomy in the Ninth Century." *Arab Sciences and Philosophy* 4, no. 1 (1994): 6, 111–139.

Rice, D. S. "Medieval Ḥarrān: Studies on Its Topography and Monuments." *Anatolian Studies* 2 (1952): 36–84. Includes a translation of Ibn-Shaddād's account of Ḥarrān.

Rudolph, Kurt. *Mandaeism*. Leiden, Netherlands: Brill, 1978.

Tardieu, Michel. "Sabiens coraniques et Sabiens de Ḥarrān." *Journal Asiatique* 274 (1986): 1–44.

CHRISTOPHER HATCH MACEVITT

SACRAMENTS AND SACRAMENTAL THEOLOGY.

Medieval sacramental theology is inseparably linked to salvation history, which recounts the divine restoration of fallen humanity through the gift of grace. Humankind was reckoned sick unto death following the Fall, and so the sacraments were a remedy to ensure the recovery of that life and peace humanity had forfeited. No mere juridic procedure but rather a restorative process, medieval theology consistently presents God as the merciful physician dispensing the medicine of grace through the sacraments, thereby providing sustenance to Christian "wayfarers" as they make their way to the Heavenly Jerusalem.

The Latin term *sacramentum* (sacrament/symbol) had originally referred to the oath soldiers swore upon their induction into the Roman army. Throughout the time of the church fathers (the patristic era) and the early

Middle Ages the term "sacrament" was used in a wide sense to denote sacred things generally. The eleventh-century scholastic Berengar of Tours (*d.* 1088) was the first to limit the term to the consecrated material and visible element, thus strictly separating this outward *sacramentum* from the *res* (reality) that it signified. Twelfth-century canon law collections, as well as theological works, adopted (and adapted) the definition of a sacrament attributed to St. Augustine by Berengar, though actually of his own creation: "a visible form of invisible grace." Though this certainly echoes similar formulas in Augustine's writings it is not authentic and is surely too confined.

While sacraments were understood, broadly speaking, as "sacred signs," around 1130 the Parisian scholar Hugh of St. Victor (1096–1141) offered a more complete definition: "A sacrament is a corporeal or material element that is set before the senses outwardly, representing through its likeness, signifying on account of its institution, and containing some invisible and spiritual grace by way of sanctification." (*De sacramentis Christiane fidei*, Book 1, part 9, ch. 2) Yet the term "sacrament" was still broad enough in the early twelfth century for Hugh to count holy water, the reception of ashes, the sign of the cross, and invocation of the Trinity as those "sacraments" upon which salvation does not necessarily depend. The anonymous writer of the *Summa sententiarum* (*ca.* 1140) states that sacraments consist of things, deeds, and words and must have both a *sacramentum* and a *res sacramenti* (reality of the sacrament) that is, some outward symbolic aspect which points to an invisible spiritual reality. Peter Lombard (*ca.* 1100–c. 1160), whose *Sentences* (*ca.* 1155) became the authoritative theological textbook throughout the later Middle Ages, notes that sacraments were not instituted simply to signify but to sanctify. And it is for this reason that he insists the sacrifices and observances of the Old Law (of the pre-Christian era) were not sacraments in the strict sense of the term, for they were only signs of a sacred reality that they could not furnish. Lombard listed what would later become the official ordering of the seven sacraments: baptism, confirmation, Eucharist, penance, unction, orders, and marriage. The sacraments all derive their power from the passion of Christ, but they were not instituted immediately after sin entered the world, says Lombard, inasmuch as Christ did not wish to arrive until the human race had concluded that neither Natural nor Written Law could bring salvation.

Lombard reflects the traditional medieval view that only the Christian sacraments could be truly effective for salvation. The Old Testament patriarchs and prophets were justified (saved) on account of their faith in what the sacrifices of their own day prefigured, not through the rites themselves. Hugh of St. Victor stands out as an exception to this rule, however, for while he insists that Christ was always the sole source of grace, he thinks that the same grace was really conferred within the sacraments of the Natural and Written Law. God the physician dispensed the sole remedy for salvation under different means, even though such means cease to be effective when the next age dawns. The Age of Grace has thus put an end to all previous sacraments. This position is clearly in contrast to Thomas Aquinas (*d.* 1274), who contends that Christ's passion would have been unnecessary were the sacraments of the Old Law able to confer justifying grace by their own power. Echoing the traditional line, then, Thomas states that the Old Testament patriarchs were saved through faith in Christ's future passion.

Everyone agreed that God could have offered salvation without the sacraments. Hugh of St. Victor presents three generally accepted reasons for their institution. They subject humankind to the humbling prospect of seeking the invisible within the material; instruct human beings to recognize the invisible power residing within the tangible elements; and exercise the human mind that it might always move forward in this pursuit. Aquinas holds that the sacraments were not necessary in the state of innocence because the higher aspects of human nature were not yet dominated by the lower nor dependent upon them.

Sacraments were understood to have material and formal components. Until the thirteenth century their matter and form usually referred to the physical element and ritual words respectively. Yet this limited conception presented difficulties for sacraments that had no material element. Thus thirteenth-century theologians appealed to a more developed hylomorphic composition for all sacraments, whereby the matter of a sacrament was no longer confined to physical objects like water or bread but could also include perceivable ritual actions awaiting formal determination through words. The matter of a deacon's ordination, for instance, would be the reception of the Gospel books and its form the accompanying words.

There was some disagreement as to whether the Christian sacraments actually contain the grace that they present to the faithful recipient. The Franciscan theologians St. Bonaventure (*d.* 1274) and Duns Scotus (*d.* 1308) maintained that created objects simply cannot contain eternal grace and so have no causal power of their own. It is by divine decree that grace is conferred on those occasions when the sacraments are duly administered. On the other hand, the Dominican Hugh of St. Cher (*d.* 1263) declared around 1230 that the sacraments of the New Law, unlike those of the Old, do in fact contain the power of sanctification, functioning as secondary causes, effecting the grace bestowed by God, the primary cause. A few decades later, the Dominican Aquinas stated that depriving the sacraments of any real causality would reduce them to mere signs of grace, like those of the Old Law. God alone produces grace as a principal cause, while the sacraments are employed as instruments to produce an effect, deriving their power from the divine principal agent. While Thomas admits that spiritual power cannot exist in a material object permanently and completely, he thinks this power can exist instrumentally in order to achieve a spiritual effect.

The church had long recognized that some sacraments imprint a permanent mark upon the soul, not unlike a sheep's brand, and by the latter part of the twelfth century theologians referred to this mark as an indelible "character." Baptism, confirmation, and orders were said to imprint such a character, designating a distinct relationship to God. Unlike the other four sacraments, they could not be repeated. Yet agreement broke down when it came to defining the nature of the character more precisely. Albert the Great (*d.* 1280), as well as St. Bonaventure, took it to be a habit that disposes the recipient to grace. Aquinas said that because divine worship involves either receiving certain divine things or handing them over to others, so the character connotes a certain spiritual power, whether passive or active. The Franciscan Peter John Olivi (*d.* 1298) denied the character was a created quality of the soul and called it instead a relation of the soul to God. Scotus saw no good reason to demand its existence at all, except for the authority he accords Pope Innocent III's 1201 decretal *Maiores,* which speaks of its reception in baptism.

The Second Council of Lyons (1274) named seven sacraments, as did the Council of Florence (1439), which also stated that the Christian sacraments truly contain grace and confer it upon those who worthily receive them. Three things are deemed necessary: the material element, the words that function as the form, and the minister conferring the sacraments with the proper intention of carrying out what the church itself does. In 1547 the Council of Trent, in response to Protestant attacks on Catholic ritual, reaffirmed that there were seven sacraments, all of which were bolstered by the claim they had been instituted by Christ. The council also affirmed the indelible spiritual character (which it did not define), as well as the notion that the sacraments of the New Law do in fact contain the grace they confer.

BAPTISM

In the Middle Ages, infant baptism was the norm. The sacrament of baptism, considered a precondition for reception of the others, rid the recipient of original or actual sin while conferring grace. The Venerable Bede (*d.* 735) speaks of receiving grace in baptism that effects the remission of sins through the water and the Spirit. It is the laver of regeneration opening up the gates of heaven. The great scholar of Charlemagne's court Alcuin of York (*d.* 804) speaks of human beings restored to the image of the Trinity in whose name they are baptized. Having fallen into death one rises again to life through grace. For Hugh of St. Victor the material element of water is sanctified through the word such that it now contains grace. The *Summa sententiarum* defines baptism as immersion made with invocation of the Trinity. In keeping with the principle that sacraments must have both a material and a formal element, the form of baptism is the name of the Trinity pronounced over the material element of the water. As the blessed water is the *sacramentum,* so its *res* is the inner cleansing from sin. Peter Lombard insists on the prescribed trinitarian formula based upon the principle that proper words must be added to the element to make a sacrament. Purification and justification are baptism's *res.* It was generally acknowledged that as every sacrament also requires proper intention, were a mother to invoke the Trinity while bathing her baby she would not baptize. Moreover, the all-important form is safeguarded by the stipulation that as long as the Latin words are not so mangled as to alter their meaning the formula is valid.

The canonists were very concerned with proper administration of the sacraments as a matter of law. So it is that Gratian's *Decretum* (*ca.* 1140) reaffirms the classic Augustinian anti-Donatist position, that baptism in the name of the Trinity must not be repeated even if administered by a heretic. For to deny this principle is to undermine the objective power of the Trinity itself. Upon confession of the church's true faith, schismatics are to be received into the church through the laying on of hands. This position was also affirmed by Peter Lombard and later theologians. Innocent III's *Maiores* (1201) states that so long as one does not thoroughly repudiate the sacrament, one will receive the impressed character. And Aquinas notes that while the justification of baptism can be lost through mortal sin, the character remains indelible.

As this sacrament is the initiation into the New Law of grace, it is only natural that theologians discussed its relationship to the great initiation rite of the Old Law: circumcision. Bede finds that circumcision worked against the wound of original sin but could not open the supernal gates prior to Christ's passion. In the meanwhile its faithful recipients would rest in the bosom of Abraham awaiting their entrance into heaven. Hugh of St. Victor says much the same. Peter Lombard, intent on preserving the unique status of New Testament sacraments, was wary of assigning too much efficacy to circumcision, arguing that it only blotted out sin without conferring grace. Thus Abraham found justification through his faith, while circumcision was only a sign that conferred nothing inwardly. Contrary to Lombard, Aquinas argues that grace was bestowed in circumcision, since grace alone remits sins. Yet this did not occur by the power of the sacrament itself, as in baptism, but instead as a sign of faith in Christ's future passion. Justification therefore came from the faith signified and not from the sign.

On a practical level, there was always the question of the unbaptized. Hugh of St. Victor reflects the general feeling that unbaptized martyrs, as well as those who have faith and a sincere desire to be baptized, will acquire the *res* even if deprived of the ritual itself, the *sacramentum*. In this vein, Lombard states that just as those who receive this sacrament without faith, or with a false faith, receive the *sacramentum tantum* (sacrament alone) and not the *res,* so too martyrs and those with faithful intent receive the *res tantum.* As for unbaptized infants, it is quite another story. The majority of theologians took the strict Augustinian line, as Lombard does when he argues that while the faith of the church suffices for infants when they are baptized, it will not suffice for children who have not received the sacrament. As such, infants who die unbaptized will be damned since they bear original sin from their conception. Roland of Bologna allows (*ca.* 1150) that the will to be baptized suffices among adults who die on the way to seek baptism but declares that infants who die on route are surely damned since they lack both the will and the reality, despite their parents' faith. As to their punishment, theologians found some consolation in Augustine's belief that it would be of the least painful sort. Aquinas thinks unbaptized infants are deprived of the beatific vision owing to their lack of sanctifying grace, while for Bonaventure and Alexander of Hales (*d.* 1245), infants suffer no pain but are still deprived of light.

Some theologians did dissent, however. Anselm of Laon (*d.* 1117) saw no reason why an infant should be punished for the sin of his negligent parents. But it was Peter Abelard (*d.* 1142), the brilliant logician and theologian, who put forward a position radically at odds with his contemporaries. Because intentionality stands at the heart of his ethics, he argues that infants do not inherit Adam's sin in the strict sense of the term. For Abelard defines sin as contempt for God, or willing consent to evil; and this cannot be attributed to infants who have not yet attained the free use of reason. Infants only contract the *poena* (penalty) for sin. That being said, he still maintains that infants who die without the grace of baptism will suffer the eternal punishment to which all are now subject on account of the *culpa* (guilt) of humanity's first parents. Abelard was attacked for this position, most notably by his indomitable Cistercian opponent, Bernard of Clairvaux (1090–1153).

The Council of Florence affirmed that the matter of baptism is water, while its form is the invocation of the Trinity. Its effect is the remission of original and actual sins, and every penalty owed to the guilt. In 1547, in response to the Protestant Anabaptists, the Council of Trent reaffirmed the efficacy of infant baptism in the faith of the church and so condemned the practice of rebaptism.

CONFIRMATION

By the fourth century, in the West, confirmation was becoming a rite unto itself, distinct from baptism; its administration was reserved for bishops. With respect to the anointing and imposition of hands involved in the sacrament, Hugh of St. Victor says the chrism (consecrated oil) is made from oil and balsam because through oil the infusion of grace is designated and through balsam the scent of good fame. By the imposition of hands the bishop imparts the Holy Spirit. As the matter of the sacrament is consecrated oil mixed with balsam, so then the form, as Peter Lombard says, consists of the words spoken by the bishop when he signs the baptized person with chrism upon the forehead. Its virtue is the gift of the Holy Spirit given to strengthen the one who has already received baptism.

There was very little controversy surrounding this sacrament, but there was some debate as to whether it had been personally instituted by Christ or by the Apostles or even by the later church. This is actually a very important question, for it speaks to the larger issue of scriptural authority with respect to later tradition and the extent to which the church can be considered a source of continuing revelation. Jacques de Vitry (*ca.* 1160–1240) declared around 1220 that the imposition of hands was of apostolic origin but that the anointing had been instituted by the later church. Albert the Great argues that the form was in fact instituted by Christ and handed down to the Apostles, even though one does not read of it in the Gospels. Bonaventure, in keeping with his high regard for extrascriptural tradition, feels free to deny that confirmation was instituted or handed down by Christ or the Apostles, insisting instead that it was the work of the Holy Spirit through the successors of the Apostles. Aquinas knew this position and rejected it on the grounds that the institution of a new sacrament pertains to the unique power of Christ, who instituted confirmation when promising the Apostles he would send them the Paraclete (John 16:7). And while Thomas says all the sacraments are in some way necessary for salvation, he adopts the traditional position that some are in fact dispensable, even while contributing to the perfection of salvation. For in confirmation the Holy Spirit is accompanied by justifying grace.

The Council of Florence offered the traditional definition of confirmation's matter, form, and effect, as well as reserving its administration for the bishop. The Council of Trent in 1547 simply reaffirmed its full sacramental status over and against any Protestant deprecation.

EUCHARIST

By the twelfth century, the church had affirmed the substantial presence of Christ's body and blood in the Eucharist. Because Christ was understood to be really present in the sacrament beneath the species (outward appearance) of bread and wine, theologians applied the *sacramentum-res* relationship in a new way, allowing for a tripartite Eucharist. Following Hugh of St. Victor's lead, the *Summa sententiarum* proposed that the *sacramentum tantum* is the visible species, while Christ's body is the *sacramentum et res* (sacrament and reality)—since it is not only the signified reality but is itself a symbol of a further reality, namely the union with Christ through faith that is the *res tantum*. This theory was widely accepted, and Peter Lombard would make use of it when explaining that while the communicant does receive Christ's whole substantial body, the fracture and division of the host affect only that first level, the sacramental symbol alone. Yet there was a problem with calling Christ's *invisible* body in the host a sacrament, precisely because even the most basic definition of a sacrament reckons it a *visible* sign. Gerhoh of Reichersberg (*d.* 1169) refused to call Christ's Eucharistic body a sacrament for this very reason. In response to this problem some argued that the Eucharistic body is in fact visible to the saints now and will be later to the faithful in heaven. Nevertheless, by 1202 Pope Innocent III (*ca.* 1161–1216; pope 1198–1216) employed the tripartite formula in his decretal *Cum Marthae,* and it became standard fare in the later Middle Ages.

The question of the sacrament's valid administration was of the utmost importance in an age concerned

with schismatics and simoniacs (those who bought or sold church offices). Lombard claims that excommunicated or manifestly heretical priests cannot consecrate despite their orders, since they do not offer them in the person of the church. Bonaventure distinguishes between the truth of the sacrament that he calls the *res prima* (first reality), and the benefit of the sacrament, the *res ultima* (final reality), which is mystical union with Christ. A sinful priest who consecrates with due form and proper intention will affect the truth and benefit for those who devoutly hear his mass, though to his own damnation. But if the priest is an excommunicate or heretic then all who knowingly participate do so to their own damnation. The true body of Christ will still be present then, though to nobody's advantage. Thomas Aquinas allows that excommunicates, heretics, and schismatics do consecrate, since this ability is based upon the power of their holy orders, having received the indelible character. Because they misuse this power when separated from the church, however, they do not receive the spiritual power of the sacrifice.

With so much emphasis on Christ's substantial presence, theologians were also forced to contend with the fate of the consecrated host in the hands of sinners, heretics, unbelievers, and even animals. Lombard states that sinners receive the true body and blood but do not reap the spiritual effect of union with Christ. As to the common question of what a mouse receives when he eats the consecrated host, Lombard pleads ignorance and leaves that to God. While Bonaventure also admits that sinful believers receive the *sacramentum et res* without the *res tantum,* he spoke for much of the tradition to that time when arguing that proper intention is essential for even sacramental communication. Thus a mouse could never receive Christ's body and would consume only the bare elements. Indeed, Thomas Aquinas did not represent the medieval consensus when he contended that infidels and mice receive Christ's body. His position was born of his desire to uphold the metaphysical integrity of the sacrament, whereby the process of transubstantiation could not be undone except by way of miracle.

Worthy reception of the sacrament was of supreme importance. The Fourth Lateran Council's decree *Omnis utriusque* (1215), which also mandated yearly confession, stated that all lay people of both sexes, having reached the age of reason (seven to ten years old), should receive communion once a year at Easter. Here the Eucharist and penance are closely bound. For only those who had first made a full confession and could be confident that their mortal sins were absolved by God might then proceed to receive his precious body. To receive communion in a state of mortal sin was a sacrilege of the worst order. None of this is to say that Eucharistic devotion declined as result of such restrictions; quite the opposite is true.

The emphasis on transubstantiation in the thirteenth and fourteenth centuries led to an increasing devotion to the host, which by this time would be elevated in the mass for the laity to gaze upon. Just the sight of the consecrated host was believed to have a genuine sacramental power. Not unlike a relic, one prayed before the host in hope of receiving the blessings of its inherent power and holiness. Placed in a monstrance (vessel), it would be carried in procession through the streets under a canopy accompanied by candles and bells. The most notable procession was the Feast of Corpus Christi, which began in thirteenth-century Liège and was celebrated throughout the West by the early fourteenth century.

Attendant to the awe surrounding the consecrated elements was the fear of damaging them. By the thirteenth century it was standard practice to withhold the chalice from the laity, though the priest still used both consecrated elements. This so-called "communion under one kind" was bolstered by the theological principle of concomitance, whereby Christ's blood is always present with his body and vice versa. As might be expected, there were some who chafed under this provision, regarding it as unscriptural and contrary to the practice of the early church. The Czech theologian Jan Hus (1369–1415) called for the restoration of the chalice to the laity and so communion under both kinds (Utraquism). While the Council of Constance burned Hus at the stake for his supposedly heretical ecclesiology, they recognized the inherent orthodoxy of Utraquism. Though withholding the chalice was passed into law on the grounds that it was a reasonable custom introduced to prevent scandal, some two decades after Hus's death the Council of Basel conceded the right of reception under both kinds to the by-then politically strong Hussites.

Also important to the penitential system was the belief that the benefits of Christ's once-and-for-all offering on the altar of the cross were applied to the church during the sacrifice of the mass. And so, despite the fact that the laity were rarely receiving the host, a person's pious devotion during the mass was considered meritorious. In 1551 the Council of Trent affirmed many late medieval Eucharistic principles including transubstantiation, communion under one kind, and the full adoration (latria) of the consecrated host. In 1562 the council also confirmed the mass as a genuine sacrifice for the remission of sins and punishments, whereby the very same Christ offered up on the altar of the cross is now sacrificed in an unbloody manner through the ministry of the priests.

PENANCE

In the early church the sacrament of penance was a once-in-a-lifetime public act whereby the penitent was set apart from the rest of the Christian community for an extended period of time. This "second plank after the shipwreck" was a unique opportunity to recover from sin after baptism. By the sixth century the Irish church was taking quite a different approach to penance. In a church dominated by abbots, as opposed to bishops, the monastic practice of regular private confession and penance was the norm. The Irish missionaries took their penitential manuals with them as they evangelized western Europe in the following centuries. And while this form of penance could meet with stiff resistance in places, by the thirteenth century private confession to a priest was standard throughout the Latin West. In the later Middle Ages penance was a sacrament of the greatest magnitude. As the means to eradicate mortal sin after baptism, it became thoroughly integrated into the whole system of merit and thus indulgences and purgatory. Almsgiving, church construction, crusades, and pilgrimages were all conducted with an anxious, if pious, eye to securing a safe and swift passage to the Heavenly Jerusalem.

Alcuin of York encouraged the boys at St. Martin's school to confess their sins. God the divine physician knows our fragile condition and bestows the remedy of penance for our wounds, which must be exposed in confession for the medicine to be effective. The Romano-Germanic Pontifical (ca. 950) directs priests to make the penitent fully aware of the magnitude of his sin, while at the same time encouraging him not to despair of God's mercy. Because penances varied depending on the precise nature of the offense, so the priest must ask someone who has committed homicide, for instance, the circumstances of the sin: whether done willingly, to avenge a parent, or at the command of his lord. In the newly Christianized lands, penances of three to five years were given to those who still made vows to trees, springs, and spirits.

Theologians and canon lawyers in the twelfth and thirteenth centuries grappled with the sacrament's necessary aspects and procedures. Peter Lombard lists three requirements: contrition, confession, and works of satisfaction. The penitent should confess if given the opportunity but will find remission of sins as long as there is the solemn intention to do so. As God alone forgives sin, so priests are only granted the power to demonstrate which people are forgiven. In other words, for Lombard, their powers are merely declarative. For Peter Abelard it is contrition that marks true repentance, and God's love itself that inspires the contrition that drives out sin. Confession is still important as a sincere act of humility but not a prerequisite for forgiveness. Everyone agreed that true contrition means sorrow for all of one's sins; a person must not be selective. Roland of Bologna observed that anyone with true contrition must have charity and thus the remission of all mortal sins, since it is impossible for love and evil to coexist.

The canon lawyers stressed the need for confession before a priest, thereby upholding clerical control over the keys to the kingdom. The *Decretum* states that sin is not remitted without confession and satisfaction (reparation achieved through good works). As God gave priests the power of binding and loosing, so nobody receives pardon except that he seeks it in the supplications of the church. The Lateran IV decree *Omnis utriusque* advises priests to inquire diligently into the circumstances of a sin. Because assurance of confidentiality is of paramount importance in eliciting a full and frank confession, any priest who would divulge the confession is threatened with deposition and perpetual penance in a monastery.

The twelfth-century theologians were quite sanguine about a penitent's ability to be genuinely contrite and thereby ready for God's forgiveness. Yet if contrition is born of charity and so is incompatible with mortal sin, how is it that someone in a state of mortal sin can express such love for God? The thirteenth-century theologians dealt with this problem by distinguishing between attrition, which is sorrow born of servile fear, and true contrition born of filial fear of God. William of Auvergne (*d.* 1249) says God turns attrition into contrition. Yet even attrition, this preliminary movement of the heart in preparation for grace, is itself a gift from God who justifies those whom he has prepared. Albert the Great calls attrition that sorrow for sin that is not informed by grace. It is a gift of the Holy Spirit, but unlike the sorrow of contrition, it is not perfected by justifying grace. For Bonaventure, attrition becomes contrition through the infusion of divine grace. There must be a movement of faith and sorrow, so that grace will find the free will prepared to be moved from attrition to contrition. As contrition can be achieved prior to confession, so too then does one find justification. But because confession is imposed upon sinners, none can be justified without it, whether in fact or in intention. Aquinas, believing that contrition must be formed by love, says that attrition is converted into contrition when the priest pronounces

absolution. Scotus held that if a person has been contrite for a period of time deemed sufficient by God, he will confess and through the priest's pronouncement of absolution receive the infusion of grace whereby his attrition is turned into full contrition, informed then by the requisite charity. Unlike Aquinas, however, Scotus says the sacrament is not an instrumental cause but simply an occasion for grace that God agrees to offer under proper conditions. On the other hand, William of Ockham (*d.* 1349) finds that while mortal sin cannot be remitted without contrition, human beings are able, apart from grace, to achieve a level of contrition sufficient for the expulsion of guilt and the infusion of grace.

God absolves people of eternal guilt, and thus eternal punishment, following a full and earnest confession, but the temporal punishment remains. Pardoned sinners must still perform works of satisfaction to make good their offenses against the divine majesty. The doctrine of purgatory came into its own during the twelfth century within this penitential context. Hugh of St. Victor and Peter Abelard both speak of purgatory for those who do not complete their works of satisfaction in this lifetime. By the fourteenth century it was fully ingrained in the entire medieval sacramental system. In 1343 Pope Clement VI (1291–1352; pope 1342–1352) issued the bull *Unigenitus Dei filius,* which established that the papacy, as keeper of St. Peter's keys, has been entrusted with the dispensation of merits accumulated by Christ and the saints, which are to be applied for the remission of temporal punishments. By 1476 Pope Sixtus IV (1414–1484; pope 1471–1484) issued *Salvator noster,* which extended indulgences to those purchased on behalf of the dead in purgatory. From here it was but a small step to the hawking of indulgences in Germany that so vexed Martin Luther.

In 1551 the Council of Trent declared that Christ himself had instituted penance (John 20:22). Attrition, ridiculed by the Protestants, was affirmed as an impulse of the Holy Spirit that disposes one to receive God's grace in the sacrament of penance. In 1563 Trent reaffirmed indulgences while condemning abuses. Purgatory is likewise reaffirmed as the place where souls are detained, and can be helped through the intercession of the faithful.

UNCTION

Anointing the sick was an ancient Christian practice, and while in the earlier Middle Ages it was most often administered by the laity it gradually became the domain of the clergy. Originally pertaining to bodily health, it was later regarded as effective for the remission of venial sins. By the ninth century the sacrament was becoming predominantly one of final anointing for those on the verge of death. Hugh of St. Victor says the "anointing of the sick" was instituted by the Apostles (James 5:14–16) for the sake of remission of sin and the alleviation of sickness. The *Summa sententiarum* also claims this sacrament was instituted by the Apostles and now terms it "extreme unction." Its *sacramentum* consists of the anointing with oil, while its *res sacramenti* is the remission of sins conferred by an interior anointing. Indebted to the *Summa*, Peter Lombard also claims an apostolic foundation for the sacrament and lists it under the title of "extreme unction." He too argues that unction can be repeated as long as there is need and, again like the *Summa*, admits that while the sacrament is not essential for salvation, omission by way of contempt or negligence is damnable.

This sacrament, like confirmation, aroused little controversy, but to the extent that it did it was for the same reason: the question of its institution. In contrast to those who claimed the Apostles had instituted the sacrament, albeit by divine inspiration and authority, Albert the Great claims Christ had done so personally (Mark 6:13). Thus James only instituted the canon by way of promulgating the rule of its observation. Bonaventure, on the other hand, argues that the Holy Spirit instituted it through the Apostles. Appealing to John 16:12–13 to support the principle that the Spirit would make further revelations after Christ's Ascension, Bonaventure states that all sacraments are instituted by God, but some through the Son and others through the Spirit. When the Apostles anointed the sick in Mark 6:13, this was principally for corporeal health, as they did not yet have the power of the keys. Aquinas, in keeping with his principle that all sacraments of the New Law were instituted by Christ, says that while Christ did institute all the sacraments, he personally promulgated only those that are especially difficult to believe. Others, such as confirmation and extreme unction, were left to the Apostles to promulgate.

The Council of Florence stated that unction is sacrament for the sick in fear of death, whose matter is olive oil blessed by a bishop and whose form is the accompanying words. Its effect is the cleansing of soul and body. The Council of Trent stated in 1551 that this sacrament was instituted by Christ for the sick and later promulgated by the Apostle James.

ORDERS

Peter Lombard counted seven grades of orders: door keeper, lector, exorcist, acolyte, subdeacon, deacon, and priest. These seven, among a few others, had been known to the church since the fifth century. And while Lombard admits that all seven are sacred, he states, in keeping with the Beneventan Council of 1091, that only the offices of deacon and priest are deemed holy orders, for they alone are read of in the primitive church and derive from the Apostles' precept. By the thirteenth century priesthood was considered the perfection of orders, whose power was bound to the sacrament of the Eucharist above all else. For Thomas Aquinas, the ordinand receives justifying grace in the sacrament through which he may then dispense the other sacraments. Like Bonaventure, Thomas finds that in the ordination of a priest the character is imprinted during the reception of the chalice under the form of the words, since the principal act of the priest is Eucharistic consecration.

By the middle of the eleventh century, clerical celibacy, lay investiture, and simony had become major issues of contention. As the Gregorian reforms pressed forward, the popes and their councils issued a series of decrees designed to improve the moral status of the clergy, while at the same time attempting to wrest the church from the hands of the lay nobility. The demand for clerical celibacy was not simply driven by the need to disentangle ecclesiastical offices from hereditary control. It was also born of a desire to instate a cultic purity among the diocesan clergy, calling them to an ideal previously expected only of monks. To the likes of two Benedictines, Pope Gregory VII (d. 1085; pope 1073–1085) and Cardinal Humbert of Silva Candida (d. 1061), the grace of ordination renders the entire priesthood a class above and apart from the laity. The hands deemed worthy to consecrate the Lord's body at the altar must remain free from the contaminations of the flesh. No less a crime against the church was the buying and selling of ecclesiastical orders, known as simony, and the investiture of church offices at the hands of laymen. Compromise on investiture was achieved by papacy and empire with the Concordat of Worms in 1122.

Clerical marriage and simony were condemned as early as 1049 at the Councils of Rheims and Mainz during the tenure of the reform-minded Pope Leo IX (1002–1054; pope 1049–1054). In 1059 Pope Nicholas II (d. 1061; pope 1058–1061) prohibited the laity from hearing mass said by a priest known to be keeping a concubine and also stated that no one may be ordained or promoted to clerical office through the simoniacal heresy. And in 1123 the First Lateran Council decreed that priests, deacons, and subdeacons are strictly forbidden to cohabitate with concubines or wives, and it refused to recognize anyone who received their office through simony. Twelfth and thirteenth-century canon law makes it quite clear that simoniacal ordination is invalid and, as such, nobody should receive ordination from a known simoniac. Convicted simoniacs are to be deposed. And with regard to priests guilty of fornication, as a matter of principle the laity should avoid their masses and refuse their sacraments. That being said, the form and effect of the sacraments will remain untainted, thereby excluding Donatism (the doctrine that the validity of a sacrament depends on the sanctity of its administrator).

Sacramental validity was always of the foremost concern when dealing with the problem of simoniacal priests and bishops. Cardinal Humbert had taken an absolutely uncompromising line, arguing that as grace is by definition free, the grace of ordination cannot be purchased, with the result that one who obtains his office through simony has received nothing at all and thus has nothing to confer. What makes this argument especially cogent is that it does not speak to the personal worthiness of the minister as such but to the proper observance of the rite itself, which he claims is corrupted from the start. As one might imagine, implementing this principle would have resulted in spiraling chaos throughout the clerical ranks. Hugh of St. Victor is aware of this very argument when he claims that those who have unwittingly been ordained by a simoniac do receive spiritual grace. Hugh separates the man from the office such that grace is given only through the ministry of the simoniac. For while the simoniac has received no grace, he has received the office through which grace will still proceed to those who worthily receive it. Peter Lombard specifically sides with the ruling of Pope Nicholas II (*ca.* 1060) that someone who unwittingly receives ordination from a simoniac is permitted to remain in office.

Albert the Great claims that among more modern theologians there is clear consensus that heretics, whether inside or outside the church, are capable of administering the sacraments as long as they preserve the intention and form of the church. In this vein, Bonaventure later affirmed that heretical bishops, preserving due form and intention, truly ordain but to no useful end outside the Catholic church. Given the indelible nature of the character they received in their own ordination, the power to confer the sacraments remains.

It must be noted that recent scholarship has shown that well into the twelfth century the terms *ordo* (order), *ordinatio* (ordination), and *ordinare* (to ordain) were in fact taken very broadly and did not always have the sacramental quality they would later acquire. Often one was "ordained" to perform some function in society, whether as priest, abbot, or king. There are numerous texts dating

to the tenth and eleventh centuries that speak of women being "ordained" as deaconesses, canonesses, and abbesses. By the middle of twelfth century, however, most canon lawyers argued that women could not be ordained, though in the early thirteenth century some still claimed that nuns are ordained and even receive the sacramental character. By the middle of the thirteenth century Bonaventure claims it is common opinion that women cannot be admitted to sacred orders. Not only a matter of law for Bonaventure, it is one of nature. In the sacrament of orders the person signifies Christ the mediator. And as the mediator is of the male gender, so only men can properly represent him.

Women often assumed leading positions among heretical and schismatic groups like the Cathars and Waldensians. Among the fifteenth-century English dissenters known as the Lollards, some thought women had the right to preach, consecrate the host, and pronounce absolution. This hinged upon the principle that any righteous Christian, male or female, is a priest and so has the power to confect Christ's body.

The Council of Florence claimed the matter of this sacrament is the way in which the order is conferred and its form the accompanying words. In 1563 Trent declared that the priesthood was instituted by Christ. While the New Testament was said to attest specifically to the offices of priest and deacon, the council stated that the other five orders were in use from the beginning of the church. Grace is conferred through sacred ordination, such that no one should doubt its status as one of the church's seven sacraments.

MARRIAGE

Roman law considered consent to be the essential element of marriage for free people. The church also recognized this requirement, thus listing coercion among the numerous impediments, including consanguinity and disparity of religion, for which a marriage could be annulled. Apart from such impediments marriage was seen as an indissoluble union. Prior to the eighth century marriage among the laity did not require the presence of a priest, but as it was brought within the domain of clerical jurisdiction it assumed a sacred quality.

Marriage was unique among the seven sacraments for having been instituted prior to the Fall. Hugh of St. Victor says it was originally instituted as an office. But as a remedy for sin after the Fall, marriage is designed to confine carnal concupiscence so that the greater evil of fornication can be avoided. The *Summa sententiarum* affirms the goodness of marriage, in opposition to the heretical Cathars who detested it along with all sexual activity. Appealing to Old and New Testament texts, the *Summa* claims for marriage a divine institution, principally for procreation and secondarily to eradicate fornication. Peter Lombard appeals to the same biblical texts in support of its goodness against the Cathars. He also notes that as woman was formed from the side, or middle part, of man, rather than the head or feet, so this is a union of fellowship and not dominance or servitude.

A problem emerges in Lombard's treatment of marriage as a sacrament. When listing the seven sacraments, he counts marriage as conferring remedy alone, as opposed to the grace conferred in the others. When treating marriage specifically he notes that because it is a sacrament it must be a sign of a sacred thing, namely the union of Christ and the church. By his own definition, however, sacraments of the New Law must confer the very grace they signify. Marriage raises difficulties precisely because it existed prior to the New Law, whose sacraments alone are said to confer grace.

Albert the Great and St. Bonaventure believe that marriage does in fact confer grace, the latter arguing that under the New Law it is not only a means to legitimize sexual intercourse but bestows a gift of grace upon those who, by the consent of love, are joined for sake of raising children to worship God. Thomas Aquinas argues that as the causality of grace belongs to the definition of a sacrament and marriage is counted as a sacrament, it must therefore confer grace. As a remedy designed to suppress concupiscence, it must possess grace to accomplish this. Thus, in keeping with Lombard's own distinction, Thomas points out that were marriage not the cause of grace but only a sign thereof, it would not surpass the rites of the Old Law. Because marriage is contracted in the faith of Christ, it can confer the grace that enables people to do the works required. He too condemns the Cathars, arguing that as the good God created the corporeal nature, then what pertains to its preservation cannot be altogether evil.

The Council of Florence stated that although adultery would be grounds for sleeping apart, neither spouse may enter into a new marriage since the bond legitimately contracted is perpetual. In an effort to support the full sacramental value of marriage, the Council of Trent in 1563 numbered it among the sacraments of the New Law inasmuch as it surpasses ancient marriages in grace through Christ. Indeed, the council claimed it was instituted by Christ and does in fact confer grace.

The level of scholastic refinement sacramental theology had undergone by the end of the fifteenth century, and thus at the dawn of the Reformation, is quite remarkable. But such refinements in the schools were also accompanied by a pervasive legalism, itself the natural concomitant of the increasing clericalization of church life that was under way by the early thirteenth century. Perhaps this was the inevitable outcome of the church's fight against heresy and its desire to establish and secure effective means for communicating God's grace to the people placed in its care. The laity had long cherished the sacraments and sought ways to express pious devotion to Christ through them. And yet while many sincere churchmen wished to accommodate such piety, they were careful to do so in a way that did not threaten clerical authority and prerogatives. The result was an unresolved tension between the divinely sanctioned dispensers of grace and those for whom this grace was intended. Indeed, many of the protests lodged by the sixteenth-century reformers were by no means new; they echoed the sentiments of previous centuries.

BIBLIOGRAPHY

PRIMARY SOURCES

Albert the Great. *Commentarii in IV libros sententiarum.* Paris: Vivès, 1894. See vols. 29–30.

Bonaventure. *Commentaria in quatuor libros sententiarum.* Florence: Quaracchi, 1889. See vol. 4.

———. *Breviloquium.* Florence: Quaracchi, 1891. See vol. 5.

Denzinger, Henry, and Adolf Schönmetzer, eds. *Enchiridion symbolorum.* 36th ed. Rome: Herder, 1976.

Friedberg, Emil, ed. *Corpus iuris canonici.* 2 vols. Graz, Austria: Akademische Druck- u. Verlagsanstalt, 1959.

Hugh of St. Victor. *De sacramentis Christiane fidei.* In *Patrologia Latina* 176: 183–618. Available as a computer database, Alexandria, Va.: Chadwick-Healey, 1995. The 217-volume *Patrologia Latina* was originally edited by Jacques-Paul Migne and published between 1844 and 1855.

Peter Lombard. *Sententiae in IV libris distinctae.* 2 vols. 3d rev. ed., edited by Ignatius C. Brady. Grottaferrata (Rome): S. Bonaventurae ad Claras aquas, 1971–1981.

Thomas Aquinas. *Summa theologiae.* 4 vols. Turin and Rome: Marietti, 1948.

SECONDARY SOURCES

Colish, Marcia. *Peter Lombard.* 2 vols. Leiden, Netherlands: E. J. Brill, 1994.

Galot, J. *La nature du caractère sacramental.* Museum Lessianum series. Paris: Desclée de Brouwer, 1956.

Ghellinck, Joseph de. "Un chapitre dans l'histoire de la définition des sacrements au XII siècle." In *Bibliothèque Thomiste* 14, no. 2 (1930): 79–96. Paris: Librairie Philosophique J. Vrin.

Haring, N. M. "Berengar's Definitions of *Sacramentum* and Their Influence on Mediaeval Sacramentology." *Mediaeval Studies* 10 (1948): 109–146.

Macy, Gary. *The Theologies of the Eucharist in the Early Scholastic Period.* Oxford: Clarendon, 1984.

———. *Treasures from the Storeroom: Medieval Religion and the Eucharist.* Collegeville, Minn.: Liturgical Press, 1999.

Osborne, Kenan. *Priesthood: A History of the Ordained Ministry in the Roman Catholic Church.* New York: Paulist Press, 1988.

Van den Eynde, Damian. "The Theory of the Composition of the Sacraments in Early Scholasticism." *Franciscan Studies* 11 (1951): 1–20; 117–144; 12 (1952): 1–26.

IAN CHRISTOPHER LEVY

[See also **DMA:** Baptism; Clergy; Confirmation; Donatism; Extreme Unction; Mass, Liturgy of the; Penance and Penitentials.]

SATAN. See **Devil**.

SATIRE is both a specific genre, attested amply in the Middle Ages in prose, verse (both quantitative and metrical), and combinations of prose and verse, and a general tone, mode of discourse, or outlook that may be an element in literature of other genres. As both a genre and a tone, satire abounds first in Latin as well as later in the vernaculars: vast lists of satiric works in English, French, Italian, Spanish, German, and other languages have been compiled—and even more remain still to be assembled. Further complicating matters, satire overlaps with other such forms and techniques as invective, comedy, parody, mock epic, irony, fable, and beast epic. The term *satira* was used routinely in Medieval Latin, but it did not become domesticated in English (either directly from Latin or indirectly through French) until the sixteenth century.

Because of the similarity in spelling, satire was sometimes confused in Roman antiquity and long afterward with the literary form "satyr play," associated with choruses of the half-men and half-animals known as satyrs. Quintilian's pronouncement that "satire is in fact all our own" (*Institutio oratoria; ca.* A.D. 95) rested on the assumption that satire as a genre was a Roman innovation, written in the dactylic hexameters and constituting a smorgasbord of criticism on different human and social failings. The choice of the word "smorgasbord" is deliberate here, since another ancient etymology for satire held it to be a metaphor for a "full plate" *(lanx satura),* which is to say, a medley of commentary on different issues. The "fullness" and concomitant variety of satire elicited comment from Isidore of Seville in the *Etymologies.*

In contrast to diatribists, satirists claim often to be motivated in their criticism by righteous indignation (*saeva indignatio,* as the Roman satirist Juvenal put it) and to seek to correct rather than merely to attack the failings they identify. The thirteenth-century Latin author John of Garland (*ca.* 1195–1272), who wrote a satire himself, differentiates in his *Parisiana Poetria* (*ca.* 1220–1235) between diatribe or invective and satire specifically on these grounds and offers a two-line digest of satire's chief features: "indignant satire derides, strips what is covered, bounds about verbally, reeks of vices, smacks of boorishness." These two lines demonstrate knowledge of Juvenalian indignation in its first clause and of the nexus between satire and satyrs in the second and third.

But the distinction between satire and diatribe or invective often blurs. To take an example from the early Middle Ages, Old Irish poets engaged in what is usually termed "satire" to shame individuals and destroy their social standing, and belief in the deadly power of such satire was so strong that satire was regulated legally. Still, the claim to indignation is what enabled commentators to subsume the satires of Horace, Juvenal, and the first-century Stoic poet Persius under the heading of ethics.

Although satiric elements can be found in Medieval Latin authors of the Carolingian period (Theodulf of Orléans is one example), the hexameter satire took wing in the eleventh century in the Norman Latin poet Warner of Rouen (each of whose unquestionably identifiable satires takes an individual antagonist as its main focus), the German Latin poet Sextus Amarcius, and a few other authors and texts. By the end of the eleventh century the investiture conflicts had generated a substantial body of satire and invective, much of it in prose. These polemics provided a foundation for later anti-ecclesiastic and anti-clerical satire.

TWELFTH-CENTURY SATIRE

One important generic connection of satire was with plaint and complaint (*planctus* in Latin, *planh* in Occitan, etc.). Two twelfth-century examples of such complaints would be the Latin verse *De contemptu mundi* (Scorn for the world; *ca.* 1140) by Bernard of Cluny (also known as Bernard of Morlaix, Morlaas, or Morval), which assails the whole gamut of human vices, and the Latin prosimetrum *De planctu naturae* (The plaint of nature) by Alan of Lille (*d.* 1203), which expresses the supposed alienation of humankind from nature by focusing upon homosexuality. The alternation of prose and verse in the latter designates it as a Menippean satire, a form that was found in the classical Latin authors Varro, Seneca, and Petronius and that enjoyed considerable popularity in the Latin Middle Ages.

Alongside the hexameter and prosimetric satires, the twelfth century saw an explosion of satires in rhythmic

Latin poetry. These rhythmic poems are often ascribed in later manuscripts to a small set of authors, many of them with pseudonyms, some of them historically attested, others quite possibly almost entirely legendary. Thus we have Hugh "Primas" of Orléans (1093–1160), the "Archpoet" (*fl.* 1159–1165), Walter of Châtillon (*ca.* 1135–*ca.* 1179), Map, Walter. (*ca.* 1140–*ca.* 1208; also known as "Mapes"), "Eraclius," and—most famously but perhaps least securely—"Golias." (Attempts have been made to etymologize Golias and its derivative Goliard with reference alternatively to the biblical figure Goliath and to the Latin noun *gula* ["throat," as in "gullet" or "gluttony"].)

Although what can be determined historically about the existences of the real individuals does not bear out modern images, illusions die hard about "Goliards" or "wandering scholars" (*vagantes* in Latin), according to which these poets, to the dismay of the ecclesiastic authorities, crisscrossed medieval Europe in search of wine, women, and song. It is true that many poems written by "Goliardic" poets satirize the church, but that fact does not mean that the authors were bohemians *avant la lettre,* scrawling poems of protest on the medieval equivalent of tablecloths as they drank the medieval equivalent of absinthe. On the contrary, these satirists had ecclesiastic affiliations themselves, and however great their facility in composing verse, they seem not to have improvised much of it. The rhythmic lines known as Goliardic and heavily employed in satire can seem simple and even superficial, but they are often complex in their rhymes, word play, and allusions to earlier literature. In particular, Walter of Châtillon made remarkable use of what is called "the Goliardic stanza *cum auctoritate,*" in which every fourth line is a hexameter drawn from classical poetry—often quoted so as to express one viewpoint when read in the context of Walter's poem alone, another when set against its original context.

These satirists directed their poems against a variety of human frailties and social inequities. In the former category greed receives a heavy dose of opprobrium: the satirists see the world as being governed by the power of the almighty *denarius.* Probably not surprisingly, since the poets were mainly clerics and since chastity was ever more prized by the church, antifeminist themes also abound. In conjunction with the antifeminism is anti-matrimonialism: misogyny leads often into misogamy. Representative texts would be the anonymous *De coniuge non ducenda* (Against taking a wife) and *Dissuasio Valerii* (A dissuasion of Valerius), eventually included in Walter Map's *De nugis curialium* (Courtiers' trifles).

SOCIAL CRITICISM

In the category of social inequities, many social classes and institutions elicit mockery and criticism. A number of the satirists were themselves at least part-time courtiers, but this fact did not restrain them from expressing frustration with the style and values (or lack thereof) of life at court: anti-curialism is a salient feature of satire in the later twelfth century. The same ambition that is faulted in courtiers comes under fire in the schools and universities, where teachers are rebuked for requiring payment for their services, students for crass careerism. The satirists lament pointedly that poetry is poorly paid, in comparison with law and medicine. Above all other institutions, the church is faulted for its financial corruption: the name of Rome is explicated as a Latin acronym for "the root of all evil is avarice"; the Latin word for "pope," as a repetition of the verb "pay!" Greed engenders a host of abuses, with simony and nepotism being two that especially rankled satirists; the notion of a young boy being consecrated bishop elicited mocking comment from many poets. Since the system of bribes was allegedly at its most heinous in connection with court cases, the lawyers who swelled the bureaucracy of the curia in Rome also came under heavy fire.

The clergy was ridiculed and reprimanded for its gluttony, lust, and hypocrisy, among other things. First the monks, especially the new orders that grew in the twelfth century, and later the friars endured their share of satire. Although no order seems to have been exempt, the Cistercians appear to have elicited the harshest criticisms (their practice of not wearing breeches is singled out for derision); they are still being attacked bitterly for greed and luxury in the second half of the thirteenth century in the Middle English *Land of Cockaygne.* At the other end of the social ladder, peasants were mocked for their lack of social graces, intelligence, and other shortcomings. By the end of the fourteenth century the satire has been redirected: in the Middle English "Piers the Plowman's Creed" (*ca.* 1394) and "London Lickpenny" (fifteenth century), a humble plowman is contrasted favorably with representatives of many different classes and occupations.

Both tendencies in social criticism, but especially the anti-monastic one, may be seen in two twelfth-century Latin epics about animals. *Ysengrimus,* often ascribed to Nivardus of Ghent, has as its central figure a wolf who gives the poem its name. One of his most memorable misadventures occurs in a monastery and gives a scathing picture of monastic life—going so far as to "name names" in its denunciation. Even outside the monastery the wolf has pretenses to being a monk. *Speculum stul-*

torum (Mirror of fools), the work of a monk of Canterbury named Nigel (Whiteacre, Wireker, of Longchamp), tells of a donkey who seeks to acquire a longer tail but ends up losing the one he had originally. It includes a systematic review of different monastic orders that points out the foibles of each.

Speculum stultorum contains a few passages in which national stereotypes are mentioned. Although satires on specific nations, ethnic groups, and places are less frequent than satires on courtiers, clerics, and monks, they should nonetheless not be overlooked as a component of medieval satire. Furthermore, the potential for satire on current events or concerns that emerged during the investiture conflicts became a steadily larger component in vernacular satire, as poems on specific political developments proliferated. Other sorts of satire reached an ever broader audience through preaching, which began to influence the vernaculars; verse sermons on the different social classes ("estates satire") appear already around 1190 as components at the opening and closing of Hélinand of Froidmont's Old French *Vers de la mort* (Verses on death). Estates satire would later receive its most important medieval expression in Geoffrey Chaucer's *Canterbury Tales* (*ca.* 1387–1400), especially in the General Prologue.

The sorts of stories incorporated in unified epic form in *Ysengrimus* enjoyed enormous success in the separate Old French *branches* of the *Roman de Renart,* composed by various authors over a seventy-year period (*ca.* 1174–1250). In the Old French *Renart,* satire is aimed at many parts of the social structure but particularly at the king, lords, and clergy. Estates satire and antifeminist satire came to the fore in both the narrative poems known as *dits* and dramatic poems called *jeux.* Of the former, the outstanding early representative would be Rutebeuf, who was active between roughly 1250 and 1280. He passed judgment on the issues that were liveliest in the world at large, such as the Crusades, but he reserved satire especially for his own milieu, where the tensions between the friars and the secular masters at the University of Paris concerned him greatly.

MEDIEVAL OCCITAN VERSE

Well before satire can be documented extensively in Old French, it is found abundantly in several genres of medieval Occitan verse. The most prominent among the earliest satiric poets would be Marcabru (*fl.* 1130–1149), whose *contemptus mundi* in his *vers* shows traits of an eclecticism comparable in its breadth to Bernard of Cluny—but the social setting that occasions Marcabru's preacherly invective is secular. In the next generation of poets Bertran de Born (*d.* before 1215) is also concerned with a secular setting, and his viewpoint in his *sirventes* (which are satiric by definition) is more clearly secular than Marcabru's, even if no more approving. In the thirteenth century Peire Cardenal (*ca.* 1180–*d.* before 1280) continued the tradition of *sirventes* but also wrote satiric verse sermons. In them he responds to the starkly different social context induced by the Albigensian Crusade in southern France.

The Occitan models influenced the subsequent development of satiric forms in other Romance languages, but all of them developed their own independent traits. Italian has satiric *canzoni, frottole,* and *novelle;* Galician-Portuguese, the self-evidently satiric *cantigas d'escarnho e de maldizer;* and so forth. If to this literature we added an enumeration of the major satiric genres recognized in Middle English, Middle High German, and medieval Dutch literature or even in medieval Scandinavian literatures, we could increase an already unmanageable corpus geometrically. Medieval authors and audiences seem to have had an insatiable appetite for righteous (and sometimes even unrighteous) indignation, at least when couched in humor.

BIBLIOGRAPHY

TRANSLATIONS

Adcock, Fleur, ed. and trans. *Hugh Primas and the Archpoet.* Cambridge, U.K., and New York: Cambridge University Press, 1994.

Alan of Lille. *The Plaint of Nature.* Translated by James J. Sheridan. Toronto: Pontifical Institute of Mediaeval Studies, 1980.

Bernard of Cluny. *Scorn for the World: Bernard of Cluny's* De contemptu mundi. Edited and translated by Ronald E. Pepin. East Lansing, Mich.: Colleagues Press, 1991.

Bertran de Born. *The Poems of the Troubadour Bertran de Born.* Edited by William D. Paden Jr., Tilde Sankovitch, and Patricia H. Stäblein. Berkeley: University of California Press, 1986.

Hélinand of Froidmont. *The Verses on Death of Hélinand of Froidmont: Les vers de la mort.* Edited and translated by Jenny Lind Porter. Kalamazoo, Mich.: Cistercian Publications, 1999.

Johannes de Hauvilla. *Johannes de Hauvilla: Architrenius.* Edited and translated by Winthrop Wetherbee. Cambridge, U.K., and New York: Cambridge University Press, 1994.

Map, Walter. *De nugis curialium=Courtiers' Trifles.* Edited and translated by M. R. James. Revised by C. N. L. Brooke and R. A. B. Mynors. Oxford: Clarendon Press; New York: Oxford University Press, 1983.

Marcabru. *Marcabru: A Critical Edition.* Edited and translated by Simon Gaunt, Ruth Harvey, and Linda Paterson. Cambridge, U.K., and Rochester, N.Y.: D. S. Brewer, 2000.

Nigel of Longchamp. *A Mirror for Fools: The Book of Burnel the Ass.* Translated by J. H. Mozley. Notre Dame, Ind.: University of Notre Dame Press, 1963.

Nivardus of Ghent. *Ysengrimus.* Edited and translated by Jill Mann. Leiden and New York: Brill, 1987.

Rigg, A. G., ed. and trans. *Gawain on Marriage: The Textual Tradition of the* De coniuge non ducenda. Toronto: Pontifical Institute of Mediaeval Studies, 1986.

Warner of Rouen. *Moriuht: A Norman Latin Poem from the Early Eleventh Century.* Edited and translated by Christopher J. McDonough. Toronto: Pontifical Institute of Mediaeval Studies, 1995.

Whicher, George F., ed. and trans. *The Goliard Poets: Medieval Latin Songs and Satires.* Westport, Conn.: Greenwood Press, 1979.

STUDIES

Bayless, Martha. *Parody in the Middle Ages: The Latin Tradition.* Ann Arbor: University of Michigan Press, 1996.

Elliott, Robert C. *The Power of Satire: Magic, Ritual, Art.* Princeton, N.J.: Princeton University Press, 1960.

Ferm, Olle, and Bridget Morris, eds. *Master Golyas and Sweden: The Transformation of Clerical Satire.* Stockholm: Sällskapet Runica et Mediævalia, 1997.

Ferruolo, Stephen C. *The Origins of the University: The Schools of Paris and Their Critics, 1100–1215.* Stanford, Calif.: Stanford University Press, 1985.

Mann, Jill. *Chaucer and Medieval Estates Satire: The Literature of Social Classes and the General Prologue to the Canterbury Tales.* Cambridge, U.K.: Cambridge University Press, 1973.

———. "Satiric Subject and Satiric Object in Goliardic Literature." *Mittellateinisches Jahrbuch* 15 (1980): 63–86.

Pepin, Ronald E. *Literature of Satire in the Twelfth Century: A Neglected Mediaeval Genre.* Lewiston, N.Y.: E. Mellen Press, 1988.

Peter, John Desmond. *Complaint and Satire in Early English Literature.* Oxford: Clarendon Press, 1956.

Rigg, A. G. "Golias and Other Pseudonyms." *Studi Medievali,* 3d ser., 18, no. 1 (1977): 65–109.

Schmidt, Paul Gerhard. "The Quotation in Goliardic Poetry: The Feast of Fools and the Goliardic Strophe *cum auctoritate.*" In *Latin Poetry and the Classical Tradition: Essays in Medieval and Renaissance Literature.* Edited by Peter Godman and Oswyn Murray. Oxford: Clarendon Press; New York: Oxford University Press, 1990.

Thomson, Rodney M. "The Origins of Latin Satire in Twelfth Century Europe." *Mittellateinisches Jahrbuch* 13 (1978): 73–83.

Witke, Charles. *Latin Satire: The Structure of Persuasion.* Leiden: Brill, 1970.

Yunck, John A. *The Lineage of Lady Meed: The Development of Mediaeval Venality Satire.* Notre Dame, Ind.: University of Notre Dame Press, 1963.

JAN M. ZIOLKOWSKI

[See also **DMA:** Alan of Lille; Antifeminism; Archpoet; Bertran de Born; *Dit;* Fables; Goliards; Hugh (Primas) of Orléans; Investiture and Investiture Conflict; Isidore of Seville, St.; John of Garland; Map, Walter; Marcabru; Nigel of Longchamp; Parody, Latin; Peire Cardenal; Renard the Fox; Rutebeuf; Sirventes; Theodulf of Orléans; Walter of Châtillon; *Ysengrimus;* **Supp:** Animals, Attitudes Toward.]

SAVONAROLA, GIROLAMO (1452–1498). The "Socrates of Ferrara," Girolamo Savonarola was born in Ferrara on 21 September 1452 and joined the Dominican order in 1475. He came to Florence in 1482 and became reader at the Convent of San Marco. He left the city in 1487 but returned three years later at the invitation of Lorenzo de' Medici. Through his preaching, he quickly rose to prominence, and on 13 August 1493 he became the vicar general of the newly formed Dominican Congregation of Tuscany, separated from the Lombard Congregation to carry out the reforms that Savonarola advocated. His sermons warned of the impending doom that would strike Florence if the city did not turn wholeheartedly toward God. As the friar established himself in Florence, he began to believe that God intended the city to be the center of a new, reformed Christianity in the coming millenarian age. The catastrophic French invasion of Italy in 1494 appeared to many citizens the doom that Savonarola had foreseen. Savonarola was a member of the embassy sent to Charles VIII's camp on 5 November 1494, and he was also part of the negotiating team when the French king entered Florence on 17 November. The friar received much of the credit for the favorable treaty signed on 25 November, which prevented the return to power of the detested Piero de' Medici.

Following the collapse of the Medici dynasty, Savonarola became the prophet and adviser of a popular regime, which maintained an alliance with the French king. Savonarola's influence transformed the public life of the city. Old festivals, such as the Palio horse race and Carnival, were canceled as insufficiently Christian. Laws were introduced to enforce morality of dress, and young men enforced the new code on the city streets. Despite his condemnation of "pagan" subjects of study, many of the intellectuals and artists who had once been a part of Lorenzo de' Medici's circle listened avidly to Savonarola's sermons, even burning their artwork in the great bonfires the friar organized.

Savonarola's sermons angered Pope Alexander VI, both because of the glorification of Charles VIII and because of Savonarola's denunciation of corruption in Rome and prophecy that the purified church would be transferred to Jerusalem or Florence. A papal letter dated 21 July 1495 ordered the friar to come to Rome, but Savonarola claimed to be too ill to travel. Attempting another tactic, the pope ordered on 7 November 1496 that the Dominican Congregation of Tuscany be joined with that of Rome, hoping thus to deprive Savonarola of his independence as well as his rank as vicar general. The friars of San Marco, however, refused to comply.

Girolamo Savonarola. *Portrait by Fra Bartolommeo della Porta (1472–1517) in the Museo di San Marco, Florence.*

A newly elected Florentine government, seeing Savonarola as a liability, forbade all public preaching beginning on 3 May 1497, Ascension Sunday. The pope followed with an excommunication on 12 May, but only five Florentine churches publicized it. On 8 April 1498, Palm Sunday, following an aborted trial-by-fire designed to test Savonarola's prophecies, the friar was arrested by the Florentine government, an action that produced riots outside the Church of San Marco. Under torture, he confessed to heresy, then stood trial in front of judges sent from Rome; he died at the stake on 23 May. He left behind him, however, a group of supporters, often called the Piagnoni, who continued to be influential in Florence until the 1540s. Savonarola's ideas were disseminated not only through his sermons but also through several texts, such as the *Compendio di rivelazioni,* published in 1495, which went through five editions in both Latin and Italian in six weeks.

BIBLIOGRAPHY

PRIMARY WORKS

Pico della Mirandola, Gianfrancesco. *Vita Hieronomyi Savonarolae.* Edited by Elisabetta Schisto. Florence: Olschki, 1999.

Savonarola, Girolamo. *Prediche sopra aggeo con il trattato circa il reggimento e governo della città di Firenze.* Edited by Luigi Firpo. Rome: Belardetti, 1965.

———. *Prediche sopra i salmi.* 2 vols. Edited by Vincenzo Romano. Rome: Belardetti, 1969.

SECONDARY WORKS

Polizzotto, Lorenzo. *The Elect Nation: The Savonarolan Movement in Florence, 1494–1545.* Oxford: Clarendon Press, 1994.

Ridolfi, Roberto, *The Life of Girolamo Savonarola,* Translated by Cecil Grayson, New York: Knopf, 1959. A solid biography from a Florentine historian who clearly admired Savonarola.

Weinstein, Donald. *Savonarola and Florence: Prophecy and Patriotism in the Renaissance.* Princeton, N.J.: Princeton University Press, 1970.

CHRISTOPHER HATCH MACEVITT

[See also **DMA:** Florence; Medici; Millennialism, Christian.]

SCHOOLS

LATE ROMAN SCHOOLING

The Roman Empire was well supplied with schools and schooling. Elementary education (reading, writing, beginning grammar, and simple arithmetic) began about age seven at home or outside the household with an independent, fee-supported teacher. More advanced grammar, learned while reading and reciting Roman authors (especially the poets, and particularly Vergil), began about age twelve. At the grammar level municipally supported schools were numerous in Italy and available in towns as far north as Britain, along the Rhine, and throughout Spain and Gaul. The seven liberal arts—the *trivium* (the verbal arts of grammar, dialectic, and rhetoric) along with the *quadrivium* (the mathematical arts of geometry, mathematics, music, and astronomy)—were carried over from the Greeks and only partly instituted within Roman schools. Influential Roman writers (Varro, St. Augustine of Hippo, Martianus Capella, Anicius Manlius Severinus Boethius, Flavius Magnus Cassiodorus, and St. Isidore of Seville), however, helped transmit the idea of the liberal arts to medieval Europe. Higher education consisted, for the most part, of legal and rhetorical studies.

Between the fourth and sixth centuries, Roman education survived in an attenuated form in the west. Public municipal schools still existed in southern Gaul, Spain, North Africa, and in the major Italian towns. There were scattered provincial schools from North Africa to Britain, and household education was still the norm among aristocratic families, but the number of students cannot have been large. Barbarian settlers did not normally educate their children alongside the romanized inhabitants. And the growing popularity of monasteries and bishoprics as centers of Christian education competed with Roman education, which, grounded as it was in pagan culture, was suspect to many Christians. The remaining public schools in the west eventually closed their doors, and schools for rhetoric ended by the late sixth century. Only scattered private education in law, medicine, and Latin poetry remained. Despite this marked decline in Roman schooling, the history of medieval education was to be one of a persistent classical, Latin educational influence within a growing variety of institutional and social frameworks and a fundamentally new Christian environment.

EDUCATION IN EUROPE, FIFTH THROUGH SEVENTH CENTURIES

In place of publicly supported education, religious institutions (especially monasteries and episcopal centers) offered elementary reading, chanting of the Psalter, memorization of scripture, study of biblical and patristic texts, and copying of manuscripts. In Gaul, for example, Lyon was one of the best-known cathedral centers of learning. According to the Council of Vaison in 529, however, even rural parish priests were to take in lectors (readers) and teach them the Psalter, holy texts, and divine law. Pierre Riché has characterized this initiative as the birth of the rural school of the Middle Ages. The goal seems to have ranged from memorizing the Psalter to reading the Bible thoroughly. A major school in Rome was the papal *schola cantorum* where aspiring clergy learned the particular modulations of Roman liturgical chants and read religious texts. Other forms of training in Rome, at the Lateran or in private homes, prepared boys for papal administrative duties.

Household education for the wealthy continued (and seems never to have disappeared completely throughout the Middle Ages), but we know little about it in this early period. One result of household education, however, was a number of women whose letters and learned reputations have survived. Finally, the royal Merovingian courts may have housed schools for aristocratic children, or they may have placed them in other households for training. Court and household educations would have included reading Latin texts, both classical and Christian, and Latin grammar (especially the *Ars grammatica* or *Ars maior* and *De partibus orationis ars minor* of the late Roman grammarian Donatus). The remainder of the liberal arts fell into desuetude, and even the memory of what they were seems to have faltered.

Barbarian households trained their sons in military expertise and heroic legends; gradually, however, descendants of these invaders gained a Latin education and en-

tered the church. This put a strain on the church, particularly in Gaul, and educational levels declined as local schools that retained little of the classical curriculum became dominant. What remained was an elementary Christian education, and pragmatic training in reading (especially legal and notarial instruments), writing (copying manuscripts and composing letters, with some sense of correct style), and numeracy. These schools taught both clergy and laity.

In certain areas, especially Spain and North Africa, antique culture and lay education survived reasonably intact. Spain and North Africa remained in closer touch with Byzantium and suffered less from invasions and wars. Both North African and Spanish monasteries retained the texts of classical antiquity and educated an elite group of laity and churchmen in profane and sacred learning. By the seventh century episcopal and parish schools had spread. There students learned to read, to chant, to write, and hopefully to master Latin grammar. This education did not include attention to the liberal arts or to classical texts and was focused on training clergy for diocesan work, although some youths educated in these schools returned to lay status. This expansion of learning was halted with the Arab invasions of the early eighth century.

Between the fifth and seventh centuries classical and Christian texts passed to Ireland. Some came from Spain, while others may have survived from sub-Roman Britain. Ireland was a nonromanized, Celtic culture, unique in the degree to which it balanced traditional vernacular with Latin learning from the fifth century onward. The *Filid*, a professional order of poets, held schools that trained students in Irish grammar and legends, genealogies, complex poetic and oratorical compositions, law, and medicine. These schools were frequented by the sons of leading families and focused on oral learning and memorization, although they produced written texts by the late sixth century. From the fifth century, the growing needs of the Irish Christian church required a trained clergy. Education in Latin took place in apprenticeship relationships with local priests, especially at the elementary level, and, increasingly, in rural monastic, anchoritic, or episcopal centers where the Bible, church fathers, hymns, and penitentials were studied. The number of monasteries was large, perhaps two hundred, and while some scholars became priests and monks and also *fili*, others returned to lay life. It was not uncommon for students to travel from one master to another, depending on Irish hospitality for bed, board, and books. By the 660s the accessibility of Irish schools attracted foreign students, particularly from Britain, who studied Latin grammar, scriptural exegesis, and perhaps some geometry and astronomy.

In England schools at Canterbury, from the time of St. Augustine, taught liturgical chant and scriptural reading. Around 670 St. Theodore of Canterbury and St. Hadrian of Canterbury had brief careers as teachers of Greek, but Greek studies did not take root. There was also training in poetry, *computus,* and astronomy. Schools following the Roman ecclesiastical traditions and the *schola cantorum* were set up at Wearmouth-Yarrow, York, Ripon, and Hexham. The high level of learning possible is exemplified by Bede (673–735), who taught at Yarrow and wrote a grammar book and a *computus* used in teaching; Bede, however, had no sympathy for the classical curriculum beyond the grammar needed to learn Latin.

THE CAROLINGIAN REVIVAL OF EDUCATION, EIGHTH AND NINTH CENTURIES

The earliest Irish monks to visit the continent, particularly St. Columbanus (*ca.* 550–615) at Luxeuil and Bobbio, brought more of an ascetic than a learned culture with them. But between the eighth and tenth centuries the Irish and English became the schoolmasters of Europe—teaching at Paris, Luttich, St. Gall, Laon, Pavia, Bobbio, Reichenau, Compiègne, Metz, and elsewhere and copying and preserving pagan classics. Insular (Celtic and English) influences in the schools of Carolingian Europe—a region under the control of a Frankish dynasty, and encompassing France, Italy, and Germany—are wide ranging but sometimes difficult to trace. Classical school texts (e.g., Vergil, Statius), grammar texts with insular scribal influences, and grammars and grammatical commentaries authored by insular, especially English, scholars were scattered throughout continental libraries. A significant corpus of early Carolingian manuscripts, often with insular elements, were copied by nuns who had learned to write either from copying exemplars or from scribal training they received before or after entering a monastery. The quality of these copies suggests that they had good Latin reading skills.

The high level of writing practiced in these nunneries compares favorably with the diffuse but relatively untrained writing that emerged in seventh- and eighth-century Italy. While writing was common among ecclesiastics as well as professional laity, the uneven quality of the more formal uncial, as opposed to the daily cursive hand, suggests that there was a dearth of writing schools in Italy and no agreed norms. Individuals seemed to have learned a variety of styles as autodidacts, perhaps by imitating models.

By the end of the seventh century, parts of Europe experienced an educational revival. By about 700 the Lombard kings at Pavia turned their attention to education. The cathedral school in Pavia began teaching the liberal arts. The monastery at Bobbio began to produce grammars, treatises on poetry, glossaries, and excerpts from classical texts. Books from Africa and Spain arrived in Italy via Sardinia. The burgeoning interest in Italy in books, education, and royal patronage of scholars provided a model for the Carolingian Franks.

Carolingian interest in education was also sparked by the influence of insular monks and nuns and by the influx of Spanish refugees and books into Gaul. In addition, the Frankish church began to revitalize and to focus on missionary efforts. Newly founded missionary monasteries required educated clerics to interact with newly converted populations.

The first Carolingian king, Pepin III (crowned in 751), sought monks and cathedral canons trained in Roman chant. His son, Charlemagne (*r.* 768–814), legislated frequently regarding the education of priests and their duty to instruct others. His major educational directive, *Admonitio generalis* (789), required clergy to teach reading not only to servile children (who more commonly entered the clergy) but also to the children of freemen and to establish reading schools and scriptoria in every monastery and cathedral. These schools were to teach the reading of Psalms, *notae* (shorthand), liturgical chant, the *computus,* grammar, writing, and the careful correcting of religious texts. Bishop Theodulf of Orléans in 798 instructed his clergy to set up free schools teaching basic literacy in towns and villages. In addition, the Council of Frankfurt in 794 and royal letters (*Epistola de litteris colendis,* drafted by Alcuin of York, and *Epistola generalis,* a preface to Paul the Deacon's homiliary) urged that grammar, literature, speaking and writing correctly, and the liberal arts be taught throughout the realm. Charlemagne particularly promoted the role of royal monasteries in education and expected them to play a key role in the standardization of Latin texts. Charlemagne and his successors (especially Charles II in the 860s and 870s) created a school within the royal palace where sons and daughters of aristocrats as well as those recommended for their talent could access court learning and culture. The result of these initiatives, reinforced by an influx of foreign scholars and continued by Charlemagne's son and grandson, was an expansion and regularization of education and a renewed attention to the study of the liberal arts.

The Carolingians saw a concentration of schools in northern and central Italy, parts of Germany, northern

France, northern Spain, eastern Ireland, and parts of England (especially Northumbria). At the turn of the ninth century, these schools numbered around eighty, rising to perhaps one hundred in the tenth century, although a particular school may have ceased functioning at times, for schools were dependent upon the presence of a competent master.

The heart of Carolingian education was *grammatica,* codified into a methodology and a body of school texts by Alcuin of York (*ca.* 731–804), court scholar and abbot of Tours, whose grammatical program strongly shaped subsequent Latin learning. Alcuin began with the simple teaching texts of Donatus, which were widely used in the ninth century. He also drew on an anonymous collection of moralizing Latin sentences entitled *Cato's Distichs (Disticha Catonis)* and on *Institutiones grammaticae,* written in the sixth century by Priscian, essentially introducing Priscian's grammar into Carolingian culture. He invoked the classical authorities Vergil, Statius, and Lucan, as well as the poems of early Christian writers such as Sedulius Scottus, Prudentius, St. Paulinus of Nola, Venantius Fortunatus, and Prosper of Aquitaine. Alcuin organized education into elementary and advanced levels, with elementary levels of reading, writing, and chant followed by more advanced grammar, literature, and scripture, and perhaps some introduction to elements of the *quadrivium.* Although Alcuin promoted the liberal arts, his focus was primarily grammar, which he defined as the science of letters and the guardian of speaking and writing correctly. He concentrated on meaning, pronunciation, and orthography. By the mid-ninth century, however, a more exegetical method of teaching grammar became common, with greater free flow of questions and debate between masters and students.

Independent of Alcuin's innovations, an elementary liturgical instruction was already available to young oblates and older novices in monasteries where they chanted psalms, canticles, hymns, and litanies and read the lessons. They also might be taught to write. Either the cantor or the librarian or their assistants taught the school or divided responsibilities for the training. Methods included oral repetition, memorization, and pronunciation, reading aloud, and silent reading, with meanings of words glossed in the vernacular.

It is unclear how many of those educated at a monastery or cathedral stayed in clerical ranks. Legislation under Louis I (the Pious, *r.* 814–840) tried to discourage cathedral canons and monasteries from educating laity, which suggests that some did so. Certainly monks continued teaching lay children, if not in the home monastery then in outlying estates. At the Council of Paris in 829 and again at Savonnières in 859 the bishops requested the emperor to set up public schools with governmental support. While there is no evidence that this advice was followed, widespread pragmatic or passive Latin lay literacy among freemen in the more fully Christianized areas of the Carolingian empire suggest that such local schools did exist.

There has been some debate as to the degree of Greek learning during this Carolingian educational revival. Greek communities of monks and scholars at Rome produced books and translated Greek texts, and a number of Irish scholars (John Scottus Eriugena being the most famous and best trained) were competent in Greek—whether they gained this competency in Ireland, in Italy, or elsewhere. But most scholars in Carolingian Europe would have had only a passing acquaintance with Greek, perhaps enough to define words or read a simple text.

EDUCATIONAL DEVELOPMENTS, TENTH AND ELEVENTH CENTURIES

By the ninth century the Carolingians were exporting scholars and influencing areas outside Francia. A capitulary (collection of ordinances) issued by King Lothar I in 825 promoted a regional system of schools for northern Italy. Roman synods in 826 and 853, noting the lack of teachers, required cathedrals and larger parishes to establish masters and teachers to instruct in letters and the liberal arts. Neither of these ambitious programs was widely applied, and the Italian clergy sunk into disarray with the difficult political situation of the late ninth and tenth centuries.

England, in contrast, experienced an educational revival in the tenth century. Spurred by King Alfred the Great's desire to promote education by providing a curriculum of Latin texts in English and influenced as well by Carolingian monastic reforms at Fleury and Gorze, Bishops Dunstan, Ethelwold, and Oswald of Ramsey initiated monastic and educational reforms that produced additional schools at Abingdon, Ramsey, Cernel, Eynsham, Worcester, and perhaps York. Latin grammar texts were supplemented with English reading, including translations of scripture; the language of instruction appears to have been English. Students also studied *computus* and liturgical texts but not the classical curriculum common on the continent. It was the goal of Alfred, reiterated in a treatise by Byrhtferth of Ramsey, to teach country priests so they could teach others. To what degree this educational program succeeded is unclear.

The history of continental schools from the mid-tenth century to the opening of the twelfth century is characterized by the prominence of elementary and secondary education within cathedrals. Monastic centers continued to provide education, particularly in grammar, liturgical chant, and *computus,* although the monastic reforms of the tenth century radiating from Cluny and Gorze were not primarily educational in focus. The depredations of the ninth and tenth centuries contributed to making some areas (parts of southern France, Italy, parts of England and Ireland) less hospitable to schools, and education in some of the traditional Carolingian cathedrals and monasteries also suffered. The greatest growth in schools came, in the tenth century, under the auspices of the Ottonians, as their need for competent administrators and ecclesiastical leaders produced an imperial church system and, within it, learning in cathedrals from Belgium and northern France down the Rhine to various German cities. Royal monasteries (including nunneries such as Quedinberg and Gandersheim) were also centers of learning, although apparently not as open to laity as had been the case with Carolingian monasteries. Also, following Carolingian and late Roman models, the German imperial court housed a palace school. These schools offered a very different ambience than those of their Carolingian predecessors. The education was primarily grammatical, rhetorical, and poetic, and the tastes of the schoolmasters decidedly classical. Separated from the pastoral and monastic concerns of the Carolingians, royal cathedral schools trained students in Vergilian verse. A canon of grammatical texts began to form that included Donatus (*Ars minor* and *Ars maior*), *Cato's Distichs,* Priscian, and their glosses. From this period comes the idea that "to study Donat" means "to study grammar." Martianus Capella's text grew in popularity, as did the works of Boethius. Terence, Horace, Lucan, Juvenal, Persius, Statius, Seneca, and Ovid became school texts, along with some Christian poets, including Prudentius, Juvencus, St. Avitus, Sedulius Scottus, and Arator. C. Stephen Jaeger has characterized this school culture as one in which a cult of charismatic personality surrounded the schoolmasters, the most famous of whom was Gerbert of Aurillac, schoolmaster at Rheims and later Pope Sylvester II (*ca.* 945–1003). Although the liberal arts were touted, grammar and rhetoric along with music and cosmology/astronomy were privileged within the *trivium* and *quadrivium.* Dialectic was rarely taught, although Gerbert of Aurillac was noted, exceptionally, for teaching logic. Rhetoric, which meant Cicero above all, was especially valued for the individual engaging in public affairs and for learning the art of living rightly. Students were trained to write elegies, dialogues, letters, invective, and laments. These schools were therefore also schools for manners, where education centered on the externalities of correct behavior as well as on an ethical training that was more classical and heroic than Christian, and that taught from personal models as well as from texts.

The paucity of sources does not allow us to document to what degree an elementary education was available at levels below a cathedral or prominent monastery. In contrast, Jewish sources tell us a great deal about the education of Jewish children and youth in this time period in the Mediterranean basin. Schooling was nearly universal for Jewish boys, including orphans and the poor. There are also instances of girls in school and women scholars, teachers, and calligraphers. Jewish schooling, which took place either in the synagogue, household, or teacher's home, enabled boys to participate in the synagogue services and to learn Jewish law. Teachers began with the alphabet and elementary biblical passages before moving on to more of the Torah and then to the Talmud. There was a great deal of memorization involved, although students also learned to write. They might also learn Arabic, Hebrew grammar and literature, and some arithmetic. By the thirteenth century there is evidence for community-supported Jewish schools in Provence and Spain. The Ashkenazi communities of northern Europe depended more on fee-paying teachers. In all Jewish communities learning continued at home and in the synagogue beyond the age of schooling.

THE EDUCATIONAL REVOLUTION OF THE TWELFTH CENTURY

While Jewish education did not change significantly by the thirteenth century, Christian schooling underwent dramatic shifts. Jacques Verger has called the twelfth century, in particular, a period of educational revolution. It is a century characterized by growing numbers of cathedral schools—particularly numerous in England, Germany, and northern France—that housed grammar schools and offered training in liturgical chant and often in one or more of the quadrivial subjects, theology, and law. By contrast, however, the great monastic schools, with some exceptions, were in decline. Advocates of a return to the original ideals of monasticism rejected the classical curriculum and any education not sufficiently grounded in scripture, while progressive educational reformers were increasingly hostile to schooling within monastic precincts. Although novices still required monastic training, and external schools, usually for poor children, remained attached to some monasteries, monastic centers were no longer the mainstay of elementary and grammar education. Instead, schools began to appear in collegiate churches of canons and larger parish churches, as well as in urban centers and smaller towns where instruction was provided by independent fee-supported teachers. Paris, for example, had at least twenty such teachers in 1140. Growing numbers of households also began to hire clergy as tutors.

There is a dearth of information regarding the curriculum in these schools. The best sources are surviving grammatical manuscripts, which tell us which texts were commonly used and offer, in the accompanying glosses, some sense of the method of instruction. These glosses suggest that schoolmasters did not clearly differentiate reading from grammar. Indeed, "grammar" appears to identify only the principal subject of study. Such schools might also teach chant, reading, perhaps writing, and accounting. Dialectic was fast becoming the dominant subject, displacing rhetoric and subordinating grammar. Instruction was primarily oral (the teacher, not the students, having access to texts) and involved extensive memorization. It was sometimes accompanied by tablets and a writing stylus and sometimes divorced from writing altogether. New versified grammars (such as Alexander de Villa Dei's *Doctrinale puerorum* and Évrard of Béthune's *Graecismus*) made memorization easier. Although most twelfth-century grammar texts were based in the classical tradition, by the thirteenth century there was a shift to texts with a Christian emphasis, the popularity of which was to dominate grammar schools to the end of the Middle Ages. Nevertheless, some classical texts continued in use. Donatus, Horace's *Satires,* and Vergil's *Aeneid* were standard school texts. Ovid, Statius, Lucan, and Juvenal were still part of the curriculum of some schools. At the advanced level Priscian's *Institutiones grammaticae* was studied and annotated by grammar masters but rarely used directly in the classroom. Besides the common texts, individual teachers often edited, adapted, compiled, and commented on the standard texts. Occasionally they wrote their own texts.

These schools were taught by secular clergy and were open to anyone (including adult students) who could pay the fees. Most students (except perhaps those taught at home) were expected to enter ecclesiastical orders. The primary impetus behind this twelfth-century expansion in education was ecclesiastical. The growing needs of parish churches and ecclesiastical administrators as well as increasing governmental demands for literate cleric-administrators promoted Latin schooling and the everyday use of ecclesiastical Latin. The dominant role of the church and of clerical schoolmasters in the twelfth century did not, however, mean that the church was able to enforce educational monopolies in particular areas. The evidence of competition between schoolmasters from the twelfth century to the end of the middle ages is too compelling and leads to the conclusion that any ecclesiastical educational monopolies were local at best and only sporadically effective.

LATE MEDIEVAL EDUCATION

By about 1300 schools began to expand in number throughout rural areas of Europe. These rural schools, however, may have been short lived, being dependent on the presence of a vicar, chantry priest, or parish clerk who had the ability and desire to teach. Such schools usually taught elementary education, although occasionally they also offered Latin grammar.

Grammar schools tended to be more long lived and were more commonly situated in urban areas. London, for example, in the fifteenth century had perhaps a dozen Latin grammar schools. There are indications that a town's investment in grammar schools was a way to attract immigrants and bolster the economy, as, for example, in Arezzo or York. In some cases, as in Venice or Florence, the motivation was commercial. In a great many instances, investment in education was motivated by the need for literate, usually Latinate, skills in legal, administrative, and governmental affairs. Increasingly this involved the education of laity and the growing involvement of literate laymen and women in the foundation and maintenance of schools, the hiring of schoolmasters, and the funding of scholars. In addition, lay schoolmasters now sometimes taught in ecclesiastical schools, while clerics might teach in lay schools or privately.

Some of the impetus for educational expansion also came from late medieval ecclesiastical reformers who pushed for better instruction of both clergy and laity. For example, John Gerson (1363–1429), chancellor of Paris, promoted synodal legislation in 1408 requiring visitations to determine whether schooling was available in the parishes. In 1484 synodal constitutions from Cuenca (Spain) stipulated that every father send at least one son to the village sacristan for an elementary education.

By the fourteenth century elementary teaching was more clearly differentiated from that at the grammar level. While some elementary instruction continued within grammar schools, much of it was now independently, in parish churches, in convents, associated with chantries or guilds, and in households with a tutor, parent, or guardian. The elementary curriculum followed was remarkably similar throughout Europe, although Italian schools included more emphasis upon arithmetic, bookkeeping, and the art of letter writing and increasingly used a parsing grammar called *Ianua* rather than Donatus's *Ars minor*. Northern schools stressed learning the liturgy for the growing number of children (including girls) in parish choirs. Some schools (*abbacus* schools in Italy, business schools in England, reading and writing schools in Spain and Germany) may have been conducted in the vernacular. Throughout much of Europe, however, primary education began with the alphabet and simple vernacular prayers and very quickly passed to Latin bits of scripture and, finally, the Latin Psalter. At this entry level some children learned to both read and sing (chant); others learned only to sing or only to read. Beginning scholars might also be taught to write, often by a separate writing master. The most common elementary Latin grammar, Donatus's *Ars minor,* was sometimes taught as part of the elementary curriculum and sometimes taught in the grammar schools. Girls could attend elementary schools, but rarely learned Latin grammar. Significantly, more and more students now had access to books, although memorization in the classroom remained important.

Those (male) students who went on to Latin grammar schools encountered a curriculum that had not changed significantly since the twelfth and thirteenth centuries, with the possible exception of the Italian schools. There, a shift in the curriculum associated with the rise of humanistic studies may have occurred in the early fifteenth century in some northern Italian household schools. If so, it spread to Latin schools throughout Italy, which had, by the fourteenth and fifteenth centuries, become overwhelmingly secular, run by towns, villages, or guilds or run privately. Humanism introduced newer, more classically oriented grammar texts and Latin sentences, Cicero (with an accompanying emphasis on rhetoric), Latin poets and playwrights (Terence, Plautus), and Latin historians (Livy, Gaius Julius Caesar, Sallust) as well as the rudiments of Greek. North of Italy this increased emphasis on Latin classics and on Greek made little impact until the late fifteenth and the sixteenth centuries. Northern schools were more commonly religious in orientation than was the case in Italy. Many were associated with chantries, parishes, or houses of canons. Although monastic schools had been in decline since the thirteenth century, some monasteries continued to house schools, and nunneries continued to serve as a place for girls (and sometimes very young boys) to receive an education that included training in Latin or the vernacular. The Dominican and Franciscan friars created school networks throughout Europe. The Franciscans, beginning in the 1240s, set up a grid of schools teaching basic Latin grammar as well as, in each ward, a school of advanced grammar, rhetoric, and logic. While these schools were for the friars, they were also open to laity. The Dominicans required every friar to attend school daily, but their convent schools emphasized higher learning, biblical studies, and theology rather than grammar. And the Augustinian friars also developed schools where instruction ranged from song and grammar to philosophy and theology. Older cathedral grammar schools, while still functioning, were mostly now offering training in song and Latin grammar. Alongside these ecclesiastically based schools were town schools, guild schools, and privately endowed schools. The children of nobility still depended on private education offered by household tutors, although some were beginning to send their children to Latin grammar schools. Finally, most schools, whether elementary or secondary, lay or ecclesiastical, private or public, charged fees. At the end of the fourteenth century in England but not until the sixteenth century in Italy, individuals began to endow schools, with the result that some scholars could attend tuition-free.

BIBLIOGRAPHY

Black, Robert. "Italian Renaissance Education: Changing Perspectives and Continuing Controversies." *Journal of the History of Ideas* 52 (1991): 315–334.

————. *Humanism and Education in Medieval and Renaissance Italy: Tradition and Innovation in Latin Schools from the Twelfth to the Fifteenth Century.* Cambridge, U.K.: Cambridge University Press, 2001.

Bonner, Stanley. *Education in Ancient Rome: From the Elder Cato to the Younger Pliny.* Berkeley: University of California Press, 1977.

Boynton, Susan. "Training for the Liturgy as a Form of Monastic Education." In *Medieval Monastic Education.* Edited by George Ferzoco and Carolyn Muessig. London: Leicester University Press, 2000.

Contreni, John J. *The Cathedral School of Laon from 850 to 930: Its Manuscripts and Masters.* Munich, Germany: Arbeo, 1978.

————. *Carolingian Learning, Masters, and Manuscripts.* Brookfield, Vt.: Variorum, 1992. A series of articles published between 1972 and 1992 that focus on education and learning in early medieval Europe, especially the Carolingian Renaissance, highlighting the Irish contribution and Laon cathedral.

Goitein, S. D. *A Mediterranean Society.* Volume 2: *The Community.* Berkeley: University of California Press, 1971. See especially chapter 6, "Education and the Professional Class."

Grendler, Paul. *Schooling in Renaissance Italy: Literacy and Learning, 1300–1600.* Baltimore: Johns Hopkins University Press, 1989.

Hildebrandt, M. M. *The External School in Carolingian Society.* Leiden, Netherlands: Brill, 1992.

Irvine, Martin. *The Making of Textual Culture: "Grammatica" and Literary Theory, 350–1100.* Cambridge, U.K.: Cambridge University Press, 1994.

Jaeger, C. Stephen. *The Envy of Angels: Cathedral Schools and Social Ideals in Medieval Europe, 950–1200.* Philadelphia: University of Pennsylvania Press, 1994.

Jones, Michael. "Education in Brittany during the Later Middle Ages: A Survey." *Nottingham Medieval Studies* 22 (1978): 58–77.

Kanarfogel, Ephraim. *Jewish Education and Society in the High Middle Ages.* Detroit, Mich.: Wayne State University Press, 1992.

Law, Vivien. *The Insular Latin Grammarians.* Woodbridge, U.K.: Boydell, 1982.

Marcus, Ivan G. *Rituals of Childhood: Jewish Acculturation in Medieval Europe.* New Haven, Conn.: Yale University Press, 1996. See especially chapter 3, "Ancient Jewish Pedagogy."

McGrath, Fergal, S. J. *Education in Ancient and Medieval Ireland.* Dublin: Studia "Special Publications," 1979.

McKitterick, Rosamund. *The Carolingians and the Written Word.* Cambridge, U.K.: Cambridge University Press, 1989.

———. "The Palace School of Charles the Bald." In *Charles the Bald: Court and Kingdom.* 2d ed. Edited by Margaret T. Gibson and Janet Nelson. Brookfield, Vt.: Variorum, 1990.

———, ed. *The Uses of Literacy in Early Medieval Europe.* Cambridge, U.K.: Cambridge University Press, 1990. Various articles that examine literacy in Europe from the sixth to the tenth centuries and which range from Ireland and Spain to Byzantium.

Moran, Jo Ann Hoeppner. *The Growth of English Schooling 1340–1548: Learning, Literacy, and Laicization in Pre-Reformation York Diocese.* Princeton, N.J.: Princeton University Press, 1985.

Morrish, Jennifer. "King Alfred's Letter as a Source on Learning in England in the Ninth Century." In *Studies in Earlier Old English Prose.* Edited by Paul E. Szarmach. Albany: State University of New York Press, 1986.

Mulchahey, M. Michèle. *"First the Bow is Bent in Study": Dominican Education before 1350.* Toronto: Pontifical Institute of Mediaeval Studies, 1998.

Orme, Nicholas. *English Schools in the Middle Ages.* London: Methuen, 1973.

———. *Education in the West of England, 1066–1548.* Exeter, U.K.: Exeter University Press, 1976.

———. "Schools and Society from the Twelfth Century to the Reformation." In his *Education and Society in Medieval and Renaissance England.* London: Hambledon, 1989.

———. *Medieval Children.* New Haven, Conn.: Yale University Press, 2001.

Petrucci, Armando. *Writer and Readers in Medieval Italy: Studies in the History of Written Culture.* Edited and translated by Charles M. Radding. New Haven, Conn.: Yale University Press, 1995.

Pryce, Huw. *Literacy in Medieval Celtic Societies.* Cambridge, U.K.: Cambridge University Press, 1998.

Riché, Pierre. *Education and Culture in the Barbarian West, Sixth through Eighth Centuries.* Translated by John J. Contreni. Columbia: University of South Carolina Press, 1976.

———. *Education et culture dans l'Occident médiéval.* Brookfield, Vt.: Variorum, 1993. A collection of articles written by Riché between 1980 and 1988, ranging from the late antique period to the twelfth century and examining, among other matters, pedagogical ideas, Gerbert of Aurillac, Benedictine schooling, and the role of the Irish.

Roest, Bert. *A History of Franciscan Education (c. 1210–1517).* Leiden, Netherlands: Brill, 2000.

Verger, Jacques. *Culture, enseignement, et société en Occident aux XIIe et XIIIe siècles.* Rennes, France: Presses Universitaires de Rennes, 1999.

JO ANN HOEPPNER MORAN CRUZ

[See also **DMA:** Schools, Cathedral; Schools, Grammar; Schools, Islamic; Schools, Jewish; Schools, Monastic; Schools, Palace; Universities; Universities, Byzantine.]

SEMIOTICS. See **Signs, Theory of.**

SERVANTS were essential at all levels of medieval society. Royal households employed five hundred or more domestic servants, and higher servants employed their own personal servants. A peasant household added a servant if at all possible; that person might be a poor relative who received no more than bed and board in return for hard labor. Because notions of hierarchy, division of labor, and the social values assigned to domestic work—indeed the very definition of domestic labor itself—differed markedly from modern times, a number of distinctions must be made to set medieval domestic servants in context.

Service held manifold meanings in medieval life. In fifth- to ninth-century kingdoms, administrative offices that governed the realm evolved out of service roles in royal households. The mayor of the palace guarded the king's door before he ascended to power in his own right; in early times a royal marshal or constable oversaw the stables, while a seneschal or steward and a chancellor or chamberlain provided for the needs of the king and his family. In southern Germany the ministerials (*ministeriales*) or knightly administrative class remained bondsmen of the crown throughout the medieval era. Service at this level of society was anything but menial, providing one indication among many that personal access to the ruler and his circle was a surer route to power than freeborn status and military prowess. In no way did this evolution of administrative offices out of service roles ennoble the hard menial labor necessary for the smooth running of a great household, nor did the language articulating feudal bonds—for example, "your humble servant, milord"—influence attitudes toward domestic servants. Vassalage, with its elaborate gestures of deference and service, was a form of dependence peculiar to the upper classes, where being the "man" of a great lord to whom one was bound to give aid and obedience was an indication of high status and conveyed no intention to perform base tasks.

Domestic servants' actual roles are best understood from the twelfth century onward. With the proliferation of household accounts, contracts, court proceedings, letters, sermons, and advice manuals a detailed picture emerges of the lives of servants and the conditions under which they lived. As towns grew so did the demand for domestic staff. Occasionally in artisan households domestic service shaded into apprenticeship, creating some opportunity to develop marketable skills. In medieval London more males than females entered apprenticeships, which were designed to fill roles in male-dominated crafts. In periods of labor shortage households resorted to hiring the sons of serfs to get the cheap labor that apprenticeship provided an artisan household. A learned skill improved an ordinary servant's prospects in life. In Paris in 1272 Orenge of Fontenay, a servant trained in wool carding, developed a right arm and elbow so inflamed that she could not work. Her labor in the house of Maurice, a weaver, was so valued that she received room and board until, four years later, she was cured by a miracle at the tomb of St. Louis and returned to her former work. In fourteenth-century Exeter households supported by women servants frequently brewed and sold ale, thereby enriching the household, which in turn bettered the relative position of servant women who brewed.

Domestic servants who performed the least skilled and most menial tasks might or might not be paid; they either worked as servants in their youth and passed on to a better life or remained servants for a lifetime, performing the skilled work they had learned on the job, like cooking or stable work. Households hired out some of the most despised tasks. In late medieval London teams of men called "gong farmers" cleaned privies at two shillings a ton, piling their refuse onto carts and sending it out of town by barge. This task had to be performed every two years or so, and it was the good fortune of household staff to avoid it. Laundresses picked up and delivered loads of laundry to urban households, taking on a task considered among the most backbreaking and undesirable household drudgery. Laundresses, whose personal lives were not overseen by a mistress and master but who instead lived independently, were frequently accused of loose living and were at times regarded as little better than prostitutes.

GENDER AND DIVISION OF LABOR

Sometimes the gender division of labor in the Middle Ages surprises. Well-born young men, usually in training to be knights, served at high table in great noble or royal households. Some acquaintance with good manners was desirable, and presenting dishes at table could teach social skills. But their time serving others was brief, and certainly it was not onerous work. The heavy work of butchering, food preparation, and cooking was handled by menial servants who labored at their jobs without respite. Women servants were not spared the heavy work of carrying firewood for the kitchens, and they often hauled goods. In the north of England a feminization of the servant population involved in the victualing and the leather-tanning trades occurred after the Black Death, when men found better jobs elsewhere. Leather workers tanned their own skin along with the hides on which they worked, so both the color of their hands and the lingering smell of the chemicals they used branded these women.

In Germany from the fourteenth century onward women's wages were usually about half of men's. This was true whether employment was in an elite house in a city, a rural estate, or an artisanal household. A feminization of service occurred in Germany and across western Europe. Very possibly the transformation of "maid" (German, *magd*), originally denoting an unmarried woman, into a synonym for a single woman employed as a domestic worker, began at this point. In tight labor markets after the Black Death men moved out of the domestic service sector and into more lucrative jobs. This resulted in a devaluation of domestic service, as women who encountered few other chances to better their position remained in service.

Perhaps the most specialized of all female servants was the wet nurse, who might perform her services within the infants' family's household or in her own home, very possibly out in the countryside. In Florence over the course of the later Middle Ages there was a movement to send children out to wet nurse. This was a change driven by a shortage of reliable wet nurses in town, as more and more wealthy households sought them for their children. A rural wet nurse living with her husband was regarded as somewhat untrustworthy, because, against strict orders, she might cohabit with her husband, become pregnant, and lose her milk. St. Catherine of Siena (1347–1380), the next-to-last of twenty-five offspring, was the first of her siblings to be nursed by her mother, while her twin was sent out to be breast-fed by a wet nurse and soon died. It is unlikely that Catherine's parents could have produced such a large family had her elder siblings been breast-fed by their own mother rather than a wet nurse. Scholars associate wet-nursing with affluent families' desire to produce as many offspring as possible during the wife's childbearing years. High priority was placed on hiring a competent, clean, and conscientious woman for the task.

SLAVERY AND CONTRACT LABOR

In the Mediterranean south, a wet nurse might be referred to as a *balia* and might be either a free or unfree

SERVICE AGREEMENT

I, Giacomo from Cremona now an inhabitant of Venice in the parish of San Paternian, make manifest with my heirs and successors that I give and affirm to you, lady Clara, a widow of sir Pietro di Avanzo of the parish of San Lorenzo, my daughter named Francesca such that from now on at your free will she must live and remain with you and in your service (and) serve you loyally and that she must maintain and keep your possessions to the best of her ability, without fraud or evil intent. For your part, you must give her food, clothing, and shoes in good measure according to your means. The girl must not leave you or your service without your consent. And if at any time I cause the girl to leave your service, then I promise and obligate myself to pay you all the expenses that you have incurred up to that day on which she is removed by me or by some other person acting on my behalf from your service. If, however, I ever try to act against this agreement, then I, with my heirs and successors, am obliged to pay you or your heirs and successors five gold lire. And this agreement remains in force.

[Venice, dated March 1407. No mention of a wage or term of service, which was likely ten years, according to a statute from 1388.]

SOURCE: Romano, *Housecraft and Statecraft*, pp. 129–130, citing Venetian State Archives CI, Notai, busta 24, notary Rolandinus de Bernardis, protocol 1406–32, fol. 58r.

woman. In thirteenth-century Dubrovnik (Ragusa) the wet nurse was likely to be a slave, and she might also live out her life as the nurse and companion of her young charge, often accompanying her to her new home upon marriage. Slavery appears to have been highly attractive to wealthy householders because of the absolute control it offered over those who provided personal services like wet-nursing and child care. At best a slave could run away, but unless there was a supportive community to which to flee, escape was seldom feasible. While close to 90 percent of slaves registered in medieval Dubrovnik were women, runaways were almost evenly divided between women and men. This suggests that enslaved men, who probably performed work outside the home, had far

better opportunities to run away than did women slaves, who lived under close surveillance.

A revived slave trade in the Mediterranean south was part of the response to the shortage of domestic servants in the late Middle Ages. Traditionally, Italian cities fulfilled their needs for domestic labor by contracting for service; this was referred to as indenture in Venice (see sidebar). If money was paid out when a service contract was drawn up, the parent or guardian of the young person very likely received it. In Florence, rural girls contracted for domestic service received room, board, and a basic wardrobe, and they worked for a protracted term of five, eight, or ten years. Contract servants remained single through their years of service, but if all went well they might receive a small dowry at the end of their term, which probably afforded them the opportunity to wed and remain in town. Dowries might also be awarded to servants in a master's or mistress's will. Servants simply did not think in terms of regular wages, and often it took a precipitous departure for a servant to collect any money. A servant's best chance to collect sums due was to force the master to close his or her account.

A household staffed by young girls working under contract might also employ some slaves purchased from Bosnia or Greece, or Tartar or Russian slaves obtained in the Crimea. Piero Guarducci and Valeria Ottaviani argue that a slave brought into an Italian household served as a warning to servants that they could be replaced, thus ensuring a docile workforce. Wealthy households throughout Europe relied on a rigid hierarchy of tasks and obligations for servants, as well as different terms of service and distinctions between free status, contract labor, and slavery. These distinctions strengthened the householder's control over domestic staff, who were seldom viewed as honest or hardworking.

MORALITY AND RELIGION

Servants were frequently characterized as untrustworthy, disrespectful, and incompetent. Indeed, advice manuals make grim reading whenever the subject of servants is raised. A wife's task was to keep servants honest, hardworking, obedient, and silent by both example and instruction, as the Goodman of Paris admonishes his young bride-to-be. Francesco Barbaro (1390–1454), a Venetian humanist, took matters one step further in "On wifely duties." Following the example of Cato the Elder, a good wife should immediately rid the household of any servant or slave too old to work, since "it [is] in no way proper to keep useless slaves in a household," Barbaro advised. On the other hand he stated that an ignorant servant might be turned into a hardworking, faithful, and diligent worker through training and the promise of promotion, and he further advised that servants should not be separated from their children and families. He noted as well that servants would be grateful for good medical care. Positive incentives were recommended to householders, but the general tenor of Barbaro's discourse is that servants are lazy, possibly slovenly, and probably immoral if left to their own devices.

On the issue of morality, town statutes, religious authority, and advice manuals all concurred: servants were to remain chaste as well as obedient. The difficulty in living up to this standard was the likelihood that a pregnant servant would bear her master's child or that of another member of his family. Through the medieval era households tended to care for the illegitimate offspring of their servants or to find them suitable mates, thus terminating their service. Generally speaking, the servant who was not chaste was regarded as the guilty party; in some towns she could be punished, branded, or even banished for fornication.

Servants working in Jewish households had to meet special conditions throughout Christian Europe. In Venice Christian servants working for Jews needed special approval from officials with jurisdiction over the Jewish population. These servants were forbidden to eat, drink, or sleep in the homes of their employers, and only mature servants were permitted to serve in Jewish homes. Servants or slaves whose religious backgrounds aroused suspicion of heresy or schism were required by the Catholic church to be baptized. The religious and moral conduct of domestic staff fell squarely on the shoulders of the Christian householder.

In the Middle Ages some women servants moved from the countryside to town to better their prospects, and some contract servants obtained dowries so they could wed and remain in town. Nevertheless menial unskilled labor in the household was increasingly devalued as the medieval world shaded into the modern. While labor shortages affected domestic service in the later Middle Ages, this failed to improve the conditions under which most servants labored. Men left domestic service, attracted by work with better prospects elsewhere; in the south the labor shortage was answered in part by a revival of the slave trade. Throughout Europe householders remained steadfastly in control of the terms under which servants rendered their labor.

BIBLIOGRAPHY

PRIMARY WORKS

Barbaro, Francesco. "On Wifely Duties." In *The Earthly Republic: Italian Humanists on Government and Society.* Edited by Benjamin G.

Kohl and Ronald G. Witt. Philadelphia: University of Pennsylvania Press, 1978. A fifteenth-century Venetian treatise informing wives of their household duties.

Power, Eileen, trans. *The Goodman of Paris (Le ménagier de Paris): A Treatise on Moral and Domestic Economy by a Citizen of Paris (c. 1393).* London: G. Routledge and Sons, Ltd., 1928. Advice manual to a young Parisian bride from her elderly groom.

Society of Antiquaries of London. *A collection of ordinances and regulations for the government of the royal Household, made in divers reigns. From King Edward III, to King William and Queen Mary. Also, receipts in ancient cookery.* London: J. Nichols, 1790. Microfilm, History of Women 519. New Haven, Conn.: Research Publications, 1975. Household accounts, rules, and some kitchen recipes from the time of King Edward III.

SECONDARY SOURCES

Bennet, Judith M., and Amy M. Froide. *Singlewomen in the European Past, 1250–1800.* Philadelphia: University of Pennsylvania Press, 1999. Some of the articles discuss women servants and slaves.

Farmer, Sharon. "Down and Out and Female in Thirteenth-Century Paris." *American Historical Review* 103, no. 2 (April 1998): 345–372. The poor in Paris included a number of single women who were domestic servants.

Freed, John B. *Noble Bondsmen: Ministerial Marriages in the Archdiocese of Salzburg, 1100–1343.* Ithaca, N.Y.: Cornell University Press, 1995. How noble bondsmen intermarried, perpetuating their unique legal status.

Goldberg, P. J. P. *Women, Work, and Life Cycle in a Medieval Economy: Women in York and Yorkshire, c. 1300–1520.* Oxford: Clarendon Press; New York: Oxford University Press, 1992. Discusses women servants in late medieval York, England.

Guarducci, Piero, and Valeria Ottanelli. *I servitori domestici della casa borghese toscana nel basso Medioevo.* Florence: Salimbeni, 1982. Discusses the relation of slavery to wage labor in Italian households.

Hanawalt, Barbara A. *Growing Up in Medieval London: The Experience of Childhood in History.* New York: Oxford University Press, 1993. Life stories of youth, including servants, who moved to or grew up in London.

———, ed. *Women and Work in Preindustrial Europe.* Bloomington: Indiana University Press, 1986. Two of the essays concern domestic service, others discuss related occupations.

Heers, Jacques. *Esclaves et domestiques au Moyen Âge dans le monde méditerranéen.* Paris: Fayard, 1981 Ties the medieval revival of the slave trade to the market for domestic servants.

Klapisch-Zuber, Christiane. *Women, Family, and Ritual in Renaissance Italy.* Trans. Lydia Cochrane. Chicago: University of Chicago Press, 1985. Articles discuss households, servants, and wet nurses.

Kowaleski, Maryanne. *Local Markets and Regional Trade in Medieval Exeter.* Cambridge, U.K., and New York: Cambridge University Press, 1995. Statistical comparisons of servants to other occupations in an English town.

Mertes, Kate. *The English Noble Household, 1250–1600: Good Governance and Politic Rule.* Oxford and New York: Basil Blackwell, 1988. Features household accounts and statistics on elite households.

Origo, Iris. "The Domestic Enemy: The Eastern Slaves in Tuscany in the Fourteenth and Fifteenth Centuries." *Speculum* 30, no. 3 (July 1955): 321–399. Older but still valuable on domestic slavery.

Romano, Dennis. *Housecraft and Statecraft: Domestic Service in Renaissance Venice, 1400–1600.* Baltimore: Johns Hopkins University Press, 1996. Servants, including gondoliers, in late medieval and Renaissance Venice.

Stuard, Susan Mosher. "Ancillary Evidence for the Decline of Medieval Slavery." *Past and Present* 149 (November 1995): 3–28. Discusses medieval chattel slavery for women domestics.

SUSAN MOSHER STUARD

[See also **DMA:** Class Structure, Western; Constable, Local; Feudalism; Guilds and Métiers; Marshal; Ministerials; Seneschal; Serfs and Serfdom: Western Europe; Slavery, Slave Trade; **Supp:** Childbirth and Infancy; Women.]

SEXUALITY. "Sexuality" refers to the set of meanings a given culture constructs around sexual behavior. The European Middle Ages had its own distinct set of sexual categories and identities. Where modern schemes of categorization put a great emphasis on the gender or age of one's partner (one is classified as a heterosexual, a pedophile, etc., based on the object of one's desire), medieval schemes put more emphasis on whether one played an active or passive role than on who one's partner was. "Active" and "passive" did not mean pursued and pursuer; a woman could be very aggressive in seducing her partner but was still considered the passive partner in intercourse because she was the one mounted and penetrated.

The history of sexuality is a history of attitudes or ways of thinking and feeling rather than a history of who did what to whom. Different people in medieval society had very different attitudes; there is no such thing as "the medieval attitude" toward sex. The leaders of the church might espouse one view, but it never completely permeated the culture, and sexual behavior may indeed have been less restricted in this supposedly church-dominated society than in more modern ones. Different kinds of writing, written for different purposes, express different ideas about sexuality. These writings rarely took into account the ways the man or woman in the street (or the field) understood sexuality. In a society where most writing was for public consumption, some aspects of intimate life never got recorded.

CHASTITY

The fundamental distinction in the Christian Middle Ages was between those who were sexually active and those who were chaste. For the majority of modern people, virginity or chastity is not an identity, orientation, or way of life but a circumstance. People may approve of those who remain virgins until marriage, but a much smaller number find it admirable to remain unmarried and virgin for one's entire life. In the Middle Ages, however, virginity was not only a life stage (although remaining a virgin until marriage was certainly valued) but also a highly respected calling, one might say a state of the soul. It was not necessarily a goal for everyone, but it was a distinct sexual identity.

Among Jews and Muslims, on the other hand, virginity before marriage was important for women, but virginity as a lifelong status was not desirable. While they feared the same desires as Christians, most Jewish authors held that marriage legitimated these desires. Marriage was required not only for the sake of procreation but also to prevent lustful thoughts. Jewish philosophers in the Mediterranean region were more ascetic than northern rabbis; the German pietists of the twelfth and thirteenth centuries (Hasidei Ashkenaz), while very concerned about the harmful effects of lust, urged marriage rather than chastity.

For many Christians, choosing chastity meant taking up a particular way of life in a religious order. Men could become monks or secular priests; both were required to be celibate (unmarried), although priestly celibacy was not fully enforced until the twelfth century. Women could become nuns. Widows or widowers as well as the unmarried could join religious orders, and even the married could do so if both spouses agreed. By the later Middle Ages, other options appeared. Men could become mendicant friars who traveled and preached. Women, especially in the Low Countries, could join the Beguines, who lived in groups without undergoing the enclosure of nuns; they could also become Franciscan or Dominican tertiaries, lay affiliates of a religious order, some of whom lived together in communities. Throughout the Middle Ages both men and women chose to become recluses or anchorites, living on their own. These options might offer women (and men) more autonomy than marriage or the cloister.

Throughout the Middle Ages—indeed, from the beginning of Christianity—Christians argued about whether sexual intercourse could ever be anything other than a sin. For some, marriage was a lesser evil, permissible because not everyone could be expected to maintain strict chastity. For others, it was a positive good, although perhaps still a lesser good than virginity.

Particularly in response to the teaching of dualist groups—the Manicheans in the fourth and fifth centuries, the Cathars in the twelfth—who claimed that the body and therefore all sexual intercourse was evil, mainstream Western Christian teaching held that sex for purposes other than pleasure—to have children, to prevent one's spouse from falling into sin—was acceptable. However, chastity was always preferable; some medieval writers believed that no sexual act, no matter how conjugal and procreative, could be accomplished without concupiscence (sinful desire), and even those canonists and theologians who argued against this position were deeply suspicious of intercourse.

The suspicion of all sexual behavior as sinful had its roots in early Christianity. Sexual asceticism became more mainstream in Christianity than it had in the ascetic movements in Hellenistic pagan and Jewish culture that influenced it. Abstinence was not for everyone, but everyone recognized the holiness of those who did take it up. While Jesus himself in the Scriptures did not put a great deal of emphasis on sexual abstinence, he did refer to "those who have made themselves eunuchs for the sake of the Kingdom of Heaven" (Matt. 19:12), implying that the rejection of sex (either literally or metaphorically) was of high spiritual value. Paul, in his epistles, paid more attention to the question of abstinence. He grudgingly allowed that "it is better to marry than to burn" (1 Cor. 7:9).

Several reasons determined the emphasis on sexual renunciation in early Christianity. Hellenistic philosophers taught that sexual relations tied one to the concerns of the body and the world and distracted one from the things of the mind. Christianity added to this the notion of purity. In early Christianity women took up the notion of virginity for another reason, independence from male domination. Because marriage was the only acceptable sexual activity for women, rejection of sex meant rejection of control by a husband. The spiritual authority chaste women amassed could help them gain their independence from fathers and brothers as well.

Augustine of Hippo was the early Christian writer who most influenced medieval thought about sexuality. He placed a high value on virginity but stressed that marriage too was an honorable status. Jerome, however, in his treatise *Against Jovinian* (393), wrote a diatribe against marriage (and against women) that also greatly influenced medieval thought about virginity. Both he and his contemporary Ambrose of Milan stressed that virginity could take women out of their socially defined gender roles.

These early Christian writers praised chaste widowhood as well as virginity. Medieval writers, too, valued the renunciation of sexual activity even among those who were not virgins: widows, repentant fornicators or prostitutes, and even the married who agreed to live chastely with their spouses. Virginity, especially for women, remained somewhat different, because it im-plied a certain bodily integrity that once lost could never be regained. Medieval texts, however, were far from unanimous in emphasizing physical integrity, and virginity as a state of the soul—what we today might call an identity—remained far more important.

Most of what we know about the chaste in the Middle Ages comes from their biographies—hagiography or saints' lives. These texts attempted to persuade the audience that their subject was indeed a saint and to provide examples for believers to emulate. Chastity constituted a common feature of a holy life.

Most early medieval saints were monks or nuns, whose chastity was assumed rather than a noteworthy achievement. For those saints in the secular world, virginity was not as important an issue as it later became. A saint engaged in sex as little as possible, but to be married and have intercourse in order to conceive children did not detract significantly from sanctity. The sixth-century Frankish queen and saint Radegunda provides a good example. Because of her family position Radegunda was too valuable a marriage prize to be allowed to remain a virgin. According to her biographers, however, she used to get up from her husband Chlothar's bed at night and pray near the privy. Eventually she fled and became a nun. Her biographers never refer to marital intercourse as having polluted or corrupted her; she wished to escape marriage because it distracted her from full concentration on God, not because it made her impure.

With the emergence of the church reform movement of the eleventh century, which promoted the enforcement of clerical celibacy, a new rhetoric of chastity emerged, drawing on early Christian writings about the evils of sex and marriage and the importance of ritual purity. Chastity now became a more important distinguishing feature of those who had chosen the religious life. Especially for secular clergy living among sexually active people, chastity of the body required constant vigilance. Although intended for the clergy, the writings that encouraged this vigilance affected the laity as well.

The stricter enforcement of clerical celibacy also promoted an already existing pattern: the division of society into those intended for marriage and those intended for chastity. Not everyone with a calling to chastity was able to maintain it—economic need or family pressures might force them into marriage—but some maintained it even within marriage, either by submitting to sexual relations only reluctantly or by persuading their spouses to forgo them altogether. (According to the doctrine of the "marriage debt," however, neither spouse was allowed to outright deny the other sexual intercourse.)

The church did not especially encourage chaste marriage, in part perhaps because it threatened the boundaries between clergy and laity. Perhaps, too, churchmen thought that the availability of this choice would encourage women to rebel against their husbands.

By the later Middle Ages, while many texts glorified virginity for women, physical intactness was generally less important than the spiritual state. For young women who were to marry, physical virginity could be important—the ritual of displaying the bloody sheet after the wedding night was not unknown in the Middle Ages, although it was not usual. For those who chose an unmarried life, it did not matter so much whether one was a virgin, a widow, or a reformed fornicator; what mattered more was the condition of one's soul.

From a medical point of view, sexual abstinence might be considered harmful, both for women and for men. Medieval medical theory stressed moderation and balance. Overindulgence in sex could be harmful, but abstinence could lead to a harmful buildup of semen (which many thought was a product of blood, secreted by both men and women). Some diseases were thought to be specific to virgins and curable by sexual intercourse.

Medical texts also provide an interesting perspective on chastity of soul. Theologians generally concluded that being raped did not make a woman unchaste, as long as she did not consent or take pleasure in it. Some medical writers believed that women emitted seed during orgasm, which was thus necessary to become pregnant. However, it was possible to receive physical pleasure from intercourse without consent of the will. Some theologians, though, held that the higher virtue was to subject one's flesh to the will so that an involuntary orgasm would not be possible. Thus a truly virtuous man would not have nocturnal emissions, and a truly virtuous woman would not experience pleasure when raped.

MARITAL SEX

The idea that women could not conceive without an orgasm is one of the few clues we have to the practice of marital sex. If a husband wanted children, he had to make sure that his wife took pleasure in sexual intercourse. Some medical manuals counseled foreplay, for example caressing the woman's breasts, for that reason. The thirteenth-century Jewish *Sefer Hasidim* suggests the man allow his wife to reach orgasm before him so that she will conceive a son. However, medical theory also held that women derived pleasure from being penetrated and from receiving the men's seed, and these ideas reinforced the notion of female passivity. Stories like the French *fabliaux* show women who exhaust their husbands with their insatiable demands for sex, but the pleasure that they lusted for was a passive rather than an active one.

For the most part, medieval texts do not spend much time describing the normal parameters of marital sex. Both texts and manuscript illuminations treat the position of man on top as considered normal and natural; indeed, the thirteenth-century writer William Peraldus referred to any other position as a form of sodomy. A Jewish midrash (a story explaining the Bible) from the ninth or tenth century recounts how Lilith, Adam's first wife before the creation of Eve, fled and was turned into a demon because Adam refused to allow her to be on top during intercourse.

Manuscript illuminations also hint that people went to bed naked, though this could be an artistic convention. The theme of one woman substituted for another on the wedding night appears in literary sources frequently enough to indicate that married people commonly had sex in the dark, but here too the needs of narrative may take precedence over actual practices. Married couples would sometimes not have had a great deal of privacy. Peasant couples might share their bed with several children. Among the aristocracy servants might sleep in the room, although bed curtains did provide some degree of privacy. Among the upper aristocracy husbands and wives had separate bedchambers, so all the servants would be aware when they were sharing a bed.

Not all medieval authorities agreed on the role of sexual intercourse in the creation of marriage. The canonist Gratian, in his great compilation the *Decretum* (mid-twelfth century) argued that the completion of marriage required consummation. On the other hand, the theologian Peter Lombard, author of the *Sentences* (1155–1157), which became the most important theology textbook of the Middle Ages, held that not intercourse but mutual consent created a marriage, which was binding even if intercourse did not take place. Both parties, however, had to be capable of contracting marriage. If one was incapable of sexual intercourse, the marriage was not valid, in the same way as it was invalid if one party had previously contracted marriage with another. The idea of marriage as constituted by consent grew out of the view that marriage was not primarily a means for engendering legitimate children, providing an outlet for lust, or creating social and economic ties between families, but a calling, an identity or status in life. Nevertheless, outside of the programmatic writings of theologians and canonists, medieval people generally understood marriage as being for the purpose of reproduction, and therefore sexual intercourse was central to it. This intercourse had to be at least potentially reproductive. Augustine had written, in a passage frequently cited in the later Middle Ages, that if a man were to have unnatural sexual intercourse it would be better to have it with a prostitute, who was already corrupt, rather than with his wife.

Although procreation was central to marriage, theologians and canon lawyers throughout the Middle Ages held that a married couple could have sex for other reasons—to pay the marriage debt when one spouse demanded it, to prevent the temptation to engage in extramarital sex, or even to increase love between the couple—as long as they did not actively do anything to prevent conception. A couple could have intercourse at times when the woman was believed to be infertile or after she had passed the age of childbearing.

No medieval Christian theologian or canonist wrote that contraception was permissible, even when the life of the woman was at risk from further childbearing; they urged abstinence instead. The practice of breast-feeding, particularly among poorer people, contributed to the limitation of family size, since lactation tends to inhibit ovulation, especially in undernourished populations. Repeated prohibitions of herbs (mainly abortifacients rather than contraceptives), amulets, and pessaries indicate that people were trying these methods as well. Some of the herbal or barrier methods may have been somewhat effective—not as effective as modern birth control methods but enough so as to have a statistically significant effect on population. Jewish authorities permitted contraception under some circumstances—for example, to protect the health of the woman.

The church hedged marital intercourse about with prohibitions relating not only to reproductive intent but also to particular times and places. The penitentials, or handbooks for confessors, of the early Middle Ages were particularly restrictive about the dates on which one could legitimately have sexual intercourse. Less than half the days in the year would have been permissible: Sundays, Wednesdays, Fridays, many holidays, and all of Lent were days for abstention, as well as the woman's periods of menstruation, pregnancy, and lactation. Later writers said that the marriage debt trumped these prohibitions, but the partner who demanded sex on a holy day still sinned even if the one who complied did not.

Although either partner was required to render the marriage debt upon demand, and women who refused their husbands sex were condemned, there is remarkably little evidence of husbands enforcing their right to marital sex by violence. Medieval lawyers would not have called this rape because the woman had no right to withhold her consent. Cruel husbands in medieval stories and

court cases beat their wives, but this mistreatment does not include sexual violence. This hardly means such violence never took place, but perhaps indicates that people did not see it as a prominent problem or simply accepted that a woman had no right to refuse.

Medieval Jewish society had different rules about opportunities for marital sex. The Talmud prohibits a man from forcing his wife to have sex with him; it also permits marital sex even when not procreative. A Jewish wife did have the right (called *onah*) to sexual intercourse with her husband; this was comparable to the Christian doctrine of the marriage debt, but only women could demand it. Jewish culture did have one very important, universally acknowledged taboo. A woman was considered unclean during her menstrual period; after her period was over she had to wait a week and undergo a ritual purification by visiting an immersion bath *(mikveh)* before she could have intercourse with her husband. Rabbis criticized women who refused to go to the *mikveh* until their husbands fulfilled some condition. When a woman visited the *mikveh,* everyone knew that she and her husband would be having sex that night (this was considered a particularly likely time for the conception of a child). This was an obligation and not considered shameful as it was in Christian society.

In both Jewish and Christian society, marital sex was understood as something that a husband did to his wife. Even when the woman took pleasure in sex, it was pleasure in receiving her husband's seed (and sometimes in emitting her own as well). The nearly unanimous use of language for intercourse in which the man is the grammatical subject and the woman the object—even when it is a woman who is speaking—reflects a pervasive understanding that the man's and the woman's experience of sex was very different.

MEN AND EXTRAMARITAL SEX

Men's and women's experiences outside of marriage were quite different also. Men's sexual transgressions were often taken far less seriously than women's. This did not mean that within medieval culture men were free to do whatever they wished sexually; many church authors condemned both men and women for sexual activity outside of marriage, and local communities might see men who had mistresses or patronized prostitutes as less than honorable. Nevertheless, at all levels and in all segments of medieval society men had considerably more latitude than women did, and women's sexual activity outside of marriage reaped more opprobrium than men's.

Literary depictions of men in love tend to be more frankly sexual than those of women: men speak of enjoying their ladies more than vice versa. This difference may reflect the power differential between men and women, where women need men for their economic support and physical protection, whereas men need women for the reproductive possibilities they provide. It may also reflect a medieval understanding of the modesty appropriate to a woman. It does not necessarily reflect the understanding of men as sexually active and women as passive because passivity in the sex act itself did not make women passive or reticent in seeking it out. However, although literature occasionally depicts women as sexual aggressors, men more often play that role. A belief that women are more lustful than men is not necessarily incompatible with a pattern in which men take the initiative; women may have much greater incentive to control their desire, such as fear of pregnancy or loss of reputation. Sex had fewer dangerous consequences for men, although medical writers did believe that overindulgence, whether due to intercourse or masturbation, could lead to illness.

The hierarchical nature of society offered some men many sexual opportunities outside of marriage. Men of the aristocracy had mistresses as well as more casual sexual encounters. Indeed, one of the ecclesiastical biographers of Henry I of England (*r.* 1100–1135) praised these liaisons, attributing them not to lust but to the wish to beget offspring and distribute the royal seed. Some scholars have confused *gynacaea,* or women's weaving workshops on large estates of the early Middle Ages, with harems because lords expected to have sexual access to the unfree women who worked there. Although the droit du seigneur, or "right of the first night," is a myth, lords could rape peasant women with impunity, and literature like the French *pastourelle* poetry celebrated these encounters. Householders or their sons often saw their domestic servants as fair game. In those medieval societies that held slaves, men often bought or used women slaves for sexual purposes. Under Muslim law, a man was permitted to have sex with his own slaves. A slave who bore a child to her master received special privileges, including her freedom at her master's death. Because Christian jurisdictions prohibited such relations (although they were still common in practice), there were no legal protections for the women involved as there were under Islam. The same sexual access to persons of lower status may have held true for male-male sexual relations, although there is much less evidence about this. It did not hold true when the woman was the party of higher status. Aristocratic women's sexual access to servants was not assumed, and indeed under some laws of the early Middle Ages a free woman who had sex with a slave could herself be enslaved.

It is not possible to determine how great a part coercion, whether economic or physical, played in relationships between men of higher status and women of lower. Medieval courts rarely heard accusations of rape of a servant by her master, but that does not mean that such relations were consensual; it could mean that the woman simply had no recourse. In situations where the couple remained sexual partners over a period of years and had children together, even if the woman must eventually have consented or at least become resigned to the situation, this does not mean that the man never brought pressure to bear.

Medieval men were not concerned with drawing a line between persuasion and coercion, seduction and rape. Rape was a concern if the victim was the wife or virgin daughter of a respectable man. Otherwise, people assumed she was sexually available and her consent did not really matter. Rape could be an assertion of the social hierarchy, in which the men at the top could do as they pleased, or it could be an assertion of the gender hierarchy, as in fifteenth-century Dijon, where an epidemic of gang rape served to punish women who had transgressed sexually in some way (including being abandoned by their husbands).

MALE SAME-SEX RELATIONS

Within most medieval understandings of sexuality, role rather than object choice defined a man's identity. It made a difference whether a man played the active (masculine) or the passive (feminine) role, but not whether he was active with men or with women. There was no category of "gay" into which all men who had sex with other men fit. Just as a man and a woman who had sex together were not understood as committing the same act, the same was true of two men who had sex together. Court records describe the act as "A committed sodomy with B," not "A and B committed sodomy." If both played an active role, they might say "A committed sodomy with B and B with A"; it was not something they did together but something they did to each other by turns.

Sodomy was, in most medieval schematizations, the worst of the sexual sins. Treatises on sin called it "the unmentionable vice" or more commonly "the sin against nature" (the latter did not always mean sodomy but was often used synonymously with it). Sodomy did not only refer to sex between two men. It was against nature because it was sterile, and it could refer to any sort of nonprocreative intercourse, occasionally including heterosexual intercourse with the woman on top, which medieval people thought inhibited conception. Sodomy not only undermined the procreative purpose of intercourse, it also upset the gender order because it put men in the passive or women in the active role.

Most of the time "sodomy" was used to mean anal sex between two men. A variety of legislation and penitentials attacked the practice in the early Middle Ages, but the medieval critique of sodomy really began with Peter Damian in the eleventh century. Damian associated sodomy particularly with the clergy. Others too made this association, perhaps because of their celibacy, perhaps because monasteries created opportunities for close relationships between men. Priests and monks throughout the Middle Ages were satirized for their heterosexual adventures but also for their love of boys, and by the fifteenth century the English heretical sect of the Lollards criticized the doctrine of clerical celibacy precisely on the grounds that it promoted sodomy.

Medical writers did not necessarily consider sodomy against nature, some holding passive sodomy to be "natural" for some men who had peculiarities of the genitalia that caused them to receive pleasure from the reception of seed. This argument, however, did not lead to an understanding of a sodomite as a biologically determined particular type of individual. For the active man, medical theory generally held that the discharge of seed in moderation was necessary for good health, but no medical theory discussed a preference for a woman or man as the receptacle.

Although any man could commit sodomy, with a man or woman as partner, and the Middle Ages had no concept of "the homosexual" as a type of person, some men had clear preferences for one gender or the other. The most famous with a preference for men was probably Edward II of England in the fourteenth century, who had notorious relationships with at least two male lovers and according to chronicles was eventually murdered by a red-hot poker up the anus. The fact that Edward was also married and fathered children does not tell us much about his sexual preferences or desires; as a king, he had an obligation to the dynasty to reproduce. But he also fathered at least one illegitimate child. This does not mean that he was "bisexual," another concept unknown to the Middle Ages. It does mean medieval people did not assume that men who desired or engaged in sex with other men had an exclusive preference. Legal records show us that not only did many married men commit sodomy but the same men had sex with men and with female prostitutes.

The Italian metropolis of Florence in the late fourteenth and fifteenth centuries provides the most information about sodomy, both from the fiery sermons of the friar Bernardino of Siena and from the records of the Office of the Night, a municipal body established in 1432 to regulate and punish what the town saw as a sodomy epidemic. As Bernardino described it, sodomy involved an older man as active partner and a teenage boy as passive partner. He accused boys of inviting sodomy by wearing effeminate and elaborate clothing and families (particularly mothers) of encouraging it by letting their sons dress up in order to gain the attentions of a wealthy lover. The Office of the Night encouraged people to place anonymous denunciations of sodomites in boxes strategically placed all over town. The resulting accusations show that active partners were typically in their very late teens or their twenties; by contrast, only 3 percent of passive partners were over twenty. The age pattern of older active partners and younger passives corresponds to the marriage pattern in Florence at this time, where men tended to marry in their thirties and women in their teens, even early teens. By their late twenties or early thirties, when men tended to marry, far fewer were accused of sodomy. In Florence, then, sodomy seems for many men to have been a life stage rather than a permanent preference. A few "inveterate" sodomites continued to be passive partners for their entire lives, but Florentines considered this much more shameful than for a boy to do so.

Oral sex complicated the dichotomy between active and passive. In vaginal, anal, or interfemoral sex, the penetrator was the active. The ancient Romans had considered the penetrator in oral sex as the active partner too, while the fellator or fellatrix was the passive partner. In Florence, however, the distinction was based on who actually did the work, not on who penetrated and ejaculated, and the fellator was considered the active partner. Thus it was permissible for an older man to fellate a boy, but not to be anally penetrated by him.

Information does not survive in as much detail from anywhere else in Europe as it does from Florence, although Venice runs a close second, and there are a number of northern European towns where some sodomy accusations survive. Because the bulk of the evidence we have is from criminal accusations and prosecutions, however, we cannot trust it as to the prevalence of the behavior. Some towns may simply have prosecuted it more strictly at some times, depending on local anxieties about the gender order and about reproduction (in the wake of the Black Death, for example, when population was low), or for political reasons.

Court records reveal more about acts than about feelings. Some poetry and letters, however, especially from monasteries in the twelfth century and before, speak of powerful emotional relationships between men. There is no direct evidence that the men were lovers, but scholars typically treat similar poetry and letters from a man to a woman as evidence of an erotic relationship, even if unconsummated. From medieval Islamic cultures there also survives love poetry from men to younger men or boys, and Jewish writers in Muslim cultures also wrote such poetry, despite the fact that Jewish and Muslim religious law condemned sexual intercourse between men much as Christian law did.

Medieval writers had little criticism of these emotional relationships, whether between two monks or between aristocrats or kings like Richard the Lionhearted of England and Philip II Augustus of France in the twelfth century, who also seem to have loved each other deeply when young. It may be that if contemporaries had really thought the latter were committing sodomy with each other, they would have reacted negatively. It may be, however, that people did not necessarily connect two men having a loving and physical relationship with sodomy, which was a rejection of God.

Indeed, medieval society celebrated a type of deep, passionate friendship between men that modern society does not. Most people today would assume that contemporary men who expressed their feelings for each other in the same way medieval men did were sexually involved with each other. Medieval people either did not believe that they were or did not think it noteworthy, because they rarely objected to it.

WOMEN AND EXTRAMARITAL SEX

Some churchmen argued that women were less responsible for their sexual lapses than men: they were not only more lustful but also weaker and therefore less able to control their lusts. This argument did not lead to toleration of women's nonmarital sexual activity but rather was a reason to keep women under strict control. Adultery was treated far more seriously for women than for men: although the church taught that it was just as bad for a man to violate his marriage vows as for a woman, usually authorities only prosecuted adultery when the woman was married, whether or not the man was. Because inheritance was so important in medieval society, a wife's adultery was especially problematic, as it cast doubt on the legitimacy of her children. Men's fear of women's adultery also formed part of a general distrust of feminine independence that emerged in a variety of misogynist diatribes.

A few texts, some written by women, hint that some people thought women's adultery might be excusable. Several of the *lais* of Marie de France, a French poet of the second half of the twelfth century, send the message that a husband who does not treat his wife well only gets what is coming to him if she is unfaithful. In other stories that make a jealous husband a figure of ridicule, it is hard to know whether a medieval audience would have sympathized with the unfaithful wife, but it is clear that they were not expected to sympathize with the husband. Older men married to much younger women were the most frequent targets of ridicule, indicating at least some sense that women were entitled to love or sexual pleasure in marriage.

At some levels of society families policed unmarried women's sexual behavior less than that of married women. Among aristocrats a daughter's virginity might be particularly important in making a good marriage. Among English villagers, however, church court records reveal that "simple fornication," between a single man and a single woman, was reasonably common and was often a prelude to marriage. Fornicating couples incurred a fine but not the outrage of the community. Wage workers or servants, who at least in some parts of Europe tended to marry later than the aristocracy and who lived with their employers or other workers rather than with their families, had opportunities both to meet potential marriage partners and to have sex with them.

Nonmarital sex was not always a prelude to marriage. Some women lived with men to whom they were not married, including priests. Medieval texts tend to call priests' partners "concubines," but in many cases the relationship was permanent, and they were wives in all but law. Although the priest was breaking a vow and his partner was not, to late medieval writers the woman was more responsible and took most of the blame.

Women whose sexual relations were with other women also could not marry their partners. Perhaps 10 percent of all women in medieval northern Europe never married. Some of these were nuns, and some would have married if they could, but some made the choice not to marry because they wanted independence or because they preferred relationships with other women. Unmarried women often lived together without arousing much comment, but we do not know whether they were friends, housemates, or lovers.

There is somewhat more evidence for loving relationships among women than there is for genital sex between them. As with men's same-sex love letters and poetry, most although not all comes from a monastic context. Visitations that commented on sexual irregularities in women's monastic houses, though, focused preponderantly on the heterosexual. The infrequency of references in the monastic visitations or in court records comes from the medieval understanding that sex was something that one person did to another, by penetrating him or her. If there was no phallus, there could be no penetration and therefore no gender transgression. Those few women who were condemned by the courts for same-sex behavior were described as usurping the role of a man, probably through the use of a dildo or cross-dressing. Medieval sources reveal little trace of a lesbian identity.

The women who appear most frequently in court records for sexual offenses were not adulteresses, concubines, or lesbians but prostitutes. Canon lawyers made promiscuity, rather than the acceptance of money for sex, the deciding feature of a prostitute; however, most of the people arrested as prostitutes were those who did take money.

The working conditions of prostitutes varied greatly. Most turned to the trade, on a casual or permanent basis, because work opportunities for women were meager and wages low; examples of what the Greeks called *hetairai* and early modern Europeans called courtesans are very few in the Middle Ages. Some prostitutes worked in official brothels, either private institutions licensed by the local authority or institutions municipally owned. The regulations of these brothels were supposed to protect the women but also severely restricted many aspects of their lives. Other prostitutes operated in a much less formal setting, as streetwalkers or out of their own homes through the use of a go-between.

Many municipal authorities took the attitude that official brothels prevented greater sin, either the rape or seduction of respectable women or sodomy between men. Although the authorities considered prostitutes already fallen and therefore appropriate outlets for sexual desires that might otherwise endanger the respectable people of the town, the prostitutes' peers among the poor or working people may not have adopted that attitude. People who believed that simple fornication was not all that bad—perhaps a venial rather than a mortal sin—might consider the prostitute just another service worker. Prostitutes participated in networks of women within towns, associating with servant women if not with elite women.

Particularly in multicultural regions of Europe, like Spain, prostitutes' activity threatened religious and ethnic boundaries. Christians, Jews, and Muslims all prohibited their women from sexual contact with men from the other groups, while concerning themselves much less with their own men's intergroup activities. In Christian Castile, for example, a Muslim or Jewish man who had sex with a Christian woman was liable to the death penalty, even if the woman was a prostitute. Authorities were especially concerned about prostitutes in this connection. Because prostitutes were "common women" available to all men of the community, for a non-Christian to have access to them was tantamount to allowing him membership in the community, a boundary that Christians did not want to break.

In medieval Europe a normative religious discourse taught that sex was basically sinful and evil (though tolerable for reproductive purposes), and yet some segments of the society chose to ignore that teaching. Sexuality related to personal identity in the Middle Ages differently than it does in the contemporary world, the relevant categories being the chaste, the married, and the sinful. Gender distinctions, too, were central to how medieval people understood sexuality: to be active was to be masculine, to be passive was to be feminine, and in any given sex act the two partners played very different roles. What we know about medieval sexuality, however, is mainly what the elites of the society thought about it, and both women and men of other social groups may have experienced it rather differently.

BIBLIOGRAPHY

Biale, David. *Eros and the Jews: From Biblical Israel to Contemporary America.* New York: Basic Books, 1992.

Boswell, John. *Christianity, Social Tolerance, and Homosexuality: Gay People in Western Europe from the Beginning of the Christian Era to the Fourteenth Century.* Chicago: University of Chicago Press, 1980.

Boureau, Alain. *The Lord's First Night: The Myth of the Droit de Cuissage.* Translated by Lydia G. Cochrane. Chicago: University of Chicago Press, 1998.

Brown, Peter. *The Body and Society: Men, Women, and Sexual Renunciation in Early Christianity.* New York: Columbia University Press, 1988.

Brundage, James A. *Law, Sex, and Christian Society in Medieval Europe.* Chicago: University of Chicago Press, 1987.

Bullough, Vern L., and James A. Brundage, eds. *Handbook of Medieval Sexuality.* New York: Garland, 1996.

Cadden, Joan. *Meanings of Sex Difference in the Middle Ages: Medicine, Science, and Culture.* Cambridge, U.K.: Cambridge University Press, 1993.

Camille, Michael. *The Medieval Art of Love: Objects and Subjects of Desire.* New York: Abrams, 1998.

Dinshaw, Carolyn. *Getting Medieval: Sexualities and Communities, Pre- and Post-Modern.* Durham, N.C.: Duke University Press, 1999.

Elliott, Dyan. *Spiritual Marriage: Sexual Abstinence in Medieval Wedlock.* Princeton, N.J.: Princeton University Press, 1993.

Goodich, Michael. *The Unmentionable Vice: Homosexuality in the Later Medieval Period.* Santa Barbara, Calif: ABC-Clio, 1979.

Gravdal, Kathryn. *Ravishing Maidens: Writing Rape in Medieval French Literature and Law.* Philadelphia: University of Pennsylvania Press, 1991.

Jaeger, C. Stephen. *Ennobling Love: in Search of a Lost Sensibility.* Philadelphia: University of Pennsylvania Press, 1999.

Jordan, Mark D. *The Invention of Sodomy in Christian Theology.* Chicago: University of Chicago Press, 1997.

Karras, Ruth Mazo. *Common Women: Prostitution and Sexuality in Medieval England.* New York: Oxford University Press, 1996.

McNamara, Jo Ann, and John E. Halborg, with E. Gordon Whatley, eds. and trans. *Sainted Women of the Dark Ages.* Durham, N.C.: Duke University Press, 1992.

Mormando, Franco. *The Preacher's Demons: Bernardino of Siena and the Social Underworld of Early Renaissance Italy.* Chicago: University of Chicago Press, 1999.

Nirenberg, David. *Communities of Violence: Persecution of Minorities in the Middle Ages.* Princeton, N.J.: Princeton University Press, 1996.

Noonan, John T., Jr. *Contraception: A History of Its Treatment by the Catholic Theologians and Canonists.* Cambridge, Mass.: Harvard University Press, 1986.

Otis, Leah Lydia. *Prostitution in Medieval Society. The History of an Urban Institution in Languedoc.* Chicago: University of Chicago Press, 1985.

Payer, Pierre J. *Sex and the Penitentials: The Development of a Sexual Code, 550–1150.* Toronto: University of Toronto Press, 1984.

Puff, Helmut. "Female Sodomy: The Trial of Katherina Hetzeldorfer (1477)." *Journal of Medieval and Early Modern Studies* 30 (2000): 41–61.

Riddle, John M. *Contraception and Abortion from the Ancient World to the Renaissance.* Cambridge: Harvard University Press, 1992.

Rocke, Michael. *Forbidden Friendships: Homosexuality and Male Culture in Renaissance Florence.* New York: Oxford University Press, 1996.

Rossiaud, Jacques. *Medieval Prostitution.* Translated by Lydia G. Cochrane. New York: Blackwell, 1988.

Sayyid-Marsot, Afaf Lufti al-, ed. *Society and the Sexes in Medieval Islam.* Malibu, Calif., Undena, 1979.

Schuster, Peter. *Das Frauenhaus: Städtische Bordelle in Deutschland (1350–1600).* Paderborn: Ferdinand Schöningh, 1992.

Wogan-Browne, Jocelyn. *Saints' Lives and Women's Literary Culture c. 1150–1300: Virginity and Its Authorizations.* New York: Oxford University Press, 2001.

RUTH MAZO KARRAS

[See also **DMA:** Cathars; Celibacy; Contraception, European; Contraception, Islamic; Family; Law, Canon; Prostitution; **Supp:** Abortion; Droit du Seigneur; Gender, Theories of; Women.]

SEXUALITY, MEDICAL. Medieval physicians and medical writers dealt with aspects of the modern category "sexuality" in the contexts of their concerns with reproductive success and general regimen. The subjects they discussed included the mechanisms of sexual experience and the ways in which sexual dynamics could affect health. Like most learned and much popular medicine in the Jewish, Christian, and Muslim societies of the period, the approach to sexual desire, pleasure, and expression depended on an understanding of anatomy, physiology, psychology, and health.

SOURCES AND CULTURAL CONTEXTS

Learned medical knowledge in this period had its origins primarily in ancient Greek medical traditions, especially those influenced by the Hippocratic writers and Rufus of Ephesus, Soranus, and, above all, Galen. The works of Aristotle also shaped medieval medical views, as did some South Asian concepts and medicinal substances. Evidence concerning the early Middle Ages is scanty. Latin versions of obstetrical material by Soranus suggested that sexual activity was not required for women's health, a notion later displaced. Surviving remedy books contain instructions that may have been intended to stimulate desire as aids to conception, such as a potion for the man and woman to drink, made with parsley seeds, the herb rue, filtered honey, and the best wine. The notion that heterosexual intercourse could be separated from procreation is suggested by the existence of recipes for contraception.

From the ninth century onward, physician-scholars of various ethnicities and religions writing in Arabic, often under the patronage of Muslim caliphs, developed a huge body of medical literature in which sexual matters occupied a place. In addition, they produced works on sexual hygiene for an elite audience, containing advice and anecdotes about erotic practices. This material, in turn, circulated in the Muslim territories from the Caucasus across the Middle East and North Africa to Spain, contributing to Hebrew and Latin medical theory and practice.

Differences in religion, social organization, and other conditions insured that medical approaches to sexuality were not uniform in the Mediterranean and European world. Physicians writing in Arabic composed far more material on sexual behavior and health than those writing in Hebrew or Latin. Cross-cultural exchange was common, however. For example, Constantine the African, a Christian monk who came from Islamic North Africa and worked in the region of Salerno in the eleventh century, translated, summarized, and borrowed from Arabic authors, notably ʿAli ibn al-ʿAbbās and Abū Bakr Muḥammad ibn Zakarīya al- Rāzī (Rhazes). Sexual subjects figure in Constantine's general works on medicine and in his separate treatise *On Coitus.* He offered explanations for the effect of mood on sexual relations and recipes for enhancing and dampening desire. A four-

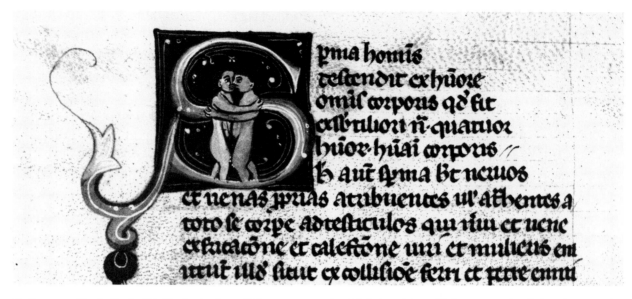

De Spermate *(On the Seed). This illumination from a 13th-century manuscript of Galen's work is notable for its image of a naked couple in a standing embrace.* INSTITUZIONE BIBLIOTECA MALETESTIANA. REPRODUCED BY PERMISSION.

teenth-century work on childlessness written in Judeo-Arabic (Arabic in Hebrew letters) borrows from Latin as well as Arabic traditions. It advises a man to make sure that his wife is awake and aroused by caresses before having intercourse with her. Scholars in Spain and southern Italy translated many Greek and Arabic medical works into Hebrew and Latin. One of the most important was the eleventh-century *Canon of Medicine* by Ibn Sīnā (Avicenna), translated into Latin in the twelfth century. It included chapters on the anatomy, functions, and pathology of the genital organs that gave direction and detail to Western authors for more than four centuries.

THEORIES CONCERNING SEXUALITY

Accounts of sexual anatomy and physiology varied. A profusion of nerves made the penis sensitive to a particular tickling in men; in women the "vulva" (which could refer to the vulva, vagina, or genitals in general) and the uterus were sensitive. But according to one view the body as a whole experienced sexual sensations since, during intercourse, the reproductive seed was drawn from all parts. At the same time, a certain type of "spirit"—a highly refined and active physiological substance that was responsible for the motion of the seed—originated in the brain and descended through certain vessels via the kidneys to the loins, reaching the male or female receptacles (called "testes" in both sexes). It often mediated between the corporeal and the mental. A third substance, called "windiness," was sometimes said to be involved, and, along with the spirit, it contributed to a man's erection and ejaculation. Pleasure was thus caused

not only by the release of seed but by the rush of contributory substances through the body. Other accounts represented the seed as the direct product of a series of "digestions" (refinements) of food that took place in the stomach, liver, heart, and testes. Many authors noted the involvement of a psychological cycle. The sight of an attractive person kindled appetite, which moved an individual toward fulfillment. The mind remembered both object and pleasure, so that sight or memory could reawaken desire.

Since, in the case of heterosexual attraction, the good of the species was involved, nature or Providence provided for sexual desires and pleasures. For the individual, the proper regulation of sexual activity, along with food, drink, exercise, baths, sleep, and emotional state, was crucial to the maintenance of the body's balance (health) or the rectification of imbalance (illness). "Regimen" or "diet," as this approach was called, was the foremost tool of medieval medicine.

According to one tradition, referred to as "Methodist" and sometimes associated with Soranus, health depended on the proper relationship between constriction, which retained substances in the body, and laxity, which released them. Reproductive material needed to be collected, and its retention gave rise to healthy sexual impulses. On the other hand, at a certain point it needed to be excreted. Emission was a cause of pleasure, and failure to achieve some form of release was harmful. According to another tradition, derived from Galen, health depended upon an equilibrium of the paired "primary" qualities of hot-cold and moist-dry. Too much or too little sexual activity could adversely affect their proper, temperate balance. Since, for example, both male and female seed were believed to be moist, too much sex could cause desiccation. People with different temperaments (proportions of the basic qualities) were understood to have different kinds and degrees of sexual appetites and experiences.

Sexual topics figure in medical texts devoted to successful and healthy procreation, a number of which were produced in Latin and Hebrew in the later Middle Ages. Since desire was associated with the buildup of reproductively necessary seed and pleasure with its similarly required emission, attention to erotic sensibilities joined the instructions about diet, timing, drugs, and charms that dominated medical discussions of fertility. Thus treatises on sterility, gynecology, and obstetrics include references to foreplay and aphrodisiacs. Concerns expressed about the relative sizes of the man's penis and woman's vulva (and measures to adjust them) may have been meant to enhance stimulation. Ointments rubbed on the genitals were sometimes said to increase desire. Some of the treatments involving sympathetic magic and spells (such as the application of wolf's testicles to a man's or woman's genitals) may have been aimed at arousal, though it is difficult to distinguish this immediate goal from more distant goals of love, marriage, fertility, or the production of sons.

These general concepts applied to both women and men. Medical writers usually emphasized women when addressing conception and took the perspective of men when discussing intercourse. Often the details of anatomy and physiology referred to men. Spirit and windiness, for example, played a specific role in erection. Medical encyclopedists included chapters on "satyriasis" and "gonorrhea" in men. They believed both sexes produced some sort of seed or "semen" necessary for procreation by refining blood. Since blood had the capacity to nourish all parts of the body, they reasoned that seed produced from it would have the potential to form a new creature. When speaking of women, however, many physicians emphasized the menses rather than seed. Menstruum, though the result of the same process as male and female seed, was not completely refined, and thus retained the properties of blood. When not providing nutriment for a fetus, menstrual blood was expelled. Menstruation thus served as an outlet for female superfluities, making sexual release a less pressing urge and health need for adult women in their prime than for men or for women before and after the age of menstruation.

The focus of sexual excitement and enjoyment in men was the nerve-filled penis and, to a lesser extent, the testicles and the anal sphincter. In women, whose erogenous areas included the breasts, sexual response was more diffuse. The uterus possessed the faculty (the tendency and power) of drawing both the man's and the woman's released seed into itself and was thus associated with desire and pleasure. Men's pleasure in intercourse was consequently more "intensive," both spatially and temporally, and women's more "extensive." Men's was concentrated in emitting seed; women's distributed between emitting and receiving. Women and men were thus not regarded as having different amounts of sexual appetite but rather as having different types. In sexual relations men were generally represented as the actors, women as those acted upon.

DIFFICULTIES AND PATHOLOGIES

Because sexual behavior was a significant axis of physiological balance and imbalance, excessive or inadequate sex, as well as sexual acts undertaken at the wrong times or under the wrong conditions, could cause illness. The result might be any number of symptoms, from headaches or melancholy to the odor of putrefying moisture. Physicians occasionally issued caveats about the circumstances for therapeutic intercourse and prescriptions or prohibitions of coital positions. Medical opinion accommodated but did not always accord with other social and cultural perspectives. A text known as *Trotula* suggested ways to restore the endangered health of women who refrained from intercourse as the result of a vow; Moses Maimonides offered aid to a male patron who felt socially required to have intercourse more often than would be healthy.

Appetites and acts themselves might be disordered in a number of ways. From the medical and broader cultural perspective, dispositions, acts, and their consequences could shade from the natural into the unnatural and harmful. Women, because of their cooler temperaments, might be naturally inclined to desire the heat of intercourse, but this disposition could become excessive. Adolescents, in transition between childhood and adulthood, experienced sexual arousal from the movement of spirit and other physiological causes before they were able to experience the pleasure of release. From the medical perspective, male and female youths who kept trying, whether by intercourse or masturbation, were neither completely temperate nor pathological.

Homosexual desires and pleasures, when mentioned at all, were usually taken to be products of an unhealthy constitution or unnatural disposition. Lesbian sexuality is almost invisible in the medical literature. One twelfth-century Arabic treatise on sexual relations by Samūʾīl ibn

Yaḥyā ibn ʿAbbās al-Maghribī al-Andalusī does mention women whose physical incompatibility with their husbands leads them to turn to other women. It also distinguishes a group of mainly intelligent, literate women who have certain masculine qualities, enjoy heterosexual intercourse only when they take the initiative, and are given to sexual relations with other women.

Arabic medical writers occasionally mention that men have intercourse with boys, but only *ubnah,* an adult man's desire to be penetrated by another man, was dealt with as a medical problem. Al-Rāzī apologized for having written a treatise about the subject; most Western authors judged homosexual acts unspeakable. Al-Rāzī and the Italian physician Pietro d'Abano described the condition as innate. It involved a slight deflection of the ordinary physiological processes, giving rise particularly to stimulation around the rectum. But al-Rāzī also implied that it could develop, and Pietro thought it could occur in adults who had experienced such pleasures when young, becoming second nature. Once fully established, the condition could not be cured, though there was some disagreement about why. Ibn Sīnā and, following him, Latin authors believed the excessive sexual appetites characteristic of such men could be calmed by privative measures, such as limiting food, drink, and sleep, that would stem the production of seed and thus the pressure to release it. Al-Rāzī suggested trying direct heterosexual stimulation, along with warming the penis and testicles while cooling the rectal area with herbs or even an ice suppository.

In addition to treatments for the general imbalance and thus illness associated with inadequate or excessive sexual activity, medical works in Arabic, Hebrew, Latin, and various vernaculars offered remedies for sexual dysfunctions, especially but not exclusively in men, including recipes for aphrodisiacs. Several other specific conditions were understood to have a sexual dimension. In women the putrefaction of trapped seed was among a number of possible causes for the dangerous condition known as suffocation of the womb, the symptoms of which could include difficulty breathing and loss of consciousness. Among the remedies suggested was rubbing the genitals with medicinal ointments to secure release. There was no corresponding disorder in men.

Conversely, women were very seldom mentioned as the victims of lovesickness, a topic discussed by a number of Arabic authors. The condition was known in Arabic as ʿishk and in the West by terms like *morbus eros* and *amor heroicus.* Its symptoms were dominated by melancholy, which, like all temperaments, had both physiological (cold and dry) and psychological dimensions. Its

causes could likewise include a superfluity of seed and disorders in the mind involving perception, imagination, and judgment. General principles of regimen dictated treatments with food, wine, and baths but also with music, pleasant company, and sweet aromas to restore the sufferer's temperament to a healthy equilibrium. In addition, to relieve the pressure of accumulated semen, medical writers prescribed intercourse. The ascetic measures proposed to control homosexual desire are absent from the medical literature on lovesickness.

BIBLIOGRAPHY

Barkaï, Ron. *A History of Jewish Gynaecological Texts in the Middle Ages.* Leiden, Netherlands: Brill, 1998. A lengthy introduction followed by six Hebrew texts with English translations.

Cadden, Joan. "Western Medicine and Natural Philosophy." In *Handbook of Medieval Sexuality.* Edited by Vern L. Bullough and James Brundage. New York: Garland, 1996.

———. "Silences/Sciences: The Natures and Languages of 'Sodomy' in Peter of Abano's *Problemata* Commentary." In *Constructing Medieval Sexuality.* Edited by Karma Locherie, Peggy McCracken, and James A. Schultz. Minneapolis: University of Minnesota Press, 1997.

Constantinus Africanus. *Liber de coitu: El tratado de andrología de Constantino el Africano.* Edited and translated into Spanish by Enrique Montero Cartelle. Santiago de Compostela, Spain: Universidad de Santiago, 1983. An English translation made from a sixteenth-century edition is available: Delany, Paul. "Constantine the African's *De coitu:* A Translation." *Chaucer Review* 4 (1969): 55–65.

Green, Monica H. "Female Sexuality in the Medieval West." *Trends in History* 4, no. 4 (1990): 127–158.

———, ed. and trans. *The Trotula: A Medieval Compendium of Women's Medicine.* Philadelphia: University of Pennsylvania Press, 2001. A substantial introduction followed by three Latin texts with English translations.

Jacquart, Danielle, and Claude Thomasset. *Sexuality and Medicine in the Middle Ages.* Translated by Matthew Adamson. Princeton, N.J.: Princeton University Press, 1988.

Maimonides, Moses. *Maimonides "On Sexual Intercourse": fī l-jimâ.* Translated with commentary by Morris Gorlin. Brooklyn, N.Y.: Rambash, 1961. Also contains a translation of a second work on the subject falsely attributed to Maimonides.

Rosenthal, Franz. "Ar-Râzî on the Hidden Illness." *Bulletin of the History of Medicine* 52 (1978): 45–60. Reprinted in Franz Rosenthal, ed., *Science and Medicine in Islam: A Collection of Essays.* Aldershot, U.K.: Variorum, 1990. Contains a translation of al-Rāzī's treatise on *ubnah.*

Wack, Mary Frances. *Lovesickness in the Middle Ages: The "Viaticum" and Its Commentaries.* Philadelphia: University of Pennsylvania Press, 1990. Includes editions and English translations of Latin texts.

JOAN CADDEN

[See also **DMA:** Constantine the African; Contraception, European; Contraception, Islamic; Medicine, History of; Rāzī, Abū Bakr Muḥammad ibn Zakarīya al- (Rhazes); Science, Islamic; Science, Jewish; Sīnā, Ibn; Trota and Trotula; **Supp:** Body, The; Gynecology; Hygiene, Personal; Medicine, Islamic; Sexuality.]

SIGNS, THEORY OF. During the Middle Ages, theoretical considerations of the sign were entertained as part of epistemological reflections on ontology, grammar, logic, human anthropology, astrology, medicine, and law. The sign was considered primarily with respect to its agency in the spheres of cognition, communication, and representation; medieval semiotics explored signs from the viewpoints of their nature, classification, and signifying process. At stake in the concept of the sign was the ontology of reality, a topic whose comprehensiveness may account for the fact that discussions of semiotics pervade an extensive body of texts though very few medieval treatises are devoted to signs per se. These include the *Commenti super Priscianum majorem extracta* attributed to Robert Kilwardby and Roger Bacon's *De signis.*

AUGUSTINE'S SEMIOTICS

The most important early medieval discussion of signs was that of St. Augustine of Hippo (*d.* A.D. 430) who, in positing an explicit fusion of the theory of signs with the theory of language, took a radical departure from antiquity. Augustine's theory of signs was forged from Platonic, Aristotelian, and Stoic elements, so as to address his concern about the ambiguous natures of words and meaning, whose deferred referentiality clashed with his metaphysical understanding of the Logos, and of truth, as the absoluteness of presence. This compelled him to search for a method by which to endow words with the ability to signify. Such ability had, in classical semiotics, solely been the property of nonlinguistic events. Only empirical occurrences—for instance, the smoke that by implication reveals a fire—had been considered to be signs. The semiotic tradition prior to Augustine considered that a sign offered access to the knowledge of the object to which it referred. If words were to be (and to act as) signs, the knowledge of a word would imply knowledge of the thing it signified. In his early treatise *De dialectica* (A.D. 387), Augustine asserted that "a word is a sign of any sort of thing, it is uttered by a speaker and can be understood by a hearer." He defined the sign as "something which is itself sensed and which indicates to the mind something beyond the sign itself." Thus, signification is the power of signs to raise in the mind a concept, a meaning, which in turn will mediate an act of reference to things. This triadic definition of the sign implied that the relation between the sign and its referent was always mediated by meaning. In revisiting the subject several times, in *De magistro* (A.D. 389) and especially in *De doctrina christiana* (A.D. 396–397, with later additions), Augustine expanded these ideas but did not depart from them, and his definition of the sign became standard throughout the Middle Ages. However,

Augustine's fusion of word and sign required him to question the informative nature of the linguistic sign, which led to a new classification distinguishing natural and instituted (or intentional) signs. Natural signs, *signa naturalia* (e.g., smoke), signify without intention, through their inferential relation to that which they signify (fire). Instituted signs, *signa data* (e.g., words), are used by beings, including God, with the direct intention of communicating their thoughts or impressions to a perceiver who must have prior knowledge of the communicated object to recognize that the word is a sign of this object. Such prior knowledge comes from the inner word imprinted in the human mind by God, either in the form of innate knowledge or as impressions imparted by the objects of knowledge, that is, the entire world through which God expresses himself (*De Trinitate,* A.D. 399–419). All created things are *vestigia Trinitatis,* and are in that capacity signs of the Creator. The Platonic overtones of the Augustinian system stress the polar distinction between sign and thing and diminish the sign, which Augustine considers to be "worth less than the thing for which it stands." In Augustine's linguistics, there is but a single true referent, God; all other referents can only be imprecise derivatives of that absolute truth. In his attempt to accommodate both a linguistics of difference and a philosophy of essence whereby truth is conceived as perfect sameness, Augustine was a semiotician preoccupied with ultimate referentiality. Margaret W. Ferguson has shown how his theology of the incarnate Word bridged the gap between sign and thing by positing a sign, Christ-Logos, that is simultaneous and consubstantial with its referent (God). With the incarnation, a new category of signs was made possible, the sacrament, which Augustine termed a *sacrum signum.*

In the matter of signs, as in so many others, the Augustinian legacy was authoritative and fundamental. First, it was Augustine who, in *De magistro,* promoted language as the semiotic paradigm on the grounds of language's unique capacity to translate other semiotic systems. Second, in insisting upon the intentionality of the *signa data* and on conceptual mediation, Augustine introduced a psychological dimension to the idea of the sign and based his semiological system on communication. Third, in assigning to all created things the status of signs, Augustine planted the seeds of universal symbolism. Fourth, in denying the linguistic sign truthful referentiality, Augustine manifested a tendency toward dualism, with the sign inevitably separated from transcendental reality. Finally, in his treatment of incarnational theology, Augustine also laid the foundation for an immanent theory of signification that sanctioned a conflation between sign and thing, conceiving the signified thing as a constitutive part of the sign.

LINGUISTIC SIGNS

Among medieval thinkers subsequent to Augustine, opinions clashed over the relationship between sign, concept, and thing, with debates focusing on the difference between signification and reference. Did signs signify ideal concepts (universals) through which to refer to particular things, or did signs directly denote specific concrete things (individuals)? By the twelfth century, this question had become particularly crucial because of its central relevance for two major debates. The first concerned the nature of the Eucharistic sign, with those in favor of the doctrine of real presence holding that the Eucharistic sign was unique in actually being what it signified as opposed to those who considered the Eucharist to have symbolic meaning. The second debate was between realism and nominalism and bore upon the ontological status of abstract concepts (universals) and of concrete objects of everyday experience (individuals). Those holding that signs signified concepts also believed in the reality of universals through which the objectivity of human knowledge was preserved. Those holding that signs referred directly to things identified reality with individuals.

In his commentary on Aristotle's *De interpretatione,* Boethius (*d.* 524/526) settled upon the conceptual mediation of signs, that is, upon a definition whereby signs signified concepts, a position retained in the twelfth century by Anselm of Canterbury and Peter Abelard and in the thirteenth century by Thomas Aquinas, all of whom further elaborated a common definition for each aspect of the sign's tripartite dynamic. *Significare* refers to the concept (or universal) generated in the mind by the linguistic sign *(vox); denotare* (or *designare)* involves the semantic relationship between a sign and its conceptual (extralinguistic) object, that is, its definition or meaning *(definitio, sententia);* and *nominare* or *appelare* concerns the sign's function of referring to a concrete individual thing. In this approach, alert to the psychological and ontological aspects of language and focused on the function of communication, meaning—that is, "definition" or *sententia*—is correlated to a sign by way of designation or denotation, while signification is an aspect of the causal relationship by which that same sign makes a person think. In this conception, universals exist neither in individual things nor separated from them but in the soul. The cognitive model implied by this approach asked what signs signify and offered a real entity (the universal) as an ontological basis for a correspondence theory of truth.

Challenges to this model took two directions. In one, where the goal was to gain freedom from ontological commitment, attention was directed away from the actual referent *(res)* toward the mode of signifying it *(modus significandi),* hence the term *Modistae* to designate the speculative grammarians Boethius of Dacia (*fl.* second half of the thirteenth century), Martin of Dacia (*d.* 1304), Thomas of Erfurt (*fl.* first quarter of the fourteenth century), and Siger of Courtrai (*ca.* 1283–1341), who were responsible for this particular doctrine of linguistic signs. Modistic theory analyzes words in sentences with respect to three modes: signifying *(modus significandi),* understanding *(modus intelligendi),* and being *(modus essendi).* The *modus significandi,* that is, a peculiar feature (noun, verb, cases, tense) of the sign (significative word), originates in the mind. The mind, by means of the *modi intelligendi,* that is, the mode by which it conceives what is then signified, reproduces in its signification process *(modus significandi)* the mode of being *(modus essendi)* belonging to the signified object. Modistic theory aimed at codifying the rules of a universal grammar on the assumption that there existed an isomorphic parallelism between linguistic structure and reality. Yet, the relationship between signs and reality was not worked out beyond the pairing which the *modus intelligendi* encoded within the word between the lexical component (e.g., man) and the mode of signifying (e.g., noun). The sign was a product of the intellect, and the thing to which it referred was not a particular extramental reality.

The second set of objections to the cognitive model of signification held by Boethius, Anselm, Abelard, and Aquinas was also directed at the modistic theory. Those who objected pointed out that, in these two models, signs signified concepts, and therefore all that could be verified were propositions (sentences) about mental entities. The concern underlying such objections was for truth and for the related issue of reference, and this prompted concentration on the sign's actual sense, that is, its semantic definition and the individual concrete thing to which it, the sign, might be properly applied. The question was no longer what but how signs signify, and the correspondence theory of truth, which helped address this question, stated that a proposition signifies as is the case, that is, by the actual presence of the signified object. Initially foreshadowed by Peter of Spain the Elder (*d.* 1277), this movement away from signification (as the relationship between signs and universals) gained strength at the universities of Paris and Oxford in the works and teaching of Roger Bacon (*d. ca* 1291), John Duns Scotus (*d.* 1308), and William of Ockham (*d.*

1347). In his *De Signis,* Bacon asserted that there was no conceptual mediation between a sign and the object it has been appointed to name and that a sign does not necessarily possess a sensible nature; he also omitted Augustine's canonical definition that a "sign causes the knowledge of something different from itself." For Bacon, the meaning of the linguistic sign depends upon a mythical *impositio,* a codified fixing of the correspondence between signs and things that rendered *significatio* a permanent property of the sign. This correspondence, that is, the meaning of the sign, is lodged in the human mind as a concept. Bacon explained the correspondence of the concept to extramental reality by fusing concept with the species (simulacra, images) which, generated by and in resemblance to every sensible object, is seen by the eye, abstracted, and imprinted in the mind. Linguistic signs (words) can point to mental objects (concepts) or to the concrete things to which concepts correspond, but the correctness of the reference is guaranteed only by the actual presence of the signified object. Objects and concepts are thus two different types of referent, each involving different semiotic processes. Signs signify things directly, as arbitrary and conventional symbols (names) applied to things with the intention to signify. Conversely, the relationship between sign and mental concept is natural (symptomatic) since it arises, not by virtue of an intention to signify, but through some natural relationship (causality, concomitance, or similarity). As for the equivalence between concept and thing, it too is based on similarity, necessity, or concomitance and thus, like the relationship between concept and sign, it is natural. Bacon's position that *significatio* indicates the relationship between signs and the actual states of the world was a drastic break from earlier tradition, which, since Plato, had vested *significatio* in the relationship between signs and concepts.

Duns Scotus, following upon Bacon's observations, theorized further about the relationship between words and concepts. He argued that the word-sign existed in subordination to the concept-sign since the word was imposed to signify the same thing that the concept signified directly and naturally. Ockham agreed that concepts are natural signs but argued that this was not on the basis of an iconic relationship to things. For were concepts to function as iconic signs of things, concepts would only be intermediate reproducers of that knowledge of the thing of which they were images and thus could not lead to a primary knowledge of that thing. Furthermore, Ockham argued that the objective relationship of resemblance, causality, or concomitance that concepts generically entertain with their objects is impossible to retrace because it is slowly built up in the mind through the ex-

perience of individual things. Ockham therefore reworked the theory of the concept as a natural sign in ways that were consistent with his nominalistic belief in the primacy of the individual and his rejection of a universal existing apart from or within things. He rejected Bacon's assimilation of concept to species, postulating that the thing itself is sufficient to be the direct cause of the act of knowledge, that is, the concept. The concept, thus, is identical with the act of knowing and is created in the mind by an inference grounded in experience of individual things. Concepts are the natural, "real" signs of things because they are the only possible signs of experienced reality. Words relate directly to those things they are imposed upon to name. Words do not signify concepts and are subordinate signs with respect to concepts, since concepts already signify directly and naturally the things that words have been imposed to name. Yet words and concepts signify the same thing. In removing any intermediary (such as mental images and simulacra) between the thing and the concept, Ockham abandoned the triadic inferential model of iconism (sign-likeness-thing) in favor of a dualistic model of linguistic symbolism whereby signs are symbols that represent things by substitution. Linguistic signs thus become bipolar instruments for representing the world and not, as in the Platonic-Augustinian model, a triadic communicative tool with which to transmit thought.

SACRUM SIGNUM

In *City of God* (*De civitate Dei;* A.D. 413–426), Augustine defined *sacramentum* as a *sacrum signum,* thus creating the particular category of the sacred sign that he characterized as showing a special resemblance (*similitudo*) to the (sacred) thing it signified. Hugh of St. Victor (*d.* 1141) further distinguished sacraments from such other sacred signs as ritual actions and instruments or holy images, by positing that sacraments were institutional signs containing and conveying that which they signify (*De sacramentis*). Peter Lombard (*d.* 1160) was responsible for introducing causality into the definition of sacraments, which, in the fourth book of his *Sentences,* he described as institutional signs (*signa data*) resembling "that which they signify and cause at the same time." Sacramental causality, that is, the sacraments' capacity to infuse grace, touched upon the issue of the agency of signs and of their effect upon the society that manipulated them. Medieval theologians, however, focused their attention not on the effects but on the modalities of sign efficacy. Some, following the lead of Thomas Aquinas, judged sacraments to be instrumental causes of grace by means of inherent virtue. Others, many of whom were associated with late medieval nominalism, judged sacramental efficacy to be covenantal, holding that "sacraments operate out of a pact of divine ordination," that they were signs rather than the cause of grace.

THE AGENCY OF SIGNS: ASTROLOGY, MEDICINE, REPRESENTATION

The issue of semiotic causality was treated variously in medieval Christian culture depending upon the extent to which such causality was seen as substituting for divine providence and human will. Patristic condemnation of astrology stemmed from a refusal to ascribe to celestial bodies any determinant influence upon the events of human life. In antiquity, the sky was considered to be a signifying space for the configuration of future events, which led to practices of divination and nativities (personal horoscopes done at birth). Even Augustine, who generally opposed such practices vehemently, accepted that constellations were signs, albeit signs "instituted by human presumption" when used to predict the future *(De doctrina christiana)*. Augustine asserted that the predictable orbit of the moon was useful to fix the date of Easter but was inefficacious for interpreting scripture. Nor would he entertain the classical hypothesis of a homologous correspondence between the microcosms and the general order of the universe (macrocosm). From the twelfth century onward, however, exposure to Aristotelian texts and to Arab scholarship on Aristotle's physical and cosmological doctrines inspired a group of theologians, including Raymond of Marseille *(fl. ca.* 1140), Gerard of Cremona *(d.* 1187), Albertus Magnus *(d.* 1280), and Roger Bacon in particular, to conceive of the heavens as a medium *(operatio caeli)* for God's actions upon terrestrial creatures. Bacon, in part 4 of his *Opus maius* (1266), claimed for stars and celestial bodies the status of *signa innuentia,* that is, of signs indicative of God's eternal knowledge of what occurs through nature or human will or by his own providence. Astral signs, thus, not only signify but cause influence as conduits of God's guidance, and as such, they imprint their properties upon inferior bodies. For Bacon and another advocate of astrology, Pierre d'Ailly *(d.* 1420), the heavens were as a system of natural signs, providing knowledge of possible future effects.

Since ancient Greek times, the practice of medicine had rested upon sign-based knowledge. In medieval medical treatises, methodology was still very much articulated around the concept of the sign, and semiotic processes remained an integral part of medical discourse and practice in Galenic texts (second century A.D.), in the *Canon* (translated by Gerard of Cremona) and *Cantica* (translated by Armengol Blasi de Montpellier) of Avicenna *(d.* 1037), in the *Conciliator controversarum quae inter*

philosophos et medicos versantur of Peter of Abano *(ca.* 1305) and in the commentaries upon the *Canon* by Gentile of Foligno *(d.* 1348). Medieval medical semiotics awaits investigation; it is not clear as yet how medieval medicine's close ties to philosophy and astrology may have influenced the structure of the medical sign, or whether particular orientations, Hippocratic, Aristotelian, Galenic, or Avicennan, contributed varied semiotic approaches. Alfonso Maierù's foray into the nature of the medieval medical *signum* permits some preliminary grasp of this complex semiotics. The observable effects of an illness were experienced empirically. They acquired *significatio* when considered mentally by the physician, thus becoming signs, *signa indicativa* (the illness itself, *accidens, passio*), or *signa prognostica* (symptoms dealing with the progress of the illness), or *signa rememorativa* (evidence concerned with the past history of the illness). *Signum* and *significatio* might therefore be used as equivalent in medical treatises, with *signum* being the sensible manifestation of illness and *significatio* the mental identification of this illness. Gentile de Foligno, however, insisted upon a distinction between these two. He considered that *accidens* (or *signum*) is material and occurs only in the patient's body, whereas *significatio* is formal and exists in the physician's mind independently of the illness. For Gentile de Foligno, medical *signa* have different natures; they may be either material or formal. Material signs, that is, symptoms, reveal the existence of a cause; the sign-*significatio* leads to the knowledge (though not to the understanding) of that cause with which it itself entertains not a causal but an inferential relationship. Medicine was thus, to paraphrase Aristotle, a science of signs and not of causes, and the issue for its medieval practitioner was how to match *signum* and *significatio,* that is, how to infer a valid cause (upon which depended proper treatment). This inference was made by implying a general rule to which medical conjecture referred the material sign that thereby acquired *significatio* as an instance of that rule and, in the case of success, became proof of that rule's validity and its applicability to other material signs. Medical semiosis offered, as a technique for interpreting an observable phenomenon, a method of hypothetical inference based on probability. In terms of this method, the material sign was not traced back to its cause but referred to a general rule; sign and rule reciprocally validated each other.

The association between signs and validation was central to the medieval system of documentary authorization, with the term *signum* referring to the various modes of authentication in use at different times and in different medieval European locations. One category of *signa* focused on the transaction itself: stones, knives, twigs, or rings stood for the thing conveyed in ceremonial transfer and, kept in archives or recorded in documents, had the effect of granting and guaranteeing the right to the thing transacted. A second category of *signa* focused on those party to the recorded deed. Early medieval charters concluded with the *signum manus* (or *manuele,* or *crucis)*, that is, the subscription of each individual involved in the transaction, authors as well as witnesses. Such *signa* included names and titles (if relevant) but were rarely autograph. The result was a loose referentiality that tended to depersonalize documents. From the eleventh century onward, the growing diffusion of two documentary formats, the notarial instrument in southern Europe and the sealed charter in the north, indicated the construction of a new referential system that incorporated personal authority within the body of the written record. The notarial sign manual *(signum meum, signum manus, signum meum authenticum)* was autograph and unique to each individual notary, who was bound to register it and to retain the same sign through his entire career. This assured validation through personal participation and objective verification. The seal *(sigillum),* bearing the name and image of its owner, was imprinted on a document with an intaglio-engraved seal matrix. As an imprint, the seal contained the trace of an origin within its very matter, which process, in the views of those scholars responsible for the diffusion of sealed charters, made the seal a sign forever indicating a radical presence. Validation was achieved by the seal's ability to mark origin and to materialize presence. This understanding of eleventh- and twelfth-century sealing semiosis emerged from the prescholastic discourse of chancery scholars, whose overlapping activities in monastic or episcopal schools and in chanceries, led them to formulate a sign theory that would address their concern for real presence (in the Eucharist) and for authoritative representation (in written records warranting personal commitment). By the thirteenth century, the discourse on seal semiotics had left the field of theology for that of the law. Subsequent sealing practices and formats indicate the existence of different signifying processes that responded to and articulated changing referential patterns. The complete history of these transformations throughout the Middle Ages has yet to be written.

Roger Kilwardby (*d.* 1279) noted that the Latin term *signum* had a wide range of uses (*signum multipliciter dicitur)*. Medieval theory was, in fact, deeply engaged in considerations of the linguistic sign and, to a lesser extent, of the sacramental sign. Momentum for medieval semiotic theory mainly derived from an interaction between two complementary traditions: one Augustinian, dealing with intentional signs, the cognitive

relation between signs and meaning, the communicative process, the other Aristotelian, dealing with natural signs, the system of signification, the relation between signs and the thing that is the case, and a truth-conditional approach for the acquisition of knowledge. Underlying all semiotic considerations was a logical concern for the nature of the relationship between sign and thing signified and an epistemological inquiry into the value to be attached to knowledge obtained by means of signs. Fluctuating between attention to meaning and a focus on truth, predicated upon metaphysics or logic, hinging on the status of universals and individuals, medieval sign theories may be said to have presented signs, variously, as vehicles for transmitting thought, as instruments for representing the world, and as operative agents. However, no evolutionary pattern seems to have directed these ideas, which remained in dialectical tension throughout the medieval period. The extent to which ideas about signs and the role of signs in medieval societies may have had reciprocal action has thus far attracted too little scholarly attention.

BIBLIOGRAPHY

PRIMARY WORKS

Abelard, Peter. *Dialectica.* Edited by L. M. de Rijk. Assen, Netherlands: Van Gorcum, 1956.

Anselm of Canterbury. *De grammatico.* In Desmond P. Henry, *The De grammatico of St. Anselm: The Theory of Paronymy.* Notre Dame, Ind.: University of Notre Dame Press, 1964.

Aquinas, Thomas. *In libros* Peri hermeneias *et* Posteriorum analyticorum expositio. Edited by Raymundi M. Spiazzi. Turin and Rome: Marietti, 1955.

Arens, Hans, ed. and trans. *Aristotle's* Theory of Language *and Its Tradition: Texts from 500 to 1750.* Amsterdam and Philadelphia: Benjamins, 1984.

Augustine. *De dialectica.* Edited by Jan Pinborg, with English translation by B. William Darrell Jackson. Dordrecht, Netherlands, and Boston: Reidel, 1975.

————. *De doctrina christiana.* Edited and translated by R. P. H. Green. Oxford: Clarendon, 1995.

Bacon, Roger. *De signis.* In Karin Margareta Fredborg, Lauge Nielsen, and Jan Pinborg, "An Unedited Part of Roger Bacon's 'Opus maius': 'De signis.'" *Traditio* 34 (1978): 75–136.

Boethius of Dacia. *Modi significandi sive quaestiones super Priscianum maiorem.* Edited by Jan Pinborg, Heinrich Roos, and Povl Johannes Jensen. Copenhagen: Gad, 1969.

Duns Scotus, John. *In primum et secundum librum Perihermeneias quaestiones.* In his *Opera Omnia.* 12 vols. Edited by Luke Wadding et al. Hildesheim, Germany: Olms, 1968–1969.

————. *Ordinatio, I–II.* Edited by Commissio Scotistica. Rome: Typis Polyglottis Vaticanis, 1954–1973.

Hugh of Saint Victor. *On the Sacraments of the Christian Faith.* Translated by Roy J. Deferrari. Cambridge, Mass.: Mediaeval Academy of America, 1951.

———. *De grammatica.* In his *Opera propaedeutica.* Edited by Roger Baron. Notre Dame, Ind.: University of Notre Dame Press, 1966.

Kilwardby, Robert [attributed to]. *Commenti super Priscianum majorem extracta.* Edited by Karin Margareta Fredborg, Niels Joergen Green-Pedersen, Lauge Nielsen, and Jan Pinborg. *Cahiers de l'Institut du Moyen Age grec et latin* 15 (1975): 1–146.

Martin of Dacia. *Modi significandi.* In his *Opera.* Edited by Heinrich Roos. Copenhagen, 1961.

Ockham,. William. *Summa logicae.* Edited by Philotheus Boehner, Gideon Gál, and Stephen Brown. St. Bonaventure, N.Y.: St. Bonaventure University, 1974.

Peter of Spain. *Tractatus, Called Afterwards "Summulae logicales."* Edited by L. M. De Rijk. Assen, Netherlands: Van Gorcum, 1972.

Thomas of Erfurt. *Grammatica speculativa.* Edited and translated by G. L. Bursill-Hall. London: Longmans, 1972.

GENERAL SECONDARY WORKS

Brind'Amour, Lucie, and Eugène Vance. *Archéologie du signe.* Toronto: Pontifical Institute of Mediaeval Studies, 1983.

Chenu, Marie-Dominique. "The Symbolist Mentality." In her *Nature, Man, and Society in the Twelfth Century.* Edited and translated by Jerome Taylor and Lester K. Little. Chicago and London: University of Chicago Press, 1968.

Chydenius, Johan. "The Theory of Medieval Symbolism." *Commentationes humanarum litterarum,* 27, no. 2 (1960): 1–42.

Colish, Marcia L. *The Mirror of Language: A Study in the Medieval Theory of Knowledge.* Rev. ed. Lincoln and London: University of Nebraska Press, 1983.

Eco, Umberto, and Costantino Marmo, eds. *On the Medieval Theory of Signs.* Amsterdam and Philadelphia: Benjamins, 1989. A collection of essays that gives an in-depth analysis of some major trends in medieval semiotics.

Evans, Jonathan D. "Medieval Studies and Semiotics: Perspectives on Research." *Semiotica* 63, nos. 1–2 (1987): 13–32.

———. "Medieval Semiotics." In *Semiotics in the Individual Sciences.* Bochum Publications in Evolutionary Cultural Semiotics 10. Vol. 1. Edited by Walter A. Koch. Bochum, Germany: Brockmeyer, 1990.

Henry, Desmond Paul. *That Most Subtle Question* (quaestio subtilissima): *The Metaphysical Bearing of Medieval and Contemporary Linguistic Disciplines.* Manchester, U.K.: Manchester University Press, 1984.

Ladner, Gerhart B. "Medieval and Modern Understanding of Symbolism: A Comparison." *Speculum* 54 (1979): 223–256.

Maierù, Alfonso. " 'Signum' dans la culture médiévale." *Miscellanea Mediaevalia* 13, no.1 (1981): 51–72.

Manetti, Giovanni. *Theories of the Sign in Classical Antiquity.* Translated by Christine Richardson. Bloomington and Indianapolis: Indiana University Press, 1993.

Parmentier, Richard J. "The Pragmatic Semiotics of Cultures." *Semiotica,* 116, no. 1 (1997): 1–113. See pp. 78–88 for a suggestive chapter on "The Typology of Medieval Realism."

Sebeok, Thomas A, ed. *Encyclopedic Dictionary of Semiotics.* Berlin, New York, and Amsterdam: Mouton de Gruyter, 1986. Contains useful entries that provide good introductions to the main aspects of medieval semiotics.

WORKS ON AUGUSTINE

Ando, Clifford. "Augustine on Language." *Revue des études augustiniennes* 40, no. 1 (1994): 45–78.

———. "Signs, Idols, and the Incarnation in Augustinian Metaphysics." *Representations* 73, no. 1 (2001): 24–53.

Dawson, David. "Sign Theory, Allegorical Reading, and the Motions of the Soul in the *De doctrina christiana.*" In *De doctrina christiana: A Classic of Western Culture.* Edited by Duane W. H. Arnold and Pamela Bright. Notre Dame, Ind., and London: University of Notre Dame Press, 1995.

Ferguson, Margaret. "Saint Augustine's Region of Unlikeness: The Crossing of Exile and Language." *Georgia Review* 29 (1975): 842–864.

Jackson, B. Darrell. "The Theory of Signs in St. Augustine's *De doctrina christiana.*" *Revue des études augustiniennes* 15 (1969): 9–49.

Jordan, M. D. "Words and Word: Incarnation and Signification in Augustine's *De doctrina christiana.*" *Augustinian Studies* 11 (1980): 177–196.

Markus, R. A. "St. Augustine on Signs." *Phronesis* 2 (1957): 60–83. Reprinted in his *Sacred and Secular: Studies on Augustine and Latin Christianity.* Aldershot, U.K.: Variorum, 1994.

———. " 'Imago' and 'similitudo' in Augustine." *Revue des études augustiniennes* 10 (1964): 125–143. Reprinted in his *Sacred and Secular: Studies on Augustine and Latin Christianity.* Aldershot, U.K.: Variorum, 1994.

———. "Signs, Communication, and Communities in Augustine's *De doctrina christiana.*" In *De doctrina christiana: A Classic of Western Culture.* Edited by Duane W. H. Arnold and Pamela Bright. Notre Dame, Ind., and London: University of Notre Dame Press, 1995.

WORKS ON SPECIFIC SIGN THEORIES

Adams, Marylin McCord. "Ockham's Theory of Natural Signification." *Monist* 61 (1978): 444–459.

Boehner, Philotheus. "Ockham's Theory of Signification." *Franciscan Studies* 6 (1946): 143–170. Reprinted in *Collected Articles on Ockham.* Edited by E. Buytaert. St. Bonaventure, N.Y.: Franciscan Institute, 1958.

Fredborg, Karin Margareta. "Universal Grammar according to Some Twelfth-Century Grammarians." *Historiographia Linguistica* 7, nos. 1–2 (1980): 69–84.

Gilson, Étienne. *Jean Duns Scot: Introduction à ses positions fondamentales.* Paris: Vrin, 1952.

Maloney, Thomas. "The Semiotics of Roger Bacon." *Mediaeval Studies* 45 (1983): 120–154.

———. "Is the *Doctrina* the Source for Bacon's Semiotics?" In *Reading and Wisdom: The* De doctrina christiana *of Augustine in the Middle Ages.* Edited by Edward D. English. Notre Dame, Ind., and London: University of Notre Dame Press, 1995.

Petrilli, Susan, and Augusto Ponzio. "Peirce and Medieval Semiotics." In *Peirce's Doctrine of Signs: Theory, Applications, and Connections.* Edited by Vincent M. Colapietro and Thomas M. Olshewsky. Berlin and New York: Mouton de Gruyter, 1996.

Rosier, Irène. *La grammaire spéculative des Modistes.* Lille, France: Presses Universitaires de Lille, 1983.

Sweeney, Eileen C. "Hugh of St. Victor: The Augustinian Tradition of Sacred and Secular Reading Revised." In *Reading and Wisdom: The*

De doctrina christiana *of Augustine in the Middle Ages.* Edited by Edward D. English. Notre Dame, Ind., and London: University of Notre Dame Press, 1995.

WORKS ON SEMIOTIC PROCESSES

Bedos-Rezak, Brigitte M. "Medieval Identity: A Sign and a Concept." *American Historical Review* 105, no. 5 (2000): 1489–1533.

Benveniste. Émile. "The Latin Vocabulary of Signs and Omens." In his *Indo-European Language and Society.* Translated by Elizabeth Palmer. London: Faber, 1973.

Camille, Michael. "The Book of Signs: Writing and Visual Difference in Gothic Manuscript Illumination." *Word and Image* 1, no. 2 (1985): 133–148.

Courtenay, William J. "The King and the Leaden Coin: The Economic Background of 'Sine qua non' Causality." *Traditio* 28 (1972): 185–209. Reprinted in his *Covenant and Causality in Medieval Thought: Studies in Philosophy, Theology, and Economic Practice.* London: Variorum, 1984.

———. "Sacrament, Symbol, and Causality in Bernard of Clairvaux." In *Bernard of Clairvaux: Studies Presented to Dom Jean Leclercq.* Edited by Basil Pennington. Washington, D.C.: Cistercian Publications, 1973. Reprinted in his *Covenant and Causality in Medieval Thought: Studies in Philosophy, Theology, and Economic Practice.* London: Variorum, 1984.

Crookshank, F. G. "The Importance of a Theory of Signs and a Critique of Language in the Study of Medicine." In *The Meaning of Meaning.* Edited by C. K. Ogden and I. A. Richards. London: Kegan Paul, 1923.

Fraenkel, Béatrice. *La signature: Genése d'un signe.* Paris: Gallimard, 1992.

Haidu, Peter. "The Semiotics of Alterity: A Comparison with Hermeneutics." *New Literary History* 21, no. 3 (1989–1990): 671–691.

Häring, Nikolaus M. "Character, Signum und Signaculum: Die Einführung in die Sakramententheologie des 12. Jarhunderts." *Scholastik* 31 (1956): 41–69.

Rosier, Irène. "Signe et sacrement." *Revue des sciences philosophiques et théologiques* 74, no. 3 (1990): 392–436.

Staiano, K. V. "Medical Semiotics: Redefining an Ancient Craft." *Semiotica* 38, nos. 3–4 (1982): 319–346.

Stock, Brian. *The Implications of Literacy: Written Language and Models of Interpretation in the Eleventh and Twelfth Centuries.* Princeton, N.J.: Princeton University Press, 1983.

Van den Eynde, Damien. *Les définitions des sacrements pendant la première période de la théologie scholastique (1050–1240).* Rome: Typo Pio X, 1950.

Vance, Eugène. *Mervelous Signals: Poetics and Sign Theory in the Middle Ages.* Lincoln: University of Nebraska Press, 1986.

BRIGITTE MIRIAM BEDOS-REZAK

[See also **DMA:** Augustine of Hippo, St.; Bacon, Roger; Dialectic; Grammar; Kilwardby, Robert; Nominalism; Philosophy and Theology, Western European; Realism; Seals and Sigillography, Western European; Universals.]

SĪRAT BANŪ HILĀL. See **Hilāl, Banū.**

SONG OF IGOR'S CAMPAIGN (Russian: *Slovo o polku Igoreve*). In 1185 Prince Igor Sviatoslavich of Novgorod-Seversky led his small retinue on a raid into pagan Polovtsian territory far into the steppe regions of Russia. The Polovtsians, socially nomadic and—partly as a consequence—masters of steppe warfare, crushingly defeated the prince, although he himself eventually escaped and was heroically welcomed back to his lands. This foray, regarded as foolhardy in the *Song* that commemorates it and by subsequent scholarly authorities, nonetheless earned Igor a place in the emerging mythography of Russian collective identity. The author of the later *Zadonshchina*, the epic commemoration of the Russian victory over the Tatars at Kulikovo Field in 1380, was inspired by his knowledge of a version of these events when he was writing.

It is not certain, however, that his knowledge came from the *Song* as we now have it, which is an edition of a unique manuscript discovered in 1795 and destroyed seventeen years later in the fire that ravaged Moscow during Napoleon's invasion of 1812. This loss would not loom so large but for other factors. Many editions of now lost manuscripts are accepted as faithful reproductions of versions of medieval works, even if the lost manuscripts were reputedly very late copies. The problem is that the *Song* is strange in many ways. It is not simple narration (a battlefield report or letter). While impressionistically it has an epic sensibility, it is not of epic length. It could be published in fifteen pages or less in any typical printer's font on standard pages. Even the *Song of Roland*, short by western medieval epic standards and concerned with an equally minor skirmish, is about ten times as long as the Russian work. As to the language, the *Song of Igor's Campaign* is lyrical prose-poetry, a fact that makes it difficult to fit it into accepted genres of medieval and early modern Russian literature. All this being conceded, however, the prevailing, though contested, opinion affirms the genuinely medieval character of the work. Most scholars prefer to see the *Song* as the work of a medieval genius who broke all the rules than as a modern forgery.

Igor's campaign probably was meant to thwart a coalition of Polovtsian clan chieftains from achieving long-term success against the Russians. The hero may have been unable to enlist the support of other Russian princes, or he may have had a quixotic sense of his own destiny. The author of the *Song* uses various episodes to slide into some extraordinarily elaborate and creative metaphorical images. It is these that contribute so powerfully to the overall lyrical quality of the text. One rhetorical figure, symbol, or personification in one metaphorical passage triggers the elaboration of either a similar or precisely contrasting figure in a subsequent passage, and then sometimes turns back upon itself: battle → wedding banquet → blood wine → battlefield → reaping of bones, etc. The sheer daring of the conceits makes one think of modern symbolist prose-poetry. The author ran the risk of overindulgence, and perhaps if the *Song* were as protracted as even the shorter of the western *chansons de geste,* he would have succumbed to that vice. But as it stands, the *Song of Igor's Campaign* is the unmatched masterpiece of medieval Russian literature.

BIBLIOGRAPHY

Howes, Robert C., trans. *Tale of the Campaign of Igor: A Russian Epic Poem of the Twelfth Century.* New York: Norton, 1973. A standard translation.

Mann, Robert. *Lances Sing: A Study of the Igor Tale.* Columbus, Ohio: Slavica, 1990. A solid scholarly study. The allusion to "singing lances" is to another striking figure in the *Song.*

Nabokov, Vladimir, trans. *The Song of Igor's Campaign: An Epic of the Twelfth Century.* New York: Vintage Books, 1960. A more famous translation.

WILLIAM CHESTER JORDAN

[See also **DMA:** Russia, Nomadic Invasions of; Slavic Languages and Literatures; **Supp:** *Zadonshchina.*]

SOUL AND BODY. The Christian tradition, in contrast to many other religions, is characterized by an understanding of the human person as constituted of two entities: soul (which reflects a sense that the person transcends corporeal limits through thought, dreams, or memory) and body (which reflects the pleasure, struggle, and limits of corporeal existence seen in, for example, sexuality, aging, and death). Although cosmic dualism (that is, the belief in two powers—good and evil—dominating the universe) was rejected, there was a sense of disjunction or incompatibility between soul and body that is sometimes labeled "practical dualism." This was not, however, a simple body-soul dichotomy, much less a rejection of the corporeal. The doctrine of the Incarnation (the claim that God was embodied in Jesus) made body crucial to theories of person. Although textbooks still sometimes see Christian asceticism as rejection of the body, most recent interpretation stresses instead the centrality of body and holy matter in medieval religion. Indeed the western Middle Ages is now understood to

be less dualistic than the early modern period, in which theories of the person stressed a split between body and mind.

Scholars in the early part of the twentieth century were mostly interested in medieval conceptions of the soul. The *Catholic Encyclopedia* of 1912, for example, has an article on "soul" but no entry for "body." Recent scholarship has concentrated on concepts of body. The volume *Critical Terms for Religious Studies* (1998) has a long article on "body" but nothing on "soul." We need to realize, however, that what medieval theorists and pious adherents alike were primarily interested in was the relationship between the two (which was often conceptualized as other than binary). This article does not cover all medieval understandings of body and soul but is rather a survey of the various conceptions of their relationship as elaborated by theorists (both theologians and natural philosophers), manifested in literature (where the body-soul relationship provided crucial metaphors), and revealed in praxis (where understandings of it are reflected in such things as burial practices and bodily signs of mystical states).

BACKGROUND: GREEK PHILOSOPHY

Medieval understandings of soul and body had roots both in Greek philosophy and in the Hebrew Scriptures. Plato saw soul as an immortal, incorruptible, intellectual principle that preexisted the human being. Its basic concepts were innate and transcendent, and it passed after the death of the body into other bodies, higher or lower, as reward or punishment (a process known as metempsychosis). The soul was incorporeal, without particular physical characteristics such as sex or race; its immortality was an intrinsic consequence of its spiritual and hence changeless nature; body was its prison or tomb, at best its instrument. Like other ancient philosophers, Plato saw philosophy as a way of life that involved bodily discipline and self-control.

To Aristotle, soul is the "first act" or vital principle of a living organism; hence the human person is a unitary being of body animated by soul. Aristotle understood natures by analyzing them as a duality of form and matter. Applied to epistemology, this made knowledge a process by which the mind abstracted concepts (forms) from evidence provided by sense data (matter); hence it stressed attention to the natural world rather than striving for the transcendent. Although Aristotle's *De anima* suggested in one passage that there might be a part of the soul that survived the individual, his biologist's understanding of the person as a living entity seemed generally to exclude the survival of anything beyond death. To Aristotle, the

The Soul Being Carried to Heaven. *Miniature of the soul (represented as a small person) being carried to heaven out of the body of St. Liudger.* STAATSBIBLIOTHEK ZU BERLIN—PREUSSISCHER KULTURBESITZ, HANDSCHRIFTEN-ABTEILUNG, MS THEOL. LAT., FOL. 323, FOLIO 20R. REPRODUCED BY PERMISSION.

act of conception produced a living being by the action of a seed (or form) from the father on matter provided by the female, a position which was modified by Galen (*d. ca.* A.D. 200), who held that two seeds (both male and female) were necessary. To later thinkers, Muslim, Jewish, and Christian, Aristotle's understanding turned human attention earthward and seemed to achieve conceptual unity of person—but some feared it did so at the expense of the possibility of survival for a separated soul.

BACKGROUND: BIBLICAL AND PATRISTIC

The early Christian sense of the human being drew more on Platonic ideas than on Aristotle. It was also influenced by the Hebrew Scriptures, which tended to speak of person rather than soul, to stress resurrection or return (of the people of Israel or of the whole human per-

son) rather than immortality, and to conceive of personal responsibility as an obligation to will the good and obey God (in contrast to the Greek emphasis on the intellect and right knowing). Although there are references to immortality in the Hebrew literature of the first centuries B.C. and A.D., it is understood less as something intrinsic to soul (in a Platonic sense) than as a gift from God.

In the New Testament, the claim that God became a complete human being in Jesus and saved humankind by his death and resurrection thrust embodiment to the center of theories of salvation, although devotion to the details of Jesus's human life would not emerge for over a thousand years. The Epistles of Paul held a trinary theory of the person, not a binary one, and spoke of *spiritus* (pneuma), *anima* (psyche), and *corpus* (soma). Augustine of Hippo reflected such ideas when he wrote that there are three sorts of visions: corporeal (bodily sight), spiritu-

The Struggle for Man's Soul. *Manuscript page from the* Carthusian Miscellany *(15th century) illustrating the stages of the struggle for the soul (represented as a small person).* THE BRITISH LIBRARY, ADD. MS 37049, FOL. 29R. REPRODUCED BY PERMISSION.

al (seeing angels, apparitions, and so forth) and intellectual (the imageless understanding of mind). Augustine also made much of reflections of the Trinity in the human psyche—for example: memory, understanding, and love. What is important to understand is not so much the variety of categories (for person or the faculties of the soul) found in the New Testament and among the Fathers but the fact that many of the models medieval thinkers inherited as tools for analyzing metaphysics, epistemology, and psychology were trinary, not binary.

Among the Fathers of the early church a consensus gradually emerged that was passed on to the Middle Ages. The Stoic idea that the soul was material (held by Tertullian) was rejected, as was the Neoplatonic idea (probably held by Origen) of salvation as a kind of cosmic return of soul. Flesh *(caro)* was often understood as concupiscence; sexual pleasure was condemned; and the monastic movement, like ancient philosophy, stressed strict discipline of body. Nonetheless, the earliest creeds affirmed bodily resurrection, and salvation was understood to be of the whole person. As Tertullian said: "The

flesh is the pivot of salvation." Origen's espousal of the Platonic idea of preexistence was rejected by the fourth century, but the earlier understanding of immortality as a reward given by God to good souls gave way to a Greek concept of soul as immortal by definition—an understanding that lasted through the Middle Ages and was not really challenged until Pietro Pomponazzi (d. 1525). In the fifth century, opinion about the origin of the soul was divided between traducianism (the idea that the soul of the child was provided in the reproductive act of the parents—a theory that linked the transmission of original sin closely to sexuality) and creationism (the theory that God created an individual soul for infusion into each embryo). By 1100 opinion had swung to creationism, which is the theory espoused in Peter Lombard's *Sententiae,* the basic textbook for medieval universities. In the early twelfth century, the person was still seen (in Platonic terms) as a soul using a body. But the importance accorded by early medieval Christianity to the presence of the divine in matter—the doctrine of the Incarnation and Resurrection of Christ, the belief in the real presence of Christ's body and blood in the Eucharist, and the cult of the relics (physical remains) of the saints—led to an increasing sense of person as a unity of body and soul and to new efforts to express how the two (or more) entities made one person.

THE HIGH MIDDLE AGES: THEORETICAL DISCUSSIONS

On the level of theory, the general development from around 1100 to the 1280s seems to be one of increasingly sophisticated efforts to express the intrinsic necessity of both body and soul in the psychosomatic entity "person," followed in the early fourteenth century by a renewed emphasis on soul, psyche, and will. On the level of praxis, however, the trend throughout the Middle Ages seems to be toward the increasing importance of bodiliness. In the twelfth century, we can see in three aspects of contemporary theory a move toward a concept of person as a tight soul-body unity. The "faculty psychology" of the Cistercians and the interest of the writers from the so-called School of Chartres in classifying the powers of the soul led to an increasing effort to theorize the nexus of body and soul, sometimes through a third element or median, and a sense of multiple layers of person between abstract thought and animal life. (Major examples of this trend are the writings of William of Conches, Isaac of Stella, and the pseudo-Augustinian *De spiritu et anima,* which is often misidentified as a work of Alcher of Clairvaux.) Among these same thinkers, theories of person as microcosm, reflecting the entire macrocosm of creation, tended to stress the human being as

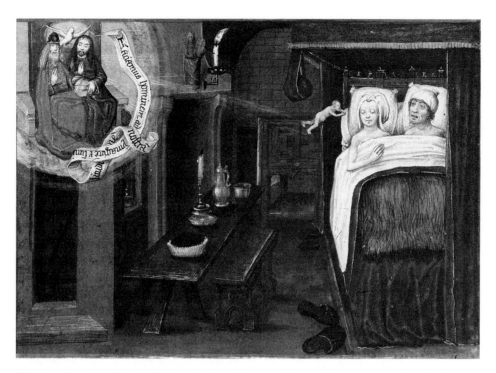

The Fetus Ensouled. *Here the Trinity sends the soul (represented as a small person, presumably a fetus being ensouled) into a bed in which a couple is resting. Bibliothèque Arsenal, Paris, Miroir d'humilité, MS 5206, fol. 174v.*
BIBLIOTHÈQUE NATIONALE DE FRANCE. REPRODUCED BY PERMISSION.

gathering up all reality into him/herself. The rise of a complicated theology around the concept of purgatory led to two developments that seemed to confuse the categories of corporeal and incorporeal: first, an emphasis on change of the (supposedly changeless) soul after death, and, second, a sense of corporeal sufferings inflicted on separated souls.

In the course of the thirteenth century, new theories of the relationship of soul and body emerged among theologians and philosophers. Three circumstances contributed to this. First, the rediscovery of Aristotle supported renewed attention to the natural world and provided, through the theory of hylomorphism (form and matter), a way of conceptualizing the person as a single entity, that is, a soul (substantial form) actualizing body (matter). Second, the rise of dualist heresy forced attention to the material and the bodily. Although scholars debate to what extent the dissident movements of the twelfth century saw matter as the creation of an evil god, some of the group known as Cathars did teach cosmic dualism, and Christian preachers understood many manifestations of anticlericalism—such as rejection of crucifixes or of the sacraments—as dualistic. Indeed Christians came increasingly to define themselves as antidualists by projecting their own fears of bodily limitation onto heretics. Third, the theory of monopsych-

ism—an interpretation of Aristotle, put forward by the Arab commentator Ibn Rushd (Averroes), that saw Aristotle's *De anima* as asserting the existence of one soul for all human beings and therefore denying personal immortality—forced university professors to find ingenious ways of integrating a sense of body as crucial to person with the idea of an individualized soul surviving between personal death and general resurrection. Theologians such as Albert the Great, Thomas Aquinas, Bonaventure, William of Baglione, Henry of Ghent, and Giles of Rome devised sophisticated theories to explain the soul-body relationship, all of which made use of Aristotelian hylomorphism. Theories differed over whether several forms or one constituted the human person, whether there was a form of bodiliness to account for the continuity of body between death and resurrection, and whether (and how) several souls succeeded each other in embryological development. In the 1280s at Oxford, the idea that only one substantial form accounts for the person was condemned; in 1311–1312 a version of the idea of several souls was condemned. What is important to understand is that, behind the opposing theories, we see a clear understanding that, as Aquinas put it, "the soul . . . is not the whole person, and I am not my soul." All theories explained the senses and sense data (hence body) as crucial to knowing, insisted both that soul survives death and that the same identical body of this life returns at resurrection, and stated clearly that body adds something to person when the resurrection comes. The consequence of such a tight union of body and soul was the lifting into heaven of human particularity: sex, race, even the scars of martyrdom, would be part of the person for all eternity.

In medical thinking, the ideas of Aristotle, which partly supplemented and partly replaced those of Galen, had two consequences for ideas of the person. First, the role of the male in the production of the fetus (the one-seed theory) was increasingly stressed. Second, human physiology was conceptualized on a male model—the so-called one-sex theory, according to which woman is seen as a defective version of man (a sort of turning outside in of male physiology). Nonetheless this tilt toward male superiority was to some extent neutralized by the doctrine of bodily resurrection: if people rose in two sexes, the female sex could not be a defect, since God repaired defects in resurrection. Male dominance in reproduction was also relativized by the idea that God creates and infuses the soul into the embryo (not, according to most theorists, at conception but at a later point); the parents produce only the body. Moreover the theory of the four humors, which accounted for temperament and character through the balance of bodily fluids, undercut any sharp line between the sexes and tended to locate in the body many aspects of what we today call psychology.

When, in the fourteenth century, attention in the universities turned away again from the thirteenth-century concern with metaphysics and back toward a twelfth-century concern with psychology and ethics, several factors contributed to a new emphasis on soul, mind, and psyche. Nominalist theologians rejected analysis of the person into entities such as form and matter and gave renewed energy to questions of the will. A controversy in the 1330s concluded with the doctrinal pronouncement that the saints could receive the beatific vision before the end of time—a position that seemed to make both body and bodily resurrection less important for salvation. A great upsurge in mystical writing—some of it stressing the encounter beyond word or image known as the "negative way"—seemed to value a spirituality cut off from body and society. Nonetheless it is not correct to see the fourteenth and fifteenth centuries as turning away from body. The understanding of person as psychosomatic unity continued. Even university theologians, with their increasingly abstruse jargon, understood their technical debates to have a context in pious practices, such as Eucharistic devotion and relic cult, in which matter and body were key.

THE HIGH MIDDLE AGES: LITERATURE AND PRAXIS

In the literature of the later Middle Ages, language reflects a sense of the bodiliness of person. What we call "mixed metaphors" (for example, the "eyes of the heart") abound; the idea of society as a body, with different statuses and roles represented by various members, was common. Folktales, sermons, and learned eschatological discussions imagined souls as body-shaped; ghost stories proliferated. Monastic, courtly, and educational treatises gave new attention to gesture and deportment, suggesting an emphasis on the expression of inner states in outward behavior. (Sophisticated analysis of the faculties and of inner spiritual states also increased.) The genre, popular in Latin and the vernacular, of "debate between the body and the soul" evidences both a continuing sense of conflict between these two constituents of person and their interdependence. Soul and body accuse each other: body sees evil lodged in will (a quality of soul) while soul blames evil on the senses. What is clear in these debates is that neither can act, for evil or good, without the other.

In medical literature and in public life, what we would call corporeal tended to be mixed with the moral or spiritual. Leprosy, for example, was seen as both a disease and a moral condition. Pain was understood to be lodged in the soul or the person (a psychosomatic unity), not the body. Doctors and lawyers paid new attention to ways in which the body might be "alive" after death (for example, by bleeding to accuse a murderer). Interest in the body led in the fourteenth century to the beginnings of autopsy and dissection, both for legal purposes and for scientific study. The rise of public executions involving dismemberment and infliction of acute pain reflects an increasing tendency to enact political judgments on the body itself.

Especially in the area of piety, a new bodiliness characterized late medieval culture. The interest in making the inner visible in the outer led in some cases to what modern psychologists call "somatization": the manifestation of religious experience in bodily phenomena, such as stigmata (the appearance of Christ's wounds on the body of an adherent) and trances. Relic veneration continued, and the practice arose of dividing and distributing the bodies of ordinary Christians for burial near the saints. Religious literature increasingly stressed the physical suffering of Christ, and devotion to his wounds and heart sometimes seemed to lodge salvation in the fact of bodily pain itself. In new ascetic practices such as extreme fasting, flagellation, and bodily mutilation, the pious punished their flesh for its sinfulness and released torrents of emotion toward God. Alongside mysticism of the "negative way," we find writing (often by and about women) in which bodily experiences, described in highly physical, even erotic, language, are major sites of encounter with the divine.

APPROACHES

In the mid-twentieth century, Catholic scholarship devoted much attention to scholastic theories and often argued that Aquinas's understanding of the soul as the single substantial form of the body was the beginning of a modern sense of unitary person. Recent work tends to concentrate less on intellectual history than on social context. Feminists have been interested both in misogynist understandings of the female body and in ways in which women writers and visionaries seem sometimes to have found empowerment in their own bodiliness. Scholars influenced by structuralist anthropology have tended to see images as expressions of social structure; they argue that those who eschew bodily images of the self in favor of a unisex, immaterial soul tend to radical rejection of status and hierarchy, whereas those who stress the specificity of a psychosomatic self tend to perpetuate social difference and inequality. No single approach can encompass the richness of the topic of soul and body. The practice of a very bodily religion and the abstruse details of philosophical theorizing about the nature of person cannot be understood apart from each other. Praxis should not, however, be seen as merely a reflection of the ideas of intellectuals nor should medieval ideas be understood as dictated by the structures of society.

BIBLIOGRAPHY

GENERAL AND CROSS-CULTURAL PERSPECTIVES

Fromaget, Michel. *Dix essais sur la conception anthropologique "corps, âme, esprit."* Collection culture et cosmologie. Paris and Montreal: L'Harmattan, 2000.

LaFleur, William R. "Body." In *Critical Terms for Religious Studies.* Edited by Mark C. Taylor. Chicago: University of Chicago Press, 1998.

GENERAL MEDIEVAL

Anime e corpo nella cultura medievale: Atti del V Convegno di Studi della Società italiana per lo Studio del Pensiero Medievale, Venezia, 25–28 Settembre 1995. Edited by Carla Casagrande and Silvana Vecchio. Tavarnuzze, Italy: Sismel edizioni del Gallazzo, 1999.

Baschet, Jérôme. "Âme et corps dans l'Occident médiéval: Une dualité dynamique, entre pluralité et dualisme." *Archives de sciences sociales des religions* 112 (2000): 5–30.

Bynum, Caroline Walker. *Fragmentation and Redemption: Essays on Gender and the Human Body in Medieval Religion.* New York: Zone, 1991. Especially chapters 6 and 7.

Schmitt, Jean-Claude. "Corps et Âme." In *Dictionnaire raisonné de l'Occident médiéval.* Edited by Jacques Le Goff and Jean-Claude Schmitt. Paris: Fayard, 1999.

BODY AND SOUL IN ESCHATOLOGY

Bynum, Caroline Walker. *The Resurrection of the Body in Western Christianity, 200–1336.* New York: Columbia University Press, 1995.

Dinzelbacher, Peter. "Reflexionen irdischer Sozialstrukturen in mittelalterlichen Jenseitsschilderungen." *Archiv für Kulturgeschichte* 61, no.1 (1979): 16–34.

Gager, John G. "Body-Symbols and Social Reality: Resurrection, Incarnation, and Asceticism in Early Christianity." *Religion* 12, no.4 (1982): 345–364.

Tugwell, Simon. *Human Immortality and the Redemption of Death.* London: Darnton, Longman, and Todd, 1990.

THEOLOGICAL AND PHILOSOPHICAL DISCUSSION

Biller, Peter, and A. J. Minnis, eds. *Medieval Theology and the Natural Body.* York Studies in Medieval Theology 1. York, U.K.: York University Press in association with Boydell and Brewer, 1997.

Chenu, Marie-Dominique. "Spiritus. Le vocabulaire de l'âme au XIIe siècle." *Revue des sciences philosophiques et théologiques* 41 (1957): 209–232.

Dales, Richard C. *The Problem of the Rational Soul in the Thirteenth Century.* Brill's Studies in Intellectual History. Leiden, New York, and Cologne: Brill, 1995.

McGinn, Bernard, ed. *Three Treatises on Man: A Cistercian Anthropology.* Translated by Benjamin Clark. Cistercian Fathers Series 24. Kalamazoo, Mich.: Cistercian Publications, 1977. See especially the introduction.

Michaud-Quantin, Pierre. "La classification des puissances de l'âme au XIIe siècle." *Revue du moyen âge latin* 5 (1949): 15–34.

Pegis, Anton C. *St. Thomas and the Problem of the Soul in the Thirteenth Century.* 1934. Reprint, Toronto: Pontifical Institute of Mediaeval Studies, 1976.

Reynolds, Philip Lyndon. *Food and the Body: Some Peculiar Questions in High Medieval Theology.* Studien und Texte zur Geistesgeschichte des Mittelalters 69. Leiden, Netherlands, and Boston: Brill, 1999.

Reypens, L. "Âme (son fond, ses puissances, et sa structure d'après les mystiques)." In *Dictionnaire de spiritualité, ascétique et mystique, doctrine et histoire.* Edited by Marcel Viller et al. Vol. 1. Paris: Beauchesne, 1937.

Wéber, Edouard-Henri, O. P. *La personne humaine au XIIIe siècle: L'avènement chez les maîtres parisiens de l'acception moderne de l'homme.* Bibliothèque Thomiste 46. Paris: Vrin, 1991.

MEDICAL DISCUSSION

Cadden, Joan M. *The Meanings of Sex Difference in the Middle Ages: Medicine, Science, and Culture.* Cambridge, U.K.: Cambridge University Press, 1993.

Jacquart, Danielle, and Claude Thomasset. *Sexuality and Medicine in the Middle Ages.* Translated by Matthew Adamson. Princeton, N.J.: Princeton University Press, 1988.

Pouchelle, Marie-Christine. *The Body and Surgery in the Middle Ages.* Translated by Rosemary Morris. New Brunswick, N.J.: Rutgers University Press, 1990.

BODY AND SOUL IN RELIGIOUS AND SOCIAL PRACTICE

Ackerman, Robert W. "The Debate of the Body and the Soul and Parochial Christianity." *Speculum* 37 (1962): 541–565.

Angenendt, Arnold. "Corpus incorruptum: Eine Leitidee der mittelalterlichen Reliquienverehrung." *Saeculum* 42, nos.3–4 (1991): 320–348.

Brown, Elizabeth A. R. "Death and the Human Body in the Later Middle Ages: The Legislation of Boniface VIII on the Division of the Corpse." *Viator* 12 (1981): 221–270.

Brown, Peter. *The Body and Society: Men, Women, and Sexual Renunciation in Early Christianity.* New York: Columbia University Press, 1988.

Ross, Ellen M. *The Grief of God: Images of the Suffering Jesus in Late Medieval England.* New York: Oxford University Press, 1997.

Schmitt, Jean-Claude. *La raison des gestes dans l'Occident médiéval.* Paris: Gallimard, 1990.

———. *Ghosts in the Middle Ages: The Living and the Dead in Medieval Society.* Translated by Teresa Lavender Fagan. Chicago: University of Chicago Press, 1998.

CAROLINE WALKER BYNUM

[See also **DMA**: Medicine, History of; **Supp**: Body, The; Disease.]

SPIRIT. See **Matter.**

STANISŁAW, ST. (*ca.* 1030–1079). No elaborate contemporary or near-contemporary life of St. Stanisław has survived, and it is doubtful that one ever existed. Scholars must argue from fragmentary chronicle sources, themselves written long after his death, or from a thirteenth-century life contemporary with his canonization, in 1253, by Pope Innocent IV. The bare facts seem to be the following: Stanisław was born near Kraków at a time not long after the initial acceptance of Christianity in Poland in 966 by King Mieszko I (962–992). The Christianization of the country was itself tenuous. Following the death of Mieszko's son Bolesław I in 1025 and the political disputes that followed, there was a pagan revival. It was put down, but the early years of Stanisław's life must have shaped his tenacious attachment to Christian life. In any case, he was raised a Catholic and evidently had some sort of formal religious education.

Influenced by the Gospel injunction to give to the poor, he gave away as alms the property he inherited from his parents. Subsequently he became a priest, and although he served a parish outside of Kraków, he was closely associated with the cathedral. Its bishop most likely ordained him and probably also employed him in various capacities at the cathedral. It was therefore understandable when the cathedral chapter, of which he was undoubtedly a canon, elected him bishop. Stanisław may have preferred otherwise, but he accepted, according to legend, when compelled to do so by one of the great reforming popes, Alexander II (*r.* 1061–1073).

The ongoing reforms in the church Universal were very slow in coming to Poland. This does not mean that Stanisław ignored practices that he deemed unChristian, insufficiently Christian, or immoral. Practices like polygamy (or concubinage) and simony, the sale and purchase of church offices, may have provoked his wrath. It would not be hard to believe that Stanisław came into conflict with King Bolesław II the Bold (*r.* 1058–1079) on these matters, except that Bolesław was an enemy of the German emperor and an ally of the reforming popes. His actual crowning took place in 1076 in the presence of a papal legate sent by the archreformer Gregory VII (*r.* 1073–1085).

Of course, the establishment of a political alliance with the papacy does not mean that Bolesław supported the papal reform program—indeed the evidence on such matters one way or the other is absent. However, the sources such as they are point to other disputes between the two men over questions of property and the treatment of nobles friendly to the see of Kraków. There may also have been wider aristocratic resentment with Bolesław's foreign policy, particularly his multiple interventions in the succession struggles then going on in Great Kiev, which appear to have triggered a rebellion against him and forced him into exile, where he died.

But before these events unfolded, the confrontation between Stanisław and the king came to crisis. Stanisław excommunicated Bolesław and effectively closed the cathedral to him. The bishop repaired to St. Michael's, a sanctuary near Kraków, presumably in the hope that the king would seek him out to be reconciled. Bolesław did seek him out but not for reconciliation. The king may have ordered his retinue to kill the bishop, but the fact seems to be that he did the deed himself (8 May 1079), possibly during the celebration of mass, though this detail—like the order to the retinue and their fearful refusal—sounds suspiciously like a topos. The martyr, later recognized as patron saint of Kraków and all Poland, was interred in St. Michael's, but his body was translated to the cathedral in 1088. Stanisław's feast day is 7 May (8 May in Kraków). The feast of his translation is celebrated on 27 September. His standard iconography features a sword, and he may be shown being martyred before the altar.

BIBLIOGRAPHY

Grudziński, Tadeusz. *Boleslaus the Bold, Called Also the Bountiful, and Bishop Stanislaus: The Story of a Conflict.* Translated by Lech Petrowicz. Warsaw: Interpress Publishers, 1985.

WILLIAM CHESTER JORDAN

[See also **DMA:** Martyrology; Poland; **Supp:** Kraków.]

STEPHEN OF ENGLAND, KING (*r.* 1135–1154).

King Henry I of England died in 1135, leaving as his only legitimate child a daughter, the empress dowager Matilda. Twice, in 1127 and again in 1133, he obliged his barons to swear to respect Matilda's claims and those of her young son, also named Henry, by her second husband, Count Geoffrey of Anjou. Stephen of Blois, the king's nephew, swore the oath on both occasions.

Stephen, born in the late 1090s, was the son of Henry's sister, Adela, and thus a grandson of William I the Conqueror. After the accidental death by drowning of Henry's only legitimate son, William, in 1120, Stephen, whom Henry liked, was treated almost like the king's son. The king employed the young knight in his wars and endowed him with extensive properties in England and the duchy of Normandy. Stephen augmented these by exchanging his inheritance claims in the lands of Blois with holdings of one of his brothers in the duchy.

Rich and affable (although mercurial in temperament) and with a solid connection to Henry I, Stephen was in a remarkable position to claim the throne on the king's death. Only his oath stood in the way, and this impediment was later laid to rest by the allegation, truthful or not, that Henry I had reconsidered the inheritance towards the end of his life, designating Stephen instead of Matilda as his heir. In any case, Stephen asserted his claim, and with the support of another brother, who was bishop of Winchester, he immediately secured the royal treasure. On or about Christmas day 1135 he was crowned king despite Matilda's appeals against him. The pope did not denounce Stephen's act.

Enemies were on all sides, however, and the years of Stephen's reign witnessed repeated outbreaks of rebellion and civil war. The Scottish king, David I, saw an opportunity in his beleaguered counterpart's woes to exact territorial grants in northern England for his family and supporters, and he did not hesitate to use force to secure his position. Earls and barons throughout the realm, but especially the earl of Gloucester, Matilda's illegitimate half-brother, challenged Stephen at various times. Matilda herself raised forces for an invasion and even achieved the upper hand in 1140–1141. Although Stephen, who had been imprisoned briefly, was exchanged and led resurgent forces successfully against Matilda's soon after, his opponents continued the civil war.

In the circumstances, both sides to the dispute took liberties with the property of the church. Sometimes, of course, churchmen, just like lay aristocrats, benefited from the disorder by throwing their support one way or the other, but the variability and volatility of the overall situation were more significant than any temporary ecclesiastical gains. Stephen's early honeymoon with the church was brief; he was often at bitter odds with clerics, including the primate, Archbishop Theobald of Canterbury, and his own brother, the bishop of Winchester, who was also papal legate. Monkish chroniclers may exaggerate the violence (so modern authorities sometimes argue), but Stephen's reign was noted for its disturbances. "Men openly said," the Anglo-Saxon chronicler wrote, "that Christ and his saints were asleep."

Meanwhile, in 1144, Matilda's husband conquered Normandy. A few years later, their son, the future Henry II, was formally invested with the duchy. In England, beginning in the 1150s, the situation deteriorated for Stephen. In 1151 Henry began to make considerable inroads into areas until then under the king's control. But the sense of hopelessness became genuinely palpable in Stephen's camp when his wife and eldest son died in 1152 and 1153, respectively. His wife had worked vigorously on his behalf, and he had endeavored, though unsuccessfully, to have his son, Eustace, crowned co-king in 1152 in order to secure a smooth succession, as the French rulers did, by associative kingship. The effort failed, because the ancient customary right to crown the English king lay with the archbishop of Canterbury, who was then in exile because of his opposition to Stephen. Both wife and son were buried at Faversham Abbey, a foundation owed to Stephen.

By the Treaty of Wallingford of 1153 Stephen agreed to recognize Henry as his heir, retaining rule for himself until his death. He also promised to help pacify the kingdom in anticipation of the succession. This settlement might not have turned out to be definitive if Stephen's younger son, William, had not been willing to go along with it, if Henry had been assassinated (there was a plot against him, hatched among Stephen's Flemish mercenaries), or if Stephen himself had lived—but the king died after a brief illness on 25 October 1154. He, too, was interred at Faversham in the company of his wife and son.

BIBLIOGRAPHY

Crouch, David. *The Reign of King Stephen, 1135–1154.* Harlow, U.K., and New York: Longman, 2000.

Davis, R. H. C. *King Stephen, 1135–1154.* Berkeley: University of California Press, 1967.

Matthew, Donald. *King Stephen.* London and New York: Hambledon and London, 2002.

WILLIAM CHESTER JORDAN

[See also **DMA:** Henry I of England; Henry II of England; Plantagenets; **Supp:** Matilda, Empress.]

SÜSSKIND VON TRIMBERG, a German poet of the mid-thirteenth century. His twelve extant lyric poems, preserved in the Manesse-Codex, treated commonplace themes like the praise of God, the plight of the poor, and the remembrance of the dead. Nothing definitive is known about his life or career.

Historical interest in Süsskind von Trimberg rests primarily on the inference that he was of Jewish descent. If this was the case, then he was the only medieval Jew to compose lyric poetry in German. The question of the poet's religious identity rests on three pieces of evidence, none of which is conclusive. First, the compiler of the Manesse-Codex listed his poems under the title "Süsskint der Jude von Trimpberg" and accompanied them with an author portrait depicting Süsskind in Jewish garb. It is improbable, however, that the compiler of the manuscript knew anything definitive about the personal or vocational history of the poet, and he likely dubbed him "the Jew" because of a reference to Jews in his work. The illuminator of the codex simply took his cue from the compiler's title. In short, the Manesse-Codex cannot provide an authoritative statement concerning the identity of the poet. Second, some scholars have understood the direct reference to Jews in one of Süsskind's poems—a rare occurrence in German lyric poetry from this period—to provide an indication of his religious background. The passage in question is a simple analogy, in which the author states that poetry is so unprofitable that he will soon be forced to wander the roads like an old Jew. This simile, however, is a rhetorical device that reveals nothing certain about the religion of the author. Finally, much has been made of the poet's name. Süsskind was a common Jewish name in the late medieval and early modern periods and may indicate that the poet was of Jewish descent. This hypothesis is the most credible of the three, but it is by no means conclusive. Until further evidence comes to light, Süsskind von Trimberg's religious identity and the historical signifi-

cance of his small corpus of lyric poetry remain open to question.

BIBLIOGRAPHY

Jahrmärker, Manuela. "Die Miniatur Süsskinds von Trimberg in der Manessischen Liederhandschrift." *Euphorion* 81 (1987): 330–346.

Kraus, Carl von, ed. *Deutsche Liederdichter des 13. Jahrhunderts.* 2 vols. Tübingen, Germany: Max Niemeyer, 1978. See vol. 1, pp. 421–425 (no. 56), and vol. 2, pp. 513–516, for a reprint of Süsskind's poems and commentary.

Straus, Raphael. "Was Süsskint von Trimperg a Jew? An Inquiry into Thirteenth-Century Cultural History." *Jewish Social Studies* 10 (1948): 19–30.

Wenzel, Edith. "Süsskind von Trimberg, ein deutsch-jüdischer Autor im europäischen Kontext." In *Interregionalität der deutschen Literatur im europäischen Mittelalter.* Edited by Hartmut Kugler. Berlin and New York: Walter de Gruyter, 1995.

SCOTT G. BRUCE

[See also **DMA:** German Literature: Lyric.]

SYRIAN CHRISTIAN ARCHITECTURE. The indigenous Christian communities of the Middle East (in this article limited to Syria, Palestine, and Mesopotamia) developed from the late-antique culture of the Roman Empire but after 626 fell under the rule of the Islamic caliphate. Ecclesiastical architecture thus drew on the public architectures of both the Roman and Sasanian empires, as well as on local traditions. Many of its most striking monuments date from late antiquity, but Christian communities—Melchite, Jacobite, and Nestorian—continued to build and restore churches to the fourteenth century. The loss of imperial patronage from Constantinople in 626 ended a longstanding link to Byzantine architecture, while the Muslim conquest of Persia emphasized cultural ties among Christian communities of Persia, Mesopotamia, and Syria. Though the great architectural historian Richard Krautheimer categorized Christian buildings of the Islamic period as "folk architecture," the surviving churches, mostly monastic, reveal sophisticated building techniques. Modern study began with the photographs and books of the intrepid Gertrude Bell, who traveled throughout Syria, Mesopotamia, and Arabia at the beginning of the twentieth century, and with Howard Crosby Butler, who studied the late-antique architecture of Syria. Recent archaeology has added to the corpus of known churches, but further study is hampered by poor conservation and limited opportunities for additional excavations.

SYRIA

While most Syrian churches rightfully belong to the late-antique or Byzantine architectural corpus, the tradition they represent was distinctly Syrian and influenced later styles. Three elements distinguished late-antique Syrian basilicas—exemplified by the church complex at Burǧ Heidar, northwest of modern Aleppo—from others in the Roman world. The entrances to Syrian churches were often from a courtyard on the southern side of the building rather than through the western end. Second, the apsed sanctuary was flanked by two square side chambers, called *pastiphoria*. In the medieval period they were used for the preparation of the Eucharistic elements before consecration; it is, however, unlikely the rooms served this period in the fifth century. The one to the left of the altar may have served as a place for the deacons (a diaconicon); the one to the right in some cases preserved the relics of the martyrs, forming a martyrium, such as at the monastery of Deir Déhès near Antioch. The third distinctive element, known as the bema or ambo, was a dais intended for the reading of scripture, which often occupied the center of the nave.

Not all churches in Syria shared these characteristics. Imperial patronage introduced architectural plans lacking the markers of indigenous Syrian architecture, particularly in cities, such as Antioch and Apamea, and at the larger shrine churches, such as the basilica of St. Simeon Stylites. While lacking the characteristic bema and side chambers, the basilica has a rich decorative style that links it to other fifth-century Syrian churches. Deep carved foliate moldings run the length of the buildings, while "windblown" acanthus leaves decorate the column capitals. Such decorative details on cornices, moldings, and entablatures continued to be used within churches into the medieval period. While most common in Syria, this decorative influence can be seen as far away as Qaṣr Serīj, some sixty miles northwest of Mosul in Iraq. Church building petered out by the end of the eighth century, partly as a result of Islamic restrictions on Christian communities and partly due to the slow impoverishment of the region.

PALESTINE

While Palestinian churches show some markers of Syrian architectural traditions, imperial concern for the Holy Places led to greater influence from outside the Middle East. Furthermore, the peculiar demands of shrine churches also led to a greater variety of styles designed to accommodate the specific *loca sancta*. Nevertheless, many churches featured *pastiphoria*, such as the church of St. Lazarus in Bethany and the first phase of the "East" church of Halutza in the Negev. The bema, however, rarely appeared. As in Syria, ecclesiastical building came to a halt during the Islamic period, with the exception of the "anchor church" near Tiberias, which was rebuilt after an earthquake in 749.

MESOPOTAMIA

The area of Mesopotamia, roughly covering modern Iraq and southeastern Turkey, was, along with Syria, Palestine, and Egypt, an influential center of Christian monasticism. Whereas Syrian masonry was largely stone with vaults or wooden roofs, northern Mesopotamian architecture commonly employed stone with brick vaulting, while in central and southern Iraq mud brick was prevalent.

Tūr ʿAbdīn, a mountainous area in southeastern Turkey, furnishes a rich inventory of late-antique churches and monasteries comparable in quality to those of Syria, such as the monastery of Qartmin (*ca.* 512). The churches of Tūr ʿAbdīn, however, most commonly terminated in three rectangular chambers, showing evolution from the apse flanked by two chambers that marked Syrian churches. Particular to the Tūr ʿAbdīn (though imitated in the al-Jazīra region) were transverse naves—that is, single-aisle naves wider than they are long—found at Qartmin, Mar Yakub at Salah, and Mar Ibrāhīm at Midyat. Other churches feature a longitudinal nave, such as those found in basilica churches. Many churches also have an apse at the east end of an outdoor courtyard, which may have been used for services in summer or for weekday services. Such outdoor apses generally date from after the ninth century, as is the case with the one at Mar ʿAzaziel in Kefr Zeh, which an inscription dates to 934. Such exterior ecclesiastical spaces often simulate the triple sanctuaries within the churches through the placement of three stone tables in front of the apse.

The monastic church at ʿAin Shaʿia in southwestern Iraq exemplifies a style of architecture found in southern Mesopotamia and the Persian Gulf region. The mud brick church, which measures 73.5 feet by 45.3 feet (22.4 meters by 13.8 meters), has a long narrow nave with no bema, flanked by two aisles separated from the nave by solid masonry pierced by three openings. Like many Syrian examples, the church was entered through a courtyard to the side of the building, while the eastern end (actually northeastern) terminated in three rectangular chambers. The construction date is uncertain, but it is known that the church went out of use in the ninth century. Similar churches have been found in Kuwait and elsewhere in southern Iraq.

The later Middle Ages brought a series of disasters upon the Middle East generally and on the Christian population specifically. The Muslims who reconquered the Levantine coast from the crusaders often considered local Christians as possible supporters of future crusader conquests, and local Christian communities shrunk under the pressures of war, conversion, plague, and the depopulation of many rural areas. Few, if any, churches were built in this period.

BIBLIOGRAPHY

Bell, Gertrude Lowthian. *The Churches and Monasteries of the Tūr 'Abdīn.* Revised by Marlia Mundell Mango. London: Pindar, 1982.

Biscop, Jean-Luc. *Deir Déhès, monastère d'Antiochène.* Beirut: Institut français d'archéologie du Proche-Orient, 1997.

Donceel-Voûte, Pauline. *Les pavements des églises byzantines de Syrie et du Liban: Décor, archéologie, et liturgie.* Louvain, Belgium: Département d'archéologie et d'histoire de l'art, 1988.

Foudrin, Jean-Pascal. "Les églises à nef transversale d'Apamène et du Tûr 'Abdîn." *Syria* 62 (1985): 319–335.

Kleinbauer, Eugene. "Aisled Tetraconchs in Syria and Northern Mesopotamia." *Dumbarton Oaks Papers* 27 (1973): 89–114.

Oates, David. "Qasr Serij—A Sixth Century Basilica in Northern Iraq." *Iraq* 24 (1962): 78–89.

Okada, Yasuyoshi. "Early Christian Architecture in the Iraqi Southwestern Desert." *al-Rafidan* 12 (1991): 71–83.

Palmer, Andrew. *Monk and Mason on the Tigris Frontier: The Early History of Tūr 'Abdīn.* Cambridge, U.K.: Cambridge University Press, 1990.

Rice, Talbot D. "The Oxford Excavations at Hira, 1931." *Antiquity* 6 (1932): 276–291.

Tchalenko, Georges. *Églises de village de la Syrie du nord.* 2 vols. Paris: Librairie orientaliste Paul Guethner, 1979–1980. An album with plans.

———. *Églises syriennes à bêma.* 3 vols. Paris: Librairie orientaliste Paul Guethner, 1979–1990.

Wiessner, Gernot. *Christliche Kultbauten im Tūr 'Abdīn.* Wiesbaden: Harrassowitz, 1981–1982.

CHRISTOPHER HATCH MACEVITT

[See also **DMA:** Syrian Christianity.]

TAKLA HAYMANOT, ST. (*ca.* 1215–*ca.* 1313), a thirteenth-century leader in the revitalization of Ethiopian monasticism and the Christianization of southern Ethiopia. Although Christianity came to Ethiopia in the fourth century and monasticism soon after, it remained confined to the northern Tigre province for the next several centuries. Dabra Asbo, the monastery Takla founded, became one of two "motherhouses" with which most Ethiopian monasteries had close ties.

Takla Haymanot was born at Silalish in the Shawa region, the southern portion of Ethiopia, which at that time remained only partially incorporated into the kingdom. His name at birth was Fesseha Seyon, and his family was one of the leading priestly families of the region, where, according to tradition, they had lived for ten generations. He was ordained a deacon as a child, but according to his vita he became a monk only after refusing to marry his family's choice of a bride. His decision was inspired by a vision from Michael the Archangel, who directed him to the monastery of St. Stephen at Lake Hayq (known as Dabra Hayk), where he took the monastic name by which he is now known. This monastery had only a short time earlier been founded by Iyasus-Mo'a and was the only monastery in southern Ethiopia. After nine years at Hayq, Takla traveled north to the monastery of Dabra Damo, where Iyasus-Mo'a had been educated. Takla remained for several years under the guidance of Yohanni, who had been the teacher of Iyasus-Mo'a.

After several years under these mentors, two of the most prominent monastic leaders in Ethiopia, Takla decided to return to his homeland, Shawa, which still held a large pagan and Muslim population. Takla began preaching in the area around his family's home, attempting to both convert non-Christians and reform the existing Christian community. He demolished pagan places of worship and, according to his hagiographer, built churches in their place. Around 1286, he established his monastery, Dabra Asbo (later called Dabra Libanos), in the pagan area of Grarya to the northwest of Silalish. The monastery contained both male and female monastics during Takla's lifetime, but after his death, the monastery was divided into separate male and female houses. Takla attracted disciples from the local area and from Dabra Damo and other monasteries in the north.

Unlike his teachers at Dabra Hayk and Dabra Damo, Takla did not maintain a close relationship with the royal Amharan dynasty, which seized the throne in 1270. Instead, Takla relied on local leaders for support, even though the Amharan dynasty had come to power with the support of the Christian communities of Shawa and of many monastic leaders, including Iyasus-Mo'a.

Thanks to Takla's efforts, Christianity dominated the region by the time he died in 1313. Many of his disciples continued his work, founding other monasteries in the region and encouraging the spread of Christianity. Takla was particularly esteemed for his ascetic devotions, which included standing on one leg for seven years after his foot rotted away. It is in this pose that he is characteristically portrayed in painting.

BIBLIOGRAPHY

SOURCES

Budge, E. A. Wallis, ed. and trans. *The Life of Takla Hâymânôt.* London: Printed privately for Lady Meux, 1906.

Conti Rossini, C. "Il'Gadla Takla Haymanot' secondo la redazione Waldebbana." *Memorie della Reale Accademia dei Lincei,* 5th ser., 2 (1896): 97–143.

STUDIES

Huntingford, G. W. B. "The Lives of Saint Takla Hāymānot." *Journal of Ethiopian Studies* 4, no. 2 (1966): 34–40.

Kaplan, Steven. *The Monastic Holy Man and the Christianization of Early Solomonic Ethiopia.* Wiesbaden: Franz Steiner Verlag, 1984.

Tamrat, Taddesse. *Church and State in Ethiopia, 1270–1527.* Oxford: Clarendon Press, 1972.

CHRISTOPHER HATCH MACEVITT

[See also **DMA:** Abyssinia (Ethiopia).]

TANNENBERG/GRUNWALD, BATTLE OF.

A terrible battle between the Teutonic Knights and armies of the Poles and Lithuanians took place in the area between two villages in eastern Prussia, Tannenberg and Grunwald, on 15 July 1410. Relations between the Teutonic Knights and other powers in central and eastern Europe—Germans, Poles, Lithuanians, and Russians—had been difficult for two centuries, and although there were many periods of peace, the so-called Order State that the Knights established in their Baltic lands came into greater and more sustained conflict with its neighbors in the late fourteenth and early fifteenth century. But the Knights were often more than a match for their rivals.

Marienburg, the monumental headquarters of the knightly order, represented in impressive physical form the intended permanence of its rule in Prussia. When war between the Knights and both the Poles and Lithuanians was renewed in the early fourteenth century, the symbolic and more-than-symbolic attraction of assaulting Marienburg was not lost on the Knights. By the late fourteenth century, Poland-Lithuania in theory constituted two states within one dynastic realm. In fact, there was little integration of the Polish and Lithuanian armies (and the various allies from a wide variety of ethnic groups) that were marshaled in 1410 and led by King Władysław II Jagiełło for a strike at Marienburg. When the Knights met them in battle on 15 July while their foes were still on the march toward Marienburg, they inflicted a stunning defeat on the Lithuanians and their auxiliaries. The Poles and their allies, however, held on.

The battle continued for hours, and the bravery on all sides was considerable, but in the end the Knights suffered a sobering and almost complete defeat. Among the casualties, besides more than two hundred knights and an unknown number of auxiliaries, were the grand master and the majority of the commanders of the Order. No genuinely satisfactory estimates of the overall number of casualties on both sides exist (and extravagant estimates have been made), but it would not be surprising if they ran into the low thousands.

The victors then proceeded to mop up. Castles belonging to the Order began to surrender as word spread of the horrific defeat and as the invading armies resumed their march on Marienburg. But Marienburg itself was not to be taken. Heinrich Reuss, Graf von Plauen, who began to serve as grand master, commanded the great fortification successfully, and as the summer waned the invaders gave up their attempt and began their retreat.

The Battle of Tannenberg/Grunwald and the campaigns that ensued until the withdrawal in September did not break the back or the heart of the Order of the Teutonic Knights, but they effectively reduced its military power for a time and prevented the further expansion of the Order State along the southeastern coast of the Baltic. In hindsight, therefore, the battle is often seen as the beginning of the decline and fall of the Teutonic Order as a territorial force, even though it would remain a significant and feared player in Baltic politics for decades thereafter and would survive, even after further battlefield defeats, for more than a century as a state authority.

BIBLIOGRAPHY

Ekdahl, Sven. *Die Schlacht bei Tannenberg 1410: Quellenkritische Untersuchungen.* Berlin: Duncker and Humblot, 1982.

Turnbull, Stephen. *Tannenberg 1410: Disaster for the Teutonic Knights.* Oxford: Osprey Publishing, 2003.

WILLIAM CHESTER JORDAN

[See also **DMA:** Chivalry, Orders of; Jagiełło Dynasty; Lithuania; Poland; **Supp:** Teutonic Knights.]

TAXATION: GERMANY, ITALY, IBERIA.

The word "taxation" as employed in this essay implies a required payment authorized by a governing authority. The amount may be assessed on people, the value of property, income, or transactions. There is no obligation for the government to repay the levy to the contributors. Thus, taxation differs from forced loans, although some scholars conflate the two. Other scholars make a distinction between customary levies, with either an explicit or implicit contractual basis (tolls, for example), and special or new levies, regarding only the latter as taxes, particularly if the institutional setting within which they are authorized is a public assembly. Still others make an analytic distinction between direct taxes on wealth and indirect taxes on consumption.

GERMANY

The history of taxation in Germany is very complex. Heinrich Mitteis long ago observed that the most successful practitioners of taxation in Germany were the territorial principalities; it is they that developed institutions "along the same lines as in England and France, although on a much smaller scale" (*The State in the Middle Ages,* p. 311). In this essay, however, the focus of attention is the kingdom and imperium of Germany, which in terms of ideological claims was the superstate of the Middle Ages—though claims and reality are two different matters. As the German tag line has it, "ohne Steuer kein Staat" ("without taxes there is no state"). The application of this phrase to the Holy Roman Empire of the German Nation may be extreme, but taxation was not the institutional strong point of governance in the Middle Ages. And this was realized already in the twelfth century, when the English king Henry I allegedly instructed the emperor Henry V, his son-in-law, about the utility of levying a tax (Arnold, *Medieval Germany,* p. 158).

The extraordinary levies that the German king-emperors imposed on their subjects varied considerably, were often directed at individual towns, and, it has been argued, were typically exacted by the implied threat of force. The income from these levies constituted part of the crown or imperial, as opposed to familial or lineage, revenues (*Krongut* or *Reichsgut* as opposed to *Hausgut*). The justifications for the levies are similar to those employed in other realms across Europe. Military necessity—an expedition against Slavic raiders or Hungarian troops, for example—was an obvious and fairly frequent one. The crown could also exact grants as a form of punishment for alleged political misbehavior on the part of an urban government. There were also grants made, as in the great monarchies of the west, originally to provide the king with hospitality on a visit, but which could be diverted to other pressing purposes. "Voluntary" gifts for some great occasion in the life of the monarch were, in this sense, a form of taxation, too. Just as the thirteenth-century French king Louis IX might request financial aid from his towns to pay for indemnities accruing from a

peace treaty with England (1259), the German ruler expected the towns to make a financial gesture to him on, say, the occasion of his coronation.

Levies of the sort described tended to become fixed by custom although nowhere in medieval Europe did they ever entirely lose their arbitrary character. In Germany such grants as were obtained in these ways supplemented the sometimes enormous income the king-emperors derived from their family property *(Hausgut)*. The family property, at least from the late tenth century when the Ottonian "state" emerged, was not a fixed entity. It grew from donations, marriage, and confiscations, and it could be and was often severely depleted as well.

Spoils of war—when military campaigns were successful, and they frequently were not—supplemented the *Krongut, Reichsgut,* and *Hausgut.* However, the decentralization of Germany, which is to say, the profound strength of the princes from the period of Frederick I Barbarossa's reign (1152–1190) until the end of the Middle Ages, meant that the royal exaction of traditional taxes on towns, classified as part of *Krongut* and *Reichsgut* revenue, probably compared unfavorably with the levels from comparable sources of income in a more centralized country like England. Not surprisingly, therefore, the German king-emperors did attempt to systematize taxation of the towns as much as possible and in a way paralleling successful attempts in other medieval principalities, namely, through negotiation in assemblies. The appropriate (and central) assembly in Germany was the Imperial Diet, which already in the twelfth century served important judicial, political, and advisory functions, in the same manner as protoparliaments elsewhere.

The great princes of the secular nobility and the church constituted the core of the Imperial Diet. To this core other groups could be added when appropriate. From about the mid-thirteenth century the bourgeois element begins to appear, comprising representatives of the imperial free towns and the episcopal cities. As a general rule, at least through the fifteenth century, representatives of towns and cities only attended when matters of taxation had to be addressed. They were deemed dispensable when the business turned, say, to advising the king about the viability of an Italian military campaign. Indeed, the routine summoning of urban representatives to the diet is characteristic rather of the sixteenth century and the religious and political issues attending the Reformation and attempts to suppress Lutheranism—and, of course, the financial exigencies these entailed.

Long before the Reformation, however, the era of the Hussite Wars (1420–1434) had brought the fiscal situation of the German monarchy to a crisis point. The crown had to mount five major military campaigns. It also had to support princes who were incapable with their own resources of resisting, let alone overcoming, the Hussites. The emergency, as severe as any military emergency ever seen in Germany before the Reformation, was the occasion for a meeting of the diet at Nuremberg in 1422. The assembly consented to a tax at the rate of 1 percent to be levied across the board—on municipalities and on individual taxpayers. It also imposed heavier obligations on the Jews of the imperial fisc. As long as the Hussite threat was strong, measures like this were at least conceivable, though it is hard to know how successfully they were enforced. What happened at the diet that met at Basel in 1433–1434 was emblematic of the future: its members were prepared to grant a tax similar to the one consented to at Nuremberg in 1422, but the vanquishment of the Hussite army at Lipany in 1434 put paid to these efforts. The Middle Ages in Germany would not see further innovations in taxation.

ITALY

Italy was a patchwork of jurisdictions throughout the Middle Ages, and no short essay can do justice to the varieties of taxation employed in the various principalities and city republics. In general the territorial city-states that emerged in north Italy have to be differentiated from the kingdom (later, kingdoms) in the south. The territorial city-states of the north (like Florence) are known as city-states not because the state coincided with the urban space, but because the urban corporation dominated a more or less large territorial agglomeration of other cities and villages. Some of these subordinate cities, such as Pisa in the Florentine state, had themselves been the centers of city-states in earlier times.

Taxes were typically imposed for the whole state by the governing oligarchy of the chief city, and urban authorities often made assessments of rural wealth themselves, rather than delegating this task to locals. This was almost inevitable since the hostility of locals was rooted in the fact that the city-states were conquest states; incorporation of subject cities and their rural hinterlands had not been accomplished by peaceful means. It is not surprising, then, that in the systems of taxation that emerged, there seems to have been a strong bias in favor of the chief city. Direct taxes on bourgeois wealth were rarely levied in the capital city; the preferred mode of taxation was on consumption. Of course, serious emergencies undercut this convention. Fourteenth-century Florence witnessed two episodes of direct taxation of its citizens, but these did not lead to the regular levying of direct taxes on the Florentines. Contrariwise, citizens of subject cities and rural landholders were obligated to pay direct taxes, assessed typically either by head or hearth. As the tax burden fell disproportionately heavily on the citizens of subject cities and on the rural population, political revolts often drew considerable strength from anger over taxes.

The kingdom of Sicily in its various manifestations is more comparable to the principalities of the west. The fundamental underlying principle in taxation was that it should be shared among the various orders in the community. Neither in Sicily nor anywhere in Europe did the superior orders—nobility and clergy—bear a tax burden proportionate to their wealth, but to some extent discontent was contained by three factors. First, taxation was authorized in the Sicilian parliament. That is to say, the representatives of the orders or estates consented to taxation after its purpose was explained and its level was negotiated. Second, distribution of the burden within communities, especially cities, was frequently left to community authorities, thus allowing elites, whose favor the crown needed, to shift the burden onto the less powerful. Third, from the time of the establishment of the Aragonese dynasty in Sicily (the island) in 1286, an upper limit of 15,000 *onze* seems to have been set to the size of the assessment. If this had actually been collected, it would have contributed to the Sicilian crown's coffers about one-tenth of the equivalent annual crown revenues in France, which would have been a good-size tax even in France. (Recall that crown revenues in France as in Sicily and other realms drew on far more sources than taxation, but taxation was a significant portion. Rulers wanted to increase its significance.) In practice, it was customary in Sicily, however, to consent to the collection of 5,000 *onze.* The trade-off for these limitations was the custom that also began to arise of granting the *donativo,* as the levy was known, automatically, rather as the English parliament granted tonnage and poundage to the English kings at the opening of their reign.

In the long run, the Sicilian crown's finances suffered from these arrangements. Royalists could always argue that emergencies necessitated higher assessments than those typically granted, but negotiations inevitably started with the question of how much more was necessary than the accustomed assessment of 5,000 *onze,* not how much more was needed than the higher theoretical assessment of 15,000. Moreover, over a long period inflation eroded the value of the customary *donativo.* Efforts to revise the system in the crown's favor collapsed after they sparked tax revolts. As a result, the traditional method of taxation continued in force in Sicily throughout the later Middle Ages.

IBERIA

In the Christian kingdoms of Iberia, the fiscal demands of wars, especially the wars of Reconquest, made the imposition of taxation a regular necessity. Jews and Muslims under Christian rule, of course, were subject to the arbitrary impositions of Christian princes, although the latter often "negotiated" the amount and terms of the contributions with the leading men of the non-Christian communities. Rulers, sometimes invoking dubious precedents, aggressively tried in the late twelfth century to increase their revenues by also imposing new levies on their Christian populations. These attempts often provoked anger and resistance that were vented and smoothed over in assemblies of nobles and churchmen called for that purpose.

As elsewhere in Europe, however, these bodies then emerged as the forums in which consent to new extraordinary levies was given. The assemblies took their name in the various Romance dialects from the first word of the Latin phrase, *curiae regis* ("the king's courts"): *cortes* (in Navarre, Portugal, Castile, and Aragon) and *corts* (in the Catalan-speaking regions). They were not always "national": Castile and León, although in union, for a time had separate *cortes*; Valencia's *corts* met separately from the *cortes* of Aragon; and so forth. The composition of these assemblies varied according to the business that was being addressed (taxation was not the only concern) or the prince's whims. There is evidence of the more or less regular meeting of some of these assemblies already in the twelfth century (and all of them by the early thirteenth) and of the presence in them quite early of representatives from towns. This evidence predates that which allows any very detailed reconstruction of the procedures followed to secure consent to taxation. Peasants "enjoyed" only virtual representation through the presence of their noble and ecclesiastical overlords at the assemblies.

The presence of representatives of the towns was crucial for taxation because the nobles and members of the upper clergy were largely exempted from extraordinary levies. In Navarre, beginning in the fourteenth century, approximately 27 free, that is, nonseigneurial, towns sent representatives to its *cortes,* but the number was not absolutely fixed and continued to grow beyond the end of the Middle Ages. In Castile upwards of 150 towns could have made a reasonable case for having sufficient importance to send representatives to the medieval *cortes,* but the crown preferred to offer the privilege to a much smaller number that became more or less fixed at 18.

On occasion—during, say, a serious emergency—consent must have been a mere formality, but usually it was a zealously insisted upon custom and implied that taxation required the give-and-take of bargaining. From the early to the mid-thirteenth century there is evidence of various rulers promising their assemblies, for example, not to debase the coinage (for a term of years) in return for the grant of a tax. In Portugal, Castile, Aragon, and Catalonia the ruler's obligation to seek consent from the assemblies was repeatedly stressed from the mid-thirteenth century, and assemblies insisted, too, that no extraordinary levies be imposed without calling them into session for the purpose of consenting to them, which is to say, every extraordinary levy was ipso facto a tax and required the consent of the representative assembly.

Achieving consent was usually possible, for it was as hard in Iberia as it was elsewhere to withhold consent. Every request for taxation was accompanied by some sort of plea about the evident dangers that the principality faced if it did not receive the money it needed. The requirement of consent made it possible to negotiate about the grant's overall size and rate (percentage of individual income). Also negotiated was the length of time the tax would be in force (one or several years). The basis of the tax was another matter for discussion: would it be apportioned on each adult male and *femme sole* (a poll or head tax), on each domicile (or, rather, hearth), on the taxpayer's chattels, on trade (surcharges on customs dues), or assessed some other way? The selection of the tax collectors was another matter often in dispute; for example, a stipulation might be made that Jews could not serve as collectors or that a collection agency be created under the assembly's formal control. In the fourteenth and fifteenth centuries such bureaus of supervision became regular institutions in the Iberian kingdoms.

The assemblies were less successful in putting effective limits on the disbursement of tax funds, which could easily be diverted by kings from the purpose for which they had been granted to other quite different purposes in rapidly changing circumstances. The assemblies' lack of effectiveness in this regard did not stop them from trying; in 1407, for example, the Castilian *cortes* tried to restrict its grants to the support of military campaigns against the Muslims.

The tax burden was especially crushing for peasants. One must always keep in mind that taxation, in the sense of extraordinary levies, fell on peasants, whose regular annual obligations were already heavy. The historian Oliveira Marques estimated (see *Daily Life in Portugal in the Late Middle Ages,* pp. 183–184) that a Portuguese peasant paid between one-tenth and one-third of his agricultural production (or its equivalent in coin) as annual rent, but also paid additional annual levies that had built up over the years and become customary (Oliveira Marques listed four of these as typical). Besides these there was the tithe to the church and forced labor (or the commuted payment of this obligation). Oliveira Marques could not be sure how much a typical farmer retained for himself and his family—to consume or sell—because of complications in the regional imposition of these levies and the prominence of sharecropping. The lower end of his estimate, however, was that only one-fourth of a farmer's total production was at his free disposal. The high-end estimate, for the most privileged peasants, was one-half. Extraordinary taxation voted by the *cortes* would have reduced this even further. Despite geographical variations, the situation in other Iberian regions, like Old Catalonia, was often as grievous.

BIBLIOGRAPHY

GERMANY

Arnold, Benjamin. *Medieval Germany, 500–1300: A Political Interpretation.* Houndmills, U.K., and London: Macmillan, 1997. Mentions Henry I of England's advice to the emperor and is representative of general surveys in its assessment of the relative unimportance of "national" taxation in Germany.

Du Boulay, F. R. H. *Germany in the Later Middle Ages.* New York: St. Martin's, 1983. Deals with taxation in Germany at the level of kingdom and empire, as opposed to the many studies of taxation in the various principalities and towns.

Mitteis, Heinrich. *The State in the Middle Ages: A Constitutional History of Feudal Europe.* Translated by H. F. Orton. Amsterdam: North-Holland Publishing, 1975.

Schwennicke, Andreas. *"Ohne Steuer kein Staat": Zur Entwicklung und politischen Funktion des Steuerrechts in den Territorien des Heiligen Römischen Reichs (1500–1800).* Frankfurt-am-Main, Germany: V. Klostermann, 1996. Covers taxation on the eve of modernity, when the story gets more interesting.

ITALY

Epstein, Stephen. "Taxation and Political Representation in Italian Territorial States." In *Public and Private Finances in the Late Middle Ages.* Edited by Marc Boone and Walter Prevenier. Louvain, Belgium: Garant, 1996. A good synthetic essay on Italian territorial taxation.

Waley, Daniel. *The Italian City-Republics.* London: Longman, 1988. A good place to start for a more detailed examination of the separate histories of the city-states.

IBERIA

Bisson, Thomas. *The Medieval Crown of Aragon: A Short History.* Oxford: Clarendon, 1986.

Boswell, John. *The Royal Treasure: Muslim Communities under the Crown of Aragon in the Fourteenth Century.* New Haven, Conn., and London: Yale University Press, 1977.

O'Callaghan, Joseph. *A History of Medieval Spain.* Ithaca, N.Y.: Cornell University Press, 1975.

Oliviera Marques, A. H. de. *Daily Life in Portugal in the Late Middle Ages.* Translated by S. S. Wyatt. Madison: University of Wisconsin Press, 1971.

WILLIAM CHESTER JORDAN

[See also **DMA:** Taxation, Byzantine; Taxation, Church; Taxation, English; Taxation, French; Taxation, Islamic.]

TEMPLARS *(Pauperes commilitones Christi templi Salomonici).* The Order of the Temple established a new ideal of Christian piety, that of the warrior-monk, which reflected new Christian ideas about war and holiness that developed in the eleventh and twelfth centuries. Hugh of Payns established the order in late 1119 to help guide and protect pilgrims in the newly founded Kingdom of Jerusalem. The new group was called the Poor Knights of Christ of the Temple of Solomon; their headquarters were in the Mosque of Al-Aqṣā (the Temple of Solomon to the Latins), and hence the knights were popularly called Templars. In the 1130s, the Templars' duties expanded to protecting the Holy Land, as the Templars received several castles to defend, including Latrun (Toron des Chevaliers), west of Jerusalem, and Baghras (Gaston), north of Antioch. In the Iberian Peninsula, the order received its first castle in Portugal in 1128. Alfonso I of Aragon (1104–1134) left his entire kingdom to the Holy Sepulcher in Jerusalem, the Hospitallers, and the Templars. Although Ramon Berenguer IV eventually inherited the kingdom, Alfonso's will shows the prominence the military orders achieved soon after they were founded. Yet the order did not have a sufficient number of knights or sergeants to protect all their new holdings and frequently employed mercenaries to augment their military strength. The new order received a written rule in 1129, perhaps written by Bernard of Clairvaux, who took an early interest in the Templars. His treatise *De laude novae militiae* (1128) popularized the Templars throughout Europe.

The support of Europe's most charismatic religious leader gave the Templars immediate appeal throughout the Catholic world, and the order grew quickly in wealth and in numbers. The Templars were divided into two main groups, knights and sergeants. The knights largely came from noble families and were the elite of the order. The majority of Templars, however, were sergeants, who managed the order's properties and fought as foot soldiers. The order also had priest-brothers to perform religious services. Unlike traditional monasticism, the order did not retain its novitiate, an introductory period common in many monastic traditions where new members join the community but do not take permanent oaths until certain of their commitment. They did, however, take oaths of poverty, obedience, and chastity. Soldiers as well as monks, the Templars were required to follow the daily liturgical hours. If a brother was in the field, he was to say the Lord's Prayer a set number of times instead. The grand master ruled the order from Jerusalem, while the properties of the Templars were divided into provinces. The master held general chapter meetings periodically, which all provincial commanders attended. On a local level, the commandery managed Templar properties in a given area, and sent the proceeds to the headquarters in the Latin East. Although the order forbade the establishment of female Templar houses, they developed anyway. The monastery of Mühlen was under their care, and evidence survives that some sisters of the order lived in commanderies with the brothers, perhaps in another building. At least one woman, Ermengarda d'Oluja, was recognized as a commander of the order, being in charge of the local commandery in Rourell in Aragon.

The Templars served various nonmilitary roles as papal chamberlains and almoners. They quickly developed a reputation for competency in financial matters, served as the royal almoners in England from 1177 to 1255, and became treasurers to the kings of France. Because they were constantly channeling money from their estates in Europe to the Latin East, "the Temple" was often viewed as safe place to keep money.

Although the Templars could probably field only approximately three hundred brothers at one time, their wealth, mercenaries, and control of important fortresses made them one of the most powerful groups in the Latin East. They participated in most of the great battles of the kingdom but sometimes were accused of valuing valor over strategy. Some blamed the Templars for the catastrophic defeat at the Horns of Ḥiṭṭīn (4 July 1187), where they advocated attacking Saladin rather than taking a defensive position. If so, they paid the price. After the battle all of the Templars, with the exception of the grand master, were executed, and most of their castles were destroyed, with the exception of Tartus (Tortosa). Despite their losses, the Templars rebuilt numerous castles, such as Safed, and established new ones, such as ʿAtlit (Château Pèlerin). At Acre, they built an enormous compound that became their new headquarters. Because of weakened royal and aristocratic power in the thirteenth century, the military orders negotiated truces with Muslim leaders independently of secular political leaders, and they were not bound by the treaties of others. However, the effectiveness of the military orders was undermined by the rivalry between them, such as in Antioch, where the Templars backed the claims of Bohemond IV of Tripoli to the throne, while the Hospitallers supported his nephew, Raymond Rupen. The fall of Acre in 1291 ended Latin rule in the Levant; a great number of Templars died defending the city. The Templars were the last to leave the Syrian coast, holding onto the island of Arwad until 1302. Those Templars who survived retreated to Cyprus, where their new grand master, Jacques de Molay, traveled to western Europe to plan a new crusade.

On 13 October 1307, Philip IV of France ordered all the Templars arrested, accusing them of heresy, sodomy, and other crimes. Many confessed after having been tortured. A month later Pope Clement V, who had just moved the papacy to Avignon under French protection, ordered that all Templars be arrested. He insisted, however, that the case be tried by papal authorities, but Philip refused. Some Templars retracted their earlier confessions and sought to defend the order in a papal court. On 12 May 1310, at Philip's order, fifty-four Templars were burned at the stake for being relapsed heretics, that is, for admitting their heresy and then returning to it. The pope summoned a council at Vienne in 1311 to consider the case, but Philip's propaganda made it difficult to rehabilitate the order. In the papal bull *Vox in excelso,* issued 22 March 1312, Clement V declared the order dissolved but stated that the Templars' guilt had not been proven. Some Templars were allowed to retire to other monastic houses, but trials still continued against some. A papal commission condemned Jacques de Molay to be burned at the stake on 18 March 1314. This series of events bewildered western Europe. Never before had such an influential and respected part of the church been so thoroughly discredited and destroyed. Modern consensus has been that Philip attacked the Templars to acquire their great wealth. Certainly the king was facing serious financial problems, and the Templars presented a rich target. In other parts of Europe, the order fared better. The English Templars were arrested, but none were tortured. In Brandenburg the order was turned into a secular order of knights under the margrave's command. The papacy ordered the belongings of the Temple be given to the Hospitallers, except in the Iberian Peninsula, where Templar property endowed local military orders under royal control.

BIBLIOGRAPHY

SOURCES

Delaville Le Roulx, Joseph. *Documents concernants les Templiers: Extraits des archives de Malte*. Paris: E. Plon, 1882.

Gilmour-Bryson, Anne, ed. and trans. *The Trial of the Templars in Cyprus*. Leiden, Netherlands, and Boston: E. J. Brill, 1998.

Hiestand, Rudolf. *Papsturkunden fur Templer und Johanniter: Archivberichte und Texte*. Göttingen, Germany: Vandenhoeck and Ruprecht, 1972.

———. *Papsturkunden fur Templer und Johanniter: Neue Folge*. Göttingen, Germany: Vandenhoeck and Ruprecht, 1984.

STUDIES

Barber, Malcolm. *The Trial of the Templars*. Cambridge, U.K., and New York: Cambridge University Press, 1978.

Nicholson, Helen. *The Knights Templar: A New History*. Stroud, U.K.: Sutton, 2001.

Selwood, Dominic. *Knights of the Cloister: Templars and Hospitallers in Central-Southern Occitania, c. 1100–c. 1300*. Woodbridge, U.K., and Rochester, N.Y.: Boydell Press, 1999.

CHRISTOPHER HATCH MACEVITT

[See also **DMA:** Acre; Chivalry, Orders of; Clement V, Pope; Crusades and Crusader States; Ḥiṭṭīn (Hattin); Philip IV the Fair; **Supp:** Hospitallers.]

TERTULLIAN (Quintus Septimus Florens Tertullianus, *ca.* A.D. 155/160–*ca.* 230/240) claims the title of the first important Christian writer in the Latin West. An educated man who was born and spent most of his life in North Africa, Tertullian wrote many theological and ethical treatises; thirty-one are extant, and at least fifteen additional works, some of which were in Greek, are now lost. Few details about Tertullian's personal background and the events of his life are known for certain. From his own writings, Jerome's account, and information from Eusebius of Caesarea, it is clear that Tertullian was born into a prosperous pagan family, received a good education, and converted to Christianity in middle age. It is also possible that the apologist started off with a career in law; in addition to Eusebius's comment that Tertullian was an expert in Roman law, much of his writing features legalistic imagery (e.g., *On the Witness of the Soul*). From *ca.* 205 onward, Tertullian joined the rigorist Montanist Christians, although it is uncertain whether he separated himself formally from the orthodox church of Carthage. Montanism began in the mid-second century A.D. in Asia Minor. Its founders, the poet Montanus, Priscilla (or Prisca), and Maximilla, believed that they received revelations that they called the New Prophecy. These teachings centered on the virtues of martyrdom and on the strict avoidance of sin, as well as the belief that the Holy Spirit continued to send prophesy. Later, Tertullian left the Montanists to start his own sect, the Tertullianists, who observed an even stricter moral code.

By the late fourth century, Tertullian's writings were well known; his association with the condemned Montanists had not prevented the circulation of his work. The treatises that survive are characterized by the educated Christian's use of polished Latin rhetoric and fierce argumentation in his articulation of Christian doctrine and morality. Most notably, Tertullian put his eloquence to use in his *Apology* of 197, which attempted to reason pagan rulers out of their policy of persecuting Christians. He disputed the rumors that Christians practiced incest, cannibalism, and treason and then criticized the illogical way the courts condemned Christians without accusing them of actual crimes. The apologist also took the offensive and attacked the pagans for their own religion's inconsistencies and scandals, accusing them of committing all of the disgraceful acts ascribed to the Christians. Tertullian wrote treatises against other groups he disagreed with—the Gnostics, the Jews, and, later, the critics of the Montanist movement. In addition to arguing against his opponents, Tertullian also dealt with topics important to the study of early Christian doctrine and liturgy, such as the resurrection, prayer, the nature of the soul, baptism, fasting, and penance. His concerns over the proper behavior of Christians produced works that provide information of interest to social historians on topics such as sexual mores and marriage, female fashion, and popular entertainment. In antiquity, Tertullian influenced prominent North African Christians, including Cyprian of Carthage, Augustine, and Lactantius, as well as the more far-flung readership of Eusebius of Caesarea, Pope Leo the Great, and Isidore of Seville, among many others. Tertullian fell out of favor in the Middle Ages, but was rediscovered by Christian humanists in the Renaissance.

BIBLIOGRAPHY

Barnes, Timothy David. *Tertullian: A Historical and Literary Study*. Rev. ed. Oxford: Clarendon Press; New York: Oxford University Press, 1985.

Dunn, G. D. "The Universal Spread of Christianity as a Rhetorical Argument in Tertullian's adversus Judaeos." *JECS* 8, no. 1 (spring 2000): 1–19.

Osborn, Eric. *Tertullian, First Theologian of the West*. Cambridge, U.K., and New York: Cambridge University Press, 1997.

Rankin, David. *Tertullian and the Church*. Cambridge, U.K., and New York: Cambridge University Press, 1995.

Sider, Robert D., ed. *Christian and Pagan in the Roman Empire: The Witness of Tertullian*. Washington D.C.: Catholic University of America Press, 2001. English translations of selected works by Tertullian.

JACLYN MAXWELL

[See also **DMA:** Eusebius of Caesarea; Jerome, St.; Latin Literature.]

TEUTONIC KNIGHTS. The Teutonic Knights, known collectively as the Teutonic Order or the German Order, originated in a German hospital established in the city of Acre during the Third Crusade. In 1193 Henry of Champagne, the ruler of Jerusalem, gave the brethren of the hospital the responsibility of maintaining a section of the city's defenses in addition to their duties of caring for the sick and the poor. Their role was soon extended to the protection of German crusaders and pilgrims. By the end of the century, they adopted the rule of the Templars and took up arms in defense of Christian interests in the Holy Land.

As their name implies, the Teutonic Knights were recruited primarily from German laymen of free status and shared a linguistic background that lent them a cultural cohesion lacking in other military orders. Their religious purpose and rules of personal discipline differed little, however, from those of their models. Like the Templars, the Teutonic Knights understood combat against non-Christians as a means of personal salvation and as an act of Christian charity. Borrowing strict rules of conduct and comportment from monastic orders, the Knights took vows of poverty, chastity, and obedience; slept and ate in communal dormitories and refectories; observed a rule of silence; and attended church services. Entry into the Order was not immediate and binding. Like cloistered communities, the Order had a novitiate, or period of probation to test the preparedness and intention of new recruits.

The administrative organization of the Teutonic Knights was also similar to that of other military orders of the time. Every convent of the Order had an administrative official known as a commander or preceptor who was responsible for the regulation of internal discipline. Individuals held this office on an annual basis. In some convents, the commander had an assistant, the cellarer, who looked after the provisioning of the community. The brethren discussed the business of the convent in a weekly meeting. Every commander answered to the provincial head of his region, the *Deutschmeister*. This administrator oversaw the convents of his district and organized the provincial chapter, an annual meeting of convent commanders to discuss the initiatives and affairs of the Order. The provincial heads answered in turn to the grand master, the supreme head of the Teutonic Knights, who was elected by a council of thirteen individuals and held his office for life.

Although founded in the Holy Land, the Teutonic Knights played their most significant role on the northeastern frontiers of Christendom, where the conquest of land went hand in hand with the subjugation and baptism of pagan peoples. In 1211, King Andrew II of Hungary gave the Knights their first foothold in central Europe when he granted them the district of Burzenland to serve as a staging ground for military campaigns against the Cumans and other pagan peoples who inhabited the lands north of the Transylvanian Alps. Around 1225–1226, Conrad of Mazovia established the Teutonic Knights in Culm to protect and assist frontier missionaries in Livonia and Prussia. There they usurped the military role of the Order of Swordbearers and the Dobriner Order and absorbed the members of these orders into their ranks. Although their numbers were never very large at any time in their history, they enjoyed considerable success in the Baltic region, building many strongholds and attracting German settlers and a steady flow of new recruits. Income from trade monopolies, land rents, and the spoils of combat increased their power and autonomy. By the end of the thirteenth century, the Teutonic Knights had formed an independent state in Prussia and established an important foothold in Livonia.

With the collapse of the Latin settlements in the Holy Land in 1291, the headquarters of the Teutonic Order moved first to Venice and then in 1309 to Marienburg in Prussia. Shortly thereafter, the Order came under the threat of dissolution because of accusations of misconduct on the Baltic frontier. In 1310, charges leveled against the Knights included the murder of Christians in Livonia, the looting and destruction of church property, and the interruption of the process of conversion. The Teutonic Order weathered this storm of controversy and made considerable gains in territory throughout the fourteenth century. Under Winrich von Kniprode, who was the grand master of the Order from 1351 to 1382, western nobles were successfully encouraged to participate in seasonal military expeditions (*reysen*) against pagan strongholds in Prussia, Livonia, and Lithuania. Henry IV, the future king of England, took part in these prestigious outings on two occasions. Campaigns to the north and east gradually increased the holdings of the Order and augmented land gains made by purchase or conquest in Pomerania and Estonia.

The Teutonic Knights ultimately suffered from their success in the field. The conversion of the Lithuanians and the consolidation of the Order's hold on Prussia and Livonia caused European nobles to lose interest in the Order's military expeditions. By the early fifteenth century, the expense of mercenaries needed to maintain a viable military presence on the frontiers began to take its toll on the Order's resources. To make matters worse, Prussian nobles resented the political autonomy of the Knights and kindled civil war against them. The German Order was dissolved in the sixteenth century. In 1525, the grand master Albrecht of Brandenburg converted to Lutheranism and ruled Prussia as a secular duke, paying homage to the king of Poland. His conversion eventually led to the secularization of the entire Order.

BIBLIOGRAPHY

Burleigh, Michael. *Prussian Society and the German Order: An Aristocratic Corporation in Crisis, c. 1410–1466.* Cambridge, U.K.: Cambridge University Press, 1984.

Christiansen, Eric. *The Northern Crusades: The Baltic and the Catholic Frontier 1100–1525.* London and Basingstoke, U.K.: Macmillan, 1980.

Forey, Alan. "Novitiate and Instruction in the Military Orders during the Twelfth and Thirteenth Centuries." *Speculum* 61 (1986): 1–17.

———. *The Military Orders: From the Twelfth to the Early Fourteenth Centuries.* Toronto and Buffalo, N.Y.: University of Toronto Press, 1992.

Nicholson, Helen. *Templars, Hospitallers, and Teutonic Knights: Images of the Military Orders, 1128–1291.* Leicester, U.K.: Leicester University Press, 1993.

Scott G. Bruce

[See also **DMA:** Chivalry, Orders of; Crusades and Crusader States; **Supp:** Cumans/Kipchaks; Hermann of Salza; Tannenberg/Grunewald, Battle of; Templars.]

TEXTILES, BYZANTINE. Symbols of status for both individuals and the state, textiles, particularly silks, also played an important economic role in Byzantium. The production of silk, linen, and wool cloth for use in garments, tapestries, and vestments was one of the mainstays of the Byzantine economy. Carpets and wall hangings were important furnishings in the home, playing both a decorative and practical role. As clothes, textiles of various styles, colors, materials, and qualities were the principal markers of status, both socially and officially, within the hierarchy of the imperial court.

Woman Playing a Kithara (Textile). *Surviving example of a late-antique tapestry.* ABEGG-STIFTUNG, CH. 3132 RIGGISBERG (FOTO CHRISTOPH VON VIRAG). REPRODUCED BY PERMISSION.

LATE ANTIQUITY AND EARLY BYZANTIUM

The Byzantines inherited much of their textile industry from the Romans, whose textile industry was based largely on wool and linen. While wool was produced throughout the empire, Gaul, Spain, Italy, and Asia Minor were areas of high production. Linen was also manufactured in many parts of the empire, but the highest quality material came from Syria and Egypt; cotton, not grown around the Mediterranean, was imported from Africa and India as a finished product. A thriving industry in Egypt and Syria turned raw silk into woven dyed textiles. The silk, however, was imported from China, where the secrets of its production were protected by imperial decree. Most late-antique textiles have been discovered in Egyptian tombs and in consequence are often called "Coptic" textiles, though their origin is not necessarily Christian. Most are linen-wool tapestries, but some silk material also survives. Decorative elements include birds and animals, as well as persons such as Dionysus, Pan, or the Virgin Mary, depicted in the fourth-century silk tapestry the "Virgin" silk. According to Procopius of Caesarea, the Byzantine empire began cultivation of silkworms and mulberry trees in the sixth century, when monks smuggled silkworms across Asia to the Mediterranean. The Muslim conquests of the seventh century captured the centers of Byzantine textile production in Syria and Egypt, and Constantinople subsequently became home to the industry.

MIDDLE BYZANTINE TEXTILES

The largest proportion of surviving textiles from the Middle Byzantine period consists of silks, often preserved as wrappings in western relic collections. Wool and linen were still used by the majority of the population, but few examples have survived from this period. The most studied and appreciated of Byzantine silk textiles were the products of imperial workshops in Constantinople. A variety of laws restricted private production of high-quality silk, beginning with the Theodosian Code in the early fifth century and continuing into the twelfth century. The use of highly valued and symbolic purple cloth, representative of royalty and divinity, was solely an imperial privilege. The introduction of the drawloom allowed the production of complex repeating patterns on silk, but the expense of the complex machinery largely limited its use to imperial workshops and a few large manufacturers. Although the imperial workshops produced the highest-quality silks, a variety of other manufacturers also flourished. Byzantine dyeing techniques shared much in common with the traditions of western Europe, with the exception of the famous purple imperial dyes. Although these are usually associated with the dye extracted from the *murex* mollusks, other purple dyes were also used, even in high-quality textiles. The Siegburg "Lion" silk, now in Berlin, though of imperial origin and perhaps an imperial gift, used madder to create its purple color.

Imperial oversight of silk production continued in the eighth and ninth centuries, when textiles, usually silk, were sent as diplomatic gifts to both the kingdoms of western Europe and the caliphate. Such gifts, which included individual high-quality silks from imperial workshops as well as bulk textiles bought on the open market in Constantinople, could serve as wedding trousseaus for Byzantine princesses, gifts to foreigner leaders, or even as part of tribute. Whatever their purpose, the quality of the textiles declared the industrial and cultural superiority of Byzantium. The ninth-century *Book of the Eparch* details the intensive imperial oversight of the silk industry by officials named *kommerkiarioi*. The regulation of private silk guilds points to a flourishing local and international trade. Restrictions on aristocratic estate workshops suggest that textiles were also produced commercially on private estates.

Increasing the demand for high-quality silks was their widespread use among Christian clergy of all denominations. Sacred images of the saints, the Virgin Mary, or even Christ appeared on late antique clerical dress but disappeared in the Greek church by the seventh century, before iconoclasm. However, historiated silk vestments were still prized among other eastern churches and reappeared in the thirteenth century among the Greeks. In the thirteenth century, embroidered textiles, particularly silks, became popular and were often used by clerics as part of their vestments and as *podeai,* or icon cloths. The images gained layers of symbolic meaning that linked the priest to the liturgy of the Mass and to the reenactment of Christ's life.

The tenth through twelfth centuries are considered the peak in Byzantine silk textile production. The tenth-century book of imperial ceremonies, *De ceremoniis,* describes the regalia, hierarchy, and ceremonies of the Byzantine court and reveals the important role silks played as markers of status. Each rank of courtier was restricted to wearing garments of a certain quality, color, and imagery. The resulting splendor not only made visible the hierarchy of the imperial court but also displayed to ambassadors and visitors its wealth and magnificence. The silk and gold trimmings of courtiers' garments were designed to enhance the magnificence of the emperor's costume, as did the tapestries of silk and wool that decorated the palace.

Evidence for the establishment of a silk industry outside of Constantinople is scarce before the twelfth century, but some evidence suggests that silk weaving flourished in parts of Greece, particularly Thebes and Corinth, as early as the ninth century. Jewish silk workers played a significant role, particularly in Thebes. By the late twelfth century, Theban silk surpassed that of Constantinople in quality and perhaps even in quantity. The later medieval name for southern Greece, the Morea, may well derive from the Greek name for the mulberry tree.

LATE BYZANTINE TEXTILES

The Fourth Crusade in 1204 effectively destroyed the Byzantine silk industry in Constantinople, but the

Theban industry continued production into the fourteenth century. Furthermore, the plundered textiles that flooded Europe as a result of the Crusade lessened the rarity and value of Byzantine work. However, Byzantine textile production continued in the successor states of Epiros, Trebizond, and Nicaea, although few surviving cloths of the later period can be attributed to these territories. Although we cannot distinguish Byzantine textiles from western productions of this period, textual and art historical material shows that textiles continued to play an important role in imperial court life.

BIBLIOGRAPHY

Jacoby, David. *Trade, Commodities and Shipping in the Medieval Mediterranean.* Brookfield, Vt.: Variorum, 1997.

Millet, Gabriel. *Broderies religieuses de style byzantin.* Paris: E. Leroux, 1939–.

Muthesius, Anna. *Byzantine Silk Weaving: A.D. 400 to A.D. 1200.* Edited by Ewald Kislinger and Johannes Koder. Vienna: Fassbaender, 1997.

Stauffer, Annemarie. *Textiles of Late Antiquity.* New York: Metropolitan Museum of Art, 1995.

CHRISTOPHER HATCH MACEVITT

[See also **DMA:** Codex Theodosianus; *Eparch, Book of the; Morea, Chronicle of;* Silk; Sumptuary Laws, European; Textile Technology; Textile Workers.]

TOLLS were renders in goods or money that were required for the exercise of certain privileges. The right to levy tolls, like many similar rights, could be construed as regalian, that is, as strictly limited to the crown. Because enormous numbers of individual lords and corporations (municipalities, cathedral chapters, monasteries, etc.) claimed and exercised such rights, jurists articulated a legal fiction, which probably does not conform to historical reality, that the crown had originally granted rights to collect tolls and use toll receipts to these holders as a reward for good service, in exchange for other rights, or for some other reason. It followed—and the doctrine became enforceable at law in the twelfth and thirteenth centuries throughout Europe—that any significant abuse in the exercise of the right to collect and dispense the income of tolls, including a holder's long failure to collect them, was justification for the crown's recovery.

Tolls were a ubiquitous feature of the medieval landscape. The income generated from their collection both gave a legitimate profit to the holder and provided funds for maintaining the institutional arrangements or physical properties for the privilege of whose enjoyment the tolls were levied. Thus, a road toll was meant to provide income to the lord who had the right to levy the toll as well as the resources to erect and keep the tollgate and booth in good repair, pay the toll keeper, and maintain the quality of the appropriate stretch of road. A market toll returned profit to the owner of the market and other monies to pay market inspectors and perhaps also to erect and maintain a covered area in the marketplace. A mill toll provided income to the lord of the mill, the wages of the miller, and expenditures for upkeep.

Various factors influenced tariffs. The amount of toll for using a bridge could be calibrated to the confession, condition, or status of the person crossing: a Jew might pay more than a Christian; an adult, more than a child; nobles, crusaders, and pilgrims might be exempt. There were other criteria, too. Two-wheeled carts paid less than wagons with four wheels; a goat-drawn conveyance, less than a horse-drawn; and a laden oxcart, more than an empty one. Large multiple-oared barges paid higher river tolls than smaller two-oared boats.

Tolls were often farmed. The holder, as it were, auctioned the toll to the highest bidder for a term of years, for life, or in perpetuity. The successful bidder or farmer typically rendered payment annually (or in partial payments throughout the year) to the holder; the farmer profited when tolls collected during the year exceeded the amount he paid. This stimulated many a farmer to maximize his income by reducing expenditures for upkeep while extorting exorbitant fees whenever it was possible to do so. The lord was responsible for seeing that the farmer remained within the limits of legality, but supervision was not always strict.

Toll in the singular (Latin, *theloneum*) was widely used to indicate the privilege of individuals and corporations to be free from the infliction of tolls in defined jurisdictions, not excluding the kingdom as a whole.

BIBLIOGRAPHY

The Coutumes de Beauvaisis of Philippe de Beaumanoir. Translated by Frank Akehurst. Philadelphia: University of Pennsylvania Press, 1992. Law book of the High Middle Ages with a section devoted to the imposition of tolls.

WILLIAM CHESTER JORDAN

[See also **DMA:** Markets, European; Mills; Roads and Bridges, Western European.]

TONSURE, from the Latin *tondere,* "to shear," typically refers to a hairstyle worn by monks and clergy in which some portion of the head is shaved. The act of tonsuring had neither any intrinsic meaning nor basis in scripture or early Christian literature. Explanations for its origins vary, but it is often suggested that the first Christian monks with tonsures were emulating the shaved heads of Roman slaves, in order to endure their own humiliation and to render themselves slaves of God.

By the end of the fifth century at the latest, even Roman lawmakers associated the tonsure with clergy, who apparently had copied the practice from monks. There was still, however, no prescribed method of tonsuring. Most early recipients of a tonsure probably had hair cropped close to the scalp, or possibly the entire head was shaved. This close-cropped style came to be associated with St. Paul, for no good reason except to distinguish it from other styles such as the one prevalent in western Europe, that of St. Peter. This latter style involved shaving the scalp except for a ring or crown of hair around the head. A third pattern—the so-called Celtic tonsure—featured a narrow band of shaved skin running from ear to ear, leaving a thin fringe of hair in front; its Irish proponents attributed it to St. John the Baptist. The Venerable Bede and other Roman Christian churchmen, however, associated the Celtic tonsure with the wicked magician of apocryphal scripture, Simon Magus. It was even believed that during the Apocalypse, the Antichrist would sport the same hairstyle. Tonsure was no small matter: along with disagreement over competing systems for establishing the date of Easter, tonsure was an issue that threatened to divide the church in Britain during the early Middle Ages. Despite the importance of tonsuring, however, it was in fact a revocable act. As long as tonsured clergy did not take monastic vows or ascend in rank, they could grow their hair back and reenter society. Thus in the Merovingian dynasty, for example, tonsure was a convenient way to disqualify members of the royal family from succession to the throne, while allowing the possibility of their reinstatement to political life if necessary.

While literary descriptions and debates over forms of tonsure allow historians to have a good idea of how various tonsure hairstyles looked throughout the Middle Ages, our knowledge of the rituals that surrounded tonsuring is more incomplete. By the thirteenth century, visual depictions of clerics getting their first tonsure begin to appear with increasing frequency. In these images, someone—usually a bishop, seated and wearing a miter—wields a large pair of shears over the head of a kneeling cleric; consecrated clerics stand behind the bishop, bearing liturgical objects, and other clerics awaiting their own tonsures sometimes appear as well. Other sources describe the accompanying investment with the surplice, or outer gown. The spiritual prestige symbolized by such ceremonies and by the tonsure itself could also be reversed, however, even if the ordination itself could not. In the case of an errant cleric, there were rituals of degradation in which the cleric's head would be shaved in order to remove any vestige of his tonsure.

BIBLIOGRAPHY

Bartlett, Robert. "Symbolic Meanings of Hair in the Middle Ages." *Transactions of the Royal Historical Society,* 6th ser., 4 (1994): 43–60.

Dykmans, M. "Le rite de la dégradation des clercs d'àpres quelques anciens manuscrits." *Gregorianum* 63 (1982): 301–331.

James, Edward. "Bede and the Tonsure Question." *Peritia* 3 (1984): 85–98.

Sayers, William. "Early Irish Attitudes toward Hair and Beards, Baldness, and Tonsure." *Zeitschrift für celtische Philologie* 44 (1991): 154–189.

KEVIN UHALDE

[See also **DMA:** Celtic Church; Clergy.]

TORQUEMADA, JUAN DE (1388–1468), the eminent fifteenth-century Spanish theologian and defender of the papacy, was born in Valladolid to a family of hidalgos (members of the lesser nobility). His father came from Torquemada in the province of Palencia, and his mother seems to have hailed from a family of New Christians (Jewish converts). In 1403 he joined the Dominican convent of S. Pablo in Valladolid. Torquemada made his first foray into the world of international church politics in 1417 when he accompanied Luis of Valladolid, the Castilian legate, to the Council of Constance. After the council elected Martin V (1417–1431) as the new pope, ending the Great Schism, Torquemada departed for Paris, where he received his master's degree in theology around 1425. After a brief stint as prior of S. Pablo of Valladolid, he assumed a similar position at St. Peter Martyr in Toledo.

The experience gained at Constance and his growing reputation led John II of Castile and León (*r.* 1406–1454) to name Torquemada as his legate to the Council of Basel in 1431. There Torquemada would step into his new role as the leading defender of the papacy against the conciliarists. His most important writing in this area (he penned over forty works) was the *Summa de ecclesia* (1449–1453), in which he defended the absolute power of the papacy. His skill and tenacity earned him the appreciation of Eugenius IV (1431–1447), who

Meditations seu Contemplationes Devotissimae. *Manuscript page from the 1479 edition of Juan de Torquemada's* Meditations seu contemplationes devotissimae, *printed in Mainz by Johann Neumeister.* THE LIBRARY OF CONGRESS.

appointed him the papal curia's chief theologian. It was in this capacity that he led the church's efforts at reconciliation with the Greek Orthodox church at the Council of Ferrara-Florence, culminating in an agreement in 1439. As his successes mounted, so too did his titles and appointments including Defender of the Faith and Cardinal Bishop of Sabina. In 1464, he became the early favorite to succeed the deceased Pius II as pope, but he refused due to his declining health. He died in Rome in 1468.

In his native Castile, Torquemada had also been a powerful force, especially in the increasingly hostile and contentious issue of New Christians and racial purity. The large number of conversions that resulted from the persecutions of 1391 and subsequent forced conversions had created a large population of New Christians, or conversos, in the Spanish kingdoms by the mid-fifteenth century. Politically and economically powerful, the conversos had slowly been drawn into a growing conflict with the old Christian families who resented the usurpation of their power and influence and accused the conversos of backsliding into Jewish practices. Torquemada came to the defense of the conversos in his *Tractatus contra Madianitas et Ismaelitas* (1449), arguing that those Old Christians who sought to hurt them were doing so out of hatred and jealousy and not for any moral or religious reason. Torquemada was convinced that the majority of New Christians were faithful to Christ and that the attacks against them were an attack against all of Christianity. Although other writers joined Torquemada in his defense of the conversos, it would all be for naught. Ten years after his death, the Inquisition was introduced in Spain to deal with the conversos, and in an ironic twist of fate, it would be Torquemada's own nephew, Tomás de Torquemada, who would become the first grand inquisitor and most zealous persecutor of the New Christians.

BIBLIOGRAPHY

PRIMARY SOURCES

Maguire, William Edward, ed. and trans. *The Antiquity of the Church.* Washington, D.C.: Catholic University of America Press, 1957. Contains some chapters of Torquemada's *Summa de ecclesia.*

———. *Tractatus contra Madianitas et Ismaelitas : Defensa de los judíos conversos.* Edited by Nicolás López Martínez and Vicente Proaño Gil. Burgos: Seminario Metropolitano de Burgos, 1957.

SECONDARY SOURCES

Izbicki, Thomas M. *Protector of the Faith: Cardinal Johannes de Turrecremata and the Defense of the Institutional Church.* Washington, D.C.: Catholic University of America Press, 1981.

Netanyahu, B. *The Origins of the Inquisition in Fifteenth-Century Spain.* New York: Random House, 1995. Very useful discussions on Torquemada, especially his activities relating to the conversos.

JARBEL RODRIGUEZ

[See also **DMA:** Conciliar Theory; Converso; Councils, Western (1311–1449); Expulsion of Jews; Ferrara-Florence, Council of; Inquisition; New Christians; Political Theory, Western: After 1100; **Supp:** Eugenius IV, Pope; Race.]

TORQUEMADA, TOMÁS DE (*ca.* 1420–1498). In late 1483 Tomás de Torquemada became grand inquisitor of the Spanish Inquisition, leading the nascent institution in its formative years, as it developed and perfected many of the methods of persecution, repression, and terror for which it would become infamous. Although scholars have gained an appreciable understanding of the

Tomás de Torquemada. *The grand inquisitor is shown in his Dominican habit.* THE GRANGER COLLECTION, NEW YORK. REPRODUCED BY PERMISSION.

Spanish Inquisition as an institution, little is known about the grand inquisitor beyond some basic facts about his life.

He was probably born around 1420 in the village of Torquemada, southwest of Burgos. He entered the church at the Dominican convent of S. Pablo in Valladolid, where his uncle, Juan de Torquemada, was prior. Tomás de Torquemada eventually became its prior and later took a similar position at the convent of Santa Cruz in Segovia (1452). It was while at Santa Cruz that he began his long relationship with the young princess (later queen) of Castile, Isabella, agreeing to become her con-

fessor. In 1482 Pope Sixtus IV made him an inquisitor, along with seven other Dominicans. The following year the Catholic monarchs, Ferdinand and Isabella, raised him to the top position of inquisitor general. In that role he was responsible for naming all the inquisitors in Spain and was the final authority in all judgments rendered by the Inquisition. During the early years at its head, Torquemada set about establishing much of the Inquisition's institutional and bureaucratic framework.

The Inquisition's main task was to discover and prosecute conversos (Jews who had converted to Christianity) suspected of Judaizing. In Torquemada, Ferdinand and Isabella found the combination of zeal, administrative capability, and hatred of Jews that would turn the Inquisition into the machine of terror it became. Not everyone agreed with the Inquisition's tactics, however, and a strong opposition rose against it, especially in the Crown of Aragon. Seeing Jewish hands behind these efforts and blaming them for encouraging conversos to Judaize but unable to attack Jews directly as they were beyond the authority of the Holy Office, Torquemada began to push for the Jews' complete expulsion from the Spanish kingdoms. He achieved limited results early on, as the Catholic monarchs agreed to expel Jews only from certain regions. Searching for popular support, the Inquisition engineered a trial in 1490–1491 over which Torquemada himself presided. Jews and conversos were accused of crucifying a Christian child, tearing its heart out, and using it with the host in an incantation aimed at destroying the power of the Inquisition. Within months of the trial's conclusion, the Catholic monarchs sealed the Edict of Expulsion (1492), forcing all Jews in Spain to leave the country.

Shortly before his death, Torquemada retired to the monastery of St. Thomas of Ávila, which he had founded years earlier. As a parting salvo against the conversos he had battled during his life, he requested and received a papal bull barring anyone with Jewish blood from joining the monastery. He died there on 16 September 1498, almost eighty years old and still inquisitor general.

BIBLIOGRAPHY

Huerga Criado, Pilar. "Fernando II y Torquemada." In *Fernando II de Aragón: El Rey Católico.* Edited by Esteban Sarasa. Saragossa: Institución Fernando el Católico, 1996.

Longhurst, John Edward. *The Age of Torquemada.* Sandoval, N.M.: Coronado Press, 1962.

Netanyahu, B. *The Origins of the Inquisition in Fifteenth-Century Spain.* New York: Random House, 1995.

JARBEL RODRIGUEZ

[See also **DMA:** Converso; Expulsion of Jews; Inquisition; Jews in Christian Spain; New Christians; **Supp:** Race.]

TOURNAI. Located at the confluence of the river Scheldt (French: Escaut) and the Roman road from Cologne to the Atlantic port of Boulogne, Tournai was the site of a Roman army camp by the first century and was already known then for its quarries. As a regional administrative and trading center, Tournai acquired an urban character during the Roman and late antique periods, including a Roman wall surrounding what was for the period a fairly substantial area on the left bank of the Scheldt. Around 431 the Salian Franks conquered the city and made it their capital. Childeric, the father of Clovis, was buried there (his tomb was discovered in 1653), and Clovis had his principal residence in the town before he began his conquest of Gaul around 486. The Merovingian kings retained substantial estates in and around Tournai until at least the late sixth century.

By the end of the fifth century the town had been elevated to a bishopric, but sometime between 626 and 638 it was joined to the noncontiguous see of Noyon, where the bishop of Noyon-Tournai henceforth kept his residence. It was only in 1146 that Tournai became once again an independent bishopric. As an episcopal center favored by the Carolingian dynasty, Tournai survived the worst period of early medieval deurbanization with its urban core intact.

As with much of the rest of Europe, Tournai experienced a surge in population and commercial activity beginning in the late eleventh century. The town's wealth is monumentalized in its spectacular cathedral. Begun around 1030 in a Romanesque style, over the two and a half centuries it took to complete, the architecture evolved into one of the most notable examples of the so-called Schelde Gothic. Both the cathedral chapter and the monastery of St. Martin had well-known schools in the twelfth and thirteenth centuries. Another symbol of the prosperity brought by the presence of the bishop, the cloth industry, and the mining of the famous local limestone was the construction after 1187 of a belfry, symbol of communal liberties and power.

But with economic expansion came increased tensions. Tournai had long sat astride the border between France and the county of Flanders. Under the Carolingians, the bishop was given ducal powers, so the city remained for a time relatively independent of its two great neighbors. In a series of expeditions beginning in 892, however, the Flemish count Baldwin II took over the territory surrounding the city, although he was not able to take the city itself. In 1187 the French king Philip II Augustus assumed direct control of the town, and it remained in French hands throughout the Middle Ages, even though all the countryside under its sway was held by the count of Flanders. Within the town, various forces competed for power. The bishop and the castellan ruled the city, but the canons of the Cathedral of Our Lady also played an important role in its governance since the bishop was often away in Noyon. As the town became an increasingly important industrial and trading center, the burghers grown wealthy in the manufacture and trading of wool and finished cloth sought to take power from the traditional rulers. They formed a merchant guild, which later became part of the city administration and in 1147 led the formation of a sworn commune.

The late thirteenth and fourteenth centuries in Tournai were marked by struggles between the merchants, who monopolized the civil government and the administration of justice, and the tradesmen and day laborers, who were also largely involved in the production of cloth. Tournai also suffered from the frequent wars between Flanders and its English allies and France. By the end of the fifteenth century, Tournai was in political and economic decline due to the effects of the Hundred Years War and the revolts of the workers against the merchant oligarchy. Paradoxically, this period also saw a flourishing of the arts. The painters Robert Campin and Rogier van der Weyden worked in Tournai, and the town was a center of tapestry, sculpture, and brass production.

BIBLIOGRAPHY

PRIMARY SOURCES

Herman of Tournai. *The Restoration of the Monastery of Saint Martin of Tournai.* Translated by Lynn H. Nelson. Washington, D.C.: Catholic University of America Press, 1996.

SECONDARY SOURCES

Châtelet, Albert, et al. *Les grands siècles de Tournai (12e–15e siècles): Recueil d'études publié à l'occasion du 20e anniversaire des Guides de Tournai.* Tournai, Belgium: Cathédral de Notre Dame, 1993.

Pycke, Jacques. "'Urbs fuerat quondam quod adhuc vestigial monstrant.' Réflexions sur l'histoire de Tournai pendant le haut moyen âge (Ve–Xe siècle)." In *La Génèse et les premiers siècles des villes médiévales dans les Pays-Bas méridionaux: Un problème archéologique et historique.* Brussels: Crédit Communal, 1990.

Rolland, Paul. *Histoire de Tournai.* Tournai, Belgium: Casterman, 1956. An accessible one-volume history of the city.

Schabacker, Peter H. *Observations on the Tournai Painters' Guild, with Special Reference to Rogier van der Weyden and Jacques Daret.* Brussels: Palais des Académies, 1982.

Verhulst, Adriaan E. *The Rise of Cities in North-West Europe*. Cambridge, U.K.: Cambridge University Press, 1999. Covers the development of the towns of Belgium until the twelfth century and provides an extensive and updated bibliography.

Verriest, Léo. *Les luttes sociales et le contrat d'apprestissage à Tournai jusqu'en 1424*. Brussels: Hayez, 1912.

EMILY KADENS

[See also **DMA:** Campin, Robert; Flanders and the Low Countries; Merovingians; Weyden, Rogier van der.]

TRANSUBSTANTIATION. Christians have held from earliest times that Jesus, after his resurrection from the dead, is present as the risen Lord in the community. Christians claim that this presence makes itself felt powerfully in the ritual meal of blessed bread and wine known as the Eucharist, or Lord's Supper. In the eleventh century Christian writers began to discuss in earnest how this presence in the Eucharist might be possible. Transubstantiation is one way of describing how it might occur. Most basically, transubstantiation posits that the *substantia* (substance) of the bread and wine are replaced by the *substantia* of the body and blood of the risen Lord during the blessing of the bread and wine in the ritual of the Eucharist. *Substantia,* although not understood uniformly by medieval theologians, generally referred to the Aristotelian category of *ousia,* or the essential reality that underlies individual things. Transubstantiation and a belief in the real presence, although sometimes confused, are quite distinct. Belief in the real presence asserts that the risen Lord is present in the Eucharist; transubstantiation attempts to explain how that is possible. Belief in the real presence was considered a requirement for orthodox Christian belief in the Middle Ages. It is not clear that belief in transubstantiation was ever so required, except when denial of transubstantiation was understood to entail denial of the real presence.

Belief in the real presence received only sporadic attention from Christian theologians until the ninth century, when the monks Paschasius Radbertus and Ratramnus of Corbie wrote conflicting treatises explaining the real presence. Ratramnus argued that the physical presence of Christ could exist only in heaven. The theology of Paschasius, which became the dominant theology by the eleventh century, insisted, on the other hand, that the body of Christ, born of the Virgin and now present in heaven, was also present in the blessed bread and wine. This understanding was challenged by Berengar, the *scholasticus* of Tours, in the mid-eleventh century. In the later stages of this controversy, the term *substantia* was introduced to describe more precisely how the risen

Lord could be present in the ritual of the Eucharist and more particularly in the blessed bread and wine. In this understanding, the *substantia* of the bread and the wine were changed into the *substantia* of the body and the blood of the risen Lord. This teaching was included in the oath taken by Berengar at the Council of Rome in 1079.

In the twelfth century, discussions about the real presence intensified, due at least in part to the challenge of the Cathars, who denied that Jesus ever had a body and that any material thing (such as bread and wine) could have a spiritual effect. The English theologian Robert Pullen is credited with coining the term *transubstantiatio* (transubstantiation) around 1140 to refer to the change in substance that took place during the Eucharist. The term gained in popularity during the twelfth century and received a form of official sanction when the Fourth Lateran Council used the term in the creed that formed its first canon. The vast majority of thirteenth-century theologians did not consider the council statement a definition, however, and only in the fourteenth century did some theologians judge the council to have defined transubstantiation as a matter of belief.

Transubstantiation was a term that covered three distinct theories concerning the change. Some theologians believed that bread and wine remained present along with the body and blood of the Lord; others felt that the substance of the bread and wine were annihilated, the substance of the body and blood alone remaining. Finally, a third group argued that the substance of bread and wine was transmuted into the substance of the body and blood at the words of consecration.

During the thirteenth century, a more refined understanding of Aristotle's metaphysics engendered more sophisticated theories of transubstantiation. The theory that the substance of the bread and wine coexists in the sacrament with the substance of the body and blood of the risen Lord came to be seen as unacceptable. The theory of annihilation was advocated particularly by the canonists and Franciscan theologians, while the Dominican theologians Albertus Magnus and Thomas Aquinas argued strenuously that the substances of bread and wine were transformed into the substance of the body and blood.

None of these theologians would have understood the change that took place as "physical" in the sense of modern physics. Indeed, transubstantiation as espoused in the later Middle Ages specifically states that a substantial change does not entail any change in the *accidentia* (accidents, or sense data) of the bread and wine. Since *substantia* was only detected by the mind, not the senses,

---

VIEWS ON TRANSUBSTANTIATION

OATH TAKEN BY BERENGAR AT THE COUNCIL OF ROME IN 1079

[T]he bread and wine which are placed on the altar ... are changed substantially into the true and proper vivifying body and blood of Jesus Christ our Lord and after the consecration there are the true body of Christ which was born of the Virgin ... and the true blood of Christ which flowed from his side, not however through sign and in the power of the sacrament, but in their real nature and true substance.

FOURTH LATERAN COUNCIL, 1215

We ... believe the body of Christ and the blood to be truly contained in the sacrament of the altar, under the species of bread and wine, the bread having been transubstantiated into the body and the wine into the blood ...

COUNCIL OF TRENT, SESSION 13, CANON 2

If any one says that in the sacred and holy sacrament of the Eucharist, the substance of the bread and wine remains conjointly with the body and blood of our Lord Jesus Christ, and denies that wonderful and singular conversion of the whole substance of the bread into the Body, and of the whole substance of the wine into the Blood—the species only of the bread and wine remaining—which conversion indeed the Catholic Church most aptly calls Transubstantiation; let him be anathema.

---

theologians could refer to transubstantiation as an intellectual or spiritual change. Indeed, the whole point of the theory of transubstantiation seems to have been to describe a change that was real but not sensed, in order to assert a real but not crassly material presence of the risen Lord in the Eucharist.

Transubstantiation in either of its two acceptable forms involved numerous metaphysical problems, however. In the beginning of the fourteenth century, the Franciscan theologian John Duns Scotus offered extensive argumentation to show that transubstantiation was contradictory to a proper understanding of Aristotelian metaphysics, although Scotus found the annihilation theory the least offensive approach. Scotus proposed that since the Fourth Lateran Council had approved transubstantiation, it had to be accepted as the teaching of the church. Later in the century, the Franciscan theologian William of Ockham continued Scotus's assault on the intelligibility of transubstantiation while asserting its validity.

In the late fourteenth century, the Oxford theologian John Wyclif rejected transubstantiation as a recent aberration of Christian tradition. His teaching was adopted and adapted by the heretical group dubbed the Lollards, who were held to deny not only transubstantiation but also the real presence. Transubstantiation was later rejected by the Reformation leaders Martin Luther, Huldrych Zwingli, and John Calvin. The Council of Trent condemned the teaching that the substance of the bread and wine remains in the Eucharist after the consecration and cautiously approved transubstantiation, dubbing it *aptissime,* a "most apt" way of explaining the real presence.

BIBLIOGRAPHY

Burr, David. "Scotus and Transubstantiation." *Mediaeval Studies* 34 (1972): 336–360.

————. *Eucharistic Presence and Conversion in Late Thirteenth-Century Franciscan Thought.* Philadelphia: American Philosophical Society, 1984.

Goering, Joseph. "The Invention of Transubstantiation." *Traditio* 46 (1991): 147–170.

Jorissen, Hans. *Die Entfaltung der Transsubstantiationslehre bis zum Beginn der Hochscholastik.* Münster, Germany: Aschendorffsche, 1965.

Levy, Ian. *John Wyclif: Scriptural Logic, Real Presence, and the Parameters of Orthodoxy.* Milwaukee, Wis.: Marquette University Press, 2003.

Macy, Gary. *Theologies of the Eucharist in the Early Scholastic Period.* Oxford: Clarendon Press, 1984.

————. "The Dogma of Transubstantiation in the Middle Ages." *Journal of Ecclesiastical History* 45 (1994): 11–41.

McCue, James F. "The Doctrine of Transubstantiation from Berengar through Trent." *Harvard Theological Review* 61 (1968): 385–430.

GARY MACY

[See also **DMA:** Berengar of Tours; Duns Scotus, John; Lollards; Mass, Liturgy of the; Paschasius Radbertus of Corbie, St.; Ratramnus of Corbie; Wyclif, John.]

TRINITARIANS (Order of the Most Holy Trinity for the Redemption of Captives). On 17 December 1198

Pope Innocent III granted a bull to the Frenchman John of Matha (*ca.* 1154–1213) officially approving the foundation of a new religious order whose primary mission was to be the ransoming of Christians held in Islamic regions. Innocent also approved a rule for the order drafted by John of Matha. The rule later underwent multiple revisions, in 1217, 1267, 1619, 1628, and 1631, the last three when the order was known as the Discalced (barefooted) Trinitarians.

The origins of the Trinitarians date back to at least the early 1190s. By 1198, the order had at least three houses, including the motherhouse of Cerfroid, northeast of Paris. Expansion came rapidly thereafter as new houses were founded in Aragon (1201), southern France (Marseilles and Arles, both in 1203), Castile (Toledo in 1206 and Burgos in 1207), and Rome (1209), where Innocent III himself donated the property. It would be in Spain, and especially in Castile, that the order would enjoy its greatest successes and provide the biggest benefits as its services became critical during the Reconquest.

Captives had become a significant problem for Spanish authorities as Muslim forces captured growing numbers of Christians during the twelfth century. Efforts to free these people included municipal and royal ransomers, merchants and, starting around 1180, the more systematic ransoming efforts of the Order of Santiago and the short-lived Order of Mountjoy. Although Santiago and Mountjoy played an important role, they were primarily military orders, not specifically dedicated to charitable ransoming. It was this role that the Trinitarians and later the Mercedarians filled.

Central to the Trinitarian mission was the tripartite division of their resources. According to the rule, Trinitarians would divide their assets into three equal parts. Two parts would go toward the upkeep of the brothers and the order's houses and properties, as well as to other charitable works. The last third was strictly set aside for the ransoming of captives. Although this division caused numerous confusions and was not always strictly adhered to, it did ensure that captives remained at the center of the order's efforts and that there was usually money for their ransom.

This money came from traditional sources: rents from properties, donations made in wills, gifts, and the collection of alms. The order helped its collection efforts by parading recently released captives—accompanied by flying pennons and blaring trumpets—through Iberian cities as a testimonial to their success. These fund-raising efforts caused significant friction not only with the Mercedarians—their main competitors—but also with other

agents of the church, as the different charitable groups fought over finite resources.

The order's success in the Middle Ages is tangible but difficult to gauge. We know that there were numerous successful ransoming missions, but it is harder to determine the number of captives involved in these efforts. The Trinitarians in Castile seem to have been the most active, but significant contributions were also made by the houses of France and Aragon, which often sent ransoming expeditions independently. The Trinitarians continued their ransoming work during the wars against the Turks and the North African principalities of the sixteenth through the eighteenth centuries, and even in the twenty-first century they remain vitally active in ransoming captives and slaves.

BIBLIOGRAPHY

Brodman, James W. "Military Redemptionism and the Castilian Reconquest, 1180–1250." *Military Affairs* 44, no. 1 (February 1980): 24–27. Good introduction to early ransoming activities.

———. *Ransoming Captives in Crusader Spain: The Order of Merced on the Christian Islamic Frontier.* Philadelphia: University of Pennsylvania Press, 1986. Best English-language introduction to the problem of captivity on the Iberian Peninsula, although its primary focus is the Mercedarians.

Cipollone, Giulio. "L'Ordre de la Sainte Trinité et de la rédemption des captifs, 1198: Les Trinitaires dans le Midi." *Cahiers de Fanjeaux* 18 (1983): 135–156.

———. *Cristianità-Islam: Cattività e liberazione in nome di Dio: Il tempo di Innocenzo III dopo "il 1187."* Rome: Editrice Pontificia Università Gregoriana, 1992.

Porres Alonso, Bonifacio. *Libertad a los cautivos: Actividad redentora de la Orden Trinitaria.* 2 vols. Córdoba: Secretariado Trinitario, 1997. Impressive history of the order including, over 350 documents from its history.

JARBEL RODRIGUEZ

[See also **DMA:** Innocent III, Pope; Reconquest; Spain, Christian-Muslim Relations; **Supp:** Mercedarians.]

TYRANTS AND TYRANNICIDE. The Greek and Roman defense of tyrannicide was generally rejected by the church fathers, who stressed the absolute Christian duty of obedience to secular rulers. St. Augustine, for example, who viewed government as a product of human sin, emphasized the rightful absolutism of secular rulers. Given that secular rulers were believed to derive their authority from God, Augustine argued that whatever such rulers decreed was lawful and must be observed. Even if a ruler were a tyrant, his Christian subjects were bound to obey his commands, so long as those commands were not contrary to God's will. Underlying Augustine's argument was his belief that God sometimes used tyrants and bad rulers as a means of punishing humans for their sins, as amply illustrated in the Hebrew Bible. Some church fathers, such as John Chrysostom, drew a distinction between the divinely ordained office of a king and the particular ruler who occupied and sometimes corrupted the office, thus raising questions about the legitimacy of a wicked king's rule. But in general, most church fathers maintained that Christians owed absolute obedience to their secular rulers and that resistance was only justified when it was the only alternative to breaking divine law.

EVOLVING THEORIES OF KINGSHIP

During the Middle Ages, theories about what constitutes a tyrant and about the types of legitimate resistance against a tyrant evolved alongside changing notions about kings and their relation to their subjects. In his *Etymologiae* (*ca.* 620–636), Isidore of Seville suggested an etymological connection between the words "rex" and "recte." According to Isidore, a king's title (*rex*) depended upon his ruling rightfully (*recte*). If a king sinned or failed to rule as a king should, he ceased to be a king and became a tyrant. This ethical understanding of rulership differed from Augustine's emphasis on a king's absolute, divinely ordained authority. "In common usage," Isidore wrote, "those who come to be called tyrants are the very worst and most vile kings, dominated by a passion for luxuries and exercising domination of the cruelest sort over their peoples." But Isidore never suggested that a tyrant be resisted. In his view, rather, as in Augustine's, a tyrant was the result of a people's wickedness, and the people had no choice but to endure the tyrannical rule they deserved.

Although there had long been expectations about a king's duties and conduct and a recognition of the need for at least some consensus on the part of a king's subjects, questions were increasingly raised during the ninth century about the relationship between a king or emperor and his subjects. Archbishop Hincmar of Rheims wrote a treatise in which he distinguished between the way kings and tyrants assumed power and ruled, but in the tradition of St. Paul and St. Augustine, he insisted that all power came from God and therefore had to be obeyed. While Hincmar and other Carolingian writers further developed the notion of the divinely ordained authority of kings and emperors, they also conceded that from a pragmatic perspective a king or emperor's political existence depended upon the support of the local aristocracy, which might include its own tyrants. According

to Hincmar, a king's best hope for maintaining his rule was to uphold the laws and statutes and seek the counsel of lay and clerical leading men. Whereas a tyrant was thought to rule his subjects the way a lord rules his slaves, a king was thought to serve his subjects by working for the common welfare.

At the end of the eleventh century, during the investiture controversy over whether bishops and abbots would be appointed by kings or the pope, Manegold of Lautenbach, an Augustinian canon and supporter of Pope Gregory VII, argued that if a king turned tyrannical and failed to perform his responsibilities, his subjects had the right to dismiss him in the same way that a negligent pig herder was dismissed for failing to look after his swine. Before the king could be deposed by the people, however, Manegold believed the pope needed to release the people from their oath of fidelity to the king. Although Manegold's notion of the king's accountability to his people was radical for its time, it reflected a growing sense in the eleventh century that the king's authority was at least provisionally subject to the consent of his subjects. The investiture controversy raised the question of whether the pope might play a role in dealing with a wayward secular ruler.

DISCUSSIONS OF TYRANNICIDE

The twelfth-century Scholastic John of Salisbury was the first medieval theorist to suggest that tyrannicide might be a legitimate political response to severe misrule. John first revealed his understanding of what constituted a tyrant in a satirical poem, *Entheticus, de dogmate philosophorum* (Indicator of wise men's doctrine), in which he described the fictitious King Hircanus, whom he labeled a tyrant. King Hircanus did not rule according to justice or reason but rather according to his own passions and raw will. By enslaving his subjects, leading a life of sin, and offending both God and his people, Hircanus was a king only in title. Thus, for John of Salisbury, kingship necessarily involved respecting the laws and just rights of people. A tyrant was a powerful and evil man who showed no scruples about governing by force and ignoring the law.

In his most famous work, *Policraticus* (1159), John broadened the concept of tyranny, saying that tyrants were not necessarily kings or even secular rulers but could just as easily be private individuals, such as magnates or even priests. In John's eyes, any excessive use of power that infringed upon the rights and liberties of others constituted tyranny. Echoing Augustine, John argued that tyrants most often emerged from communities corrupted by sin. A tyrant, John believed, was both a divinely ordained punishment and the product of a corrupted body politic.

It appears difficult to reconcile John's belief that a tyrant often represented a divine means of communal punishment on the one hand with his defense of tyrannicide on the other. It is important to note, however, that *Policraticus* was a theoretical work (in which the subject of tyrants and tyrannicide took up a relatively small space) and that John only defended tyrannicide as necessary in certain limited situations. For instance, the killing of a tyrant might be permissible in a just community that did not deserve a tyrant in the first place or in a sinful community that had changed and repented for its previously evil ways. Even in these cases, John maintained that tyrannicide should serve as a last resort. Prayer was the best way to deal with a tyrant, he argued, since God would eventually dispose of any tyrant either by his own means (such as through a natural disaster) or through human instruments. John advocated tolerating a tyrant whenever that was at all possible. Even in cases where tyrannicide appeared necessary, John stipulated that it was impermissible to use poison, that anyone bound by fealty to the tyrant could not carry out the murder, and that no one should kill the tyrant if he would lose honor or religion as a result. *Policraticus* appeared so cautionary in its defense of tyrannicide that Coluccio Salutati, the fourteenth-century chancellor of Florence, did not even believe that John had argued tyrannicide was just, only that there were historical examples of its being practiced. Some contemporary scholars have also questioned whether John advanced a particular argument on behalf of tyrannicide or whether he simply maintained (as Aristotle had) that tyrants were bound to fall.

Thomas Aquinas, generally considered a moderate monarchist, nonetheless conceded that public resistance was sometimes legitimate in the face of a tyrant who made demands outside his legitimate authority or contrary to fundamental law. Agreeing with Aristotle, Aquinas called tyranny the worst form of government and noted the injustice of a tyrant putting his private interests above the common good. It was no mortal sin to overthrow a tyrant, Aquinas argued in his *Summa theologiae,* so long as the consequences of overthrowing the tyrant were better for the community than permitting the tyrannical rule to continue. By using the examples of lesser rulers as opposed to kings, Aquinas dodged the question of whether it was ever legitimate to overthrow or murder a tyrannical king. He made it clear, however, that he believed there was justification in overthrowing a ruler whose power was acquired illicitly. A ruler also lost all claims to the obedience of his subjects,

according to Aquinas, when he made demands that were contrary to virtue or beyond his rights as ruler. But a ruler did not lose his claims to authority through mere personal unworthiness.

The author of the first two books of *De regimine principum* (On the government of rulers), whose former attribution to Aquinas is now doubted by some scholars, argued that tyranny was bound to fall because "what is opposed to the wishes of many cannot last long." Under the presupposition that any tyrant's rule would be short-lived, the author of the early books of *De regimine* argued that tyrannical rule should be endured for as long as possible. If the community appointed the king, it had the right to depose him, since the king, by becoming tyrannical, had already broken the *pactum* with his subjects. If the king had been appointed by a superior, the people should seek help from him. If no human recourse were available, the people should turn to God and repent for their sins, which, according to the author, had probably given rise to the tyrant in the first place.

Often tyranny was invoked to warn kings of their duties, especially since many believed that tyrannical regimes were inherently unstable and bound to fall. Unpopular kings, such as King John of England, were denounced by contemporaries as tyrants. In a highly polemical work, Gerald of Wales described France as the home of liberty in contrast to England, the seat of tyrants. In the fourteenth and fifteenth centuries, French writers criticized the tyrannical regimes of Italy, stressing that the signori such as Gian Galeazzo Visconti, the duke of Milan, relied on force rather than consent, placed their private interests over the common good, and instilled fear in their subjects, whereas the French kings earned their subjects' love.

Fourteenth-century jurists, such as Bartolo da Sassoferrato and Baldus de Ubaldis, distinguished between different forms of tyranny, arguing that it was as possible for a pope to be tyrannical as it was for an emperor or king. As Bartolo conceded in his *De tyranno,* tyrannical elements were often present in nontyrannical forms of government. He maintained that it was unrealistic to expect that rulers would always place their subjects' interests above their own. At the same time, true tyrants were those whose rule was invalid and who showed a total disregard for the public's well-being. Both jurists drew on Aquinas in arguing that the harmful costs to society that might result from attempting to overthrow a tyrant might not be worth the benefits of ending his rule. In general, fourteenth-century academics sounded a note of caution when discussing the theoretical overthrow of tyrannical governments by private individuals. But the fourteenth century was also marked by a new theory of politics, in which the people were increasingly viewed as the source of a government's authority. In *Defensor pacis* (Defender of peace; 1324), Marsilius of Padua addressed a corporate community's need for the authority to correct and punish a bad ruler. Instead of theorizing about what a private individual could do to resist a tyrant's rule, academics increasingly discussed institutional and constitutional mechanisms for making rulers responsible to their communities.

There is debate among scholars about the relationship between the constitutional acts of the deposition of kings in the Middle Ages and the developing theories on resistance to tyranny. It may be significant that both Kings Edward II and Richard II were forced to abdicate the English throne (in 1327 and 1399 respectively) because of their "insufficiency" to govern. In other words, it was royal inadequacy and not tyranny that led to their downfall. Neither king's murder was understood at the time as tyrannicide. In France, however, questions about the legitimacy of tyrannicide did not disappear. In 1408 a significant defense of tyrannicide (although it did not involve a tyrannical king) was put forth by the Franciscan Jean Petit, who defended the duke of Burgundy's assassination of Louis of Orléans, the brother of the French king Charles VI. Petit not only lost his case, but after his death, John Gerson, chancellor of the University of Paris, denounced the errors in Petit's doctrine and sought to have the Council of Constance condemn them. Although the council did not address Petit's case in particular, it did condemn as heretical a statement that justified tyrannicide.

BIBLIOGRAPHY

Burns, J. H., ed. *The Cambridge History of Medieval Political Thought, c. 350–c. 1450.* Cambridge, U.K.: Cambridge University Press, 1988.

Guenée, Bernard. *Un meurtre, une société: L'assassinat du duc d'Orléans, 23 novembre 1407.* Paris: Gallimard, 1992.

John of Salisbury. *Policraticus.* Edited and translated by Cary J. Nederman. Cambridge, U.K.: Cambridge University Press, 1990.

———. *Policraticus.* Edited by K. S. B. Keats-Rohan. Turnholt, Belgium: Brepols, 1993.

Nederman, Cary J. "A Duty to Kill: John of Salisbury's Theory of Tyrannicide." *The Review of Politics* 50 (1988): 365–389.

———. "The Changing Face of Tyranny: The Reign of King Stephen in John of Salisbury's Political Thought." *Nottingham Medieval Studies* 33 (1989): 1–20.

Nederman, Cary J., and Catherine Campbell. "Priests, Kings, and Tyrants: Spiritual and Temporal Power in John of Salisbury's *Policraticus.*" *Speculum* 66 (1991): 572–590.

Parsons, Wilfrid. "The Mediaeval Theory of the Tyrant." *The Review of Politics* 4 (1942): 128–143.

Rouse, Richard, and Mary Rouse. "John of Salisbury and the Doctrine of Tyrannicide." *Speculum* 42 (1967): 693–709.

Turchetti, Mario. *Tyrannie et tyrannicide de l'Antiquité à nos jours.* Paris: Presses Universitaires de France, 2001.

Van Laarhoven, Jan. "Thou Shalt Not Slay a Tyrant! The So-Called Theory of John of Salisbury." In *The World of John of Salisbury.* Edited by Michael Wilks. Oxford: Basil Blackwell, 1984.

ADAM JEFFREY DAVIS

[See also **DMA:** Aquinas, St. Thomas; Augustine of Hippo, St.; Hincmar of Rheims; Isidore of Seville, St.; John of Salisbury; Kingship, Theories of; Manegold of Lautenbach.]

ULFILA (Wulfila, *ca.* 311–383), bishop of the Goths, is known for his translation of the Bible into Gothic and his role in spreading Arian Christianity to the Goths. Despite his importance in the events of the fourth century, little else is known about him. The surviving accounts of Ulfila's life are from fragmentary Arian sources—the fifth-century church history of Philostorgios, which exists only in an epitome by the ninth-century patriarch of Constantinople Photios, and a letter by Ulfila's student Auxentius, an Arian bishop of Milan. Although Ulfila's name is Gothic, meaning "little wolf," his family was originally from Cappadocia and had been captured by the Goths, probably in the third century; they had settled north of the Danube River. According to Philostorgios, numerous Christian captives lived amid the Goths in this period and played a role in the spread of Christianity among them.

Gothic leaders chose Ulfila to serve as an ambassador to the emperor Constantius II. At this point, in either 336 or 341, the Arian bishop of Constantinople, Eusebius of Nicomedia, ordained Ulfila as bishop of the Goths. He was not the first to hold this title, however, since a Bishop Theodore of the Goths had attended the Council of Nicaea in 325. Not all Goths, however, were eager to accept Christianity. Gothic leaders conducted two persecutions of Christians in the fourth century. When Ulfila and his followers were driven out of Gothic lands by persecutions in the late 340s, Constantius II allowed them to settle in the Roman province Moesia, south of the Danube (present-day Bulgaria). According to both Philostorgios and Auxentius, Constantius supported Ulfila's missionary work, dubbing Ulfila "the Moses of our times." After settling in Roman territory, Ulfila served as bishop to the Goths for more than thirty years. It is most likely during this period that Ulfila translated the Bible into Gothic. According to fifth-century accounts, Ulfila invented the Gothic alphabet, which is based primarily on Greek letters, for this project. The sources note that he translated the entire Bible, leaving out only the Book of Kings because of its glorification of military prowess. It is quite possible, though, that the translation was a group effort. Substantial portions of the Gothic New Testament survive, but only fragments of Ezra and Nehemiah remain from the Hebrew Scriptures.

At the Council of Constantinople in 360, with the approval of the emperor Constantius II, Ulfila signed the creed of the Homoeans, which viewed God the Father and Christ as "alike" *(homoios)* but not of the same substance *(homoousios)*. Ulfila's creed rejected the Nicene concept of "substance" *(ousios)* altogether, emphasizing instead the different functions of the persons of the Trinity. Although a range of Trinitarian doctrines vied for prominence in this period, all of the non-Nicene creeds were later lumped together as "Arian." Indeed orthodox authorities branded Ulfila and his followers as such, which ultimately led to the destruction of most of the texts about him and his circle. Later in life, the bishop of the Goths became more involved with doctrinal controversies. In 383, he died in Constantinople, where he had promoted the cause of the non-Nicene Christians to the orthodox emperor Theodosius I.

BIBLIOGRAPHY

Friedrichsen, G. W. S. *The Gothic Version of the Gospels: A Study of Its Style and Textual History.* London: Oxford University Press/ H. Milford, 1926.

Heather, Peter, and John Matthews. *The Goths in the Fourth Century.* Liverpool, U.K.: Liverpool University Press, 1991. Introductions to and translations of relevant texts.

Sivan, Hagith. "Ulfila's Own Conversion: The Formation of Nicene and Arianized Historiographical Traditions in Late Antiquity." *Harvard Theological Review* 89 (4): 373–386.

Thompson, E. A. *The Visigoths in the Time of Ulfila.* Oxford: Clarendon Press, 1966.

JACLYN MAXWELL

[See also **DMA:** Arianism; Philostorgios.]

UPPSALA. Old Uppsala *(Ubsola)* was renowned in the early Middle Ages as the most important center for pagan cultic practice in Scandinavia. Located in the Uppland region of Sweden near the modern city of Uppsala, the shrine boasted an impressive temple dedicated to three gods of the Norse pantheon. The eleventh-century chronicler Adam of Bremen provided a detailed description of the place and the rituals performed there in the fourth book of his *Gesta Hammaburgensis ecclesiae pontificum* (History of the archbishops of Hamburg-Bremen, *ca.* 1073–1076), in which he gave an account of the geography and inhabitants of Scandinavia.

According to Adam's *Gesta,* the temple at Old Uppsala was an impressive structure adorned with gold and encircled by a gold chain. The main chamber housed three statues of pagan deities: Thor, the god of thunder; Odin, the god of war; and Freyr, the god of earthly pleasure. Attendant priests made sacrifices to these gods to gain their favorable attention at specific times. Thor protected his worshipers from famine and plague, Odin lent his strength during wars, and Freyr smiled upon marriage celebrations. In addition, every nine years the king of Scandinavia and his subjects gathered for a general religious festival at the temple. Attendance at the event was considered mandatory for the peoples of Sweden. Adam of Bremen expressed considerable dismay at the participation of recent converts to Christianity in the festivities, which involved blood sacrifice. During the nine-day festival, worshipers presented the gods with the heads of male animals of every kind, including human beings, and then hung the decapitated bodies to rot in a sacred grove alongside the temple. The efforts of Christian missionaries to destroy the shrine met with significant opposition and were not successful until the twelfth century. In 1164, Old Uppsala became the seat of the first archbishopric in Sweden, and a stone cathedral replaced the old wooden church there. A century later, fire destroyed the cathedral, forcing the archbishop to move to the nearby city of Uppsala.

Historians have recently cast doubt on the credibility of Adam of Breman's account of the pagan cult at Old Uppsala and have even questioned the existence of the shrine itself. No other eleventh-century source mentions it. Archaeological finds suggest that the site had been inhabited since the third century A.D. but provide no evidence of a temple structure. A royal hall excavated nearby may have provided the focus for the pagan practices that figure so prominently in the episode, but the very presence of such an influential cultic center seems incongruous with the many hundreds of Christian runic inscriptions erected by Scandinavian landowners in the Uppland region in the eleventh century. It has been suggested that Adam of Bremen employed the episode as a literary device to emphasize the challenges facing the Christian mission based in Hamburg-Bremen or, less plausibly, to make an allegorical statement about his imperial allegiances in the investiture conflict. Answers to these questions await the discovery of corroborating evidence for the activities and influence of the pagan cult at Old Uppsala.

BIBLIOGRAPHY

Adam of Bremen. *Hamburgische Kirchengeschichte*. Edited by Bernhard Schmeidler. Scriptores rerum Germanicarum in usum scholarum ex Monumentis Germaniae historicis. Hannover and Leipzig, Germany: Hohnsche, 1917. Edition with German translation of *Gesta Hammaburgensis ecclesiae pontificum*.

————. *History of the Archbishops of Hamburg-Bremen*. Translated by Francis J. Tschan. New York: Columbia University Press, 1959. English translation of *Gesta Hammaburgensis ecclesiae pontificum*.

Armstrong, Guyda, and Ian N. Wood, eds. *Christianizing Peoples and Converting Individuals*. Turnhout, Belgium: Brepols, 2000. The chapters by Anne-Sofie Gräslund and Henrik Janson are relevant to Uppsala.

SCOTT G. BRUCE

[See also **DMA:** Adam of Bremen; Missions and Missionaries, Christian; Scandinavian Mythology; Scandinavian Temples; Sweden; **Supp:** Paganism and Pagan Gods, Survival of.]

URBAN IV, POPE (d. 1264). Jacques Pantaléon, the son of a cobbler, was born in Troyes toward the end of the twelfth century. He became a canon of Laon and attended the First Council of Lyons. His abilities impressed Innocent IV, who sent him to Silesia in 1247 to restore ecclesiastical discipline and negotiate a compromise between the Teutonic Knights and their vassals. In 1249 he became archdeacon of Liège and in 1251 went to Germany to recruit soldiers for William of Holland, the papally approved candidate for emperor. In 1253 he became bishop of Verdun, and Alexander IV appointed him patriarch of Jerusalem in 1255. He took up residence in Acre in June 1256 and supported the Venetian colony of the city in the war of St. Sabas against the Genoese. The arrival of a papal legate prompted Pantaléon's departure for Rome; he little appreciated the competing claims to ecclesiastical authority in Acre. Once pope, he arranged for his successor as patriarch to enjoy the temporalities of the bishopric of Acre and to be papal legate, simplifying the hierarchy of Latin Palestine.

He was thus in Italy when Alexander IV died, and after three months' deliberation by the eight cardinals of the Sacred College, he was elected pope on 29 August 1261. Through concerted negotiations with Charles of Anjou and his brother, King Louis IX of France, Urban found a means to counter the threat posed by the ambitious king of Sicily, Manfred. Charles would conquer Sicily from Manfred and rule it as a papal fief. Urban initially forbade Charles from becoming senator of Rome or holding any equivalent mayoral position in an Italian city but later only restricted him from holding such a position for life. Urban then preached a crusade against Manfred in 1264, with much of the crusade taxes going to Charles. Urban's decision to replace Manfred with Charles was momentous; it led to the establishment of an Angevin dynasty in southern Italy, with a profound impact on politics both in Italy and throughout the Mediterranean world.

Urban also transformed the character of the Sacred College by creating fourteen new cardinals, seven of whom were French. Three of these would go on to become pope themselves (Clement IV, Martin IV, and Honorius IV), and this group effectively formed the nucleus of a French faction among the cardinals—a faction that would have increasing influence in the late thirteenth and early fourteenth centuries. Urban also instituted the churchwide feast of Corpus Christi to encourage Eucharistic piety, a local tradition he may have become familiar with while in Liège. Urban spent most of his papacy in Orvieto, avoiding the political turbulence of Rome, though the city accepted his authority. He sponsored the construction of the great gothic church of St.-Urbain in his native Troyes and died 2 October 1264 in Perugia.

BIBLIOGRAPHY

Gobry, Ivan. *Deux papes champenois: Urban II, Urban IV*. Troyes, France: Librairie bleue, 1994.

Guiraud, Jean, ed. *Les registres d'Urbain IV (1261–1264)*. 4 vols. Paris: A. Fontemoing, 1901.

Hampe, Karl. *Urban IV und Manfred (1261–1264)*. Heidelberg: C. Winter's Universitätbuchhandlung, 1905.

CHRISTOPHER HATCH MACEVITT

[See also **DMA:** Angevins: France, England, Sicily; Corpus Christi, Feast of; **Supp:** Manfred of Sicily, King.]

UTRAQUISM is both a set of beliefs about proper ritual practice and a broader sectarian ideology that, in the later Middle Ages, was regarded as a heretical deviation from Roman Catholicism. Coming from the Latin *utraque* ("both"), the word denotes the taking by the laity of communion in both kinds—bread and wine. The general practice up to and even deep into the twelfth century seems to have been to allow the laity to do so, and there had never been an absolute prohibition to the contrary. But in the twelfth century and generally thereafter in the Middle Ages, the practice arose of restricting the chalice to the clergy, with some exceptions, such as anointed kings.

This evolution has been variously explained. One of the most persuasive suggestions is that because of the investiture conflict, the clergy came to be represented as a far more distinct—and special—order of society, and taking communion underscored that difference. It has also been suggested that laypeople's (especially laywomen's) habit of taking communion more and more often, not simply once a year at Easter (the minimum mandated by the Fourth Lateran Council), reinforced the clergy's unwillingness to offer the cup. What might strike modern secularists as a minor concern, the fear of spilling the precious sacrament of Christ, may actually have played an important role here. In any case, the orthodox view was that transubstantiation effected the change of both the bread and wine into the real body and blood of Christ. To receive the wafer was to receive body and blood, just as to receive the liquid in the chalice was to obtain body and blood. It was not necessary for salvation to take communion in both kinds.

In the fourteenth century, as Eucharistic devotion intensified, laypeople's desire to receive in both kinds became more strident. This intensification, however, was not the basis on which theologians such as John Wyclif at Oxford or, following in his path, Jakob von Mies and Jan Hus at Prague, argued for the utraquist position. Especially in the work of Jakob (1414) and his later interpreters, the issue was not popular desire, but salvation. A key text was Jesus's words as reported in the Gospel of John 6:53–56:

> Verily, verily, I say unto you, Except ye eat the flesh of the Son of Man, and drink his blood, ye have no life in you. Whoso eateth my flesh, and drinketh my blood, hath eternal life; and I will raise him up at the last day. For my flesh is meat indeed, and my blood is drink indeed. He that eateth my flesh, and drinketh my blood, dwelleth in me, and I in him.

It is possible to interpret these words to mean that the flesh of Jesus is the wafer and the blood the liquid in the chalice. Moreover, the text can be read as conditioning the possibility of salvation (having eternal life, being raised up at the last day, dwelling in Christ) on receiving in both kinds. Here, too, is where history (tradition) could be used as evidence against contemporary so-called orthodox practice: if the church practiced giving communion in both kinds to the laity for a millennium, it must have seen the practice as more than just a custom.

The orthodox party replied repeatedly that these interpretations were incorrect, and its spokesmen could draw on other texts that appeared to endorse its view. The very continuation of the Johannine text quoted above might be read as a confirmation that receiving the wafer alone was sufficient: "As the living Father hath sent me, and I live by the Father: so he that eateth me, even he shall live by me" (John 6:57).

Although only one factor among many in precipitating and sustaining the Hussite Rebellion, utraquism was so directly a challenge to the magisterium of the church, instantiated in the Papacy and the councils and their right to define the Catholic faith, that the need was felt to extirpate it. The Council of Basel (1431–1449), under considerable pressure from Hussite representatives who had been invited to the proceedings, implicitly made a distinction in a session held in January 1433 between communion in both kinds as a practice and an ideology. As a practice, it was not forbidden, provided that those who defended and indulged in the practice accepted two points: (1) The body *and* blood of Christ were "contained" under both species, bread and wine. How else could the *real* Christ be present in each, if he was but flesh in one and blood in the other, when real men are flesh and blood? (2) Receiving in only one kind did not sacramentally compromise the hope of salvation. Those who subscribed to these two conditions of belief remained orthodox in the council's view. A distinction is usually made between these "moderate" utraquists and others who refused to be reconciled, the former being known as Calixtin(e)s, from the Latin word for chalice, and the latter as Taborites, whose increasingly apocalyptic views and willingness to fight stamped them as a dangerous enemy to Catholic orthodoxy. (Not all those who refused to subscribe, however, resorted to violence.)

It is fair to say that many of the moderate utraquists were as hostile to the Taborites as were non-utraquist Catholics. The defeat of the Taborites at the Battle of Lipany in 1434, as well as further defeats inflicted on them up until 1453, were the achievements of an alliance of these two groups. Nonetheless, Catholic authority over the moderate utraquists was rarely as effective as the ecclesiastical establishment wished. There continued to be apprehension about the practice of utraquism and suspicion about its underlying belief system among the people who practiced it. To this extent, it may be said that churches in which utraquism was practiced and the clergy that celebrated in these churches and both commended and defended the practice thought of themselves and their lay congregants as a kind of self-contained institution. The orthodox, including orthodox clergy who ordained the utraquist priests, perceived an erosion of distinction between clergy and laypeople and often viewed them as the same entity. It was inevitable that some moderate utraquists were not considered moderate enough by the orthodox party and suffered savagely for it. Therefore, many utraquists welcomed the rise of reformist (Protestant) ideas in the sixteenth century, one of which was the commending of communion in both kinds.

BIBLIOGRAPHY

Zdeněk, David V. *Finding the Middle Way: The Utraquists' Liberal Challenge to Rome and Luther.* Baltimore: Johns Hopkins University Press, 2003). This will become the standard study.

WILLIAM CHESTER JORDAN

[See also **DMA:** Councils, Western; Eucharist; Hussites.]

VATICAN LIBRARY. A library and an archival collection of the popes probably existed from the earliest days of the church in Rome. Scholars have traditionally divided the history of this library into five periods. The first was a pre-Lateran period, which has only vague surviving traces of collections of books and documents. That was followed by an era when books and documents were kept in the Lateran Palace in Rome. That institutional period lasted to the end of the thirteenth century and the reign of Pope Boniface VIII (1294–1303). This was followed by the great book collecting and massive growth in record keeping by the popes who took up residence in Avignon in southern France soon after the death of Boniface. From the papal return to Rome in the 1370s and the ensuing Great Schism after 1378, the library of the Avignonese popes was scattered, with only a small part of it returning in the Middle Ages to the restored papacy in Rome. This fourth era is often called the pre-Vatican. It is only with the initial efforts of Pope Nicholas V (1447–1455) and the consolidation and institutionalization by Pope Sixtus IV (1471–1484) that one can begin a more or less continuous history of the present-day collection in the Vatican Library.

Throughout these earlier periods the contents of the library were only irregularly divided between a collection of manuscript books and one of administrative documents. The books were usually of a legal and theological nature and viewed as necessary aspects of the pastoral role of the pope. The secret archives were only separated and given their own building under Pope Paul V in 1610. The care of all this material varied according to the interests and needs of the pope and his administrative staff. Clerics functioning as formal librarians were rare before the reign of Sixtus IV. The contents of a pope's library were usually considered his personal property and thus subject to familial inheritance and despoiling until the fourteenth century. In addition, while many popes remained resident in Rome, others had to move their court around. When they were not in Rome, the collection in the papal Lateran Palace was neglected and periodically looted.

Clearly the great legalistically minded popes of the thirteenth century such as Innocent III and Boniface VIII cultivated manuscript collections in order to accomplish their political and canonistic programs of reform. The registers of Innocent III are the oldest to survive. The oldest surviving library catalog, from the reign of Boniface VIII, records that he possessed 443 items at his death. His implacable enemies plundered this collection in 1303. Most of the popes in Avignon between John XXII (1316–1334) and Gregory XI (1370–1378) made strong efforts to collect, and even have copied, manuscripts that came to be stored in a large collection in the Angels' Tower of the Papal Palace. This library, probably the richest in Europe, was maintained by the antipope Benedict XIII (1394–1423) and mostly removed to where he had to seek refuge, at Peñiscola on the Mediterranean coast between Barcelona and Valencia. There are numerous and detailed published inventories of all of these collections from Avignon.

After the end of the schism in 1417, Popes Martin V and Eugenius IV made efforts to rebuild the manuscript collection by purchasing manuscripts and bringing books back from Avignon and elsewhere. Nicholas V, however, was an ardent bibliophile and laid the foundation for the revived library after 1450, even using some of the proceeds from the jubilee that year to buy books. He believed and proclaimed that the library of the popes should be among the finest in Europe and open to scholars "for the common convenience of the learned." On his death in 1455, an inventory of the library contained some 1,200 entries, including 800 in Latin and 400 in Greek. The contents of the library did not grow under the next two popes, and its facilities were neglected.

Seeking to establish the Holy See at the center of the contemporary intellectual and humanist world, Sixtus IV transformed this collection of manuscripts into a functioning and accessible library in 1475. He also appointed the first two real librarians, Giovanni Andrea Bussi and Bartolomeo Platina. Regular provision was made for acquiring, copying, and lending manuscripts. Platina's catalog of 1481 shows that the collection had expanded to encompass some 3,500 items. As the borrowing records show, numerous scholars and members of the higher clergy took out books and visited the collection.

From Sixtus's reign the library was maintained continuously. Later popes did not always demonstrate an ardent interest in its fortunes, and the sack of Rome in 1527 led to some losses. There were, however, major additions to its medieval holdings from the sixteenth century to the present. Many of the manuscripts from its days in Avignon returned to the Vatican through acquisitions of the collections. These rich collections are associated with the confiscated Palatine Library from Heidelberg, with the dukes of Urbino, with Queen Christina of Sweden, and with the Ottoboni, Borghese, Barberini, and Chigi families. The collection continues to grow and has more than 75,000 manuscripts in Latin, Greek, Hebrew, Arabic, Syriac, Coptic, and many other languages. As part of his effort to come to terms with the modern world and demonstrate the intellectual vitality of the church, Pope Leo XIII gave scholars much wider and more regular access to the library in the late nineteenth century. The popes and librarians since his time have supported and maintained this most important manuscript library of manuscripts from the medieval world.

BIBLIOGRAPHY

Biblioteca apostolica vaticana. *The Vatican Library: Its History and Treasures.* Edited under the patronage of Alfons Maria Cardinal Stickler and Leonard E. Boyle. Text: Maria Siponta De Salvia. English text: Brigitte Weitbrecht. Yorktown Heights, N.Y.: Belser, 1989.

Bignami Odier, Jeanne. *La bibliothèque Vaticane de Sixte IV à Pie XI: Recherches sur l'histoire des collections de manuscrits.* Vatican City: Biblioteca apostolica vaticana, 1973.

Blouin, Francis X., Jr., ed. *Vatican Archives: An Inventory and Guide to Historical Documents of the Holy See.* New York: Oxford University Press, 1998.

Boyle, Leonard E. *A Survey of the Vatican Archives and of Its Medieval Holdings.* Rev. ed. Toronto: Pontifical Institute of Mediaeval Studies, 2001.

Chadwick, Owen. *Catholicism and History: The Opening of the Vatican Archives.* Cambridge, U.K.: Cambridge University Press, 1978.

Faucon, Maurice. *La librairie des papes d'Avignon: Sa formation, sa composition, ses catalogues (1316–1420) d'après les registres de comptes et d'inventaires des archives Vaticanes.* 2 vols. Paris: E. Thorin, 1886–1887.

Grafton, Anthony, ed. *Rome Reborn: The Vatican Library and Renaissance Culture.* Washington, D.C.: Library of Congress, 1993.

Jullien de Pommerol, Marie-Henriette, and Jacques Monfrin. *La bibliothèque pontificale à Avignon et à Peñiscola pendant le grand schisme d'Occident et sa dispersion: Inventaires et concordances.* 2 vols. Rome: École française de Rome, 1991.

Müntz, Eugène, and Paul Fabre. *La bibliothèque du Vatican au XVe siècle.* Paris: E. Thorin, 1887.

EDWARD D. ENGLISH

[See also **DMA:** Libraries; Papacy, Origins and Development of; Schism, Great.]

VICES. See **Virtues and Vices.**

VIOLENCE. The Middle Ages have frequently been portrayed as uniquely violent. In the seventeenth century, Giambattista Vico wrote: "everywhere violence, rapine, and murder were rampant, because of the extreme ferocity and savagery of these most barbarous centuries." Such views, however, are nothing more than an ideological strategy by which successive modernities have defined themselves. Casting the Middle Ages as the violent, inverted mirror image of modernity implies the innate peaceability and rationality of the "modern," a claim that even a passing examination of postmedieval history renders preposterous.

Violence nonetheless remains as a central question in medieval society: it was a topic of continuing concern to medievals themselves. The violence that concerned them was not an exception to normative laws but a structural violence, an integral part of concrete social processes: the routine use of brutal force to impose and maintain the social order, as well as its symbolic repercussions and representations. Violence was functional or could be. In a primarily agricultural economy, peasants were the overwhelming majority, producing the food and surplus value for the rest of society. Wealth and status, military force and political power, finally depended on peasant productivity and its control: kings, princes, and nobles at the apex of society were its ultimate beneficiaries. Control depended on a complex intermediary class of sheriffs, provosts, bailiffs, *châtelains* (local masters of one or several fortresses), and the knights at their command who actually applied force. The violence of these intermediaries of power was ambiguous: it could function as an instrument of social control and productivity; it could also be an obstacle to productivity. The cycle of noble vengeance, for example, could be endless, as reflected in the late medieval epic *Raoul de Cambrai* (ca. 1200).

Counterviolence occurred more frequently than commonly appreciated. The English peasant rebellion of 1381 is well known; other revolts also left documentary traces. A "savage insurrection of the people" occurred in Merovingian France in the sixth century. In eastern Europe slaves revolted repeatedly against Saxon domination (ninth to eleventh centuries). The Norman peasant revolt (end of the tenth century), written up by the Latin chronicler William of Jumièges (late eleventh century), was retold and amplified in vernacular verse histories by the twelfth-century court poets Wace and Benoît de Sainte-Maure, inscribing a permanent threat to governance that resonated across at least 150 years. Urban analogues exist: Guibert of Nogent recounts the murderous revolt of Laon (1112). The murder of lords was frequent enough to be standardized and even ritualized. It was not necessarily thought extraordinary: punishment was sometimes surprisingly light. In the later Middle Ages rebellion enters into the political arsenal of the urban bourgeoisie, as popular revolts were led by Wat Tyler in England (1380–1381) and Étienne Marcel (1357–1358) and Simon Caboche (1413) in Paris.

Violence often marked encounters of social, economic, political, religious, and gender differences. Accusers and accused often belonged to different social groups, with different interests, value systems, and perspectives. The privileging of any one voice is reductive, and the documentation historians must rely on for a history of violence is inherently ambiguous. In early histories written by educated Romans or churchmen, for example, violence is attributed to nomads they call "barbarians." These barbarians left virtually no written records, so the representations modernity inherits are ineluctably skewed. Since World War II a revisionist historiography has downplayed the violence of these nomadic groups. Alongside invasions—Attila's ravages in northern France (A.D. 451), the sack of Rome by the Vandals (A.D. 455), etc.—this scholarship emphasizes peaceful migrations of families seeking arable land.

Some evidence concerning knightly violence is arguable. It is sometimes contained in documents that seek to protect clerical lands and interests. Since it occurs in both clerical and secular archives, however, the polemical purposes it may have served do not cancel its evidentiary value. Peace served the concrete interests of large sections of the population, in whose name churchmen organized a peace movement. The tenth- and eleventh-century Peace of God movement in France held large-scale meetings that united clerics and peasants (including women) and called on local knights to abjure violence against certain categories of victims (priests, peasants, and women). In the variant Truce of God movement, aggressions during certain days of the week around the Sabbath were the target. No one imagined the disappearance of violence, only its limitation and discipline. At its most successful, the peace movement in France obtained respites from violence. It influenced later history by placing peace once again on the monarchical agenda as of the twelfth century: royal coronation rituals incorporated its discourse.

The increasing consolidation of monarchical power throughout the Middle Ages had paradoxical results for peace, even when kings embraced their pastoral responsibilities sincerely. The means available to monarchical governance for the enforcement of peace were the weap-

Knight Spearing a Dragon. *The ideal of the noble knight is depicted in this early-12th-century mosaic. Moisenay, Monastre Notre-Dame de Ganagobie.* © GAULT-77350 MOISENAY-FRANCE. REPRODUCED BY PERMISSION.

ons of war. The consolidation of monarchical powers of war and taxation produced greater financial resources and the greater projection of royal power. Increased income permitted the construction of more imposing military facilities like castles built of stone rather than wood and greater reliance on mercenaries, which only worsened the periodic devastations visited on the countryside. The expulsion of the Jews from France in 1182 allowed for confiscations of their wealth to finance wars of conquest, which aggrandized French royal lands and financed yet further aggressions. Later regimes tempered the ferocity of war somewhat; its savagery rebounded during the Hundred Years War, which overlay an Anglo-French conflict with civil war.

The development of nascent state bureaucracies was accompanied by the "formation of a persecuting society" and identitarian categories of exclusion (heretics, Jews, homosexuals, prostitutes, etc.). While crossing the

Knight Descending into Hell. *This sculpture from the tympanum of the abbey of Conques shows a knight being damned for his violent acts.* PHOTOGRAPH BY PETER HAIDU. REPRODUCED BY PERMISSION.

Rhineland on their way to Jerusalem, Crusaders in 1096 massacred Jews in small-scale genocides in Mainz, Speyer, and Cologne. Three years later, the Jews crowded into the synagogue of Jerusalem were incinerated. All forms of incorrect belief were attacked. In Béziers, a Cathar stronghold in the crusade against "Albigensians," the massacre of *all* inhabitants was ordered by a papal nuncio who specified the inclusion of women and children (1209). Rigorous persecutorial practices were legitimated by the Fourth Lateran Council (1215). Increasingly sophisticated torture became an instrument of judicial interrogation.

War was the most extreme form of the violence that characterized permanent, structural social conflicts. The actual conduct of war showed no regard for "just-war" theories or fictive principles of "chivalry." Nobles tended to spare each other for the sake of ransom but wreaked violence on civilian populations, with regular recourse to treachery, arson, and pillage. War, short of an ultimate battle *(proelium)* that risked everything on a single encounter, was a "normal," seasonal activity (spring was the preferred season).

Even as it attempted to rein in the power of the knights, the church remilitarized, creating new orders of "warrior-monks" (Knights Templar, Hospitallers, Teutonic Knights), and encouraged the crusades. In preaching the First Crusade (begun in 1095), Urban II gave religious warrant not only to the export of surplus violence but to a political and economic expansionism that implanted Christian colonies in Arab lands and Muslim populations. Ideologized as a "pilgrimage" to the Holy Land and a form of "holy war," the Christian Crusades were counterpart to the Muslim jihad. The cross Crusaders wore legitimated a violence against others who saw it as aggressive expansionism.

LITERARY REPRESENTATIONS OF VIOLENCE

Medieval literature is an essential source for a study of violence in the Middle Ages. Literature itself often stages conflicts between dissenting ideologies. Representations of violence are ubiquitous, traversing texts of all types. Saints' lives, with clerical, Latin origins, reenact Jesus's rejection as disciple of any who "does not hate father and mother, wife and children" (Luke 14:26). The troubadour Bertran de Born (*ca.* 1140–*ca.* 1215) sings of war with subjective glee (in a passage adapted from Blackburn, *Proensa*):

> I love beyond all pleasure
> Maces smashing painted helms,
> sword-strokes descending, riven shields,
> . . . bursting blood on the broken harness,
> horses of the wounded and killed.

Violence is the central narrative material of epic, though not necessarily affirmed as a positive value. The *Charroi de Nîmes* (mid-twelfth century) describes war with sadism, pity, and perhaps some guilt:

> I saw the entire land filled with enemies,
> burning towns, violating churches,
> chapel roofs melted down, bell-towers
>   tumbled,
> twisting the breasts of noble women:
> so great a pity overwhelmed my heart
> I wept tenderly from the eyes of my head.

War's devastations became narrative convention. Descriptions of combat in the *Song of Roland* (*ca.* 1100) have been read both as forming a how-to-kill handbook and as a plea for a monarchical solution to the self-destructiveness of feudalism. The extraordinary *Raoul de cambrai* (*ca.* 1200) is more an exploration of the disastrous effects of cyclical feudal vengeance than its praise.

Romances, associated with noble courts, focus on the individual, but combat remains their central narrative coin, even when carnal love and social advancement are portrayed. The *Roman de Thèbes* (*ca.* 1150) follows a single knight "who loves a starting war," as he rides down into a valley of battle joyfully:

> There you would have seen lances lowered,
> gonfanons unfurled,
> shields crack open, hauberks split,
> lances break, fragments fly off,
> great sword-strokes struck,
> and many a head cut off its trunk.

Motivation is unambiguous: "noble knights had come to other lands for conquest." The poem insists, however, on the necessity of the leader's self-control and presents extensive debates in councils of war as integral to the decision-making process. Violence is a problem narrative addresses, not a joy it glorifies.

Love does not supplant violence. In Chrétien de Troyes's world of romance, a maiden explains "ancient customs": a woman traveling under escort risked having to endure the will of any knight who fought and defeated her escort (*Lancelot, ca.* 1177–1181). With bitter irony,

Perceval's mother calls knights "the angels people complain about, who kill everything they see" (*Perceval,* before 1191). Throughout Chrétien de Troyes's writing, as in much medieval literature, episodic construction continually reinscribes combat as the deciding factor in constituting individual value and achieving social ends.

The fabliau (thirteenth and fourteenth centuries), was associated with the rise of the middle class, urban development, and investment capitalism, reveled in fetishizing dismemberment of sexual parts and the pursuit of dominance by force or deceit. Late theatrical mysteries insistently represent the sacrifices of Christ and his saints.

Violence inheres in the narratives of women authors as well. An essential narrative element in the *lais* of Marie de France (twelfth century), it joins feminism as a recurrent concern in Christine de Pizan's political texts, written in the context of the Hundred Years War.

CONCLUSION

The violence of medieval society was not natural or genetic or a moral failing: it was ideologically linked to socioeconomic structures and political goals, which joined self-interest and gratification. Partly sublimating its violences, the Middle Ages constructed the foundations of the modern state, with its social ideal of peace, and the accompanying vernacular culture, with its ideals of secular love and social equality, while leaving behind an enduring heritage of ideological and social conflict. The central symbol of Christianity—the Crucifixion—symbolized not beatific contentment but the harrowing death by extended torture of a human body as the expression of the Creator's love for his creation.

BIBLIOGRAPHY

PRIMARY WORKS

Blackburn, Paul. *Proensa: An Anthology of Troubadour Poetry.* Berkeley: University of California Press, 1978.

Chrétien de Troyes. *Complete Romances.* Translated by David Staines. Bloomington: Indiana University Press, 1990.

Christine de Pizan. *Selected Writings.* Translated by Renate Blumenfeld-Kosinski and Kevin Brownlee. New York: Norton, 1997.

Kay, Sarah, ed. and trans. *Raoul de Cambrai.* Oxford: Clarendon Press, 1992.

Marie de France. *Lais.* Translated by Robert Hanning and Joan Ferrante. Durham, N.C.: Labyrinth, 1982.

Terry, Patricia, trans. *The Song of Roland.* New York: Bobbs-Merrill, 1965.

HISTORY AND CRITICISM

Barthélemy, Dominique. *L'an mil et la paix de Dieu: La France chrétienne et féodale, 980–1060.* Paris: Fayard, 1999.

Bartlett, Robert. *The Making of Europe: Conquest, Colonization, and Cultural Change, 950–1350.* Princeton, N.J.: Princeton University Press, 1993.

Bloch, Marc. *Feudal Society.* Translated by L. A. Manyon. London: Routledge and Kegan Paul, 1961.

Contamine, Philippe. *War in the Middle Ages.* Translated by Michael Jones. Oxford: Blackwell, 1984.

Duby, Georges. *The Early Growth of the European Economy: Warriors and Peasants from the Seventh to the Twelfth Century.* Translated by Howard B. Clarke. Ithaca, N.Y.: Cornell University Press, 1974.

Freedman, Paul. *Images of the Medieval Peasant.* Stanford, Calif.: Stanford University Press, 1999.

Haidu, Peter. *The Subject of Violence:* The Song of Roland *and the Birth of the State.* Bloomington: Indiana University Press, 1993.

———. *The Subject: Medieval/Modern. Text and Governance in the Middle Ages.* Stanford, Calif.: Stanford University Press, in press.

Head, Thomas, and Richard Landes. *The Peace of God: Social Violence and Religious Response in France around the Year 1000.* Ithaca, N.Y.: Cornell University Press, 1992.

Hilton, Rodney. *Bond Men Made Free: Medieval Peasant Movements and the English Rising of 1381.* New York: Viking, 1973.

Jordan, William Chester. *The French Monarchy and the Jews: From Philip Augustus to the Last Capetians.* Philadelphia: University of Pennsylvania Press, 1989.

Le Patourel, John. *The Norman Empire.* Oxford: Clarendon Press, 1976.

Maalouf, Amin. *The Crusades through Arab Eyes.* Translated by Jon Rothschild. New York: Schocken, 1985.

Moore, Robert I. *The Formation of a Persecuting Society: Power and Deviance in Western Europe, 950–1250.* Oxford: Blackwell, 1987.

Nirenberg, David. *Communities of Violence: Persecution of Minorities in the Middle Ages.* Princeton, N.J.: Princeton University Press, 1996.

Past and Present 142 (1994) and 152 (1996).

Strayer, Joseph R. *On the Medieval Origins of the Modern State.* Princeton, N.J.: Princeton University Press, 1970.

PETER HAIDU

[See also **DMA:** Chansons de Geste; Crusades and Crusader States; Expulsion of Jews; Knights and Knight Service; Peace of God, Truce of God; Peasants' Rebellion; Warfare, Western European.]

VIRTUES AND VICES

ETHICS AND CULTURE

In the Middle Ages sacred time, space, and work were organized at least partially as a means to acknowledge and expiate sin in human existence. The liturgical calendar or the Last Judgment, the physical space in which confession was made or the cosmic spaces of heaven and hell, the activity of hearing confession or of doing penance—these helped define the borders outside of which behavior was no longer accepted as morally legitimate. Building on the thought of St. Augustine of Hippo (354–430), early medieval theologians in particular often viewed sin as a misdirected love, an ego-driven separation of the self from both God and the community of faith. Scholastic theologians preferred a different Augustinian definition according to which sin is a word, act, or desire governed by the will and contrary to God's law (*Contra Faustum,* 22.27). Augustine also supplied one of the basic definitions of virtue as a habit of the mind consonant with human nature and reason (*De 83 diversis quaestionibus,* 31); from Anicius Manlius Severinus Boethius (*ca.* 480–524/526), twelfth-century theologians in particular culled another definition of virtue as the disposition of a well-ordered mind (*De differentiis topicis,* 2).

Sin viewed as a retreat from the love of God and one's neighbor into a self-referential concupiscence or as a violation of divine law and virtue understood as an acculturated habit acquired with grace demonstrate how the community in which they are located can be described in terms of desire: the vices, then, become the discrete forms of an interrupted actualization of accepted forms of desire; the virtues, ideals of the socialization of desire. Variations in the appearance of both occur along lines of class and gender. Insofar as pastoral considerations, the monastic concern with meditation, and scholastic analysis were often informed by speculation on the physiological or psychological causes of sin and virtue, treatises of moral theology became the vehicle for a scrutiny of humanity that has been termed a form of "paleopsychology." Sin was not considered a cause of insanity, but treatises on the vices and virtues may fairly be understood as handbooks of abnormal psychology and their therapeutic counterparts; both reflect a sometimes implicit statement of behavioral norms.

These social, psychological, and spiritual considerations resulted in a complex mixture of systems of vices, virtues, and accompanying moral qualities. In the first four Christian centuries, vices were comprehended within the "deadly sin" tradition—generally unsystematic gatherings of sinful acts that were thought to lead to the death of the soul. Written analyses of the deadly sin tradition begin in rabbinic literature as early as the first century B.C. The variability of the contents of these groupings is analogous to nontheological lists that one finds in works on comportment, courtesy books for gentlemen, and the like, especially in the late Middle Ages when the observation of manners began to encroach on the hegemony of moral theology. Theological and worldly value systems were often interrelated: near the beginning of the *Roman de la Rose*, for example, the wall surrounding the garden of pleasure contains images of attributes to be eschewed by a courtly lover. These range from theologically defined sins such as covetousness, avarice, and religious hypocrisy, to undesirable traits conceived in plainly secular terms, such as old age and poverty.

SACRED ARITHMETIC: TAXONOMIES OF GOOD AND EVIL

The capital vices, later identified as the seven deadly sins (pride, envy, wrath, avarice, sloth, gluttony, lust—in their most frequent order), are the most familiar system of medieval moral thought on the vices, as the cardinal and theological virtues are of the virtues, but these were supplemented, in particular in the later Middle Ages, by other numerical groupings. Permutations of the lists of these vices and virtues—their number and order, the designation of a chief or root sin or virtue among them, and a varying emphasis on one or the other of the vices or virtues—characterize the changing history of these lists' functions. Systems of morally negative qualities included the four "sins that cry to heaven" (murder; sodomy; oppression of the poor, widows, and orphans; withholding justly earned wages); six "sins against the Holy Spirit" (presumption of God's mercy, despair of receiving mercy, impugning Christian truth, envy of another's spiritual good, obstinacy in sinning, stubborn impenitence); nine "accessory sins" (causing someone else to sin or supporting that sinner by commanding, advising, consenting, praising, protecting, participating, concealing, not opposing, not revealing); and varying groupings of sins of the tongue emphasized in treatises from the thirteenth century on. Systems of morally positive qualities included the seven gifts of the Holy Spirit (wisdom, understanding, knowledge, counsel, fortitude, piety, fear of God—derived from Is. 11:1–3); seven corporal works of mercy (feeding the hungry, giving drink to the thirsty, housing strangers, clothing the naked, visiting the sick, attending to prisoners, burying the dead); seven spiritual works of mercy (correcting sinners, teaching the ignorant, counseling the doubtful, comforting the afflicted, bearing wrongs in patience, forgiving offenses willingly, praying for the living and the dead); seven petitions of the Lord's Prayer (derived from Matt. 6:9–15 [Luke 11:2–4]); eight beatitudes (Matt. 5:3–10); and Ten Commandments (Exod. 20:2–17, Deut. 5:6–21). They also included the virtues, strictly speaking: three theological virtues (important, broadly speaking, as spiritual categories: faith, hope, *caritas* [1 Cor. 13:13]); four cardinal virtues (moral/political categories above all: prudence, justice, temperance, fortitude [see

Plato, *Republic,* 4.427e; Cicero, *De finibus,* 5.23.67; Ambrose, *De excessu fratris Satyri,* 1.56]); and lists of remedial virtues developed as the therapeutic opposites to lists of sins.

From its limited and technical origins in late antiquity, by the end of the Middle Ages the teaching on the capital vices had become the most widespread articulation of the moral tradition of Latin Christendom. The centrality of the capital vices is all the more remarkable considering that many of the most authoritative writers in the West gave little or no attention to this doctrine. Augustine developed a different triad of sins on the basis of 1 John 2:16 that he termed the "origins of evil" (*Confessions,* 3.8.16, see also 10.30.41; *De vera religione,* 38.70; *Enarrationes in Psalmos,* 8.13): pride, curiosity, and sins of the flesh. Though the titles of two of St. Bernard of Clairvaux's *Sententiae* (*De septem vitiis principalibus* and *De septem vitiis*) indicate that they deal with the seven capital vices, these works are in fact analyses of stages in the psychological development of sinfulness that Bernard (1090–1153) suggests are counteracted by the gifts of the Holy Spirit. In *Liber de gradibus superbiae et humilitatis,* Bernard developed twelve "steps" of pride as opposites to the stages of perfect humility in the Benedictine rule. Nowhere does Augustine or Bernard draw on a list of the capital vices to articulate a moral position. Though St. Thomas Aquinas (1224–1274) referred to the capital vices several times, his moral thought was based on Aristotle's *Nichomachean Ethics,* which is organized around a wide list of virtues in which pairs of vices appear as opposite extremes to the virtue that forms the "golden mean" between them. Aquinas accepted the list of seven vices as traditional moral thought, but his analysis superseded them in many ways.

VICES, VIRTUES, AND HISTORY

The longevity and centrality of the capital vices testifies, nevertheless, to the authoritativeness and versatility of what began as an element of monastic education. Their origin is found in the list of eight "evil thoughts" (gluttony, lust, avarice, wrath, sadness, sloth, vainglory, pride) that developed in the hermit communities of northern Egypt. These eight *logismoi* may have been common in the oral teaching of the Egyptian monks, but in written form they are found earliest in the Greek works of Evagrius Ponticus (346–399). Evagrius adopted many of the components of the octad and their order from the Alexandrian theologian Origen (*ca.* 185–*ca.* 254). Hellenistic texts like the Pseudo-Aristotelian *On Virtues and Vices,* a popular synthesis of antique moral thought, also inspired him in developing the eight *logis-*

moi and in relating a list of eight virtues, including the cardinal virtues, to the Platonic model of the tripartite soul (*Praktikos,* p. 89ff.). In the octad, Evagrius systematized the theory of demonic intrusions on the contemplative work of the anchorite so that the monk would be better armed to defeat the demons who used temptations to hinder his attainment of *apatheia* (passionlessness). John Cassian (*ca.* 360–432/435) learned of the octad from Evagrius and made the order of *logismoi* in Evagrius's *De octo spiritibus malitiae* central to his Latin works written for cenobitic monasteries in Marseille. Here the "evil thoughts" were now termed *vitia,* each with a list of sub-sins to which it gives rise. Cassian emphasized the concatenation (linking together) of the first six vices, a sequential relationship in which an excess of one vice becomes the foundation for the subsequent one. Vainglory and pride become dangerous precisely when the previous six have been extirpated. The ascetic orientation of these early monastic octads, written for communities of holy men, can be seen in the way control of bodily desires lays the foundation for the defeat of more spiritual temptations.

The sin octad remained important in monastic literature throughout the Middle Ages—it helped shape the early penitentials and influenced the late-medieval spirituality of the *devotio moderna*—but it was not the only important early-medieval analysis of the combat against evil: Prudentius's *Psychomachia* (*ca.* 405) adopted classical ethics and became the source for much visual and textual iconography of the battle between personified vices and virtues throughout the Middle Ages.

Pope Gregory I the Great (*ca.* 540–604) synthesized Cassian's monastic thought with Augustine's view of sin as reflective of the will. Using most of the octad's components, Gregory reversed the order of vices—what he explicitly called two "carnal sins" come after five spiritual ones, with pride serving as the root of all seven "principle vices": vainglory, envy, wrath, sadness, avarice, gluttony, lust (see *Moralia in Job,* 31.45.87–90). When pride itself was included in the list, the result could be understood as a variant of a sin octad, but in either case, Gregory considered these vices the origins of all sinfulness. The excesses of the ego depicted in the heptad's spiritual sins emphasize the importance of humility for Gregory as the central virtue of active obedience to authority within the community in moral, monastic, and secular political terms. Pride was most commonly (though not exclusively) considered the foundation of sinfulness in the early Middle Ages. Gregory asserts that the determination of intention in any act necessitates close examination of motives that may reveal a gap between the appearance

of virtue and its origin in the impulses of vice. He presupposes, thus, a certain amount of moral ambiguity in any act.

The heptad reflects the social values of a hierarchical society and theologically sanctions the aspirations of the powerful in the existing social order. In the early Middle Ages, however, many other presentations of vices and virtues were addressed to the needs of the nobility as well: St. Martin of Braga (*ca.* 515–579) composed the very popular *Formula vitae honestae* (570–579), a treatise on the cardinal virtues, for the moral instruction of the Suevic King Miro I and his court. Typical of the aristocrats directly involved in the ethical renewal of the Carolingian reforms is Wido, margrave of the Marca Britanniae, to whom Alcuin of York (*ca.* 730–804) addressed his influential *Liber de virtutibus et vitiis* (*ca.* 800). The reformers emphasized *ethica,* the study of virtue leading to correct living, along with the liberal arts and logic as the disciplines of philosophy: Alcuin frames his treatise with systems of virtue (at the beginning, theological virtues; at the end, cardinal). His compilation of scriptural and patristic texts as governing authorities served the further end of aiding uniformity in the Carolingian church, which allies his and other Carolingian and post-Carolingian treatises on moral theology with the genre of the *florilegium.* Typical examples are the recensions of Adalgerus's *Admonitio ad Nonswindam reclusam* on the virtues and vices assembled by Albuin (d. 1031).

The internalization of concepts of the individual and spirituality in the late eleventh and twelfth centuries anchored moral theology in psychological processes. Hugh of St. Victor (d. 1141) reinterpreted concatenation as a description of developing sinfulness that began with the common classification of sin according to the subject it is directed against: pride removes the sinner from God, envy from his neighbor, wrath from himself. The last four vices marked stages in the sinner's descent into slavery to sin (see *De quinque septenis*). The intended audience of this view of the vices now includes new classes of an urban population. The renewal of interest in Augustinian theology can be seen in the *Liber de humanis moribus* (reworked as the influential *De similitudinibus*), reporting the words of Anselm of Canterbury (1033–1109): here, Augustine's sin-triad is analyzed according to the combinations of the physical senses each vice involves. The Augustinian revival also marks a tendency to see *caritas* (Christian love) as the most important virtue, in opposition to Gregory the Great's focus on humility. The *Ethica* of Peter Abelard (*ca.* 1079–*ca.* 1142) for the first time systematically analyzed the importance of intention and conscience—that is, the inner disposition of each human being—in the determination of what constitutes vice and virtue. The interconnection between monastic theology and the developing "theology of the schools" produced many other presentations using the symmetry of vices and virtues (or related qualities, especially the gifts of the Holy Spirit). For example, the *Liber de fructu carnis et spiritus* by Conrad of Hirsau (*ca.* 1070–*ca.* 1150) treats the Gregorian heptad and an opposed list (theological plus cardinal virtues) and was influential in the development of illuminations of matching trees of vices and virtues; Alan of Lille's *De virtutibus et de vitiis et de donis Spiritus sancti* (*ca.* 1170–1180) examines the gifts of the Holy Spirit, defines the vices and their progeny, and makes the theological virtues a category of one of the cardinal virtues; and the façade of Notre Dame cathedral in Paris (early thirteenth century) arranges personifications of virtues with roundels of exemplified vices in a way that summarizes types of representation of both. With the shift to a growing profit economy in the eleventh and twelfth centuries, treatments of avarice and its sub-sins (usury, illicit merchant practices, etc.) began to vie with pride more frequently in discussions of which sin is the root of all others.

Early scholastic literature began to treat sin and virtue within a wider approach to systematic theology, though attempts to adduce a theoretical rationale for a system of sins (generally as aberrations of the human will) produced any number of classifications of the vices. Peter Lombard's *Sententiae* (1155–1158), the standard textbook for scholastic education in theology, had suggested four: Augustine's distinction of sins by their origin in cupidity or fear; Jerome's classification of sins of thought, word, or deed; the distinction according to the subject sin is directed against; and the Gregorian heptad (*Senteniae*, 2.30–44). The capital vices could not easily be justified as the most important or the most serious sins. The phenomenology of sin and virtue became central to theology as a discipline, but this opened up new avenues of classification. The use of Aristotle's *Nichomachean Ethics* reinforced academic moral theology's move beyond its focus on vice (and interest in only seven capital vices) to instead become a theory of virtue, devoted to questions touching the divisions of the virtues (intellectual, moral, theological), their causes, and their interconnection. Beginning in the second half of the twelfth century, theologians also developed the category of natural virtues, positive traits acquired without the action of grace that facilitated social life, so that they were called civil or political virtues. Aquinas still discussed the capital vices at some length; John Duns Scotus (*ca.* 1266–1308) treated them fleetingly as "occasions" for

sinfulness; William of Ockham (*ca.* 1285–1347) did not treat them at all.

The importance of the sacrament of penance influenced frequent scholastic attempts to distinguish between explicit violations of God's law (deadly sins) and acts that do not directly breach this law (venial sins). The attempts to define venial sin also included the idea of a diminution of any inherent human sinfulness due in part to the imperfect nature of human intention or human knowledge, as one can see, for example, in "Le profit de savoir quel est péché mortel et véniel" and other works by John (Jean) Gerson (1363–1429). The capital vices no longer suffice as a schematic organization of the multitude of errors that Gerson discusses, which in one treatise amount to fifty-eight different kinds of deception by the devil (i.e., vices disguised as virtues). With an endless choice of feigned virtues that self-examination will expose as vices, Gerson's sinner has arrived at what has been described as a "paralysis of the soul" typical of late-medieval guilt culture. An interest in the Jewish scriptures that had begun in the twelfth century, uneasiness with the lack of a biblical foundation for the capital vices, and a concern to bind morality into a juridical system resulted in the emergence of the Ten Commandments, especially among Franciscan theologians beginning with Duns Scotus, as the moral system that would be universally taught after the sixteenth century.

In pastoral theology, art, and literature, the capital vice tradition remained dominant through the sixteenth century. The reforming efforts of the church to control the content of catechesis (elementary education in matters of the faith) by reinstructing congregations at all social levels in matters of the faith culminated in canon 21 of the Fourth Lateran Council (1215), which legislated confession for all Christians at least once a year. Many regional councils demanded that clergy preach on vices and virtues, as well. The examination of the conscience envisioned here included material specific to women and all classes of society. The question of how to organize the sins to be confessed and preached on was answered very early by drawing on the capital vices, which now became the seven deadly sins. Robert of Flamborough's early thirteenth-century *Liber poenitentialis* recommended the heptad precisely because the genetic relationship of the vices (and their progeny) facilitated confession. Eventually, the number of progeny was vastly expanded, but the basic classification of seven chief sins and their chief remedies remained, though often in tandem with other catechetical systems. The outpouring of penitential and homiletic texts treating vice and virtue, initially addressed to the clergy, was the work especially of the Dominicans and Franciscans, and it influenced the development of vernacular works on morality, now addressed to the laity. William Peraldus's widely transmitted *Summa virtutum ac vitiorum* (1236–1250), which played a seminal role in the development of the sins of the tongue, influenced important vernacular treatments of the vices and virtues such as Friar Lorens d'Orléans's *Somme le roi* (*ca.* 1279) and (indirectly) Geoffrey Chaucer's "Parson's Tale" (late fourteenth century). The use of images for educating pious Christians drew in the late Middle Ages on pastoral literature, the natural-philosophical understanding of animals, and traditional moral iconography to produce emblematic presentations of the vices and virtues in many media and for many functions, from supporting the Benedictine reform to promoting civic ethics (as in the Regensburg tapestry of the vices and virtues, *ca.* 1400). The confluence of pastoral literature and pervasive emblematic iconography also characterizes late-medieval and Renaissance literary treatments of the vices and virtues, from the *Divine Comedy* of Dante Alighieri (1265–1321), to morality plays, and to Book I of Edmund Spenser's *Faerie Queene* (1590), with its personified virtues such as Holiness and its procession of vices.

BIBLIOGRAPHY

PRIMARY WORKS

Abelard, Peter. *Peter Abelard's Ethics*. Edited by D. E. Luscombe. Oxford: Clarendon, 1971.

Alan of Lille. *De virtutibus et de vitiis et de donis Spiritus sancti*. Edited by Odo Lottin. In Lottin's *Psychologie et morale aux XIIe et XIIIe siècles*, Vol. 6. Gembloux, Belgium: Duculot, 1948–1960.

Alcuin. *Liber de virtutibus et vitiis*. In *Patrologia Latina*. Edited by Jacques-Paul Migne. Vol. 101. Paris. (Originally printed in 217 volumes from 1844 to 1855, the *Patrologia Latina* is also available as a computer database, published by Chadwick-Healey, Alexandria, Va., 1995.)

Anselm of Canterbury. *Liber de humanis moribus*. In *Memorials of St. Anselm*. Edited by R. W. Southern and F. S. Schmitt. Auctores Britannici Medii Aevi, 1. London: Oxford University Press, 1969.

Cassian, John. *Collationes patrum*. Edited and translated by E. Pichery. 3 vols. Paris: Cerf, 1955–1959.

———. *De institutis coenobiorum*. Edited and translated by Jean-Claude Guy. 2d ed. Paris: Cerf, 2001. The original edition was published in 1965.

Conrad of Hirsau. *Liber de fructu carnis et spiritus*. In *Patrologia Latina*. Edited by Jacques-Paul Migne. Vol. 176. Paris. (Also available in the *Patrologia Latina* computer database, Alexandria, Va.: Chadwick-Healey, 1995.)

Evagrius Ponticus. *Praktikos*. In *Évagre le Pontique: Traité pratique ou le moine*. Edited and translated by Antoine Guillaumont and Claire Guillaumont. 2 vols. Paris: Cerf, 1971.

———. *De malignis cogitationibus*. In *Évagre le Pontique: Sur les pensées*. Edited by Paul Géhin, Claire Guillaumont, and Antoine Guillaumont. Paris: Cerf, 1998.

———. *De octo spiritibus malitiae*. In *Patrologia Graeca*. Edited by Jacques-Paul Migne. Vol. 79. Paris: 1863. (Originally published in 161 volumes from 1857 to 1866, *Patrologia Graeca* is also available as a computer database, published by the Religion and Technology Center, Stone Mountain, Ga., 2003.)

———. *De vitiis quae opposita sunt virtutibus*. In *Patrologia Graeca*. Vol. 79. Paris: 1863. (Also available in the *Patrologia Graeca* computer database, Stone Mountain, Ga.: Religion and Technology Center, 2003.)

Gerson, Jean. "Le profit de savoir quel est péché mortel et véniel." In *Jean Gerson: Oeuvres complètes*. Edited by Palémon Glorieux. Vol. 7. Paris: Desclée, 1966.

Gregory the Great. *Moralia in Iob*. Edited by Marci Adriaen. 3 vols. Turnhout, Belgium: Brepols, 1979–1985.

Hugh of St. Victor. *De quinque septenis*. In his *Six opuscules spirituels*. Edited by Roger Baron. Paris: Cerf, 1969.

Martin of Braga. *Formula vitae honestae*. In *Martini episcopi Bracarensis opera omnia*. Edited by Claude W. Barlow. Papers and Monographs of the American Academy in Rome, 12. New Haven, Conn.: Yale University Press, 1950.

Peraldus, William. *Summa virtutum ac vitiorum Guilhelmi Paraldi Episcopi Lugdunensis de ordine predicatorum*. Paris: 1512.

Peter Lombard. *Magistri Petri Lombardi Parisiensis episcopi "Sententiae in IV libris distinctae."* 2 vols. 3d ed. Spicilegium Bonaventurianum, 4–5. Grottaferrata, Rome: Collegium S. Bonaventurae, 1971–1981.

Prudentius. *Psychomachia*. In *Aurelii Prudentii Clementis carmina*. Edited by M. P. Cunningham. Turnhout, Belgium: Brepols, 1966.

Robert of Flamborough. *Liber poenitentialis*. Edited by J. J. Francis Firth. Studies and Texts, 18. Toronto: Pontifical Institute of Mediaeval Studies, 1971.

Thomas Aquinas. *Summa theologiae*. 9 vols. In *Sancti Thomae Aquinatis doctoris angelici opera omnia iussu impensaque Leonis XIII P. M. edita*. Vols. 4–12. Rome: Typographia Polyglotta S. C. de Propaganda Fide, 1888–1906.

SECONDARY WORKS

Bejczy István P., and Richard G. Newhauser, eds. *Virtue and Ethics in the Twelfth Century*. Forthcoming.

Biller, Peter, and A. J. Minnis, eds. *Handling Sin: Confession in the Middle Ages*. York, U.K.: York Medieval Press, 1998.

Bloomfield, Morton W. *The Seven Deadly Sins: An Introduction to the History of a Religious Concept, with Special Reference to Medieval English Literature*. 1952. Reprint, East Lansing: Michigan State University Press, 1967.

Bossy, John. "Moral Arithmetic: Seven Sins into Ten Commandments." In *Conscience and Casuistry in Early Modern Europe*. Edited by Edmund Leites. Cambridge, U.K.: Cambridge University Press, 1988.

Casagrande, Carla, and Silvana Vecchio. *I sette vizi capitali: Storia dei peccati nel Medioevo*. Saggi, 832. Turin, Italy: Einaudi, 2000.

Delumeau, Jean. *Sin and Fear: The Emergence of a Western Guilt Culture, Thirteenth–Eighteenth Centuries*. Translated by Eric Nicholson. New York: St. Martin's, 1990.

Hourihane, Colum, ed. *Virtue and Vice: The Personifications in the Index of Christian Art*. Princeton, N.J.: Princeton University Press, 2000.

Howard, Donald R. *The Three Temptations: Medieval Man in Search of the World.* Princeton, N.J.: Princeton University Press, 1966.

Jehl, Rainer. "Die Geschichte des Lasterschemas und seiner Funktion." *Franziskanische Studien* 64 (1982): 261–359.

Katzenellenbogen, Adolf. *Allegories of the Virtues and Vices in Mediaeval Art from Early Christian Times to the Thirteenth Century.* Translated by Alan J. P. Crick. 1939. Reprint, Toronto: University of Toronto Press, 1989.

Kent, Bonnie. *Virtues of the Will: The Transformation of Ethics in the Late Thirteenth Century.* Washington, D.C.: Catholic University of America Press, 1995.

Little, Lester K. "Pride Goes before Avarice: Social Change and the Vices in Latin Christendom." *American Historical Review* 76 (1971): 16–49.

Lottin, Odon. *Psychologie et morale aux XIIe et XIIIe siècles.* 6 vols. Gembloux, Belgium: J. Duculot, 1942–1960.

MacIntyre, Alasdair C. *After Virtue: A Study in Moral Theory.* 2d ed. Notre Dame, Ind.: University of Notre Dame Press, 1984.

Newhauser, Richard G. "From Treatise to Sermon: Johannes Herolt on the *novem peccata aliena.*" In *De ore domini: Preacher and Word in the Middle Ages.* Edited by Thomas L. Amos et al. Studies in Medieval Culture, 27. Kalamazoo, Mich.: Medieval Institute Press, 1989.

———. *The Treatise on Vices and Virtues in Latin and the Vernacular.* Typologie des sources du moyen âge occidental, 68. Turnhout, Belgium: Brepols, 1993.

———. *The Early History of Greed: The Sin of Avarice in Early Medieval Thought and Literature.* Cambridge Studies in Medieval Literature, 41. Cambridge, U.K.: Cambridge University Press, 2000.

———, ed. *In the Garden of Evil: The Vices and Culture in the Middle Ages.* Forthcoming.

O'Reilly, Jennifer. *Studies in the Iconography of the Virtues and Vices in the Middle Ages.* New York and London: Garland, 1988.

Rosenwein, Barbara, ed. *Anger's Past: The Social Uses of an Emotion in the Middle Ages.* Ithaca and London: Cornell University Press, 1998.

Solignac, Aimé. "Péchés capitaux." In *Dictionnaire de Spiritualité.* Vol. 12. Paris: Beauchesne, 1986.

Tuve, Rosamond. "Notes on the Virtues and Vices." *Journal of the Warburg and Courtauld Institutes* 26 (1963): 264–303; 27 (1964): 42–72.

Utley, Francis L. "The Seven Deadly Sins: Then and Now." *Indiana Social Studies Quarterly* 25 (1975): 31–50.

Wenzel, Siegfried. *The Sin of Sloth: Acedia in Medieval Thought and Literature.* Chapel Hill, N.C.: University of North Carolina Press, 1967.

———. "The Seven Deadly Sins: Some Problems of Research." *Speculum* 43 (1968): 1–22.

RICHARD G. NEWHAUSER

[See also **DMA**: Penance and Penitentials; Seven Deadly Sins.]

VOIVODE is a common English spelling of a word that entered the language around 1560, just as the British, in their "age of exploration," became more familiar with the governmental and administrative arrangements in eastern and southeastern Europe. One of the earliest uses of the term is in Hakluyt's *Voyages* (1570), a foundational text of travel literature. It was not merely the curious sound of the word that encouraged writers to employ rather than translate the word (though the spellings "waywode" and "vaivode" suggest that contemporary pronunciation was curious indeed). The truth was that a voivode did not seem to have a precise equivalent in English insular experience. The word itself seems to have been common to the Slavic languages (its root may be *voi*, army) and was early on adopted into Magyar, Romanian, and Greek.

The meanings given to the term include district or battlefield military commander; deputy or governor appointed by a king, emperor or sultan; and hereditary lesser noble (petty prince, petty king) with circumscribed territorial jurisdiction. During the long period of Hungarian hegemony in Romania from roughly the millennium to the close of the Middle Ages, the Magyar king ruled through a voivode. Very frequently early modern western discourse, however, makes voivode equivalent to warlord, a ruler who is in merely formal dependence on a sovereign prince.

Medieval voivodes appear, insofar as the evidence permits us to know, rather like medieval aristocrats elsewhere in Europe, but the military and arbitrary powers they wielded did tend to be greater than they were in the west. Their power in eastern Europe was probably the result of the savage and seemingly ceaseless wars across confessional and ethnic lines, the central states' only intermittent success in enforcing political and social discipline in the region, and, toward the end of the Middle Ages, the peculiarly degrading forms of serfdom that arose there and required brute force to sustain them. Under such conditions there was also a tendency toward conspicuous consumption and display. Power was "performed" in order to impress one's peers as well as the dependent or subjugated population. About the most ruthless and ostentatious of these figures, grotesque and gruesome legends arose—sometimes with more than a grain of truth to them.

In the west the periods when local notables most resemble voivodes occur, not surprisingly, when central power breaks down—France in the Hundred Years War, for example. Dracula, or Vlad III Țepeș of Walachia (*d.* 1476), was a voivode of Walachia in Romania, and the Breton Gilles de Rais, or Bluebeard (1404–1440), was a westerner whose life and afterlife fit the type.

BIBLIOGRAPHY

There is no specialized comprehensive study in English of the term "voivode" in its various usages in central, eastern, and southeastern Europe, but most of the major dictionaries established on historical principles provide valuable examples of usages.

WILLIAM CHESTER JORDAN

VOYTECH. See **Adalbert, St.**

WALLACE, WILLIAM (?–1305), a leader in the Scottish fight against English occupation under Edward I. In the spring of 1286, the king of Scotland, Alexander III, died leaving behind a troubled succession. By 1292, one of the claimants, John Balliol, had gathered enough support to claim the crown. His success, however, was occurring in the shadow of Edward I of England's claims to overlordship over Scotland. Barely had the new king been crowned when Edward made such onerous demands on him that John had little choice but to refuse if Scottish independence was to be maintained. In 1296, war broke out, and almost immediately the Scottish side began to feel the superiority of English arms, highlighted by the capture of John himself at the Battle of Dunbar and his subsequent imprisonment in the Tower of London. English armies followed up their victories by occupying much of Scotland. The ravages of the English soldiers, however, hardened the resolve of the Scots to remove them, and much of this resolve coalesced around the figure of a young member of the lesser aristocracy named William Wallace.

Poor records and myths shroud Wallace's life before the war. He may have been a vassal of the great noble James the Stewart, but even this is not certain. The English invasion of 1296 lifted Wallace from obscurity, as he emerged as the leader of a popular movement in southern Scotland challenging English oppression. In May 1297, Wallace slew the sheriff of Lanark, signaling the beginning of the revolt—popular legend claimed that Wallace was avenging the execution by the English of his love Marion Bradfute.

During the summer of 1297, Wallace's ranks continued to swell, and he began to harass and drive out the occupying English forces. In September, in conjunction with Andrew de Moray, who was leading a similar revolt in the north, Wallace and his forces dealt Edward's Scottish aspirations a blow when they crushed an English army at Stirling Bridge. He followed up the victory with an invasion of Northumbria on the English side of the border. His success prompted the Scottish nobles to knight Wallace and to appoint him as guardian of Scotland, acting as regent on behalf of the imprisoned King John. In this capacity, Wallace made treaties, issued writs, distributed land, and even appointed a new bishop of St. Andrews.

By the following summer, however, Edward had raised another powerful army that he personally led north, routing Wallace and the Scots at Falkirk. Wallace escaped with a few men and resigned the guardianship. For the following seven years he continued to wage a guerrilla war on the English as they tried to consolidate their gains in Scotland. Some reports suggest that during this time he may have gone to France and perhaps even to visit the pope. In 1305, extensive (and expensive) English efforts to capture Wallace came to fruition as he was captured near Glasgow. He was taken to London, tried as an outlaw and a traitor, and beheaded, his head placed above London Bridge.

His death, however, did not diminish his fame, and legends about his deeds and personal traits soon began to replace the historical facts. His legend received a boost in the fifteenth century when Blind Harry, a minstrel, wrote a lengthy and barely historical poem about his life. The historical Wallace disappeared further in 1995 with the release of the film *Braveheart*.

BIBLIOGRAPHY

Barrow, G. W. S. *Robert Bruce and the Community of the Realm of Scotland.* 3d ed. Edinburgh: Edinburgh University Press, 1988.

Keen, Maurice Hugh. *The Outlaws of Medieval Legend.* London: Routledge and Kegan Paul, 1961.

Reese, Peter. *Wallace: A Biography.* Edinburgh: Canongate, 1996.

JARBEL RODRIGUEZ

[See also **DMA:** Edward I of England; Robert I of Scotland; Scotland: History; Treason.]

WENCESLAS, ST. (*ca.* 907–929). Born near Prague around the year 907, Wenceslas (Václav) was heir to the principality of Bohemia. His childhood was marked by his own mother's alleged murder of his Christian grandmother, (later St.) Ludmilla. When precisely Wenceslas inherited the throne is in doubt, but it is certain that Dragomir (Drahomíra), his pagan mother, ruled in his name until at least 924 or 925, whereupon the adolescent boy took power, probably with the support of his more important Christian nobles. He himself was Christian, but Bohemia was deeply divided along confessional lines, and paganism was very strong. The challenge of completing the conversion of Bohemia excited his support of Catholic missions in the country, which issued mostly from his powerful neighbor, Germany.

The relations of Bohemian nobles with the Frankish aristocracy had often been mutually beneficial, with the Bohemians allying with various German lineages in order to stabilize their own power and enrich themselves through contacts with the wider central and western European Christian world. These relationships, however, were established on the principle that Bohemia was one of the subordinate members in a loose confederation of duchies. Primacy lay in the early tenth century with Henry I the Fowler, king of Germany (r. 919–936), whose power really rested on his control of Saxony. His reign was a long process of reducing the duchies, like Swabia and Bavaria, to subordination, and he tried to do the same, though not always successfully, to his Danish, Slavic, and Magyar neighbors.

Relations between Henry I and the Bohemian nobility became fractious in 929, and the king felt obliged to put down the "rebellion" by force. Wenceslas's attempt to save the situation by assuming the traditional role of subordination to the Saxon ruler did allow the rebellion to be crushed, but his gesture also had an unexpected effect. It is almost certain that Wenceslas's earlier support of German missionaries in Bohemia and his continual efforts to spread Christianity among the pagan nobility and their subjects combined with his submission to Henry to precipitate a coup. His own brother Bolesław was a party to the plot and in fact carried out the brutal murder (that Wenceslas was hacked to death is perhaps a martyrological convention). The deed took place directly in front of the church where Wenceslas was intending to hear mass, a detail that also seems too nice to be quite true. In any case, Bolesław, who was destined for a long reign of more than thirty years, appears to have been remorseful, and he had his brother's body translated to Prague in 932. Miracles, which had commenced at the site of Wenceslas's slaying, continued in Prague. The church of St. Vitus, where "Good King Wenceslas" (the hero of the nineteenth-century carol) was interred, became one of the greatest Catholic shrines in central Europe. The martyr is considered the patron saint of Bohemia. His feast day is 28 September.

BIBLIOGRAPHY

Dvornik, Francis. *The Life of Saint Wenceslas.* Prague: State Printing Office, 1929. The best English-language discussion of Wenceslas's life and rule.

WILLIAM CHESTER JORDAN

[See also **DMA:** Bohemia-Moravia; Martyrology.]

WIDOWHOOD. The widow is a ubiquitous figure in medieval society, but even the briefest analysis shows a considerable diversity in how widows lived their lives or were viewed by the law, custom, or religion across time and between different cultures or levels of society. Though widows tend to be more visible than wives in documentary records, some widows are more visible than others, and many are comparatively invisible. Any discussion of widowhood, moreover, is complicated by the tendency for those who have written on the subject either to characterize widows as vulnerable and impoverished or as empowered and "liberated." The widow's experience is not so easily characterized—the widow begging alms coexisted with the powerful noble or royal dowager. It is nevertheless possible to explore issues relating to differing cultural perspectives on widows, the material welfare of widows, and widow remarriage.

CONTRASTING CULTURAL PATTERNS

The society of southern or Mediterranean Europe placed particular emphasis on the "honor" of women, understood in terms of sexual reputation. Within this broad cultural context brides were expected to be virgins, wives chaste, and widows celibate. Widow remarriage was frowned upon, and only some young widows would normally have remarried. Given that this cultural region was characterized, possibly from Roman times, by a significant age gap between spouses, with the man some ten years or more the senior of his bride, it follows that the population of widows was quite substantial. Widows were considered to belong to their natal families and so were not considered the responsibility of the families into which they had been married. Although some later medieval evidence suggests that groups of well-born widows may have lived together following a devout life, most widows were expected to either return to their natal families, usually without their children, or support themselves as well as they could from their dowry. Many dowries, however, would have been insufficient, and there were in any case difficulties in persuading the late husband's family to return the value of dowry, especially where it had been invested in the family business. Numbers of widows lost out and were obliged to work as unpaid servants in return for their employer's support when they ceased to be able to continue working. Nevertheless, a small proportion of households were in fact headed by widows, though this was more marked in urban than rural communities. Some urban widows were supported or at least assisted by alms from confraternities such as the wealthy Florentine guild of Or San Michele that identified poor widows as an especially deserving cause. In Reconquest Spain grown-up children were expected to provide for their widowed mothers where necessary, although the need to reinforce this in law would suggest such aid could not be counted on.

We know from English legal records that in peasant society widows enjoyed customary rights of dower whereby they would have use of a third and sometimes half of the land their husbands had previously held. These "customary" arrangements are clearly of some antiquity, but they were limited protection. In the land-hungry years of the thirteenth and early fourteenth centuries, when average holdings tended to contract in size, the widow's third might not offer any real livelihood. Moreover, because the widow did not have title to the tenancy as such, merely a life interest in the dower part, she could sometimes face real difficulties in asserting her rights over resentful heirs. Over the same period, villein (servile) widows with more substantial dower rights sometimes found themselves pressed by their lords to remarry, taking as their new husbands younger men anxious to obtain land and willing to pay the lord a substantial marriage fine (*merchet*) and entry fine for the privilege. It is against these pressures that we find a growing tendency for husbands to provide for their wives by renegotiating the title to their tenancies by having their lord regrant it in the name of both husband and wife. This jointure arrangement guaranteed the widow full control over the entire holding without her having to ask within the customary court and even allowed her to sell the holding or take it with her into a new marriage if she so wanted, even if this disinherited any heir. Another way in which peasant husbands provided for wives as widows was to arrange for the transfer of their holding premortem to a younger generation, perhaps a married daughter or sometimes even someone unrelated—and again sometimes to the loss of any heir—in return for maintenance in form of living accommodation, clothing, fuel, and regular supplies of food. Such arrangements would continue until the widow's eventual demise and, if registered in the manor court, could be enforced in case of dispute. In the era following the Black Death such maintenance agreements may have become less common, and numbers of older widows appear instead to have supported themselves either by retaining the labor of older children—there is a particular tendency for widows to live with older daughters—or by employing live-in servants. The proportion of peasant holdings controlled by widows probably increased after the plague, and this may suggest that society was more accepting of women as property holders and heads of households. Much the same point may be made of later medieval urban society in much of northwestern Europe, particularly in relation to the widows of artisans managing their own workshops. Here widows were often able to take over workshops from their late husbands and continue to run businesses, train apprentices, and be recognized as members of their craft guild or as burgesses or citizens within their respective communities. It is only by the later fifteenth century that we find increasing social pressure, sometimes formalized in actual guild ordinances, for such widows to surrender workshops. This pressure goes hand in hand with a more general marginalization of women within the economy and a growing trend for males only to be employed in craft workshops.

Two points follow. Just as male workers were increasingly reluctant to work alongside females or to work under a female employer, so women and widows found their role increasingly consigned to "the domestic." Widows might thus become more dependent on earning a sometimes precarious livelihood from work activities that were an extension of their domestic identity, such as by spinning, laundry work, sewing, and selling ale, or by marrying again, especially when they had young children to support. The widow of an artisan, prevented by social convention and even sometimes guild regulation from continuing the business in her own right, might opt to marry her apprentice to retain de facto control of the workshop, but her action could be construed as subversive of the "natural" order and hence open to ridicule or worse at the hands of groups of young men. For lower echelons of both urban and rural society, the lot of the widow was probably even harder. As in Byzantium and in southern Europe, however, the poor widow was identified as a legitimate object of charity, and the period saw a proliferation of almshouses, some of which catered especially to poor women, most of whom would presumably have been widowed. After the grain harvest in peasant society, the poor widow's right to glean was protected by custom. It was also poor widows who were employed to prepare the bodies of the dead for burial.

Some other cultural and regional outlines may be suggested. Within northern Jewish society from the High Middle Ages, a widow from a more well-to-do background enjoyed a degree of security from her rights to her *ketubbah,* in effect, a substantial portion of her late husband's assets. She would have guardianship over her children, so long as they were underage, and might continue her late husband's trade. Numbers of Jewish widows, however, chose moneylending as an effective way of turning the *ketubbah* into a regular source of income. (Moneylending was also sometimes practiced by gentile peasant widows, no doubt for much the same reason.) Jewish custom permitted the remarriage of widows, but poorer widows, though particularly identified as objects of charity, were, as elsewhere, probably particularly likely to remain single and to face growing hardship in old age. Wherever a multiple or complex householding system may have prevailed, as in parts of the Balkans and perhaps more widely within Slavic society, older widows would have been supported by the wider kin group, but the headship of the household passed from husband to son and would invariably have bypassed the widow. Younger widows would no doubt have contributed to the broad range of tasks defined as "women's work."

REMARRIAGE

The propensity of widows to remarry or remain single varied enormously between cultures and across time. As already noticed, some cultures disapproved of the remarriage of widows, preferring, as in Byzantine society, to identify the widow as a worthy object of charity. Even where the remarriage of widows was socially acceptable, as in Germanic or Islamic society, only some widows would have actually preferred to remarry. In feudal societies, however, the temptation for kings, lords, or even male kin to marry off landed widows for political or economic gain was great. In England the custom of widows being allowed a year's mourning before they might contemplate remarriage can be traced back to at least the early eleventh century. Such customs protected widows from pressure to remarry immediately. To retreat into a nunnery or to take vows of chastity were more certain ways by which well-to-do widows were able to opt out of a second marriage. Where remarriage tended to be frowned upon, as in Byzantium, entry into the religious life was actively promoted. The chaste widow leading a devout life within the world was a paradigm that had its roots in the early church. In later medieval England numbers of gentry and a few mercantile widows but also higher-status women became vowesses, adopting sober dress and a devout lifestyle while remaining within secular society, often as affluent dowagers. Much the same is true of the Florentine *pinzochere*. In this way they were able to protect themselves from familial pressures to remarry, from accusations of unchastity, and perhaps also from political intrigue. Such options hardly existed for lower-status women, although such widows probably faced less pressure to remarry. Widows with young children were perhaps most anxious to find a new husband, but it was wealthy merchants' widows who were most attractive to men, and it is at this level of society that women who were widowed more than once may sometimes be found. A like propensity for wealthier widows

to remarry has been described within the Jewish communities of late medieval Umbria. Here the occasional widow even converted in order to marry a gentile suitor.

Widows of laborers and the landless were perhaps least likely to remarry and were the most vulnerable to extreme hardship. It is certainly possible to find examples of such poor widows begging alms, hawking cheap goods, or doing odd jobs. In the hungry decades before the Black Death, some are even described dying of exposure. In towns it is sometimes possible to find groups of women living in close proximity to one another, perhaps for reasons of sociability, perhaps for security, sometimes even for devotional reasons. Although it is rarely possible to determine marital status, such women are more likely to be widowed than never married. Although poor widows were often identified as appropriate objects of almsgiving and even of institutional provision, it does not follow that the widow was always the object of sympathy or pity. The targeting of poor widows as witches belongs to a later era, but the older widow was subject to a long tradition of misogynistic suspicion and disparagement, as is reflected in the literary tradition of the old hag, such as La Vieille from the *Roman de la Rose*. The wider conclusion must be that widowhood was often a time of increasing hardship and that notions of widows' "liberation" are to no small extent anachronisms.

BIBLIOGRAPHY

Burguière, André, et al., ed. *A History of the Family.* Volume 1: *Distant Worlds, Ancient Worlds.* Translated by Sarah Hanbury Tenison, Rosemary Morris, and Andrew Wilson. Cambridge, U.K.: Polity Press, 1996.

Goldberg, P. J. P., ed. *Woman Is a Worthy Wight: Women in English Society c. 1200–1500.* Stroud, U.K., and Wolfeboro Falls, N.H.: Alan Sutton, 1992.

Klapisch-Zuber, Christiane. *Women, Family, and Ritual in Renaissance Florence.* Translated by Lydia Cochrane. Chicago: University of Chicago Press, 1985.

Mate, Mavis E. *Women in Medieval English Society.* Cambridge, U.K.: Cambridge University Press, 1999.

Walker, Sue Sheridan, ed. *Wife and Widow in Medieval England.* Ann Arbor: University of Michigan Press, 1993.

P. J. P. GOLDBERG

[See also **DMA:** Family, Byzantine; Family and Family Law, Jewish; Family and Marriage, Western European; **Supp:** Marriage, Christian; Women.]

WILLIAM OF DROGHEDA (*d.* 1245), the foremost English canon lawyer of the earlier thirteenth century

and author of the unfinished *Summa aurea* (*ca.* 1239), a manual of English ecclesiastical practice.

The circumstances of William's education and early career are not known, nor is there evidence about his connection with the Irish market town by which he is identified. But charter evidence suggests a familial connection with Hampshire. The same evidence and the text of the *Summa* itself place William in Oxford, where he taught, practiced as an advocate, and perhaps had studied. As for his skills as an advocate, the chronicler Matthew Paris relates that William of Montpellier, whose election to the see of Coventry and Lichfield was contested, dropped his litigation on learning that his lawyer William had died.

As a procedural manual, the *Summa aurea* was learned, up-to-date, technical, and devoid of jurisprudential concerns. It was a practical text addressing such matters as the formulary to be used in commencing suits against different defendants, the appointment, qualifications, and obligations of advocates, defense tactics, contumacy, legal fees, and the role of judges delegate and ordinary, assessors, and arbitrators. In collecting libel formulas, the *Summa* borrowed from Roffredus de Epiphaniis of Benevento but also offered shrewd tactical advice and pleading tips, for which it was praised a century later by Johannes Andreae. Yet with the advent of notarial practice in England around 1280, the *Summa* was superseded.

F. W. Maitland, the first modern scholar to study the *Summa* systematically, reprinted excerpts but concluded that "what we have of his work is perhaps too fragmentary and too technical to deserve an edition in the England of today"; elsewhere, citing William, he said that "England produced no canonist of first-rate rank." In response H. G. Richardson suggested that "one can well understand that a fastidiously upright man [Maitland] might be repelled by the none-too-honest devices which William of Drogheda regarded as a matter of course." Maitland notwithstanding, Ludwig Wahrmund published a modern edition of the *Summa* in 1914.

Maitland used the *Summa aurea* largely to support his argument that medieval English canon law became tied to Rome, for the *Summa* assumed that, as S. E. Thorne put it, "all large and much small litigation will be brought in the first instance to a court constituted for the occasion by a papal *breve*," rather than to the local ordinary. But William's work was only a small part of Maitland's argument, and because discussion of English practice necessarily focused on William Lyndwood's *Provinciale* (first published *ca.* 1483–1485), William of Drogheda escaped being made a major figure in the debate about the autonomy of the English church.

The *Summa* could not as easily escape the debates over the influences on and composition of Henry de Bracton's treatise *De legibus Angliae*. Here, Bracton's apparent use of William's *Summa,* both as model for a suitable introduction and as illustration of church procedures, was used to argue for the breadth of Bracton's Roman learning and against an early date of composition. More recent scholarship has broadened the inquiry from Bracton to the flourishing networks of civil and canon law jurists in Oxford and elsewhere, of whom Vacarius and William of Drogheda are only the best known.

William's *Summa* enjoyed longevity, but its author was not so fortunate. Matthew Paris's reference to William's tragic death alluded to his murder at the hands of his squire around 1245, by which time William probably had already abandoned work on his treatise.

BIBLIOGRAPHY

Helmholz, Richard H. *Canon Law and the Law of England.* London: Hambledon, 1987. Uses William of Drogheda's text in examining impartiality.

Maitland, Frederic William. "William of Drogheda and the Universal Ordinary." *English Historical Review* 12 (1897): 625–658. The leading work on William and his text.

Richardson, H. G. "Azo, Drogheda, and Bracton." *English Historical Review* 59 (1944): 22–47. Discusses the relationship of William and his *Summa* to Bracton.

Salter, H. E., ed. *Cartulary of the Abbey of Eynsham.* Vol. 2. Oxford: Clarendon, for the Oxford Historical Society, 1908. Pages 174–176 provide an account of William's death.

Sayers, Jane E. *Law and Records in Medieval England: Studies on the Medieval Papacy, Monasteries, and Records.* London: Variorum, 1988. Uses William of Drogheda's text in examining canon law procedure.

Thorne, S. E. *Essays in English Legal History.* London: Hambledon, 1985. Pages 51–59 and 93–110 are relevant to William of Drogheda and Henry de Bracton.

William of Drogheda. "Summa Aurea." In *Quellen zür Geschichte des Romisch-Kanonischen Processes im Mittelalter.* Vol. 2. Edited by Ludwig Wahrmund. Innsbruck, Austria: 1914.

Zulueta, F. de. "William of Drogheda." In *Mélanges de Droit Romain dédiés a Georges Cornil.* Edited by Paul Collinet and Fernand de Visscher. Vol. 2. Ghent, Belgium: Vanderpoorten, 1926. Best survey of William's life and text.

JONATHAN A. BUSH

[See also **DMA:** Bracton, Henry de; Law, Canon: After Gratian; Matthew Paris; Roffredus de Epiphaniis of Benevento; Vacarius.]

WILLIAM OF ST. AMOUR (1200–1272) was born in the southern French town from which he takes his surname. A canonist and theologian who studied at the University of Paris, he also taught philosophy and theology there. He was admired for his intellectual and administrative abilities and was honored by his elevation to the dignity of dean of the masters of theology around the mid-thirteenth century. He would be well known as a philosopher, owing to his book *On the Prior and Posterior Analytics,* a commentary on Aristotle's logical works, but his oeuvre as a professional scholar was eclipsed by his central and obsessive involvement in the struggle between mendicant friars and secular masters at the university in the 1250s and 1260s.

It is no surprise that the Dominicans would want a foot in the university faculty at Paris, the intellectual center of theological studies in Europe. Founded to be an order of brothers well-trained in doctrine in order that they might confute, through their preaching and missionary work, heretical and ignorant interpretations of scripture, the Dominicans had emphasized education from their very inception. It is somewhat more surprising that the Franciscans, with their stress on simplicity and exemplary evangelical living, came to see higher education as important to their training or the articulation of their theology. (In fact, there were divisions in the order on this and many other points.) Nonetheless, the Franciscans needed, like the Dominicans, to be able to counter badly informed interpretations of scripture, and as they were drawn into the bureaucracy of the church, they required the kind of education that made advancement possible.

For several reasons William of St. Amour found the mendicant friars' presence at the university distasteful and their very existence dangerous. His critique in part spoke to the concern of other secular masters and would-be masters that the mendicant friars were becoming competitors for plum positions and were refusing to join and accept the direction of the Masters' Guild. The fact that many Franciscans idolized their founder as the herald of a new spiritual age and that the mystical theology of the Calabrian monk Joachim of Fiore was employed in defense of this view also irritated William, for he regarded the anti-institutional bent of Joachim's theology as heterodox.

William succeeded in 1254 in persuading the pope to suspend the mendicant masters from preaching and to limit their number, when they resumed, to one for each of the two orders. In December 1254, however, a new pope, Alexander IV, thought better of some of these policies. Enraged at this turn of events, William spoke,

sermonized, and wrote against the mendicant orders and criticized the French royal family who patronized them. As far as he was concerned, the friars were drummer boys for the coming Antichrist (*Liber de Antichristo et eiusdem ministris,* 1255). The pope reacted with equal vigor to this activity, placed William under censure in 1256, including suspension from his diaconal, teaching, and clerical dignities, with the ultimate threat being expulsion from the university and the kingdom.

William formally capitulated by promising an episcopal commission that had been set up to investigate his works in 1256 to remove all errors, but he nonetheless enlisted the support of other secular masters at the university in the publication of a diatribe against the mendicant orders that included subversive aspersions on the king's favor towards them (*De periculis novissimorum temporum,* 1256). Alexander had had enough, and he denounced the *De periculis* as error-ridden, a judgment he later confirmed despite William's efforts to have him lift it. Expulsion from the university and exile from France followed in 1257.

Many years later, in 1266, Pope Clement IV (King Louis IX's close friend, but a southerner like William) allowed the exiled professor to return to St. Amour on condition that he make no further public denunciations of the mendicant orders. He lived the remainder of his life in uneventful circumstances, dying in September 1272. His antifraternal works, however, continued to be pillaged for arguments against the mendicant orders, certain versions of their theology (particularly as embodied in spiritual Franciscanism), and their alleged hypocrisy in getting around their vow of apostolic poverty.

BIBLIOGRAPHY

Douie, Decima L. *The Conflict between the Seculars and the Mendicants at the University of Paris in the Thirteenth Century: A Paper Read to the Aquinas Society of London on 22nd June, 1949.* London: Blackfriars, 1954.

Dufeil, Michel-Marie. *Guillaume de Saint-Amour et la polémique universitaire parisienne, 1250–1259.* Paris: A. et. J. Picard, 1972.

Perrod, Maurice. *Étude sur la vie et sur les oeuvres de Guillaume de Saint-Amour.* Lons-le-Saunier: L. Declume, 1902.

WILLIAM CHESTER JORDAN

[See also **DMA:** Dominicans; Franciscans; Joachim of Fiore; Paris, University of.]

WILLIAM II (RUFUS) OF ENGLAND, KING (*b.* 1056; *r.* 1087–1100). Of William the Conqueror's four sons and the three who lived long enough to have a significant influence on Anglo-Norman politics, William "Rufus" (he of the ruddy complexion) is the most enigmatic. Trusted by his father as a consequence of his firm support when other family members tried to encroach on the Conqueror's power, Rufus was designated his successor in England, even though the king did not disinherit his eldest son, Robert Curthose, duke of Normandy. Some statements attributed to Rufus in various sources make him appear a religious skeptic or at least hostile to the Catholic faith; yet for two or three months in 1093, when he thought he was dying, he made promises and carried through on ecclesiastical appointments that suggest a genuine, if fear-motivated, religiosity. No sooner had he recovered than he resumed his old habits. His often tense relations with the church, especially with Archbishop Anselm of Canterbury, one of the appointees of 1093, disposed many contemporary ecclesiastical and non-ecclesiastical authors to write against him. That all the charges they levied are true, including the alleged sexual orientation of this bachelor king, may be doubted. Relentless in his exaction of fiscal resources from his subjects, he was also extremely openhanded to those in his circle, many of whom were fiercely loyal to him.

Three issues dominated William Rufus's reign—the hostility of the Celtic principalities north and west, the status of Normandy, and the liberty of the church. The first was intractable despite what seems like effective action in Rufus's time. Repeatedly English and Scottish forces squared off in small battles and sieges or raided each other's territories. At times, large royal armies or baronial contingents on both sides, acting as surrogates, engaged in more widespread violence. The same was true, mutatis mutandis, of the English encounter with the Welsh. The balance sheet was clearly in favor of the English in their struggles with both in Rufus's reign, but claims that the Welsh were pacified or that the Scots accepted English overlordship, while true, rest on ephemeral successes. William Rufus achieved no definitive pacification of Wales, and claims to English overlordship over the kingdom of Scotland remained contested.

As for Normandy, from the beginning of his reign in England, William coveted Normandy, his desire fueled perhaps by that of barons holding lands on both sides of the Channel. William exploited numerous pretexts to intervene in Norman affairs. His brother, Robert, resisted him ineffectually but also sometimes encouraged the intervention, because the third brother, Henry, also seemed disappointed in the Conqueror's settlement and wanted to reconfigure the holding of lands. In the course of the period from soon after his accession in En-

gland until 1096, William steadily encroached on Robert's power in the duchy. In 1096 he translated power into authority by lending money to Robert to go on the First Crusade. Robert's pledge was the duchy itself, which thus passed to Rufus's rule. That the transfer of authority was intended to be temporary was Robert's understanding, although the sources are inconsistent or uninformative on how long it was supposed to last.

The re-creation of an Anglo-Norman domain by Robert's pledge to William occasioned the king's wider involvement in continental politics. He attempted to re-enact his father's territorial policies by reconquering the county of Maine and by wresting the Vexin (the Norman-French borderlands) from the Capetians. He had designs, too, on the lands around Poitou, expecting that he might receive them in pledge when their ruler went on crusade. This expectation was not vain. Magnates in west-central France were often in conflict with their Capetian overlords, and William had allied with them for his own benefit. These magnates could not have anticipated that the agreements worked out between William and Robert would fail to be respected by the former. Rather, those agreements looked like a promising strategy for cash-strapped lords seeking to join the crusade.

The crusade was occasioned by a sermon preached in November 1095 by Pope Urban II in Clermont in southern France. Urban's situation was not entirely secure. There was another claimant to the papal throne supported by the German emperor, because Urban represented the so-called Gregorian reform party that, among other things, opposed the emperor's investiture of prelates. William's archbishop of Canterbury identified with the reformers and did so with greater and greater enthusiasm over the course of his archiepiscopate. He expressed the wish to acknowledge Urban II as the true pope several months before the famous sermon at Clermont, but William regarded an independent acknowledgement as an infringement on royal prerogatives, and Anselm did not receive the support he had hoped for from senior churchmen.

After increasing numbers of European nobles vowed to go on crusade, however, the prestige of Urban's pontificate gained in prominence. (Even William Rufus informally negotiated with him as if he were the true pope.) Anselm pressed his cause once more in October 1097, but William cautioned the archbishop that if he left the realm to do obeisance to Urban, he would be doing so at the risk of the crown's seizure of the temporal income of the see of Canterbury. This lucrative source of revenue for the crown—legitimate during the vacancy following any bishop's death or resignation but subject to abuse—was often collected from various sees Rufus kept vacant. Anselm decided nonetheless to depart. He did not return to England until after Rufus's death in the year 1100; the temporalities of Canterbury were accounted to the royal treasury in the interim.

No long-lasting solutions to the Welsh and Scottish problems, the conflicts with the Capetians, the disposition of Normandy after Robert's return, or the dispute with Anselm were achieved in Rufus's lifetime. In the year 1100, while still a relatively young man, perhaps a little over forty (he was born between 1056 and 1060), he was killed in a hunting accident in the New Forest. The hunting party dispersed immediately, and the king's brother, Henry, rode off to Winchester to seize the royal treasure and soon thereafter arranged for his own coronation as Henry I. In his coronation proclamation or charter, he blackened his brother's memory with notice of his alleged misdeeds and promised good government and generous treatment of the church. That no one was prosecuted for William's death has given rise to speculation as to whether "accident" is a misnomer for the cause of the king's death. Rustics took William's body to Winchester the day after he died, and without benefit of formal obsequies, he was interred in the cathedral.

BIBLIOGRAPHY

Barlow, Frank. *William Rufus.* London: Methuen, 1983. The standard biography.

Golding, Brian. *Conquest and Colonisation: The Normans in Britain, 1066–1100.* New York: St. Martin's Press, 1994. Places Rufus's reign in a broad context.

WILLIAM CHESTER JORDAN

[See also **DMA:** Anselm of Canterbury, St.; Crusades and Crusader States: To 1192; Henry I of England; Urban II, Pope; William I of England.]

WILLIAM I OF SICILY, KING (called Guglielmo il Malo [William the Bad]) (*ca.* 1120–1166). The youngest son of Roger II, William inherited the throne to become the second Norman king of Sicily after the premature deaths of his three older brothers. William's family, the Hautevilles, had come to southern Italy in the early eleventh century from Normandy, and through intermarriage with the Lombard aristocracy, exploitation of local conflict, and a tempestuous alliance with the papacy, managed to conquer southern Italy and Sicily in the course of two generations. In 1151, when William was approximately thirty years old, he was crowned coruler with his father. Although his older brothers had partici-

pated in governing the kingdom alongside their father, William did not take an active role in ruling Taranto, where he had been prince since *ca.* 1140, nor in the other principalities with which he was subsequently invested. His father's death in February 1154 left him the sole ruler. In the summer of 1155, William faced an invasion by a combined papal-Byzantine army, as well as a baronial revolt. By the treaty of Constance (1153), Holy Roman Emperor Frederick I Barbarossa was obliged to help the papacy against William, but Frederick's barons refused to accompany him to Italy. After recovering from a serious illness in the winter, William led his army against the invaders and rebels in the spring of 1156, defeating both. He negotiated an agreement (the Concordat of Benevento) with Pope Adrian IV the same year, in which he recognized the papacy as overlord, while Adrian confirmed him as king and recognized him as apostolic legate for Sicily. William soon became the protector of the papacy against Barbarossa, who sought to control both the papacy and southern Italy and sponsored the election of an antipope in 1159. While succeeding in Italy, William lost control over the North African ports conquered by his father, losing Tripoli, Mahdia (al-Mahdīya), and Sfax by 1160.

Another aristocratic revolt in 1160 succeeded in killing William's chief minister, Maio of Bari, and temporarily seizing the king and the royal family. The rebellion was accompanied by widespread attacks on Muslim communities throughout Sicily, which were usually under royal protection. These massacres may have prompted the geographer al-Idrīsī and other Muslim intellectuals to flee Sicily. With the help of his Muslim soldiers, the Latin bishops, and the citizens of Palermo, William escaped and defeated the rebels, but his eldest son, Roger, was killed in the revolt. The death of Maio also brought to end the era of the single chief minister, often called the *ammiratus* (or *amiratus*), who controlled the royal administration. Instead, William entrusted the government to a group of three *familiares regis,* who were usually Latin bishops and aristocrats but also included converted Muslim palace officials. William died on 7 May 1166, leaving behind two sons who were still minors—William II, his heir, and Henry, whom he made prince of Capua—as well as his wife, Margaret of Navarre (married *ca.* 1150), who became regent for young William.

The contemporary chronicler Hugo Falcandus considered William I a "bad" king, since he left important decisions to his ministers and abandoned himself to the luxuries of Palermo. Certainly, William was a less capable ruler than his father, but he also had to confront the aristocratic resentments that had built up over the course of his father's reign. Despite the baronial revolts and the death of Maio of Bari, the royal government maintained its authority and financial solvency.

BIBLIOGRAPHY

Loud, G. A. "William the Bad or William the Unlucky? Kingship in Sicily, 1154–1166." *Haskins Society Journal* 8 (1998): 99–113.

Matthew, Donald. *The Norman Kingdom of Sicily.* Cambridge, U.K., and New York: Cambridge University Press, 1992.

Pio, Berardo. *Guglielmo I d'Altavilla: Gestione del potere e lotta politica nell'Italia normanna: 1154–1169.* Bologna: Pàtron, 1996.

Takayama, Hiroshi. *The Administration of the Norman Kingdom of Sicily.* Leiden, Netherlands, and New York: E. J. Brill, 1993.

CHRISTOPHER HATCH MACEVITT

[See also **DMA:** Adrian IV, Pope; Frederick I Barbarossa; Roger II of Sicily; Sicily, Kingdom of.]

WILLIAM II OF SICILY, KING (called Guglielmo il Buono [William the Good]) (*ca.* 1154–1189), third in the line of the Norman kings of Sicily, succeeded to the throne of Sicily following the death of his father William I on 7 May 1166. Because William was still a minor, his mother, Margaret of Navarre, served as regent until William turned nineteen in 1172. She initially entrusted the government to Qa'id Peter, a eunuch and former Muslim who had been one of the chief ministers in her husband's administration. After only a few months, Qa'id Peter fled to Tunis, and Count Richard of Molise took over. The queen's cousin Stephen of Perche succeeded him in 1167 but fled the following year after riots broke out. This administrative instability ceased in 1169 when Gualterio (Walter) Offamilio, William II's tutor, became archbishop of Palermo and chief minister. After having been exiled for participating in a revolt in 1161, William's illegitimate cousin Tancred returned to Sicily under Margaret's regency and was made count of Lecce in 1169.

William came of age in 1172, but Offamilio remained the chief minister throughout his reign. Despite its rocky beginning, William's reign was peaceful and prosperous. Later generations named him "the Good," while his father received the epithet "the Bad." Although not particularly pious, William II built many churches, including the impressive Benedictine monastery at Monreale, with its magnificent mosaics in the Byzantine style. The monastery became an archbishopric, though only five miles from Palermo. William also built on the out-

William II Presenting Church to the Virgin Mary. *This mosaic is from the monastery church of Monreale, one of William's most famous endowments.* © SCALA/ART RESOURCE, NY.

skirts of Palermo the palaces known as the "Cuba" and the "Zisa," which were Islamic-style pleasure palaces with gardens and fountains.

The Byzantine emperor Manuel I Komnenos proposed that William marry his daughter Maria in 1172, an opportunity William accepted. Manuel, however, changed his mind, and when William traveled to Bari to meet his bride, she was not there. With peace established between the papacy and the emperor Frederick I Barbarossa in 1177, William came to terms with the emperor as well, agreeing to the marriage of his young aunt, Constance, to Frederick's son Henry. This marriage had profound implications for Sicily, Italy, and much of western Christendom, for Constance's son Frederick II inherited Sicily, thus potentially uniting Italy as both Holy Roman Emperor and king of Sicily, a circumstance that horrified the papacy and engendered decades of conflict in Italy and Sicily in the thirteenth century. For William, however, it brought peace to Italy, leaving William free to focus on the Mediterranean, where the waning of Byzantine power left an opening William was keen to exploit. With Tancred of Lecce commanding the fleet, William attacked Alexandria in 1174. He turned his attention to Byzantium next, long the desideratum of the Norman kings, and in 1185 briefly captured Dyrrachium (Durazzo) and Thessaloniki, before being defeated. Although William did not join the Third Crusade as he had hoped, the Sicilian fleet participated, defeating a Turkish armada off the coast of Latakia. William died on 18 November 1189, leaving behind a widow, Joan of England (married 1177), sister of Richard I the Lionhearted, but no children. His designated successor was Constance, whose husband was now the emperor Henry VI, but Tancred of Lecce seized power and was crowned king.

BIBLIOGRAPHY

Enzensberger, Horst. "Der 'böse' und der 'gute' Wilhelm: Zur Kirchenpolitik der normannischen Könige von Sizilien nach dem Vertrag von Benevent (1156)." *Deutsches Archiv für Erforschung des Mittelalters* 36, no. 2 (1980): 385–432.

Matthew, Donald. *The Norman Kingdom of Sicily.* Cambridge, U.K., and New York: Cambridge University Press, 1992.

Romuald of Salerno. *Chronicon.* Edited by C. A. Garufi. Rerum italicarum scriptores, Vol. 7, pt. 1. Città di Castello/Bologna: S. Lapi, 1914–1935.

Takayama, Hiroshi. *The Administration of the Norman Kingdom of Sicily.* Leiden, Netherlands, and New York: E. J. Brill, 1993.

CHRISTOPHER HATCH MACEVITT

[See also **DMA:** Manuel I Komnenos; Sicily, Kingdom of; **Supp:** Henry VI of Germany, Emperor.]

WOMEN. Women's position in the Middle Ages had many dimensions. To gain a full picture requires examining their political power, economic importance, spiritual leadership, authority within the family, and cultural impact. The position of women varied across different time periods, geographical regions, ethnic or cultural backgrounds, and social statuses. Nevertheless, all women in the Middle Ages had a great deal in common; medieval texts usually categorized men by social status or occupation but women simply as "women" or by marital status (virgin, wife, or widow; any other possibility was unmentionable). In practice women's social and economic position might differ, but medieval writings tended to treat them as a group. Within any given subgroup in medieval society, the women's position tended to be subordinate to that of the men, and women performed many of the same tasks (child care, provision of food and clothing) across all of medieval society. Some of these similarities hold for Jewish and Muslim as well as Christian women. Because the vast majority of women in medieval Europe were Christian, this article focuses on them, but it occasionally notes differences among Jewish and Muslim women.

LAW

No medieval society offered women equality under the law, but none offered men equality either; it would have been an alien concept to medieval people that people who were manifestly different in status should be treated legally as though they were the same. Women did not serve as judges or jurors, local officials (with few exceptions), or legislators.

Different weights accorded to different individuals become obvious in rules about compensation found in early medieval law codes (for example, those of the Burgundians, the Salian Franks, and various Anglo-Saxon kingdoms). These laws prescribe compensation payments for killing or wounding another person. The amount of the payment varies not only by the nature of the injury but also by the status of the individual. For women the level of compensation varied, however, not only by social level (noble, free, or slave), as it did for men, but also by marital status: virgin, wife, or widow. In the Salic law, the compensation for a woman was the same as for a man of her social class, but if she was of childbearing age, the compensation tripled. A woman's value was related to her capacity for motherhood.

In practice people probably did not adhere strictly to the compensation levels set in the early medieval laws; they were merely guidelines for levels of monetary payment sufficient to ward off feud. They had less to do with the economic value of the individual than they did with honor. Harm to a person of the highest social level (especially by someone not of the same level) caused a greater loss of honor than harm to someone lower. In the case of a woman, not only she herself but also the man responsible for her—usually her father, brother, or husband—lost honor. Compensation payments for harm to women generally went not to the woman herself but to her male guardian, even in cases of rape; this was also true of compensation for harm to male dependents.

By the central Middle Ages in most parts of Europe, action by royal officials had replaced the compensation system found in early medieval law codes; fines for various offenses went to the crown rather than to the victim of the offense, and central or local authorities imposed other punishments. This meant that the social level or gender of the victim played less of an official role (although it may still have helped authorities decide which offenses to prosecute). Gender still made a difference to some crimes, like rape. It could also make a difference to punishments: different sorts of shame punishments and, sometimes, different means of capital punishments applied to men and women.

In early medieval laws, as in their Roman antecedents, a woman had a guardian, tutor, or *mundwald* who was responsible for her. Guardianship passed from father to husband upon the woman's marriage; in her widowhood a son or brother might serve as guardian. Under these laws a woman could not act legally for herself. By the central and later Middle Ages, however, many jurisdictions stipulated circumstances under which a woman could take legal action on her own behalf. Widows tended to have the most freedom of legal action; wives and never-married women often required the participation or at least consent of husband or father. These rights varied by whether a particular jurisdiction used common law (as in England), Roman law (as in many Mediterranean polities), or regional customary law. Legal records do show instances in which even married women became involved in legal action on their own.

It was difficult for a woman not only to bring a legal action on her own but even to testify in court. Some jurisdictions did not allow women's testimony except in particular kinds of cases—for example, in the case of a death in childbirth, which only women attended. It could make a big difference to inheritance whether the mother died before or after the child or indeed whether the child was born dead or born alive and then died (in England, for example, a widower had the right to a life interest in his wife's property only if a living child had been born from the marriage). Under Islamic law, women could testify in most cases, with two women's testimony valued as that of one man.

Outside the criminal law, most medieval law dealt with the inheritance and transfer of property. Again, this law varied between common law and Roman law jurisdictions, and between real property (land) and personal property (money and goods). Women in the Middle Ages could own property; even if a woman's husband had the right to control it during the marriage, it did not necessarily become his. Although in continental Europe land acquired during the marriage could be treated as communal, in England the property that each partner brought to the marriage never merged. Upon the death of one partner, the other might get a life interest in the dead partner's land or in a portion of it, but upon the

death of the second partner, the first partner's property would go to the heirs of the first partner, not of the second. This was not the case for personal property: under English common law the wife's personal property became the husband's upon marriage, and she did not get it back even after his death. Where there were children from the marriage the details of marital property law did not matter; they got the property whether it had originally belonged to their mother or their father. Stepchildren, however, inherited only from their birth parent, so for them it mattered whether that parent owned the property or not.

Under Jewish law, a married woman's rights to property were specified in her *ketubah*, or marriage contract. Jewish women, particularly in Ashkenaz (northwestern Europe), tended to bring a large dowry to their marriage; this acted as a safeguard against divorce, since the dowry would be difficult for the husband to repay, as was his obligation if he divorced her.

Christian women brought property into a marriage because of their dowry, but also sometimes because they themselves inherited property. Inheritance laws varied greatly across Europe. Much land was transmitted according to regional customs and could not be bequeathed according to the wishes of the donor. The most common rule for inheritance of land on the level of the aristocracy was primogeniture, in which all the land went to the eldest son. In some places the custom was partible inheritance, with the land divided among all sons. Nowhere did the law allocate a share in the patrimony to daughters if there was a surviving son. However, fathers often gave land before their death to sons and daughters, the latter usually as a dowry.

Inheritance customs differed greatly in what happened to the land if there were no sons. The difference depended not only on region but also on the type of land tenure. In some cases land went to the eldest daughter, in others (as in Norman England) it was divided among all daughters, thus creating more opportunities for profitable marriages, and in yet others most went to the nearest surviving male heir. Justification for the last rule, at least with regard to land held by military tenure, was that a woman could not be expected to do the military service required. In cases where women could inherit, their overlord might retain the right to approve or even choose a husband for them, for the same reason.

A widow inherited only a life interest in a husband's land or a portion of it, but she might actually wield active control of all of it as guardian of a minor child. A lord had a good deal of influence as to the choice of a guardian, but it was not at all uncommon for a woman, Christian or Jewish, to end up as guardian or one of several guardians of her children and actively manage the child's property during his or her minority.

Women who held property and wielded authority in medieval society tended to be widows, though scholars have cited them as examples of how women generally could hold power. Many widows, however, were left poor, and even if they did have property, they might easily fall victim to those who tried to dispossess them; without a powerful man to back them, they might be unable to exert effectively what legal rights they did have.

During a woman's marriage she usually had little control over what property she did own. Although the church supported a woman's right to make a will to dispose of her own personal property, under English law her goods were her husband's so she had nothing to bequeath. Even when a married woman had few formal rights, however, she might exercise effective control of her husband's property in his absence and might be legally recognized as his representative. In England, a married woman could operate a business as *femme sole,* as if she were unmarried; the advantage to her husband was that he would not be liable for her debts. Women who did not marry could operate independently in the same way.

Although it restricted women's opportunities, medieval law did not consider women the property of husbands. Laws, especially in the early Middle Ages, compensated men for damage to their wives in the same manner that they compensated them for damage to their slaves and livestock, but no medieval European legal system actually equated women with real or personal property. Even where (as in Scandinavia) a bride price was paid to a woman's family upon marriage, that purchase of a bride did not make her a slave: in fact the very payment of a bride price distinguished her from a slave concubine. Even when women's legal rights were quite limited compared with those of men, the law recognized that free women were persons—it did not always recognize for enslaved men and women as such.

ROYAL WOMEN

Rules of inheritance applied not only to land but also to titles. Two separate questions bore on royal inheritance: whether a woman could rule, and whether a woman could transmit the title to the throne. The answers varied in various parts of Europe. In England, for example, Matilda, daughter of Henry I (*r.* 1100–1135), ended up fighting a bloody civil war against her cousin Stephen (*r.* 1135–1154). The struggle was fought on the battlefield more than in the courts or in political theory,

and so there was not a great deal of discussion over whether a woman could rule; the war was eventually settled with a treaty making Matilda's son Stephen's heir (Henry II, *r.* 1154–1189). But it was quite clear that in England, a woman could transmit a claim to the throne. Stephen was the son of Henry I's sister, therefore the grandson of William the Conqueror in the female line. The issue arose again in the fifteenth century in the Wars of the Roses but once again was determined mainly on the basis of military power rather than argument about women's legal status.

On the other hand, legal arguments about the ability of women to inherit the crown became very important in France in the fourteenth century. The three sons of Philip the Fair (*r.* 1285–1314) died without male heirs; one of them left a daughter, but political rivals cast doubt on her legitimacy. Philip also had a daughter, Isabelle (1292–1358), and she had sons. However, it was politically highly undesirable that her descendants be able to inherit the kingdom of France, because she was married to Edward II of England (*r.* 1307–1327). Her descendants, starting with her son Edward III (*r.* 1327–1377), did indeed claim the throne of France by inheritance through Isabelle, resulting in the Hundred Years War. The French countered not just on the battlefield but also with learned legal arguments, claiming that the law of the Salic Franks declared that "no woman may inherit Salic land." They held that this barred women not only from inheriting lands and titles themselves but also from transmitting a claim to them to their male heirs.

In other places women's ability to inherit titles or a throne went largely unchallenged. In Spain, women did inherit the throne; Queen Urraca of Castile-León (*r.* 1109–1126) and Isabella of Castile (*r.* 1474–1504) are two examples (Isabella married Ferdinand of Aragon and thus joined the two crowns, but she ruled Castile in her own right). Eleanor of Aquitaine (1122–1204), the daughter of the deceased son of the duke of Aquitaine, was heiress of his title and lands; this, rather than her famous beauty and personality, are the real reasons the future kings of France and of England sought to marry her. Matilda of Tuscany (1046–1114), a countess in her own right, exerted great influence in the struggle between the papacy and the German Empire.

Queens wielded power as regents for their sons, either during their minority or (as with Eleanor of Aquitaine and her son Richard I, *r.* 1189–1199) during the son's absence from the kingdom. This power is all the more remarkable since kings tended to marry foreign princesses and these women were therefore strangers to the kingdoms they ruled. Isabelle of France, mother of

Edward III, along with her lover Roger Mortimer (1287–1330), helped depose her husband and place her fifteen-year-old son on the throne, only to see her son three years later kill Mortimer and deny her any power. She was known to English schoolboys in later centuries as the "She-Wolf of France." On the other hand, the Spanish princess Blanche of Castile (1188–1252), mother of St. Louis (r. 1226–1270), was an effective regent in France both during her son's minority and during his absence on crusade.

Foreign queens or noblewomen, when they arrived in their new home, often brought with them a household including servants, clerics, and aristocratic attendants. This often meant new fashions at the court and new styles of devotion. In the late sixth century, for example, the Frankish princess Bertha married Aethelbert of Kent (r. ca. 560–616), and the marriage treaty specifically allowed her to bring clergy and practice Christianity at that pagan court. She played a major role in her husband's decision to welcome Christian missionaries who eventually converted Kent. A queen could also commission works of literature or art in languages or styles with which she was familiar, thus functioning as a vector of cultural change.

WOMEN'S WORK

The gender division of labor within peasant households was fairly similar across most of medieval Europe. Women tended to do the indoor tasks and tasks that could be done closer to home—brewing, baking, cooking, dairying, tending the kitchen garden, preparing fiber, weaving cloth, and sewing garments—as well as some gathering of food. Men worked in the fields or herded livestock. The division of labor came about in part because medieval society saw women as the main caregivers for children, and their tasks had to be compatible with this. Women were not secluded in the home; they took produce to market and helped in the fields at harvest time, as well as interacting with other women and men within the village. But, in general, they did not do the same tasks as men. Widowed or single landholders, male or female, might hire servants to do the tasks inappropriate to their gender, or family members might help.

Because of the demands of running a household and the gender division of labor, medieval society expected most people to marry. Marriage was not just for love, for a legitimate sexual outlet, or for the begetting of children (although it was those things as well); it was also an economic partnership. At the aristocratic level, the lady had to manage the household, in essence a full-time adminis-

trative job. Among urban craft workers, family members, including the wife, might provide unskilled or even skilled labor, or the wife might handle the retail end of the business while the husband took care of production.

Even if the wife's work was mainly domestic, feeding and clothing the family, it was often essential to the husband's occupation, whether agricultural or manufacturing. The family included not just the children or other relatives of the household but also domestic servants or hired labor. Without someone to see to the daily maintenance of the labor force—sometimes called "social reproduction"—the husband/entrepreneur would not be able to carry out his duties.

Women's contribution to the household labor unit was always important, if perhaps not measurable. But women also did skilled and unskilled labor for pay in their own right. Most employed women were domestic workers, but others worked in craft production (indeed, there was not always a sharp line, because a servant in the home of a master craftsman would likely become a skilled, though not highly paid, worker).

In the early Middle Ages, a great number of women worked in textile production, many of them in *gynecaea,* or weaving workshops on great estates. By the thirteenth century, following the development of the horizontal loom and the consequent professionalization of weaving, most weavers in the more urbanized parts of Europe were men, and women's contributions to textile production were limited either to spinning and other auxiliary crafts or to cloth manufacture for household use rather than for the market. Women continued, however, to weave for the market in places like Iceland, where woven cloth was a major export.

As with weaving, so with the craft of brewing. When brewing was done locally, women brewed for the market; they became skilled craftswomen but not usually entrepreneurs on a large scale. In the later Middle Ages, as the brewing industry became more capitalized and professionalized, men took over more and more. Women did not lose control of a lucrative industry; rather, men assumed control when it became lucrative.

A few women did remain brewers and weavers, and indeed the records of most towns in the later Middle Ages show that a few women participated in just about any craft. Most of these, however, were widows. The guilds that controlled craft production in most medieval cities tended to exclude women except as wives or widows of members. Some allowed widows to continue to practice the craft of a late husband, as long as they did not remarry outside the craft. Even in those guilds that women could join in their own right, they could rarely hold leadership positions. A few towns had craft guilds exclusively for women, especially in the luxury crafts, such as silk work or embroidery. In most places, however, these feminine crafts did not have a formal guild structure.

Midwifery also remained exclusively feminine but for the most part without corporate structure. Most people considered childbirth a feminine matter; male doctors did not generally attend. Midwives not only dealt with obstetric and gynecological matters but also could treat other medical conditions; given their empirical training and the state of academic medical knowledge at the time, the care they provided was probably no worse than that of male doctors and sometimes better. After the establishment of formal medical education in the universities, however, doctors did not want the competition. The medical faculty at the University of Paris, for example, prosecuted Jacoba Felicie in 1322 for unauthorized practice of medicine.

In discussing women's role work in the Middle Ages, it is important to remember that the opportunity to work outside the home, however liberating in the 1970s, was not necessarily so in other time periods. The work women did, whether in their own home or for others, was hard; men's work was hard, too, but not quite so ill paid. Women who worked for wages were subject to the sexual predations of their employers or their employers' sons, and servants who became pregnant were often dismissed. Although some women did develop craft skills, most tended to move from one occupation to another, sometimes including occupations that were considered suspect, like regrating (buying wholesale and selling retail) or prostitution. They were generally unable to enter occupations that required capital. Those who did engage in capital-intensive activity—for example, mercantile activity, of which there are isolated examples, or moneylending, in which some Jewish women participated—generally acquired that capital from a husband or father rather than from their own accumulation.

Because so much of medieval industrial work was conducted within the household, some scholars have suggested that women were better off in the Middle Ages than in the early modern period. When crafts were based in the household, men and women could work collaboratively, and the money they received for the goods they produced was household income. Later, on the other hand, when men worked for wages, the money came to them, not to the household, and women's contributions became less visible, even though they worked to reproduce the household as they always had by feeding and clothing its members. It is unclear, however, how much change in women's status this economic shift actually brought. There were always many men in the Middle Ages who worked for wages, whether in the agricultural or manufacturing sector; not everyone was a small producer. By the later Middle Ages in Florence, for example, even master craftsmen like weavers were in the position of employees, working for the great cloth merchants for wages. Furthermore, even in household production, law and custom considered the husband the producer, even if the wife made his work possible or even did much of the actual work. Men appear in the records listed by occupation, whereas women appear as wives or widows. In terms of public attitudes, women's work did not receive as much acknowledgment as the value it produced.

The relation of women's work to marriage remains another crux of historians' debate. After the Black Death (1349) in the north of England, for example, some have suggested that labor shortages opened up new job opportunities for women and that the ability to support themselves may have led women to choose not to marry. However, others point out that women's wages were never very high, and as women still outnumbered men in towns, many women may simply have been unable to find husbands.

The religious life was the main institutional alternative for women who chose not to marry and who did not need to support themselves. However, the best estimate is that across Europe about 10 percent of both men and women never married, and not all of these took up the religious life. Some single women lived with a sibling or other family member; some lived alone; and others lived together, whether for companionship or out of economic necessity (on lesbian relationships, see **Sexuality**). In general their economic position was fairly precarious, since women's wages were so much lower than men's.

MARRIAGE AND FAMILY

The family was a locus of economic production, but it was also many other things. Women's primary purpose, in the view of many medieval authors, was the bearing of children, and the family setting legitimized this. On the aristocratic level, particularly in the early Middle Ages when bilateral tracing of kinship was more important, the choice of a wife was also a choice of what in-laws one wanted and what maternal relatives one wanted one's children to have. Marriage in medieval Europe, at least among Christians, was either neolocal or virilocal: the couple set up a household of their own or lived with the husband's family. (Among Jews it was not uncommon for married couples to live with the wife's family.) The Christian wife was thus often an outsider in her new environment. Among aristocrats and royalty a wife might be chosen to create a link between two families—a "peace-weaver" as the Anglo-Saxons called her. This was an important social role but could be a difficult one if peace failed and she found herself married to the enemy of her natal family.

During the early Middle Ages the church and secular authorities contested the legal basis of marriage. Merovingian kings (and probably other men also) had more than one wife at a time, but the church would only recognize one as a legal wife and only her children as legal heirs. Especially after the church managed to enforce the rule of monogamy in the Carolingian period, kings insisted on the right to repudiate a wife to whom they no longer wished to be married, often because there had been no sons born from the union. It was not until the twelfth century that the church definitively won the battle to control the definition of marriage.

The indissolubility of Christian marriage had important consequences for both men and women. It could be annulled if one party could prove that it had not been valid in the first place (because, for example, of a previous marriage contracted by one partner or because the spouses were too closely related). If it was a valid marriage, however, it could not be dissolved. In cases of adultery (usually by the wife) or cruelty the church courts might decree a separation, but this did not normally permit the parties to remarry. It is hard to say whether the permanence of marriage affected men or women more. Christian men did not have the legal option that Muslim and Jewish men had to divorce their wives at will, and this could have benefited the wives, but only if they wished to stay in the marriage. The Qur'an urged men to divorce their wives rather than treat them badly, but Christians were forced to remain in an unhappy marriage, which no doubt led to some domestic abuse.

Jewish law in the rabbinic period permitted both polygyny and divorce. During the Middle Ages the practice among Jews living in Christian lands began to diverge; since Islam permitted polygyny and divorce, Jews under Islam were not under the same pressure to abandon them. In Ashkenaz, though, polygyny was uncommon by the end of the tenth century (restricted largely to men whose wife had not borne a child in ten years of marriage; such men were required to marry another) and forbidden in a text attributed to the eleventh century. Similarly, Ashkenazic rabbis held that a woman should not be divorced without her consent, except in cases of misconduct. Although in the Talmud only a man had the right to divorce, a woman could come before a religious court and ask that her husband be compelled to divorce her. The courts granted these requests in the case of beating or other mistreatment.

The degree of choice that Christian women (and men) had in marriage varied greatly. From the twelfth century on, as it began to develop its doctrines on marriage, the church insisted that the consent of both parties was required. It backed up that insistence with decisions declaring invalid marriages where one party (usually the woman) had not consented, as well as decisions validating marriages to which the parties had consented but their families had not. Of course, since the age of consent to marriage was twelve for girls and fourteen for boys, and since among the aristocracy (and among all social classes in some parts of Europe) women tended to marry very young, it would be a rare girl who was strong enough to refuse her parents' choice of marriage partner and maintain that refusal in the church courts.

Among members of the high aristocracy, whose marriages often involved issues of land and political power, it was common for the parents of both parties to negotiate marriage. For those outside the aristocracy the best evidence comes from the later Middle Ages. In late-medieval Tuscany, where the average age of marriage was in the teens for women but in the thirties for men, men negotiated marriage themselves, with the father of their prospective partner. People at a lower social level may have had more choice of marriage partner simply because there were fewer financial considerations involved, although the low age at marriage for women and a trend of dowry inflation meant that Italian women, even peasants or domestic servants, had little say. In England, by contrast, both men and women tended to marry in their twenties, at a point by which many women had already left home to go into domestic service, and they had an opportunity to meet prospective marriage partners and make their own choice. Even here, family and friends often cared a great deal about choice of marriage partner—but the couple could overrule them. Among the gentry, where land and financial considerations were important, the fifteenth-century Paston letters indicate that the couple negotiated about marriage themselves, although the man also negotiated with the woman's parents (not just her father).

In fifteenth-century England, courting couples wrote love letters to each other. Elsewhere, too, romance stories told of love culminating in marriage (though they told of adulterous love as well). Certainly from the way married couples worked together as a team in their craft or in agriculture and from the way they grieved over each other's death and prayed for the soul of a departed spouse, it seems likely that many marriages were companionate. However, medieval people for the most part did not enter marriage expecting that it would be the defining emotional attachment of their lives. Women had their own networks of companionship with their women friends, and men with theirs.

Many people married more than once, and stepfamilies often complicated marriages. Because of high mortality rates, the chance of a child's reaching age twenty-one with both of his or her birth parents still living in the same household were no higher than in the contemporary world with its high divorce rates. Because women married so young in southern Europe, even a teenager might be on her second marriage and have children from a previous marriage.

The rearing of all children, whether her own or the result of such a blended family, largely fell to the mother. She might nurse her children for several years—usually longer for boys than for girls. If the family were wealthy they might use a wet nurse. Medieval people believed that sexual intercourse would harm a woman's milk, so a man who wanted to resume sexual relations with his wife had to provide other means for nourishing the children. For families who could not afford a wet nurse or chose not to employ one, nursing a child may have provided a moderately effective means of contraception.

Bernard of Clairvaux (1090–1153) commented with approval that his mother, unlike other twelfth-century aristocratic women, chose to nurse her own children. Religious men and women often remembered their mother as virtuous: not only their nurturing of infants but also their efforts at educating their offspring. Not all religious tales about mothers, however, spoke of devoted love and self-sacrifice. Some writers praised women who cared about God more than about their children or cared about their children's souls more than about their bodies. Children could distract women from focusing on their salvation as they should. If a woman paid too much attention to her children, she might be a bad Christian, but if she paid more attention to God, her secular acquaintances might accuse her of neglecting her children.

Mothers were often responsible for the moral upbringing of their children, sons as well as daughters. An aristocratic Frankish woman, Dhuoda, wrote a book of advice to her son in 841/43; Christine de Pizan (1364–1430) wrote another for hers. These works, especially Christine's, were intended for public consumption as well as for the individual addressee, which indicates

an expectation that others would see a mother's advice as valuable.

Women's importance in the upbringing of their children also promoted cultural exchange. As western Europeans colonized various areas—the Baltic region, the Mediterranean islands, the Balkans, Ireland—there was substantial intermarriage or interethnic domestic partnerships without benefit of marriage, almost always between women of the colonized group and men of the colonizers. The children of these relationships, if acknowledged by their fathers, constituted important links between cultures, as they claimed their father's lineage but bore with them their mothers' acculturation. Iceland, for example, was unpopulated when colonized by Norwegians; but DNA studies indicate that the female ancestors of the modern Icelandic population included a quite substantial Celtic component, which probably consisted both of captured Irish slaves and of wives that the Norwegians married during sojourns in the Scottish isles before settling in Iceland. It is very difficult to link particular DNA patterns with particular cultural patterns, but it is clear that to speak of Scandinavian colonization of Iceland is to ignore the maternal ancestry.

RELIGION

Some mothers gave up their maternal responsibilities to take up a religious life. For most women, however, the religious life meant renouncing marriage and motherhood in the first place. From the early Middle Ages, monasteries provided a place in which women could live independently of men, become educated, and exercise power and influence. Most early medieval female monasteries were headed by aristocratic women, either unmarried daughters or widows. Some of them may have had the religious life chosen for them, but many did choose it themselves. Nuns, like monks, copied books and wrote their own. They conducted and supported missionary activities. In Anglo-Saxon England and Merovingian Gaul, double monastic houses included both men and women. Women's houses enjoyed a great deal of independence, at least in the earliest period. Carolingian monastic reforms on the Continent and their echoes in England reduced the leadership role of women.

Church reform in the twelfth century diminished the role of abbess further—she remained important within the monastery itself but less so in the world outside—and nuns were no longer able to do the same sorts of things as monks. Monks could travel to cathedral schools or to universities to study; nuns could not. Several of the new orders founded in the twelfth century involved double houses in which the men's main purpose was to assist and support the women—the Gilbertines and the order of Fontevrault are examples. The Premonstratensians welcomed women's participation in the order at first but eventually began to discourage new women's houses. The Cistercians grudgingly allowed women's houses to affiliate with their order but placed severe restrictions on them. Whether this was because they did not want the administrative burden (as they saw it) of caring for the women or for some other reason, women were not seen as an asset to their orders.

Existing orders also placed greater restrictions on their female members from the twelfth century on, requiring their supervision by men and limiting their activities outside the cloister in conformity with admonitions about enclosure that had previously been more flexibly enforced. These restrictions corresponded with the new reformist emphasis on clerical celibacy; the maintenance of nuns' chastity became a high priority both to prevent their "pollution" and to make them a scapegoat for men's difficulties over celibacy. A further step in controlling the religious life of women came in a papal decree of 1298 that provided that all nuns of all orders must remain cloistered and that unauthorized outsiders could not enter. The prohibition on leaving their monasteries and receiving visitors put a serious limitation on nuns' abilities to conduct the legal and business affairs of their house, solicit funds from donors, run schools, play a leadership role in their order, or advise secular leaders.

If they were willing to accept enclosure, monasticism remained a viable option for women throughout the later Middle Ages. Women's monastic houses tended to be less wealthy than men's; with a few notable exceptions, they did not attract the major donors. However, having a local rather than a regional or national donor base gave them close ties to their communities. No nun in the later Middle Ages produced major works of theology or science, as Hildegard of Bingen (1098–1179) did in the twelfth century. But (particularly in Germany) they did produce many works of personal devotion, both literary and artistic.

During the central and later Middle Ages, too, other forms of devotion developed for women (and men) besides the monastery. Most women who became nuns were aristocrats or at least from well-to-do gentry or merchant families; the monasteries demanded dowries. Poorer women had to look elsewhere. When the mendicant orders for men developed in the thirteenth century, they did not provide a real alternative for women as they did for men. Both the Dominicans and Franciscans established associated orders for women, but they were little different from other nuns, whereas the preaching friars were quite distinct from monks. However, the option of becoming an anchoress or recluse was open to women. These recluses lived on their own or sometimes in very small communities with a servant or companion. In general they lived lives of prayer and asceticism, but they also served as spiritual advisers to other women or to men who sought them out. Christina of Markyate (ca. 1097–1161) was a good friend to Abbot Geoffrey of St. Albans; Juliana of Cornillon (1192–1258) wrote a liturgical office for the feast of Corpus Christi that influenced the one Thomas Aquinas wrote a few years later; Julian of Norwich (1342–ca. 1416) wrote several influential books of meditations on the life of Christ. These women, who often lived in a cell built next to a church, remained in some ways part of the community in which they lived, unlike nuns who withdrew.

In the late Middle Ages another form of religious life became available to women. Particularly in Italy, they could become members of a Franciscan or Dominican "third order," taking lesser vows than those of monasticism. Some of these tertiaries were married, and some remained in the secular life; others lived in communities of their own. Catherine of Siena (1347–1380), the only medieval woman to have been named a doctor of the church, was a Dominican tertiary; she not only provided a role model for other religious women, she also played a major role in the ecclesiastical politics of the day, writing copious letters of advice to the pope. The Beguines, found mainly though not exclusively in the Low Countries, were similar in some ways to those tertiaries living in communities. They lived in houses together, working with their hands to support themselves, and a number of them wrote religious tracts. Women living on their own like this were often suspect; the Beguine Marguerite Porete was burned in Paris in 1310 for her writings, which were considered heretical although they later circulated anonymously as a popular devotional manual.

Groups like the Beguines served a number of social functions for women as well as providing an outlet for their religious enthusiasm. In many late medieval towns—which generally had more women than men and in which not all women were able to marry (or wished to do so)—religious communities offered an alternative form of life more socially acceptable than simply living alone and also provided companionship and care when needed. Such groups, however, were not simply demographic safety valves. The religious impulses involved were very real. Elsewhere these impulses might take other forms—for example in England, where there were no Beguines or tertiaries but a number of anchoresses and where the late-medieval heretical movement of Lollardy also allowed an outlet for religious expression for both women and men who were dissatisfied with the hierarchical church.

Women mystics were found among all these groups: nuns, recluses, Beguines, and tertiaries. The characteristic feature of mysticism is a personal, emotional relationship with the divinity. In the case of women, while this relationship did not supplant the mediated relation to God provided by the priest as administrator of the sacraments, it supplemented it, allowing them to relate to God without a male mediator. Eucharistic mysticism was particularly common among women in the High to late Middle Ages: they desired frequent communion and sometimes had visions in which they received communion directly from God or the Holy Spirit. Their visions also frequently involved an ecstatic experience of divine love. These visions were by no means limited to women but were more characteristic of them than of men. Many women mystics, especially in the later Middle Ages, were highly respected and demonstrated how women could wield power in an institutional church where they could not be priests.

Women participated in a variety of heretical movements—the Albigensians (or Cathars), the Waldensians, the Lollards, the Hussites, even the Protestant Reformation in its early years. These movements did not, for the most part, allot to women a fundamentally larger spiritual role than did orthodox Catholicism. To the extent they repudiated the church's all-male hierarchy and allowed a greater leadership role for lay people, both men and women could participate; but to the extent that they established hierarchies of their own, these tended to replicate the hierarchies in the wider society and exclude women.

Judaism and Islam gave women less of a formal leadership role than did Christianity; because there was no monasticism, there was no role equivalent to that of an abbess. However, both these religions had forms of private devotion in which women participated heavily. Much Jewish prayer and ceremony, for example, took place in the home rather than the synagogue. Muslim women played a role in devotion to saints, including pilgrimages; they would also become sufis.

Some scholars have argued that Judaism was more favorable to women than Christianity, because it valued marriage, motherhood, and the family more consistently than did Christianity with its praise of virginity and distrust of sex. But a closer look at medieval Jewish and Muslim cultures reveals complexities in women's status and in attitudes to women similar to those found in medieval Christian culture.

CULTURE

Women's most significant contributions to learned culture came from within the religious life—as nuns, recluses, Beguines, or tertiaries. They wrote copiously: prayers and other devotional works, lives of saints (especially women who had been their sisters), and letters to spiritual advisers and other friends. The German nun Hrotsvit (930/940–ca. 1002) wrote a series of Latin plays, modeled after the comedies of Terence but with Christian stories. Some were lives of saints, others were stories of heroic virtue.

Secular women, too, contributed to medieval literary culture. Many or most medieval texts that survive are anonymous, and many of those may have been written by women. Indeed, women may even have written some of those attributed to men and given a false authorship in order to make them more acceptable. Scholars have been too quick to doubt authorship of anything attributed to a woman. For example, the corpus of gynecological texts known as the *Trotula,* attributed to Trota, a twelfth-century healer from Salerno, was long thought to be the work of a man. Modern scholarship has shown that the text clearly could have been written by a woman. There is no absolute evidence that it was, but then again there is no absolute evidence that many of the texts we have with the names of male authors on them were actually written by men.

Some of the most poignant writing by medieval women consists of their letters. Those of Heloise, written sometime after 1132 as she reflected on the end of her marriage to Abelard and her life as a nun, give a picture from her own point of view to supplement that from Abelard's own memoirs. Her adoption of antifeminist commonplaces about how marriage distracts a man from the important things in life led some scholars to doubt that the letters could have been written by a woman, but one can also read this as her attempt to put a brave face on the situation in which she found herself. The Paston family in fifteenth-century England wrote business letters to each other but also love letters; we see mothers caring for their sons and wives for their husbands, as well as family conflict. The Paston women probably dictated their letters, but their voices still come through.

The twelfth century brought a flowering of vernacular culture, especially in France, and women participated as both patrons and authors. The lyric poetry of the Occitan troubadours had its counterpart in that of the trobairitz (women troubadours). Many of the themes of trobairitz poetry resemble those found in poems written by men, but they tend to deal less with nature and beauty and more with human feeling. In northern France,

Marie de France wrote fables and *lais* that rank with the best of medieval narrative literature, most focusing on love and some dealing with the plight of unhappily married women.

Poetry that was written by men was often dedicated to women. In the south of France inheritance customs were such that women could wield a great deal of political power, and when a poet dedicated a love poem to Ermengarde of Narbonne (1127/29–1196/97), for example, it was not just her beauty, but her very real authority, that attracted him. The dedication of poetry to Ermengarde is part of a twelfth-century phenomenon modern scholars have called "courtly love" in which men wrote poetry or otherwise expressed their love for women whom they place in a position of power over them. Some of this poetry also praised extramarital liaisons. Scholars have debated for years whether this literature reflects actual social practice—did people really conduct love affairs according to rules by which a man earned a woman's love?—or merely a game and whether or not it accorded women any real or symbolic power.

Women as well as men at court enjoyed hearing not only lyric poetry but also romances and helped reward those who composed and told them well. Women also acted as patrons for writers of all kinds. Aristocratic or royal women also acted as transmitters of culture between one part of Europe and another when they married and brought books, courtiers, and even artists or poets with them to their new home. Women's patronage extended beyond literature and art: they founded monasteries and other ecclesiastical institutions, including colleges.

The fifteenth century is particularly notable for women writers. Margery Kempe (*ca.* 1373–1438), an Englishwoman, wrote the first autobiography in the English language (the text claims to have been dictated by her to a male cleric, although this could be an effort on Margery's part to give the text more authority). Margery, a very devout woman, never took up a formal religious life; the book gives an account of her visions, her pilgrimages, and the mistreatment she received from those who thought her a heretic or a lunatic. Christine de Pizan, who wrote to support herself, her widowed mother, and her children after the early death of her husband, is sometimes considered the "first feminist" because of her book *The City of Ladies* (1405), which uses examples of illustrious women throughout history to make a case in favor of women, responding to a long history of misogynist or antifeminist writing especially by clerics (see **Gender, theories of** for further discussion). She also wrote a variety of other works, including a poem on Joan of Arc.

Joan of Arc (1412–1431), another French woman of the fifteenth century, shows some of the possibilities for women in the late Middle Ages but also the limitations. A peasant girl from Lorraine, she saw a vision instructing her to go to the French dauphin for an army to raise the siege of Orléans, under attack by the English. She was militarily successful for some time, though she was eventually captured and put to death by an ecclesiastical court allied with the English. Her remarkable story indicates that a woman could succeed in a man's world, even as a military leader, if people saw them as having sufficient charisma. However, the prosecutors at her trial stressed the weakness of women and Joan's inability to discern whether the spirits commanding her were good or evil. Christine de Pizan praised the divine intervention that let France be saved by a woman, but once Joan's military victories evaporated, it was easy to deploy the common antifeminine stereotypes against her.

Joan's story, like those of many other medieval women, reveals the complexity of women's roles in the Middle Ages. Women were not merely passive objects exchanged within a male-dominated system of property and inheritance nor meek followers doing whatever men told them nor secluded wives who cleaned the house while men went out and did important things. They seized opportunities and took action, wielded political power, worked at all kinds of jobs, and created their own approaches to religious life. And yet, no matter what they accomplished, it never fundamentally challenged the prevailing gender hierarchy. Medieval people, whether or not they espoused the more vitriolic misogynist diatribes of some texts, lived within a system that accepted male dominance as natural. At some times women enjoyed certain rights and privileges more than at others; some women, because of their social standing or the accident of widowhood or inheritance, had more opportunity than others to achieve wealth and influence. Never, however, was their gender irrelevant to their opportunities and achievements.

BIBLIOGRAPHY

PRIMARY WORKS

Amt, Emilie, ed. *Women's Lives in Medieval Europe: A Sourcebook.* New York: Routledge, 1993.

Green, Monica H., ed. and trans. *The Trotula: A Medieval Compendium of Women's Medicine.* Philadelphia: University of Pennsylvania Press, 2001.

Larrington, Carolyne, ed. *Women and Writing in Medieval Europe: A Sourcebook.* London: Routledge, 1995.

Petroff, Elizabeth A., ed. *Medieval Women's Visionary Literature.* New York: Oxford University Press, 1986.

SECONDARY WORKS

Atkinson, Clarissa W. *The Oldest Vocation: Christian Motherhood in the Middle Ages.* Ithaca, N.Y.: Cornell University Press, 1991.

Baskin, Judith, ed. *Jewish Women in Historical Perspective.* 2d ed. Detroit, Mich.: Wayne State University Press, 1998.

Bennett, Judith M. *Ale, Beer, and Brewsters in England: Women's Work in a Changing World, 1300–1600.* Oxford: Oxford University Press, 1996.

Bitel, Lisa M. *Women in Early Medieval Europe 400–1100.* Cambridge, U.K.: Cambridge University Press, 2002.

Burns, E. Jane. "Courtly Love: Who Needs It? Recent Feminist Work in the Medieval French Tradition." *Signs: Journal of Women in Culture and Society* 27 (2001): 23–57.

Bynum, Caroline. *Holy Feast and Holy Fast: The Religious Significance of Food to Medieval Women.* Berkeley: University of California Press, 1987.

Dillard, Heath. *Daughters of the Reconquest: Women in Castilian Town Society, 1100–1300.* Cambridge, U.K.: Cambridge University Press, 1984.

Duby, Georges. *The Knight, the Lady, and the Priest: The Making of Modern Marriage in Medieval France.* Translated by Barbara Bray. New York: Pantheon, 1983.

Evergates, Theodore, ed. *Aristocratic Women in Medieval France.* Philadelphia: University of Pennsylvania Press, 1999.

Gilchrist, Roberta. *Gender and Material Culture: The Archaeology of Religious Women.* London: Routledge, 1994.

Goldberg, P. J. P. *Women, Work, and Life Cycle in a Medieval Economy: Women in York and Yorkshire c. 1300–1520.* Oxford: Clarendon, 1992.

Hambly, Gavin R. G., ed. *Women in the Medieval Islamic World: Power, Patronage, and Piety.* New Middle Ages Series. New York: St. Martin's, 1998.

Hanawalt, Barbara A., ed. *Women and Work in Preindustrial Europe.* Bloomington: Indiana University Press, 1986.

Herlihy, David. *Opera Muliebria: Women and Work in Medieval Europe.* Philadelphia: Temple University Press, 1990.

Howell, Martha C. *The Marriage Exchange: Property, Social Place, and Gender in Cities of the Low Countries, 1300–1550.* Chicago: University of Chicago Press, 1998.

Jochens, Jenny. *Women in Old Norse Society.* Ithaca, N.Y.: Cornell University Press, 1995.

Johnson, Penelope D. *Equal in Monastic Profession: Religious Women in Medieval France.* Chicago: University of Chicago Press, 1991.

LaBarge, Margaret Wade. *A Small Sound of the Trumpet: Women in Medieval Life.* Boston: Beacon, 1986.

McNamara, Jo Ann Kay. *Sisters in Arms: Catholic Nuns through Two Millennia.* Cambridge, Mass.: Harvard University Press, 1996.

McSheffrey, Shannon. *Gender and Heresy: Women and Men in Lollard Communities, 1420–1530.* Philadelphia: University of Pennsylvania Press, 1995.

Newman, Barbara. *From Virile Woman to WomanChrist: Studies in Medieval Religion and Literature.* Philadelphia: University of Pennsylvania Press, 1995.

Parsons, John Carmi, ed. *Medieval Queenship.* New York: St. Martin's, 1993.

Rosenthal, Joel T., ed. *Medieval Women and the Sources of Medieval History.* Athens: University of Georgia Press, 1990.

Shahar, Shulamith. *The Fourth Estate: A History of Women in the Middle Ages.* Translated by Chaya Galai. London: Methuen, 1983.

Simons, Walter. *Cities of Ladies: Beguine Communities in the Medieval Low Countries, 1200–1565.* Philadelphia: University of Pennsylvania Press, 2001.

Stafford, Pauline. *Queens, Concubines, and Dowagers: The King's Wife in the Early Middle Ages.* Athens: University of Georgia Press, 1983.

Stuard, Susan Mosher. "Ancillary Evidence for the Decline of Medieval Slavery." *Past and Present* 149 (1995): 3–28.

Wemple, Suzanne Fonay. *Women in Frankish Society: Marriage and the Cloister 500 to 900.* Philadelphia: University of Pennsylvania Press, 1985.

RUTH MAZO KARRAS

[See also **DMA:** Courtly Love; Family; Women's Religious Orders; **Supp:** Abortion; Body, The; Childbirth and Infancy; Gynecology; Love and Courtship; Marriage, Christian; Pornography; Rape; Sexuality; Sexuality, Medical; Widowhood.]

WOYCIECH. See **Adalbert, St.**

WULFILA. See **Ulfila.**

ZADONSHCHINA ("The Battle beyond the Don"), a long prose epic penned soon after the Battle of Kulikovo Field in 1380, where Russian forces defeated the Tatar commander, Mamai. The earliest manuscript of the six extant dating before the eighteenth century comes from the 1400s and tells the story of two Russian princes, brothers, being informed of the Tatar invasion while banqueting. This is the occasion for several word pictures, some of which describe the Russian landscape, others of which, the series of humbling defeats Rus had endured from the time of the initial Mongol conquest of the 1220s.

Dmitrii and Volodimir, the brothers, set off like eagles to face the invaders, having gathered together other Russian princes and their retinues for the task. Despite their hopes, Dmitrii, who leads the initial attack, is defeated. This bitter outcome is the occasion for a series of lamentations put in the mouths of the narrator and various characters. But a second attack carries the day against Mamai, who flees the field of battle. Prince Dmitrii, vindicated by victory, remembers with praise the Russian princes, living and dead, who brought about the victory and praises God for permitting the defeat of unbelievers on Russian soil.

The manuscripts of the *Zadonshchina* differ considerably, although the simplified outline of the story given above is more or less common to them all. More difficult to answer are questions involving authorship, historicity, relationship to the "national epic," the *Song of Igor's Campaign,* and literary merit.

Two manuscripts refer to Sofonii of Riazan in the heading of the text; three others refer to him in the text itself. But none does so unequivocally as the author, and it is possible to interpret the references in a different way, namely, as an invocation of a previous prose author (and his work) as a model for the present (different) author (and his work). It is therefore best to be agnostic on authorship.

As to historicity, the fact that the description of the battle occurs in an almost contemporary manuscript suggests that the author could not have played loose with the simpler details of the encounter, such as the two-phase (initial defeat, subsequent victory) scenario of the battle. The princes' speeches and the laments of the wives of the warriors dead on the battlefield mean to capture a different kind of reality. These passages make sense because of the Russian victory: whatever really happened when the two princes banqueted or the whole host gathered, what is preserved for posterity are those sentiments, among many others no doubt expressed, that lent themselves to a triumphalist and redemptive interpretation of the battle's outcome.

The relationship of the *Zadonshchina* to the *Song of Igor's Campaign,* which treats events far more remote in time than the Battle of Kulikovo Field, remains in dispute. Presuming the *Song* or something like it predated the *Zadonshchina* in written form, the uncanny similarities between the two amount almost to quotation and extended paraphrase. Inevitably, too, the memory of Igor's "heroic" defeat by Polovtsian pagans plays a shaping role in the anonymous author of the *Zadonshchina's* understanding of the previous woes of Rus. Why would he not consult an earlier source that movingly recounted the defeat, memorialized it in an effective way, and provided a general blueprint about how to write in an epic fashion? Yet the author of the *Zadonshchina* often departed from his putative model, and most students regard the finished product as derivative in the pejorative sense where it imitates the *Song* and, worse still, condescending gestures to a few lyrical passages notwithstanding, where it does not.

BIBLIOGRAPHY

Jakobson, Roman, and Dean S. Worth, eds. *Sofonija's Tale of the Russian-Tatar Battle on the Kulikovo Field.* The Hague: Mouton, 1963. Translation and commentary.

WILLIAM CHESTER JORDAN

[See also **DMA:** Mongol Empire; Slavic Languages and Literatures; **Supp:** *Song of Igor's Campaign.*]

ZURARA, GOMES EANES DE (1410/1420–1473/ 1474). Little is known about the early life of the Portuguese chronicler Gomes Eanes de Zurara. He was probably born in the early years of the fifteenth century and may have come from a well-to-do family. He seems to have entered the military Order of Christ as a young man and eventually rose to its highest levels as a commander of the order. His youth was, consequently, spent in a military career, and he likely received the extensive education that would later serve him so well as an older man in the thriving literary world of fifteenth-century Portugal. In the late 1430s he secured a position in the Royal Library, eventually becoming its director. His earliest writings, a miracle collection, date from this period.

It was with the *Chronicle of the Capture of Ceuta* (written from 1449 to 1450) that his reputation as a historian began to grow. The account depicts the capture of that city by the Portuguese from Morocco in 1415 and displays not only Zurara's impressive command of history but also his extensive knowledge of literature and religious writings.

In 1452, the king of Portugal, Afonso V (*r.* 1438–1481), charged Zurara with writing another historical work and to continue the recording of national history begun by Fernão Lopes (who served as chief chronicler of the realm until 1454). This time it was to be a record of the deeds of Prince Henry the Navigator, the great patron of Portuguese expansion and exploration and Afonso's uncle. *The Chronicle of Guinea,* as the work is known, although sometimes filled with effusive praise for Henry, whom Zurara knew and admired, is also a remarkable and reliable source for these early years of Portuguese exploration of West Africa. Presenting much of its material as a chivalric crusade, the *Chronicle of Guinea* includes among its more notable contributions descriptions of the rounding of Cape Bojador in 1434, the colonization of the Madeiras and Azores island groups, and the first seizure of African captives by Portuguese adventurers in 1441. Modern scholars have viewed this last event as the opening act of the Atlantic slave trade, making *The Chronicle of Guinea* a vital documentary source for its early stages.

Afonso rewarded Zurara handsomely for his work, appointing him keeper of the royal archives (chief chronicler of the realm) in 1454. In this capacity he presided over a restructuring of the royal archives, but his attempt to streamline them resulted in the destruction of many older and seemingly less important registers, thereby leaving a blemish on Zurara's career. He also continued to write, most notably a second book on Ceuta, the *Chronicle of Count Pedro de Meneses* (finished in 1463), describing the first twenty years of Portuguese control. In 1467 Zurara traveled to North Africa, the location of many of his writings, to learn more about it and the native Muslims firsthand and to collect information for another book, the *Chronicle of Count Duarte de Meneses* (probably finished in 1468).

Ironically for one who took such pains to record the lives of others, very little is known about the last years of Zurara's life or his death, sometime in the mid-1470s. However, he left behind a vast collection of historical works describing, explaining, and commenting on the critical years when Portugal took its first tentative steps of exploration and expansion.

BIBLIOGRAPHY

Blackburn, Robin. *The Making of New World Slavery: From the Baroque to the Modern, 1492–1800.* London and New York: Verso, 1997. See especially chapter 2. An excellent introduction to the Atlantic slave trade, including the crucial Portuguese role, of which Zurara was the main chronicler.

Russell, Peter. *Prince Henry "the Navigator": A Life.* New Haven, Conn.: Yale University Press, 2000. The most recent biography of Henry; includes discussion of Zurara's role in the shaping of his myth and image.

Zurara, Gomes Eanes de. *The Chronicle of the Discovery and Conquest of Guinea.* Edited and translated by Charles Raymond Beazley and Edgar Prestage. 2 vols. New York: B. Franklin, 1963. Translation of Zurara's most important work as well as good biography.

JARBEL RODRIGUEZ

[See also **DMA:** Exploration by Western Europeans; Lopes, Fernão; Portugal: 1279–1481; Slavery, Slave Trade; **Supp:** Henry the Navigator of Portugal, Prince.]

Contributors

DOMINIC D. ALEXANDER
St. Mary's College, London
GODRIC OF FINCHALE, ST.

KATHLEEN ASHLEY
University of Southern Maine
ETIQUETTE AND MANNERS

MARTIN AURELL
Université de Poitiers—C.E.S.C.M.
PATRONAGE, LITERARY

CLIFFORD R. BACKMAN
Boston University
PIRATES AND PIRACY

BRIGITTE MIRIAM BEDOS-REZAK
New York University
SIGNS, THEORY OF

J. L. BERGGREN
Simon Fraser University
MATHEMATICS, ISLAMIC

ANNE BERTHELOT
University of Connecticut
NUMEROLOGY

RENATE BLUMENFELD-KOSINSKI
University of Pittsburgh
CATHERINE OF SIENA, ST.

KIM BOWES
Yale University
ARCHITECTURE, DOMESTIC

RICHARD BRITNELL
University of Durham
COMMERCIALIZATION

SCOTT G. BRUCE
University of Colorado
ANSGAR, ST.; CHARLES IV, EMPEROR;
 CONRAD III OF GERMANY, EMPEROR;
 CONRAD IV OF GERMANY, EMPEROR;
 CONRADIN; CORBIE, ABBEY OF;
 CORVEY, ABBEY OF; FRAXINETUM;
 HENRY VII OF GERMANY, KING;

IDUNG OF PRÜFENING; JEROME OF
 PRAGUE; LOUIS IV THE BAVARIAN,
 EMPEROR; MAIOLUS; OBLATES AND
 OBLATION; RUDOLF OF HABSBURG;
 SÜSSKIND VON TRIMBERG; TEUTONIC
 KNIGHTS; UPPSALA

JAMES A. BRUNDAGE
University of Kansas
MARRIAGE, CHRISTIAN

JONATHAN A. BUSH
Washington, D.C.
CINQUE PORTS; HUBERT DE BURGH;
 PETER DES ROCHES; WILLIAM OF
 DROGHEDA

CAROLINE WALKER BYNUM
Institute for Advanced Study, Princeton, N.J.
SOUL AND BODY

JOAN CADDEN
University of California at Davis
SEXUALITY, MEDICAL

ELSPETH JANE CARRUTHERS
University of Illinois at Chicago
ADALBERT, ST.; BOLESŁAW I CHROBRY
 OF POLAND, KING ; BOLESŁAW III
 KRZYWOUSTY OF POLAND, KING;
 CONRAD I OF GERMANY, EMPEROR;
 HENRY I OF GERMANY, EMPEROR;
 HENRY II OF GERMANY, EMPEROR;
 HENRY V OF GERMANY, EMPEROR;
 HENRY VI OF GERMANY, EMPEROR;
 MIESZKO I OF POLAND, KING; OTTO II
 OF GERMANY, EMPEROR; OTTO IV OF
 GERMANY, EMPEROR

CELIA CHAZELLE
The College of New Jersey
ORIGINALITY IN ARTS AND LETTERS

CHRISTINE CHISM
Rutgers University
ALLITERATIVE LITERATURE

ALICE V. CLARK
Loyola University, New Orleans, La.
MUSICUS; PLANCTUS MARIAE

JEFFREY J. COHEN
George Washington University
RACE

PATRICK W. CONNER
West Virginia University
EXETER BOOK

PAM J. CRABTREE
New York University
ARCHAEOLOGY

JO ANN HOEPPNER MORAN CRUZ
Georgetown University
SCHOOLS

ALEXANDRA CUFFEL
Virginia Polytechnic Institute and State University
IMMACULATE CONCEPTION OF THE
 VIRGIN

ADAM JEFFREY DAVIS
Denison University
ACCIAIUOLI; ALEXANDER DE VILLA DEI;
 ANDREA DA BARBERINO; ASTRAL
 MAGIC; ATHEISM; BARTHOLOMAEUS
 ANGLICUS; BOBBIO; BOETHIUS OF
 DACIA; BOGURODZICA; CLARE, ST.;
 DEMANDA DO SANTO GRAAL; DIES
 IRAE; DURAND OF HUESCA; ELIAS OF
 CORTONA; FALL, THE; FITZRALPH,
 RICHARD; GENIUS; HUMBERT OF
 ROMANS; JEAN RENART; JOHANNES DE
 LIGNANO; JOHN OF SACROBOSCO;
 JOHN XXIII, ANTIPOPE; OLEŚNICKI,
 ZBIGNIEW; TYRANTS AND
 TYRANNICIDE

LAURENCE DE LOOZE
University of Western Ontario
AUTOBIOGRAPHY AND CONFESSIONAL
 LITERATURE

ISABEL DE SENA
Sarah Lawrence College
PORTUGUESE LITERATURE

GEORGE E. DEMACOPOULOS
Fordham University
LITURGICAL YEAR, EASTERN

KELLY DEVRIES
Loyola College in Maryland
FIREARMS

PETER DINZELBACHER
*Institut für Wirtschafts- und
Sozialgeschichte der universität*
PAGANISM AND PAGAN GODS, SURVIVAL
OF

SUSAN L. EINBINDER
Hebrew Union College
HAGIOGRAPHY, JEWISH

IVANA ELBL
Trent University
ESPIONAGE

RICHARD K. EMMERSON
The Medieval Academy of America
HELL, CONCEPTS OF

EDWARD D. ENGLISH
Santa Barbara, Calif.
VATICAN LIBRARY

STEVEN A. EPSTEIN
University of Kansas
COMMUNES, 1200–1500

PAUL FREEDMAN
Yale University
MEDIEVAL STUDIES

JOHN BLOCK FRIEDMAN
Kent State University
DEMONS; DEVIL; MONSTERS AND THE
MONSTROUS

KARLFRIED FROEHLICH
Princeton Theological Seminary
BIBLICAL COMMENTARIES

GUY GELTNER
Princeton University
NATURE

C. M. GILLMOR
Salt Lake City, Ut.
HORSES AND HORSEMANSHIP

P. J. P. GOLDBERG
University of York
WIDOWHOOD

MONICA H. GREEN
Arizona State University
CHILDBIRTH AND INFANCY;
GYNECOLOGY

GUY GULDENTOPS
Katholieke Universiteit Leuven
MATTER

THOMAS HAHN
University of Rochester
ARTHURIAN ROMANCES

PETER HAIDU
University of California, Los Angeles
VIOLENCE

PAUL ANTONY HAYWARD
University of Otago
GOSCELIN OF ST. BERTIN

THOMAS J. HEFFERNAN
University of Tennessee, Knoxville
BIOGRAPHY

RICHARD C. HOFFMANN
York University
ECOLOGY

LOIS L. HUNEYCUTT
University of Missouri–Columbia
MATILDA, EMPRESS; QUEENS AND
QUEENSHIP

DANIELLE JACQUART
École Pratique des Hautes Études, Paris
MEDICINE, ISLAMIC

KATHERINE LUDWIG JANSEN
The Catholic University of America
POOR CLARES

ELIZABETH JEFFREYS
Exeter College, University of Oxford
PRODROMIC POEMS

WILLIAM CHESTER JORDAN
Princeton University
ANNE OF BOHEMIA; BANNOCKBURN,
BATTLE OF; BYLINY; CASIMIR III THE
GREAT OF POLAND, KING; CASIMIR IV
THE JAGIELLONIAN OF POLAND, KING;
CHASTITY BELT; CUMANS/KIPCHAKS;
DALIMIL'S CHRONICLE; DROIT DU
SEIGNEUR; EDMUND OF ABINGDON,
ST.; ELIZABETH OF HUNGARY, ST.;
GUESCLIN, BERTRAND DU; JOAN,
POPE; KALISZ, STATUTES OF; KRAKÓW;
LUND; MANOR AND MANORIALISM;
PIERRE DE BELLEPERCHE; ROUTIERS;
SONG OF IGOR'S CAMPAIGN;
STANISŁAW, ST.; STEPHEN OF
ENGLAND, KING; TANNENBERG/
GRUNWALD, BATTLE OF; TAXATION:
GERMANY, ITALY, IBERIA; TOLLS;
UTRAQUISM; VOIVODE; WENCESLAS,
ST.; WILLIAM OF ST. AMOUR; WILLIAM
II (RUFUS) OF ENGLAND, KING;
ZADONSHCHINA

EMILY KADENS
University of Chicago Law School
ACCURSIUS; AMSTERDAM; ANTWERP;
BERNARD OF PARMA; BERNARD OF
PAVIA; BULGARUS; CALUMNY OATH;
CAPITAL PUNISHMENT; DIPLOMATICS;
DIRC VAN DELFT; JACQUES DE
RÉVIGNY; LIBRI FEUDORUM; MIDDLE
AGES; RICARDUS ANGLICUS; TOURNAI

RUTH MAZO KARRAS
University of Minnesota
GENDER, THEORIES OF; SEXUALITY;
WOMEN

JOEL KAYE
Barnard College
JUST PRICE

HENRY ANSGAR KELLY
University of California, Los Angeles
RAPE

LISA J. KISER
The Ohio State University
ANIMALS, ATTITUDES TOWARD

GEOFFREY KOZIOL
University of California, Berkeley
PEACEMAKING

STEPHEN LAHEY
University of Nebraska
PHILOSOPHICAL GENRES

ANNE E. LESTER
Princeton University
CHILDHOOD AND ADOLESCENCE

IAN CHRISTOPHER LEVY
Lexington Theological Seminary
SACRAMENTS AND SACRAMENTAL
THEOLOGY

JOYCE TALLY LIONARONS
Ursinus College
EPIC GENRE

CHRISTOPHER HATCH MACEVITT
Dartmouth College
ALEXANDER IV, POPE; 'ANTAR;
ASTROLOGICAL ICONOGRAPHY;
ATHENS; BATHS AND BATHING;
BEDOUIN; BLUES AND GREENS;
CAROLINGIAN RENAISSANCE; CASTLE-
GUARD; CHRISTOPHER, ST.; CIOMPI,
REVOLT OF THE; COLONNA FAMILY;
COMITATUS; DANDOLO, ENRICO;
EDESSA, COUNTY OF; EUGENIUS III,
POPE; EUGENIUS IV, POPE; EZZELINO
DA ROMANO; FRANKS; GODFREY OF
BOUILLON; GREGORY X, POPE;
HERMANN OF SALZA; HILĀL, BANŪ

(SĪRAT BANŪ HILĀL); HONORIUS III,
POPE; HOSPITALLERS; KALĪLA WA-
DIMNA; MANFRED OF SICILY, KING;
NICHOLAS II, POPE; NICHOLAS III,
POPE; NICHOLAS IV, POPE; ORSINI
FAMILY; RIBĀṬ; SABIANS;
SAVONAROLA, GIROLAMO; SYRIAN
CHRISTIAN ARCHITECTURE; TAKLA
HAYMANOT, ST.; TEMPLARS;
TEXTILES, BYZANTINE; URBAN IV,
POPE; WILLIAM I OF SICILY, KING;
WILLIAM II OF SICILY, KING

GARY MACY
University of San Diego
TRANSUBSTANTIATION

JACLYN MAXWELL
Ohio University
ANTHONY OF EGYPT, ST.; TERTULLIAN;
ULFILA

MICHAEL MCVAUGH
*University of North Carolina at Chapel
Hill*
DISEASE; HYGIENE, PERSONAL;
PHYSICIANS

JOSEF W. MERI
Institute of Ismaili Studies, London
HAGIOGRAPHY, ISLAMIC

MARK D. MEYERSON
University of Toronto
MORISCOS

RACHEL MILSTEIN
Hebrew University of Jerusalem
OTTOMAN ART AND ARCHITECTURE

ELIZABETH J. MOODEY
New York Public Library
PATRONAGE, ARTISTIC

VERA B. MOREEN
Bala Cynwyd, Pa.
PERSIAN LANGUAGE

JAMES MULDOON
*The John Carter Brown Library,
Brown University*
CONVERSION

JOHN H. MUNRO
University of Toronto
MANUFACTURING AND INDUSTRY

JAMES M. MURRAY
University of Cincinnati
INSURANCE

STEPHEN MURRAY
Columbia University
GOTHIC ARCHITECTURE

LEONORA NEVILLE
The Catholic University of America
NOVEL (BYZANTINE LAW)

RICHARD G. NEWHAUSER
Trinity University, San Antonio, Tex.
VIRTUES AND VICES

DÁIBHÍ Ó CRÓINÍN
National University of Ireland
BRIAN BORU

GEORGI PARPULOV
*The Walters Art Museum, University of
Chicago*
MANUSCRIPT ILLUMINATION,
BYZANTINE

MARK GREGORY PEGG
Washington University
GHOSTS; GNOSTICISM; POLLUTION AND
TABOO

KENNETH PENNINGTON
The Catholic University of America
ALBERICUS DE ROSATE; GRATIAN;
JOHANNES BASSIANUS; LAW, CRIMINAL
PROCEDURE; LAW, FEUDAL; NATURAL
LAW; OLDRADUS DE PONTE;
ROLANDINUS DE PASSAGERIS

RICHARD W. PFAFF
*University of North Carolina at Chapel
Hill*
LITURGICAL YEAR, WESTERN

JAMES M. POWELL
Syracuse University
ALBERTANO DA BRESCIA

WALTER PREVENIER
Universiteit Ghent
RITUAL, CIVIC

KATHRYN L. REYERSON
University of Minnesota
MERCHANTS; NOTARIES

JARBEL RODRIGUEZ
San Francisco State University
ADMIRAL; ALFONSO V OF ARAGON;
BURSFELD, ABBEY OF; CAPITULATIONS;
CASPE, COMPROMISE OF;
DEGUILEVILLE, GUILLAUME DE;
DRACONTIUS, BLOSSIUS AEMILIUS;
FERDINAND III OF CASTILE, KING;
FINNSBURH FRAGMENT; GRÁGÁS;
HENRY THE NAVIGATOR OF
PORTUGAL, PRINCE; JAMES I OF
ARAGON, KING; JUGLARÍA; LAS NAVAS
DE TOLOSA, BATTLE OF; LE FRANC,
MARTIN; LISBON; MERCEDARIANS;
PEDRO III "THE GREAT" OF ARAGON,

KING; PERAULT, WILLIAM; PETRUS
ALFONSI; TORQUEMADA, JUAN DE;
TORQUEMADA, TOMÁS DE;
TRINITARIANS; WALLACE, WILLIAM;
ZURARA, GOMES EANES DE

JOEL T. ROSENTHAL
*State University of New York at Stony
Brook*
OLD AGE

TEOFILO F. RUIZ
University of California, Los Angeles
POVERTY

NEIL S. RUSHTON
Trinity College, Cambridge University
CHARITY

JAMES D. RYAN
*Bronx Community College, City
University of New York*
CHINA

ANGEL SÁENZ-BADILLOS
Universidad Complutense de Madrid
HEBREW LANGUAGE

PAULA SANDERS
Rice University
DHIMMĪS; EUNUCHS

MARGARET SCHLEISSNER
Rider University
ABORTION

M. B. SHEPARD
Corpus Vitrearum, USA
GOTHIC ART

JOHN SHINNERS
*Saint Mary's College, Notre Dame,
Ind.*
RELIGION, POPULAR

JAMES SIMPSON
University of Cambridge
HUMANISM

DON C. SKEMER
Princeton University
MANUSCRIPT COLLECTIONS

T. ALLAN SMITH
*University of St. Michael's College,
Toronto*
JOSEPH OF VOLOKOLAMSK, ST.

LYNN STALEY
Colgate University
LOVE AND COURTSHIP

SARAH STANBURY
*College of the Holy Cross, Worcester,
Mass.*
BODY, THE

CARLOS STEEL
Katholieke Universiteit Leuven
MATTER

MATTHEW STRICKLAND
University of Glasgow
PERCY FAMILY

SUSAN MOSHER STUARD
Haverford College
SERVANTS

EDITH DUDLEY SYLLA
North Carolina State University
MERTON CALCULATORS; PROBABILITY

PAUL E. SZARMACH
Western Michigan University
DUNSTAN, ST.

MICHAEL UEBEL
University of Kentucky
PORNOGRAPHY

KEVIN UHALDE
Ohio University
BRUNHILD; EUSKARA; FREDEGUNDA;
HYPATIA; LATIFUNDIA; MARTIN OF
TOURS, ST.; ORIGINAL SIN; OVENS;
RADEGUNDA, ST.; TONSURE

KATHLEEN VERDUIN
Hope College
MEDIEVALISM

OEBELE VRIES
Rijksuniversiteit Groningen
FRISIAN LITERATURE

DIANA WEBB
King's College, London
PILGRIM SOUVENIRS; PILGRIMAGE,
CELTIC

BENJAMIN WEISS
*Burndy Library, Massachusetts Institute
of Technology*
CARTOGRAPHY

EVELIN WETTER
*Geisteswissenschaftliches Zentrum
Geschichte und Kultur
Ostmitteleuropas e.V. Leipzig*
BOHEMIAN ART

JAN M. ZIOLKOWSKI
Harvard University
HILARY OF ORLÉANS; LATIN
LITERATURE: SECULAR LYRICS; SATIRE

Index

*References to main entries are in **boldface**. References to illustrations are followed by (illus.). References to sidebars are followed by (sidebar).*

A

Aachen
  palace in, 33b
  scholarship in, 89b
Abaco, Paolo dell', 400b
ʿAbbās, ʿAlī ibn al-
  al-Kitāb al-malakī, 380b
  Kitāb Kāmil as-sināʿ at at-tibbiya, 283b
  on sexuality, 577b
Abbasids, 188b
  Bedouin poetry and, 52a
  medicine under, 380a
  pact of ʿUmar and, 158b
Abbey, Edwin Austin
  murals of, 394b, 395 (illus.)
Abbeys. See Monasteries
ʿAbd al-Raḥmān III, Andalusian Umayyad calliph, 260a
Abelard, Peter, 58b, 387b, 437a
  abilities of, 211b
  consequences literature of, 473b
  cult of, 390b
  Ethica, 630b
  Hilary of Orléans and, 272a
  Historia calamitatum, 46b, 211b, 334a–335a
  humanism and, 281a
  on sacraments, 547a–b, 550a, 550b
  on signs, 582a, 582b
Abortion, **1a–2b,** 252a
  gynecology and, 250b
  prohibition of, 572a
Abraham (patriarch)
  Sabians and, 543b
  sacraments and, 547a
Abraham ben Meïr ibn Ezra, 60a, 257b, 260b
Absalon, archbishop
  Lund cathedral and, 340b–341a
Abū al-Faḍl ibn Turk, 371a
Abū Kāmil, 372a
Abū Naṣr Manṣūr ibn ʿIrāq, 373b
Abū Nuʿaym al-Iṣfahānī
  Ḥilyat al-awliyā, 255a
Abu ʾl-Qāsim al-Zahrāwī (Albucasis), 109a, 381b

Abū ʾl Qāsim Firdawsī
  Shāhnāma, 180b
Abū Yaʿqūb Yūsuf ibn Nuḥ
  al-Diqduq, 259b
Accedens. See Innocent III, pope
Acciaiuoli, **2b–3b,** 403a
Acciaiuoli, Antonio, 45a
Acciaiuoli, Donato, 3a–b
Acciaiuoli, Nerio, 45a
Acciaiuoli, Niccolò, 3a, 3b (illus.)
Accursius, **4a–b**
  Glossa ordinaria (Magna glossa), 4a, 318a, 322a
  on Libri feudorum, 322a
Accursius, Franciscus, 4b
Achaemenids
  Persians under, 466b
Acre, 132b, 424a
  fall of (1291), 604b
  Hospitallers headquarters in, 276b
  Teutonic Order and, 270b
Acts of John, 62a
Acts of Mercy, 432a
Acts of Paul and Thecla, 62a
Acts of Peter, 62a
Acts of Pilate, 154b
Ad Lucilium. See Seneca
Adalbert, St., **4b–5b**
  poetry by, 72a
  relics of, 78b
Adalhard, abbot, 145a–b
Adalugerus
  Admonitio ad Nonswindam reclusam, 630b
Adam and Eve, 194a–196a, 207b
  in drama and art, 195a–196a
  gift of esoteric revelation, 213b
  original sin and, 194a–b, 434b–435a, 436b
  stories of, 194b–196a
Adam of Bremen, 620a–b
  Gesta Hammaburgensis ecclesiae, 620b
Adamnan of Iona
  Life of Columba, 480a
  on pilgrimages, 480a, 480b
Adams, Henry
  Education of Henry Adams, The, 395a
  as medievalist, 394b

  Mont Saint-Michel and Chartres, 385a, 395a
Adams, John
  Dissertation on Canon and Feudal Law, 394a
Adelaide of Maurienne, 513a
Adelard of Bath
  Questiones naturales, 421a
Adelard of Ghent, 168b
Adelbertus of Constance
  on excommunication, 317b
Adenet le Rois, 16b
Administration, Western European
  admiral in, 5b
  of Amsterdam, 16a
  of Catholic Church, 424a
  naval, 6a
  queenship and, 513b–514a
  service roles and, 565a
  of Sicily, 642a
Admiral, **5b–7a**
  duties of, 5b–6a
  origin of term, 5b
Admonitio ad Nonswindam reclusam. See Adalugerus
Admonitio generalis. See Charlemagne
Adolescence. See Childhood and adolescence
Adolf of Nassau, count, 542b
Adoptionism, Spanish, 420b
Adoration of the Lamb. See Eyck, Hubert van
Adrian IV, pope, 641b
Adrianople
  crusader defeat at (1205), 149a
ʿAḍud al-Dawla, 380b
Adultery. See Marriage, Christian
Advent
  Eastern liturgical year and, 329a, 329b
  Western liturgical year and, 331a, 331b
Advent Lyrics, 191b
Adversus haereses. See Irenaeus
Aegean Sea, 201b
Aelfric of Eynsham, abbot
  alliterative literature and, 12b, 15a
  De falsis deis, 14b
Aeneid. See Vergil

Aethelbert of Kent, 646a
Afonso I of Portugal, king, 201b, 326b
   Crónica geral de Espanha de 1344 on,
     495a
Afonso III of Portugal, king, 327a
Afonso V of Portugal, king, 654b
Africa. *See* North Africa
Africa. See Petrarch
Against Jovinian. See Jerome, St.
Agesilaus. See Xenophon
Aghlabids, 381a
Agilulph
   conversion of, 66b
Agnes of Bohemia
   Poor Clares and, 488b
Agnes of Meran, queen, 368b
Agricola (Georg Bauer)
   De re metallica, 348a
Agriculture, 170a–171a
   Amsterdam and, 16a
   animals and, 17b–18a
   cereal grains in, 170a–171a
   Christianization and, 141b, 143b
   commercialization and, 129b–130a
   history of, 408a
   innovations in, 171a
   markets in, 171a
   in Mediterranean, 170b
   poverty and, 501a–502b
   sustainability of, 171a
   See also Ecology
Agroecosystem. *See* Agriculture; Ecology
Aḥima ʿats ben Paltiel
   Megillat aḥima ʿats, 256b
Ahl-al-dhimma. *See* Dhimmīs
Ahl-al-kitāb (people of the book), 158a
Aḥsān al-Taqā sīm fī ma ʿrifat al-aqālīm.
   See Muqaddasī, al-
Ailly, Pierre d'
   astrology and, 41a, 584a
   Imago mundi, 120a
   John XXIII, antipope, and, 298b
   De legibus et sectis contra superstitiosos
     astronomos, 41a
Ailred of Rievaulx, 216a
ʿAin Shaʿia (monastic church: Iraq), 597b
Aiol, 17a
"Airs, waters, and places." *See*
   Hippocrates
Aix-la-Chapelle, court of
   literary patronage at, 457a–b
Akathistos Hymn Moscow
   manuscript of, 362b
Akiba, 257a
Al-. *See* Next element of name
Alan of Lille, 211a
   Anticlaudianus, 281a
   humanism and, 281a
   De planctu naturae, 337b, 421a, 554b
   De virtutibus et de vitiis et de donis
     Spiritus sancti, 631a
Alarcos, Battle of, 305b
Alard, Gervase, 6a

Alaric I, Visigothic king
   Athens and, 44b
   Galla Placidia and, 511b–512a
Álava, 190a
Alberich da Romano, 9a
Albericus de Rosate, **7a–8a**
   Dictionarium iuris tam civilis quam
     canonici, 7b
Albert of Bavaria, duke, 163b
Albert of Habsburg, king, 542b
Albert of Saxony, 406b
Albert the Great. *See* Albertus Magnus
Albertano da Brescia, **8a–b**
   De amore et dilectione Dei et proximi et
     aliarum rerum et de forma vitae, 8a
   De doctrina dicendi et tacendi, 8a
   Liber consolationis et consilii, 8a
Albertus Magnus, 59a, 436b
   De animalibus, 411a
   animals and, 18b
   on Aristotle, 378a
   on Aristotle and monsters, 411a
   on astrology, 584a
   on gender difference, 208a
   gunpowder recipes of, 198a
   Immaculate Conception and, 289a
   on sacraments, 546a, 550a, 551a,
     552a, 553a
   Secreta mulierum, 2a, 411b, 412a
   on sexuality, 492b
   soul and body and, 591b
   on transubstantiation, 614b
Albigensian Crusade, 556b
   songs about, 458a
Albigensians, 213a, 227b
   devil and, 156a–b
   massacre of, 626a
   popular religion and, 528b
   See also Cathars
Albizzi family
   Acciaiuoli and, 3a
Albrecht IV of Habsburg, 542b
Albrecht of Brandenburg, 607a
Albucasis. *See* Abu 'l-Quāsim al-Zahrāwī
Albuin, 630b
Alcher of Clairvaux
   Liber de spiritu et anima, 212b
   on soul and body, 590b
Alcuin of York, 57b *(illus.)*
   Charlemagne and, 457a
   Epistola de litteris colendis, 560b
   Liber de virtutibus et vitiis, 630b
   on sacraments, 546b, 549b
   schools and, 561a
   study of logic and, 89a
Aldus, Peter, abbot, 67a
Ale and beer. *See* Brewing
Aleppo
   trading colonies, 202a
Alexander II, pope, 422b
   St. Stanisław and, 594b
Alexander III, pope, 193b
   heresy and, 314a

   inquisitorial procedure and, 312b
   on marriage, 336a, 367a–b
Alexander IV, pope, **8b–9b,** 621a,
   639a–b
   excommuncation of Manfred of Sicily
     by, 342b
Alexander de Villa Dei, **9b–10a**
   Carmen de algorismo, 10a
   Doctrinale puerorum, 9b, 563a
   Ecclesiale, 10a
   Massa compoti, 10a
   Summarium biblicum, 10a
Alexander fragments, 13b
Alexander III (the Great) of Macedon,
   king, 180a
Alexander of Bonaventure, 59a
Alexander of Hales, 59a
   on sacraments, 547a
Alexander III of Scotland, king, 634a
Alexander the Great. *See* Alexander III
   (the Great) of Macedon, king
Alexander VI, pope, 440b
   pornographic entertainments of, 491a
   Savonarola and, 557b–558a
Alexandreis. See Walter of Châtillon
Alexandria
   attack of, 643a
   Museum of, 286b
   trading colonies in, 202a
Alexiad. See Anna Komnena
Alexios I Komnenos, 360b
Alexios III Angelos, Byzantine emperor,
   149a
Alexios IV, Byzantine emperor, 149a
Alexios V Doukas, Byzantine emperor,
   149a
Alf Trisar Shiala ("Thousand and Twelve
   Questions"), 544a
Alfaquis (Morisco Islamic teachers), 415b
Ælfgyva, abbess, 217a
Alfonso I of Aragon, king, 184b, 603b
   Petrus Alfonsi and, 471b
Alfonso V of Aragon, king, **10a–11a**
Alfonso II of Asturias, king
   Lisbon and, 326b
Alfonso VIII of Castile, king, 150b, 196a,
   196b
   Battle of Las Navas de Tolosa and,
     306a
Alfonso IX of León, king, 196a, 196b
Alfonso X of Castile and León, king,
   196b, 419b
   astrology and, 40b
   Holy Roman Empire and, 542a, 542b
   patronage by, 459a
   poetry under, 494b
   poverty classification under, 499b–500a
Alfonso XI of Castile and León, king
   begging licenses under, 500b
Alfonso of Gandia, duke
   as contender to throne of Aragon, 94b
Alfred the Great
   cult of, 392b

patronage by, 457b
schools and, 561b
Algebra, 371a–372b
  See also Mathematics, Islamic
Algebra. See Khwārizmī, Muḥammad ibn
  Mūsā al-
Algeria
  Muslims in, 416a
ʿAlī ibn Abī Ṭālib, 253b, 254b
Aljamiado literature, 415a–b
Allegory, 149b–150a, 154b–155a, 155a
  (illus.)
  biblical commentaries and, 54b
  pagan gods interpreted as, 452a–b
Alliterative literature, **11a–15b**
  audience for, 12b–13a, 15a
  authorship of, 12a–b
  gaps in history of, 13a–b
  medieval views of, 11a–12a
  in Old English, 11a, 12a–15a, 192a
  poetry and, 14a–b
  Revival of, 13b
  rhythmic prose and, 11a, 14b–15a
Almagest. See Ptolemy
Almericus, abbot, 82b
Almohads, 196b
  in Iberian Peninsula, 305b–306a
  in North Africa, 196b
Almsgiving, 99b–100b
  penance and, 549b
  See also Charity
Alnwick castle, 464b, 465 *(illus.)*
Alps, 170a, 172b
  passes, 202b, 203a
Alpujarras mountains
  Morisco rebels in, 414b
Altar
  Gothic art and, 239b–240a, 241a
  in Kraków, 305b
Altdorfer, Albrecht
  pilgrim souvenir painting by, 479a
Altenberg, Cistecian monastery at, 236a
Althing, 245a
Alvares, João
  Vida do Infante D. Fernando, 496b
Amadeo VIII of Savoy, pope, 188a
Amadís de Gaula, 495a
Amalfi
  merchants of, 402a
Amand, St., 24a
Amaury of Bène
  atheism and, 44a
Ambrose, St., 54b
  on sexuality, 570a
Ambrosiana (library: Milan), 358b, 359a
Amharan dynasty, 598b
Ami et Amile, 181a
Amiens (cathedral: France), 219a,
  222a–b, 226b
  choir of, 227b
  Gothic reconstruction of, 227a
Amorion
  public baths in, 50a

Ampullae
  as pilgrim souvenirs, 477b, 479a
Amstel River, 15b
Amsterdam, **15b–16b**
Amulets
  in popular religion, 527b–528a
Anagogy
  biblical commentaries and, 54b
Anatomy
  sexuality and, 578a, 579a
  study of, 380a, 381a, 382a
Anchorites
  women as, 569b
Ancient English Metrical Romances. See
  Ritson, Joseph
Ancrene Riwle, 115b
Andalusī, Samūʾil ibn Yaḥyā ibn ʿAbbās
  al-Maghribī al-
  on sexual pathologies, 579b–580a
Andalusia
  Ferdinand III of Castile and, 196b
  Hebrew language in, 260a–261a
András II of Hungary, king
  Teutonic Order and, 270b
Andrea da Barberino, **16b–17b**
  Aspramonte, 17a
  Guerrino il meschino, 17a
  I reali di Francia, 16b, 17a
  Prima Spagna, 17a
  Rinaldo, 17a
  Secondo Spagna, 17a
  La storia del re Ansuigi, 17a
  La storia di Aiolfo del Barbicone, 17a
  La storia di Ugone d'Avernia, 17a
  Storie di Rinaldo da Montalbano, 17a
  Storie Nerbonesi, 17a
Andrea del Castagno
  Niccolò Acciaiuoli, 3b *(illus.)*
Andreae, Johannes, 638a
Andreas Capellanus. *See* Capellanus,
  Andreas
Andrew de Moray, 634a
Andrew II of Hungary, king, 606b
Andrew of Caesarea, 55a
Andrew of St. Victor, 58a, 59b
Anegenge, 195a
Angela of Foligno
  union with Christ by, 69a
Angelomus of Luxeuil, 57a
Angels
  demons and, 151a–152a, 154a, 156a
Angels' Tower of the Papal Palace. *See*
  Vatican Library
Angevins
  establishment of, 621b
  factions, 423b
Anglica historia (History of England). *See*
  Vergil, Polydore
Anglo-Norman literature, 219b
  alliterative literature and, 11a, 13a
  Arthurian romances and, 37b
  drama of, 195a–b

Anglo-Saxon poetry, 191b–192b, 192a
  alliterative literature and, 13b, 14a,
    14b
Anglo-Saxons
  archaeology of, 25b, 26a–b, 27b
  comitatus and, 129a–b
  domestic architecture of, 31b *(illus.),*
    32 *(illus.)*
Animal husbandry, 170a–171a
  attitudes toward animals and, 18a
  domestic architecture and, 33a
Animals
  anthropomorphization of, 19a, 20b
  in the Exeter Book, 192a
  exotics in ecosystem, 173b
  extinction of, 173a
  fallow deer, 173a–b
  in illuminated manuscripts, 359a, 360b
  as marvels, 410b
  symbolism of, 18a, 20a
Animals, attitudes toward, **17b–21a**
  bestiaries and, 18b–19a
  fables and epics and, 19a–b, 180a
  falconry and, 20a
  hagiography and, 19b–20a
  heraldry and, 20a
  hunting and, 20a, 173a, 360b
  social rank and, 173a–b
  theological writings and, 18a–20a
Anna Komnena
  Alexiad, 63b
Anna Selbdritt, 242a
Annales (journal), 533b
Annales rerum gestarum Alfredi. See Asser
Annals. See Tacitus
Anne of Bohemia, **21a–b**
  influence of, 514a
Annonce faite à Marie, L' (The tidings
  brought to Mary). *See* Claudel, Paul
Anṣārī, Abū Ayyūb al-, 253b
Anselm of Canterbury, St., 436b–437a,
  437a, 640a
  atheism and, 44a
  England, departure from, 641a
  Liber de humanis moribus, 630b
  Proslogion, 43b
  reformers and, 640b
  on signs, 582a, 582b
Anselm of Laon, 547a
Anselm of Lucca, 422b
Ansgar, St., **21b–22a**, 146a
ʿAntar, **22a–23a**
Anthony of Egypt, St., **23a–24a**
  demons and, 23b *(illus.)*
  temptations of, 151b, 156b–157a
  Vita, 156b
Anti-Semitism, 388a
  Petrus Alfonsi on, 471a–472b
  pollution and taboo and, 485a
Antichrist
  Satan and, 157a
Anticlaudianus. See Alan of Lille

Anticlericalism
   atheism and, 43b
   soul and body and, 591a
Antifeminism
   Eve and, 195b–196a
   satire and, 555a, 556a
Antiheresis. See Durand of Huesca
Antioch, 174a–b, 175a, 201b
Antiphonary of Bangor, 66b
Antiquities laws
   archaeology and, 28a
Antoninus of Florence, St., 400a
   price formation and, 303a
   voluntary poverty and, 100b
Antwerp, **24a–25a**
Anuario de estudios medievales (journal), 384b
Anziani (elders), 134a
Aphorisms. See Maimonides, Moses
Aphorisms (Kitāb al-Nawādir al-ṭibbîya).
   See Māsawayh, Yūḥannā ibn
Aphrodisiacs, 580a
Apocalypse, 262a
Apocalypse of Baruch, 194b
Apocalypse of Paul, 262b
Apocrypha, 151a–b, 152b *(illus.),* 154b
Apollonius, 371a–b
   Conics, 286b
Apologetics
   Portuguese, 496b
   See also Polemics
Apologia. See Guy de Bazoches
Apology. See Tertullian
Apostles of Gaul, 222a, 224a–b
Apothecaries, 476a
Apparition of St. Michael, The. See
   Bonaguida, Pacino di
Apparitions. See Ghosts
Apprenticeship
   adolescence and, 116a–b
   beginning of, 115a
   for merchants, 400b
   servants and, 566a
Apulia, 170b, 422b
Aqṣā, al- (mosque: Jerusalem), 603b
Aquamanilia, 244a
Aquileia, Diet of
   Henry VII of Germany and, 269a
Aquinas, Thomas, St., 57a, 59a, 207b,
   208a, 419b, 420b, 436b, 650b
   animals and, 18a–b
   atheism and, 43b, 44a
   on capital vice, 629b, 631a
   Catena aurea, 57a
   Expositio in Job ad litteram, 59a
   humanism and, 281b
   Immaculate Conception and, 289a,
     290a
   just price and, 302a–b
   on matter, 378a–b
   on merchants, 399a
   natural law and, 418b–419b
   original sin and, 434b, 436b, 437a

   on probability, 509a
De regimine principum, 618b
   on resurrection, 70b–71a
   on sacraments, 545b–548b, 550a–
     551b, 553a, 583b
   on sexuality, 492b
   on signs, 582a, 582b
   soul and body and, 591b, 593a
   Summa theologiae, 98b, 163b, 302a,
     419a, 618a
   on transubstantiation, 614b
   on tyranny, 618a–b
Aquitanians, 190a
Arabia
   contact with China and, 117a–118a
Arabic language, 191a
   administrative terms from, 5b
   Hebrew language and, 260a–261a
   Persian language influenced by,
     467a–b, 467b–468a
   in schools, 562b
   writings on sexuality in, 577b, 580a
Arabic literature
   epic poetry, 22a
Arabic medicine. See Medicine, Islamic
Arabs
   invasions of, 559b
   in Islamic world, 158a–158b
   piracy among, 482b
   See also Bedouins
Aragon, Crown of, 413a–b, 612b
Aragon, kingdom of
   Admiral in, 6a
   Athens and, 45a
   Mercedarians in, 397b
   Moriscos in, 414a
   Sicily and, 601b
Aramaic language, 259b, 261b
   Mandaic dialect, 544a
Arator
   used in schools, 562a
Aratus
   Phainomena, 42a
Archaeology, **25a–30b**
   architecture and, 30b
   domestic architecture and, 31b, 33a
   early medieval, 26b–28a
   environmental, 25a, 29a–b
   future of, 29b–30a
   "gray literature" of, 29b–30a
   history of, 25a–26b
   medieval architecture and, 28b–29a
   new directions in, 29a–b
   urban, 28a–b, 29a
Archaeoscience, 170a
Archimedes, 371a–b, 373a
   Sphere and Cylinder, 543b
Architecture
   Anglo-Saxon, 35b
   archaeology and, 26a, 28b–29a
   Byzantine, 596b–597a
   Christian, 596b
   defensive, 34a, 34b

   French Romanesque, 153a, 154a, 154b
     (illus.), 155b, 155b *(illus.)*
   Italian, 231a
   Mesopotamian Christian, 597b
   Ottonian, 218b
   Palestinian Christian, 597a–b
   patronage in, 456a
   Poor Clares and, 489b
   Roman domestic, 30b
   Romanesque, 34a
   urban identity and, 538a–b
   See also Gothic architecture; Ottoman
     art and architecture; Syrian Christian
     architecture
Architecture, domestic, **30b–36b**
   in Carolingian period, 33b–34a
   in late antiquity, 30b–31b
   late medieval, 36a
   rural, 30b, 33b–34a, 35a–b, 36a
   in sixth to ninth century, 32a–34a
   in tenth to fourteenth century, 34a–
     36a
   urban, 30b, 31a, 33a–b, 34a–b, 36a
Architrenius (Archlamenter). *See* John de
   Hauville
Archpoet, 555a
   Prodromic poetry and, 510b
Ardizone, Jacob de, 325a
Arechis II of Salerno
   public baths and, 50b
Arethras of Casesarea, 55a
Aretino, Leonardo Bruni
   biography of Dante by, 64a
Argenteuil (abbey), 46b
Argumenta. See Ricardus Anglicus
Argumentum super quatuor questionibus.
   See Idung of Prüfening
Arianism, 420b, 620a
   Dracontius and, 167a
   St. Anthony and, 23b
   spread of, 619b
Ariosto, Ludovico, 17b, 390a
   Orlando furioso, 181b
Aristotelianism, heterodox
   leader of, 71b
Aristotle, 417a
   on abortion, 1a
   De anima, 588b, 591b
   on astrology, 584a
   atheism and, 43b
   biography and, 61a–b
   commentaries on, 3b, 71b, 411a–b,
     473a, 639a
   on four qualities, 207b
   gender differences and, 68b
   humanism and, 281b
   De interpretatione, 582a
   Libri naturales, 411a
   on matter, 377a–379a
   medicine and, 381b
   Metaphysics, 377a–378b, 411a–b
   on metaphysics, 614b, 615b
   on monsters, 409b

on nature, 420a
Nicomachean Ethics, 296b, 301b, 629b, 631a
Peripatetic school under, 61a
Physics, 377a–378b
on physics, 406a
Poetics, 178b–179b
political theory of, 134b–135a
on probability, 508a, 509a
on profit, 399a
semiotics of, 581a, 582a, 584b, 585b
on sexuality, 577b
on soul and body, 588b, 589a, 591a, 591b, 592a
teachings of, 210a
transubstantiation and, 614a
on tyranny, 618a
works of, 411a
Arithmetic. See Khwārizmī, Muḥammad ibn Mūsā al-
Arles
raids on, 202b
Armagh, archbishop of. *See* Fitzralph, Richard
Armengol Blasi de Montpellier, 584a
Armenia
biblical commentaries in, 55a–b
Armenian Gospels Venice, 360a
Armenians, 174a–b, 175a, 202a
Arnade, Peter
on civic ritual, 533b, 538a
Arnald of Villanova, 164a–b, 165b
on personal hygiene, 285b–286a
Arnim, Achim von, 393a
Arnold of Brescia, 139a, 187b
Arnolfo di Cambio, 240b
Arnulf of Carinthia, duke, 137b–138a
Arnulf of Orléans
Hilary of Orléans and, 272a
Arpâd, Maria
Poor Clares and, 488b
Arras
communes of, 135b
Congress of, 323b
Arrazi, Ahmed
Crónica do Mouro Rasis, 495a
Arrian, on horsemanship, 275b
Ars dictaminisi school
Vigna and, 458b
Ars grammatica (Ars maior). See Donatus
Ars nova, 427b
Arson. *See* Violence
Art
images of the Fall and, 195b
pornographic, 492a–b
See also Bohemian art; Gothic art; Islamic art and architecture; Ottoman art and architecture
"Art of Medicine." *See* Galen
Arte de trovar, 494a
Arte della Lana, 402b
Arte della Seta, 399b
Arte di Calimala, 402b

Artevelde, Jacob van, 136a, 404a
Artevelde, Philip van, 404a
Arthur, king, 389b–390a
in myth, 392b, 396a
Arthurian romances, **36b–40a,** 393a, 395b–396b
adaptations of, 38b–39b
Idylls of the King, 392a
Lady of the Lake, The, 391b, 392a (*illus.*)
Perceval in, 184a–b
Portuguese, 150b–151a, 494b–495a
reassessments of major texts of, 37a–38b
Spanish, 150b–151a, 151a
Artillery, 198a–b
transportation of, 199b–200a
See also Firearms
Artisans
servants and, 566a
Arts and Crafts movement, 392b–393a
Arundel, duke of, 6a
Arwad, island of, 604b
Aryans, 466a
Asceticism
Christian, 23a–24a, 588a
Islamic, 68b
repression of the body and, 68a
of St. Catherine of Siena, 96a
Asega (law-sayer), 205a–206a
Asegabuch (book of the *asega*), 205a–b
Ashkenaz
divorce and, 648a–b
Hebrew language and, 261a–b
literary traditions and, 256b
marriage and, 644b, 648a–b
Asia
trade with, 118a
Aspramonte. See Andrea da Barberino
Asser
Annales rerum gestarum Alfredi, 63a
Assisi, basilica of, 176b, 177a–b
Assize of Clarendon, 315b
Assizes of Romania, 44b
Astral magic, **40a–41b**
Astrological iconography, **41b–43a**
Astrology
vs. astral magic, 40a–b
Oresme on, 509b
semiotics and, 584b
signs and, 584a
Astronomy
astrology and, 41b
John of Sacrobosco and, 296b–298a
mathematics of, 373a–b
pagan images in manuscripts on, 453a
Petrus Alfonsi and, 471b
Sabians and, 543b
See also Mathematics, Islamic
Atala, St., abbot, 66b
Ataulf
Galla Placidia and, 511b–512a

Athanasius of Alexandria, St.
on fasting, 329a
Life of St. Anthony, 23a, 62a, 153a
Atharib, al-, 174b
Atheism, **43a–44a**
Athens, **44b–45a**
Athos, Mount
illuminated manuscripts on, 359b–360a (*sidebar*), 360b, 362a–b
ʿAtlit (Château Pèlerin), 604a
Attila the Hun, 625a
Aubigné, Agrippa d'
on poverty, 502b
Audience
of Arthurian romances, 36b, 37a, 37b, 38a
Audovera, 203b
Auerbach, Erich, 386b
August II, duke
manuscript collection of, 355b
Augustine of Hippo, St., 54b, 434b, 605b
on abortion, 1a
animals and, 18a–b
astrology and, 41b, 42a, 584a
Canterbury and, 228b
City of God, 62a, 221a–b, 262a, 583b
Confessions, 45a–46a, 45b–46a, 46b, 114a, 143b, 333b
De cura pro mortuis gerenda, 212b
De dialectica, 581a
distinction of sin, 631a
on divorce, 364a
De doctrina christiana, 18b, 581a, 584a
Enchiridion, 409b
on gender difference, 208a
on ghosts, 212b
on government, 616b
influence of, 8a
vs. Julian Eclanum, 436a
De libero arbitrio, 212b
life stages and, 430b
De magistro, 581a, 581b
on matter, 377b
numeric philosophy and, 427b
on original sin, 67a, 194b, 288a, 434b, 435b, 436a–b, 437a
on origins of evil, 629b
on peace, 461b, 462a
vs. Pelagius, 435b–436a
De quantitate animae, 212b
on sacraments, 545a
St. Anthony and, 23a
semiotics of, 581a–582a, 583a, 583b
on sexuality, 570a, 572a
signs and, 585a
on sin, 630a–b
on soul and body, 589b–590a
De Trinitate, 581b
on tyrants, 616b–617b
used in schools, 558b
on virtue, 628b
Augustine of Kent, 143a–b

Augustinian Rule
  hospitals and, 104a
  Humbert of Romans commentary on,
    283a
Augustinians
  biblical studies and, 59a
  Mercedarians and, 397b
  schools and, 564b
Augustodunensis, Honorius, 154b–155a
  Sigillum Sanctae Mariae, 58a
Augustus, Roman emperor
  astrology and, 42b
Austrasia
  Brunhild and, 81a–b
Austria, duchy of, 542b
Austro-Hungarian Empire, 542b
Authenticum, 322a
Authority
  obedience to, 616b–617a
  people as source of, 619a
  power to rule, origins of, 617a–b
Autobiography and confessional literature,
  45a–48a
  Boethius and, 46a
  in literature, 47a–b
  medieval, 46a–b
  St. Augustine and, 45b–46a
Autopsy
  causes of death, 252b
  soul and body and, 592b
Autun, cathedral of, 153a *(illus.),* 154a,
  154b *(illus.)*
Auxentius of Milan, bishop, 619b
Averroës. *See* Rushd, Ibn
Avesta
  Zoroastrians and, 158a
Avestan language, 468a
Avicebron. *See* Solomon ben Judah ibn
  Gabirol
Avicenna. *See* Sīnā, Ibn
Avignon
  Florentine merchants in, 3a
  papal court in, 7a, 136a
  St. Catherine of Siena and, 96b
Avitus, St.
  used in schools, 562a
Awntyrs of Arthure, The, 14b
Aymard, abbot
  Maiolus and, 341b
Ayyubids
  medical practice under, 381a
Azo, 4a
Azores
  colonization of, 655a
  Portuguese colonization and, 269b
Azzo d'Este VII, 193b

B

"B" (biographer of St. Dunstan), 168a,
  168b
Baba Naqqāsh (Old Master Designer),
  447a

Babenberg family, 542b
Babylonian Talmud, 214b
Bacon, Roger, 197b
  on astrology, 584a
  on disease, 165a–b
  *Epistola de secretis operibus artis et
    naturae et de nullitate magiae,* 197b
  Opus maius, 584a
  De Signis, 582b–583b
Baden-Powell, Lord, 392b
Badges
  as pilgrim souvenirs, 478b, 478 *(illus.),*
    479a
Baghdad
  as center of science, 371a, 373b,
    380a–b, 382a
  dhimmīs in, 158b
Bagrat (of Armenia), 174a
Bailiff
  of communes, 135b
Baiṭār, Ibn al-, 381b
Bakhtin, Mikhail
  Rabelais and His World, 539a
Balak, 174b
Balbus. *See* Bernard of Pavia
Baldus, 134b, 618b
  on feudal law, 322b–323a
Baldwin I, Latin emperor of
  Constantinople, 149a
Baldwin II of Flanders, count, 613a–b
Baldwin I of Jerusalem, king, 174a, 174b,
  215a, 271a–b
  as count of Edessa, 215b
Baldwin II of Jerusalem, king, 174a, 175a
Baldwin of Boulogne. *See* Baldwin I of
  Jerusalem, king
Baldwin of Bourg. *See* Baldwin II of
  Jerusalem, king
Baldwin of Edessa, count. *See* Baldwin I
  of Jerusalem, king
Baldwin of Flanders, count. *See* Baldwin
  I, Latin emperor of Constantinople
Bale, John, 389b
Balkans
  Byzantine control of, 132b
  Muslims in, 416a
Balliol, John, 634a–b
  capture of, 634a
Balthild, queen, 145a
Baltic Sea
  piracy in, 481a
Bamberg
  Henry II of Germany and, 266b
Bamberg Cathedral, 230a
Banal (feudal) rights
  ovens and, 449b–450a
Bandelli, Vincent
  Immaculate Conception and, 290a
Banking
  merchants and, 398b, 399b, 400b,
    402b, 403a, 404a
Bannā', Ibn al-, 375a
Bannockburn, Battle of, **48a–b,** 63a

Banū Mūsā
  *On Knowledge of the Measurement of
    Plane and Spherical Figures,* 372a
Baptism, 112 *(illus.),* 436a, 545a
  conversion and, 140b–142a, 143a,
    144a
  of infants, 114b
  newborns and, 109b–110a
  in peacemaking, 460b–461a
  race and, 515b
  Sabians and, 544a
  as sacrament, 546a, 546b–547b
Barbara, St., 200a
Barbarigo, Andrea, 403b
Barbaro, Francesco
  "On wifely duties," 567b–568a
Barbarossa, Frederick of Germany. *See*
  Frederick I Barbarossa of Germany,
  emperor
Barber-surgeons, 476a
Barberini family, 624a
Barč, prince, 147a
Barcelona
  communal government in, 136b
  James I of Aragon and, 293a
  law code of, 44b
  trade in, 133b
Bardi company, 2b, 3b, 400b, 403a
Barhebraeus, 55b
Bari
  merchants in, 402a
Barlaão e Josafate, 496a
Baron, Hans, 386a
Barsegh I, Armenian patriarch, 175a
Bartholomaeus Anglicus, **49a–b**
  animals and, 18b
  De proprietatibus rerum, 49a–b, 114a
  on race, 516b–517a
Bartlett, Robert
  on race, 515a–b
Bartolo da Sassoferrato
  De tyranno, 618b
Bartolomeo Prignano of Bari. *See* Urban
  VI, pope
Basel, Council of (1431–1449), 187b–
  188a, 610b, 622b
  Bursfeld Abbey and, 83a
  deposition of Pope Eugenius IV and,
    323b
  Immaculate Conception and, 290a
  on sacraments, 549a
Basil I, Byzantine emperor, 359a
Basil II, Byzantine emperor, 360b
Basil (the Great) of Caesarea, St., 59b
Basilics (Basilica), 426b–427a
Basilios of Neopatria, 55a
Basques, 190a–191b
Bassano, 193b
Bassianus, Johannes, 4a, 82a
Baswell, Christopher, 179b
Bartholomew of Pisa (de Rinonico), 159b

Baths and bathing, **49b–51b,** 283b
(*illus.*)
personal hygiene and, 285a–b
Battle of Maldon, The, 129a
Baṭṭūṭa, Ibn, 399b
Baudoin de Guînes, Comte
Lambert genealogy of, 457b–458a
Baudonivia
Radegunda biography by, 518b
Baudri of Bourgueil, 308b
Bavaria
Henry II of Germany and, 266a
Bāyāzīd I, Ottoman sultan, 442b
Bāyāzīd II, Ottoman sultan
mosque complex of, 443a
Bayeux Tapestry
horses and, 274b
Bazianus, 295b
Beardsley, Aubrey, 392a (*illus.*), 393a
Beatrice (wife of Joscelin II), 175a
Beatrice of Swabia, 196a
Beatrice of Wormgay
Hubert de Burgh and, 278a
Beaufort, Thomas, duke of Exeter, 6a
Beauvais (cathedral: France), 219b, 222a,
226b
Gothic reconstruction of, 227a
transept of, 233b
upper choir of, 227b
Becket, Thomas, St., 29b, 228a–b, 229a
Henry II and, 458b
pilgrim souvenirs and, 478b–479a, 478
(*illus.*)
Bede, 56b, 179b, 421a, 610a
autobiography by, 45b
*Ecclesiastical History of the English
Church and People,* 56a (*illus.*),
143a–b, 365a
on merchants, 399a
on pilgrimages, 480b
poverty and, 499b
on sacraments, 546b–547a
schools and, 560a
Bédier, Joseph, 383b, 393b
Bedouins, **51b–52b**
Beelzebub. *See* Devil
Beggars
charity and, 503b–504b
in England, 499b, 500b
Beguines, 529a, 569b, 650b
mystic love poetry and, 339a
Behar, Ruth, 502b
Behavior, codes of, 183b–184b
Behemoth. *See* Devil
Beit Alpha (synagogue: Palestine), 41b
Béla IV of Hungary, king, 147a
Belgium
cities of, 24a
schools in, 562a
Bell, Catherine
Ritual Theory, Ritual Practice, 532a–b
Bell, Gertrude
travels of, 596b

Bella Brigata (followers of Catherine of
Siena), 96a
Belloc, Hilaire, 395a
Bembo, Francesco, bishop, 97a
Benedict Biscop, St.
abbeys founded by, 56b
pilgrim souvenirs of, 477b
Benedict of Aniane, 62b
Benedict of Nursia, St.
animals and, 19b
on monastic tradition, 62b
temptations of, 151b–152a
on wandering monks, 479b–480a
Benedict X, pope, 422a, 422b
Benedict XII, pope
China missions and, 119a
Benedict XIII, antipope, 439b, 440b,
623b
Alfonso V and, 10b
throne or Aragon and, 94b–95a
Benedictine Rule, 145a, 429a, 432a
Benedictine Revival and, 168a–b
at Bobbio abbey, 66b
in France, 89a
regula mixta and, 145a
Regularis concordia, 168b
St. Clare and, 126a–127a
Benedictines
monasteries of, 82b–83a
Westminster Abbey charitable
distributions and, 102b–103a
Benevento, Battle of (1266), 342b
Benevento, Concordat of, 641b
Benevento, Council of (1091)
on sacraments, 551b
Benoît de Sainte-Maure, 624b
Henry II and, 458a
Beowulf, 129a, 179a, 180a–b, 390a, 391a
alliterative literature and, 12a
Finnsburh Episode of, 197a
queen in, 512a
Berengar of Tours, 545a, 614a–615a
papal condemnation of, 422a
Berenguela of Castile, 196a
Beresford, Maurice, 26b
Bergamo, 7a
Bergman, Ingmar
Seventh Seal, The, 396b
Virgin Spring, The, 396b
Bern of Sweden, king, 21b
Bernadette, St. *See* Soubirous, Marie-
Bernarde
Bernard of Chartres
humanism and, 281a
on matter, 377b
Bernard of Clairvaux, St., 57b, 138b,
187a, 387b, 649a
on art, 454b
De consideratione
on Immaculate Conception, 288b
language of spiritual friendship and,
338b
De laude novae militiae, 603b

*Liber de gradibus superbiae et
humilitatis,* 629b
on monasticism, 62b, 287b
Sententiae, 629b
Bernard of Cluny
De contemptu mundi, 554b
satire and, 556a
Bernard of Gui. *See* Gui, Bernard
Bernard of Parma, **52b–53a**
Casus longi, 53a
Summa super titulis decretalium, 53a
Bernard of Pavia (Balbus), **53a–54a,** 84b
Brevarium extravigantium, 53b
Collection in Ninety-five Titles, 53b
Compilatio prima, 84b
Parisiensis secunda, 53b
Summa decretalium, 53b
Bernard Silvester, 211a
Cosmographia, 421a
humanism and, 281a
De mundi universitate, 421a
Bernardino of Siena, St., 400a, 574b
on contraception, 252a
Poor Clares and, 488b, 489a
voluntary poverty and, 100b
Bernhardus of Heldesheim
on excommunication, 317b
Bernoldus of Constance
on excommunication, 317b
Bersuire, Pierre
Reductorium morale, 411a
Bertha of Kent, queen, 143a, 646a
Bertran de Born
satire and, 556b
on war, 627b
Bertulf, St., 66b
Bessarion, Johannes, cardinal
manuscript collection of, 356a
Bestiaries
Andrea da Barberino and, 16b
attitudes toward animals and, 18b–19a
Betrothal, contract of, 363b, 364b, 367a
Beverlai, Johanna, 239b
Bevershoutsveld, Battle of (1382), 198b
Bible
on abortion, 1a
attitudes toward animals and, 18a
concept of soul and body in, 588b
criminal procedure and, 311b–312a,
313a–b
in *disputatio,* 472b
due process and, 318b
Genesis, 45b–46b, 214a–b, 434b–435a
Hebrew, 620a
manuscript illumination and, 357b
New Testament, 194a, 213b, 590a,
620a
numerology in, 427b
Old Testament, 154a–b, 179b, 428b–
429a
Septuagint, 1a
on soul and body, 589a–b, 590a
as source of *Dies irae,* 158b

standardized version of, 89a
Ten Commandments, 631b
translations of, 142a–b
Vivian, 42a
Biblical commentaries, **54a–61a**
by Bernard of Pavia, 53b
of early Middle Ages, 55b–57a
eastern Christian, 54b–55b
of High Middle Ages, 57b–59a
Jewish, 60a–b
of later Middle Ages, 59b–60a
patristic, 54b–55b
Biblioteca Marciana, Venice, 359a
Bibliothèque bleue, 390b
Bibliothèque nationale, Paris, 359a
Bicchieri, Guala, 273a
Biddle, Martin, 28a
Biga party (Spain), 136b
Bigamy, 364a
Biography, **61a–64b**
of abbots, 62b
of ascetics, 62a–b
of bishops, 62b
Christian, 61b
classical, 61a–b
of martyrs, 61b–62a
royal, 62b–64a
sexuality in, 570b
See also Hagiography
Biringuccio, Vannocia, 345b
Birka (Sweden), 27a
Bīrūnī, Muḥammad ibn Aḥmad Abū
’l-Rayḥān al-, 373a, 373b
Biscay, 190a
Bishoprics
schools in, 558b–559a
Bishops
authority of, 133b–134a, 134b
Henry V of Germany and, 267a–b
Black Death, 172a, 398a, 636a, 637b
charity and, 101a–b, 103a, 105b–106a
civic ritual and, 534b
homosexuality and, 574b
labor shortage after, 566b, 647b
Lisbon and, 327a
poverty and, 499b
rural depopulation and, 26b
See also Bubonic plague
Black Sea
piracy in, 481a
Blackstone, Sir William
Commentaries on the Laws of England,
390b
Blanche of Castile, queen of France,
178b, 232b–233a, 646a
as regent, 513b
Blanche of Savoy
Poor Clares and, 488b
Blast furnaces, 347a–b
Blessings, books of, 528a
Blind, hospitals for, 104a
Blind Harry, 634b

Bloch, Marc
on civic ritual, 534a
Les rois thaumaturges, 533b
Bloy, Léon, 395a
Bluebeard. *See* Gilles de Rais
Blues and Greens, **65a–66b**
Bobbio, **66b–67a**
library of, 66b–67a
monastery at, 560a, 560b
Bobbio Missal, 66b
Bobone, Giacinto, 440a
Bobone, Orso di, 440a
Boccaccio, Giovanni
Genealogia deorum gentilium, 452a
pornography in, 491b
Teseida, 180b
Trattatello in laude de Dante, 64a
Boccanegra, Guglielmo, 134b
Bochove, Thomas Ernst van, 426b
Bodleian Library, Oxford, 360b
Bodmer, Johann Jakob, 391b
Body, the, **67a–71b**
of Christ, in late Middle ages, 69b–
70b
class and, 68b–69b
gender and, 68b–69b
in medieval Christianity, 68b–69b
in medieval Islam, 68b
resurrection of, 70b–71a
Body language, as ritual, 533b–540a
Boethius, Anicius Manlius Severinus,
417a, 427b, 628b
Consolation of Philosophy, 46a, 281a
Contra Eutychen et Nestorium, 420b
De institutione musica, 416b
on matter, 377b
De musica, 417a
philosophy of music, 416b
on signs, 582a
used in schools, 558b, 562a
Boethius of Dacia, **71b–72a**
De aeternitate mundi, 71b
De modis significandi, 71b
on signs, 582b
De summo bono, 71b
Theodoric and, 457a
Bogurodzica (Mother of God; Polish
hymn), **72a–73a**
Bohemia, 408b, 409a
Bartholomaeus Anglicus and, 49a
history of, 147b
king of, 542a
nobles of, 635a
St. Adalbert and, 5a
Bohemian art, **73a–78b**
Beautiful Style era and, 76a–b
Hussite rebellion and, 76b
Jagiellonian kings period and, 76b–78a
Luxembourg house era and, 74a–76a
Prague and, 76a–b
Přemyslid dynasty and, 73a–b
Reformation art and, 76b
Bohemond IV of Tripoli, 604b

Bohemond of Antioch, prince, 215b
Boiardo, Matteo, 17b, 390a
Boileau, Étienne, 135a
Boleslav II of Bohemia, duke, 4b
Bolesław of Bohemia (brother of St.
Wenceslas), 635a
Bolesław I Chrobry of Poland, king, 5a,
78b–79b, 266b, 305a, 409a
St. Stanisław and, 594a, 594b
Bolesław III Krzywousty of Poland, king,
79b–80a
Bolesław V the Pious, 304b
Bolingbroke, Henry. *See* Henry IV of
England, king
Bolland, John, 389b
Bollandist project, 383b
Bologna
feudal law and, 324b–325a
podesta in, 134a
Bologna, University of, 8a
notaries and, 540a–541a
Bombarone, Elias. *See* Elias of Cortona
Bonaguida, Pacino di
Apparition of St. Michael, The, 241a,
242a *(illus.),* 243b
Tree of Life, 489b
Bonaventure, St., 159b
on demons, 527b
Immaculate Conception and, 289a
on ordination of women, 552b
on sacraments, 545b, 546a, 547a,
548b, 550a, 551a, 551b, 552a, 553a
soul and body and, 591b
Boniface, abbot, 62b
Boniface of Montferrat
Athens and, 44b
Dandolo and, 149a
Boniface of Wessex
pilgrimages of, 480b
Boniface VIII, pope, 387b, 440a, 623a
Colonna family and, 128a
glosses on decretal of, 318b
indulgences of, 528a
Liber sextus, 7b
library catalog of, 623b
manuscript collections of, 623b
Bonis brothers, 400b
Bonusbaro, Elias. *See* Elias of Cortona
Books. *See* Manuscript books
Book of Armagh, 80b
Book of Courtesy. See Caxton, William
*Book of Deeds of Arms and of Chivalry,
The. See* Christine de Pizan
Book of Enoch, 151a
Book of hours, 264a
monasticism and, 242b–243a
popular religion and, 529a
Très riches heures, 42b
Book of Job, 179b
Book of Jubilees, 152b
Book of Kings. See Abū ’l Qāsim Firdawsī
Book of Margery Kempe, 47b
Book of Rudolph, 206a

Book of Sinbad, The, 471b
Book of the Eparch, 608b
Book of the Knight of the Tower, 185b
Book of Vices and Virtues, 100a
Book on the Conditions of Women, 1b
Boorman, John
   Excalibur, 396b
Borchling, Conrad, 205b
Bordes, Charles, 396a
Borghese family, 624a
Borgia, Cesare, 440b
Borgia d'Este, Lucrezia
   Poor Clares and, 488b
Borroff, Marie, 14a
Borromeo, Federico, cardinal
   manuscript collection of, 356a
Bosch, Hieronymus
   Last Judgement triptych by, 265a
Bosco deleitoso, 496a
Bosnia
   slaves from, 567b
Bosworth, Battle of (1483)
   Percy and, 465b–466a
Botone, de. *See* Bernard of Parma
Bottono. *See* Bernard of Parma
Boucicaut Hours, 243a
Bourg
   siege of, 198b
Bourges Cathedral, 227a
Bouts, Dirk
   Brotherhood of the Holy Sacrament
     altarpiece, 455b–456a
Bouvines, Battle of (1214)
   Peter des Roches and, 469a
Boy's King Arthur, The. See Lanier, Sidney
Brabant, 24b
Bracciolini, Poggio, 51a
Bracton, Henry de
   criminal procedure and, 316a
   on English law, 419b
   De ligibus Angliae, 638b
   on natural law, 417a
Bradford, William, 394a
Bradfute, Marion, 634a
Bradley, Marion Zimmer
   Arthurian romances and, 36b
   Mists of Avalon, The, 396b
Bradwardine, Thomas, 405a, 421a
   De proportionibus velocitatum in
     motibus, 406a
   on semantics, 473b
Brahmagupta, 371a
Braine, Jehan de
   Par dessor l'ombre d'un bois, 72b
Brancaleone, 9a
Brandenburg, margrave of, 542a
Brandenburg ad der Havel Cathedral,
   altarpiece of, 75b
Braveheart, 634b
Bréauté, Fawkes de, 278a
Bredon, Simon, 405b
Brendan, St., voyage of, 480a–b

Brentano, Clemens
   Des Knaben Wunderhorn, 393a
Brescia, 193b
   communal life in, 8a
Břetislav of Bohemia, duke, 5a
Brevarium extravigantium. See Bernard of
   Pavia
Breviary of St. Clare, 158b
Brewing, 646b
   ale, 171a
Brian Boru, **80a–81a**
Brie, Simon de. *See* Martin IV, pope
Brigid, St.
   pilgrimages to church of, 480b
Britain, 171b
   domestic architecture in, 30b, 31a
     (illus.), 32b, 33a
   schools in, 558b, 559b
Britannia. See Camden, William
Brito, William, 58b
Broad Stone of Honour, The. See Digby,
   Kenelm
Brocarda. See Ricardus Anglicus
Brokers
   merchants and, 399b
Brokmer Manuscripts, 205a
Brooke, A. N.
   Prospects of Medieval History, The, 383a
Brown, Peter, 408a
Bruce, Edward
   invasion of Ireland by, 48b
Bruce, Robert. *See* Robert I (the Bruce)
   of Scotland
Bruegel, Pieter the Elder, 24a
   The Beggars, 500 *(illus.)*
   Caritas (etching), 101 *(illus.)*
   on carnival, 539a
Bruges
   Antwerp and, 24b
   communes and, 136a
Brun, Rudolph, 136a
Brunhild of Austrasia, queen, **81a–82a,**
   203b, 512a
Bruni, Leonardo
   Historia Florentini populi (History of
     the Florentine people), 3b
Bruno of Segni, 57b
Brussels
   Antwerp and, 24b
Brut, the, 13b, 14b–15a, 181a
Bubonic plague, 135b, 136a, 136b, 164a,
   381b
   public bathing and, 51a
   See also Black Death; Disease; Plagues
Buc, Philippe
   Dangers of Ritual, The, 532b
Buch der Natur. See Conrad of
   Megenberg
Budziszyn, treaty of (1018), 79a, 266b
Buhske di Remmer, 206b
Bulgaria, 424a
Bulgarian Tomich Psalter, 358b
Bulgarians, 408b

Bulgarus, 4a, **82a–b,** 311a
   Quaestiones disputatae, 82b
Bunyan, John, 150a
Buonaccorsi, Phillip
   Polish monarchy and, 434a
Burchard of Worms
   on sexuality, 493a
Burğ Heidar (church)
   distinctive elements of, 597a
Bürger, Gottfried August
   "Lenore," 391b
Burgh, Hubert de
   Peter des Roches and, 469a, 470a,
     470b, 471a
Burgos Cathedral (Spain), 233a
Burgundio of Pisa
   De regimine sanitatis, 284a
   translation of *Peri hygieion* by, 284a
Burgundy
   Antwerp and, 24b–25a
   Code of, 310a
   Henry II of Germany and, 266a
Burgundy, duke of, 619a
Burial. *See* Death and burial
Buridan, Jean
   consequences literature of, 473b
   economic analysis by, 301b–302a
   insurance and, 291a
   Summulae de dialectica, 509a
Buridan, John. *See* Buridan, Jean
Burkard of Hall, 222b
Burke, Edmund, 392a
Burley, Walter, 405a
   consequences literature of, 473b
   De intensione et remissione formarum,
     406a
   De primo ultimo instanti, 406a
   Tractatus primus, 406a
Burne-Jones, Edward, 392b, 393a
Bursfeld, abbey of, **82b–83b**
Burzōe (physician), 303b
Busca party (Spain), 136b
Bussi, Giovanni Andrea, 623b
Buṭlān, Ibn
   Tacuini sanitatis (Taqwīm al-ṣiḥḥa or
     Almanac of Health), 284b, 380b–
     381a
Butler, Alban, 392b
Butler, Howard Crosby, 596b
Butler, Robert, 191b
Būzjānī, Abū al-Wafāʾ al-, 373b
Byland (abbey church: England), 228a
Byliny (Russian stories), **83b–84a**
Bynum, Caroline
   on Christ's genitals images, 493a
Byrhtferth of Ramsey, 168a, 561b
Byzantine architecture, 596b–597a
   Ottoman architecture and, 443a
Byzantine church, 187b–188a, 423a
   Immaculate Conception and, 288b
   liturgy from, 72b
   papal supremacy and, 247b
   union with Roman church, 188a

Byzantine Empire, 201b
  archaeology of, 25b
  astrology in, 41b
  espionage in, 182a–b
  Fourth Crusade and, 148a–149a
  Mamlūk quassad of, 182a
  new legislation in, 426a–427a
  rape in, 520a
  role of eunuchs in, 188a–190a
  Roman law in, 426b
  schools and, 559b
  secret police in, 182a
  slavery in, 188a–189b
  social history of, 427a
  state control within, 132b
  trade with, 402a
Byzantine literature
  Prodromic poetry, 510a–b
Byzantium
  adolescents in, 116a–b
  contact with China and, 117a–118a
  education in, 115b
  oblation and, 116a
  public baths in, 50a
  See also Constantinople

C

Cable, Thomas, 14a
Caboche, Simon, 625a
Cædmon
  Hymn, 11a
Caesar, Gaius Julius, 190a
  used in schools, 564a
Caesarius Coppula of Salerno
  on uterine suffocation, 251a
Caesarius of Arles
  on abortion, 1a
Caffarelli, Thomas
  Legenda minor, 94a
Cairo
  Genizah community in, 399b
  medical practice in, 380b–382a
Calabria, 422b
Calafato, Eustochia
  Poor Clares and, 489a
Calcidius
  on matter, 377b
  on *Timaeus,* 281a
Calculations. See Swineshead, Richard
Calendar
  Julian, 327a
Calixtines
  on utraquism, 622b
Calixtus II, pope
  on criminal procedure, 317a–b
  Henry V and, 267b
Calligraphy
  illuminated manuscripts and, 359b,
    361 *(illus.),* 362a–b
  Islamic, 468a
  Perlschrift style, 359b, 362a–b
  Persian, 468a

Calumny oath, **84a–85a**
Calvin, John, 389b, 434b, 437a, 615b
Cambridge Songs, 308a
Camden, William
  Britannia, 25a–b, 390a
Camden Society, 392b
Camelot, 396b
Camilla Battista of Varano
  I dolori mentali di Gesù, 489a
  Vita spiritualis, 489a
Campbell, Alistair, 206a
Campin, Robert, 613b
Cams, 346b–347a
  shipbuilding and, 349a
  textile manufacturing and, 349a
Cancioneiro da Ajuda, 494a, 494b
*Cancioneiro da Biblioteca Nacional de
    Lisboa,* 494a, 494b
Cancioneiro da Vaticana, 494a
Cancioneiro de Colocci-Brancuti, 494a,
    494b
Cancioneiro general. See Castillo,
    Hernando del; Resende, Garcia de
Cannon, 197b, 198a–b, 198b, 199b–
    200a
Canon of Medicine. See Sīnā, Ibn
Canonization
  papal control of, 332a
  of St. Catherine of Siena, 97a
Cantar de Mío Cid, 179a, 180b
Canterbury, 175b–176a
  archaeology of, 29b
  schools in, 560a
Canterbury Cathedral, 176a, 191b
  construction of, 228a–b
  St. Dunstan and, 168b
Canterbury Tales. See Chaucer, Geoffrey
Cantica. See Sīnā, Ibn
Cantigas, 494a–b
Capellanus, Andreas
  De amore, 184a, 338a
Capetians, 219b, 223b, 232b–233a
  conflict with, 640b
Capital punishment, **85a–86b**
  criminal procedure and, 310a–b
Capitulations, **86b–87b**
Capua, John
  Directorium vitae humanae, 303a
Caravans
  ribāṭ and, 530b–531a
  vulnerability of, 203a
Caravel
  industrial revolution and, 348b–349a
Carcassonne
  rebuilding of, 393a
Carding, 349a–351a
Carinthia, duchy of, 542b
Carl of Carlisle, The, 38b
Carloman of Austrasia, 88a
Carlyle, Thomas
  Past and Present, 392b
Carmelites
  Honorius III and, 274a

Carmen de algorismo. See Alexander de
  Villa Dei
Carmen pascale. See Sedulius
Carmina Burana, 308b–309a, 491b
  Hilary of Orléans and, 272a
  page from, 307b *(illus.)*
Carmina figurata
  of Hrabanus Maurus, 438a
Carniola, duchy of, 542b
Carnival
  as ritual, 539a
Carolina (legal code), 2a
Carolingian Empire, 408a, 437b–438b
  archaeology of, 27a
  astrology in, 42a
  capital punishment and, 85b
  Conrad I of Germany and, 137b–138a
  divorce in in, 365b
  East Franks and, 137b–138a
  longevity in, 431b
  merchant houses in, 401b
  monasticism and, 145a–b, 146b
  on moral theology, 630b
  ordeals in, 536a
  patronage in, 457a–b
  peacemaking in, 462a
  queenship in, 511a, 512b–513a
  reform of, 630a
  rulers of, 85b, 613a
  satire in, 554b
  West Franks and, 138a
  See also Charlemagne
Carolingian miniscule, 89b
Carolingian renaissance, **88a–90b**
  ecclesiastical reforms and, 88a–89a
  humanism and, 280b
  Latin literature and, 308b
  scholarship of, 89a–90a
Carr, J. Comyns
  King Arthur, 393a
Carrack
  industrial revolution and, 348b–349a
Carta Pisana, 91b
Carthusian Miscellany, 590a *(illus.)*
Carthusians, 429b
Cartography, **90b–93a**
  China and, 119b–120a
  in early Middle Ages, 91a–92a
  during fifteenth century, 92a–b
  in High Middle Ages, 91a–92a
  mathematics of, 373b
  Ottoman, 446a
  world maps and, 90b–92a, 411a
Casamari (church), 231a
Casimir III (the Great) of Poland, king,
  93a–b, 304b
Casimir IV (the Jagiellonian) of Poland,
  king, **93b–94b**
Caspe, Compromise of (1412), 10b,
  94b–95a
Cassian, John, 54b, 630a
  manuscript of, 55b *(illus.)*

Cassiodorus, Senator, Flavius Magnus, 56a
  autobiography by, 45b
  Institutiones, 146a
  used in schools, 558b
Castellan
  vs. castle-guard, 95a
Castile, 413a–b
  Admiral in, 6a
  Alfonso V and, 10b, 11a
  Christianization of, 413b
  civil war in, 248b
  vs. France, 423a, 423b
  Moriscos in, 414a
  prostitution in, 576a
  self-government within, 132b
  Siete partidas, 499b–500a
Castillo, Hernando del
  Cancioneiro general, 494b
Castle-guard, **95a–96a**
Castle Karlštejn
  Chapel of the Holy Cross, 74 *(illus.),* 75a
  renovation of, 75a
Castle of Perseverance (drama), 153b
Castles and fortifications, 34a, 34b
  construction of, 219b–220a
  innovations to, 219b–220a
Castration and Islam, 188b
  See also Eunuchs
Casus decretalium. See Ricardus Anglicus
Casus longi. See Bernard of Parma
Catalan atlas, 92a
Catalan Company
  Athens and, 44b
Catalans, 201b
Catalonia, 413a, 413b
  Alfonso V and, 10b, 11a
  Aragon throne and, 94b
  Moriscos in, 414a
Catani, Peter, 176b
Categorematics, in philosophy, 473b
Catena aurea. See Aquinas, Thomas, St.
Catenae (chains), biblical commentary as, 54b–55a
Cathars, 169a–b, 614b, 626a
  atheism and, 43b, 44a
  body of Christ and, 70a–b
  popular religion and, 528b
  poverty and, 505a
  on sacraments, 552b–553a
  sexuality and, 569b
  soul and body and, 591a
  See also Albigensians
Cathedral, 153a *(illus.)*
  age of, 235a
  celebration of Mass and, 240b–241a
  French Romanesque, 153a, 154a, 154b *(illus.),* 155b, 155b *(illus.)*
  Gothic art and, 236b–239a
  preservation of, 393a
  schools in, 562a, 562b, 564b
  See also particular cathedrals

Catherine of Alexandria, St., martyrdom of, 76b
Catherine of Bologna, St.
  Le sette armi spirituali, 489a–b
Catherine of Siena, St., **96a–98a,** 566b
  Dialogue of Divine Providence, 96b, 97b
  as doctor of church, 650b
  Letters, 96b
  Prayers, 96b
  stigmata of, 96a, 97a *(illus.)*
Catherine of Valois, marriage of, 514a
Catholic Encyclopedia, 588b
Cato the Elder
  on wifely duties, 567b
Cato's Distichs (Disticha Catonis), 561a, 562a
Catullus, Manutius edition of, 491b
Causidici (professional legal counselors), 8a
Cavalry, European
  horsemanship and, 274b–275a
Caxton, William, 431a
  Book of Courtesy, 185a
Ceffons, Pierre
  on probability, 509b
Čelebi, ʿĂrif
  Süleymanname, 446b
Celestine III, pope, 439b
  child oblate consent and, 429b
Celestis altitudo potentie. See Nicholas IV, pope
Celibacy
  clerical, 68a–b, 209b, 422a, 422b, 569b, 570b
  homosexuality and, 574a
  orders and, 551b
  rape and, 571a
  repression of the body and, 68a–b
Cellarius, Christoph, 407b
Celtic mythology
  animals in, 18a
  Arthurian romances and, 36b, 37a
  Christianity and survival of, 453a
  medievalism and, 395b
Cencius Savelli. *See* Honorius III, pope
Centre National de la Recherche Scientifique, 383a
Ceremonies
  dancing, 538b
  joyous entry, 534b–535b, 539b
Cervantes, Miguel de
  Don Quixote, 390b
Český Krumlov
  Beautiful Madonna sculpture, 76b
Ceuta, 654b, 655a
  Portuguese spies and, 182a–b
Chalcedon, Council of, 420b
Chalice, design of, 240b, 244a
Chambers, R. W., 11b, 13a
  The Exeter Book of Old English Poetry, 192b, 193a

Champagne
  fairs, 131b, 399a, 402b
Champion des dames, Le. See Le Franc, Martin
Chancery
  signs and, 585a
Chanson de Guillaume, 181a
Chanson de Roland. See Roland, Song of
Chansons de geste
  epic romance and, 16b, 17a
  Song of Igor's Campaign and, 588a
Charcoal
  in gunpowder, 198a
Chariot races
  political power and, 65a–b
Chariton (scribe), 362b
Charity, **98a–106b**
  Castilian guidelines on, 500a
  concepts of poor and, 98a–102a
  deserving vs. undeserving poor and, 499b–501a
  just price and, 302a
  poverty and, 497b–508b
  provisions for, 102a–106a
  social welfare programs and, 504a
  See also Almsgiving
Charivari, 539a
Charlemagne, Holy Roman Emperor, 145a, 201b, 206a
  Admonitio generalis, 88b, 560b
  biography of, 62b–63a
  concubines of, 365b
  education and, 56b–57a
  library of, 89b
  in literature, 17a, 432a
  longevity of, 431b
  patronage by, 456a, 457a
  renovatio Romani imperii, 456a
  schools and, 560b
  standardized version of the Bible and, 89a
  See also Carolingian Empire
Charles IV, Holy Roman Emperor, 21a, **107a–b,** 333a
  extension of jurisdiction by, 75b
  Golden Bull, 107a
Charles V, Holy Roman Emperor, 413b, 432a, 440b
  legal codes of, 2a
  literary patronage by, 459a
Charles I of Anjou, king of Naples and Sicily, 139b, 140a–b, 440a, 621a
  defeat of Conradin by, 247b
  defeat of Manfred of Sicily by, 342b
  Pedro III and, 463a
Charles II of Anjou, king of Naples, 423a, 423b–424a
Charles IV of France, king, 619a
  emperor Charles IV and, 107a
Charles V of France, king
  biography of, 63b–64a
  manuscript collection of, 355b
Charles VII of France, king, 198b, 404a

Charles VIII of France, king
  Savonarola and, 557b
Charles II (the Bald), Holy Roman
    Emperor
  astrology and, 42a
  longevity of, 431a, 431b
  patronage by, 457b
Charles III (the Fat), Holy Roman
    Emperor, 137b
Charles Martel, 424a
Charles of Orléans, 47a
Charles of Valois, 463a
Charles VIII of Sweden, king
  sack of Lund by, 341b
Charroi de Nîmes, 627a
Charter, 160b–163a
Chartres, school of
  on soul and body, 590b
Chartres Cathedral, 220a, 226b–227a
  description of, 226b
  Gothic art and, 236a
  sculpture in, 236a–b, 238b
  stained-glass windows in, 237a
Chastity, 569a–571a
  See also Celibacy
Chastity belt, **107b–108a**
Chastoiement des dames. See Robert of
    Blois
Château Gaillard (castle: Normandy),
    220a, 220a *(illus.)*
Château Pèlerin. *See* ʿAtlit
Chateaubriand, François-Auguste René
    de, 395a
  Le génie du Christianisme, (The genius
      of Christianity), 393a
  medievalism and, 393b
Chatterton, Thomas
  "Rowley Poems," 391a
Chaucer, Geoffrey, 391a
  alliterative literature and, 11b
  Anne of Bohemia and, 21a
  Arthurian romances and, 39a
  Canterbury Tales, 11b, 39a, 40b, 47a,
      208b–209a, 430b, 556a, 632a
  humanism and, 282a
  influences on, 8b, 150a
  Parliament of Fowls, 421a
  Perault and, 464a
  the poor represented in, 504b
  pornography in, 491b
  Troilus and Criseyde, 181a
Checchini, Aldo, 8a
Chesterton, G. K., 392b, 395a
Chiaravalle Milanese (church: Italy), 231a
Chiffoleau, Jacques, 534b
Chigi family, 624a
Child oblation. *See* oblates and oblation
Childbirth and infancy, **108b–113b,** 112
    (illus.), 431a
  Cesarean section, 110a, 110a *(illus.)*
  conduct of birth and, 110b–111a
  dangers of, 108b
  fetus, 109b *(illus.)*

infant mortality, 430a
medical interventions and, 110b
medical knowledge and, 108b–110a
paraphernalia, 110b
postpartum seclusion and, 111a–113a
professional care and, 108b–110a
purification ritual, 538b
Childebert II of Austrasia, king, 81b
Childeric I, Merovingian king, 25b, 613a
Childhood and adolescence, **113b–117b**
  abandonment and, 115a–116a
  stages of, 114b–115b
Children
  hospitals for, 104a
  royal, 115a
  upbringing of, 649a
Chilperic I, Merovingian king, 81a,
    203a–b, 512a
  assassination of, 203b
  children of, 203b
  wives of, 203a–b
Chin dynasty (China), 117b
  Mongol invasion of, 118b
China, **117b–120b,** 424a
  Arab contact with, 117a–118b
  Byzantine contact with, 117a–118b
  European contact with, 118a–b, 118b–
      119a
  European knowledge of, 119b–120a
  invention of gunpowder in, 197b
  missionary activity in, 119a–b
  Roman contact with, 117a–118b
Chirograph, 161b
Chivalry, 184a
  Arthurian romances and, 37b, 39a
  cult of, 394a–b, 395a
  Gothic revival and, 391a, 392a–b
  in Portuguese literature, 496a
  See also Arthurian Romances
Chlothar II, Frankish king, 81a, 203b
Chlothar III, Frankish king, 145a
Chludov Psalter, 359a
Choiroboskos, Georgios, 55a
Chrétien de Troyes, 184a, 428b, 627a–b
  Arthurian romances of, 36b, 37a, 37b–
      38a, 38b
  Cligès, 17a
  Conte de la Charette, 17b
  Érec and Énide, 184a, 338a, 428b
  use of numeric measurements, 428b
Christ. *See* Jesus Christ
Christ (Exeter Book), 191b, 192b
Christ Church (Canterbury). *See*
    Canterbury Cathedral
Christ on the Mount of Olives (Trebon
    Altarpiece), 76a *(illus.)*
Christian-Muslim relations, 196b
  medieval studies and, 388a
  in Spain, 397b–398a
  trade and, 403b
Christian of Prussia, bishop
  Teutonic Order and, 270b
Christian of Stavelot, 57a

Christianity, 407a, 407b
  afterlife in popular, 521a
  art patronage and, 454a–455a
  Arthurian romances and, 39a
  astrology and, 41a, 42b
  atheism and, 43a–44b
  concept of soul in, 588a–594a
  early culture of, 407a
  in Ireland, 559b
  movement of, 218a
  nature and, 420b
  peacemaking and baptism in, 460b–
      461a
  periods of, 407b
  Petrus Alfonsi on, 471a–472a
  on pornography, 492b–493a
  Portuguese apologetics for, 496b
  prostitution and, 576a–b
  queens in, 512b
  as race, 515b–516a
  reinterpretation of pagan gods in,
      450b–452a
  ritual and, 539b
  in schools, 559a, 563a
  on sex with slaves, 573a
  sexuality as sin in, 569b–570a, 576b
  on women, 651a
  See also Philosophy and theology,
      Western European
Christianization
  in Americas, 144a–b
  of Europe, 141a–144b
  See also Conversion; Missions and
      missionaries; Paganism
Christians
  capitulations and, 86b–87b
  in Islamic world, 158a–159b
  persecution of, 142a
Christina of Markyate, 650b
Christina of Sweden, queen, 624a
Christine de Pizan
  autobiography of, 47b
  *The Book of Deeds of Arms and of
      Chivalry,* 183a
  Cité des dames, 63b–64a, 652b
  Le ditié de Jehanne d'Arc, 63b–64a
  as first feminist, 47b
  influences on, 8b
  *Livre des fais et bonnes meurs du sage
      roy Charles V,* 63b
  Livre des trois vertus, 111a
  Livre du trésor de la cité des dames,
      186a
  on motherhood, 649a–b
  political texts, 627b
  on poverty, 502a
  on *Roman de la Rose,* 492a
  story of Eve and, 195b–196a
  on treatment of women, 209b, 210a
  writings of, 652a–b
Christology, 420b

Christopher, St., **120b–121b,** 121a
  (illus.)
  legend of, 524a, 524 (illus.)
Chronica Fiorentina. See Villani, Giovanni
Chronicle. See Fredegarius; Gervase of
  Canterbury
Chronicle of Count Duarte de Meneses. See
  Zurara, Gomes Eanes de
Chronicle of Count Pedro de Meneses. See
  Zurara, Gomes Eanes de
Chronicle of Guinea, The. See Zurara,
  Gomes Eanes de
Chronicle of the Capture of Ceuta. See
  Zurara, Gomes Eanes de
Chronicles, 147b–148a
  alliterative literature and, 11a
Chrysobull, 427a
Chrysostom, John, St. See John
  Chrysostom, St.
Chrysostom manuscript, Athens, 359a
Chrysostom Paris, 360b
Church, 169a
  on abortion, 1a
  alliterative literature and, 13a
  animals and, 19a
  astrology and, 40b–41a
  authority of Roman, 218b
  centralization of, 218a–b
  early, 1a
  economics of, 223b
  English, 228a
  expansion of, 218a
  financial administration of, 424a
  in Gaul, 88a
  Greek, 200b
  King Stephen and, 595b
  medieval aspects of, 389b, 392b, 393a,
    395a–b
  natural law and, 418a
  organization of, 141a, 141b, 143b
  original sin and, 437a
  reform of, 570b, 594b
  Slavonic rite in, 5a
  Spanish counter-reformation in, 414a
  state and, 7b, 19a
  teachings of, 141a
Church architecture, 596b
  astrological symbols on, 42a
  Gothic art and, 236b–239a
  See also Gothic architecture
Church fathers
  sacraments and, 544b
  in schools, 559b
  soul and body and, 590a
Churching (purification), 111b, 113a
"Church's Time and Merchant's Time."
  See Le Goff, Jacques
Cicero
  influence of, 8a
  De officiis, 281a
  De re publica, 281a, 417b
  De senectute, 430b, 431a, 431b
  used in schools, 562a, 564a

Cid, El, 300b, 393b
  See also Cantar de Mío Cid
Cingulum castitatis, 108a
Cinque Ports, **121b–124a,** 122 (map)
Ciompi, revolt of the (1378), **124a–
  125b,** 136b, 506b
Circumcision, 546b–547a
Circus Maximus, 65a
Cisneros, Francisco Ximénez de, cardinal.
  See Ximénez de Cisneros, Francisco,
  cardinal
Cistercian order, 186b–187a
  Athens and, 44b
  building program of, 220a
  Chaalis monastery (France), 149b
  convent of, 73b
  Idung of Prüfening and, 287b
  in Italy, 231a
  pope Eugenius III and, 186b–187a
  satire of, 555b
  on soul and body, 590b
  texts from, 208b
Citadel (Cairo), 189a
Cité des dames. See Christine de Pizan
Cities. See Urbanism
City of God (De civitate Dei). See
  Augustine of Hippo, St.
City of Ladies, The. See Christine de Pizan
Civic Ritual. See Ritual, Civic
Civilizing Process, The. See Elias, Norbert
Clare, St., **126a–127b**
  Alexander IV and, 9a
  Breviary of, 158b
  Poor Clares and, 126a–127a, 485b–
    490b
  Rule or Form of Life, 127a, 487b, 489a
Clarissans. See Poor Clares
Claros varones de Castilla. See Pulgar,
  Hernando del
Class, social
  abortion and, 1a
  animals and, 19a
  archaeology and, 29a
  domestic architecture and, 31a
  servants and, 565a
Claudel, Paul
  L'annonce faite à Marie, (The tidings
    brought to Mary), 393b
Claudius of Turin, 57a
Claver, Alice, 398b
Clemence of Burgundy, 252a
Clement III, pope
  child oblate consent and, 429b
Clement IV, pope, 621b, 639b
  Conradin and, 140a
Clement V, pope, 119a, 440b
  legislation of, 433b
  Saepe contingit, 314b
  Vox in excelso, 604b
Clement VI, pope
  Unigenitus Dei filius, 550b
Clement VII, pope, 440b
  Great Schism and, 96b

Immaculate Conception and, 290a
Clement X, pope, 196b
Clement of Alexandria, St.
  repression of the body and, 68a
  Stromateis, 213b
Clergy
  as healers, 474b–475a
  homosexuality and, 574a
  Latin, Athens and, 44b
  marriage of, 484b
  pollution and taboo among, 484b
  poverty and, 505a–b
  satire of, 555b, 556a
  See also Celibacy, clerical
Clermont-Ferrand (church: France), 227b
Cligès. See Chrétien de Troyes
Climate, 170a–b
  agriculture and, 170b–171a
  changes in, 171b–172b
Cloisters, New York, 383b
  Play of Daniel performance at, 396a
Clontarf, Battle of (1014), 80b
Cloth industry. See Textile industry
Clothar I, Merovingian king
  Radegunda and, 518b
Clothar II, Merovingian king
  patronage by, 457a
Clotilda, queen, 143a
Clovis, Frankish king, 143a, 201a–b,
  613a
Cluny Abbey, 429a
  abbots of, 341b, 431b
  Cluny III, 227a
  monastic reforms at, 562a
  monks of, 203a
  town house in, 34a, 34 (illus.)
Cnut I (the Great) of Denmark, king,
  340b
Coats of arms
  Gothic art and, 244a
  See also Heraldry
Cocherel, Battle of
  Bertrand du Guesclin and, 248a
Codex Justinianus, 310a, 426a
Codex Theodosianus, 426a, 608a
Cohen, Gustave
  Miracle de Théophile, 395b–396a
Cola di Rienzo, 136a, 440b
Colette of Corbie, St.
  Poor Clares and, 488a, 488b–489a
Collection in Ninety-five Titles. See
  Bernard of Pavia
Collège de France, 384b
College of Cardinals, 423b
  imprisonment of, 440a
Colman, St.
  animals and, 19b
Cologne
  town council of, 139a–b
  university of, 163b
Cologne, archbishopric
  Holy Roman Empire and, 542a
Cologne Cathedral, 230b

Colonna, Ascanio, 128b
Colonna, Giacomo, cardinal, 127b–128a
Colonna, Giovanni, 127b
    *Lives of the Roman Pontiffs from St.
    Peter to Boniface VIII,* 128b
Colonna, Lorenzo Oddone, 128b
Colonna, Marcantonio, 128b
Colonna, Margherita, 127b
Colonna, Pietro, cardinal, 433a
Colonna, Sciarra, 128a, 440b
Colonna, Stefano, 128a
Colonna, Vittoria, 128b
Colonna family, **127b–129a,** 187b,
    423b, 424a, 439b–440b
    pope Nicholas IV and, 423b
Columba, St.
    on monastic tradition, 62b
    pilgrimage of, 480a
Columbanus, St., 81b, 560a
    founding of Bobbio abbey by, 66b
    on monastic tradition, 62b
    pilgrimages of, 480a
    rule of, 145a
Comestor, Peter
    Historia scholastica, 58b
Comitatus, **129a–b**
Commedia. See Dante Alighieri
Commenda, 400b
Commentaries
    as philosophical genre, 472b–473a
    probability and, 509a
Commentaries on the Laws of England. See
    Blackstone, Sir William
Commercialization, **129a–132a**
    economic development and, 129b–
        131a
    effects of, 131a–132a
Common law *(ius commune),* 318b–319a,
    321a, 322a–323a
    See also English common law
Communes, **132b–137b**
    consuls and, 133b–134a
    definition of, 132b–133a
    economics of, 133a–b
    factionalism and, 134a–b, 135a, 136b,
        137a, 404a
    law and, 132b, 134b–135a
    liberties in, 133a–b
    monarchical resistance to, 135a, 136b–
        137a
    oligarchy and, 135b–136b
    urbanization and, 132b, 403b
Communion, 240b
Compass, 91b
Compendio di rivelazioni, 558a
Compendium theologicae veritatis. See
    Ripelin, Hugh
Compilatio antiqua. See Obertus de Orto
Compilatio prima. See Bernard of Pavia;
    Ricardus Anglicus
Compline, 328a
Composition payments vs. capital
    punishment, 85b

Compostela (Spain)
    archaeology of, 29b
Computus (book on how to reckon
    church festivals), 10a
Comynes
    spying and, 182b
Conciliarists
    in Poland, 434a
*Conciliator controversarum quae inter
    philosophos et medicos versantur. See*
    Peter of Abano
Concordat of Benevento, 641b
Concubinage, 364a, 364b, 365b
Conduct books, 183b–186b
    social structure and, 185b–186a
    for women, 185a–b, 186a
Condulmaro, Gabriel. *See* Eugenius IV,
    pope
Confession
    in early church, 45b–46a
    Eucharist and, 548b–549a
    penance and, 549b, 550a
    See also Autobiography and
        confessional literature
Confirmation, 545a, 546a
Confiscation of property. *See* Property
Confraternities, 8b
    charity of, 105a–b
    popular religion and, 529a
Conics, The. See Apollonius
*Connecticut Yankee in King Arthur's
    Court, A. See* Twain, Mark
Conner, Patrick W., 191b, 192b, 193a
Conques cathedral, 155b, 155b *(illus.)*
Conrad I of Germany, emperor, **137b–
    138b**
    goals of, 138a
    Henry I of Germany and, 265b
Conrad III of Germany, emperor, **138b–
    139a**
Conrad IV of Germany, emperor, **139a–
    140a,** 542a
    Alexander IV and, 9a
    See also Carolingian Empire
Conrad of Franconia, duke. *See* Conrad I
    of Germany, emperor
Conrad of Hirsau
    Liber de fructu carnis et spiritus, 631a
Conrad of Marburg, 178a
Conrad of Mazovia, duke, 606b
    Teutonic Order and, 270b
Conrad of Megenberg
    Buch der Natur (1349), 51a, 411b
Conradin of Germany, king, 139b,
    140a–140b
    Alexander IV and, 9a
    defeat of, by Charles of Anjou, 247b
Consequentia (consequences literature),
    473b
Consilia, 433a–b
    age of, 433a
    legal genres and, 433a

Consolation of Philosophy. See Boethius,
    Anicius Manlius Severinus
Constance, Council of (1414–1418), 76b,
    187b, 434a, 619a
    Bursfeld Abbey and, 83a
    election of Martin V as pope at, 128a
    Jerome of Prague and, 294a–b
    John XXIII, antipope, and, 298b
    on sacraments, 549a
Constance, treaty of (1153), 641b
Constance (daughter of Manfred
    Hohenstaufen)
    Pedro III and, 462b
Constance of Hungary
    founding of convent by, 73b
Constans II, Byzantine emperor
    Athens and, 44b
Constantine (scribe), 360b
Constantine V, Byzantine emperor, 426b
Constantine I (the Great), Roman
    emperor, 142a, 144b, 407a–b, 426a
    on divorce, 364a–b
    patronage by, 454a
Constantine the African
    on abortion, 2a
    De coitu, 493a
    on contraception, 252a
    on sexuality, 577b
    translations by, 293b
Constantinople, 174b, 407b
    census in (602), 66a
    conquest of (1203–1204), 148a–149a,
        361
    illuminated manuscripts in, 359a,
        360b–362b
    Prodromic poetry and, 510a–b
    trading colonies in, 202a
    See also Byzantium
Constantinople, Council of (360), 620a
Constantius II, Byzantine emperor,
    619b–620a
Constitutional History of England. See
    Stubbs, William
Constitutions of Hugolino, 487b
Construction
    castles and fortifications, 219b–220a
    church, 549b, 642a
    symbolic, 224a–b
Consuls
    communes and, 133b–134a
Conte du Graal. See Chrétien de Troyes;
    Grail, legend of
Contes moralisés, Les. See Nicole Bozon
Conti, Rainaldo dei. *See* Alexander IV,
    pope
"Conto de Amaro," 496b
Contra Eutychen et Nestorium. See
    Boethius, Anicius Manlius Severinus
Contraception, 250b, 252a, 572a, 577b
Contracts
    between artists and patrons, 455a–b
    betrothal, 363b, 364b, 367a
    marriage, 336a–b

merchant, 400b
under natural law, 419a
notarial, 425a
Contrafactum, 458a
Convents
in Ghent, 163b
schools in, 564a, 564b
in Ypres, 163b
Conversion, 140b–145a, **140b–145a**
during adolescence, 116b
baptism and, 140b–142a, 143a, 144a
Franciscans and, 424a
to Islam, 543b
of Jews, 611a–b
to monasticism, 116b, 429a
of Muslims, 144a, 413a–415a
of Prussians, 5a
in Reconquista Spain, 258a
of Sabians, 543a, 543b, 544a
strategies of, 21b–22a
Conversos, 413a–b
Conybeare, John Josias, 192b
Cooper, Susan
Dark Is Rising, The, 396b
Copernicus, Nicholas, 375a
Copper
mining of, 348a–b
Copyhold, 344b
Corbechon, Jean, 49b
Corbie, abbey of, **145a–b**
Córdoba
fall of, 196b
Coronation
as civic ritual, 534a
of queens, 512b–513a
Corpus Christi, Feast of, 526a–b, 549a,
621b, 650b
Corpus iuris civilis, 426a–b
additions to, 433a
Greek translations of, 426b
Oldradus de Ponte and, 433a
Pierre de Belleperche on, 476b–477a
Correr, Angel (pope Gregory XII), 187b
Correspondence
political, 458b
of St. Catherine of Siena, 96b
Corsairs, 481b
See also Pirates and Piracy
Corsica
Alfonso V and, 10b
Corte Imperial, 496b
Cortenuova, Battle of (1237), 193b
Cortes (corts)
Pedro III and, 463a
Corvey, abbey of, 82b, **145b–146b,** 429a
Cosmographia. See Bernard Silvester;
Ptolemy
Cossa, Baldassare. *See* John XXIII,
antipope
Cotton, Sir Robert, 390a
manuscript collection of, 356a
Cotton Map, 91b

Councils, 144a
abortion and, 1a
See also Lateran Councils; *individual
councils, under name of city*
Counter-Reformation, 156a, 389b
autobiography and, 47b
Court of Shepway, 123a
Courtesy books, 183b, 184b
Courtier bishops, 183b
Courtiers, satire of, 556a
Courtly love, 383b
Courts of law. *See* Law
Courtship. *See* Love and courtship
Coutrai, Battle of (1302), 136a
Cowdery's Down, Hampshire, 33a
Anglo-Saxon house from, 31b *(illus.),*
32 *(illus.)*
Crafts production
archaeology of, 27b, 28a, 28b, 29a
Cram, Ralph Adams, 394a, 395a
Cranach, Lucas, 430b
Crane, Susan, 538b
Creationism, 590b
Credit, commercialization and, 131a,
131b
Crete
Athens and, 44b
Venetian control of, 149a
Cribs, miniature
Gothic art and, 242b
Criminal justice
penal code, 53b
ritual in, 535b–538a
trials and, 316b–319b
Criminality
poverty as, 504b
rape and, 519a–520b
Critical Terms for Religious Studies, 588b
Crónica da Guiné. See Zurara, Gomes
Eanes de
Crónica de D. Duarte. See Lopes, Fernão
Crónica de D. Fernando. See Lopes,
Fernão
Crónica de D. João I. See Lopes, Fernão
Crónica de D. Pedro I. See Lopes, Fernão
Crónica de Portugal de 1419. See Lopes,
Fernão
Crónica do condestabre, 496a
Crónica do Mouro Rasis. See Arrazi,
Ahmed
Crónica geral de Espanha de 1344. See
Pedro of Barcelos
Crowned King, The, 15a
Crucifixion
in art, 75b *(illus.)*
Crusader states, 174a–175a, 201b
Crusades
First, 201a–201b, 215a–b, 402a, 626b,
640b
Second, 138b–139a, 174b–175a,
186b–187a
Third, 643a
Fourth, 44b, 148a–149a, 361b

achievements of, 201a–b
Albigensian, 169b
Henry the Navigator of Portugal and,
270a
Henry VI of Germany and, 268a
Hermann of Salza and, 270b
Honorius III, pope, and, 273a–b
Hospitallers and, 277a
indulgences and, 187a
Jewish martyrs and, 257b
against Mongols, 9a
nomadism during, 52a
Pedro III and, 463a
penance and, 549b
Peter des Roches and, 470a–b
piracy and, 482b
race and, 515b
satire on, 556a
Cuenca (Spain), 563b
Cuerda seca
in Ottoman ceramics, 447a, 447b
Cueta
Portuguese conquest of, 269b–270a
Culture in Mind. See Shore, Bradd
Cum causam. See Lucius III, pope
Cum Marthae. See Innocent III, pope
Cumans/Kipchaks, **146b–147b,** 423a,
606b
Cuthbert of Lindisfarne, St., 523b
Cynewulf
Christ II, 191b, 192a
Juliana, 192a, 192a *(illus.)*
Cyprian, St., 605b
on original sin, 435b
Cyprian of Carthage, bishop. *See*
Cyprian, St.
Cyril of Alexandria, St.
Hypatia and, 287a
Cyropaedia. See Xenophon
Czechoslovakia
Dalimil's Chronicle and, 147b–148a
St. Adalbert and, 5a

D

Da Ponte, Lorenzo, 385b
Dabra Asbo (monastery), 598a–b
Dabra Damo (monastery), 598b
Dabra Hayk. *See* St. Stephen
Dabra Libanos. *See* Dabra Asbo
Dagobert I, Merovingian king, 224a,
457a
Dagome iudex, 78b, 409a
Daimbert of Pisa, 215b
Dál Cais (Déis Tuaiscirt) family, 80a–b
Dalimil's Chronicle, **147b–148a**
Damascus, 174b–175a
conversion of St. Paul, 140b
as medical center, 381a, 382a
seige of (1148), 139a
Umayyad Mosque of, 373b
Dame Ragnelle, 38b, 39a
Damian, Peter. *See* Peter Damian, St.

Dancing ceremonies, 538b
Dandolo, Domenico, 148a
Dandolo, Enrico, **148a–149b**
Dandolo, Vitale, 148a
Danes
  conversion of, 21b–22a
  in Finnsburh Fragment, 197a–b
  Gothic revival and, 391a
Dangers of Ritual, The. See Buc, Philippe
Danica literatura antiquissima (Danish
  antiquities). See Worm, Ole
Dante Alighieri, 407a, 438b, 632a
  biographies of, 64a
  cult of, 392b, 393b
  Divine Comedy, 7a, 47a, 153b, 180a,
    181a, 263a, 264b, 335a, 394b,
    423a, 632a
  humanism and, 282a
  Latin literature and, 309a
  De monarchia, 7b
  numerology and, 428a
Dante Society of America, 385a–b
Darī language, 466b–468a
Dark Is Rising, The. See Cooper, Susan
Darnton, Robert, 533b
Datheus of Milan, archbishop, 116a
Datini, Francesco, 290b–291a, 401a
David, Gerard
  Judge Cambyses diptych by, 537a
  Judgment of Cambyses, 455a
David of Dinant
  on Aristotle, 378a
  atheism and, 44a
David I of Scotland, king, 376b
  King Stephen and, 595a
Davis, Alexander Jackson, 394a
Davis, Natalie, 533b, 538a, 539a
De aeternitate mundi. See Boethius of
  Dacia
De amicitia. See Johannes de Lignano
De amore. See Capellanus, Andreas
De amore et dilectione Dei et proximi et
  aliarum rerum et de forma vitae. See
  Albertano da Brescia
De anima. See Aristotle
De animalibus. See Albertus Magnus
De bello. See Johannes de Lignano
De ceremoniis, 66a, 606b
De coitu. See Constantine the African
De coniuge non ducenda, 555a
De consideratione. See Bernard of
  Clairvaux
De contemptu mundi. See Bernard of
  Cluny
De corpore et sanguine Domini. See
  Paschasius Radbertus of Corbie
De cura pro mortuis gerenda. See
  Augustine of Hippo, St.
De curis mulierum. See Trota
De dialectica. See Augustine of Hippo, St.
De diversis regulis iuris antiqui. See
  Justinian

De divisione naturae. See John Scottus
  Eriugena
De docta ignorantia. See Nicholas of Cusa
De doctrina christiana. See Augustine of
  Hippo, St.
De doctrina dicendi et tacendi. See
  Albertano da Brescia
De eruditione praedicatorum. See Humbert
  of Romans
De falsis deis. See Aelfric
De fide orthodoxa. See John of Damascus
De fletu ecclesiae. See Johannes de Lignano
De impregnatione, 251b
De institutione musica. See Boethius,
  Anicius Manlius Severinus
De intensione et remissione formarum. See
  Burley, Walter
De interpretatione. See Aristotle
De iride. See Theodoric of Freiberg
De l'Allemagne. See Staël, Germaine de
De laude novae militiae. See Bernard of
  Clairvaux
De laudibus Dei. See Dracontius, Blossius
  Aemilius
De legibus et sectis contra superstitiosos
  astronomos. See Ailly, Pierre d'
De libero arbitrio. See Augustine of
  Hippo. St.
De ligibus Angliae. See Bracton, Henry de
De magistro. See Augustine of Hippo, St.
De miseria humanae conditionis. See
  Innocent III, pope
De modis significandi. See Boethius of
  Dacia
De mundi universitate. See Bernard
  Silvester
De natura daemonum. See Witelo
De natura rerum. See Thomas of
  Cantimpré
De nobilitatibus, sapientiis et prudentiis
  regum. See Walter de Milemete
"De notulis." See Rolandinus de
  Passageris
De nugis curialium. See Map, Walter
De nuptiis Philologiae et Mercurii. See
  Martianus Capella.
De octo spiritibus malitiae. See Evagrius
  Ponticus
De officiis. See Cicero
"De officio tabellionatus in villis vel
  castris." See Rolandinus de Passageris
De pace. See Johannes de Lignano
De partibus orationis ars minor. See
  Donatus
De passionibus mulierum. See Trota
De pauperie Salvatoris. See Fitzralph,
  Richard
De periculis novissimorum temporum. See
  William of St. Amour
De planctu naturae. See Alan of Lille
De praestigiis daemonum. See Weyer,
  Johann

De primo ultimo instanti. See Burley,
  Walter
De proportionibus velocitatum in motibus.
  See Bradwardine, Thomas
De proprietatibus rerum. See
  Bartholomaeus Anglicus
De quantitate animae. See Augustine of
  Hippo, St.
De radiis. See Kindī, Abū Yūsuf Yaʿqūb
  ibn Isḥāq al-
De raptu Helenae. See Dracontius,
  Blossius Aemilius
De raptu virginum. See Justinian I,
  Byzantine emperor
De re diplomatica. See Mabillon, Jean
De re metallica. See Agricola
De re publica. See Cicero
De rectoribus christianis. See Sedulius
  Scottus
De regia potestate et papali. See John of
  Paris
De regimine principum. See Aquinas,
  Thomas, St.; Egidius Colonna
De regimine sanitatis. See Burgundio of
  Pisa
De regulis iuris. See Johannes Bassianus
De sacramentis. See Hugh of St. Victor
De Sancta Trinitate et operibus eius. See
  Rupert of Deutz
De secretis secretorum Aristotelis. See
  Walter de Milemete
De senectute. See Cicero
De Signis. See Bacon, Roger
De situ orbis. See Fillastre, Guillaume
De spiritu et anima, 590b
De sterilitate, 251b
De substantia orbis. See Rushd, Ibn
De summo bono. See Boethius of Dacia
De Trinitate. See Augustine of Hippo, St.
De tyranno. See Bartolo da Sassoferrato
De viris illustribus. See Jerome, St.; Nepo,
  Cornelius; Suetonius
De virtutibus et de vitiis et de donis
  Spiritus sancti. See Alan of Lille
Death and burial, 430a, 431a
  mourning and, 539a
  pilgrim souvenirs in, 479a
  ribāṭ and, 531a
Death penalty. See Capital punishment
Decameron. See Boccaccio, Giovanni
Decimal system, 372a–b
Declaration of Independence, 419b–420a
Decretalists, 53b
Decretum. See Gratian
Dede Korkut, 180b
Dederoth, John
  Bursfeld Abbey and, 83a
Defensor pacis. See Marsilius of Padua
Deguileville, Guillaume de, **149b–150b**
  Pèlerinage de Jhesucrist, 150a
  Pèlerinage de la vie humaine, 149b, 156
    (illus.)

Pèlerinage de l'âme, (Pilgrimage of the Soul), 149b, 263a, 264b
Deir Déhès (monastery: Antioch), 597a
Deir Mar Antonios (monastery: Egypt), 24a
Della Porta, Fra Bartolommeo
   Girolamo Savonarola, 558a *(illus.)*
Della Vigna, Pietro
   Frederick II and, 458b
Demanda del Sancto Grial, 151a
Demanda do Santo Graal, **150b–151a,** 495a
Demesne
   manors and, 343b
Demetrios Palaiologos, 362b
Demons, **151a–154a**
   concepts of hell and, 262a–263b
   descriptions of, 153a–b, 154a–b, 155a–b
   Germanic tradition of, 153b
   modern imagery of, 396 *(illus.)*
   pagan gods as, 451b–452a, 452 *(illus.)*
   in popular religion, 527a
   St. Anthony and, 23b *(illus.)*
Denis, St., 218a, 223b, 225a
Denis (Dinis) I of Portugal, king
   poetry of, 494a, 494b
Denis the Carthusian, 59b
Denmark
   missionaries in, 21b–22a, 146a
   Teutonic Order and, 270b
Dent, J. M.
   Birth, Life and Acts of King Arthur, 392a *(illus.)*
"Deor" (poem: Exeter book), 192a, 192b
Dervishes, Ottoman architecture and, 443a
Des Knaben Wunderhorn. See Brentano, Clemens
Descensus ad inferos (Harrowing of Hell), 154b
Deschamps, Eustache, 47a
Desco da parto (birthing plate), 453a
Description of the World. See Polo, Marco
Desert Fathers, pilgrimages of, 480a
Desiderius of Vienne, bishop
   stoning death of, 81b
D'Este family, 193b
Destruction of Troy, The, 15a
Déus Tuaiscirt (Dál Cais) family, 80a–b
Deutsche Grammatik. See Grimm, Jacob
Deutsche Mythologie. See Grimm, Jacob
Devil, **154a–157b**
   concepts of hell and, 262a–263b
   St. Dunstan and, 168a
   scatology and, 155b–156a
   See also Demons; Satan
Devotio Moderna (New Devotion), 529a
Dézières, Philippe de
   Charles V and, 459a
Dhimmīs, **158a–159b**
Dhuoda (Frankish woman), 649a–b
Di Segni family, 8b

Dialectic, 509a, 581a
   See also Schools; Signs, theory of
Dialogue of Divine Providence. See Catherine of Siena, St.
Dialogues. See Gregory I (the Great), pope
Dialogus contra Judaeos. See Petrus Alfonsi
Dialogus duorum monachorum. See Idung of Prüfening
Dicksee, Frank, 392a
Dictionarium iuris tam civilis quam canonici. See Albericus de Rosate
Dictus papae. See Gregory VII, pope
Didache, 328a
Dido and Aeneas, 179b–180a
Dies irae, **159b–160a**
Diet, and medicine, 380a
Digby, Kenelm
   Broad Stone of Honour, The, 392a
Digest. See Justinian
Dijon
   gang rape in, 573b
   mortuary chapel at, 238a
Dinant
   siege of, 198b
Diocletian, Roman emperor, 142a, 432a
Dionysiou Monastery, 359b, 360b
Dionysius Bar Ṣalibi, 55b
Dionysius Exiguus
   Western liturgical year and, 330a
Dionysus, as tapestry subject, 608a
Diophantus of Alexandria, 371a
Dioscorides Paris, 359a, 361 *(illus.),* 381b
Diplomacy
   espionage and, 182a–b
Diplomatics, **160a–163a,** 389b
Diqduq, al-. See Abū Yaʿqūb Yūsuf ibn Nuḥ
Dirc van Delft, **163b–164a**
   Tafel van den Kersten Ghelove, 163b–164a
Directorium vitae humanae. See Capua, John
Discalced Trinitarians. *See* Trinitarians
Disciplina clericalis. See Petrus Alfonsi
Disease, **164a–166b**
   causes of, 164a–b, 381b
   diagnosis of, 165a–b, 382a–b
   kinds of, 164b–165a
   public bathing and, 51a
   See also Black Death; Medicine; Physicians; Plagues
Disputatio
   obligationes literature on, 473b–474a
   in philosophy, 472a–b
   See also Polemics
Dissertation on Canon and Feudal Law. See Adams, John
Dissuasio Valerii (A dissuasion of Valerius), 555a
Distaff, 350a–b
Distinctiones decretorum. See Ricardus Anglicus

Ditié de Jehanne d'Arc, Le. See Christine de Pizan
Dits (narrative poems), 556a
Divination
   Ottoman, 446b
   Raynes on, 522 *(illus.)*
Divine law, just price and, 302a
Divorce
   church teaching on, 141a, 143b
   papal reforms on, 513a–b
   See also Marriage
Ḍiyā al-Dīn al-Maqdisī, 255a
Długosz, Jan, 434b
Dobbie, E. V. K., 192b
Dobriner Order, 606b
Docking, Thomas, 59a
Doctrinale puerorum. See Alexander de Villa Dei
Documents
   archaeology and, 26a, 26b, 28b, 29a
   astrological, 41b
   signs and validation of, 584b–585a
   See also Diplomatics
Dodici avvertimenti che deve dare la madre alla figliuola quando la manda a marito, 185a
Doge, 134a, 148a–149b
Domenico Lenzi, 103b *(illus.),* 105b
Domesday Book
   water wheels in, 346a
Dominicans, 147b, 159b, 631b–632a
   biblical studies and, 59a
   Dirc van Delft of, 163b
   encyclopedias of, 49a, 411a
   Honorius III, pope, and, 274a
   master generals of, 282b
   Perault, 463b–464a
   Peter des Roches and, 469a
   schools and, 564a–b
   Third Order of, 96a
   at University of Paris, 639a
   women as tertiaries of, 569b
Don Quixote. See Cervantes, Miguel de
Donatism, 169a, 546b, 552a
Donatus (Aelius Donatus), 9b
   Ars grammatica (Ars maior), 559a
   Ars minor, 564a
   De partibus orationis ars minor, 559a
   used in schools, 559a, 561a, 562a, 563a, 564a
Donatus of Fiesole, 341a
Doon de Maïence, legend of, 16b
Dorestad (Netherlands), 27a, 28a
Dormition (monastery: Nicaea), 299a
Dorson, Richard, 180a
Dorst, Tankred
   Merlin oder Das Wüste Land (Merlin, or the waste land), 396b
Downing, Andrew Jackson, 394a
Dowry, 364a, 365b, 366b, 368a, 368b
   monte delle doti, 368b–369a

Dracontius, Blossius Aemilius, **166b–167b**
  De laudibus Dei, 167a, 180a
  Romulea, 167a
  Satisfactio ad regem Gunthamundum, 167a
Dracula. *See* Vlad III Ţepeş of Walachia; voivode
Dragomir (Drahomíra), 634b
Drama, Western European
  alliterative literature and, 12a
  Anglo-Norman, 195a
  English, 153b, 195b
  passion plays, 483b
  satyr plays, 554a, 554b
Drang nach Osten, 304a
Dreams. *See* Ghosts
Dresdener Bilderhanschrift des Sachsenspiegels, 345b–346a
Dress and Habits of the People of England (Strutt), 390 *(illus.),* 391b
Dressage, 275a–b
Dreyer, Carl Theodor
  Passion of Joan of Arc, The, 396b
Droit du seigneur, **167b–168a,** 573a
Druidism, revival of, 397a
Drungarios, John, 55a
Drünkrut, Battle of, 542b
Du Cange, Charles, 383b
Dualism, 154a, 156a–b
  of soul and body, 588a, 591a
Duarte of Portugal
  Livro de Montaria, 496b–497a
Dubravka (daughter of duke of Přemyslid), 409a
Dubrovnik
  Florentine merchants in, 3a
  slaves in, 567a
Duccio di Buoninsegna
  Madonna and Child, 241a
Due process
  criminal trials and, 316b–317a
  Magna Carta and, 316b
  right to, 318a–319a
  See also Law
Duels, 536b
Dufresne, Charles, 389b
Duggan, Hoyt, 14a
Dumbleton, John, 405a
Dümmler, Ernst, 438b
Dunash ben Labrat, 260a
Dunbar, Battle of, 634a
Duns Scotus, John, 379a, 615a–b
  atheism and, 44a
  Immaculate Conception and, 289b–290a
  obligationes literature of, 474a
  price formation and, 303a
  on sacraments, 545b, 546a, 550b
  on signs, 582b, 583a
  on vice, 631a–b
Dunstable Annals
  Ricardus Anglicus and, 531b

Dunstan, St., **168a–b**, 561b
Durand, Guillaume, 52b, 522a
  Rolandinus de Passageris and, 541a
  Speculum iudiciale, 52b, 318b, 541a
Durand of Huesca, **168b–169b**
  Antiheresis, 169b
  Liber contra Manicheos, 169a–b
Durham, 13b
Durham Cathedral, 228a
Durkheim, Émile
  on civic ritual, 532a
  Elementary Forms of Religious Life, 532a
Dutch literature
  Middle, 163b
  satire in, 556b
Dwy, Owain Glyn, 465a–b
Dyrrachium (Durazzo), capture of, 643a

E

Eadmer of Canterbury, 168b
  Life of Anselm, 114a
Early Medieval Art. See Nees, Lawrence
Earthquakes
  Lisbon and, 327a
East Anglia (kingdom: England), 27b
Easter
  Western liturgical year and, 330b, 331b
Ebo of Rheims, 21b
Ebstorf map, 411a
Ecbasis captivi, 180a
Ecclesiale. See Alexander de Villa Dei
Ecclesiastical History of the English Church and People. See Bede
Eckhart, Meister, 59b
Ecloga. See Leo the Isaurian
Ecloga ton nomon, 426b
Eco, Umberto
  Name of the Rose, The, 397a
École des Chartes, 383a
Ecology, **169b–174a**
  disruptions of, 171b–173b
  effect of agriculture on, 172b–173a
  human impacts on, 173a–b
  population and, 172a
  sociopolitical changes and, 170a–173b
  tree ring sequences and, 171b
  See also Agriculture
Economic depressions, 3a
Economic development
  archaeology and, 29b–30a
  domestic architecture and, 31b
  medieval, 129a–131a
Economic production
  animals and, 17b–18a
  archaeology of, 26a–b, 29a
  Athens and, 44b
Eden, Garden of, 194a
Edessa, county of, 139a, **174a–175b**, 187a, 201b
  architectural surveys of, 175a
Edict of Expulsion (1492), 612b

Edict of Milan (313), 142a
Edmund of Abingdon, St., **175b–176a**
Edmund of England, prince
  Alexander IV and, 9a
Education
  in Byzantium, 115b
  Charlemagne and, 56b–57a
  disputatio in, 472a–b
  Franciscans and, 639a
  literacy and, 115b
  of physicians, 474b
  popular religion and, 522a
  religious, 522a
  of surgeons, 475a
  See also Schools
Education of Henry Adams, The. See Adams, Henry
Edward I of England, king, 634a
  admirals of, 6a
  children of, 115a
  Cinque Ports and, 123a
Edward II of England, king, 645b
  Battle of Bannockburn and, 48a–b
  homosexuality of, 574a
  inadequacy of, 619a
  statue of, 239a
Edward III of England, king, 431a–b, 645b
  corsairing statutes of, 481b
  criminal procedure and, 316a
  default on loans of, 3a
Edward IV of England, king
  marriage of, 514a
  Percy and, 465b
Edward the Black Prince, 335a
Edward the Confessor, St., 229a
  pilgrimages to, 526 *(illus.)*
Edwy of England, king, 168a
Egidius Colonna (Giles of Rome), 128b, 378b–379a, 591b
  De regimine principum, 458b–459a
Egils saga Skallagrímssonar, 512a–b
Egypt
  dhimmīs in, 158b
  medicine in, 382a
  Muslims in, 416a
Einhard
  Vita Caroli Magni, 62b–63a
Eisagoge tou nomou, 426b
Ekkehard of Aura, 201b
Eleanor of Aquitaine, 368b, 645b
  longevity of, 432a
  as queen, 513b
Eleanor of Castile, queen of England
  children of, 115a
  influence of, 514a
  statue of, 239a
Eleanor of England (queen of Alfonso VIII), 150b
Elegies, Anglo-Saxon, 192a–b
Elementary Forms of Religious Life. See Durkheim, Émile
Elements. See Euclid

Eleutherius, St., 224a
Elias, Norbert
   Civilizing Process, The, 533b
Elias of Cortona, **176b–177b**
Eligius, St., 24a
Eliot, T. S.
   Murder in the Cathedral, 395b
   Waste Land, The, 395b
Ełišē, 55a
Elite identity, 185b–186a
Elizabeth I of England, queen
   Percy and, 466a
Elizabeth of Bavaria, 140a
Elizabeth of Hungary, St., **177b–178b**
Ellis, George
   Specimens of Early English Metrical
     Romances, 391a
Ely Cathedral, 228a
Enamel
   basse-taille, 240b
Enchiridion. See Augustine of Hippo, St.
Enclosure
   More, Thomas, on, 502a, 507a
   poverty and, 502a, 507a
   rural depopulation and, 26b
Encyclopedias
   by Bartholomaeus Anglicus, 49a
   Dominican, 411a
   by Isidore of Seville, 49b
   by Thomas of Cantimpré, 49a
   by Vincent of Beauvais, 49a
Enéas, 281b
Engelbert of Cologne, 268b
England
   Admiral in, 6a
   Alexander IV and, 9a
   Anglo-Saxon, 32b
   archaeology of, 25b, 26a
   baronial resistance to monarchy in,
     11b
   beggar permits in, 499b, 500b
   communes in, 135a
   criminal procedure in, 315a–316b
   domestic architecture in, 36a
   Florentine merchants in, 3a
   garrison duty in, 95b
   Jews persecuted in, 517a–518a
   kilns in, 449b
   love days in, 461a
   manorialism and, 343a–344b
   nationalism in, 11b
   Peasants' Revolt in (1381), 136b
   popular religion in, 528b–529a
   race in, 517a–518a
   schools in, 560a, 561a–562b, 563b,
     564a, 564b
   self-government within, 132b
   wool trade in, 399a
English architecture
   Gothic, 228a–230a
English common law
   Bracton on, 419b
   marriage and, 367b, 369a

English drama, 153b, 195b
   the Fall and, 195b
English language
   Henry IV and, 13a
English literature
   alliterative, 11a–15a, 192a
   autobiography in, 47a
   Beowulf, 179a, 180b
   the Exeter Book and, 191b
   Faerie Queene, The 181b
   Morte Arthure, 179b
   Paradise Lost, 181b
   poetry, 14a
   satire in, 554a
   Troilus and Criseyde, 181a
   See also Medievalism; Middle English
     literature; Old English literature
Enlightenment, the, 407b
Ensoulment, 589a, 591 *(illus.)*
   abortion and, 1a
   soul and body and, 592a
Entheticus, de dogmate philosophorum. See
   John of Salisbury
Eoforwic (Anglian York, England), 27a
Epanagoge. See Eisagoge tou nomou
Ephraem, 55a, 359b
Epic and Romance. See Ker, W. P.
Epic genre, **179a–181b**
   Arabic, 22a
   attitudes toward animals and, 19a–b
   Carolingian-cycle, 16b
   Greek vernacular, 180b
   hero in, 179b
   Italian, 180b
   Koranic influence and, 180b
   Latin, 179a–180a
   literary, 179a
   medieval Latin, 179a
   oral folk, 179a
   in Persian tradition, 180b
   poetic stories in, 83b–84a
   Portuguese, 494b–495a
   Russian, 587b
   secondary, 180b
   vernacular, 179a, 180a
   See also Zadonshchina
Epidemics. *See* Bubonic plague; Disease
Epistola de litteris colendis. See Alcuin of
   York
Epistola de secretis artis et naturae et de
   nullitate magiae. See Bacon, Roger
Epistola generalis, 560b
Epistula Apostolorum, 62a
Eraclius, 555a
Érec and Énide. See Chrétien de Troyes
Erfurt, University of, 163b
Ermengarda d'Oluja, 604a
Ermengarde of Narbonne, 652a
Ernst (Ernest) of Pardubice, archbishop
   Madonna painting commissioned by,
     75b
Eschatology, 157a

Eskil, archbishop
   Lund cathedral and, 340b
Espinas, Georges, 402a
Espionage, **182a–183b**
   agents of, 182b
   by diplomats, 182a
   during Hundred Years War, 183a
   by Islamic states, 182a, 182b
   punishment for, 182b–183a
Esprit des lois, L'. See Montesquieu,
   Charles-Louis de
Essen Minster, church of, 226a
Estoire del Saint Graal, 150b
Estrif de fortune et virtu, L'. See Le Franc,
   Martin
Établissements de St. Louis, 84b, 322b
Ethelbert of Kent, king, 143a
Ethelhelm of Canterbury, archbishop,
   168a
Ethelred of Rievaulx, St., 421a
Ethelstan of England, king, 168a
Ethelwold, 168a–b, 561b
Ethica. See Abelard, Peter
Ethics
   animal symbolism and, 18b, 19a
   probability and, 508a
Ethiopia, 424a
   Christianization of, 598a
Etiquette and manners, **183b–186b**
   codes of, 183b–186a
   manuals of, 184b
   social structure and, 184a, 185b–186a
Etymologiae. See Isidore of Seville
Eucharist, 545a, 548a–549b
   cult of, 70a–b
   Eastern liturgical year and, 328a
   semiotics and, 582a
   signs and, 585a
   soul and body and, 590b, 592a
   stained-glass windows and, 237a
   See also Transubstantiation; Utraquism
Euclid, 371a
   Elements, 371b
Eugenius II, pope, 365b
Eugenius III, pope, **186b–187b**
   Conrad III and, 139a
   Divina dispensatione, 187a
   Hospitallers and, 276a
   Quantum praedecessores, 187a
   Second Crusade and, 186b–187a
Eugenius IV, pope, **187b–188a,** 434a,
   610b–611a, 623b
   Colonna family and, 128b
   Martin Le Franc and, 323b
   unity of Christian churches and, 188a
Eugenius of Palermo, 6a
Eugenius II of Toledo, bishop, 167a
Euhemerism, 452b–453a
Eunuchs, **188a–190a**
   as educators, 189a–b
   freedmen, 189a
   under Mamluk sultanate, 189a
   roles of, 188b–189b

Euphrates River, 174a
Europe
    agricultural transformation of, 172b–
        173a
    archaeology of, 25b
    Christianization of, 141a–144b
    before industrial revolution, 408a
    kingdoms of northern, 27a
    markets in, 131b
    modern period and, 408a
    periodization of, 408a
    trade in northern, 27a–28a
Eusebius of Caesarea, 142a, 605a–b
Eusebius of Nicomedia, 619b
Euskal Herria, 190a
Euskara, **190a–191b**
Eustace II of Boulogne, 215a
Euthymios Zigabenos, 55a
Evagoras. See Isocrates
Evagrius Ponticus, 629b
    De octo spiritibus malitiae, 630a
Eve, 207b, 210a
    depictions of, 195b–196a
    misogyny and, 195b–196a
    sensuality of, 69a
    symbolism of, 195b–196a
    women's subjection and, 195a
Everyman, 395b
Evil eye
    menstruation and, 249b
Evil magic (*maleficium*)
    abortion and, 1a, 2a
Évrard of Béthune
    Graecismus, 9b, 563a
Evrenoz Bey, 45a
Excalibur. See Boorman, John
Excommunication
    of German bishops, 317b
Execution
    as civic ritual, 537a
    soul and body and, 592b
Exegesis, 195a
Exempla
    Perault on, 463b–464a
Exeter Book, **191b–193a,** 192a (*illus.*)
Exeter Cathedral, 191b
Exiit qui seminat. See Nicholas II, pope
Exorcism, 151b
Expositio in Job ad litteram. See Aquinas,
    Thomas, St.
Extepare, Bernard
    Linguae vasconum primitiae, 190b
Eyck, Hubert van
    Adoration of the Lamb, 534b
Eyck, Jan van, 265a
    Adoration of the Lamb, 534b
Eyvān (hall), 443a
Ezra, Fourth Book of, 194b
Ezzelino da Romano, 9a, **193b–194a**
    crusade against, 193b

F

Fables
    Aesopic, 19a
    attitudes toward animals and, 19a–b
    in Sanskrit language, 303b–304a
Fables of Bidpai, 303b
Fabliau
    sexuality in, 491b, 492a, 571a–b
Facetus moribus et vita, 184a
Factionalism, 133b, 134a–b, 135a, 136b,
    137a
Faerie Queene, The. See Spenser, Edmund
"Fair of Lincoln" (1217)
    Peter des Roches and, 470a
Fairs
    Champagne, 399a, 402b
    commercialization and, 131b
Falcandus, Hugo, 641b
Fall, the, 154a, **194a–196a**
    Eve's role in, 195b–196a
    free will and, 194b
    in German literature, 195a
    interpretaions of, 194a–b
    Jewish concept of, 194b
    sexual desire and, 194b
    theological implications of, 195a
    visual images of, 195b
Family
    architecture and, 30b, 36a
    in peacemaking, 460b–461a
    ties of queens to, 514b
Famine
    14th century, 135b
    poverty and, 499b, 501a–502b
Fan dae koningen Kaerle ende Redbad,
    206a
Farīd al-Dīn al-ʿAṭṭār, 254b, 255a
Fārisī, Kamāl al Dīn al-, 372b, 375a
    (*sidebar*)
Farmer, Sharon, 505a
Farming. *See* Agriculture
Fasting, 328b–329b
Fāṭima, as Islamic saint, 254b
Fatimids, 188b
Fauchet, Claude, 390b
Faust. See Goethe, Johann von
Faversham Abbey, 595b
Fayreford, Thomas, 251a
Fazārī, al-, 371a
Feast days
    Eastern liturgical year and, 328b–329b
Feast of the Pheasant (1454), 535b
Feasts and festivals
    Savonarola and, 557b
Febvre, Lucien, 533b
Felicianus, 166b
Felicie, Jacoba, 647a
Felix V, pope, 188
    Martin Le Franc and, 323b–324a
Felony
    criminal procedure and, 315a–316a
    manorialism and, 343b

Ferdinand II of Aragon, king, 413a,
    612b, 645b
    Poor Clares and, 488b
Ferdinand III of Castile, king, 191a,
    196a–197a
    Andalusia and, 196b
    Battle of Las Navas de Tolosa and,
        306a
Ferdinand V of Castile, king, 413a–b
Ferdinand de Antequera (Ferdinand of
    Aragon, Valencia, and Catalonia), king,
    10a–b
Ferdinand of Trastámara
    as contender for throne of Aragon, 94b
Ferguson, Margaret W., 581b
Ferrara-Florence, Council of (1439),
    188a, 611a
*Feschichte der romanischen und
    germanischen Völker von 1494 bis 1514*
    (History of the Romantic and
    Germanic peoples). *See* Waitz, Georg
Feudalism, 321a
    castle-guard and, 95a
    comitatus and, 129a
    Portuguese literature on, 496a
    See also Law, feudal
Feuds, 460a, 465b
Fibonacci, Leonardo, 400b
Ficino, Marsilio, 41a
Figure poems. *See carmina figurata*
Filelfo, Francesco
    biography of Dante by, 64a
Filid (Irish order of poets), 559b
Fillastre, Guillaume, 92b, 298b
    De situ orbis, 92b
Film, 396b
    Arthurian romances in, 36b
Fin 'amors
    in Portuguese poetry, 494a
Finchale, 216a–b
Finn of Frisia, king, 197a
Finnsburh Episode, 197a–197b
Finnsburh Fragment, **197a–b**
Firdaws al-ḥikmah. See Tabarī, ʿAlī ibn
    Sahl Rabbān al-
Firearms, **197b–200a**
    gunpowder in, 198b–200a
    invention of, 198a
    manufacture of, 198a, 199b
    uses of, 198a–b
Fireworks, 197b
First Riustring Codex (*asegabuch*), 205a–b
Fisheries, 170a
Fishing for Leviathan, 155a (*illus.*)
Fitz Nigel, Richard
    on the *murdrum,* 515b
Fitzralph, Richard, bishop of Armagh,
    100b, 200b, **200b–201a**
    diary of, 200b
    De pauperie Salvatoris, 200b
    on poverty, 200b–201a
    Proposicio, 200b

Summa de quaestionibus Armenorum, 200b
Flaccus. *See* Alcuin
Flagellants
  plague and, 534b
  soul and body and, 592b
Flambard, Ranulf, 216a
Flanders, county of
  Antwerp and, 24b
  blue nails in, 503b
  cloth industry in, 136a
  communes in, 137a
  count of, 24b
  Karls rebellion, 506b
Flaubert, Gustave
  La Legénde de Saint Julien l'Hospitalier, 393b
  La Tentation de Saint Antoine, (The Temptation of Saint Anthony), 393b
Flete fideles animae, 483b
Fleury, monastic reforms at, 561b
Florence
  blue nails in, 503b
  charitable giving in, 103b *(illus.),* 105a–b
  childbirth in, 108b
  Ciompi revolt, 124a–125b, 503b
  cloth industry of, 136b, 402b, 403a
  commune in, 134b, 136a, 137a
  contract labor in, 567b
  Council of, 137a, 546a, 548a, 551a, 552b, 553a
  economic depression in, 3a
  foundling hospital in, 113a
  homosexuality in, 574a–b
  Mercanzia of, 403b
  merchants of, 2b–3b, 399b, 402b, 403b
  ministates of, 132b, 137a
  Savonarola and, 557b
  wet nurses in, 566b
Florian Gate, 305b
Flos sanctorum em linguagê portugues, 496b
"Flos ultimarum voluntatum." *See* Rolandinus de Passageris
Foliot, Gilbert, bishop of London, 458b
Folksongs, 393a
Fon alra Fresena fridome, 206a
Fontana, Filippo, archbishop of Ravenna, 193b
Fontana, Philip, 193b
Food
  distribution of, 499b
  personal hygiene and, 284b–285a
Forest of Symbols, The. See Turner, Victor
Forestry, plantation, 171b
Forlì, Ranieri di, 7a
Formula vitae honestae. See Martin of Braga, St.
Forum of Nerva, Rome, 33b, 33 *(illus.)*
Fossanova (church: Italy), 231a

Fosterage, peacemaking through, 460b
Fouqué, Friedrich de La Motte, 393a
Four Books of Sentences. See Peter Lombard
"Four Doctors," 82a
Fournier, Jacques, 212a
Foxe, John, 389b
France
  admiral in, 6a
  astrology in, 42a
  commercialization and, 132a
  communes of, 135a
  domestic architecture in, 30b, 36a
  feudal law in, 322b
  Florentine merchants in, 3a
  garrison duty in, 95b
  Hebrew language in, 261a
  humanism and, 280b–281a
  insurance and, 290b
  language of love and, 337a–b
  manorialism and, 344b
  monasteries in, 145a–146b
  Muslims in, 416a
  patron saints of, 370b
  Salian (Salic) law, 514a
  schools in, 560a, 561a, 562a, 562b, 563a
  self-government within, 132b
  silk manufacturing in, 353b
Francien dialect. *See* French language
Francis II of Alençon, duke
  pornographic entertainments of, 491a
Francis of Assisi, St., 169b, 176b–177b, 393b
  animals and, 20a
  biography of, 158b
  imitation of Christ by, 484b–485a
  piety of, 209a
  poverty and, 505a–b, 506a
  St. Clare and, 126a, 485b–486a
  stigmata of, 70a
Franciscan Rule, 177a, 423a
  Poor Clares and, 488a
  St. Clare and, 127a
Franciscans, 176a–177b, 178a, 423a, 423b, 632a
  Alexander IV and, 9a
  in Armagh, 201a
  biblical studies and, 59a
  China missions and, 119a–b
  conversion of Middle East and, 424a
  as delegates to China, 118b–119a
  Dies irae and, 158b
  on education, 639a
  Honorius III, pope, and, 274a
  influence of, 70a
  Pauperes Christi concept and, 98b
  Poor Clares, 485b–490b
  in Saxony, 49a
  schools and, 564a
  Spirituals and, 177b, 440a–b
  theologians of, 378a–b
  on usury, 400a

women as tertiaries of, 569b
Frankfurt, Council of (794), 560b
Frankish church
  council of (742), 88a
  reform movement and, 88a
Frankish states, 201b
  unification of, 203b
Frankl, Paul, 223b
Frankoi. See Franks
Franks, 174a–175a, **201b–202b**
  archaeology of, 26b, 27b
  aristocracy of, 635a
  conquest of Frisians, 204a
  courage of, 202a
  as crusaders, 201b
  diversity within, 201b
  ethnic identity, application of, 201b–202a
  gens francorum, 201b
  greed of, 202a
  intelligence of, 202a
  meanings of, 201b–202a
  negative connotations of, 202a
  schools and, 560b
Frauendienst, 47a
Fraxinetum, **202b–203a**
  Muslims at, 202b, 203a, 342a
  See also Maiolus
Frazer, Sir James
  Golden Bough, The, 395b
Fredegarius
  Chronicle, 203b
Frédégonde et Brunehaut, 203b
Fredegunda, Merovingian queen, 81a–b, **203a–204a,** 512a
Frederick II Babenberg of Austria, duke, 304b
Frederick I Barbarossa of Germany, emperor, 139a, 187b, 196a, 600b, 642b
  ambitions of, 641b
  heresy and, 314a
  longevity of, 431a
  papacy, aid to, 641b
Frederick II of Germany, emperor, 8a, 44, 139a–b, 177a, 193b, 423a, 440a, 441b, 442a, 642b
  Alexander IV and, 9a
  Colonna family and, 127b
  "Golden Bull of Rimini," 270b
  Henry VII of Germany and, 268b–269a
  Honorius III, pope, and, 273b
  Peter des Roches and, 470a
  physician qualification under, 475b
  Pope Innocent III and, 442a
  Sicilian feudal law and, 322b
  Vigna and, 458b
Frederick II of Swabia, king, 138b
Freeman, Edward A.
  History of the Norman Conquest, 392b
Freiburg-im-Breisgau (cathedral: Germany), 230b

Freiburg Münster (cathedral: Germany), 230b
French architecture. *See* Gothic architecture; Romanesque architecture
French Blockbook Apocalypse, 152b (*illus.*)
French language, Francien dialect of, 293b
French literature
　alliterative literature and, 11a, 12b, 13a
　Arthurian romances and, 38b
　autobiography in, 47a
　chansons de geste, 16b, 17a, 588a
　pastourelle, 573a
　poetry, 293b
　satire in, 554a, 556a
　sexuality in, 571a–b
Freyr (god), 620b
Friars
　celibacy of, 569b
　mendicant, 569b
　satire of, 555b, 556a
　voluntary poverty of, 100b
Friday Mosque (*Ulu Cami;* Bursa), 442b
Friedrich, Caspar David, 393a
Friesland, "Great Drowning" in, 172b
Frisia, 205 (map)
Frisian literature, **204a–207a**
　characteristics of, 204a–b
　development, lack of, 204a–b
　Finnsburh Fragment and, 197a–b
　glosses, 206a–b
　heroic poetry in, 206a
　ideological themes in, 206a
　legal poetry in, 205a–b
　legal writings, 204a–205b
　rhyming poetry in, 206a
　See also Alliterative literature
Frisians, 197a–b, 204a–207a, 411a
　Christianization of, 204a
　as traders, 401b
Frit-ware, Ottoman, 447a
Froissart, Jehan
　La prison amoureuse, 47a
From Ritual to Romance. See Weston, Jessie L.
Frugardi, Ruggiero
　medical texts of, 475a
Frumentarii tradition, 182a
Fulbert of Chartres
　feudal law and, 321a–b
　as healer, 474b
　on *Libri feudorum,* 322a
Fulda, 429b
Fulk of Anjou, count
　pilgrim souvenir of, 477b
Fulk of Jerusalem, king
　Hospitallers and, 276a
　Melisende and, 513b
Fulling
　industrial revolution and, 352a–353b
Funeral Oration. See Joseph of Volokolamsk, St.

Funerary rituals, 534a–b
Furness (abbey church: England), 228a
Furs (legal code) of Valencia, 475b

G

Gaimar, Geffrei, 457b
Gaius
　Institutes, 417b, 418a, 426a
Galbert of Bruges, 536a
Galen, 377a–b
　on abortion, 1b
　"Art of Medicine," 380b
　medical tradition of, 380a, 381a–382a
　Peri hygieion, 284a
　physician education and, 474b
　on sexuality, 577b, 578b, 578 (*illus.*)
　on signs, 584a
　on soul and body, 589a, 592a
　De Spermate, 578 (*illus.*)
Galesiotes, George, 362a
Galician-Portuguese literature
　satire in, 556b
Galilei, Galileo, 509b
Gall, St. (Gallus), 480a
Galla Placidia, Roman empress, 511b–512a
Gallus Anonymous, 78b
Galswintha, 203b, 512a
Games, gladiatorial, 65b
Gameson, Richard, 191b
Garden of Eden, 194a
Gasthaüser, 105a
Gaul
　conquest of, 613a
　domestic architecture in, 31a, 32a
　Roman, 201a
　schools in, 558b, 559a, 559b, 560b
Gavardo (town), 8a
Gaveston, Piers, 464b
Gawain, legend of, 39a
Geertz, Clifford, 532a, 532b, 533b, 535b
Gelasius I, pope, 519a–b
Gender, theories of, 188a–189b, **207a–210b**
　abortion and, 1a
　adolescence and, 116a–b
　animals and, 19a
　application of law, 209a–b
　archaeology and, 29b
　arguments on, 208a–b
　Arthurian romances and, 38b
　causes, 207b–208a
　distinction between sex and, 207a–b
　hierarchical evaluation of, 209a
　nature of, 207a
　origins of, 207a–208a
　questions of, 209a
　of saints, 209a
　structural antifeminism, 210a
　universities, access to, 210a
　See also Sexuality; Sexuality, Medical; Women

Gender roles
　homosexuality and, 574a, 574b
　norms of, 209b
　sexuality and, 570a, 576b
Genealogia deorum gentilium. See Boccaccio, Giovanni
Generaciones y semblanzas. See Pérez de Guzmán, Fernán
Generalia. See Ricardus Anglicus
Genesis. *See* Bible
Genghis Khan, 118a–b
Génie du Christianisme, Le. See Chateaubriand, François-Auguste René de
Genius, **210b–212a**
　concept of, 211a–b
　interpretation of, 210b–211a
Genizah community, Cairo, 399b
Gennep, Arnold van
　Rites de passage, 533a–b
Genoa
　Alfonso V and, 10b
　foreign control of, 137a
　insurance and, 290b–291a
　merchants of, 399b–400a, 402a, 402b, 403a–b
　podesta in, 134a
　public debt of, 296a
Gens francorum. See Franks
Gentile da Foligno, 584b
Gentiles, conversion of, 141a
Geoffrey V Plantagenet, count of Anjou, 376b, 595a
　tomb of, 239a
Geoffrey of Monmouth
　alliterative literature and, 15a
　Historia regum Britanniae, 15a, 37a–b, 38b, 389b–390a
　Robert of Gloucester and, 457b
Geoffrey of St. Albans, abbot, 650b
Geoffrey of St. Victor
　Planctus ante nescia, 483b
Geoffroy de la Tour-Landry. *See Book of the Knight of the Tower*
Geographical coordinate system, 90b
Geography. See Ptolemy
Geography in literature, 16b
Geometry. *See* Mathematics, Islamic
George of Antioch, 6a
Georgian Lapskaldi Gospels, 360b
Georgian Vani Gospels, 361a
Gerald of Wales, 20a, 47b, 618b
　History and Topography of Ireland, 516a
Gerard of Burgundy. *See* Nicholas II, pope
Gerard of Cremona, 584a
Gerbert of Aurillac, 66b, 562a
　See also Sylvester II, pope
Geremek, Bronislaw, 504b
Gerhoh of Reichersberg, 58a, 548a
German law
　on marriage, 364b–365b
　peacemaking and, 460a

German literature, 179a, 179b, 180a, 180b, 181a
  autobiography in, 47a
  satire in, 554a
German Order. *See* Teutonic Knights
German towns, 542b
Germania. See Tacitus
Germanias (Valencian brotherhoods), 413b
Germanic peoples, 197a–b
  folklore of, 18a, 197a–b
  warriors, 201a
  See also Franks
Germany
  Alexander IV and, 9a
  astrology in, 41b
  communes in, 132b, 135a–b, 137a
  under Conrad III, 138b–139a
  under Conrad IV, 139a–140a
  customs of, 309b–310a
  domestic architecture in, 32b, 33a, 33b, 36a
  electors, 542a–b
  émigré scholars from, 386a
  emperor of, 7b
  Hohenstaufen dynasty and, 138b–140b
  interregnum period in (1257–1273), 542a
  manorialism and, 344b
  ministerials in, 565a
  minnesong of, 337b
  Ottonian dynasty and, 137b, 146b
  Salian dynasty and, 138b, 146b
  schools in, 560a, 560b, 562a, 562b, 564a
  taxation in, 600a–601a
Gero of Saxony, count, 408b
Gerona (cathedral: Spain), 233a
Gerson, John, 619a
  astrology and, 41a
  Le profit de savoir quel est péché mortel et véniel, 631b
  on *Roman de la Rose,* 492a
  schools and, 563b
  vice as virtue, 631b
Gerusalemme liberata. See Tasso, Torquato
Gervase of Canterbury
  Chronicle, 223b–224a, 228a–b
  History of the Archbishops of Canterbury, 62b
  Life of St. Thomas of Canterbury, 62b
Gervase of Tilbury, 410b–411a
  Otia imperialia, 213a
Geschichte der Deutschen Sprache. See Grimm, Jacob
Gesta, described, 63a
Gesta Friderici. See Otto of Freising
Gesta Guillelmi ducis Normannorum. See William of Poitiers
Gesta Hammaburgensis ecclesiae. See Adam of Bremen

Gesta pontificum anglorum. See William of Malmesbury
Gesta rerum anglorum. See William of Malmesbury
Gesta Roberti Wiscardi. See William of Apulia
Ghayat al-ḥakīm. See Majrīṭī, Maslama al-
Ghazālī, al-, 115b
Ghent
  Antwerp and, 24b
  communes and, 133b, 135b, 136a
  Dominican convent of, 163b
  St. Peter's abbey, 168a
  secular schools of, 400b
Ghibellines. *See* Guelphs and Ghibellines
Ghifārī, Abū Dharr al-, 253b
Ghosts, **212a–213a**
  See also Demons; Hell, concepts of; Soul and body
Gibbon, Edward, 391b
Gilbert of Hastings, 326b
Gilchrist, Roberta, 29b
Giles of Rome. *See* Egidius Colonna
Gill, Eric, 395a
Gilles de Rais (Bluebeard), 633b
Gilson, Étienne, 384b
Ginza (*Sidra rba;* "the great book"), 544a
Ginzburg, Carlo, 43a
Giordano da Rivalto, 43a
Giotto di Bondone, 407a
  Poor Clares Grieving over the Body of St. Francis, 486 *(illus.)*
Giovanna II of Naples, queen, 10b
Giovanni de Legnano. *See* Johannes de Lignano
Giovanni of Capistrano, St., 489a
Girart de Roussillon, 181a
Girolamo Savonarola. See Della Porta, Fra Bartolommeo
Girone il Cortese, 17a
Gislebertus, 264b–265a
Glass, stained, 392b, 394b
  Gothic art and, 236a, 237a
Glastonbury Abbey, 168a, 191b
  Irish monks at, 168a
Glenn Máma, Battle of (997), 80b
Glosas Emilianenses, 190b
Glossa ordinaria, 58a–b, 476b–477a
  See also Accursius
Glosses
  as biblical commentaries, described, 56b, 58b–59a
  Roman law and, 82a–b
Gnosticism, 213b, **213b–215a,** 214a
  manuscripts on, 214a–b
  vision of, 213b
  See also Fall, The; Matter; Soul and Body
Godfrey of Bouillon, 174a, **215a–215b**
  as crusader, 215a–b
  as ruler of Jerusalem, 215b
Godfrey of Fontaines, 378b

Godfrey of Lorraine and Tuscany, 422a
Godric of Finchale, St., **215b–216b,** 402a
  miracles attributed to, 216b
Goethe, Johann von
  Faust, 391b
Golden Bough, The. See Frazer, Sir James
Golden Bull. *See* Charles IV, Holy Roman Emperor
"Golden Bull of Rimini." *See* Frederick II of Germany, emperor
Golden Horn. *See* Constantinople
Golden Legend. See Jacobus de Varagine
Goliardic verse
  satire in, 555a
Golias, 308a, 555a
Gologras and Gawain, 11a
Gomes Eanes de Zurara. *See* Zurara, Gomes Eanes de
Goodhue, Bertram, 394a
Goodman of Paris, 567b
Gorze
  monastic reforms at, 266b, 561b, 562a
Goscelin of St. Bertin, **216b–217b**
  Historia translationis S. Augustini, 217a
  Libellus de adventu beati Adriani abbatis in Angliam, 217a
  Liber confortatorius, 216b–217a
Gosforth Cross, 453 *(illus.)*
Gospel of Nicodemus, 154b, 263a
Gospel of Truth, 214a
Gospels
  biography and, 61b
  illumination of, 358a–b, 359b, 360a–b, 361a–b, 362a *(illus.),* 362b
Gospels Mount Athos, 359b, 362a, 362b
Gospels Paris, 362b
Gospels St. Petersburg, 362b
Gospels Sinai, 362a–b
Gospels Vatican, 360b
Gothic architecture, 34a, **217b–235a,** 407b
  Abbotsford, 391 *(illus.)*
  in America, 385a, 394a–b
  as barbaric, 390a
  in cathedrals, 220b, 222a
  characteristics of, 218a–b
  in churches, 392b, 393a
  classification of, 217b–218a
  domestic, 32a
  economics and, 219a–b, 228a
  employment and, 220a–b
  English, 228a–230a
  financing of, 219a–b
  French, 220b, 223a–228a
  German, 230a–230b
  Houses of Parliament and, 392b
  Italian, 230b–232a
  Late, 233a–233b
  modern aspects of, 218b–219a
  nature used in, 219a
  Neuschwanstein Castle, 394 *(illus.)*
  popularity of, 385a

preservation of, 393a
production, factors of, 219a
Pugin and, 392b
Rayonnant design, 227a–b, 230a
St.-Denis as first, 454b–455a
Schelde, 613a
Strawberry Hill, 390b
Sunnyside, 394a
term for, 218a
variety of edifices, 218a, 219a
See also Architecture, Domestic
Gothic art, **235a–245a**
Heavenly Jerusalem and, 236b–241b
personal devotion and, 241b–243b
secularism and, 243b–244a
style and, 236a–b
Gothic literature, 389b–392b, 394a–396a
See also Romance literature
Goths, 235b, 407b
conversion of, 142a–b
Gottfried von Strassburg, 37b
Gottschalk (peasant), vision of, 451a
Gottschalk of Orbais, 429b, 436b
Government
joyous entry ceremonies and, 534b–535b
literature on, 458b–459a
mirrors of princes on, 496b–497a
social welfare programs by, 506a–507a
Gower, John, 211a–b, 309a
Confessio Amantis, 47a, 211b
influences on, 8b
Gozzoli, Benozzo, 455b
Grace, divine
vs. original sin, 436a
Graecismus. See Évrard of Béthune
Grágás, **245a–b**
Grail, legend of
Arthurian romances and, 36b, 37a, 38b, 39a
cult of, 151a, 394b, 395 *(illus.),* 396b
Grain crops, 170a–b, 171a
dietary culture and, 172b
supplies of, 170b–171a
Grammar, 393b, 563b
See also Schools *and frontispiece*
Granada, kingdom of, 196b, 381b, 413b
Christianization of, 413b, 414b
Muslim surrender of, 413a
Grand testament. See Villon, François
Grande Encyclopédie, 541b
Grandes chroniques de France, 459a
Gratian, **246a–247a,** 418a
Decretum, 52b, 53a–b, 109a, 246a–247a, 246b *(illus.),* 317a–b, 321b, 336a, 366a–b, 399a, 418a–b, 546b, 550a, 571b
definition of natural law by, 418a
on marriage, 571b
on merchants, 399a
on rape, 519b
Raptus quoque, 519b
Ricardus Anglicus on, 531a–b

Great Drowning, 172b
Greece
archaeology of, 25b
astrology in, 41b
eunuchs in, 188a–190a
learning of ancient, 561b, 564a, 590b
marvel writers of, 410a
scholarly attention to, 437b–438b
slaves from, 567b
Turks in, 45a
Greek law. *See* Novel
Greek literature, 180b
epic, 180b
Greek Orthodox Church. *See* Byzantine church
Greeks, as administrators, 5b
Green Tomb (Bursa), 443a, 443 (illus.)
Greenberg, Noah, 396a
Greenland
archaeology in, 29a
climate change in, 29a, 172b
Gregorian chant
in France, 89a
Gregorian decretals. *See* Bernard of Parma; Gregory IX, pope
Gregory I (the Great), pope, 54b, 143a–b, 144b, 159b
Dialogues, 152a
humility, focus on, 630b
on missions, 522b–523a
Moralia in Job, 56a, 154b, 157a, 464a
Perault on, 464a
poverty and, 499b
praise of Brunhild by, 81b
seven-degree rule and, 365a
Gregory II, pope, 365b
Gregory VII, pope, 422a, 617b
Dictus papae, 311a
excommunication of German bishops by, 317b
Gregorian reforms of, 422b
on pollution and taboo, 484b
on sacraments, 551b
St. Stanisław and, 594b
Gregory IX, pope, 8b, 9a, 176b–177a, 440a
on canonization, 525a
Decretals, 52b, 84b
Honorius III, pope, and, 274a
inquisitors of heretical depravity and, 314a
Liber extra, 52b–53a
Mercedarians and, 397b
Peter des Roches and, 470b, 471a
Poor Clares and, 487a–b
St. Clare and, 126b, 127a
Gregory X, pope, **247a–248a,** 423a, 423b
Gregory XI, pope
Great Schism and, 96b
manuscript collections of, 623b
Gregory XII, pope, 187b
Gregory of Akragas, 55a

Gregory of Nazianzus, St., 358a, 360a *(sidebar)*
Gregory of Nyssa, St., 59b, 377b
Gregory of Tours, St., 203a–b, 401a
autobiography by, 45b
biography of St. Martin of Tours, 370b
elevation of, 81a
on poverty, 499b
on Radegunda, 518b
texts of, 145b
Grigor Tatʿewacʿi, 55a
Grima, Dominic, 59a
Grimm, Jacob, 205b
Deutsche Grammatik, 393b
Deutsche Mytholoige, 393b
Geschichte der Deutschen Sprache, 393b
Kinder-und Hausmärchen, 393b
Teutonic Mythology, 450b
Grimm, Wilhelm, 393a
Grisone, Federico
Ordini del cavalcare, 275b
Grosseteste, Robert, 59a, 492b
Grundtvig, N. S. F., 395b
Nordens Mytologi (Norse mythology), 393b
Grunwald, Battle of. *See* Tannenberg/Grunwald, Battle of (1410)
Gualo (papal legate), 278a
Guanilo (monk), 43b
Guarducci, Piero, 567b
Guelphs and Ghibellines, 134a–b, 140a, 404a, 423a, 439b
Charles of Anjou and, 247b
Manfred of Sicily and, 342b
Parte Guelfa and, 124b
Guerric of St. Quentin, 59a
Guerrilla warfare, 634b
Guerrino il meschino. See Andrea da Barberino
Guesclin, Bertrand du, **248a–b,** 542a
Guestlings, 123a
Guglielmo il Buono. *See* William II of Sicily, King
Guglielmo il Malo. *See* William I of Sicily, King
Gui, Bernard, 387b
Guibert of Nogent, 625a
Memoirs, 114a
Monodiae (Vita sua; Memoirs), 46b
Guide for the Perplexed. See Maimonides, Moses
Guido d'Arezzo, 417a
Guido of Milan, archbishop, 422b
Guilds
Barcelona and, 136b
in England, 135a, 403b
Flanders and, 136a, 403b–404a
in Florence, 124b–125b, 136a, 136b, 399b, 402b, 403b–404a
in Germany, 403b–404a
in Kraków, 305a
in London, 135a

mercantile trade and, 133b, 403b–404a
Paris and, 135a
patronage and, 455a–b
political aspect of, 134b, 137a
popular religion and, 529a
revival of, 392b
strength of, 136a
textiles and, 352b
Guillaume de Deguileville. *See*
Deguileville, Guillaume de
Guillaume de Dôle. See Renart, Jean
Guillaume de Lorris
Roman de la Rose, 47a, 338a
Guillaume d'Orange, legend of, 16b, 17a
Guipúzcoa, 190a, 191a
Guizot, François, 392a
Guns and gunpowder
invention of, 197b
military potential of, 198a
recipes for, 198a, 199b
unconventional uses of, 200a
Gunthamund (Vandal ruler), 166b–167a
Guntram of Burgundy, king, 81b, 203b
Guthlac, 191b, 192b
Guy II of Athens, duke, 44b
Guy de Bazoches
Apologia, 412a
Guy of Montpellier
founding of Order of Holy Spirit by,
116a
Gymnasium, 50a, 65b
Gynacaea (women's weaving workshops),
573a
Gynaecia. See Muscio
Gynecology, **249a–253a,** 249b *(illus.)*
contraception, 252a
dissemination of knowledge about,
252b–253a
fertility and, 251a–b
See also Abortion; Childbirth and
infancy

H

Habsburg dynasty
first ruler of, 542b
Hadewijch of Brabant, 339a–b
Ḥadīth, 158a
on eunuchs, 188b
Hadrian, abbot (Ireland), 56b
Hadrian of Canterbury, St., 560a
Hagiography, Islamic, **253a–256a**
Hagiography, Jewish, **256a–259a**
Hagiography, Western European, 438a
attitudes toward animals and, 19b–20a
described, 61b
illuminated manuscripts and, 359a,
360b
medieval revival and, 393b
in popular religion, 521a, 523b–525b
Portuguese, 496a–b
St. Anthony and, 23a
sexuality in, 570b

Haimeric, 311a
Hainsworth, J. B., 180a
Haithabu (Germany), 27a
Ḥajjāj ibn Maṭar, al-, 371b
Hakluyt, Richard, 633b
Voyages, 633b
Halberstadt Cathedral, 239a
Hallam, Henry
*View of the State of Europe in the
Middle Ages,* 391b–392a
Halls, in domestic architecture, 31a, 33a,
33b, 34a–b, 35 *(illus.),* 36a, 443a
Halutza (church: Negev), 597b
Hamburg
diocese of, 21b
Viking sack of, 22a
Hamburg-Bremen (mission), 620b
Hamilton Psalter, 362b
Hammat Tiberias (synagogue: Palestine),
41b
Hamwih (Saxon Southampton, England),
27a, 27b
Hanafī legal school, 158a
Hananiah ben Teradion, 257a
Hand-washing rituals, 244a
Handlyng Synne. See Mannyng, Robert
Hangchow (China)
Franciscan missionaries in, 119a
Hanka, Venceslav, 148b
Hanna, Ralph, 14a
Hanseatic League, 398b, 399b, 400b,
401a, 402b
Amsterdam and, 16a
archaeology of, 29a
Kraków becomes member of, 305a
Hansen's disease. *See* Leprosy
Harald Klak of Denmark, king, 21b
Ḥarbīs (outside lands of Islam), 158a
Hardenberg, Friedrich von. *See* Novalis
Harley, Edward, 356a
Harley, Robert, 356a
Harmscara, 461b
Harran, Battle of, 174a
Ḥarrān, Sabians of, 543a–b
Harrowing of Hell, 154b, 263a
Hartlieb, Johannes, 2a
Hartmann von Aue
Iwein, 181a
Hārūn al-Rashīd, caliph, 380a
oldest hospital and, 382a
of *Thousand and One Nights,* 371b
Harvard University, medieval studies at,
385a–b, 394b–395a
Ḥasdai ibn Shaprūt, 260a
Haskins, Charles Homer
Renaissance of the Twelfth Century, The,
385b
Hatayi motif, 447a
Ḥaṭīb, Ibn al-, 381b
Ḥātima, Ibn, 381b
Hautevilles, the. *See* William I of Sicily,
King

Ḥāwī, al-. See Rāzī, Abū Bakr
Muḥammad ibn Zakarīya' al-
Ḥawrānī, Ibn
al-ishārāt ilāziyārāt, 255b
Haymo of Faversham, 57a, 177a
Haytham, Ḥasan ibn al-, 371b, 372b
Optics (Kitāb al-manāẓir), 373a, 375a
(sidebar)
Heart on the Cross, in Gothic art, 242b
Heavenly Jerusalem, Gothic churches as,
236b–237a
Heavenly Ladder. See John Klimakos
Hebrew language, 191a, **259a–262a**
in al-Andalus, 260a–261a
Bible in, 620a
in European kingdoms, 261a–b
in Islamic empire, 260a–261a
medieval studies on, 259b–260a
Persian scripts in, 467b
in schools, 562b
writings on sexuality in, 577b, 578a,
579a, 580a
Hedwig of Kiburg, 542b
Hein, Christoph
Die Ritter der Tafelrunde, 396b
Heiric, 57a
Helena, St., 142a
Heliand, 205b–206a
Hélinand of Froidmont, 214b
Vers de la mort, 556a
Hell, concepts of, 153b–154b, 156a,
156a *(illus.),* 156 *(illus.),* 160a, **262a–
265b**
medieval art and, 263b–265a
theater and, 263a–b
tours of hell and, 262b–263a
Hellenism
sexuality and, 570a
Helm, Joan, 428b
Heloise
Peter Abelard and, 46b, 334a–335a,
651b
writings of, 651b
Hengest of the Danes, 197a–b
Henry Bate of Malines
Speculum divinorum, 378b
Henry I of Castile, king
Henry II of Castile, king, 248b
Henry III of Castile, king, 10b
Henry I of England, king, 184b, 217a,
376a–b, 600a, 645a–b
coronation of, 641a
King Stephen and, 595a
Petrus Alfonsi and, 471b
queen of, 513a
sexuality of, 573a
succession of, 513b
Henry II of England, king, 368b, 376b,
645b
Becket and, 458b
King Stephen and, 595b
patronage by, 458a

public prosecution of criminals and, 315b
Henry III of England, king, 175b–176a, 222b, 223a, 227b, 229a, 423a, 431a
  Alexander IV and, 9a
  Honorius III, pope, and, 273a
  Peter des Roches and, 470a, 471a
Henry IV of England, king
  English language and, 13a
  Percy and, 465a–b
  Teutonic Knights, relationship to, 606b
Henry V of England, king
  admirals of, 6a
  marriage of, 514a
Henry VII of England, king
  Percy and, 466a
Henry VIII of England, king
  Cinque Ports and, 123b
  dissolution of monasteries and, 389b
  suppression of religious houses by, 355b
Henry I (the Fowler) of Germany, king, 635a
Henry I of Germany, emperor, 138a, 146a, **265b–266a**
Henry II of Germany, emperor, 79a, **266a–267a**
  astrology and, 42a
  monasticism and, 146b
Henry IV of Germany, emperor, 215a, 441b
  conflict with Pope Gregory VII and, 317b
Henry V of Germany, emperor, 79b, **264a–b**, 376b, 600a
Henry VI of Germany, emperor, **268a–b**, 433a–b, 442a, 642b–643a
Henry VII of Germany, emperor, 139b, **268b–269b**
Henry (the Lion) of Bavaria and Saxony, duke, 138b, 140a, 441b
  longevity of, 431b
Henry X (the Proud) of Bavaria and Saxony, duke, 138b
Henry of Burgundy, count of Portucale, 326b
Henry of Capua, prince, 641b
Henry of Champagne, 606a
Henry of Ghent, 591b
Henry of Huntingdon, 308b, 516b
Henry of Langenstein, 41a
Henry of Nordheim, duke, 82b
Henry of Saxony, duke, 138a
  See also Henry I of Germany, emperor
Henry of Silesia, 118b
Henry of Trastámara. See Henry II of Castile, king
Henry of Warnsdorf, 147b
Henry Raspe of Thuringia, landgrave, 139b

Henry the Navigator of Portugal, prince, **269b–270a**
  biography of, 654b
Henry the Wrangler of Bavaria, duke, 409a
Heracleon, 54a
Heraldry
  attitudes toward animals and, 20a
  Gothic art and, 244a
Herbert of Bosham, 59b
Herder, Johann Gottfried von
  Stimmen der Völker (Voices of the people), 393a–b
Hereford map, 411a
Heresies, Christian, 169a
  adolescent conversion and, 116b
  Albigensian, 156a–b
  Arianism, 167a
  atheism and, 43b–44a
  criminal procedure and, 313b–314a
  dualism, 154a, 156a–b
  Gnostic influences in, 156a, 214b–215a
  Pelagianism, 154a
  pollution and taboo and, 485a
  pornography and, 491b
  punishment for, 86a
  sacraments and, 548b, 552a, 552b, 553b
  of Savonarola, 558a
  of servants, 568a
  soul and body and, 591a
Herman of Sherborne, bishop, 216b
Herman of Tournai, 252a
Hermann of Salza, **270a–271a**
Hermann I of Swabia, duke, 266a
Hermes Trismegistus, 40a
Heroic Epic and Saga. See Oinas, Felix
Herrad of Hohenberg, abbess
  Hortus deliciarum, 155a, 155a (illus.)
Hetairai (courtesans), 576a
Hexabiblos. See Basilics
Heytesbury, William, 406a, 406b
  Regulae solvendi sophismata (Rules for solving sophismata), 405a–406a
  on semantics, 473b
Ḥibbur yafeh min ha-yeshuʿa. See Nissim ben Jacob ben Nissim Ibn Shahin
Hierarchy
  peacemaking and, 461b–462a
  servants and, 565a, 567b
  sexuality and, 573a–b
  soul and body and, 593a
Higden, Ranulf
  Historia Polychronica, 421a
Hilāl, Banū (Sīrat Banū Hilāl), 22b, **271a–b**
Hilary of Orléans, **271b–272b**, 308b
Hilary of Poitiers, St., 370a
Hildebert of Lavardin, 280a, 308b
Hildebrand. See Gregory VII, pope
Hildeburh (sister of Hnaef), 197a

Hildegard of Bingen, 207b–208a, 650a
  gynecological knowledge and, 252b
  Liber Scivias, 155b
  longevity of, 432a
Hill, Geoffrey, 395a
Hill Monastic Manuscript project, Minnesota, 383b
Ḥilyat al-awliyā. See Abū Nuʿaym al-Iṣfahānī
Hincmar of Rheims, 436b, 617a–b
  on marriage, 365b, 366a
Hippocrates
  "Airs, waters, and places," 380b
  disease and, 165a
  doctrine of, 208a
  medical tradition of, 380a, 382a
  semiotics and, 584b
  on sexuality, 577b
Hippocratic oath, 1b
Hippodrome
  circus factions and, 65b–66a
  political power and, 66a
Hippolytis of Rome, 214a
Hispanus, Laurentius, 52b
Hispanus, Vincentius, 52b
Histoire de St. Louis. See Joinville, Jean de
Historia calamitatum. See Abelard, Peter
Historia Florentini populi. See Bruni, Leonardo
Historia naturalis. See Pliny the Elder
Historia novella. See William of Malmesbury
Historia orientalis. See Jacques de Vitry
Historia Polychronica. See Higden, Ranulf
Historia regum Britanniae. See Geoffrey of Monmouth
Historia scholastica. See Comestor, Peter
Historia translationis S. Augustini. See Goscelin of St. Bertin
Historiography
  agricultural, 408a
  Portuguese, 495a–496a
  of poverty, 498b–499a
  preindustrial, 170b
History and Topography of Ireland. See Gerald of Wales
History of Latin Christianity. See Milman, Henry
History of the Anglo-Saxons. See Turner, Sharon
History of the Archbishops of Canterbury. See Gervase of Canterbury
History of the Mongols. See John of Plano Carpini
History of the Norman Conquest. See Freeman, Edward A.
Hitler, Adolf
  in medieval armor, 395a
Hnaef of Denmark, 197a
Hoccleve, Thomas, 47a
Hodegon Monastery, 362b
Hodges, Richard, 401a
Hodgson, Marshall G., 467b

Hodo of Germany, margrave, 409a
Hoe dae Fresen toe fridom koemen, 206a
Hoe dae Friesen Roem wonnen, 206a
Hoffmann, E. T. A., 393a
Hoffmannstahl, Hugo von, 395b
Hofstaðir (Iceland), 29b
Hohenstaufen dynasty, 138b–140b,
    268a–b, 441b–442a, 542a, 542b
    Alexander IV and, 9a
    last of the, 247b, 343a
    Pedro III and, 462b
Holcot, Robert, 59a
Holkham Bible Picture Book, 155b, 157a
    (illus.), 264b
Holland. *See* Low Countries
Holland, Thomas, 335a–b
Holy Roman Empire, 196b, 441b–442a
    Antwerp and, 24a–b
    Conrad III and, 138b–139a
    Conrad IV and, 139a–140a
    Diet of, 600b
    Frederick II and, 139a–140a, 273b
    Golden Bull of Emperor Charles IV
        and, 107a
    interregnum period in (1257–1273),
        542a
    law of, 427a
    Prague as artistic center of, 74a–b
Holy Rood, legends of, 195a
Holy Sepulcher (church: Jerusalem), 603b
Holy Spirit, sacraments and, 548a, 551a
Homer, 179a–179b
    Iliad, 179a
    Odyssey, 179a
Homildon Hill, Battle of (1401)
    Percy and, 465a
Homiletic literature
    alliterative literature and, 13b, 14b
Homily on the Fall of Idols. See Jacob of
    Serugh
Homoeans, creed of, 620a
Homosexuality, 573b–575a
    as disease, 579b–580a
    oral sex and, 574b
    satire on, 554b
Honorius III, pope, 8b–9a, **272b–274b**
    Athens and, 44b
    on clerical healers, 474b
    Liber censuum, 273a
    "Ordo Romanus," 273a
    Super specula, 474b
Honorius IV, pope, 423a, 621b
Horace
    satire of, 554b
    Satires, 563a
    used in schools, 562a, 563a
Horns of Ḥiṭṭīn (1187), 604a
Horses and horsemanship, **274a–275b**
Hortus deliciarum. See Herrad of
    Hohenberg
Hospices
    charity and, 504a
    Poor Clares and, 485b–486a

Hospitallers, **276a–277a,** 424a, 603b,
    604b, 626b
    commandery, 276b
    Hospitaller Commanderie of Zittau,
        147b
Hospitals, 165b–166a
    for the blind, 104a
    charity and, 103b–104a, 504a
    childbirth and, 111a
    for foundlings, 113a, 116a
    Manṣūrī, Cairo, 382a
    Nūrī, Damascus, 381a, 382a
    poor relief and, 502b
Host
    locking up, 526b–527a
    in popular religion, 521a
    veneration of, 525b–527a
    See also Eucharist
Hostiensis, 317b, 400a
Hours of Catherine of Cleves, 264a
House of the Valerii, Caelian Hill
    (Rome), 31a
How the Good Wife Taught Her Daughter,
    185a
How the Wise Man Taught His Son, 185a
Hrabanus Maurus, abbot of Fulda, 57a,
    179b, 429b
    carmina figurata of, 438a
    In honorem sanctae crucis, 437b *(illus.),*
        438a
    Liber de oblatione peurorum, 429b
    Louanges de la sainte croix, 457b
Hradčany castle complex, 73a, 73b
Hrotsvit, 651b
Ḥubaish al-Ibādī, 380a–b
Hubert de Burgh, **277a–279b**
Hugh of Fleury, 217a
Hugh (Primas) of Orléans, 308a, 555a
Hugh of Payns, 603b
Hugh of St. Cher, 546a
    Postilla super totam Bibliam, 58b
Hugh of St. Victor, 58a, 207b
    on concatenation, 630b
    De sacramentis, 583b
    on sacraments, 545a, 545b, 546b,
        547a, 548a, 550b, 551a, 552a,
        552b, 583b
Hughes, Thomas, 392a
Hugo, Victor
    Notre-Dame de Paris, 393a
Hugo da Porta Ravennate, 82a
Hugolino. *See* Gregory IX, pope
Hugolinus, 4a
Huguccio
    feudal law and, 321b
    origin of natural law and, 418b
Huizinga, Johan, 408a
    Waning of the Middle Ages, 533b
Hulagu
    creation of Persian *il-khânate* by, 118b
Hulbert, James Root, 11b
Humanism, **279b–282b**
    during fifteenth century, 279b–280b

in Italy, 407a
medieval, 280b–282a
of Renaissance, 407b
in schools, 564a
Humbert of Romans, 159b, **282b–283a**
    De eruditione praedicatorum, 283a
    Opusculum tripartitum, 283a
    Perault and, 464a
Humbert of Silva Candida, 551b, 552a
Humors (physiology), 164b
    astrology and, 42b
    race and, 516b–517a
    soul and body and, 592a
    See also Disease
Humphrey of Gloucester, duke, 355b
Ḥunain ibn Isḥāq al-Ibādī
    al-Masā' il fī l-ṭibb (Questions of
        medicine), 380a–b
    Isagoge, 283a–b, 285a–b
Hundred Years War, 233b, 404a, 613b,
    627b
    cause of, 645b
    espionage in, 183a
    France in, 633b
    poverty and, 502a
    routiers in, 541b–542a
    savagery in, 625b
Hüner-nāme, 446b
Hungarians
    Cumans and, 147a–147b
Hungary
    castle-guard and, 95b
    Mongol invasion of, 118b, 147a, 147b
    royal succession in, 79b
Huns
    archaeology of, 27a
Hunting and fowling, Western European
    attitudes toward animals and, 19b, 20a
    game preserves, 173a–b
    as identity ritual, 538b–539a
    in illuminated manuscripts, 360b
    social rank and, 173a
Huon d'Auvergne, legend of, 16b
Hurd, Richard
    Letters on Chivalry and Romance, 391a
Hurst, John, 26b
Hus, John (Jan)
    death of, 76b
    Jerome of Prague and, 294a–b
    on sacraments, 549a
    on utraquism, 622a
Ḥusayn ibn Jamāl al-Dīn al-Khazrajī, al-
    Sīrat al-awliyā' fī-al-qarn al-sābi'
        al-Hijrī, 255a
Husayn Wā,'iz Kāshifī, 303b
Husband's Message, The, 192a
Hussite Wars, 600b–601a
Hussites, 210a
    decorative art and, 76b
    defeat of, 601a
    rebellion of, 76b, 622b
    on sacraments, 549a
Huzvāresh script, 467b

Hygelac, mythical king, 410a
Hygiene, personal, **283a–286b**
　air and, 284b
Hylas. See Dracontius, Blossius Aemilius
Hylomorphism, 591a, 591b
Hymn. See Cædmon
Hypatia, **286b–287a**
Hypocaust, 50a

I

I dolori mentali di Gesù. See Camilla
　Battista of Varano
I reali di Francia. See Andrea da
　Barberino
Iamblichus, 286b
Ianua (grammar book), 563b
Iberian Peninsula
　battles for control of, 305b
　capitulations and, 86b
　Euskara languagae and, 190b–191a
　Ferdinand III and, 196b
　Hebrew language in, 260a–261a
　Lisbon and, 326a
　Muslims in, 305b–306a
　reconquest of, 196b
　taxation in, 602a–603a
　See also Portugal; Spain
Ibn. *See* Next element of name
Ibrāhīm ibn Yaʿqūb, 51a, 408b
Ice Age
　climate changes of Little Ice Age,
　　172a–b
Iceland
　archaeology of, 29b
　climate changes and, 172b
　laws of, 245a–b
　peacemaking in, 460b
　towns in, 132b
Icelandic literature, 180a, 191a
Iconoclasm, Christian
　Charlemagne and, 457a
Ida of Bouillon, 215a
Idley, Peter
　Instructions to His Son, 185a
Idrīsī, al-, 641b
Idung of Prüfening, **287a–288a**
　Argumentum super quatuor questionibus,
　　287b
　Dialogus duorum monachorum, 287b
Idylls of the King. See Tennyson, Alfred
　Lord
Ifranj, Al-. See Franks
Ifrīqiya
　capture of, 271a–b
Igor Sviatoslavich, prince of Novgorod-
　Seversky, 587b
Il-khânate, 118b–119a
Île-de-France, 218b, 223a–b
　edifices in, 226b
Illustrations of Anglo-Saxon Poesie, 192b
Ilya of Murom, 84a
Imago mundi. See Ailly, Pierre d'

Imam
　tradition and, 253b
Immaculate Conception of the Virgin,
　288a–290b, 289 *(illus.)*
Imrān, Ishāq ibn
　on melancholy, 381a
In honorem sanctae crucis. See Hrabanus
　Maurus
Incarnation
　soul and body and, 588a, 589b, 590b
Incubi, 152b
　See also Demons
Indenture, 567b
Index of Christian Art, Princeton, 383b
India
　Muslim conquest of, 158a
　trade in, 399b
Individual, concept of
　architecture and, 30b
　autobiography and, 45a–b
Indo-European languages, 190a
Indulgences
　in popular religion, 528a–b, 529a–b
　sale of, 294b, 550b
Infancy. *See* Childbirth and infancy
Infancy Gospel of Thomas, 62a
Infant mortality. *See* Childbirth and
　infancy
Ingeborg of Denmark, queen, 368b
Ingelheim palace, 33b
Inheritance
　sexuality and, 575a
Innkeepers
　merchants and, 399b, 401a
Innocent I, pope, 435b
Innocent III, pope, 8b, 196a, 431b,
　442a, 616a
　Accedens, 519b
　Cum Marthae, 548a
　Dandolo and, 148b
　ecclesiastical vs. secular authority and,
　　442a
　foundling hospitals and, 116a
　on heresy, 156b
　Honorius III, pope, and, 273a
　inquisitorial procedure and, 312b–
　　313a, 315a
　Maiores, 546b
　manuscript collections of, 623b
　on marriage, 367b
　De miseria humanae conditionis, 430b
　Peter des Roches and, 469a
　on pilgrim souvenirs, 478b
　plenary indulgences from, 306a
　Poor Clares and, 487a
　Privilege of Poverty, 487a, 487b, 489a
　Qualiter et quando, 313a
　on rape, 519b
　registers of, 623b
　on sacraments, 548a
　Venerabilem, 317b

Innocent IV, pope, 9a, 139b, 423a, 621a
　deposition of emperor Frederick II by,
　　317b
　investigation of Mongols by, 118b
　Manfred of Sicily and, 342b
　St. Stanisław and, 594a
Innocent VIII, pope, 440b
Inquisition, 394b
　Boethius of Dacia and, 71b
　criminal procedure and, 312a–315a,
　　316b
　in Spain, 414a, 414b, 415a
Insolubilia literature, 473b
Institoris, Henry
　Malleus maleficarum, 2a
Institute of Mediaeval Studies. *See*
　Pontifical Institute of Mediaeval
　Studies
Institutes. See Gaius
Institutio oratoria. See Quintilian
Institutiones. See Cassiodorus
Institutiones grammaticae. See Priscian
Instructions to His Son. See Idley, Peter
Insulae (apartment buildings), 33b
Insurance, **290b–291b**
International Boethius Society, 387a
International Congress on Medieval
　Studies, 386b, 389b
Interpretatio Christiana, 450b–452a
Investiture conflict
　satire on, 554b, 556a
Iolanthe of Castile, queen
　Poor Clares and, 488b
Ipswich (England), 27a, 27b–28a
Iran
　conquest by Muslims, 158a
　Sabians of, 543a, 544a
Iraq
　Sabians of, 543a, 544a
Ireland
　archaeology in, 29b
　biblical commentaries and, 56a–b
　conversion of, 142b–143a, 143b
　high-king of *(ard-rí Érenn)*, 80b
　schools in, 559b, 561a, 561b, 562a
Irenaeus, St., 214a, 435a
　Adversus haereses, 214a
　on gnosis, 214a
Irish church
　on sacraments, 549b
Irish literature
　bardic poetry, 12a–b
　Táin bó Cúailgne, 180a
Irnerius, 4a
Iron
　water power and, 346b–347b
Irving, Sir Henry, 393a
Irving, Washington, 394a
Isaac II Angelos, Byzantine emperor,
　149a
Isaac of Stella, 590b
Isaac Palaiologos Asan, prince, 362a
Isabel de la Cavalleria, 110b

Isabel of France, 488b
Isabella of Castile, queen, 95b, 413a–b,
    612a–b, 645b
    Poor Clares and, 488b
Isabella of Gloucester, 278a
Isabelle, queen (wife of Edward II),
    645b–646a
Isabelle II of Jerusalem, queen, 139a
    Hermann of Salza and, 270b
    marriage of, 273a
Isagoge. See Ḥunain ibn Isḥāq al-Ibādī
Iṣfahānī, al-, 254b, 255a
Isḥāq ibn Ḥunain, 371b, 380a
Ishārāt ilāziyārāt, al-. See Ḥawrānī, ibn
    al-
Ishōʿdad of Merv, 55b
Isidore of Seville, St., 56a, 179b, 421a,
    605b
    animals and, 18b
    on astrology, 40a
    cartography and, 91a
    definition of natural law by, 418a
    Etymologies, 46a, 46b, 56a, 118a, 418a,
        457a, 554a, 617a
    life stages and, 430b
    numerology and, 427b
    patronage of, 457a
    peacemaking and, 460a
    on the power of words, 515a
    on race, 516b–517a
    Treaty on Natural History, 457a
    used in schools, 558b
Islam
    age of discernment and, 115b
    astrology in, 41b
    atheism and, 43b
    the body and, 68b
    calligraphy in, 468a
    conquests of, 27a, 158a
    conversion of Sabians to, 543b
    dhimmīs and, 158a–159a
    hagiography of, 253a–256a
    homosexuality in, 575a
    Jewish communities under, 258a
    marriage and, 336b
    Persian language and, 466b
    Petrus Alfonsi on, 471b–472a
    piracy and, 482a
    pollution and taboo and, 485a
    public baths and, 50a–b
    ribāṭ and, 530b–531a
    right to practice, 413a
    Sabians and, 543a–b
    saints of, 253a–255b
    on soul and body, 589a
    in Spain, 415a–b
    suppression of, 414a
Islamic administration, 596b
    espionage activities of, 182a–b
    eunuchs under, 188a–189a
    Hebrew language under, 259b, 260a–
        261a
    slavery under, 188a–189b

Islamic art and architecture
    calligraphy, 468a
Islamic literature
    folklore and, 22a
Ismāʿīlīya, 543b
Isocrates
    Evagoras, 61a
Isrāʾīlī, Isḥāq al-, 381a
Italian literature
    chivalric, 17a
    fantasy in, 16b
    satire in, 554a, 556b
Italy
    admiral in, 6a
    archaeology of, 25b
    astrology in, 41b, 42a
    city-states, 6a
    commercialization and, 131b
    communes in, 132b, 403b
    contract labor in, 567b
    criminal procedure and, 309b
    domestic architecture in, 30b, 32a
    Hebrew language in, 261a
    Henry VI of Germany and, 268a–b
    humanism and, 279b–280a, 281b
    invasion of (1254), 139b
    latifundia in, 306b–307a
    medical writers in, 578a
    merchants of, 399b, 400b–403b
    potential unification of, 642b–643a
    public baths and, 50b
    schools in, 558b, 560a, 560b, 561b,
        562a, 563b, 564a, 564b
    Sicily and, 601a–b
    silk manufacturing in, 353b
    taxation in, 601a–601b, 601a–b
Iter italicum. See Kristeller, Paul Oskar
Itinerarius. See Johannes Witte of Hese
Ius commune (common law), 318b–319a,
    321a, 322a–323a, 419a–b
Ivanhoe. See Scott, Sir Walter
Iviron Monastery, 359b–360a *(sidebar),*
    362a
Iwein. See Hartmann von Aue
Iyasus-Moʾa, 598b
Iznik
    pottery production in, 447a–b

J

Jacob, E. F., 464b
Jacob of Serugh
    Homily on the Fall of Idols, 543a
Jacobite Christians (Monophysites), 202a
Jacobus Columbi, 325a
Jacobus de Porta Ravennate, 82a
Jacobus de Varagine
    Golden Legend, 121a, 151b, 154b,
        156b–157a
Jacopo della Lana, 7a
Jacopone da Todi
    Stabat mater dolorosa, 483b
Jacquerie uprising, 506b

Jacques Coeur, 399b, 403b, 404a
Jacques de Molay, 604b
Jacques de Révigny, **291b–292b**
    Pierre de Belleperche and, 476b–477a
Jacques de Vitry, 486b
    Historia orientalis, 410a
Jaeger, C. Stephen, 562a
Jaén, fall of, 196b
Jagiełło dynasty, 76b–78a
James, earl of Douglas, 465a
James, St. (apostle), 551a
    sepulcher of (Compostela), 29b
James I (the Conqueror) of Aragon and
    Catalonia, king, **292b–293a,** 397b
    Battle of Las Navas de Tolosa and,
        306a
    capitulations and, 86b
    Libre des feyts, 292b–293a
    Pedro III and, 462b
James II of Aragon, king, 423b–424a
    personal hygiene of, 285b–286a
James of Urgell
    as contender for throne of Aragon,
        94b–95a
James of Viterbo, 134a
    Liber de regimine civitatum, 134a
    on matter, 378b
James the Monk, 360b, 361a
James the Stewart, 634a
Japheth ben Ali, 60a
Játiva, capitulation of (1244), 87a
Jawzī, Ibn al-
    Manāqib al-Imām Aḥmad ibn Ḥanbal,
        255a
    Manāqib ʿUmar ibn ʿAbd al-ʿAzīz,
        255a
Jazzār, Ibn al-
    Zād al-musāfir, 381a
Jean de Chelles, 227b
Jean d'Erlée, 457b
Jean de Mailly
    Life of St. Dominic, 62b
Jean de Meun, 208b, 211b
    humanism and, 282a
    Roman de la Rose, 47a, 153b, 208b,
        211b, 338a–b, 421a, 629a, 637b
Jean des Champs, 227b
Jean of Berry, duke, 242b
Jean Petit, 619a
Jean Renart, **293b–294a**
Jeanne d'Évreux, queen, 236a, 242b
Jedermann, 395b
Jefferson, Thomas
    on Anglo-Saxons, 394a
    Declaration of Independence, 419b–
        420a
    natural law and, 420a
Jerome, St., 54b, 605a
    on abortion, 1a
    Against Jovinian, 570a
    classification of sin, 631a
    on Lucifer, 154a
    prologue to Pentateuch, 42a

on sexuality, 570a
De viris illustribus, 62a–b
Jerome of Prague, **294a–b**
Jerusalem
  Hospitallers headquarters in, 276b
  siege of (1099), 215a–b
Jerusalem, Kingdom of, 174a–175a,
  201b, 217a, 603b
  archaeology of, 28b–29a
  Hohenstaufen dynasty and, 139a–140b
  self-government in, 132b
Jesus Christ
  Adam and, 194a
  animal symbolism and, 18a, 20a, 20b
  arrival of, 214a
  blasphemy against, 214a
  body of, 69b–70b
  cosmic dualism and, 213b
  divinity of, 61b
  gift of esoteric revelation, 213b
  Gothic sculpture and, 239a–240a
  heresies and, 43b
  images of, 529a
  images of genitals of, 493a
  imitation of, 484b–485a, 486a, 487a
  incarnation of, 194b
  as a mother, 208b
  Pietà and, 241a–b
  popular religion and, 529a–b
  rejection of humanity, 214b
  representation by poor and, 98b
  soul and body and, 590b
  universal salvation and, 194a
  wounds of, 521 *(illus.)*
Jesus Tempted by Satan in the Desert,
  154a, 154b *(illus.)*
Jeux (dramatic poems), 556a
Jewish communities
  public baths and, 50a–b
Jewish Gnostics, 214b
Jewish law
  divorce, and, 648a–b
  marriage, and, 364a, 648a–b
Jews
  Ashkenazi, 562b
  astrology and, 42b
  biblical commentary by, 60a–b
  chastity and, 569b
  Christian prostitutes and, 576a–b
  Christian servants of, 568a
  in Christian Spain, 413a
  conversion of, 611a–b
  in England, 470b, 517a–518a
  in Islamic world, 158a–159b
  languages of, 259a–b
  legal status of, 433b
  Lisbon and, 327a
  marriage law and, 364a
  massacre of, 626a
  persecution of, 517a–518a, 612b
  Peter des Roches and, 470b
  race and, 515b
  Radhanite, 399b, 401b

right to due process and, 319a
rights of, 133b
ritual and, 539b
schools of, 562b
violence against, 625b
wet nurses and, 113a
on women, 651a–b
Jihad
  ribāṭ and, 530b
Jiménez de Rada, Rodrigo
  Battle of Las Navas de Tolosa and,
  306a
Jizya (poll tax), 158a–159a
Joachim of Fiore, 59a, 639a
  atheism and, 44a
Joan, pope, **294b–295a**
Joan of Arc, 652b
  canonization of, 393b
  cult of, 396a–b
  prosecution of, 652b
  success of, 652b
Joan of England, 643a
Joan of Kent, 335a–b
Joanna I of Anjou, queen of Naples, 3a
Joanna of Constantinople, 536 *(illus.)*
Joasaph (scribe), 359b *(illus.)*
Job Jerusalem MS, 362a
Johannes Andreae
  on *Libri feudorum,* 322a
  on torture, 315a
Johannes Bassianus, **295a–296a**
  De regulis iuris, 295b
Johannes de Lignano, **296a–b**
  De amicitia, 296a
  De bello, 296a
  De fletu ecclesiae, 296b
  De pace, 296a
  Somnium, 296a
  tomb of, 297 *(illus.)*
Johannes Teutonicus, 53b
Johannes Witte of Hese
  Itinerarius, 411a
Johannitius. *See* Ḥunain ibn Isḥāq
  al-Ibādī
John XXI, pope, 423a
John XXII, pope, 440b
  Colonna family and, 128a
  excommunication of Louis IV the
  Bavarian by, 332b–333a
  manuscript collections of, 623b
John XXIII, antipope, **298a–299a**
John II Komnenos, Byzantine emperor,
  174b, 360b
  Prodromic poetry and, 510b
John VI Kantakouzenos, Byzantine
  emperor, 362b
John VIII Palaiologos, Byzantine
  emperor, 362b
John I (the Great) of Portugal, king,
  327a
  Livro de Montaria, 496b
John II of Aragon, king
  Alfonso V and, 10b, 11a

John II of Castile and León, king, 610b
John Chrysostom, St., 100b, 617a
  on pornography, 492b
  on poverty, 501a
John de Hauville
  Architrenius, 180a
John II of France, king
  capture of, 136b
  ransom of, 403b
John of Damascus, St., 55a
  De fide orthodoxa, 288b
John of England, king, 618b
  Honorius III, pope, and, 273a
  Peter des Roches and, 469a
  Ricardus Anglicus and, 531b
John of Garland
  Parisiana Poetria, 554b
John of Hagen, 59b
  monastic reformation and, 83a
John Klimakos
  Heavenly Ladder, 358b, 359b *(illus.),*
  360b
John of La Rochelle, 59a
John of Lodi
  Life of St. Peter Damian, 114a
John (Jan) of Luxembourg, king
  Bohemian crown and, 74a
John of Marignolli
  China missions and, 119a
John of Matha, 616a
John of Mirecourt
  on probability, 509b
John of Monte Corvino, 424a
  in China, 119a
John of Montesono
  Immaculate Conception and, 290a
John of Paris
  De regia potestate et papali, 7b
John of Parma
  Humbert of Romans and, 282b
John of Plano Carpini, 410b
  History of the Mongols, 118b
John of Sacrobosco, **296b–298a**
  Tractatus de algorismo, 298a
  Tractatus de computo, 298a
  Tractatus de sphaera, 296b–297b
John of Salisbury, 387b, 421a
  Entheticus, de dogmate philosophorum,
  617b
  humanism and, 281a
  Nugae, 47b
  Policraticus, 458b, 617b
  on tyrannicide, 618a
  on tyranny, 617b–618a
  on the Welsh, 517a
John of Segovia
  Immaculate Conception and, 290a
John of Varzy, 59a
John Philoponus of Alexandria
  on matter, 378a
John Scottus Eriugena, 57a, 421a, 436b,
  561b
  Carolingian renaissance and, 89a

De divisione naturae, 57a
Periphyseon, 89a, 377b
John the Baptist, St., 610a
  relics of, 75a
  Sabians and, 544a
John the Evangelist, St., 221b
Joinville, Jean de, 178b, 390b
  Histoire de St. Louis, 63a
Jones, David, 395b
Joscelin II, 174b–175a
Joscelin of Courtenay, 174b
José de Arimateia, 495a
Joseph of Arimathea, legend of, 150b
Joseph of Arimathie, 13b, 14a
Joseph of Exeter
  Ylias, 180a
Joseph of Volokolamsk, St., **299a–300a**
  Funeral Oration, 299b
  Lives, 299b
  Monastic Rule, 299a–b
  Paterikon, 299b
  Prosvetitel, 299b
Josephus Scottus, 57a
Jour du Judgement, 263b
Judah ben Samuel he-Hasid, 257b
Judah ben Samuel ibn Balʿam, 60a
Judah Halevi
  Hebrew poetry and, 260b
Judaism
  on abortion, 1a
  adolescent conversion and, 116b
  atheism and, 43b
  consequences of sin in, 194b
  contraception in, 572a
  conversion to Chrisitanity and,
    141a–b, 144a
  demons and, 151a–152b
  Gnosticism in relation to, 214a–b
  hagiography of, 256a–258b
  homosexuality in, 575a
  on marital sex, 572b
  marriage and, 336b
  numeric concepts in, 427b
  original sin in, 435a
  Petrus Alfonsi on, 471a–472a
  Sabians and, 544a
  in schools, 562b
  sexuality and, 570a, 571a, 571b, 572a,
    572b
  on soul and body, 589a
Judaizing heresy, 299b
Judeo-Arabic language, 578a
Judges. *See* Justices
Judicial combat, 310a
Judicial procedure
  criminal procedure and, 310b
  under natural law, 419a
Judith of Bavaria
  patronage by, 457b
Juglaría, **300a–b**
Julian of Norwich, 47b, 650b
Juliana, 192a, 192a (*illus.*)

Juliana of Liège (Cornillon), St., 526a–b,
  650b
Julius II, pope
  Colonna family and, 128b
Julius of Braunschweig-Wolfenbüttel
  manuscript collection of, 355b
Julius Paulus, 1a
Juljul, Ibn
  Ṭabaqāt al-aṭibbāʾ (Generations of the
    physicians and the wise), 381b
Jung, Carl, 214a
Jung Codex, 214a
Jungfrau von Orleans, Die. See Schiller,
  Friedrich von
Jurisprudence
  Pierre de Belleperche on, 476b–477a
  probability in, 508a–509b
  Ricardus Anglicus on, 531a–b
Jury trials
  criminal procedure and, 315b–316a
Just price, **300b–303b**
  determination of, 301a–302a
  theologians and, 302a–303a
Justice
  podestaria and, 134a
Justices
  criminal procedure and, 309b–310b,
    313b–315a
Justin Martyr, 214a
Justinian I, Byzantine emperor, 182a,
  426a
  Athens and, 44b
  codification of Roman Law by, 417b
  Corpus iuris civilis, 433a, 519a–520b
  Digest, 310a, 318a, 426a
  De diversis regulis iuris antiqui, 82a–b
  marriage law and, 367a
  Nika riot and, 66a
  piracy under, 482a
  Procopius on, 492a
Juvenal
  satire of, 554a–b
  used in schools, 562a, 563a
Juvencus, 180a
  used in schools, 562a

K

Kalīla wa-Dimna, **303b–304a**
Kalisz
  Jewish settlers in, 304b
  statutes of, **304a–305a**
Kamil, al-, Ayyubid sultan, 470b
Kāmil al-ziyārāt. See Qūlūya, Ibn
Kanonarion, 327a
Kantorowicz, Ernst, 386b, 534a, 539b
Kara, Joseph, 60b
Karahissar Gospels, 361b
Karaites
  Hebrew language and, 259b
Karajī, Abū Bakr ibn Muḥammad ibn
  al-Ḥusayn al-
    Pascal's triangle and, 372a–b, 375b

Karakī, Ibn al-Quff al-
  manual on surgery and, 381a
Karls rebellion, 506b
Karlstein Castle. *See* Castle Karlštejn
Kāshī, Jamshīd ibn Masʿud al-, 375b
Kemble, John Mitchell
  Saxons of England, The, 392b
Kempe, Margery, 652a
Kent
  Hubert de Burgh and, 278a
Ker, W. P.
  Epic and Romance, 180a, 180b, 181a
Kertzer, David
  Ritual, Politics, and Power, 532a
Khaldūn, Ibn, 52a
Khanbalik (Beijing)
  missionaries in, 119a
Khwārizmī, Muḥammad ibn Mūsā al-,
  371a–b, 372a
  Algebra, 371b
  Arithmetic, 371b
  on fractions, 373a *sidebar*
  *Kitāb al mukhtaṣar fīh-isāb al-jabr
    w'al-muqābala,* 10a
Kidnapping, 202b, 519a–520b
Kiev
  St. Stanisław and, 594b
Kievan Rus, 408b
Kilvington, Richard
  obligationes literature of, 474a
  Sophismata, 406a
Kilwardby, Roger, 585a
Kimḥi, David, 60b
Kimḥi, Joseph, 60b
Kindī, Abū Yūsuf Yaʿqūb ibn Isḥaq al-
  De radiis, 411b
King Arthur. See Carr, J. Comyns
King of Tars, The, 515b
King's College Chapel (England), 233b
Kingship, 11b, 135a
Kingsley, Charles, 392a
Kinship. *See* Family
Kipchaks. *See* Cumans/Kipchaks
Kirkstall (abbey church: England), 228a
Kitāb al-malakī, al-. See ʿAbbās, ʿAlī ibn
  al-
Kitāb al-manāẓir (Optics). *See* Haytham,
  Ḥasan ibn al-
Kitāb al-Mazār. See Shaykh al-Mufīd, al-
*Kitāb al-Taisīr fī l-mudāwāt wa l-tadbīr.
  See* Zuhr, Abū Marwān ʿAbd al-Mālik
  ibn
Kitāb al-ṭibb al-Manṣūrī. See Rāzī, Abū
  Bakr Muḥammad ibn Zakarīyaʾ al-
Kitāb Faṣīḥ al-ʿibrāniyyīn. See Saadiah
  Gaon
Kitāb fī l-jadarīwa l-ḥaṣba. See Rāzī, Abū
  Bakr Muḥammad ibn Zakarīyaʾ al-
*Kitāb ʿuyūn al-anbāʾ fī ṭabaqāt al-aṭibbāʾ.
  See* Uṣaybiʿa, Ibn Abī
Kitāb Kāmil as-sināʿ at at-tibbiya. See
  ʿAbbās, ʿAlī ibn al-
Kitzinger, Ernst, 386b

Klimakos Milan, 358b
Klopstock, Friedrich Gottlieb, 391b
Klosterneuburg
  Gothic art and, 236a
Knight Errant, The (periodical), 395a
Knight of the Tower. *See Book of the*
  Knight of the Tower
Knighthood
  as identity ritual, 538b–539a
Knights of Malta. *See* Hospitallers
Kniprode, Winrich von, 606b
Knowing of Woman's Kind in Childing,
  The, 110b, 113a
Knowles, David
  Prospects of Medieval Studies, The, 383a
Kokkinobaphos. *See* James the Monk
Kokkinos, Philotheos, patriarch, 362b
Komnenoi, 188b
Konrad von Hochstaden, archbishop,
  230b
Konrad von Megenberg. *See* Conrad of
  Megenberg
Koran
  on dhimmīs, 158a
  among Moriscos, 415b
  traditions and, 253b
Koreses, Michael, 361a
Kosmoteira monastary
  public baths in, 50a
Koziol, Geoffrey, 533b, 537a, 538a
Krak des Chevaliers
  Hospitallers and, 276a
Kraków, **305a–b**
  episcopal see in, 434a
  St. Stanisław and, 594a, 594b
Kraków university, 433b, 434b
Krapp, G. P., 192b
Krautheimer, Richard, 596b
Kristeller, Paul Oskar
  Iter italicum, 386a
Kristin Lavransdatter. See Undset, Sigrid
Ku Klux Klan, 394b
Kublai Khan
  missionaries and, 118b–119a
Kudrun, 179b
Kūhī, Abū Ṣahl al-, 373a–b
Kulikovo Field, Battle of (1380), 653b,
  654a
Kulliyāt fī l-ṭibb. See Rushd, Ibn
Kunigunde, St., 266b
Kunnāsh, lesser and greater, 380a
Kutná Hora, decorative art in, 78a

L

La Farge, John, 394b
La Martorana, church of (Palermo), 6a
La Rochelle, Battle of (1372), 6b
La Tour-Landry, Geoffroy de. *See Book of*
  the Knight of the Tower
Labor
  contract, 567b, 568a
  division of servants', 565a

domestic, 567b, 568a
feminization of servant, 566b
poverty and, 503a–b
shortages of, 566a, 566b, 568a
Labourd, 190a
Lactantius, 605b
Ladislas IV of Hungary, king, 147a
Lady of the Lake, The. See Scott, Sir
  Walter
Lagny
  siege of, 198b
Lai, lay
  planctus Mariae and, 483b
Lai de Lanval. See Marie de France
Lai de l'ombre, Le. See Renart, Jean
Laleli mosque, 445a
Lambert of Ardres, curé
  Baudoin genealogy by, 457b–458a
Lancelot, legend of, 39a
Lancia, Conrad, 6b
Land, reclamation of, 15b, 16a
Land of Cockaygne, 555b
Land ownership
  architecture and, 30b
  novels on, 427a
Lanfranc of Bec, St., archbishop of
  Canterbury, 57b, 228a
  biography of, 53b
Lanfranc of Milan
  medical texts of, 475a
Langland, William
  alliterative literature and, 12a, 13b,
    14a, 15a
  Piers Plowman, 12a, 13b, 14a, 15a, 47a
Langton, Stephen
  biblical teaching and, 58b
  Peter des Roches and, 469a
Language
  modistic theory and, 582b
  race and, 515b
  semiotics and, 581b, 582a–583b
Languedoc
  language of love and, 337a–b
Lanier, Sidney
  Boy's King Arthur, The, 394b
Laon, revolt of (1112), 625a
Laon Cathedral, 230a
Las Navas de Tolosa, Battle of (1212),
  196b, 232b–233a, **305a–306b**
Łaski, Jan
  Statutes of the Polish Kingdom, 72b
Last Judgment
  biblical source of, 262a
  See also Hell, concepts of
Lateran (basilica: Rome), 454a
Lateran Councils
  First (1123), 551b
  Second (1139), 474b
  Third (1179), 169a, 314a, 400a
  Fourth (1215), 104a, 109b, 144a,
    166a, 273a, 310b, 313a–b, 315b,
    367b–368a, 420a, 442a, 484a, 487a,

  525b, 527a, 531b, 536a, 548b,
  550a, 614b–615a, 622a, 626a, 631b
Lateran Palace (Rome), 623a–b
Lathcen, 56b
Latifundia, **306b–307a**
Latin language, 190a
  Andrea da Barberino and, 17b
  Carolingian renaissance and, 88b–89a
  schools and, 559b, 560a, 561a, 563a,
    564a
  study of, 384b, 386b, 388a
  translations from Arabic into, 40a
  writings on sexuality in, 577b, 578a,
    579a, 580a
Latin literature
  Aeneid, 179a, 179b, 180a, 181a
  alliterative literature and, 11a, 11b,
    12b, 13a
  Dracontius and, 166b–167a
  epic poetry, 179b–180a
  evaluation of, 438a
  humanism and, 280a
  monasteries and, 146a
  pagan gods in, 452a–b
  poetry, 166b–167a, 555a
  rhetoric and, 162a–b, 163b, 166b
  satire in, 554a, 554b
  schools and, 559a, 560a, 564a
  secular lyrics, **307a–309b**
  vs. vernacular, 17a, 180a
Latini, Brunetto, 8b
Latitude, cartography and, 90b
Laudario of the Compagnia di Sant'Agnese,
  241a
Laude, Oldradus de. *See* Oldradus de
  Ponte
Lauria, Roger de, 6b, 482a
Law
  admiral and, 6a
  animals in, 20b
  on antiquities, 28a
  asega (law-sayer), 205a–206a
  common, 318b–319a, 321a, 322a–
    323a, 419a–b
  communes and, 132b, 134b–135a
  courts of, 461a
  divine, 302a
  Frankish, 44b
  gender and, 209a–b
  German, 1a, 364b–365b, 460a
  of Holy Roman Empire, 427a
  Jewish, 364a, 648a–b
  marriage and, 363a, 367a
  oaths and, 84a–b
  positive, 318a
  praetorian, 318a
  race and, 515b–515b
  ritual in, 535b–538a
  signs and, 585a
  soul and body and, 592b
  women and, 21a, 572b, 643b–645a
  See also Natural law; Novel (Byzantine
    law); Roman law

Law, canon
    after twelfth century, 322a–b
    Bernard of Parma and, 52b–53a
    Bernard of Pavia and, 53a–b
    commentaries on, 7a–b, 364a, 365a–
        368b
    Decretum and, 246a, 336a
    emergence of, 310b–311a
    feudal law and, 324b–325a
    just price and, 301b
    marriage and, 336a
    Ricardus Anglicus on, 531a–b
    teachers of, 295b, 296a
Law, civil
    prerogatives of the prince and, 318a–b
Law, criminal procedure, **309b–320b**
    in England, 315a–316b
    revolution of, during twelfth century,
        310b–315a
    trials and, 316b–319b
Law, feudal, **320b–323b**
    Accursius and, 4a
    after twelfth century, 322a–323a
    basic texts on, 321b–322a, 323a
    communal liberties and, 133a
    droit du seigneur and, 167b
    on ovens, 449b–450a
    See also Droit du seigneur
Law codes
    of Alfonso X, 459a
    anti-poor legislation in, 504a
    of Barcelona, 44b
    peacemaking in, 461a
    physician qualification under, 475b
    on piracy, 481a
    on poverty, 499b–500a
    probability in, 508a–509b
    on rape, 519a–520b
Lawton, David, 14a
Lawyers
    satire of, 555b
Lay of the Last Minstrel, The. See Scott,
    Sir Walter
Layamon
    Brut and, 13b, 14b–15a, 181a
Lazario, 314b
Le Bec Monastery, 376b
Le Franc, Martin, **323b–324b**
    Le champion des dames, 323b–324a
    L'estrif de fortune et virtu, 324a
Le Goff, Jacques, 408a
    on property, 505a
    on time perception, 502b–503b
Lea, Henry C., 394b
Lebecq, Stéphane, 401a
Lechfeld, Battle of, 265b
Lectio divina, 57b
Lectionary Athos, 360a
Legal briefs. *See* consilia
Legenda maior. See Raymond of Capua
Legenda minor. See Caffarelli, Thomas
La Legénde de Saint Julien l'Hospitalier.
    See Flaubert, Gustave

Leibniz, Gottfried Wilhelm, 406b
Leixa-prem, 494b
Leizarraga, Joannes de, 190b
Leland, John, 390a
"Lenda de Santa Iria," 496b
Lenoir, Alexandre
    Musée des Mounments Français and,
        393a
"Lenore." *See* Bürger, Gottfried August
Lent
    Eastern liturgical year and, 329a
    Western liturgical year and, 330a–b
Leo III, Byzantine emperor, 426b
Leo VI, Byzantine emperor, 426b–427a
Leo I (the Great), pope, 605b
Leo IX, pope, 551b
Leo X, pope, 217b–218a, 440b
Leo XIII, pope, 393b, 624a
Leo the Isaurian
    Ecloga, 520a
León, 610b
Leonor of Portugal, queen, 182b
Lepanto, Battle of, 128b
Lepers, pollution and, 485a
Leprosaria, 104a, 105a
Leprosy, 165b–166a, 592b
Lerner, Alan Jay
    Camelot, 396b
Lesbianism, 575b–576a
    as disease, 579b–580a
Lesser Rogation. *See* Rogation
Lestoquoy, Jean, 402a
Letters. See Catherine of Siena, St.
Letters of marque, 481b
Letters on Chivalry and Romance. See
    Hurd, Richard
Levant, 174a, 201b
    Latin rule in, 604b
    trade in, 399b, 402a, 403a
Leversedge, Edmund
    Vision, 152a
Leviathan. *See* Devil
Lévy-Brühl, Lucien
    La Mentalité primitive, 533a–b
Lewis, C. S.
    Arthurian trilogy of, 396a
*Libellus de adventu beati Adriani abbatis
    in Angliam. See* Goscelin of St. Bertin
Liber almansoris. See Rāzī, Abū Bakr
    Muḥammad ibn Zakarīya al-
Liber calculationum. See Swineshead,
    Richard
Liber censuum. See Honorius III, pope
Liber Conformitatum. See Batholomew of
    Pisa
Liber confortatorius. See Goscelin of St.
    Bertin
Liber consolationis et consilii. See
    Albertano da Brescia
Liber contra Manicheos. See Durand of
    Huesca
Liber de Antichristo et eiusdem ministris.
    See William of St. Amour

Liber de fructu carnis et spiritus. See
    Conrad of Hirsau
Liber de gradibus superbiae et humilitatis.
    See Bernard of Clairvaux, St.
Liber de humanis moribus. See Anselm of
    Canterbury
Liber de infantia Salvatoris de Maria,
    288b
Liber de oblatione puerorum. See Hrabanus
    Maurus
Liber de regimine civitatum. See James of
    Viterbo
Liber de sinthomatibus mulierum, 249a
Liber de spiritu et anima. See Alcher of
    Clairvaux
Liber de virtutibus et vitiis. See Alcuin of
    York
Liber extra. See Gregory IX, pope
Liber Historiae Francorum, 203b
Liber monstrorum, 409b–410a
Liber poenitentialis. See Robert of
    Flamborough
Liber Scivia. See Hildegard of Bingen
Liber sextus. See Boniface VIII, pope
Libergier, Hugues
    tomb of, 239a
Liberty and liberties
    in communes, 132b–137a
Libraries
    Ambrosiana, Milan, 358b, 359a
    Bodleian, Oxford, 360b, 362b
    Boston Public, 394b
    British, London, 360b
    at cathedral of York, 89b
    of Charlemagne, 89b
    illuminated manuscripts in, 358a–
        359a, 360b, 362b
    Marciana, Venice, 359a, 360a
    Morgan, New York, 383b
    National Library of Russia, 358b
    Newberry, New York, 383b
    Topkapi Sarāy, Istanbul, 360b
    University of Chicago, 361b
    Vatican, 359a, 360b, 362b
    See also Manuscript collections
Libre des feyts. See James I (the
    Conqueror) of Aragon and Catalonia,
    king
Libri feudorum, 4a, 321b–323a, 324b–
    325b, **324b–326a**
Libri naturales. See Aristotle
Libro de buen amor. See Ruiz, Juan
Licensing
    of corsairs, 481b
    physician, 475b–476a
Liebfraukirche (church: Trier), 230a
Liège
    blast furnace at, 347a
Life cycle, 430a–b
    rites of, 538b–539a
Life of Anselm. See Eadmer of Canterbury
Life of Anthony. See Athanasius of
    Alexandria, St.

Life of Apollonius of Tyana. See
Philostratus
Life of Augustus. See Suetonius
Life of Columba. See Adamnan of Iona
Life of St. Ansgar. See Rimbert
Life of St. Anthony. See Athanasius of
Alexandria, St.
Life of St. Dominic. See Jean de Mailly
Life of St. Eustace and His Companions,
62a
Life of St. Gregory the Decapolite, 482b
"Life of St. Kenelm" *(South English
Legendary),* 11a, 11b
"Life of St. Lubin, The," 240 *(illus.)*
Life of St. Peter Damian. See John of Lodi
Life of St. Thomas of Canterbury. See
Gervase of Canterbury
Life of the Virgin Apparels, 241b *(illus.)*
Life on the Mississippi. See Twain, Mark
Ligugé Monastery, 370a
Limassol
Hospitallers headquarters in, 276b
Limbo, concepts of hell and, 263a
Limbourg, Herman, 242b
Limbourg an der Lahn (cathedral:
Germany), 230a
Limoges
candlesticks made in, 239b
Gothic art in, 235b
Lincoln Cathedral, 228b
Angel Choir in, 230a
innovations in, 228b
Lingard, John, 392b
Linguistics
Hebrew language and, 259a–260b
signification and, 71b
Lipany, Battle of (1434), 622b
Lipsius, Justus, 24a
Lisbon, **326a–327b**
Christian, 326b–327a
under Muslims, 326b
Literacy
alliterative literature and, 12b
of clerics, 89b–90a
diplomatics and, 161a–162a
education and, 115b
gynecological texts, 252b
popular religion and, 529a
pornography and, 491a–b
schools and, 560a, 561b, 563b
storytelling and, 83b–84a
Literature
autobiography in, 46b–47b
chivalric prose, 16b–17b
devotional, 529a
invective (diatribe) in, 554a, 554b
medieval studies and, 383a–384a
paganism and pagan gods in, 452a–
453a
patronage in, 456b–459b
Poor Clares and, 489a–b
the poor represented in, 504b
rape in, 520a–b

soul and body in, 588b
in violence, 626b–627a
See also Satire, *national literatures, and
individual authors and works*
Lithuania
defeat of at Marienburg, 599a
grand dukes of, 93b–94a
Little, Lester
on property, 505a
Liturgical year, Eastern, **327b–330a**
calendars for, 327b–328a
daily and weekly cycles of, 328a
fasting and, 328b–329b
feasting and, 328b–329b
worship and, 328a–b
Liturgical year, Western, **330a–332b**
commemorations of saints, 331a–b
fixed commemorations, 330a–331a
yearly circle, 331b–332b
Liturgy, Catholic
Dies irae and, 159b–160a
study of, 384a, 386a–b
Liudger, St., 589 *(illus.)*
Liuro de Josep Abaramatia, 150b
Liutprand of Cremona, 202b
Lives. See Joseph of Volokolamsk, St.
*Lives of the Roman Pontiffs from St. Peter
to Boniface VIII. See* Colonna,
Giovanni
Livre de chasse, 20a
*Livre des fais et bonnes meurs du sage roy
Charles V. See* Christine de Pizan
Livre des mestiers, 350b
Livre des trois vertus. See Christine de
Pizan
Livre dou voir dit. See Machaut,
Guillaume de
Livro da Virtuosa Bemfeitoria. See Pedro
of Portugal, Infante
Livro de Alveitaria, 496b
Livro de Falcoaria. See Menino, Pero
Livro de Linhagens. See Pedro of Barcelos
Livro e legende dos santos martires, 496b
Livro Velho de Linhagens, 495a
Livy, 145b, 564a
Ljuitizi, 266b
Llywelyn of Wales, prince
Hubert de Burgh and, 278b
Lodi. See Oldradus de Ponte
Loewe, Frederick
Camelot, 396b
Logic
Christian doctrine and, 89a
study of, 89a, 405b–406a
See also Philosophical genres
Lohengrin. See Wagner, Richard
Loire Valley poets, 308b
Lollards, 210b
heretical movement of, 650b–651a
homosexuality and, 574a
popular religion and, 528b–529a
poverty and, 100b
repression of, 70b

sacraments and, 552b
sola scriptura, 201a
on transubstantiation, 615b
Lombard, Peter. *See* Peter Lombard
Lombard League, 8a, 193b, 269a
Lombards
domestic architecture of, 32a
Lombards, kingdom of, 89b
Lombardy
feudal law and, 325a–b
schools in, 560b
Lombe, Thomas, 353b
London
archaeology of, 27a, 29b
city government and, 133b, 135a
revolt in, 136b
schools in, 563b
servants in, 566a
"London Lickpenny," 555b
London Merchant Adventurers
Antwerp and, 24b
Longevity, 431a–b
Longfellow, Henry Wadsworth
Poets and Poetry of Europe, The, 394b
translation of *Divine Comedy,* 385b
Longitude, cartography and, 90b
Loom
industrial revolution and, 351a–352a
Lopes, Fernão, 654b
Crónica de D. Duarte, 495b
Crónica de D. Fernando, 495b
Crónica de D. João I, 495b
Crónica de D. Pedro I, 495b
Crónica de Portugal de 1419, 495b
Lopez, Robert, 401a, 403b
commercial revolution and, 400b
López de Tovar, Gregorio, 419b
Loqmān, 446b
Lord of the Rings, The, 396 *(illus.)*
Lorens d'Orléans (Gallus)
Somme le roi, 632a
Lorraine, 138a
Lothar I, Holy Roman Emperor, 561b
longevity of, 431b
Lothar III, Holy Roman Emperor, 138b
Lothar of Supplinburg, 267a–b
Lotharingia
Henry II of Germany and, 266a
Louanges de la sainte croix. See Hrabanus
Maurus
Louis, St. *See* Louis IX of France, king
Louis I (the Pious), Holy Roman
Emperor, 178b, 365b, 401b, 429b
longevity of, 431b
monasteries and, 21b, 145b–146a
patronage by, 457b
schools and, 561a
Louis II the German, East Frankish king,
431b
Louis I of Bavaria, duke, 268b
Louis II of Bavaria, king
medievalism of, 394 *(illus.)*

Louis VI (the Fat) of France, king
biography of, 63a
queen's influence with, 513a
Louis VII of France, king, 368b
Second Crusade and, 138b–139a
Louis VIII of France, king, 232b–233a
marriage of, 513b
Louis IX of France, king, 135a, 139b,
178b, 219b, 222b, 233a, 423a,
600a–b, 621a, 639b, 646a
biography of, 63a
letters of, 184b
poor relief under, 504a
poverty classification under, 499b
regency of, 513b
routiers under, 541b
Louis IV (the Bavarian) of Germany,
emperor, **332b–333b**, 440a–b
Colonna family and, 128a
excommuniation of, 107a
Louis II of Hungary, 77b
Louis of Anjou, 94b
Louis of Orléans, 619a
Louis of Thuringia, 177b–178a, 270b
Louis the Child, East Frankish king, 138a
Lourdes, 393b
Louvain
Antwerp and, 24b
Love and courtship, 184a, 185a–b,
333b–340b, 334 (illus.), 335a–b
experience of, 333b–366b
literature of, 336b–339b
Low Countries
communes in, 132b
domestic architecture of, 32b, 33a
tapestry production in, 456a–b
wetland changes in, 173a
Low Navarre, 190a
Lowell, James Russell, 385b
Lübeck
archaeology of, 28b, 29a
town council of, 135a
trade in, 133b
Lubin, St., 237a
Lucan
Pharsalia, 179b
used in schools, 561a, 562a, 563a
Lucifer. See Devil
Lucius II, pope, 187a
Lucius III, pope
Cum causam, 519b
heresy and, 314a
on rape, 519b
Lucy, Thomas
Percy and, 464b
Ludmilla, St., 634b
burial site of, 73b
mural of life of, 75a
Ludwig. See Louis
Luis of Valladolid, 610b
Lullingstone, Kent
villa at, 31a (illus.)
Lund, **340b–341b**

Lund Cathedral, 341a (illus.)
Luther, Martin, 407b, 434b, 437a, 550b,
615b
civic ritual and, 533a
on devils, 452a
on the poor, 506b
Lutheranism
Counter-Reformation and, 156a
suppression of, 600b
Lutici, 409a
Luttrell Psalter, 516 (illus.)
water wheels in, 345b
Luxembourg dynasty
decorative art during, 74a–76a
Luxeuil (monastery: Burgundy), 145a
Luzzatto, Gino, 401a
Lydgate, John
translations in Middle English, 150a
Lyndwood, William, 638a
Provinciale, 638a
Lyons
purgatory, concept of, 99b
schools in, 559a
Lyons, Councils of
First (1245), 139b, 317b, 621a
Second (1274), 202a, 400a, 423a,
423b, 546a

M

"Ma vile chanson engagée, facile et
vulgaire." See Peire Duran
Maʿaseh-Buch, 257a
Maastricht
siege of, 198a
Mabillon, Jean, 145b
De re diplomatica, 383b
Mac Domniall, Máelsechlainn, 80b
Macedonian legislation, 427a
Machaut, Guillaume de
Livre dou voir dit, 47a
Machiavelli, Niccolò, 137a
Mackie, William S.
The Exeter Book, 192b
Macpherson, James
Poems of Ossian, 391a
Macrobius
on De re publica, 281a
Madeira Islands, 269b, 655a
Madiis, Emmanuel de (di Maggi), 8a
Madonna and Child. See Duccio
Máelsechnaill II of Ireland, king, 80b
Magdeburg, law code of, 305a
Maghribi mathematicians, 375a–b, 375b
(illus.)
Magic, in popular religion, 521a, 523a–b,
527a–528a
Magna Carta, 390a
Cinque Ports and, 123a
due process and, 316b
Hubert de Burgh and, 278a
Percy and, 464b
Peter des Roches and, 471a

Magnet, 410b–411a
Magyars
Conrad I of Germany and, 138a
defeat at Lechfeld, 401b
Henry I of Germany and, 265b
Mahābhārata, 303a
Maḥberet. See Mehaḥem ibn Sārūq
Mahdia (al-Mahdīya), 641b
Maierù, Alfonso, 584b
Maimonides, Abraham ben Moses, 257a
Maimonides, Moses, 60a
Aphorisms, 381b
Guide for the Perplexed, 60a
Regimen of Health, 381b
Sabians and, 544a
on sexual pathologies, 579b
Mainz
Holy Roman Empire and, 542a
synod of, 429b
Mainz, Council of
on sacraments, 551b
Mainz Cathedral, 230a
Maio of Bari, 6a
death of, 641b–642a
Maiolus, 202b–203a, **341b–342a**
Maiores. See Innocent III, pope
Mairano, Romano, 403a
Maitland, F. W., 638a
Majorca, 292b–293a
Majrītī, Maslama al-
Picatrix (Ghayat al-ḥakīm), 40b
Maller, Paul-Henri
Northern Antiquities, 391a
Malleus maleficarum. See Institoris, Henry
Malory, Sir Thomas, 36b, 392a
Morte Darthur, 38b, 392a (illus.)
Malta
Hospitallers and, 277a
Malthus, Thomas, 135b
Malumbra, Riccardus, 7a
Mamai, emir, 653b
Mamluk dynasty
conquests of, 202a
quassad of, 182a
Maʾmūn, al-, Abbasid caliph, 371b
Man price. See Wergild
Manāqib al-Imām Aḥmad ibn Ḥanbal. See
Jawzī, Ibn al-
Manāqib ʿUmar ibn ʿAbd al-ʿAzīz. See
Jawzī, Ibn al-
Mandaeans, 544a
Mandeville, Sir John
Travels, 20a, 119b
Manegold of Lautenbach, 617b
Manesse-Codex, 596a
Manetti, Giannozzo
biography of Dante by, 64a
Manfred of Sicily, king, 193b, **342a–
343a,** 621a
Alexander IV and, 9a–b
Conradin and, 140a
Mani, 214b
Manichaeaism, 377b

Manichaeans
  sexuality and, 569b
Mannyng, Robert, of Brunne
  almsgiving and, 99b
  Handlyng Synne, 98a
Manor and manorialism, **343a–345a**
Manṣūr, Abū Jaʿfar ʿAbd Allāh ibn
  Muḥammad al-, Abbasid caliph
  Sindhind and, 371a
Manṣūrī hospital, Cairo, 382a
Manuel I Komnenos, Byzantine emperor,
  148b, 427a, 642b
  Prodromic poetry and, 510b
Manufacturing and industry, **345a–355a**
  Florentine merchants and, 3a
  in North Sea-Baltic area, 402b
  shipbuilding and, 348b–349a
  silk industrial revolution, 353b–354a
  textile industrial revolution and, 349a–
    353b
  water power and, 345a–348b
Manuscript books
  Carolingian renaissance and, 89b
  copying of, 439a
  devil in, 152b *(illus.),* 155a *(illus.),* 156
    (illus.), 157a *(illus.)*
  Dies irae and, 158b
  "Hand D" and, 168b
  interpretation of, 38a
  monastaries and, 145a–b
  sexuality in, 571b, 578 *(illus.)*
Manuscript collections, **355a–357b**
Manuscript illumination, 150a, 457a
  sexuality and, 571b, 578 *(illus.)*
Manuscript illumination, Byzantine,
  357b–363a
  styles of, 359b–360a, 361b
Manuscripts of Chrétien de Troyes, The,
  37b
Manutius, Aldus
  Catullus edition by, 491b
Map, Walter (Mapes)
  De nugis curialium, 555a
  satire of, 555a
Mappae mundi, 91b–92a
Maps. *See* Cartography
Mar ʿAzaziel (church: Kefr Zeh), 597b
Mar Ibrāhīm (church: Midyat), 597b
Mar Yakub (church: Salah), 597b
Marbod of Rennes, 308b
Marburg, hospice of, 178a–b
Marca Britanniae, margrave of, 630b
Marcabru
  pornography by, 492a
  satire and, 556a–b
Marcel, Étienne, 136b, 625a
Marciana Library, Venice, 359a, 360a
Marcus, Ivan, 539b
Marcus Graecus, 198a
Margaret, St., 111b *(illus.)*
Margaret I of Denmark, queen, 341a
Margaret of Austria
  Henry VII of Germany and, 268b

Margaret of Cleves, 163b
Margaret of Navarre
  as regent, 641b, 642a
Margaret of Scotland, St., 278a
  biography of, 63a
Margaret of York
  Poor Clares and, 488b
Margaritus of Brindisi, 6a
Marginalia
  in books of hours, 243a
Marie de France, 339a, 627b
  on infidelity, 575a–b
  Lai de Lanval, 17a–b
  language of love and, 338a
  writings of, 652a
Marienklagen. See Planctus Mariae
Maritain, Jacques, 395b
Markets, 398b–399a
  agricultural, 171a
  commercialization and, 131b
  just price and, 302b
Marmoutier, Abbey of, 370a
Marques, Oliveira, 602b–603a
Marriage, 647b–649b
  abortion and, 1a
  age of consent, 648b
  annulment of, 552b
  betrothal contract and, 363b, 364b
  of clergy, 484b
  consent in, 571b
  considerations for, 648b
  contracts of, 336a–b
  conversion and, 141b–142a, 143a
  courtship and, 335a–b
  cross-cultural, 649b
  divorce and, 648a
  Jewish law and, 364a, 648a–b
  legal basis of, 648a
  love and, 648b–649a
  multiple, 649a
  papal reforms on, 513a–b
  peacemaking through, 460b, 514a
  procreation in, 572a
  prostitution and, 576a
  queens and, 512b
  rape and, 519a–520b
  as rite of passage, 538b
  during Roman Empire, 363b–364b
  as sacrament, 545a, 552b–553a
  sexuality in, 571a–572b
  strategy of, 647b–648a
Marriage, Christian, 141a, 143b, **363a–
  370a**
  alimony and, 368a
  annulments and, 368b
  banns of, 367b
  child support and, 368a, 369b
  church teaching on, 141a, 143b, 364a,
    365a–368b
  community property and, 369a
  conditions for, 363b, 364b, 365b,
    366b, 367a
  four-degree rule and, 368a

  remarriage and, 364a–b, 365a–b, 366a
  Roman Rota and, 368a–b
  as sacrament, 366b
  seven-degree rule and, 365a
Marriage Act of 1753, 367b
Marriage of Philology and Mercury. See
  Martianus Capella
Marseilles, 202b
Marshal, Richard
  Peter des Roches and, 470b, 471a
Marshal, William. *See* William Marshal
Marsilius of Inghen, 379a
Marsilius of Padua, 387b
  Defensor pacis, 333a, 619a
Martelli, Roberto
  as Medici agent, 455b
Martianus Capella, 558b
  De nuptiis Philologiae et Mercurii,
    (Marriage of Philology and
    Mercury), 146a, 281a
  used in schools, 562a
Martim Codax
  poetry of, 494a
Martin IV, pope, 621b
  Pedro III and, 463a
Martin V, pope, 187b, 610b, 623b
  Great Schism and, 128a–b
Martin I of Aragon, king of Sicily, 10b
  death of, 94b
Martin of Braga, St.
  Formula vitae honestae, 630b
Martin of Dacia, 582b
Martin of Tours, St., 99 *(illus.),* **370a–
  371a**
  animals and, 20a
  charity of, 99a
  miracles of, 370b
  Radegunda compared with, 518b
Martines, Lauro, 538b
Martini, Raymond, 59b
Martinus Gosia, 82a
Martyrdom of Polycarp, 62a
Martyrs
  biographies of, 61b–62a
  in Bohemia, 76b
  Jewish, 256a–b, 257b–258a
  Western liturgical year and, 330b
Marvels, collections of, 410b
Marx, Karl, 392b
Mary. *See* Virgin Mary
Masada, martyrs of, 257b
Masā ʾil fī l-ṭibb, al-, 380a–b
Māsawayh, Yūḥannā ibn
  *Aphorisms (Kitāb al-Nawādir
    al-ṭibbīya),* 380a
Masci, Girolamo. *See* Nicholas IV, pope
Masoretes of Tiberias, 259a
Mass
  altars and, 239b–240a
  cathedrals and, 240b–241a
  Gothic art and, 240a–b
  liturgy of, 158b–159a
Massa compoti. See Alexander de Villa Dei

Masters' Guild, University of Paris, 639a
Masturbation, 492b–493a
Mater dolorosa, 529b
Mathematics
   physics and, 406a–b
   Sabians and, 543b
Mathematics, Islamic, **371a–376a,** 543a,
   543b
   Indian influences on, 371a, 372 *(illus.)*
   number theory and, 372a–373a
   origins of, 371a
   parabolas and, 371b, 374 *(illus.)*
   pi, 373b, 375b
   trigonometry and, 373b
   See also Algebra
Mathgamain of Munster, king
   Dál Cais and, 80a–b
Mathieu d'Arras
   St. Vitus's Cathedral and, 74b
Mathilda of Scotland, 376b
Matilda (Maud), Empress, **376a–377a,**
   645a
   influence of, 645b
   King Stephen and, 595a–b
   longevity of, 432a
Matilda of Boulogne, 513a
Matilda of Tuscany, countess, 267b
Matins, 328a
Matraqi, Nasuh, 446a
Matsys, Quinten, 24a
Matter, **377a–379b**
Matthew of Aquasparta, 59a, 159b
Matthew Paris, 638a–b
Matthias I Corvinus of Hungary, king
   literary patronage by, 459a
   manuscript collection of, 356a
Mattias Rajsek
   Powder Tower of, 77a
Maurdramnus, abbot, 145a
Maurice, bishop, 217a
Maurice, Byzantine emperor
   dethronement of, 66a
Mauro, Fra, 92b
   mappa mundi, 119b
Mausoleum
   ribāṭ as, 531a
Mavillon, Jean, 389b
Max-Planck Institutes, 383a
Maximilla (Montanist), 605a
Mayeul. *See* Maiolus
McCormick, Michael, 401a
McGovern, Thomas, 29a
Mecca, maps of, 373b
Mechthild von Magdeburg, 47b
   mystic love poetry and, 339a
Mediaeval Studies (journal), 384a
Medici, Cosimo de'
   Acciaiuoli and, 3a–b
   manuscript collection of, 355b–356a
Medici, Lorenzo de'
   Savonarola and, 557b
Medici, Piero de'
   patronage by, 455b

Savonarola and, 557b
Medici, Salvestro de'
   Ciompi revolt and, 124b, 125b
Medici company, 400b
   banking and, 403a
Medici family
   Acciaiuoli and, 3a–b
   vs. communes, 137a
Medicine, Greek
   abortion and, 1b
   sexuality and, 577b, 578a
Medicine, Indian, 380a
Medicine, Islamic, **379b–382b**
   abortion and, 1b
   on homosexuality, 580a
   hospitals and, 381a, 382a
   Koran and, 382a
   mental illness and, 382a
   sexuality and, 577b, 578a, 580a
Medicine, Jewish
   sexuality and, 577b, 578a, 580a
Medicine, Western European
   abortion and, 1b, 2a
   Arab authors and, 165a–b
   astrology and, 40b, 42b
   bathing and, 51a
   gunshot wounds, 200a
   homosexuality and, 574a
   humoral, 1b, 42b, 164b, 377b
   manuscripts of, 361 *(illus.)*
   Methodist tradition in, 578b
   patronage of, 459a
   physicians and, 474a–476b
   pilgrim souvenirs and, 478b–479a
   popular religion on, 527 *(illus.)*
   pornographic illustrations in, 493a
   regimen in, 578b
   saints and relics in, 523b–525b
   sexuality and, 571a, 573a, 577a–580b,
     577b
   signs in, 584a–b
   soul and body and, 592a, 592b
   See also Disease; Physicians
Medieval Academy of America, 384a–b,
   386b–387a, 395a
Medieval studies, **383a–389a**
   Annaliste approach to, 383b
   art history and, 383a, 384a, 386a–b,
     388b
   in Europe, 383a, 384a–b, 388a
   German émigré scholars and, 386a–b
   interdisciplinary approach to, 383b–
     384b, 386a, 387a, 389b
   in North America, 383a–b, 384b–388b
   postmodernism and, 387b–388a
   textuality and, 384a, 386a, 387b, 393b
Médiévales (journal), 384a
Medievalism, **389a–397b**
   in 20th century, 395a–397a
   in America, 394a–395a
   definition of, 389a–b
   in France, 393a–b
   in Germany, 393a–b

in Scandinavia, 393b
   in Victorian England, 392a–393a
Medievistik (journal), 384a
Meditations seu Contemplationes
   Devotissimae. See Torquemada, Juan de
Mediterranean region, 170a–b, 171b,
   172a–b, 173a–b
   archaeology in, 25b
   culture of, 141a–b
   revival of slavery in, 566b–567b
   trade in, 399a–404a
Mediterranean Sea
   navigational charts of, 91b
   piracy in, 481a, 482a
Megillat aḥima ʿats. See Aḥima ʿats ben
   Paltiel
Mehaḥem ibn Sārūq
   Maḥberet, 260a
Mehmed II, Ottoman sultan
   architecture under, 443a
   patronage by, 445b–446b
   portrait of, 446 *(illus.)*
Meinwerk of Paderborn, bishop, 146b
Meissen, fortress at, 265b
Mela, Pomponius, 92b
   writings on Asia by, 118a
Melfi
   Constitutions of, 322b
   Council of, 422b
Melisende of Jerusalem, 513b
Mellitus, monk, 143b
Melun, siege of
   Bertrand du Guesclin and, 248a
Mémoire sur L'ancienne chevalerie. See
   Sainte-Palaye, Jean-Baptiste de La
   Curne de
Memoirs. See Guibert of Nogent
Ménagier de Paris, 8b, 185b
Menaion, 328a
Menas, St., 120b
   pilgrim souvenirs from shrine of, 477b
Mendicant orders
   biblical studies and, 59a
   restricted number of, 247b
Mengart de Pomiès, 212a
Mengho (criminal), 314b
Menino, Pero
   Livro de Falcoaria, 496b
Menologion London, 358a, 360b
   See also Oxford Menologion
Menstruation
   abortion and, 1b
   gynecology and, 249a
   as purgative process, 249a–251a
   sexuality and, 579a
Mentalité primitive, La. See Lévy-Brühl,
   Lucien
Mercator, Gerardus, 24a
Mercedarians, **397b–398b**
   role of, 616a
Merchants, **398b–405a**
   Amsterdam and, 16a
   Antwerp and, 24b

Arab, 399b
Arras and, 135b
branch offices and, 403a
corsairing by, 481b
disdain for, 398b, 399a
documents of, 400b–401a, 403b
factors and, 403a
Florentine, 2b–3b, 133b
Ghent and, 133b, 135b
innkeepers and, 399b, 401a
insurance and, 290b–291a
long-distance trade and, 399a–400a,
  401a–403b
missionaries and, 22a
protectionism and, 399b
royal support for, 401b, 403a–b, 404a
training of, 400a–401a
See also Trade
Mercy
categories of, 629a
seven works of, 99b
Mérimée, Prosper, 393a
Merlin oder Das Wüste Land. See Dorst,
  Tankred
Merovich, Merovingian ruler, 203b
Merovingians, 203a
archaeology of, 26b
dynasty of, 218b, 610a
marriage laws of, 365a
merchant houses in, 401a–b
queens, 512a
royal authority under, 88a
schools and, 559a
in Tournai, 613a
Merseburg agreement (1135), 80a
Merton Calculators, **405a–407a,** 421a
Mesopotamia, 174a
Metallurgy, 348b
water wheels and, 347a
Metamorphoses. See Ovid
Metaphor
in *Song of Igor's Campaign,* 588a
of soul and body, 588b
Metaphysics. See Aristotle
Metempsychosis, 588b
Michael, St., 213a
Michael (archangel), 154a, 598b
Michael Choniates, 44b
Michael IV, Byzantine emperor, 360b
Michael VII, Byzantine emperor, 360b
Michael VIII Palaiologos, Byzantine
  emperor, 247b
Michaud, Joseph-François, 393a
Michele di Lando, 125a, 136b
Michelet, Jules, 393a
Micrologus (journal), 384a
Middle Ages, **407a–408b**
cultural diversity and innovation in,
  438a
periodization of, 408a
romantic notion of, 407b
Middle English literature, 11b, 12b, 13a,
  14a, 150a, 555b, 556b

Middle High German literature, satire in,
  556b
Midrashic period, 152b
Midwives
abortion and, 2a
childbirth and, 108b–111a
function of, 647a
gynecological information and, 252b
Mies, Jakob von
on utraquism, 622a
Mieszko I of Poland, king, 5a, 305a,
  408b–409b
Bohemian alliance of, 409a
Dagome Iudex, 78b, 409a
death of, 78b
religious conversion of, 409a
St. Stanisław and, 594a
Mieszko II of Poland, king, 5a
Migne, Jacques-Paul, 393b
Migration period
archaeology of, 25b, 26a, 26b–27a
Miḥrabs (niches), 443a
Milan, 193b
duke of, 10b
feudal law and, 324b
power of, 137a
statutes of, 322b
Visconti family in, 134b
Milan Cathedral, 456a
Milan Gregory, 359a
Military. *See* Warfare
Millais, John Everett, 392a
Miller's Tale. See Chaucer, Geoffrey
Mills, 345a–b, 346a–b
Milman, Henry
History of Latin Christianity, 392b
Milner, John, 392b
Milton, John
influences on, 150a
Paradise Lost, 181b
Milvian Bridge, Battle of (312), 142a
Mining
copper, 348a–b
water power and, 347b–348b
Minnesong, 337b
Minstrels
alliterative literature and, 12b
Minstrelsy of the Scottish Border. See Scott,
  Sir Walter
Mints and money
commercialization and, 130b, 131a,
  132a
Venetian currency, 148b
Minuccio da Siena
Gothic art and, 236a
Miracle de Théophile. See Cohen, Gustave
Miracles
of Martin of Tours, St., 370b
in popular religion, 521a
of St. Clare, 158b
Miro I, Suevic king, 630b
Mirrors of princes, Portuguese, 496b–
  497a

Misch, Georg, 45b
Misericordia (confraternity), 105a
Misogyny
Eve and, 195b–196a
repression of the body and, 68b
sexuality and, 570a, 575a
soul and body and, 593a
Missal of Sbinko of Hasenburg, 75b
  (illus.), 76b
Missions and missionaries, 169a
in Americas, 144a–b
in Antwerp, 24a
atheism and, 43b
Celtic pilgrimage and, 479b–480a
in China, 119a–b
in Denmark and Sweden, 21b–22a
Irish, 549b, 560a
to pagan Europe, 141b, 142a–144b
in Scandinavia, 146a
schools and, 560b
strategies of, 522a–523b
See also Christianization
Mists of Avalon, The. See Bradley, Marion
  Zimmer
Mithraism, astrology and, 41b
Mitteis, Heinrich, 600a
Mladá Maria
founding of convent by, 73b
Mobility
geographic, 499b, 500b, 502a
social, 541b
Modern Language Association, 384b
Modistic theory, 582b
Mohács, Battle of (1526), 77b
Mohammed. *See* Muḥammad
Mollat, Michel, 503a–b, 504a
Monarchia. See Dante Alighieri
Monarchy. *See* Kingship
Monasteries, 149b, 359b, 360b, 361a,
  362a, 362b, 370a, 376b
adult conversions to, 429a
biblical studies in, 57b
in Bohemia, 73b
children in, 428b–430a
dissolution of, 389b
in France, 145a–146b
homosexuality and, 574a, 574b–575a
manuscripts of, 358a–b, 359b–362b,
  361a
oblates in, 116a
reforms of, 83a, 266b, 561b, 562a,
  562b
restoration of, 341b
schools in, 558b–559a, 559b, 560b,
  561a, 562a, 562b, 564a
Monastic Rule. See Joseph of
  Volokolamsk, St.
Monasticism
adolescent conversion to, 116b
Benedictine Revival, 168a
charity and, 103b, 504a
Christian, 23a
Dominican order and, 147b

Eastern Orthodox, 24a
Gothic art and, 242b
humanism and, 281a
Idung of Prüfening on, 287a–288a
influences on, 23a
in Ireland, 56a–b
lay orders and, 529a
medical care and, 474b–475a
in peacemaking, 461a
pilgrim souvenirs in, 477b
Poor Clares, 485b–490b
pornography about, 491b
poverty and, 505a–b
proliferation of, 487a
Radegunda in, 518b
ribāṭ and, 530b–531a
royal support for, 145b–146b
satire of, 555b, 556a
scriptoriums and, 145a–146a
soul and body and, 590a
wandering, 479b–480a
Money changing
Florentine merchants and, 3a
Mongol empire
crusades against, 9a
European contact with, 118a–b
invasion of Hungary (1240–1241),
147a, 147b
trade with, 400a
Monks, satire of, 555b, 556a
Monodiae (Vita sua; Memoirs). See
Guibert of Nogent
Monophysitism, 202a
Monopsychism, 591a–b
Monsters and the monstrous, **409b–412b**
Aristotle's views of, 411a, 412a
astrological causes of, 411b
climatic explanations for, 411b–412a
as entertainment, 409b–412b
human responses to, 411a–412b
in nature, 410b–412b
in the *Secrets of Women,* 411b
variety of effects of, 409b
See also Demons
Monstrance, Gothic art and, 241a
Mont Saint-Michel and Chartres. See
Adams, Henry
Montague, William, 335a
Montalembert, Charles de, 393a
Montanist Christians, 605a–b
Montanus, Priscilla, 605a
Montaperti, Battle of (1260), 9a, 342b
Monte (Florentine civic debt), 125a
Monte Barro (Italy), 32a
Monte delle doti, 368b–369a
Montesquieu, Charles-Louis de
L'esprit des lois (The spirit of laws),
390b
Montiel, Battle of, 248b
Montmartre
as pagan holy place, 451a
Montpellier
town council of, 135a

Monty Python and the Holy Grail, 396b
Monumenta Germaniae Historica, 383a,
393a
Moralia in Job. See Gregory I (the Great),
pope
More, Sir Thomas
on enclosure, 502a
on the poor, 506b
Utopia, 502a
Moreau, Gustave, 393b
Morgan Library, 383b
Moriaen, 39a
Morisco literature, 415b
Moriscos, **413a–416b**
crypto-Islam of, 414a
expulsion from Spain of, 416a
Granada revolt of, 414b
Muslim identity of, 415a–b
religion and culture of, 415a–b
Morocco, Muslims in, 416a
Morris, William
Arts and Crafts movement and, 392b
Mort Artu, 151a
See also Arthurian Romances
Mortality. *See* Death and burial
Morte Arthure (Middle English alliterative
poem), 12a, 14a, 15a, 179b, 393a
See also Arthurian Romances
Morte Darthur, Le. See Malory, Sir
Thomas
Mortimer, Edmund, 465a
Mortimer, Roger, 646a
Mosaics
in domestic architecture, 31a
San Apollinare Nuovo, 153a
Moscow, Napoleon's invasion of, 587b
Moses
covenant with, 435a
Hebrew poetry and, 260b
Mosque of Three Galleries (Edirne), 443a
Mosques
Ottoman, 442b–445b, 444 *(illus.),* 445
(illus.)
Mother of God. *See* Virgin Mary
Mothers, 649a
in autobiography, 46b
See also Women
Motley, John Lothrop, 394a
Mourning. *See* Death and burial
Mozarabs
Lisbon and, 326b
Muchembled, Robert, 533b
Mudejars, 413a–b
Muḥammad, 188b, 214b
on dhimmīs, 158a
Islamic hagiography and, 253b, 254b
Muḥammad al-Nāṣir, 305b–306b
Muḥammad ibn Idrīs al-Shāfiʿī. *See*
Shāfiʿī, Muḥammad ibn Idrīs al-
Muhassin, Abū ʿAli al-, 543a
Mühldorf, Battle of (1322), 332b
Mühlen (monastery), 604a
Muir, Bernard J., 192b, 193a

Muʿizz, al-, Fatimid caliph, 271a
Mum and the Sothsegger, 15a
Munʿim, Ibn, 375a
Münster Cathedral, 230a
Muqaddasī, al-
*Aḥsān al-Taqā sīm fī ma ʿrifat
al-aqālīm,* 467a
Muqaffaʿ, ʿAbd Allāh ibn al-, 303a, 467a
Mural painting
in Bohemia, 73b, 75a
Muratori, Ludovico, 389b
Murder in the Cathedral. See Eliot, T. S.
Murdrum fine, 515b
Murethach, 57a
Murray, Margaret, 451a
Murshid al-zuwwār ilā al-abrār. See
ʿUthmān, Ibn
Murshid al-zuwwār ilā qubūr al-abrār. See
ʿUthmān, Ibn
Muschg, Adolf
Der rote Ritter (The red knight), 396b
Muscio
Gynaecia, 109a
Muscovy
expansion of power by, 94a
Musée des Mounuments Français, 393a
Music
medieval revival of, 396a
patronage and, 458a
planctus Mariae, 483a–b
in Poland, 72a–b
of war, 627a
Musical instruments, archaeology of, 28b
Musicus, **416b–417a**
definition of, 416a–417a
Muslims, 201b
as brigands, 202b
capitulations and, 86b–87b
chastity and, 569b
Christian prostitutes and, 576a
conquest of Persia, 596b
conversion of, 144a
crusaders and, 138b–139a, 139a,
148a–149a, 361b, 402a
expulsion from Spain of, 413a, 413b,
416a
forced conversion of, 413a–415a
in Iberia, 196a–b, 305b–306a, 413a–
416b
legal status of, 433b
legal system of, 158a
in North Africa, 414a, 415b
ransom from, 397b–398a
revolt of, 413a
rights of, 133b
sexuality and, 573a
Sicily and, 641b
slavery and, 573a
in Valencia, 293a
wet nurses and, 113a
See also Islam
Mustaʾmins (lands of Islam), 158a
Mustanṣir, al-, Abbasid caliph, 271a

Muʿtaḍid al-, Abbasid caliph, 372a
Mutawakkil al-, Abbasid caliph, 380a
*Muwallah*s (holy men and women), 254a
Mystère d'Adam, 195a–b
Mystery religions, 141b
Mysticism
  autobiography and, 47b
  devotional practices by, 69a–b
  medievalism and, 393a, 395a
  Portuguese, 496a–b
  Sabians and, 543a, 543b
  of St. Catherine of Siena, 96a
  soul and body and, 592b–593a

N

Nadīm, Ibn al-, 543a
Nafīs, Ibn al-
  on anatomy, 381a, 382a
Nag Hammadi
  on Gnosticism, 214a
Naḥmanides, Moses
  Zohar, 60a
Najd, 271b
Name of the Rose, The. See Eco, Umberto
Naples
  Acciaiuoli in, 3a
  Alfonso V and, 10b
  merchants in, 2b, 402a
  self-government within, 132b
Narsai, 55b
Natio, race and, 517a–518a
Nationalism
  archaeology and, 25b
  medievalism and, 393a–b
  peacemaking and, 460a
Natural History. See Pliny the Elder
Natural law, **417b–420a**
  Declaration of Independence and, 420a
  eternal truths, 419b
  human behavior and, 417b
  legal systems and, 419b
  ordo iudicarius and, 318a–b
  sacraments and, 545a, 545b
  theology and, 418b–419b
  western jurisprudence and, 417b
Nature, **420a–422a**
  diversity in, 421b
  Eurocentric view of, 421a
  explanations found in, 411a
  humanism and, 281a
  philosophical concepts of, 420a, 420b
  theology and, 18b
Nature of Body and Soul, The. See
  William of St. Thierry
"Nature of Gothic, The." *See* Ruskin,
  John
Naumburg Cathedral, choir screen in,
  238b–239a
Navarre, kingdom of, 190a, 641b, 642a
Navegação de São Brandão, 496a–b
Navies, Western
  admiral in, 6a–7a

Navigation, charts for, 91b–92a
Nazarenes, 393a
Neck verse, 86a
Neckham, Alexander, 18b
Nees, Lawrence
  Early Medieval Art, 439a *(illus.)*
Negev Desert
  nomadism and, 51b–52a
Neoplatonism, 211a, 377a–378a, 421a
  astrology and, 42b
  Hypatia and, 286b
  Sabians and, 543b
  on soul and body, 590a
Nepo, Cornelius
  De viris illustribus, 61a
Népomucène Lemercier, Louise-Jean
  Frédégonde et Brunehaut, 203b
Nepotism, satire of, 555b
Nero. See Suetonius
Nersēs Lambronacʿi, 55a
Nersēs Šnorhali, 55a
Netherlands. *See* Low Countries
Neuschwanstein Castle, 394 *(illus.)*
Neville family
  Percy feud with, 465b
New Christians, 144a
  conversion of, 611a–b
  persecution of, 611a–b
New Testament. *See* Bible
New Testament Codex Ebnerianus, 360b
New York Pro Musica, 396a
Newberry Library, 383b
Newcastle upon Tyne, 130b
Newfoundland, 191a
Newman, John Cardinal
  Tracts for the Times, 392b
News from Nowhere. See Ruskin, John
Newspapers, 24a
Niall of the Nine Hostages (Noígiallach),
  80b
Nibelungenlied, 179a, 180b
Nicaea
  siege of, 215a
Nicaea, Empire of
  Alexander IV and, 9a
Nicaea, First Council of (325), 142a,
  619b
Nicasius, St., 218a
Niccolò III d'Este of Ferrara, duke
  manuscript collection of, 355b
Nicholas II, pope, **422a–b**
  Exiit qui seminat, 423a
  reforms of, 422a–b
  on sacraments, 551b, 552a
Nicholas III, pope, **422b–423b,** 439b,
  440a
  Colonna family and, 127b
  office of senator and, 440a
Nicholas IV, pope, **423b–424a**
  Colonna family and, 423b
  delegation of Franciscans to China
    and, 119a
  Franciscan Order and, 423b

  Jacques de Révigny and, 291b
Nicholas V, pope, 623a, 623b
  election of, 333a
  Martin Le Franc and, 324a
  private library of, 355b
Nicholas of Cusa, 83a
  atheism and, 44a
  De docta ignorantia (On learned
    ignorance), 379a
  hospice of, 432a
Nicholas of Gorran, 58b
Nicholas of Lyra, 59b
  Postilla moralis, 59b
  Postillae perpetuae super totam Bibliam,
    59b
Nicholas of Verdun
  Gothic art and, 236a
Nichols, Stephen, 439a
  "Introduction: Philology in a
    Manuscript Culture," 438b *(sidebar)*
Nichomachean Ethics. See Aristotle
Nicodemus
  Apocryphal Gospel of, 154b, 263a
Nicole Bozon
  Les Contes moralisés, 100a
Nidaros, 28b
Nigel (Whiteacre, Wireker) of
  Longchamp/Canterbury
  Speculum stultorum, 180a, 555b–556a
Nika Revolt (532), 66a
Nikephoros III Botaneiates, Byzantine
  emperor, 360b
Niketas Choniates, 482b
Niketas of Herakleia, 55a
Nîmes
  town council of, 135a
Nissim ben Jacob ben Nissim ibn Shahin
  Ḥibbur yafeh min ha-yeshuʿa, 256b,
    257a
Nivardus of Ghent, 555b
Noah, 220b
Nobility and nobles
  animals and, 20a
  feuds among, 460a
  patronage by, 455a–459b
  Portuguese, 495a–b
  poverty among, 499a
  women, 21a
Nodier, Charles, 393a
Nogaret, Guillaume de, 128a
Nolasc, Pere, 397b
Nomadism, 141b, 147a, 170b
  Bedouin, 51b–52a
Nominalism
  semiotics and, 582a, 583b
  soul and body and, 592a
Nonpossessors, 299b
Nordens Mytologi. See Grundtvig, N. S. F.
Normandy, duchy of
  conquest of England, 219b, 228a
  as English holding, 376b
  Matilda and, 595b

Normans, 201b
  culture of, 390a, 402a
  in Italy, 422b
  in Sicily, 402a
Norns, 451a
Norse mythology, 393b, 395b
North Africa, 196b
  Alhomads in, 196b
  schools in, 558b, 559b, 560b
  trade with, 399b, 402a, 403a
North Atlantic Biocultural Organization
  (NABO), 29b
North Sea, piracy in, 481a
North Sea-Baltic Zone
  merchant houses within, 401b, 402b
  shipping in, 401a
  trade in, 399a–404a
Northern Antiquities. See Maller, Paul-
  Henri
Northumbria
  invasion of, 634a
  renaissance in, 89b
  schools in, 561a
Norton, Charles Eliot, 385b
  studies on Dante, 394b–395a
Norwich (cathedral: England), 228a
Notabilia decretorum. See Ricardus
  Anglicus
Notaries, 8a, 161b, 362a, **424a–426a**
  contracts, 425a
  marriage separation and, 369a
  merchants and, 399b
  as public scribes, 424b
  as register of public deeds, 424b
  registers, 425a
  Rolandinus de Passageris and, 540a–
    541a
  signs and, 585a
Notre-Dame at Lausanne (cathedral),
  237b
Notre-Dame de Paris. See Hugo, Victor
Notre Dame of Paris (cathedral: France),
  218b, 225a–226a
  emulation of, 227a
  personification of virtue, 631a
  transept of, 227b
Notre Dame of Senlis (cathedral: France),
  225a
Notre Dame of Soissons (cathedral:
  France), 219b, 222b, 226b
Novalis, 393a
Novel (Byzantine law), **426a–427b**
  in Constantinople, 427a
  on land ownership, 427a
  reasons for, 426a
  See also Macedonian legislation
Novgorod
  archaeology in, 28b
Noyon Cathedral (France), 225b, 226a
Nugae. See John of Salisbury
Number theory, 372a–373a
Numentanum, conquest of, 422b

Numerology, **427b–428b**
  in literature, 428a
  in the quadrivium, 427b
  in Western thought, 427b
Numismatics
  medieval studies and, 383b, 386a,
    390a
  minting of gold and, 401a
Nuns
  amenorrhea and, 251a
  celibacy of, 569b
  literacy of, 560a
  mystical union with Christ and, 242b
  ordination of, 552b
  sexuality and, 575b
  See also Women: religion and
Nūr-al-Dīn, 174b–175a
Nuremburg
  metallurgy in, 348b
Nūrī hospital, Damascus, 381a, 382a
Nursing horns, 114b
Nuruosmaniye mosque, 445a

O

O-T maps, 91a–b
Oakden, J. P., 13a
Oasthouses, 450a
Oath
  of canonical purgation, 312b, 313b
  capitulations and, 87a
  of compurgation, 310a, 312a–b, 343b
  of loyalty, 129a
  to pope, 321b
  Roman law and, 84a–b
  by vassals to lords, 322b
  of verity, 84b
  of wickedness, 84b
Oberammergau, 395b
Obertus de Orto, 321a, 324b
  Compilatio antiqua, 324b–325a
  Libri feudorum, 324b
Oblates and oblation, 146a, **428b–430a**
  in High Middle Ages, 429b
  legality of, 429b
  liturgical role of, 429a
  in monasteries, 116a
  personal consent and, 429b
Obligationes literature, 473b–474a
Obodrites, 408b, 409a
Observations on the Faerie Queene. See
  Warton, Thomas
Occitan literature. *See* Provençal literature
Occitania. *See* Languedoc
Ockham, William of, 421a, 615b
  atheism and, 44a
  consequences literature of, 473b
  on matter, 379a
  obligationes literature of, 474a
  on sacraments, 550b
  on signs, 582b, 583a–b
  on vice, 631b
Octateuch, 360b, 361a, 362a

Odense, as pagan holy place, 451a
Odin (god), 620b
Odo of Deuil, 139a
Odocacer (Vandal ruler), 166b
Odoric of Pordenone
  China missions and, 119a
  Relatio, 119b
Offamilio, Gualterio, 642a
"Offering of the Heart," 243 *(illus.),* 244a
Office of the Night (Florence), 574b
Ögödai, Great Khan
  invasion of Europe by, 118b
Oikoumenios, 55a
Oinas, Felix
  Heroic Epic and Saga, 180a
Öja Church
  Gothic art and, 239a
Oktechos, 328a–b
Old age, **430a–432b**
  coping with, 431b–432a
  negative view of, 430b–431a
  provisions for, 432a
  response to, 430a
Old Christians, 413b, 414a–415a
Old English literature
  alliterative literature and, 13a, 192a
  the Exeter Book and, 191b–192b
  Finnsburh Fragment of, 197a–b
Old Frisian, 205a–205b, 206b
  development of, 205a
  locations spoken, 205a
  music in, 206b
  replacing Latin, 205a
  wedding speeches in, 206b
Old Frisian law, 205a–205b
Old Mosque (*Eski Cami;* Edirne), 442b
Old St. Paul's Cathedral (England), 230a
Old St. Peter's (church: Rome), 227a,
  230b
Old Testament. *See* Bible
Old Uppsala. *See* Uppsala
Oldradus de Ponte, 7a, **433a–b**
  consilia of, 433a–b
  quaestiones and *consilia* of, 433a
Oleśnicki, Zbigniew, bishop of Kraków,
  433b–434b
Oligarchy
  communes and, 135b–137a
Olisipo, 326a
Olivi, Peter John, 59a, 400a
  insurance and, 291a
  on price formation in marketplace,
    302b–303a
  on sacraments, 546a
Ollivier, Jacme, 400b
Ollazabal monastery, 191a
Olympiodorus, 358b
O'Malley, Grace, 482b
Omnis utriusque. See Lateran Councils:
  Fourth
On Christian Doctrine. See Augustine, St.
On Coitus. See Rāzī, Abū Abkr
  Muḥammad ibn Zakarīya' al-

On Knowledge of the Measurement of Plane and Spherical Figures. See Banū Mūsā
On Spiritual Friendship. See Ethelred of Rievaulx
On the Nature of the Child, 1b
On the Prior and Posterior Analytics. See William of St. Amour
On the Witness of the Soul. See Tertullian
On Virtues and Vices, 629b
"On wifely duties." *See* Barbaro, Francesco
Once and Future King, The. See White, T. H.
Ongles bleu (blue nails), 503a–b
Opthalmology
  treatise on, 380a
Opus anglicanum, 235b, 239b
Opus francigenum, 235a
Opus lemonvicense, 235b
Opus maius. See Bacon, Roger
Opusculum tripartitum. See Humbert of Romans
Or San Michele (guild), 636a
Oral tradition
  alliterative literature and, 13a
  animals in, 18a, 19a
  Arabic literature and, 22a–b
  Avesta, the, 158a
  in schools, 559b
  troubadour poetry and, 150b
Oran, mufti of, 415a
Orange, council at
  Pelagius and, 436a
Orbais (abbey church), 226b
Ordeal
  criminal procedure and, 309b–311a
  due process and, 317a
  as ritual, 536a–b
  trial by, 526b
Ordene de chevalerie, 184a
Order of Mountjoy, 616a
Order of S. Damiano, 127a
Order of Santiago, 398a, 616a
Order of St. Clare (O.S.C.). *See* Poor Clares
Order of Swordbearers, 606b
Order of the Holy Spirit, 116a
Order of the Temple, 603b
Orders, 545a, 551a–552b
  as sacrament, 546a
Ordinances of Justice (1293), 136a
Ordinancy of Labourers (1349), 101b
Ordinarius of Bursdfeld, 83a
Ordinary
  Eastern liturgical year and, 328
Ordinatio, 472b
Ordini del cavalcare. See Grisone, Federico
Ordo iudicarius, 310b–312a
  natural law and, 318a–b
  See also Ricardus Anglicus
Orenge of Fontenay, 566a

Oresme, Nicole, 406b
  on astrology, 41a, 509b
  De causis mirabilium, 412a
  Charles V and, 459a
  on demons, 153b
  insurance and, 291a
  on probability, 509a
Orestes of Egypt, imperial prefect
  Hypatia and, 287a
Orestis tragoedia. See Dracontius, Blossius Aemilius
Origen, 629b
  biblical commentaries by, 54a–b
  on punishment, 262a
  on soul and body, 590a, 590b
Original sin, 194a–b, **434b–437a**
  free will and, 435a–b
  Islam and, 68b
  Jewish thought and, 194b
  Paul's letter to the Romans and, 435b
  in rabbinical literature, 435a
  sacraments and, 547a
  soul and body and, 590b
  unbaptized infants and, 436a–b
  Virgin Mary and, 288a–b
  See also Sin
Originality in arts and letters, **437a–439b**
  barbarian and classical influences on, 439a
  classicizing traits in, 439a
  figure poems and, 438a
Orlando furioso. See Ariosto, Ludovico
Orléans, 476b–477a
  siege of, 652b
Orphans
  civic care for, 116a
  slavery and, 116b
Orsanmichele, Madonna di, 105a–b
Orsini, Bertoldo, 440a
Orsini, Giordano, cardinal, 440a
Orsini, Giovanni, Gaetano. *See* Nicholas III, pope
Orsini, Latino, cardinal, 159b
Orsini, Lorenzo, 440b
Orsini, Matteo Rossi, 423a, 440b
  Colonna family and, 127b
Orsini, Napoleone, cardinal, 440a
Orsini, Rainaldo, cardinal, 440a
Orsini family, 423a, **439b–441a**
  vs. Colonna family, 127a, 128b, 439b
  the papacy and, 439b–440b
  in Rome, 439b–440a–b
Ortelius, 24a
Orto do Esposo, 496a
Osbern of Canterbury, 168b
Osmund, bishop, 216b
Oswald of Ramsey, 561b
Oswald of Worcester, 168a–b
Otho de la Roche
  Athens and, 44b
Otia imperialia. See Gervase of Tilbury
Ottaviani, Valeria, 567b

Otto I (the Great) of Germany, emperor, 137b, 409a
  history of, 146a
  patronage by, 457b
  royal authority of, 266a
  Slavic rebellion and, 265b
Otto II of Germany, emperor, 4b, 5a, 409a, **441a–b**
  Antwerp and, 24b
Otto III of Germany, emperor, 409a
  imperial renewal program of, 78b
Otto IV of Germany, emperor, 410b, **441b–442b**
Otto of Bamberg, St., 79b
Otto of Brunswick, 441b
  Bursfeld Abbey and, 83a
Otto of Freising
  Gesta Friderici, 63a
Ottoboni family, 624a
Ottokar II of Bohemia, king, 542b
Ottoman art and architecture, **442b–449b**
  architecture, 442b–445b
  baroque style in, 445a
  ceramics, 447a–447b
  decorative arts, 447a
  painting, 445b–446b
  rugs, 447b–448b
Ottomans, 414a, 415b
  conquests of, 202a
Ottonians. *See* Saxon dynasty
Our Lady, Cathedral of (Tournai), 613b
Our Lady (church: Antwerp), 24b
Ovens, **449b–450a**
Ovid (Publius Ovidius Naso)
  humanism and, 282a
  language of love and, 338a
  Metamorphoses, 452b
  rape in, 520a–b
  used in schools, 562a, 563a
Owl and the Nightingale, The, 20a
Oxford Calculators, 378b–379a
Oxford Menologion, 362b
  See also Menologion London
Oxford University, 200b
  medieval ritual and, 392b
  Merton Calculators of, 405a–407a
Ozanam, Antoine-Frédéric, 393a

P

Pachomius, St., 23a
Pacioli, Luca, 400b
Pact of 'Umar, 158b
Padua, 193b
Paganelli di Montemagno
  pope Eugenius III and, 186b–187a
Paganism
  archaeology of, 26b
  astrology and, 41a
  atheism and, 43a, 43b
  conversion from, 140b–143b
  Cumans and, 147a

folklore and, 22a
  missionaries and, 21b–22a, 141b–143b
  mystery religions and, 141b
  Sabians and, 543a, 543b, 544a
  St. Adalbert and, 4b, 5a
  Savonarola and, 557b
  schools and, 559a
  sexuality and, 570a
  See also Christianization
Paganism and pagan gods, survival of,
  450b–454a, 594a
  in literature, 452a–453a
Painting
  mural, 73b, 75a
  Ottoman, 445b–446b
  pagan gods in, 453a
  Poor Clares and, 489b
  pornographic, 491a
  topographical, 446a
Palaces
  Ottoman, 445a–b
Palatina Psalter, 362a
Palatine Chapel (Aachen), 226a
Palatine Library (Heidelberg), 624a
Paleography, 160b, 161a, 389b
Palestine
  hierarchy of Latin, 621a
Pallavicino, Uberto da, 193b
Palma Cathedral (Mallorca), 233a
Panchatantra, 303a
Pandulf, papal legate, 278a, 470a
Panizzi, Antonio, 356a
Panofsky, Erwin, 222a, 386b
Pantaléon, Jacques. *See* Urban IV, pope
Panther, The, 192a
Pantokrator (monastery: Constantinople),
  361a
Papacy, 623b
  Alfonso V and, 10b
  in Avignon, 7a, 440b
  election of pope, 247b
  Frederick II and, 440a
  Hohenstaufen dynasty and, 138b–139b
  judicial court of, 433a
  legal authority of, 7b
  literary patronage and, 458b, 459a
  papal supremacy, 247b
  peacemaking by, 461a
  political control of, 132b
  queenship and, 513a–b
  reform of elections, 422a
  relations with Florence of, 3a
  Roman revolt and, 136a–b
  sharing income of, 424a
Papal States, 424a
Paper, manufacture of, 349a
Papinianus
  on praetorian law, 318a
Par dessor l'ombre d'un bois. See Braine,
  Jehan de
Parabola (geometry), 371b, 374 *(illus.)*
Paraclete, 548a
Paradise Lost. See Milton, John

Paradox (philosophy), 473b
Paradoxography, 421a
Paralelismo, 494b
Parallel Lives. See Plutarch
Parchment, 358b
Pardon
  civic rituals of, 537a–538a, 537 *(illus.)*
  concept of, 85a
Parenti, Giovanni, 176b
Paris
  city government and, 135a, 136b
  guilds of, 135a
  Place de Grève, 538b
  schools in, 563a
  tapestry production in, 456a
Paris, Council of (829), 561b
Paris, Gaston, 383b, 393b
Paris, Matthew. *See* Matthew Paris
Paris, Paulin, 393b
Paris, University of
  friars' right to teach at, 9a–9b
  satire and, 556a
Paris Gregory, 359a
Paris Psalter, 359b
Paris Sacra Parallela, 359a
Parish, 141a, 141b, 143b
Parisiana Poetria. See John of Garland
Parisiensis secunda. See Bernard of Pavia
Parker, Matthew, archbishop of
  Canterbury, 355b, 389b
Parkin, David
  Sacred Void, 540a
Parlement of the Thre Ages, The, 12b
Parler, Peter, 74b
Parler family, 76b
Parliament of Fowls. See Chaucer,
  Geoffrey
Parsifal. See Wagner, Richard
Parsival, legend of, 39a
Parthenon, 45a
Partridge, The, 192a
Parvulus, 114b
Parzival. See Wolfram von Eschenbach
Pascal, Blaise, 372b
Pascha (Easter), 327b, 329a–b
Paschal II, pope
  excommunication of Henry IV of
    Germany by, 267a
Paschasius Radbertus of Corbie, St., 57a,
  145b, 614a
  De corpore et sanguine Domini, 145b
Pashto language, 468b
Pasquier, Estienne, 390b
Passio Perpetuae et Felicitatis, 62a
Passion of Joan of Arc, The. See Dreyer,
  Carl Theodor
Passion plays
  planctus Mariae and, 483b
Passover
  Eastern liturgical year and, 327b
Past and Present. See Carlyle, Thomas
Paston family, 651b
  courtship and marriage and, 335b

Pastoreaux uprising, 506b
Patarine movement, 422b
Paterikon. See Joseph of Volokolamsk, St.
Paternoster beads, 242a
Patriarch
  Islam and, 254b
Patrick, St., 142b–143a
Patronage, artistic, **454a–456b**
  by the church, 454a–455a
  influence of, 456a–b
  intermediaries in, 455b–456a
  operation of, 455a–b
  Peter des Roches and, 469a
  queens in, 512b
Patronage, literary, **456b–459b**
  alliterative literature and, 12b
  Germanic and Carolingian, 457a–b
  later Middle Ages, 459a
  twelfth and thirteenth century, 457b–
    459a
Patton, George S., 395a
Paucapalea (jurist), 318b
Paul, St., 194a, 610a, 617a
  on celibacy, 364a
  conversion of, 140b
  cosmic dualism and, 213b
  Epistles, 589b
  gift of esoteric revelation, 213b
  on original sin, 435b
  on sexuality, 570a
  soul and body and, 589b
Paul II, pope
  on Jewish rights, 319a
Paul III, pope
  on law of nature, 319a
Paul V, pope, 623a
Paul of Aegina, 381b
Paul of Burgos, 59b
Paul the Deacon, 560b
  at Aachen, 89b
Paulinus of Nola, St., 212b, 561a
Paulinus of Périgueux
  biography of St. Martin of Tours,
    370b
Pauperes Christi, 98b
Pauperes commilitones Christi templi
  Salomonici. *See* Templars
Paupers
  definition of, 499a
  See also Poverty
Pavia, 560b
Peace of God, 461b
  reconciliation rituals and, 537a
Peace of God movement, 625a
Peace of Toruň, 434a
Peacemaking, **459b–462b**
  bilateral peace in, 460a–461a
  Pierre de Belleperche in, 477a
  queens in, 512a–b, 514a
  restoring the order through, 461a–462a
Pearl, 12a, 47a
Pearl Poet, the
  Anne of Bohemia and, 21a

Pearl Poet Society, 387a
Peasants
  feudal society and, 133a
  hunting and, 173a
  manorialism and, 343a–b
  poverty among, 501a–502b
  as routiers, 541b–542a
Peasants' rebellions, 502a, 506b, 624b–625a
  14th century, 135b–136b
  England (1381), 136b
  France (1358), 136b
Peckham, John
  beginning of the world and, 72a
  on matter, 378b
Pedro II of Aragon, king, 150b
  Battle of Las Navas de Tolosa and, 306a
Pedro III (the Great) of Aragon, king, **462b–463b**
Pedro I (the Cruel) of Castile, king, 248b
Pedro de Portugal, Dom
  Sátira de la infelice e felice vida, 493b–494a
Pedro of Barcelos
  Crónica geral de Espanha de 1344, 495a, 495b
  lais of, 494b
  Livro de Linhagens, 495a–b
  Primera crónica general, 495b
Pedro of Portugal, Infante
  Livro da Virtuosa Bemfeitoria, 496b, 497a
Pegolotti, Francesco di Balduccio
  La practica della mercatura, 400b
Péguy, Charles, 395a
Peire Cardenal, 556b
Peire Duran, 458a
  "Ma vile chanson engagée, facile et vulgaire," 458a
Pelagianism, 154a
  original sin and, 435b–436a
Pelagius, 435b–436a
Pèlerinage de Charlemagne, 181a
Pèlerinage de Jhesucrist. See Deguileville, Guillaume de
Pèlerinage de la vie humaine. See Deguileville, Guillaume de
Pèlerinage de l'âme. See Deguileville, Guillaume de
Penal code. *See* Criminal justice
Penance, 545a, 549b–550b
  church construction as, 549b
  public rituals of, 536b–537a
Penitentials
  abortion and, 1a
  Celtic pilgrimage and, 479b–481a
  homosexuality and, 574a
  peacemaking and, 461b–462a
  pollution and taboo and, 484a–485a
  pornographic illustrations in, 492b–493a
  on sexuality, 572a

Penitents
  Poor Clares and, 486a
Penniless Prodromos, 510a–b
Penshurst, Kent, Great Hall at, 35a, 35 (*illus.*), 36a
Pentateuch
  Jerome's prologue to, 42a
Pentekonstarion, 328b
Peperit charm, 110b
Pepin III (the Short), mayor of the palace, 88a, 560b
Pepsyan Model Book, 236a
Peraldus, William. *See* Perault, William.
Perault, William, **463b–464a**
  on sexuality, 571b
  Summa de vitiis et virtutibus, 463a–464a, 632a
Perceval le Gallois. See Rohmer, Eric
Percy, Henry, earl of Northumberland, 464b–465a
Percy, Henry (Hotspur), 465a–b
Percy, Henry II, 464b
Percy, Henry III, 464b
Percy, Richard, 464b
Percy, Thomas, 465b
  Reliques of Antient English Poetry, 391a
Percy, William I de, 464a–b
Percy, William II de, 464b
Percy family, **464a–466a**
Pere II of Catalonia. *See* Pedro III (the Great) of Aragon, king
Peregrinus. See Pilgrimage
Pereira, Nuno Álvares
  in *Crónica do condestabre,* 496a
Pérez, Ferrán, 502a
Pérez de Guzmán, Fernán
  Generaciones y semblanzas, 63b
Pérez de Herrera, Cristóbal, 506b
Peri hygieion. See Galen
Perjury, criminal procedure and, 310a
Perpetuus of Tours, bishop, 370b
Persecuting society, 485a
Persian folklore, 22a
Persian language, **466a–469a**
  Arabic influences in, 467a–b
  Iranian dialects in, 468a
  New Persian or *darī,* 466b–468a
  scripts in, 467b–468a
Persius, 554b, 562a
Peruzzi company, 2b, 3b, 400b
  banking and, 403a
Peter, St., 610a
Peter III of Aragon, king, 6b
Peter Chrysologus, St., 98b
Peter Damian, St., 422b
  homosexuality and, 574a
Peter de Maulay, 278a
  Peter des Roches and, 470a
Peter des Roches, **469a–471a**
  Hubert de Burgh and, 278a–279a
Peter Lombard, 58b, 436b
  atheism and, 44a

"French model" of marriage and, 366b–367a
  on marriage, 571b
  on sacraments, 545a, 546b, 547a, 548a, 548b, 549b–550a, 551a–b, 552a, 553a, 583b
  Sentences, 58b, 200b, 207b, 288b, 336a, 366b, 472b, 473a, 492b, 545a, 571b, 583b, 590b, 631a
  Sententiae in IV libris distinctae, 336a
  on sexuality, 492b
  on soul and body, 590b
Peter of Abano
  Conciliator controversarum quae inter philosophos et medicos versantur, 584a–b
Peter of Blois, 308a
  letters of, 458b
  sermons of, 100a
Peter of Corvaro, 333a
Peter of Courtenay
  Honorius III, pope, and, 274a
Peter of Eboli
  public baths and, 51a
Peter of Langtoft
  Chronicle, 12b
Peter of Lucalongo, 119a
Peter of Scala, 59a
Peter of Spain the Elder, 582b
Peter of Tarentaise, 59a
Peter the Chanter, 222a
  "Summa Abel," 58b
Peter the Venerable, abbot of Cluny
  Heloise and, 335a
  language of spiritual friendship and, 338b
  on monasticism, 287b
Peterborough *Chronicle,* 13b
Peters, Ellis, 397a
Petrarch (Francesco Petrarca), 47a, 407a
  Africa, 458b
  in Portuguese literature, 496a
  "Rotta è l'alta Colonna," 128b
Petronius
  satire of, 554b
Petrus Alfonsi, **471a–472a**
  Dialogus contra Judaeos, 471b, 472a
  Disciplina clericalis, 184b, 471b, 472a
Petrus Crassus
  defense of Henry IV by, 317b
Petrus de Bella Pertica. *See* Pierre de Belleperche
Petty jury
  evolution of, 316a
Phainomena. See Aratus
Pharmacology, 382a
Pharsalia. See Lucan
Philibiblon. See Richard de Bury
Philip, duke of Swabia, 441b, 442a
Philip II (the Bold) of Burgundy, duke
  manuscript collection of, 355b
  mausoleum of, 534b, 535 (*illus.*)

Philip III (the Good) of Burgundy, duke
  entry into Ghent of, 534b
  Feast of the Pheasant and, 535b
Philip II Augustus of France, king, 220a,
  368b, 442a, 613b
  Peter des Roches and, 469a
  Richard the Lionhearted and, 575a
  routiers under, 541b
Philip III of France, king
  Pedro III and, 463a
Philip IV (the Fair) of France, king,
  604b, 645b
  daughter Isabelle, 645b
  patronage by, 458b–459a
  Pierre de Belleperche, 477a
  succession of, 514a
Philip II of Spain, king, 414a, 414b,
  416a
Philip III of Spain, king, 416a
  Moriscos and, 416a
Philip the Chancellor, 308a, 309a
Philippa of Hainault, 514a
Phillippe de Commines, 182a
Phillipps, Thomas
  manuscript collection of, 355b
Philo of Alexandria
  on abortion, 1a
  biblical interpretation by, 54a
  on biography, 61b
Philology
  medieval studies and, 383b–384b,
    387b, 393b, 395b, 396b
Philoponus. See John Philoponus of
  Alexandria
Philosophical genres, **472a–474a**
Philosophy and theology, Greek
  original sin and, 435a–b
Philosophy and theology, Islamic, 377b–
  378a
  original sin and, 435a
Philosophy and theology, Western
  European
  on abortion, 1a
  Christ's incarnation and, 194b
  the Fall and, 194a
  God of, 281a–b
  natural law and, 418b–419b
  nature and, 420a–421a
  numeric concepts in, 427b
  numerology and, 428a
  original sin and, 194b, 435a
  Oxford Calculators and, 378b–379a
  Peripatetic thinkers and, 377b–378a
  philosophy and, 472a–474a
  in popular religion, 521a–529b
  on poverty, 497b–508b
  probability in, 508a–509b
  race and, 515b
  semiotics and, 584b
Philostorgios
  history of, 619b
Philostratus
  Life of Apollonius of Tyana, 61a–b

Philoxenus of Mabbug, 55b
Phocaea
  alum industry of, 403b
Phoenix, The, 191b
Phokas, Byzantine emperor, 66a
Photios, patriarch, 426b, 619b
Physicians, **474a–476b**
  licit vs. illicit, 475a–476a
  as professionals, 165b–166a
  See also Disease; Medicine
Physics
  Merton calculators and, 406a–b
Physics. See Aristotle
Physiologus, 18b
Pi, value of, 373b, 375b
Piagnoni, the, 558a
Piast dynasty, 78b–79b, 408b, 409a
Picardy, 226b
Picatrix (Ghayat al-ḥakīm). See Majrīṭī,
  Maslama al-
Picaud, Aymeri
  Codex Calixtinus, 191a
Pico della Mirandola, Giovanni
  astronomy and, 41a
Pictish language, 190a–b
Pierce the Ploughman's Crede, 15a, 555b
Pierre de Belleperche, **476b–477b**
Pierre de Montreuil, 227b
Pierre Le Moyne
  Saint Louis (poem), 390b
Piers Plowman. See Langland, William
Piers the Plowman's Creed. See Pierce the
  Ploughman's Crede
Pietà, 69 (illus.), 239b (illus.), 529b
  development of, 241a–b
  popularity of, 69a
Pietists, German (Hasidei Ashkenaz),
  569b
Pietro d'Abano, 580a
Pilgrim souvenirs, **477b–479b,** 478
  (illus.), 524b–525a
Pilgrimage, 479b–480b
  archaeology of, 26a, 27b, 29b
  avoiding imprisonment through, 537a
  certificates of, 479a
  indulgences and, 528a
  Islam and, 253a, 255b
  Jewish saints and, 258b
  to Lourdes, 393b
  narrative of, 411a
  Ottoman, 446b
  penance and, 549b
  saints and relics in, 524b–525a
Pilgrimage, Celtic, **479b–481a**
Pilgrimage of Grace (1536)
  Percy and, 466a
Pilgrimage of the Soul. See Deguileville,
  Guillaume de
Pilgrim's Guide, 226a
  on pilgrim souvenirs, 477b–478a
Pillage. See Violence
Pillius de Medicina, 4a
  on Libri feudorum, 322a, 325a

Pirates and piracy, **481a–483a**
  corsairs in, 481b
  naval administration and, 6a
  prevalence of, 482a–b
  targets of, 481b–482a
Pirenne, Henri, 27a, 28a, 401a, 402a,
  408a
Pirkei de Rabbi Eliezer, 152b
Pisa
  as Florentine ministate, 137a
  merchants of, 402a
Pisa, Council of
  John XXIII, antipope, and, 298b
Pistoia
  factionalism in, 134a
Pius II, pope, 611a
Pla de Nadal (Spain), 32a
Placentinus, 4a
Plagues, 172a
  bubonic, 51a, 135b, 136a, 136b, 164a,
    381b
  Chinese trade and, 119b
  Ciompi revolt and, 124a–b
  civic ritual and, 534b
  poverty and, 499b, 502a
  urban poor and, 503a–b
  See also Black Death
Planctus ante nescia. See Geoffrey of St.
  Victor
Planctus Mariae (Marienklagen), **483a–
  484a**
Planetary motion, 297b–298a
Plantagenet, Geoffrey. See Geoffrey V
  Plantagenet, count of Anjou
Plantagenets, 223a
Plantin, Christopher, 24a
Platina, Bartolomeo, 623b
Plato
  definition of nature and, 420a–b
  semiotics of, 581a, 581b, 583a, 583b
  on soul and body, 588b, 589a, 589b,
    590b
  Timaeus, 222b, 281a, 377a–377b
Plato and Platonism
  humanists and, 421a
  numeric concepts in, 427b
Plautus, 564a
Play of Daniel, 272a, 396a
Pliny the Elder, 409b
  cartography and, 91a
  on latifundia, 306b
  Natural History, 118a
  writings on Asia by, 118a
Plotinus
  Gnostics, attack of, 214a
  Hypatia and, 286b
Plow, moldboard, 170b–171a
Plutarch
  Lives, 3b
  Parallel Lives, 61a
Podesta
  authority of, 134a, 135a
  as profession, 134a

Poe, Edgar Allan, 391b
Poel, William
  revival of *Everyman,* 395b
Poems of Ossian. See Macpherson, James
Poetics. See Aristotle
Poetry
  of Alcuin, 89b
  alliterative, 14a–15a
  animals in debate, 20a
  of Banū Hilāl, 271a–b
  of Bedouin, 52a
  carmina figurata, 438a
  Carolingian Latin, 192b
  concepts of hell and, 263a
  epic, 627a, 653b
  Exeter Book and, 191b–192b
  in Hebrew, 260b
  heroic, 17a, 206a
  by Hilary of Orléans, 272a–b
  humanism and, 281a–282a
  by Jean Renart, 293b
  Jewish, 256b
  of juglars, 300b
  language of love and, 337a–338a
  in Latin literature, 307a–309a
  love of, 652a
  lyric, 596a, 651b–652a
  macaronic, 309a
  Old English, 191b
  of Poland, 72a–b
  Portuguese, 494a–b
  prodromic, **510a–511a**
  satire in Irish, 554b
  of Tosafists, 258a
  of war, 627a
  See also Anglo-Saxon poetry;
    Troubadours, poetry of
Poets and Poetry of Europe, The. See
  Longfellow, Henry Wadsworth
Poitiers, Battle of (1356), 136b, 403b
Poland
  Bartholomaeus Anglicus and, 49a
  Jewish migration into, 304a–305a
  markets in, 131b
  medieval period of, 408b
  Mongol invasion of, 118b
  poetry from, 72a–b
  St. Adalbert and, 5a
  Slavonic rite in, 5a
Polani, Pietro, doge, 148a
Polemics
  on Gnosticism, 214a
  Petrus Alfonsi on, 471b–472a
Policraticus. See John of Salisbury
Polihistor. See Solinus, Gaius Julius
Polish army
  victory at Marienburg, 599a–b
Politics
  correspondence on, 458b
  satire on, 556a
Pollution and taboo, **484a–485b**
Polo, Maffeo, 118b

Polo, Marco, 400a
  in China, 118b–119a
  Description of the World, 119b, 120a
Polo, Niccolo, 118b
Polovtsians, 587b
  See also Cumans/Kipchaks
Polygamy
  church teaching on, 141a
  St. Stanisław and, 594b
Pomerania
  Polish control over, 79b–80a
Pomponazzi, Pietro, 590b
Pomponius
  on positive law, 318a
Pontifical Institute of Mediaeval Studies,
  384b–385a
Pontigny, abbey of, 176a
Ponza, island of, Mithraic shrine on, 41b
Poor Catholics, 169a–b
  See also Waldensians
Poor Clares, 126a–127a, **485b–490b**
  art and, 489a–b
  convent founders of, 488a–b
  formalization of, 487a–488a
  growth of, 488a
  Observant, 488b, 489a
  reforms of, 488a, 488b–489a
  St. Francis and, 485b–486a, 486
    (*illus.*)
  work of, 486a–487a
*Poor Clares Grieving over the Body of St.
  Francis. See* Giotto
Poor Knights of Christ. *See* Templars
Poorhouses, 504a
  See also Charity
Pope, John, 192b
Popolo minuto, 124b–125a
Population
  declines in, 26b
  growth in, 130a, 135b, 402a–b
Populo
  guilds and, 404a
  rise of, 134b
Porete, Marguerite, 47b, 339a, 650b
Pornography, **490b–493b**
  defining, 490a–491b
  types of, 491b–493a
Porphyry of Tyre, 214a
Port Coeli convent
  founding of, 73b
Portolan chart, 91b
Portugal
  exploration and, 269b–270a
  shipbuilding in, 348b–349a
Portuguese literature, **493b–497b**
  Demanda do Santo Graal, 150b–151a
  poetry, 494a–b
  prose, 494b–497a
Possessors vs. Nonpossessors, 299b
Possidius of Calama
  Vita Augustini, 62b
Postglossators
  Pierre de Belleperche, 476b–477a

Postilla moralis. See Nicholas of Lyra
Postilla super totam Bibliam. See Hugh of
  St. Cher
*Postillae perpetuae super totam Bibliam.
  See* Nicholas of Lyra
Pottery, production of
  archaeology of, 27b, 29a
  Ottoman, 447a–b
  ovens in, 449b
Poverty, **497b–508b**
  beggars and, 503b–504b
  charity and, 98a–102a
  classifications of, 499b–501a
  geographic differences in, 498b
  historiography of, 498b–499a
  marginalization and, 504a–b
  perception of the poor and, 506b–507a
  Poor Clares and, 485a–489b
  rural vs. urban, 501a–503b
  St. Clare and, 126a–127a
  as social and economic category, 499a–
    501a
  social welfare programs and, 499a
  the state and, 506a–b
  voluntary vs. involuntary, 504b–506a
Power
  potestas absoluta (absolute), 7b
  rituals and, 540a–541b
Practica della mercatura, La. See Pegolotti,
  Francesco di Balduccio
Praeneste, 422b
Praetextatus,
  exile and murder of, 203b
Praetorian law, 318a
Prague
  archaeology in, 28b
  bishop of, 4b–5a
  decorative art in, 73a–77b
  urban renewal in, 107a
Prague, University of
  founding of, 107a
Prague Castle
  Władislaw (Wenceslas) Hall in, 77
    (*illus.*)
Prato
  merchants of, 400b–401a
Praxapostolos Moscow, 358b
Prayer
  astrology and, 40b
  atheism and, 43a
Prayers. See Catherine of Siena, St.
Pre-Raphaelites, 392b
  Arthurian romances and, 36b
  Ruskin on, 389a
Preaching
  Perault on, 463a–464a
Přemsyl Otokar II of Bohemia, king, 73b
Přemyslid dynasty
  decorative art during, 73a–b
Prescott, William Hickling, 394a
Prester John
  Arthurian romances and, 39a

Priesthood
    celibacy and, 569b
    sexuality and, 575b
Prima Spagna. See Andrea da Barberino
Primas, Hugh. *See* Hugh (Primas) of
    Orléans
Primera crónica general. See Pedro of
    Barcelos
Prince Valiant (comic strip), 396a
Princeps
    in Poland, 79b–80a
Printing
    in Antwerp, 24a, 25a
    humanism and, 280a
    pornography and, 491a–b
Priscian, 9b
    Institutiones grammaticae, 561a, 563a
    used in schools, 561a, 562a, 563a
Prison amoureuse, La. See Froissart, Jehan
Privacy
    architecture and, 30b
    pornography and, 491a–b
Privilege of Poverty. See Innocent III, pope
Privileges of Ghent and Flanders, 536
    (illus.)
Privilegium paupertatis, 126b–127a
Probability, **508b–510a**
Processo castellano, 97a
Procheiron (procheiros nomos), 426b
Procopius of Caesarea
    Secret History (Anecdota), 492a
Procopius of Gaza, 55a
Prodromic poems, **510a–511a**
Prodromos, Manganeios, 510a
Prodromos, Theodore, 510a
Proemio e carta al condestable de Portugal.
    See Santillana, Marqués de
Profit de savoir quel est péché mortel et
    véniel, Le. See Gerson, John
Property
    confiscation of, 315b
    just price and, 301a
    salvation and, 505a, 506a
Property rights, 132b, 419a
Prophets
    Islam and, 254b
Proposicio. See Fitzralph, Richard
Prose, rhythmic
    alliterative literature and, 11a, 13b,
    14b–15a
Proslogion. See Anselm of Canterbury
Prosopography, 160b
Prospects of Medieval History, The. See
    Brooke, A. N.
Prospects of Medieval Studies, The. See
    Knowles, David
Prosper of Aquitaine
    used in schools, 561a
Prostagma, 427a
Prostitution, 576a–b
    public penances for, 537a
Prosvetitel. See Joseph of Volokolamsk, St.

Protestantism, 144b, 407a, 623a
    sacraments and, 548a, 550b
    See also Reformation
Protoevangelium of James, 288b
Provençal literature
    satire in, 556a–b
    troubadours and, 651b
Provence
    Hebrew language in, 261a
    Muslims in, 202b
    schools in, 562b
Provinciale. See Lyndwood, William
Provins, commune of, 135a
Provision of the Voyager (Viaticum). See
    Razzāz al-Jazarī˒, Ibn al-
Provisions, ecclesiastical
    Alexander IV and, 9a
Prudentius (Aurelius Prudentius Clemens)
    Psychomachia, 180a, 630a
    used in schools, 561a, 562a
Prussia
    Teutonic Knights in, 94a
Prussians
    conversion of, 5a
Psalter
    illumination of, 153a, 358a–b, 359a–b,
    360a, 362a–b
Psalter and New Testament Sinai, 362b
Psalter in Venice, 360a
Psalter map, 91a
Psalter St. Petersburg, 358b
Pseudo-Boron cycle, 495a
Pseudo-Dionysius the Areopagite, 222a,
    428a
    on matter, 377b
Pseudo-Map cycle, 495a
Pseudo-Matthew, 288b
Psychology
    semiotics and, 581b, 582a
    soul and body and, 592a, 592b
Psychomachia. See Prudentius
Ptochoprodromos, 510a–b
Ptolemy, Claudius, 373b
    Almagest, 286b
    Asian geography and, 118a
    astronomy of, 371a, 375a
    cartography and, 90b
    Cosmographia, 16b, 17b
    Geography, 92a–b
    Tetrabiblos, 412a
Public baths. *See* Baths and bathing
Public Life in Renaissance Florence. See
    Trexler, Richard
Public registers, 424b, 425a
Public sphere
    domestic architecture and, 31a
Pucelle, Jean, 242b
Pugin, A. W. N., 395a
    Gothic architecture of, 392b
Pulgar, Hernando del
    Claros varones de Castilla, 63b
Pullen, Robert, 614b
Pulteney, Sir John de, 35 *(illus.)*

Punishment
    for espionage, 182b–183a
    for heresies, 86a
    Origen on, 262a
    peacemaking and, 461b–462a
    See also Capital punishment
Purgation, canonical, 312b, 313b
Purgatory, 550b
    almsgiving and, 99a–b
    charity and, 98b
    concept of, 262b
    Masses to shorten time in, 528b
    in popular religion, 528a–b
    poverty and, 505a, 506a
    soul and body and, 591a
Pythagorean theory
    numeric concepts in, 427b

Q

Qa˒id Peter, 642a
Qartmin (monastery), 597b
Qayrawān, al-
    capture of, 271a
    circle (Kairouan), 381a
Qiftī, Ibn al-, 381a
Quadrivium, 416b, 427b
Quaestiones, 472b
Quaestiones decretales. See Ricardus
    Anglicus
Quaestiones disputatae. See Bulgarus
Qualiter et quando. See Innocent III, pope
Quantum praedecessores. See Eugenius III,
    pope
Queens and queenship, **511a–515a**
    Carolingian era, 512b–513a
    central Middle Ages, 513a–514a
    early Middle Ages, 511b–512b
    later Middle Ages, 514a–b
    succession and, 511b
Quentovic, 27a, 27b
Queste del Saint Graal, 151a
Questiones naturales. See Adelard of Bath
"Questions on Medicine," 380a–b
Qūhī, al-, parabola and, 374 *(illus.)*
Quinque compilationes, 53b
Quintilian (Marcus Fabius Quintilianus)
    Institutio oratoria, 554a
Qūlūya, Ibn
    Kāmil al-ziyārāt, 255b
Qūmisī, Daniel al-, 60a
Qunfudh, Ibn, 375b
Quodlibet, 472b
Qurashī, al-
    on toy markets, 115b
Quṣayr ˒Amra (Umayyad palace), 41b
Qutra, Thabit ibn, 40b
Qvarnström, Gunnar, 427b

R

Rabelais, François, 191a
    Gargantua and Pantagruel, 390b

Rabelais and His World. See Bakhtin, Mikhail

Rābiʿa al-ʿAdaawīya, 254b

Race, **515a–518a**
　Arthurian romances and, 39a
　as construct, 515a–516b
　ethnicity and, 516b–517a
　medievalism and, 387b, 394b
　natio concept and, 517a–518a
　ritual and, 539b

Radegunda, St., **518b–519a,** 570b

Radulfus Tortarius, 308b

Radulphus Glaber, 203a

Rafn, Carl Christian, 393b

Raigern Altarpiece, 76b

Ralph, archbishop of Canterbury, 217a

Ramadan
　among Moriscos, 415b

Rambaldo, 17a

Ramon Berenguer IV of Barcelona, count, 603b

Ramsey Abbey
　Gothic art and, 241a

Rand, E. K., 384a

Ranke, Leopold von, 392a

Raoul de Cambrai, 624b, 627a

Raoul de Presles
　Charles V and, 459a

Rape, **519a–520b**
　in Byzantine law, 520a
　in literature, 520a–b
　within marriage, 572a–b

Raphael, 217b–218a

Raptus quoque. See Gratian

Rashbam, 60b

Rashi, 60a, 257a, 261b

Rask, Rasmus, 393b

Rather of Verona, 114b

Ratramnus of Corbie, 614a

Ravenna
　mosaics in, 153a
　palace of Theodoric in, 32a

Raymond of Antioch, 174b

Raymond of Capua
　Legenda maior, 94a
　St. Catherine of Siena and, 96a–97a

Raymond of Marseille
　on astrology, 584a

Raymond IV of Toulouse, count, 215a–b

Rāzī, Abū Bakr Muḥammad ibn Zakarīyaʾ al- (Rhazes), 165a–b, 377b
　on abortion, 1b
　al-Ḥāwī, 380b, 381a
　On Coitus, 577b
　Kitāb al-ṭibb al-Manṣūrī, 380b
　Kitāb fī l-jadarī wa l-ḥaṣba, 380b
　Liber almansoris, 284b
　on sexuality, 577b, 580a
　on swaddling of newborns, 113a

Razzāz al-Jazarīʿ, Ibn al-
　Provision of the Voyager (Viaticum), 2a

Realism
　semiotics and, 582a

Reconquest, 616a
　battles of, 305b
　wars of, 602a

Recopolis (Spain), 32a

Record keeping. *See* notaries

Redbad, king, 206a

Rede, William, 405b

Reductorium morale. See Bersuire, Pierre

Reform
　Church, 88a–89a, 422a–b
　in Gaul, 88a
　of marriage laws, 513a–b
　monastic, 266b, 561b, 562a
　on pollution and taboo, 484b
　queens in, 512b

Reformation, 389b, 407a–b, 600b–601a
　civic ritual and, 533a
　popular religion and, 529b
　See also Protestantism

Regimen of Health. See Maimonides, Moses

Reginald the monk
　Vita Godrici, 216a–b

Regino of Prüm (Regino Prumiensis)
　on abortion, 1a
　on race, 515a–b

Registers, public, 424b–425a

Regula mixta, 145a

Regulae solvendi sophismata. See Heytesbury, William

Regularis concordia. See Benedictine rule

Reichenau (monastery), 429a

Reihengräber (graves in rows: Germany), 26b

Reinfrid von Braunschweig, 411b

Reinhausen, abbey of, 83a

Reʾis, Pīrī, 446a

Reja de San Millán, 191a

Relatio, 119b

Relics
　cult of, 523b–525b
　in Gniezno, 78b
　in Karlšsejn castle, 75a
　miracles and, 523b
　as pilgrim souvenirs, 477b
　pilgrimages and, 480a
　in popular religion, 521a, 523b–525b
　power of, 70a–b
　Radegunda as collector of, 518b
　of St. James, 239b
　of St. John the Baptist, 75a
　of St. Stanislaw, 305a
　soul and body and, 590b, 592a, 592b

Religion, popular, **520b–530b**
　civic ritual and, 532a–533a
　cult of saints in, 523b–525b
　magic in, 527a–528a
　missions in, 522a–523b
　movements in, 528b–529b
　of servants, 567b–568a
　veneration of the host in, 525b–527a

Religious Drama Society, 395b

Reliquary
　Arm Reliquary of the Apostles, 67b *(illus.)*
　Gothic art and, 241a

Reliques of Antient English Poetry. See Percy, Thomas

Remigius, 57a, 218a

Renaissance of the Twelfth Century, The. See Haskins, Charles Homer

Renaissances, 437b–439a
　of 12th century, 407b–408a
　astrology and, 42b

Renart, Jean
　Guillaume de Dôle, 293b–294a
　Le lai de l'ombre, 293b

Renaud de Cambrai, 181a

Renault de Cormont, 227b

Renaut, legend of, 16b

Repgowe, Eike von
　Sachsenspiegel, 116a

Reportatio, 472b

Res gestae Saxonicae. See Widukind of Corvey

Resende, Garcia de
　Cancioneiro general, 494b

Resurrection
　soul and body and, 592a

Reuss, Heinrich, Graf von Plauen, 599b

Revolts. *See* Peasants' rebellions

Reynolds, Robert L., 403a

Rhazes. *See* Rāzī, Abū Bakr Muḥammad ibn Zakarīyaʾ al-

Rheims, Council of (1119)
　on sacraments, 551b

Rheims Cathedral, 219b, 222a, 223a, 226b
　choir of, 227a–b
　Gothic reconstruction of, 227a

Rhetoric, 163b, 166b
　charters and, 162a–b
　See also Schools

Rhine, count-palatine of the, 542a

Rhodes
　Hospitallers headquarters on, 276b–277a
　siege of, 198b

Rhumb lines, 91b

Riade
　defeat of Magyars at, 265b

Rib vault. *See* Vault, ribbed

Ribāṭ, **530b–531a**

Ribe, 27a

Ricardus Anglicus, **531a–532a**

Ricciardi company of Lucca
　banking and, 403a, 404a

Rich, Edmund, 175b

Richard I (the Lionhearted) of England, king, 220a, 442a, 643a, 645b
　Henry VI of Germany and, 268a
　Peter des Roches and, 469a
　Philip II Augustus of France and, 575a
　songs by, 458a

Richard II of England, king
Anne of Bohemia and, 21a
English language and, 13a
inadequacy of, 619a
Percy and, 464b–465a
Richard III of England, king
Percy and, 465b–466a
Richard III Society, 387a
Richard de Bury
Philibiblon, 355a
Richard of Cornwall, earl, 139b, 542a
Alexander IV and, 9a
Richard of Maidstone
almsgiving and, 100b
Richard of Molise, count, 642a
Richard of Salerno, 174b
Richard the Redeless, 15a
Richardson, H. G., 638a
Richardson, Henry Hobson, 394a
Riché, Pierre, 559a
Richer of Rheims, 474b
Ricold of Monte Croce, 412a
Riddles
in Exeter Book, 192a
pornographic, 491b
Riḍwān, ʿAlī ibn, 380b
Ried, Benedikt, 77a–b, 78a
Rights
banal (feudal), 449b–450a
of Muslims, 133b
property, 132b, 419a
to trial, 317a, 318a–319a
against tyranny, 617b
of women, 133b, 644a
Rimbert, St.
Life of St. Ansgar (Vita Anskarii), 21b, 22a, 146a
Riming Poem, the (Exeter Book), 192a
Rinaldo. See Andrea da Barberino
Ring of the Nibelung. See Wagner, Richard
Ripelin, Hugh
Compendium theologicae veritatis, 163b
Rites de passage. See Gennep, Arnold van
Ritson, Joseph
Ancient English Metrical Romances, 391a
Ritter der Tafelrunde, Die. See Hein, Christoph
Ritual, civic, **532a–540a**
fusion among, 539b
historiography on, 533a–b
sociology of religion and, 532a–533a
types of, 533b–539a
Ritual, Politics, and Power. See Kertzer, David
Ritual Theory, Ritual Practice. See Bell, Catherine
Robb, Candace, 397a
Robert I (Curthose) of Normandy, duke, 640a–b
Robert I (the Bruce) of Scotland, king
Battle of Bannockburn and, 48a–b

biography of, 63a
Robert Guiscard, 422b
Robert of Anjou, king of Sicily, 433b, 440b
Petrarch and, 458b
Poor Clares and, 488b
Robert of Blois
Chastoiement des dames, 185b
Robert of Flamborough, 631b
Liber poenitentialis, 631b
Robert of Geneva. *See* Clement VII, pope
Robert of Gloucester, 376b
patronage by, 457b
Robert of Naples, king. *See* Robert of Anjou, king of Sicily
Robin Hood, 391a, 394a, 396a
Roche (abbey church: England), 228a
Rockefeller McCormick New Testament, 361b
Rockets
use of gunpowder in, 197b
Rodríguez de Montalvo, Garcí
Amadís de Gaula and, 495a
Roffredus de Epiphaniis of Benevento, 638a
Rogation Days, 332a
Greater and Lesser, 523a
Roger of Parma. *See* Frugardi, Ruggiero
Roger II of Sicily, king, 187b, 641a
Rohmer, Eric
Perceval le Gallois, 396b
Roʾie, David, 258b
Rois thaumaturges, Les. See Bloch, Marc
Roland, legend of, 16b
Roland, Song of, 179a, 181a, 300b, 383b, 393b, 432a, 587b, 627a
Roland of Bologna. *See* Roland of Cremona
Roland of Cremona, 59a
on sacraments, 547a, 550a
Rolandinus de Passageris, **540a–541b**
tomb of, 540 *(illus.)*
Rolandus
canon law and, 246b
Rolle, Richard
alliterative literature and, 12b
Rolls series, 392b
Romagna, 423a
Roman Catholic church. *See* Church
Roman de la Rose, 184a, 324a
autobiography in, 47a
influence of, 149b
Jean de Meun as author of, 47a, 153b
pagan images in, 453a
pornographic illustrations of, 491a, 492a
on poverty, 502a
See also Guillaume de Lorris; Jean de Meun
Roman de Renart, 556a
Roman de Rou. See Wace
Roman de Thèbes, 281b, 627a
Roman de Troie, 281b

Roman Empire, 408a
archaeology of, 25b, 26a, 27a, 30a
aristocracy of, 439b–440b
barbarian period of, 408a
Christian, 142a–b, 143a, 437b–438b
Christianization of, 407a
destruction of, 235b
espionage in, 182a
eunuchs in, 188b
Germanic emulation of, 457a
homosexuality and, 574b
ius gentium of, 417a
ius naturale and, 417b
kilns in, 449b
Late, 218a
marriage in, 363b–364b, 367a
missions in, 523a
natural law and, 417b
scholarly attention to, 437b–438b
schools in, 558b
social welfare programs in, 499a
Roman law, 82a–b, 417b, 427a
on abortion, 1a
Accursian gloss on, 4a–b
additions to, 426a
Bologna school of, 4a
calumny oaths and, 84a–b
commentaries on, 7a–b
criminal procedure and, 309a–310b
Decretum and, 246a, 247a
feudal law and, 320b, 324b–325a
just price and, 30ab
Justinian codified, 310a
on marriage, 552b
merchant contracts and, 400b
peacemaking and, 460a
Pierre de Belleperche on, 476b–477a
right to trial and, 317a
teachers of, 82a, 291b–292a
Romance literature, 16b–17b, 180b–181b, 184a–b, 383b, 389b–390b
alliterative literature and, 11a
animals in, 20a
epic, 180b–181b
See also Gothic literature
Romance of Barlaam and Josaphat, 358b
Romance of the Rose. See Roman de la Rose
Romanesque architecture, 34a
French, 153a, 154a, 154b *(illus.),* 155b, 155b *(illus.)*
Romano-Germanic Pontifical
on sacraments, 549b
Rome, 407a
archaeology of, 29b
biography and, 61a–b
chariot races in, 65a–b
Cola di Rienzo government of, 440b
commune in, 9a, 132b, 136a–b
contact with China and, 117a–118a
domestic architecture in, 31a, 33 *(illus.)*
Honorius III, pope, and, 274a
markets in, 131b

public baths and, 50a
relations with Florence of, 3a
Rienzo and, 136a–b
riots in, 66a
sack of (1527), 624a
schools in, 559a
senator of, 440a
Rome, Council of (1079), 614b
Romulea. See Dracontius, Blossius
    Aemilius
Roncaglia, Diet of (1158), 82a
Rosary
    Paternoster beads and, 242a
Rosenwein, Barbara, 538a
Rossetti, Dante Gabriel, 392b
Rota
    Roman, 368a–b
Rote Ritter, Der. See Muschg, Adolf
"Rotta è l'alta Colonna." *See* Petrarch
Rouen
    commune of, 135a
Rouen Cathedral, 376b–377a
Rougiers site (France)
    domestic architecture at, 35b–36a
Routiers, **541b–542a**
Rowley Poems. *See* Chatterton, Thomas
Royal Danish Society of Antiquities,
    393b
Royal Library, the, 654b
Rudolf I of Habsburg, Holy Roman
    Emperor, 423a, 424a, **542a–543a**
Rudolf II of Habsburg, Holy Roman
    Emperor, 542b
Rudolf IV of Hapsburg, Holy Roman
    Emperor, 247b
Rufus of Ephesus
    on sexuality, 577b
Rugs and carpets
    Ottoman, 447b–448b
Rui de Pina
    historiography by, 496a
Ruin, the, 192a
Ruiz, Juan
    Libro de buen amor, 47a, 338a, 504b
Rule of St. Francis. *See* Franciscan Rule
Rūmī
    repression of the body and, 68b
Rūmī motif, 447a, 448a
Ruodlieb, 181a
Rupen, Raymond, 604b
Rupert of Deutz, 57b–58a
    De Sancta Trinitate et operibus eius,
    57b–58a
Rural areas
    archaeology of, 26b
    depopulation of, 26b
    poverty in, 501a–502b
    schools in, 563b
Rus
    expansion of power by, 94a
    fur trade and, 402b
    people of, 147a

Rushd, Ibn (Averroes)
    Kulliyāt fī l-ṭibb, 381b
    on matter, 377b–378b, 379a
    soul and body and, 591b
    De substantia orbis, 378a
Ruskin, John, 389a
    "Nature of Gothic, The," 392b
    News from Nowhere, 392b
    Stones of Venice, The, 392b
Russia
    National Library of, 358b
    slaves from, 567b
    storytelling in, 83b–84a
Russian literature
    prose-poetry in, 587b–588a
Rusticello da Pisa, 119b
Rusticus, St., 224a
Rutebeuf, 47a, 556a

S

Saadiah Gaon (Saʿadya ibn Yūsuf al
    Fayyūmī), 60a
    Kitāb Faṣīḥ al-ʿibrāniyyīn, 260a
    Sefer ha-agron, 260a
Saba (Sheba), 543a
Sabatier, Paul, 393b
Sabians (Sabaeans), **543a–544b**
    of Ḥarrān, 543a–b
    Mandaeans, 543a, 544a
Ṣābiʾ ūn (Sabians), 543a, 544a
Sachsenspiegel. See Repgowe, Eike von
Sacraments and sacramental theology,
    544b–554a
    confirmation, 547b–548a
    Eucharist, 548a–549b
    marriage, 366b, 552b–553a
    orders, 551a–552b
    penance, 549b–550b
    semiotics and, 581b, 583b–584a
    signs and, 585a
    unction, 550b–551a
Sacred College
    cardinals of, 621a
    structure of, 621b
Sacred Void. See Parkin, David
Saepe contingit. See Clement V, pope
Safed (castle), 604a
Safety-valve model of misrule, 539a
Ṣāghānī, Abū Ḥāmid al-, 373b
Saiger smelting process, 348b
St. Apolostolen (cathedral: Cologne),
    230a
St. Augustine's Abbey, 217a
St. Barbara Church, 78a
Saint Bernard Pass, Great, 202b–203a
St. Catherine of Znojmo Chapel, 73b
St. Cécile (cathedral: Albi), 227b–228a
Ste. Chapelle (chapel: Paris), 223a, 227b
St. Damiano (church), Assisi, 158b
S. Damiano monastery, 126a–127a

St. Denis (abbey church: Paris), 146a,
    218a, 223b–225b, 225b *(illus.)*
    features of, 224a–b
    frontispiece of, 224a
    Gothic art and, 235b, 236b, 244a
    Gothic sculpture and, 237a–b
    nave of, 227b
    reconstruction of, 223b–224b
    retrochoir, 221 *(illus.),* 224a–b
    shrine of saints, 224b
    Suger and, 454b–455a
    symbolic construction in, 224a–b
    transept of, 227b
    upper choir of, 227b
St. Dorothy Church (Wrocław), 236b
St. Elisabeth (church: Marburg), 230b,
    231 *(illus.)*
St. Erkenwald, 12a
St. Étienne (church: Paris), 218b, 227b
St. Felicity (church: Rome), 41b
St. Florian, church of, 434a
St. Fortunato (church: Todi), 232a
St. Francesco (basilica: Assisi)
St. Gall (monastery: Switzerland), 146a,
    429a
    public baths and, 50b
St. George Convent, 73b
St. Germaine des Prés (abbey church:
    Paris), 225a, 225b
St. Germer de Fly (abbey church:
    France), 225b, 226a
St. Gothard pass, 402b
St. Jacques monastery (Paris), 58b
St. John's Christians. *See* Sabians
St. Just (church: Narbonne), 227b
St. Lazarus (church: Bethany), 597a
St. Lorenzo (church: Naples), 232a
Saint Louis (poem). *See* Le Moyne, Pierre
St. Louis University
    Vatican Library manuscripts in, 383b
St. Madeleine (church: Vézelay), 151b
    (illus.), 152a *(illus.)*
S. Marco (cathedral: Venice)
    mosaics in, 451 *(illus.)*
St. María del Mar (church: Barcelona),
    233a
S. Maria Maggiore, Basilica of, 424a
St. Maria Novella (church: Florence),
    231a, 232 *(illus.)*
St. Maria sopra Minerva (church: Rome),
    231b
St. Martin (church: Wharram Percy,
    England), 26b
St. Martin des Champs (abbey church:
    France), 224a, 225b
St. Mary (church: Athens, Parthenon),
    45a
St. Mary of the Latins monastery
    Hospitallers and, 276a
St. Michael's College, Toronto, 384b
St. Nazaire (church: Carcassone)
St. Nicaise of Rheims (abbey church:
    France), 227b

St. Nicholas (church: Carcere Tulliano), 423a
St. Nicholas Church (Amsterdam), 16a
St. Omer (commune: Flanders), 135b
St. Pablo (convent: Valladolid), 610b, 612a
St. Paolo fuori le Mura church, 240b–241a
St. Patrick's Purgatory, 262b
St. Peter Martyr (convent: Toledo), 610b
St. Peter's (abbey), 168a
St. Peter's Basilica
    Constantine's gifts to, 454a
St. Peter's Church (Leuven)
    Brotherhood of the Holy Sacrament altarpiece in, 455b–456a
St. Peter's Church (Rome), 410b
St. Peter's Yard (Novgorod), 402b
St. Pierre de Montmartre (church: France), 224a
St. Remi (abbey church: Rheims), 146a
St. Sabas, war of, 621a
St. Séverin (cathedral: Paris)
    choir of, 233b
St. Simeon Stylites (basilica), 597a
St. Stephen (monastery: Lake Hayq), 598b
St. Thomas (monastery: Ávila), 612b
St. Urbain (church: Troyes), 227b, 621b
St. Victor abbey (Paris), 58a
St. Vitus (cathedral: Prague), 635a
    as burial place of rulers, 73a
    construction of, 74b–75a
    described, 73a
    St. Wenceslas chapel in, 107a
St. Wenceslas Chapel
    decoration of, 75a
    redecoration of, 77a
St. Yved (church: Braine), 226b, 230a
Sainte-Palaye, Jean-Baptiste de La Curne de
    Mémoire sur L'ancienne chevalerie (Memoir of ancient chivalry), 391a
Saints
    canonization of, 525a
    commemorations of, 327b–329b, 331a–b
    cult of, 523b–525b
    images of Ottoman, 446b
    Jewish, 256a–258b
    Muslim, 253a–255b
    in popular religion, 523b–525b
    Portuguese literature on, 496b
    reinterpretation of pagan gods as, 450b–452a
Saladin, 604a
Salah al-din al-Safadi, 257a
Salian dynasty, 542b
Salian Franks, 613a
Salian (Salic) Law, 310a, 514a, 645b
Salimbene, 176a
Salimbeni of Siena
    banking and, 403a, 403b

Salisbury Cathedral (England), 228b
Sallust (Gaius Sallustius Crispus), 564a
Salter, Elizabeth, 13b
Saltpeter, in gunpowder, 198a
Salutati, Coluccio, 618a
Salvador, Mercedes, 192b
Salvatierra, castle at, 305b
Salvation
    poverty and, 505a–b, 506a
    soul and body and, 589b
Salvator noster. See Sixtus IV, pope
Samaw'al, al-, 372a
Samhain, Christianization of, 523a
Samuel ben Meir (grandson of Rashi). *See* Rashbam
Samuel ha-Nagid (Ismail ibn Nagrela), 260b
San Apollinare Nuovo (church: Ravenna)
    mosaics in, 153a
San Bernardino of Siena
    price formation and, 303a
San Cataldo (church), 6a
San Germano, Treaty of (1230), 270b–271a
Sancho VII (the Strong) of Navarre, king
    Battle of Las Navas de Tolosa and, 306a
Sancia of Mallorca, queen
    Poor Clares and, 488a, 488b
Sanctitatis nova signa. See Thomas of Celano
Sanglier, Henri de, 225a
Sanskrit language
    fables in, 303b–304a
Santa Chiara Dossal, 126b *(illus.),* 489b
Santa Cruz (convent: Segovia), 612a
Santiago de Compostela, 191a
    pilgrim souvenirs from, 478a
    Pilgrim's Guide, 226a
Santillana, Marqués de
    Proemio e carta al condestable de Portugal, 493a
Sapori, Armando, 401a
Sarābiyūn, Yūḥannā ibn, 380a
Saracens
    defeat at La Garde-Freinet, 401b
    race and, 515b
Sardinia, 171b
    Alfonso V and, 10b
    schools in, 560b
Sardis
    public baths in, 50a
Sarperia, Jacop d'Angelo da
    translations by, 92a
Sasanian dynasty
    Persians under, 466b
Sassoferrato, Bartolo de, 7a
Satan, 195a
    concepts of hell and, 263b
    demons and, 151a–b, 152a
    See also Devil; Witchcraft
Sátira de la infelice e felice vida. See Pedro de Portugal, Dom

Satire, **554a–557a**
    anti-clerical, 554b, 555b
    anti-curial, 555a, 555b
    anti-ecclesiastical, 554b, 555b
    antifeminist, 555a, 556a
    estates, 556a
    in medieval Occitan verse, 556a–b
    Menippean, 554b
    as social criticism, 555a–556a
    twelfth-century, 554b–555a
Satires. See Horace
Satisfactio ad regem Gunthamundum. See Dracontius, Blossius Aemilius
Sator arepo tenet opera rotas, 110b
Satyr plays, 554a, 554b
Savonarola, Girolamo, **557a–558b,** 558a *(illus.)*
Savonnières, Council of (859), 561b
Saxon dynasty, 265b, 408b, 441a–442a, 562a, 600b
Saxons of England, The. See Kemble, John Mitchell
Saxony
    abbeys of, 145b–146b
    castle-guard and, 95b
    dukes of, 138a–b, 542a
    Henry II of Germany and, 266a–b
Saxony wheel, 351a
Saz (reed) motif, 447a, 447b, 448b
Scandinavia
    archaeology of, 25b, 26a
    domestic architecture of, 32b, 33a, 33b
    towns in, 132b
Scandinavian literature
    satire in, 556b
Scatology, devil and, 155b–156a
Schering, Arnold, 396a
Schiller, Friedrich von
    Die Jungfrau von Orleans, 391b
    Wilhelm Tell, 391b
Schism, Great, 187b, 623a
    Alfonso V and, 10b
    end of, 128a, 610b
    John XXIII, antipope, and, 298b
    St. Catherine of Siena and, 96b
Schlegel, August, 393a
Schlegel, Friedrich, 393a
Schminck, Andreas, 426b
Schola cantorum, 559a, 560a
Scholasticism, 377b–378a
    humanism and, 281b
    at Louvain, 393b
Schongauer, Martin
    Temptation of St. Anthony, 23b *(illus.)*
Schools, **558b–565b**
    Carolingian (eighth-ninth centuries), 560a–561b
    fifth-seventh centuries, 559a–560a
    Jewish, 562b
    late medieval, 563b–564b
    late Roman, 558a–559a
    tenth-eleventh centuries, 561b–562b
    twelfth century, 562b–563b

Schorne, John
  cult of, 479a–b
Science, Islamic
  astrology and, 40a, 41a
  medicine and, 165a–b
  Sabians and, 543a, 543b
  translations of, 40a
Scolland, abbot, 217a
Scotland
  Battle of Bannockburn and, 48a–b
  occupation of, 634a
Scott, Sir Walter, 391b–392a,
    391 (illus.), 393a, 394b
  Ivanhoe, 392a
  Lady of the Lake, The, 391b, 392a
    (illus.)
  Lay of the Last Minstrel, The, 391b
  Minstrelsy of the Scottish Border, 391b
Scottish literature
  alliterative literature and, 12a
Scottus. See John Scottus Eriugena;
    Josephus Scottus; Sedulius Scottus
Scotus. See Duns Scotus, John
Scriba, Giovanni, 425a
Scribes
  Chariton, 362b
  Chrysostom Initialer, the, 359a
  Constantine, 360b
  Ephraem, 359b
  function of, 161a, 162a
  Galesiotes, George, 362a
  handwriting traits of, 359a
  Joasaph, 359b (illus.), 362b
  manuscript illumination and, 358a,
    359a–b, 360b, 362a
  Theodore Hagiopetritis, 360b
Scriptoria, 145a–146a, 161a
Sculpture
  Beautiful Madonna, 76b
  in Chartres Cathedral, 236a–b, 238b
  demons in, 151b (illus.), 152a (illus.),
    153a, 153a (illus.), 154b (illus.),
    155b (illus.)
  Gothic, 237a–241b, 237a–b, 239a–
    240a
  pagan, 453a
  pornographic, 492b
Seafarer, The, 192a
Seals and sigillography, 160b, 161b, 162a
  signs and, 585a
Sebokht, Severus, bishop, 371b
Second Merseburg Charm, 451a
Secondo Spagna. See Andrea da Barberino
Secret History (Anecdota). See Procopius of
  Caesarea
Secreta mulierum. See Albertus Magnus
Secretz de la nature or Merveilles du
  monde, 411a
Sedulius Scottus, 57a
  Carmen pascale, 180a
  De rectoribus christianis, 512b
  used in schools, 561a, 562a
Sefardi, Moisés. See Petrus Alfonsi

Sefer ha-agron. See Saadiah Gaon
Sefer Hasidim, 571a
Sefer Josippon, 256b, 257b
Selīmiye mosque, 444b–445a, 445
  (illus.), 447 (illus.), 448 (illus.)
Semiotics. See Signs, theory of
Semiramis, 209b
Senatusconsultum Velleianum
  women and, 425b
Seneca
  Ad Lucilium, 8a
  satire of, 554b
  used in schools, 562a
Senna knots, 448b
Sens Cathedral (France), 226b
  rebuilding of, 225a
  specifications of, 225a
Sentence literature
  commentaries, 473a
  as philosophical genre, 472b
Sentences. See Peter Lombard
Sententiae. See Bernard of Clairvaux, St.;
  Peter Lombard; Sentence literature
Sententiae in IV libris distinctae. See Peter
  Lombard
Sepharad. See Iberian Peninsula
Septizonium palace scandal, 440a
Septuagint. See Bible, Septuagint
Serapion of Novgorod, bishop
  St. Joseph of Volokolamsk, and, 299b
Serfs and serfdom
  manorialism and, 344a
Sermons
  atheism and, 43a, 43b
  satire in, 556a, 556b
  of Savonarola, 557b, 558a
Servants, 565b–569a
  contract labor and, 566b–567b
  division of labor and, 566a–b
  domestic, 566a, 568a
  gender and, 566a–b
  prostitution and, 576a
  as sexual objects, 573a–b
  sexuality of, 575b
  slavery and, 566b–567b
Sette armi spirituali, Le. See Catherine of
  Bologna, St.
Seven Deadly Sins
  Perault on, 463a–464a
Seventh Seal, The. See Bergman, Ingmar
Sevet Yehuday. See Solomon ibn Verga
Seville
  fall of, 196b
Seville Cathedral, 233b
Sextus Amarcius
  satire of, 554b
Sexuality, 188a–189b, 569a–577a
  in autobiography, 46b
  Catharism on, 552b–553a
  chastity and, 569a–571a
  consummation of marriage and, 364b,
    366a–367a
  the Fall and, 194b, 195b–196a

  language of love and, 338a
  lesbian, 575b–576a
  male-male, 573b–575a
  in marriage, 571a–572b
  marriage debt and, 570b, 572a, 572b
  men's extramarital, 572b–573b
  pollution and taboo and, 484a
  pornography and, 490a–493a, 492b–
    493a
  public baths and, 50a, 50b
  rape and, 519a–520b
  repression of the body and, 68b–69a
  satire and, 555a
  servants and, 568a
  soul and body and, 590a, 590b
  women's extramarital, 575a–576b
  See also Abortion
Sexuality, medical, 577a–580b
  lovesickness and, 580a–b
  pathologies and, 579b–580b
  psychology and, 580a–b
  sources for, 577b–578a
  theories on, 578a–579b
Seyon, Fessēha. See Takla Haymanot, St.
Sfar Malwasha, 544a
Sfax, 641b
Shaddād of Aleppo, Ibn-, 543b
Shāfiʿī, Muḥammad ibn Idrīs al-, 188b
Shāhnāma. See Abū 'l Qāsim Firdawsī
Shaizar, 174b
Shakespeare, William
  life stages and, 430b
  Percy and, 465a
Shalshelet ha-Qabbala. See Yahya,
  Gedaliah ibn
Shams al-Dīn al-Khalīlī, 373b
Sharaf al-Dīn al-Tūsī, 372b
Sharḥ tashrīḥ al Qānūn. See Sīnā, Ibn
  (Avicenna)
Shaykh al-Mufīd, al-
  Kitāb al-Mazār, 255b
She-Wolf of France. See Isabel of France
Shīʿa
  Islamic hagiography and, 253b
Shifāʾ. See Sīnā, Ibn (Avicenna)
Ships and shipbuilding
  Amsterdam and, 16a
  Cinque Ports and, 123a
  revolution in, 348b–349a
Shor, Joseph Bekhor, 60b
Shore, Bradd
  Culture in Mind, 532a
Sicilian Vespers, War of (1282), 6b
Sicily, 170b, 423b
  Alexander IV and, 9a
  conquer of, 621a
  feudal law and, 322b
  Henry VI of Germany and, 268a
  Hohenstaufen Dynasty and, 139a–
    140b
  invasion of, 641b
  latifundia in, 306b–307a
  merchants in, 2b

Muslims, attacks on, 641b
term admiral in, 5b–6a
Siculo, Lucio Marineo, 191a
Sidonius Apollinaris, 370b
Sieciech, 79b
Siege of Jerusalem, The, 14a, 15a
Siege warfare, 198a, 198b, 215a–b, 274b
Siegfried III of Mainz, archbishop, 139b
Siena
commune in, 134b
Ghibellines of, 342b
Siete partidas, 322b, 419b
Siger of Courtrai
on signs, 582b
Sigibert I of Austrasia, king, 203a–b
assassination of (575), 203b
Sigillography. *See* Signs, theory of
Sigillum Sanctae Mariae. See
Augustodunensis, Honorius
Sigismund of Luxembourg, 434a
Signori, 193b
Florentine, 133b, 137a
Signoria, 125a
Signs, theory of, **581a–587a**
in astrology, 584a
Augustinian, 581a–582a
in documentary validation, 584b–585a
linguistic, 582a–583b
in medicine, 584a–b
sacrum signum and, 583b–584a
Silk
industrial revolution and, 353b–354a
manufacture of, 349b, 353b–354a,
608a–b
trade with China and, 118a
water power and, 349b
Silos Beatus Apocalypse, 264a
Silsilnâme (Genealogy), 446b
Silver mining, 348a–b
Simon Chèvre d'Or
Ylias, 180a
Simon Magus, 610a
Simon de Montfort, 458a
capture of James I of Aragon by, 292b
Simony
clerical, 422a, 422b, 423b
orders and, 551b–552a
sacraments and, 548b
St. Stanisław and, 594b
satire of, 555b
Simson, Otto von, 222a
Sin
categories of, 629a
causes of, 628b
deadly, 629a, 631b
definition of, 628b
peacemaking and, 461b–462a
Perault on, 463a–464a
pollution and taboo and, 484a–485a
venial, 631b
See also Original sin
Sīnā, Ibn (Avicenna)
abortion and, 1b
Canon of Medicine (Qānūn fīl-ṭibb),
284a, 380b, 474b, 578a, 584a, 584b
Cantica, 584a
disease and, 165a
on homosexuality, 580a
on matter, 377b, 379a
medicine and, 380b–381b
on sexuality, 578a
Sharḥ tashrīḥ al Qānūn, 381a
Shifā', 378a
on signs in medicine, 584a–b
Sinān, 443b–445a, 448 (*illus.*)
Sinhind (mathematical text), 371a
Sir Gawain and the Green Knight, 38b,
390a
alliterative literature and, 12a, 13b,
14a, 15a
Sir Tristrem, 38b
Sīra, 253b
Sīrat al-awliyāʾ fi-al-qarn al-sābiʿ al-Hijrī.
See Ḥusayn ibn Jamāl al-Dīn
al-Khazrajī, al-
Sīrat ʿAntar, 22a–23a
Sīrat Banū Hilāl. See Hilāl, Banū
Sirventes, 458a
Sisam, Kenneth, 192b
Sisebut, Visigothic king, 457a
Sixtus IV, pope, 440b, 612b, 623a–b
Colonna family and, 128b
on Jewish rights, 319a
Salvator noster, 550b
Sixtus VI, pope
Immaculate Conception and, 290a
indulgences and, 528b
Skeltana Riucht, 205b
Skripou, Battle of (1311), 44b
Slavery and slave trade, 188a–189b,
401b, 419a
capital punishment and, 85b
Henry the Navigator of Portugal and,
270a
latifundia and, 306b
medievalism and, 387b
orphans as, 116b
race and, 517a
revival of, 566b–567b, 568a
sexuality and, 573a
Slavic folklore
animals in, 18a
Slavic languages
archaeology and, 28b
Slavs
archaeology of, 25b, 27a
Henry I of Germany and, 265b–266a
Sloane, Hans
manuscript collection of, 356a
Sluter, Claus, 238a
Philip the Bold mausoleum by, 534b,
535 (*illus.*)
Smith, John, 394a
Smyrna
Hospitallers and, 277a
Smyrna Physiologus, 360b
Social structure
architecture and, 30b
Arthurian romances and, 37b
charity and, 503b–504a
codes of etiquette and, 184a, 185b–
186a
peacemaking and, 460a–461a, 461b,
462a
pirates in, 482a
pornography and, 491a
Socialist League, 392b
Society for Creative Anachronism, 397a
Society for Medieval Feminist
Scholarship, 387a
Society of Antiquaries, 390a
Sodomy, 571b, 573b–574a
prostitution and, 576a
Soissons, kingdom of, 203a
Soisy, priory of, 176a
Sokhasteri Monastery, 361a
Sol Invictus, 142a
Solinus, Gaius Julius
Polihistor, 118a
Solomon, Temple of. *See* Aqṣā, al-
(mosque: Jerusalem)
Solomon ben Isaac. *See* Rashi
Solomon ben Judah ibn Gabirol, 260b,
377b–378a
Solomon ibn Verga
Sevet Yehuday, 2567a
Somatization, 592b
Somer Sonday, 14b
Somme le roi. See Lorens d'Orléans
Somnium. See Johannes de Lignano
Song of Igor's Campaign (Slovo o polku
Igoreve), **587b–588a**
Song of Roland. See Roland, Song of
Song of Solomon, 337a
Song of Songs, 57b–58a
Songe du vergier
Charles V and, 459a
Sophismata, 405a–406a, 473b
See also Kilvington, Richard
Soranus
abortion and, 1b
on sexuality, 577b, 578b
Sorsky, Nil, 299b
Soto, Domingo de
on the poor, 506b
Soto, Dominic, 437a
Soubirous, Marie-Bernarde
Lourdes and, 393b
Soul and body, **588a–594a,** 589 (*illus.*),
590a (*illus.*), 591 (*illus.*)
Bible on, 589a–b
Church Fathers on, 589b–590b
in Greek philosophy, 588b–589a
in literature and praxis, 592b–593a
medieval theories of, 590b–592a
See also Body, the; Ghosts
Soule, 190a
Soul's Address to the Body, The, 13b
South Asia, medical theories from, 577b

South English Legendary
  "Life of St. Kenelm," 11a, 11b
Southey, Robert, 392a
Southwell (cathedral: England), 219a
Spain, 413a–416b
  castle-guard and, 95b
  domestic architecture in, 30b, 31a, 32a
  feudal law in, 322b
  Jewish intellectual life in, 60a
  medical practice in, 381a–b
  medical writers in, 578a
  Nasrid kingdom of Granada and, 381b
  prostitution in, 576a
  resistance to Christianity, 144a
  schools in, 558b, 559b, 560b, 561a,
    562b, 563b, 564a
Spanish adoptionism, 420b
Spanish Inquisition, 414a, 414b, 611b–
  612b
  function of, 612b
  motives of, 612b
Spanish literature
  autobiography in, 47a, 47b
  Cantar de Mío Cid, 179a, 180b
  satire in, 554a
*Specimens of Early English Metrical
  Romances. See* Ellis, George
Speculum (journal), 384a, 387b
Speculum al foderi, 493a
Speculum divinorum. See Henry Bate of
  Malines
Speculum iudiciale. See Durand,
  Guillaume
Speculum naturale. See Vincent of
  Beauvais
Speculum stultorum. See Nigel (Whiteacre,
  Wireker) of Longchamp
Spedale del Bigallo, 105a
Spenser, Edmund
  Arthurian romances and, 36b
  Faerie Queene, The, 181b, 390a, 632a
  influences on, 150a
  poetry of, 211a
Sphere and Cylinder. See Archimedes
Spiesz, Hans, 77a
Spinning, 349a–351a
  spindle whorl, 350a–b
  wheels, 350b–351a
Spirits. *See* Ghosts
Sprenger, James
  Malleus maleficarum, 2a
Spying. *See* espionage
Stabat mater dolorosa. See Jacopone da
  Todi
Staël, Germaine de
  De l'Allemagne (Germany), 393a
Stained glass. *See* Glass, stained
Stanisław, St., **594a–595a**
  relics of, 305a
Stanley, Eric, 205b
Stans puer ad mensam, 185a
Staraya Logoda (Russia), 27a

Statius
  Thebaid, 179b, 272b
  used in schools, 560a, 561a, 562a,
    563a
Status
  of queens, 511b
  race and, 515b–516a
  ritual and, 539b
Statutes of the Polish Kingdom. See Łaski,
  Jan
Stavronikita Monastery, 359b
Steinberg, Leo
  on Christ's genitals images, 493a
Stephanites and Ischnelates. See Symeon
  Seth
Stephen V of Hungary, king, 147a
Stephen IX (or X), pope, 422a
Stephen of Blois. *See* Stephen of England,
  king
Stephen of Bourbon, 525a
Stephen of England, king, 187a–b, 376b,
  595a–596b
Stephen of Perche, 642a
Stephen of Tournai, 311b–312a
  judicial process and, 318b
Sticca, Sandro
  on *planctus Mariae,* 483b
Stigmata
  of St. Catherine of Siena, 96a, 97a
    (illus.)
  of St. Francis, 70a
  soul and body and, 592b
  women and, 69b
Stimmen der Völker. See Herder, Johann
  Gottfried von
Stirling Bridge, Battle of (1297), 634a
Stoicism
  semiotics in, 581a
  soul and body and, 590a
Stones of Venice, The. See Ruskin, John
Storia del re Ansuigi, La. See Andrea da
  Barberino
Storia di Aiolfo del Barbicone, La. See
  Andrea da Barberino
Storia di Ugone d'Avernia, La. See Andrea
  da Barberino
Storie di Rinaldo da Montalbano. See
  Andrea da Barberino
Storie Nerbonesi. See Andrea da Barberino
Stories and storytelling
  in poetic form, 83b–84a
  in Russia, 83b–84a
Stoss, Veit, 305b
Stoudiou Monastery, 360b
Strabo, 190a
Strabo, Walafrid
  on St. Gall, 480a
Strasbourg Cathedral, 230a–b
Stromateis. See Clement of Alexandria
Strutt, Joseph
  *Dress and Habits of the People of
    England,* 390 *(illus.),* 391b

Stubbs, William
  Constitutional History of England, 392b
Studi medievali (journal), 384a
Studies in Medievalism (journal), 389b
Stuttgart Psalter, 153a
Styria, duchy of, 542b
Succession, political. *See* Kingship;
  Queens and queenship
Succubi, 152b
  See also Demons
Suetonius
  Life of Augustus, 63a
  Nero, 61b
  De viris illustribus, 61a
Suffolk, duke of, 6a
Sufism
  repression of the body and, 68b
  saints and, 254a
Suger of St. Denis, 222a, 223b–225a
  art patronage by, 454b–455a
  autobiography by, 45b
  Gothic art and, 236a, 244a
  Vita Ludovici Grossi, 63a
Sulamī, al-, 254b
Süleyman I (the Magnificent), Ottoman
  sultan
  mosque complex of, 443b–444b, 444
    (illus.), 447b
  painting under, 446a
  Topkapi palace and, 445a–b
Sullivan, Arthur, 393a
Sulphur
  in gunpowder, 198a
Sulpicius Severus, 370b
"Summa Abel." *See* Peter the Chanter
Summa artis notariae. See Rolandinus de
  Passageris
Summa aurea. See William of Drogheda
Summa brevis. See Ricardus Anglicus
Summa casinensis, 295b
Summa de ecclesia. See Torquemada, Juan
  de
Summa de quaestionibus Armenorum. See
  Fitzralph, Richard
Summa de vitiis et virtutibus. See Perault,
  William
Summa decretalium. See Bernard of Pavia
Summa musice, 417a
Summa sententiarum
  on sacraments, 545a, 546b, 548a,
    551a, 552b, 553a
Summa super titulis decretalium. See
  Bernard of Parma
Summa theologica. See Aquinas, Thomas
Summa virtutum ac vitiorum. See Perault,
  William
Summae
  of Accursius, 4a
  philosophical, 473a
Summae confessorum
  on sexuality, 493a
Summarium biblicum. See Alexander de
  Villa Dei

Summulae de Dialectica. See Buridan, Jean
Sung dynasty (China)
  conquest of, 118b
  invention of printing during, 117a
Sunni Muslims
  Islamic hagiography and, 253b
Super specula. See Honorius III, pope
Superstition
  humanism and, 280b
Sūr-nāme (Book of descriptions), 446b
Surgeons
  physicians compared with, 475a, 476a
  women as, 476b
Surgery, 475a, 475 *(illus.)*
  Muslim writings on, 381a–b
Süsskind von Trimberg, **596a–b**
Süsskint der Jude von Trimpburg. *See*
  Süsskind von Trimberg
Sutton, Thomas, 378b
Sutton Hoo, 27b
Sweden
  missionaries in, 21b–22a, 146a
Swedes
  conversion of, 21b–22a
Swineshead, Richard, 406a, 406b
  Calculations, 378b–379a
  Liber calculationum, 405a–b
  obligationes literature of, 474a
  on semantics, 473b
Swineshead, Roger
  obligationes literature of, 474a
  on semantics, 473b
Switzerland
  communes in, 137a
Syllogisms, probability and, 509a
Sylvester II, pope, 562a
  See also Gerbert of Aurillac
Symbolism
  astrological, 41a–42b
Symeon Seth
  Stephanites and Ischnelates, 303a
Synaxarion, 327a
Syncategorematics, 473b
Synesius of Cyrene, bishop
  on Hypatia, 286b
Syria, 174a–b
  conquering of, 215a
  Muslims in, 416a
  Sabians of, 543a–b
Syriac language, 371b
  medical encyclopedia in, 380a
Syrian Christian architecture, **596b–598a**
  basilicas, late, elements of, 597a
  churches, builders and restorers of,
    596b
  decline of, 598a
  masonry of, 597b
  study of, 596b

T

Ṭabaqāt al-aṭibbā'. See Juljul, ibn

Tabarī, ʿAlī ibn Sahl Rabbān al-
  Firdaws al-Ḥikmah, 380a
"Table of God," 239b–240a
Table settings
  Gothic art and, 244a
Tableaux vivants, 534b
Tabernacle of the Holy Corporal. See Vieri,
  Ugolino di
Taboo. *See* Pollution and taboo
Taborites
  on utraquism, 622b
Tacitus, Cornelius, 146a
  Germania, 129a, 390a
Tacuinum sanitatis. See Buṭlān, Ibn
Taddeo di Bartolo, 264b
Tadhkirat al-awliyā'. See Farīd al-Dīn
  al-ʿAṭṭār
Tafel van den Kersten Ghelove. See Dirc
  van Delft
Taghrībat Banī Hilāl, 271a
Tagliacozzo, Battle of (1268), 140a, 247b
Táin bó Cúailnge (Cattle raid of Cooley),
  180a
Takla Haymanot, St., **598a–599a**
Tales of the Prophets, 446b
Talmud, 562b
  Babylonian, 214b
  commentaries on, 60a–b
  on marital sex, 572b
  on marriage, 648b
Tancred of Antioch, 174b
Tancred of Bologna, 52b
Tancred of Lecce, 642a
  as fleet commander, 643a
  Henry VI of Germany and, 268a
  power, seizure of, 643a
Tang dynasty (China)
  Constantinople and, 118a
Tannenberg/Grunwald, Battle of (1410),
  434a, **599a–599b**
Tannhäuser. See Wagner, Richard
Tanning industry
  women in, 566b
Tapestry
  Gothic art and, 244a
Taprobane people, 411a
Taqīya, Islamic, 415a
Tara
  St. Patrick at, 142b–143a
Tardieu, Michel, 543b
Tariffs
  communal liberties and, 133b
Tarragona, 187a
Tarsus, 215a
Tartar
  slaves from, 567b
Tartus (castle), 604a
Tasso, Torquato, 17b, 390a
  Arthurian romances and, 36b
  Gerusalemme liberata, 181b
Tatars
  Russian victory over, 587b
Tavola ritonda, 17b

Ṭawāshī, 188b
Taxation, **599b–603b**
  communal liberties and, 133a, 135b
  definition of, 599b–600a
  in Florence, 3a
  in Germany, 600a–601a
  in Iberia, 602a–603a
  in Italy, 601a–601b, 601a–b
  manorialism and, 344b
Technology
  archaeology of, 26a, 28b
  crankshafts, 346b–347a
Tell Bashir, 174a, 175a
Tempier, Étienne, bishop of Paris
  royal inquisition and, 71b
Templars, 424a, **603a–605a,** 603b, 626b
  at Acre, 604a–b
  arrest of, 604b
  Cyprus, retreat to, 604b
  downfall of, 604b
  executions of, 604a
  financial competency of, 604a
  guidelines of, 604a
  orders against, 604b
  popularity of, 603b
  structure of, 604a
  trials against, 604b
  See also Teutonic Knights
Temptation of St. Anthony. See
  Schongauer, Martin
Temptations
  of Jesus, 154a, 154b, 154b *(illus.)*
  of St. Anthony, 151b, 156b–157a
  of St. Benedict, 151b–152a
  of St. Dunstan, 168a
Temur Oljeitu (Chenzong), 119a
Ten Commandments. *See* Bible
Tenant labor
  latifundia and, 306b
Tennyson, Alfred Lord
  Arthurian romances and, 36b
  Idylls of the King, 392a
Tentation de Saint Antoine, La. See
  Flaubert, Gustave
Tenure of land
  communal liberties and, 133a
Terah, Ugo, 400b
Terence, 651b
  used in schools, 562a, 564a
Teresa of Ávila
  autobiography of, 47b
Tertullian, **605a–606a**
  Apology, 605b
  Gnosis, views on, 214a
  influence of, 605b
  On the Witness of the Soul, 605a
  on original sin, 435b
  on soul and body, 590a
  treatises of, 605a
  writings, topics of, 605b
Tertullianists, 605b
Teseida. See Boccaccio
Tetrabiblos. See Ptolemy, Claudius

Teutonic Knights, 434a, **606a–607a,**
    626b
  accusations toward, 606b
  conquests of, 606b
  culture of, 606a
  headquarters of, 606b
  Hermann of Salza and, 270a–b
  Order State of, 599a
  origins of, 606a
  power and autonomy of, 606b
  in Prussia, 94a
  reduction of power and influence,
    599b
  relationships of, 599a
  role of, 606a–b
  secularization of, 607a
  structure of, 606a–b
  See also Cumans/Kipchaks; Hermann
    of Salza; Tannennberg/Grunwald,
    Battle of; Templars; Urban IV, pope
Teutonic Mythology. See Grimm, Jacob
Teutsch Kalender, 492b
Textile industry, 133b, 135b, 136b
  Antwerp and, 24b
  Ottoman, 447b–448b
  silk, 398b, 402a, 403a
  wool, 399a, 401b, 402b, 403a, 403b,
    404a
Textiles
  astrological symbols on, 42a
  industrial revolution in, 349a–353b
  production of, 646b
Textiles, Byzantine, **607a–609a**
  Fourth Crusade, effects from, 609a
  functions of, 607a
  as gifts, 608a–b
  industry, origins of, 607b
  manufacture, process of, 608a
  raw materials for, 607b
  as status symbols, 608b
  subject matter of, 608a
  Woman Playing a Kithara, 607b *(illus.)*
Thābit ibn Qurra, 371b, 372a–b, 543b
Thebaid. See Statius
Theobald of Canterbury, archbishop,
    187a–b
  King Stephen and, 595b
Theodebert II, Frankish king, 81b
Theodofrid, abbot, 145a
Theodora I, Byzantine empress, 182a
  Procopius on, 492a
Theodore, bishop, 56b, 619b
Theodore bar Konai, 55b
Theodore Hagiopetritis (scribe), 360b
Theodore of Canterbury, St., 560a
Theodore of Mopsuestia, 55b
Theodoric, Master
  panel paintings by, 75a
Theodoric II of Burgundy, 81b
Theodoric of Freiberg
  De iride, 375a *(sidebar)*
Theodoric the Ostrogoth
  Boethius and, 457a

Theodorus Priscianus, 1b
Theodosian Code. *See Codex Theodosianus*
Theodosius I (the Great), western Roman
    emperor, 142a, 620a
Theodotus, 213b
Theodulf of Orléans, 554b
  Charlemagne and, 457a
  schools and, 560b
Theophylact of Ochrid, archbiship, 55a
Theophylactus Simocatta
  accurate description of China by, 118a
Thessaloniki, 44b, 149a
  capture of, 643a
  Ottoman conquest of, 362b
Thet Freske Riim, 206a
Thibaut of Champagne, count, 47a
Thierry, Augustin, 393a
Thierry of Chartres, 377b, 428a
Thirty-Nine, the, 135b
Thomas, Alvarus, 406b
Thomas Agni of Lentini
  on St. Dominic, 62b
Thomas de Bretagne
  Tristan, 38b
Thomas de Courcelles, 64a
Thomas of Canterbury,
  Bertrand du Guesclin and, 248a
Thomas of Cantimpré
  animals and, 18b
  De natura rerum, 410a, 411b
  on obstetrical care, 109b
Thomas of Celano
  biographer of St. Francis, 158b
  Vita prima, 176b
Thomas of Erfurt
  on signs, 582b
Thomas of Savoy
  humiliation ritual and, 536 *(illus.)*
Thompson, Edward P.
  on civic ritual, 533b, 539a
Thomson, S. Harrison, 385b–386a
Thor (god), 620b
Thorkelin, Grimur, 391a
Thorne, S. E., 638a
Thousand and One Nights, 371b
  in Petrus Alfonsi, 471b
  as pornography, 492a
Thrasamund (Vandal ruler), 167a
Three Dead Kings, The, 14b
Thuringia
  landgrave of, 177b
Tibbonid family
  Hebrew translations and, 261a
Tieck, Ludwig, 393a
Tiffany, Louis Comfort, 394b
Timaeus. See Plato
Time, concept of
  astrology and, 42a
  poverty and, 502b–503a
Titone, Virgilio, 538b
Todot Yeshu, 258a
Toledo (cathedral: Spain), 233a

Tolkien, J. R. R.
  Lord of the Rings, The, 396b, 396
    (illus.)
Tolls, **609a–b**
  definition of, 609a
  implementation of, 609a–b
  influences upon, 609b
  subcontracting of, 609b
Tolomei of Siena
  banking and, 403a
Tombs
  Gothic art and, 239a
Tonsure, **609b–610b**
  British church and, 610a
  description of, 609b–610a
  process of, 610a–b
  purpose of, 610a
  types of, 610a
Topkapi palace, 445a–b
  Circumcision Room in, 447a–b
Topkapi Sarāy Library, Istanbul, 360b
Torah, 562b
  hagiographical traditions and, 258a
Torcello
  basilica of, 264a
Torquemada, Juan de, **610b–611b**
  influences of, 611a–b
  *Meditations seu Contemplationes
    Devotissimae,* 611a *(illus.)*
  Summa de ecclesia, 610b
  *Tractatus contra Madianitas et
    Ismaelitas,* 611b
  See also Eugenius IV, pope; Race
Torquemada, Tomás de, **611b–613a**
  as inquisitor general, 612b
  See also Race
Tortosa, 187a
Torture
  criminal procedure and, 309b, 315a
Tosafists
  poetry of, 258a
Toulouse
  commune of, 135a
Tournai, **613a–614a**
  architecture of, 613a
  attributes of, 613a
  decline of, 613b
  goods produced, 613b
  industry of, 613a
  location of, 613a
  prosperity of, 613a
Tournament
  horsemanship and, 274b–275a
Tours
  archaeology in, 28b
Tower of London, 634a
Tower of the Winds (Athens), 41b
Town councils, 135a–b
Tractates, philosophical, 473a
*Tractatus contra Madianitas et Ismaelitas.
  See* Torquemada, Juan de
Tractatus de algorismo. See John of
  Sacrobosco

Tractatus de computo. See John of
Sacrobosco
Tractatus primus (First treatise). See
Burley, Walter
Tracts for the Times. See Newman, John
Cardinal
Tractus criminum, 311a
Trade
Amsterdam and, 16a
Antwerp and, 24b
archaeology of, 27a–28a, 28a, 28b, 29a
in Athens, 45a
in Barcelona, 133b
between China and Byzantium, 118a
commercialization and, 129a
Florentine merchants and, 2b–3a
growth of international, 130b
in Lübeck, 133b
in luxury goods, 401b, 402a, 402b
maritime, 27a, 401a
Mediterranean region and, 399a–404a
Mongolian invasion of Europe and,
118b
North Sea-Baltic Zone and, 399a–404a
organization of, 131a–b
piracy and, 481a–b, 482b
in Venice, 133b
See also Merchants
Traditio (journal), 384a
Tradition
civic ritual and, 532b–539a
descent of, 438a
preservation of, 437a–438a
Traducianism, 435b
Trans tombs
resurrection and, 70b
Transhumance, horizontal (nomadism),
170b
Translatio studii, 457a
Transubstantiation, 420b, 548b–549a,
614a–615b
belief in, 614a
controversy toward, 614a–615b
described, 70a–b
theory of, 614a–b
veneration of the host and, 525b–527a
views on, 615a
See also Eucharist
Transversal Figure. See Tūsī, Naṣīr
al-Dīn al-
Transylvania
Teutonic Order and, 270b
Transylvanian Alps, 606b
Trastámara, House of, 95b
Trattatello in laude di Dante. See
Boccaccio
Travel literature
animals in, 20a
of China, 119b–120a
Travels. See Mandeville, Sir John
Tre Fontane, Cistercian monastery, 187a,
429b
Treachery. *See* Violence

Treason
criminal procedure and, 316b
Treaty on Natural History. See Isidore of
Seville
Třebíč monastery basilica, 73b
Trebon Altarpiece, 76a *(illus.)*
Tree of Life. See Bonaguida, Pacino di
Trent
hydraulic bellows at, 347a
Trent, Council of (1545–1563), 367b,
434b, 437a, 615a–b
on probability, 509b
on sacraments, 546a, 548a, 549a,
550b, 551a, 552b, 553a
Tres matres, 451a
Très riches heures
astrology in, 42b
Trevet, Nicholas, 59a
Trevisa, John, 49b
Trexler, Richard
on civic ritual, 533b, 538a
Public Life in Renaissance Florence,
532b
Trier, archbishopric
Holy Roman Empire and, 542a
Trigonometry. *See* Mathematics, Islamic
Trinitarian doctrine, 620a
Trinitarians, **615b–616b**
activities at present, 616b
atheism and, 44a
collection of assets, 616a–b
locations of, 616a
Mercedarians and, 398a
origins of, 616a
Trinity
numerology and, 427b, 428a
soul and body and, 590a, 591 *(illus.)*
Triodion, 328b
Tripoli, 201b, 641b
Hospitallers and, 277a
Tristan. See Gottfried von Strassburg;
Thomas de Bretagne
Tristan, legend of, 39a
Tristan and Isolde, 383b
Tristan cycle, 495a
Tristan und Isolde. See Wagner, Richard
Trobairitz, 337b–338a
Troilus and Criseyde. See Chaucer,
Geoffrey
Trondheim, 28b
Tropology
biblical commentaries and, 54b
Trota
De curis mulierum, 111a, 252a
gynecological knowledge and, 252b
De passionibus mulierum, 493a
Trotula treatises and, 1b, 2a, 249a,
251a, 253a, 579b, 651b
Trotula treatises. *See* Trota
Troubadours
vs. juglars, 300a
language of love and, 337a–338a
poetry of, 47a, 150b, 492a

Trovadores, 150b
Troyes
commune of, 135a
Troyes, Treaty of (1420)
Henry V marriage in, 514a
Troyes Cathedral
upper choir of, 227b
Truce of God movement, 625a
Tudor dynasty, 389b
Tumulto, il. See Ciompi, revolt of the
Tundale's Vision, 262b, 264b
Tunisia
astrology in, 41b
Muslims in, 416a
Tūr ʿAbdīn
churches and monasteries of, 597b
Turgot, bishop of St. Andrews, 63a
Turkey, 174a, 175a
Turkish literature
Dede Korkut, 180b
Turks
Athens and, 45a
Turner, Sharon
History of the Anglo-Saxons, 391b
Turner, Victor
The Forest of Symbols, 532a
Turville-Petre, Thorlac, 14a
Tusculum, 422b
Tūsī, Naṣīr al-Dīn al-
Transversal Figure, 375a
Twain, Mark
*Connecticut Yankee in King Arthur's
Court, A,* 394b
Life on the Mississippi, 394b
Twenty-Four Statutes, 205b
Typikon, 328b
Tyrants and tyrannicide, **616b–619b**
conditions acceptable for tyrannicide,
618a
defense of, 616b–617a
in other areas, 618b–619a
safeguards against, 619a
situations of, 619a
subjects' rights against, 617b
view of, 617a–b
Tyre, 132b
Venetians and, 148a
Tyrolean King, The, 459a
Tyrwhitt, Thomas, 391a

U

Ulfila, 142a–b, **619b–620a**
Bible, translation of, 619b, 620a
Gothic alphabet, invention of, 619b
Ulixbone, 326a
Ulpian
natural law and, 417b, 418a
Ulugh-Beg of Samarkand, sultan, 375b
ʿUmar I ibn al-Khaṭṭāb, Umayyad caliph
on dhimmīs, 158a–b
ʿUmar Khayyām, 372b

Umayyad Mosque (Damascus), 373b
Unction, 545a, 550b–551a
Undset, Sigrid
    Kristin Lavransdatter, 395b
Unicorn Tapestries, 235b
Unigenitus Dei filius. See Clement VI,
    pope
Universals
    signs and, 582a, 585b
Universities
    biblical studies in, 58b–59a
    of Cologne, 163b
    emergence of, 58a
    of Erfurt, 163b
    humanism and, 280a
    in Portugal, 327a
University Library, Moscow, 358b
University of Aarhus (Denmark), 26a
University of Louvain
    chair of Scholasticism at, 393b
University of Toronto
    medieval studies at, 383a, 384b
Uppsala, **620a–621a**
    location of, 620a
    pagan cult at, 620b
    religious festival at, 620b
    temple at, 620b
Urbain le courtois, 185a
Urban II, pope
    First Crusade, 626b, 640b
Urban IV, pope, 423a, 440a, **621a–621b**
    Charles of Anjou and, 140a
    on Corpus Christi, 526b
    Poor Clares and, 485b, 488a
Urban VI, pope
    Great Schism and, 96b
    Immaculate Conception and, 290a
Urbanism, 132b–133a
    archaeology and, 26a, 27a, 28a–b, 29a,
        30a
    civic rituals and, 538a–b
    communal liberties and, 133a
    communes and, 132b–137b
    merchants and, 398b, 399a, 402a–b
    Ottoman, 442b–443a
    peacemaking and, 462a
    poverty and, 502b–503b
    schools and, 563b
    vendettas in, 8b
Urbanus magnus, 184b
Urbino, dukes of, 624a
Urraca of Castile, queen, 513b, 645b
Usaybiʿa, Ibn Abī
    *Kitāb ʿuyūn al-anbāʾ fī tabaqāt
        al-atibbāʾ,* 381a
Usury, 400a
Uterine suffocation, 251a, 251b *(illus.)*
ʿUthmān, Ibn
    Murshid al-zuwwār ilā al-abrār, 255b
    Murshid al-zuwwār ilā qubūr al-abrār,
        255b
Utopia. See More, Sir Thomas

Utraquism, 549a, **621b–623a**
    basis of, 621b
    Catholic authority over, 622b
    controversy of, 621b–622a
    interpretation of, 622a
Utrect
    town council of, 135a

V

Vacarius, 638b
Vaison, Council of (529), 559a
Valdès, Peter
    popular religion and, 528b
    poverty and, 505a, 505b
Valencia
    Alfonso V and, 10b
    conquest of, by James I of Aragon,
        292b–293a
    Germanias in, 413b
    Moriscos in, 413b–414a
Valentinus, 213b–215a
Valor Ecclesiasticus, 103b
Vandals, 166b–167a, 625a
Váradi, Péter
    Matthias I Corvinus and, 459a
Vardan Arewelcʿi, 55a
Varro
    satire of, 554b
    used in schools, 558b
Vasari, Giorgio, 389b
Vasco-Iberist theory, 190b, 191a
    See also Euskara
Vasil (Armenian leader), 175a
Vasilievich, Boris
    founding of Dormition monastery by,
        299a
Vasilii III Ivanovich of Muscovy, grand
    prince
    St. Joseph of Volokolamsk and, 299b
Vassalage
    comitatus and, 129a
    servants and, 565a
Vatican Library, **623a–624a**
    access to, 623b, 624a
    expansion of, 623b
    illuminated manuscripts in, 359a, 360b
    inconsistency of, 623a–b
    maintenance of, 623a–624a
    period of literature in, 623a
    at present, 624a
    rebuilding collection of, 623b
    role of pope and, 623a
Vatican Ptolemy, 359a
Vatopedi Monastery, 362b
Vault, ribbed
    history of, 223b
Vecto of Bologna, judge, 314b–315a
Veleti tribe, 408b, 409a
Venantius Fortunatus, 308b, 370b
    Carolingian renaissance and, 89b
    Radegunda and, 518b
    used in schools, 561a

Vendetta, 8b
Venerabilem. See Innocent III, pope
Venerable Bede. *See* Bede
Venice
    admiral in, 6a
    Athens and, 45a
    commercialization and, 130b
    communal government of, 137a, 403b
    contract labor in, 567b
    currency of, 148b
    doges of, 134a, 148a–149b
    espionage of, 182b
    Great Council of, 136a
    homosexuality in, 574b
    insurance and, 290b
    servants in, 568a
    trade in, 133b, 400a, 403a–b
Venta Belgarum (Winchester, England),
    28a
Verdun
    bishopric of, 291b
Verger, Jacques, 562b
Vergil, Polydore
    Anglica historia (History of England),
        389b–390a
Vergil (Publius Vergilius Maro), 179a,
    179b
    Aeneid, 179a, 179b, 181a, 563a
    humanism and, 282a
    used in schools, 558b, 560a, 561a,
        562a, 563a
Vernacular literature
    alliterative literature and, 12a, 12b
    vs. Latin, 17a
    noble women and, 21a
    patronage and, 458a
    Portuguese, 496b
Verona
    Accursian gloss and, 4a
    d'Este family and, 193b
Veronica, Veil of, 410b
Vers de la mort. See Hélinand of
    Froidmont
Versailles, Treaty of, 385b
Vesconte, Pedro, 92a
Vespers, 328a
Vézelay, 151b *(illus.),* 152a, 152a *(illus.)*
Viaticum. See Razzāz al-Jazarīʿ, Ibn al-
Viator (journal), 384a
Vices. *See* Sin; Virtues and vices
Vico, Giambattista, 624b
Victorinus of Pettau, 54b
*Vida e milagres de Dona Isabel, Rainha de
    Portugal,* 496b
Vido do Infante D. Fernando. See Alvares,
    João
Vieri, Ugolino di
    Tablernacle of the Holy Corporal, 241a
*View of the State of Europe in the Middle
    Ages. See* Hallam, Henry
Vikings
    in Antwerp, 24a
    archaeology of, 25b, 26a, 29b

cult of, 392b
of Dublin, 80b
in Greenland, 29a
in Iceland, 29b
of Limerick, 80b
marriage by kidnapping by, 519b
raid targets of, 481b–482a
sack of Hamburg by, 22a
sack of Lisbon by, 326b
trade and, 401b
Villages
manors and, 343a–b
Villani, Filippo
biography of Dante by, 64a
Villani, Giovanni, 2b
Chronica Fiorentina, 64a
Villani, Matteo, 101a
Villard de Honnecourt, 227b
Gothic art and, 236a
Villon, François
Grand testament, 47a–b
Vincent of Beauvais, 410a–b
animals and, 18b
encyclopedia of, 49a
Vincent Ferrer, St., 95a
Violence, **624b–628a**
aspects of control of, 624b
attempts to moderate, 625a
beliefs against specific, 626a
in Christianity, 627a
on civilians, 626a
counterviolence, 624b–625a
definition of, 624b
dramatization of, 627b
effect on productivity, 624b
financing of, 625b
image of Middle Ages, 624b
against Jews, 625b–626a
knights and, 625a, 625b (*illus.*), 626
    (*illus.*)
literature in, 626b–627a
music of, 627a
rebellions and revolts, 624b–625a
rites of, 539a
significance of, 625a
in war, 626a
Viollet-le-Duc, Eugène, 393a
Virgilius of Salzburg, 421a
Virgin and Child, 237b (*illus.*)
Virgin Mary
Beautiful Madonna sculpture, 76b
cantigas de Santa María, 494b
churches dedicated to, 238b
commemorations of, 331a–b
consecration of churches to, 87b
cult of, 525b
feast days of, 331b
Immaculate Conception of, 288a–290a
as mother, 208b
as Muslim saint, 254b
Pietà and, 241a–b
popular religion and, 529a–b
rejection of humanity, 214b

statues of, 236a–b
as tapestry subject, 608a
virginal maternity of, 69a, 69b
Virgin Spring, The. See Bergman, Ingmar
Virtues and vices, **628a–633a**
capital, origin of, 629b
capital, tradition of, 631b
categories of, 629a–b
causes of, 628b
definition of, 628b
divisions of, 631a
monastic theology, approach of, 631a
moral theology, approach of, 630b
natural, 631a
Regensburg tapestry, 632a
relationships between, 630a
study of, 630b
systematic theology, approach of,
    631a–b
volume of text on, 631b–632a
Visaõ de Tündalo, 496a
Visconti, Gian Galeazzo, duke of Milan,
    618b
on feudal law, 322b–323a
patronage by, 456a
Visconti, Tedaldo. *See* Gregory X, pope
Visconti family, 134b
Visigoths
domestic architecture of, 32a
Vision. See Leversedge, Edmund
Vision of Tundale, 155a–b
Visions
of St. Catherine of Siena, 96a
Visitation, 238a (*illus.*)
Gothic art and, 242b
Vita Adae et Evae, 195a
Vita Anskarii. See Rimbert, St.
Vita Augustini. See Possidius of Calama
Vita Caroli Magni. See Einhard
Vita Godrici. See Reginald the monk
Vita Liudgeri, 205b
Vita Ludovici Grossi. See Suger of St.
    Denis
Vita prima. See Thomas of Celano
Vita spiritualis. See Camilla Battista of
    Varano
Viterbo, Battle of, 471a
Vitéz, Johannes, 459a
Vitoria, Francisco de, 419a
Vitus, St.
relics of, 146a
Vivas, João, 150b
Vives, Joan Lluís, 506b
Vlad III Ţepeş of Walachia, 633b
Vladimir I of Russia, prince, 84a
Vladislav II of Bohemia, king, 76b–77a
Voivode, **633a–634a**
meanings of, 633b
power of, 633b
Vojtěch. *See* Adalbert, St.
Voltaire, 390b
Voluptas (Pleasure), 68a (*illus.*)
Vorauer Genesis, 195a

Vox in excelso. See Clement V, pope
Voyages. See Hakluyt
Voytech. *See* Adalbert, St.
Vratislav II of Bohemia, king, 73a
Vroedschap, the, 16a
Vulgate cycle, 495a
Vyšehrad Codex, 73a
Vyšší Brod monastery, 73b

W

Wace
Brut and, 15a
on Norman peasant revolt, 624b
Roman de Rou, 458a
Wadding, Luke, 159b
Wages
of servants, 566b
Wagner, Richard
operas of, 393b, 394 (*illus.*)
Wahrmund, Ludwig, 638a
Waitz, Georg
*Feschichte der romanischen und
    germanischen Völker von 1494 bis
    1540,* 393a
Wakefield Master
alliterative literature and, 12a
Walafrid Strabo of Reichenau, 57a
Waldebert of Luzeuil, abbot, 145a
Waldemar II of Denmark, king, 270b
Waldensians, 168b–169b
atheism and, 44a
capital punishment and, 86a
popular religion and, 528b
poverty and, 505a
sacraments and, 552b
Waldes, 169a–b
Wales
Hubert de Burgh and, 278b
Wallace, William, **634a–b**
death of, 634b
knighting of, 634a–b
myths surrounding, 634a
Wallingford, Treaty of (1153), 595b
Walpole, Horace
Castle of Otranto, The, 390b–391a
Walram of Limburg, 270b
Walsperger, Andreas
map by, 412a
Walter de Milemete, 198a
*De nobilitatibus, sapientiis et prudentiis
    regum,* 198a
De secretis secretorum Aristotelis, 198a
Walter of Brienne, 44b
Walter of Châtillon, 308a, 555a
Alexandreis, 180a
Waltharius, 180a
Wanderer, The, 192a
Wandering poets, 308a
Wandering womb theory, 251a
Waning of the Middle Ages. See Huizinga,
    Johan

Warfare
  capitulations and, 86b–87b
  corsairs in, 481b
  naval, 6b–7a
  poverty and, 499b
  ribāṭ and, 530b–531a
  routiers in, 541b–542a
Warner of Rouen
  satire of, 554b
Wars of Alexander, The, 15a
Wars of the Roses, 465b, 645b
Wartburg castle, 177b
Warton, Thomas
  Observations on The Faerie Queene,
    391a
Waste Land, The. See Eliot, T. S.
Water
  industialization and, 345a–348b
  ordeal of, 315b
Water wheels, 345a–346a
Watts, George Frederick, 392a
Weaponry, handheld, 198a, 198b, 199b
  See also Artillery; Cannon; Firearms
Weaving, 646b
  industrial revolution and, 351a–352a
Wechssler, Eduard
  on *planctus Mariae,* 483a–b
Wedding. *See* Marriage
Weiner Genesis, 195a
Welfescholz, Battle of, 267a–b
Wells (cathedral: England), 228b
Welsh literature
  alliterative literature and, 12a
Wenceslas, St., **634b–635b**
  burial site of, 73a
  German missionaries, support of, 635a
  mural of life of, 75a
  murder of, 635a
  as patron saint of Bohemia, 635a
  as ruler, 634b
Wenceslas Bible, 76a
Wenceslas IV of Germany, emperor,
    76a–b
Wenceslas Hall (Prague), 233b
Wends
  Second Crusade and, 187a
Werewolves, 410b
Wergild, 85b
Werve, Claus de
  Philip the Bold mausoleum by, 535
    (illus.)
West Stow site (England), 26a–b
Western Schism. *See* Schism, Great
Westminster, Statute of (1219), 315b
Westminster Abbey, 229b–230a
  changing ratios of charitable provision
    at, 102 *(illus.)*
Weston, Jessie L.
  From Ritual to Romance, 36b–37a,
    395b
Wet nurses, 113a, 566b–567a
Wetlands
  in Holland, 173a

  human effects on, 173a
Weyden, Rogier van der, 265a, 613b
Weyer, Johann, 152a
  De praestigiis daemonum, 151a, 153b
Whale, The, 192a
Wharram Percy site (England), 26a, 26b,
    35b
White, T. H.
  Arthurian romances and, 36b
  Once and Future King, The, 396b
Whitehouse, David, 401a
Whittington, Dick, 133b
Wicca, 397a
Wichmann of Saxony, 409a
Wido, abbot, 217a, 630b
Widowhood, **635a–637b**
  cultural outlines, 636b–637a
  dowry and, 635b–636a
  legal issues of, 636a
  means of support, 635b–637a
  mourning period, 637a
  provisions for, 636a
  quantity of, 635b
  regional outlines, 636b–637a
  religious life and, 637a
  remarriage of, 635b, 637a–b
  as workshop owners, 636b
Widsith, 192a
Widukind of Corvey, 408b
  Res gestae Saxonicae, 146a
"Wife's Lament, The" (poem; Exeter
  Book), 192a, 192b
Wigbodus, 56b–57b
Wild hunt (witchcraft), 450b–451a
Wilfrid of York, St., 477b
Wilgefortis, St., 525a
Wilhelm Tell. See Schiller, Friedrich von
Will, the
  soul and body and, 592a, 592b
Will (testament)
  charity in, 505b
  communal liberties and, 133a
William V of Aquitane, duke, 321a–b
William IX of Aquitane, duke
  pornography by, 492a
William de la Mare, 59b
William de la Pole, 399a
William I (the Conquerer) of England,
  king, 645b
  murdrum fine by, 515b
  queen of, 513a
  sons of, 639b–640a
William II (Rufus) of England, king,
  639b–641a
  crown, revenue of, 640b–641a
  death of, 641a
  power, acquisition of, 640a–b
  on religion, 640a
William Marshal, 278a
  patronage by, 457b
  Peter des Roches and, 469b–470a
William of Alton, 59a

William of Apulia
  Gesta Roberti Wiscardi, 63a
William of Arles, count, 203a
William of Auvergne, 152b
  on sacraments, 550a
William of Baglione, 591b
William of Conches
  humanism and, 281a
  on matter, 377b
  on soul and body, 590b
William of Drogheda, **637b–638b**
  law writings of, 638a
  murder of, 638b
  Summa aurea, 638a
William of Holland, 139b, 621a
William of Jumièges, 624b
William of Malmesbury, 168b, 216b
  allegiance of, 516b
  Gesta pontificum anglorum, 63b
  Gesta rerum anglorum, 63b
  Historia novella, 63b
  Robert of Gloucester and, 457b
William of Middleton, 59a
William of Montpellier, 638a
William of Ockham. *See* Ockham,
  William of
William of Poitiers
  Gesta Guillelmi ducis Normannorum,
    63a
William of Raleigh, 279a
William of Rubruck, 118b
William of St. Amour, **639a–b**
  exile of, 9b, 639b
  on mendicant orders, 639a
  De periculis novissimorum temporum,
    639b
  On the Prior and Posterior Analytics,
    639a
  voluntary poverty of, 100b
William of St. Thierry, 421a, 454b
  The Nature of Body and Soul, 421a
William of Sens, 223a, 228b
William of Tyre, 202a, 272a
William of Ware, 289b
William of Wykeham, 239a
William VII of Poitiers, count, 47a
William I of Sicily, king, **641a–642a**
  antipope, election of, 641b
  death of, 641b, 642a
  Italy and Sicily, conquering of, 641a
  opinions on, 641b
William II of Sicily, king, **642a–643a**
  administrative instability, 642a
  *William II Presenting Church to the
    Virgin Mary,* 642b *(illus.)*
William the Bad. *See* William I of Sicily,
  king
William the Englishman, 228b
William the Good. *See* William II of
  Sicily, King
Willibrord, St., 24a
Wilton Diptych, 21a

Winchester
   archaeological excavations at, 28a–b
Winchester, Treaty of (1153), 376b
Winchester Psalter, 263b
Windeatt, Barry, 181a
Winsbeke, Der, 185a
Winsbekin, Die, 185a
Wisdom literature, 8a
Witchcraft
   abortion and, 2a
   demons and, 153b
   medievalism and, 394b
   pollution and taboo and, 485a
Witelo
   De natura daemonum, 153b
Witmar (monk), 21b
Władysław II Jagiełło of Poland, king,
   434a, 599a
Władysław III of Poland, king, 434a
   crusade against the Turks by, 93b–94a
   See also Jagiełło dynasty
Wolf, Kenneth, 506a
Wolf, Philippe, 503a–b
Wolfram von Eschenbach, 36b, 37b
   Parzival, 39a, 181a
Wolin (Poland), 27a
Women, **643a–653b**
   ailments of, 250 *(illus.)*
   almsgiving to, 105b
   in Arabic literature, 22b
   autobiographies by, 47a, 47b
   as biographers, 63b–64a
   in business, 646b
   celibacy of, 569b, 570a
   characteristics of, 207b–208b
   chastity belts and, 107b–108a
   childbearing, importance of, 643b
   as Christian intermediaries, 141b, 143a
   cloistered, 287b
   contributions to household by, 646b
   culture and, 651b–652b
   death penalty for, 365a
   devotional practices of, 69a
   dimensions of, 643a
   experience of the divine by, 485a
   extramarital sex of, 575a–576b
   in guilds, 646b–647a
   hostility to, 570a
   independence of, 570a, 571a, 575a,
      575b
   in Jewish law, 572b
   law and, 21a, 643b–645a
   lay monastics, 529a
   marriage and, 336a–b, 363b, 365a,
      553a, 646a–b
   in medieval Jewish hagiographical
      writing, 258a
   midwives and, 109a
   as military leaders, 652b
   as Muslim saints, 254b
   nomadism and, 52a
   non-married, 647b
   ordination of, 552b

papacy and, 295a
pardons and, 538a
passivity of, 571a
as penitents, 486a
as physicians, 252b, 476a–b
pilgrimages of, 480b
in pornography, 492a
rape and, 573b
religion and, 647b, 649b–651a
repression of the body and, 68b–69a
reproductive tract of, 249b *(illus.)*
rights of, 133b
royal, 645a–646a
satire of, 555a
schools and, 559a, 562b, 564a
as servants, 566b, 568a
sexual dysfunctions of, 580a
sexuality and, 579a–b
as slaves, 567a–b
soul and body and, 593a
supervision of servants by, 567b
as troubadors, 337b–338a
vernacular literature and, 21a
virginity of, 571a, 575b
as wet nurses, 566b–567a
work of, 646a–647b
See also Abortion; Body, the;
   Childbirth and infancy; Gynecology;
   Love and courtship; Marriage,
   Christian; Pornography; Rape;
   Sexuality; Sexuality, medical;
   Widowhood
Women's religious orders
   Cistercians, 650a
   Dominicans, 650a–b
   Fontevrault, 650a
   Franciscans, 650a–b
   Premonstratensians, 650a
   Radegunda in, 518b–519a
   See also Poor Clares
Wonder, analysis of, 410b–411a
Wood, Ian, 141a
Woodlands
   agricultural transformation of, 172b–
      173a
   animals and, 171a
   coppice from, 171b
   exploitation of, 171a–b
   in Northern Europe, 171b
   pollarding in, 171b
   timber in, 171a–b
Woodville, Elizabeth, 514a
Wool
   industrial revolution and, 349b–350a
Wool manufacturing. *See* Textile industry
Worcester Fragments, 13b
Workman, Leslie J., 389b
World War II
   archaeology and, 25b, 28a
Worm, Ole
   Danica literatura antiquissima (Danish
      antiquities), 390b

Worms, Concordat of (1122)
   investiture issue and, 267b
   on sacraments, 551b
Woyciech. *See* Adalbert, St.
Writing, 359a
   Carolingian miniscule, 89b
   Persian scripts, 467b–468a
   teaching of, 560a
Wrocław, St. Dorothy's Church in, 236b,
   241b
"Wulf and Eadwacer" (poem; Exeter
   Book), 192a, 192b
Wulfila. *See* Ulfila
Wulfstan
   alliterative literature and, 12b, 13b,
      14b
Wyclif, John, 201a
   Anne of Bohemia and, 21a
   Jerome of Prague and, 294a–b
   on transubstantiation, 615b
   on utraquism, 622a

X

Xenophon
   Agesilaus, 61a
   Cyropaedia, 61a
   on horsemanship, 275b
Ximénez de Cisneros, Francisco, cardinal,
   413a

Y

Yahya, Gedaliah ibn
   Shalshelet ha-Qabbala, 257a
Yangchow (China)
   Franciscan missionaries in, 119a
Yearley, Janthia
   on *planctus Mariae,* 483b
Yeats, William Butler, 395b
Yehiel of Paris, 257a
Yiddish language
   formation of, 261a
Ylias. See Simon Chèvre d'Or
Yohanni, 598b
York Plays
   alliterative literature and, 12a
Ypres
   Dominican convent of, 163b
Ysengrimus, 180a, 555b, 556a
Yuan dynasty (China)
   founder of, 118b
Yūnus, Ibn, 373b

Z

Zabarella, Francesco, 296a, 298b
Zaccaria, Benedetto, 403a–b
Zād al-musāfir. See Jazzār, Ibn al-
Zadonshchina, 587b, **653a–654b**
   author of, 654a
   story of, 653b–654a
   style of, 654a

See also Song of Igor's Campaign
Zaitun
    Franciscan missionaries in, 119a
Zangī, atabeg of Mosul, 174b, 187a
Zara, conquest of, 148b–149a
Zaynab, 254b
Ždár nad Sázavou monastery, 73b
Zdislava of Lemberk, duchess, 147b
Zeno the Isaurian, Byzantine emperor,
    166b
Zero, concept of, 371a
Zibaldone da Canal, 400b
Ziyādat Allāh III, 381a
Ziyāra, 253a, 255b

Zlatá Koruna monastery, 73b
Zodiac
    iconography of, 41b–42b
    See also Astrological iconography
Zohar. See Naḥmanides, Moses
Zoroastrianism
    dhimmīs and, 158a
    Persian language and, 466b
    Sabians and, 544a
Zübdetü᾿ t-tewārikh, 446b
Zuhr, Abū Marwān ʿAbd al-Mālīk
    ibn
    *Kitāb al-Taisīr fī l-mudāwāt wa
        l-tadbīr,* 381b

Zunnār (belt), 158b
Zurara, Gomes Eanes de, **654b–655b**
    Chronicle of Count Duarte de Meneses,
        655a
    Chronicle of Count Pedro de Meneses,
        655a
    Chronicle of Guinea, 496a, 654b
    Chronicle of the Capture of Ceuta,
        654b
    as historian, 654b–655b
    military career of, 654b
Zurich, 136a
Zwingli, Huldrych, 615b

ISBN 0-684-80642-8

90000

DATE DUE